Frommer's®

AUSTRALIA
FROM $50 A DAY

Here's what the critics say about Frommer's:

"Amazingly easy to use. Very portable, very complete."
— *Booklist*

♦

"The only mainstream guide to list specific prices. The Walter Cronkite of guidebooks—with all that implies."
— *Travel & Leisure*

♦

"Complete, concise, and filled with useful information."
— *New York Daily News*

♦

"Hotel information is close to encyclopedic."
— *Des Moines Sunday Register*

Other Great Guides for Your Trip:

Frommer's Portable Sydney

Frommer's Australia

Frommer's New Zealand from $50 a Day

Frommer's® 11th Edition

AUSTRALIA
FROM $50 A DAY

The Ultimate Guide to
Comfortable Low-Cost Travel

by Natalie Kruger & Marc Llewellyn

MACMILLAN • USA

ABOUT THE AUTHORS

Sydney resident **Marc Llewellyn** (chapters 2, 4, 5, 6, 12, 13, 14, 15, and 16) is one of Australia's premier travel writers and a regular contributor to all of Australia's leading newspaper travel sections and travel magazines. As a member of the Australian Travel Writers' Association, he keeps his suitcase ready, packed beneath his bed. He is also the author of *Frommer's Portable Sydney* and co-author of *Frommer's Australia.*

Natalie Kruger (chapters 3, 7, 8, 9, 10, and 11), another Sydneysider, used to be a public relations consultant for international and Australian airlines, hotel chains, tourist promotion boards, and tourist industry organizations until she realized it is more fun to be a travel writer because you get to say what you *really* think. She contributes to the travel pages of national Australian newspapers and is co-author of *Frommer's Australia.*

MACMILLAN TRAVEL USA

A Pearson Education Macmillan Company
1633 Broadway
New York, NY 10019

Macmillan Publishing books may be purchased for business or sales promotional use. For information please write: Special Markets Department, Macmillan Publishing USA, 1633 Broadway, New York, NY 10019.

Find us online at **www.frommers.com**

ISBN 0-02-863045-9
ISSN 8755-5425

Editor: Suzanne Roe Jannetta
Production Editor: Suzanne Snyder
Design by Michele Laseau
Staff Cartographers: John DeCamillis, Roberta Stockwell
Photo Editor: Richard Fox
Page Creation: Melissa Auciello–Brogan, Ellen Considine, Laura Goetz, Sean Monkhouse, and Linda Quigley

SPECIAL SALES

Bulk purchases (10+ copies) of Frommer's and selected Macmillan travel guides are available to corporations, organizations, mail-order catalogs, institutions, and charities at special discounts, and can be customized to suit individual needs. For more information write to Special Sales, Macmillan General Reference, 1633 Broadway, New York, NY 10019.

Manufactured in the United States of America.

Contents

List of Maps

An Invitation to the Reader

In researching this book, we discovered many wonderful places—hotels, restaurants, shops, and more. We're sure you'll find others. Please tell us about them, so we can share the information with your fellow travelers in upcoming editions. If you were disappointed with a recommendation, we'd love to know that, too. Please write to:

Frommer's Australia from $50 a Day, 11th Edition
Macmillan Travel
1633 Broadway
New York, NY 10019

An Additional Note

Please be advised that travel information is subject to change at any time—and this is especially true of prices. We therefore suggest that you write or call ahead for confirmation when making your travel plans. The authors, editors, and Publisher cannot be held responsible for the experiences of readers while traveling. Your safety is important to us, however, so we encourage you to stay alert and be aware of your surroundings. Keep a close eye on cameras, purses, and wallets, all favorite targets of thieves and pickpockets.

What the Symbols Mean

✪ **Frommer's Favorites**

Our favorite places and experiences—outstanding for quality, value, or both.

The following abbreviations are used for credit cards:

AE	American Express	ER	enRoute
BC	Bankcard	EURO	Eurocard
CB	Carte Blanche	JCB	Japan Credit Bank
DC	Diners Club	MC	MasterCard
DISC	Discover	V	Visa

Find Frommer's Online

Arthur Frommer's Budget Travel Online (**www.frommers.com**) offers more than 6,000 pages of up-to-the-minute travel information—including the latest bargains and candid, personal articles updated daily by Arthur Frommer himself. No other Web site offers such comprehensive and timely coverage of the world of travel.

The Best of Australia

by Natalie Kruger & Marc Llewellyn

Maybe we shouldn't say so, being Aussies ourselves, but Australia has a lot of bests. World bests, that is. It's got some of the best natural scenery, the weirdest wildlife, certainly the most brilliant scuba diving and snorkeling, the best beaches (shut up, California), the oldest rain forest (110 million years and counting), the world's oldest human civilization (some archaeologists say 40,000 years, some say 120,000—who cares? it's old), the best wines (OK, OK, stop browsing the Napa or Bordeaux and come see what we mean), the world's most laid-back people when they're not from Melbourne and watching Aussie Rules football), the best weather (give or take the odd Wet Season in northern parts), the most innovative east-meets-west-meets-someplace-else cuisine—all bathed in the world's most pervasive white sunlight that brings everything up in Technicolor.

"Best" means different things to different people, but scarcely a visitor lands on these shores without having the Great Barrier Reef at the top of their "Best Things to See in Australia" list. So they should, because it really is the Eighth Wonder of the World, a glorious natural masterpiece no one should die without seeing. Also high on most folks' must-see list is Ayers Rock. This monolith must have some kind of magnet inside it designed to attract planeloads of tourists. We're not saying the Rock isn't special, but we think the vast Australian desert all around it is even more special. Sure, come and gawk at the Rock, but spend a bit of time chilling out in the Red Centre wilderness, too. The third attraction on most visitors' lists is Sydney, the Emerald City that glitters in the Antipodean sunshine on—here we go with the "bests" again—the best harbor spanned by the best bridge in the world (shut up, San Francisco).

These "big three" attractions are understandably popular with travelers. What the TV commercials or the travel agent window displays don't show, however, is how much else there is to see. Like the World Heritage wetlands and Aboriginal rock art of Kakadu National Park, the second Great Barrier Reef on the western coast, and the snowy mountain hiking trails of Tasmania. As planes zoom overhead delivering visitors to the Reef, the Rock, and Sydney, Aussies in charming country towns, on far-flung beaches, on rustic sheep stations, in rain-forest villages, and in mountain lodges shake their heads and say sadly, "They don't know what they're missin'." Well, the aim of this chapter is to show you "what you're missin'." Of course, you will no doubt find your own "bests" as you travel, and we would like to hear about them when you do. All of the country's major attractions are included in our recommendations here, but we've compiled this list in the belief that you will have a better vacation if you take the road less traveled once or twice.

In these lists, NSW stands for New South Wales, QLD for Queensland, NT for the Northern Territory, WA for Western Australia, SA for South Australia, VIC for Victoria, TAS for Tasmania, and ACT for the Australian Capital Territory.

1 The Top Travel Experiences

- **Experiencing Sydney** (NSW): Consistently voted the best city in the world by noted travel publications, Sydney is more than just the magnificent Harbour Bridge and Opera House. For one thing, no other city has beaches in such abundance and few have such a magnificently scenic harbor. Our advice is to get aboard a ferry, walk from one side of the bridge to the other, and plan to spend at least a week here, because you're going to need it. See chapters 4 and 5.
- **Seeing the Great Barrier Reef** (QLD): It is hard to believe God would create such a glorious underwater fairyland, a 2,000-kilometer-long (1,200-mile-long) coral garden with electric colors and bizarre fish life, and have the grace to stick it all somewhere with warm water and year-round sunshine. This is what you came to Australia to see. See chapter 8.
- **Exploring the Wet Tropics Rain Forest** (QLD): Folk who come from skyscraper-packed cities like Manhattan or L.A. can't get over the moisture-dripping ferns, the butterflies, and the peace-filled bliss of this World Heritage patch of rain forest stretching north, south, and west from Cairns. Hike it, 4WD (four-wheel drive) it, or glide over the treetops in the Skyrail gondola from Cairns. See chapter 8.
- **Bareboat Sailing in the Whitsunday Islands** (QLD): *Bareboat* means unskippered—that's right, even if you think port is an after-dinner drink you can charter a yacht, pay for a day's instruction from a skipper, then take over the helm yourself to explore these 74 island gems. It's scary how easy it is, really—and surprisingly affordable in the off-season, especially if you have friends to pair up with. If your budget is a bit tighter, join an inexpensive 3-day, 2-night organized sailing trip instead. See chapter 8.
- **Exploring the Olgas (Kata Tjuta) and Ayers Rock (Uluru)** (NT): Just why everyone comes thousands of miles to see the big red stone of Ayers Rock is a mystery—that's probably why they come, because the Rock is a mystery. Just 50 kilometers (30 miles) from Ayers Rock are the round red heads of the Olgas, a second rock formation more significant to Aborigines and more intriguing to many visitors than Uluru. See chapter 9.
- **Taking an Aboriginal Desert Discovery Tour** (Alice Springs, NT): Eating wasps, considering a hill to be a giant caterpillar at rest, and seeing in the stars your grandmother smiling down at you all give you a new perspective on your own culture. See what we mean on this half-day tour from the Aboriginal Art and Culture Centre. See chapter 9.
- **Enjoying the "Sounds of Silence"** (Ayers Rock, NT): Billed as a "million-star restaurant" because it's outdoors under the Milky Way, this three-course dinner in the desert near Ayers Rock is not the cheapest meal you will have in Oz, but it is a must. Sip champagne to the twang of the didgeridoo, then feast on bush tucker such as emu, kangaroo, and crocodile at white-clothed tables as waiters pour Aussie wines. Some guests even don black tie for the occasion, but with

sneakers instead of stilettos. Then it's lights out, the music stops, and you hear it—the eerie sound of silence. See chapter 9.

- **Exploring Kakadu National Park** (NT): Australia's biggest national park is a wild wonderland of lily-clad wetlands, looming red escarpments, fabulous Aboriginal rock art, fern-fringed water holes, and countless birds, fish, and menacing crocodiles. Cruise it, hike it, 4WD it. See chapter 10.
- **Cruising the Kimberley** (WA): Australia's last frontier, the Kimberley is a romantic cocktail of South Sea pearls, deadly crocodiles, priceless Aboriginal rock art, and million-acre farms in a never-ending wilderness. Cross it by 4WD on the adventurous Gibb River Road, stay at a cattle station camp, or base yourself on glamorous Cable Beach in Broome. See chapter 10.
- **Rolling in Wildflowers** (WA): Imagine Texas three times over and covered in wildflowers. That's what happens in the state of Western Australia every spring from August to October when pink, mauve, red, white, yellow, and blue wildflowers bloom their hearts out. Aussies flock to the state big-time for this spectacle, so make your travel plans in advance. See chapter 11.
- **Wine Tasting in the Barossa Valley** (SA): One of Australia's four largest wine-producing areas, this German-speaking region less than an hour's drive from Adelaide is also one of the prettiest. Adelaide's restaurants happen to be some of the country's best, too, so test out your wine purchases on the city's terrific Modern Australian cuisine. See chapter 12.
- **Visiting with the Sea Lions on Kangaroo Island** (SA): Walk along a beach where these giant sea mammals lounge, and you'll believe you've never been so close to nature. Sit in the sand and watch them play before you head off on the trail of koalas, possums, seals, and far more wildlife than you can swing a cat at. See chapter 12.
- **Seeing the Sights along the Great Ocean Road** (VIC): This 106-kilometer (63½-mile) coastal road carries you past wild and stunning beaches, forests, and dramatic cliffs—including the Twelve Apostles, 12 pillars of red rock standing in splendid isolation in the foaming Southern Ocean. See chapter 14.
- **Driving Around Tasmania:** The "Apple Isle" is Australia's prettiest state, a picturesque Eden of snow-topped granite tors, white-water wildernesses, and haunting historic prisons. A bonus is that it's small enough to drive around in a few days. See chapter 16.

2 The Best Adventures That Won't Cost You a Fortune

- **Abseiling in the Blue Mountains** (NSW): Careering backward down a cliff face with the smell of gum trees in your nostrils is not everyone's idea of fun, but you sure know you're alive. Several operators welcome both novices and the more experienced, but if you just want to walk, well, the hiking also is superb here. See chapter 6.
- **Playing a Round of Night Golf** (White Cliffs, NSW): The locals around here play golf in the dark with fluorescent golf balls on "greens" that are no more than strips of dust. Lightning Ridge offers dust golf, too. See chapter 6.
- **White-Water Rafting the Nymboida River** (NSW): The Grade 5 Nymboida River near Coffs Harbour is a terrific challenge for the experienced and the beginner. **Wow Rafting** (☎ **1800/640 330** in Australia, or 02/6654 4066) offers day trips and longer adventures. See chapter 6. The Grade 3 to 4 Tully

River near Mission Beach in north Queensland is also big on the rafting map. See chapter 8.

- **Canoeing the Top End** (NT): Paddling down sun-drenched Katherine Gorge really sharpens the senses, especially when a freshwater crocodile pops its head up! The Ord River in the Kimberley is another breathtaking backdrop, rich with birds, red cliffs, and yep, more freshwater crocs. Canoe it for an afternoon, or take a three-day self-guided camp-canoe safari. See chapter 10.

- **Surfing in Margaret River** (WA): A 90-minute surf lesson with four-time and current Western Australia surf champ Josh Parmateer is a great introduction to the sport—if only to hear Josh's you-beaut Aussie accent! See chapter 11.

- **Sea Kayaking with Sea Lions** (WA and SA): Take a sea-kayaking day trip from Perth with **Rivergods** (☎ **08/9259 0749TK**) and you'll get to snorkel with sea lions and watch penguins feed. The company also runs multiday sea kayak expeditions past whales, dolphins, and sharks in Shark Bay, and over the brilliant coral of Ningaloo Reef on the Northwest Cape in Western Australia. See chapter 11. Kayaking is also a great way to explore the Whitsunday Islands, the Cairns coastline, and Dunk Island off Mission Beach in Queensland. See chapter 8.

- **Going on Camel Safari** (SA and NT): Trek the Flinders Ranges in South Australia with **Kev's Kamel Kapers** (☎ **08/8648 4299TK**). You can either trot through the semidesert range on a two-hour sunset trip or take an overnight safari, camping beside a gum-wood fire. See chapter 12. You can also amble on camelback down a dry riverbed in the center of Alice Springs, and roll up to Ayers Rock astride one, à la Lawrence of Arabia. See chapter 9.

- **Hiking Cradle Mountain National Park** (TAS): The 80-kilometer (48-mile) Overland Track is known as the best bushwalking (hiking) trail in Australia. The trek, from Lake St. Clair to Cradle Mountain, takes anywhere from 5 to 10 days, depending on your fitness level. Shorter walks, some lasting just half an hour, are also accessible. See chapter 16.

3 The Best Things to Do for Free

- **Hitting the Beach:** Australia's coastline is really just one big white sandy beach, and it's all free. Just remember to slip, slop, slap—slip on a shirt, slop on sunscreen, and slap on a hat.

- **Whale Watching:** Playful 40-ton humpbacks ply the east and west coasts of the continent from June to October, later in southern parts. Good free vantage points include the whale-watch lookout at Cape Naturaliste in Western Australia (see chapter 11), and the cliffs at Byron Bay in New South Wales (see chapter 6).

- **Wine Tasting:** Australia makes a very good drop indeed, and most wineries charge you nothing to taste their produce at the cellar door. The main wine regions are the Hunter Valley (see chapter 6), the Barossa Valley (see chapter 12), Margaret River (see chapter 11), and the Yarra Valley (see chapter 13).

- **Walking Across the Sydney Harbour Bridge:** Start your journey from The Rocks and walk across the bridge to Milsons Point CityRail station, where you can catch a train back to the city center. The car fumes and the height can be a little much for some, but the views of the city, the harbor, the ferry terminals, and the Sydney Opera House are magnificent. See chapter 5.

- **Exploring the Blue Mountains** (NSW): Head for the hills to one of the best bushwalking areas in the world. There are plenty of fabulous walks to choose from; most offer incredible views, waterfalls, and wildlife. See chapter 6.

- **Taking a Bath in Lightning Ridge** (NSW): Wallow up to your neck—along with local opal miners—in the hot waters of the town's Bore Baths. The water comes direct from the Artesian Basin, so it's rich in mineral deposits and very hot. The best time to bathe is at night, with a bucketload of stars above your head. See chapter 6.
- **Cruising the Blackall Range Tourist Drive 23** (Sunshine Coast, QLD): Leave the touristy Sunshine Coast behind and drive along the winding green ridge tops of the Blackall Ranges. Cute villages are lined with craft shops and galleries, parrots play in the trees, and the views to the coast are sensational. Drive right on to Mary Cairncross Park to see the wacky Glasshouse Mountains poking out of the plain. See chapter 8.
- **Soaking up the Scenery at Lamington National Park** (The Gold Coast Hinterland, QLD): Even if you can't afford to stay at either of the park's two lodges, Binnaburra Mountain Lodge or O'Reilly's Rainforest Guesthouse (see "The Best Alternative Accommodations," below, for both), you can still visit for the day. Set off early, so you have plenty of time to hike one of the 20 or so trails that meander through subtropical rain forest, past waterfalls and ancient Antarctic beeches. See chapter 8.
- **Hiking in the Outback** (Red Centre, NT): Feel the spirit of the Outback on a hiking trail. Walk the almost-complete 220-kilometer (132-mile) Larapinta Trail through the West MacDonnell Ranges from Alice Springs, or tackle one of its shortest sections (8km/5 miles). You can also choose from several trails of up to half a day's duration in pretty Trephina Gorge Nature Park in the East MacDonnell Ranges, or just take a path from the Old Telegraph Station picnic grounds in Alice Springs. See chapter 9.
- **Experiencing a Darwin Sunset** (NT): Darwin's superb sunsets arrive on cue every night in the Dry Season from April to October. Good vantage points include the Wharf, where you can also watch the fishermen reel in their catches; the Darwin Sailing Club; and Mindil Beach, where the fabulous markets are located. On Sunday, the free Sunset Jazz concert by the sea in the gardens of the MGM Grand Casino is the best spot of all. See chapter 10.
- **Taking a Dip in Hot Springs** (NT): Soak your travel aches and pains away in the warm, clean waters of the Hot Springs in the Katherine River in Katherine. See chapter 10. Another free hot bath is waiting for you at Mataranka, en route between Alice Springs and Darwin, where flying foxes hang in the lush tropical foliage around the pool. See chapter 9.
- **Wandering Around Fremantle** (WA): Perth's bustling port of Fremantle is full of wonderfully ornate warehouses and offices. Sit and watch the sailing and fishing vessels come in, or people-watch over a coffee at the busy cappuccino strip on South Terrace. See chapter 11.

4 The Best Places to Experience the Outback

- **Broken Hill** (NSW): There's no better place to experience real Outback life than in Broken Hill. There's the city itself, with it's thriving art scene and the Royal Flying Doctor Service; a historic ghost town on its fringe; a national park with Aboriginal wall paintings; an opal-mining town nearby; and plenty of kangaroos, emus, and giant wedge-tailed eagles. See chapter 6.
- **Lightning Ridge** (NSW): This opal-mining town is as rough and ready as the stones they pull out of the ground. Meet amazing characters, share in the

eccentricity of the place, and visit opal rush areas where you can search for stones in the sun-bleached mine tailings. See chapter 6.

- **Ayers Rock (Uluru)** (NT): This magical monolith will enthrall you with its eerie, still beauty. Hike around Uluru's base, ride a camel to it, or climb it if you must. The nearby Olgas (Kata Tjuta) are even more soothing and visually arresting than Uluru, and are actually taller than the Rock. Don't go home until you have stood still in all that sand and felt the powerful heartbeat of the desert. See chapter 9.

- **The MacDonnell Ranges** (NT): These red rocky hills that stretch along either side of Alice Springs were formed by the Aboriginal Caterpillar Dreaming that wriggled from the Earth in the dawn of time. To the west are dramatic gorges, idyllic (and bloody cold) water holes, and cute wallabies. To the east are Aboriginal rock carvings, bird-filled walking trails, and the Ross River Homestead where you can crack a stock whip, throw a boomerang, feast on damper and billy tea, and ride horses through the bush. See chapter 9.

- **Kings Canyon** (NT): Anyone who saw the cult flick *The Adventures of Priscilla, Queen of the Desert* will remember the scene where the transvestites climb a soaring cliff and survey the desert floor. That was Kings Canyon, about 300 kilometers (180 miles) from Alice Springs. Climb and walk the dramatic rim or take the easier shady route along the canyon floor. Don't forget your lipstick, guys. See chapter 9.

- **Finke Gorge National Park** (NT): If you like your wilderness scenic and ancient, come here. Finke Gorge is home to "living fossil" palm trees that survived the ice ages and to what scientists think may be the world's oldest river course. Camp, hike, or just soak up the timeless bush. Visit for a day from Alice Springs or camp out. See chapter 9.

- **Elsey Station** (NT): This vast farm was made famous as the setting of the Australian book *We of the Never-Never,* an account of isolated Outback life written in 1902. The title came from visitors' desire to "never, never" leave such remote beauty. Visit for a day and meet the resident Aboriginal kids, or stay longer and canoe the isolated Roper River to Red Lily Lagoon. **Far Out Adventures** (☎ **08/ 8972 2552**) runs trips to the station. See chapter 10.

- **The Northwest Cape** (WA): This treeless moonscape of red anthills, spiky spinifex, and blazing heat seems to go on forever, so it is all the more amazing to find a beautiful coral reef gracing the shore. Ride in a 4WD over the rugged hills, dodge kangaroos, cruise the green waters of an ochre-walled gorge, spot your constellation at night in a sky unspoiled by city lights, scuba dive the reef, and laze on deserted white beaches where the Outback meets the sea. See chapter 11.

5 The Best Places for Viewing Wildlife

- **Montague Island** (Narooma, NSW): This little island just offshore from the seaside town of Narooma, on the south coast, is a haven for nesting seabirds, but it's the water around it that's home to the main attractions. Dolphins are common, fairy penguins, too, and during whale-watching season you are almost sure to spot humpback and southern right whales, some with their calves. See chapter 6.

- **Jervis Bay** (NSW): This is probably the nearest place to Sydney where you are certain to see kangaroos in the wild and where you can pat them, too. The national park here is home to plenty of possums, as well as hundreds of bird species, including black cockatoos. See chapter 6.

- **Lone Pine Koala Sanctuary** (Brisbane, QLD): Cuddle a koala (and have your photo taken doing it) at this Brisbane park, the world's first and largest koala sanctuary. Apart from 130 koalas, you can see lots of other Aussie wildlife—including lizards, frogs, 'roos, wallabies (which you can hand-feed), and colorful parakeets. See chapter 7.
- **Rainforest Habitat Wildlife Sanctuary** (Port Douglas, QLD): More than 150 animal species from the Wet Tropics rain forests of north Queensland are gathered in two walk-through cages at this excellent sanctuary in Port Douglas. Get face-to-beak with rain-forest birds, hand-feed big red kangaroos, and get close, but not too close, to saltwater crocodiles. See chapter 8.
- **Daintree River** (QLD): The murky green water of the Daintree hides thrillingly life-threatening saltwater crocodiles, while its thickly rain-forested banks shelter dozens of species of less-terrifying Australian birds, best seen in the early morning. Wildlife-spotting cruises at night reveal possums, frogs, and more crocs. See chapter 8.
- **Australian Butterfly Sanctuary** (Kuranda, near Cairns, QLD): Walk through the biggest butterfly "aviary" in Australia and see some of Australia's most gorgeous butterflies, including the electric-blue Ulysses. Wear pink, red, or white to encourage them to land on you. See chapter 8.
- **Birdworld and the Aviary** (Kuranda, near Cairns, QLD): These almost identical sanctuaries have dozens of species of native Aussie birds in walk-through aviaries, with a big emphasis on Australia's boldly colored parrots. See chapter 8.
- **Mission Beach** (QLD): The rain forests of Mission Beach are among the last wild habitats for the endangered cassowary, a prehistoric-looking ostrich-like creature with black feathers and a bony blue crest on its head. You can easily spot them on a hiking trail or just crossing the road. They're cute, but can disembowel you with the spurs on their dinosaur-like feet, so be wary. See chapter 8.
- **Mon Repos Turtle Rookery** (Bundaberg, QLD): Most nights from November to January, giant green loggerhead, and hawksbill turtles crawl up Mon Repos Beach in Bundaberg to lay their eggs. From late January to March, the babies hatch and scamper down the beach to the water. Join rangers from the Visitor Centre to see them by torchlight (flashlight). Heron Island in Queensland and the Northwest Cape in Western Australia are two other excellent turtle-viewing sites. See chapters 8 and 11.
- **David Fleay Wildlife Park** (The Gold Coast, QLD): This small park on the Gold Coast was founded by a pioneering zoologist and is home to all kinds of Aussie mammals, birds, crocs, and other reptiles in natural free-roaming settings. See chapter 8.
- **Currumbin Bird Sanctuary** (The Gold Coast, QLD): Tens of thousands of unbelievably pretty red, blue, green, and yellow rainbow lorikeets have been screeching into this park on the Gold Coast for generations, to be hand-fed by delighted visitors every morning and afternoon. There are 'roos, wombats, and other Australian animals at the sanctuary, too, but the birds steal the show. See chapter 8.
- **Lamington National Park** (The Gold Coast Hinterland, QLD): Every day brilliant black-and-gold Regent bowerbirds, satin bowerbirds, crimson-and-cobalt rosellas, and loads of other wild rain-forest birds feed right out of your hand at O'Reilly Rainforest Guesthouse (☎ 07/5544 0644), located in this mountainous national park a 90-minute drive inland from the Gold Coast. Hike the trails and soak up the cool mountain air while you're here. See chapter 8.
- **Desert Park** (Alice Springs, NT): All kinds of rarely seen marsupials with big ears and big eyes, bizarre thorny devil lizards, striped numbats, finches, and ven-

omous snakes are on show at this Alice Springs park. Desert wildlife is hard to spot in the wild, so this park combines animals from three Australian desert habitats into one location. Don't miss the daily birds-of-prey show. See chapter 9.

- **Kakadu National Park** (NT): One-third of Australia's bird species live in Kakadu; so do dingoes, snakes, frogs, and lots of dangerous saltwater crocs. A cruise on the Yellow Waters billabong is like cruising through a wetlands theme park, especially in the Dry Season, when wildlife converges around this shrinking water source. See chapter 10.

- **Northwest Cape** (WA): For the thrill of a lifetime, go snorkeling with a whale shark. No one knows where they come from, but these mysterious monsters up to 18 meters (56 feet) long surface in these remote Outback waters every March to May. A mini-industry has sprung up, taking snorkelers out to swim alongside the sharks as they feed (on plankton, not snorkelers). See chapter 11.

- **Monkey Mia** (WA): Almost every day wild bottle-nose dolphins swim into this remote Outback shore to say hello to visitors. You'll have to join the queue, as this place gets worldwide publicity, but it's worth it when these gentle creatures cruise past and look up at you with those intelligent eyes. While you're here, don't miss a cruise on the *Shotover* catamaran to spot dugongs (manatees), turtles, sea snakes, and sharks. See chapter 11.

- **Kangaroo Island** (SA): You are sure to see more native animals here—including koalas, wallabies, birds, echidnas, reptiles, seals, and sea lions—than anywhere else in the country, apart from a wildlife park. Another plus: The distances between major points of interest are not great, so you won't spend half the day just getting from place to place. See chapter 12.

6 The Best Beaches

- **Palm Beach** (Sydney, NSW): At the end of a long string of beaches north of Sydney Harbour, Palm Beach is long and very white, with some good surfing and a golf course nestled between it and the secluded beach and shallows of Pittwater. See chapter 5.

- **Hyams Beach** (Jervis Bay, NSW): This beach, south of Sydney along the Princes Highway that runs along the coast to Melbourne, is said to have the whitest sand in the world—and it squeaks when you walk on it. (The reflection off the sand can give you a sunburn in minutes, even on a cloudy day). See chapter 6.

- **Four Mile Beach** (Port Douglas, QLD): The sea is turquoise, the sun is warm, and the low-rise hotels that are starting to line this tropical strand can't spoil the feeling that it's a million miles from anywhere. See chapter 8.

- **Mission Beach** (North Coast, QLD): Azure sea, beautiful coral, tropical isles looming offshore, and lush white sand edged by dense tangled-vine forests make this beach a real winner. So does the fact that hardly anyone ever comes here. Cassowaries hide out in the rain forest, and the neat town of Mission Beach politely makes itself invisible behind the leaves. See chapter 8.

- **Whitehaven Beach** (on Whitsunday Island, QLD): It's not a great surf beach, but this 6-kilometer (3½-mile) stretch of silica sand is pristine, peaceful, and as white as snow. Bring a book, curl up under the rain forest bordering the beach, and fantasize that the cruise boat is going to leave without you. See chapter 8.

- **Main Beach** (The Sunshine Coast, QLD): The trendy shops on Hastings Street line the white sand and gently rolling surf of this pretty beach. Dust off your designer swimsuit for this one. When you tire of the scene and the sun, you can hike the green walking trails of Noosa National Park nearby. See chapter 8.

- **Surfers Paradise Beach** (The Gold Coast, QLD): Surfers Paradise may be the most famous, but actually all the beaches that stretch end to end along the 30-kilometer (18-mile) Gold Coast, in southern Queensland, are worthy of inclusion here. Every one of them has squeaky-clean sand, great surf, fresh breezes, and an air of freedom. Just ignore the tacky high-rises behind you. See chapter 8.
- **Cottesloe Beach** (Perth, WA): Perth has 19 great beaches, but this petite crescent is the prettiest. After you have been seen being seen on the sand, join the fashionable set for a caffe latte in the quaint Indiana Tea House, a mock-Edwardian bathhouse fronting the sea. See chapter 11.
- **Cable Beach** (Broome, WA): Is it the South Sea pearls they pull out of the Indian Ocean, the camels loping along the sand at sunset, or the red earth that comes down to meet the green sea that gives this beach its exotic appeal? Maybe it's just the 26 kilometers (15½ miles) of glorious white sand. See chapter 10.

7 The Best Affordable Diving & Snorkeling Sites

- **Port Douglas** (QLD): Port Douglas, north of Cairns, offers dozens of fabulous dive sites where you'll swim among delicate fan corals, spectacular coral gardens, and giant clams. Snorkelers can take in the abundant marine life of Agincourt Reef, where the 440-passenger Quicksilver catamaran moors daily, or sail in a smaller crowd to the coral-rich cays of the Low Isles just an hour offshore. An all-inclusive day trip aboard the Quicksilver cat will cost about A$135 (U.S.$95), while a trip aboard the smaller *Wavelength* will set you back about A$103 (U.S.$72). See chapter 8.
- **Green Island** (QLD): This island is made of coral, so you'd expect the snorkeling to be good. Plunge off the beach just about anywhere and marvel at the never-ending coral. If you tire of snorkeling, you can take a stroll through the rain forest. A half-day trip from Cairns costs less than A$50 (U.S.$35). See chapter 8.
- **Cairns** (QLD): In addition to Green Island (above), Moore, Norman, Hardy, Saxon, and Arlington Reefs and Michaelmas and Upolu Cay are all about 90 minutes off Cairns. Every one offers great snorkeling and endless dive sites— all at prices that won't bust your budget. See chapter 8.
- **The *Yongala* Wreck** (QLD): Sunk by a cyclone in 1911, the 120-meter (394-ft.) S.S. *Yongala* lies in the Coral Sea off Townsville. Big schools of trevally, kingfish, barracuda, and batfish surround the wreckage; giant Queensland grouper live under the bow; turtles graze on the hull; and hard and soft corals make their home on it. **Mike Ball Dive Expeditions** (☎ 07/4772 3022) runs 3-day trips to the wreck that cost about A$143 (U.S.$100) per person per day, including a total of six dives. See chapter 8.
- **The Whitsunday Islands** (QLD): These 74 breathtaking islands offer countless dive sites, both among the islands themselves and on the outer Great Barrier Reef, 90 minutes away. The underwater life is as varied and stunning here as anywhere else along the Great Barrier Reef, and when you're not diving or snorkeling, the above-the-water island-scape is a terrific playground. Most day trips from the mainland include free snorkeling gear, or you can rent gear at the island resorts for about A$10 (U.S.$7) a day. See chapter 8.
- **Rottnest Island** (WA): Just 19 kilometers (11½ miles) off Perth, excellent snorkeling and more than 100 dive sites await you in the turquoise, sheltered bays of this former prison island. Wrecks, limestone overhangs, and myriad fish entertain

divers. There are no cars on the island, so snorkelers should rent a bike and snorkel gear, grab a laminated snorkel-trail map, and head off to find their own private coral garden. See chapter 11.

• **Ningaloo Reef** (WA): A stunningly well-kept secret is the way we'd describe Australia's second Great Barrier Reef, stretching 260 kilometers (156 miles) along the Northwest Cape, halfway up Western Australia. Dazzling coral starts right onshore, not 90 minutes out to sea like the Great Barrier Reef. Snorkel or dive with giant manta rays, and dive to see sharks, angel fish, turtles, eels, grouper, potato cod, and much more. You can even snorkel with whale sharks (see "The Best Places for Viewing Wildlife," above). An adventure here may cost a little bit more, but it's definitely worth the splurge. See chapter 11.

8 The Best Places to Learn About Aboriginal Culture

• **The Umbarra Aboriginal Cultural Centre** (Wallaga Lake, near Narooma, NSW): This center offers boomerang- and spear-throwing instruction, painting with natural ochres, discussions on Aboriginal culture, and guided walking tours of Aboriginal sacred sites. See chapter 6.

• **Tjapukai Aboriginal Cultural Centre** (Cairns, QLD): This multimillion-dollar center showcases the history of the local Tjapukai people—their creation story (called the "Dreamtime") and their often harrowing experiences since Europeans arrived—using a film, a superb theatrical work, and a dance performance. You can also find out how to cure a snake bite or asthma, learn to play the didgeridoo, or have a go at throwing a boomerang. See chapter 8.

• **Native Guide Safari Tours** (Port Douglas, QLD): Hazel Douglas, who was brought up in the 110-million-year-old rain forest of the Daintree and Cape Tribulation area north of Port Douglas, takes you on a full-day 4WD safari in which she explains Aboriginal legends, points out what different plants are used for, and teaches you how to know when a crocodile is in the water. See chapter 8.

• **Aboriginal Art and Culture Park** (Alice Springs, NT): You'll get to taste bush food, see traditional houses, throw boomerangs and spears, and experience an insightful glimpse into Aboriginal family values in one action-packed half-day tour of the center. A 1-hour didgeridoo class rounds off the morning. See chapter 9.

• **Lilla Aboriginal Tours** (Kings Canyon, NT): Take a short walk with an Aboriginal guide to sacred paintings in Watarrka National Park, learn the Dreamtime significance of the paintings in the area, taste bush food, throw a boomerang, and ask questions of your guide about local Aboriginal ways. See chapter 9.

• **Anangu Tours** (Ayers Rock, NT): The Anangu are the owners of Ayers Rock, or Uluru, as it is called in their native tongue. Join them for walks around the Rock as you learn about their creation stories (poisonous snake men once fought battles here), pick bush food off the trees, throw spears, visit rock paintings, and watch the sunset over the monolith. The Anangu's Uluru–Kata Tjuta Cultural Centre near the base of Ayers Rock has good displays of cultural and Dreamtime life. See chapter 9.

• **Manyallaluk Tours** (near Katherine, NT): This Aboriginal community welcomes visitors to their bush home for the day and teaches them to paint, weave, throw boomerangs, and do other tasks of daily life. Get involved as little or as much as you want. See chapter 10.

- **Katherine** (NT): Mike Keighley of Far Out Adventures is an honorary member of the Jilkminggan Aboriginal community on Elsey Station near Katherine. Join him on a visit to the community to meet the kids, talk about Dreamtime legends or modern-day issues, maybe sample bush tucker, and chill out by the rain forest–lined river here. See chapter 10.
- **Yamatji Bitja Aboriginal Bush Tours** (Kalgoorlie, WA): Geoffrey Stokes, who was brought up the traditional Aboriginal way in the bush near Kalgoorlie, takes you tracking animals, foraging for bush food, and even hunting a kangaroo for dinner (with a gun, not a boomerang!). Explore the bush, learn about creation myths, and find out what his childhood was like. See chapter 11.
- **Tandanya Aboriginal Cultural Institute** (Adelaide, SA): This place offers a great opportunity to experience Aboriginal life through Aboriginal eyes. You might catch one of the dance or other performances staged here, although there are plenty of other opportunities to find out more about Aboriginal culture. See chapter 12.

9 The Best of Small-Town Australia

- **Central Tilba** (NSW): Just inland from Narooma on the south coast, this tiny historic hamlet is one of the cutest you'll ever see, complete with its own black-smiths and leather-work outlets. The ABC cheese factory here offers visitors free tastings, while you can spend hours browsing the antiques stalls or simply admiring the period buildings. See chapter 6.
- **Broken Hill** (NSW): Known for its giant silver mines, the quirky town of Broken Hill has more pubs per capita than just about anywhere else. It's also the home of the School of the Air—a "classroom" that transmits its lessons by radio to isolated communities spread over thousands of miles of Outback. Here you'll also find the eccentric Palace Hotel, made famous in the movie *The Adventures of Priscilla, Queen of the Desert*, as well as plenty of colonial mansions and her-itage homes. See chapter 6.
- **Port Douglas** (QLD): What happens when trendy Sydneysiders and Melbur-nites discover a quaint one-street fishing village in tropical north Queensland? Come to Port Douglas and find out. A strip of groovy restaurants and a cham-pionship golf course have not diminished "Port's" old-fashioned air. Stunning Four Mile Beach (see "The Best Beaches," above) is at the end of the main street, and the Quicksilver high-speed catamaran departs daily for the Great Barrier Reef. See chapter 8.
- **Mission Beach** (QLD): You'd never know that this tidy village, hidden in lush rain forest off the highway, existed if you weren't a well-informed traveler. Aussies know it's here, but few of them bother to patronize its dazzling beach, cute restaurants, and secluded rain-forest trails, so you'll have the place all to yourself. There's great white-water rafting on the nearby Tully River, too. See chapter 8.
- **Broome** (WA): This romantic pearling port on the far-flung Kimberley coast on the Indian Ocean blends Australian corrugated iron architecture with Chinese pagoda roofs left by the Asian pearl divers who settled here. Its streets are a mix-ture of sophisticated international ambience and rough Outback attitude. Beau-tiful Cable Beach (see "The Best Beaches," above) is just outside town. See chapter 10.
- **Kalgoorlie** (WA): This is it, the real McCoy, the iconic Australian gold-mining boom town sitting on what used to be the richest square mile of gold-bearing

earth ever to see the light of day. Upwards of 2,000 ounces a day are still pulled out of that square mile. Wander the wide dusty streets, have a drink in one of the many gracious 19th-century pubs, descend a mine shaft and pan for riches, and play "two-up" in a rusting corrugated-iron gambling ring. See chapter 11.

- **Hahndorf** (SA): A group of Lutheran settlers founded this German-style town, located in the Adelaide Hills, just outside Adelaide, in the 1830s. You'll love the churches, the wool factory and craft shops, and the delicious German food served up in the local cafes, restaurants, and bakeries. See chapter 12.

- **Coober Pedy** (SA): For a fair dinkum (that means "genuine") Outback experience, few places are as weird and wonderful as this opal-mining town in the middle of nowhere. You can visit mines and wacky museums, and stay in a hotel underground—which is not really that unusual, considering all the locals live like moles anyway. See chapter 12.

- **Launceston** (TAS): Tasmania's second city is not much larger than your average European or American small town, but it's packed with Victorian and Georgian architecture and plenty of remnants of Australia's convict days. Spend a couple of days here discovering the town and the local scenery, and splurge a little on a stay in a historic hotel. See chapter 16.

10 The Best Museums

- **Australian National Maritime Museum** (Sydney): The best things about this museum are the ships and submarines often docked in the harbor out front. You can climb aboard and explore what it's like to be a sailor. Inside are some fascinating displays relating to Australia's dependence on the oceans. See chapter 5.

- **Old Telegraph Station Historical Reserve** (Alice Springs, NT): It's not called a museum, but that's what this restored telegraph repeater station out in the picturesque hills near Alice Springs really is. From the hot biscuits turned out of the wood-fired oven to the old telegraph equipment tapping away, this 1870s settlement is as real as history can get and offers a great snapshot of pioneering Australian life. See chapter 9.

- **Australian Aviation Heritage Centre** (Darwin, NT): Pride of place in this hangar is a B-52 bomber on permanent loan from the United States. But there's loads more—not just heaps of planes, engines, and other aviation paraphernalia, but detailed stories, jokes, and anecdotes associated with the exhibits—put together by enthusiastic members of the Aviation Historical Society of the Northern Territory. See chapter 10.

- **Western Australian Museum** (Perth): Skip the natural history displays endemic to state museums the world over and head straight to the country's best display of Aboriginal culture. Evocative photographs, artifacts, and display boards draw a sad and thoughtful picture of Australia before and after the arrival of Europeans. See chapter 11.

- **Western. Australian. Maritime Museum** (Perth): Housed in a two-level warehouse in the historic port city of Fremantle, this excellent museum tells tales of the Western Australian coastline, beginning with when the Dutch first bumped into it in the 1600s and promptly abandoned it as useless. There are also some good displays of treasure recovered from the deep. See chapter 11.

- **York Motor Museum** (WA): This multimillion dollar collection of veteran, vintage, classic, and racing cars is one of the most wide ranging in the country. If you're a car buff, don't hang around Perth—get yourself the 99 kilometers

(59½ miles) to the charming historic country town of York and make a day of it. See chapter 11.

- **New Norcia Museum and Art Gallery** (WA): The collection of European Renaissance art works in this tiny country museum in the Spanish Benedictine monastery town of New Norcia is mind-boggling. It also has all kinds of memorabilia from the monks' past—including manuscripts, clothing, and musical instruments—and gifts from Queen Isabella of Spain. See chapter 11.

- **Migration Museum** (Adelaide, SA): This fascinating museum gives visitors insight into the people who came to Australia, how and where they settled, and how many suffered getting here. Don't expect a lot of musty displays, either, as this museum is full of hands-on activities. See chapter 12.

- **Australian War Memorial** (Canberra, ACT): Given its name, you might expect this museum to be a bleak sort of place, but you'd be wrong. The museum gives important insight into the ANZAC (Australian and New Zealand Army Corps) spirit, including an evocative exhibit on the tragic battle of Gallipoli. There's also a pretty good art collection. See chapter 15.

11 The Best Moderately Priced Hotels

- **The Russell** (Sydney, NSW; ☎ 02/9241 3543): Located right in the heart of the historic district called The Rocks, this gorgeous property has delightful rooms, brightly painted walls, creaking floorboards, and a cozy atmosphere. If you don't mind sharing a bath, you can have a charming room at a great price. See chapter 4.

- **Waverley** (Brisbane, QLD; ☎ 07/3369 8973): The cool deck within earshot of rainbow lorikeets and the warm hospitality from your hostess, Annette Henry, make this gorgeous old Queenslander house decorated with lots of homey touches a truly lovely place to stay. The cute shops and galleries of fashionable Paddington are right outside your door. See chapter 7.

- **Absolute Beachfront B&B** (Cairns, QLD; ☎ 07/4055 6664): Sporting timber and limestone floors, a beachfront dining room, and a pool by the sea, this glamour-puss B&B looks as though it was lifted from the pages of a glossy interior design magazine and set down on the white sandy crescent and swaying palms of Trinity Beach. It's absolute perfection—and guess what? It's only A$80 (U.S.$56) double, A$100 (U.S.$70) if you splurge on the room with the Jacuzzi. See chapter 8.

- **Lilybank Bed & Breakfast** (Cairns, QLD; ☎ 07/4055 1123): Mike and Pat Woolford are charming, fun-loving hosts who know everything there is to know about exploring Cairns and the Reef. Oh, and their house ain't bad either—a 100-year-old timber tropical mansion that used to be the mayor's residence. See chapter 8.

- **The Summer House** (Darwin, NT; ☎ 08/8981 9992): Sleek white rooms adorned with eight-foot-high tropical flower arrangements, hip mosaic bathrooms, and glass-louvered windows at this cool, stylish B&B are the ideal haven from which to explore tropical Darwin. See chapter 10.

- **Miss Maud's Swedish Hotel** (Perth, WA; ☎ 1800/998 022 in Australia, or 08/9325 3900): Staying at this slightly musty hotel in the heart of Perth is like staying at grandma's—even if your grandma's house doesn't have Swedish murals on the walls as this place does. Friendly staff members—who actually look pleased to see you—and great food complete the picture. See chapter 11.

- **Robinson's by the Sea** (Melbourne, VIC; ☎ **03/9534 2683**). If you want something very special, this 1870s heritage B&B just across the road from the beach has a comfortable, antique-filled living room, homey bedrooms, and friendly hosts. See chapter 13.

12 The Best Places to Stay on a Shoestring

- **Sydney Central YHA** (Sydney, NSW; ☎ **02/9281 9111**): One of the biggest, busiest youth hostels in the world, this place has a popular night spot, a bistro selling cheap meals, a convenience store, pool tables, a movie room, a heated swimming pool, and a sauna—all in the center of Sydney. See chapter 4.
- **Holiday Village Backpackers** (Byron Bay, NSW; ☎ **02/6685 8888**): For a bohemian kind of place, Byron Bay is pretty luxurious when it comes to budget accommodations, and this place is about as good as it gets. You can stay in a dorm room if you want, but for a couple of dollars more you can get a fully self-contained unit with a separate bedroom, lounge, and kitchen area. There's also a volleyball court, a spa and pool, and a TV and video lounge with a video library. Cool. See chapter 6.
- **Explorers Inn** (☎ **1800/623 288** in Australia, or 07/3211 3488) and **Hotel George Williams** (☎ **1800/064 858** in Australia, or 07/3308 0700; both in Brisbane, QLD): These two hotels, just around the corner from each other, are shining examples of what cheap hotels should be—trendy, clean, and bright with useful features like electronic keys. See chapter 7.
- **Halse Lodge** (Sunshine Coast, QLD; **1800/242 567** in Australia, or 07/5447 3377): How many backpacker lodges do you know located in Heritage-listed Queenslander houses, with neat private rooms, meals for less than A$7.15 (U.S.$5), a wide verandah with attractive furniture and garden views, an atmospheric bar and courtyard, and free surfboards to use at the (excellent) beach just a stroll away? None? Well, now you know one. See chapter 8.
- **Inn the Tropics** (Cairns, QLD; ☎ **1800/807 055** in Australia, or 07/4031 1088): Cheery private rooms (some with attached bathrooms, a TV, and tea and coffee), a pleasant pool and courtyard, super-clean shared bathrooms, and friendly management make this YWCA property in the heart of Cairns a winner. See chapter 8.
- **Beachcomber Coconut Caravan Village** (Mission Beach, QLD; ☎ **07/ 4068 8129**): Right across the road from what is arguably the prettiest beach in Australia, this oh-so-pretty campground has freshly painted cabins with little balconies, en suite bathrooms, cooking facilities, and even separate bedrooms for you and the kids. Cassowaries wander out of the dense jungle at the back and come right up to you. See chapter 8.
- **The Kimberley Club** (Broome, WA; ☎ **08/9192 3233**): Low-slung Outback architecture, trendy blue walls and yellow curtains in the private rooms, a rustic open-sided bar and restaurant serving great food, and a rock-lined swimming pool make this one of the coolest places to stay in pricey Broome. See chapter 10.
- **Adelaide City Backpackers** (Adelaide, SA; ☎ **08/8212 2668**): This family-owned backpackers place is located in a historic 19th-century, two-story building in a nice area of town (just 2 minutes from the bus station). It offers home-cooked dinners for just A$4 (U.S.$2.80)—included free for your first night's stay! A Sunday evening barbecue will ensure that you meet some new friends. See chapter 12.

• **Toad Hall** (Melbourne, VIC; ☎ **03/9600 9010**): Well-traveled budget travelers consider Toad Hall one of the best places to stay in Australia. The 1858 mansion is an excellent value and centrally located. See chapter 13.

13 The Best Alternative Accommodations

• **Barrington Guest House** (Barrington Tops National Park, NSW; ☎ **02/4995 3212**): You can either stay in the main building of this traditional guest house or in one of 20 new luxury huts in the rain forest—either way, the trails through the rain forest and the abundance of wild animals and birds on your doorstep will make a stay here a memorable experience. See chapter 6.

• **Caves Beach, Jervis Bay** (Bouderee National Park, NSW): If you have access to a tent and a car, then make the 3-hour journey from Sydney and camp out for a night or two at Caves Beach campsite, home to kangaroos and lots of bird life. During the day, lounge around on the whitest beach in the world or hike through the Australian bush daubed in plenty of insect repellent. See chapter 6.

• **Underground Motel** (White Cliffs, NSW; ☎ **1800/021 154** in Australia, or 08/8091 6677): All but two of this motel's rooms are underground in this fascinating opal-mining town. Rooms are reached by a maze of spacious tunnels dug out of the rock. See chapter 6.

• **TENTative Nests** (Kuranda, QLD; ☎ **07/4093 9555**): These six permanent tent "nests" tucked away in exquisite World Heritage rain forest behind Cairns have mattresses, lanterns, table and chairs, and a hammock on the balcony. You meet other ecologically minded guests for gourmet bush tucker meals in an open-sided pole cabin in the jungle, when you're not hiking the trails to spectacular Barron Falls nearby. See chapter 8.

• **Binnaburra Mountain Lodge** (☎ **1800/074 260** in Australia, or 07/5533 3622) and **O'Reilly's Rainforest Guesthouse** (☎ **1800/688 722** in Australia, or 07/5544 0644; both in the Gold Coast Hinterland, QLD): These two retreats, tucked snugly almost 1,000 meters (3,000 feet) up on rain-forested ridges, offer fresh mountain air and instant access to the hiking trails of Lamington National Park, where 2,000-year-old Antarctic beech trees loom up in the mist. If the resorts are too pricey, opt for the safari tents at **Binnaburra Campsite** (☎ **1800/ 074 260** in Australia, or 07/5533 3758), which have wonderful views over the valley. See chapter 8.

• **Emma Gorge Resort** (near Kununurra, WA; ☎ **08/9169 1777**): These cute timber-floored safari tents on one million-acre El Questro Station are almost as comfortable as a hotel room, and the food is darn good, too. An easy hiking trail leads beneath towering red cliffs into the exquisite natural swimming rock pool of Emma Gorge. This is a great and inexpensive place to soak up the Australian wilderness. See chapter 10.

• **Prairie Hotel** (Flinders Ranges, SA; ☎ **08/8648 4895**): This remarkable tin-roofed, stone-walled Outback pub in the Flinders Ranges has quaint rooms, a great bar out front where you can meet the locals, and some of the best food in Australia. See chapter 12.

• **Freycinet Lodge** (Freycinet National Park, Coles Bay, TAS; ☎ **03/6257 0101**): These ecofriendly bush cabins are right next to one of the nation's best walking tracks. The ocean views from the magnificent restaurant and the surrounding balconies are spectacular. This place is definitely worth the splurge. See chapter 16.

14 The Best Worth-a-Splurge Restaurants

- **Mezzaluna** (Sydney, NSW; ☎ **02/9357 1988**): Come here for truly exquisite food, flawless service, and a great view across the city's western skyline. The main dining room opens onto a huge, all-weather terrace kept warm in winter by giant, overhead fan heaters. Don't miss it. See chapter 4.
- **Fishlips Bar & Bistro** (Cairns, QLD; ☎ **07/4041 1700**): Clever ways with fresh seafood and other Aussie ingredients, like crocodile, make this cheerful blue beach house the pick of the bunch in Cairns. Don't miss the homemade ice cream. See chapter 8.
- **Zouí Alto** (Townsville, QLD; ☎ **07/4721 4700**): Townsville is not a place that springs to mind when compiling a "Best Restaurants" list, but this rooftop venue fully deserves to be here for its faultlessly turned-out fare using robust Mediterranean ingredients. The views of Castle Hill on one side and the bay on the other are great. See chapter 8.
- **Nautilus** (Port Douglas, QLD; ☎ **07/4099 5330**): Bill and Hillary Clinton ate at this pretty restaurant outdoors under the trees and the Milky Way during their visit Down Under in November 1996. Fresh seafood gets a modern tropical twist with exotic-sounding fruit and veggies. See chapter 8.
- **The Tree House at Silky Oaks Lodge** (Mossman, QLD; ☎ **07/4098 1666**): What better place to enjoy elegant modern Australian fare than on this open-sided verandah restaurant overhanging the gushing boulder-strewn Mossman River with views into the vines and rain forest? See chapter 8.
- **Fraser's** (Perth, WA; (☎ **08/9481 7100**): The city center and Swan River sparkling in the sunshine seem close enough to touch from the terrace at this parkland restaurant. Superb Mod Oz food turned out with flare and flavor is what you come here for. Go for a bike ride in Kings Park afterward to work off your meal. See chapter 11.
- **Newtown House** (Vasse, near Margaret River, WA; ☎ **08/9755 4485**): Chef Stephen Reagan makes intelligent, flavorsome food that beautifully partners the premium Margaret River wines being made all around him. Stay in his homestead B&B overnight and explore the wineries the next day. See chapter 11.
- **Lamont's** (Swan Valley, near Perth, WA; ☎ **08/9296 4485**): Hearty country fare with lots of sophistication is what this rustic restaurant in the vineyards is all about. It's worth the 20-minute drive from Perth, but if you can't make it, the chef does a mean take-out from her Perth city outlet. See chapter 11.
- **Jolleys Boathouse Restaurant** (Adelaide, SA; ☎ **08/8223 2891**): Situated on the banks of the River Torrens, Jolleys has views of boats, ducks, and black swans from its alfresco dining spots. It's a fabulous place to relax and watch the world float by. See chapter 12.
- **Prairie Hotel** (Flinders Ranges, SA; ☎ **08/8648 4895**): Chef Darren ("Bart") Brooks serves up some very high-class cuisine in the middle of nowhere. His so-called "feral" food dishes—such as kangaroo tail soup and a mixed grill of emu sausages, camel steak, and kangaroo—are remarkable. See chapter 12.
- **The Mirrabook** (Canberra, ACT; ☎ **02/6273 2836**): This unique restaurant is located in the beautiful Sculpture Garden of the National Gallery of Australia. It's perched on a goldfish-filled lake surrounded by sculpture. As you dine, a "fog sculpture"—created by smoke machines on the far side of the lake—rolls across the water toward your table. See chapter 15.
- **Mures Upper Deck** (Hobart, TAS; ☎ **03/6231 2121**): This large and bustling waterfront restaurant offers great views of yachts in the city's colorful harbor,

as well as fine seafood caught on the owner's very own fishing boats. See chapter 16.

15 The Best Dining Bargains

- **Returned Services League (RSL) Clubs:** RSL clubs, or their equivalent, can be found in most cities and towns throughout Australia. Just sign in at the door and you enter a world of cheap drinks at the bar and inexpensive meals at the bistro. You'll probably find a couple of pool or billiards tables too, as well as an atmosphere unique to Australia.
- **Fish-and-Chips:** This quintessentially English staple stowed away with the first convicts to settle Australia and is still alive and well Down Under. This dish is about as unsophisticated as a meal can get, but who cares when it tastes good? They are best done soggy, wrapped in newspaper, and eaten on a beach, any beach, at sunset.
- **The Great Aussie BBQ:** Australian parks are full of public barbecues, often in scenic settings, that are free or cost just a couple of dollars to coin operate. Stock up on meat, veggies, paper plates and plastic glasses, and the cheapest cooking utensils you can buy from the supermarket, and cook yourself up a storm. Hand the utensils on to someone else if you can't be bothered carrying them in your suitcase.
- **Govindas** (Sydney, NSW; ☎ 02/9380 5155): Eat as much as you want at this Hare Krishna vegetarian restaurant in Kings Cross, and then take in a free movie in the theatre upstairs. See chapter 4.
- **No Names** (Sydney, NSW; ☎ 02/9360 4711). Choose between plates of spaghetti, fish, or meats and fill yourself up on the cheap at this Italian-style cafeteria. Just order off the blackboard. Be sure to bring your own wine, or quaff the free fruit cordial drinks. See chapter 4.
- **Bowen Mangoes:** Queensland produces the best mangoes in Australia, and Bowen, a small coastal town between the Whitsundays and Townsville, produces the best mangoes in Queensland. Look for the mangoes in supermarkets. If you are lucky enough to be driving through north Queensland in summer, you might snare some from roadside sellers at a good price: A$3 (U.S.$2.10) per mango is expensive, A$2 (U.S.$1.40) is fine, A$1 (U.S.70¢) is a steal. See chapter 8.
- **The Pioneer Barbecue and Bar** (Ayers Rock Resort, NT; ☎ 1800/089 622 in Australia, or 08/8956 2170): Forget the mostly expensive restaurants at Ayers Rock Resort and join the happy crowds at this rollicking bar-cum-shearer's mess. Throw your shrimp, steak, or emu sausage on the barbie yourself, order a beer or two, and you're still looking at a tab of less than A$28.60 (U.S.$20). See chapter 9.
- **A Picnic on the Grounds of the Old Telegraph Station** (Alice Springs, NT): What could be more enjoyable (and affordable) than an alfresco spread at the serene grounds of this historic site. You'll be surrounded by river red gums, green lawns, and a few historic cottages. Admission to the picnic grounds is free. See chapter 9.
- **Mindil Beach Markets** (Darwin, NT): Every Thursday night between May and October, thousands of Darwin folk pack wine and beach blankets and flock to this city beach to feast at food stalls from every Asian cuisine you can name, and a few you can't. Eat Vietnamese, Cambodian, Singaporean, Malaysian, Indonesian, and more, and then shop the 200 arts-and-crafts stalls, get a Chinese head massage, or have your tarot cards read. See chapter 10.

- **North Cott Express Café** (Perth, WA; ☎ **08/9385 0338**): The terrific sea views are free at this modest beach shack. Don't expect anything fancy—you sit at plastic tables and chairs—but the cafe-style food is unexpectedly good. If you find the atmosphere too casual, head next door to the more upscale Blue Duck, or wander down the street to the groovy Indiana Tea House, where coffee and pastries won't cost the earth. See chapter 11.
- **Queen Victoria Market** (Melbourne, VIC): These markets are the heart of this vibrant city, and there's nowhere better to pick up a satisfying snack. The pizzas on sale at Café Bianca are some of the best in Australia, and there are plenty of stalls selling fresh bread and deli produce for a sandwich to take away. See chapter 13.
- **Chinatown** (Melbourne, VIC): Head to this colorful part of town, centered on Little Bourke Street, for super-cheap ethnic eats. You'll be hard-pressed to find a lunch costing more than A$5 (U.S.$3.50). This is where the locals go, so you know it's got be good (and authentic). See chapter 13.

Introducing Oz 2

by Marc Llewellyn

The land "Down Under" is a modern nation coming to terms with its identity. The umbilical cord with mother England has been cut, and the nation is still trying to find its position within Asia. One thing it realized early on, though, was the importance of tourism to its economy. Millions of visitors flock to Australia every year; after all it has some of the biggest tourist icons in the world—you won't find a building like the Sydney Opera House anywhere but Sydney, you certainly can't find a coral reef the size of the Great Barrier Reef anywhere else, and Ayers Rock in the Red Center is as Australian as the didgeridoo.

It doesn't have to cost the earth either. Once you've paid for your airfare, things settle down in terms of price. With Australia's low-cost lodging options, cheap coach and train fares, and good quality food that won't break the bank, you can easily get around and still keep to a limited budget. Indeed, you probably won't find a country anywhere so geared toward keeping the independent tourist happy. After all, tourism is Australia's biggest export, and the independent traveler is the most valued of all visitors—there are more of them, they stay longer, they spend more than people in a group, and they spread that money more evenly throughout the community.

As Sydney and Australia gear up for the Sydney 2000 Olympic Games, the emphasis on promoting tourism—and ensuring that everyone has a fabulous and safe time while traveling through this huge continent—is at the forefront of everyone's mind. You'll find Aussies generally impressively helpful and friendly; and services, tours, and food and drink the rival of any in the world. And then, of course, there's the landscape, the native Australian culture, the sunshine, the animals, and some of the world's best cities—what more could you ask for? Or, more to the point, what are you waiting for?

Whether you are planning a week's visit or an extensive road trip, this chapter will give you a taste of what to expect before you leave home and once you arrive.

1 The Regions in Brief

People who have never visited Australia always wonder why such a huge country has a population of just 18 million people. The truth is, Australia can barely support that many. The vast majority of Australia is harsh **Outback** country, characterized by salt bush plains, arid

Australia

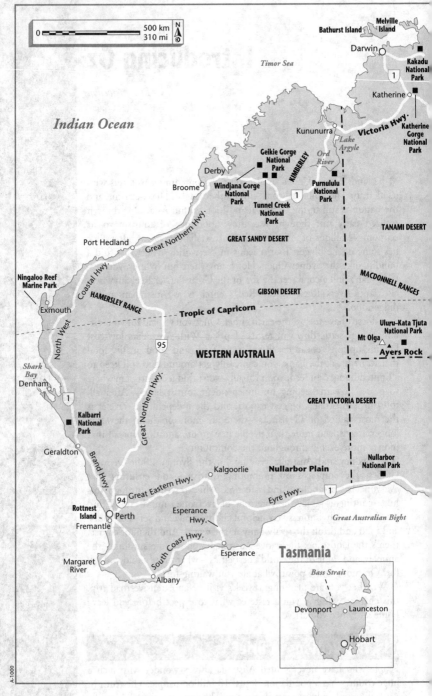

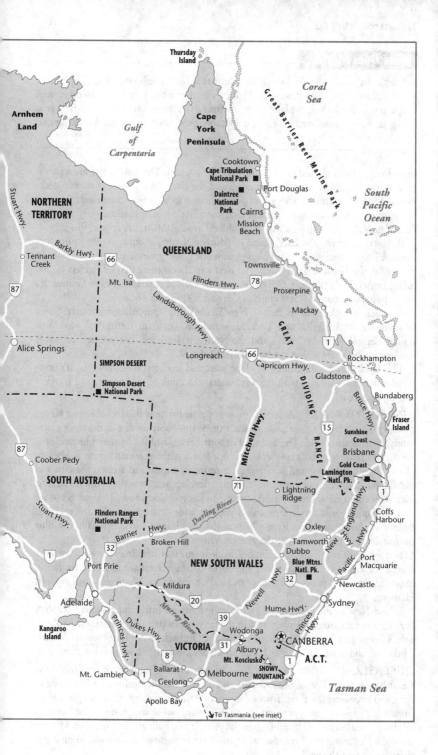

Size Does Matter

People are often surprised when they hear that both Melbourne and Brisbane are more than a long day's drive from Sydney, and that it takes three days to drive from Sydney to Perth. When planning your itinerary, keep in mind that Australia is as big as the whole of western Europe and about the same size as the 48 contiguous U.S. states.

brown crags, shifting sand deserts, and salt lake country. The soil for the most part is poor in the Outback; it hardly ever rains, and the rivers barely make it to the ocean. Nearly 90% of Australia's 18 million people live in an area that covers only 2.6% of the continent. Climatic and physical land conditions ensure that the only relatively decent rainfall occurs along a thin strip of land around Australia's coastal fringe.

If Australia knows the harsh hand of Mother Nature, though, it also knows her bounty. The Queensland coast is blessed with one of the greatest natural attractions in the world: the **Great Barrier Reef.** The Reef stretches some 2,000 kilometers (1,200 miles) from off Gladstone in Queensland, to the Gulf of Papua, near New Guinea. It's home to approximately 1,500 kinds of fish and 400 species of corals.

Australia is made up of six states—New South Wales, Queensland, Victoria, South Australia, West Australia, and Tasmania—and two internal "territories"—the Australian Capital Territory (ACT) and the Northern Territory. The political capital is Canberra, which lies within the boundaries of the ACT.

This book isn't organized strictly along state and territory lines, however. It's organized more in accordance with the way Australians think of the country and travelers will experience it.

NEW SOUTH WALES   Australia's most populated state is also the one most visited by tourists. Principally they come to see Sydney, undoubtedly one of the most glamorous cities in the world. The Sydney Harbour Bridge and the Sydney Opera House are major drawing cards of course, but no one leaves without remarking on the beauty of the dozens of harbor and ocean beaches scattered within and around the city, and the dramatic mixture of bushland and city development around Sydney Harbour itself. You could easily spend months getting to know Sydney, and you won't get to see all the major tourist attractions unless you set aside at least a week for exploring. Sydney is also a good base from which to discover inland areas, especially the Blue Mountains and the wineries of the Hunter Valley.

Farther afield is a string of quaint beachside towns that stretch all the way down the southern coast into Victoria. Along the north coast are remnant areas of rain forest, impressive national parks, and a more tropical air, in laid-back hangouts such as Coffs Harbour.

Inland New South Wales is dry and sparsely forested. Intriguing regions to explore here are the area around Broken Hill in the far western part of the state, for its abundant wildlife and Aboriginal influences, and the Outback opal-mining towns of White Cliffs and Lightning Ridge, which exist in a wacky, underground world of their own.

QUEENSLAND   Without a doubt, the biggest drawing card in Queensland is the Great Barrier Reef. Coming to Australia and not visiting the Reef is a bit like going to Paris and bypassing the Eiffel Tower. Anywhere from Bundaberg north is a good place from which to explore it. Ogling the tropical fish, weird sea creatures, and endless rainbow-hued corals will be a highlight of your Aussie holiday. Alluring island resorts are dotted all along the Reef, and while most are expensive, we clue you in on a few that won't break the bank.

Aside from the Reef, Queensland is also known for its numerous white-sand beaches. The best are on the Gold Coast in the state's south, and the Sunshine Coast has some lovely ones, too. Cairns and Port Douglas in the north have more than their fair share of beaches, too, but unfortunately, deadly box jellyfish call a halt to all ocean swimming from October to May anywhere north of Gladstone. Queensland has yet another aquatic playground—the 74 tropical Whitsunday Islands. These mostly uninhabited islands are a paradise for water sports, sea kayaking, diving, fishing, hiking through rain forest, and, best of all, sailing.

Away from the coast, the biggest attraction in the state is the lush 110-million-year-old Daintree Rain Forest, just north of Port Douglas. The capital, Brisbane, has Australia's largest koala sanctuary.

THE RED CENTRE   The eerie silence of Uluru, more commonly known as Ayers Rock, is what pulls everyone to the sprawling crimson sands of the Red Centre, the heart of the Northern Territory. Most folks discover that they like a nearby giant pebble even more—the towering domes of Kata Tjuta, also known as the Olgas. A half-day's drive from the Rock brings you to Kings Canyon, a sheer orange desert gorge popular with hikers. If you visit the Red Centre, try to schedule some time in Alice Springs. This laid-back Outback town has the best Aboriginal arts-and-crafts shopping in Australia, some fun Aboriginal tours, a good desert wildlife park, wonderful scenery, a little local history to explore, hikes through the stark MacDonnell Ranges, and, of all things, camel rides down a dry river bed.

Don't make the common mistake of flying into the Rock one day and flying out the next. Give yourself time to soak up the timeless peace of the Aussie desert. One of the best ways to appreciate the Red Centre is on a 3-day 4WD safari, where you camp out under the Southern Cross and cook around a campfire.

THE TOP END   The northwest reaches of Oz, from the dramatic Kimberley in Western Australia to the northern third of the Northern Territory, encompasses what Aussies eloquently dub "the Top End." This is Mick "Crocodile" Dundee territory, a remote, vast, hot semidesert region where men are heroes and cows probably outnumber the people. Near Darwin, the state's capital, is Kakadu National Park, where you can cruise past crocodiles on inland billabongs, bird-watch, and visit ancient Aboriginal rock art sites. Even closer to Darwin is Litchfield National Park, where you can take a dip in fern-fringed water holes surrounded by majestic red cliffs—stuff straight from Eden. You can cruise the orange walls of Katherine Gorge, a few hours south of Darwin, or explore them by canoe. You can even make your own dot painting at an Aboriginal community near Katherine.

In the Western Australia–section of the Top End, you can visit age-old Geikie and Windjana Gorges, pearl farms where the world's best South Sea pearls grow, and the

Impressions

> *I love a sunburnt country,*
> *A land of sweeping plains,*
> *Of ragged mountain ranges,*
> *Of drought and flooding rains.*
> *I love her far horizons, I love her jewel sea,*
> *Her beauty and her terror—*
> *The wide brown land for me!*

—Dorothy Mackellar, *"My Country"* (1911)

charming—in a corrugated-iron sort of way—city of Broome. This tract of the country is so remote and wild that most Aussies think of it almost as a foreign land. Near Kununurra, on the eastern edge of the Kimberley, is a 1-million-acre cattle station, El Questro, where you can camp in comfy safari tents, fish for barramundi, hike through the bush to Aboriginal rock art, and dine every night on terrific modern Oz cuisine. In Kununurra you can cruise on the bird-rich and croc-infested Ord River and tour the Argyle Diamond Mine, the world's biggest.

WESTERN AUSTRALIA   One of the least visited states (largely because airfares are so expensive), Western Australia is also the state with the most untamed natural beauty. The seas here team with whales, and thrill-seekers can swim alongside gentle giant whale sharks on the Northwest Cape every April. Snorkelers gawk at corals and fish on Rottnest Island, 19 kilometers (11½ miles) off Perth; and on the 260-kilometer (156-mile) Ningaloo Reef on the Northwest Cape, tourists greet wild dolphins at Monkey Mia.

In the southwest hook of the continent lies the Margaret River wine region. Its wild forests, thundering surf, dramatic cliffs, rich bird life and wild 'roos make it one of the country's most attractive wine regions. The state's capital, Perth, is one of the most interesting cities to visit in Australia, especially for its beaches and its wonderfully restored 19th-century port of Fremantle. An hour or two's drive from the city brings you to some lovely towns, such as charming York, the state's oldest inland settlement, and the monastery town of New Norcia. Inland, the state is mostly wheat fields and desert, but if you have the time and inclination, head west 600 kilometers (360 miles) from Perth to the gold-mining boomtown of Kalgoorlie. With its gracious old pubs lining the wide, bustling streets, it's just like what you think the perfect Aussie country town should be.

SOUTH AUSTRALIA   Stretched out between Western Australia and Victoria is the nation's breadbasket: South Australia. The capital, Adelaide, is a stately affair known for its conservatism, parks, and churches. It's a delightful stopover, offering some magnificent accommodation options, and it's the base for exploring the giant water-bird sanctuary called the Coorong—the south's version of Kakadu. The other big attraction is the South Australian Outback, where you can stay in an underground hotel in the offbeat opal-mining town of Coober Pedy, or ride a camel through the craggy, ancient arid lands of the Flinders Ranges.

But the greatest of South Australia's attractions is Kangaroo Island, likely the best place in Australia to see native animals. In a single day—with the right guide—you can spot wallabies, rare birds, sea eagles, echidnas, seals, penguins, and even walk along a beach loaded with sea lions. It's a must-see.

VICTORIA   Australia's second largest city, Melbourne, is the capital of Victoria. Melbourne is far more stately than Sydney (in terms of being more Old World rather than Californian) and offers an exciting mix of ethnicity and fashion. Around Melbourne there's plenty to see and to do, too, including Phillip Island, world famous for its Penguin Parade, where hundreds of tiny penguins dash up the beach to their burrows at dusk and the historic gold-mining city of Ballarat. Victoria is also the site of one of Australia's greatest road trips, which stretches for some 106 kilometers (63½ miles) along some of the most scenic coastline you will ever experience. Then there's the inland, which in Victoria is mostly high country, the stuff of legends, à la *The Man from Snowy River*. The skiing's pretty good around here as well, if you're visiting during the Down Under winter.

AUSTRALIAN CAPITAL TERRITORY (ACT)   Surrounded entirely by New South Wales is the tiny Australian Capital Territory. The ACT is made up of bushland

and the nation's capital, Canberra, an architecturally orchestrated city very similar in concept to Washington, D.C. As the capital, Canberra has the country's best museums, although many outsiders consider it rather boring. It could surprise you, though, so don't automatically exclude it from your itinerary.

TASMANIA   Finally, there's the last port before Antarctica, Hobart: capital of the island state of Tasmania. Visit the Apple Isle for its beautiful national parks, enormous stretches of wilderness, the world's best trout fishing, and a relaxed pace of life rarely experienced anywhere else. If you're up to it, you could tackle the most well-known hiking trail in Australia, the Overland Track, an 85-kilometer (51-mile) route between Cradle Mountain and Lake St. Clair that passes through highland moors and dense rain forests and traverses several mountains. Another option is a more leisurely visit to Port Arthur, Australia's version of Devil's Island, where thousands of convicts brought in to settle the new British colony were imprisoned and died. All of Tasmania is spectacular, but you haven't seen anything until you've experienced Freycinet National Park, with its pink granite outcrops set against an emerald-green sea.

2 The People of Oz

It's generally believed that more races live in Australia at the present time than anywhere else in the world, including America. Eighteen million people, from some 165 nations, make the country their home. In general, relations between the different ethnic groups have been peaceful. Australia is a shining example of a multicultural society, despite an increasingly vocal minority that believes Australia has come too far in welcoming people from races other than their own.

ABORIGINAL AUSTRALIA   When Captain James Cook landed at Botany Bay in 1770 determined to claim the land he surveyed for the British Empire, at least 300,000 Aborigines were already living on the continent. Whether you consider as true a version of history that suggests the Aboriginal people were descendants of migrants from Indonesia to the north, or the Aboriginal belief that they have occupied Australia since the beginning of time, there is scientific evidence that people were using fire for cooking in present-day New South Wales at least 120,000 years ago.

At the time of the white invasion of their lands, there were in Australia at least 600 different largely nomadic tribal communities, each linked to their ancestral land by *sacred sites* (certain features of the land, such as hills or rock formations). They were hunter-gatherers, spending about 20 hours a week harvesting the resources of the land, rivers, and the ocean. Much of the rest of the time was taken up by a complex social and belief system, as well as the practicalities of life, such as making utensils, weapons, and unique musical instruments such as didgeridoos and clapsticks.

The basis of Aboriginal spirituality rests in the **Dreamtime** stories, in which everything, including the land, stars, mountains, the moon, the sun, the oceans, water holes, and both animals and humans, were created by spirits. Much Aboriginal art is related to the land and the sacred sites where the Dreamtime spirits reside. Some Aboriginal groups believe these spirits came in giant human form, others believe they were animals, still others believe they were huge snakes. Some even believe in a single Western God–like figure. According to Aboriginal custom, individuals can draw on the power of the Dreamtime spirits by reenacting various stories and practicing certain ceremonies.

Dream On: Aboriginal Art in Australia

The first works of art in Australia may not have been created by the Aborigines, as is commonly believed. Ancient, strange-looking stick figures, totally dissimilar to the Aboriginal cave paintings that are often found on rock overhangs across the country, were discovered in Western Australia. Although we'll probably never know who painted these, we know a fair bit about what remains of age-old Aboriginal artistic creations. Aborigines used natural pigments produced from charcoal, clays, plants, and ochre from iron ore to create their artwork. Often they would spray paint from their mouths over their hands to leave a stencil mark on a wall face—the painting would show that they belonged to that land. Some paintings told stories of the Dreamtime, some marked sacred places, and others were used as maps to show what animals were around and where the water holes were. Aborigines also used quartz to chip at rocks, forming picture engravings, some of which survive to this day.

Most of the best rock art is in the north and central districts of the country. Kakadu National Park (see chapter 10) has some of the best rock art sites in Australia. Only a few of the more than 5,000 sites scattered across the park's 4.3 million acres are open to the public, but what sites they are! One of the best is the striped Dreamtime figure of Namarrgon, the "Lightning Man," at Nourlangie. It sits alongside distinctive X-ray-style paintings of animals and fish—an art form that was first practiced in this region of Australia.

The Kimberley region (see chapter 10) is renowned for "Wandjina" art, which features large figures with halo-like hairdos. Even more mysterious in this part of Australia, though, are the "Bradshaw" figures—long, thin figures in a style very different from other Aboriginal art. The El Questro Station has many rock art sites open to visitors across its 1 million acres.

On a walk around Uluru (Ayers Rock) in the Red Centre (see chapter 9), you will discover rock art in caves and overhangs. At N'Dhala Gorge Nature Park, a couple of hours' drive east of Alice Springs, are up to 6,000 Aboriginal rock carvings, some of which you can explore via a 1.5-kilometer (1-mile) signposted trail. In our time, Aboriginal people have taken to portraying their inner life and tribal land maps on canvas. Many of the best paintings cost a fortune and are sold to collectors from all over the world.

Aboriginal groups had encountered people from other lands before the British arrived. Dutch records from 1451 show that the Macassans, from islands now belonging to Indonesia, had a long relationship trading Dutch glass, smoking pipes, and liqueur for edible sea slugs from Australia's northern coastal waters, which they sold to the Chinese in the Canton markets. Dutch, Portuguese, French, and Chinese vessels also encountered Australia—with the Dutch fashion for pointy beards catching on through northern Australia long before the invasion of 1770.

When the British came, they brought with them diseases that the Aborigines had never encountered, and thus had no natural defenses against. Entire coastal communities were virtually wiped out by smallpox. Even as late as the 1950s, large numbers of Aborigines in remote regions of South Australia and the Northern Territory succumbed to deadly influenza and measles outbreaks.

Although it seems relationships were initially peaceful between the settlers and local Aborigines, conflicts over land and food soon led to skirmishes in which Aborigines were massacred and settlers and convicts turned on—even the colony's first governor, Arthur Phillip, who had been the commander of the First Fleet, was speared in the back by an Aborigine in 1790.

Within a few years, some 10,000 Aborigines and 1,000 Europeans were killed in Queensland alone, while in Tasmania a campaign to rid the island entirely of local Aborigines was ultimately successful. By the turn of the century it was widely thought that the Aboriginal people were a race doomed for extinction. Most of those left alive were living in government-owned reserves or Church-controlled missions.

Massacres of Aborigines continued to go largely or wholly unpunished into the 1920s, by which time it became official government policy to remove light-skinned Aboriginal children from their families and to forcibly sterilize young women. Many children of this stolen generation were brought up in white foster homes or church refuges and were never reunited with their parents.

Today, there are some 283,000 Aborigines living in Australia, and the great divide still exists between them and the rest of the population. Aboriginal life expectancy is up to 20 times lower than that of other Australians, with overall death rates between two and four times higher. A far higher percentage of Aboriginal people than other Australians fill Australian prisons, and despite a Royal Commission into Aboriginal Deaths in Custody, Aborigines continue to die while incarcerated.

A landmark in Aboriginal affairs occurred in 1992 when the High Court determined that Australia was not an empty land (*terra nullius*) as it had been seen officially since the British invasion. The "Mabo" decision resulted in the 1993 Native Title Act, which allowed Aboriginal groups, and the ethnically distinct people living in the Torres Strait islands off northern Queensland, to claim government-owned land if they could prove continual association with it since 1788. The later "Wik" decision determined that Aborigines could make claims on Government land leased to agriculturists.

At the time this book went to press, the federal government curtailed these rights following pressure from powerful farming and mining interests. In response, Aboriginal groups were threatening major demonstrations during the Sydney 2000 Olympic Games.

THE REST OF AUSTRALIA   "White Australia" was the term always used to distinguish the Anglo-Saxon population from that of the Aboriginal population. These days, though, a walk through any of the major cities would show that things have changed dramatically. On average, around 100,000 people emigrate to Australia each year. Of these, approximately 12% were born in the U.K. or Ireland; 11% in New Zealand; and more than 21% in China, Hong Kong, Vietnam, or the Phillipines. Waves of immigration have brought in millions of people since the end of World War II. At the last census, in 1996, for example, more than a quarter of a million Australia residents were born in Italy, some 186,000 in the former Yugoslavia, 144,000 in Greece, 118,000 in Germany, and 103,000 in China. So what's the typical Australian like? Well, it's hardly Crocodile Dundee.

If it's fair enough to judge a society by its values, then in broad terms Australian society evokes certain principles. For one, it's part of the Australian psyche to believe in a "fair go"—in other words, an unhindered right to be oneself. Another principle adhered to is "mateship," a particularly male phenomenon born no doubt from days spent struggling against the elements of a hostile new country, laboring together as convicts, fighting at Gallipoli and in the trenches during World War I, and reinforced by sports—rugby league and Aussie Rules Football, in particular—and booze ups down at the local pub as adolescents.

Impressions

If you want to know what it is like to feel the "correct" social world fizzle into nothing, you should come to Australia. It is a weird place. In the established sense it is socially nil. Happy-go-lucky, don't-you-bother, we're-in-Australia. But also there seems to be no inside life of any sort: just a long lapse and a drift . . . It really is a weird show. The country has an extraordinary hoary, weird attraction. As you get used to it, it seems so old, as if it had missed all this Semite-Egyptian-Indo-European vast area of history, and was a coal age, the age of great ferns, and mosses.

—D. H. Lawrence, 1922.

One Japanese guidebook shows its version of the average Australian male in a photograph. There, naked to the waist, is an overweight, pink-fleshed Aussie, resting a glass of Fosters on the upswell of his beer belly. Rather unfair I thought—what about all those pumped up Bondi lifeguards? Don't they deserve a stake in the running for the Aussie cliché? The average Australian woman is often portrayed as carefree and topless on Bondi Beach—a "surf chick" grown brown and brazen with the sun. Don't believe any of it. The average Australian doesn't exist—although it's fair to say, as a whole, that most don't bite.

3 History 101

Dateline

- **120,000 B.C.** Evidence suggests Aborigines living in Australia.
- **60,000 B.C.** Aborigines living in Arnham Land in the far north fashion stone tools.
- **24,500 B.C.** The world's oldest known ritual cremation takes place at Lake Mungo.
- **1606 A.D.** Dutch explorer Willem Jansz lands on the far north coast of Van Diemen's Land (Tasmania).
- **1622** First English ship to reach Australia wrecks on the west coast.
- **1642** Abel Tasman charts the Tasmanian coast.
- **1688** Englishman William Dampier lands at Shark Bay in Western Australia.
- **1770** Capt. James Cook lands at Botany Bay.
- **1787** Capt. Arthur Phillip's First Fleet leaves England with convicts aboard.

continues

IN THE BEGINNING In the beginning there was The Dreamtime—at least according to the Aborigines of Australia. Between then and now, perhaps, the supercontinent referred to as Pangaea split into two huge continents called Laurasia and Gondwanaland. Over millions of years continental drift carried the landmasses apart. Laurasia gradually broke up and formed North America, Europe, and most of Asia. Meanwhile, Gondwanaland divided into South America, Africa, India, Australia and New Guinea, and Antarctica. Giant marsupials evolved to roam the continent of Australia: Among them were a plant-eating animal that looked like a wombat the size of a rhinoceros, a giant squashed-face kangaroo standing three meters (10 feet) high, a giant wombat the size of a donkey, and a flightless bird the same size as an emu, but four times heavier. The last of these giant marsupials are believed to have died out some 40,000 years ago.

EARLY EXPLORERS The existence of Australia had been in the minds of Europeans since about A.D. 150, when the Ancient Greek astronomer, Ptolemy, drew a map of the world showing a large land mass in the south, which he believed had to be there to balance out the land in the northern hemisphere. He called it *Terra Australia Incognita*—the unknown south land.

There's evidence to suggest that Portuguese ships reached Australia at least as early as 1536 and even charted part of its coastline. In 1606 William Jansz was sent by the Dutch East India Company to open up a new route to the spice islands, and to find New Guinea, which was supposed to be rich in gold. He landed on the north coast of Queensland, and fought with local Aborigines. Between 1616 and 1640, many more Dutch ships made contact with Australia as they hugged the west coast of what they called "New Holland," after sailing with the westerlies from the Cape of Good Hope.

In 1642 the Dutch East India Company, through the Governor General of the Indies, Anthony Van Diemen, sent Abel Tasman to search out and map the great south land. During two voyages he charted the northern Australian coastline and discovered Tasmania, which he named Van Diemen's Land after the Governor General.

THE ARRIVAL OF THE BRITISH—In 1697 the English pirate William Dampier published a book about his adventures. In it he mentions Shark Beach on the northwest coast of Australia as the place the pirate ship he sailed on made its repairs after robbing ships on the Pacific Ocean. The king of England was so impressed with Dampier that he sent him back to Australia to find out more. On his return, Dampier reported that he found little to recommend.

Captain James Cook turned up more than 70 years later, in 1770, and charted the whole east coast, claiming it for Britain and naming it New South Wales. On the 29th of April, Cook landed at Botany Bay, which he named after the plant-collecting expedition led by ship's botanist Joseph Banks. Back in Britain, King George III was convinced Australia could make a good colony. It would also help reduce Britain's overflowing prison population, caused by the refusal of the new United States of America to take any more transported British convicts following the War of Independence.

In May 1787 the First Fleet, led by Arthur Phillip and made up of 11 store and transport ships, left England. (It's interesting to note that none of these ships was bigger than the regular passenger ferries that ply modern-day Sydney Harbour from Circular Quay to Manly.) Aboard were 1,480 people, including 759 convicts. Phillip's flagship, *The Supply*, reached Botany Bay in January 1788, but Phillip decided the soil was poor and the surrounds too swampy. On January 26th, now celebrated as Australia Day, he settled for Port Jackson (Sydney Harbour) instead.

- **1788** Captain Phillip raises British flag at Port Jackson (Sydney Harbour).
- **1788–1868** Convicts are transported from England to the colony of Australia.
- **1793** The first free settlers arrive.
- **1813** Explorers Blaxland, Wentworth, and Lawson cross the Blue Mountains.
- **1830** Governor Arthur lines up 5,000 settlers across Van Diemen's Land to walk the length of the island to capture and rid it of all Aborigines.
- **1841** Explorer Edward Eyre travels overland from Adelaide to Perth.
- **1850** Gold discovered in Bathurst, New South Wales.
- **1852** Gold rush begins in Ballarat, Victoria.
- **1853** The last convict arrives in Van Diemen's Land; to celebrate, the colony is renamed Tasmania, after Abel Tasman.
- **1860** The white population of Australia jumps to more than one million.
- **1861** Explorer John Stuart travels overland from Adelaide to Northern Territory coast.
- **1861** Explorers Burke and Wills perish at Coopers Creek.
- **1872** England and Australia exchange their first telephone call.
- **1875** Silver found at Broken Hill, New South Wales.
- **1880** Bushranger Ned Kelly hanged.
- **1886** The Duke of Edinburgh wounded by a shot in the back in Sydney.
- **1892** Massive gold reef found at Kalgoorlie, Western Australia.
- **1895** Banjo Patterson's *The Man from Snowy River* published.

continues

- **1889** Australian troops fight in the Boer War in South Africa.
- **1901** The six states join together to become the Commonwealth of Australia.
- **1902** Women gain the right to vote.
- **1908** Canberra is chosen as the site of the federal capital.
- **1911** Australian (non-Aboriginal) population reaches 4,455,005.
- **1915** Australian and New Zealand troops massacred at Gallipoli.
- **1920** Qantas airline founded.
- **1923** Police strike in Victoria leads to mass rioting in Melbourne.
- **1927** Federal capital is moved from Melbourne to Canberra.
- **1931** First airmail letters are delivered to England by Charles Kingsford Smith and Charles Ulm.
- **1931** The Arnham Land Aboriginal Reserve is proclaimed.
- **1932** The Sydney Harbour Bridge opens.
- **1942** Darwin bombed, and Japanese minisubmarines found in Sydney Harbour.
- **1942** Australian volunteers hold back Japanese invasion of New Guinea on the Kokoda Trail—Australia's Alamo.
- **1950** Australian troops fight alongside Americans in Korea.
- **1953** British nuclear tests at Emu in South Australia lead to a radioactive cloud killing and injuring many Aborigines.
- **1956** Olympic Games held in Melbourne.
- **1957** British atomic tests conducted at Maralinga, South Australia. Aborigines again affected by radiation.

SETTLING DOWN The convicts were immediately put to work clearing land, planting crops, and constructing buildings. The early food harvests were failures, and by early 1790 the fledgling colony was facing starvation.

Phillip decided to give some convicts pardons if they were good and worked hard, and even grant small land parcels to those who were really industrious. In 1795 coal was discovered; in 1810 Governor Macquarie began extensive city-building projects; and in 1813 the explorers Gregory Blaxland, William Charles Wentworth, and William Lawson forged a passage over the Blue Mountains to the fertile plains beyond.

When gold was discovered in Victoria in 1852, and in Western Australia 12 years later, hundreds of thousands of immigrants from Europe, America, and China flooded into the country in search of their fortunes. By 1860 more than a million non-Aboriginal people were living in Australia.

The last 10,000 convicts were transported to Western Australia between 1850 and 1868, bringing the total shipped out to Australia to 168,000.

FEDERATION & THE GREAT WARS On January 1, 1901, the six states that made up Australia proclaimed themselves to be part of one nation, and the Commonwealth of Australia was formed. In the same ceremony the first Governor General was sworn in as the representative of the Queen, who remained head of state. In 1914 Australia joined the mother country in war. In April of the following year, the Australian and New Zealand Army Corps (ANZAC) formed a beachhead on the peninsula of Gallipoli in Turkey. The Turkish troops had been prewarned, and eight months of fighting ended with 8,587 Australians dead and more than 19,000 wounded.

Australians were fighting again in World War II, this time in North Africa, Greece, and the Middle East. In March 1942 Japanese aircraft bombed Broome in Western Australia and Darwin in the Northern Territory. In May of that year Japanese midget submarines entered Sydney Harbour and torpedoed a ferry before being destroyed. Later that year Australian volunteers waged a fighting retreat through the jungles of Papua New Guinea on the Kokoda Trail against superior Japanese forces. Australian troops fought alongside Americans in subsequent wars in Korea and Vietnam and sent military support to the Persian Gulf conflicts.

continues

RECENT TIMES   Following World War II, mass immigration to Australia, primarily from Europe, boosted the population. In 1974 the left-of-center Whitlam government put an end to the White Australia policy that had largely restricted black and Asian immigration since 1901. In 1986 the official umbilical cord to Britain was cut when the Australian Constitution was separated from that of the motherland. Australia had begun the march to complete independence.

In 1992 the High Court handed down the "Mabo" decision, which ruled that Aborigines had a right to claim government-owned land if they could prove a continued connection with it. The following year, huge crowds filled Sydney's Circular Quay to hear that the city had won the 2000 Olympic Games. In 1998 debate began to rage over continued Asian immigration, Aboriginal land claims, restrictive gun laws (following a 1996 massacre in which gunman Martin Bryant killed 35 people in Port Arthur, Tasmania), and a feeling among parts of the community that the government was ignoring the electorate. As the world looked on with concern at the events unfolding in Australia, a new right-wing political party, called One Nation, began to make stunning electoral gains. The party won more than 10% of the vote in Queensland during the 1998 general election, in which the Liberal/National Party Coalition was returned, with John Howard as Prime Minister. We shall see what is in store for the "lucky country."

4 Aussie Eats & Drinks

THE EATS

It took a long time for the average Australian to realize there was more to food than English-style sausage and mashed potatoes, "meat and three veg," lamb chops, and a good old Sunday roast. It wasn't so long ago that spaghetti was something foreigners ate, and zucchini and eggplant were considered exotic vegetables. Then came mass immigration, and with it all sorts of foods that people had only read about in *National Geographic.*

The first big wave of Italian immigrants in the 1950s caused a national scandal. The great Aussie dream was to have a quarter-acre block of land with a Hills Hoist (one of those circular revolving clothesline implements) in the backyard. When the Italians started hanging their freshly made pasta out to dry

- **1962** Commonwealth government gives Aborigines the right to vote.
- **1965** Australian troops start fighting in Vietnam.
- **1967** Aborigines granted Australian citizenship and counted in census.
- **1968** Australia's population passes 12 million following heavy immigration.
- **1971** Australia pulls out of Vietnam following mass demonstrations the previous year.
- **1971** The black, red, and yellow Aboriginal flag flown for the first time.
- **1972** White Australia policy formally ended.
- **1972** Aboriginal Tent Embassy erected outside Parliament House in Canberra.
- **1973** The Sydney Opera House completed.
- **1974** Cyclone Tracy devastates Darwin.
- **1976** The Aboriginal Land Rights (Northern Territory) Act gives some land back to native people.
- **1983** Ayres Rock given back to local Aborigines, who rename it Uluru.
- **1983** Australia wins the Americas Cup, ending 112 years of American domination of the event.
- **1984** "Advance Australia Fair" made Australian national anthem following referendum.
- **1986** Queen Elizabeth II severs the Australian Constitution from Great Britain's.
- **1988** Aborigines demonstrate as Australia celebrates its Bicentennial with a reenactment of the First Fleet's entry into Sydney Harbour.
- **1991** Australia's population reaches 17 million.

continues

- **1993** Sydney chosen as the site of 2000 Olympic Games.
- **1994** High Court "Mabo" decision overturns the principle of *Terra Nullius,* which suggested Australia was unoccupied at time of white settlement.
- **1995** Australians protest as France explodes nuclear weapons in the South Pacific.
- **1996** Severe bushfires destroy many national parks, and charcoal leaves rain down across Sydney.
- **1996** Gunman Martin Bryant kills 35 people in Port Arthur, Tasmania.
- **1996** High Court hands down "Wik" decision, which allows Aborigines the right to claim some Commonwealth land.
- **1998** Prime Minister John Howard attempts to reverse Wik decision in favor of lease-holding pastoralists.
- **1998** The right-wing One Nation Party, led by former fish-and-chip shop owner Pauline Hanson, holds the balance of power in Queensland elections on a platform of antiimmigration and anti-Aboriginal policies

on this Aussie icon, it caused a national uproar, and more than a few clamored for the new arrivals to be shipped back home. As Australia matured, Southern European cuisine became increasingly popular, until olive oil was greasing frying pans the way only lard had previously done.

The 1970s brought the great Aussie barbecue into fashion. (It was during this time that rising comedian Paul Hogan—later of *Crocodile Dundee* fame—uttered the immortal phrase "throw another shrimp on the barbie.") In the 1980s, everything was turned on its head again, this time as waves of Asian immigrants hit Australia's shores. Suddenly, everyone was cooking with woks, and newly discovered spices and herbs were causing a sensation at dinner parties across the land. These days, this fusion of flavors and styles has melded into what's commonly referred to as Modern Australian, or Mod Oz—a distinctive cuisine blending the spices of the East with the flavors of the West.

Aboriginal people, of course, have been living off the land for tens of thousands of years, but it was only recently that Australian restaurateurs began looking into the possibilities of native foods (bush tucker). See the box below for an introduction to the most common bush tucker. Kangaroo is now a common sight on menus around the country, with wallaby, emu, and crocodile also making regular appearances. Native berries and nuts, such as the *quandong* (a tart-tasting fruit the size of a grape) and the now world-famous macadamia nut, commonly find their way into new wave Australian cuisine. Less widely eaten by squeamish Australians are *witchetty grubs*—large white insect larvae that look like puffed-up bald caterpillars, that Aborigines traditionally eat raw. Australia's introduced species have also become semipopular to eat, with Northern Territory buffalo, in particular, lumbering onto restaurant menus.

<hr />

Impressions

This country will become the most valuable acquisition Great Britain has ever made.

—Arthur Phillip, the colony's first Governor General.

There was not a single article in the whole country that could prove of the smallest use to the mother country.

—John White, a doctor on the First Fleet.

From Lilli-Pillies to Witchetty Grubs

Soon after the First Fleet of European convicts and settlers landed in Sydney Cove on January 26, 1788, they starved. They believed the Australian bush to be empty of nourishment, despite evidence to the contrary in the well-fed, healthy, and happy Aborigines all around them. Only in the past 10 years or so, a mere 200 years after landing, have Europeans finally started to wake up to the dazzling variety and wonderful tastes of *bush tucker,* native Aussie food. These days bush tucker is all the rage, and it's a rare fashionable restaurant that hasn't worked wattle-seed, lemon myrtle, or some other native taste sensation onto its menu.

To help you make sense of it all, here's a list of the native foods you are likely to encounter in trend-setting restaurants around the country:

Bunya nut   Crunchy nut, about the same size as a macadamia nut; comes from the Bunya pine.

Illawarra plums   Dark berries with a rich, strong, tangy taste.

Kakadu plum   Wonderfully sharp, tangy, green fruit that boasts the highest recorded vitamin C level of any food in the world.

Lemon aspene   Citrusy, light-yellow fruit with a sharp tangy flavor.

Lemon myrtle   Gum leaves with a fresh, lemony tang; often used to flavor white meat.

Lilly-pilly   Delicious juicy sweet pink berry; also called a riberry.

Rosella   Spiky red petal of a flower; it has a rich, berry flavor; traditionally used by Europeans to make rosella jam.

Wattle-seed   Roasted ground acacia seeds that taste a little like bitter coffee; commonly used by Europeans in pasta or desserts.

Wild limes   Smaller and sourer than regular limes; good in salads.

Witchetty grubs   This is one ingredient you probably won't see on any restaurant menus, because most people are too squeamish to eat these fat slimy white critters. They live in the soil or in old dead tree trunks and are a common source of protein for Aborigines. You only eat them alive, not cooked. If you get offered one to eat in the Outback, you can do what most folks do and freak out, or eat the thing and enjoy its pleasantly nutty taste as a reward for your bravery!

THE DRINKS

THE AMBER NECTAR   The great Aussie drink is a *tinnie* (a can) of beer. Barbecues would not be the same without a case of tinnies, or *stubbies* (small bottles). In the hotter parts of the country, you may be offered a plastic-foam cup in which to place your beer to keep it cool. *Warning:* Don't pour the beer into the cup and expect to get away without everyone collapsing into laughter—place your tinnie or stubbie into it instead.

Australian beers vary considerably in quality but, of course, there's no accounting for tastes. Among the most popular are Victoria Bitter (known as VB), XXXX (pronounced "four ex"), Fosters, and various brews produced by the Tooheys company. All are popular in cans, bottles, or on tap (draft). If I had to recommend a choice brew, I'd go for the XXXX (popular in Queensland) in a can or draft and Tooheys Red from the bottle. If you prefer slightly darker beers, then go for Tooheys Old. My favorite beer is Cascade, a German-style beer usually found only in a bottle. It's light in color, strong in taste, and is made from Tasmanian water straight off a mountain. If you want to get

Australian Pub Culture & Other After-Dark Fun

Australian **pubs** are uniquely ugly by tradition. The walls are often tiled like a bathroom (so you can hose them down at the end of the night), and the bar area is an often far-too-large circular contraption that pins thirsty patrons onto uncomfortable bar stools around its edge. Traditionally, too, the Aussie pub was also the local hotel (in fact, pubs are most commonly referred to as "hotels"). It was a sign of the times, when the only place to stay as a traveler, or to recover from an almighty hangover if you'd had one too many, was the hostelry above the bar. (It's fortunate that the Irish are slowly infiltrating the pub scene, bringing with them more comfortable venues, with a bit more atmosphere. If you spot a shamrock on a pub-lined street, make a beeline for it.) That said, Aussies are friendly pub-goers. They chat away merrily (often disconcertingly in the bathroom), shake hands after playing pool, and are generally jolly drunks.

Pub opening times vary significantly depending on their licenses. But as a rule, most are open from around 10am to midnight most nights, with many extending their drinking hours to the small hours on Friday and Saturday nights. A few pubs in major cities are open 24-hours.

Most Australian capital cities now have a **casino** to soak up any spare cash you might be carrying around. Generally, casinos stay open until the wee hours of the morning and impose a "smart but casual" dress code.

If you're not ready to hit the high-stakes tables of a casino, you could patronize a traditional Aussie **club** instead. Every town and city has at least one, and often several, of these ostensibly private clubs, which are usually ex-servicemen's clubs, workers' clubs, bowling clubs, ethnic clubs, or sporting leagues clubs. Most offer essentially the same things—cheap drinks, a bistro, sometimes a quality restaurant, plenty of *pokies* (poker machines, or one-armed-bandits), and a billiards table or two. On weekends, there might be entertainment or a disco. Some clubs can be enormous, with tens of thousands of registered members and a huge patronage every day of the week. The club is the social heart of many small towns. Although technically private, nonmembers usually have no trouble gaining admission; they are just asked to sign a form when they enter the club, to comply with government licensing laws.

plastered, try Coopers—it's rather cloudy in looks, very strong, and usually ends up causing a terrific hangover. Most Australian beers range from 4.8% to 5.2% alcohol.

In New South Wales, beer is served by the glass in a schooner or a smaller "midi"— although in a few places it's also sold in British measurements, by pints and half pints. In Victoria, you should ask for a "pot," or the less copious glass. Elsewhere in the country, the terminology differs, sometimes from town to town. My advice is to ask for a beer and gesture with your hands like a local to show whether you want a small glass or a larger one.

THE VINO   Australian wine making has come a long way since the first grape vines were brought to Australia on the First Fleet in 1788. These days, more than 550 major companies and small wine makers produce wine commercially in Australia. It comes as no surprise—at least not to Australians, anyway—that vintages from Down Under consistently beat competitors from other wine-producing nations in major international shows. It's widely believed, and not without justification, that it takes a very good bottle of old-world wine to beat an average bottle from Australia. The demand for Australian wine overseas has increased so dramatically in the past few years that domestic prices have risen, and new vineyards are being planted at a frantic pace.

Australian wines are generally named after the grape varieties from which they are made. Of the white wines, the fruity chardonnay and Riesling varieties, the "herbaceous" or "grassy" sauvignon blanc, and the dry semillon are big favorites. Of the reds, the dry cabernet sauvignon, the fruity merlot, the burgundy-type pinot noir, and the big and bold shiraz come out tops.

5 Australia in Print & on the Silver Screen

BOOKS

One of the best ways to get to the heart of a nation is through its books. The earliest Australian literature consists mostly of poems and shanties that generally go on about how difficult it was to travel all the way over to the new land to find it full of flies, dusty plains, and hard work. Of the 19th-century writers, the one that stands head and shoulders above anyone else is the poet Banjo Patterson, whose epic poem *The Man from Snowy River* hit the best-seller list in 1895.

A big name of the 20th century is Miles Franklin, who wrote *My Brilliant Career* (1901), which tells the story of a young woman faced with the dilemma of choosing between marriage and a career. Outback adventures were at the heart of three classic Australian books printed later in the century. Colleen McCullough's *Thorn Birds* is a romantic epic about a Catholic priest who falls in love with a girl; *We of the Never Never* tells the story of a young woman who leaves the comfort of her Melbourne home to live on a cattle station in the Northern Territory; and *Walkabout*, by James V. Marshall, shows the relationship between an Aborigine and two children who get lost in the bush. *Walkabout* was later made into one of Australia's most influential films.

The critics choice, and the winner of the Nobel Prize for Literature in 1973 for *The Eye of the Storm*, is novelist and scholar Patrick White, who also wrote *Voss*. Though not Australian, D. H. Lawrence spent a lot of time Down Under, and his novel *Kangaroo* is worth a read.

Travel writer Bruce Chatwin really got to the heart of Australia with his book, *Songlines*, while another travel scribe, Jan Morris, summed up the Emerald City well in her book, *Sydney*. If you can find it anywhere, *The Long Farewell*, by Don Charlwood holds amazing firsthand diary accounts of long journeys from Europe to Australia in the last century.

Sailing to Australia, by Andrew Hassan, relays diary extracts from convicts and settlers who sailed to Australia in the 19th century. William Dampier's *A New Voyage Around the World*, a classic of Australian travel writing, was written by one of the first Western sailors to make it as far as the Australian coast. *Discovery: The Quest for the Great South Land*, by Miriam Estensen, is another book worth reading if you're interested in accounts of the first trips to the land Down Under.

The Explorers, by Tim Flannery, is one of the best accounts yet of the early pioneers and what they saw when they set out on their great voyages of discovery across the continent.

Additional modern novelists of note include David Ireland, Elizabeth Jolley, Helen Garner, Sue Woolfe, and Peter Carey (who wrote the classic *Oscar and Lucinda*).

FILMS

Australia's movie industry has never been a slouch when it comes to producing beautifully made, intelligent dramas, as well as quirky, off-beat comedies. All of the following films are available on video. If you plan to buy any of them in Australia, note that Australia uses the PAL system, whereas the United States used the NTSC system—which means you'll have to get your videos converted.

COMEDY

- *The Adventures of Priscilla, Queen of the Desert* (1994). Terrence Stamp, Hugo Weaving, and Guy Pearce star as three transsexuals who set out from Sydney in a bus called Priscilla to work their way across Australia. Thanks to their outrageously funny exploits the movie is far from a drag. The costumes won an Oscar.
- *Babe* (1994). Starring a young pig, this cute and eminently rewatchable porcine masterpiece cried out for a string of Oscars when it hit the world's screens. Indulge yourself in a movie that caused a generation of children to push aside their bacon. A sequel, *Babe: Pig in the City,* came out in 1998.
- *Bad Boy Bubby* (1994). Starring Nick Hope, this strange comedy-drama is about a man in his 30s who's never left his mother's apartment. When he finally finds his way out, he discovers he has a fascination for disposing of cats and people by winding them up in plastic food wrap.
- *Malcolm* (1986). Colin Friels and John Hargreaves are excellent in this off-beat comedy about a slow-witted man who is a genius at inventing mechanical gadgets.
- *Muriel's Wedding* (1994). Toni Collette, Rachel Griffith, and Bill Hunter combine in this tremendously quirky comedy about a plain-looking girl from suburbia who leaves it all behind to find the man of her dreams in the big city.
- *Reckless Kelly* (1993). Yahoo Serious is a wacky version of the notorious Australian bush-ranging bandit Ned Kelly. Yahoo's 1988 hit *Young Einstein* was a strange tale of a Tasmanian apple farmer who plans to split the beer atom.
- *Strictly Ballroom* (1992). Paul Mercurio hotfoots it around the ballroom dance floor as he breaks all tradition by introducing his own steps. A romantic comedy well worth watching.

DRAMA

- *Bliss* (1985). This wonderfully entertaining movie is about a successful Sydney businessman whose life changes after he dies for a few moments. It was adapted from a novel by Australian writer Peter Carey.
- *The Boys* (1998). This brutally realistic film tells of the events leading up to a horrendous crime—and in the process reveals the underbelly of Australian society.
- *Breaker Morant* (1980). Aussie icons Edward Woodward, Jack Thompson, and Bryan Brown star in a true story of three mates who find themselves in the Boer War. Many consider this to be one of the best dramas ever made.
- *Gallipoli* (1981). Mel Gibson and Mark Lee are two young runners who join the army amid the jingoism surrounding World War I. They find themselves facing their toughest moment when going over the top of the trenches means running for their lives.
- *Mad Max* (1979). The first of a trilogy of Mad Max films based on a futuristic world controlled by roving gangs. Mel Gibson comes of age as an ex-cop. The sequel, *Mad Max II–The Road Warrior* (1981) carried on the tradition, which ended with *Mad Max Beyond Thunderdome* (1985), the best of the three movies.
- *The Man from Snowy River* (1982). Kirk Douglas and Jack Thompson ride the ranges in a remake of Banjo Patterson's famous poem about the chase of an escaped colt.
- *The Piano* (1993). This joint Australian-New Zealand-French production starring Holly Hunter, Harvey Keitel, and Sam Neill, is a wonderfully filmed yarn

about a Scottish mute who comes to live in New Zealand with a man she has never met. An unsettling love triangle turns the moody landscape sour.

- *Picnic at Hanging Rock* (1975). Rachel Roberts is one of three girls and a teacher who disappear while on a school trip into the bush. The images are hauntingly beautiful.
- *Proof* (1991). Hugo Weaving, Genevieve Picot, and Russell Crowe star in an eccentric drama about a blind photographer who composes his shots through the eyes of a young kitchen-hand. When his assistant falls in love with his housemaid the problems really begin.
- *Romper Stomper* (1992). Russell Crowe is a skinhead who, along with his gang, takes to beating up Melbourne's Asian youth. Very controversial and very violent, it's an interesting sociological study of a youth culture.
- *Storm Boy* (1976). Set in the Coorong in South Australia, this delightful film stars Greg Rowe as a kid who develops a friendship with a pelican and an Aborigine (played by David Gulpilil) who teaches him how to love his environment.
- *Walkabout* (1976). Jenny Agutter and David Gulpilil are the stars of this visually evocative movie about a young girl who gets lost in the desert and is befriended by a traditional Aborigine. It was rereleased in 1998.

3 Planning an Affordable Trip to Australia

by Natalie Kruger

This chapter aims to answer all those practical questions that pop up as you plan your trip—How will I get there? How much will it cost? What should I see? How will I get around?—and many other pesky details. Australia's a big country, and you probably won't be able to see all of it, so in this chapter and throughout the book we also give you no-nonsense advice on what's worth your time and money and what's not. In other words, we've done all the legwork—ferreting out the best deals on airfares, package deals, outdoor adventures, accommodations, and more—so you won't have to.

1 How This Guide Can Save You Money

Now, I know what you're thinking—is it really possible to travel around a country like Australia (it's the same size as the continental United States) for as little as U.S.$50 a day per person? Absolutely! In fact, given Australia's abundance of family-run motels, authentic country pubs, cute B&Bs, and inexpensive ethnic restaurants, traveling on a budget won't seem a chore at all.

First, let me explain the "fifty-dollars-a-day" premise. It's based on the assumption that two adults are traveling together and that between the two of you, you have at least U.S.$100, or U.S.$50 per person, to spend per a day on accommodations and meals. (We used a conservative calculation in this book of U.S.$100 equals A$143. Take note of the actual exchange rate when you travel, as it may go up or down; see "Money," below, for more information.) Sightseeing, entertainment, and transportation costs are extra, but we have unearthed loads of free and next-to-free ways for you to see the sights and get around without having to remortgage your house. Because airfare is likely to be the most expensive part of your trip, we provide helpful tips on nailing down low-cost air deals and packages.

This isn't a backpackers guide to Oz. Although the book includes the very best backpacker-style accommodations and hostels, its aim is to suggest the best places to stay and dine at the best price, not necessarily the cheapest dive in town. In fact, if you stay and dine at the places recommended in this guide and follow its money-saving tips on transportation and sightseeing, you'll be traveling around the country the same way most average Australians do. Most Aussies would rather stay in a midpriced country guesthouse that has a bit of charm, and eat at the cheap and fabulous Thai nosh-house down the road, than pay a fortune to sit around a five-star resort's swimming pool eating $15 hamburgers.

2 Fifty Money-Saving Tips

This entire book is loaded with money-saving tips, but here's a handy round-up of 50 tips to help you keep your traveling costs to a minimum:

GENERAL TRAVEL

1. Even if you never set foot in a youth hostel, the all-time great buy Down Under is membership in the Australian Youth Hostels Association (AYHA), or its sibling in the United States, Hostelling International. Membership costs just U.S.$25, U.S.$15 if you're a senior, and entitles you to a huge array of discounts on car rental (30% off at Avis, for example), train travel, bus passes, tours, outdoor-gear purchases, Sydney Harbour cruises, museum admission—the list goes on and on and on. See "Youth Hostels and Backpacker Lodges" in "Tips on Accommodations," later in this chapter.

2. Book directly. Many companies, particularly airline ticket consolidators who buy tickets wholesale and some Australian tour companies, offer discounts for booking straight with them, rather than through a travel agent, to whom they must pay commission. Of course, it makes sense to check with the travel agent, too, just to make sure you're getting the best deal.

3. When booking a hotel room at a major chain or renting a car from a major car-rental agency, be sure to mention which frequent-flier programs you belong to and ask whether you qualify for miles. If you have already racked up a load of frequent-flier miles, don't forget that they may be redeemable for free hotel nights, free air tickets, and other travel-related rewards.

4. If you are a senior or student, be sure to ask about discounts at every opportunity—when booking your airfare, hotel, rental car, or sightseeing tour; when purchasing theater tickets; or when visiting any museum or attraction.

5. Hotels, museums, cafes, stores and other businesses displaying the **International Youth Travel Card** (ITYC) logo offer discounts to cardholders. The card is available to anyone under 26, student or not, and is issued by the Federation of International Youth Travel Organizations for U.S.$15. Get it from **STA Travel** (☎ **800/781 4040** in the U.S., 800/836-4115 in Canada, 020/7361-6262 in the U.K., and 1300/360 960 in Australia).

6. Full-time students should not leave home without an **International Student Identification Card,** available from **STA Travel** (see no. 5 above). For just U.S.$20, you get free or discounted access to tours, attractions, action pursuits, and even cafes.

7. Before you purchase travel insurance, check that you do not already have it as part of your credit card agreement or existing health insurance policy. If your current health insurance policy covers you fully for medical treatment and evacuation anywhere in the world and if your credit card company insures you against travel accidents if you buy plane, train, or bus tickets with its card (see "Health & Insurance" later in this chapter), why duplicate the coverage? Your homeowner's insurance should cover stolen luggage. However, if you have paid a large portion of your vacation expenses up front, it might be a good idea to buy trip cancellation insurance.

AIR TRAVEL

8. In terms of airfares to Australia, the off-season runs from mid-April to the end of August. This is not only the cheapest time to fly from America, but it's also the best time to visit Australia! That's because Down Under winter (June, July, and August), when the days are balmy and nice, is more pleasant than the too-hot summer (Dec, Jan, and Feb).

9. Traveling on certain days of the week can save you money. You can shave an extra U.S.$60 off your Qantas airfare if you depart Monday to Thursday.

10. Take a package. Whether you opt for an independent or group tour, package deals are terrific values because they typically include airfares (usually from Los Angeles), a decent standard of accommodations, some or all meals, tours, transfers, and other extras. The per-day price of a package (including airfare) can work out to be about the same as a night's accommodation in a midrange hotel.

11. Shop around for travel agents and consolidators that specialize in cheap fares to Australia. See "Flying to Australia," later in this chapter for a list of companies.

12. The quickest way between two points is not always the cheapest. Sometimes airlines and travel agents release spot specials for people prepared to travel via a lengthier route, or at short notice. If this is you, scour travel agents' windows and the travel sections of newspapers for the latest deals. Canada 3000 is such an airline; it flies to Australia via Honolulu and Fiji, and in the low season, it may be worth forking out the money for airfare from your hometown to Vancouver to catch its Sydney-bound flight.

13. The cheapest fares are usually the ones with the most restrictions. With Qantas's 21-day advance purchase Super-Apex fare, for example, you must pay for the ticket within 21 days after booking it, you must stay at least a week and no more than a month in Australia, you are not allowed to make stopovers, and you cannot change the routing once you have paid for the ticket. All these conditions are pretty easy to meet for many people.

14. Flying within Australia is horrifyingly expensive—*but* not if you prepurchase coupons from Qantas or Australia's other national airline, Ansett. The coupons can cost less than half the regular fares. Only non-Australians can buy them, and you must buy them before you leave home.

15. Because air travel within Australia is so expensive, Ansett and Qantas offer special discounts of around 30% off regular fares for non-Australian passport holders. To obtain the discount, quote your passport number when booking your flight.

16. If you belong to a frequent-flier club, use your points to contribute toward your airfare. If you are not already a frequent-flier member, join when you buy your ticket. It won't save you money on this trip, but the long flight to Australia could earn you a wheelbarrow-load of points to use when you get home.

17. To rack up even more frequent-flier miles, pay for your airline ticket on a credit card that lets you earn miles for every dollar you spend. Just be sure you don't get zapped with sky-high interest charges.

ACCOMMODATIONS

18. Airfare and accommodations will take the biggest bite out of your travel budget, so remember to investigate money-saving package tours that include both your plane ticket and five or more nights' accommodations—often at substantial savings for both.

19. If you get an apartment with a full kitchen, you can save money by not eating out at every darn meal, as long as you don't mind doing a little cooking (well, microwaving, at least). Australian cities and holiday destinations are awash with

this kind of accommodation. Even if you only cook yourself breakfast every morning, you could save enough to splurge on one really special meal.

20. Hotel and apartment rates in popular coastal vacation spots like the Gold Coast, the Sunshine Coast, and Cairns in Queensland increase dramatically during the Australian school vacations. Even motel rates will rise by as much as A$20 (U.S.$14) a night, and most apartments will only rent by the week at this time. It really is worth trying to avoid visiting Australia during the country's school holidays (see "When to Go" section later in this chapter).

21. Many accommodation chains offer discounted rates for customers of a particular car-rental company with which the hotel chain is partnered. When making your reservation or checking in, it never hurts to ask whether you qualify for a discount.

22. Bed-and-breakfasts are a friendly alternative to a cheerless motel room, and in Oz they're often incredibly cheap. Many pretty B&Bs charge A$75 (U.S.$52.50) or less for a double room with breakfast—about the same as a motel room without breakfast. This book recommends many; see "Bed & Breakfast Inns," later in this chapter for details on how to find more.

23. Don't think that youth hostels and backpacker lodges are just for youths and backpackers. Some are almost as good as resorts, with a pool, a tour desk, Internet access, and often a very cheap but good restaurant attached. Many have basic but clean private rooms for well under A$50 (U.S.$35) for a double. As long as you can handle sharing a bathroom, these rooms are often the cheapest comfortable bed in town.

24. **YWCA** (☎ **1800/249 124** in Australia, or 03/9329 2184) has eight comfortable budget hotels around Australia with private rooms a cut above the average backpacker digs. Rates range from A$40 (U.S.$28) to A$89 (U.S.$62.30) double. There is one in Alice Springs, one in Cairns, and one in all state capitals except Adelaide and Hobart.

25. Many pubs in Australia, especially those in the country, offer a bed for the night as well as a pint of your favorite grog. Staying in a pub can be a money-saving option if you don't mind sharing a bathroom (some have private bathrooms, but don't expect it) and coping with the din of farmers drinking—loudly—in the bar downstairs (often until midnight on Friday and Saturday). The quality varies, but most rooms have a measure of historical charm. Rates can be as little as A$40 (U.S.$28) for a double and are rarely more than A$75 (U.S.$52.50); most include breakfast.

26. Most hotels in Australia accommodate kids up to age 12 (and even older) free of charge in your room if they use existing beds; if a hotel does charge extra for a child, it's usually only A$10 (U.S.$7), or A$20 (U.S. $14) at most.

LOCAL TRANSPORTATION

27. Coach travel in Oz is not the low-rent form of transport it typically is in the United States—the buses are clean, the seats are comfortable, and you sometimes even get a video onboard. Passes from the two national coach companies, Greyhound Pioneer and McCafferty's, represent great value, especially as some of them include tours.

28. Train fares in Australia cost about the same as bus fares, if you travel in a sitting berth on the train. If you want a sleeper cabin, train fares get expensive fast. Check out the money-saving passes Rail Australia offers, which are outlined in "Getting Around," later in this chapter.

29. Countrylink, the rail organization overseeing rail travel in New South Wales, Victoria, and Queensland, offers advance-purchase discounts of up to 40%.

30. Before you automatically book a rental car in Australia, think seriously about whether you really need one. In major tourist towns like Alice Springs and Cairns, travelers fall into the trap of renting a car and then letting it sit outside their hotel the whole vacation, because every local tour company picked them up at the door. If you really need a car only to drive into town for dinner, take a cab.

31. When you return a rental car, fill up the tank at a nearby gas station. The gas from the car-rental depot's pump is a complete rip-off. The front desk staff even admits it.

32. Gas in cities is often cheaper on Monday, since most people fill up their tanks before the weekend.

33. Whether you are getting around by air, rail, bus, or car, try not to backtrack. In a country as big as Australia, you can waste a lot of money retracing your steps.

34. Don't buy expensive maps. Most visitor centers dispense free or next-to-free maps of the local area. If you are a member of an automobile club with which the Australian Automobile Association (AAA) has a reciprocal agreement, you can often obtain free state, regional, and city road maps. The American Automobile Association, the Canadian Automobile Association, the Automobile Association in the United Kingdom, and the New Zealand Automobile Association, Inc., all have such an arrangement with Australia. Pick up the maps from your home auto club before you leave, or collect them at the AAA offices in Australia. See "Getting Around: By Car" for locations.

WINING & DINING

35. The key letters to look for when dining out in Oz are *BYO,* which stands for Bring Your Own, and means you buy your own wine or beer at the cheapest bottle shop ("liquor store" to American readers, "off-license" to Brits) you can find, and take it along to the restaurant to drink with your meal. That way you avoid the mark-up of 100%, 200%, or even 300% that restaurateurs are so fond of adding to their liquor prices. All you will pay is a corkage charge of around A$1 (U.S.70¢) to A$3 (U.S.$2.10) per person. BYO doesn't mean the food is iffy, either. Most excellent ethnic restaurants are uniformly BYO, and so are some cutting-edge Modern Australian restaurants in trendy locales.

36. Go ethnic and you're almost guaranteed great food at low prices—Indian, Cambodian, Malaysian, Vietnamese, Italian, and Thai are all pretty sure bets. The smarter Chinese restaurants are good, but often a tad pricey, and not always BYO.

37. An advantage of going out for Asian food is that dishes are usually shared at the table, so small eaters can get away with not ordering a whole meal for themselves (great for families). Because one Asian main course is often enough for two people, the golden rule is to order and eat one dish first, then order a second if you need it.

38. In cities, head to an Italian sidewalk cafe for tasty pasta and stylish sandwiches. A tummy-filling foccacia sandwich with salami, provolone cheese, sun-dried tomatoes, and arugula (rocket) will set you back around A$8 (U.S.$5.60) and keep you going 'til dinner.

39. Backpacker lodges, youth hostels, and universities (colleges) almost always have dirt-cheap restaurants or cafes attached, which serve up big portions of tasty, healthy food.

40. Tipping is not necessary in Australia, although it is common to tip 5 to 10% in restaurants and to round cab fares up to the nearest A$1. Plenty of Aussies don't tip, so you needn't be embarrassed about hanging on to your coins.

41. If you are traveling by car, keep a box of cereal and long-life milk in the trunk and use the hotel coffee cups as bowls. It beats paying A$10 (U.S.$7) for the same thing in the hotel restaurant.

42. RSL (Returned and Services League) clubs and League clubs (as in Rugby League football) serve hearty meals—along the roast, chicken kiev, and steak lines, with vegetables or salad, and bread and potato included—for around A$10 (U.S.$7). You will have to sign in before you enter the club and put up with their uniquely lurid brand of neon-lit decor, but so what? Kids' meals are about A$5 (U.S.$3.50).

TOURS & SIGHTSEEING

43. Australian city councils are big on providing free entertainment—for example, Sydney has free dance performances or concerts at Darling Harbour many weekends, and free lunchtime concerts in Martin Place most days; Brisbane has street performers at South Bank Parklands most weekends; and Darwin has free Sunday Jazz by the sea at the MGM Grand Casino in Dry Season. Check local newspapers for details.

44. You can often get half-price theater tickets on the day of the performance. We've listed half-price ticket agencies in the "After Dark" sections of each chapter, where relevant. Matinees are often around A$8 (U.S.$5.60) cheaper than evening shows.

45. Walking tours are often up to one-half the price of bus tours, and they give you a good close-up view of the city and sights.

SHOPPING

46. Skin-care products, cosmetics, perfume, electronic equipment, imported designer accessories, liquor, cigarettes and other luxury items attract high duty in Australia. If you need to buy these products, get them in a duty-free store, which can be found in all capital cities and major tourist destinations. You will need to show your airline ticket and passport to enter the store.

47. If you find yourself buying anything expensive in Australia—jewelry, for example—ask if there is a tax-free (that is, duty-free) price for international travelers. Most regular non-duty-free stores selling jewelry, electronic equipment, and other high-ticket items offer tax-free prices to international travelers who show their airline ticket and passport.

48. Aboriginal artifacts make great souvenirs and gifts, but don't necessarily buy them from the shops on main street or in the city mall. The shops just a block or two away from the center of town sell the same items a good bit cheaper.

NIGHTLIFE

49. There's no cover charge at pubs, and drinks here are always cheaper than in nightclubs. Some pubs have live entertainment, pool tables, and sports video screens.

50. Aussies love a beer any time, but it never tastes better than during happy hour, that idyllic period from around 4pm to 6pm when many city bars and pubs mark drinks down to half price or less. Happy hours are especially common Thursday and Friday, but any time of the week you are never far from a pub that makes an art form of brand-based specials—"A$1 (U.S.70¢) Stolis (Stolichnaya vodka) until 9pm Tuesdays," "A$2 (U.S.$1.40) Crown Lagers All Nite Wednesdays," "A$1 (U.S.70¢) VBs (Victoria Bitter beer) for Students," and so on.

3 Visitor Information

AUSTRALIAN TOURIST COMMISSION   The Australian Tourist Commission (ATC) offers several ways to help you plan your trip Down Under. You can also write to the Australian Tourist Commission at Level 4, 80 William St., Woolloomooloo, Sydney NSW 2011 (☎ **02/9360 1111;** fax 02/9331 2538).

Aussie Helpline   For help with piecing together an itinerary, or to find out more about any aspect of traveling in Australia, contact the ATC's **Aussie Helpline** at ☎ **805/775 2000,** or fax 805/775-4448 in the United States and Canada; ☎ **0990/ 022 000** and fax 0171/940 5221 in the United Kingdom and Ireland; or to simply order brochures, call ☎ **0990/561 434,** in the U.K., and 01/402 6896 in Ireland; and ☎ **0800/65 0303,** or fax 09/527 1629 in New Zealand.

When you call, request a copy of the ATC's comprehensive brochure, the *Australian Traveller's Guide.* The ATC also publishes *Australia Unplugged,* an excellent, hip guide to the country's coolest offerings.

You can access an on-line version of Aussie Helpline, and order brochures at the ATC's Web site: www.aussie.net.au.

Aussie Specialists   The ATC maintains a network of "Aussie Specialist" travel agents in several hundred cities across North America, the United Kingdom, and New Zealand, who are committed to a continuous training program on the best destinations, hotels, deals, and tours in Oz. They will know better than most agents how to package an itinerary that's right for you. To find the Aussie Specialist nearest you, call the Aussie Helpline or check the ATC Web site.

On the Web   The Australian Tourist Commission's excellent Web site, www.aussie.net.au, has more than 10,000 pages of listings for tour operators, hotels, car-rental companies, specialist travel outfitters, public holidays, maps, distance charts, and much more. Press the Customise button on the bottom tool bar of the home page to use the version of the site tailored for your country—that way, if you're Canadian you'll see the latest deals from Canada, not from Sweden, for example.

STATE TOURIST OFFICES   Another great source of information can be the state tourist bureaus. I find that the more targeted your request for information—ask for "diving in the Whitsunday Islands," for example, rather than saying "send me stuff on Queensland"—the more useful the response. Here are the addresses:

- **Tourism New South Wales,** Tourism House, 55 Harrington St., The Rocks, Sydney NSW 2000 (☎ **02/9931 1111,** fax 02/9931 1490, www.tourism. nsw. gov.au).
- **Queensland Tourist and Travel Corporation,** Level 36, Riverside Centre, 123 Eagle St., Brisbane, QLD 4000 (☎ **07/3406 5400**, fax 07/3406 5246, www. queensland-holidays.com.au).
- **Northern Territory Tourist Commission,** Tourism House, 43 Mitchell St., Darwin, NT 0800 (☎ **08/8999 3900,** fax 08/8999 3888, www.nttc.com.au).
- **Western Australian Tourism Commission,** 16 St. George's Terrace, Perth, WA 6000 (☎ **08/9220 1700,** fax 08/9220 1702, www.wa.gov.au/watc).
- **South Australian Tourism Commission,** Terrace Towers, 178 North Terrace, Adelaide, SA 5000 (☎ **08/8303 2222,** fax 08/8303 2295, www.visit-southaustralia.com.au.
- **Tourism Victoria,** 55 Collins St., Melbourne, VIC 3000 (☎ **03/9653 9777,** fax 03/9653 9744, www.tourism.vic.gov.au).
- **Canberra Tourism & Events Corporation,** Locked Bag 2001, Civic Square, Canberra, ACT 2608 (☎ **02/6205 0044,** fax 02/6205 0776, www. canberratourism.com.au).

- **Tourism Tasmania,** Trafalgar Centre, Floors 13–15, 110 Collins St., Hobart TAS 7000 (☎ **03/6230 8169,** fax 03/6230 8353, www.tourism.tas.gov.au).

OTHER USEFUL WEB SITES

- The Australian Embassy in Washington, D.C., has a handy Web site at www.austemb.org. The site posts loads of links to sites on tourism; cultural and educational matters; briefings on the economy, trade, sports, geography, and the people; and lists of events. It's written with North Americans in mind, though much of the information is relevant no matter where you are traveling from.
- All Australian telephone numbers are listed in the Telstra White Pages (search by name) and Yellow Pages (search by subject): www.whitepages.com.au and www.yellowpages.com.au, respectively.
- For the latest on the Sydney 2000 Olympic Games, visit the official site at www.sydney.olympic.org.
- Check out the latest weather forecasts and research average temperature, rainfall, and humidity on the Australian Bureau of Meteorology's site at www.bom.gov.au.
- Pick up cool suggestions for sporting activities, restaurants, shops, attractions, and festivals as well as current film and other cultural listings, an extensive accommodations directory, and lifestyle feature stories about Sydney and Melbourne at sydney.citysearch.com.au and melbourne.citysearch.com.au.

4 Entry Requirements & Customs

ENTRY REQUIREMENTS   Along with a current **passport,** valid for the duration of your stay, the Australian government requires a **visa** from visitors of every nation (New Zealand citizens are issued a visa on arrival in Australia). This bothers the United States and other countries that do not make reciprocal demands on Australians, so the Australian government has introduced the **Electronic Travel Authority (ETA)**—an electronic or "paperless" visa that takes the place of a rubber stamp in your passport.

This is how the ETA works: you give your passport details in person or over the phone to your travel agent or your airline reservationist at the time you book your air travel. This information is entered into the travel agent's or airline's reservations system, which is linked to the Australian Department of Immigration and Multicultural Affairs' computer system. Assuming you are not wanted by Interpol, your ETA should be approved in about six to eight seconds, while you wait. The beauty of this system is that you can do the work over the telephone without having to stand in a line at the embassy or mail your passport to the embassy with a visa application. You can also apply for an ETA at Australian embassies, high commissions, and consulates (see below).

Tourists apply for a **Tourist ETA.** It's free and is valid for as many visits to Australia of up to 3 months each as you like, within a one-year period. Tourists may not work in Australia, so if you are visiting for business, you pay A$50 (U.S.$35) for a **Long Validity Business ETA** that entitles you to as many 3-month stays as you like for the life of your passport. Business travelers who are U.S., Canadian, French, or Spanish citizens can apply for a free **Short Validity Business ETA,** which is valid for a single visit of 3 months within a one-year period.

In certain situations you still must apply for a visa the old-fashioned way—by taking or mailing your passport with a visa application form, and with payment, to your nearest Australian embassy or consulate. This will be the case if your travel agent or airline (or cruise ship, if you plan to arrive in Australia by sea) is not connected to the ETA system. In the United States, Canada, and the United Kingdom, most agents and major airlines are ETA-compatible, but few cruise lines are. There is a A$50 (U.S.$35) processing fee for non-ETA tourist and business visas for stays of up to three months, and A$145 (U.S.$101.50) for business visas for stays of between three months and four years. Applications to extend most kinds of visas entail a processing fee of A$110 (U.S.$77), whether or not your application is successful.

You will also need to apply for a visa the old-fashioned way if you plan to enter Australia as something other than a tourist or a business traveler—for example, as a student, long-term resident, sportsperson, performer, or member of a social group or cultural exchange. In any of these categories you need what is called a **Temporary Residence visa.**

You can apply for non-ETA visas at Australian embassies, consulates, and high commissions. In the **United States,** contact the Australian Embassy, 1601 Massachusetts Ave. NW, Washington, DC 20036–2273 (☎ **202/797-3000**), or the Australian Consulate-General, 2049 Century Park E., Level 19, Los Angeles, CA 90067–3238 (☎ **310/229-4840**). In **Canada,** contact the Australian High Commission, 50 O'Connor St., #710, Ottawa, ON K1P6L2 (☎ **613/783 7619**). For visa inquiries in the U.S. and Canada call ☎ **800/579 7664.** In the **United Kingdom,** contact the Australian High Commission, Australia House, The Strand, London WC2B 4LA (☎ **020/7465 8218**), or the Australian Consulate, Chatsworth House, Lever St., Manchester M1 2QL (☎ 0161/228 1344). In **Ireland,** contact the Australian Embassy, Fitzwilton House, Wilton Terrace, Dublin 2, Ireland (☎ **1/676 3576**).

You can also apply for non-ETA visas via the Internet at the **Australian Department of Immigration and Multicultural Affair's Web site** (www.immi.gov.au). This site also has a good explanation of the ETA system.

Allow a month or more for processing of non-ETA visas.

CUSTOMS & QUARANTINE Anyone over age 18 can bring into Australia no more than 250 cigarettes or 250 grams of cigars or other tobacco products, 1.125 liters (41 fl. oz.) of alcohol, and "dutiable goods" to the value of A$400 (U.S.$280), or A$200 (U.S. $140) if you are under age 18. Broadly speaking, "dutiable goods" are luxury items such as perfume concentrate, watches, jewelry, furs, and gifts of any kind. Keep this in mind if you intend to come bearing presents for family and friends in Australia. If the items are your own personal goods and you're taking them with you when you leave, they are usually exempt from duty. If you are not sure what is dutiable and what's not, contact the nearest Australian embassy or consulate (see above).

Because Australia is an island, it is free of many agricultural and livestock diseases. To keep it that way, strict quarantine applies to importing plants, animals, and their products, including food. Don't be alarmed if, just before landing, the flight attendants spray the aircraft cabin (with products approved by the World Health Organization) to kill flying insects that entered the plane in a foreign country. For more information on what is and is not allowed entry, contact the nearest Australian embassy or the Australian Quarantine and Inspection Service in Sydney (☎ **02/ 9364 7222**).

For U.S. Citizens Returning U.S. citizens who have been away for 48 hours or more are allowed to bring back into the United States, once every 30 days, U.S.$400 worth of merchandise duty-free. You'll be charged a flat rate of 10% duty on the next U.S.$1,000 worth of purchases. Be sure to have your receipts handy. On gifts, the duty-free limit is U.S.$100. You cannot bring fresh foodstuffs into the United States, but tinned foods are allowed. There are a few restrictions on amount: one liter of alcohol (you must be over age 21), 200 cigarettes, and 100 cigars. Antiques (over 100 years old) and works of art are exempt from the U.S.$400 limit, as are gifts you mail home. Once a day you can mail U.S.$100 worth of gifts duty-free; label each package "unsolicited gift." On the exterior of any package you must describe the contents and their value. You cannot mail alcohol, perfume (it contains alcohol), or tobacco products. For more information, contact the **U.S. Customs Service,** 1301 Constitution Ave. (P.O. Box 7407), Washington, DC 20044 (☎ **202/927-6724**) and request the free pamphlet *Know Before You Go.* It's also available on the Web at www.customs.ustreas.gov/travel/kbygo.htm.

For U.K. Citizens British citizens returning home from a non-EC country have a customs allowance of 200 cigarettes; 50 cigars; 250 grams of smoking tobacco; 2 liters of still table wine; 1 liter of spirits or strong liqueurs (over 22% volume); 2 liters of fortified wine, sparkling wine or other liqueurs; 60cc (ml) of perfume; 250cc (ml) of toilet water; and £145 worth of all other goods, including gifts and souvenirs. People under age 17 cannot have the tobacco or alcohol allowance. Meat and poultry products and some plants are also banned or restricted. For more information, contact **HM Customs & Excise,** Passenger Enquiry Point, 2nd Floor Wayfarer House, Great South West Road, Feltham, Middlesex, TW14 8NP (☎ **0181/910-3744,** from outside the U.K. 44/181-910-3744), or consult their Web site at www.open.gov.uk.

For Canadian Citizens For a clear summary of Canadian rules, write for the booklet *I Declare,* issued by **Revenue Canada,** 2265 St. Laurent Blvd., Ottawa K1G 4K3 (☎ **800/461-9999** or 613/993-0534, www.rc.gc.ca). Canada allows its citizens a Can$500 exemption, and you're allowed to bring back duty-free 200 cigarettes, 2.2 pounds of tobacco, 40 imperial ounces of liquor, and 50 cigars. In addition, you're allowed to mail gifts to Canada from abroad at the rate of Can$60 a day, provided they're unsolicited and aren't alcohol or tobacco (write on the package: "Unsolicited gift, under $60 value"). Restrictions apply to animal, plant, and biological products.

For New Zealand Citizens The duty-free allowance for New Zealand is NZ$700. Citizens over age 17 can bring in 200 cigarettes, 50 cigars, or 250 grams of tobacco (or a mixture of all three if their combined weight doesn't exceed 250 grams); plus 4.5 liters of wine and beer, or 1.125 liters of liquor. New Zealand currency does not carry import or export restrictions. Fill out a certificate of export, listing the valuables you are taking out of the country; that way, you can bring them back without paying duty. Most questions are answered in a free pamphlet available at New Zealand consulates and Customs offices: *New Zealand Customs Guide for Travellers, Notice no. 4.* For more information, contact **New Zealand Customs,** 50 Anzac Ave., P.O. Box 29, Auckland (☎ **0800/428 786** or 09/359-6655).

5 Money

CASH & CURRENCY The Australian dollar is divided into 100 cents. Coins come in 5¢, 10¢, 20¢ and 50¢ pieces (all silver in color) and $1 and $2 pieces (gold in color). The 50-cent piece is 12-sided. Prices in Australia often end in a variant of 1¢ and 2¢ (for example, 78 cents or $2.71), a relic from the days before 1¢ and 2¢ pieces were phased out (prices are rounded to the nearest 5¢). Bank notes come in denominations of $5, $10, $20, $50 and $100.

ATMS, CREDIT CARDS & TRAVELER'S CHECKS One of the fastest, safest, and easiest methods of managing money Down Under is to withdraw money directly from your home bank account at an Australian automatic-teller machine (ATM). That way you can get cash when banks and currency exchanges are closed, and your money resides safely in your bank account back home until you withdraw it. Also, you get the bank exchange rate, not the higher commercial rate charged at currency exchanges. You will be charged a fee for each withdrawal, usually A$4 (U.S. $2.80) or so. It's your bank that charges this, not the Aussie bank, so ask your bank what the fee is.

The Australian Dollar, the U.S. Dollar & the British Pound

For U.S. Readers   The rate of exchange used to calculate the dollar values given in this book was U.S.$1 = approximately A$1.43 (or A$1 = U.S.70¢).

For British Readers   The rate of exchange used to calculate the pound values in the accompanying table was 1 British pound = A$2.50 (or A$1 = 40p).

Note: International exchange rates can fluctuate markedly. Check the latest rate when you plan your trip. This table should be used only as a guide.

A$	U.S.$	U.K.£	A$	U.S.$	U.K.£
0.25	0.17	0.10	30.00	21.00	12.00
0.50	0.35	0.20	35.00	24.50	14.00
1.00	0.70	0.40	40.00	28.00	16.00
2.00	1.40	0.80	45.00	31.50	18.00
3.00	2.10	1.20	50.00	35.00	20.00
4.00	2.80	1.60	55.00	38.50	22.00
5.00	3.50	2.00	60.00	42.00	24.00
6.00	4.20	2.40	65.00	45.50	26.00
7.00	4.90	2.80	70.00	49.00	28.00
8.00	5.60	3.20	75.00	52.50	30.00
9.00	6.30	3.60	80.00	56.00	32.00
10.00	7.00	4.00	85.00	59.50	34.00
15.00	10.50	6.00	90.00	63.00	36.00
20.00	14.00	8.00	95.00	66.50	38.00
25.00	17.50	10.00	100.00	70.00	40.00

All of the biggest banks in Australia—ANZ, Commonwealth, National, and Westpac—are connected to the Cirrus network. ANZ, Commonwealth, and National are also connected to Maestro. Only ANZ and National take Plus. Ask your bank at home for a directory of international ATM locations where your card is accepted. Both **Cirrus** (☎ 800/424-7787; www.mastercard.com/atm) and **Plus** (☎ 800/843-7587; www.visa.com) networks have automated ATM locators that list the banks in each country that will accept your card. Most ATMs in Australia accept both four- and six-digit PINs (personal identification numbers), but it's a good idea to request a four-digit PIN from your bank, as these are the most common, not just in Australia, but in the rest of the world as well.

Credit Cards   Definitely get a **Visa** or **MasterCard** before you leave home. Visa and MasterCard are universally accepted in Australia; American Express and Diners Club

Travel Tip

In Outback areas carry cash (several hundred dollars) and a credit card. ATMs are widely available in cities and towns, but in remote parts of the country and in small Outback towns they can be conspicuous by their absence. Small merchants in remote parts may not cash traveler's checks.

What Things Cost in Sydney, NSW	A$	U.S.$	U.K.£
Taxi from airport to city center	12.60	8.80	5.00
Bus from Central Station to downtown	.85	.60	35p
Local telephone call from pay phone	.28	.20	12p
Double at Buena Vista Hotel (cheap)	52.50	36.75	21.00
Double at Ravesi's on Bondi Beach (affordable)	69.30	48.65	27.80
Double at Tricketts Luxury Bed & Breakfast (pricey)	98.00	68.60	39.20
Lunch for one at The Olive (cheap)	5.40	3.80	2.10
Lunch for one at Arizona (moderate)	16.80	11.75	6.55
Dinner for one, without wine, at No Names (cheap)	9.45	6.60	3.70
Dinner for one, without wine, at Old Saigon (affordable)	15.15	10.60	6.00
Dinner for one, without wine, at MCA Café (pricey)	24.50	17.15	9.80
Beer (285ml)	1.45	1.00	50p
Coca-Cola (375ml)	.90	.65	40p
Roll of Kodak ASA 100 film, 36 exposures	4.25	3.00	1.70
Adult admission to Taronga Zoo	11.20	7.85	4.45
Movie ticket	8.75	6.15	3.50

What Things Cost in Townsville, QLD	A$	U.S.$	U.K.£
Taxi from airport to city center	7.70	5.40	3.05
Local telephone call from pay phone	.28	.20	12p
Double at Coral Lodge Bed & Breakfast Inn (cheap)	42.00	29.40	16.80
Double at Seagulls Resort (affordable)	65.10	45.60	26.05
Lunch for one at Thai Exchange (cheap)	5.25	3.70	2.10
Lunch for one at Michel's (affordable)	16.00	11.20	6.40
Dinner for one, without wine, at Zoui Alto's (pricey)	17.50	12.25	7.00
Beer (285ml)	1.35	.95	55p
Coca-Cola (375ml)	.84	.60	35p
Roll of ASA 100 Kodak film, 36 exposures	6.25	4.40	2.50
Admission to Great Barrier Reef Aquarium	10.35	7.20	4.10
Movie ticket	5.25	3.70	2.10

are accepted less often, particularly by many of the low-cost accommodations and restaurants in this book—they cannot afford the higher merchant fees charged by those two cards. Always have some cash on your person, as many merchants in Australia will not take cards for purchases under A$5 (U.S.$3.50) or A$10 (U.S.$7). If your credit card is linked to your bank account, you can use it to withdraw cash from an ATM (just keep in mind that interest starts accruing immediately on credit-card cash advances).

Sydney 2000 Olympic Games Update

The Games of the XXVIIth Olympiad will be held in Sydney from September 15 to October 1, 2000. Approximately 10,000 athletes from some 200 countries will vie for gold, silver, and bronze in 28 sports. Events will be held primarily in two major Olympic "zones"—the Sydney Olympic Park and the Sydney Harbour Zone.

The Sydney Olympic Park, at Homebush Bay, a 30-minute drive from downtown Sydney, will be the site of the new 110,000-seat Stadium Australia (where the opening and closing ceremonies and soccer and track-and-field events will be held) and the Athletes' Village. Other venues constructed or under construction here include an indoor arena, a velodrome, and centers for tennis, baseball, and archery. Already open and in use at Homebush Bay are the Sydney Showground (where baseball, rhythmic gymnastics, and basketball preliminaries will be held, among other events), the Sydney International Athletic Centre, and the Sydney International Aquatic Centre. (Public tours of these facilities are offered from Sydney; see chapter 5, "What to See & Do in Sydney.")

Events to be held in the Sydney Harbour Zone include portions of the marathon, which will begin in North Sydney and head across the Harbour Bridge and through The Rocks, the Botanic Garden, and Darling Harbour before finishing at Stadium Australia; basketball, boxing, and weightlifting at Darling Harbour; and yachting in Sydney Harbour. Sydney's famous Bondi Beach will be the venue for beach volleyball, which was first introduced in Olympic competition in 1996 at the Atlanta Olympic Games.

Traveler's Checks   Traveler's checks are something of an anachronism from the days before ATMs made cash accessible at any time. The only sound alternative to traveling with dangerously large amounts of cash, traveler's checks were as reliable as currency, unlike personal checks, but could be replaced if lost or stolen, unlike cash. These days, traveler's checks seem less necessary because most cities have 24-hour ATMs and most establishments accept credit cards. Still, they are a safe means of carrying money.

You can get traveler's checks at almost any bank. Get the checks in Australian dollars. While U.S.-dollar traveler's checks are widely accepted at banks, big hotels, and currency exchanges, many smaller hotels, restaurants, and businesses will have no idea what the current exchange rate is when you present a U.S. check. Another plus of Australian-dollar traveler's checks is that two of the largest Aussie banks, ANZ and Westpac, cash them for free. If you bring checks in U.S. dollars, pounds Sterling, or any other foreign currency, each transaction will cost you A$7 (U.S.$4.90) at Westpac, A$6.50 (U.S.$4.55) for amounts under A$3,000 (U.S.$2,100) at ANZ, A$7 (U.S.$4.90) at Commonwealth, and A$5 (U.S.$3.50) at National.

You can get **American Express** traveler's checks over the phone by calling ☎ **800/ 221-7282;** by using this number, Amex gold and platinum cardholders are exempt from the 1% fee. AAA members can obtain checks without a fee at most AAA offices in the United States.

Visa offers traveler's checks at Citibank locations nationwide, as well as several other banks. The service charge ranges between 1.5 and 2%; checks come in denominations of $20, $50, $100, $500, and $1,000. **MasterCard** also offers traveler's checks. Call ☎ **800/223-9920** for a location near you.

What's a major sporting event without a mascot? The Sydney 2000 Olympic Games will have three critters to embody the spirit of the Games (merchandising?). All three are cuddly versions of native Aussie animals: Olly, a kookaburra; Millie, an echidna (it's like a spiny-coated anteater); and Syd, a platypus.

Getting Tickets   Details on how Australians can apply for (or, more likely, since the demand for tickets will no doubt be high, enter a national ballot for) Sydney 2000 tickets will be released by the **Sydney Organising Committee for the Olympic Games (SOCOG)** in May 1999. For more information, check out SOCOG's Web site at www.sydney.olympic.org.

Eighty percent of the approximately 5.5 million tickets will be sold in Australia; residents of other countries should check with their country's National Olympic Committee for details on obtaining tickets.

In the United States, **Cartan Tours,** Inc., 1334 Parkview Ave., Suite 210, Manhattan Beach, CA 90266 (☎ **800/818-1998** or 310/546-9662; fax 310/546-8433), is the official ticket agent responsible for the exclusive sale of tickets to the general public. To request information or to receive Cartan's Olympic brochure, call or visit the agency's Web site at www.cartan.com or contact them via e-mail at sales@cartan.com. Cartan will also offer a variety of exclusive travel packages.

Of course, several events, including the marathon, are open to spectators free of charge.

For tips on finding accommodations during the Games, see the "Finding a Room During the Sydney 2000 Olympic Games" box in chapter 4.

THEFT   Almost every credit card company has an emergency 800 number that you can call if your wallet or purse is stolen. **MasterCard's** emergency toll-free number in Australia is ☎ **1800/120-113,** and **Visa's** number is ☎ **1800/125-440.** To report a lost **American Express** card, call ☎ **1800/230 100** anywhere in Australia outside Sydney, or 02/9271 8666 in Sydney from 8:30am to 7pm, or 1800/642 227 from anywhere in Australia after hours.

If you opt to carry traveler's checks, be sure to keep a record of their serial numbers—separately from the checks, of course—so you're ensured a refund if the checks are lost or stolen. To report lost or stolen American Express traveler's checks call ☎ **1800/25 1902** anywhere in Australia, or 02/9271 8689 in Sydney.

Odds are that if your wallet is gone, the police won't be able to recover it for you. However, after you cancel your credit cards, it is still worth informing the police, since your credit card company or insurer may require a police report number.

6 When to Go

There are a couple of things to keep in mind when deciding when to travel to Australia. The first, of course, is the climate. Because seasons are created by the earth tilting on its axis, when countries in the Northern Hemisphere have winter, Australia and the Southern Hemisphere have summer, and vice versa. And, unlike the Northern Hemisphere, the farther south you go in Australia, the colder it gets. Second, you need to take into account the country's high and low travel seasons, which will determine when you're most likely to get the best deal on airfare, say, and when you'll have to pay top dollar for a hotel room.

THE CLIMATE & HIGH/LOW TRAVEL SEASONS

HIGH SEASON   The peak travel season in Australia is **winter.** In most parts of the country, summer is just too darn hot, too darn humid, too darn wet, or all three, especially in the northern part of the country—Queensland from north of around Townsville, all of the Top End and the Red Centre, and most of Western Australia. The most pleasant time to travel in these parts is April to September—when daytime temperatures are 19°C to 31°C (66°F to 89°F). June, July, and August are the busiest months in the Red Centre and the Top End; you'll need to book accommodations and tours way in advance during these months. Many hotels and resorts, especially those along the north Queensland coast, charge higher rates in winter, especially during Australia's school holidays (see below).

LOW SEASON   From October to March, fierce sunlight and intense heat can make touring outdoors all but impossible in the Northern Territory and northern Western Australia. In the Top End, which includes Darwin, Kakadu National Park, and the Kimberley, an intensely hot, humid **Wet Season** lasts from November or December to March or April, preceded by an even hotter and stickier build-up in October and November. Some attractions and tour companies even close up shop. Touring in the Wet can be a delightful experience, though, as waterfalls swell, lakes stretch to the horizon, and the land turns green. Just be prepared to change plans to suit the flood-waters, and be prepared for intense humidity. You usually can get significant discounts on accommodations during the off-season.

On the other hand, summer (December, January, and February) is the nicest time to visit the southern states—New South Wales, Victoria, South Australia, Western Australia from Perth on south, and Tasmania. Even in winter, however, the temperature rarely dips below freezing in these parts, and snow falls only in parts of Tasmania, in the ski fields of Victoria, and in the Snowy Mountains in southern New South Wales.

HOLIDAYS

In addition to the period from December 26 to the end of January, when Aussies take their summer vacations, the four days at **Easter** (from Good Friday through Easter Monday) and all school holiday periods are also very busy, so book ahead. Almost everything shuts down on Good Friday, and much is closed Easter Sunday and Monday. Most places are closed until 1pm, if not all day, on **ANZAC Day,** a World War I commemorative day on April 25.

More Secrets of the Seasons

If I had to pick the one best month to visit Australia, I'd say **September,** when it's usually warm enough to hit the beach in the southern states, but the humidity and rains haven't hit Cairns and the Top End yet.

Surprisingly, the *low season* for flights to Australia from the United States actually corresponds to Australia's peak travel season. Airfares on U.S. airlines are lowest from mid-April to late August, or, in other words, from the middle of Australia's autumn through the winter.

Try to stay away from Australia from Boxing Day (December 26) to the end of January, which is when Aussies take their summer vacations. Hotel rooms and seats on planes get scarce as hen's teeth, and not a single airline or hotel will discount one dollar off their full fares in that month.

Australia's Average Temperatures (°F) and Rainfall

	Jan	Feb	Mar	Apr	May	June	July	Aug	Sept	Oct	Nov	Dec
Adelaide												
Max	86	86	81	73	66	61	59	62	66	73	79	83
Min	61	62	59	55	50	47	45	46	48	51	55	59
Days of rain	2.8	2.5	8.5	9.4	10.3	8.4	7.6	7.6	6	4.9	3.2	3.2
Alice Springs												
Max	97	95	90	81	73	67	67	73	81	88	93	96
Min	70	69	63	54	46	41	39	43	49	58	64	68
Days of rain	4.8	3.9	8.6	7.8	8	2.6	2.1	2.1	0.6	1.9	3.5	4.4
Brisbane												
Max	85	85	82	79	74	69	68	71	76	80	82	85
Min	69	68	66	61	56	51	49	50	55	60	64	67
Days of rain	12.4	12.3	12.8	11.2	10.4	7.6	6.8	6.1	5.4	7	9.6	10.6
Cairns												
Max	90	89	87	85	81	79	78	80	83	86	88	90
Min	74	74	73	70	66	64	61	62	64	68	70	73
Days of rain	18.5	18.2	19.7	16.1	11.8	8.2	5.4	5.7	4.9	6.0	10.0	14.7
Canberra												
Max	82	82	76	67	60	53	52	55	61	68	75	80
Min	55	55	5	44	37	34	33	35	38	43	48	53
Days of rain	5.2	4.8	9.8	9.2	9.4	6.6	5.9	6.8	4.6	6.2	5.4	5.4
Darwin												
Max	90	90	91	92	91	88	87	89	91	93	94	92
Min	77	77	77	76	73	69	67	70	74	77	78	78
Days of rain	18	16.9	15.5	11.3	8.0	1.5	1.3	1.5	1.2	5.7	11.4	15.2
Hobart												
Max	71	71	68	63	58	53	52	55	59	63	66	69
Min	53	53	51	48	44	41	40	41	43	46	48	51
Days of rain	5.2	4.4	9.4	9.5	9.4	6.8	6.6	6.1	6.0	6.5	6.7	5.6
Melbourne												
Max	78	78	75	68	62	57	56	59	63	67	71	75
Min	57	57	55	51	47	44	42	43	46	48	51	54
Days of rain	5.2	5.0	9.8	9.9	9.7	6.6	6.1	6.1	6.5	7.2	6.5	6.1
Perth												
Max	85	85	81	76	69	64	63	67	70	76	81	73
Min	63	63	61	57	53	50	48	48	50	53	57	61
Days of rain	1.5	1.8	8.3	9.3	12.4	13.8	13.4	12.4	9.0	6.2	2.2	2.0
Sydney												
Max	78	78	76	71	66	61	60	63	67	71	74	77
Min	65	65	63	58	52	48	46	48	51	56	60	63
Days of Rain	8.3	9.1	12.3	12.5	12.3	11.0	11.0	8.4	7.9	7.7	7.9	7.2

Source: Australian Tourist Commission Australia Vacation Planner.

MAJOR NATIONAL HOLIDAYS

New Year's Day	January 1
Australia Day	January 26
Labour Day	First Monday in March (WA)
Eight Hour Day	First Monday in March (TAS)
Labour Day	Second Monday in March (VIC)

Canberra Day	Third Monday in March (ACT)
Good Friday	Varies
Easter Sunday	Varies
Easter Monday	Varies
ANZAC Day	April 25
May Day	First Monday in May (NT)
Labour Day	First Monday in May (QLD)
Adelaide Cup	Third Monday in May (SA)
Foundation Day	First Monday in June (WA)
Queen's Birthday	Second Monday in June (except WA)
Royal National Show Day	Second or third Wednesday in August (QLD)
Queen's Birthday	Monday in late Sept/early Oct (WA)
Labour Day	First Monday in October (NSW, SA)
Melbourne Cup Day	First Tuesday in November (Melbourne only)
Christmas Day	December 25
Boxing Day	December 26

SCHOOL HOLIDAYS

The school year in Australia is broken into four semesters, with 2-week holidays falling around the last half of April, the last week of June and the first week of July, and the last week of September and the first week of October. There's a 6-week summer/ Christmas vacation from mid-December to the end of January.

AUSTRALIA CALENDAR OF EVENTS

January

- **New Year's Eve.** The big treat on this day is to watch the Sydney Harbour Bridge light up with fireworks. The main show is at 9pm, not midnight, so young kids don't miss out. Pack a picnic and snag a harborside spot by 4pm, or even earlier at the best vantage points: Mrs. Macquarie's Point in the Royal Botanic Gardens, Cremorne Point on the North Shore (take the ferry), and the Sydney Opera House.
- **Sydney Festival.** A summertime visual and performing arts festival, with impromptu nightclubs, outdoor cinema by the Opera House, and more. Highlights are the free concerts held outdoors Saturday nights in the Domain, near the Botanic Gardens. Contact the **Sydney Festival,** 36–38 Young St., Sydney, NSW 2000 (☎ **02/8248 6500,** fax 02/8248 6599). For three weeks in January.
- **Hyundai Hopman Cup,** Perth. Tennis greats from the world's nine top tennis nations are invited to battle it out in an 11-day mixed-doubles competition. Contact the Cup's offices at ☎ **08/9380 4000,** or fax 08/9388 1436. Early January.
- **Tamworth Country Music Festival,** Tamworth, New South Wales. It may look like an Akubra Hat Convention, but this gathering of rural folk and city folk who would like to be rural folk is Australia's biggest country music festival. Aussie stars perform alongside international guests in this country town. The Tamworth Information Centre (☎ **02/6755 4300,** fax 02/6755 4312) takes bookings. Held over 10 days in the second half of January.
- **Australia Day.** Australia's answer to the Fourth of July marks the landing of the First Fleet at Sydney Cove in 1788. Most Aussies celebrate by heading to the nearest beach, but every large town and city has some kind of celebration. In Sydney there are ferry races and tall ships on the harbor, free performing arts at Darling Harbour, a vintage car festival, and fireworks in the evening. January 26.

- **Heineken Classic,** on Perth's outskirts. The country's richest golf tournament draws players like Daly, Els, Montgomerie, and Nobilo to the Novotel Vines Resort in the Swan Valley wine region, a 20-minute drive from Perth. Call the Classic's office (☎ **08/9297 3399,** fax 08/9297 3311). Last week of January.

February

- **Adelaide Festival.** This huge event on the international arts scene features enthusiastic performance art, music, dance, and outdoor concerts, as well as an associated Fringe Festival and a writers' week (1998's authors included Julian Barnes and Booker Prize–winner Arundhati Roy). A summer party atmosphere takes over Adelaide's city streets every night until late. Contact Adelaide Festival, 105 Hindley St., Adelaide, SA 5000 (☎ **08/8216 4444,** fax 08/8216 4455, www.festivals.on.net/adelaide.html). For two and a half weeks in March, every second year. The next festival is in 2000.

March

- **Qantas Australian Grand Prix,** Melbourne. The first Grand Prix of the year on the international FIA Formula One World Championship circuit takes place in Melbourne. Contact Australian Grand Prix Corporation, 220 Albert Rd., South Melbourne, VIC 3205 (☎ **03/9258 7100,** fax 03/9699 3727). Usually the first week of March.

- **Sydney Gay & Lesbian Mardi Gras.** A spectacular parade of floats, costumes, and dancers. Contact Sydney Gay & Lesbian Mardi Gras Ltd., 21–23 Erskineville Rd., Erskineville, NSW 2043 (☎ **02/9557 4332,** fax 02/9516 4446, e-mail: mardigras@mardigras.com.au). Usually the last Saturday night in February; occasionally the first Saturday in March.

April

- **Australian Surf Life Saving Championships,** Kurrawa Beach, Queensland. As many as 6,000 bronzed Aussie men and women swim, ski paddle, board paddle, sprint relay, pilot inflatable rescue boats through the surf, perform march-pasts, and resuscitate "drowning" swimmers in this annual event on the Gold Coast. Join 45,000 Aussies on the beach to watch them over a 4-day period every late March or early April. Contact Surf Life Saving Australia (☎ **02/9597 5588,** fax 02/9599 4809).

June

- **Sydney International Film Festival.** World and Australian premieres of leading Aussie and international flicks are shown in the ornate State Theatre. Tickets start at A$21 (U.S.$14.70) for any three films, or you can pay up to A$250 (U.S.$175) for a 2-week subscription to the best seats in the house. Contact the Sydney Film Festival, 405 Glebe Point Rd., Glebe, NSW 2037 (☎ **02/9660 3844,** fax 02/9692 8793; www.sydfilm-fest.com.au). Runs for 2 weeks from first or second Friday in June.

August

- **Sun-Herald City to Surf,** Sydney. Fifty thousand Sydneysiders pound the pavement annually in this 14-kilometer (8½-mile) "fun run" from the city to Bondi Beach. There are also walking and wheelchair categories. Entry is around A$20 (U.S.$14) for adults and A$15 (U.S.$10.50) for kids. For an entry form, write to Sun-Herald City to Surf, 201 Sussex St., Sydney, NSW 2000 (☎ **02/9282 2822,** fax 02/9282 2360), or enter on the day of the race. Usually the second Sunday in August, but it may be a month earlier in 2000 to avoid clashing with the Olympics.

September

- **Australian Rules Grand Final,** Melbourne. The closest thing Australia has to the Super Bowl. Late September/early October.
- **Floriade,** Canberra. The banks of Lake Burley Griffin become covered with living flower-bed designs at this spring celebration, to which a little spice is added with performing arts, as well as gourmet food and wine tastings. Contact the Canberra Tourism & Events Corporation (☎ **02/6205 0044,** fax 02/6205 0776). Held from the second or third week of September for a month.

October

- **Henley-on-Todd Regatta,** Alice Springs. Sounds oh-so-sophisticated, doesn't it? It's actually a harum-scarum race down the dry Todd River bed in hilarious home-made "boats." The only liquid flowing for miles around is the beer at the pub afterward. Contact the Central Australian Tourism Industry Association (☎ **08/ 8952 5800,** fax 08/8953 0295). Late September or early October.
- **Indy Carnival,** Surfers Paradise, Queensland. The world's best Indy-car drivers race a street circuit around Surfers Paradise on the glitzy Gold Coast. Contact the Gold Coast Tourism Bureau (☎ **07/5538 4419,** fax 07/5570 3259). Four days in mid-October.
- **Lizard Island Black Marlin Classic,** Great Barrier Reef, Queensland. Potential world record–sized giant black marlin swim in these waters, and every year anglers look for them at this event. Lizard Island, which is near Cairns, also hosts a 3-day Halloween Billfish Shootout, ending with a party on October 31. Contact Lizard Island Lodge (☎ **1800/676 134** in Australia, or 07/4060 3999). Runs for a week in mid-October.

November

- **Melbourne Cup.** If you aren't glued to the TV to watch this million-dollar 3,200-meter (2-mile) horserace, well, you're probably not an Australian. First Tuesday in November.

December

- **Sydney to Hobart Yacht Race.** Find a clifftop spot near the Heads to watch the glorious show of spinnakers as 100 or so yachts leave Sydney Harbour for this grueling world-class event. Contact Tourism New South Wales (☎ **02/ 9931 1111,** fax 02/9931 1490) or Tourism Tasmania (☎ **03/6230 8169,** fax 03/6230 8353). Starts December 26.

7 The Active-Vacation Planner

Australia's warm weather, sporty people, and natural scenery are perfect for active vacations. The good news is that organized active vacations are among the most affordable, with all activities, meals, camping gear or accommodations (generally basic but clean), and any sporting equipment included in the price.

Most of the operators and outfitters listed here specialize in adventure vacations for small groups. As a rule, their packages include meals, accommodations, equipment rental, camping gear where appropriate, and guides. International airfares are *not* included unless otherwise noted. The place you spend the night can vary depending on the type of package you select—for example, on a sea-kayaking trip you almost always camp on the beach, on a hiking expedition you may stay at anything from a campsite to a wilderness lodge, while on a biking trip you often stop over at charming B&B-style lodgings. If your trip is camping-based you may need to bring your own sleeping bag or rent one from the adventure operator.

You will find additional information on the outdoor activities discussed below in the relevant regional chapters. Before you hit the outdoors, review the tips on safety later in this section.

DIVING

Diving Down Under is one of the best travel experiences you can have anywhere. The Great Barrier Reef alone consists of 2,900 coral reefs, 400 kinds of coral, and 1,500 kinds of fish. Don't think all of Australia's dive spots are on the Great Barrier Reef, though. First-rate sites are found all around the coastline. A second barrier reef in Ningaloo Marine Park stretches 260 kilometers (156 miles) off the coast of Western Australia (see chapter 11 or check out Exmouth Diving Centre's Web site: www.exmouthdiving.com.au). For a rundown on the country's truly outstanding dive areas, see "The Best Affordable Diving & Snorkeling Sites" in chapter 1.

Wherever you find coral in Australia you will find dive companies offering learn-to-dive courses, day trips, and, in some cases, extended journeys on live-aboard vessels. Most international dive certificates, including PADI, NAUI, SSI, and BSAC, are recognized. It's easy to rent gear and wet suits for around A$20 (U.S.$14) per day wherever you go, or you can bring your own. Open-water certification courses range from an intensive three days to a more relaxed five days, for which you can expect to pay between A$320 (U.S.$224) and A$600 (U.S.$420). Most operators offer courses right up to instructor level. A one-day dive trip including two dives usually costs about A$110 to $140 (U.S.$77 to $98) dollars, including gear rental.

If you are a certified diver, remember to bring your C card. It's also a good idea to bring your log book. If you are going to do a dive course, you will need two passport photos and a medical certificate that meets Australian standard AS4005.1 and specifically states you are fit for scuba diving (an all-purpose medical is not enough). Your dive operator can fax the standard's requirements to your doctor at home so you can have the physical before you leave; some states, such as Queensland, require the medical to be done on their home soil. For A$35 to 50 (U.S.$24.50 to $35), virtually all dive operators can arrange with an Australian doctor a medical exam for you that fits the standard. Remember, for medical reasons you can fly before you dive, but you must complete your last dive 24 hours before you fly in an aircraft. This catches a lot of people off guard when they are preparing to fly after a day on the Reef. Check to see whether your travel insurance covers diving.

If you've never dived before, you can see what all the fuss is about on a "resort" or "introductory" dive. Most Great Barrier Reef day-trip cruise boats and dive operators offer them for around A$55 to 85 (U.S.$38.50 to $59.50). After a short briefing, followed by a practical lesson in the resort swimming pool or on the cruise boat's pontoon, you are ready for a 20-minute foray into a magical underwater world. An instructor is beside you the whole time.

Diving Tip

August to January is peak visibility time on the Great Barrier Reef, but the marine life will wow you any time of year.

For information on dive sites, operators, and courses, contact the **Australian Tourist Commission** for diving anywhere in Australia, or the **Queensland Tourist & Travel Corporation** for diving the Great Barrier Reef (see "Visitor Information" earlier in this chapter); their Web sites have plentiful links to dive operators all over the country. Also check out www.queensland-holidays.com.au. **Dive Queensland** (the Queensland Dive Tourism Association), P.O. Box 5120, Cairns, QLD 4870 (☎ 07/ 4051 1510; fax 07/4051 1519; wwww.great-barreir-reef.net.au), is a one-stop shop for getting in touch with member dive operators in that state who stick to a code of ethics.

Peter Stone's Dive Australia, by Peter Stone, is a comprehensive 608-page guidebook to more than 2,000 dive sites, plus dive operators, all over Australia. It is published by Ocean Publications, 303 Commercial Rd., Yarram, VIC 3971 (☎ 03/5182 5108; fax 03/5182 5823; www.netspace.net.au/~oceans/oe.html). You can mail-order it for A$36 (U.S.$25.20) plus postage or buy it from **Best Publications** in Arizona (☎ **520/527 1055**).

The **National Parks & Wildlife** offices listed in the following "Bushwalking" section can also be good sources of information, as many Marine Parks with good diving come under their jurisdiction.

BUSHWALKING (HIKING)

With so much unique scenery and so many rare animals and plants to protect, it's not surprising that Australia is full of national parks crisscrossed with hiking trails. You're never far from a park with a bushwalk, whether it's an easy 300-meter (⅓-mile) stroll to a lookout or a 650-kilometer (390-mile) odyssey.

Australia's official bushwalking Web page is at www.bushwalking.org.au. The best place to get information about bushwalking before you leave home is the **National Parks & Wildlife Service,** or its equivalent, in each state:

- **National Parks & Wildlife Service (NSW) Information Centre,** Level 1, 43 Bridge St., Hurstville, NSW 2220 (☎ **02/9585 6333,** or 02/9585 6444; fax 02/9585 6527; www.npws.nsw.gov.au/).
- **Naturally Queensland Information Centre,** Department of Environment (QLD), 160 Ann St., Brisbane, QLD 4000 (☎ **07/3227 8186;** fax 07/ 3227 8749; www.env.qld.gov.au).
- **Parks & Wildlife Commission of the Northern Territory,** Goyder Centre, 25 Chung Wah Terrace, Palmerston NT 0830 (☎ **08/8999 5511;** fax 08/ 8932 3849). The Northern Territory Tourist Commission (see "Visitor Information" earlier in this chapter) is the official dispenser of information on parks and wildlife matters.
- **Department of Conservation and Land Management (CALM),** Western Australia Naturally Information Centre, 47 Henry St., Fremantle, WA 6160 (☎ **08/ 9430 8600;** fax 08/9430 8699; www.calm.wa.gov.au).
- **Department of Environment, Heritage and Aboriginal Affairs (SA) Information Centre,** Ground Floor, 77 Grenfell St., Adelaide, SA 5000 (☎ **08/ 8204 1910;** fax 08/8204 1919; www.denr.sa.gov.au).
- **Parks Victoria,** 35 Whitehorse Rd. Deepdene, VIC 3013 (☎ **13 19 63** in Australia, or 03/9816 7066; fax 03/9817 6459; www.nre.gov.au/parks).
- **Tasmania Parks & Wildlife Service,** GPO Box 44a, Hobart, TAS 7001 (☎ **03/ 6233 3382** for the information officer, or 03/6233 2189 for administration; fax 03/6223 2158; www.parks.tas.gov.au).

Some parks charge a daily or one-time entry fee; it's usually around A$5 to $8 (U.S.$3.50 to $5.60), but is occasionally as much as A$15 (U.S.$10.50).

North by Northwest, 52 Tierra Montanosa, Rancho Santa Margarita, CA 92688 (☎ and fax **949/858-1073;** www.north-by-northwest.com), conducts 9- and 12-day bushwalks through the alpine wilds of Tasmania's Cradle Mountain and Lake St. Clair regions and the lofty peaks of the state's Walls of Jerusalem.

MORE ACTIVE VACATIONS FROM A TO Z

ABSEILING   Rapelling is another name for this sport, which involves backing down vertical cliff faces in a rope and harness. The ruggedly beautiful Blue Mountains (see chapter 6) are Australia's abseiling capital. In the Margaret River region (see chapter 11) you can do it as mighty breakers crash on the cliffs below. You can even do it in Brisbane on river cliffs in the heart of the city (see chapter 7).

BIKING   Cycling is a well-developed sport in Australia. On Rottnest Island off Perth (see chapter 11), it's the only mode of transport. The rain-forest hills behind Cairns recently hosted the world mountain biking championships, and Sydney's Blue Mountains have excellent mountain-biking terrain and marked trails. Australia's flat countryside is ideal for cycling, but consider the heat and the *v-a-s-t* distances before trying to cycle from point to point. All major towns and most resort centers rent regular bikes and mountain bikes.

If you are interested in taking an extended biking trip, get a copy of *Cycling Australia: Bicycle Touring Throughout the Sunny Continent,* by Australian Ian Duckworth (Bicycle Books). This 224-page touring guide outlines eight long bike trips, with maps and detailed route descriptions. Any large bookstore can order it, and it is available for U.S.$14.95 (C$19.95) from the **Adventurous Traveler Bookstore** (☎ **800/ 282-3963** in the U.S. and Canada; www.adventuroustraveler.com), or for £9.95 from the **Cycling Bookshop,** Teignmouth, England TQ14 8DE (☎ **01626/77-5436**).

Boomerang Bicycle Tours, P.O. Box 267, Forestville, NSW 2087 (☎ **02/ 9975 4251;** fax 02/9975 6082; www.ozemail.com.au/~ozbike) does multiday tours of the Hunter Valley wine region north of Sydney, New South Wales' Southern Highlands, and the Snowy Mountains (see chapter 6); Queensland's Gold Coast (see chapter 8); and Victoria's Great Ocean Road and picturesque northeast country (see chapter 14). You stay in comfortable guesthouses and wilderness lodges.

Remote Outback Cycle Tours, P.O. Box 1179, West Leederville, WA 6901 (☎ **08/9244 4614;** fax 08/9244 4615; www.omen.com.au/~roc), takes novice and expert bike riders, young and old, on extended biking tours through the Outback. Itineraries include a 5-day Margaret River Forest and Wine sojourn in Western Australia; a 5-day trip from Alice Springs through the MacDonnell Ranges; and an epic 14-day expedition across the Gibb River Road in the Kimberley.

Rolling On . . . Mountain Bike Tours, P.O. Box 19, Hove, SA 5048 (☎ **08/ 8358 2401;** www.rolling.mtx.net), runs 1- to 16-day scenic mountain bike tours from Adelaide throughout South Australia. Itineraries include the rugged Flinders Ranges and the Barossa Valley wine region. Nights are spent camping or in basic accommodations.

Mountain Logistix, P.O. Box 49, Tawonga South, VIC 3698 (☎ **03/5754 1676;** fax 03/5754-1644; www.mtbeauty.albury.net.au/~mtlgx), runs multiday mountain-biking trips in Victoria's picturesque High Country. Camp or upgrade to motel-style lodgings. **Bicycle Victoria** (☎ **03/9328 3000;** fax 03/9328 2288) runs several major cycling tours every year throughout the state.

BIRD-WATCHING   Australia has a rich range of bird life, and its unique position as an island continent ensures it has species you won't see anywhere else. Australia is probably best known for its wide variety of brilliant parrots, but over the continent you will see species from the wetlands, savannah, mulga scrub, desert, oceans, dense bushland, rain forest, mangroves, rivers, and other habitats. More than half the country's species have been spotted in the Daintree Rainforest area in north Queensland (see chapter 8), and one-third of Australia's species live in wetlands-rich Kakadu National Park in the Northern Territory (see chapter 10). The Coorong in South Australia (see chapter 12) and Broome (see chapter 10) are home to marvelous waterfowl populations.

To get in touch with bird-watching clubs all over Australia, contact **Birds Australia** (formerly the Royal Australasian Ornithologists' Union), 415 Riversdale Rd., Hawthorn East, VIC 3123 (☎ **03/9882 2622;** fax 03/9882 2677).

Kirrama Wildlife Tours, P.O. Box 133, Silkwood, QLD 4856 (☎ **07/4065 5181;** fax 07/4065 5197; www.gspeak.com.au/kirrama/), operates extended birding expeditions to remote rain-forest, arid, monsoon, and mangrove regions in northern Australia. The company is based near Cairns.

Australian Ornithological Services, P.O. Box 385, South Yarra, VIC 3141 (☎ and fax **03/ 9820 4223**), conducts tailor-made bird-watching tours all over Australia.

CANOEING & SEA KAYAKING   Katherine Gorge in the Northern Territory (see chapter 10) is probably the most spectacular flat canoeing in the country, through a series of red-walled ravines and forested banks, although the Gorge demands more than its fair share of fording. You'll find delightful flat canoeing on the magnificent Ord River (see chapter 10), and on numerous broad, peaceful rivers running down from the Great Dividing Range all along the continent's east coast. Katherine Gorge and the Ord are full of generally harmless freshwater crocodiles, but *never* canoe in saltwater crocodile territory. White-water canoeing can be found in Barrington Tops National Park north of Sydney (see chapter 6).

Australia's long coastline and rich warm seas are tailor-made for sea kayaking. Several companies rent kayaks or offer guided expeditions against the backdrop of the Whitsunday Islands (see chapter 8); to Dunk Island off Mission Beach (see chapter 8); and in Perth, Monkey Mia, and the Northwest Cape in Western Australia (see chapter 11).

Rivergods, 5 Ziera Place, Parkwood, Perth, WA 6147 (☎ **08/9259 0749;** fax 08/9259 0902; www.ca.com.au/rivergod), conducts 1-day and multiday sea kayaking, canoeing, and white-water rafting adventures throughout Western Australia's pristine ocean and rivers, in which whales, sharks, dugongs (manatees), sea snakes, turtles, and dolphins abound.

CANYONING   A mixture of abseiling down canyon walls, swimming through waterholes, floating down a river at the canyon floor on an air mattress, and hiking or rock-climbing back out of the canyon is the assorted disciplines that make up this unusual sport. The rugged plateaus and deep ravines of Sydney's Blue Mountains are a plum spot for it in summer (the canyon water is too icy in winter).

Something Different: Camel Trekking

It might sound strange, but Australia has one of the world's largest camel populations. Camels were imported to negotiate waterless deserts in the 1900s, but were later set free. They are now making a comeback as a popular way to trek the country. One-hour rambles in Alice Springs and Ayers Rock are a novel way to see the Outback (see chapter 9). Several companies in Broome lead guided rides along Cable Beach (see chapter 10). You can also camel trek through Flinders Ranges National Park in South Australia (see chapter 12).

CAVING   Australia doesn't have a lot of caves, but the ones it has are spectacular. The best are the Jenolan Caves in the Blue Mountains west of Sydney, a honeycomb of stunningly beautiful limestone caverns that have been forming intricate stalactite and stalagmite patterns for millions of years (see chapter 6). The Margaret River region in Western Australia (see chapter 11) has about 350 limestone caves, two of which, Moondyne and Ngilgi, can be explored on a regular half-day adventure tour by folk who've never been spelunking. In Australia, spelunking is called speliology.

FISHING   Reef, game, deep sea, beach, estuary, river, and trout fishing—Australia's massive coastline lets you do it all. Drop a line for coral trout on the Great Barrier Reef; go for the world record in the Lizard Island Black Marlin Classic near Cairns; hook a fighting "barra," short for barramundi, in the Northern Territory or the Kimberley; or cast for trout in Tasmania's highland lakes. You can rent fishing tackle and bait in any coastal town, and most have at least one fishing tour operator running half-day or full-day guided trips.

GOLF   Australians are almost as passionate about golf as they are about footy (football) and cricket—after all, before Greg Norman was a Yank he was an Aussie! Thanks to an equable climate, you can golf year-round. There's no shortage of world-class championship courses, many the handiwork of star-quality designers like the Thomson-Wolveridge team, as well as humbler but pleasant community fairways all over the country. Queensland has the lion's share of the most stunning resort courses, such as the Sheraton Mirage in Port Douglas, Laguna Quays Resort near the Whitsundays, and Hyatt Regency Sanctuary Cove Resort on the Gold Coast (see chapter 8). The Gold Coast alone is studded with more than 40 courses. These championship courses will cost you, though; we also recommend some less-expensive courses. The Novotel Vines Resort in the Swan Valley near Perth is another outstanding resort course (see chapter 11). One of the top 10 desert courses in the world is at Alice Springs (see chapter 9). You can play a round of bush golf in Broken Hill—it's played at night when it's cool, with fluorescent golf balls (see chapter 6); or hit the links in Lightning Ridge (see chapter 6) where the greens are dusty browns.

Most courses rent clubs for around A$30 (U.S.$21). Greens fees start at around A$20 (U.S.$14) for 18 holes, but average A$60 (U.S.$42) on a championship course.

HORSEBACK RIDING   Horseback-riding operators are readily found throughout Australia, but keen riders should consider a multiday riding and camping trek out in the Snowy Mountains in New South Wales (see chapter 6). This is "The Man from Snowy River" country, and a beautiful place to explore in the saddle.

ROCK CLIMBING   Australia doesn't have a lot of mountains, but it has enough sheer cliff faces to support a healthy number of people who like climbing them. Surmounting the Three Sisters rock formation in the Blue Mountains is one popular challenge for climbers (see chapter 6); another is scaling the towering cliffs of Western Australia's Margaret River as mighty breakers crash below you (see chapter 11).

SAILING   The 74 island gems of the Whitsundays in Queensland (see chapter 8) are an out-of-this-world backdrop for sailing. And no, you don't have to know how to sail—plenty of operators charter *bareboat* yachts (that means unskippered) by the day or the week, even to folk like me with not a stitch of sailing experience. Sailors will find plenty of companies all around the coast at which to charter a suitable vessel for a day or more.

Sydney and Perth have twilight races most summer evenings, and it's usually okay to front up to any of the numerous sailing clubs to try to get a place on a boat for an afternoon.

Skiing, Anyone?

Australia is never going to be the ski capital of the universe, but if you find yourself on vacation in the Aussie winter, you might want to try Thredbo and Perisher Valley in the Snowy Mountains in southern New South Wales (see chapter 6) or the High Country of inland Victoria. The season is short—June to September, with the best falls in July and August.

SURFING   You'll have no trouble finding a good surf beach anywhere around the Australian coast, so prolific are they. Perth and Sydney are blessed with loads of good surf beaches right in the city. Other popular spots include Kirra at Coolangatta on the Gold Coast (see chapter 8), the legendary Southern Ocean swells along Victoria's southern coast (see chapter 14), and the magnificent sets off Margaret River in Western Australia (see chapter 11). Just don't take your board much north of the Sunshine Coast in Queensland—the Great Barrier Reef puts a stop to the swell from there all the way to the northern tip of Queensland. In any surfing town, you can rent a Malibu and a wet suit for between A$25 (U.S.$17.50) and A$45 (U.S.$31.50) a day. Surf schools in all the big surfing centers give beginner's classes in which they guarantee to have you standing in 90 minutes.

WHITE-WATER RAFTING   The best rapids are the Grade 5 torrents on the Nymboida and Gwydir Rivers behind Coffs Harbour in New South Wales (see chapter 6). Grade 5 rapids can also be found on the Johnstone River in north Queensland, which must be accessed by helicopter. Loads of tourists who have never held a paddle hurtle down the Grade 3 to 4 Tully River near Mission Beach and the gentler Grade 2 to 3 Barron River near Cairns (see chapter 8). The Snowy River National Park in Victoria is another spot popular with rafters.

Peregrine Adventures, 258 Lonsdale St., Melbourne VIC 3000 (☎ 03/9662 2800; fax 03/9662 2422; www.peregrine.net.au), runs rafting expeditions in Victoria and on the mighty Franklin River in the wilds of Tasmania. It is represented in the United States by **Himalayan Travel** (☎ 800/225-2380), in Canada by several companies including **Westcan Edmonton** (☎ 800/267-3347), and in the United Kingdom by **Guerba Expeditions** (☎ 01373/82-6611).

See also "Canoeing and Sea Kayaking," above.

WINDSURFING   Most summer evenings and weekends, Sydney Harbour is alive with windsurfers nimbly dodging the ferries. Many coastal towns have windsurfers for rent, and no self-respecting island resort in Queensland would be without them. Many rental outfits and resorts throw in a free lessons for beginners. Fremantle in Western Australia (see chapter 11) is a world windsurfing center thanks to fairly calm waters and strong, regular winds.

MORE OUTFITTERS & ADVENTURE-TRAVEL OPERATORS
AUSTRALIA-BASED OPERATORS

Landscope Expeditions, the tourism arm of the Western Australian Department of Conservation and Land Management (CALM), runs a terrific program whereby you get to help naturalists, marine biologists, and other scientists in their work and have fun at the same time. The 1998–99 program included Project Eden, in which participants helped reintroduce endangered Australian reptiles and mammals to the Outback area around Shark Bay in Western Australia. For a brochure, contact Landscope Expeditions, UWA Extension, University of Western Australia, Nedlands, WA 6907 (☎ 08/9380 2433; fax 08/9380 1066; www.calm.wa.gov.au).

Morrell Adventure Travel, 57 Oliver St., Berridale, NSW 2029 (☎ **1800/ 066 126** in Australia, or 02/6456 3681; fax 02/6456 3679; www.morrell.com) takes you mountain biking, bushwalking, cross-country and adventure skiing, or white-water rafting in the Snowy Mountains' Kosciusco National Park and other beauty spots in southern New South Wales. Pick one sport or do them all in a combo.

MudMaps Australia, P.O. Box 31, Campbell, ACT 2612 (☎ **1800/803 565** in Australia, or 02/6257 4796; fax 888/MUD-MAPS in the United States; www.mudmaps.com), offers 1- to 4-day wilderness tours from Canberra to the nearby Snowy Mountains and as far afield as Sydney and Melbourne. The groups are small, your guide is a bushman, the transport is 4WD, and you stay at farms and B&B-style accommodations.

Tasmanian Expeditions, 110 George St., Launceston, TAS 7250 (☎ **03/ 6334 3477;** fax 03/6334 3463; www.tassie.net.au/tas_ex/index.html), conducts hiking, cycling, rafting, abseiling, and rock-climbing trips throughout Tasmania's national parks. Day trips are also available.

U.S.–Based Operators

In addition to the operators listed here, two Web sites are very useful for locating adventure tour operators: *USA Today's* **travel** Web site at http://usatoday.travelon.com allows you to find to all kinds of adventure packages to Australia at a travel date and price to suit you; the site also has links to the company organizing the trip. The **Great Outdoor Recreation Pages** (G.O.R.P.) site at www.gorp.com not only has links to heaps of adventure tour operators but also contains articles, sells books and maps, and has links with an action slant to all kinds of sites in Australia.

Adventure Express Travel, 650 Fifth St., Suite 505, San Francisco, CA 94107 (☎ **800/443-0799** or 415/442-0799; www.adventureexpress.com), sells scuba-diving packages on the Great Barrier Reef, including day dives, extended live-aboard trips, and learn-to-dive courses. It also custom-builds independent multisport itineraries in and around Sydney and North Queensland. The company claims to meet or beat any competitor's price.

Down Under Answers, 12727 NE 20th St., Suite 5, Bellevue, WA 98005 (☎ **800/ 788-6685** or 425/895-0895; www.adventour.com), sells diving packages in North Queensland, sea-kayaking trips from Cairns, and biking trips in a range of scenic spots throughout the country. A 7-day multisport option combines canoeing, hiking, biking, and snorkeling the Great Barrier Reef from Cairns.

Outer Edge Expeditions, 45500 Pontiac Trail, Walled Lake, MI 48390-4036 (☎ **800/322-5235** or 248/624-5140; www.outer-edge.com), specializes in ecologically minded camping, diving, hiking, mountain-biking, canoeing, and sea-kayaking packages to such places as the Great Barrier Reef, Ayers Rock, and Kangaroo Island off South Australia.

Roads Less Traveled, 2480 Wilderness Place, #F, Boulder, CO 80301 (☎ **800/ 488-8483** or 303/413-0938; www.roadslesstraveled.com), runs combined hiking, mountain-biking, canoeing, snorkeling, and diving packages in the Great Barrier Reef and North Queensland. Itineraries range from 7 to 11 days for a maximum 14 travelers.

World Traveler's Club, 1475 Polk St., Level 2, San Francisco, CA 94109 (☎ **800/ 693-0411** or 415/447-6112; www.around-the-world.com), offers a range of hiking, Great Barrier Reef–diving, rafting, sea-kayaking, and biking packages to popular parts of the country.

TIPS ON HEALTH, SAFETY & OUTDOOR ETIQUETTE DOWN UNDER

Australia has a lot of rough, remote territory typified by incredibly high temperatures, no water, little shade, flash floods, and bushfires. Add to that the deadly snakes and spiders you might meet, and the thought that the nearest gas station, telephone, or person could be hundreds of miles away, and it's a wonder anyone ventures 10 miles from the airport! Extreme heat and ultraviolet rays can lead quickly to exhaustion, dehydration, sunstroke, and severe sunburn, even if you are expending only a small amount of energy. Follow the tips below and you should make it back home unscathed.

SOME GENERAL RULES OF THUMB

- Don't disturb wildlife, take plant cuttings, or remove rocks, shells, coral, or other pieces of the wilderness. It is seen as bad form to impact on the environment like this, and it is an offense in national and marine parks.
- Tell someone where you are going, whether you're taking a 2-hour hike or a 3-week 4WD trip across the country. If you are hiking in a national park, leave your details with someone at the ranger station. On a longer trip, leave your travel plans with friends, relatives, or the police.
- Carry extra water. It's easy to dehydrate without even knowing it. Two liters per person per day should be your minimum ration; 2 liters per person per hour is the rule in the Outback and the Top End in summer.
- Don't feed animals, birds, and fish. It makes them unhealthy and causes them to lose their hunting skills.
- Obey fire restrictions. In hot dry weather, a total fire ban may apply, which means you cannot light a naked flame. Many national parks permit camp-ovens only, not campfires. If you use a campfire, burn only fallen wood, not standing dead trees that could house animals. Thoroughly extinguish all campfires.
- Look at but don't touch historical Aboriginal sites such as rock art walls and *middens* (shell mounds). It can be an offense to disturb them.

BASICS FOR BUSHWALKERS

- Stay on the track. Cutting corners can damage vegetation and cause erosion.
- Whatever you take in, take out. Leave no rubbish, even organic stuff like an apple core (it takes a long time to degrade, it's not the right food for native animals, and it might self-seed and become a pest among native vegetation). For the same reason don't bury your rubbish.
- Check track conditions and the weather forecast before you go.
- Register in the National Parks & Wildlife Service logbook if there is one placed at the start of the walk (don't forget to indicate in the register that you've returned, or a search party will be out looking for you while you're having dinner back at your hotel).
- Wear a broad-brimmed hat, sunglasses, sunscreen, sturdy shoes, and a comfortable backpack. Insect repellent should be a key item on your list, as flies can reach plague proportions in dry areas and mosquitoes are common in rain forests.

BEACH SAVVY FOR SWIMMERS & SURFERS

- Never swim alone at beaches not patrolled by lifesavers (lifeguards).
- Always swim between the red and yellow flags denoting a safe swimming zone. Crossed flagpoles or a red flag mean the beach is closed due to extremely dangerous swimming conditions. A yellow flag means conditions are dangerous and swimming is not advised.

What About Sharks?

"If you knew the danger out there, you'd never leave the safety of your hotel," a tourist said to me as he went for a swim off Sydney's Manly Beach. The day before, a helicopter had been called in to fire warning shots across the noses of a school of 3-meter (9.8-foot) hammerhead sharks that had come too close to shore for comfort. Fortunately, shark attacks are extremely rare; only 190 people have been killed, and 263 people injured, by sharks since the first death in 1791.

- *Rips* are powerful currents that can carry even a strong swimmer out to sea. If caught in one, don't fatigue yourself by struggling. Remain calm, raise one arm high above your head, and wait for help. Try to swim diagonally against the current to shore.
- If you get a cramp, raise one arm to signal "help," and keep the cramped part still.

DANGEROUS AUSSIE WILDLIFE

Spiders are common all over Australia, with the funnel web spider and the red-back spider being the most aggressive. Funnel webs live in holes in the ground (they spin their webs around the entrance to the hole) and stand on their back legs when they're about to attack. Red-backs have a habit of resting under toilet seats and in *boots* (car trunks), generally outside the main cities.

Fish to avoid are stingrays, porcupine fish, stonefish, lion fish, and puffer fish. Never touch an octopus if it has blue rings on it, or a cone shell, and be wary of the very painful and sometimes deadly tentacles of the **box jelly fish** (also called marine stingers) found along the northern Queensland coast in summer. If you happen to brush past one of these creatures, pour vinegar over the affected site immediately—local councils leave bottles of vinegar on the beach specifically for this purpose. In Sydney, you might come across **blue bottles**—long-tentacled blue jellyfish that can inflict a nasty stinging burn that lasts for hours. Sometimes you'll see warning signs on patrolled beaches. The best remedy if you are stung is to apply vinegar or have a very hot shower.

8 Health & Insurance

You don't have a lot to worry about health-wise on a trip to Australia. Hygiene standards are high, hospitals are modern, and doctors and dentists are all well educated. Australia's great distances mean you can sometimes be a long way from a hospital or a doctor, but help is never far away, thanks to the Royal Flying Doctor Service. No vaccinations are needed to enter the country unless you have been in a yellow fever danger zone—that is, South America or Africa—in the past six days.

It's a long trip Down Under (no matter where you're coming from!) so ask your doctor to recommend treatments for such common problems as travel sickness, insomnia, jet lag, constipation, and diarrhea. Drink plenty of water on the plane, as the air-conditioning dehydrates you quickly.

WHAT TO DO IF YOU GET SICK AWAY FROM HOME

It can be hard to find a doctor you can trust when you're in an unfamiliar place. Try to take proper precautions the week before you depart, to avoid falling ill while you're away from home. Amid the last-minute frenzy that often precedes a vacation break, make an extra effort to eat and sleep well—especially if you feel an illness coming on.

If you worry about getting sick away from home, you may want to consider **medical travel insurance** (see the section on travel insurance later in this chapter). In most cases, however, your existing health plan will provide all the coverage you need. Be sure to carry your identification card in your wallet.

If you suffer from a chronic illness, consult your doctor before your departure. For conditions like epilepsy, diabetes, or heart problems, wear a **Medic Alert Identification Tag** (☎ 800/825-3785; www.commedicalert.org), which will immediately alert doctors to your condition and give them access to your records through Medic Alert's 24-hour hot line. Membership is $35, plus a $15 annual fee.

Pack **prescription medications** in your carry-on luggage. Carry written prescriptions in generic not brand-name form, and dispense all prescription medications from their original labeled vials. Also bring along copies of your prescriptions in case you lose your pills or run out. Usually a 3-month supply is the maximum quantity of prescription drugs you are permitted to carry in Australia, so if you are carrying large amounts of medication, it's a good idea to contact the Australian embassy or consulate in your home country just to check that your supply does not exceed the maximum. If you need more medication while you're in Australia, an Australian doctor will have to write the prescription for you.

If you wear contact lenses, pack an extra pair in case you lose one.

Contact the **International Association for Medical Assistance to Travelers (IAMAT)** (☎ 716/754-4883 or 416/652-0137; www.sentex.net/~iamat). This organization offers tips on travel and health concerns in the countries you'll be visiting, and lists many local doctors. The United States **Centers for Disease Control and Prevention** (☎ 404/332-4559; www.cdc.gov) provides up-to-date information on necessary vaccines and health hazards by region or country (by mail, their booklet is U.S.$20; on the Internet, it's free). When you're abroad, any local consulate can provide a list of area doctors. If you do get sick, you may want to ask the concierge at your hotel to recommend a local doctor—even his or her own. If you can't find a doctor who can help you right away, try the emergency room at the local hospital.

WARNING: SUNSHINE MAY BE HAZADOUS TO YOUR HEALTH

There's a reason Australians have the world's highest skin cancer death rate—the country's intense sunlight. Limit your exposure to the sun, especially during the first few days of your trip and, thereafter, from 11am to 3pm in summer and 10am to 2pm in winter. Keep in mind that scattered UV rays that bounce off surfaces such city walls, the water, and even the ground can burn you, too. Use a broad-spectrum sunscreen with a high protection factor (SPF 30+) and apply it liberally. It's also a good idea to wear a broad-brimmed hat that covers the back of your neck, your ears, and your face (not a baseball cap); and a long-sleeved shirt to cover your forearms. Remember that children need more protection than adults do.

A Word About Smoking

Smoking in many public areas, such as museums, cinemas, and theaters is restricted if not banned. Smokers can take heart that few Oz restaurants are totally nonsmoking yet; they just have smoking and nonsmoking sections. Pubs are a territorial victory for smokers; after a night in an Aussie pub nonsmokers go home smelling as though they had smoked the whole pack (which they probably did, albeit passively). Most hotels have smoking and nonsmoking rooms. Australian aircraft on all domestic and international routes are completely nonsmoking, even on long-haul flights to the United States and Europe.

Don't even think about coming to Oz without sunglasses, or you'll spend your entire vacation with your eyes shut against Australia's hard, bright "diamond light," which cuts your eyes like, well, a diamond.

INSURANCE

There are three kinds of travel insurance: trip cancellation, medical, and lost-luggage coverage. **Trip cancellation insurance** is a good idea if you have paid a large portion of your vacation expenses up front. The other two types of insurance, however, don't make sense for most travelers. Rule number one: check your existing policies before you buy any additional coverage.

Your existing health insurance should cover you if you get sick while on vacation (although if you belong to an HMO, you should check to see whether you are fully covered when away from home). If you need hospital treatment, most health insurance plans and HMOs will cover out-of-country hospital visits and procedures, at least to some extent. Most, however, make you pay the bills up front at the time of care; you'll get a refund after you've returned and filed all the paperwork. Members of **Blue Cross/Blue Shield** can now use their cards at select hospitals in most major cities worldwide (☎ **800/810-BLUE,** or check www.bluecares.com/blue/bluecard/wwn for a list of hospitals). Check to see exactly what your existing health insurance covers, though. For example, your policy may not cover helicopter or Royal Flying Doctor Service airlift, which you might well need if you become sick or injured in the Outback. Your policy should also cover the cost to fly you back home in a stretcher, along with a nurse, should that be necessary. A stretcher takes up three coach-class seats, and you might need extra seats for a nurse and medical equipment. **Medicare** covers U.S. citizens traveling in Mexico and Canada only.

If you hold **British or New Zealand citizenship,** you are covered for most medical expenses for immediately necessary treatment (but not evacuation, ambulances, funerals, dental care, and other expenses) by Australia's national health system. It's still a good idea to buy insurance, though, as Australia's national health-care system typically covers only 85%, sometimes much less, of treatment. Foreign students of any nationality must take out the Australian government's Overseas Student Health Cover as a condition of entry.

For independent travel health-insurance providers, see below.

Your homeowner's insurance should cover **stolen luggage.** The airlines are responsible for U.S.$1,250 on domestic flights if they lose your luggage; if you plan to carry anything more valuable than that, keep it in your carry-on bag.

The differences between **travel assistance** and **insurance** are often blurred, but in general the former offers on-the-spot assistance and 24-hour hot lines (mostly oriented toward medical problems), whereas the latter reimburses you for travel problems (medical, travel, or otherwise) after you have filed the paperwork. The coverage you should consider will depend on how much protection is already contained in your existing health insurance or other policies. Some credit- and charge-card companies may insure you against travel accidents if you buy plane, train, or bus tickets with their cards. Before purchasing additional insurance, read your policies and agreements carefully. Call your insurers or credit-/charge-card companies if you have any questions.

Some credit cards (American Express and certain gold and platinum Visa and MasterCards, for example) offer automatic flight insurance against death or dismemberment in case of an airplane crash.

If you do require additional insurance, try one of the companies listed here. Don't pay for more than you need. For example, if you need only trip-cancellation insurance, don't purchase coverage for lost or stolen property. Trip-cancellation insurance costs approximately 6 to 8% of the total value of your vacation.

Reputable issuers of **travel insurance** include the following:
- **Access America,** 6600 W. Broad St., Richmond, VA 23230 (☎ **800/284-8300**).
- **Travel Guard International,** 1145 Clark St., Stevens Point, WI 54481 (☎ **800/826-1300**).
- **Travel Insured International,** Inc., P.O. Box 280568, East Hartford, CT 06128 (☎ **800/243-3174**).
- **Columbus Travel Insurance,** 279 High St., Croydon CR0 1QH (☎ **0171/375-0011** in London; www2.columbusdirect.com/columbusdirect).
- **Travelex Insurance Services,** P.O. Box 9408, Garden City, NY 11530-9408 (☎ **800/228-9792**).

Companies specializing in **accident and medical care** include:
- **MEDEX International,** P.O. Box 5375, Timonium, MD 21094-5375 (☎ **888/MEDEX-00** or 410/453-6300; fax 410/453-6301; www.medexassist.com).
- **Travel Assistance International** (Worldwide Assistance Services, Inc.), 1133 15th St. NW, Suite 400, Washington, DC 20005 (☎ **800/821-2828,** or 202/828-5894; fax 202/828-5896).
- **The Divers Alert Network** (DAN) (☎ **800/446-2671,** or 919/684-2948) insures scuba divers.

9 Tips for Travelers with Special Needs

FOR TRAVELERS WITH DISABILITIES   Most public hotels, major stores, museums, attractions, and public restrooms have wheelchair access. Many smaller lodges and even B&Bs are starting to cater to guests with disabilities. National parks make a big effort to include wheelchair-friendly pathways through their more picturesque scenery.

An excellent source of information on all kinds of facilities and services in Australia for people with disabilities is the **National Information Communication Awareness Network (NICAN),** P.O. Box 407, Curtin ACT 2605 (☎ **1800/806 769** in Australia, or 02/6285 3713; fax 02/6285 3714; e-mail nican@spirit.com.au). This free service can put you in touch with accessible accommodations and attractions throughout Australia, as well as with travel agents and tour operators who understand your needs. Taxi companies in bigger cities can usually supply a cab equipped for wheelchairs.

A World of Options, a 658-page book of resources for travelers with disabilities, covers everything from biking trips to scuba outfitters. It costs $35 ($30 for members) and is available from **Mobility International USA,** P.O. Box 10767, Eugene, OR 97440 (☎ **541/343-1284,** voice and TDD; www.miusa.org). Annual membership for Mobility International is $35, which includes the quarterly newsletter, *Over the Rainbow.* In addition, **Twin Peaks Press,** P.O. Box 129, Vancouver, WA 98666 (☎ **360/694-2462**), publishes travel-related books for people with disabilities.

FOR GAY & LESBIAN TRAVELERS   Sydney is probably the biggest gay city in the world after San Francisco, and across most of Australia, the gay community has a high profile and lots of support services. The annual Sydney Gay & Lesbian Mardi Gras, culminating in a huge street parade and gay-only party on the last Saturday in February, is a high point on the city's calendar for people of all sexual persuasions, and attracts thousands of gay visitors from around the world.

The International Gay & Lesbian Travel Association (IGLTA), (☎ **800/448-8550** or 954/776-2626; fax 954/776-3303; www.iglta.org), links up travelers with the appropriate gay-friendly service organization or tour specialist. With around

1,200 members, it offers quarterly newsletters, marketing mailings, and a membership directory that's updated quarterly. Membership often includes gay or lesbian businesses but is open to individuals for $150 yearly, plus a $100 administration fee for new members. Members are kept informed of gay and gay-friendly hoteliers, tour operators, and airline and cruise-line representatives. Contact the IGLTA for a list of its member agencies, who will be tied into IGLTA's information resources.

One of the biggest travel agencies specializing in gay travel in Australia is **Jornada,** 263 Liverpool St., Darlinghurst, NSW 2010 (☎ **1800/672 120** in Australia, or 02/9360 9611; fax 02/9326 0199; www.jornada.com.au).

Australia has several gay publications, including the *Sydney Star Observer,* a free weekly newspaper available from newsagents, clubs, and cafes, and glossy mags *Outrage* and *Campaign* sold by newsagents. Some services you may find useful are the **Gay & Lesbian Counselling Service of NSW** (☎ **02/9207 2888** for the administration office), which runs a hot line daily from 4pm to midnight (☎ **02/9207 2800**). The **Albion Street Centre** (☎ **1800/451 600** in Australia, 02/9332 4000 for the information lines, or 02/9332 1090 for administration) in Sydney is an AIDS clinic and information service.

FOR SENIORS   Seniors—often referred to as pensioners by Aussies—visiting Australia from other countries don't always qualify for the discounted entry prices to tours, attractions, and events that Australian seniors enjoy, but mostly they do. The best ID to bring is something that shows your date of birth, or something that marks you as an "official" senior, such as a membership card from the **American Association of Retired Persons (AARP)** (☎ **800/424-3410** in the U.S.; www.aarp.org). Membership in AARP is open to working or retired people over age 50 and costs U.S.$8 a year. AARP members, or anyone over age 60 for that matter, get a 10% discount at Best Western hotels in Australia.

Elderhostel (☎ **877/426 8056** toll-free in the U.S. and Canada; www.elderhostel.org), is a nonprofit organization that sells educational package tours, including ones to Australia, for travelers age 55 and over. Recent itineraries in Australia included Great Barrier Reef study cruises, Outback camping trips, bushwalking tours in Tasmania, and visits to Lord Howe Island off the east coast of Australia and Kangaroo Island off the south coast.

The **Australian College for Seniors** at the University of Wollongong, south of Sydney (☎ **02/4221 3531;** fax 02/4226 2521; e-mail acfs@uow.edu.au) runs about 20 trips a year within Australia for people over age 50 under the "Odyssey Travel" name. Many trips have heritage, ecotourism, or soft-adventure themes. The college is the Australian program coordinator for Elderhostel.

Senior Tours, Level 2, 32 York St., Sydney, NSW 2000 (☎ **02/9262 6140;** fax 02/9262 2085), is a travel company specializing in vacations for seniors in Australia.

FOR FAMILIES   Australia is a great destination for kids. Lots of the sorts of things kids like to do, such as playing in the park and building sand castles at the beach, are widely available and free in Australia. Australians travel widely with their own kids, so facilities for families, including family passes to attractions, are common.

Most hotels in Australia accommodate kids up to age 12 (and even older kids) free in your room if they use existing beds; if a hotel does charge extra for a child, it's usually only A$10 (U.S.$7), or A$20 (U.S. $14) at most. Kids age 12 and under stay free at Best Western properties. Some motels have family rooms that sleep three, four, or even more, and these often have kitchenettes. Interconnecting rooms are often discounted as much as 50% for families. Many hotels will arrange baby-sitting, given a day's notice.

Aussie families often stay in serviced apartments, which frequently cost considerably less than a hotel room yet have a living room, a kitchen (to keep meal costs down), often two bathrooms, and the privacy of a separate bedroom for adults.

International airlines and domestic airlines within Australia charge 67% of the adult fare for kids under age 12. Most charge 10% for infants under age two not occupying a seat. Australian coach and rail companies often charge around half price for kids, as do most attractions and tours throughout the country.

Rascals in Paradise (☎ **800/U RASCAL** in the U.S., or 415/978 9800; www. RascalsInParadise.com), tailors family vacation packages to Australia.

FOR SINGLES   Striking up a conversation with friendly Aussies is very easy when you're traveling solo, and single women will be glad to know the crime rate is low, even in major cities. When it comes to accommodations for singles, pricing policies vary widely. Many hotels charge singles the full room rate, a very few charge singles at half the room rate, and the majority charge a "single rate" of about three-quarters of the full room rate. Pubs and hostels often charge a flat per person rate whether there is one, two, or more of you, so they are a good option. B&Bs usually charge slightly less for a single person than for a couple. Many package- and adventure-tour operators are happy to pair you up with another solo traveler in a twin-bed room, if you do not mind sharing a room with someone you've just met. Then each of you pays for the whole tour at the twin-share rate, not the more-expensive single rate.

FOR STUDENTS   Australia is cheap, sporty, and laid back, has stunning scenery, great weather, fun pubs, and beautiful beaches—in other words, it's paradise for students. The Australian Tourist Commission publishes a groovy vacation guide just for students called *Australia Unplugged* (see "Visitor Information," earlier in this chapter).

STA Travel (☎ **800/781 4040** in the U.S., 171/361 6262 in the U.K., and 1300/360 960 in Australia) is a good source of tips and advice for students traveling Down Under. It specializes in discounted airfares for students and any traveler under age 26, sells its own brand of travel insurance, and, most important of all, issues **International Student Identification Cards (ISIC).** The ISIC is the most widely recognized proof in Australia that you really are a student, ensuring you discounts to a wide variety of tours and attractions. In the United States, it costs U.S.$20 and is available to any student over age 12 enrolled in a diploma or degree program at an accredited secondary or tertiary institution. Check out STA Travel's Web site at www.statravel. com in the U.S., or www.statravel.com.au in Australia. The company has loads of offices across Australia and throughout the world.

You can also obtain an ISIC from the **Council on International Educational Exchange** (CIEE), another excellent source for students. Its travel branch, **Council Travel Service** (☎ **800/226-8624;** www.ciee.com), is the biggest student travel–agency operation in the world. It can get you discounts on plane tickets, rail passes, and the like. Ask them for a list of CTS offices in major cities so you can keep the discounts flowing (and aid lines open) as you travel.

Connection Holidays (☎ **02/9262 2444;** fax 02/9290 3159) and **Contiki Holidays** (☎ **800/CONTIKI** in the U.S. and Canada, 0181/290 6677 in the U.K., or 02/9511 2200 in Australia) specialize in package tours for 18- to 35-year-olds. These trips attract a lot of Australians, too, so they are a good way to meet locals.

The "Tips on Accommodation" section later in this chapter has details on how to join Hostelling International to take advantage of Australia's excellent youth hostels.

The **Homestay Network** (see "Tips on Accommodations") specializes in placing students with Sydney families on a self-catered or three-meals-a-day basis. Student placements cost around A$185 (U.S.$129.50) a week with all meals, plus a A$120 (U.S.$84) booking fee. This is ideal for long-term stays.

10 Booking a Package or Escorted Tour

It's possible to buy a package tour to Australia that includes airfare and, say, five nights' accommodations in a decent hotel for less than the cost of the airfare alone. When this book went to press, **United Vacations** (www.unitedvacations.com) offered just such a five-night package for U.S.$1,119 from Los Angeles or $1,499 from New York to Sydney on a twin-share basis, with some conditions attached. Because each element of a package—airfare, hotel, tour, car rental—costs the package company less than if you had booked the same components yourself, packages are a terrific value and well worth investigating.

There are two kinds of package tours—independent and escorted—and each has its pros and cons. **Independent packages** usually include some combination of airfare, accommodations, and car rental, with an occasional tour or shopping discount-voucher book thrown in. The main advantage is that you travel at your own pace and according to your own interests, rather than sticking to a group schedule. Your car and hotel arrangements are already booked, leaving you free to get on with your day instead of fussing about finding a hotel for the night.

Escorted tours have different advantages—you don't have to carry your own luggage, for starters. Nor do you need to constantly plan ahead, and if you have free time, there is someone to advise you on fun things to do and even to make your tour bookings for you. A significant argument for escorted tours is that you usually have a well-informed guide who can offer interesting tidbits about the country as you go along, so that you'll probably learn more than you would on your own. You also get to meet and travel with other people. Escorted tours tend to be more expensive because you're paying for the guide, but most meals are included.

And what are the cons of each? If you fancy an independent tour, think about whether you really want to book your own tours day after day, do all the driving yourself (on the wrong side of the road, don't forget!), and schlep up the stairs carrying your own luggage. If you're considering an escorted tour, do you really want your magical bushwalk in the Blue Mountains cut short because the schedule says at noon we all have to be back in Sydney for opal shopping? And can you stand the thought of traveling with strangers for days or weeks on end?

The airlines themselves are often a good source of package tours. Check newspaper ads, the Internet, or your travel agent. The following U.S. companies also offer affordable independent packages Down Under: **Austravel** (☎ 800/633-3404 in the U.S. and Canada), **Destinations Downunder** (☎ 773/832-1699), **Inta-Aussie South Pacific** (☎ 800/531-9222), **Sunmakers Tours** (☎ 800/841-4321), and **United Vacations** (☎ 800/32-TOURS in the U.S. and Canada).

Escorted tours are available from **Collette Tours** (☎ 800/340 5158 in the U.S. and Canada), **Globus & Cosmos** (☎ 800/338-7092), **Maupintour** (☎ 800/255-4266), and **Sunbeam Tours** (☎ 800/955 1818 in the U.S.).

The following companies offer both independent and escorted tours: **ANZA Travel** (☎ 888/699 6179 in the U.S. and Canada), **ATS Tours** (☎ 800/423-2880 in the U.S.), **Goway** (☎ 800/387-8850 in the U.S. and Canada), **Jetset Vacations** (☎ 800/4JETSET in the U.S., 800/663 5522 in Canada), **Kristensen International Travel & Tours** (☎ 800/635-5488 in the U.S. and Canada), **Qantas Vacations** (☎ 800/348 8139 in the U.S., and 800/268-7525 in Canada), and **Swain Australia Tours** (☎ 800/22-SWAIN). Swain Australia is owned and largely staffed by Aussies.

11 Flying to Australia

Note: Be sure to read "Fifty Money-Saving Tips" earlier in this chapter for advice on how to save on airfare.

There's no doubt about it—Australia is a looong flight from anywhere except New Zealand. Sydney is a 14-hour nonstop flight from Los Angeles, longer if your flight stops in Honolulu. From the East Coast, add 5½ hours. If you're coming from the States via Auckland, add transit time in New Zealand plus another 3 hours for the Auckland–Sydney leg. The real killer, though, is coming from the U.K. Prepare yourself for a flight of more or less 12 hours from London to Asia; then a long day in transit, as flights to Australia have a nasty habit of arriving in Asia early in the morning and departing around midnight; and finally the 8- to 9-hour flight to Sydney!

Sydney, Cairns, Melbourne, Brisbane, Adelaide, Darwin, and Perth are all international gateways, but most airlines fly into Sydney only—perhaps also into Melbourne.

THE MAJOR CARRIERS   Here are toll-free reservations numbers and Web sites for the major international airlines serving Australia. The 13 prefix in Australia means the number is charged at the cost of a local call from anywhere in the country.

MAJOR CARRIERS FLYING FROM NORTH AMERICA
- **Air New Zealand** (☎ 800/262-1234 in the U.S., 800/663-5494 in English and 800/799-5494 in French in Canada, 0800/737 000 in New Zealand, or 13 24 76 in Australia; www.airnewzealand.co.nz/)
- **Canada 3000** (☎ 1877/FLY CAN3 in Canada, 416/674 3000 in the United States, or 02/9567 9631 in Australia); www.canada3000.com)
- **Canadian Airlines** (☎ 800/665-1177 in Canada, 800/363 7530 in French in Canada outside Quebec, 800/426 7000 in the U.S., or 1300/655 767 in Australia; www.cdnair.ca)
- **Qantas** (☎ 800/227 4500 in the U.S. and Canada, or 13 13 13 in Australia; www.qantas.com.au)
- **United Airlines** (☎ 800/241-6522 in the U.S. and Canada, or 13 17 77 in Australia; www.ual.com)

MAJOR CARRIERS FLYING FROM THE U.K.
- **British Airways** (☎ 0345/222-111 in the U.K., or 02/8904 8800 in Sydney, 07/3223 3123 in Brisbane, 1800/113 7222 in Canberra, 03/9603 1133 in Melbourne, and 08/9425 7711 in Perth; www.british-airways.com)
- **Cathay Pacific** (☎ 0345/581-581 in the U.K., or 13 17 47 in Australia; www.cathaypacific.com)
- **Malaysia Airlines** (☎ 0171/341-2020 or 0181/740-2626 in the U.K., 13 26 27 in Australia; www.malaysiaairlines.com.my).
- **Qantas** (☎ 0345/747-767 in the U.K., or 13 13 13 in Australia; www.qantas.com.au)
- **Singapore Airlines** (☎ 020/8747-0007 in London, 0161/830-8888 in Manchester, 0121/233-2066 in Birmingham, 0141/204-0656 in Glasgow, or 13 10 11 in Australia, 07/4031 7538 in Cairns; www.citechco.net/singaporeair.com.bd)
- **Thai Airways International** (☎ 020/7499-9113 in London, 0161/831-7861 in Manchester, or 1300/651 960 in Australia; www.thaiair.com)

FINDING THE BEST AIRFARE   If you are flying from America, keep in mind that the airlines' **low season** is mid-April to the end of August—this is when you'll

Money-Saving Tip

Consolidators, also known as bucket shops, are another good source for low fares. Consolidators buy seats in bulk from the airlines and then sell them back to the public at prices below even the airlines' discounted rates. Their small boxed ads usually run in the newspaper's Sunday travel section, at the bottom of the page. Before you pay, however, ask for a confirmation number from the consolidator and then call the airline itself to confirm your seat. Be prepared to book your ticket with a different consolidator—there are many to choose from—if the airline can't confirm your reservation. Also be aware that bucket shop tickets are usually nonrefundable or rigged with stiff cancellation penalties, often as high as 50 to 75% of the ticket price.

find the cheapest fares, even though this happens to be the *best* time to travel most parts of Australia. **High season** is December through February, and **shoulder season** is September through November and again from March to mid-April. Keep an eye out for special deals offered throughout the year. Unexpected lows in airline passenger loads often lead airlines to put cheap offers on the market. The catch is that these offers usually have a short lead time, requiring you to travel in the next six weeks or so. Some deals involve taking a circuitous route, via Fiji or Japan, for instance. **Canada 3000** has good rates from Vancouver in low season and often has promotional specials. Some travel agents specializing in cheap fares to Australia include **Austravel** (☎ 800/633-3404 in the U.S. and Canada); **DownUnder Direct,** which is a division of Swain Australia (☎ 800/22-SWAIN in the U.S.); **Goway** (☎ 800/387-8850 in the U.S. and Canada); and **South Pacific Travel Shops** (☎ 800/894-7722 in the U.S.).

Council Travel (☎ 800/226-8624; www.counciltravel.com) and **STA Travel** (☎ 800/781-4040; www.sta.travel.com) cater especially to young travelers, but their bargain-basement prices are available to people of all ages. Other reliable consolidators include **1-800-FLY-CHEAP** (www.1800flycheap.com); **TFI Tours International** (☎ 800/745-8000 or 212/736-1140), which serves as a clearinghouse for unused seats; or "rebators" such as **Travel Avenue** (☎ 800/333-3335 or 312/876-1116) and the **Smart Traveller** (☎ 800/448-3338 in the U.S., or 305/448-3338), which rebate part of their commissions to you.

You can also search **the Internet** for cheap fares—although it's still best to compare your findings with the research of a dedicated travel agent, if you're lucky enough to have one, especially when you're booking more than just a flight. A few of the better-respected virtual travel agents are **Travelocity** (www.travelocity.com) and **Microsoft Expedia** (www.expedia.com). Just enter the dates you want to fly and the cities you want to visit, and the computer roots out the lowest fares. Expedia's site will e-mail you the best airfare deal once a week if you want. Travelocity uses the SABRE computer reservations system that most travel agents use, and has a Last Minute Deals database that advertises really cheap fares for those who can get away at a moment's notice.

IN-FLIGHT COMFORT   To relieve the discomfort of this long-distance flight, wear loose clothing and a roomy pair of shoes because your feet will swell en route. Drink plenty of water and go easy on the free alcohol. To while away the hours, consider traveling with an airline that offers in-seat videos. Requesting a bulkhead or exit-door seat will give you more legroom. Some airlines allow you to request seats when you book, but others allocate seats only at check-in—in that case, be early to beat savvy Aussies queuing for the same thing!

Jet lag is a foregone conclusion on such a long trip, so don't plan to climb Ayers Rock the first morning you arrive or book opera tickets for your first evening. There is no cure for jet lag, but you can help fight it by getting as much sleep as possible on the flight and not overeating. Try to acclimate yourself to the local time as quickly as possible. Stay up as long as you can the first day, then try to wake up at a normal hour the next morning.

On such a long journey, it makes sense to break the trip with a one-night stopover if you have time. If you're coming from America, this will probably be Honolulu; if you're coming from Europe, you have any number of exciting Asian cities—Bangkok, Singapore, Hong Kong—in which to spend a night or two. If you're coming from Europe and you have a long layover in Asia, it's a very good idea to book a day room at a hotel, with a 6pm checkout. Wandering around a humid, crowded city at 2pm when your body thinks it's 3am is not fun.

12 Getting Around

The one big mistake many tourists make when traveling Down Under (apart from getting sunburned) is failing to understand the distances between attractions and regions. Every Sydney hotelier has a tale to tell about the Japanese, American, or European tourists who come down to the front desk complaining that their room doesn't have a view of Ayers Rock (a mere 2,841 kilometers/1,704½ miles away), or asking what time the afternoon boat to the Great Barrier Reef leaves. Distances between the most popular spots can be vast, so don't try to cram too much into one trip.

While traveling overland may make sense in Europe or North America, flying in Australia is the best way to go. People who go by train, bus, or car are often disappointed by Australia's flat unchanging vistas of desert, wheat fields, and gum trees—and this dull scenery can literally go on for days. A good compromise is to take to the air for long trips and save the land travel for short hops of no more than a few hours. Try not to backtrack, as doing so eats up valuable time and money.

BY PLANE

Australia is a big country with a small population to support its air routes, hence the big airfares. But there are ways for international travelers to beat 'em.

Domestic travel is almost entirely operated by **Qantas** (☎ **800/227-4500** in the U.S. and Canada, 0345/747 767 in the U.K., and 13 13 13 in Australia; www.qantas. com.au) and **Ansett** (☎ **13 13 00** for domestic flights and 13 14 14 for international flights in Australia; www.ansett.com.au). Ansett's overseas representation is handled by **Air New Zealand** (☎**888/4-ANSETT** in the U.S. or Canada, and 020/8741 2299 in the U.K.).

Most of the time Qantas and Ansett airfares are the same, to within a dollar for the same route, and both airlines maintain virtually identical standards of in-flight service and safety. Both own or are affiliated with a number of regional airlines whose schedules and fares are all linked into the parent airline's reservations systems. Australia's air network is not as well developed as that of North America's, so don't assume there is a direct flight to your chosen destination or that there is a flight every day. *Note:* All flights in Australia are nonsmoking.

FARES FOR INTERNATIONAL TRAVELERS   Qantas and Ansett typically offer international travelers a 30% discount off full fares for domestic flights. So, if the full fare for Australians is A$1,000 (U.S.$700), international visitors pay only A$700—which works out to U.S.$490! Not bad. To qualify for these fares, simply quote your passport number to the reservationist.

Sample Flying Times & Airfares

This list of some commonly flown routes gives you an idea of typical flying times and costs. The times are those on the shortest route available, and the fares are one-way at the full coach rate (21-, 14-, and 7-day advance-purchase fares, air pass coupons, or fares for international travelers are much cheaper):

Route	Travel Time	Fare
Sydney to Cairns	3 hrs	A$559 (U.S. $419.30)
Cairns to Ayers Rock	3 hrs, 45 min.	A$516 (U.S. $361.20)
Sydney to Melbourne	1 hr, 5 min.	A$228 (U.S. $201.60)
Alice Springs to Darwin	2 hrs	A$392 (U.S. $274.40)
Perth to Broome	2 hrs, 45 min.	A$537 (U.S. $375.90)

AIR PASSES   If you are planning to whip around to more than one city, purchasing an Air Pass from either Qantas or Ansett is loads cheaper than buying a number of regular-fare tickets. You must buy these passes before you arrive in Australia; residents of Australia and New Zealand cannot purchase them.

With Qantas' **Boomerang Pass,** for example, you must purchase a minimum of two coupons priced at U.S.$175/C$240 per coupon for travel within a zone, or U.S.$220/C$300 per coupon for travel between zones. That's a great value when you consider that the regular Sydney–Cairns fare is A$599, which works out to U.S.$419.30, compared to the coupon fare of just U.S.$175! Coupons are also good for travel to and from New Zealand and to the most popular South Pacific nations. The pass is also good for domestic travel within New Zealand aboard Ansett New Zealand, and around the South Pacific with Air Pacific. Zone 1 covers Western Australia; Zone 2 covers the Red Centre and Darwin; and Zone 3 covers South Australia (Adelaide), Tasmania, Victoria, New South Wales, and Queensland. You must book your first coupon destination before you arrive, but you can book the rest as you go.

Ansett's air passes are similar, although the pricing and zone structure may differ somewhat. Many small towns, some island resorts, and many airports served by subsidiaries of Qantas and Ansett are not covered by the air passes.

BY TRAIN

The rail network in Australia is mostly used for long-distance travel between state capitals and the points in between. Taking the train is a good deal cheaper than flying; it's safe, and it's comfortable, especially if you buy a sleeper, although sleepers often cost considerably more than a seat. Service standards and facilities are more than adequate on most trains.

Most long-distance trains have smart sleepers with big windows, electric outlets, wardrobes, washbasins, and fresh sheets and blankets. First-class sleepers have en suite bathrooms, and meals are often included in the fare. Second-class sleepers use shared shower facilities, and meals are not included; some second-class sleepers are private cabins, but on other trains you share with strangers. Single cabins are usually of broom-closet dimensions but surprisingly comfy. The food on all trains ranges from okay to pretty darn good, and the club cars are a sociable place to meet other travelers. You can smoke in some trains in the club cars, but rarely in the dining car or in your sleeper. In some trains smoking is prohibited altogether.

Australian rail schedules are no match for the snappy convenience of European rail travel—some trains operate once a week only—so check the timetable before you get your other travel arrangements in place.

Australia's rail routes are managed either by the private enterprise **Great Southern Railway** (☎ **13 21 47** in Australia, or 08/8213 4592), which runs the *Indian Pacific,* the *Overlander,* and the *Ghan,* or by one of the following government bodies: **Queensland Rail** (☎ **13 22 32** in Australia, or 07/3235 1122) which handles rail within that state; **Countrylink** (☎ **13 22 32** in Australia, or 02/9379 1298) which manages travel within New South Wales and to Canberra, Melbourne, and Brisbane; and **Westrail** (☎ **13 10 53** in Western Australia, or 08/9326 2244), which operates trains in Western Australia. The Umbrella organization **Rail Australia** (☎ **08/8213 4429**) handles inquiries and makes reservations for all long-distance trains in Australia, with the exception of Westrail services. Outside Australia, call Rail Australia's overseas agents: **ATS Tours** (☎ **800/423-2880**) in the United States, **Goway** (☎ **800/ 387-8850**) in Canada, and **Leisurail** (☎ **1733/505 453**) in the United Kingdom.

The only train linking Sydney, Adelaide, and Perth is the luxury *Indian Pacific,* a train most folk take for the experience rather than as a way to get to Perth. Unless you are prepared to sit up for the 3 days it takes to reach Perth, consider another mode of transport, as the sleepers are prohibitively expensive. The *Overland* links Adelaide and Melbourne. The *Ghan* traverses the desert between Melbourne, Adelaide, and Alice Springs. Countrylink runs fast **XPTs** (Express Passenger Trains, which despite their name stop at points en route) linking Sydney with Melbourne, Canberra, and Brisbane; and **Explorer** trains to Broken Hill in Outback New South Wales.

You have a choice of several trains most days on the Brisbane–Cairns route, including the very expensive first-class-only *Queenslander;* the comfortable *Sunlander,* with sitting berths and economy-class sleepers you share with strangers; and the *Spirit of the Tropics,* a sitting-car-only train with a "disco on the rails" for young travelers. The *Spirit of the Tropics* runs only as far as Proserpine in the Whitsundays.

RAIL PASSES National and state rail passes are available from **Rail Australia's** overseas agents (see above)—and only to nonresidents of Australia—before you arrive.

The national **Austrailpass** is good for economy seats on intrastate, interstate, and even suburban city train networks around the country. A 14-day pass is A$545 (U.S.$381.50), a 21-day pass is A$705 (U.S.$493.50) and a 30-day pass is A$850 (U.S.$595); you can buy 7-day extensions for A$250 (U.S.$175). An alternative pass, the **Austrail Flexipass,** allows you to travel for any 8, 15, 22, or 29 days, consecutive or not, within a 6-month period. An 8-day Flexipass is A$450 (U.S.$315), with the price going up to A$1,175 (U.S.$822.50) for a 29-day Flexipass. *Note:* You cannot use the 8-day pass on the Adelaide–Perth route or the Adelaide–Alice Springs route.

State passes are available in New South Wales, Victoria, Queensland, and Western Australia, and can be purchased after you arrive in Australia. The **New South Wales Discovery Pass** is good for unlimited travel for 1 calendar month on all long-distance trains in New South Wales in economy-class seats (not sleepers); it costs A$249 (U.S.$174.30), or A$199 (U.S.$139.30) for YHA (Youth Hostels Association/ Hostelling International) members.

Queensland's **Sunshine Rail Pass** is valid for intrastate and suburban economy-class seats (not interstate routes or sleepers); a 14-day pass costs A$267 (U.S.$186.90), a 21-day pass goes for A$309 (U.S.$216.30), and a 30-day pass is A$388 (U.S.$271.60). A first-class-seat version is available, and upgrades to sleepers are available for a surcharge.

Train Travel Tip

Because Australia does not have many trains, those it does have are often fully booked; make reservations in advance whenever you can.

Sample Travel Times & Rail Fares

To give you an idea of fares and distances, here are some examples of one-way, full-price fares on major routes. Countrylink offers discounts of up to 40% for advance bookings.

Route	Travel Time	Sitting Car	2nd-Class Sleeper
Brisbane–Cairns	32 hrs	A$135(U.S.$94.50)	A$165 (U.S.$115.50)
Sydney–Perth	64 hrs	A$400 (U.S.$280)	A$823 (U.S.$576.10)
Adelaide–Alice Springs	20 hrs	A$170 (U.S.$119)	A$351 (U.S.$245.70)

Queensland's **Road & Rail Pass** is good for travel in an economy-class sitting berth on intrastate long-distance trains and for travel on McCafferty's buses; it costs A$269 (U.S.$188.30) for 10 journeys over a 60-day period, or A$349 (U.S.$244.30) for 20 journeys over a 90-day period. Its use is subject to availability during Queensland school-holiday periods, however. Unlike the Sunshine Railpass, it cannot be used on suburban trains or the Kuranda Scenic Railway.

The **East Coast Discovery Pass** allows you to travel one-way (north or south) in economy-class seats between Melbourne, Canberra, Sydney, Brisbane, and Cairns; you can hop on and off as you please within a 6-month period. You buy this pass in sectors: the cheapest is the Sydney–Brisbane sector, for A$76 (U.S.$53.20); the most expensive is the entire Melbourne–Cairns run, for A$275 (U.S.$192.50). Some legs are available only to non-Australian residents.

Upgrades to an economy-class sleeper on all the passes described above are available for a surcharge of between A$30 (U.S.$21) and A$105 (U.S.$73.50) per journey.

RAIL PACKAGES   Both Countrylink and Queensland Rail (see above) offer a wide range of rail packages that include accommodations and sightseeing throughout New South Wales, as far south as Canberra and Melbourne, and throughout Queensland.

BY BUS

Bus travel in Australia is a big step up from the low-rent affair it can be in the United States. Terminals are centrally located and well lit, the coaches are clean and air-conditioned, you sit in comfy adjustable seats, the drivers are polite and comment on points of interest along the way. Videos are shown onboard, and some buses even have bathrooms. Unlike Australia's train service, there are few places the extensive bus network won't take you. Buses are totally nonsmoking.

Greyhound Pioneer Australia (☎ **13 20 30** in Australia, or 07/3258 1737; www.mccaffertys.com.au) and **McCafferty's** (☎ **13 14 99** in Australia, or 07/4690 9888; www.greyhound.com.au) are the two big national coach operators. McCafferty's has many international agents, including **Inta Aussie South Pacific** (☎ **310/568-2060**) in the United States, **Goway** (☎ **800/387-8850** in the U.S. or Canada) in Canada, and **Bridge the World** (☎ **020/7209 9459**) in the United Kingdom. Greyhound Pioneer has offices in the United States (☎ **310/578 5455**) and the United Kingdom (☎ **020/7291 4590**).

BUS PASSES   Bus passes are a great value. **Day Passes** are good for 7, 10, 15, 21, or 30 days of travel, consecutive or not, within a 1- to 3-month period. Fares range from A$499 (U.S.$349.30) for a Greyhound Pioneer 7-day pass to A$1,245 (U.S.$871.50) for a McCafferty's 30-day pass. The passes are valid for travel in any direction, and backtracking is allowed. The McCafferty's pass must be bought before you arrive in Australia, while Greyhound Pioneer's passes are available only in Oz.

Sample Travel Times & Bus Fares

Here are some sample bus fares and travel times, to give you an idea of what you're getting yourself into as you step aboard. All fares and travel times are one-way.

Route	Travel Time	Fare
Broome to Darwin	25 hrs	A$220 (U.S. $151.40)
Sydney to Melbourne	13 hrs	A$71 (U.S. $49.70)
Cairns to Brisbane	28^1/₂ hrs	A$144 (U.S. $100.80)

Note: These are the fares you'll pay if you buy your ticket in Australia—fares and passes can be considerably cheaper if you buy them before you leave home. If you're a student, a senior, or a YHA/Hostelling International member, fares will be cheaper still.

If you know where you are going and are willing to obey a no-backtracking rule, a better deal is a **Travel Australia** (McCafferty's) or **Aussie Explorer** (Greyhound Pioneer) pass. These allow unlimited stops in a generous time frame on a preset one-way route (although you can sometimes travel the route in either direction). You can choose from a dazzling array of routes all over the country, with names like "Best of the East and Centre," "Reef & Rock," "Follow the Sun," "Outback Wanderer," and "Top End Safari."

As an example, McCafferty's **Sun and Centre Pass** takes in Ayers Rock, Alice Springs, Kings Canyon, Katherine, Darwin, Kakadu National Park, Mt. Isa, Cairns, and the whole east coast down to Sydney. The pass is valid for 6 months and costs a terrifically low A$670 (U.S.$469) for travel only, or A$750 (U.S.$525) with three full-day tours in a choice of 11 popular destinations. McCafferty's does not serve Western Australia, so if you want a pass that covers the whole country, go for Greyhound Pioneer's **All Australian Pass** for A$1,555 (U.S.$1,088.50).

Greyhound Pioneer's **Aussie Kilometre Pass** and McCafferty's **Australian Roamer Pass** both allow unlimited stops in any direction within the mileage you buy. For example, a 3,000-kilometer (1,8005-mile) pass—enough to get you from Cairns to Sydney with McCafferty's—is A$228 (U.S.$159.60). Passes are available in increments of 1,000 kilometers (600 miles) with Greyhound, and 2,000 kilometers (1,200 miles) with McCafferty's. Prices range from A$165 (U.S.$115.50) for 2,000 kilometers (1,200 miles) with McCafferty's to A$1,400 (U.S.$980) for a whopping 20,000 kilometers (12,000 miles) with Greyhound.

BUS PACKAGES   Greyhound Pioneer Touring (☎ 1800/800 260 in Australia) sells a wide range of day tours and coach holidays to popular destinations. Packages include coach travel, basic but comfortable accommodations, and some meals and sightseeing. Packages are currently offered for travel in the Northern Territory and Queensland, with other states to follow.

GETTING AROUND BY ALTERNATIVE BUS

Beloved of backpackers but fabulous for any fun-loving independent traveler are Australia's two alternative bus companies. **Oz Experience** (☎ 1300/300 028 in Australia, or 02/9368 1766; fax 02/9368 0908; www.ozex.com.au) has a fleet of brightly painted air-conditioned coaches that link scenic popular and off-the-beaten-path spots. They travel at a more leisurely pace than Greyhound's and McCafferty's and zigzag to interesting places in search of beauty and adventure, with a commentary from the driver.

Bus Travel Tip

Traveling overnight by bus is almost unavoidable, given Australia's vast distances. The upside to this is that you save on hotel accommodations for the night.

You get plenty of time to bungee jump, swim in a fern-fringed rock hole, or take a hike in a national park. There is something free to do at every stop, and passengers often get discounts to attractions and activities nearby. The driver often cooks dinners for A$3 (U.S.$2.10) to A$7 (U.S.$4.90), and the company will book you into the next YHA hostel, or drop you and pick you up wherever you're staying. You hop on and off wherever you want. The only restriction is that you must book your next leg 48 hours in advance. Fares range from A$165 (U.S.$115.50) for the Brisbane–Sydney leg to A$1,275 (U.S.$892.50) for the full circuit, including a flight between Cairns and Darwin. YHA/Hostelling International members and International Student Identification Card holders get a 5% discount. The company also offers an array of air-bus passes with Qantas.

Similar in spirit but less backpacker-oriented, hence better for families and seniors, is the **Wayward Bus** (☎ **1800/882 823** in Australia, or 08/8232 6646; fax 08/8232 1455; www.waywardbus.com.au) which meanders all over southeast Australia between Sydney and Adelaide, and up to Alice Springs, in air-conditioned coaches and minicoaches. You get friendly commentary from the driver, and there's plenty of time to stop and do things. You can use the bus simply as transport on some routes and get on and off as much as you like, but the company's focus is on leisurely 3- to 8-day tours for small groups. Fares are very reasonable—the Sydney–Melbourne leg via the Blue Mountains, Jenolan Caves, and Canberra is just A$140 (U.S.$98).

BY CAR

Getting around by car in Australia can be expensive because of the long distances you have to cover. Car rental is not particularly cheap.

Australia's roads are not great. The taxes of the population of 18 million people get spread pretty thin when it comes to maintaining roads in a country roughly the size of the continental United States. Most highways are two-lane affairs with the occasional rut, pothole, often no outside line markings, and sometimes no shoulders to speak of. You will hit the odd fabulous stretch, but not often.

When you are poring over the map of Australia, remember that what looks like a road may be an *unsealed* (unpaved) track suitable for 4WD vehicles only; many roads in the Top End are passable only in Dry Season. If you plan to do some serious long-distance driving, get a proper road map from your automobile club, or write to the Australian clubs listed below.

You cannot drive across the middle of the country (except the north-south Stuart Highway that links Adelaide and Darwin) because most of it is desert. Instead, in most places you must travel around the edge. The map on the inside front cover of this book marks the major highways.

Your current **driver's license** or **international driver's permit** is fine in every state of Australia. By law you must carry your license with you when driving. The minimum driving age is 16 or 17, depending on which state you visit, but some car-rental companies require you to be 21, or even 26, particularly if you want to rent a 4WD vehicle.

Sample Driving Distances & Times

Here are a few sample road distances between popular points and the time it takes to drive between them.

Route	Distance	Approx. Driving Time
Cairns to Sydney	2,495 kilometers (1,559 miles)	29 hrs (allow 5 days)
Sydney to Melbourne	873 kilometers (546 miles)	15 hrs (allow 2 days)
Sydney to Perth	4,131 kilometers (2,582 miles)	51 hrs (allow 6 days)
Adelaide to Darwin	3,024 kilometers (1,890 miles)	31 hrs (allow 4 days)
Perth to Darwin	4,163 kilometers (2,602 miles)	49 hrs (allow 6 days)

CAR RENTALS

Think twice about renting a car in big cities and in tourist hot spots such as Cairns, for in cities a judicious mix of public transport and taxis may be better value, and in big tourist areas most tour operators pick you up at your hotel door.

The "big four" companies all have extensive networks across Australia:

- **Avis** (☎ **1800/22 5533** in Australia, or 02/9353 9000 in Sydney; 800/ 230-4898 in the U.S.; 800/272-5871 in Canada; 01344/70 7070 or 0990/ 900-500 in the U.K.)
- **Budget** (☎ **1300/36 2848** in Australia, or 13 27 27, which puts you through to the nearest Budget office; 800/472-3325 in the U.S.; 800/268-8900 in Canada; 1442/276-266 in the U.K.)
- **Hertz** (☎ **13 30 39** in Australia; 800/654-3001 in the U.S.; 800/263-0600 in English, 800/263-0678 in French in Canada, or 416/620-9620 if calling from Toronto; 020/8679-1799 in the U.K.)
- **Thrifty** (☎ **1300/367 2277** in Australia; 800/367-2277 in the U.S. and Canada; 1494/44 2110 in the U.K.)

A small sedan good for zipping around a city or touring a wine region will cost around A$70 (U.S.$49) a day or around A$65 (U.S.$45.50) a day for rentals of a week or longer. A feistier vehicle with enough grunt to get you hundreds of miles from state to state will cost around A$100 (U.S.$70) a day or around A$95 (U.S. $66.50) a day for rentals of a week or longer.

Because of the high number of unsealed roads in Australia, it can make sense to rent a **four-wheel-drive** (4WD) vehicle. All the "big four" companies rent them, but they are more expensive than a regular car at around A$150 (U.S.$105) a day, or around A$130 (U.S.$91) a day for rentals of a week or longer.

All rates quoted here are only a guide. You can often get cheaper rates from small local companies, many of which are listed in the regional chapters of this guide. Even the big guys sometimes offer specials, especially in tourist areas with distinct off-seasons. Advance-purchase rates—usually 7 to 21 days—can offer a significant savings.

INSURANCE   Insurance for theft, loss, or damage to the car, and third-party insurance are usually included in the rate, but always have the rental company spell out exactly what kinds of insurance are and are not covered in the quoted rate. For example, damage to the car body may be covered, but not damage to the windscreen or tires, or damage caused by water. Damage to the car caused by an animal (see below) is rarely covered, nor is driving on an unpaved road.

The deductible, known as "excess" in Australia, on insurance may be as high as A$2,000 (U.S.$1,400) for regular cars and considerably more for 4WDs. You can reduce or avoid the deductible by paying a premium of around A$6 to $15 (U.S. $4.20 to $10.50) per day. Again, check the conditions; some reduction payments do not reduce excesses on single-vehicle accidents, for example.

ONE-WAY RENTALS   One drawback to renting a car in Australia is that the great distances often make one-way rentals a necessity. Car rental companies commonly charge a hefty penalty for one-way rentals. This penalty can amount to many hundreds of dollars, even when you want to drop off the car within the same state. Campervan renters (see below) are luckier—Maui and Budget Campervans don't charge extra for one-way rentals, and Britz charges a reasonable A$150 (U.S.$105) on one-way rentals on most routes, although you must rent for 7 days or more.

Another thing to take into account when planning your trip is that most renters will not insure you for driving 2WD vehicles on unpaved roads—and remote parts of Australia have a lot of those. This restriction applies to 2WD campervans, too.

CAMPERVANS   *Campervans* (the Aussie term for motor homes) are a great way to roam across this wide continent. Campervans generally are smaller than the enormous RVs in the United States. They come in two-, three-, four-, or six-berth versions, and usually have everything you need, such as a minifridge (an icebox in the smaller versions), cooking utensils, sleeping bags or linen, pillows, towels, and maps. Many have showers and toilets. Australia's biggest campervan rental company is **Britz Australia** (☎ **1800/331 454** in Australia, or 03/9483 1888, 0990/143 609 in the United Kingdom; www.britz.com); other major national operators include **Maui** (☎ **1300/ 363 800** in Australia, or 02/9597 6155, 818/981 1270 in the U.S.; www. maui-rentals.com), and **Hertz Campervans** (☎ **1800/33 5888** in Australia, or Auto-Rent Hertz 1800/030500 in Tasmania). Britz Australia manages a fleet of campervans on behalf of Budget in Australia, so you can book a Brits or Budget campervan by calling **Budget Rent-A-Car** ☎ **800/472 3325** in the United States, 1800/268 8900 in Canada, 0800/181 1891 in the United Kingdom, or 1800/643 985 in Australia.

Frustratingly, most local councils take a dim view of your pulling over by the roadside to camp for the night. Instead, you will likely have to stay in a campground, so factor around A$20 (U.S.$14) per night into your budget for a motorized campsite.

For a two-berth campervan without shower or toilet, expect to pay between A$60 (U.S.$42) and A$130 (U.S.$91) per day, depending on the season, and for a four-berth with shower and toilet, between A$125 (U.S.$87.50) and A$215 (U.S.$150.50) per day. May and June are the slowest months; December and January are the peak season. It is sometimes possible to get better rates by booking in your home country before departure. Renting for longer than 3 weeks knocks around A$10 (U.S.$7) or more off the daily rate. Check specifics of the insurance; damage to the car and third party is usually included, but the excess, or deductible, may be as much as A$5,000 (U.S.$3,500), reducible by a payment, usually between A$18 (U.S.$12.60) and A$40 (U.S.$28) a day. Most companies will demand a minimum 4- or 5-day rental.

Money-Saving Tip

One nifty way to cut an average of 30% off your car-rental rate is to join the Australian Youth Hostels Association (YHA) or Hostelling International (see "Tips on Accommodations " below). Along with a host of other discounts, membership entitles you to discounts from Avis, Budget, and Hertz.

ON THE ROAD IN AUSTRALIA

GAS   The price of *petrol* (gasoline) will elicit a cry of dismay from Americans and a whoop of delight from Brits. Prices go up and down a lot, but expect to pay about A79¢ a liter (or U.S.$2.12 per U.S. gallon) for unleaded petrol in New South Wales, as little as A60¢ a liter (or U.S.$2.27 per U.S. gallon) in Queensland, and as much as A95¢ a liter (or U.S.$3.65 per U.S. gallon) in the Outback. One liter equals .26 U.S. gallons. Petrol stations can be few and far between in the Outback, so fill up at every opportunity.

DRIVING RULES   Australians **drive on the left,** which means you give way to the right. Left turns on a red light are not permitted unless a sign says so. Roundabouts are common at intersections; approach them slowly enough so you can stop if you have to, and give way to all traffic on the roundabout. It is illegal not to indicate as you leave the roundabout, even if you're going straight ahead, although you will notice most Aussies never do it.

The maximum permitted **blood alcohol level** when driving is 0.05, which equals approximately two 200ml (6.6 fl. oz.) drinks in the first hour for men, one for women, and one drink per hour for both sexes after that. The police set up random breath-testing units (RBTs) in cunningly disguised and unlikely places all the time, so it is easy to get caught. You will face a court appearance if you do.

The **speed limit** is 60kmph (36 m.p.h.) in urban areas and a frustratingly low 100kmph (60 m.p.h.) or 110kmph (66 m.p.h.) in most country areas. Speed limit signs are black numbers circled in red on a white background.

Drivers and passengers must wear a **seatbelt** at all times when the car or campervan is moving forward. Young children must sit in a child safety seat or wear a safety harness; car-rental companies will rent these to you when you rent your car.

MAPS   The best sources for maps are the state automobile clubs listed in "Auto Clubs & Breakdown Services" below. Most petrol stations stock a limited range of maps relating to the route they are on, and bigger newsagents can be a good source.

HEMA Maps (☎ 07/3290 0322; fax 07/3290 0478; www.hemamaps.com) pub-lishes a wide range of useful, easy-to-read touring and four-wheel-drive road maps of Australia, including state, city, and many regional maps. HEMA also publishes maps to some major national parks, including Kakadu.

Gregory's is the country's leading brand of street directories in capital cities; it also issues state directories that map the streets of all major towns in the state, as well as country, state, capital-city, and touring maps of popular regions such as the Blue Mountains. Gregory's products are published by **Universal Press** (☎ 02/9857 3700; fax 02/9888 9850).

Both HEMA and Gregory's maps are distributed in the United States by **Map Link** (☎ 805/692 6777; www.maplink.com); you may find them in Barnes & Noble or other major bookstores or travel stores.

ROAD SIGNS   Australians navigate by road name, not road number. The easiest way to get where you're going is to familiarize yourself with the major towns along your route and follow the signs toward them. For instance, if you're driving from Sydney to Wagga Wagga, which is between Sydney and Melbourne, follow the signs from Sydney that say MELBOURNE. Closer to your destination you will start seeing signs for Wagga Wagga.

ROAD CONDITIONS & SAFETY   Long distances, roads of dubious quality, and wildlife are all potential hazards. Here are some of the most common dangers and ways to avoid them:

Fatigue   Third on the list of factors responsible for deaths on Australia's roads, fatigue is the biggest killer after driving while intoxicated and speeding. Be sure to take a break whenever you begin to feel tired.

Kangaroos & Other Wildlife   Yep, Skippy is a road hazard. Avoid driving between dusk and dawn at all costs in country areas, for this is when 'roos feed and are most active. If you hit one, always stop and check its pouch for live joeys (baby kangaroos) as females usually have one in the pouch. Wrap the joey tightly in a towel or old sweater, don't feed or overhandle it, and take it to a vet in the nearest town or call one of the following wildlife care groups: **Wildlife Information & Rescue Service** in New South Wales (☎ 1800/641 188 or 02/9975 1633); **Wildlife Care Network** in Victoria (☎ 0500/540 000 or 03/9663 9211); **Wildcare** in Queensland (☎ 07/5527 2444); **Wildlife Foundation Inc.,** in the ACT (☎ 02/6296 3114); **Department of Conservation and Land Management** in Western Australia (☎ 08/9334 0333); **Parks and Wildlife Commission** in the Northern Territory (☎ 08/8999 4536); or **Wildcare** in Tasmania (☎ 03/6248 4053). Most vets will treat native wildlife free of charge.

Some major highways run through unfenced *stations* (ranches), where sheep and cattle pose a threat. Cattle like to rest on the warm bitumen road at night, so put your lights on high beam to spot them. If an animal does loom up in the lights, slow down but never swerve, and, if you have to, hit it. Tell station owners within 24 hours if you have hit their livestock.

Most car-rental companies will not insure you for animal damage to the car, which should give you an inkling of just how common an occurrence this is.

Road Trains   Also known as semitrailers, *road trains* consist of as many as three big truck carriages linked together to make a "train" up to 53.5 meters (175 feet) long. If you're driving in front of one, give them plenty of warning when you brake, as they need a lot of distance in which to slow down. Allow at least 1 clear kilometer (over half a mile) before you attempt to pass a road train, but don't expect the driver to make it easy for you—"truckies" are notorious for their lack of concern for motorists.

Unsealed Roads   Many of Australia's country roads are unsealed (unpaved). Travel at a moderate speed on unpaved roads—about 35kmph (21 m.p.h.) is not too cautious—and do not overcorrect if you veer to one side. Keep well behind any vehicles in front of you so the thick dust they throw up will not block your vision.

Floods   This is a common road hazard in the Top End and north of Cairns from December to March or April (the Wet Season). Never cross a flooded road unless you are sure of its depth. Crocodiles may be in the water, so do not wade in to test it! Fast-flowing water is particularly dangerous, even when very shallow. When in doubt, stay where you are and wait for the water to drop, as most flash floods subside in 24 hours. Check the road conditions ahead at least once a day in Wet Season.

WHAT TO DO IF YOU BREAK DOWN   If you break down or get lost, the golden rule is *never* leave your vehicle. Many a motorist, often an Aussie who should know better, has died wandering off on some crazy quest for help or water, knowing full well that neither is to be found for hundreds of miles. Conserve your body's moisture level by doing as little as possible and staying in the shade of your car. Put out distress signals in patterns of three—three yells, three columns of smoke, and so on. The traditional Aussie "coo-ee," yodeled in a high pitch, travels a surprisingly long way.

Auto Clubs & Breakdown Services   Every state has its own automobile club that provides free breakdown emergency assistance and maps to members of other automobile associations around the world. Ask your association whether it has such a reciprocal agreement with Australian clubs, and don't forget to bring your membership

Emergency Breakdown Assistance

The emergency breakdown assistance telephone number for every Australian auto club is ☎ **13 11 11** from anywhere in Australia. If you are not a member of an auto club back home that has a reciprocal agreement with an Australian club, you'll have to join the Australian club on the spot before they will come tow/repair your car. This costs only around A$60 (U.S.$42), which is not a big price to pay when you're stranded! In the Outback this charge may be considerably higher. Most rental-car companies also have emergency assistance numbers.

card. Even if you are not a member, the clubs are a good source of advice on local traffic regulations, general motoring concerns, touring advice, road conditions, traveling in remote areas, and other motoring questions you may have. They sell maps to nonmembers at reasonable prices. You can drop into numerous regional offices as well as the head office locations listed here:

- **New South Wales & ACT:** National Roads and Motorists' Association (NRMA), 74–76 King St. at George St., Sydney, NSW 2000 (☎ **13 21 32** in New South Wales, or 02/13 2132; fax 02/9292 8472).
- **Victoria:** Royal Automobile Club of Victoria (RACV), 550 Princes Hwy., Noble Park, VIC 3174 (☎ **13 19 55** in Victoria, or 03/9790 2211; fax 03/ 9790 2628). A more convenient city office is located at 360 Bourke St., Melbourne.
- **Queensland:** Royal Automobile Club of Queensland (RACQ), 300 St. Pauls Terrace, Fortitude Valley QLD 4006 (☎ **13 19 05** in Queensland, or 07/ 3361 2444; fax 07/3257 1863). A more convenient city office is in the General Post Office building at 261 Queen St., Brisbane.
- **Western Australia:** Royal Automobile Club of Western Australia (RACWA), 228 Adelaide Terrace, Perth, WA 6000 (☎ **08/9421 4444;** fax 08/9221 2708).
- **South Australia:** Royal Automobile Association of South Australia (RAA), 41 Hindmarsh Sq., Adelaide, SA 5000 (☎ **08/8202 4500;** fax 08/8202 4520).
- **Northern Territory:** Automobile Association of the Northern Territory (AANT), 79–81 Smith St., Darwin, NT 0800 (☎ **08/8981 3837;** fax 08/ 8941 2965).
- **Tasmania:** Royal Automobile Club of Tasmania (RACT), Corner of Murray and Patrick Streets, Hobart TAS 7000 (☎ **13 27 22** in Tasmania, or 03/ 6232 6300; fax 03/6234 8784).

TIPS FOR FOUR-WHEEL DRIVERS   If you are traveling off-road on 4WD trails beyond the areas covered by this book, always keep to the track and leave gates as you found them. Carry 5 liters (around 1 gallon) of drinking water per person per day; enough food to last 3 or 4 days more than you think you will need; a first-aid kit; spare fuel; a jack and two spare tires; spare fan belts, radiator hoses and air-conditioner hoses; a tow rope; and a good map that marks all gas stations. If you're traveling in seriously remote areas, carry a high-frequency and CB radio. When traveling on private station (ranch) roads, obtain permission from the owners. Advise a friend or a police station of your route and your expected time of arrival at your destination.

13 Tips on Accommodations

You'll find loads of inexpensive accommodation choices in Australia, even in the cities. Some of the terms used in Australia may not be familiar to international visitors, so here's a brief rundown.

HOTELS   You will recognize many of the major hotel chains in Australia, including the following:

- **Holiday Inn** (☎ **800/HOLIDAY** in the U.S. and Canada, 0800/897 121 in the U.K., 0800/442 888 in New Zealand, or 1800/553 888 in Australia; www.holiday-inn.com).
- **Marriott,** including the more affordable Courtyard brand, in Surfers Paradise, Cairns, and Sydney (☎ **800/MARRIOTT** in the U.S. and Canada, 0800/221 222 in the U.K., 0800/441 035 in New Zealand, 1800/251 259 in Australia outside Sydney or 02/9299 1614 in Sydney; www.marriott.com).
- **Ramada International Hotels & Resorts** (Marriott Hotels handles bookings for Ramada properties in Australia).
- **Travelodge,** a two-star product but smarter than its American counterpart (☎ **1300/363 300** in Australia, 800/835-7742 in the U.S. and Canada, 0800/801 111 in New Zealand, 0345/581-666 in the U.K. outside London, or 020/8335-1304 in London).

Australia has a few hotel chains of its own, including **All Seasons** (☎ **02/9272 8800**), which has practical hotels and resorts in popular Outback and central city locations, and the honest and affordable **Country Comfort** (call Touraust Hotels ☎ **1800/065 064** in Australia).

If you are prepared to forgo the convenience and predictability of a chain, there are any number of moderately priced, individually run hotels that often offer a little more personal warmth and style than the big guys.

It's a rare hotel room that does not have reverse-cycle air-conditioning for heating and cooling, a telephone, color TV, clock-radio, a minirefrigerator if not a minibar, an iron and ironing board, and self-serve tea and coffee. Private bathrooms are standard, although they often have only a shower, not a tub.

SERVICED APARTMENTS   This type of accommodation is very popular with Aussies, for not only do you get a fully furnished apartment with one, two, or three separate bedrooms and a spacious living room, you also get a full kitchen and often two bathrooms. In other words, you're getting all the facilities and more of a hotel suite—and often for less than the cost of a standard hotel room. Serviced apartments are great for families, and for anyone prepared to save money by cooking their own meals. The apartment inventory in Australia ranges from clean and comfortable to quite luxurious, and rates vary accordingly. You can find a nice two-bedroom apartment for A$120 (U.S.$84). Most can be rented for just one night, but some proprietors may insist on a minimum 3-night stay, or even a week in high season in popular vacations spots.

MOTELS & MOTOR INNS   You can usually rely on Australia's plentiful motels to be neat and clean, if a little dated. You can count on them having air-conditioning, a telephone, color TV, clock-radio, a minirefrigerator or minibar, and self-serve tea and coffee. Most have only showers, not bathtubs. Some have a restaurant attached, and many have a swimming pool. Motor inns offer a greater range of facilities, and fancier rooms than motels, without losing their down-to-earth touch or affordability. Rates average A$70 to $90 (U.S.$49 to $63) double, although in low season you can score rooms for as low as A$50 (U.S.$35) double.

The leading chains in Australia include **Best Western,** with 265 locations (☎ **800/780-7234** in the U.S. and Canada, 0800/39 3130 in the U.K., 0800/237 893 in New Zealand, 13 17 79 in Australia); **Flag** (☎ **800/624-3524** in the U.S. and Canada, 0800/892 407 in the U.K., 0800/803 524 in New Zealand, 13 24 00 in Australia); and **Budget,** a slightly less spiffy but always affordable chain (☎ **03/ 5143 1077**). The Country Comfort chain listed above in "Hotels" also has nice motor inns.

BED & BREAKFAST INNS   B&Bs in Australia are a fabulous value—it is easy to find charming rooms for A$75 (U.S.$52.50) or less for a double, and rarely will you pay more than A$100 (U.S.$70) for a double per night. Some B&Bs are modest suburban homes whose owners rent out a room to travelers; others are charming historical houses converted to accommodations; still others are purpose-built homes with several rooms designed for traveling guests, often with private bathrooms. Some larger commercial inns, with maybe 10 or 15 rooms, also call themselves B&Bs. Whatever the style of building, the accommodation is usually cozy and the welcome warm. Staying in B&Bs is a terrific way to meet other travelers, and of course you get to meet your real Aussie hosts. There are a few considerations to take into account—you probably won't have access to a telephone unless the hosts let you use theirs; you may not have a TV, clock-radio, minibar, or other accoutrements you are used to in hotels and motels; the place may not take credit cards; and your hosts, who have their own lives to live, may not be there to receive you 24 hours a day. Bath facilities are often shared, although quite a few B&Bs these days have private bathrooms.

Travel agents rarely list B&Bs because the establishments are not big enough to pay commission, so they can be hard to find. One excellent source is **Bed & Breakfast Australia,** P.O. Box 408, Gordon, NSW 2072 (☎ **02/9498 5344,** fax 02/9498 6438; e-mail bnb@bnba.com.au; www.bnba.com.au). This Sydney-based booking service has hundreds of B&Bs on its books in cities, on farms, near beaches, and in wine regions all over the country. Rates range from A$85 (U.S.$59.50) to A$120 (U.S.$84) for a double, including breakfast. Owners Carolyn and Cory Moore know their properties well and try to suit you to compatible hosts, houses, and locations. They can also find you lodgings in larger guesthouses, inns, or self-catering cottages; suggest itineraries; and make car-rental bookings for you. The company requires a minimum booking of two nights, which can be spent at two separate locations, or a minimum A$130 (U.S.$91) booking. Cory and Carolyn also arrange Home Hosted Dinners, where you enjoy a three-course meal with wine, cooked by an Aussie host at his or her home, for A$70 (U.S.$49) per person.

Another good source is *The Australian Bed & Breakfast Book* (Moonshine Press). It's distributed by **South Pacific Traveler's Booksource,** Box 55, Wooster, OH 44691 (☎ **800/234-4552,** fax 330/262-7821) and retails for U.S.$16.95. In the United Kingdom, contact **The Bed & Breakfast Book,** 16 Blenheim St., Hebden Bridge, West Yorkshire, HX7 8BU (☎ **01422/845 085,** fax 01422/845 875).

What Next? Productions Pty Ltd, 24 Mitford St., St. Kilda, Melbourne, VIC 3182 (☎ **03/9537 0833,** fax 03/9537 0922), publishes two exquisite color guides of almost 200 pages each to Victoria and Tasmania, both titled *Beautiful B&Bs & Small Hotels.* The properties listed are more upscale than most, roughly in the A$100-to-$200 (U.S.$70-to-$140) price range for a double. Guides to South Australia and New South Wales will be added to the series soon. The guides sell for A$24.95 (U.S.$17.50).

The **Bed & Breakfast and Farmstay Association of Far North Queensland,** 75 Kamerunga Rd., Stratford, Cairns, QLD 4870 (☎ **07/4058 1227,** fax 07/4058 1990; e-mail: bbnetwork@internetnorth.com.au), can send you a brochure listing nearly 100 properties in and around Cairns, Mission Beach, Port Douglas, and Townsville.

Another Web site listing Australian B&Bs is **BABS (Bed and Breakfast Site)** at www.babs.com.au.

PUBS   Aussie pubs are really made for having a drink, not spending the night, but many offer rooms upstairs, usually with shared facilities. Because most pubs are over 100 years old, the rooms are often either old-fashioned in a cute kind of way—

wrought-iron beds, pretty lace bedcovers, dark wood furniture, French doors opening onto wide verandahs—or just plain old. Pub accommodations are dying out in the cities, but are a common enough place to stay in the country. Australians are rowdy drinkers, so sleeping over the front bar can be hellishly noisy, but the pub's saving grace is incredibly low rates. Most charge per person, not per room, and you will rarely pay more than A$50 (U.S.$35) per person a night. It is not hard to find a bed for as little as A$20 (U.S.$14) a night.

HOMESTAYS   If you want to stay with an Aussie family and really get involved in their life, even down to sitting at their table, **Homestay Network,** 5 Locksley St., Killara, NSW 2071 (☎ **02/9498 4400;** fax 02/9498 8324; e-mail: thenetwork@ bigpond.com; www.sydney.citysearch.com.au—you will find it under "Staying in Sydney," then "Where to Stay," then "Guesthouses") can place you in one of 1,400 homes in the wider Sydney area. Prices vary widely, but as a rough guide expect to pay about A$150 (U.S.$105) double with breakfast.

FARMSTAYS   The Aussie answer to the dude ranch is a farmstay, where you spend anywhere from one night to several weeks getting involved in farm duties, touring the property, or just relaxing under a gum tree with a cold beer. Accommodations on farms can be anything from a basic bunkhouse (ask whether it's air-conditioned, because most farms are in very hot areas) to a rustically luxurious lodge that would do Ralph Lauren proud. Do some research on your chosen farm—many activities are seasonal, some farmers will not want you getting involved in dangerous work, and "farm" can mean different things in different parts of Australia. If you like green fields and cute black-and-white dairy cows, Victoria is the place for you. If checking fences on a dusty 500,000-acre Outback station (ranch) sounds wildly romantic, not only are you crazy, but you should head to Western Australia or the Northern Territory.

The **Host Farms Association,** Level 6, 230 Collins St., Melbourne, VIC 3000 (☎ **03/ 9650 2922,** fax 03/9650 9434), makes free bookings for a huge range of farmstay properties in Victoria, New South Wales, Queensland, South Australia, and Western Australia. Ask for their color brochures, one for each state, that detail the style of accommodation, activities, and rates at each property. Rates vary, but expect to pay about A$85 (U.S.$59.50) double without meals.

Bed & Breakfast Australia (see "Bed & Breakfasts" above) also books farmstay properties all over the country.

YOUTH HOSTELS & BACKPACKER LODGES   Australia has oodles of backpacker hostels. Some are little more than grim dormitories (sometimes not airconditioned) with few facilities, others are spiffy new complexes with cheerily painted rooms, a swimming pool, a tour desk, a restaurant and bar, communal kitchens, and Internet access. If you like the idea of traveling on the cheap, but aren't wild about bunking with strangers, opt for one of the many hostels that offer private double rooms or family rooms. Some hostels will impose a maximum stay of 3 nights, others are happy to accommodate you for a week or more. Blankets and pillows are provided, but you may need to rent bed linens for an extra two or three dollars per stay; bring your own towel. Look for hostels that have lockers, as the backpacker circuit has more than its fair share of petty thieves. Hostels typically charge between A$11 (U.S.$7.70) and A$18 (U.S.$12.60) per dorm bed per night, and between A$38 (U.S.$26.60) and $45 (U.S.$31.50) for a twin/double private room. These rooms are in high demand, so book ahead.

The **Australian Youth Hostels Association (YHA),** 422 Kent St., Sydney, NSW 2000 (☎ **02/9261 1111,** fax 02/9261 1969; www.yha.org.au) is the Australian arm of Hostelling International, and has more than 140 hostels in Australia. Despite the name, people of any age can stay at them. Quality and facilities vary, but all YHA hostels are clean, and have communal kitchens and 24-hour access. You don't have to join the association to stay at its hostels, but members receive discounted rates and are entitled to myriad other discounts—on car rental, bus travel, and tours, for example—that can repay the membership fee many times over.

It is best to join before you arrive in Australia. In the United States, contact **Hostelling International,** 733 15th St. NW, Suite 840, Washington, DC 20005 (☎ **202/783-6161;** www.hiayh.org) or join at any of the approximately 150 hostels in the United States. The 12-month membership is free if you are 17 or under, U.S.$25 if you are 18 to 54, and U.S.$15 if you are 55 years or older. Hostelling International sells a directory of all Australian youth hostels for U.S.$5.50.

In Canada, contact **Hostelling International–Canada,** 205 Catherine St., Suite 400, Ottawa, Ontario, K2P 1C3 (☎ 613/237 7884; www.hostellingintl.ca). In England and Wales, contact **Youth Hostels Association** (England and Wales), Trevelyan House, 8 St. Stephen's Hill, St. Albans, Hertfordshire AL1 2DY (☎ 1727/855 215). In Scotland, contact the **Scottish Youth Hostels Association,** 7 Glebe Crescent, Stirling FK8 2JA (☎ 1786/891 400). In Ireland, contact **Hostelling International– Northern Ireland,** 22 Donegall Rd., Belfast BT12 5JN (☎ 1232/315 435). All of these offices are accessible at www.iyhf.org.

It is possible to join after you arrive in Oz, at some (but not all) Australian hostels and at YHA Membership and Travel Centres in all state-capital cities.

Note: YHA properties are nonsmoking.

YWCA (☎ **1800/249 124** in Australia, or 03/9329 2184; www.ywca.org. au/travel) has eight comfortable budget hotels with private rooms, and sometimes also dormitories, that are a cut above the average backpacker hostel. Rates for a double range from A$40 to A$89 (U.S.$28 to $62.30). There is a YWCA in Alice Springs, Cairns, and in all state capitals except Adelaide and Hobart.

CAMPING & CARAVAN PARKS   Australians camp everywhere year-round, even in remote desert outposts and even in winter. The only places you might want to avoid are Tasmania and the mountainous areas of New South Wales and Victoria in winter, when it's a bit too nippy, and the Top End in the summer Wet Season.

Campsites are attached to nearly all the country's numerous caravan (camper) parks, and many lodges offer associated campgrounds. Camping in national parks does entail some restrictions—usually you can camp only at designated campsites; occasionally, bookings may be required 24 hours in advance. Quite often fires are banned, so you will need to rely on a gas barbecue or, if none is supplied, your own camping stove.

Expect to pay A$3 (U.S.$2.10) to A$8 (U.S.$5.60) per adult in a tent, A$8 (U.S.$5.60) to A$11 (U.S.$7.70) for a powered campsite, and about half price for kids. Book ahead during school vacations and peak season.

FAST FACTS: Australia

American Express   For all travel-related customer inquiries regarding any American Express service, including reporting a lost card, call ☎ **1800/230 100** anywhere in Australia outside Sydney, or 02/9271 8666 in Sydney. These lines are staffed between 8:30am and 7pm. After hours, the authorizations line handles emergencies (1800/642 227) from anywhere in Australia. To report lost or stolen traveler's checks there is a separate line (1800/251 902 anywhere in Australia, or 02/9271 8689 in Sydney).

Banks/ATM Networks   See "Money" earlier in this chapter.

Business Hours Banks are open Monday through Thursday from 9:30am to 4pm, and until 5pm on Friday. General **business hours** are Monday through Friday from 8:30am to 5:30pm. **Shopping hours** are usually 8:30am to 5pm weekdays, and 9am to 4pm Saturday. Many shops close Sunday, although major department stores and shops aimed at tourists, like opal stores, are open seven days.

Car Rentals   See "Getting Around" earlier in this chapter.

Climate   See "When to Go" earlier in this chapter.

Currency   See "Money" earlier in this chapter.

Customs   See "Entry Requirements" earlier in this chapter.

Dates   Australians write their dates day, month, year: for example, January 5, 1968, is written 05/01/68.

Documents Required   See "Visitor Information & Entry Requirements" earlier in this chapter.

Driving Rules   See "Getting Around" earlier in this chapter.

Drugstores   These are called "chemists" or "pharmacies." Australian pharmacists are permitted to fill only prescriptions written by Australian doctors.

Electricity   The current is 240 volts AC, 50 Hertz. Sockets take two or three flat, not rounded, prongs. North Americans and Europeans will need to buy a converter before they leave home (don't wait until you get to Australia, because Australian stores only sell converters for Aussie appliances to fit American and European outlets). Some hotels have 110-volt outlets for electric shavers, or dual-voltage, and some will lend converters, but don't count on it. Power does not start automatically when you plug in an appliance; you need to flick the switch located beside the socket to the on position.

Embassies/Consulates   Most diplomatic posts are in Canberra, the nation's capital: **British High Commission,** Commonwealth Ave., Canberra, ACT 2600 (☎ 02/6270 6666); **High Commission of Canada,** Commonwealth Ave., Yarralumla, ACT 2600 (☎ 02/6273 3844); **New Zealand High Commission,** Commonwealth Ave., Canberra ACT 2600 (☎ 02/6270 4211); and the **United States Embassy,** 21 Moonah Place, Yarralumla, ACT 2600 (☎ 02/6214 5600). Embassies or consulates with posts in state capitals are listed in "Fast Facts" in the relevant state chapters.

For Australian embassies abroad, see "Entry Requirements & Customs" earlier in this chapter.

Emergencies   Dial ☎ **000** anywhere in Australia for police, ambulance, or the fire department. This is a free call from public and private telephones, and needs no coins.

Etiquette   Australia's laid-back disposition means it's first names from the start, handshakes all round, and no standing on ceremony, mate. Always return a "shout" (round) at the pub, and don't butt in if there's a queue (line). Avoid using a mobile telephone in a restaurant if you can, and turn it off in the theater.

Holidays   See "When to Go" earlier in this chapter.

Information   See "Visitor Information" earlier in this chapter.

Language   Australians speak English—kind of. The "Aussie-Yankee Lexicon" at the end of this book may help you decipher the lingo.

Liquor Laws   Pub (bar) hours vary from pub to pub, but most are open Monday through Saturday from around 10am to 10pm or midnight. The minimum drinking age is 18. Random breath tests to catch drunk drivers are common, and drunk-driving laws are strictly enforced. The maximum permitted blood alcohol level is 0.05. Alcohol is sold only in liquor stores, or "bottle shops" attached to a pub, and rarely in supermarkets.

Mail   Australia's single postal service, **Australia Post** (☎ **13 13 17** in Australia) has a post office in every suburb. Every state capital has a central General Post Office (GPO) offering a complete range of services. Some newsagents sell stamps. A postcard costs A95¢ (U.S.67¢) to the United States or Canada, A$1 (U.S.70¢ to the United Kingdom, and A70¢ (U.S.49¢) to New Zealand. American Express cardholders can have mail sent to any American Express office in Australia for collection.

Maps   See "Getting Around" earlier in this chapter.

Newspapers/Magazines   National newspapers are *The Australian* (Monday through Friday) and *The Weekend Australian* (Saturday), plus the *Australian Financial Review* (Monday through Saturday). *Time* magazine publishes a weekly Australian edition. *The Bulletin* is Australia's own weekly news magazine.

Pets   Leave 'em at home. You will be back home planning your next vacation before Fluffy clears quarantine in Oz.

Police   Dial ☎ **000** anywhere in Australia. This is a free call from public and private telephones, and requires no coins.

Safety   Violent crime is uncommon. Semiautomatic and automatic weapons are banned, and handguns are strictly controlled. Purse-snatchers are the same threat in capital cities and tourist areas that they are all over the world.

Taxes   Sales tax is built into most prices, and while there is no way to claim a refund on most day-to-day items, you can obtain tax-free prices on big-ticket luxury purchases such as electrical goods, perfume, and jewelry by showing your passport and return international airline ticket. Sales tax varies from item to item, but it can be as much as 42% on luxury items, so always ask about tax-free prices for travelers. Other taxes are departure tax of A$30 (U.S.$21), which is included in the price of your ticket; landing and departure taxes at many airports, also included in the price of your ticket; accommodation tax of 10% in central Sydney and 5% in the Northern Territory; "reef tax," or Environmental Management Charge of A$4 (U.S.$2.80) for every person over the age of four every time he or she enters the Great Barrier Reef Marine Park (this charge goes toward park upkeep); and a minimal 1 or 2%, varying from state to state, on rental cars.

After July 2000, should the government in power when this was written still be in power, expect a GST (Goods and Services Tax, or consumption tax) of around 8% on most products and services. This is likely to partly or totally replace many existing taxes, including the sales tax mentioned above.

Telephone & Fax   **To call Australia from North America,** dial the international access code 011; then **Australia's country code (61);** then the area code (we've given the area code for every number listed in this book); then the local number. The local area codes found throughout this book all begin with "0"; you drop the "0" if you're calling from outside Australia, but you need to dial it along with the area code if you're calling long distance within Australia. For example, to ring the Sydney Opera House (☎ **02/9250 7111**) from the United States, dial 011-61-2-9250-7111.

To call Australia from Britain, dial the international access code 00, and then follow the instructions above.

To make an international call from Australia, dial the international access code 0011 (note it has two zeros, not one like the international access code from North America); then the country code, then the area code, and finally the local number. Dial 0012 instead of 0011, and the operator will ring back within minutes of the call to tell you what it cost. To find out a country code, call ☎ 1222 or look in the back of the Australian White Pages. Common country codes are: USA and Canada, 1; United Kingdom, 44; New Zealand, 64; and South Africa, 27.

To make an international credit card or collect call from Australia, dial one of the following access codes to your country:

- **United States:** AT&T Direct ☎ 1800/881 011, Sprint ☎ 1800/881 877, MCI ☎ 1800/881 100, Worldcom ☎ 1800/881 212, or Bell Atlantic ☎ 1800/881 152
- **United Kingdom:** BT ☎ 1800/881 441, or Mercury ☎ 1800/881 417
- **New Zealand:** ☎ 1800/881 640

To use a calling card from some pay phones, you will need to deposit A40¢ to put the call through, but this is usually refunded when you hang up.

To make a long-distance call within Australia, dial the area code, including the initial zero, followed by the number you are calling. Australia's area codes are in the process of being switched from a plethora of two- and three- digit codes to a uniform two-digit code in each state, followed by an eight-digit number. The new codes are: New South Wales and the A.C.T., 02; Victoria and Tasmania, 03; Queensland, 07; and South Australia, Western Australia, and the Northern Territory, 08. Long-distance calls within Australia on Telstra's network are half price before 7am and after 7pm Monday through Friday and anytime on weekends.

Local calls in Australia are untimed and cost a flat A40¢ from a public telephone, or A25¢ (U.S.18¢) from a private phone in a home or office.

Newsagents and some tourist information booths sell Smart Phonecards (which you swipe in the pay phone) and PhoneAway cards (which you use by dialing access codes printed on the card) containing a prepaid allotment of call time; not all public telephones take these cards yet.

Cellular or "mobile" telephones are hugely popular in Australia and are available for daily rental in major cities. For any information on mobile phones, call ☎ **1800/018 111** in Australia.

To reach the operator for help making a call, dial ☎ **1234.** To make a collect or "reverse charges" call, dial the operator at ☎ **12550.**

To find out a telephone number, call **Directory Assistance** at ☎ **1223** for numbers within Australia, or ☎ **1225** for overseas numbers.

Time   Australia crosses three time zones. When it is noon in New South Wales, the A.C.T., Victoria, Queensland, and Tasmania, it is 11:30am in South Australia and the Northern Territory and 10am in Western Australia. All states except Queensland, the Northern Territory, and Western Australia observe daylight saving time from around the last Sunday in October (the first Sunday in October, in Tasmania) to around the first Sunday in March. To confuse things, not all states switch over to daylight saving time on the same day or even in the same week.

The east coast of Australia is GMT (Greenwich Mean Time) plus 10 hours. When it is noon (Eastern Standard Time, or EST) on the east coast, it is 2am in London that morning, and 6pm in Los Angeles, and 9pm in New York the previous night. These times are based on standard time, so allow for daylight saving in the Australian summer, or in the country you are calling. New Zealand is two hours ahead of the east coast of Australia.

For the exact local time in Australia, call ☎ **1194;** call ☎ **1222** for the exact local time overseas. For national and international time zones, ring ☎ **1900/ 937 106.**

Tipping   Once almost unheard of in Australia, these days it is customary to tip 10% for a substantial meal in a restaurant (but not for a casual sandwich and cup of coffee). Some passengers round up to the nearest dollar in a cab, but it's OK to insist on every last 5¢ piece of change back from the driver. Tipping bellboys and porters is sometimes done, but not mandatory. No one tips bar staff, barbers, or hairdressers.

Water   Water is fine to drink everywhere except Port Douglas, where you should stick to the bottled variety. In the Outback, the taps may carry slightly salty underground bore water for showers and laundry, while drinking water is collected in rainwater tanks.

Settling into Sydney

4

by Marc Llewellyn

Sydney, the "emerald" city, sits majestically around the greenest, most beautiful urban harbor in the world. It's at its best approached at night from the air, when you'll see a million twinkling lights, a vast swath of fluorescence spreading across the water, and the Sydney Opera House and Harbour Bridge lit up like Christmas. And this is not just one Sydneysider's opinion of the city, either. In October 1996 *Condé Naste Traveler* voted Sydney the World's Best City Destination for the second year running, and in 1997 the magazine's readers voted it the World's Friendliest City. In 1998 *Travel & Leisure* readers gave it the thumbs up as the Best Value City in the World. Beat that Paris, Venice, Melbourne, or myriad other hopefuls.

Sydney has something for everyone: miles of beaches, from world-famous Bondi just south of the city to pretty little Shelly Beach on the North Shore; world-class cuisine that combines the very best of many cultures; outdoor adventures literally at the city's back door, in the Blue Mountains and beyond; historic pubs where you can buy a "shout" for your new Aussie mates; city strolls; Harbour cruises; and more.

Sydney is also, of course, gearing up for the 2000 Olympic Games, when the city will be the focus of the world's attention. The city has been going through a major upheaval ever since it was announced that Sydney had won the right to host the Games. Virtually every sidewalk in the city center has been pulled up and renewed, and there has been major disruption all across town as new office blocks, retail plazas, and hotels spring up on sites vacant for years. The arrival and departure areas of Sydney International Airport have been completely overhauled, and a rail link from the airport to Central Railway Station is under construction. It hasn't always been easy for Sydney residents, but one hopes they'll get a better city out of it in the end.

In addition to hosting the Olympic Games, Sydney is also hosting the XI Paralympic Games in the year 2000 (October 18 to 24), when some 4,000 athletes from 125 countries will take part in some 18 sports—making it the largest games of this sort ever held. What's more, from the August 2000 Olympic Games to the conclusion of the Paralympic Games on October 24, Sydney will come alive to the sights and sounds of the Olympic Arts Festival. The festival, which will be concentrated around the city center and the Sydney Olympic Park in Homebush Bay, will include a series of outdoor concerts and cultural activities, and a whole range of events aimed at celebrating 2000.

The frugal traveler will find that, compared to other major cities around the world, Sydney offers good value for money spent. Food and public transport are quite cheap, and attractions are generally not prohibitively expensive (senior citizen and student prices are almost always available if you have identification). The price of a hotel room is far cheaper than in other major population centers, such as New York and London.

1 Orientation

ARRIVING

BY PLANE   Sydney International Airport (also known as Kingsford Smith Airport) is 8 kilometers (about 5 miles) from the city center. The International and Domestic terminals are separate, but are linked by regular free shuttle buses. In both terminals, you'll find free luggage carts, wheelchairs, a post office (open Monday through Friday 9am to 5pm), mailboxes, duty-free shops (including one before you go through customs on arrival), restaurants, bars, stores, showers, luggage lockers, and tourist information desks. Caffè Italia on the Departures Level regularly wins awards for the best coffee in Sydney. There is also an Olympic Store here selling Sydney 2000 Olympic Games–related goods; a State Transit Kiosk selling bus, train, and ferry tickets; and a New South Wales Travel Centre desk offering cheap deals on hotels as well as a whole range of travel-related services (see "Accommodations You Can Afford" later in this chapter). Smoking is prohibited throughout the airport.

Getting into Town: Fast and comfortable green and yellow **Airport Express buses** operated by State Transit travel to and from the city center and both the International and Domestic terminals from 5am to 11pm, stopping at various points along the way. The number 300 bus runs to and from Circular Quay, The Rocks, Wynyard, and Town Hall every 15 minutes Monday to Friday and approximately every 30 minutes early mornings, nights, weekends, and public holidays. The trip to Circular Quay takes about 45 minutes. The number 350 bus runs to and from Kings Cross, Potts Point, and Elizabeth Bay every 20 minutes and takes around 30 minutes to reach Kings Cross. Both buses travel via Central Station (around 20 minutes from the International terminal).

The new Airport Express bus number 351 leaves for Coogee, Bronte, and Bondi beaches every 30 minutes. The trip from the International terminal to Bondi Beach takes approximately 55 minutes. The number 352 bus travels between Central Station, Chinatown, Darling Harbour, the Star City casino, Sydney Fish Markets, and Glebe, approximately every 30 minutes. Trip time is about 30 minutes to Darling Harbour, and 50 minutes to Glebe.

One-way tickets for all buses cost A$6 (U.S.$4.20) for adults, A$4 (U.S.$2.80) for kids under 16, and A$15 (U.S.$10.50) for a family (any number of children); a round-trip ticket costs A$10 (U.S.$7) for adults, A$5 (U.S.$3.50) for kids, and A$25 (U.S.$17.50) for a family. You must use the return portion within 2 months. Buy your tickets from the Airport Express booth outside the airport terminal, or on the bus. Airport Express buses also travel to and from the International and Domestic terminals. An interterminal ticket costs A$2.50 (U.S.$1.75) for adults, A$1.50 (U.S.$1.05)for children, and A$6.50 (U.S.$4.55) for a family.

State Transit bus number 100 provides new rapid service from the airport to the northern suburbs of Neutral Bay, Cremorne, Manly Vale (not Manly beach), and Dee Why.

The **Kingsford Smith Airport Coach** also operates to the city center, from bus stops outside the terminals. This service will drop you off (and pick you up) at your hotel (pickups require at least 1 hour's advance notice; call ☎ **02/9667 3221**). Tickets cost A$6 (U.S.$4.20) one-way and A$11 (U.S.$7.70) round-trip (the return portion can be used at any time in the future).

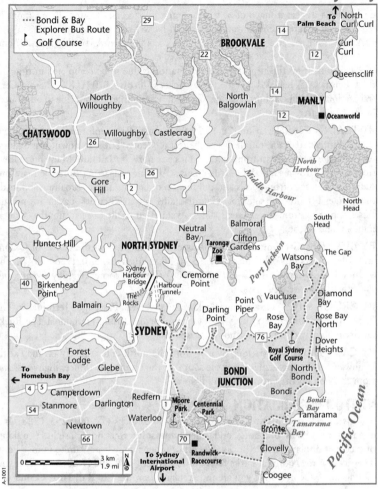

Greater Sydney

Legend:
···· Bondi & Bay Explorer Bus Route
⛳ Golf Course

BROOKVALE

To Palm Beach
North Curl Curl
Curl Curl
Queenscliff
MANLY
■ Oceanworld

North Willoughby
North Balgowlah

CHATSWOOD
Willoughby
Castlecrag
North Harbour
North Head

Gore Hill

Neutral Bay
Balmoral
Clifton Gardens
South Head
The Gap

Hunters Hill
NORTH SYDNEY
Taronga Zoo
Middle Harbour
Watsons Bay

Sydney Harbour Bridge
Cremorne Point
Port Jackson

Birkenhead Point
Harbour Tunnel
The Rocks
Darling Point
Point Piper
Vaucluse
Diamond Bay
Rose Bay North

Balmain
SYDNEY
Rose Bay
Dover Heights

Forest Lodge
Glebe
Royal Sydney Golf Course
North Bondi

To Homebush Bay
BONDI JUNCTION
Bondi
Bondi Bay

Camperdown
Redfern
Moore Park
Centennial Park
Tamarama
Tamarama Bay

Stanmore
Darlington
Waterloo
Bronte

Newtown
Clovelly

To Sydney International Airport
Randwick Racecourse
Coogee

Pacific Ocean

0   3 km
     1.9 mi

Privately operated shuttle buses also connect the airport with the city center, Kings Cross, Darling Harbour, and Glebe hotels. These buses depart when they're full, and run from the city to the airport between 5am and 8pm, and from the airport to the city between the first and last flights each day. Each company requires advance reservations for pickups from your hotel to the airport. One company you could try is **Silks Sydney Airport-Hotel Transfers** (☎ **02/9371 4466;** e-mail: Silksydtransfer@seltek.com.au). The fare is A$6 (U.S.$4.20) one-way for adults and A$4.50 (U.S.$3.15) for children 5 to 11.

The **Bondi Jetbus** (☎ **0500 886008;** fax 02/9487 3554) will take you to any of the eastern beaches, including Bondi and Bronte. The trip costs A$8 (U.S.$5.60) for adults and A$4 (U.S.$2.80) for children. Call when you arrive at the airport, and they'll come pick you up within 15 minutes. The **Pittwater Airport Shuttle** (☎ and fax **02/9973 1877**) will take you to any of the northern beaches. A trip to Manly, for example, costs A$20 (U.S.$14) for the first person, A$10 (U.S.$7) for the second, and A$5 (U.S.$3.50) for each subsequent passenger. The shuttle makes approximately six departures a day, so it may not be worth your while to hang around. Reservations (a day in advance) are essential; travel agents can make reservations.

A **taxi** from the airport to the city center costs between A$16 (U.S.$11.20) and A$20 (U.S.$14).

A **rail link** from the airport to Central Station is due to be completed in time for the Olympics. It's believed that a one-way ticket will cost A$10 (U.S.$7). From Central Station, it will be a short taxi ride, CityRail train journey, or bus ride to other areas of the city center.

BY TRAIN   Central Station (☎ **13 15 00** in Australia for information) is the main city and interstate train station. It's at the top of George Street in downtown Sydney. All interstate trains depart from here, and it's a major CityRail hub. Many buses leave from here for Town Hall and Circular Quay. All buses departing from the main bus station on George Street (locals also call the top of George Street "Broadway") outside the main exit (follow the signs for "Countrytrains") go to Circular Quay or Town Hall. Buses departing from the side exit (Eddy Avenue) go to the eastern suburbs (such as Balmain and Glebe).

BY BUS   The **Greyhound-Pioneer Australia** terminal is on the corner of Oxford and Riley streets in Darlinghurst (☎ **13 20 30** in Australia, or 02/9283 5977). The **Sydney Coach Terminal** (☎ **02/9281 9366**) is on the corner of Eddy Avenue and Pitt Street, near Central Station.

BY CRUISE SHIP   Cruise ships dock at the **Overseas Passenger Terminal** in The Rocks, just opposite the Sydney Opera House, or in Darling Harbour if The Rocks facility is already occupied by another vessel.

BY CAR   Drivers approaching Sydney from the north enter the city on the Pacific Highway, those approaching from the south on the Hume and Princes highways, and from the west on the Great Western Highway.

VISITOR INFORMATION

The **Sydney Visitor Center,** 106 George St., The Rocks (☎ **02/9255 1788**), is a good place for maps, brochures, and general tourist information. It also has two floors of excellent displays on The Rocks. The office is open daily from 9am to 6pm. Also in The Rocks is the **National Parks & Wildlife Center** (☎ **02/9247 8861**) in Cadmans Cottage, 110 George St. If you are in Circular Quay, the **CityRail Host Center** (no phone), opposite No. 5 jetty, has a wide range of brochures and a staff member on hand to help with general inquiries. It's open daily 9am to 5pm. The **Manly Visitors Information Bureau** (☎ **02/9977 1088**), right opposite Manly beach near the Corso, offers general information but specializes in Manly and the northern beaches. If you want to inquire about destinations and holidays within Sydney or the rest of

---

A Taxi Tip

Especially in busy periods, cab drivers may try to insist that you share a cab with other passengers waiting in line at the airport. After dropping off the other passengers at their various stops, the cab driver will attempt to charge you the full price of the journey, despite the fact that the other passengers paid for their sections. If this happens you certainly won't save any money by sharing a cab, and your journey will be a long one. It's better to wait until you can get your own cab, or catch an airport bus to the city center (and then take a taxi from there to your hotel, if necessary). If you are first in line in the taxi rank, the law states that you can refuse to share the cab.

New South Wales, call Tourism, New South Wales' help line, at ☎ **13 20 77** in Australia.

Electronic information on cinema, theater, exhibitions, and other events can be accessed through Talking Guides (☎ **13 16 20** in Australia). You'll need a code number for each topic, which you can find on page 3 of the A–K section of the Sydney Yellow Pages phone directory. The service costs the same as a local call.

In the United States, **Tourism New South Wales** has an office in Marina Del Rey, California (☎ **310/301-1904;** fax 310/301 0913; e-mail: tnswla@earthlink.net).

Good **web sites** on the city include **CitySearch Sydney** (www.sydney.citysearch. com.au), for events, entertainment, dining, and shopping; and **City of Sydney** (www. sydneycity.nsw.gov.au), the official information site, which includes updates on the Olympic Games.

CITY LAYOUT

Sydney is one of the largest cities in the world by area, covering more than 1,730 square kilometers (668 sq. miles) from the sea to the foothills of the Blue Mountains. The jewel in Sydney's crown is its harbor, which empties into the South Pacific Ocean though the headlands known simply as North Head and South Head. On the southern side of the harbor are the city center, a string of beaches, and the inner-city suburbs. The Sydney Harbour Bridge and a tunnel take you northward past the North Sydney business district to the affluent northern suburbs and a series of beautiful ocean beaches, including the oceanfront resort suburb of Manly.

MAIN ARTERIES & STREETS   The city's main thoroughfare, **George Street,** runs up from Circular Quay (pronounced "key"), past Town Hall and on past Central Station. A host of streets bisect the city parallel to George, including Pitt, Elizabeth, and Macquarie streets. **Macquarie Street** runs from the Sydney Opera House past the Royal Botanic Gardens, colonial architecture, and Hyde Park. **Martin Place** is a long pedestrian thoroughfare that stretches from Macquarie to George streets. It's about halfway between Circular Quay and Town Hall—in the heart of the city center. The easy-to-spot **Centerpoint Tower,** facing the pedestrian-only Pitt Street Mall, is the main city-center landmark.

NEIGHBORHOODS IN BRIEF

SOUTH OF THE HARBOR

Circular Quay   This transport hub for ferries, buses, and CityRail trains is tucked between the Harbour Bridge and the Sydney Opera House. The Quay, as it's known to the locals, is a good spot for a stroll, and its outdoor eateries and *buskers* (street musicians/performers) are very popular. The Rocks, the Royal Botanic Gardens, and the start of the city's main shopping district are all just a short walk away. To reach the area via public transportation, take a CityRail train, ferry, or city-bound bus to Circular Quay.

The Rocks   This historic area, just a short stroll west of Circular Quay, is closely packed with colonial stone buildings, intriguing back streets, boutiques, popular pubs, tourist stores, and top-notch restaurants and hotels. It's the most expensive area to stay in because of its beauty and its proximity to the Opera House. You won't find many shopping bargains here, either—The Rocks is geared mostly towards Sydney's yuppies and wealthy Asian tourists. On weekends a portion of George Street is blocked off for The Rocks Market, with its many street stalls selling tourist-orientated souvenirs and handicrafts. To reach the area via public transportation, take any bus bound for Circular Quay or The Rocks (via George Street) or a CityRail train or ferry to Circular Quay.

Sydney at a Glance

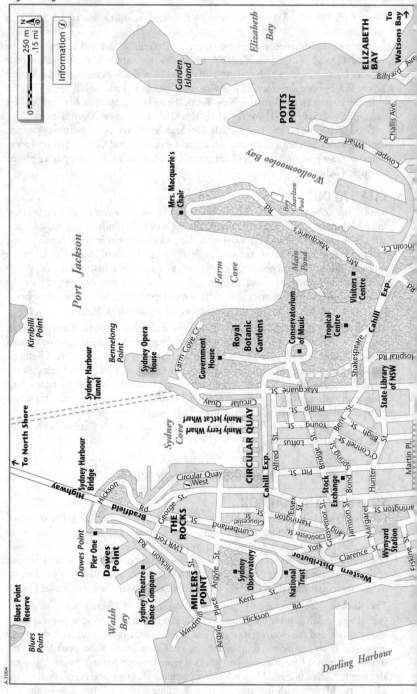

N

0 — 250 m
0 — .15 mil

ⓘ Information

Port Jackson

Elizabeth Bay

Garden Island

POTTS POINT

To Watsons Bay

Billyard Ave.

Cowper Wharf Rd.

Challis Ave.

ELIZABETH BAY

Woolloomooloo Bay

Mrs. Macquarie's Chair

Boy Charlton Pool

Mrs. Macquarie's Rd.

Lincoln Cr.

Visitors Centre

Cahill Exp.

Rd.

Hospital Rd.

Farm Cove

Main Pond

Royal Botanic Gardens

Conservatorium of Music

Tropical Centre

Shakespeare

State Library of NSW

Bennelong Point

Government House

Sydney Opera House

Farm Cove Cr.

Macquarie St.

Phillip St.

Young St.

Bligh St.

Bent St.

Martin Pl.

Kirribilli Point

Sydney Harbour Tunnel

Circular Quay

Manly Jetcat Wharf

Manly Ferry Wharf

Sydney Cove

CIRCULAR QUAY

Cahill Exp.

Alfred St.

Loftus St.

O'Connell St.

Spring St.

Bridge St.

Hunter

To North Shore

Highway

Sydney Harbour Bridge

Hickson

Bradfield

George St.

Circular Quay West

Pitt St.

Essex St.

Harrington St.

Bond St.

Stock Exchange

Margaret

Carrington St.

Blues Point Reserve

Blues Point

Walsh Bay

Dawes Point

Pier One

Dawes Point

Sydney Theatre Dance Company

MILLERS POINT

THE ROCKS

LWR Fort St.

Cumberland St.

Gloucester St.

Grosvenor St.

Jamison St.

York

Clarence St.

Wynyard Station

Erskine St.

Hickson Rd.

Windmill

Argyle Place

Argyle St.

Kent St.

Sydney Observatory

National Trust

Hickson Rd.

Western Distributor

Lang St.

Darling Harbour

A-1004

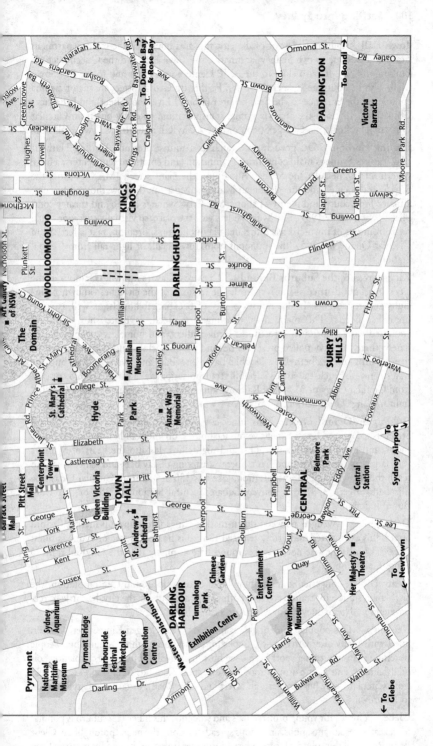

Town Hall   Right in the heart of the city, this area houses all the main department stores and is home to two Sydney landmarks, the Town Hall and the Queen Victoria Building (QVB). It's also close to the AMP Centerpoint Tower and to the Pitt Street Mall, with its boutique-style chain stores. Farther up George Street are major cinema complexes, the entrance to the Spanish area (around Liverpool Street), and the city's Chinatown. To reach the area via public transportation, take any bus from Circular Quay or The Rocks via George Street, or take a CityRail train to the Town Hall stop.

Darling Harbour   Designed from scratch as a tourist precinct, Darling Harbour now features Sydney's main convention, exhibition, and entertainment centers; a huge waterfront promenade; the Sydney Aquarium; the giant screen IMAX Theatre; the Sega World theme park; the Australian Maritime Museum; the Powerhouse Museum; a major food court; and plenty of shops. Star City, Sydney's casino and theater complex, opened in late 1997. Few Sydneysiders visit the place, so virtually everyone you'll see is from out of town. To reach the area via public transportation, take a ferry from Circular Quay (Wharf 5), the monorail from Town Hall, or light rail from Central Station.

Kings Cross & the Suburbs Beyond   "The Cross," as it's known, is famous as the city's "red light district"—but it's also home to some of the city's best-known nightclubs and restaurants. It also houses plenty of backpacker hostels, as well as some upmarket hotels. The main drag, Darlinghurst Road, is quite short—but it's crammed with strip joints, prostitutes, drug addicts, and homeless people. Fortunately, there's a heavy police presence. Beyond the strip clubs and glitter, the attractive suburbs of Elizabeth Bay, Double Bay, Rose Bay, and Watsons Bay hug the waterfront. To reach the area via public transportation, take bus 324, 325, or 327 from Circular Quay or 311 from Railway Square, Central Station; or take a CityRail train to Kings Cross station.

Paddington/Oxford Street   This inner-city suburb, centered on trendy Oxford Street, is recognized for its expensive terrace houses, off-the-wall boutiques and bookshops, and popular restaurants, pubs, and nightclubs. It's also the heart of Sydney's very large gay community and has a liberal scattering of gay bars and dance spots. To reach the area via public transportation, take bus 380 or 382 from Circular Quay (via Elizabeth Street); 378 from Railway Square, Central Station; or 380 or 382 from Bondi Junction.

Darlinghurst   Wedged between down-market Kings Cross and up-market Oxford Street, this extroverted and grimy terraced suburb is home to some of Sydney's finest cafes. It's probably wise not to walk around here at night. Take the CityRail train to Kings Cross stop.

Central   The congested and badly polluted crossroads around Central Station, the city's main station for trains traveling both within and outside the city, has little to recommend it. The Sydney Central YHA is located here.

Newtown   This popular student area is focused on car-clogged King Street, which is lined with many alternative shops, bookshops, and cheap ethnic restaurants. People watching is an interesting sport here—see how many belly-button rings, violently colored hairdos, and Celtic arm tattoos you can spot. Take bus 422, 423, 426, or 428 from Circular Quay (via Castlereagh Street and City Road), or take the CityRail train to Newtown.

Glebe   A mecca for young professionals and students, this inner-city suburb is popular for its cafes, restaurants, pubs, and shops spread out along the main thoroughfare, Glebe Point Road. All this, plus its location just 15 minutes from the city and 30 minutes from

Circular Quay make it a good place to stay for budget-conscious travelers. Take bus 431, 433, or 434 from Millers Point, The Rocks (via George Street), or 459 from behind Town Hall.

Bondi & Other Southern Beaches   Some of Sydney's most glamorous surf beaches—Bondi, Bronte, and Coogee—can be found basking along the South Pacific Ocean coastline southeast of the city center. Bondi is a disappointment to many tourists who have built up more in their imagination than the former working-class suburb has to offer. If you want to stay on the beach, though, this (or Manly) is your best bet—the long beach has good sand, and there are some good restaurants. To reach the beaches via public transportation, take bus 380 or 382 to Bondi Beach from Circular Quay or a CityRail train to Bondi Junction to connect with these buses; bus 378 to Bronte from Railway Square, Central Station (via Oxford Street); or bus 373 or 374 to Coogee from Circular Quay.

Watsons Bay   Watsons Bay is known for The Gap—a section of dramatic sea cliffs—as well as for several good restaurants, such as Doyles on the Beach, and the popular Watsons Bay Hotel beer garden. It's a good spot for an afternoon outing. Take bus 324 or 325 from Circular Quay, or a ferry from Circular Quay (Wharf 2) on Saturdays and Sundays.

NORTH OF THE HARBOR

North Sydney   Just across the Harbour Bridge, the high-rises of North Sydney attest to its prominence as a major business area. That said, there's little for tourists here except the possibility of being knocked down on some extremely busy thoroughfares. Take the train to the North Sydney stop.

North Shore   Ferries and buses provide good access to these wealthy neighborhoods across the Harbour Bridge. Balmoral Beach, Taronga Zoo, and up-market boutiques are the main attractions in Mosman, while Chatswood is a good bet for more general shopping. Take bus 250 from North Sydney to Taronga Zoo or a ferry from Circular Quay (Wharf 4). Take the train from Central or Wynyard stations to Chatswood.

Manly & the Northern Beaches   Half an hour away by ferry, or just 15 minutes by the faster JetCat, Manly is famous for its beautiful ocean beach and scores of cheap food outlets. Farther north are more magnificent beaches popular with surfers. Unfortunately, there is no CityRail train line to the northern beaches. The farthest beach from the city, Palm Beach, has both magnificent surf and lagoon beaches, nice walks, and a scenic golf course. To reach the area via public transportation, take the ferry or JetCat from Circular Quay (wharves 2 and 3) to Manly. Change at Manly interchange for various northern beach buses, numbers 148 and 154 through 159. You can also take bus L90 from Wynyard Station.

WEST OF THE CITY CENTER

Balmain   Located west of the city center, a short ferry ride from Circular Quay, Balmain was once Sydney's main shipbuilding area. In the last few decades the area has become trendy and expensive. The suburb has a village feel about it, is filled with restaurants and pubs, and hosts a popular Saturday market. Take bus 441, 442, or 432 from Town Hall or George Street, or a ferry from Circular Quay (Wharf 5).

Homebush Bay   This is the site of the Sydney 2000 Olympic Games. Here you'll find the Olympic Stadium, the Aquatic Center, and the Homebush Bay Information Center, as well as parklands and a waterbird reserve. To reach the area via public transportation, take a train to the new Olympic Park CityRail station.

2 Getting Around

BY PUBLIC TRANSPORTATION

State Transit operates the city's buses and the ferry network, CityRail runs the urban and suburban trains, and Sydney Ferries runs the public passenger ferries. Some private bus lines operate buses in the outer suburbs. For timetable information on buses, ferries, and trains, call the **Infoline** at ☎ **13 15 00** in Australia (daily 6am to 10pm). Other modes of transport in the city include a monorail that connects the city center to Darling Harbour and a light rail line that runs between Central Station and Wentworth Park in Pyrmont. Pick up a **Sydney Transport Map** (a guide to train, bus, and ferry services) at any rail, bus, or ferry information office.

BY PUBLIC BUS   Buses are frequent and fairly reliable and cover a wide area of metropolitan Sydney—though you might find the system a little difficult to navigate if you're visiting some of the outer suburbs. The minimum **fare** (which covers most short hops within the city) is A$1.20 (U.S.85¢) for a 4km (2.5-mile) section. The farther you go, the cheaper each section is. For example, the 44km (27-mile) trip to beautiful Palm Beach, way past Manly on the North Shore, costs just A$4.40 (U.S.$3.10). Sections are marked on bus stand signs (though most Sydneysiders are as confused about them as you are sure to be). Basically, short city hops such as Circular Quay to Town Hall cost A$1.20 (U.S.85¢), and slightly longer ones, say Circular Quay to Central Station, cost A$2.50 (U.S.$1.75). You can purchase single tickets onboard from the driver; exact change is not required. You can tell the driver where you want to go, and he or she will tell you the correct fare.

Most buses bound for the northern suburbs, including night buses to Manly and the bus to Taronga Zoo, leave from Wynyard Park on Carrington Street, behind the main Wynyard CityRail station on George Street. Buses going to the southern beaches, such as Bondi and Bronte, and the western and eastern suburbs leave from Circular Quay. Buses to Balmain leave from behind the Queen Victoria Building. Call ☎ **13 15 00** for timetable and fare information, or ask the staff at the bus information kiosk on the corner of Alfred and Loftus streets, just behind Circular Quay railway station (☎ **02/9219 1680**). The kiosk is open Monday through Saturday 8am to 8pm and Sunday 8am to 6pm.

Buses run from 4am to around midnight during the week, less frequently on weekends and public holidays. Some night buses to outer suburbs run after midnight and throughout the night.

BY RED SYDNEY EXPLORER BUS   These bright red buses travel a 35km (22-mile) circuit with 22 stops at top sightseeing attractions throughout the city. Passengers can get on and off anytime they like. Buses run every 20 minutes between 9am and 3pm. One-day tickets cost A$25 (U.S.$17.50) for adults, A$18 (U.S.$12.60) for children under 16, and A$60 (U.S.$42) for a family of two adults with two or more children. Tickets are sold onboard and are valid only on the day of purchase—so start early. Bus stops are marked with red-and-green Sydney Explorer signs. The same ticket allows free travel on any State Transit bus within the boundaries of the Explorer circuit until midnight on the day of purchase.

BY BLUE BONDI & BAY EXPLORER BUS   This bus operates on the same principle as the Red Sydney Explorer Bus, but visits Sydney's famous Bondi Beach and the scenic harbor suburbs of Double Bay, Rose Bay, and Watsons Bay. The bus covers a route of 45 kilometers (27 miles) in all and stops at 20 locations, including Circular Quay, the oceanfront suburbs of Bronte and Clovelly, the Royal Randwick Racecourse, and the Sydney Cricket Ground. Buses leave every 30 minutes between 9am and 6pm. The one-day fare is A$25 (U.S.$17.50) for adults, A$18 (U.S.$12.60) for a child under 16, and A$68 (U.S.$47.60) for a family.

BY FERRY & JETCAT   The best way to get a taste of a city that revolves around its harbor is to jump aboard a ferry. The main ferry terminal is at Circular Quay. Tickets can be bought at machines at each wharf (there are also change machines) or at the main Circular Quay ticket offices. For ferry information call ☎ **13 15 00** in Australia, or visit the ferry information office located opposite Wharf 4. Timetables are available for all routes.

Journeys within the inner harbor (virtually everywhere except Manly and Parramatta) cost A$3.20 (U.S.$2.25) for adults one-way and A$1.60 (U.S. $1.10) for children. The ferry to Manly takes 30 minutes and costs A$4 (U.S.$2.80) for adults and A$2.40 (U.S.$1.70) for children, one-way. It leaves from Wharf 3. The rapid JetCat service to Manly takes 15 minutes and costs A$5.20 (U.S.$3.65) for adults and children alike, one-way. After 7pm all trips to and from Manly are by JetCat at ferry prices.

You can also take a ferry to Taronga Zoo, just across the harbor. At the Taronga Zoo wharf, a bus will take you to the upper zoo entrance for A$1.20 (U.S.85¢), or you can take a cable car to the top for A$2.50 (U.S.$1.75). The lower entrance is 2 minutes up the hill. A combined ferry, bus, and zoo admission ticket, which also includes an aerial safari ride in the zoo, costs A$21 (U.S.$14.70) for adults and A$10.50 (U.S.$7.35) for children.

Other places that can be reached by ferry include Darling Harbour, the Star City Casino, Neutral Bay, Watsons Bay, Kirribilli, Cremorne, Balmain, Greenwich, Cockatoo Island, Hunters Hill, Meadowbank, and Parramatta. Ferries run from 6am to midnight, although the frequency of services varies

Sydney Ferries also operates a special **Summer Harbour Beaches** service between Manly, Watsons Bay, and Balmoral on weekends only, November through March. This loop service allows you to get off when you want and rejoin a later ferry. Tickets, valid for one day, cost A$10 (U.S.$7) for adults and A$5 (U.S.$3.50) for children and include the return fare to Circular Quay. Timetables are available from the ferry information office opposite Wharf 4.

BY HARBOUR EXPRESS   Matilda Cruises (☎ **02/9264 7377**) operates the high-speed **Rocket Ferry** that runs between Darling Harbour and Circular Quay daily from 9am to 7pm. It costs A$3.25 (U.S.$2.30) for adults and A$1.60 (U.S.$1.15) for children, one-way. One-hour cruises on the **Rocket Harbour Express** run daily from 9:30am to 4:30pm. The Rocket Harbour Express leaves Darling Harbour Aquarium Wharf on the half hour and Circular Quay Commissioner Steps (a small wharf opposite the Museum of Contemporary Art) at a quarter to the hour. The boat stops at the

Tour the Olympic Venues

Want to get a sneak peek at the Sydney 2000 Olympic Games? Tours of **Homebush Bay,** the site of the new Olympic Park, include transport to the site on a Rivercat ferry up the Parramatta River. Tours depart Circular Quay Monday through Friday at 10am, 11am, noon, 1pm, and 1:30pm, and Saturday and Sunday at 10:35am and 12:25pm. Weekday tours cost A$15 (U.S.$10.50) per person; weekend tours cost A$22 (U.S.$15.40) per person and include an extra tour of the Aquatic Center, built specifically for the Sydney 2000 Olympic Games. Buy tickets at Wharf 5 before departure. Contact **State Transit** at ☎ **02/9207 3170** for more details. The ferry trip to Homebush Bay is pleasant, and the tour is interesting if you're into the Olympics.

Sydney Transportation Systems

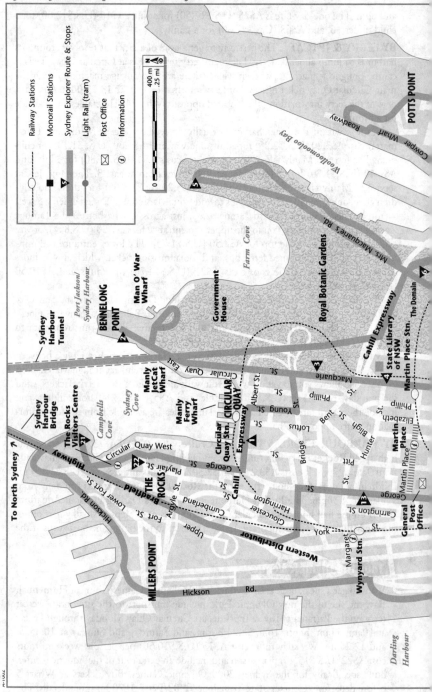

Legend:
- Railway Stations
- Monorail Stations
- Sydney Explorer Route & Stops
- Light Rail (tram)
- ⊠ Post Office
- ⓘ Information

0 400 m
.25 mi
N

To North Sydney ↑

Sydney Harbour Bridge
Bradfield Highway
Sydney Harbour Tunnel
Port Jackson/Sydney Harbour
BENNELONG POINT
Man O' War Wharf
Farm Cove
Government House
Royal Botanic Gardens
Woolloomooloo Bay
Cowper Wharf Roadway
POTTS POINT
Mrs. Macquarie's Rd.

The Rocks Visitors Centre
Campbells Cove
Sydney Cove
Manly JetCat Wharf
Manly Ferry Wharf
CIRCULAR QUAY
Circular Quay East
Circular Quay West
Circular Quay Stn.

THE ROCKS
MILLERS POINT
Hickson Rd.
Hickson Rd.
Lower Fort St.
Upper Fort St.
Fort St.
Argyle St.
Playfair St.
George St.
Cumberland St.
Gloucester St.
Harrington St.
Cahill Expressway
Cahill Expressway

Western Distributor
York St.
Carrington St.
George St.
Pitt St.
Bridge St.
Loftus St.
Young St.
Phillip St.
Albert St.
Macquarie St.
Bligh St.
Hunter St.
Bent St.
Elizabeth St.
Phillip St.

Margaret St.
Wynyard Stn.
General Post Office
Martin Place
Martin Place Stn.
State Library of NSW
The Domain

Darling Harbour

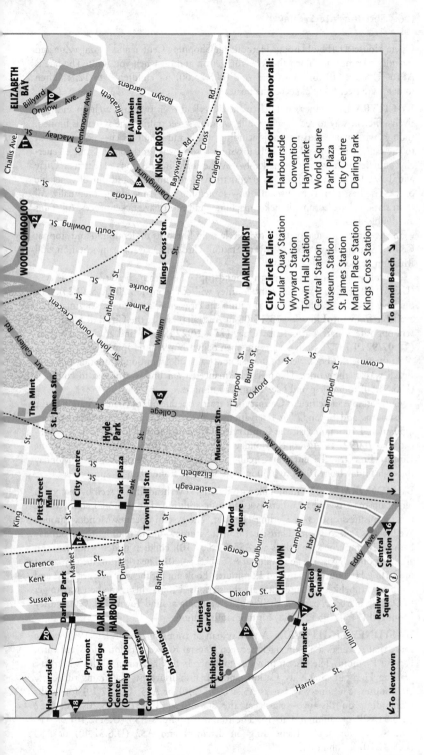

City Circle Line:
Circular Quay Station
Wynyard Station
Town Hall Station
Central Station
Museum Station
St. James Station
Martin Place Station
Kings Cross Station

TNT Harborlink Monorail:
Harbourside
Convention
Haymarket
World Square
Park Plaza
City Centre
Darling Park

To Bondi Beach ↗

ELIZABETH BAY

WOOLLOOMOOLOO

KINGS CROSS

DARLINGHURST

DARLING HARBOUR

CHINATOWN

Hyde Park

Chinese Garden

El Alamein Fountain

The Mint

Pyrmont Bridge

Convention Center (Darling Harbour)

Harbourside

Pitt Street Mall

City Centre

Park Plaza

World Square

Capitol Square

Exhibition Centre

Railway Square

Central Station

→ To Redfern
↓ To Newtown

↓ (downward arrow near Wentworth Ave.)

105

Opera House, Darling Harbour Harbourside Shopping Center, and Taronga Zoo and includes commentary along the way. You get on and off when you want. The fare is A$16 (U.S.$11.20) for adults and A$8 (U.S.$5.60) for children 5 to 12; children under 5 are free. Buy tickets on the boat.

BY CITYRAIL   Sydney's publicly owned CityRail train system is a cheap and relatively efficient way to see the city while avoiding street traffic. The system is limited, though, with many tourist areas—including Manly and Bondi Beach—not connected to the railway network. The CityRail system is somewhat antiquated, signage generally poor (especially—and remarkably—at the main intersections of Circular Quay and Town Hall), and trains have a reputation of running late and out of timetable order. The best plan is to just turn up—something will come along, eventually. All train stations have automatic ticket machines, and most have ticket offices. All trains are double-decker.

In the center of the city, the **City Circle** train line runs underground and stops at Central Station, Town Hall, Wynyard Station, Circular Quay, St. James Station, and Museum Station.

The off-peak (after 9am) return (round-trip) fare within the city center is A$2 (U.S.$1.40). Before 9am, the same journey will cost you A$3.20 (U.S.$2.25). The one-way fare is A$1.60 (U.S.$1.15) within the city center at all times. Information is available from **InfoLine** (☎ **13 15 00** in Australia) and at the **CityRail Host Centers** opposite Wharf 4 at Circular Quay (☎ **02/9224 2649**) and at Central Station (☎ **02/9219 1977**); both centers are open daily from 9am to 5pm.

At the time this book went to press, a new train link from Bondi Junction to Bondi Beach was in the works. The privately financed train line is expected to cost A$5 (U.S.$3.50) round-trip and take around 10 minutes.

Comfortable and efficient **Countrylink trains** operate out of Central Station to the far suburbs and beyond. For reservations call ☎ **13 22 32** in Australia between 6:30am and 10pm, or visit the **Countrylink Travel Center** at 11–31 York St., Wynyard (☎ **02/92244744**), open Monday through Friday from 8:30am to 5pm, or the **Countrylink Travel Center** at Circular Quay (☎ **02/9224 3400**), open Monday through Friday from 10am to 5:30pm and Saturday from 10am to 2pm.

BY MONORAIL   The monorail, with its single overhead line, is seen by many as a blight on the city and by others as a futuristic addition. The monorail connects the central business district to Darling Harbour. The system operates Monday through Wednesday 7am to 10pm, Thursday through Saturday 7am to midnight, and Sunday 8am to 10pm. One-way tickets are A$3 (U.S.$2.10); children under 5 ride free. An all-day monorail pass is a good value at A$6 (U.S.$4.20). The trip from the city center to Darling Harbour takes around 12 minutes. Look out for the gray overhead line and the plastic tubelike structures that are the stations. I think this is the best way to get to Darling Harbour, particularly if you are shopping around Town Hall. Call **Sydney Monorail** (☎ **02/9552 2288**) for more information.

BY SYDNEY LIGHT RAIL   A new system of **trams** opened in late 1997 with a route that traverses a 3.6km track between Central Railway Station and Wentworth Park in Pyrmont. The system provides good access to Chinatown, Paddy's Markets, Darling Harbour, Star City Casino, and the Fish Markets. The trams run every 10 minutes. The one-way fare is A$2 (U.S.$1.40) or A$3 (U.S.$2.10) for adults (depending on distance—check at the station) and A$1 (U.S.70¢) or A$2 (U.S.$1.40) for children 4 to 15. The round-trip fare is A$3 (U.S.$2.10) or A$4 (U.S.$2.80) for adults (depending on distance) and A$2 (U.S.$1.40) or A$3 (U.S.$2.10) for children.

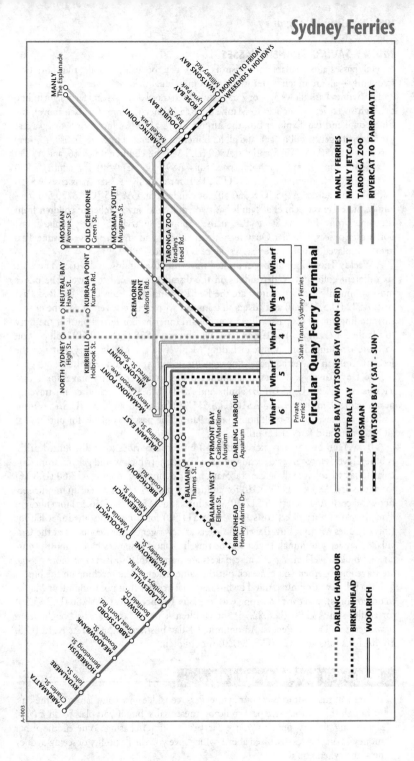

Sydney Ferries

MANLY
The Esplanade

WATSONS BAY
Military Rd.

ROSE BAY
Lyne Park

MONDAY TO FRIDAY

WEEKENDS & HOLIDAYS

DOUBLE BAY
Bay St.

DARLING POINT
McKell Park

MOSMAN
Avenue St.

OLD CREMORNE
Green St.

MOSMAN SOUTH
Musgrave St.

TARONGA ZOO
Bradleys Head Rd.

NEUTRAL BAY
Hayes St.

KURRABA POINT
Kurraba Rd.

CREMORNE POINT
Milsons Rd.

NORTH SYDNEY
High St.

KIRRIBILLI
Holbrook St.

MILSONS POINT
Alfred St. South

McMAHONS POINT
Henry Lawson Ave.

BALMAIN EAST
Darling St.

PYRMONT BAY
Casino/Maritime Museum

DARLING HARBOUR
Aquarium

BIRCHGROVE
Louisa Rd.

BALMAIN
Thames St.

GREENWICH
Mitchell St.

BALMAIN WEST
Elliott St.

WOOLWICH
Valentia St.

BIRKENHEAD
Henley Marine Dr.

DRUMMOYNE
Wolseley St.

GLADESVILLE
Punt Rd.

CHISWICK
Blackwall Point Rd.

ABBOTSFORD
Great North Rd.

MEADOWBANK
Bowden St.

HOMEBUSH
Bennelong St.

RYDALMERE
John St.

PARRAMATTA
Charles St.

Wharf 2

Wharf 3

Wharf 4

Wharf 5

Wharf 6

State Transit Sydney Ferries

Circular Quay Ferry Terminal

Private Ferries

MANLY FERRIES

MANLY JETCAT

TARONGA ZOO

RIVERCAT TO PARRAMATTA

ROSE BAY/WATSONS BAY (MON - FRI)

NEUTRAL BAY

MOSMAN

WATSONS BAY (SAT - SUN)

DARLING HARBOUR

BIRKENHEAD

WOOLRICH

A-1003

107

MONEY-SAVING TRANSIT PASSES

Several passes are available for visitors who will be using public transportation frequently—all are much better values than individual tickets.

The **SydneyPass** allows 3, 5, or 7 days' unlimited travel on buses and ferries, including the high-speed JetCat services to Manly, the Red Sydney Explorer Bus (see above), the Blue Bondi and Bay Explorer Bus, the Airport Express Bus (so, buy your SydneyPass at the airport to get its full usage), and all harbor cruises operated by State Transit. A 3-day pass costs A$70 (U.S.$49) for adults, A$60 (U.S.$42) for children under 16, and A$200 (U.S.$140) for a family; a 5-day pass runs A$95 (U.S.$66.50) for adults, A$80 (U.S.$56) for children, and A$270 (U.S.$189) for a family; a 7-day pass costs A$110 (U.S.$77) for adults, A$95 (U.S.$66.50) for children, and A$315 (U.S.$220.50) for a family. State Transit defines a "family" as two adults and any number of children from the same family. Buy the SydneyPass at the airport, Countrylink offices, Public Transport ticket offices, Circular Quay ferry ticket offices, and anywhere else a SydneyPass logo is displayed; proof of overseas residence is required.

A **Weekly Travel Pass** allows unlimited travel on buses, trains, and ferries. There are six different color passes, depending on the distance you need to travel. The passes most commonly used by visitors are the Red Pass and the Green Pass. The **Red Pass** costs A$22 (U.S.$15.40) and covers all transport within the city center and the nearby surrounding area. This pass will get you aboard inner harbor ferries but not the ferry to Manly, for example. The **Green Pass,** which costs A$28 (U.S.$19.60), will get you to more far-flung destinations, including Manly (via the Manly Ferry, but not the JetCat). You can buy either pass at newsagents or bus, train, and ferry ticket outlets.

The **Day Rover** pass gives you unlimited bus, train, and ferry travel for 1 day. Tickets cost A$20 (U.S.$14) for adults and A$10 (U.S.$7) for children for travel in peak (before 9am) hours, and A$16 (U.S.$11.20) for adults and A$8 (U.S.$5.60) for children for travel in off-peak hours (after 9am). The pass is available for purchase at all bus, train, and ferry ticket offices.

A **TravelTen** bus or ferry ticket offers 10 bus or ferry rides for a discounted price. A **blue** TravelTen covers two sections on the bus route (which would get you from Circular Quay to Town Hall or Central Station, for example) and costs A$8.60 (U.S.$6) for adults and A$4.40 (U.S.$3.10) for children; a **red** TravelTen covers up to nine sections and costs A$17.60 (U.S.$12.30) for adults and A$8.80 (U.S.$6.15) for children. The TravelTen ferry ticket costs A$17 (U.S.$11.90) for trips within the inner harbor (this excludes Manly). Buy TravelTen tickets at newsagents, bus depots, or at the Circular Quay ferry terminal. If you will be traveling short distances by bus mostly, purchase a blue TravelTen. *Note:* These tickets are transferable, so if two or more people are traveling together, you can each put the same ticket in the machine on the bus.

For a full day's unlimited travel by bus in the city center (but not to Bondi or Manly, in other words), you can't go wrong with the **Bus Tripper.** It costs A$7.80 (U.S.$5.50) for adults and A$3.90 (U.S.$2.75) for children 4 to 15, and can be bought from newsagents and at bus depots. An unlimited 1-day bus/ferry tripper costs A$12 (U.S. $8.40) for adults and A$6 (U.S. $4.20) for children.

Before You Buy the SydneyPass . . .

Before you rush out to buy your SydneyPass, consider how you plan to see the city. Although this all-inclusive pass could be a reasonable buy if you plan to do *a lot* of sightseeing, in my opinion you're far better off purchasing some of the other money-saving passes discussed above, which give you the flexibility of seeing Sydney how and when you want.

BY TAXI

Several taxi companies service the city center and suburbs. All journeys are metered and cost A$3 (U.S.$2.10) when you get in and A$1.07 (U.S.75¢) per kilometer thereafter. It costs an extra A$1 (U.S.70¢) if you call for a cab. You must also pay extra for waiting time, luggage weighing over 25kg (55 lb.), and if you cross either way on the Harbour Bridge or through the Harbour Tunnel (A$2/U.S.$1.40). An extra 10% will be added to your fare if you use a credit card to pay.

Taxis line up at ranks in the city, such as those found opposite Circular Quay and Central Station, and frequently hang around hotels. A small yellow light on top of the cab means it's vacant. Cabs can be particularly hard to get on Friday and Saturday nights and between 2pm and 3pm every day, when tired cabbies are changing shift after 12 hours on the road. Tipping is not necessary, but appreciated. Some people prefer to sit up front with the driver, but it's certainly not considered rude if you don't. It is compulsory for all passengers to wear seat belts in Australia. The **Taxi Complaints Hotline** (☎ **02/9549 3722**) deals with problem taxi drivers.

The main cab companies are **Taxis Combined Services** (☎ **02/9332 8888**); **RSL Taxis** (☎ **02/9581 1111**); **Legion Cabs** (☎ **13 14 51** in Australia); and **Premier** (☎ **13 10 17** in Australia).

BY CAR

Traffic restrictions, parking problems, and congestion can make getting around the city center by car a frustrating experience, but if you plan to visit some of the outer suburbs or take excursions elsewhere in New South Wales, then renting a car will give you more flexibility.

Car rental agencies in Sydney include **Avis,** 214 William St. (☎ 02/9357 2000); **Budget,** 93 William St. (☎ 13 28 48 or 02/9339 8888); **Dollar,** Domain Car Park, Sir John Young Car Park (☎ 02/9223 1444); **Hertz,** Corner of William and Riley streets (☎ 02/9360 6621); and **Thrifty,** 75 William St. (☎ 02/9380 5399). Avis, Budget, Hertz, and Thrifty also have desks at the airport. Rental rates average about A$30 (U.S.$21) per day for weekly rentals and A$90 (U.S.$63) for single-day rentals.

If you're going into the bush (Aussie lingo for "the country") for a few days, you can rent an economy campervan from **Campervan Rentals** (☎ **1800/246 869** in Australia or 02/9797 8027; fax 02/9716 5087) for A$35 to $55 (U.S.$24.50 to $38.50) per day, including insurance and unlimited kilometers. **Brits Campervans,** 182 O'Riordan St., Mascot 2020 (☎ **1800/331 454** in Australia or 02/9667 0402) is a very reputable company with good air-conditioned vans that cost from A$65 (U.S.$45.50) per day in June and July, rising progressively to A$115 (U.S.$80.50) in the peak period over Christmas. Both companies allow you to drop off your van at most state capitals elsewhere in Australia and in Cairns, though Brits charges an extra A$150 (U.S.$105) for the convenience.

Yo, Water Taxi!

Harbour Taxis, as they are called, operate 24-hours a day and are a quick and convenient way to get to waterfront restaurants, harbor attractions, and some suburbs. They can also be hired for private cruises of the harbor. A journey from Circular Quay to Watsons Bay, for example, costs A$40 (U.S.$28) for two. An hour's sightseeing excursion around the harbor costs A$150 (U.S.$105) for two. The two main operators are **Taxis Afloat** (☎ **02/9955 3222**) and **Water Taxis Combined** (☎ **02/9810 5010**).

Help!

If you encounter trouble on the road, the **NRMA's** (National Roads and Motorists' Association—the New South Wales auto club) emergency breakdown service can be contacted at ☎ **13 11 11** in Australia.

FAST FACTS: Sydney

American Express   The main AMEX office is at 92 Pitt St., near Martin Place (☎ **02/9239 0666**). It's open Monday through Friday 8:30am to 5:30pm and Saturday 9am to noon.

Baby-Sitters   Dial an Angel (☎ **02/9416 7511** or 02/9362 4225) offers a well-regarded baby-sitting service. Charges for one or two children are as follows: daytime, A$48 (U.S.$33.60) for the first three hours, then A$11 (U.S.$7.70) for each hour thereafter; evening, A$45 (U.S.$31.50) for the first three hours then A$10 (U.S.$7) for each hour thereafter. Extra charges apply after midnight and on Sundays.

Business Hours   General office and banking hours are 9am to 5pm Monday through Friday. Many banks are also open from approximately 9:30am to 12:30pm on Saturdays. Shopping hours are usually 8:30am to 5:30pm daily, though most stores stay open until 9pm on Thursdays. Stores outside main areas are either closed or open for limited periods on Sundays.

Car Rentals   See "Getting Around" earlier in this chapter.

Currency Exchange   Most major bank branches offer currency exchange services. Small foreign currency exchange offices are clustered at the airport and around Circular Quay and Kings Cross. **Thomas Cook** foreign exchange offices can be found at the airport; at 175 Pitt St. (☎ **02/9231 2877**); in the Kingsgate Shopping Center, Kings Cross (☎ **02/9356 221**); and on the lower ground floor of the Queen Victoria Building, Town Hall (☎ **02/9264 1133**).

Dentist   A well-respected dentist office in the city is **City Dental Practice,** Level 2, 229 Macquarie St. (near Martin Place) (☎ **02/9221 3300**). For dental problems after hours call **Dental Emergency Information** (☎ **02/9369 7050**).

Doctor   The Park Medical Centre, Shop 4, 27 Park St. (☎ **02/ 9264 4488**), in the city center near Town Hall, is open Monday through Friday 8am to 6pm; consultations cost $35 (U.S.$24.50) for 15 minutes. The **Kings Cross Travelers' Clinic,** Suite 1, 13 Springfield Ave., Kings Cross (☎ **1300/369 359** in Australia, or 02/9358 3066), located just off the Darlinghurst Road main drag opposite Hungry Jacks, is a great place for travel medicines and emergency contraception pills, among other things. Hotel visits in the Kings Cross area cost A$60 (U.S.$42) to $80 (U.S.$56). Consultations cost A$35 (U.S.$24.50). The **Travelers' Medical & Vaccination Centre**, Level 7, 428 George St. (☎ **02/ 9221 7133**), in the city center, stocks and administers all travel-related vaccinations and medications.

Drugstores   Most suburbs have pharmacies that are open late. For after-hours referral, contact the **Emergency Prescription Service** (☎ **02/9235 0333**).

Embassies/Consulates   All foreign embassies are based in Canberra; see "Fast Facts: Australia" in chapter 3 for a list. You'll find the following consulates in Sydney: **United Kingdom,** Level 16, Gateway Building, 1 Macquarie Place,

Circular Quay (☎ **02/9247 7521**); **New Zealand,** 1 Alfred St., Circular Quay (☎ **02/9247 1999**); **United States,** 19–29 Martin Place (☎ **02/9373 9200**); **Canada,** Level 5, 111 Harrington St., The Rocks (☎ **02/9364 3000**).

E-mail   Global Gossip, at 770 George St. (☎ **02/9212 1466**), near Central Station, and 111 Darlinghurst Rd., Kings Cross (☎ **02/9326 9777**), offers Internet, e-mail and computer access for A$2 (U.S.$1.40) for 10 minutes or A$10 (U.S.$7) an hour. It's open daily from 8am to midnight. Elsewhere, find the **Surfnet Café** (☎ **02/9976 0808**), next to the public library in Manly, open Monday through Saturday 9am to 9pm and Sunday 9am to 7pm; the **Internet Café**, Level 3, Hotel Sweeney, 236 Clarence St. (☎ **02/9261 5666**), open Monday through Friday 10am to 9pm and Saturday noon to 6pm; and the **Well Connected Café,** 35 Glebe Point Rd., Glebe (☎ **02/9566 2655**), open Monday through Thursday 10am to 11pm, Friday and Saturday 10am to 6pm, and Sunday noon to 10pm.

Emergencies   Dial ☎ **000** to call the police, the fire service, or an ambulance. Call the **Emergency Prescription Service** (☎ **02/9235 0333**) for emergency drug prescriptions, and the National Roads and Motorists' Association (NRMA) for car breakdowns (☎ **13 11 11**). Contact the **Poisons Information Center** at ☎ **13 11 26.**

Holidays   See "When to Go" in chapter 3. New South Wales also observes Labour Day on the first Monday in October.

Hospitals   Make your way to **Sydney Hospital,** on Macquarie Street, at the top end of Martin Place (☎ **02/9382 7111** for emergencies). **St. Vincents Hospital** (☎ **02/9339 1111**) is on Victoria and Burton streets in Darlinghurst (near Kings Cross).

Hotlines   Contact the **Rape Crisis Center** at ☎ **02/9819 6565,** and the **Crisis Center** at ☎ **02/9358 6577.**

Lost Property   There is no general lost property bureau in Sydney. Contact the nearest police station if you think you've lost something. For items lost on trains, buses, and ferries, contact the **Lost Property Office,** 490 Pitt St. (☎ **02/ 9211 4535** or 02/9211 1176), near Central Railway Station. The office is open Monday through Friday 8:30am to 4:30pm. For items left behind on planes or lost at the airport, go to the Federal Airport Corporation's administration office (☎ 02/9667 9583), on the top floor of the International Terminal. Each taxi company has its own lost property office; see "Getting Around," above for names and numbers.

Luggage Storage   You can leave your bags at the **International Terminal** at the airport. A locker costs A$4 (U.S.$2.80) per day, or you can put them in the storage room for A$6 (U.S.$4.20) per day per piece. The storage room is open from 4:30am to the last flight of the day. Call ☎ **02/9667 9848** for information. You can also leave luggage at the Cloakroom at **Central Station,** near the front of the main building off George Street in the Countrytrains section (☎ **02/ 9219 4395**). Storage at the rail station costs A$1.50 (U.S.$1.05) per article until 10:30pm the following evening and A$4.50 (U.S.$3.15) per article every day thereafter. **Travelers Contact Point** 7th floor, 428 George St. (☎ **02/ 9221 8744**), stores luggage for A$10 (U.S.$7) per piece per month.

Newspapers   The *Sydney Morning Herald* is considered one of the world's best newspapers and is available throughout metropolitan Sydney. The equally prestigious *Australian* is available nationwide. The metropolitan *Telegraph Mirror* is a more casual read. The *International Herald Tribune, USA Today,* the *British Guardian Weekly,* and other U.K. newspapers can be found at Circular Quay newspaper stands and most newsagencies.

Photographic Needs   **Fletchers Fotographics,** 317 Pitt St. (☎ **02/9267 6146**), near Town Hall, is a quality photographic store selling cameras, films, and accessories. **Paxton's,** 285 George St., (☎ **02/9299 2999**) is also good. The **Camera Service Centre,** 1st Floor, 203 Castlereagh St. (☎ **02/9264 7091**), is a tiny place up a flight of stairs not far from the Town Hall station. It repairs all kinds of cameras on the spot, or within a couple of days if parts are needed.

Police   In an emergency dial ☎ **000.**

Post Office   The General Post Office (GPO) is at 130 Pitt St. (☎ **13 13 17** in Australia). It's open Monday through Friday 8:30am to 5:30pm and Saturday 8am to noon. Letters can be sent c/o Poste Restante, GPO, Sydney, 2000, Australia (☎ **02/9244 3733**), and collected Monday through Friday 8:15am to 5:30pm at 310 George St., on the 3rd floor of the Hunter Connection shopping center. For directions to the nearest post office, call ☎ **1800/043 300** in Australia.

Rest Rooms   These can be found in the Queen Victoria Building (2nd floor), most department stores, at Central Station and Circular Quay, and in the Harbourside marketplace in Darling Harbour.

Safety   Be wary in Kings Cross and Redfern at all hours and around the cinema street near Town Hall station in the evenings—it's a hangout for local gangs. If traveling by train at night, travel in the cars next to the guard's van, marked with a blue light on the outside.

Taxes   As yet, there is no GST in Australia. A 10 percent state government Bed Tax was introduced in September 1998 for all hotels except backpacker accommodations.

Taxis   See "Getting Around" earlier in this chapter.

Telephones   Sydney's public phone boxes take coins (A40¢ for local calls); many also take credit cards and phonecards A$10 (U.S.$7) available from newsagencies. **Global Gossip,** at 770 George St., near Central Station (☎ **02/ 9212 1466**), and 111 Darlinghurst Rd., Kings Cross (☎ **02/9326 9777**), offers cheap international telephone calls, such as A59¢ (U.S. 41¢) a minute to the USA and Canada, A75¢ to the UK, and A65¢ to New Zealand. An A30¢ connection fee applies.

For phone directory/assistance, dial ☎ 013 for local numbers, ☎ 0175 for interstate numbers, or ☎ 0103 for international numbers.

Transit Information   Call the **InfoLine** at ☎ **13 15 00** (daily 6am to 10pm).

Phoning Around

To call Australia from the United States, dial the international access code 011, then Australia's country code (61), then the area code; but be sure to drop the first zero of the area code, then the number you want to call. For example, to ring the Sydney Opera House (☎ 02/9250 7111) from the United States, dial 011 61 2 9250 7111.

To call the United States from Australia, dial the international access code 0011 (note it has two zeros, not one like the international access code from the United States), then the country code for the United States (1), then the area code, then the number you want to call.

Get to the Point

One handy organization travelers will want to know about is **Travelers Contact Point,** at Level 7, 428 George St. (☎ **02/9221 8744,** fax 02/9221 3746). It offers an in-house employment agency for working holiday jobs, an Australia-wide mail-forwarding service costing A$40 (U.S.$28), Internet access, and short-term mobile phones.

Useful Telephone Numbers   For news, dial ☎ **1199;** for the time, ☎ **1194;** for Sydney entertainment, ☎ **11 688;** for Travelers Aid Society, ☎ **02/9211 2469.**

Travel Agents   STA Travel (☎ **13 17 76** in Australia) has several branches throughout Sydney and offers the best prices, including student discounts, for travel within and outside Australia.

Weather   For the local forecast call ☎ **1196.**

3 Accommodations You Can Afford

Sydney's success in winning the 2000 Olympic Games, and the increased media exposure the city has received as a result, have led to more visitors to the city and more hotels to cater to them. Although it's unlikely you'll find the city's hotels completely booked if you simply turn up looking for a bed for the night, it's probably wise to reserve rooms in advance. Most hotel rooms are also much cheaper when bought as part of a **package** before you leave home (see the section on package deals in chapter 3, "Planning an Affordable Trip to Australia").

In addition, you should always ask for "specials" when booking a hotel, especially if you are traveling in winter (June, July, and August) when hotels are less likely to be full. Some hotels also offer packages based on the length of time you stay, but you'll never get them if you don't ask.

Serviced apartments are well worth considering because they mean big savings on meals, and you can eat exactly what you want. Many also have free laundry facilities.

DECIDING WHERE TO STAY   The choice location for lodging in Sydney is in The Rocks and around Circular Quay, just a short stroll from the Sydney Opera House, the Harbour Bridge, the Royal Botanic Gardens, the ferry terminals, and the train station, and close to main shopping areas. Don't expect many bargains here, however.

Hotels around Darling Harbour offer good access to the local facilities, including museums, the Sydney Aquarium, the Star City casino, the IMAX Theatre, and Sega World. Most Darling Harbour hotels are a 15-minute walk, or a short monorail or light rail trip, from Town Hall and the central shopping district in and around Centerpoint Tower and Pitt Street Mall.

Last-Minute Room Deals

If you turn up in town without a reservation, you should definitely make use of the **New South Wales Travel Centre desk** (☎ **02/9667 6050**) on the Arrivals Level of the airport's International Terminal. It represents every Sydney hotel and offers exceptional value discounts on rooms that haven't been filled that day—you can save up to 50% on a room this way. The desk is open from 6am to the last flight of the day and also offers discounts on tours (to the Blue Mountains, for example), and cheap tickets for flights within Australia.

Back to School

Another option for frugal travelers is to stay at a university. The **University of Sydney** (☎ **02/9351 2222**), close to the inner-city suburbs of Glebe and Newtown, offers good-sized rooms with TV in a lovely old building at **St. John's College,** Missenden Road, Camperdown, NSW 2000 (☎ **02/9394 5200;** fax 02/9550 6303). Rooms are generally available year-round, for A$67 (U.S.$47) for a single and A$93 (U.S.$65.10) for a double. Weekly rates are also available. The college on the main campus is surrounded by gardens, and has a very peaceful atmosphere. Right next door is the equally nice **Sancta Sophia College** (☎ **02/ 9577 2333,** or 0419/479 832 mobile phone; fax 02/9577 2388), where singles are A$50 (U.S.$35) and doubles A$80 (U.S.$56), including breakfast. Rooms here are only available during college breaks, generally from December to the last week in February, over Easter week, from the end of June to the end of July, and from the last week in September to the first weekend in October.

More hotels are grouped around Kings Cross, Sydney's red-light district. While some of the hotels found here are among the city' best, in this area you'll also find a range of cheaper lodgings, including several backpacker hostels. Kings Cross can be unnerving at any time, but especially so on Friday and Saturday nights when the area's strip joints and nightclubs are doing their best business. Staying here does have it's advantages, though: you get a real inner-city feel and it's close to some excellent restaurants and cafes centered around the Kings Cross/Darlinghurst and Oxford Street areas. Glebe, with its many ethnic restaurants, is another inner-city suburb popular with tourists. It's well served by local bus, as well as Airport Express Bus route 352.

If you want to stay near the beach, check out the options in Manly and Bondi, though you should consider their distance from the city and the lack of CityRail trains to these areas. If you stay out after midnight, you will have to rely on getting back from the city by night bus or taxi. The latter option is expensive—a taxi to Manly from the city will cost around A$30 (U.S.$21), and to Bondi around A$20 (U.S.$14).

IN THE ROCKS

The Lord Nelson Brewery Hotel. At the corner of Kent and Argyle sts., The Rocks, Sydney, NSW 2000. ☎ **02/9251 4044.** Fax 02/9251 1532. 10 units, 8 with bathroom (shower only). TV TEL. A$150 (U.S.$105) double without bathroom; A$180 (U.S.$126) double with bathroom. Additional person A$15 (U.S.$10.50) extra. Rates include continental breakfast. AE, BC, DC, MC, V. No parking available. CityRail or ferry: Circular Quay.

From its creaky floorboards and bedroom walls made from convict-hewn sandstone blocks, to the narrow corridors and the wood fire and homemade beer down in the bar, Sydney's oldest pub positively wallows in atmosphere. It's an attractive, three-floor sandstone building with a busy pub on the ground floor, a good brasserie on the second, and hotel accommodations on the third. The "small" rooms are true to their name, with room for not much more than a bed and a small TV. For the extra A$30 (U.S.$21) you get far more space to stretch out. All rooms were totally upgraded and refurbished in late 1998. Bathrooms are small and basic with a shower only.

✪ **The Russell.** 143A George St., The Rocks, Sydney, NSW 2000. ☎ **02/9241 3543.** Fax 02/9252 1652. 29 units, 18 with bathroom. TV TEL. A$110–$150 (U.S.$77–$105) double without bathroom; A$180–$220 (U.S.$126–$154) double with bathroom; A$230 (U.S.$161) suite. Additional person A$15 (U.S.$10.50) extra. Rates include continental breakfast. AE, BC, DC, MC, V. No parking available. CityRail or ferry: Circular Quay.

Finding a Room During the Sydney 2000 Olympic Games

At the time this book went to press, the **Sydney Organising Committee for the Olympic Games (SOCOG)** did not have a central reservation line to book hotels during the Games, which will be held September 15 to October 1, 2000. I've discovered that by early 1999 most hotels throughout Sydney were already booked out by corporate sponsors of the Games or were awaiting the allocation of rooms to visiting dignitaries and officials by SOCOG.

A major real estate agency, **Ray White Real Estate,** is the official agency for finding rooms for visitors during the Games via its **Residential Accommodation Program** (☎ **02/9262 3700**. Fax 02/9262 3737. E-mail: accomm@ raywhite.net). The program offers two categories of accommodation: Homestay, in which guests stay in vacant, furnished homes; and Homehost, in which guests stay with an Australian family (breakfast is provided). Accommodations are expected to range from A$90 (U.S.$63) to A$500+ (U.S.$350+) per bedroom per night. Prices vary according to the quality of the accommodation and the distance from events. The minimum booking period is one week for Homehost accommodations, three weeks for Homestay accommodations. Contact the agency's Web site at www.raywhite.com.au for complete details.

International visitors should also contact their country's National Olympic Committee for the name of the officially appointed tour operator responsible for ticket sales and package tours to the Games. For the names and numbers of Olympic Committees, go to www.olympic.org/family. U.S. residents should contact Cartan Tours, Inc., 1334 Parkview Ave., Suite 210, Manhattan Beach, CA 90266 (☎ 800/818-1998 or 310/546-9662; fax 310/546-8433; e-mail: sales@cartan. com; www.cartan.com. British residents should contact Sportsworld Travel, New Abbey Court, Stert Street, Abingdon OX143JZ (☎ 01235 554844; fax 01235 554841).

The Russell is the coziest place to stay in The Rocks, and perhaps in the whole of Sydney. The 100-year-old bed-and-breakfast inn shows its age wonderfully in the creak of floorboards and the ramshackle feel of its brightly painted corridors. Every room is totally different in style, size, and shape; all come with a queen-size bed, half the rooms have cable TV (others can have a TV moved in, if requested). All have immense character, including a series of rooms added above the Fortune of War Hotel next door in 1990. There are no harbor views, but from some rooms you can see the tops of the ferry terminals at Circular Quay. Guests have the use of a comfortable sitting room, a living room scattered with magazines and books, and a rooftop garden. Boulders restaurant serves good food on the ground floor.

WORTH A SPLURGE

The Stafford. 75 Harrington St., The Rocks, Sydney, NSW 2000. ☎ **02/9251 6711.** Fax 02/9251 3458. 61 apts. A/C TV TEL. A$210–$245 (U.S. $147–$171.50) studio double; A$250 (U.S.$175) 1-bedroom apt; A$280 (U.S.$196) executive 1-bedroom apt; A$265 (U.S.$185.50) terrace house; A$335 (U.S.$234.50) 1-bedroom penthouse. Additional person A$15 (U.S.$10.50) extra. Children under 16 free in parents' room. Ask about lower weekly and weekend rates. AE, BC, DC, MC, V. Parking A$15 (U.S.$10.50). CityRail or ferry: Circular Quay.

This place is definitely a splurge, but you might be able to save money on meals if you stay in one of these serviced apartments, located right in the heart of The Rocks, very

Central Sydney Accommodations

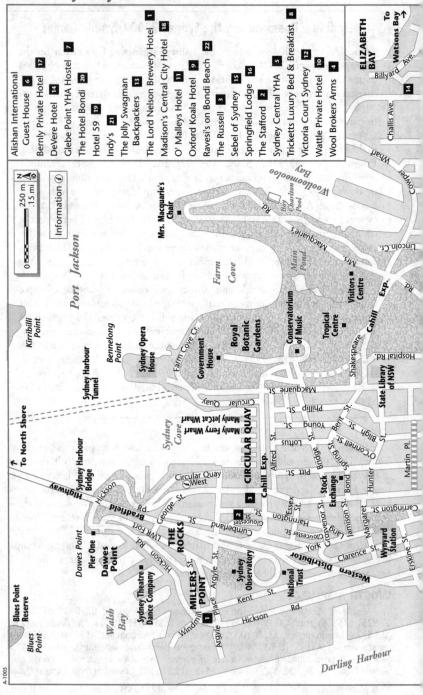

Alishan International Guest House **6**
Bernly Private Hotel **17**
DeVere Hotel **14**
Glebe Point YHA Hostel **7**
The Hotel Bondi **20**
Hotel 59 **19**
Indy's **21**
The Jolly Swagman Backpackers **13**
The Lord Nelson Brewery Hotel **1**
Madison's Central City Hotel **18**
O'Malleys Hotel **11**
Oxford Koala Hotel **9**
Ravesi's on Bondi Beach **22**
The Russell **3**
Sebel of Sydney **15**
Springfield Lodge **16**
The Stafford **2**
Sydney Central YHA **5**
Tricketts Luxury Bed & Breakfast **8**
Victoria Court Sydney **12**
Wattle Private Hotel **10**
Wool Brokers Arms **4**

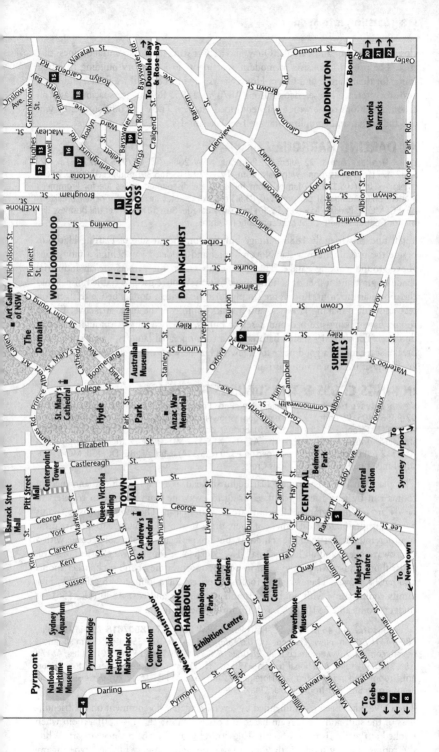

close to the harbor and Circular Quay, and a short stroll from the central business district. The property consists of modern apartments in a six-story building (the best units, for their harbor and Opera House views, are on the top three floors) and seven two-story terrace houses dating from 1870 to 1895. Rooms are spacious, and all accommodations come with a fully equipped kitchen. There's an outdoor pool, gym, spa and sauna, and complimentary self-service laundry.

AT DARLING HARBOUR

Wool Brokers Arms. 22 Allen St., Pyrmont, NSW 2009. ☎ **02/9552 4773.** Fax 02/9552 4771. 26 units, none with bathroom. TV. A$79 (U.S.$55.30) double; A$90 (U.S.$63) triple; A$105 (U.S.$73.50) family room for 4. These discounted prices are for Frommer's readers only. Additional person A$20 (U.S.$14) extra. Rates include continental breakfast. AE, BC, MC, V. Parking A$9 (U.S.$6.30) in nearby garage. Bus: 501 from central business district or Central Station. Light rail: Convention Centre.

You'll find this friendly 1886 heritage building on the far side of Darling Harbour, beside the prominent four-star Novotel hotel and hidden away behind a monstrous above-ground parking garage. The floorboards creak, the carpets are an industrial shade of gray, and it's set on a noisy road, so unless you're used to traffic noise, avoid the rooms at the front. Rooms are simply furnished with a double bed, a refrigerator, tea- and coffee-making facilities, and a sink. Room 3 is the most attractive. Family rooms have a king-size bed and a set of bunks, and two singles through an open doorway. There are 19 shared bathrooms, a coin-operated laundry, and a self-service breakfast room. It's a good place for a few nights. Stay anywhere else around here and you'll pay at least three times as much.

IN KINGS CROSS & THE SUBURBS BEYOND

Bernly Private Hotel. 15 Springfield Ave., Potts Point, NSW 2011. ☎ **02/9358 3122.** Fax 02/9356 4405. 95 units, 12 with bathroom (shower only). TV. A$50 (U.S.$35) budget double without bathroom; A$55 (U.S.$38.50) budget double with bathroom; A$85 (U.S.$59.50) standard double with bathroom; A$105 (U.S.$73.50) triple with bathroom. A$18 (U.S.$12.60) dorm bed. Additional person A$20 (U.S.$14) extra. AE, BC, DC, JCB, MC, V. On-street meter parking. CityRail: Kings Cross.

This place, tucked away just off Darlinghurst Road, is a real find. It's an ants' nest of rooms run by very friendly staff, catering to everyone from short-term travelers to newly arrived immigrants. All rooms are new and clean. The more expensive rooms here are superior to most others of their price in the area. Budget rooms are a bit scruffier and smaller than the standards, but are perfectly livable. Some come with a microwave oven, and all have a small TV. Backpacker rooms have two sets of bunk beds, though just two people seem to occupy most. Some of the backpacker rooms also have a shower. There's a good rooftop sundeck and a lounge with cable TV. Five family rooms come with double beds and two singles and cost A$80 (U.S.$56) for budget rooms and A$105 (U.S.$73.50) for a superior room.

DeVere Hotel. 44–46 Macleay St., Potts Point, NSW 2011. ☎ **1800/818 790** in Australia, 0800/441 779 in New Zealand, or 02/9358 1211. Fax 02/9358 4685. E-mail: info@devere.com.au. www.devere.com.au. 98 units. A/C TV TEL. A$99 (U.S.$69.30) double; A$179 (U.S.$125.30) suite. Additional person A$30 (U.S.$21) extra. Children under 12 free in parents' room. Parking at Landmark Hotel across the road A$11 (U.S.$7.70) per exit. CityRail: Kings Cross. Bus: 311 from Circular Quay.

The DeVere has been recommended by several readers who comment on the friendliness of the staff and the bargain-basement price of A$65 (U.S.$45.50) a room when booked at the Tourism New South Wales Travel Centre at the Sydney airport. While the rooms are very modern, they are a little too standard-gray business-type for my

In case you want to see the world.

At American Express, we're here to make your journey a smooth one. So we have over 1,700 travel service locations in over 130 countries ready to help. What else would you expect from the world's largest travel agency?

do more AMERICAN EXPRESS

Travel

Call 1 800 AXP-3429 or visit
www.americanexpress.com/travel

In case you want to be welcomed there.

We're here to see that you're always welcomed at establishments everywhere. That's why millions of people carry the American Express® Card – for peace of mind, confidence, and security, around the world or just around the corner.

do more AMERICAN EXPRESS

Cards

In case you're running low.

We're here to help with more than 190,000 Express Cash locations around the world. In order to enroll, just call American Express at 1 800 CASH-NOW before you start your vacation.

do more

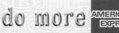

Express Cash

And in case you'd rather be safe than sorry.

We're here with American Express® Travelers Cheques. They're the safe way to carry money on your vacation, because if they're ever lost or stolen you can get a refund, practically anywhere or anytime. To find the nearest place to buy Travelers Cheques, call 1 800 495-1153. Another way we help you do more.

do more | AMERICAN EXPRESS

Travelers Cheques

liking. However, they are certainly a bargain compared to similar, but far more expensive, versions found elsewhere in Sydney. The suites have views of Elizabeth Bay, a spa bath, and a king- rather than a queen-size bed. Some have a pretty useless kitchenette with no cooking facilities. Some standard rooms have an extra single bed. Breakfast is available from A$8 (U.S.$5.60).

✪ **Hotel 59.** 59 Bayswater Rd., Kings Cross, NSW 2011. ☎ **02/9360 5900.** Fax 02/9360 1828. E-mail: hotel59@enternet.com.au. 8 units (some with shower only). A/C TV TEL. A$100–$125 (U.S.$70–$87.50) double. Rates include full breakfast. Additional person A$15 (U.S.$10.50) extra; children 2–12 A$10 (U.S.$7). BC, MC, V. Limited parking A$5 (U.S.$3.50). CityRail: Kings Cross.

This popular and friendly B&B is well worth considering if you want to be near the Kings Cross action but just far enough away to get a decent night's sleep. Deluxe rooms have either a queen- or king-size bed and a combined shower and tub, while the noticeably smaller standard rooms come with a double bed and a shower. As with any hotel in the Kings Cross area, if you don't mind your children getting an eyeful of prostitutes and sex bars on the way to and from the CityRail station, then this could be a good place to bring the family. Two large superior rooms come with a bedroom with two single beds and two more that can be locked together to form a king, as well as a separate living room. One superior room comes with a small kitchen with a microwave and hot plates. All rooms are very clean and comfortable. The small guest lounge has a TV and a "revolving" library (you take one and donate another). A full breakfast is served in the cafe below, where good main meals such as Thai curry, rainbow trout, and steak and chips go for A$6.90 to $8.50 (U.S.$4.80 to $5.95). Guests also receive 10% off meals at the adjoining Thai and Japanese steakhouse restaurants. Flights of stairs and no elevator (lift) make this a bad choice for travelers with disabilities.

Madison's Central City Hotel. 6 Ward Ave., Elizabeth Bay, NSW 2011. ☎ **1800/060 118** in Australia, or 02/9357 1155. Fax 02/9357 1193. 39 units. A/C TV TEL. A$95 (U.S.$66.50) double; A$115 (U.S.$80.50) suite. Additional person A$10 (U.S.$7) extra. AE, BC, DC, MC, V. Free covered parking. CityRail: Kings Cross.

Madison's is about a five-minute walk from Kings Cross CityRail station. It's modern, clean, and well priced, but in my opinion a bit soulless. The standard rooms resemble typical motel rooms and are significantly smaller than the suites. Each room has a combined tub and shower; the tub is quite deep, though, and there's no step to help you climb in. Rooms are interconnecting and thus suitable for families, though full room rates would apply for each room. All rooms come with either a queen-size bed or a set of twins. A coin-operated laundry is on the premises.

O' Malleys Hotel. 228 William St., corner of Brougham St. (P.O. Box 468), Kings Cross, NSW 2011. ☎ **02/9357 2211.** Fax 02/9357 2656. E-mail: bookings@omalleyshotel.com.au. 14 units. A/C TV TEL. A$72–$121 (U.S.$50.40–$84.70) double. Rates include continental breakfast. AE, BC, MC, V. On-street parking, or parking garage available for A$8 (U.S.$5.60) overnight. CityRail: Kings Cross.

If you don't mind a short stagger up the stairs from the popular "backpackers" Irish Pub below, then you'll enjoy this place. It's just a two-minute stroll from the main Kings Cross drag and has standard-size three-star rooms. The rooms on the first floor are cheaper because they are right above the bar—and the cheery hum of drinkers below could keep you awake. (The bar is open 11am to 3am Monday through Saturday, and noon to midnight on Sunday.) Rooms on the second floor are much quieter and a good value. All the country-style rooms have natural wood trim and a private bathroom (although bathrooms for rooms on the first floor are across the corridor).

Springfield Lodge. 9 Springfield Ave., Kings Cross, NSW 2011. ☎ **02/9358 3222.** Fax 02/9357 4742. 77 units, 46 with bathroom (shower only). TV. A$45 (U.S.$31.50) double without bathroom; A$65 (U.S.$45.50) double with bathroom. Additional person A$20 (U.S.$14) extra; children under 12 A$10 (U.S.$7). BC, JCB, MC, V. 24-hour secured parking 2 minutes away for around A$10 (U.S.$7) a day. CityRail: Kings Cross.

The lobby of this surprising lodge just off the main Kings Cross strip doesn't inspire much confidence, but the refurbished rooms are clean and certainly pleasant enough for a few days' stay. Standard rooms are small and dark with a small TV, a double bed, sink, and refrigerator. En suite rooms, also dark but somehow comforting, are a little larger, have both a double and a single bed and a small bathroom with shower. The wooden floorboards in all rooms are a nice touch. You need to pay a A$10 (U.S.$7) deposit for your room key.

Victoria Court Sydney. 122 Victoria St., Potts Point, NSW 2011. ☎ **1800/630 505** in Australia, or 02/9357 3200. Fax 02/9357 7606. E-mail: info@victoriacourt.com.au. www.victoriacourt.com.au. 22 units (some with shower only). TV TEL. A$99–$115 double (U.S.$69.30–$80.50) (rates vary seasonally); A$165 (U.S.$115.50) deluxe double with sun-deck or honeymoon suite with balcony. Additional person A$20 (U.S.$14) extra. Rates include buffet breakfast. AE, BC, DC, MC, V. Free secured parking. CityRail: Kings Cross.

This cute little place is made up of two 1881 terrace houses joined together. It is situated near a string of backpacker hostels and popular cafes on a leafy street that runs parallel to sleazy Darlinghurst Road. The glass-roofed breakfast room on the ground floor is a work of art, decked out with hanging ferns, giant bamboo, wrought-iron tables and chairs, and a fountain. Just off this is a peaceful guest lounge stacked with books and newspapers. Rooms, which come with either king- or queen-size beds as standard, are very plush but lack a tub in the bathroom. There's a coin-op laundry just down the road.

SUPER-CHEAP SLEEPS
The Jolly Swagman Backpackers. 27 Orwell St., Kings Cross, NSW 2011. ☎ **1800/805 870** in Australia, or 02/9358 6400. Fax 02/9331 0125. www.backpackers-world.com.au/jolly. 53 units. A$20 (U.S.$14) per person single or double. A$14 (U.S.$9.80) dorm bed. Ask about 3-day, 5-day, and weekly deals. MC, V. On-street meter parking. CityRail: Kings Cross.

This is one of the best of the backpacker hostels that dot the area between Darlinghurst Road and Victoria Street in Kings Cross. The good thing about this place is that it has two sister properties nearby, so you are almost certain to get a room. With only two sets of bunk beds in each, the 18 dorm rooms here don't get too crowded, and couples traveling together will often find they have the room to themselves. There are also plenty of twin and double rooms to go around, as well as two female-only dorms. The atmosphere is young and typical backpacker, with cheap meals (all under A$5/U.S.$3.50) served in the ground floor cafe. There's a guest kitchen, two TV rooms, a laundry, an ironing room, bag storage, free Foxtel movies, 24-hour Internet access available, and a 24-hour travel agency. Each room is spotlessly clean and has a security locker.

WORTH A SPLURGE
Sebel of Sydney. 23 Elizabeth Bay Rd., Elizabeth Bay, NSW 2011. ☎ **1800/222 266** in Australia, or 02/9358 3244. Fax 02/9357 1926. 189 units. A/C MINIBAR TV TEL. A$225–$235 (U.S.$157.50–$164.50) standard double; A$285–$295 (U.S.$199.50–$206.50) superior double; from A$319 (U.S.$223.30) suite. Additional person A$25 (U.S.$17.50) extra. Children under 12 free in parents' room. Rates include breakfast. Ask about cheaper weekend and off-season rates. AE, BC, DC, JCB, MC, V. Free parking. CityRail: Kings Cross.

Just a block away from the bright lights and sleazy sights of Kings Cross' Darlinghurst Road, the Sebel is an upmarket boutique hotel known for its theatrical theme. It's long

> **⊕ Family-Friendly Accommodations**
>
> **Hotel 59** (see page 119). This popular and friendly B&B has superior family-style rooms, which come with two single beds and two more that can be locked together to form a king. There's a separate living room, too, so there's plenty of space for everyone to spread out.
>
> **Manly Lodge** (see page 124). This ramshackle old place near the beach has great family rooms as well as table tennis and an Olympic-size trampoline. In-line skates and body boards can be rented on the beachfront.

been the hotel of choice for such international celebs as Elton John, Richard Harris, Cliff Richard, Phil Collins, Rex Harrison, Lauren Bacall, and Rod Stewart, and remains a place in which to see and be seen. To make guests feel at home, they're called by name, and the restaurant and bar close only when the last person leaves. Rooms are good value for the price and come with either queen- or king-size beds and traditional furniture. Half the rooms overlook the picturesque marina at Rushcutters Bay—and cost just A$10 (U.S.$7) more (money well spent). Suites have VCRs and CD players, as well as microwaves. The Encore Restaurant offers semifine dining, serving up everything from steaks to stir-fries. The cocktail bar is a favorite with local actors and performers. Amenities include a rooftop outdoor pool, gym, sauna, concierge, 24-hour room service, free daily newspaper, nightly turndown, shoe shine, laundry, valet, baby-sitting, business center, and gift shop.

IN DARLINGHURST

Oxford Koala Hotel. Corner of Oxford & Pelican sts., Darlinghurst (P.O. Box 535, Darlinghurst, NSW 2010). ☎ **1800/222 144** in Australia (outside Sydney), or 02/9269 0645. Fax 02/9283 2741. 330 units (including 78 apts). A/C TV TEL. A$120–$140 (U.S. $84–$98) double; A$160 (U.S.$112) 1-bedroom apt. Additional person A$25 (U.S.$17.50) extra. Children under 12 free in parents' room. AE, BC, DC, JCB, MC, V. Free parking. Bus: 380 or any bus traveling via Taylor Square.

You won't find many three-star hotels that offer as much value for your dollar as the Oxford Koala. A very popular tourist hotel, it is well placed just off trendy Oxford Street, a 5- to 10-minute bus trip from the city center and Circular Quay. There are 13 floors of rooms in this tower block; rooms on the top floor have reasonable views over the city. Superior rooms (A$140/U.S.$98) are very comfortable, with more space and better furniture than standard rooms. All come with a shower/tub combination or just a shower. The apartments are good-sized, come with a full kitchen, and are serviced daily. On the premises are a swimming pool, a restaurant, and a cocktail bar.

Wattle Private Hotel. 108 Oxford St. (corner of Palmer St.), Darlinghurst, NSW 2010. ☎ **02/9332 4118.** Fax 02/9331 2074. 12 units (some with shower only). MINIBAR TV TEL. A$99 (U.S.$69.30) double. Additional person A$11 (U.S.$7.70) extra. Rates include continental breakfast. BC, MC, V. Parking not available. Bus: Any to Taylor Square from Circular Quay.

This attractive Edwardian-style house, built between 1900 and 1910, offers homey accommodations in the increasingly fashionable inner-city suburb of Darlinghurst, known for its great cafes, nightlife, and restaurants. Rooms are on four stories, but there's no elevator (lift)—so if you don't fancy too many stairs, try to get a room on a lower floor. Rooms are smallish, but are opened up by large windows. Twin rooms have a better bathroom, with tub. The decor is a jumble of Chinese vases, ceiling fans, and contemporary bedspreads. Laundry facilities are on the premises.

IN GLEBE

SUPER-CHEAP SLEEPS

Glebe Point YHA Hostel. 262–264 Glebe Point Rd., Glebe, NSW 2037. ☎ **02/ 9692 8418.** Fax 02/9660 0431. 49 units, none with bathroom. A$25 (U.S.$17.50) per person double. A$19–$21 (U.S.$13.30–$14.70) dorm bed. Non-YHA members A$3 (U.S.$2.10) extra. Children half price. BC, JCB, MC, V. Free on-street parking. Bus: 431, 433 from George Street, or Airport Express bus 352 from Sydney Airport.

This quiet and very clean youth hostel is perfect for those not looking for the party atmosphere of many busier hostels, but who are still into a bit of socializing and a cheap room for the night. It's popular with young professionals, older adventurous travelers, and backpackers alike. On the ground floor are a pool room, dining room, self-catering kitchen, TV room, and a large laundry. Dorms usually sleep four in two sets of bunks, while double rooms come with a single and a double in a bunk-style setup, a washbasin, and an armchair. There are lockers in all dorms and a safety deposit at reception.

Alishan International Guest House. 100 Glebe Point Rd., Glebe, NSW 2037. ☎ **02/ 9566 4048.** Fax 02/9525 4686. E-mail: kevin@alishan.com.au. www.alishan.com.au. 19 units, some with bathroom (shower only). TV. A$85 (U.S.$59.50) double; A$95 (U.S.$66.50) family room. A$20 (U.S.$14) dorm bed. Additional person A$15 (U.S.$10.50) extra. AE, BC, MC, V. Secure parking available for 6 cars, otherwise free on-street parking. Bus: 431, 433 from George Street, or Airport Express bus 352 from Sydney Airport.

The Alishan is another quiet place with a real Aussie feel. It's at the city end of Glebe Point Road, just 10 minutes by bus from the shops around Town Hall. Standard dorm rooms are spotless, light, and bright, and come with two sets of bunks. Doubles have a double bed, a sofa, an armchair, and an en suite shower. Grab room 9 if you fancy sleeping on one of two single mattresses on the tatami mat floor, Japanese-style. You'll find a BBQ area, a TV room, a laundry, and Internet access on the premises.

WORTH A SPLURGE

✪ Tricketts Luxury Bed & Breakfast. 270 Glebe Point Rd., Glebe, NSW 2037. ☎ **02/ 9552 1141.** Fax 02/9692 9462. 7 units (all with shower only). A$140 (U.S.$98) double; A$175 (U.S.$122.50) honeymoon suite. Rates include continental breakfast. No credit cards. Free parking. Bus: 431 from George Street, or Airport Express bus 352 from Sydney Airport.

As soon as I walked into this atmospheric Victorian mansion, I wanted to ditch my modern Sydney apartment and move in. Your first impression as you enter is the amazing jumble of plants and ornaments, as well as the high ceilings, Oriental rugs, leaded windows, and shelves and nooks crammed with antique goodies. Guests play billiards over a decanter of port, or relax among magazines and wicker furniture on the balcony overlooking the fairly busy Glebe Point Road. The bedrooms are quiet and homey, with my favorites being number 2, with its wooden floorboards and king-size bed; and number 7, with its queen-size bed, extra single bed, and very large bathroom. All rooms have showers; none have a TV. There's a nice courtyard out back with a BBQ.

NEAR CENTRAL STATION

✪ Sydney Central YHA. 11 Rawson Place, Sydney, NSW 2000. ☎ **02/9281 9111.** Fax 02/9281 9199. 151 units, 32 with bathroom. A$58 (U.S.$40.60) double without bathroom; A$66 (U.S.$46.20) double with bathroom. A$20–$23 (U.S.$14–16.10) dorm bed. Non-YHA members A$3 (U.S.$2.10) extra. BC, JCB, MC, V. On-street parking. CityRail: Central.

This youth hostel is considered one of the biggest and busiest in the world. With a 98% year-round occupancy rate, you'll have to book early to be assured of a place. Opened in 1987 in an historic nine-story building, it offers far more than standard basic accommodations. In the basement is the Scu Bar, a very popular drinking hole with pool tables and occasional entertainment. There's also a bistro selling cheap meals, a convenience store, two fully equipped kitchens, and an entertainment room with more pool tables and e-mail facilities, TV rooms on every floor, and an audio-visual room showing movies. If you want more, try the heated swimming pool and the sauna! Rooms are clean and basic, with the single and double rooms just a touch classier. The YHA is completely accessible to travelers with disabilities.

IN BONDI

Bondi Beach is a good place to stay if you want to be close to the surf and sand, though if you're getting around by public transport you'll need to catch a bus to Bondi Junction, then a train to the city center (you can stay on the bus all the way, but it takes forever).

As well as the properties recommended below, there's a good backpacker hostel called **Indy's** (☎ **02/9365 4900**), at 35a Hall St., which offers four- to eight-person dorm rooms for A$16 (U.S.$11.20) in winter and A$20 (U.S.$14) in summer, and double rooms in a separate building opposite North Bondi Surf Club for the same price per person.

The Hotel Bondi. 178 Campbell Parade, Bondi Beach, NSW 2026. ☎ **02/9130 3271.** Fax 02/9130 7974. 50 units (all with shower only). TV. A$95 (U.S.$66.50) double; A$110–$140 (U.S.$77–$98) suite. AE, BC, MC, V. Free secure parking. CityRail: Bondi Junction, then bus 380. Bus: 380 from Circular Quay or George Street, or Airport Express bus 351 from Sydney Airport.

This white-stucco Bondi landmark is adequate for a few days stay if you don't mind the creaks of the vintage wooden elevator and the brusque service at the front desk. The corridors are generally in need of a lick of paint, and the rooms are slightly disheveled, but overall it still retains a fairly healthy slap of 1920s grandeur. Double rooms are basic and small, with a springy double bed, a shower, and a small refrigerator and TV. You pay $A10 (U.S.$7) extra to have a view of the ocean. The six suites are nicer and have their own balconies looking out to sea. Three of these are suitable as family rooms. Downstairs are seven bars, which frequently seem to attract aggressive drunks. Given the choice (Bondi hotels are often booked out well in advance), I'd stay at the far friendlier Ravesi's, recommended below.

Ravesi's on Bondi Beach. Corner of Hall St. and Campbell Parade, Bondi Beach (P.O. Box 198, Bondi Junction 2022). ☎ **02/9365 4422.** Fax 02/9365 1481. 16 units. A/C TV TEL. A$99 (U.S.$69.30) standard double; A$140–$145 (U.S.$98–$101.50) double with side view; A$170 (U.S.$119) 1-bedroom suite; A$195 (U.S.$136.50) split-level 1-bedroom; A$170–$195 (U.S.$119–$136.50) ocean view. Additional person A$20 (U.S.$14) extra. 2 children under 12 free in parents' room. AE, DC, MC, V. Free parking. CityRail: Bondi Junction, then bus 380. Bus: 380 from Circular Quay.

Situated right on Australia's most famous golden sands, this art deco boutique property offers Mediterranean-influenced rooms with a beachy decor. Standard doubles are spacious, quite basic, and don't have air-conditioning—though you'd hardly need it with the ocean breeze. The one-bedroom suite is good for families, having two sofa beds in the living room. The split-level room has a bedroom upstairs and a single sofa bed in the living area. Rooms 5 and 6 and the split-level suite have the best views of the ocean. All rooms have Juliet balconies, and the split-level suite has its own terrace. It's best to request a room on the top floor because the popular Ravesi's Restaurant can cook up quite a bit of noise on busy nights.

IN MANLY

If you decide to stay at my favorite beachside suburb, then you'll need to be aware that ferries from the city stop running at midnight. If you get stranded, you'll be facing either an expensive taxi fare (around A$30/U.S.$21), or you'll need to make your way to the bus stand behind Wynyard CityRail station to catch a night bus. Consider buying a Ferry Ten or JetCat Ten ticket, which will save you quite a bit of money in commuting expenses if you're staying in Manly for a few days.

As well as the recommendations below, Manly has several backpacker places worth checking out. The best of the bunch are **Manly Backpackers Beachside,** 28 Ragland St., (☎ **02/9977 3411**), which offers dorm beds for A$19 (U.S.$13.30), singles for A$50 (U.S.$35), and a double with a bathroom for A$55 (U.S.$38.50); and the ✪ **Wharf Backpackers,** 48 East Esplanade, opposite the ferry terminal (☎ **02/ 9977 2800**), which has dorm beds for A$17 and $18 (U.S.$11.90 and $12.60) and doubles for A$40 (U.S.$28).

Manly Lodge. 22 Victoria Parade, Manly, NSW 2095. ☎ **02/9977 8655.** Fax 02/ 9976 2090. 24 units (some with shower only). A/C TV. A$89–$140 (U.S.$62.30–$98) double; A$110–$140 (U.S.$77–$98) family room; A$125–$160 (U.S.$87.50–$112) honeymoon suite with spa; A$145–$240 (U.S.$101.50–$168) family suite with spa (sleeps 4–8). Rates depend on season. Peak season Christmas, Easter, and school holidays. Additional person A$28 (U.S.$19.60) extra; children under 10 A$15 (U.S.$10.50). Rates include continental breakfast. Ask about weekly rates; management will also negotiate off-season prices. AE, BC, MC, V. Free parking. Ferry or JetCat: Manly.

At first sight this ramshackle building halfway between the main beach and the harbor doesn't look like much—especially the cramped youth-hostel foyer bristling with tourist brochures. But don't let the taint of tattiness put you off. Some of the rooms here are really lovely, and the whole place has a nice atmosphere and plenty of character. Double rooms are not exceptional, and come with a double bed, stone or carpeted floors, a TV and VCR, and a small kitchen area; some have spas. Family rooms have a set of bunk beds and a double in one room, and a shower. Family suites are very classy, come with a small kitchen area, one double and three singles in the bedroom, and two sofa beds in the living area. The lodge also has a communal spa, sauna, gym, laundry, table tennis, and even an Olympic-size trampoline.

Manly Paradise Motel and Beach Plaza Apartments. 54 North Steyne, Manly, NSW 2095. ☎ **1800/815 789** in Australia, or 02/9977 5799. Fax 02/9977 6848. 59 units (some with shower only). A/C TV TEL. A$90–$125 (U.S.$63–$87.50) double motel unit; A$225 (U.S.$157.50) 2-bedroom apt. Additional person A$20 (U.S.$14) extra. Ask about lower long-stay rates. AE, BC, DC, MC, V. Free parking, with undercover security. Ferry or JetCat: Manly.

I walked into this place and immediately felt at home. The motel and the apartment complex are separate from each other, but share the same reception area. Though there is one motel room that goes for A$90 (U.S.$63), it's a bit small, but the rest of the irregularly shaped rooms are big yet cozy, and come with a shower (no tub) and a springy double bed. Though there is no restaurant, you can get breakfast in bed. My only concern is that the traffic outside can make it a little noisy during the day. Some rooms have sea glimpses. A swimming pool (with views) on the roof is shared with the apartment complex.

The apartments are magnificent—very roomy, with thick carpets. They're stocked with everything you need, including a private laundry, a full kitchen with dishwasher, and two bathrooms (one with a tub). The sea views from the main front balcony are heart stopping.

Periwinkle-Manly Cove Guesthouse. 18–19 East Esplanade, Manly, NSW 2095. ☎ **02/ 9977 4668.** Fax 02/9977 6308. 18 units, 11 with bathroom (most with shower only). TV. A$110 (U.S.$77) double without bathroom; A$130 (U.S.$91) double with bathroom. Units with harbor views A$10 (U.S.$7) extra. Additional person A$20 (U.S.$14) extra. Rates include continental breakfast. BC, MC, V. Free parking. Ferry or JetCat: Manly.

The Periwinkle remains a favorite with return visitors to Sydney. Nicely positioned just across the road from one of Manly's two harbor beaches, it's just a short walk from the ferry, the shops on the Corso, and the main ocean beach. Rooms are small and come with a double bed, a small TV, and a refrigerator. Some have a shower and toilet attached, but otherwise you'll have to make do with one of four separate bathrooms (one has a tub). A full kitchen next to a pleasant enough communal lounge means you could save money by not eating out. Rooms 5 and 10 are the nicest; both come with a closed-in balcony overlooking the harbor, but no bathroom. There's a courtyard out back and in the front, with BBQ facilities. For atmosphere, I prefer the Manly Lodge, above.

WORTH A SPLURGE

Manly Pacific Parkroyal. 55 North Steyne, Manly, NSW 2095. ☎ **02/9977 7666.** Fax 02/9977 7822. Reservations can be made through Southern Pacific Hotels at 800/835-7742 in the U.S. and Canada. 169 units. A/C MINIBAR TV TEL. A$260–$300 (U.S.$182–$210) double (depending on views); A$470 (U.S.$329) suite. Ask about special deals. Additional person A$25 (U.S.$17.50) extra. AE, BC, DC, MC, JCB, V. Ferry or JetCat: Manly.

If you could bottle the views from this top-class hotel, you'd make a fortune. Standing on your private balcony in the evening with the sea breeze in your nostrils and the chirping of hundreds of lorikeets in the trees is nothing short of heaven. The Manly Pacific is the only hotel of its class in this wonderful beachside suburb. Views over the ocean are really worth paying extra for (check in advance for special deals), but in any case each standard room is light and modern with two double beds, a balcony, limited cable TV, and everything necessary from robes to ironing board. The hotel is less than a 10-minute walk (or a A$4/U.S.$2.80 taxi fare) from the ferry.

Gilbert's Restaurant has fine dining and views of the Pacific. Nells Brasserie & Cocktail Bar serves a buffet breakfast and dinner daily, with a menu ranging from complete meals to snacks. The Charlton Bar and Grill has live bands every evening from Wednesday to Sunday and attracts a young crowd. Services and facilities include 24-hour room service, a concierge, laundry, a rooftop spa, a pool, a gym, and a sauna.

IN MOSMAN

✪ **Buena Vista Hotel.** 76 Middle Head Rd., Mosman, NSW 2095. ☎ **02/9969 7022.** Fax 02/9968 2879. 13 units, none with bathroom. TV. A$75 (U.S.$52.50) double, A$90 (U.S.$63) over the Christmas/New Year holiday; A$90 (U.S.$63) family room, A$110 (U.S.$77) over Christmas/New Year holiday. Prices include continental breakfast. AE, BC, DC, MC, V. Bus: Taronga Zoo from Wynyard. Ferry: Taronga Zoo, then 5-minute bus ride.

If you want to see how wealthy Sydneysiders live, then come and stay in this exclusive suburb just a 10-minute walk from Taronga Zoo, and a 5-minute bus trip and 10-minute ferry journey from Circular Quay. The rooms above this popular local pub just down the road from some of Sydney's most exclusive boutiques are clean and comfortable, and a bargain by Sydney standards. Each comes with a springy queen-size bed or two twins, a small TV, and a sink; a few have balconies. All except room 13 have good city views. The best among them is room 1, which is larger and brighter than the rest and comes with a large balcony with good views. Family rooms come with a double bed, a fold-out sofa bed, and a trundle bed—all in one room. All rooms share nice bathrooms. The fabulous Balmoral Beach is a 10-minute walk away.

A COUNTRY RETREAT

Wisemans Ferry Country Retreat. Old Northern Rd., Wisemans Ferry, NSW 2775. ☎ **02/ 4566 4422.** Fax 02/4566 4613. 54 units. A/C TV TEL. A$120 (U.S.$84) double; A$160 (U.S.$112) suite. BC, MC, V. Located 1½ hours from Sydney on the Pacific Hwy.; follow signs to Wisemans Ferry.

If you want to taste a bit of rural Australia not far from Sydney, but want the comforts of a resort, spend a night or two here. The retreat is best reached by car. (To attempt to make it here otherwise would mean a CityRail train to Pennant Hills station, then a taxi fare of around A$40/U.S.$28.) The nine-hole golf course is popular with Sydneysiders who come up for the weekend (a round of golf will cost you A$12/U.S.$8.40; club rental is an extra A$12/U.S.$8.40). The retreat also has a nice outdoor swimming pool, two tennis courts, volleyball nets, and a croquet lawn. Rooms are compact but comfortable, with a shower, a queen-size bed, and a sofa bed. Suites are similar, but come with a separate bedroom. An interesting outing nearby is to the convict-hewn Old Great North Road, which takes around 2 hours to walk (no cars are allowed on the road). To reach the road you need to cross the Hawkesbury River on the Wisemans Ferry, a couple of minutes walk from the retreat. The ferry works 24-hours a day on demand. The Riverbend Restaurant serves good modern Australian food, with lunch coming in at around A$15 (U.S.$10.50) per person, and a three-course dinner costing A$37.50 (U.S.$26.25).

4 Great Deals on Dining

Sydney is a gourmet paradise, with an abundance of fresh seafood, a vast range of vegetables and fruit always in season, prime meats at inexpensive prices, and top-quality chefs making an international name for themselves. You'll find that Asian and Mediterranean cuisine have had a major influence on Australian cooking, with spices and herbs finding their way into most dishes. Immigration has brought with it almost every type of cuisine you could imagine, from African to Tibetan, from Russian to Vietnamese, with whole areas of the city dedicated to one type of food, while other areas are a true melting pot of styles.

Food is generally far cheaper in Sydney, and consistently of better quality, than in many other major cities of the world. Though you can certainly fill up for A$10 (U.S.$7) or less, or drop a cool hundred splurging at one of the city's top-class restaurants, a two-course meal in a standard restaurant will cost around A$18 to $20 (U.S.$12.60 to $14) a person. Add a bottle of very reasonable Australian wine, at around A$12 (U.S.$8.40) a bottle, and you can eat and drink to your heart's content for around A$45 (U.S.$31.50) a couple.

Cheap eats in Sydney are congregated in inner-city areas, such as along Kings Street in Newtown, Crown Street in Darlinghurst, Glebe Point Road in Glebe, and scattered among the more upscale dining spots in Kings Cross and on Oxford Street. There are some good food courts around Chinatown, including the **Sussex Street Food Court,** on Sussex Street, which offers Chinese, Malay, Thai, Japanese, and Vietnamese meals for A$4 to $7 (U.S.$2.80 to $4.90).

I would avoid, however, the take-away booths found along the ferry wharves at Circular Quay, after revelations showed that some of them harbored nasty bugs. The

What to Know about BYO

Most moderate and inexpensive restaurants in Sydney are **BYO,** as in "bring your own" bottle, though some may also have extensive wine and beer lists of their own. More and more moderately priced restaurants are introducing corkage fees, which means you pay anywhere from A$1 to $4 (U.S.70¢ to $2.80) per person for the privilege of having the waiter open your bottle of wine. Very expensive restaurants discourage BYO.

Before You Light Up . . .

Smoking is allowed in the vast majority of Sydney's restaurants, but if you do light up you'll find you won't be the most popular person in the place. Some restaurants have a nonsmoking section.

---

fish-and-chip shop opposite the bottle shop is an exception—it also has some of the best French fries (chips) in Sydney.

NEAR CIRCULAR QUAY

City Extra. Shop E4, Circular Quay. ☎ **02/9241 1422**. Main courses A$10.30–$17.65 (U.S.$7.20–$12.35). 10% surcharge midnight–6am, Sundays and public holidays. Daily 24-hours. AE, BC, DC, MC, V. CityRail, bus, or ferry: Circular Quay. ITALIAN/AUSTRALIAN.

Because this place stays open 24 hours, it's convenient if you get the munchies at a ridiculous hour. It's also conveniently located right next to the Manly ferry terminal. The plastic chairs and tables placed outside make it a pleasant spot to while away an inexpensive meal. A range of pastas are offered as well as salads, pies, steaks, ribs, fish, and Asian-influenced dishes. There's also a fat selection of deserts. That said, I agree with several friends of mine who believe the food's much nicer and a better value next door at Rossini's.

Portobello Caffè. No.1 Eastern Esplanade, Circular Quay East. ☎ **02/9247 8548**. Main courses A$8 (U.S.$5.60). 10% surcharge Sundays and public holidays. AE, BC, DC, MC, JCB, V. Credit card minimum purchase A$30 (U.S.$21). Daily 8am–11:50pm. CityRail, bus, or ferry: Circular Quay. PIZZA/SANDWICH.

Sharing the same address as the Sydney Cove Oyster Bar (and the same priceless views), the Portobello Caffè offers first-class gourmet sandwiches on Italian wood-fired bread, small but delicious gourmet pizzas, breakfast croissants, snacks, cakes, and hot and cold drinks. Walk off with sensational ice cream in a cone for around A$3 (U.S.$2.10).

✪ **Rossini.** Shop W5, Circular Quay. ☎ **02/9247 8026**. Main courses A$7–$14 (U.S.$4.90–$9.80). Cash only. Daily 7am–10:30pm. CityRail, bus, or ferry: Circular Quay. ITALIAN.

This cafeteria-style Italian restaurant opposite ferry Wharf 5 at Circular Quay is wonderfully positioned for people watching. The outside tables make it a perfect spot for breakfast or a quick bite before a show at the Opera House. Breakfast croissants, Italian donuts, muffins, and gorgeous Danish pastries cost just A$2 (U.S.$1.40) and bacon and eggs just A$8 (U.S.$5.60). Dinner main courses include veal parmigiana, cannelloni, ravioli, chicken crêpes, and octopus salad, all of which are large and tasty. Coffee fanatics I know rate the Rossini brew as only average.

Sketches Bar and Bistro. In the Hotel Inter-Continental. 117 Macquarie St. (enter from Bridge St.). ☎ **02/9230 0200**. Reservations recommended. Pasta A$10.90–$12.90 (U.S.$8.35–$9.05) Help-yourself salads A$4.10 (U.S.$2.90). Pastas and salads an extra A$2 (U.S.$1.40) each on weekends. AE, BC, DC, MC, V. Mon–Fri 5:30–9:30pm, Sat 5:30–10pm. CityRail, bus, or ferry: Circular Quay. PASTA.

Sketches is a favorite with people on their way to the Opera House and those who really know a good cheap meal when they taste one. After getting the barman's attention, point at one of three different-sized plates stuck to the bar above your head—a small size is adequate if you're an average eater, a medium is good for filling up after a hard day of sightseeing (and no lunch), while I've yet to meet a man who can handle the large serving with its accompanying bread, pine nuts, and Parmesan cheese. Then, with ticket in hand, head toward the chefs in white hats and place your order. There

Central Sydney Dining

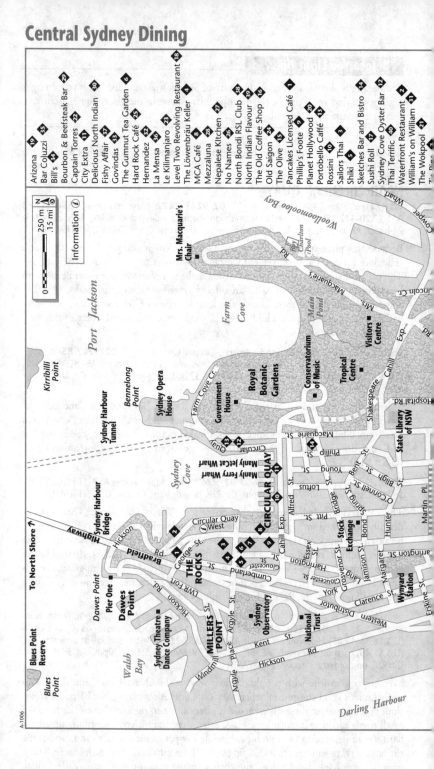

Arizona 19
Bar Coluzzi 35
Bill's 34
Bourbon & Beefsteak Bar 22
Captain Torres 22
City Extra 14
Delicious North Indian 20
Fishy Affair 37
Govindas 33
The Gumnut Tea Garden 6
Hard Rock Café 25
Hernandez 36
La Mensa 32
Le Kilimanjaro 23
Level Two Revolving Restaurant 18
The Löwenbräu Keller 4
MCA Café 8
Mezzaluna 27
Nepalese Kitchen 28
No Names 24
North Bondi RSL Club 38
North Indian Flavour 39
The Old Coffee Shop 16
Old Saigon 7
The Olive 15
Pancakes Licensed Café 1
Phillip's Foote 9
Planet Hollywood 20
Portobello Caffé 13
Rossini 10
Sailors Thai 3
Shiki 5
Sketches Bar and Bistro 26
Sushi Roll 17
Sydney Cove Oyster Bar 12
Thai Terrific 2
Waterfront Restaurant 31
William's on William 30
The Wokpool 11
Zia Pina ...

A-1006

128

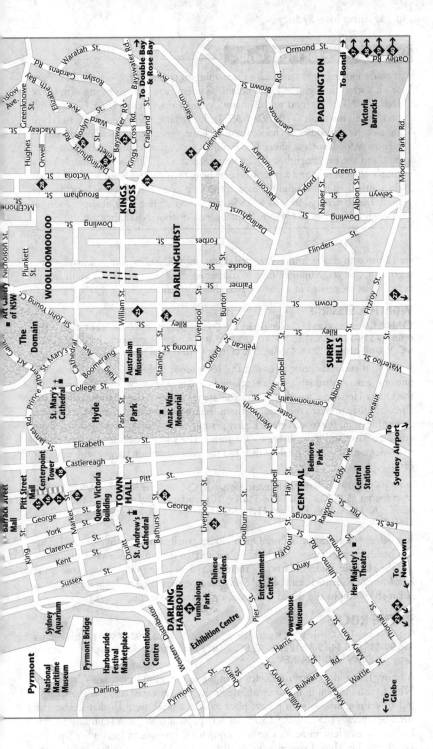

A Great Place for Picnic Grub

If you're looking for a sandwich or something to take with you on a harbor cruise or on a stroll through the Royal Botanic Gardens, you can't go wrong with **Quay Deli,** E5 Alfred St. (next to the pharmacy under the Circular Quay CityRail station, facing the road; ☎ **02/9241 3571**). Everything is fresh and tasty, and there are all sorts of goodies to choose from, including gourmet sandwiches and simple take-away foods such as olives, Greek dishes, pasta, fruit salads, green salads, meat pies, and the best English-style custard tarts around. Plenty of folks simply buy a couple of fresh rolls and a piece of cheese here, then pick up a bottle of wine from the bottle shop just around the corner, and then take off somewhere for a cheerful meal. Lunch items go for A$1.80 to $4.50 (U.S.$1.25 to $3.15). It's open Monday through Friday 5am to 6:45pm, Saturday 9am to 4pm. No credit cards.

are 12 pastas to choose from and several sauces, including carbonara, marinara, pesto, vegetarian, and some unusual ones to dishearten pasta purists, such as south Indian curry. Meals are cooked in a few minutes while you wait.

WORTH A SPLURGE

✪ **MCA Café.** Museum of Contemporary Art, Circular Quay West. ☎ **02/9241 4253.** Main courses A$19–$20 (U.S.$13.30–$14). 10% surcharge weekends and public holidays. AE, BC, MC, V. Daily noon–2:30pm. CityRail, bus, or ferry: Circular Quay. SEAFOOD.

If you find yourself sitting at one of the 16 outdoor tables here, count yourself as one of the most fortunate people lunching in Sydney. The views over the ferries and the Opera House are wonderful, and you are far enough away from the crowds at Circular Quay to watch the action without feeling a spectacle yourself. Whether you sit outside or in, the food is great. Eighty percent of the dishes are seafood, but there are some pasta and meat dishes on the menu. The signature dishes are the trevally with a lemon, olive, and parsley salad, and the smoked salmon lasagna with eggplant caviar.

Sydney Cove Oyster Bar. No.1 Eastern Esplanade, Circular Quay East. ☎ **02/9247 2937.** Main courses A$20–$23.50 (U.S.$14–$16.45). 10% surcharge weekends and public holidays. AE, BC, DC, MC, V. Mon–Sat 11am–11pm; Sun 11am–8pm. Train, bus, or ferry: Circular Quay. SEAFOOD.

Just before you reach the Sydney Opera House, you'll notice a couple of small shed-like buildings with tables and chairs set out to take in stunning views of the harbor and the Harbour Bridge. The first of these is a Sydney institution, serving some of the best Mornay, Kilpatrick, and natural Sydney rock oysters in town. Light meals such as Asian-style octopus and seared tuna steak are also on the menu.

IN THE ROCKS

The Gumnut Tea Garden. 28 Harrington St., The Rocks. ☎ **02/9247 9591.** Main courses A$6.90–$13 (U.S.$4.85–$9.10). AE, BC, DC, V. Daily 8am–5pm. CityRail, bus, or ferry: Circular Quay. MODERN MEDITERRANEAN.

A hearty lunch in a courtyard shaded from the sun by giant umbrellas—ah, heaven. With a great location in the heart of The Rocks, this restaurant also has an extensive indoor seating area, so it's a perfect place to take a break from all that sightseeing. Breakfast specials (A$7.50/U.S.$5.25) are very popular with guests from surrounding hotels, while at lunchtime it's always bustling with tourists and local office workers. Lunchtime blackboard specials cost A$10 (U.S.$7). More regular fare includes the

The Best Places for a Picnic

A good thing about Sydney is that there are plenty of places to take a ready-packed lunch or a cheap take-away meal. Some of my favorite spots for a picnic are around **Circular Quay,** where you can either sit on the grass outside the Museum of Contemporary Art (the huge sandstone building to the left of the ferry wharves as you face them) or on the benches provided around the water-front itself (where you might be approached by the occasional panhandler). From Circular Quay, you could also walk toward the Sydney Opera House and make your way into the **Royal Botanic Gardens** or hop aboard a public **ferry** to, say, Darling Harbour, and eat lunch on the water. Pick up some of the best French fries in Sydney from the excellent fish-and-chips booth opposite the bottle shop in Circular Quay, or a bite to eat from the **Quay Deli** (*see* p. 130).

Another of my favorite lunch spots is **Hyde Park,** reached via Town Hall, Museum, or St. James station. The grass and benches are popular for people-watching, and there are plenty of shade trees to keep you cool on a hot summer day. Pick up some sushi at **Sushi Roll** (see p. 135), or a gourmet Italian-style sandwich from **The Olive** (see p. 134).

You can't go wrong having lunch overlooking the waves at Bondi or Manly, either. At Bondi try the **North Indian Flavour** (see p. 141) for a cheap take-away curry on the grass, and in Manly pick up a packet of fish-and-chips from **Manly Ocean Foods** (see p. 141).

disappointing Ploughman's Lunch (why spoil a traditional English meal of bread, cheese, and pickles by limiting the bread and adding unappealing vegetables and salad?), the better chicken and leek pies, and pasta and noodle dishes. Filling Turkish bread sandwiches cost between A$6.90 and $8.20 (U.S.$4.85 and $5.75).

The Löwenbräu Keller. 18 Argyle St., The Rocks. ☎ **02/9247 7785**. Reservations recommended. Main courses A$15–$21.50 (U.S. $10.50–$15.05). AE, BC, DC, JCB, MC, V. Daily 9:30am–2am (kitchen closes 11pm). CityRail, bus, or ferry: Circular Quay. BAVARIAN.

Renowned for celebrating Oktoberfest every day for the past 20 years, this is the place to come to watch Aussies let their hair down. You can come for lunch and munch a club sandwich or focaccia in the glassed-off atrium while watching the daytime action of The Rocks. For a livelier scene, head here on a Friday or Saturday night, when mass beer-sculling (chugging) and yodeling are accompanied by a brass band, and costumed waitresses ferry foaming beer steins about the atmospheric, cellarlike bowels. Hearty southern German and Austrian fare and no less than 17 varieties of German beers in bottle or on draught (tap) are served. There's a good wine list, and, surprisingly, vegetarians also are well-catered to.

Pancakes Licensed Café. 10 Hickson Rd. (enter from Hickson Rd. or George St.), The Rocks. ☎ **02/9247 6371**. Reservations not accepted. Main courses A$12.95–$21.95 (U.S.$9.10–$15.40); breakfast (served 24-hours) A$8.95–$11.95 (U.S.$6.25–$8.35); children's menu A$4.95–$5.55 (U.S.$3.45–$3.90). AE, BC, DC, JCB, MC, V. Daily 24-hours. CityRail, bus, or ferry: Circular Quay. COFFEE SHOP/PANCAKES.

Buttermilk and chocolate pancakes and French crêpes filled with seafood, chicken, and mushrooms, vegetables in a basil-cream sauce, or smoked ham and cheese are the most popular dishes served up in this old warehouse done up in art deco style. The beef ribs, pastas, and pizzas are also best-sellers.

ⓘ Family-Friendly Restaurants

Rossini. This indoor/outdoor dining spot right next door to the ferry terminals on Circular Quay offers authentic Italian food with small pizzas and half-portion pastas perfect for children.

The Gumnet Tea Garden. Take a break from sightseeing around The Rocks at this delightful little cafe/restaurant. Cheap lunches appealing to both adults and children are served in a leafy courtyard.

Level Two Revolving Restaurant. This rotating eagle's-nest restaurant is located atop the impossible-to-miss Centerpoint Tower. Kids 3 to 12 can munch on discounted lunch and early dinner portions as they stare wide-eyed at the views across the city.

Phillip's Foote. 101 George St., The Rocks. ☎ **02/9241 1485.** Main courses A$17.50 (U.S.$12.25). AE, BC, MC, JCB, V. Mon–Sat noon–midnight, Sun noon–10pm. CityRail, bus, or ferry: Circular Quay. BARBECUE.

Venture back into the courtyard behind this historic pub and you'll find a popular courtyard strung with tables and benches and large barbecues. Choose your own steak, lemon sole, trout, chicken, or pork and throw it on the "barbie." It's fun, it's filling, and you might even meet some new friends while your meal's sizzling.

Sailors Thai. 106 George St., The Rocks. ☎ **02/9251 2466.** Reservations required well in advance in restaurant; not accepted in canteen. Main courses A$14–$26 (U.S.$9.80–$18.20) in restaurant, A$11–$16 (U.S.$7.70–$11.20) in canteen. AE, BC, DC, MC, V. Restaurant Mon–Fri noon–2pm, Mon–Sat 6–11pm; canteen daily noon–8pm. CityRail, bus, ferry: Circular Quay. THAI.

With a reputation as hot as the chilies in its jungle curry, Sailors Thai canteen attracts lunchtime crowds who come to eat noodles, clams, curries, and Thai salads at its single stainless steel table lined with more than 40 chairs. Four other tables overlook the cruise ship terminal and the quay. Downstairs, the à la carte restaurant serves simple and cutting-edge food, like a pineapple curry of mussels and a steamed duck soup with pickles.

Shiki. Clock Tower Square (corner of Argyle and Harrington sts.), The Rocks. ☎ **02/ 9252 2431.** Reservations recommended well in advance. Meals around A$30 (U.S.$21). AE, BC, DC, MC, JCB, V. Mon–Fri noon–2:30pm; Mon–Sun 6–10pm. TRADITIONAL JAPANESE.

Shiki is making a name for itself for top-flight traditional Japanese. Though you can eat at Western-style tables or the sushi bar, there are also five *tatami* rooms available, where you sit on Japanese mats around a raised table. Either way you can enjoy some good views over The Rocks (it's especially magical at night when the ferry lights strung across the area's trees are lit up). The menu includes plenty of sushi, sashimi, and sukiyaki dishes, but "pot-cooking" at the table is very popular. Of these, the Tobanyaki, where customers simmer a combination of beef and seafood on their own burner, steals the show. If you want your main meal during the day, consider the lunch menu. The sushi plate, with seven pieces of sushi, six pieces of tuna roll, a salad, and miso soup, costs A$20 (U.S.$14). Main courses at lunch go for A$13.50 to $20 (U.S.$9.45 to $14).

Zia Pina. 93 George St., The Rocks. ☎ **02/9247 2255.** Reservations recommended well in advance. Main courses A$7.80–$19 (U.S.$5.50–$13.30). AE, BC, DC, V, JCB. Daily noon–3pm, Sun–Mon 5–9pm; Tues–Thurs 5–10pm, Fri–Sat 5–11:30pm. CityRail, bus, or ferry: Circular Quay. PIZZA/PASTA.

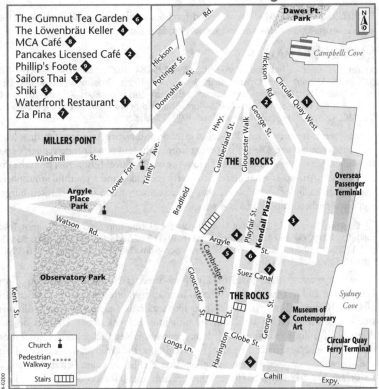

The Gumnut Tea Garden **6**
The Löwenbräu Keller **4**
MCA Café **8**
Pancakes Licensed Café **2**
Phillip's Foote **9**
Sailors Thai **3**
Shiki **5**
Waterfront Restaurant **1**
Zia Pina **7**

MILLERS POINT

Windmill   St.

Argyle
Place
Park

Watson   Rd.

Observatory Park

Kent St.

Church †
Pedestrian ..... Walkway
Stairs ▯▯▯▯

Rd.

Hickson St.
Pottinger St.
Downshire St.

Hickson Rd.
Hwy.
Lower Fort St.
Trinity Ave.
Bradfield

Cumberland St.
Gloucester Walk
George St.

THE ROCKS

Playfair St.
Kendall Plaza
Argyle   St.

Cambridge St.
Gloucester St.

Suez Canal

THE ROCKS

Harrington St.
Globe St.
George St.

Longs Ln.

Cahill   Expy.

Dawes Pt.
Park

Campbells Cove

Circular Quay West

Overseas
Passenger
Terminal

Sydney
Cove

Circular Quay
Ferry Terminal

Museum of
Contemporary
Art

4-0200

With 10 tables crammed downstairs and another 24 upstairs, there's not much room to breathe in this cramped traditional pizzeria and spaghetti house. But squeeze in between the close-fit bare-brick walls and wallow in the clashes and clangs coming from the hard-working chefs in the kitchen. Pizzas come in two sizes; the larger feeds two people. Delicious gelato goes for a cool A$4 (U.S.$2.80).

WORTH A SPLURGE

Waterfront Restaurant. In Campbell's Storehouse, 27 Circular Quay West, The Rocks. ☎ **02/9247 3666.** Reservations recommended. Main courses A$23.90–$42.50 (U.S.$16.75–$29.75). A$3 (U.S.$2.10) per person surcharge weekends and public holidays. AE, BC, DC, MC, V. Daily noon to about 11pm. CityRail, bus, or ferry: Circular Quay.

You can't help but notice the mast, rigging, and sails that distinguish this restaurant in the line of four right on the water below the main spread of The Rocks. It's very popular at lunch, when business people snap up the best seats outside in the sunshine; but at night, with the colors of the city washing over the harbor, it can be magical. Most main courses cost a hefty A$25 (U.S.$17.50) or so, but for that you get a choice of such hearty meals as steaks, mud crab, fish fillets, prawns, and a seafood platter. The food is nice and simple, with the markup added for the glorious position and views.

In the same building you'll find the Waterfront's sister restaurants: **Wolfie's Grill** (☎ **02/9241 5577**), which serves good char-grilled beef and seafood dishes for around A$23 (U.S.$16.10), and **The Italian Village** (☎ **02/9247 6111**), which serves regional Italian cuisine for A$22 to A$30 (U.S.$15.40 to $21). The other restaurant in the line is an excellent Chinese spot called the **Imperial Peking**

(☎ 02/9247 7073), which serves good food for similar prices. All four restaurants offer fantastic water views and indoor and outdoor dining.

NEAR TOWN HALL

Arizona. Corner of Pitt and Market sts. ☎ **02/9261 1077.** Main courses A$12–$18 (U.S.$8.40–$12.60). The Cowboy Bar: Mon noon–10pm, Tues noon–10:30pm, Wed noon–11pm, Thurs–Fri noon–2am, Sat noon–3:30am, Sun noon–8pm. Arizona 101 Bar & Grill: Mon–Sat noon–3pm, Mon–Wed 5–9pm, Thurs–Fri noon–10pm, Sat 5–10pm. AE, BC, DC, MC, V. CityRail, bus, or monorail: Town Hall. TEX-MEX.

Cactus-strewn frescoes, a split log–cabin exterior, and Native American figurines leave no doubt about where Arizona is coming from. Split into two separate venues, opposite each other on the second floor of a low-rise on Pitt Street (just across from the Pitt Street Mall), Arizona is a fun place with pretty good food and a youthful atmosphere. Main meals include T-bone steak, char-grilled salmon steak, Cajun chicken burger, and Texas barbecued pork ribs and wings.

✪ **Capitan Torres.** 73 Liverpool St. (just past the cinema strip on George St., near Town Hall). ☎ **02/9264 5574.** Main courses A$16.50–$19 (U.S.$11.55–$13.30). Tapas A$5–$9 (U.S.$3.50–$6.30). AE, BC, D, MC, V. Daily noon–3pm, Mon–Sat 6–11pm, Sun 6–10pm. CityRail: Town Hall. SPANISH.

Sydney's Spanish quarter, based on Liverpool Street (a 10-minute walk from Town Hall station and just past Sydney's main cinema strip), offers some great restaurants, of which Capitan Torres is my favorite. Downstairs is a tapas bar with traditional stools, a Spanish serving staff, and an authentic dark-oak decor. Upstairs on two floors is a fabulous restaurant with heavy wooden tables and chairs and an atmosphere thick with sangria and regional food. Upstairs, the garlic prawns are incredible, and the whole snapper a memorable experience. The tapas are better, though, at **Asturiana** (☎ 02/ 9264 1010), another Spanish restaurant a couple of doors down on the same street.

SUPER-CHEAP EATS

The Olive. Shop 18, Strand Arcade. ☎ **02/9231 2962.** Main courses A$4–$6.30 (U.S.$2.80–$4.40). Cash only. Mon–Sat 6am–4pm. CityRail, bus, or monorail: Town Hall. ITALIAN/SANDWICHES.

This tiny sandwich shop in the Strand Arcade, just off the Pitt Street Mall between Town Hall and the AMP Centerpoint Tower, is a wonderful place for a tasty, cheap lunch in the city center. Authentic pastas, pizzas, focaccias, and spicy rissoles are on offer. The gourmet sandwiches are filling enough to last you through an afternoon of sightseeing. You can get cheaper sandwiches in the city (simple filled rolls cost just A$2.20/U.S.$1.40 downstairs in the **Woolworth's** directly opposite Town Hall on George St.), but none are as delicious as the ones here.

Happy Hour!

Head to **Arizona** for happy hour (Monday to Friday 5pm to 8pm), when bottles of local beer, house spirits, and cheap wine go for A$2.50 (U.S.$1.75). On Friday nights and Saturdays from 6pm to 11pm cocktails are also reduced to A$3 (U.S.$2.10). A DJ spins tunes Thursday to Saturday evenings, playing modern dance and well-known classics. There's free pool on one of four tables (and free nachos) during happy hour on Thursdays. If you want to grab some grub in the bar, the nachos or a burger and fries will set you back A$7.50 (U.S.$5.25).

Planet You-Know-What

You can't miss Sydney's branch of the **Planet Hollywood** chain, 600 George St. (☎ **02/9267 7827**). Just look for the oversized globe opposite the main cinema complexes on George Street (in the opposite direction from the Queen Victoria Building and Circular Quay). If you've been to a Planet Hollywood before, expect few surprises here, just the usual TV and Hollywood memorabilia scattered around and plenty of burgers and the like on the menu. Two Australian touches are the grilled barramundi fish marinated in limes, and the ground Tasmanian salmon burger. It's open daily 11:30am to 1am (bar open daily 11:30am to 2am). Main courses go for A$10 to $18 (U.S.$7 to $12.60). Reservations not accepted.

✪ **Sushi Roll.** Sydney Central Plaza, downstairs in food hall, next to Grace Brothers on Pitt Street Mall. Sushi rolls A$1.50 (U.S.$1.05) each. No credit cards. Mon–Wed and Sat 8am–7pm, Thurs 8am–10pm, Sun 10am–6pm. JAPANESE.

The fresh and simple food served up at bargain-basement prices in this take-out booth is certainly a healthy alternative to the greasy fare many diners-on-the-dash fill up on. A wide range of sushi peeks out from behind the counter here. You can dine at the tables provided.

WORTH A SPLURGE

Level Two Revolving Restaurant. In Centerpoint Tower, Market St. (between Pitt and Castlereigh sts.). ☎ **02/9233 3722.** Reservations recommended. Lunch Mon–Sat A$34 (U.S.$23.80); lunch Sun A$37 (U.S.$25.90); early dinner A$37 (U.S.$25.90); regular dinner A$40 (U.S.$28). A$15 (U.S.$10.50) for children 3–12 at lunch and early dinner. 10% surcharge (on drinks only) weekends and public holidays. AE, BC, DC, MC, V. Daily 11:30am–2:15pm and 5–11:45pm. CityRail: St. James. Monorail: City Centre. GRILLS/ROASTS/SEAFOOD/ASIAN.

For those not scared of heights, Level Two offers a self-service all-you-can-eat buffet—ideal for those who don't want to pay for the à la carte goodies a floor down at its sister restaurant, Level One. This place is very popular with tourists, who come here for the stupendous views right across Sydney and, on a clear day, as far as the Blue Mountains. The dining area takes about an hour to fully rotate, but even going this slowly I find it a bit off-putting—especially when you're some 250 meters up. You can heap your plate with a selection of five appetizers, then choose between 15 main courses, including steaks, roasts, pork knuckles, beef stroganoff, seafood, and Asian dishes. There are also five desserts to choose from.

AT DARLING HARBOUR

The Wokpool. In the IMAX Theatre building, Southern Promenade, Darling Harbour. ☎ **02/9211 9888.** Main courses A$22–$38 (U.S.$15.40–$26.60) upstairs. Noodle bar dishes A$8–$16 (U.S.$5.60–$11.20) AE, BC, DC, MC, JCB, V. Daily noon–3pm, Sun–Fri 6–10pm, Sat 6–11pm. Monorail: Convention Center. Ferry: Darling Harbour. MODERN ASIAN.

The best restaurant with the best views in Darling Harbour, this adventuresome child of co-owners Neil Perry and chef Kylie Kwong has taken off big-time. Upstairs, the main dining room is light and spacious with glass walls opening up across the water. The essence up here is Chinese with a twist, and the Sichuan duck and stir-fried spanner crab omelet are always on the menu. Other dishes to go for are the whole steamed snapper with ginger and shallot, the rock lobster, and the mud crab. Downstairs, the noodle bar is always happening, with travelers, locals, and businessmen crunched up along the bar or around the tables and digging into such dishes as beef curry or seafood sausages with a pork and peanut relish.

Something Fishy

If you like fresh seafood at cheap prices, then saunter down to **Sydney Fish-market,** on the corner of Bank Street and Pyrmont Bridge Road, Pyrmont (☎ **02/9660 1611,** or the Fishline at 02/9552 2180 for information on special events such as seafood cooking classes). The major fish retailers here sell sashimi at the cheapest prices in Sydney, but if you prefer your seafood fresh, then don't miss out on these two fabulous outlets.

First off, there's **Musumeci Seafoods,** found outside the large blue retail arcade. It's little more than a stall with an attached hot plate, but you won't find baby octopus cooked better in any of Sydney's glitzy restaurants. Seafood combinations also are offered, with a small plate (easily enough for one person) costing just A$5 (U.S.$3.50) and a large plate going for A$10 (U.S.$7). Musumeci's is open from 7am to 4pm on Fridays and Sundays, and from 6am to 4pm on Saturdays.

Another mouthwatering option is the nearby **Christies,** a seafood retailer inside the main retail building. Here, you pick your own seafood, such as fresh calamari or mussels, and your own sauce, and they just throw it straight into a wok and cook it for you on the spot. Stir-fries, or a great Asian-style seafood noodle dish, cost just A$5 (U.S.$3.50). Christies cooks are on the job daily from 7am to 7pm.

To get to the Fishmarket, take the light rail from Central Station, Chinatown, or Darling Harbour to the Fishmarket stop, or take the pleasant walk from Darling Harbour (look for the signs).

IN KINGS CROSS & THE SUBURBS BEYOND

Bourbon & Beefsteak Bar. 24 Darlinghurst Rd., Kings Cross. ☎ **02/9358 1144.** Reservations recommended Fri–Sun. Main courses A$8.50–$23.95 (U.S.$5.95–$16.80). A$2 (U.S. $1.40) surcharge weekends and public holidays. AE, BC, DC, MC, V. Daily 24-hours (happy hour 4–7pm). CityRail: Kings Cross. INTERNATIONAL.

The Bourbon & Beefsteak has been a popular Kings Cross institution for more than 30 years. It attracts everyone from visiting U.S. sailors and tourists to businessmen and ravers. The fact that it's open 24 hours means many people never seem to leave—occasionally you'll even find someone taking a nap in a toilet cubicle. The American-themed restaurant here is busy at all hours, churning out steaks, seafood, salads, Tex-Mex, ribs, and pasta. Breakfast is served daily from 6 to 11am—the American-style pancakes are good at A$8.50 (U.S.$5.95).

Every night there's live music in the Piano Bar from 5 to 9pm, followed by a mixture of jazz, Top 40, and rock and roll until 5am. A disco downstairs starts at 11pm nightly, and a larger one takes off in The Penthouse at the Bourbon bar on Friday and Saturday nights. The music is very much geared toward the 18- to 25-year-old crowd of locals and backpackers.

✪ **Govindas.** 112 Darlinghurst Rd., Darlinghurst. ☎ **02/9380 5155.** Dinner A$13.90 (U.S.$9.75), including free movie. BC, MC, V. Daily 6–11pm. CityRail: Kings Cross. VEGETARIAN.

When I think of Govindas, I can't help smiling. Perhaps it's because I'm reliving the happy vibes from the Hare Krishna center it's based in, or maybe it's because the food is so cheap! Or perhaps it's because they even throw in a decent movie with the meal (the movie theater is on a different floor). The food is simple (sometimes bland) Indian-style vegetarian, eaten in a basic room off black lacquer tables. Typical dishes include pastas, salads, lentil dishes, soups, and casseroles. It's BYO and doctrine free.

SUPER-CHEAP EATS

Delicious North Indian. 62A Darlinghurst Rd., Kings Cross. ☎ **02/9357 4226.** Main courses A$4.50–$10.50 (U.S.$3.15–$7.35). AE, BC, DC, MC, V. Sun–Thurs 11:30am–11:30pm, Fri and Sat 11:30am–4am. CityRail: Kings Cross. NORTHERN INDIAN.

The bargain curries served here are worth tucking into at this Indian fast-food house located on the main Kings Cross drag. The curries aren't the best in the world, but they are spicy enough and very filling. You can choose a mixture of any three vegetarian curries with rice for just A$4.50 (U.S.$3.15). Meat curries cost A$6.50 (U.S.$4.55). A more formal meal with just one main dish will cost a little more.

William's on William. 242 William St., Kings Cross. ☎ **02/9358 6680.** Main courses A$3.90–$11.90 (U.S.$2.75–$8.35). AE, MC, V. Daily 7:30am–11pm. CityRail: Kings Cross. CAFE/PASTA.

Just around the corner from the Kings-X Hotel, which itself is right opposite the huge Coca-Cola sign, you'll come across this remarkably scruffy little eatery. The walls need a bit of a paint, the floors need to be swept, and the tacky plastic tablecloths look like they survived the last war. If you can get past all this, though, you'll be very satisfied. The pastas at A$5 to $6 (U.S.$3.50 to $4.20) are huge and delicious, and the all-day breakfast of bacon, egg, toast, and homemade French fries is a fantastic value at A$3.90 (U.S.$2.75). Tea and coffee come in at a very cheap A$1.50 (U.S.$1.05).

WORTH A SPLURGE

✪ **Mezzaluna.** 123 Victoria St., Potts Point. ☎ **02/9357 1988.** Reservations recommended. Main courses A$19.50–$31 (U.S.$13.65–$21.70). A$2.90 (U.S.$2.05) surcharge Sun. AE, BC, DC, MC, V. Tues–Sun noon–3pm, Tues–Sat 6–11pm, Sun 6–10pm. Closed public holidays. CityRail: Kings Cross. MODERN ITALIAN.

Exquisite food, flawless service, and an almost unbeatable view across the city's western skyline have all helped Mezzaluna position itself firmly among Sydney's top restaurants. A cozy, candlelit place with plain white walls and polished wooden floors, the main dining room opens up onto a huge, all-weather terrace kept warm in winter by giant overhead fan heaters. The restaurant's owner, well-known Sydney culinary icon Beppi Polesi, provides an exceptional wine list to complement an extravagant menu that changes daily. You could indulge in an unbeatable salmon risotto to start, followed by fillets of fish with scampi, scallops, mussels, oysters, and Morton Bay bugs, or succulent roasted lamb with grilled eggplant and sheep's yogurt. Whatever you choose, you can't go wrong. I highly recommend this place.

IN PADDINGTON

The top end of Oxford Street, which runs from Hyde Park in central Sydney toward Bondi, has a profusion of trendy bars and cafes and a scattering of cheaper eateries among the more glamorous ones.

Laksa House. In the Windsor Castle Hotel, 72 Windsor St. (corner of Elizabeth St.). ☎ **02/9328 0741.** Reservations not accepted. Main courses A$6–$9 (U.S.$4.20–$6.30). No credit cards. Open daily noon–3pm and 6–9:30pm. Bus: Oxford St. MALAYSIAN.

The dining room here is simple but friendly, and the food is wonderfully authentic. The specialty is *laksa*, a spicy Asian soup cooked with coconut milk with chicken, prawn, vegetables, or tofu. You can also try the peanut-sauce satays, the Singapore noodles, the Indonesian rice and noodle staples of *nasi goreng* and *gado gado*, as well as a range of spicy curries.

La Mensa. 257 Oxford St., Paddington. ☎ **02/9332 2963.** Reservations recommended. Main courses A$14.50–$19.50. (U.S.$10.15–$13.65). AE, BC, DC, MC, V. Mon–Thurs 11am–10pm, Fri 11am–11pm, Sat 9am–11pm, Sun 9am–10pm. Bus: Oxford St. MEDITERRANEAN.

Cafe Culture

Debate rages over which cafe serves the best coffee in Sydney, which has the best atmosphere, and which has the tastiest snacks. The main cafe scenes are centered around Victoria Street in Darlinghurst, Stanley Street in East Sydney, and King Street in Newtown. Other places, including Balmoral Beach on the north shore, Bondi Beach, and Paddington, all have their favored hangouts as well.

Note: Americans will be sorry to learn that, unlike in the States, free refills of coffee are rare in Australian restaurants and cafes. Sip slowly.

Here are a few of my favorites around town:

✪ Balmoral Boatshed Kiosk. 2 The Esplanade, Balmoral Beach. ☎ **02/9968 4412.** Daily 8am–7pm in summer, 8am–6pm in winter. Ferry to Taronga Zoo, then bus to Balmoral Beach.

A real find, this beautiful rustic cafe is right on the water beside the dinghies and sailing craft of the wooden Balmoral Boatshed. It's a heavenly place for enjoying a breakfast muffin or a ham-and-cheese croissant while basking in the sun. This place is popular with families on weekend mornings, so if you hate kids, find another place.

Bar Coluzzi. 322 Victoria St., Darlinghurst. ☎ **02/9380 5420.** Daily 4:45am–7:30pm. CityRail: Kings Cross.

Although it may no longer serve the best coffee in Sydney, this cafe's claim to fame is that long ago it served up real espresso when the rest of the city was still drinking Nescafe. Watching the street life (and being seen doing it) is still a

---

The clean-cut, minimal interior here is made a little livelier by the gourmet food and vegetable store tacked on. One communal table seats around 20 people, and other tables are both inside and out. The standout mains are the roast beef rib eye with lentils and garlic puree, the veal with spinach and onions, and the braised lamb shanks with soft polenta. The few vegetarian items on the menu include roasted banana chilies filled with risotto.

IN DARLINGHURST

Hard Rock Cafe. 121–129 Crown St., Darlinghurst. ☎ **02/9331 1116.** Reservations not accepted. Main courses A$9.95–$19.95 (U.S.$6.95–$13.95). 10% surcharge weekends and public holidays. AE, BC, DC, JCB, MC, V. Daily noon–midnight. Closed Christmas Day. CityRail: Museum, then walk across Hyde Park, head downhill past the Australian Museum on William St., and turn right onto Crown St.). Bus: Sydney Explorer Bus stop no. 7. AMERICAN.

The obligatory half a Cadillac through the wall beckons you into this shrine to rock and roll. Among the items on display are costumes worn by Elvis, John Lennon, and Elton John, as well as guitars from Sting and the Bee Gees, drums from Phil Collins and The Beatles, and one of Madonna's bras. The mainstays here are the burgers, but ribs, chicken, fish, salads, and T-bone steaks also are on the menu. Most meals come with French fries or baked potatoes and a salad. It's really busy on Friday and Saturday evenings from around 7:30pm to 10:30pm, when you might have to queue to get a seat.

Nepalese Kitchen. 481 Crown St., Surry Hills. ☎ **02/9319 4264.** Main courses A$8–$12 (U.S.$5.60–$8.40); 2-course meal A$18 (U.S.$12.60). AE, BC, DC, MC, V. Daily 6pm–11pm. CityRail: Central, then a 10-minute walk up Devonshire St. NEPALESE.

favorite hobby at this fashionably worn-around-the edges spot in the heart of Sydney's cafe district.

✪ **Bill's.** 433 Liverpool St., Darlinghurst. ☎ **02/9360 9631.** Mon–Sat 7:30am–3pm. CityRail: Kings Cross.

Bill's is on everyone's lips. The bright and airy place, strewn with flowers and magazines, serves fantastic nouveau cafe–style food. It's so popular, you might have trouble finding a seat. The signature breakfast dishes—including ricotta hot cakes with honeycomb butter and banana, and sweet corn fritters with roast tomatoes and bacon—are the stuff of legends.

Hernandez. 60 Kings Cross Rd., Potts Point. ☎ **02/9331 2343.** Daily 24 hours. CityRail: Kings Cross.

The walls of this tiny, cluttered cafe are crammed with eccentric fake masterpieces, and the air is permeated with the aroma of 20 types of coffee roasted and ground on the premises. It's almost a religious experience for discerning inner-city coffee addicts. The Spanish espresso is a treat.

The Old Coffee Shop. Ground floor, The Strand Arcade. ☎ **02/9231 3002.** Mon–Fri 7:30am–5:30pm, Sat 8:30am–5pm, Sun 10:30am–4pm. CityRail: Town Hall.

Sydney's oldest coffee shop opened in the charming Victorian Strand Arcade in 1891. The shop may or may not serve Sydney's best java, but the old-world feel of the place and the sugary snacks, cakes, and pastries make up for it. It's a good place to take a break from shopping and sightseeing.

Adventurous gourmands around here dig into this somewhat mildly spiced cuisine, which is something like a mixture of Indian and Chinese. Steamed dumplings, called "momo," and stuffed crispy pancakes made with black lentil flour are interesting to start with, and the goat curry is the pick of the main courses. Also popular is the char-grilled lamb or chicken marinated in roasted spices. The curries are very tasty, and there's a large selection of vegetarian dishes, including flavorsome eggplant curry. Accompany your food with "achars," or relishes, to highlight the flavors of your dishes.

A GREAT SPOT FOR SUPER-CHEAP PASTA

✪ **No Names.** 2 Chapel St. (or 81 Stanley St.), Darlinghurst. ☎ **02/9360 4711.** Main courses A$6–$8.50 (U.S.$4.20–$5.95). Cash only. Daily noon–2:30pm and 6–10pm. CityRail: Kings Cross or Town Hall, then a 10-minute walk. ITALIAN.

This fabulous Italian cafeteria-style joint is *the* place in Sydney to go for a cheap and cheerful meal. Downstairs you can nibble on cakes or drink good coffee, but upstairs you have a choice between spaghetti Bolognese or Neapolitana, and several meat dishes, which usually include fish, beef, and veal. The servings are enormous and often far more than you can eat. You get free bread, and simple salads are cheap. Help yourself to water and cordials. There are similar eateries in Bondi.

IN NEWTOWN: GREAT ETHNIC EATS

Inner-city Newtown is three stops from Central Station on CityRail, and 10 minutes by bus from central Sydney. On Newtown's main drag, King Street, many inexpensive restaurants offer food from all over the world.

Le Kilimanjaro. 280 King St., Newtown. ☎ **02/9557 4565.** Reservations recommended. Main courses A$8.50–$9.50 (U.S.$5.95–$6.65) No credit cards. CityRail: Newtown. AFRICAN.

With so many excellent restaurants to choose from in Newtown—they close down or improve quickly if they're bad—I picked Kilimanjaro because it's the most unusual. It's a tiny place, with very limited seating on two floors. You enter, choose a dish off the blackboard menu (while standing), and then one of the waiters escorts you to your seat. On a recent visit I had couscous, some African bread (similar to an Indian chapatti), and the *Saussou-gor di guan* (tuna in a rich sauce). Another favorite dish is the *Yassa* (chicken in a rich African sauce). All meals are served on traditional wooden plates.

Old Saigon. 107 King St., Newtown. ☎ **02/9519 5931.** Reservations recommended. Main courses A$10–$13 (U.S.$7–$9.10). BYO only. AE, BC, DC, MC, V. Wed–Fri noon–3pm; Tues–Sun 6–11pm. CityRail: Newtown. VIETNAMESE.

Another Newtown establishment bursting with atmosphere, the Old Saigon was owned until 1998 by a former American Vietnam War correspondent, who ended up living in Vietnam and marrying a local before coming to Australia. His own photos line the walls, and homemade tin helicopters hang over diners' heads. His Vietnamese brother-in-law has taken over the show, but the food is still glorious, with the spicy squid dishes among my favorites. A popular pastime is to grill thin strips of venison, beef, wild boar, or crocodile over a burner at your table, then wrap the meat in rice paper with lettuce and mint, and then dip it in a chili sauce. I highly recommend this place for a cheap night out.

AT BONDI BEACH

The seafront drag of Campbell Parade is packed with restaurants. For a super-cheap meal at the beach, you could try the bistro at the **North Bondi R.S.L. Club,** located at 120 Ramsgate Ave., North Bondi, at the far end of Bondi Beach to your left as you look at the ocean (☎ **02/9130 3152**). Daily lunches—including fish-and-chips, roast meats, and schnitzel—served between noon and 2:30pm, go for just A$3 (U.S.$2.10). The dinner menu, offered from 5 to 8:30pm daily, is good value, too. Because of its special "club" status, alcohol is very cheap in the bar here.

Fishy Affair. 152–162 Campbell Parade, Bondi Beach. ☎ **02/9300 0494.** Main courses A$14.40–$21 (U.S.$10.10–$14.70). AE, BC, JCB, MC, V. Mon–Thurs noon–3pm and 6–10pm; Fri–Sat noon–3pm and 6–10:30pm; Sun noon–10pm. Bus: Bondi Beach. SEAFOOD.

Just one of many good restaurants, cafes, and take-out joints along the beach's main drag, the Fishy Affair is nevertheless a standout. Sitting outside and munching on tasty fish-and-chips while watching the beach bums saunter past is a great way to spend an hour or so. The herb-crusted Atlantic salmon steak and the smoked salmon salad are both truly delicious.

✪ **Thai Terrific.** 147 Curlewis St., Bondi Beach. ☎ **02/9365 7794**. Reservations recommended Fri and Sat nights. Main courses A$10–$18 (U.S.$7–$12.60). AE, BC, DC, MC, V. Daily noon–11pm. Bus 380 to Bondi Beach. THAI.

Thai Terrific by name, terrific Thai by nature. This truly superb place just around the corner from the Bondi Hotel is run with flair and coolly efficient service. The large back room can be very noisy, so if you prefer less din with your dinner, sit at one of the small sidewalk tables. The servings here are enormous—three people could easily fill up on just two mains. The *tom yum* soups and the prawn or seafood *laksa* noodle soups (spicy soup made with coconut milk) are the best I've tasted in Australia and are very filling. I also highly recommend the red curries.

Equally as nice (and quieter) is the Bangkok-style **Nina's Ploy Thai Restaurant,** at 132 Wairoa Ave. (☎ **02/9365 1118**), at the corner of Warners Ave. at the end of the main Campbell Parade strip. Main courses here cost between A$8 and $12.50 (U.S.$5.60 and $8.75); cash only.

North Indian Flavour. 138 Campbell Parade, Bondi Beach. ☎ **02/9365 6239.** Main courses A$4.90–$7.90 (U.S.$3.45–$5.55). No credit cards. Mon–Fri noon–11pm, Sat–Sun 11:30am–11:30pm. NORTH INDIAN.

I've lost count of the times the North Indian Flavour restaurants around Sydney have satisfied a curry craving. Don't expect first-class Indian food, but it'll do if you really want to fill up on something a little spicy. The curries and breads are displayed just inside the doorway, and you can either eat on the premises or take your food down to the grassy strip in front of the beach. Most people tend to choose a selection of three curries on rice and mop it up with naan bread. A medium-sized serving is big enough to plug a very large appetite. Wash it down with a mango *lassi* yogurt drink for A$1.70 (U.S.$1.20). You'll find almost identical outlets on King Street in Newtown (☎ **02/ 9550 3928**), under the Grace Brothers department store on Pitt Street Mall (☎ **02/ 9221 4715**), and on Broadway opposite Central Station (☎ **02/9212 3535**).

IN MANLY

Manly is 30 minutes from Circular Quay by ferry, or 15 minutes by JetCat. The take-out shops that line the Corso, the pedestrian mall that runs between the ferry terminal and the main Manly Beach, offer everything from Turkish kebabs to Japanese noodles.

✪ **Ashiana.** 2 Sydney Rd., Manly. ☎ **02/9977 3466.** Reservations recommended. Main courses A$9.90–$15.90 (U.S.$6.95–$11.15). AE, BC, MC, V. Daily 5:30–11pm. Ferry or JetCat: Manly. INDIAN.

You'll be hard-pressed to find a better cheap Indian restaurant in Sydney. Tucked away up a staircase next to the Steyne Hotel (just off the Corso and near the main beach), Ashiana has won a few prizes for its traditional spicy cooking. Portions are large and filling, and the service is very friendly. The butter chicken is magnificent, while the *Malai Kofta* (cheese and potato dumplings in a mild, creamy sauce) is the best this side of Bombay. Beer is the best drink with everything. My only gripe is that it's hard to avoid cigarette smoke in such a cozy place, especially on Friday and Saturday nights when the place is packed. Clear your lungs and work off the heavy load in your stomach with a beachside stroll afterwards. Check out the soda machine in Wool-worth's just across the road for A80¢ (U.S.56¢) cold drinks—the cheapest in Sydney.

Café Tunis. 30/31 South Steyne, Manly. ☎ **02/9976 2805.** Main courses (big enough for two) A$17–$21 (U.S.$11.90–$14.70). AE, BC, DC, MC, V. Daily 7am–10pm. Ferry or JetCat: Manly. TUNISIAN.

Situated right on the beachfront with fabulous views across the ocean, Café Tunis dishes out huge, value-for-the-money portions of North African specialties. My favorite dish to start is the fresh tuna, with vegetables and egg deep-fried in pastry. It's big enough for a main dish. Real mains include couscous royale, with lamb, chicken,

Sydney's Best Fries

If you're looking for the best French fries in Sydney, head to **Manly Ocean Foods,** three shops down from the main beach on the Corso. Avoid the fish-and-chips here, though (the shark is not the best in my opinion), and spend a couple of dollars extra on barramundi, salmon, perch, or snapper.

and spicy sausage—it's large enough for two. The grilled seafood platter at A$35 (U.S.$24.50) is very popular, and is also big enough for you and a friend. Café Tunis is open for breakfast—the eggs Benedict is a specialty—and at lunchtime for fish-and-chips (but you can still try the authentic Tunisian desserts).

Howe's Restaurant. 33 South Steyne, Manly. ☎ **02/9977 1877.** Reservations required Fri and Sat nights. Main courses A$6.20–$9.90 (U.S.$4.35–$6.95). AE, BC, MC, V. Tues–Sun 5–11:30pm. Closed Mondays except national holiday weekends. Ferry or JetCat: Manly. THAI/INDONESIAN/MALAYSIAN.

Mr. Howe has been phenomenally successful on the Manly food circuit with his cram 'em in and keep it cheap philosophy. The restaurant is right across from Manly's main beach (to the right as you leave the Corso), but it makes no use of its position at all. What it does do is serve excellent, simple Southeast Asian dishes, including various curries, noodles, and rice-based dishes. Mr. Howe himself is generally around offering huge smiles. Tables are lined up in long rows, so don't be surprised if you are elbow to elbow with strangers. On weekend evenings, the place is swamped with a generally young crowd. Don't leave without tasting the sticky rice with mango desert.

SUPER-CHEAP VEGETARIAN

Green's Eatery. 1–3 Sydney Rd., Manly. ☎ **02/9977 1904.** Main courses A$2–$6.20 (U.S.$1.40–$4.35). Cash only. Daily 8am–6pm. Ferry or JetCat: Manly. VEGETARIAN.

Of the many restaurants in Manly, this nice little vegetarian place, just off the Corso on the turnoff just before the Steyne Hotel pub, does the best lunchtime business. The food is healthy and good quality. The menu includes 11 different vegetarian burgers, vegetable curries, noodle dishes, salads, soups, smoothies, and "roll-ups" (patties wrapped in pita bread). The cakes here are surprisingly tasty despite being incredibly wholesome.

IN NORTH SYDNEY

Shehnei. 16 Ennis Rd., Milsons Point. ☎ **02/9955 2775.** Reservations recommended Fri evening. Main courses A$9.50–$12.50 (U.S.$6.65–$8.75). AE, BC, DC, MC, V. Mon–Fri noon–3pm, daily 5:30pm–midnight. CityRail or ferry: Milsons Point. Take the left exit from Milsons Point CityRail station, and it's just up the hill to your left. INDIAN.

Traditional Indian decor is not a high point at Shehnei, but the food is good enough to make it one of my top three cheap Indian restaurants in Sydney. Just about anything on the menu is worth exploring, but if you like things a bit spicier than your average diner, you'll need to request extra chilies. Plenty of vegetarian options are available. Lunch boxes, including a curry off the menu and rice for just A$5 (U.S.$3.50), are a terrific value—eat on the grass beneath the Harbour Bridge, or alternatively walk down the street to the Milsons Point ferry wharf and eat your curry as you chug back across the harbor to Circular Quay.

SUPER-CHEAP EATS

✪ **Freckle Face Café.** 32A Burton St., Kirribilli. ☎ **02/9957 2116.** Main courses A$6.50 (U.S.$4.55) eat-in or A$5.90 (U.S.$4.15) take-out. No credit cards. Mon–Sat 7am–4pm. CityRail or ferry: Milsons Point. Take the left exit from Milsons Point CityRail station, walk downhill to the traffic light, cross the road, and it's on the street opposite. CAFE.

There's no better place to refuel after a walk across Harbour Bridge than this intimate little cafe close to the Milsons Point CityRail station. Freckle Face specializes in sandwiches, bagels, Turkish bread, and foccacia—and very good coffee. The smoked salmon, baby spinach, and cream cheese on toasted Turkish bread is one of my favorites, and the biscuits and cakes (especially the flourless orange and almond cake) are gorgeous. Yummy breakfasts go for A$6.90 (U.S.$4.85), including fruit salads, muesli, fruit bread, and egg dishes. Everything is made on the premises. The staff is very friendly, so say hello to Jackie and Victoria—two sisters with freckles on their faces.

WORTH A SPLURGE

✪ **L'Incontro Italian Restaurant.** 196 Miller St. (corner of McLaren St.), North Sydney. ☎ **02/9957 2274.** Reservations recommended. Main courses A$21.50–$32.50 (U.S.$15.05–$22.75). AE, DC, MC, V. Mon–Fri noon–3pm and 6–10pm; Sat 6–10pm. CityRail: North Sydney. NORTHERN ITALIAN.

Less than 10 minutes by train from the city center—plus a five-minute stroll up Miller Street (turn right up the hill as you exit the train station and take the first right)—this little beauty in an easy-to-miss turn-of-the-century house is a good place for moderately priced Italian. Dishes are beautifully prepared and well served in a stylish setting as far removed from the modern yuppie bistro as you can get. The food is exquisite. The courtyard, with its vines and ferns, is delightful in summer. Menus change regularly, so pray for the baked rainbow trout cooked with almonds and red-wine butter—simply the best fish I have ever tasted.

5

What to See & Do in Sydney

by Marc Llewellyn

The only problem with visiting Sydney is fitting in everything you want to do and see. A well-planned itinerary can easily be upset by the countless sights and experiences that suddenly become "must-sees" and "must-dos" after you arrive. Whatever happens, you won't have enough time. So don't be surprised if you find yourself planning ahead for your next visit, before you've even finished your first visit. Budget travelers should note that many places worth visiting offer substantial discounts for students and senior citizens with identification.

SIGHTSEEING SUGGESTIONS FOR FIRST-TIME VISITORS

If You Have 1 Day   In the morning, make your way down to **Circular Quay** to look around the Opera House and admire the Sydney Harbour Bridge. Then head over to **The Rocks,** stopping off at The Rocks Visitors Centre to pick up maps and extra information; be sure to check out the fascinating exhibits on the top two floors. Have lunch around Circular Quay or The Rocks, or jump on a ferry, to Darling Harbour or Manly perhaps, and eat onboard. A guided **walking tour** around The Rocks should be at the top of your agenda for the early afternoon. You can either follow the self-guided walking tour described later in this chapter, or book ahead for one of The Rocks Walking Tours (see "Organized Tours" below). The rest of the afternoon I'd spend browsing around the stores, or I'd head to **Taronga Zoo** by ferry to at least get a glimpse of some Australian wildlife. An option for the late afternoon, or dinner, is to take a harbor cruise.

If You Have 2 Days   On the second day, head down to Circular Quay again and take the ferry that travels beneath the Harbour Bridge and across to Darling Harbour. At Darling Harbour, visit **Sydney Aquarium** for its giant sharks, seals, underwater ocean tunnels, and Great Barrier Reef displays. Then visit the **National Maritime Museum** or one of the other attractions that dot this tourist precinct. Take the monorail to Town Hall in time to see the sunset at the top of the **AMP Centerpoint Tower.**

If You Have 3 Days   If the weather's fine, head to the beach. Go to either **Bondi Beach,** where you can take the cliff walk to Bronte Beach and back, or take the ferry to **Manly** (see "Getting Around" in chapter 4). If you have time in the afternoon, I highly recommend a visit to Featherdale Wildlife Park—it's out in the suburbs but really worth the

---

Great Deals on Sightseeing

The **Privileges Card** is a great way to save money if you plan to be out and about visiting the main attractions. The card costs A$25 (U.S.$17.50), is good for one month, and can be used in Sydney, Canberra, and Melbourne. In Sydney, for example, all the major attractions offer some sort of discount when you show a Privileges Card—usually you get two entry tickets for the price of one (or, if you're traveling alone, you can often buy an entry ticket for a reduced rate). The card also gives you discounts on harbor cruises (typically 20%), as well as on meals in certain restaurants (sometimes a free main course if two of you are dining, or a 20% rebate on the total bill for the cardholder and three others). You'll need to fill out an application form (available on the Internet at www.privilegescard.com, or you can obtain one at one of the tourist information centers when you arrive), and you'll receive a booklet with details of where you can save. Call Privileges at ☎ **02/6254 1375** or 02/6282 5181, or fax them at 02/6254 8788. If you book in advance, the company can arrange to have the card sent to your hotel.

Another money-saving option is the **Sydney Bonus Ticket,** which allows you entry to the AMP Centerpoint Tower and the Sydney Aquarium, as well as a morning or afternoon harbor cruise with Captain Cook Cruises. You can also use the card to receive discounts in the AMP Centerpoint Tower shopping complex. The card costs A$39 (U.S.$27.30) for adults and A$29 (U.S.$20.30) for children; get the card from any of the participating operators or at the desk as you enter Centerpoint from Pitt Street Mall. The separate charges for the three attractions at the time of publication totaled A$58.90 (U.S.$41.25) for adults—which means you save A$19.90 (U.S.$13.95).

---

trek. Have dinner at Circular Quay with a view of the harbor and the lights of the Opera House and Harbour Bridge.

If You Have 4 Days or more   If you have four days, get out of town. Head out to either the **Blue Mountains** for spectacular views and great bushwalking (hiking) or the vineyards of the **Hunter Valley** for wine tasting. See chapter 6 for details.

1 The Opera House & Sydney Harbour

✪ **Sydney Opera House.** Bennelong Point. ☎ **02/9250 7111** for guided tours and inquiries. Fax 02/9250 7624. www.soh.nsw.gov.au. For bookings call ☎ 02/9250 7777. Fax 02/9251 3943. E-mail for bookings: bookings@soh.nsw.gov.au. E-mail for general information: infodesk@soh.nsw.gov.au. Box office open Mon–Sat 9am–8:30pm, Sun 2 hours before performance. Tour prices A$10 (U.S.$7) adults, A$7 (U.S.$4.90) children (family prices available on application). Regular 1-hour tours Mon–Sat 9am–4pm, subject to theater availability (places are limited; be prepared to wait). Tours include approx. 200 stairs (tours for people with disabilities can be arranged). Parking daytime A$9 (U.S.$6.30) per hour; evening A$19 (U.S.$13.30) flat rate. CityRail, bus, or ferry: Circular Quay. Sydney Explorer bus: Stop 2.

Only a handful of buildings around the world have an architectural and cultural significance as great as the Sydney Opera House. But the difference between it and, say, the Taj Mahal, the Eiffel Tower, and the Great Pyramids of Egypt, is that this great, white-sailed construction caught midbillow over the waters of Sydney Cove is a working building, not just a monument. Most people are surprised to learn that it's not just an Opera House, but a full-scale performing arts complex with five major

Central Sydney Attractions

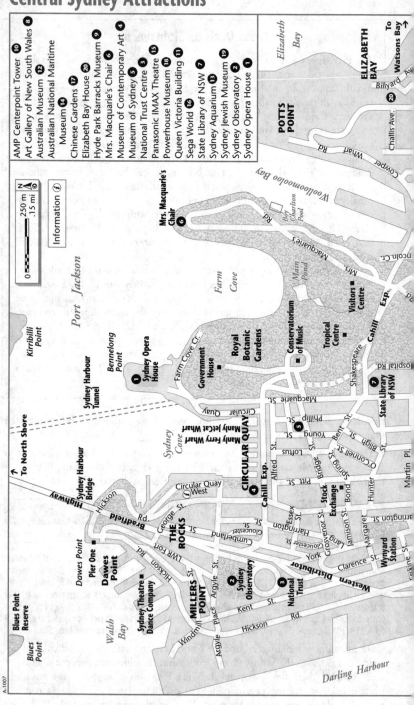

AMP Centerpoint Tower **10**
Art Gallery of New South Wales **8**
Australian Museum **12**
Australian National Maritime Museum **14**
Chinese Gardens **17**
Elizabeth Bay House **20**
Hyde Park Barracks Museum **9**
Mrs. Macquarie's Chair **6**
Museum of Contemporary Art **4**
Museum of Sydney **5**
National Trust Centre **3**
Panasonic IMAX Theatre **15**
Powerhouse Museum **18**
Queen Victoria Building **11**
Sega World **16**
State Library of NSW **7**
Sydney Aquarium **13**
Sydney Jewish Museum **19**
Sydney Observatory **2**
Sydney Opera House **1**

Information ⓘ

0 — 250 m
0 — .15 mi

N

Port Jackson

Kirribilli Point

Bennelong Point

Sydney Harbour Tunnel

Sydney Opera House **1**

To North Shore

Sydney Cove

Sydney Harbour Bridge

Blues Point Reserve

Blues Point

Walsh Bay

Dawes Point

Pier One

Dawes Point

Sydney Theatre ■ Dance Company

MILLERS POINT

Bradfield Highway

Hickson Rd.

George St.

Cumberland St.

Gloucester St.

LWR Fort St.

THE ROCKS

Sydney Observatory **2**

National Trust **3**

Windmill

Argyle Place

Kent St.

Hickson Rd.

Argyle St.

Darling Harbour

Circular Quay West ⓘ

Circular Quay

Manly Jetcat Wharf

Manly Ferry Wharf

CIRCULAR QUAY

Cahill Exp.

Museum of Contemporary Art **4**

Alfred St.

Loftus St.

Pitt St.

Essex St.

Harrington St.

York St.

Clarence St.

Western Distributor

Bridge St.

O'Connell St.

Spring St.

Grosvenor St.

Jamison St.

Lang St.

Bond St.

Margaret St.

Hunter St.

Clarence St.

Erskine St.

Wynyard Station

Stock Exchange ■

Museum of Sydney **5**

Phillip St.

Young St.

Bent St.

Bligh St.

Martin Pl.

Farrington St.

Macquarie St.

State Library of NSW **7**

Hospital Rd.

Shakespeare

Cahill Exp.

Government House ■

Royal Botanic Gardens

Farm Cove Cr.

Farm Cove

Main Pond

Conservatorium of Music

Tropical Centre ■

Visitors ■ Centre

Mrs. Macquarie's Chair **6**

Mrs. Macquaries Rd.

Boy Charlton Pool

Woolloomooloo Bay

Elizabeth Bay

ELIZABETH BAY

To Watsons Bay →

Billyard Ave.

POTTS POINT

Cowper Wharf Rd.

Challis Ave.

Lincoln Cr.

20

A-1007

146

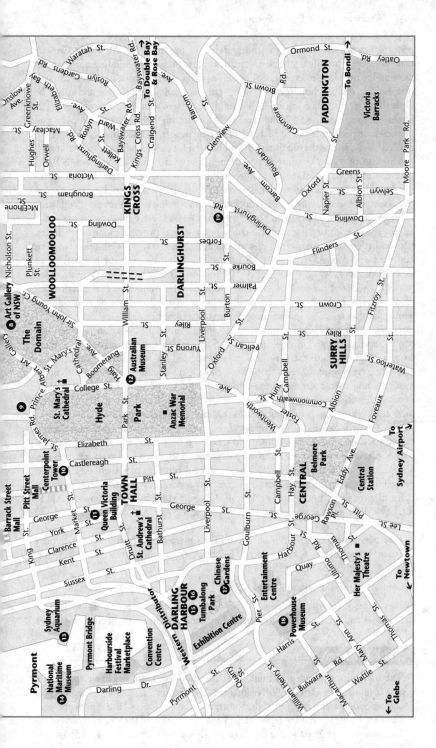

performance spaces. The biggest and grandest of the lot is the 2,690-seat Concert Hall, which has just about the best acoustics of any man-made building of its type in the world. Come here to experience not only opera, of course, but also chamber music, symphonies, dance, choral performances, and even on occasion rock and roll. The Opera Theatre is smaller, seating 1,547, and is home to operas, ballets, and dance. The Drama Theatre, seating 544, and the Playhouse, seating 398, specialize in plays and smaller-scale performances. In March 1999 a new theater, the Boardwalk, seating 300, opened on the site of the old library. It will be used for dance and experimental music.

The history of the building is as intriguing as the design. The New South Wales government raised the money needed to build it with a public lottery. Danish Architect Jôrn Utzon won an international competition to design it. From the start, the project was controversial, with many Sydneysiders considering it a monstrosity. Following a disagreement, Utzon returned home without ever seeing his finished project—and leaving the interior to fall victim to a compromise design (which, among other things, left too little space to perform full-scale operas). And the cost? Well, initially it was budgeted at a cool A$7 million (U.S.$4.9 million); but by the time it was finished in 1973, the cost was a staggering A$102 million (U.S.$71.4 million), most raised through a series of lotteries. Since then, continual refurbishment and the major task of replacing the asbestos-infected grouting between the hundreds of thousands of white tiles that make up its shell have cost many millions more.

Tours & Tickets: Guided tours of the Opera House last about an hour and are conducted daily from 9am to 4pm, except Good Friday and Christmas Day. Guides try to take groups into the main theaters and around the foyers, but if you can't see everything you want to see, it's because the Opera House is a workplace, not a museum, and there's almost always some performance, practice, or setting up to be done. Reservations are essential. Specialized tours, based on the building's architectural and engineering configurations, for example, can be arranged also.

The **Tourism Services Department** at the Sydney Opera House can book combination packages, including a dinner and show; a tour, dinner, and show; or a champagne interval performance. Prices vary depending on shows and restaurant venues. Visitors from overseas can buy tickets by credit card and then pick them up at the box office on arrival, or contact a local tour company specializing in Australia. Tickets for performances vary from as little as A$9.50 (U.S.$6.65) for children's shows to A$150 (U.S.$105) for good seats at the opera. Plays cost between A$35 to $45 (U.S.$24.50 to $31.50) on average.

Free performances are given outside on the Opera House boardwalks on Sunday afternoons and during festival times. The shows range from musicians and performance artists to school groups.

Sydney Harbour. Officially called Port Jackson.

Sydney Harbour is the focal point of Sydney and one of the things—along with the beaches and the easy access to surrounding national parks—that makes this city so

"The Toaster"

The incongruous residential building facing the Opera House as you approach it was completed in early 1999. Nicknamed "the Toaster," it's caused general uproar among Sydneysiders, with mass demonstrations on the Opera House steps and constant media criticism. One report contrasted "the purity" of the Opera House to the "worst aspects of greed"—the top-floor penthouse sold for more than A$5 million (U.S.$3.5 million).

A Bridge to Cross, Mate

One thing so few tourists do, but which only takes an hour or so, is to walk right across the Harbour Bridge. The bridge, completed in 1932, is 1,150 meters (3,795 ft.) long and spans the 503-meter (1,600-ft.) distance from the south shore to the north. It accommodates pedestrian walkways, two railway lines, and an eight-lane road. The 30-minute stroll across offers some excellent harbor views. Once on the other side, you can take a CityRail train from Milsons Point train station back to the city (to Wynyard, Town Hall, or Central stations).

As you walk across the bridge, you should stop off at the **Pylon Lookout** (☎ **02/9247 3408**), located at the southeastern pylon. From the top of this bridge support, you are 89 meters (591 ft.) above the water and get excellent views of Sydney Harbour, the ferry terminals of Circular Quay, and beyond. An interesting museum here charts the building of the bridge. Approach the pylon by walking to the far end of George Street in The Rocks, toward the Harbour Bridge. Just past the Mercantile Pub on your left you'll see some stone steps, which bring you onto Cumberland Street. From there, it's a two-minute walk to the steps underneath the bridge on your right. Climb four flights of stairs to reach the bridge's Western Footway, then walk along to the first pylon. *Note:* Climbing up inside the pylon involves 200 steps. Admission to the pylon is A$2 (U.S.$1.40) adults, and A$1 (U.S.70¢) children. It's open daily from 10am to 5pm (closed Christmas Day).

Once, only bridge workers employed in the full-time job of painting the Harbour Bridge had the opportunity to view Sydney from the top of the main bridge arch. But since October 1998, Sydneysiders and tourists have been able to experience the spectacular view and the exhilarating achievement of climbing to the top of one of Australia's icons. The experience takes three hours from check-in at the **BridgeClimb** base at 5 Cumberland Street, The Rocks (☎ **02/9250 0077;** fax 02/9240 1122; e-mail: admin@bridgeclimb.com), to the completion of the climb. The office is open from 8am to 6pm daily, and climbers leave in groups of 10 every 20 minutes or so. Climbers wear specially designed "Bridge Suits" and are harnessed to a static line. Climbers are also breath-tested, and are banned from carrying anything, including cameras or video recorders. Tickets cost A$98 (U.S.$68.60) adults, and A$79 (U.S.$55.30) children 12 to 16; children under 12 are not allowed to climb.

---

special. It's entered through the Heads, two bush-topped outcrops (you'll see them if you take a ferry or JetCat to Manly), beyond which the harbor laps at some 240 kilometers (144 miles) of shoreline before stretching itself out into the Parramatta River. Visitors are often awestruck by its beauty, especially at night when the sails of the Opera House and the girders of the Harbour Bridge are lit up and the waters swirl with the reflection of lights from the abutting high-rises—reds, greens, blues, yellows, and oranges.

During the day the harbor buzzes with green-and-yellow ferries pulling in and out of busy Circular Quay, sleek tourist craft, tall ships, giant container vessels making their way to and from the wharves of Darling Harbour, and hundreds of white-sailed yachts. The greenery along its edges, perhaps a surprising feature, is thanks to the **Sydney Harbour National Park,** a haven for native trees and plants, and a feeding and breeding ground for lorikeets and nectar-eating bird life. In the center of the

The Harbour on the Cheap

The best way to see the harbor, of course, is from the water. Several companies operate tourist craft for fare-paying customers (see "Organized Tours" later in this chapter), but it's easy enough just to hop on a regular passenger ferry (one-way tickets are just $A3.20/U.S.$2.25; see "Getting Around" in chapter 4). The best ferry excursions are over to the beachside suburb of **Manly** (come back after dusk to see the lights ablaze around The Rocks and Circular Quay); to **Watsons Bay,** where you can have lunch and wander along the cliffs; to **Darling Harbour,** for all the area's entertainment and the fact that you travel right under the Harbour Bridge; and to **Mosman,** just for the ride and to see the grand houses overlooking exclusive harbor inlets.

harbor is a series of islands, the most impressive being the tiny isle supporting **Fort Denison,** which once housed convicts and acted as part of the city's defense.

2 Attractions at Darling Harbour

Many tourists head to Darling Harbour for the **Harbourside Festival Marketplace,** a huge structure beside the Pyrmont pedestrian and monorail bridge, which is crammed full of cheap eateries and a few interesting shops. Sydney's main tourist precinct has a lot more to offer, however.

✪ **Australian National Maritime Museum.** Darling Harbour. ☎ **02/9552 7777.** Admission A$9 (U.S.$6.30) adults, A$4.50 (U.S.$3.15) children, A$19.50 (U.S.$13.65) family. Daily 9:30am–5pm (to 6:30pm in Jan). Monorail: Harbourside. Sydney Explorer bus: Stop 18. Ferry: Darling Harbour.

Modern Australia owes almost everything to the sea, so it's not surprising that there's a museum dedicated to the ships that overcame the tyranny of the waves, from Aboriginal vessels to submarines. Here you'll also find ships' logs, all sorts of things to pull and tug, as well as the Americas Cup–winning vessel *Australia II.* Docked outside is an Australian Naval Destroyer, *The Vampire,* which you can clamber all over, and an Oberon Class submarine. Two fully rigged tall ships will be installed in 1999. Allow at least two hours.

Chinese Garden. Darling Harbour (adjacent to the Entertainment Centre). ☎ **02/ 9281 6863.** A$4 (U.S.$2.80) adults, A$2 (U.S.$1.40) children, A$10 (U.S.$7) family. Daily 9:30am–dusk. Monorail: Convention. Sydney Explorer bus: Stop 19. Ferry: Darling Harbour.

The largest Chinese garden of its type outside China offers a pleasant escape from city concrete. It was designed by expert gardeners from China's Guangdong Province to embody principles of garden design dating back to the 5th century.

A Super Deal

Here's a good sightseeing deal for you: For A$29.90 (U.S.$20.95) adults and A$19.90 (U.S.$13.95) children 3 to 15, the Super Ticket gives you a ride on the monorail, entry to both the Sydney Aquarium and the Chinese Garden, a 2-hour cruise on the Matilda Harbour Express, a meal at the Sydney Aquarium cafe, and discounts on a coach tour of the site of the Sydney 2000 Olympic Games at Homebush Bay. Tickets are available at monorail stations, the Sydney Aquarium, and Darling Harbour information booths.

It takes
hard work
and dedication to get to
Sydney,

but it's
no
sweat
getting home.

It's all within your reach.

The Aquarium Link

The Aquarium Link ticket, available from CityRail train stations, is a combi 'd rail and Aquarium ticket that also includes a ferry ride on the harbor. It costs A. 5.90 (U.S.$11.15) for adults, A$8.20 (U.S.$5.75) for children, and A$42 (U.S.$2 50) for a family.

Panasonic IMAX Theatre. Southern Promenade, Darling Harbour. ☎ **02/9281 330**
Admission A$13.95 (U.S.$9.75) adults, A$9.95 (U.S.$6.95) children 3–15, A$42.95 (U.S.$30, family. Sun–Thurs 9:45am–10pm, Fri–Sat 9:45am–11:30pm. Monorail: Convention. Sydney Explorer bus: Stop 20. Ferry: Darling Harbour.

Four IMAX films, each lasting around 50 minutes, are usually showing on the gigantic eight-story-high screen. As you watch, your mind is tricked into feeling it's right in the heart of the action (that drop from the rooftop onto the street below looks realistically dangerous).

Powerhouse Museum. 500 Harris St., Ultimo (near Darling Harbour). ☎ **02/9217 0111.** Admission A$8 (U.S.$5.60) adults, A$2 (U.S.$1.40) children, A$18 (U.S.$12.60) family. Free admission first Sat of every month. Daily 10am–5pm. Monorail: Harbourside. Sydney Explorer bus: Stop 17. Ferry: Darling Harbour.

Sydney's most interactive museum is also one of the Southern Hemisphere's largest. Inside the postmodern industrial interior you'll find all sorts of displays and gadgets relating to the sciences, transportation, human achievement, decorative art, and social history. The many hands-on exhibits make this fascinating museum worthy of a couple of hours of your time.

Sega World. Darling Harbour (between IMAX Theatre and Chinese Garden). ☎ **02/ 9273 9273.** www.segaworld.com.au. Admission Mon–Fri A$22 (U.S.$15.40) adults, A$15 (U.S.$10.50) children; Sat–Sun A$25 (U.S.$17.50) adults, A$20 (U.S.$14) children. Entry includes all rides. Mon–Fri 11am–10pm, Sat–Sun 10am–10pm. Monorail: Convention. Ferry: Darling Harbour.

If you fancy a few hours' break from the kids, if you're just a big kid yourself, or if it's raining outside, then try out this indoor theme park. Simulators, 3-D rides, computer games and the like are fun (but occasionally a little limp). It's good for a couple of hours. Avoid the huge queues on Friday nights and weekends.

✪ **Sydney Aquarium.** Aquarium Pier, Darling Harbour. ☎ **02/9262 2300.** Admission A$15.90 (U.S.$11.15) adults, A$8 (U.S.$5.60) children. Daily 9:30am–10pm. Seal Sanctuary closes at 7pm in summer. CityRail: Town Hall. Sydney Explorer bus: Stop 20. Ferry: Darling Harbour.

This is one of the world's best aquariums and should be near the top of any Sydney itinerary. The main attractions are the underwater walkways, especially one containing giant rays and enormous gray nurse sharks. Other excellent exhibits include a giant Plexiglas room suspended inside a pool patrolled by rescued seals, and good displays of fish from the Great Barrier Reef. To avoid the crowds, try to visit during the week.

3 Other Top Attractions: A Spectacular View, Sydney's Convict History & More

AMP Centerpoint Tower. Pitt and Market sts. ☎ **02/9229 7444.** Admission A$10 (U.S.$7) adults, A$4.50 (U.S.$3.15) children. Sun–Fri 9am–10:30pm, Sat 9am–11:30pm. CityRail: St. James or Town Hall. Sydney Explorer bus: Stop 14.

Travel Tip

For attractions beyond central Sydney, refer to the "Greater Sydney" map in chapter 4, "Settling into Sydney."

The tallest building in the Southern Hemisphere is not hard to miss—it resembles a giant steel pole skewering a golden marshmallow. Standing more than 300 meters (1,860 ft.) tall, it offers stupendous 360° views across Sydney and as far as the Blue Mountains. Fortunately, an elevator takes you to the indoor viewing platform. Don't be too concerned if you feel the building tremble slightly, especially in a stiff breeze—I'm told it's perfectly natural. Below the tower are three floors of stores and restaurants. The giant figures on top of the tower are temporary constructions celebrating the Sydney 2000 Olympic Games.

Hyde Park Barracks Museum. Queens Square, Macquarie St. ☎ **02/9223 8922.** Admission A$6 (U.S.$4.20) adults, A$3 (U.S.$2.10) children, A$15 (U.S.$10.50) family. Daily 9:30–5pm. CityRail: St. James or Martin Place. Sydney Explorer bus: Stop 4.

These Georgian-style barracks were designed in 1819 by the convict architect Francis Greenway. They were built by convicts and inhabited by fellow prisoners. These days they house interesting, modern displays of relics from those early days, including log books, early settlement artifacts, and a room full of ships' hammocks in which visitors can lie and listen to fragments of prisoner conversation. If you are interested in Sydney's early days, then I highly recommend a visit. The courtyard cafe is excellent.

Museum of Contemporary Art (MCA). 140 George St., Circular Quay West. ☎ **02/9252 4033.** Admission A$9 (U.S.$7.60) adults, A$6 (U.S.$4.20) children, A$18 (U.S.$12.60) family. Daily 10am–6pm (5pm in winter). CityRail, bus, or ferry: Circular Quay. Sydney Explorer bus: Stop 1.

This imposing sandstone museum set back from the water on The Rocks–side of Circular Quay offers wacky, entertaining, inspiring, and befuddling displays of what's new (and dated) in modern art. It houses the J. W. Power Collection of more than 4,000 pieces, including works by Andy Warhol, Christo, Marcel Duchamp, and Robert Rauschenberg, as well as temporary exhibits. Guided tours are offered Monday through Saturday at noon and 2pm, and Sunday at 2pm.

Gledswood Homestead. Camden Valley Way, Catherine Field. ☎ **02/9606 5111.** Fax 02/9606 5897. Farm activities A$12 (U.S.$8.40) adults, A$6 (U.S.$4.20) children, A$20 (U.S.$14) family. Homestead tour A$6 (U.S.$4.20) adults, A$4.50 (U.S.$3.15) children. Horseback riding A$16 (U.S.$11.20) for 30 min. Daily 10am–4pm. Several tour operators offer trips from Sydney. By car: M5 to Camden Valley Way (Exit 89), an hour from Sydney. CityRail: Campbelltown station, then transfer to local Busways service 891 from outside station (20-minute trip).

Tour the Sydney 2000 Olympic Site

A tour of the best Olympic swimming complex in the world, as well as the athletic center where Olympic athletes will train, is fast becoming an essential thing to do for any visitor to Sydney. Ninety-minute tours of the **Sydney International Aquatic and Athletic Centres** (☎ 02/9752 3666) in the Olympic Park in Homebush Bay are offered Monday through Friday at 10am, noon, and 2pm, and Saturday and Sunday at noon and 2pm. Tours cost A$14 (U.S.$9.80) adults, A$9 (U.S.$6.30) children, A$40 (U.S.$28) family. If you fancy putting in a few laps afterward, then be prepared to pay an additional A$4.50 (U.S.$3.15) for adults, and A$3.50 (U.S.$2.45) for children. Take the CityRail to Olympic Park.

Cheap Thrills: What to See & Do for Free (or Almost) in Sydney

- **Soak up some rays on the beach.** In the summer, or on a nice winter day, Sydney's beaches are always popular. You can get to most of them via an inexpensive train, bus, or ferry ride.
- **Walk across the Sydney Harbour Bridge.** If you want to do something a little more daring than sitting on the sand, the Harbour Bridge offers the stroll of a lifetime. See the box "A Bridge to Cross, Mate" in section 1 earlier in this chapter.
- **Stop & smell the roses.** If you want to escape the city fumes, then a stroll through the **Royal Botanic Gardens** is a must.
- **Get a dose of culture.** Check out the free galleries at the **Art Gallery of New South Wales** and the new **Customs House,** opposite the ferries in Circular Quay. The **Powerhouse Museum** in Darling Harbour is free on the first Saturday of every month. Free art exhibitions are often on display at the **New South Wales State Library.**
- **Listen to some tunes.** At lunchtime, check out the free bands at the **Martin Place amphitheater.** There's more free music at the **Conservatorium of Music,** beside the Royal Botanic Gardens, Wednesday through Friday. You also can enjoy free music in front of the **Sydney Opera House** on Sunday afternoons.
- **Watch the politicians in action.** See parliament sitting at the **New South Wales State Parliament** on Macquarie Street. Question time, starting at 2:15pm on Tuesdays, Wednesdays, and Thursdays, is the best time to visit, but you must book in advance. Free guided tours are available on nonsitting days at 10am, 11am, and 2pm. Bookings are essential, call ☎ **02/9230 2111.**

If you have a day to spare and want a good dose of rural Australia, then consider making the long trek to Gledswood, a sort of theme agricultural property set on 61.5 hectares (150 acres). You can try your hand at boomerang throwing, catch a sheep-shearing demonstration, learn how to crack a stockman's whip, watch working sheepdogs in action, and milk a cow. The homestead tour can be interesting if you're into colonial relics and architecture, and the gardens are nice (take a hat in summer). A hearty lunch and snacks are served by costumed staff in the restaurant. You can also sample billy tea and damper (bread made in the embers of a campfire).

✪ **Old Sydney Town.** Pacific Hwy., Somersby. ☎ **02/4340 1104.** Admission A$17 (U.S.$11.90) adults, A$10 (U.S.$7) children. Wed–Sun 10am–4pm; daily during school holidays. Somersby is near the town of Gosford, 84km (50½ miles) north of Sydney. By car, take Pacific Hwy and Sydney-Newcastle Freeway (F3) to Gosford—about 1 hr. CityRail: trains leave Central Station for Gosford every 30 min. From Gosford, take Old Sydney Town bus (15-min. ride).

On a nice day you can spend several hours wandering around this outdoor theme park bustling with actors dressed as convicts, sailors, and the like. You'll see plenty of stores, buildings, and ships from the old days of the colony, and performances are staged throughout the day. It's the Australian version of a American Wild West theme town.

Wonderland Sydney. Wallgrove Rd., Eastern Creek. ☎ **02/9830 9100.** Admission (includes all rides and entrance to Australian Wildlife Park) A$37 (U.S.$25.90) adults, A$26 (U.S.$18.20) children, A$115 (U.S.$80.50) family. Daily 10am–5pm. CityRail: Rooty Hill (trip time: less than an hour); Australia Wonderland bus: Rooty Hill every ½ -hr. weekends; at 8:55am, 9:32am, 10:10am, 11:35am, and 12:14pm weekdays.

If you're used to big Disneyesque extravaganzas, then this theme park (until recently called Australia's Wonderland) might be a bit of a disappointment—though I guarantee "The Demon" roller coaster will more than satisfy in the terror department. Other big rides are the heart-stopping Space Probe 7, and a cute and rattly wooden roller coaster called the Bush Beast. Live shows and bands round out the entertainment options. The entry ticket also includes admission to a reasonable wildlife park, with all the Aussie favorites—koalas, wombats, kangaroos, wallabies, and more.

4 Where to See 'Roos, Koalas & Other Aussie Wildlife

The world-class **Sydney Aquarium** is discussed in this chapter's section 2, "Attractions at Darling Harbour."

Australian Reptile Park. Pacific Hwy., Somersby. ☎ **02/4340 1022.** Admission A$10.95 (U.S.$7.70) adults, A$5.50 (U.S.$3.85) children. Daily 9am–5pm. Closed Christmas Day. Somersby is near Gosford, 84km (50½ miles) north of Sydney. By car: Pacific Hwy. and Sydney-Newcastle Freeway (F3) about 1 hr. to Gosford. CityRail: Central Station (trains leave for Gosford every 30 min.). From Gosford, take Australian Wildlife Park bus 10-min. ride).

What started as a one-man operation supplying deadly snake antivenom in the early 1950s is now a nature park teeming with the slippery-looking creatures. But it's not all snakes and lizards here. You'll also find Eric, a 15-foot-long saltwater crocodile; an alligator lagoon with some 50 American alligators; and plenty of somewhat cuddlier creatures, such as koalas, platypus, wallabies, dingoes, and flying foxes. The park is set in beautiful bushland dissected by nature trails.

✪ **Featherdale Wildlife Park.** 217 Kildare Rd., West Pennant Hills. ☎ **02/9622 1644.** Admission A$12 (U.S.$8.40) adults, A$6 (U.S.$4.20) children 4–14. Daily 9am–5pm. By car: M4 motorway to Reservoir Rd. turnoff, travel 4km (2½ miles), then turn left at Kildare Rd. CityRail: Blacktown station, then take bus 725 to park (ask driver to tell you where to get off).

If you have time to visit only one wildlife park in Sydney, make it this one. The selection of native Australian animals is excellent, and—most important—the animals are very well cared for. You could easily spend a couple of hours here despite the park's compact size. You'll have the chance to hand-feed friendly kangaroos and wallabies, and have your photo taken next to a koala (there are many here, both the New South Wales variety and the much larger Victorian type). **Tranquility Tours** (☎ 02/ **4736 7760;** fax 02/4736 1334) runs afternoon tours to Featherdale that include a 90-minute guided tour of the park, as well as a visit to Mananura (an Aboriginal cultural center at Penrith) and to the Penrith Olympic Rowing Site. Daily tours cost A$48 (U.S.$33.60) adults, and A$34 (U.S.$23.80) children 4–14.

Koala Park. 84 Castle Hill Rd., West Pennant Hills. ☎ **02/9484 3141,** or 02/9875 2777. Admission A$10 (U.S.$7) adults, A$5 (U.S.$3.50) children. Daily 9am–5pm. Closed Christmas Day. CityRail: Pennant Hills station via North Strathfield (45 min.), then take bus 651–655 to park.

Unless you want to go all the way to Kangaroo Island in South Australia, it's unlikely you're going to spot as many koalas in the trees as you can find here. In all, there are around 55 koalas roaming within the park's leafy boundaries. Koala-cuddling sessions are free, and take place daily at 10:20am, 11:45am, 2pm, and 3pm. There are also wombats, dingoes, kangaroos, wallabies, emus, and native birds here. You can hire a private guide to take you around for A$70 (U.S.$49) for a 2-hour session, or join one of the free "hostess" guides who wander around like Pied Pipers.

Oceanworld. West Esplanade, Manly. ☎ **02/9949 2644.** Admission A$14.50 (U.S.$10.15) adults, A$7.50 (U.S.$5.25) children, A$39 (U.S.$27.30) family. Daily 10am–5:30pm. Ferry or JetCat: Manly.

Though not as impressive as the Sydney Aquarium, Oceanworld can be combined with the wonderful Manly beach for a nice day's outing. There's a pretty good display of Great Barrier Reef fish, a pool of giant saltwater turtles, and yet more giant sharks. For added thrills, you can swim with the seals and dive with the sharks. Seal swims run daily and cost A$65 (U.S.$45.50) for 20 minutes. Daily shark dives cost A$75 (U.S.$52.50) for a 45-minute dive for qualified divers (bring your own gear, or rent it for A$30/U.S.$21), and A$115 (U.S.$80.50) for a 20-minute basic training dive for unqualified divers (price includes gear rental).

Taronga Zoo. Bradley's Head Rd., Mosman. ☎ **02/9969 2777.** Admission A$16 (U.S.$11.20) adults, A$8.50 (U.S.$5.95) children 4–15, and A$41.50 (U.S.$29.05) family. Zoopass (includes entry, round-trip ferry from Circular Quay, and Aerial Safari cable car ride from ferry terminal to upper entrance) A$21 (U.S.$14.70) adult, A$10.50 (U.S.$7.35) seniors and children. Daily 9am–5pm (January 9am–9pm). Ferry: Circular Quay.

Taronga has the best view of any zoo in the world. Set on a hill, it looks out over Sydney Harbour, the Opera House, and the Harbour Bridge. The main attractions here are the fabulous chimpanzee exhibit, the gorilla enclosure, and the Nocturnal Houses, where you can see some of Australia's many nighttime marsupials out and about, including the platypus and the cuter-than-cute bilby (the official Australian Easter bunny). There's an interesting reptile display, a couple of rather impressive Komodo dragons, a scattering of indigenous Australian beasties—including a few koalas, echidnas, kangaroos, dingoes, and wombats—and lots more. The kangaroo and wallaby exhibit is very unimaginative; you'd be better off going to Featherdale Wildlife Park (see above) for happier-looking animals. Animals are fed at various times during the day. To avoid the big weekend crowds, visit during the week or go very early in the morning on weekends. Interestingly, the three sun bears near the lower ferry entrance/exit were rescued by an Australian businessman, John Stephens, from a restaurant in Cambodia, where they were to have their paws cut off one by one and served up as an expensive soup.

5 Hitting the Beach

One of the big bonuses of visiting Sydney in the summer months (December, January, and February) is that you get to experience the beaches in their full glory.

SOUTH OF SYDNEY HARBOUR   Sydney's most famous beach is **Bondi.** In many ways it's a raffish version of a Californian beach, with plenty of tanned skin and in-line skaters. Though the beach is nice, it's cut off from the cafe and restaurant strip by a big, ugly road that pedestrians have to funnel across in order to reach the sand. To reach Bondi Beach, take the CityRail train from the city to Bondi Junction, then transfer to bus number 380. Or catch the 380 bus directly from Circular Quay.

Sharks?

One of the first things visitors wonder when they hit the water is, "Are there sharks?" The answer is yes, but fortunately they are rarely spotted inshore. In reality, sharks have more reason to be scared of us than we of them, as most of them end up as the fish portion in your average packet of fish-and-chips (you might see shark fillets sold as "flake"). Some beaches, such as the small beach next to the Manly ferry wharf in Manly and a section of Balmoral Beach, have permanent shark nets, but most rely on portable nets that are moved periodically from beach to beach to prevent territorial sharks from setting up home alongside bathers.

Grin & Bare It

If getting an all-over tan is your scene, then head for the nudist beaches of **Lady Jane Bay,** a short walk from Camp Cove beach (accessed from Cliff Street, Watsons Bay), or **Cobblers Beach,** which is accessed via a short but steep bush track on the far side of the playing field oval next to the main HMAS Penguin naval base at the end of Bradley's Head Road, Mosman. Be prepared for a largely male-oriented scene—as well as the odd boatload of beer-swigging Peeping Toms.

If you follow the water along to your right, you'll come to a scenic **cliff-top track** that takes you to **Bronte** Beach (a 20-minute walk) via gorgeous little **Tamarama,** a boutique beach known for its dangerous rips. Bronte has better swimming. To get to Bronte, catch bus 378 from Circular Quay, or pick up the bus at the Bondi Junction CityRail station.

Clovelly Beach, farther along the coast, is blessed with a large rock pool carved into a rock platform and sheltered from the force of the Tasman Sea. This beach is accessible for visitors in wheelchairs, via a series of ramps. To reach Clovelly, take bus 339 from Circular Quay.

The cliff walk from Bondi will eventually bring you to **Coogee,** which has a pleasant strip of sand with a couple of hostels and hotels nearby. To reach Coogee, take bus 373 or 374 from Circular Quay (via Pitt, George, and Castlereagh streets, and Taylor Square on Oxford Street) or bus 314 or 315 from Bondi Junction.

NORTH OF SYDNEY HARBOUR   On the north shore you'll find **Manly,** a long curve of golden sand edged with Norfolk Island Pines (don't be fooled by the small beaches alongside the ferry terminal—some people have been!). To reach the beach, walk straight ahead from the ferry terminal, cross the road, and follow the crowds straight through The Corso shopping area; the walk is less then five minutes. Once at Manly Beach, you can follow the beachfront along to your right; it will lead you to the small and sheltered **Shelly Beach,** one of Sydney's best. Above the beach, and a parking lot, a path cuts into the Sydney Harbour National Park, where there are some spectacular coastal views. The best way to reach Manly is by ferry or JetCat from Circular Quay (see "Getting Around" in chapter 4).

Farther along the north coast are a string of ocean beaches, including the surf spots of **Curl Curl**, **Dee Why**, **Narrabeen**, **Mona Vale**, **Newport**, **Avalon,** and finally ✪ **Palm Beach,** a very long and beautiful strip of sand. Here you'll also find the **Barrenjoey Lighthouse,** which offers fine views along the coast. Buses 136 and 139 run from Manly to Curl Curl, while bus L90 runs from Wynyard to Newport and to the other northern beaches as far as Palm Beach. There's no direct bus from Manly to Palm Beach, although you can take bus 132, 155, 156, or 169 to Warringah Mall (ask the drive to tell you when to get off) and catch the L90 from there.

INSIDE SYDNEY HARBOUR   The best harbor beach is at **Balmoral,** a wealthy North Shore hangout complete with its own little island, some excellent cafes, and an upscale restaurant. The beach itself is split into three separate parts. As you look toward the sea, the middle section is the most popular with sunbathers, while the wide expanse of sand to your left and the sweep of surreally beautiful sand to your right have a mere scattering of people. Reach Balmoral via a ferry to Taronga Zoo and then a 5-minute ride on a connecting bus from the ferry wharf.

6 Historic Houses

Elizabeth Bay House. 7 Onslow Ave., Elizabeth Bay. ☎ **02/9356 3022.** Admission A$6 (U.S.$4.20) adults, A$3 (U.S.$2.10) children, A$15 (U.S.$10.50) family. Tues–Sun 10am–4:30pm. Closed Good Friday and Christmas. Bus: 311 from Circular Quay. Sydney Explorer bus: Stop 10.

This magnificent example of colonial architecture was built in 1835 and described at the time as the "finest house in the colony." Visitors can tour the whole house and get a real feel for the history of the fledgling settlement. The house is situated on a headland and has some of the best harbor views in Sydney.

Vaucluse House. Wentworth Rd., Vaucluse. ☎ **02/9337 1957.** Admission A$6 (U.S.$4.20) adults, A$3 (U.S.$2.10) children, A$15 (U.S.$10.50) family. House Tues–Sun 10am–4:30pm. Grounds daily 7am–5pm. Free guided tours. Closed Good Friday and Christmas. Bus: 325 from Circular Quay.

Also overlooking Sydney Harbour, this house includes lavish entertainment rooms and impressive stables and outbuildings. Built in 1803, it was later the home of Charles Wentworth, the architect of the Australian Constitution. It's set in 27 acres of gardens, bushland, and beach frontage—perfect for picnics.

7 Museums & Galleries

Art Gallery of New South Wales. Art Gallery Rd., The Domain. ☎ **02/9225 1744.** Free admission to most galleries. Special exhibitions vary, but expect about A$12 (U.S.$8.40) adults, A$7 (U.S.$4.90) children. Daily 10am–5pm. Tours of general exhibits Tues–Fri 11am, noon, 1pm, and 2pm. Call for weekend times. Tours of Aboriginal galleries Tues–Fri 11am. Free Aboriginal performance Tues–Sat at noon. CityRail: St. James. Sydney Explorer bus: Stop 6.

The numerous galleries here present some of the best of Australian art and many fine examples by international artists, including good displays of Aboriginal and Asian art. You enter the museum on the third floor, from The Domain parklands. On the fourth floor is an expensive restaurant and a gallery that often shows free photography displays. On the second floor is a wonderful cafe that overlooks the wharves and warships of Wooloomooloo. Every January and February there is a fabulous display of the best work created by school students throughout the state.

Australian Museum. 6 College St. ☎ **02/9320 6000.** Admission A$5 (U.S.$3.50) adults, A$2 (U.S.$1.40) children, A$12 (U.S.$8.40) family. Special exhibits cost extra. Daily 9:30am– 5pm. Closed Christmas Day. CityRail: Museum, St. James, or Town Hall. Sydney Explorer bus: Stop 15.

Although nowhere near as impressive as, say, the Natural History Museum in London, or similar museums in Washington or New York, Sydney's premier natural history museum still ranks in the top five of its kind in the world. Displays are presented thematically, the best of them being the Aboriginal section with its traditional clothing, weapons, and everyday implements. There are some sorry examples of stuffed Australian wildlife, too. Temporary exhibits run from time to time.

Customs House. Alfred St., Circular Quay. ☎ **02/9320 6429.** Free general admission. Admission to Djamu Gallery A$8 (U.S.$5.60) adults, A$2 (U.S.$1.40) children. Daily 9:30am–5pm. CityRail, bus, or ferry: Circular Quay.

This new museum, across the large square opposite the Circular Quay CityRail station and the ferry wharves, opened in December 1998. It's worthwhile looking inside just for the stunning architecture, and once inside I'm sure you'll be hooked on the interesting series of modern art objects on display on the ground floor, and the traveling exhibits on the third floor (the history of chairs was the big thing in early 1999). The

Djamu Gallery, on the second floor, has four small rooms of Aboriginal and South Pacific items—overspill from the Australian Museum. It's very interesting, albeit expensive at the present price (which is likely to have fallen by the time you visit). Outside in the square an interesting-looking cafe sells coffees, cakes, sandwiches, foccacias, and the like at reasonable prices.

Museum of Sydney. 37 Phillip St. ☎ **02/9251 5988.** Admission A$6 (U.S.$4.20) adults, A$3 (U.S.$2.10) children under 15, A$15 (U.S.$10.50) family. Daily 9:30am–5pm. CityRail, bus, or ferry: Circular Quay. Sydney Explorer bus: Stop 3.

You'll need your brain in full working order to make the best of the contents of this three-story postmodern building, which encompasses the remnants of Sydney's first Government House. This place is far from being a conventional showcase of history; instead, it's a rather minimalist collection of first-settler and Aboriginal objects and multimedia displays that invite museumgoers to discover Sydney's past for themselves. By the way, that forest of poles filled with hair, oyster shells, and crab claws in the courtyard adjacent to the industrial-design cafe tables, is called *Edge of Trees*. It's a metaphor for the first contact between Aborigines and the British.

State Library of NSW. Macquarie St. ☎ **02/9273 1414.** Free admission. Mon–Fri 9am–9pm; Sat, Sun, and selected holidays 11am–5pm. Closed New Year's Day, Good Friday, Christmas, and Boxing Day (Dec 26). CityRail: Martin Place. Sydney Explorer bus: Stop 4.

The state's main library is divided into two sections, located next door to one another. The newer reference library complex has two floors of reference materials, local newspapers, and microfiche viewers. Leave your bags in free lockers downstairs. If you are over in this area of town at lunchtime, I highly recommend the library's leafy Glasshouse Café, one of the best lunch spots in Sydney. The older building contains many older and more valuable books on the ground floor, and often hosts free art and photography displays in the upstairs galleries. A small library section in the Sydney Town Hall building has international newspapers.

Sydney Jewish Museum. 148 Darlinghurst Rd. (at Burton St.), Darlinghurst. ☎ **02/ 9360 7999.** Admission A$6 (U.S.$4.20) adults, A$3 (U.S.$2.10) children, A$15 (U.S.$10.50) family. Mon–Thurs 10am–4pm; Fri 10am–2pm; Sun 11am–5pm. Closed Jewish holidays, Christmas Day, and Good Friday. CityRail: Kings Cross.

Harrowing exhibits here include documents and objects relating to the Holocaust and to Jewish culture, mixed with soundscapes, audiovisual displays, and interactive media. There's also a museum shop, a resource center, a theatrette, and a traditional kosher cafe. It's considered to be one of the best museums of its type in the world.

Sydney Observatory. Observatory Hill, Watson Rd., Millers Point. ☎ **02/9217 0485.** Free admission in daytime; guided night tours (reservations essential), A$8 (U.S.$5.60) adults, A$3 (U.S.$2.10) children, and A$18 (U.S.$12.60) family. Daily 10am–5pm. CityRail, bus, or ferry: Circular Quay.

The city's only major museum of astronomy offers visitors a chance to see the southern skies through modern and historic telescopes. The best time to visit is during the night on a guided tour, when you can take a close-up look at some of the planets. A planetarium and a hands-on exhibition are also interesting.

8 Parks & Gardens

IN SYDNEY

ROYAL BOTANIC GARDENS   If you are going to spend time in one of Sydney's green spaces, then make it the Royal Botanic Gardens (☎ 02/9231 8111), next to Sydney Opera House. The gardens were laid out in 1816 on the site of a farm dedicated to supplying food for the fledgling colony. It's informal in appearance with a scattering of duck ponds and open spaces, although there are several areas dedicated to particular plant species, such as the rose garden, the cacti and succulent display, and the central palm and the rain forest groves. Also interesting is the pyramidal **Tropical Centre**—admission is A$5 (U.S.$3.50) for adults, A$2 (U.S.$1.40) for children, and A$12 (U.S.$8.40) per family—and the **fernery** (which is free). **Mrs. Macquarie's Chair,** along the coast path, offers superb views of the Opera House and Harbour Bridge (it's a favorite stop for bus tours). The giant sandstone building dominating the gardens nearest to the Opera House is **Government House,** which was once the official residence of the Governor of New South Wales (he moved out in 1996 in the spirit of republicanism). The pleasant Government House gardens are open daily from 10am to 4pm, and Government House is open Friday to Sunday from 10am to 3pm. Entrance to both is free. If you plan to park around here, note that parking meters cost upward of A$3 (U.S.$2.10) per hour.

A popular walk takes you through the Royal Botanic Gardens to the **Art Gallery of New South Wales** (see above). The Botanic Gardens are open daily from 6:30am to dusk. Admission is free.

HYDE PARK   In the center of the city is Hyde Park, a favorite with lunching businesspeople. Of note here are the **ANZAC Memorial** to Australian and New Zealand troops killed in the wars, and the **Archibald Fountain,** complete with spitting turtles and sculptures of Diana and Apollo. At night, avenues of trees are festooned with fairy lights, giving the place a magical appearance.

MORE CITY PARKS   Another Sydney favorite is the giant **Centennial Park** (☎ 02/9339 6699), usually accessed from the top of Oxford Street. It was opened in 1888 to celebrate the centenary of European settlement, and today encompasses huge areas of lawn, several lakes, picnic areas with outdoor grills, cycling and running paths, and a cafe. It's open from sunrise to sunset. To get there, take bus 373, 374, 377, 380, 396, or 398 from the city.

A hundred years later, **Bicentennial Park,** at Australia Avenue in Homebush Bay, came along. Forty percent of the park's total 100 hectares (247 acres) is general parkland reclaimed from a city rubbish heap; the rest is the largest remaining piece of wetlands on the Parramatta River and home to many species of both local and migratory wading birds, cormorants, and pelicans. At 1:30pm Monday through Friday, a tractor train takes visitors around the park on a 1- to 1½-hour guided trip. It costs A$6 (U.S.$4.20) per person. Follow park signs to the visitor information office (☎ 02/ 9763 1844), open Monday through Friday 10am to 4pm, and Saturday and Sunday 9:30am to 4:30pm. To reach the park, you can either take a CityRail train to Strathfield and then take bus 401 to Homebush Bay (ask the driver when to get off), or take a CityRail train directly to the Homebush CityRail station.

BEYOND SYDNEY

SYDNEY HARBOUR NATIONAL PARK   You don't need to go far to experience Sydney's nearest national park—the Sydney Harbour National Park stretches around parts of the inner harbor and includes several small harbor islands (many first-time visitors are surprised at the amount of bushland still remaining in prime real estate territory). The best walk through the Sydney Harbour National Park is the **Manly to Spit Bridge Scenic Walkway** (☎ 02/9977 6522). This 10-kilometer (6-mile) track winds its way from Manly (it starts near the Oceanarium), via Dobroyd Head, to Spit Bridge (where you can catch a bus back to the city). The walk takes between 3 and 4 hours, and the views across busy Sydney Harbour are fabulous. Maps are available from the **Manly Visitors Information Bureau** (☎ 02/9977 1088), right opposite the main beach.

Other access points include tracks around Taronga Zoo (ask zoo staff to point you toward the rather concealed entrances) and above tiny Shelly Beach, opposite the main beach at Manly. Also part of the national park is **Fort Denison,** the easily recognizable fortified outcrop in the middle of the harbor between Circular Quay and Manly. The fort was built during the Crimean War in the midst of fears of a Russian invasion, and later served as a penal colony. Restoration work is due to be completed by mid-1999. One- to two-hour **Heritage Tours** of the island leave from Cadman's Cottage (☎ 02/9247 5033), on The Rocks foreshore Saturday at 2pm and Sunday at noon and 2pm. Tours cost A$12 (U.S.$8.40) for adults, A$8 (U.S.$5.60) for children, and A$32 (U.S.$22.40) for a family of four. Sunset Tours leave at 5:30pm on Thursday and Friday, and 6pm on Saturday; they cost A$14 (U.S.$9.80) for adults, A$11 (U.S.$7.70) for children, and A$41 (U.S.$28.70) for a family. Pick up maps of Sydney Harbour National Park at Cadman's Cottage.

MORE NATIONAL PARKS   Forming a semicircle around the city are Sydney's biggest parks of all. To the west is the **Blue Mountains National Park** (see chapter 6), to the northeast is **Ku-ring-gai Chase National Park,** and to the south is the magnificent **Royal National Park.** All three are home to marsupials such as echidnas and wallabies, numerous bird and reptile species, and a broad range of native plant life. Walking tracks, whether they stretch for half an hour or a few days, make each park accessible to the visitor.

Ku-ring-gai Chase National Park (☎ 02/9457 9322, or 02/ 9457 9310), is a great place for a bushwalk through gum trees and rain forest, on the lookout for wildflowers, sandstone rock formations, and Aboriginal art. There are plenty of tracks throughout the park, but one of my favorites is a relatively easy 2.5km (1½ miles) tramp to **the Basin** (Track 12). The well-graded dirt path takes you down to a popular estuary with a beach and passes some significant Aboriginal engravings. It also offers some wonderful water views over Pittwater from the picnic areas at West Head. Pick up a free walking guide at the park entrance, or gather maps and information in Sydney at the **National Parks & Wildlife Service's** center at Cadman's Cottage, 110 George St., The Rocks (☎ 02/9247 8861).

The park is open from sunrise to sunset, and admission is A$9 (U.S.$6.30) per car. You can either drive to the park or use the **Palm Beach Ferry Service** (☎ 02/ 9918 2747) from Palm Beach to McMasters Beach or the Basin (both inside the park). Ferries run on the hour (except at 1pm) from 9am to 5pm daily and cost A$7 (U.S.$4.90) one way. **Shorelink** (☎ 02/9457 8888) bus 577 runs between the Turramurra CityRail station and the park entrance every hour on weekdays and every two hours on weekends; there's no train service directly to the park. To drive to the park, head north from the city center over the Harbour Bridge, and follow the signs toward Manly. After crossing the Spit Bridge, take the first left onto Sydney Road and follow the signs to French's Forest along the Wakehurst Parkway. Turn left at Warringah Road, then right onto Forest Way, and then right at Mona Vale Road. Then turn left into McCarrs Creek Road and follow the signs to West Head.

Camping is allowed only at the Basin (☎ 02/9457 9853) and costs A$10 (U.S.$7) for two people, booked in advance.

While in the area you could visit the **Ku-ring-gai Wildflower Garden,** 420 Mona Vale Rd., St. Ives (☎ 02/9440 8609), a huge area of natural bushland and a center for urban bushland education. There are plenty of bushwalking tracks, self-guided walks, and a number of nature-based activities. It's open daily from 8am to 4pm. Admission is A$2.50 (U.S.$1.75) for adults, A$1 (U.S.70¢) for children, and A$6 (U.S.$4.20) for a family.

Bushwalking Safety Tips

Bushwalking (hiking) in Australia can be a tough business. You'll need to take plenty of water, a hat, sunscreen, and an insect repellent to ward off the flies in summer. And it's always wise to tell someone where you're going.

To the south of Sydney is the remarkable **Royal National Park,** Farrell Ave., Sutherland (☎ **02/9542 0648**). It's the world's oldest national park, having been gazetted as such in 1879 (the main competitor to the title is Yellowstone in the United States, which was established in 1872 but not designated as a National Park until 1883). Severe bush fires almost totally destroyed the whole lot in early 1994, but the trees and bush plants have recovered remarkably. There's no visitor center, but you can pick up park information at park entrances, where you'll have to pay an entry fee of A$9 (U.S.$6.30) per car.

There are several ways to access the park, but my favorites are the little-known access points from Bundeena and Otford. To get to Bundeena, take a CityRail train from Central Station to Cronulla. Just below the train station you'll find Cronulla Wharf. From there, hop on the delightful ferry run by **National Park Ferries** (☎ **02/9523 2990**) to Bundeena; it runs hourly on the half hour (except 12:30pm). After you get off the ferry, the first turn on your left just up the hill will take you to Bundeena Beach. It's another 5 kilometers (3 miles) or so to the wonderfully remote Little Marley Beach, via Marley Beach (which has dangerous surf). The ferry returns to Cronulla from Bundeena hourly on the hour (except 1pm). The fare is A$2.40 (U.S.$1.70) one way. It takes about an hour to reach the park by car or train. You could easily spend an entire day here bushwalking.

An alternative way to reach the park is take the train from Central Station (or drive) to Otford, then climb the hill up to the sea cliffs. If you're driving, you might want to follow the scenic cliff-edge road down into Wollongong (see "Wollongong" later in this chapter). The entrance to the national park is a little tricky to find, so you may have to ask directions. A fabulous walk from here takes you for 2 hours down to Burning Palms beach. There is no water along the route. The walk back up is steep, so only attempt this trek if you're reasonably fit.

Trains to the area are irregular, and the last one departs around 4pm, so give yourself at least 2½ hours for the return trip to the station to make sure you don't get stranded. It's possible to walk the 26 kilometers (15½ miles) from Otford to Bundeena, or vice versa, in 2 days (take all your food, water, and camping gear).

9 Especially for Kids

There are plenty of places kids can have fun in Sydney, but the recommendations below are particularly suitable for youngsters (all of the places are reviewed in full earlier in this chapter).

Taronga Zoo (see p. 155) is an all-time favorite with kids, and the barnyard animals, surprisingly, get as much attention as the koalas. If your kids want hands-on contact with the animals, though, you'd better head to **Featherdale Wildlife Park** (see p. 154), where they can get their photo taken next to a koala, and hand-feed and stroke kangaroos and wallabies.

Sega World (see p. 151) in Darling Harbour will no doubt entertain kids for a few hours, but the trouble is—adults can't resist the rides, either. Just as interactive are the exhibits just crying out to be touched and bashed at the **Powerhouse Museum** (see p. 151).

The sharks at **Oceanworld** (see p. 154) in Manly and at the **Sydney Aquarium** (see p. 151) in Darling Harbour are a big lure for kids, too. The thrill of walking through a long Plexiglas tunnel as giant manta rays glide overhead will lead to squeals of excitement.

Another fascinating outing for both adults and children is to crawl around inside a navy destroyer at the **National Maritime Museum** (see p. 150)—if you're lucky, there may even be a submarine to explore.

And, of course, what kid wouldn't enjoy a day at the **beach?** Sydney's got plenty to choose from, like Bondi or Manly.

10 A Stroll through The Rocks

Sydney is relatively compact, so it's a wonderful city to explore on foot. The first walk I outline, through The Rocks, is pretty much a must-do for any visitor to Sydney. The second stroll, down George, Pitt, and Macquarie streets, provides a good mix of history and shopping.

WALKING TOUR
On The Rocks

Start: The Rocks Visitor Centre and Exhibition Gallery, 106 George St.
Finish: George Street.
Time: Allow around one hour; longer if you stop off to shop.
Best time: Any day, though Saturday brings The Rocks Market and big crowds on George Street.

The Rocks is the site of the oldest settlement in Australia. Initially, convict-built timber houses lined the rocky ridge that gave the area its name, and dockyard buildings lined the water's edge. In the 1840s a range of more permanent stone buildings was erected, including most of the pubs and shops still standing today. Slums grew up, too, and when the bubonic plague came to Sydney in 1900, the government set about demolishing most of the shanties. Between 1923 and 1932 many of the historic stone cottages in the area were pulled down to make way for construction of the Harbour Bridge. In the 1970s the government decided to pull the lot down and replace them with giant "international" office blocks and a hotel. Local residents resisted, though, and following a 2-year "Green Ban" by the Builders' Labourers Federation, during which they refused to touch any historic building, the government relented and the historic area was preserved.

Start your walk at:
1. **The Sydney Visitor Centre,** 106 George St., The Rocks (☎ **02/9255 1788**), open daily from 9am to 6pm. This excellent visitor center has not only plenty of information on Sydney, but also a whole range of Australiana books. Upstairs, on two levels, is a fascinating gallery of photographs, explanatory texts, an audiovisual presentation, and objects relating to The Rocks. The building itself is part of the former Sydney Sailors' Home, built in the 1860s.

   Outside on George Street, turn left, then turn left again at the first small avenue you come to. Walking down toward the water you'll see:
2. **Cadman's Cottage,** built in 1816. This small white building was the headquarters of the government body that regulated the colony's waterways. It's named after John Cadman, a pardoned convict who became the government coxswain, and who lived here from 1827 to 1846. It's interesting to note that before a land reclamation scheme, the water once lapped at its front door.

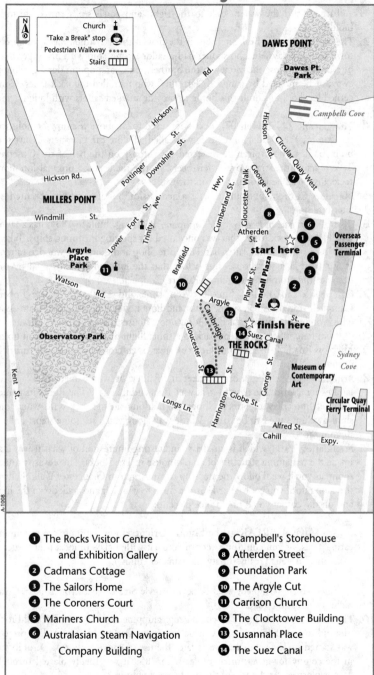

Legend:
- Church ✝
- "Take a Break" stop
- Pedestrian Walkway ••••
- Stairs ▭▭▭▭

N

DAWES POINT

Dawes Pt. Park

Campbells Cove

Hickson Rd.

Circular Quay West

Hickson St.

Pottinger St.

Downshire St.

Hickson Rd.

MILLERS POINT

Windmill St.

Lower Fort St.

Trinity Ave.

Argyle Place Park

Hwy.

Cumberland St.

Gloucester Walk

George St.

Atherden St.

start here

Overseas Passenger Terminal

Watson Rd.

Bradfield

Playfair St.

Kendall Plaza

Observatory Park

Argyle St.

Cambridge St.

finish here

Suez Canal

THE ROCKS

Gloucester St.

Sydney Cove

Kent St.

Longs Ln.

Harrington St.

Globe St.

George St.

Museum of Contemporary Art

Circular Quay Ferry Terminal

Alfred St.

Cahill Expy.

A-1008

1. The Rocks Visitor Centre and Exhibition Gallery
2. Cadmans Cottage
3. The Sailors Home
4. The Coroners Court
5. Mariners Church
6. Australasian Steam Navigation Company Building
7. Campbell's Storehouse
8. Atherden Street
9. Foundation Park
10. The Argyle Cut
11. Garrison Church
12. The Clocktower Building
13. Susannah Place
14. The Suez Canal

Turn toward the water, look to the right, and you'll see a row of historic buildings:

3. The Sailors Home, built in 1864, is the first of them. Sydney was a rough old town in those days, and no sooner had a sailor left his ship with his wages than he was likely to lose the money in the brothels, pubs, and opium dens; gamble it away; or be mugged by gangs of "larrikins" who patrolled the back lanes. Concerned local citizens built this home to provide stricken sailors with lodging and food.

4. The Coroners Court (1907), next door, used to sit above the now-demolished morgue (or the Dead House, as it was called). Before the Coroners Court was built, bodies would often be dissected for autopsy on the bar of the Observer Tavern across the street, over a few beers. Notice the exposed original foreshore rocks displayed beneath an arch on the wall.

5. Mariners Church, built in 1856, is a neoclassical building mostly obscured by later buildings.

6. Australasian Steam Navigation Company Building, built in 1884, has a fabulous Flemish clock tower that was once used for spotting incoming ships. Take a look inside the Natural Australian Furniture Shop at the amazing wooden rafters. It was used as a storehouse, but before that the location was occupied by the home of the prominent merchant Robert Campbell.

7. Campbell's Storehouse, built between 1838 and 1890, was where Robert Campbell stored his tea, sugar, cloth, and liquor, which he imported from Asia. This wonderful pair of gabled buildings now houses four popular restaurants.

From here, trace your steps back to a short flight of stairs that take you up to Hickson Road. Turn left onto George Street, then cross the road, and turn left onto:

8. Atherden Street, the shortest street in Sydney; it was named after a local landowner. Notice the natural rock wall at its end that gave The Rocks its name. Turn left into Playfair Street. Notice the markings in the rock walls where old slum dwellings used to be fixed. A little way along you'll see some steps. Follow them up to:

9. Foundation Park, which is an artist's interesting impression of what it was like inside the remaining structure of an old house in The Rocks. There wasn't much room, as you'll see. Follow the steps up to your right to Gloucester Walk. Follow this along until you get to Argyle Street. Turn to your left and walk down the hill, and on the corner you'll find a nice place to:

 TAKE A BREAK at the historic **Orient Hotel.** Upstairs are restaurant eating areas, or you could just refresh yourself with a glass of local beer (order a "schooner" if you're really thirsty, or a smaller "midi").

When you're refreshed, head back up Argyle Street, where you'll find a great archway across the road.

10. The Argyle Cut was made by chain gangs chipping away at a mass of solid rock in a bid to link The Rocks to Cockle Bay (now Darling Harbour). The project was started in 1843, but two years later the use of convict labor was prohibited in the colony for government projects. In 1859 it was finally blasted through with explosives. At the top of the hill to your right is:

11. Garrison Church, built in 1839, a wonderful little Anglican church with stained-glass windows engraved at the base with the names of children who died prematurely. In the early years of the colony, the soldiers sat on one side and the free settlers sat on the other. To keep the riffraff out, people had to pay for their pew, which was then name-tagged. Return back along Argyle Street the way you came and turn right into Harrington Street.

12. **The Clocktower Building,** on the corner of Harrington and Argyle streets, was built on the site of demolished cottages as the government stepped up its plans to clear the area of its historic buildings. After construction, the building lay empty for five years as people displayed their displeasure. Ironically, perhaps, it's now the home of Tourism New South Wales, the government tourism promotion office.

Continue down Harrington Street and take a set of steep stairs to your right. At the top you'll find:

13. **Susannah Place,** 58–64 Gloucester St., a small terrace of four historic houses built in 1844, which give visitors a glimpse into the life of working-class families of the period and later. The houses are all part of the Historic Trust of New South Wales. Guided tours of the houses are offered 10am to 5pm Saturday and Sunday year-round, and daily 10am to 5pm in January. Tours cost A$5 (U.S.$3.50) for adults, and A$3 (U.S.$2.10) for children. Call the **Historic Trust** (☎ **02/ 9241 1893**) for details.

Go back down the stairs and backtrack on Harrington Street until you spot a thin lane on your left next to a craft shop selling didgeridoos. The lane is:

14. **The Suez Canal,** which was created in the 1840s and became notorious as a place for prostitutes and the so-called "Rocks Push"—hoodlums who commonly dressed up as dandies in satin waistcoats, tight flared pants, a bandanna around their necks, and a jaunty hat. Looking good, they'd pounce on unwary sailors and citizens and mug them. Finish the walk on George Street.

11 Harbor Cruises & Other Organized Tours

For details on the Red Sydney Explorer bus, see "Getting Around" in chapter 4, "Settling into Sydney."

WALKING TOURS

The center of Sydney is surprisingly compact, and you can see a lot in a day on foot. If you want to learn more about Sydney's early history, book a guided tour with **The Rocks Walking Tour** (☎ **02/9247 6678**), based at the Sydney Visitor Centre, 106 George St. The excellent walking tours leave Monday through Friday at 10:30am, 12:30pm, and 2:30pm, and Saturday and Sunday at 11:30am and 2pm. The 1½-hour tour costs A$11 (U.S.$7.70) for adults and A$7.50 (U.S.$5.25) for children 10 to 16. Accompanied children under 10 are free.

For other historical walks contact **Sydney Guided Tours** (☎ **02/9660 7157;** fax 02/9660 0805). The company's owner, Maureen Fry, has been in the business for over 12 years and employs trained guides qualified in specific disciplines, such as history, architecture, and botany. She offers a range of tours including an introductory tour of Sydney, a tour of historical Macquarie Street, and many others. Group walking tours cost A$15 (U.S.$10.50) for 2 hours (call in advance to find out what's available).

A walking tour with a difference is **Unseen Sydney's History, Convicts, and Murder Most Foul** (☎ **02/9555 2700**). The tour is fascinating and fun, with the guide dressed in old-time gear and theatrical storytellers spinning yarns about Sydney's mysteries and intrigue. The 1½-hour tour leaves at 6:30pm sharp from Circular Quay Tuesday and Thursday through Sunday. It costs A$15 (U.S.$10.50) for adults and A$10 (U.S.$7) for children.

HARBOR CRUISES

The best thing about Sydney is the harbor, so you shouldn't leave without taking a harbor cruise. **Sydney Ferries** (☎ **13 15 00** in Australia) offers several good-value cruises. A 1-hour morning harbor cruise with commentary departs Circular Quay, Wharf 4, daily at 10am and 11:15am. It costs A$12 (U.S.$8.40) for adults, A$8 (U.S.$5.60) for children under 16, and A$32 (U.S.$22.40) for a family (any number of children under 16). A 2½-hour afternoon cruise explores more of the harbor and leaves from Wharf 4 at 1pm weekdays and 1:30pm weekends and public holidays. This tour costs A$17.50 (U.S.$12.25) for adults, A$12 (U.S.$8.40) for children, and A$47 (U.S.$32.90) for a family. The highly recommended 1½-hour ✪ **evening harbor tour,** which takes in the city lights, leaves Monday through Saturday at 8pm from Wharf 5. This cruise costs A$15 (U.S.$10.50) for adults, A$10 (U.S.$7) for children, and A$40 (U.S.$28) for a family.

If you are missing the Mississippi, another option includes a trip on the *Sydney Showboat* paddle steamer (☎ 02/9552 2722; fax 02/9552 1934), which departs from Campbell's Cove in The Rocks. A daily lunch cruise, running from 12:30pm to 2pm, includes a good buffet lunch, a jazz band, and commentary, and costs A$50 (U.S.$35) for adults and A$30 (U.S.$21) for children 5 to 12. Less-expensive coffee cruises leave daily at 10:30am, 2:30pm, and 5:15pm, and cost A$17 (U.S.$11.90) for adults, and A$11 (U.S.$7.70) for children. Dinner cruises also are offered. You can buy tickets at the no. 2 Jetty in Circular Quay.

If you're going to splurge on a lunch cruise, however, the best is aboard the fully rigged replica of Captain Bligh's *Bounty* (☎ 02/9247 1789). The boat was built to star in the remake of the movie *Mutiny on the Bounty.* Standard 2-hour lunch cruises run Monday through Friday and cost A$52 (U.S.$36.40) for adults (after October 1999, A$55/U.S.$38.50), and A$31 (U.S.$21.70) for children. Dinner and Saturday and Sunday brunch cruises also are offered. A 1½-hour before-dinner sail (with one free glass of champagne) costs A$45 (U.S.$31.50) for adults and A$27 (U.S.$18.90) for children. Buy tickets at the departure point at Campbell's Cove in The Rocks, or over the phone.

Captain Cook Cruises. Departs Jetty no. 6, Circular Quay. ☎ **02/9206 1111.** Fax 02/9251 1281. www.captcookcrus.com.au.

This major cruise company offers several harbor excursions on its sleek vessels, with commentary along the way. The Harbour Highlights cruise departs at 9:30am, 11am, 12:30pm, 2:30pm, and 4pm daily and takes in most of the main points of interest in 1¼ hours. It costs A$18 (U.S.$12.60) for adults and A$13 (U.S.$9.10) for children. The 1½-hour Sundowner cruise takes in the last of the sun's rays, starting out at 5:30pm daily; it costs the same as the Harbour Highlights cruise.

The Sydney Harbour Explorer leaves at 9:30am, 11:30am, 1:30pm, and 3:30pm, and combines visits to five major Sydney attractions with a 2-hour cruise. Get off where you want and join the boat again later. Tickets cost A$20 (U.S.$14) for adults

Harbor Cruise Tickets & Info

The one-stop shop for tickets and information on all harbor cruises is the **Australian Travel Specialists** (☎ 02/9247 5151; www.atstravel.com.au). Find outlets at Jetties no. 2 and no. 6 at Circular Quay, at Manly Wharf in Manly, at the Harbourside Festival Marketplace, at Darling Harbour; and inside the Oxford Koala Hotel on Oxford Street.

and A$12 (U.S.$8.40) for children. An Aquarium Cruise, costing A$32 (U.S.$22.40) for adults and A$18 (U.S.$12.60) for children, includes the Sydney Harbour Explorer cruise and the admission fee to the Sydney Aquarium.

Morning and afternoon coffee cruises, a luncheon cruise, and a dinner cruise with cabaret also are offered.

Matilda Cruises. Departs Aquarium Wharf, Darling Harbour. ☎ **02/9264 7377.** Fax 02/9261 8483. www.matilda.com.au.

The modern Matilda fleet, based in Darling Harbour, offers 1-hour sightseeing tours, morning and afternoon coffee cruises, and daily lunch and dinner cruises. One-hour sightseeing cruises leave Darling Harbour eight times daily and cost A$18 (U.S.$12.60) for adults, A$9 (U.S.$6.30) for children 5 to 12. All boats dock at Circular Quay's Eastern Pontoon (near The Oyster Bar) 20 minutes after picking up passengers at Darling Harbour.

12 Staying Active

CYCLING   The best place to cycle in Sydney is in **Centennial Park.** Rent bikes from **Centennial Park Cycles,** 50 Clovelly Rd., Randwick (☎ 02/9398 5027), which is 200 meters from the Musgrave Avenue entrance. (The park has five main entrances). Standard bikes cost A$6 (U.S.$4.20) for the first hour, A$10 (U.S.$7) for 2 hours, and A$14 (U.S.$9.80) for 3 or 4 hours. Mountain bikes can be hired for the day to take on bush trails elsewhere. They cost A$30 (U.S.$21) for 8 hours, or A$40 (U.S.$28) for 24 hours.

Bicycles & Adventure Sports Equipment, Pier One, The Rocks (☎ 02/ 9252 2229), rents mountain bikes from A$5 (U.S.$3.50) per hour, or A$15 (U.S.$10.50) a day. You can rent in-line skates here, too, for A$15 (U.S.$10.50) per day with all protective clothing.

GOLF   Sydney has more than 90 golf courses and plenty of fine weather. The 18-hole championship course at **Moore Park Golf Club,** at Cleveland Street and Anzac Parade, Waterloo (☎ 02/9663 1064), is the nearest to the city. Visitors are welcome every day except Sunday mornings and all day Friday. Greens fees are a reasonable A$24 (U.S.$16.80) Monday through Friday, and A$27 (U.S.$18.90) Saturday and Sunday. Club rental is A$25 (U.S.$17.50).

One of my favorite courses is **Long Reef Golf Club,** Anzac Avenue, Colloroy (☎ 02/9982 2943). This course on the northern beaches is surrounded on three sides by the Tasman Sea and has gorgeous views. Green fees are A$25 (U.S.$17.50) daily.

For general information on courses call the **New South Wales Golf Association** (☎ 02/9264 8433).

FITNESS CLUBS   The City Gym, 107 Crown St., East Sydney (☎ 02/ 9360 6247), is a busy gym near Kings Cross. Its ground-floor windows look directly onto staring pedestrians (though you can hide in the back if you prefer). Drop-in visits are A$8 (U.S.$5.60), and it's open 24 hours daily.

IN-LINE SKATING   The best places to go in-line skating are the beachside promenades at Bondi and Manly and throughout Centennial Park. **Manly Blades,** 49 North Steyne (☎ 02/9976 3833), rents skates for A$10 (U.S.$7) for the first hour, and A$5 (U.S.$3.50) for each subsequent hour, or A$20 (U.S.$14) per day. Lessons are A$20 (U.S.$14), including 1-hour skate rental and a half-hour lesson. **Bondi Boards & Blades,** 148 Curlewis St., Bondi Beach (☎ 02/9365 6555), offers the same hourly rates, with daily rental for A$28 (U.S.$19.60). There's a free lesson here every Tuesday afternoon. **Total Skate,** 36 Oxford St., Paddington, near Centennial

Park (☎ **02/9380 6356**), also has the same hourly rates, with a whole day costing A$30 (U.S.$21). Lessons at 5pm on Sundays are free if you rent skates.

JOGGING The **Royal Botanic Gardens, Centennial Park,** or any beach are the best places to kick-start your body. You can also run across the Harbour Bridge, but you'll have to put up with the car fumes. Another popular spot is along the sea cliffs from Bondi Beach to Bronte Beach.

SURFING **Bondi Beach** and **Tamarama** are the best surf beaches in the south, while **Manly, Narrabeen, Bilgola, Colloroy, Long Reef,** and **Palm Beach** are the most popular to the north. Most beach suburbs have surf shops where you can rent a board. At Bondi Beach, the **Bondi Surf Co.,** 72 Campbell Parade (☎ **02/9365 0870**), rents surfboards and body boards for A$20 (U.S.$14) for 3 hours. In Manly, **Aloha Surf,** 44 Pittwater Rd. (☎ **02/9977 3777**) rents surfboards for A$30 (U.S.$21) a day. Call the **Manly Surf School** (☎ **0418/717 313** mobile phone) for information on surfing lessons.

SWIMMING The best place to swim indoors in Sydney is the **Sydney International Aquatic Centre,** at Olympic Park, Homebush Bay (☎ **02/9752 3666**). Juan Antonio Samaranch, the president of the International Olympic Committee, called it "the best swimming pool in the world." It's open Monday through Friday 5am to 9:45pm, and Saturday, Sunday, and public holidays 7am to 7pm. Entry costs A$4.50 (U.S.$3.15) for adults, A$3.50 (U.S.$2.45) for children.

Another popular place is the **Andrew (Boy) Charlton Pool,** Mrs. Macquarie's Point (☎ **02/9358 6686**)—near the Art Gallery of New South Wales. It has great views over the finger wharves of Wooloomooloo. The pool is open in summer only, Monday through Friday from 6am to 8pm, and Saturday and Sunday 6am to 7pm. Entry costs A$2.50 (U.S.$1.75) for adults, A$1.20 (U.S.85¢) for children.

Another good bet is the **North Sydney Olympic Pool,** Alfred South St., Milsons Point (☎ **02/9955 2309**). Swimming here costs A$3 (U.S.$2.10) for adults and A$1.40 (U.S.$1) for children. By the way, more world records have been broken in this pool than in any other in the world.

TENNIS There are hundreds of places around the city to play one of Australia's most popular sports. A nice one is the **Miller's Point Tennis Court,** Kent St., The Rocks (☎ **02/9256 2222**). It's run by the Observatory Hotel and is open daily from 8am to 9:30pm. The court costs A$20 (U.S.$14) per hour. The **North Sydney Tennis Centre,** 1a Little Alfred St., North Sydney (☎ **02/9371 9952**) has three courts available from 7am to 10pm daily. They cost A$14 (U.S.$9.80) per hour until 5pm weekdays, and A$18 (U.S.$12.60) at other times.

WINDSURFING My favorite spot to learn to windsurf or to set out onto the harbor is at Balmoral Beach, in Mosman on the North Shore. Rent boards at **Balmoral Windsurfing, Sailing and Kayaking School & Hire,** 3 The Esplanade, Balmoral Beach (☎ **02/9960 5344**). Windsurfers cost A$25 (U.S.$17.50) per hour, and lessons cost A$145 (U.S.$101.50) for 5 hours of teaching over a weekend. This place also rents fishing boats.

YACHTING **Balmoral Boat Shed,** Balmoral Beach (☎ **02/9969 6006**) rents catamarans, 12-foot aluminum runabouts, canoes, and surf skis. The catamarans and runabouts cost A$30 (U.S.$21) per hour (with an A$80/U.S.$56 deposit), and go down in price for additional hours (a full-day costs A$110/U.S.$77). Other vessels cost A$10 (U.S.$7) an hour with an A$10 (U.S.$7) deposit. **Sydney by Sail** (☎ **02/9552 7561,** or 0419/367 180 mobile phone) offers daily introductory sailing cruises on the harbor aboard luxurious 34- and 38-foot yachts. A maximum of six people sail aboard each boat; they leave from the National Maritime Museum at Darling

Harbour. Introductory sails run for 90 minutes and cost A$39 (U.S.$27.30) per person. Reservations are essential. **Elizabeth Bay Marina** (☎ **02/9358 2057**), close to Kings Cross, rents boats with outboard motors for A$65 (U.S.$45.50) for half a day.

13 Catching a Cricket Match & Other Spectator Sports

CRICKET   The **Sydney Cricket Ground,** at the corner of Moore Park and Driver Avenue, is famous for its 1-day and test matches, played generally from October to March. Phone the **New South Wales Cricket Association** at ☎ **02/9261 5155** for match details. **Sportspace Tours** (☎ **02/9380 0383**) run tours of the stadium, the Sydney Cricket Ground Museum, and the Football (rugby league) Stadium next door. Tours run Monday through Saturday at 10am, 1pm, and 3pm, and cost A$18 (U.S.$12.60) for adults, A$12 (U.S.$8.40) for children, and A$48 (U.S.$33.60) for a family.

FOOTBALL   In this city, "football" means rugby league. If you want to see burly chaps pound into each other while chasing an oval ball, then be here between May and September. The biggest venue is the **Sydney Football Stadium,** Moore Park Rd., Paddington (☎ **02/9360 6601**). Match information is available at ☎ **0055 63 133.** Buy tickets through Ticketek (☎ **02/9266 4800**).

HORSE RACING   Sydney has four racetracks: Randwick, Canterbury, Rosehill, and Warwick Farm. The most central and best known is **Randwick Racecourse,** Alison St., Randwick (☎ **02/9663 8400**). The biggest race day of the week is Saturday. Entry costs A$6 (U.S.$4.20) per person. Call the **Sydney Turf Club** at ☎ **02/ 9799 8000** with questions about Rosehill and Canterbury, and the Randwick number above for Warwick Farm.

SURFING CARNIVALS   Every summer these uniquely Australian competitions bring large crowds to Sydney's beaches, as surf clubs compete against each other in various water sports. Contact the **Surf Lifesaving Association** (☎ **02/9663 4298;** fax 02/9662 2394) for times and locations. Other beach events include Iron Man and Iron Woman competitions, during which Australia's fittest struggle it out in combined swimming, running, and surfing events.

YACHT RACING   While sailing competitions take place on the harbor most summer weekends, the start of the Sydney-to-Hobart Yacht Race on Boxing Day (December 26) is something not to be missed. The race starts from the harbor near the Royal Botanic Gardens.

14 The Shopping Scene

Sydney's extensive shopping, though not as good as Melbourne's, still attracts many visitors. Most shops of interest to the visitor are located in The Rocks, and along George and Pitt streets (including the shops below the AMP Centerpoint Tower and along the Pitt Street Mall). For bargains and a little local color, check out the various weekend markets (listed below).

Shopping Hours

Regular shopping hours generally are Monday to Wednesday and Friday from 8:30 or 9am to 6pm, Thursday from 8:30 or 9am to 9pm, Saturday from 9am to 5 or 5:30pm, and Sunday from 10 or 10:30am to 5pm. Exceptions are noted in the store descriptions below.

Discount Shopping

If you're looking for bargains, head to Foveraux Street between Elizabeth and Waterloo streets in Surry Hills for Sydney's factory clearance shops. These shops sell end-of-the-run, last season's fashions, and seconds, for a fraction of the price of retail. If you're really keen on bargain shopping, you might want to take a shopping jaunt with **Shopping Spree Tours** (☎ **1800/625 969** in Australia, or 02/ 9360 6220; fax 02/9332 2641). For A$50 (U.S.$35) per adult and A$15 (U.S.$10.50) for children 3 to 12, the company's pink minibus will pick you up from your hotel, take you on a full-day tour of 8 to 10 factory outlets and warehouses (selling everything from clothes to cookware to electrical appliances), and throw in a two-course lunch at a good restaurant. Tours depart at 8:15am Monday through Saturday.

Don't miss the **Queen Victoria Building (QVB),** on the corner of Market and George streets. This Victorian shopping arcade is one of the prettiest in the world and is home to some 200 boutiques—mostly men's and women's fashion—on four levels. Most of the shops are on the expensive side, but window-shopping is free. The arcade is open 24 hours, but the shops do business Monday through Saturday 9am to 6pm (Thursday to 9pm) and Sunday 11am to 5pm.

Several other arcades in the city center also offer good shopping potential, including the **Royal Arcade** under the Hilton Hotel; the **Imperial Arcade** near the AMP Centerpoint Tower; **Sydney Central Plaza,** beside the Grace Brothers department store on Pitt Street Mall; and the **Skygarden Arcade,** which runs from Pitt Street Mall to Castlereagh Street. The **Strand Arcade** (which runs between Pitt Street Mall and George Street), was built in 1892, and is interesting for its architecture and small boutique shops, food stores and cafes, and the Downtown Duty Free store on the basement level. On **Pitt Street Mall** you'll find record shops, including HMV; The Body Shop, selling quality cosmetics and toiletries; and fashion boutiques such as Just Jeans, Jeans West, Katies, and Esprit.

SHOPPING A TO Z
ABORIGINAL ARTIFACTS & CRAFTS

Gavala Aboriginal Art & Cultural Education Centre. Harbourside, Darling Harbour. ☎ **02/9212 7232**.

If you're looking for a decent boomerang or didgeridoo, head first to this store, at the main Darling Harbour shopping center. Gavala is entirely owned and operated by Aborigines, and there are plenty of authentic Aboriginal crafts for sale, including carved emu eggs, grass baskets, cards, and books. A first-rate painted didgeridoo will cost anywhere from A$160 (U.S.$112) to A$265 (U.S.$185.50). Gavala also runs cultural talks, didgeridoo-making and emu egg–carving lessons, storytelling sessions, and dances. Open daily 10am to 9pm.

Coo-ee Aboriginal Art Gallery and Shop. 98 Oxford St., Paddington. ☎ **02/9332 1544**.

The proprietors of Coo-ee collect artifacts and fine art from more than 30 Aboriginal communities and dozens of individual artists throughout Australia. The gallery also stocks the largest collection of limited-edition prints in Australia. There are also plenty of hand-painted fabrics, T-shirts, didgeridoos, boomerangs, sculpture, bark paintings, jewelry, music, and books. Don't expect it to be cheap, however. Open Monday to Saturday from 10am to 6pm, and Sunday from 11am to 5pm.

Aboriginal & Tribal Art Centre. First floor, 117 George St., The Rocks. ☎ **02/9247 9625.**

This center carries a wide range of desert paintings and bark paintings, mostly of very high quality. Collectibles such as didgeridoos, fabrics, books, and boomerangs are on sale, too. Open daily from 10am to 5pm.

Original & Authentic Aboriginal Art. 79 George St., The Rocks. ☎ **02/9251 4222**.

On offer here is quality Aboriginal art from some of Australia's best-known painters, among them Paddy Fordham Wainburranga, whose paintings hang in the White House in Washington, D.C., and Janet Forrester Nangala, whose work has been exhibited in the Australian National Gallery in Canberra. Expect to pay in the range of A$1,000 (U.S.$700) to A$4,000 (U.S.$2,800) for the larger paintings. There are some nice painted pots here, too, from A$30 to $80 (U.S.$21 to $56). Open daily from 9:30am to 7pm.

ART PRINTS & ORIGINALS

Done Art and Design. 123–125 George St. The Rocks. ☎ **02/9251 6099**. Fax 02/9235 2153.

The art is by Ken Done (he's well known for having designed his own Australian flag, which he hopes to raise over Australia should it abandon its present one following the formation of a republic). The clothing design is by his wife Judy. The shop is open Monday to Friday from 9:30am to 7pm, Saturday from 9:30am to 6:30pm, and Sunday from 10am to 6pm. Ken Done's Gallery is in Hickson Road, just off George Street, in the Rocks. It's open daily from 10am to 5:30pm.

Ken Duncan Gallery. 73 George St., The Rocks (across from The Rocks Visitor Centre). ☎ **02/9241 3460.** Fax 02/9241 3462.

This photographer-turned-salesman is making a killing from his exquisitely produced large-scale photographs of Australian scenery. Open daily from 9am to 8pm.

BOOKS

You'll find a good selection of specialized books on Sydney and Australia for sale at the **Art Gallery of New South Wales,** the **Garden Shop** in the Royal Botanic Gardens, the **Museum of Sydney,** the **Australian Museum,** and the **State Library of New South Wales.**

Dymocks. 424–428 George St. (just north of Market St.) ☎ **02/9235 0155.**

The largest of four book stores in the city, Dymocks has three levels of general books and stationary. There's a reasonable travel section here with plenty of guides.

Abbey's Bookshop. 131 York St. (behind the Queen Victoria Building). ☎ **02/9264 3111.**

This interesting, centrally located bookshop specializes in literature, history, crime, and mystery, and has a whole floor on language and education. Open Monday to Wednesday and Friday from 8:30am to 6pm, Thursday from 8:30am to 9pm, Saturday from 9am to 5pm, and Sunday 10am to 5pm.

Gleebooks Bookshop. 49 Glebe Point Rd., Glebe. ☎ **02/9660 2333.**

Specializing in art, general literature, psychology, sociology, and women's studies, Gleebooks also has a secondhand store (with a large children's department) down the road at 191 Glebe Point Rd. Open daily from 8am to 9pm.

✪ **Goulds Book Arcade.** 32–38 King St., Newtown. ☎ **02/9519 8947.**

Come here to search for unusual dusty volumes. Located about a 10-minute walk from the Newtown CityRail station, this place is bursting at the seams with many thousands of secondhand and new books. You can browse for hours. Open daily from 8am to midnight.

✪ **Travel Bookshop.** Shop 3, 175 Liverpool St. (across from southern end of Hyde Park, near Museum CityRail station). ☎ **02/9261 8200.**

Hundreds of travel guides, maps, Australiana titles, coffee-table books, and travel accessories line the shelves of this excellent bookshop. Open Monday to Friday from 9am to 6pm, Saturday from 10am to 5pm.

Angus & Robertson Bookworld. Pitt Street Mall, 168 Pitt St. ☎ **02/9235 1188.**

One of Australia's biggest bookshops, with games and two stories of books—including a good guidebook and Australiana section.

CRAFTS

Australian Craftworks. 127 George St., The Rocks. ☎ **02/9247 7156.**

This place showcases some of Australia's best arts and crafts, from some 300 Australian artists. It's all displayed in a former police station, built in 1882. The cells and administration areas are today used as gallery spaces. Open daily from 9am to 7pm.

✪ **The puppet shop at the rocks.** 77 George St., The Rocks. ☎ **02/9247 9137.**

I can't believe I kept walking past this shop's sign for so many years without looking in. Deep down in the bowels of a historic building I eventually came across several cramped rooms absolutely packed with puppets, each costing from a couple of dollars to a couple of hundred. The owners make their own puppets—mostly Australian in style (emus and koalas and that sort of thing)—and also import things from all over the world. Wooden toys abound, too. It's the best shop in Sydney! Open daily from 10am to 5:30pm.

Telopea Gallery. Shop 2 in the Metcalfe Arcade, 80–84 George St., The Rocks. ☎ **02/ 9241 1673.**

This shop is run by the New South Wales Society of Arts and Crafts, which exhibits works made by its members. Some wonderful glass, textiles, ceramics, jewelry, fine metals, spinning, weaving, and wood-turned items are for sale. Open daily from 9:30am to 5:30pm.

DEPARTMENT STORES

The two big names in Sydney shopping are David Jones and Grace Bros. **David Jones** (☎ **02/9266 5544**) is the city's largest department store, selling everything from fashion to designer furniture. You'll find the women's section on the corner of Elizabeth and Market streets and the men's section on the corner of Castlereagh and Market streets. **Grace Bros.** (☎ **02/9238 9111**) is along the same lines and is located at the corner of George and Market streets.

Where to Load Up On Olympic Games Gear

A monopoly is good for business, and the organizing committee of the Sydney 2000 Olympic Games has things wrapped up nicely with the outrageously priced **Olympic Store** (☎ **02/9232 3099**) in the AMP Centerpoint Tower complex on the Pitt Street Mall. Everything from sweatshirts to socks has the copyrighted Olympic logo on it. Designer T-shirts go for up to A$32.95 (U.S.$23). Low-quality versions cost A$19.95 (U.S.$14).

DUTY-FREE SHOPS

Sydney has several duty-free shops selling goods at a discount. To take advantage of the bargains, you need a passport and flight ticket, and you must export what you buy. The duty-free shop with the best buys is **Downtown Duty Free,** which has two city outlets, one on the basement level of the Strand Arcade, off Pitt Street Mall (☎ **02/9233 3166**), and one at 105 Pitt St. (☎ **02/9221 4444**). Five more stores are located at Sydney International Airport.

FASHION
Aussie Outback Clothing
R.M. Williams. 389 George St., between Town Hall and Central CityRail stations. ☎ **02/9262 2228.**

Moleskin trousers may not be the height of fashion at the moment, but you never know. R.M. Williams boots are famous for being both tough and fashionable. Akubra hats, Driza-bone coats, and kangaroo-skin belts are for sale here, too.

Thomas Cook Boot & Clothing Company. 790 George St., Haymarket. ☎ **02/9212 6616.**

Located on George Street between Town Hall and Central CityRail stations, this place specializes in Australian boots, Driza-bone coats, and Akubra hats.

Unisex Fashions
Country Road. 142–146 Pitt St. ☎ **02/9394 1818.**

This chain store has outlets all across Australia as well as in the United States. The clothes, for both men and women, are good quality but tend to be quite expensive. You'll find other branches in the Queen Victoria Building, Skygarden, Bondi Junction, Darling Harbour, Double Bay, Mosman, and Chatswood.

Mostrada. Store 15G, Sydney Central Plaza, 450 George St. ☎ **02/9221 0133.**

If you're looking for good-quality leather items at very reasonable prices, then make this your first stop. Leather jackets for men and women go for A$189 (U.S.$132.30) to A$899 (U.S.$629.30), with an average price of around A$400 (U.S.$280). There are also bags, belts, and other leather accessories on offer.

Men's Fashions
Gowings. 45 Market St. ☎ **02/9264 6321.**

This is probably the best all-round men's clothing store in Sydney. More formal attire is sold in the basement, whereas upstairs things go weird, with an eclectic mix of gardening equipment, gourmet camping gear, odds and ends for the extrovert, a good range of Australian bush hats, and R.M. Williams boots (well-priced at around A$200/U.S.$140 a pair). There's a similar store at 319 George St., near Wynyard CityRail station.

Esprit Mens. Shop 10G, Sydney Central Plaza (ground floor of mall, next to Grace Bros. on Pitt St. Mall). ☎ **02/9233 7349.**

Not so cheap, but certainly colorful clothes come out of this designer store, where bold hues and fruity patterns are the in thing. Quality designer shirts cost around A$60 (U.S.$42).

Outdoor Heritage. Shop 13G, Sydney Central Plaza, 450 George St. ☎ **02/9235 1560.**

Quality clothing with a yachting influence is the theme at this good-looking store specializing in casual, colorful gear.

Women's Fashions
Dotti. Pitt St. Mall. ☎ **02/9223 4028.**

One of Sydney's most fashionable shops, Dotti offers trendy fashions at reasonable prices. There are other Dotti stores in Paddington (☎ 02/9332 1659) and in Bondi Junction ☎ 02/9389 0526).

Dorian Scott. 105 George St., The Rocks. ☎ **02/9221 8145.**

This is probably the best place to go for hand-knit sweaters (called "jumpers" in Australia). Dorian Scott has a wide range of colorful garments from more than 200 leading Australian designers. While some go for A$80 (U.S.$56), others will set you back several hundred. You'll also find clothing accessories for men, women, and children in this two-story emporium, including Hot Tuna surfware and Thomas Cook adventure clothing. There are also two Dorian Scott stores at Sydney International Airport and another at the Inter-Continental Hotel, 117 Macquarie St.

FOOD

The goodies you'll find in the downstairs food section of the **David Jones** department store on Castlereagh Street (the men's section) are enough to tempt anyone off a diet. It sells the best of local and imported products to the rich and famous.

Darrell Lea Chocolates. Corner of King and George sts. ☎ **02/9232 2899.**

This is the oldest location of Australia's most famous chocolate shop. Pick up some wonderful handmade chocolate, and lots of unusual candy, including the best licorice this side of the Kasbah.

Woolworth's Metro. Directly opposite Town Hall on George St. ☎ **02/9323 1700.**

Whenever I'm traveling in a new city on a budget, I find I make good use of the local supermarkets. This scruffy, crowded little place on the basement floor (also accessible from Town Hall CityRail station) is one of the only ones in the city center. It's open Monday to Friday from 7am to 9pm, and Saturday and Sunday from 8am to 7pm.

Coles. Wynyard Station, Castlereagh St., Wynyard (directly opposite the Menzies Hotel and the public bus stands). ☎ **02/9299 4769.**

The only other supermarket that I know of in the city center is a good bet if you want to cater for yourself or are after ready-made food (including good sandwiches) and cheap soft drinks. This place is more upscale than the Woolworth's Metro store listed above. Open daily from 6am to midnight.

GIFTS & SOUVENIRS

The shops at **Taronga Zoo,** the **Oceanareum** in Manly, the **Sydney Aquarium,** and the **Australian Museum** are all good sources for gifts and souvenirs. There are many shops around The Rocks worth browsing, too.

National Trust Gift and Bookshop. Observatory Hill, The Rocks. ☎ **02/9258 0173.**

You can pick up some nice souvenirs, including books, Australiana, crafts, and indigenous foodstuffs here. An art gallery on the premises presents changing exhibits of paintings and sculpture by Australians. There's also a cafe. Open Tuesday to Friday from 9am to 5pm, and Saturday and Sunday from noon to 5pm.

✪ **Australian Geographic.** Harbourside Shopping Centre, Darling Harbour (☎ **02/9212 6539;** AMP Centerpoint Tower, Pitt St. (☎ 02/9231 5055).

A spin-off from the Australian version of *National Geographic* magazine, the Australian Geographic store sells good quality crafts and Australiana. On offer are camping gadgets, telescopes and binoculars, garden utensils, scientific oddities, woodcraft, books and calendars, videos, music, toys, and lots more.

Dinosaur Designs. 339 Oxford St., Paddington. ☎ **02/9361 3776;** on the ground floor of the Argyle Department Store, Argyle St., The Rocks. ☎ 02/9251 5500; and Shop 73, 1st floor, The Strand Arcade. ☎ 02/9223 2953.

The high-fashion jewelry and housewares of this Australian company are extremely fashionable in Australia, Japan, and elsewhere. They make a range of modern resin, silver, and ceramic items in bold colors.

✪ **The Wilderness Society Shop.** AMP Centerpoint Tower, Castlereagh St. ☎ **02/ 9233 4674.**

Australiana is crawling out of the woodwork at this cute little craft emporium dedicated to spending all its profits on saving the few remaining untouched forests and wilderness areas of Australia. You'll find quality craft items, cute children's clothes, books, cards, and knickknacks, all based on wilderness and native animal themes.

MARKETS

The Rocks Market. On George St., The Rocks. ☎ **02/9255 1717.**

Held every Saturday and Sunday, this very touristy market has more than 100 stalls selling everything: crafts, housewares, posters, jewelry, and curios. The main street is closed to traffic from 10am to 4pm to make it easier to stroll around.

Paddington Bazaar. On grounds of St. John's Church on Oxford St., corner of Newcombe St. (just follow the crowds). ☎ **02/9258 0173.**

At this Saturday-only market you'll find everything from essential oils and designer clothes to New Age jewelry and Mexican hammocks. Expect things to be busy from 10am to 4pm. Take bus 380 or 389 from Circular Quay.

Balmain Market. On grounds of St. Andrew's Church, Darling St., Balmain. No phone.

Active from 8:30am to 4pm every Saturday, this popular market has some 140 stalls selling crafts, jewelry, and knickknacks. Take the ferry to Balmain (Darling St.); the market is a 10-minute walk up Darling St.

Paddy's Markets. Corner of Thomas and Hay sts., in Haymarket, near Chinatown. ☎ **1300/361589** in Australia.

A Sydney institution, Paddy's Markets has hundreds of stalls selling everything from cheap clothes and plants to chickens and general merchandise. It's open Friday to Sunday from 9am to 4:30pm. Above Paddy's Market is **Market City** (☎ **02/ 9212 1388**), which has 3 floors of fashion stalls, food courts, and specialty shops. Of particular interest is the largest Asian-European supermarket in Australia, on level 1, and the **Kam Fook** yum cha Chinese restaurant on level 3, also the largest in Australia.

Sydney Fishmarket. Corner of Bank St. and Pyrmont Bridge Rd., Pyrmont. ☎ **02/ 9660 1611.**

Learning about what people eat can be a good introduction to a new country and, in my opinion, nowhere is this more fascinating than at the local fishmarket. Here you'll find seven major fish retailers selling everything from shark to Balmain bugs (a kind of squat crayfish), with hundreds of species in between. Watch out for the local pelicans being fed the fishy leftovers. There's also a Doyles restaurant and sushi bar, a couple of cheap seafood eateries (see "Great Deals on Dining"), a fruit market, and a good deli. The retail sections are open from 7am to 4pm daily. Get here by Light Rail (get off at the Fishmarket stop), or walk from Darling Harbour. Parking costs A$2 (U.S.$1.40) for the first 3 hours.

MUSIC

HMV Music Stores. Pitt Street Mall. ☎ **02/9221 2311.**

This is one of the best music stores in Sydney. The jazz section is impressive. CDs in Australia are not cheap, with most new releases costing around A$30 to $35 (U.S.$21 to $24.50).

Sounds Australian. Shop 33, upstairs in The Rocks Centre, 10–26 Playfair St. (near Argyle St.), The Rocks. ☎ **02/9247 7290.**

Anything you've ever heard that sounds Australian you can find here. From rock and pop to didgeridoo and country, it's all here. Fortunately, if you haven't a clue what's good and what's bad you can spend some time listening before you buy. The management is extremely knowledgeable.

OPALS

ANA House Sydney. 37 Pitt St. ☎ **02/9251 2833.**

When buying good opals, it's always a good idea to bargain. This is one of the best city stalls to do it in. It sells some good stones, as well as all the usual touristy trinkets. There's a special VIP viewing room off to the side of the main sales floor if you're interested in buying real quality. Upstairs is a pretty good souvenir shop.

Australian Opal Cutters. Suite 10, Level 4, National Building, 250 Pitt St. ☎ **02/9261 2442.**

Learn more about opals before you buy at this shop. The staff will give you lessons about opals to help you compare pieces.

WINE

Australian Wine Centre. 1 Alfred St., Shop 3 in Goldfields House, Circular Quay. ☎ **02/9247 2755.**

This is one of the best places in the country to pick up some Australian wine by the bottle or the case. A large range of wines from all over Australia is stocked, including bottles from small boutique wineries you're unlikely to find anywhere else. Individual tastings are possible at any time, and there are formal tastings Thursday and Friday afternoons between 4 and 6pm. Wine is exported all over the world from here, so if you want to send home a crate of your favorite, you can be assured it will arrive in one piece.

15 Sydney After Dark

Australian's can be party animals when they're in the mood. Whether its a few beers around the barbecue, a few bottles of red over a dinner table with friends, or an all-night rage in a trendy dance club, they're always on the lookout for the next event. You'll find that alcohol plays a big part in the Aussie culture.

THE PERFORMING ARTS

If you have an opportunity to see a performance in the ✪ **Sydney Opera House,** jump at it. The "House" is not that impressive inside, but the walk back after the show toward the ferry terminals at Circular Quay, with Sydney Harbour Bridge lit up to your right and the departing crowd all around you debating the best part of this play or who dropped a beat in that performance—well, it's like riding around the pyramids on a horse, or hearing Gershwin on the streets of New York—you'll want the moment to stay with you forever. For details on Sydney's most famous performing arts venue, see section 1 at the beginning of this chapter.

Where to Find out What's On

The best way to find out what's on is to get hold of the "Metro" section of the Friday *Sydney Morning Herald* or the "7 Days" pullout from the Thursday *Daily Telegraph*.

Opera Australia, 480 Elizabeth St., Surry Hills (☎ **02/9319 6333;** bookings 02/9319 1088) performs at the Opera House's Opera Theatre. The opera seasons in Sydney run January to March and June to November. Some recent productions included *Carmen,* the *Barber of Seville, Falstaff,* and *Madame Butterfly.* The well-known **Australian Chamber Orchestra,** 50 Darlinghurst Rd., Darlinghurst(☎ **02/ 9357 4111;** box office 02/93681712), performs at various venues around the city, from nightclubs to specialized music venues, including the Concert Hall in the Opera House. Based in Melbourne, the **Australian Ballet,** Level 15, 115 Pitt St. (☎ **02/ 9223 9522**), tours the country with its performances. The Sydney season, at the Opera House, is from mid-March until the end of April. A second Sydney season runs from November to December.

Sydney's finest symphony orchestra, **Sydney Symphony Orchestra,** Level 5, 52 William St., East Sydney (☎ **02/9334 4644;** box office 02/9264 4600), is conducted by the renowned Edo de Waart. It performs throughout the year in the Opera House's Concert Hall. The main symphony season is from March to November; there's a summer season in February.

THEATER

Sydney's blessed with plenty of theaters, many more than we have space for here—check the *Sydney Morning Herald,* especially the Friday edition, for information on what's currently in production.

Belvoir Street Theatre. 25 Belvoir St., Surry Hills. ☎ **02/9699 3444.** Tickets around A$34 (U.S.$23.80)

The hallowed boards of the Belvoir are home to Company B, which pumps out powerful local and international plays upstairs in a wonderfully moody main theater, formerly part of a tomato sauce factory. Downstairs a smaller venue generally shows more experimental productions, such as Aboriginal performances and dance.

Capital Theatre. 13–17 Campbell St., Haymarket (near Town Hall). ☎ **02/9320 5000.** Ticket prices vary.

Sydney's grandest theater plays host to major international and local productions like—cough—Australian singing superstar Kylie Minogue. It's also been the Sydney home of musicals such as *Miss Saigon* and *My Fair Lady.*

Her Majesty's Theatre. 107 Quay St., Haymarket (near Town Hall). ☎ **02/9212 3411.** Ticket prices average A$45–$65 (U.S.$31.50–$45.50).

A quarter of a century old, this large theater is still reeling in the big musicals. Huge productions that have run here include *Evita* and *Phantom of the Opera.*

Wharf Theatre. Pier 4, Hickson Rd., The Rocks. ☎ **02/9250 1700.** Ticket prices vary.

This wonderful theater is situated on a refurbished wharf on the edge of Sydney Harbour, just beyond the Harbour Bridge. The long walk from the entrance of the pier to the theater along old creaky wooden floorboards builds up excitement for the show. The Sydney Theatre Company is based here, a group well worth seeing no matter what production is running. Dinner before the show at the Wharf's restaurant offers special views of the harbor.

A CASINO

Star City. 80 Pyrmont St., Pyrmont (adjacent to Darling Harbour). ☎ **02/9777 9000.** Free admission. Open 24 hours. Monorail: Casino. Ferry: Pyrmont (Darling Harbour).

This huge entertainment complex, which opened in 1997, has 15 main bars, 12 restaurants, two theaters—the Showroom, which presents Las Vegas–style revues, and the Lyric, Sydney's largest theater—and a huge complex of retail shops. All the usual gambling tables are here, in four main gambling areas; there are also several private gambling rooms. Each of the four gaming rooms has a different color scheme, reflecting various areas of Australia. The "desert" gaming room features a man-made rock with a bar beneath a tumbling waterfall. In all, there are 2,500 slot machines ready to gobble your change.

THE MUSIC SCENE

ROCK

Metro. 624 George St. ☎ **02/9264 2666.** Cover varies.

A medium-sized rock venue with space for 1,000, the Metro is the best place in Sydney to see local and international acts. Tickets sell out quickly.

The Coogee Bay Hotel. Corner of Coogee Bay Rd. and Arden St., Coogee. ☎ **02/ 9665 0000.** No cover.

One of the city's most intense rock music venues, this beachside pub has numerous bars and lounges, with live music in the Beach Bar from Wednesday to Sunday evenings.

JAZZ, FOLK & BLUES

✪ **The Basement.** 29 Reisby St., Circular Quay. ☎ **02/9251 2797.** Cover A$9–$10 (U.S.$6.30–$7) for local acts, A$20–$25 (U.S.$14–$17.50) for international performers.

Australia's hottest jazz club also manages to squeeze in plenty of blues, folk, and funk. At the door, pick up a leaflet showing who's playing when. A new Blue Note Bar specializing in jazz opened in July 1998. Acts appear every night.

The Harbourside Brasserie. Pier One, Hickson Rd., Walsh Bay (behind The Rocks). ☎ **02/ 9252 3000.** Cover A$8–$20 (U.S.$5.60–$14), depending on performer.

Eat to the beat of soul and rhythm and blues at this not-bad eatery. Comedy nights attract big acts. Drinks are expensive.

The Bridge Hotel & Brasserie. 135 Victoria St., Rozelle. ☎ **02/9810 1260.** Cover A$5–$25 (U.S.$3.50–$17.50).

Come on a Sunday afternoon, when you're assured of getting the blues. Friday and Saturday nights offer either blues, rock, or house music, depending on their whim. The three-level beer garden out back is nice on a sunny day.

Round Midnight. 2 Roslyn St., Kings Cross. ☎ **02/9356 4045.** Cover A$5 (U.S.$3.50) Tues–Thurs, A$10 (U.S.$7) Fri–Sun.

Come here to see live jazz New Orleans style. At this small, smoky, cozy joint groups of two and three squeeze around small round tables. It's reminiscent of New York's Cotton Club.

Soup Plus. 383 George St., (near the Queen Victoria Building). ☎ **02/9299 7728.** Cover A$5 (U.S.$3.50) Mon–Thurs; A$20 (U.S.$14) Fri and Sat, including a 2-course meal.

On my last visit to this cavernous jazz bar it seemed a pity that the cover charge forced me to eat the bistro-style food on offer, which really was poor. In the end, however, some mellow blues cheered our nonplussed group.

DANCE CLUBS

Blackmarket. 111–113 Regent St., Chippendale (corner of Meagher St., a 5-minute walk from Central Station). ☎ **02/9698 8863.** Cover A$10 (U.S.$7).

This wacky place is known for its Friday night Hellfire Club, where Sydneysiders of all persuasions hang out to watch jelly wrestling and live sadomasochism shows. It's all in (relatively) good taste though, with nothing too brutal, and it attracts a fun-loving crowd, from students to office workers (about half male and half female). Some people make the effort to dress up. There's some good music on offer, too, in the dark and moody interior. Ravers continue on, or drop in (after working nightshift elsewhere) at the Day Club, which offers dance music Saturday from 4am to 2pm (you can stay on for free after the Hellfire Club) and Sunday from 4am to 6pm.

Bourbon & Beefsteak Bar. 24 Darlinghurst Rd., Kings Cross. ☎ **02/9358 1144.** Cover A$5 (U.S.$3.50) Fri–Sat.

Right in the middle of the red-light district, this 24-hour restaurant and nightspot freaks out to dance music downstairs nightly from 11pm to 5am. It's popular with both younger backpackers and the 25 to 35 crowd.

Byblos. 169 Oxford St., Darlinghurst. ☎ **02/9331 7729.** Cover A$10 (U.S.$7).

"Upmarket nightclubbing for the likes of models and beautiful people from the [affluent] north shore of Sydney," is the way the manager described this place to me. The interior is pseudo-Roman, with lots of pillars, and it offers hard-core club/dance music. Dress code is fashionable, with a shirt collar for men and no sneakers. Greek music is on tap Wednesdays.

Cauldron. 207 Darlinghurst Rd., Darlinghurst. ☎ **02/9331 1523.** Cover A$10 (U.S.$7) Tues–Sat 10:30pm–5am.

This intimate and trendsetting nightclub is firmly established as part of the Sydney scene. Tuesday night offers retro tunes, on Wednesday and Saturday it's house, and on Thursday and Friday it's funk/R&B. A stylish dress code applies.

Mister Goodbar. 11a Oxford St., Paddington. ☎ **02/9360 6759.** Cover A$10 (U.S.$7) Fri–Sat.

A young, trendy, local crowd inhabits Mister Goodbar's two good-sized dance floors, with reggae on one floor and hip-hop on the other on Wednesdays, and disco and funk other days.

Riche Nightclub. In the Sydney Hilton, 259 Pitt St. ☎ **02/9266 0610.** No cover for hotel guests; others pay A$12 (U.S.$8.40) Fri and Sun, A$15 (U.S.$10.50) Sat.

This hot spot for dancing is popular with the local over-25 club set, as well as with hotel guests who want to shake their bootie to typical dance music.

GAY & LESBIAN CLUBS

With Sydney having the largest gay community outside San Francisco, it's no wonder there's such a happening scene here. The center of it all is Oxford Street, although Newtown has established itself as a major gay hangout, too. For information on news and events concerning gays and lesbians pick up a copy of the *Sydney Star Observer*, available at art house cinemas and many cafes and stores around Oxford Street.

✪ **Albury Hotel.** 2–6 Oxford St. (near Barcom Ave.). ☎ **02/9361 6555.**

An institution, the Albury is a grande dame offering drag shows nightly in the public bar, and knockout Bloody Marys in the cocktail lounge.

⊙ **Imperial Hotel.** 35–37 Erskineville Rd., Erskineville (near Union St.). ☎ **02/9519 9899.** No cover.

A couple of minutes' walk from King Street in Newtown, the Imperial is a no-attitude gay venue with a pool and cocktail bar out front and a raging cabaret venue out back. Sydney's best full-production drag shows happen late Thursday, Friday, and Saturday nights, with dancing in between.

Midnight Shift. 85 Oxford St. (near Crown St.). ☎ **02/9360 4319.**

The beat here is sleazy, groovy, and dance party. A favorite with the denim-and-leather set, and the odd drag queen, this place gets more energetic as night becomes day.

Newtown Hotel. 174 King St., Newtown. ☎ **02/9557 1329.**

The octagonal bar here is the center of a casual drinking and cruising scene. The place kicks up its heels during late-night drag shows and powerfully camp discos.

77. 77 William St., East Sydney. ☎ **02/9361 4981.** Cover A$5 (U.S.$3.50) Thurs and Sun, A$7 (U.S.$4.90) Fri, A$6 (U.S.$4.20) Sat.

This basement venue, beneath a tower block and prestige car salesroom, is in an odd location, but its moody interior is a hot spot for alternative, dance, progressive house, and jungle music.

Taxi Club. 40 Flinders St., (near Taylor Sq., Oxford St.) Darlinghurst. ☎ **02/9331 4256.** Cover A$10 (U.S.$7) Fri–Sat.

"Tacky Club," as it's affectionately known, is good for commercial dance music and midweek cabaret shows. It's open 24 hours.

THE BAR SCENE

Most of Australia's drinking holes are known as "hotels," after the tradition of providing room and board alongside a good drink in the old days. Occasionally you might hear them referred to as "pubs," with the term "bar" used in upscale hotels and trendy establishments.

Bondi Hotel. 178 Campbell Parade, Bondi Beach. ☎ **02/9130 3271.** Cover A$5 (U.S.$3.50) Sat.

This huge, whitewashed conglomerate across the road from Bondi Beach offers pool upstairs, a casual beer garden outside, and a resident DJ Thursday to Sunday from 8pm to 4am. There's also a free nightclub on Friday nights. Watch yourself—too much drink and sun turns some people nasty here.

A Night at the Movies

The city's major movie houses, **Hoyts** (☎ **13 27 00** in Australia), **Greater Union** (☎ **02/9267 8666**), and **Village** (☎ **02/9264 6701**), are right next to each other on George Street, just past Town Hall. They tend to show big-budget movie releases. For something different, head to one of Sydney's best art house cinemas. The best is the ⊙ **Hayden Orpheum Picture Palace,** 380 Military Rd., Cremorne (☎ **02/9908 4344**). This six-screen art deco gem is an experience in itself, especially on Saturday and Sunday evenings when a Wurlitzer pops up from the center of the Cinema 2 stage, and a musician in a tux gives a stirring rendition of times gone by. Eat "Jaffas," round candy-coated chocolates, if you want to fit in. Tickets are A$11.50 (U.S.$8.05) adults, A$7.50 (U.S.$5.25) children; Tuesday A$7.50 (U.S.$5.25) adults, A$4.50 (U.S.$3.15) children.

The Friend in Hand. 58 Cowper St., Glebe. ☎ **02/9660 2326.**

In the same location as the fantastically cheap Caesar's No Names spaghetti house, The Friend in Hand offers cheap drinks, poetry readings on Monday evenings from 8:30pm, a trivia night on Thursday evenings from 8:30pm, an Irish band Sunday from 4pm to 7pm, and the distinctly unusual Crab Racing Party every Thursday from around 8pm.

Henry the Ninth Bar. In the Sydney Hilton, 259 Pitt St. ☎ **02/9266 0610.**

This mock-Tudor drinking hole gets very busy on Friday and Saturday nights. They serve up some good ales in an oaky atmosphere. An Irish band whips up the patrons on Thursday and Friday nights, and a cover band does the same on Wednesday and Saturday nights. Good-value happy hours bring beer prices tumbling Monday to Thursday from 5:30 to 7:30pm, Friday from 5:30 to 8:30pm, and Saturday from 8 to 10pm.

Hero of Waterloo Hotel. 81 Lower Fort St., The Rocks. ☎ **02/9252 4553.**

This sandstone landmark, built in 1845, was once allegedly the stalking ground of press gangs, who'd whack unsuspecting landlubbers on the head, push them down a trapdoor out the back, and cart them out to sea. Today, this strange-shaped sandstone drinking hole is popular with the locals, and hosts old-time jazz bands (the musicians are often in their 70s and 80s) on Saturday and Sunday from 1:30 to 6:30pm, and Irish and cover bands Friday to Sunday from 8:30pm.

Jacksons on George. 178 George St., The Rocks. ☎ **02/9247 2727.** Cover A$5 (U.S.$3.50) for nightclub Fri–Sat after 10pm.

A popular drinking spot, this place has four floors of drinking, eating, dancing, and pool playing. It's a popular haunt with both tourists and after-work office staff. Pool is expensive here, at A$3 (U.S.$2.10) a game (you'll need to ask the rules, as Australians have their own), and the price of drinks has a nasty habit of going up without warning later in the evening. The nightclub plays commercial dance, and there's a smart/casual dress code. Drinks are one-third off during happy hour Monday to Friday from 5pm to 7pm.

✪ **Lord Dudley Hotel.** 236 Jersey Rd., Woollahra. ☎ **02/9327 5399.**

The best way to get to this great English-style pub is via the Edgecliff CityRail Station (between Kings Cross and Bondi Junction). From there it's a 5-minute walk up the hill outside the station and right into Jersey Road. The atmosphere is one of the best you'll find in Sydney, with log fires in winter, couches to relax in, three bars, and a restaurant.

✪ **Lord Nelson Hotel.** At Kent and Argyle sts., The Rocks. ☎ **02/9251 4044.**

Another Sydney sandstone landmark, the Lord Nelson rivals the Hero of Waterloo for the title of "Sydney's oldest pub." A drink here is a must for any visitor. The drinks are sold English-style, in pints and half pints, and the landlord even makes his own prize-winning beers (costing between A$5.50/U.S.$3.85 and A$5.90/U.S.$4.15, depending on strength). Of these beers, Three Sheets is the most popular, but if you can handle falling over on your way home you might want to try a drop of Quail (a pale beer), Victory (based on an English bitter), and a dark beer called Admiral. You can buy some good pub grub here, such as pies and mashed potatoes. Upstairs there's a more formal brasserie.

✪ **Marble Bar.** In the Sydney Hilton, 259 Pitt St. ☎ **02/9266 0610.**

Once part of a hotel demolished in the 1970s, the Marble Bar is unique in that it's the only Central Europeanish grand cafe–style drinking hole in Australia. With oil paintings,

A Night at the Races, Sort of

Every Thursday night, the Friend in Hand bar sponsors a wacky **Crab Racing Party.** Crab fanciers buy a crustacean for A$3 (U.S.$2.10), give it a name, and send it off to do battle in a race against around 30 others. There are heats and finals, and victorious crustaceans win prizes for their owners.

marble columns, and brass everywhere, it's the very picture of 15th-century Italian Renaissance architecture. It's a tourist attraction in itself. Live music, generally jazz or soul, is played Tuesday through Saturday beginning at 8:30pm. Dress smart on Friday and Saturday evenings. Last time I was here a peaceful-looking fellow was refused entry because he was wearing "unsuitable shoes." Drinks are normally very expensive, but the happy hour (daily from 7 to 9pm) cuts prices down to what you'd pay during normal drinking hours elsewhere.

The Mercantile. 25 George St., The Rocks. ☎ **02/9247 3570.**

Sydney's original Irish bar is scruffy and loud when the Irish music's playing in the evening, but it's an essential stop on any self-respecting pub crawl in The Rocks. The Guinness is some of the best you'll taste in Sydney. Irish bands kick off every night at around 8pm.

✪ **Watsons Bay Hotel.** 1 Military Rd., Watsons Bay. ☎ **02/9337 4299.**

If it's a sunny afternoon, don't waste it—get over to Watsons Bay for the best food you'll find in the sun anywhere. The beer garden serves very good seafood and barbecue meat dishes while you sip your wine or beer overlooking the harbor. Fish and steaks go for A$14.80 (U.S.$10.35), lobster for A$17.80 (U.S.$12.45), and barramundi fish-and-chips for A$11.50 (U.S.$8.05). Nearby are the fabulous Doyles Wharf Restaurant and Doyles at the Beach take-away.

6

New South Wales: The Seven Wonders State

by Marc Llewellyn

Mountains, forests, beaches, Outback, rivers, country, and Sydney—these are the seven wonders of New South Wales. With so much to see in such a big state, you're probably not going to be able to cover all the major attractions in one hit, so as with any trip to Australia, you must prioritize. If you have just a few days to spare, you should certainly head out to the Blue Mountains, and perhaps spend a day in the lower Hunter (also known as the Hunter Valley) among the vineyards. If you have a few more days, I would strongly recommend a jaunt to Barrington Tops National Park in the north of the Hunter for a taste of rain forest and native animals in the wild, or down to the pristine beaches of Jervis Bay on the south coast for gorgeous scenery and some great bushwalks.

If you are planning a longer touring trip, then you have three main options. You can head **north** toward the Queensland border on the 964-kilometer (578-mile) route to Brisbane (and then perhaps on to Cairns and the Great Barrier Reef). On the way you'll pass through pretty seaside towns and skirt an increasingly tropical hinterland.

Another option is to travel along the **south** coast 1,032 kilometers (619 miles) to Melbourne. Along the way are some of the country's most spectacular beaches, quaint hamlets, some good opportunities to spot dolphins and whales, and extensive national parks.

If you want to experience another side of Australia—the **Outback**—then you need to head **west** across the Blue Mountains. You're sure to see plenty of kangaroos, emus, reptiles, and giant wedge-tailed eagles out here. If you only have a few days, I'd advise you spend an interesting 9 hours (each way) driving to the extraordinary opal mining town of Lightning Ridge, where you can meet some of the most eccentric "fair-dinkum" (that means "authentic" or "genuine") Aussies you'll come across anywhere. If you have extra time, travel due west to Broken Hill to experience the Outback with this modern arid-land city as your base. Then there's the snow country, where summers are meant for walking and the winters for downhill skiing. It will be a wonder if you don't want to come back for more.

EXPLORING THE STATE

From Sydney, the **Pacific Highway** heads along the north coast into Queensland, and the **Princes Highway** hugs the south coast and runs into Victoria. The **Sydney–Newcastle Freeway** connects Sydney with its industrial neighbor and the vineyards of the Hunter. The **Great**

Western Highway and the M4 Motorway head west to the Blue Mountains, while the M5 Motorway and the **Hume Highway** are the quickest (and least interesting) ways to get to Melbourne. The state's automobile association, the **National Roads and Motorists' Association (NRMA),** 151 Clarence St., Sydney (☎ **13 11 22** in Australia, or 02/9260 9222), offers free maps and touring guides to members of overseas motoring associations, including the AAA in the U.S., the CAA in Canada, the AA and RAC in the U.K., and the NZAA in New Zealand.

    Countrylink (☎ **13 22 32** in Australia) and **CityRail** (☎ **13 15 00** in Australia) trains cover most points of interest within the state (see "Getting Around" in chapter 4). **Ansett** (☎ 13 13 00 in Australia), **Qantas** (☎ 13 13 13 in Australia), **Hazelton Airlines** (☎ 13 17 13 in Australia), **Kendell Airlines** (☎ 1800/338 8894 in Australia) and **Eastern Australia Airlines** (book through Qantas, ☎ 13 13 13 in Australia) fly to most major cities and towns within the state. **McCafferty's** (☎ 13 14 99 in Australia) and **Greyhound Pioneer** (☎ 13 20 30 in Australia) have coach service throughout the state.

VISITOR INFORMATION There's no central place for information on the whole of New South Wales, though if you call **Tourism New South Wales** (☎ **02/ 9931 1111**), it will direct you to the regional tourist office in the town or area you are interested in.

1 The Blue Mountains

Although the Blue Mountains today are where Sydneysiders go to escape the humidity and crowds of the city and suburbs, in the fledgling days of the colony the mountains posed one of the most difficult barriers to early exploration of the interior. In 1813 three explorers—Gregory Blaxland, William Charles Wentworth, and William Lawson—managed to conquer the sheer cliffs, valleys, and dense forest, and cross the mountains (which are hardly mountains at all, but rather a series of hills covered in bush and ancient fern trees) to the plains beyond. There they found land urgently needed for grazing and farming. The Great Western Highway and Bells Line of Road are the access roads through the region today—winding and steep in places, they are surrounded by Blue Mountains and Wollemi National Parks.

    The area is known for its spectacular scenery, particularly the cliff-top views into the valleys of gum trees and across to craggy outcrops that tower from the valley floor. It's colder up here than down on the plains, and the clouds can sweep in and fill the canyons with mist in minutes, while waterfalls cascade down sheer drops, spraying the dripping fern trees that cling to the gullies.

    ✪ The Blue Mountains area is also one of Australia's best-known adventure playgrounds. Rock climbing, caving, abseiling, bushwalking, mountain biking, horseback riding, and canoeing are all practiced here throughout the year.

    Katoomba (pop. 11,200) is the largest town in the Blue Mountains and the main tourist center. En route to Katoomba on the Great Western Highway from Sydney, you pass through the charming small towns of Wentworth Falls and Leura, which offer quaint cafes and scenic vistas.

Factoid

The Blue Mountains derive their name from the ever-present blue haze caused by light striking the droplets of eucalyptus oil that evaporate from the leaves of the dense surrounding forest.

New South Wales

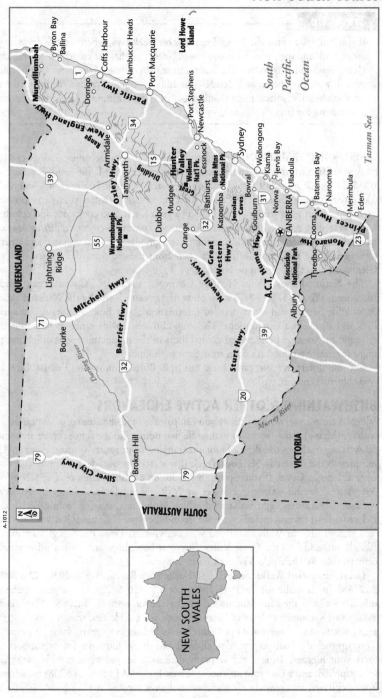

A-1012

NEW SOUTH WALES

Travel Tip

If you can, try to visit the Blue Mountains on **weekdays,** when most Sydneysiders are at work and the prices are much lower. Note, too, that the colder winter months (June, July, and August) are the busiest time in the Blue Mountains. During this period, which is known as **Yuletide**—the Blue Mountains version of the northern hemisphere's Christmas period—most places offer traditional Christmas dinners and roaring log fires.

VISITOR INFORMATION   Information is available and accommodations can be booked at **Blue Mountains Tourism,** with locations at Echo Point Road, Katoomba, NSW 2780 (☎ 02/4739 6266) and on the Great Western Highway at Glenbrook (same telephone number). The first of these information centers is an attraction in itself, with giant glass windows overlooking a gum forest, and cockatoos and colorful lorikeets feeding on seed dispensers. Make sure you pick up a copy of the *Blue Mountains Pocket Guide,* a free guide to dining, accommodations, bushwalking, and entertainment in the area. Both offices are open from 9am to 5pm daily (the office at Glenbrook closes at 4:30pm on Sunday).

The **National Park Shop,** Heritage Centre, at the end of Govetts Leap Road, Blackheath (☎ 02/4787 8877; www.npws.nsw.gov.au), is run by the National Parks & Wildlife Service and offers detailed information about Blue Mountains National Park and its bushwalking options. The shop also sells a wide range of nature-based gifts and can arrange personalized guided tours of the mountains and spotlighting at night for native animals. It's open from 9am to 4:30pm.

On the Internet, you can check out the **Blue Mountains Tourist Site** at www.bluemts.com.au.

BUSHWALKING & OTHER ACTIVE ENDEAVORS

Whereas almost every other activity you can partake of in the area costs money, *bushwalking* (hiking) is the exception to the rule that nothing in life is free. There are some 50 walking tracks in the Blue Mountains, ranging from routes you can cover in 15 minutes to the three-day **Six Foot Track** that starts just outside Katoomba and finishes at Jenolan Caves. If you're planning to do some bushwalking, pick up a copy of *Sydney and Beyond—Eighty-Six Walks in NSW* (Macstyle Publishing) by Andrew Mevissen. It features eight walks in the Blue Mountains, ranging from easy 1-hour treks to 6-hour tramps, including a walk around the Ruined Castle at Katoomba; a less well-known hike to Walls Cave; and walks at Govetts Leap, the Grand Canyon at Blackheath, and into the Grose Valley. Buy it at bookshops and tourist information centers, such as The Rocks Visitors Centre in Sydney.

Great Australian Walks, Suite 2, 637 Darling St., Rozelle, NSW 2030 (☎ **1800/ 242 461** in Australia, or 02/9555 7580; fax 02/9810 6429), is a superb operator offering walks in the Blue Mountains. I had great fun on their 3-day Six Foot Track Walk from Katoomba to Jenolan Caves. Though not a wilderness trek, it goes through nice pockets of rain forest and open gum forests and traverses pretty farming country. The trip includes transport, guides, all food and drink, four-wheel-drive support to carry your luggage, 1-night hut accommodations, a second night camping with all gear supplied, and a cave tour at Jenolan Caves. It costs A$340 (U.S.$238) for adults. Young children are allowed only on school holidays, for A$189 (U.S.$132.30).

One of the best adventure operators in the area is the **Blue Mountains Adventure Company,** P.O. Box 242, Katoomba, NSW 2780 (☎ **02/4782 1271** or 0418/210 743

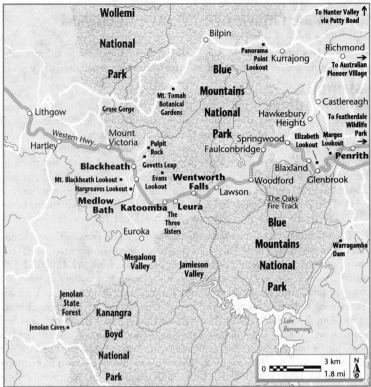

mobile phone; fax 02/4782 1277), located in Katoomba at 84a Main St. (above Elders Real Estate). Another well-known operator is the **Australian School of Moun-taineering,** 166b Katoomba St., Katoomba, NSW 2780 (☎ **02/4782 2014;** fax 02/4782 5787). Both operators can organize rock climbing, abseiling, and canyoning expeditions; the Blue Mountains Adventure Company also offers caving and moun-tain biking, and the Australian School of Mountaineering offers bushcraft and survival training. Expect to pay around A$95 (U.S.$66.50) for a full-day's introductory rock-climbing course (including abseiling), and between A$95 (U.S.$66.50) and A$125 (U.S.$87.50) for a day's canyoning.

If you feel like some adventure on your own, you could always hire a mountain bike from **Cycletech,** 3 Gang Gang St., Katoomba (☎ 02/4782 2800). Bikes cost A$15 (U.S.$10.50) for half a day and A$25 (U.S.$17.50) for a full day (superior front-suspension mountain bikes cost A$40/U.S.$28 a day). Cycletech can supply you with a regional map with bike trails marked for A$4.95 (U.S.$3.50). This company was also gearing up to do guided cycle tours.

Bushwalking Safety Tip

Before setting off on a bushwalk, always tell someone where you are going—plenty of people get lost every year. For other outdoor safety advice, see "Tips on Health, Safety & Outdoor Etiquette Down Under" in section 7 of chapter 3.

KATOOMBA: GATEWAY TO THE BLUE MOUNTAINS
114km (68½ miles) W of Sydney

It used to be a hard journey by horse and cart up to Katoomba from Sydney in the 1870s, but these days it's a far easier 1½- to 2-hour trip by train, bus, or car.

ESSENTIALS
GETTING THERE   If you decide to drive, the journey will take you around 1½ hours (longer during rush hours). From Sydney, travel along Parramatta Road and turn off onto the M4 Motorway (the Great Western Highway). You'll have to pay a A$1.50/U.S.$1.05 toll each way. Frequent CityRail and Countrylink rail service (see chapter 4) connects Sydney to Katoomba. The trip takes 2 hours, and trains leave from platforms 12 and 13 of Central Station. Trains leave almost hourly, stopping at Katoomba, Mt. Victoria, and Lithgow. An adult day-return round-trip ticket costs A$12.40 (U.S.$8.70) off-peak and A$20.80 (U.S.$14.60) during commuter hours. A child's day-return round-trip ticket costs A$2.40 (U.S.$1.70).

GETTING AROUND   If you take the train to Katoomba from Sydney, walk up the stairs from the station onto Katoomba Street; at the top of the street you'll see the Savoy, a former theatre but now a restaurant. **Mountain Link** (☎ **1800/801 577** in Australia, or 02/4782 3333) coaches meet most trains from Sydney in front of the Savoy or the Carrington Hotel across the street (check the signs for your particular destination) and take passengers to the main Blue Mountains attractions, including Echo Point, the Three Sisters, the Skyway, Leura Village, the Gordon Falls, and Black-heath, as well as other drop-off points for good views. Numerous buses run each way daily. Single-ride tickets to one destination cost between A$1.80 (U.S.$1.25) and A$3.60 (U.S.$2.50), depending on the distance. The **Blue Mountains Bus Company** (☎ **02/4782 4213**) also runs buses between Katoomba, Leura, Wentworth Falls, and as far as Woodford. Buses leave around every half hour from either the Carrington Hotel at the top of Katoomba Street or from the Savoy (to the Skyway and Echo Point). Fares are similar to Mountain Link's.

Alternatively, you can connect with the **Blue Mountains Explorer Bus.** This red double-decker bus departs Katoomba train station at 9:30am, 10:30am, 11:30am, 12:20pm, 1:40pm, 2:30pm, 3:30pm, and 4:30pm on weekends, public holidays, and during NSW school holidays. It stops at 18 major attractions between Katoomba and Leura, including the Three Sisters, the Scenic Railway & Skyway, Echo Point, Katoomba Falls, Leura Cascades, Gordon Falls Reserve, the MAXIVISION cinema, and various resorts, arts and crafts galleries, and tearooms. You can get on and off as often as you want. It costs A$18 (U.S.$12.60) for adults, A$9 (U.S.$6.30) for children, and A$45 (U.S.$31.50) for a family of 5. Monday through Friday year-round you have the option of the 3-hour **Blue Mountains Highlights Tour,** which costs A$34 (U.S.23.80) for adults, A$17 (U.S.11.90) for children, and A$80 (U.S.$56) for a family. The tour leaves Katoomba train station Monday through Friday at 10:30am, 11:30am, and 2pm. **Fantastic Aussie Tours** (☎ **1300/300 915** in Australia, or 02/4782 1866) operates both tours. Combined rail/bus tours from Sydney can be purchased at any CityRail (☎ **13 15 00** in Australia) station and cost a couple of dollars less than when you buy the tickets separately.

EXPLORING THE AREA
The most visited and photographed attraction in the Blue Mountains is the unusual rock formation known as the **Three Sisters.** The best place to view these astonishing-looking pinnacles is from **Echo Point Road,** just across from the Blue

Get on the Bus, Gus

Many private bus operators offer day trips to the Blue Mountains from Sydney, but it's important to decide what kind of experience you want and to shop around. If you're interested in hiking, for example, know that some companies offer a guided coach tour where you just stretch your legs occasionally, while others let you get the cobwebs out of your lungs with a couple of longish bushwalks.

One very popular and highly recommended operator—and a good value, too—is **Oz Trek Adventure Tours,** P.O. Box 1328, Darlinghurst, NSW 2010 (☎ **02/9360 3444;** fax 02/9331 1113; e-mail: oztrek@mpx.com.au). Their trip includes a tour of the Sydney 2000 Olympic Games Site in Homebush Bay, a visit to Glenbrook National Park (where it's possible to see kangaroos and wallabies in the wild), tours of all the major Blue Mountain sites, and a 1½-hour bushwalk—all for just A\$49 (U.S.\$34.30) for adults, A\$36 (\$25.20) for children. The company also offers fun 3-day camping trips in the mountains for A\$195 (U.S.\$136.50) per person, including food and camping gear.

Tours offered aboard **The Wonderbus** (☎ **02/9555 9800;** fax 02/9555 1345; e-mail: dave@wonderbus.com au; www.wonderbus.com.au) are good fun for all ages and include most of the major sites and a short bushwalk. Day tours leave Sydney at approximately 7:45am from Circular Quay and 8:15am from Central Station (Bay 15 on Pitt Street) and return after 7pm; the cost is A\$60 (U.S.\$42) for adults and A\$48 (U.S.\$33.60) for children. (YHA members and students with an ISIC card pay A\$48/U.S.\$33.60). Overnight packages, with accommodations in the YHA hostel in Katoomba, are also available.

Cox's River Escapes, P.O. Box 81, Leura, NSW 2780 (☎ **02/4784 1621** or mobile phone 015/400 121; fax 02/4784 2450), offers highly recommended tours off the beaten track. Operator Ted Taylor picks up clients at the Rivercat ferry stop at Parramatta or from Blue Mountains accommodations and transports them around in six-passenger, air-conditioned, four-wheel-drive vehicles. Half-day tours visit remote areas and travel through private property in and around the Megalong Valley. Full-day tours travel either around the Megalong Valley, the Garden of Stone National Park, and along the edge of wilderness areas (a 2½-hour bushwalk is optional), or through areas of the Blue Mountains in search of remote lookouts. Half-day trips with morning or afternoon tea cost A\$95 (U.S.\$66.50); full-day trips with morning tea, lunch, and afternoon refreshments cost A\$150 (U.S.\$105).

AAT Kings, Shop 1, corner of Alfred Street and ferry wharf no. 1, Circular Quay (☎ **02/9252 2788;** fax 03/9274 7400), runs a typical big bus tour of the mountains, taking in all the usual sights, with a couple of short walks included. It costs A\$66 (U.S.\$46.20) for adults and A\$33 (U.S.\$23.10) for children. Another large operator, **Australian Pacific Tours,** 102 George St., The Rocks (☎ **02/9252 2988;** fax 02/9247 2052), offers a similar trip with a visit to the Australian Wildlife Park (see "Wildlife Parks, Aquariums & More" in chapter 5) and a quick visit to the Sydney 2000 Olympic Games Site at Homebush Bay. This tour costs A\$78 (U.S.\$54.60) for adults and A\$39 (U.S.\$27.30) for children.

A Shopping Stop

If you're into hats, then you shouldn't miss **The Hattery,** 171 Lurline St., Katoomba (☎ **02/4782 5003**). One of Australia's leading hat retailers, it stocks more than 25 styles, from famous Akubra bush hats to women's hats, English tweeds, and Panama straws. The shop is open daily from 9am to 5pm.

Mountains Tourism office in Katoomba. Other good lookouts include Evans Lookout, Govetts Leap, and Hargreaves Lookout, all at Blackheath (see below).

One thing you must do in the Blue Mountains is take a ride on the **Scenic Railway,** the world's steepest. It consists of a carriage on rails that is lowered 415 meters (more than 1,000 ft.) down into the **Jamison Valley** at a maximum incline of 52°. Originally it was used in the 1880s to transport coal and shale from the mines below. The trip there and back takes only a few minutes; at the bottom there are some excellent walks through forests of ancient tree ferns. Another popular attraction is the **Skyway,** a cable car that travels 300 meters (990 ft.) above the Jamison Valley. The round-trip takes 6 minutes. The Scenic Railway and Skyway (☎ **02/4782 2699**) each cost A$5 round-trip for adults and A$2 (U.S.$1.40) for children, and operate daily from 9am to 5pm (last trip at 4:50pm).

Canyons, waterfalls, underground rivers—the Blue Mountains has them all, and before you experience them in person you can catch them on the (giant) silver screen in *The Edge* at the **MAXVISION Cinema,** 225–237 Great Western Hwy., Katoomba (☎ **02/4782 8900,** or 02/4782 8928). The special effects shown on the screen 18 meters (59 ft.) high and 24 meters (79 ft.) wide make you feel like part of the action. The 38-minute film is shown at 10am, 11:45am, 12:30pm, 1:15pm, 3pm, and 5:15pm. Another movie (titles vary) is shown between screenings of *The Edge.* Tickets are A$12 (U.S.$8.40) for adults, A$8 (U.S.$5.60) for children, and A$35 (U.S.$24.50) for a family. The cinema is open daily from 9am to 11pm and is a 5- to 10-minute walk from the train station. Recent-release movies are shown on part of the giant screen in the evenings.

WHERE TO STAY

There are plenty of places to stay throughout the Blue Mountains, including historic guest houses, B&Bs, resorts, motels, and homestays. Room rates are highest in the mountains on Friday and Saturday nights, during the Christmas and New Year holiday period, and other public holidays. Weekday stays are far cheaper.

The Cecil. 108 Katoomba St., Katoomba, NSW 2780. ☎ **02/4782 1411.** Fax 02/4782 5364. 23 units, 5 with bathroom. Midweek A$90 (U.S.$63) double; weekend A$110 (U.S.$77) double. Rates include substantial breakfast. Additional person A$20 (U.S.$14) extra. Ask about multinight midweek discounts and tour packages. AE, BC, MC, V.

Right in the center of town, this lovely old property has comfortable rooms. Rooms above the second floor (numbers 30 to 35) on the east side have great views; the best are from room 33, which offers a breathtaking vista across the mountains. Five rooms renovated in 1988 have a small, attached bathroom with shower. There's a cozy lounge area with a TV, a game room with pool and Ping-Pong tables, a good library, and a small terraced garden out back. Three-course dinners, which could include a country roast, a casserole, meat pies, and apple crumble, cost A$22.50 (U.S.$15.75). The breakfasts are huge enough to sustain you for a whole day's walking.

Echo Point Holiday Villas. 36 Echo Point Rd., Katoomba, NSW 2780. ☎ **02/4782 3275.** Fax 02/4782 7030. 5 villas, 1 cottage (all with shower only). TV. Sun–Thurs A$95 (U.S.$66.50) villa; Fri, Sat, & public holidays A$110 (U.S.$77) villa. Sun–Thurs A$175 (U.S.$122.50) cottage; weekend A$200 (U.S.$140) cottage. Linen A$6 (U.S.$4.20) per person extra for villas. Minimum 2-night stay. Additional person A$10 (U.S.$7) extra. AE, BC, DC, MC, V.

These are the closest self-contained accommodations to the Three Sisters Lookout. The two front-facing villas are the best because of their beautiful mountain views. The villas sleep 5 or 6 people, and each comes with a modern kitchen. In the bathroom are a shower, washing machine, and dryer. There are barbecue facilities in the backyard. The cottage is also fully self-contained and has a bath and access to nice gardens.

Three Explorers Motel. 197 Lurline St., Katoomba, NSW 2780. ☎ and fax **02/ 4782 1733.** 14 units (most with shower only). TV. Sun–Thurs A$89 (U.S.$62.30) double; Fri–Sat A$109 (U.S.$76.30) double; public holidays A$117 (U.S.81.90) double. Sun–Thurs A$145 (U.S.$101.50) spa suite; Fri–Sat A$200 (U.S.$140) spa suite. Ask about packages and discounts for Aussie auto club members. Additional person A$16 (U.S.$11.20) extra in double, A$22 (U.S.$15.40) extra in spa suite. Children under 13 A$12 (U.S.$8.40) extra. AE, BC, DC, MC, V.

Staying in a motel isn't the ideal Blue Mountains experience, but it does offer some advantages. Rooms here vary in size, from those just large enough to fit one queen-size bed to large family units with six beds. The main selling point of the motel is that it's just a 5-minute walk from Echo Point; it's also very quiet. Standard rooms are comfy and have an attached bathroom with shower. The spa suites have a queen-size bed in the main living area and a separate bedroom with a second queen-size bed. The spa suite bathrooms are quite large. Breakfast can be served in your room, and each night you have a choice of four main courses costing from A$13.50 to $14 (U.S.$9.45 to $9.80). There's also a laundry, and videos can be rented.

Super-Cheap Sleeps

Katoomba Mountain Lodge. 31 Lurline St., Katoomba, NSW 2780. ☎ and fax **02/ 4782 3933.** 23 units, none with bathroom. Sun, Mon–Thurs A$40–$48 (U.S.$28–$33.60) single or double; Fri & Sat (2-night package) A$128 (U.S.$89.60) single or double. A$10–$15 (U.S.$7–$10.50) dorm bed, depending on season (May–Sept is low season). AE, BC, DC, MC, V.

This 2½-star property is quite cozy, with rooms looking out across the mountains. Dorm rooms are clean, with three to six beds. Singles and doubles are basic and lack a TV, but are certainly adequate for a couple of nights. All share bathrooms. On the premises you'll find a TV lounge with a log fire, a BYO dining room, a laundry, and a game room. The staff can arrange tour packages. Breakfast costs an additional A$5 to $7 (U.S.$3.50 to $4.90) per person; additional cost for both dinner and breakfast is A$20 (U.S.$14) per person.

Katoomba YHA Hostel. 66 Waratah St. (at Lurline St.), Katoomba, NSW 2780. ☎ **02/ 4782 1416.** Fax 02/4782 6203. 16 units, most with bathroom. A$50 (U.S.$35) single or double. A$14–$19 (U.S.$9.80–$13.30) dorm bed. Family rates available. Children under 18 half price. BC, MC, V.

This former guest house is fine for a couple of nights if you don't mind things a little less than luxurious. It's friendly, clean, comfortable, well located, and has log fires in the living areas, a communal kitchen and dining room, and a laundry. The double rooms are simple, with either a double, twin, or bunk beds and not much else but a small bathroom. Dorm rooms accommodate from 4 to 12 people; the cheaper dorm rooms on the top floor share bathrooms.

Worth a Splurge

Avonleigh Guest House. 174 Lurline St., Katoomba, NSW 2780. ☎ **02/4782 1534.** Fax 02/4782 5688. 12 units (some with shower only). Midweek A$65 (U.S.$45.50) per person double with breakfast, A$105 (U.S.$73.50) per person double with breakfast and dinner.

Weekend A$135 (U.S.$94.50) per person double with breakfast and dinner. AE, BC, DC, MC, V. Children not encouraged.

This three-star, 1902 property is a cozy mountain hangout with a Victorian feel about it. The rooms are comfortable and varied, with antique furniture, either a queen-size or double bed, and a nice size bathroom with either a shower and tub or just a shower. The living room has high ceilings, velvet chairs, double cameo couches, and sprays of dried flowers. Free tea and coffee are served in the lounge all day, and in cooler months open fires supplement the central heating. When I last visited, I found plenty of American and German guests (the former studiously engrossed in a previous edition of *Frommer's Australia*). The stairs here could be difficult for travelers with disabilities.

WHERE TO DINE

Katoomba Street has many ethnic dining choices, whether you're hungry for Greek, Chinese, or Thai. Restaurants in the Blue Mountains are generally more expensive than equivalent places in Sydney.

Paragon Cafée. 65 Katoomba St., Katoomba. ☎ **02/4782 2928.** Menu items vary in price. AE, MC, V. Tues–Fri 10am–3:30pm, Sat and Sun 10am–4pm. CAFE.

The Paragon has been a Blue Mountains' institution since it opened for business in 1916. Inside, it's decked out with dark wood paneling, bas-relief figures guarding the booths, and chandeliers. The homemade soups are delicious. The cafe also serves pies, pastas, grills, seafood, waffles, cakes, and a Devonshire tea of scones and cream.

The Pavilion at Echo Point. 35 Echo Point Rd., Katoomba. ☎ **02/4782 7055.** Main courses A$10.95–$16.50 (U.S.$7.70–$11.55). AE, BC, DC, JCB, MC, V. Sun–Fri 10am–4:30pm, Sat 10am–7:30pm. MODERN AUSTRALIAN/SNACKS

This miniature version of Sydney's Queen Victoria Building is so close to Echo Point that it looks like a shove will send it tumbling over the edge. Light fills the three-story building through a rooftop glass atrium and huge windows on the top two floors. On the ground level are a few stores; on the middle level is a food court with a burger/pie outlet, a bakery, and an ice-cream counter; and on the top level is a cafe serving dishes such as baked Camembert in puff pastry, battered fillets of trout on a vegetable fritter, and oven-baked baby barramundi with lemon and parsley butter. The food is good for the price, but the views from the terrace and balcony are even better.

TrisElies. 287 Main St., Katoomba. ☎ **02/4782 4026.** Reservations recommended. Main courses A$12–$19.50 (U.S.$8.40–$13.65). Daily noon–midnight. BC, MC, V. TRADITIONAL GREEK.

Perhaps it's the belly dancers and plate smashing, or the smell of moussaka, but as soon as you walk through the door of this lively place you'll feel you've been transported around the world to an authentic Athenian taverna. The restaurant's three tiers of tables all have a good view of the stage, where Greek or international performances take place nightly. The food is solid Greek fare, such as souvlaki, traditional dips, fried haloumi cheese, Greek salads, casseroles, whitebait, and sausages in red wine. If it's winter, come in to warm up beside one of the two log fires.

LEURA

107km (64 miles) W of Sydney, 3km (2 miles) W of Katoomba

The fashionable capital of the Blue Mountains, Leura is known for its gardens, its pretty old buildings (many of them holiday homes for Sydneysiders), and its cafes and restaurants. Just outside Leura is the **Sublime Point Lookout,** which has spectacular and unusual views of the Three Sisters formation in Katoomba.

A Must-Do Scenic Drive

From the southern end of Leura Mall, a **cliff drive** takes you all the way back to Echo Point in Katoomba. Along the way, you'll get some spectacular views over the Jamison Valley.

A RESORT WORTH A SPLURGE

Fairmont Resort. 1 Sublime Point Rd., Leura, NSW 2780. ☎ **1800/786 640** in Australia, or 02/4782 5222. Fax 02/4784 1685. 230 units. A/C MINIBAR TV TEL. Midweek A$136–$210 (U.S.$95.20–$147) double; A$258–$472 (U.S.$180.60–$330.40) suite. Weekend A$174–$246 (U.S.$121.80–$172.20) double; A$302–$530 (U.S.$211.40–$371) suite. Additional person A$35 (U.S.$24.50) extra. Children under 16 free in parents' room. Ask about discounts for Aussie auto club members. 2-night minimum stay on weekends. AE, BC, DC, JCB, MC, V. Free parking.

If the more personalized attention of a B&B or guest house is not your scene, then you could always opt for this award-winning resort. It opened in 1988 as the Blue Mountains' only deluxe hotel–style accommodation. Rooms are pretty luxurious and come with either twins, queen-size, or king-size beds. The valley-view rooms on the upper floors have the best outlooks and cost the most. The resort is popular with Sydneysiders who come up to enjoy the recreational facilities and the Blue Mountain's best golf course, which is just across the road. Misty's and the Terrace offer exquisite fine dining with excellent service; the resort also has a bistro.

Amenities include indoor and outdoor swimming pools, health club, gym, spa, sauna, four floodlit tennis courts, two squash courts, adjacent Leura Golf Course, children's center and supervised activity program, concierge, 24-hour room service, laundry, valet, nightly turndown, massage, baby-sitting, business center, gift shop.

A TEA ROOM

Bygone Beautys Tea Room. 20–22 Grose St., Leura. ☎ **02/4784 3117.** Daily 10am–5pm. Closed Christmas Day and New Year's Day. Devonshire teas A$5.50 (U.S.$3.85); light meals around A$8 (U.S.$5.60); afternoon tea A$12.50 (U.S.$8.75) per person or A$22 (U.S.$15.40) for 2 people. BC, MC, V. LIGHT MEALS/DEVONSHIRE TEAS.

Everyone has to try a Devonshire tea in the Blue Mountains. It's just part of the experience. This is one of the more unusual places to partake. It's set in the midst of the largest private antiques emporium in the Blue Mountains, yet it's still cozy in an Edwardian kind of way. As well as your scones and cream, you can treat yourself to a light lunch of soup, a chicken casserole, a beef curry with rice, or a traditional afternoon tea with sandwiches, scones, homemade biscuits and cakes, all served on fine china and silver. What's more, you can browse through the antiques when you finish dining.

WENTWORTH FALLS

103km (62 miles) from Sydney, 7km (4 miles) from Katoomba

This pretty little town has numerous crafts and antiques shops, but the area is principally known for its magnificent 935-feet-high waterfall, situated in **Falls Reserve.** On the far side of the falls is the **National Pass Walk**—one of the best in the Blue Mountains. It's cut into a cliff face with overhanging rock faces on one side and sheer drops on the other. The views over the Jamison Valley are spectacular. The track takes you down to the base of the falls, to the **Valley of the Waters.** Climbing up out of the valley is quite a bit more difficult, but just as rewarding.

WHERE TO STAY

If you want to stay in a historical cottage, then consider **Bygone Beautys Cottages,** 20–22 Grose St., Leura, NSW 2780 (☎ **02/4784 3117,** fax 02/47813078). Nine of the 17 self-contained cottages the group owns are in Wentworth Falls; the others are in Leura and Bullaburra. Prices range from A$62 to $90 (U.S.$43.40 to $63) per person midweek, and A$75 to $120 (U.S.$52.50 to $84) per person on weekends (with a minimum two-night stay).

✪ **Whispering Pines, The Sandpatch & Woodlands.** 178–186 Falls Rd., Wentworth Falls, NSW 2782. ☎ **02/4757 1449.** Fax 03/4757 1219. 4 units in main building, 1 4-bedroom cottage at Sandpatch; 1 3-bedroom cottage at Woodlands. TV TEL. Whispering Pines: midweek A$100–$150 (U.S.$70–$105) double; weekend A$160–$220 (U.S.$112–$154) double. Sandpatch: A$180 (U.S.$126) per couple per night additional person A$25 (U.S.$17.50) extra (minimum of 4 people). Woodlands: midweek A$120 (U.S.$84) for 2 people, additional person A$25 (U.S.$17.50) extra; weekend A$150 (U.S.$105) for 2 people, additional person A$25 (U.S.$17.50) extra (minimum of 4 people on weekends). All properties require a 2-night minimum stay on weekends. AE, BC, DC, MC, V. Free parking.

Whispering Pines is a grand heritage mountain guest house set in 4 acres of rambling woodland gardens right at the head of Wentworth Falls. Built in 1898, it continues to foster the kind of Victorian luxury that attracted visitors a century ago. Rooms are cozy and filled with period antiques. If you really want to get away from it all, then Sandpatch property just down the road is perfect. It offers two large bedrooms and guest living rooms with Persian rugs, polished wood floors, and all the antiques and added modern luxuries you could ask for. The cottage sleeps eight people. (Two people can rent the cottage, but they have to pay for four people.) There's a full kitchen, a CD player, and a VCR. Woodlands is a wood cottage tucked away in the bush, with three bedrooms sleeping six, a lounge room with fireplace, a spa bath, laundry, and full kitchen. There's lots of bird life around here.

A NICE SPOT FOR LUNCH

Conservation Hut Café. End of Fletcher St., Wentworth Falls. ☎ **02/4757 3827.** Menu items A$6–$12 (U.S.$4.20–$8.40). BC, MC, V. Daily 9am–5pm. LIGHT MEALS.

This pleasant cafe is in the national park itself, on top of a cliff overlooking the Jamison Valley. It's a good place for a bit of lunch on the balcony if you're famished after the Valley of the Waters walk, which leaves from just outside. It serves all the usual cafe fare—burgers, salads, sandwiches, and pastas. There are plenty of vegetarian options, too. There's a nice log fire inside in winter.

MEDLOW BATH

150km (90 miles) W of Sydney, 6 km (3½ miles) W of Katoomba

A cozy place, with its own railway station, a secondhand bookstore, and a few properties hidden between the trees, Medlow Bath has one claim to fame—the ✪ **Hydro Majestic Hotel** (☎ 02/4788 1002), a must-see for any visitor to the Blue Mountains. The huge, historic Hydro Majestic has fabulous views over the Megalong Valley; the best time to appreciate the views is at sunset, with a drink on the terrace. Also, drop into Medlow Bath's **Old Post Office,** now a musty secondhand bookshop and antiques store, where you can interrupt your browsing with freshly brewed coffee among the bookshelves.

WHERE TO STAY

The Chalet. 46–50 Portland Rd., Medlow Bath, NSW 2780. ☎ **02/4788 1122.** Fax 02/4788 1064. 8 units, 4 with bathroom. TV TEL. Weekdays A$50–$60 (U.S.$35–$42) per person with breakfast; weekends $A240–$280 (U.S.$168–$196) per person for 2-night stay, including dinner and breakfast. Restaurant open Wed–Sat. AE, BC, DC, MC, V. Free parking.

Built in 1892, this recently renovated guest house is far from your average motel. When you stay at the Chalet, you are buying a bit of a bygone era. The heritage-listed cottage is set away from the main road through the Blue Mountains in three acres of gardens and lawns. Inside, it is split in two by a long chessboard-tiled hallway. On one side is a grandma's lounge, with a fireplace, flowery sofas, lace curtains, doilies, and arrangements of plastic flowers. Next door is an impressive wood-paneled dining room, with a beamed ceiling and crisp linen tablecloths, a blazing fireplace, and jazz on Saturday evenings. Guests also have the use of the clay tennis court outside. Four of the eight rooms are suitable for families, and four have private bathrooms. All are comfortable and homey. The Chalet prides itself on its contemporary food, and although the menu is small and lacks a vegetarian option, it's excellent. The Chalet is strictly BYO (bring your own) when it comes to alcohol.

BLACKHEATH
114km (68½ miles) W of Sydney, 14km (8½ miles) W of Katoomba

The **Three Brothers** at Blackheath are not as big as their more-famous Three Sisters in Katoomba, but you can climb two of them for fabulous views. More magnificent views, over Grose Valley and Bridal Veil Falls, await you on the **Cliff Walk** from Evans Lookout to Govetts Leap. The 1½-hour tramp passes through a banksia, gum, and wattle forest, with spectacular views of peaks and valleys.

GETTING THERE   The Great Western Highway takes motorists west from Katoomba to Blackheath. CityRail trains also stop at Blackheath.

WHERE TO STAY

✪ **Jemby-Rinjah Lodge.** 336 Evans Lookout Rd., Blackheath, NSW 2785. ☎ 02/ **4787 7622.** Fax 02/4787 6230. 10 cabins, 3 lodges. A$98 (U.S.$68.60) cabin for up to 2 adults and 2 children Mon–Thurs; A$135 (U.S.$94.50) Fri–Sun and public holidays. A$140 (U.S.$98) Treetops deluxe cabin Mon–Thurs; A$190 (U.S.$133) Fri–Sun and public holidays. Additional adult A$20 (U.S.$14) extra, additional child A$10 (U.S.$7) extra. A$58 (U.S.$40.60) per person in lodge, including breakfast. AE, BC, MC, V. Free parking.

The Blue Mountains National Park is just a short walk away from this collection of cabins and pole-frame lodges. If you like hiking—come here, because the nearby walking tracks take you to the spectacular Grand Canyon; the Grose Valley Blue Gum forests; and Walls Cave, a resting place for local Aborigines 10,000 years ago. The cabins are right in the bush, can sleep up to six people, and are well spaced. Each has a slow combustion heater, carpets, a bathroom, a fully equipped kitchen, and a lounge and dining area. There are also automatic laundry and barbecue areas nearby. The lodges each have five bedrooms, two bathrooms, and a common lounge area with a circular fireplace. Composting toilets, walkways, and solar heating help protect the environment. You can rent linens, but bring your own food. Free pickup can be arranged from Blackheath train station. The deluxe cabin, called Treetops Retreat, has a Japanese hot tub, TV and VCR, stereo, and three private balconies with bush views. It sleeps two, making it perfect for a romantic getaway.

JENOLAN CAVES
182km (109 miles) W of Sydney. 70km (42 miles) W of Katoomba

The winding road from Katoomba eventually takes you to a spur of the Great Dividing Range and a series of underground limestone caves, considered among the world's best. Known to the local Aborigines as "Binoomea," meaning "dark place,"

Jenolan Caves were opened to the public in 1866 and have since attracted millions of people to see the amazing stalactites, stalagmites, and underground rivers and pools.

GETTING THERE It's a 1½-hour drive from Katoomba to the caves. CityRail trains run to Katoomba, where you can link up with the daily excursions to Jenolan Caves excursions run by **Fantastic Aussie Tours** (☎ 02/4782 1866). The CityRail Link Ticket, which is a combination train ticket/bus tour, costs A$60 (U.S.$42) for adults and A$30 (U.S.$21) for children. The tour alone from Katoomba costs A$64 (U.S.$44.80) for adults and A$32 (U.S.$22.40) for children, so the Link Ticket is well worth buying. These prices include cave entry. You can purchase Link Tickets at any rail station.

Day trips to Jenolan Cavers from Sydney are operated by **AAT King's** (☎ 02/9252 2788; fax 03/9274 7400) and **Australian Pacific Tours** (☎ 02/9252 2988; fax 02/9247 2052). Coach tours depart the coach terminal at Circular Quay. Since you end up spending 6 hours on a coach on these day trips, I recommend staying overnight in either Jenolan Village or somewhere else in the Blue Mountains.

EXPLORING THE CAVES

Nine caves are open to the public, with guided tours conducted by the **Jenolan Caves Reserves Trust** (☎ 02/6359 3311; e-mail: jencaves@jenolan.org.au). The first cave tour starts at 10am weekdays and at 9:30am weekends and holidays. The final tour departs at 4:30pm (5pm in warmer months). Tours last 1 to 2 hours, and each costs from A$12 to $25 (U.S.$8.40 to $17.50) for adults, and A$8 to $10 (U.S.$5.60 to $7) for children under 15. Family concessions and multiple cave packages are available. The best all-round cave is Lucas Cave; Imperial Cave is best for seniors. Adventure Cave Tours (in which you don a hard hat and go down the shafts on your belly) last from 3 hours to all day and cost from A$40 to $100 (U.S.$28 to $70) per person.

WHERE TO STAY & DINE

Jenolan Caves House. Jenolan Caves Village, NSW 2790. ☎ 1800/068 050 in Australia, or 02/6359 3322. Fax 02/6359 3227. E-mail: bookings@jenolancaves.com. jenolancaves.com. 101 units, some with bathroom. TV TEL. A$50 (U.S.$35) budget room. Midweek A$110 (U.S.$77) double without bathroom, A$150 (U.S.$105) double with bathroom. Weekend A$120 (U.S.$84) double without bathroom, A$170 (U.S.$119) double with bathroom. Family rooms also available. Special packages available. AE, BC, DC, MC, V. Free parking.

This heritage-listed hotel was built between 1888 and 1906 and remains one of the most outstanding pieces of architecture in New South Wales. The main part of the enormous three-story building is constructed of sandstone and fashioned in a Tudor-style black and white. Around it are scattered several outbuildings, cottages, and former servants quarters. Rooms in the main house vary from simple budget-style bunk rooms to "Traditional" rooms with shared bathrooms and "Classic" rooms with private bathrooms. Traditional and Classic rooms are both old-world and cozy, with heavy furniture and views over red-tile rooftops or steep vegetated slopes. Mountain Lodge rooms are in a separate building behind the main house and are more motel-like. The lodge's bar fills up inside and out on summer weekends; Trails Bistro sells snacks (bring your own if you're a vegetarian, though), milk, and bread. Chisolms at Jenolan is a fine-dining restaurant serving very good Modern Australian cuisine.

The Gatehouse Jenolan. Jenolan Caves Village, NSW 2790. ☎ 1800/068 050 in Australia, or 02/6359 3322. Fax 02/6359 3227. E-mail: bookings@jenolancaves.com. 13 units. A$60 (U.S.$42) double; A$90 (U.S.$63) dorm room (sleeps 6). A$20 (U.S.$14) dorm bed. AE, BC, MC, V. Free parking.

The Gatehouse is a clean and cozy budget-style lodge opposite the caves themselves. It sleeps 66 people in all, in seven six-bed rooms and six rooms sleeping four. There are also two common rooms, lockers, washing machines and dryers, basic kitchen facilities, and a barbecue area, and apparently at least one ghost. Four family rooms come with a double bed and a set of bunk beds.

2 The Hunter Valley: Wine Tasting & More

Cessnock: 190km (114 miles) N of Sydney

The Hunter Valley (or The Hunter as it's also called) is the oldest commercial wine-producing area in Australia, as well as being a major site for coal mining. Internationally acclaimed wines have been pouring out of the area since the early 1800s. Although the region trails the major wine-producing areas of Victoria in terms of volume, it has the advantage, from the traveler's point of view, of being just 2 hours from Sydney.

People come here to visit the vineyards' "cellar doors" for ✪ **free wine tasting,** to enjoy the rural scenery, to sample the area's highly regarded cuisine, or to escape from the city for a romantic weekend. The whole area is dedicated to the grape and the plate, and you'll find many superb restaurants hidden away between the vineyards and farmland.

The Lower Hunter, as it's called, is centered around the towns of Cessnock and Pokolbin. More than 50 wineries dot the valley, including well-known producers such as Tyrell, Rothbury, Lindemans, Draytons, McGuigans, and McWilliams. The many varieties of wine produced here include semillon, shiraz, chardonnay, cabernet sauvignon, and pinot noir.

Farther north, the Upper Hunter offers the very essence of Australian rural life, with its sheep and cattle farms, historic homesteads, wineries, and rugged bushland. The vineyards here tend to be larger than those in the south and produce more aromatic varieties, such as traminers and Rieslings. This being the Southern Hemisphere, the harvest months are February to March.

The Upper Hunter eventually gives way to the forests of the Barrington Tops National Park, the nearest World Heritage–listed site to Sydney. The park is ruggedly beautiful and is home to some of the highest Antarctic Beech trees in the country. Animals, including several marsupial species, and bird life abound.

Day Trips from Sydney

Several companies offer day trips to the Hunter Valley from Sydney. The **Scenic Wine Tasting Tour** (☎ **02/0418 232646** mobile phone; fax 02/9746 5724) offers trips for groups of 15 or fewer, including a guided tour of the Pepper Tree Winery, wine tasting at three other wineries, morning tea, and lunch. Tours cost A$95 (U.S.$ 66.50) for adults and A$85 (U.S.$59.50) for children.

Wonderbus Tours (☎ **02/9555 9800;** fax 02/9555 1345; e-mail: dave@ wonderbus.com au; Web site: www.wonderbus.com.au) operates a fun "serious wine-tasting tour" to the Hunter Valley that includes a visit to Oakdale Farm (a native animal reserve) near Port Stephens (for A$6/U.S.$4.20 extra) and a stop at Port Stephens (see below) for dolphin spotting. The trip costs A$129 (U.S.$90.30) for adults and A$115 (U.S.$80.50) for children 5 to 12, including lunch and wine. Overnight packages are also available.

Don't Drink & Drive

Australia's drunk-driving laws are strict and rigidly enforced. If you're interested in tasting some grape in the Hunter Valley, choose a designated driver or take a guided tour (see above). Both easily identifiable and unmarked police cars regularly patrol the vineyard regions.

HUNTER VALLEY ESSENTIALS

GETTING THERE   To get to the wine-producing regions of the Hunter, leave Sydney via the Harbour Bridge or Harbour Tunnel and follow the signs for Newcastle. Just before Hornsby, turn off the highway and follow the signs for Cessnock. The trip will take about 2½ hours. Barrington Tops National Park is reached via the Upper Hunter town of Dungog.

Keynes Buses (☎ **1800/043 339** in Australia, or 02/6543 1322) runs coaches to Cessnock daily, leaving Sydney at 3pm and arriving at 5:30pm. A one-way ticket costs A$24 (U.S.$16.80) for adults and A$12 (U.S.$8.40) for children.

A rental car could cost you as little as A$35 (U.S.$24.50) a day from Sydney (see "Getting Around" in chapter 4 for names and numbers of car rental agencies in Sydney), and you might spend around A$40 (U.S.$28) on petrol for a couple of days' touring.

VISITOR INFORMATION   Wine Country Tourism, Turner Park, Aberdare Road, Cessnock, NSW 2325 (☎ **02/4990 4477;** fax 02/4991 4518; e-mail: info@winecountry.com.au; Web site: www.winecountry.com.au), is open Monday to Friday from 9am to 5pm, Saturday 9:30am to 5pm, and Sunday 9:30am to 3:30pm. The staff can make accommodations bookings and answer any questions. The **Dungog Visitors Information Centre,** on Dowling Street, Dungog (☎ **02/4992 2212**), has plenty of information on the Barrington Tops area.

VISITING THE WINERIES

Many people start their journey through the Hunter by popping into the **Hunter Valley Wine Society,** at the corner of Broke and Branxton roads in Pokolbin (☎ **02/4998 7397**). The society acts as a Hunter Valley wine clearinghouse, sending bottles and cases of wine to its members all over Australia, and some overseas. It's also a good place to talk to the experts about the area's wines, and to taste a few of them. It's open daily from 9am to 5pm.

Most of the wineries in the region are open for cellar-door tastings, and it's perfectly acceptable just to turn up, taste a couple of wines, and then say your good-byes without buying anything. Note also that 1988 was the best year for wines in Australia, with a long, hot summer producing fewer, but more intensely flavored grapes—so stock up on anything you can find from this vintage. 1997 was a very bad year in the Hunter Valley, and 1996 produced an average vintage.

The wineries in the Lower Hunter are concentrated in certain areas. The "Inner Circle" is the Pokolbin/Rothbury area, which includes two of the Hunter's most famous wine-making family dynasties: **Draytons Family Wines,** Oakley Creek Road, Pokolbin (☎ **02/4998 7513**), produces some spectacular shiraz; it's open daily from 10am to 4:30pm. **McWilliams Mount Pleasant,** Marrowbone Road, Pokolbin (☎ **02/4998 7505**), is famous for its Elizabeth semillon, which has won 15 trophies and 134 gold medals over 12 years, and the Lovedale semillon, which has won 24 trophies and 38 gold medals. McWilliams is open daily from 10am to 4:30pm for tastings and offers guided winery tours Monday through Friday at 11 am.

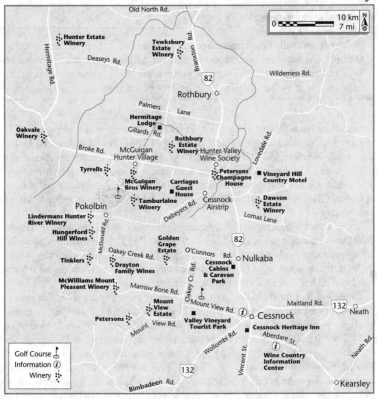

The Hunter's largest winery is the **Hunter Estate,** Hermitage Road, Pokolbin (☎ **02/4998 7777**). It crushes some 6,500 tons of grapes a year and is open for cellar-door sales daily from 10am to 5pm. Winery tours also take place daily at 11am and 2pm. Come here for excellent semillon and shiraz.

Another winery worth visiting is **Tyrell's Vineyards,** Broke Road, Pokolbin (☎ **02/4998 7509**). It has produced some famous wines and exports all over the world. Wine tours take place daily at 1:30pm.

Nearby is the very friendly ✪ **Rothbury Estate,** Broke Road, Pokolbin (☎ **02/4998 7555**). The Brokenback shiraz produced here is magnificent, and the Mudgee shiraz is nice, too. Cellar-door tastings are daily from 9:30am to 4:30pm, and the Rothbury Cafe (see below) serves meals.

You might like to visit the **Small Winemakers Centre,** McDonalds Road, Pokolbin (☎ 02/4998 7668). At any one time it represents around six of the region's smaller producers. Also in the area is **Peterson's Champagne House,** at the corner of Broke and Branxton Roads, Pokolbin (☎ **02/4998 7539**). It's the only specialist champagne winery in the Hunter and is open daily for tastings.

Another winery worth visiting in this area is **McGuigan Brothers,** McDonalds Road, Pokolbin (☎ **02/4998 7402**). It's open daily for tastings and has winery tours at noon. A cheese factory and bakery are also on the site.

A boutique winery I wouldn't miss is **Tamburlaine,** McDonalds Road, Pokolbin (☎ **02/4998 7570**), the winner of many wine and tourism awards; it's open for

---

Wine-Buying Tip

Although you will come across some unusual vintages in the Hunter, especially at the boutique wineries, don't expect to find any bargains—city bottle shops buy in bulk and at trade price, which means you're more likely to find the same bottle of wine for less in Sydney than at the cellar door in the Hunter.

---

tastings daily from 9:30am to 5pm. Other famous wineries include **Hungerford Hill Wines,** McDonalds Hill, Pokolbin (☎ **02/4998 7666**); and **Lindemans,** McDonalds Road, Pokolbin (☎ **02/4998 7684**), which offers an interesting sparkling red shiraz variety. Hungerford Hill is open for tastings Monday to Friday from 9am to 4:30pm; weekends and holidays from 10am to 4:30pm. Lindeman's cellar door is open from 9am to 4:30pm Monday to Friday, and from 10am to 4:30pm Saturday and Sunday.

If you want to taste the grapes in season (December to March) head to **Tinklers,** Pokolbin Mountains Road, Pokolbin (☎ **02/4998 7435**). It sells some 30 varieties of eating grapes, as well as nectarines, plums, peaches, and vegetables at other times of the year. It also offers wine tasting and free vineyard walks at 11am on Saturday and Sunday. Tinklers is open daily from 9am to 5pm.

To the south of the main Pokolbin area is Mount View, a small valley that runs into the foothills of the Brokenback Range. Here you can find a number of excellent boutique wineries, including **Peterson's Vineyard,** Mount View Road, Mount View (☎ **02/4990 1704**), which produces fine chardonnay, semillon, and shiraz; it's open Monday to Saturday from 9am to 5pm and Sunday from 10am to 5pm. Nearby, **Mount View Estate,** Mount View Road (☎ **02/4990 3307**), is famous as the pioneer of Verdelho wine, a very crisp and dry white that's good with seafood. Mount View is open weekends from 10am to 4pm (you must call in advance to visit weekdays).

DAY TOURS, HOT-AIR BALLOON RIDES & OTHER FUN STUFF

If you don't have a car, you'll have to get around the region with a tour group, as there is no public transportation between the wineries.

Hunter Valley Day Tours, P.O. Box 59, Paterson, NSW 2421 (☎ and fax **02/4938 5031**), offers a wine and cheese tour with pick up from your Hunter accommodations. The tour, which runs from 10:30am to 3:30pm and includes as many wineries as they can fit in, costs A$70 (U.S.$49) for adults, A$25 (U.S.$17.50) for children, and A$165 (U.S.$115.50) for a family; lunch and cheese tasting are included. A longer rain forest and winery tour includes a walk and lunch in the Watagan Mountains, followed by an afternoon of wine tasting. The tour costs A$90 (U.S.$63) for adults, A$25 (U.S.$17.50) for children, and A$205 (U.S.$143.50) for a family, and includes lunch and morning tea.

If you like adventure, try **Grapemobile Bicycle and Walking Tours** (☎ and fax **02/4991 2339**). This company supplies you with a mountain bike, helmet, guide, and support bus, and takes you on a peaceful meander through the wineries. The price, including a restaurant lunch, is A$98 (U.S.$68.60). An overnight version, including motel accommodations, evening meal, and country breakfast, costs A$189 (U.S.$132.30). Walking tours, traversing mostly private property and including wine tasting and lunch, are A$89 (U.S.$62.30). An overnight version costs A$179 (U.S.$125.30).

Another tranquil—if pricey—way to see the wineries is from above. **Balloon Aloft,** in Cessnock (☎ **1800/028 568** in Australia, or 02/4938 1955; fax 02/6344 1852),

Caravan, Man

Two caravan parks in the area offer reasonably comfortable accommodations in caravans (campers) and cabins. **Cessnock Cabins and Caravan Park,** Allandale/Branxton Road, Nulkaba (2km/1 mile north of Cessnock) (☎ **02/4990 5819;** fax 0249912944), has four on-site vans for A$30 to $40 (U.S.$21 to $28) and 12 cabins with shower for A$48 to $69 (U.S.33.60 to 48.30); the higher prices are for weekends. Camping sites here go for A$14 (U.S.$9.80), powered sites for A$16 (U.S.$11.20).

The **Valley Vineyard Tourist Park** (☎ and fax **02/4990 2573**) on Mount View Road (on the way to the vineyards) has five caravans for A$35 (U.S.$24.50) and 12 cabins with shower for A$55 (U.S.$38.50). Two two-bedroom units cost A$75 (U.S.52.50). Powered sites cost A$16 to 20 (U.S.$11.20 to $14); a camping site is A$12 (U.S.$8.40). A BYO restaurant, a camper's kitchen, and a swimming pool are on the site.

offers year-round dawn balloon flights that include a post-flight champagne breakfast. Flights last about an hour and cost A$185 (U.S.$129.50) for adults on weekdays, A$200 (U.S.$140) on weekends. Children ages 7 to 12 fly for A$130 (U.S.$91) daily.

WHERE TO STAY

Travelers on a budget will probably want to avoid the Hunter Valley on weekends and during public holidays, when the price of rooms jumps significantly and some properties insist on a two-night stay. It's worthwhile to check the information board located inside the Wine Country Tourism center for special offers.

IN CESSNOCK

Staying in Cessnock is a good idea if you don't have a car and are relying on local tour companies to pick you up and show you around the area.

Cessnock Heritage Inn. Vincent St. (P.O. Box 714), Cessnock, NSW 2325. ☎ **02/4991 2744.** Fax 02/4991 2720. E-mail: heritageinn@hunterweb.com.au. Web site: www.hunterweb.com.au/heritageinn.html. 13 units. TV TEL. Midweek A$55 (U.S.$38.50) double without breakfast, A$75 (U.S.$52.50) double with full breakfast. Weekend A$50 (U.S.$35) per person with breakfast. AE, BC, MC, V. Dinner A$8–$12.50 (U.S.$5.60–$8.75). Free parking.

This 1920s building, built as a pub, is right in the center of Cessnock, so there's easy access to all the local pubs and restaurants. All the rooms are done in country style, with dried grasses, floral drapes, and the like. All are quite large with high ceilings but differ greatly, with a mixture of singles, doubles, and queens. All have ceiling fans and free video movies. There's a guest lounge where you can meet other travelers.

IN ELLALONG

Ellalong Hotel. 80 Helena St., Ellalong, NSW 2325. ☎ and fax **02/4998 1217.** 9 units, none with bathroom. Sun–Thurs A$55 (U.S.$38.50) per person, Fri A$65 (U.S.$45.50) per person, Sat A$75 (U.S.$52.50) per person. Rates include country breakfast. No credit cards. Inquire about dinner packages.

This used to be a super-cheap place to stay, but prices went up when the hotel won an award in 1996 for best country accommodation in NSW. Although it's no longer the bargain it once was, this 1924 pub, located only 11 kilometers (6½ miles) from Cessnock, still has a good Aussie country atmosphere. All rooms have a real out-in-the-country style, with solid wood dressers and bouquets of dried flowers. Some have just a double bed, while others squeeze in an extra single. Rooms 1 and 2 are the best, with fantastic views across to the Brokenback Range from their veran-dahs. Lunch and dinner are served in the restaurant (main courses average A\$15/U.S.\$10.50), and counter meals with the locals are served up in the bistro (main courses average A\$9/U.S.\$6.30).

In Allandale

Vineyard Hill Country Motel. Lovedale Rd., Pokolbin, NSW 2321. ☎ **02/4990 4166.** Fax 02/4991 4431. 8 units. A/C MINIBAR TV TEL. Midweek A\$88 (U.S.\$61.60) 1-bedroom unit, A\$150 (U.S.\$105) 2-bedroom unit. Weekend A\$128 (U.S.\$89.60) 1-bedroom unit, A\$198 (U.S.\$138.60) 2-bedroom unit. Additional person A\$15 (U.S.\$10.50) extra. Ask about mid-week and long weekend packages. AE, BC, MC, V.

Motel is a bit of a misnomer for this place; it's more aptly described as a "fully self-contained chalet." Units are modern, with a separate bedroom, lounge and dining area, a full kitchen, and a balcony with views across a valley of vineyards to the Bro-kenback Mountain Range in the distance. It's all terrifically rural, with cows wan-dering about and kangaroos and possums creeping around come dusk. There's no restaurant, but a gourmet deli on the premises features home-cooked dishes such as curries and lasagnas. You choose your food, take it to your room, and heat it up in the microwave. In the garden you'll find a large swimming pool and a spa.

In Pokolbin

Hermitage Lodge. At Gillards and McDonalds Rds., Pokolbin, NSW 2320. ☎ **02/4998 7639.** Fax 02/4998 7818. E-mail: hlodge@ozemail.com.au. Web site: www.ozemail. com.au/~hlodge. 10 units (most have shower only). A/C TV TEL. Midweek A\$75 (U.S.\$52.50) double, A\$110–\$130 (U.S.\$77–\$91) spa suites. Additional person A\$10 (U.S.\$7) extra. Rates higher weekends, with 2-day minimum stay required. Ask about midweek multinight dis-counts. Rates include continental breakfast. AE, BC, MC, V.

There are few better places to stay if you want to position yourself right in the middle of vineyard country. The property is surrounded by vineyards and there's a great Italian restaurant, Il Cacciatore, on the premises (mains go for around A\$19.95/U.S.\$13.95). Standard rooms are large, sunny, and nicely decorated with queen-size beds and a double sofa bed, an iron and ironing board, a hair dryer, fridge, and tea- and coffee-making facilities. There's a shower attached. Spa suites are larger, with queen-size beds and double sofas, cathedral ceilings, spa baths, and separate showers. The more expen-sive suites have a separate bedroom, bathrobes, and a daily newspaper. Breakfast is served in all rooms. Frommer's readers can hire bicycles at no cost. An outdoor swim-ming pool was installed in early 1999. Laundry facilities are free.

Worth a Splurge

✪ **Carriages Guest House.** Halls Rd., Pokolbin, NSW 2321. ☎ **02/4998 7591.** Fax 02/4998 7839. 10 units. A/C TV TEL. A\$140 (U.S.\$98) double; A\$185–\$205 (U.S.\$129.50–\$143.50) suite; A\$235 (U.S.\$164.50) cottage suite. Minimum 2-night stay on weekends. Ask about 10–20% discounts midweek. Rates include breakfast. AE, BC, DC, MC, V.

Tucked away on 36 acres, a kilometer (½ mile) off the main road, Carriages is a good-value retreat, secluded yet still right in the heart of Pokolbin. The main house is a two-story double-gabled building, and there's a new two-suite cottage, called the Gatehouse, on a separate part of the grounds. In the main house, downstairs rooms open onto a verandah and are furnished with antique country pine. Upstairs, the two lofty gable suites are centered around huge fireplaces. The Gatehouse suites offer five-star luxury; although they're new, the stained-glass windows and rescued timber give them a rustic feel. Breakfast is served in the rooms, and Robert's restaurant (☎ **02/4998 7330**), which serves French/Mediterranean cuisine (main courses around A\$29), is just next door. The friendly owner, Ben Dawson, enthuses that he'll take Frommer's readers to the top of a nearby hill where they can see plenty of wild kangaroos.

IN THE UPPER HUNTER

✪ **Barrington Guest House.** Salisbury (via Dungog), NSW 2420. ☎ **02/4995 3212.** Fax 02/ 953 248. 20 rain-forest cottages, 25 guest-house units, 13 with bathroom. $129 (U.S.$90.30) per person in cottage, includes meals; A$195 (U.S.$136.50) self-catering in cottage. A$79 (U.S.$55.30) guest-house room without bathroom, includes meals; A$99 (U.S.$69.30) guest-house room with bathroom, includes meals. Rates include activities. Ask about packages. AE, BC, MC, V. About 3½ hours from Sydney and 1½ hours from the main Hunter wine region. Free pickup from Dungog railway station.

Barrington Guest House is nestled in a valley just outside the Barrington Tops National Park. It retains an old-world charm, with bacon and eggs for breakfast, scones and cream, and vegetables boiled soft enough for your dentures. The place has lace tablecloths in the dining room, a log fire beneath a higgledy-piggledy brick chimney, dark mahogany walls, high ceilings, and personalized service—despite the communal mealtimes and the lack of a menu. Rooms range from the original guest-house chambers adjoining the dining room, to new and almost luxurious self-contained two-story cottages (sleeping up to 5) that cling to a hillside. Very popular with older people midweek, the guest house attracts a range of ages on weekends, and the communal atmosphere makes meeting people easy. The guest house's grounds attract plenty of animals from the surrounding national park and act as a wildlife reserve for several rescued kangaroos. Activities include horseback riding, guided walks through the magnificent rain forest, "billy tea" tours, and night spotting for quolls (native cats) and possums. There are several marked walking tracks through the rain forest, with some circuit walks up to 2-hours long. Then there's bush dancing and tennis and film evenings and laser clay-pigeon shooting—no wonder it has an extraordinarily high rebooking rate.

WHERE TO DINE IN CESSNOCK

Amicos. 138 Wollombi Rd. ☎ **02/4991 1995.** Reservations recommended. Main courses A$8.90–$15.90 (U.S.$6.25–$11.15); pizza A$12.50–$16.50 (U.S.$8.75–$11.55). 10% discount for take-out orders. BC, MC, V. MEXICAN/ITALIAN PIZZERIA.

You can't mistake the Mexican influence in the decor, with bunches of chili peppers, cow skulls, ponchos, masks, and frescoes, but the Mediterranean/Italian connection is more evident in the menu. Mexican dishes include the usual nachos, enchiladas, burritos, barbecued chicken and the like, and there are also a few pastas and Mediterranean dishes, such as crumbed lamb brains. The pizzas are pretty good, and one could serve about four people.

Café Enzo. Corner of Broke and Ekerts rds., Pokolbin, adjacent to Peppers Creek Antiques, near Peppers Guest House. ☎ **02/4998 7233.** Fax 02/4998 7531. Main courses A$10–$18 (U.S.$7–$12.60). Devonshire tea A$5 (U.S.$3.50). AE, BC, DC, MC, V. Wed–Sun 10am–5pm. TUSCAN.

This charming little cafe offers Tuscan ambience and cuisine. Pastas, pizzettas, antipasti, and steaks dominate the menu. The pizzetta with char-grilled baby octopus, squid, and king prawns, kalamata olives, fresh chili and onion, and freshly shaved Parmesan is particularly nice. Cakes and cheese plates are a specialty.

Chang Ho's Restaurant. In the Cessnock Rugby League Supporters Club, 1 Darwin St. ☎ **02/4990 5655.** Main courses A$6–$10 (U.S.$4.20–$7) in bistro, A$10–$18 (U.S.$7–$12.60) in restaurant. AE, BC, DC, MC, V. Daily noon–2pm and 5:30–8:30pm. CHINESE.

Small-town Australia isn't very adventurous on the whole. You won't find much more than substandard fishburgers or hamburgers and bad French fries straight out of the freezer in most take-out joints, but almost every town has at least one Chinese restaurant (it's still considered exotic in some parts, it seems). The food is filling, but not great.

Something Special: A Cattle Station in the Upper Hunter

Located just off the Golden Highway, 1 hour north of Mudgee, 2½ hours west of Cessnock, and 4 hours northwest of Sydney, this 2,000-acre sheep-and-cattle station is a perfect place to experience Australia's agricultural side. You could organize a nice little trip, taking in the Hunter Valley vineyards, followed by a night at this property, and then a visit to the food and wine town of Mudgee, located on the plains west of the Blue Mountains before heading back to Sydney via the Blue Mountains.

Runnymeade. Hwy. 84, Runnymeade, Cassilis, NSW 2329. ☎ 02/6376 1183. Fax 02/6376 1187. 3 units, 2 with bathroom. A$80–$90 (U.S.$56–$63) double. Rates include breakfast. No credit cards. Dinner A$20 (U.S.$14) per person extra. BYO wine or beer.

The property offers farm-style lodgings in a 1930s California bungalow. Two rooms have an en suite shower, while the third shares the hosts' bath down the hall. The homestead offers an open fire in the living room (and a rarely used TV). There are plenty of native birds in the gardens, and kangaroos are common. May is the best time to see sheep-shearing, and August is the best time to witness lambing and calving. The hosts, Libby and David Morrow, are very good company, and guests rave about them. David offers 1-hour tours of the property for around A$30 (U.S.$21) "a Toyota-load," and other tours throughout the district.

The Rothbury Café. Upstairs at the Rothbury Estate, Broke Rd., Pokolbin. ☎ **02/4998 7363.** Main courses A$15–$16.50 (U.S.$10.50–$11.55). AE, BC, DC, MC, V. Daily noon–3pm. MODERN AUSTRALIAN.

This second-floor cafe has some of the best views across the valley, and occasionally you can even spot kangaroos grazing in the farmers' fields. The cafe has a Mediterranean feel about it, with timber tables loaded with bread and olives. Signature dishes are the chickpea-battered squid with yogurt and eggplant relish for a first course, and the venison and beetroot pie or the braised oxtail with oranges, walnuts, olives, and polenta for a main course. Desserts include a fabulously rich chocolate-chestnut torte with berries.

WORTH A SPLURGE

Casuarina Restaurant. Hermitage Rd., Pokolbin. ☎ **02/4998 7888.** Reservations recommended. Main courses A$27–$34 (U.S.$18.90–$23.80). 2-course children's meals A$15 (U.S.$10.50). A$3 (U.S.$2.10) per person surcharge weekends and public holidays. AE, DC, BC, MC, V. Mon–Sat 7pm–late; Sun noon–4pm and 7pm–late. MODERN AUSTRALIAN.

This superb restaurant has taken a slew of awards for its cooking in recent years, including Best Restaurant awards from American Express. The surroundings are elegant, with everything antique below the very high wooden ceilings. The restaurant specializes in flambés, with its signature dish being the flambé of chili lobster and prawn (for two people). Other meals to write home about are the Thai-style chicken curry and the Caesar salad.

3 Port Stephens

209km (131½ miles) N of Sydney

Port Stephen's Bay, just 2½ hours north of Sydney, should be right at the top of any New South Wales itinerary. It's a perfect add-on to a trip to the Hunter Valley.

Although you can come up from Sydney for the day, I highly recommend staying over at least one night. The sheltered bay itself is more than twice the size of Sydney Harbour, and as clean as a newly drawn bath. The sea literally jumps with fish, and the creamy islands and surrounding Tomaree National Park boast more species of birds than even Kakadu. There are two pods of bottle-nosed dolphins in the bay, around 70 individuals in all, and you are almost certain to see some on a dolphin-watch cruise. Port Stephens is also a fabulous place to watch whales during their migration to the breeding grounds farther north. There is also a large breeding colony of koalas in Lemon Tree Passage on the south side of the Tomaree Peninsula, which makes up the southern shoreline of the bay.

The main town, Nelson Bay (pop. 7,000) is on the northern side of the peninsula. The township of Shoal Bay, farther along, has a nice beach edged with wildflowers. Another small resort town, Anna Bay, is the largest development on the southern side of the peninsula, and has good surf beaches nearby. The Stockton Bight stretches some 35 kilometers (21 miles) from Anna Bay south to the large industrial town of Newcastle. The beach here is popular with ocean fishermen, who have the awful habit of driving their four-wheel drives along it. The Stockton Sand Dunes, which run along behind it, are the longest in the Southern Hemisphere.

Opposite the Tomaree Peninsula, across the bay, are the small tourist townships of Tea Gardens and Hawks Nest, both at the mouth of the Myall River.

ESSENTIALS

GETTING THERE   To get to Port Stephens, take the Sydney–Newcastle Freeway (F3) right to its end, then follow the Pacific Highway signs to Hexham and Port Stephens. **Port Stephens Coaches** (☎ 1800/045 949 in Sydney, or 02/4982 2940; fax 02/4982 2940), travel between Port Stephens and Newcastle, and to Nelson Bay from Sydney daily at 2pm. Buses from Sydney leave from Eddy Avenue, near Central Station, and the journey takes 3½ hours. A one-way ticket costs A$22 (U.S.$15.40) for adults and A$15 (U.S.$10.50) for children.

The **Wonderbus** (☎ 02/9555 9800; fax 02/9555 1345; e-mail: dave@ wonderbus.com au; Web site: www.wonderbus.com.au) combines a wine-tasting tour of the Hunter Valley with a dolphin-spotting trip at Port Stephens. The trip costs A$129 (U.S.$90.30) for adults and A$115 (U.S.$80.50) for children 5 to 12, with lunch and wine. The trip is free for kids under 5, but you'll have to bring along a lunch for them or buy it at the kiosk before you get on the bus. Overnight packages also are available.

VISITOR INFORMATION   The **Port Stephens Visitor Information Centre,** Victoria Parade, Nelson Bay (☎ 1800/808 900 in Australia, or 02/4981 1579; e-mail: tops@hunterlink.net.au; Web site: www.portstephens.org.au), is open Monday to Friday from 9am to 5pm and Saturday and Sunday from 9am to 4pm. The office can book accommodations and dolphin-spotting tours.

SEEING THE AREA

Several operators have vessels offering **dolphin- and whale-watching cruises.** One of the best is the large catamaran called *Imagine* (☎ and fax 02/4984 9000; www. imagineportstephens.hunterlink.au). Frank Future and Yves Papin are real characters, and both operate the 50-foot-long boat. Their daily Island Discovery Trip includes dolphin watching and a trip around the offshore islands. (In summer the trip sometimes includes swimming and snorkeling around a wreck.) The cruises leave Nelson Bay's **D'Albora Marina** daily at 11am daily year-round and return at 3pm; they cost $54 ($37.80) for adults and A$34 (U.S.$23.80) for a children 4 to 14, including lunch. The cruise is free for kids under 4.

A Camel Ride Through the Dunes

Another way to explore the Port Stephens area is on camelback. **Walkabout Camel Adventures** (☎ 02/4964 8996) offers 25- to 30-minute rides through the dunes for A$14 (U.S.$9.80) for adults and A$12 (U.S.$8.40) for children. These rides are offered only during school holidays and long weekends. A 6-hour camel ride through the dunes with a barbecue lunch is available at all other times for A$80 (U.S.$56) per person (but you'll need to put together a group of at least eight people yourself). You can ride a horse through the dunes with **Sahara Horse Trails** (☎ 02/4981 9077); a 2-hour trip costs A$35 (U.S.$24.50) and a half-day excursion A$60 (U.S.$42.70).

Four-hour whale-watching tours cost the same as the cruises (a A$159/U.S.$111.30 family package is also available) and leave at 11am from June 1 to November 15. You are most likely to spot humpback whales, but there's also a chance you'll see minke and southern right whales. A morning dolphin-watching cruise runs daily during summer from 9am to 10:30am; it costs A$15 (U.S.$10.50) for adults, A$7 (U.S.$4.90) for children, and A$38 (U.S.$26.60) for a family.

If you happen to be in Port Stephens on the weekend nearest a full moon, you could join one of *Imagine's* **Full Moon Tours.** The tour, A$135 (U.S.$94.50) for adults and A$95 (U.S.$66.50) for children, includes a dolphin tour, beach camping overnight on an island, and meals. Tours depart 3pm on Saturday and return 6pm Sunday.

Advance II (☎ 02/4981 0399) offers 2-hour dolphin cruises for A$15 (U.S.$10.50), a 3-hour dolphin cruise for A$22 (U.S.$15.40), and a seafood luncheon cruise for A$35 (U.S.$24.50). The **Port Stephens Ferry Service** (☎ 02/4981 3798, or 0419/417 689 mobile phone) operates a daily 2½-hour Early-Bird Dolphin Watch cruise, departing at 8:30am, that includes a stop at the township of Tea Gardens. A similar 3½-hour cruise departs at noon (you can eat lunch at Tea Gardens). There's a 2-hour dolphin-watch cruise at 3:30pm. All cruises cost A$15 (U.S.$10.50) for adults, A$8 (U.S.$5.60) for children, and A$35 (U.S.$24.50) for a family.

WHERE TO STAY

Port Stephens is very popular with Sydneysiders, especially during the Christmas holidays, the month of January, and Easter, so you'll need to book well in advance at those times.

Salamanda Shores. 147 Soldiers Point Rd., Soldiers Point, NSW 2317. ☎ **1800/655 029** in Australia, or 02/4982 7210. Fax 02/4982 7890. E-mail: salamanda@fastlink.com.au. 90 units. A/C TV TEL. A$89 (U.S.$62.30) standard double; A$169 (U.S.$118.30) sea-view room with spa; $179 (U.S.$125.30) family suite; $229 (U.S.$160.30) penthouse. Ask about packages. AE, BC, DC, MC, V.

Salamander Shores looks like a beached, ramshackle paddle steamer; all white-painted bricks, rails, and stairs, fixed to the bay by a jetty. Set in a well-tended, sloping garden of giant gums and geraniums, this five-story hotel retains a certain 1960s charm despite having undergone selective modernization. Many of the renovated rooms have spas and large balconies with sweeping views of the bay.

There are three bars and two restaurants, one serving simple, well-priced seafood and the other with a piano player and candles for more intimate dining. There's also an outdoor pool, a sauna, and a bottle shop and pub. My only complaint is that it seems a little understaffed for such a large place. Salamanda Shores is a short drive from Nelson Bay.

Port Stephens Motor Lodge. 44 Mangus St., Nelson Bay, NSW 2315. ☎ **02/ 4981 3366.**
Fax 02/4984 1655. A/C TV TEL. 17 units. A$60–$110 (U.S.$42–$77) standard double
(depending on season); weekdays A$80 (U.S.$56) family unit, weekends A$100 (U.S.$70).
Additional adult A$10 (U.S.$7) extra; additional child under 15 A$5 (U.S.$3.50) extra. AE, BC,
DC, MC, V.

Surrounded by tall trees and gardens, this motor lodge is a peaceful place to stay and
a short stroll from the main township. The standard rooms are quite plain with raw-
brick walls, a comfy double bed (and an extra single bed in most rooms), a private
balcony, and an attached shower with hip-tub. Adjacent to the lodge is a fully self-
contained family unit with two bedrooms, an internal laundry, and water views. A
swimming pool, barbecue area, and coin-op laundry are on the grounds.

Samurai Beach Bungalows Backpackers. Frost Rd., Anna Bay, NSW 2316. ☎ and
fax **02/4982 1921.** 8 units, 2 with bathroom. A$40 (U.S.$28) standard double; A$65
(U.S.$45.50) deluxe double; A$50 (U.S.$35) family room for 4. A$15 (U.S.$10.50) dorm bed.
BC, MC, V.

These bungalows are nicely positioned between gum trees, tree ferns, and
bougainvillea. Each standard two-room bungalow shares a bathroom, and six units
have a small refrigerator, a fan, and tea- and coffee-making facilities. Each bungalow
comes with either bunk or double beds. Room 8 gets the morning sun, and rooms 4,
5, and 6 get the afternoon sun. Two new deluxe rooms have private balconies (from
which you can sometimes spot koalas), an attached bathroom with shower, a TV, and
towels. There are communal cooking facilities in a separate covered area, a TV room,
and a game room with pool table. Guests have free use of surfboards, and can rent
bikes. The staff will take care of your laundry for A$2 (U.S.$1.40) a load. Public buses
going to Newcastle or Nelson Bay stop outside the door about every hour (weekend
service is more restricted). A free connecting bus meets buses from Sydney, but if
you're loaded down with luggage the hostel staff will pick you up.

WHERE TO DINE

Most people head down to Nelson Bay for their meals because of the great views across
the water. You'll also find a host of cheap take-out joints here.

The Pure Pizza Cafe. D'Albora Marina, Nelson Bay. ☎ **02/4984 2800.** Main courses
A$9–$16.50 (U.S.$6.30–$11.55). Daily 11am–10pm. AE, BC, DC, MC, V. PIZZA & PASTA.

Perfect for take-out, this pizza and pasta place offers a lunchtime pizza for one,
regular-size pizzas suitable for two, and family-size pizzas. Also on offer are filling
pastas, as well as ribs and chicken wings.

Rob's on the Boardwalk. D'Albora Marina, Nelson Bay. ☎ **02/4984 4444.** Main courses
A$16.50–$17.50 (U.S.$11.55–$12.25). Daily 8am–until last customer leaves. AE, BC, DC,
MC, V. CAFE.

You can pick up a hearty American breakfast (A$8/U.S.$5.60) at this busy cafe overlooking the bay, or get a snack throughout the day. The Caesar salad is popular, as are
the half-dozen oysters for A$13.50 (U.S.$9.45). While the food is not super cheap, it's
very good. One of the best main courses is the mixed seafood bouillabaisse. The prime
scotch fillet with sautéed forest mushrooms, Jerusalem artichokes, gratin potatoes, and
a red wine sauce is also tempting.

Rock Lobster. D'Albora Marina, Nelson Bay. ☎ **02/4981 1813.** Main courses A$9.95–
$12.96 (U.S.$6.95–$9.10). Daily 11am–10pm. AE, BC, DC, MC, V. SEAFOOD.

Eat inside or out at this peaceful restaurant with stylish, aluminum-clean atmosphere.
The plump Port Stephens Oysters should be enough to tempt you to start, while

mains such as smoked salmon in layers of wonton pastry with salad and wasabi sauce, or the calamari flavored with chili and coriander in breadcrumbs with spicy passion-fruit dip should fill you up. The menu usually includes a couple of meat dishes and a vegetarian option, too.

4 The Western Plains

Travel across the Blue Mountains and the road swoops down into the wheat, cotton, wool, and cattle country of the great western plains. Here you'll find major agricultural communities, former gold mining towns, and the rocky outcrops and deep gorges of the Warrumbungle National Park. Food and wine are easy to come by around here, with the city of Orange strangely enough the center of Australia's apple-growing region, and Mudgee an important grape-growing area. The area is well served with standard roadside motels.

BATHURST

211km (126½ miles) W of Sydney

If you're heading west from Sydney into the center of the country or down to Adelaide, this farming center (pop. 27,500) is worth a quick stop off, mainly so you can take a spin around the racing circuit.

GETTING THERE   The **Great Western Highway** cuts through the Blue Mountains and leads on down into Bathurst. Hazelton Airlines has flights from Sydney. Countrylink (see chapter 4) offers a direct rail link from the Country Trains section of Sydney's Central Station. Greyhound-Pioneer has daily buses.

VISITOR INFORMATION   The **Bathurst Visitors' Centre,** 28 William St., Bathurst, NSW 2795 (☎ **02/6332 1444;** fax 02/6332 2333), is open daily from 9am to 5pm.

SEEING THE TOWN

The most famous attraction here is the **Mount Panorama Motor Racing Circuit,** which hosts the annual Toohey's 1000 Touring Car Championships in late September or October (☎ **02/6332 1444**). Visitors can drive around the circuit free of charge when there are no races on, and visit the **National Motor Racing Museum (☎ 02/6332 1872)** located in the pit area. It's open daily from 9am to 4:30pm and costs A$5 (U.S.$3.50) for adults and A$1.50 (U.S.$1.05) for children.

If you're interested in a 1½-hour tour of Bathurst's many historic properties, you should pick up a free **Heritage Trail** brochure at the visitors' center.

Escorted Tours of the Western Plains

Countrylink Holidays (☎ 13 28 29 in Australia; e-mail: holidays@countrylink. nsw.gov.au) offers an overnight trip to Dubbo at A$195 (U.S.$136.50) for adults and A$150 (U.S.$105) for children ages 4 to 14; a 2-night trip to the Warrumbungles and Dubbo costs A$273 (U.S.$191.10) for adults and A$234 (U.S.$163.80) for children; and a 3-night trip around the western plains area costs A$425 (U.S.$297.50) for adults and A$400 (U.S.$280) for children. Prices include accommodations, train travel transfers, admission fees, coach tours, and some meals.

WHERE TO STAY & DINE

Sundowner Governor Macquarie Motor Inn. 19 Charlotte St., Bathurst, NSW 2795. ☎ **02/6331 2211.** Fax 02/6331 4754. 37 units. A/C TV TEL. A$95–$100 (U.S.$66.50–$70) double; A$135 (U.S.$94.50) suite. Additional person A$10 (U.S.$7) extra. AE, BC, DC, MC, V.

This typical motor inn is one of the nicest of the many in the area. All rooms are pleasant and comfortable, but the suites have a nicer decor, a queen-size bed instead of a double, and a separate lounge with two sofa lounges. There's a swimming pool. At a restaurant on the premises main courses average A$17 (U.S.$11.90). You can pick up a large serving of pasta or a pizza (from A$8/U.S.$5.60) at Uncle Joe's Pizza, across from the post office on Howick Street.

DUBBO

420km (252 miles) NW of Sydney

The regional capital, Dubbo (pop. 35,000), is situated on the banks of the Macquarie River. This historical town is best known as the home of the Western Plains Zoo. Dubbo is a traditional refueling and stop-off point on the journey to Broken Hill in far-western NSW or to Lightning Ridge in northern NSW.

GETTING THERE   Eastern Australia Airlines and Hazelton Airlines provide an air link between Sydney and Dubbo. The flight takes around 55 minutes. Countrylink (see chapter 4) trains take 6½ hours from Sydney. The town is a popular stopover point for coach companies, including Greyhound-Pioneer, on routes between Adelaide and Brisbane, Melbourne and Brisbane, and Sydney and Adelaide. **Rendell's Coaches** (☎ **1800 02 3328** in Australia, or 02/6884 4199) runs daily coaches to Dubbo leaving at 3pm from Bay 9, Eddy Avenue, Central Station, Sydney. The 6½-hour trip costs A$45 (U.S.$31.50) one-way for adults and A$23 (U.S.$16.10) for children under 9.

VISITOR INFORMATION   Brochures and a hotel booking service are available at the **Dubbo Visitors Centre,** at the corner of Macquarie and Erskine sts., Dubbo, NSW 2830 (☎ **02/6884 1422;** fax 02/6884 1445). It's open daily from 9am to 5pm. Closed Christmas Day. You can find motor information at the **Dubbo Museum and Historical Society,** 232–234 Macquarie St. (☎ **02/6882 5359**).

SEEING THE TOP ATTRACTIONS

Western Plains Zoo. Obley Rd., 5km (3 miles) south of town. ☎ **02/6882 5888.** Admission A$16 (U.S.$11.20) adults, A$8.50 (U.S.$5.95) children 4–16, A$41.50 (U.S.$29.05) family. Daily 9am–5pm. Take the Newell Highway south and turn left onto Obley Rd.

Having heard about the Western Plains Zoo for years, I had in mind that it was a safari park. I was disappointed when I eventually reached it and found the animals wandering around in pretty small paddocks. Nevertheless, it's interesting enough to drive around slowly in your car, or pedal around on a bicycle rented at the entrance booth. There are plenty of African and Asian animals here, and a selection of marsupials such as kangaroos, koalas, dingoes, and emus. The most interesting exhibits I saw were the hippo pools. Allow 2 to 3 hours.

Old Dubbo Gaol (Jail). Macquarie St. ☎ **02/6882 8122.** Admission A$6 (U.S.$4.20) for adults, A$3 (U.S.$2.10) for children. Daily 9am–5pm (no admission after 4:30pm). Closed Good Friday and Christmas Day.

The old city jail was once the lockup for bushrangers and murderers. Today, the original gallows are on display and animatronic figures tell about the brutal lifestyles. You can take a walk around the cells, kitchen, and hospital facilities.

5 South of Sydney Along the Princes Highway

Two main roads lead south out of Sydney: the Hume Highway and the Princes Highway. Both routes connect Sydney to Melbourne, but the Hume Highway is quicker. A favorite with truckers and anyone in a hurry, the Hume Highway will get you to Melbourne in about 12 hours. The Princes Highway is a much more scenic coastal route that can get you to Melbourne in two days, although the many attractions along the route make it well worth spending even longer.

KIAMA
119km (71½ miles) S of Sydney

Kiama (pop. 10, 300) is famous throughout the nation for its **blowhole.** In fact there are two—one large and the other smaller—and both spurt sea water several meters into the air. The larger of the two can jet water up to 60 meters (195 ft.), but you need a large swell and strong southeasterly winds to force the sea through the rock fissure with enough force to achieve those kinds of heights. The smaller of the two is more consistent, but fares better with a good northeasterly wind.

Pick up a map from the Kiama Visitors Centre (see below) to guide you around a **Heritage Walk** that takes in the historic precinct of this pretty harborside village, including a row of National Trust workers' cottages built in 1896 and available for inspection from 10am to 5pm daily.

GETTING THERE From Sydney, travel south on the Princes Highway via the steelworks city of Wollongong. There's also regular train service from Sydney, as well as Greyhound-Pioneer coach service. The trip by coach takes about 2 hours.

VISITOR INFORMATION The **Kiama Visitors Centre** at Blowhole Point, Kiama (☎ **02/4232 3322;** fax 0242 263 260; e-mail: kiamatourism@ozemail.com.au; Web site: www.kiama.net/tourism.htm), is open daily from 9am to 5pm.

WHERE TO STAY & DINE

Kiama Terrace Motor Lodge. 51 Collins St., Kiama, NSW 2533. ☎ **02/4233 1100.** Fax 02/4233 1235. 50 units (3 with shower only). A/C TV TEL. A$95–$135 (U.S.$66.50–$94.50) double. Additional person A$10 (U.S.$7) extra. Reservations can be made through Best Western (☎ 800/780-7234 in the U.S. and Canada, 0800/39 3130 in the U.K., 0800/237 893 in New Zealand, 13 17 79 in Australia). Ask about weekend packages and lower rates through Aussie auto clubs. AE, BC, DC, MC, V.

The town's only four-star motel has pleasant rooms; 22 of the more expensive ones have a spa bath. Two rooms offer facilities for travelers with disabilities. Meals can be brought to your room or eaten in a roadside restaurant that serves up good seafood. Facilities include a self-service laundry, a barbecue, and a saltwater pool.

JERVIS BAY: AN OFF-THE-BEATEN TRACK GEM
182km (109¼ miles) S of Sydney

Bouderee National Park at Jervis Bay is nothing short of spectacular. You should make a trip here even if you have to miss some of Sydney's treasures. How does this grab you—miles of deserted beaches, the whitest sand in the world, kangaroos you can stroke, lorikeets that mob you for food during the day and possums that do the same at night, pods of dolphins, some great walks through gorgeous bushland, and a real Aboriginal spirituality-of-place? I could go on, but it's best you see it for yourself.

GETTING THERE The best way to reach Jervis Bay is via Huskisson, 24 kilometers (14½ miles) southeast of Nowra on the Princes Highway. Approximately 16 kilometers (9½ miles) south of Nowra, turn left onto the Jervis Bay Road to Huskisson. The entrance to Bouderee National Park is just after Huskisson. It's about a 3-hour drive from Sydney.

Australian Pacific Tours (☎ **02/9252 2988;** fax 02/9247 2052; e-mail day. tours@apt.otc.au) runs a dolphin-watching cruise to Jervis Bay from Sydney every Tuesday and Thursday through Saturday between early October and mid-April. The trip (approximately 12 hours, 7 of which are on the coach) includes a visit to the Kiama blowhole, a 3-hour luncheon cruise looking for bottlenose dolphins, and on the way back a stop at the 80-meter-tall Fitzroy Falls in the Southern Highlands. The trip costs A$96 (U.S.$67.20) for adults and A$79 (U.S.$55.30) for children. (It's an awfully long time on a coach, though.)

VISITOR INFORMATION   For information on the area, try **Shoalhaven Visitors Centre,** 254 Princes Hwy., Bomaderry (just north of Nowra) (☎ **1800/024 261** in Australia, or 02/4421 0778; www.shoalhaven.nsw.gov.au). Pick up maps and book camping sites at the **Bouderee National Park office** (☎ **02/4443 0977**), located just beyond Huskisson; it's open daily from 9am to 4pm.

EXPLORING THE PARK: BEACHES, DOLPHINS & MORE

To see the best spots, you'll need to pay the park entrance fee of A$5 (U.S.$3.50). The entrance sticker lasts 7 days. Park highlights include ✪ **Hyams Beach,** reputed to have the whitest sand in the world. Notice how it squeaks as you walk on it. *Note:* Wear sunscreen! The reflection off the beach can give you a sunburn in minutes on a sunny day. **Hole in the Wall Beach** has interesting rock formations and a lingering smell of natural sulfur. **Summer Cloud Bay** is secluded and offers excellent fishing.

Dolphin Watch Cruises, 74 Owen St., Huskisson (☎ **1800/246 010** in Australia, or 02/4441 6311,) runs a hardy vessel out of Huskisson on the lookout for the resident pod of bottlenose dolphins—you have "more than a 95% chance of seeing them," the company claims. Lunch cruises run daily at 1pm, and a coffee cruise runs at 11am on Sundays, public holidays, and school holidays. The 2-hour lunch cruise costs A$39 (U.S.$27.30) for adults, and A$29 (U.S.$20.30) for children. The 2-hour coffee cruise costs A$25 (U.S.$17.50) for adults, and A$17.50 (U.S.$12.25) for children. It's possible to see humpback and southern right whales in June, July, September, and October.

WHERE TO STAY & DINE

If you have a tent and camping gear, all the better. **Caves Beach** is a quiet spot (except when the birds chorus at dawn) located just a stroll away from a good beach; it's home to resident eastern grey kangaroos. A campsite here costs A$8 (U.S.$5.60) per tent in winter and A$10 (U.S.$7) in summer and on public holidays. It's about a 250-meter (¼-mile) walk from the parking lot to the campground. **Greenpatch** is more dirt than grass, but you get your own area and it's suitable for campervans. It's infested with over-friendly possums around dusk. A camp spot here costs A$13 (U.S.$9.10) in winter and A$16 (U.S.$11.20) in summer.

For supplies, head to the area's main towns, Huskisson (pop. 930) and Vincentia (pop. 2,350). The **Huskisson RSL Club,** overlooking the wharf area on Owen Street (☎ **02/4441 5282**), has a good cheap bistro, and the bar serves inexpensive drinks. You'll have to sign in just inside the main entrance.

Jervis Bay Hotel. Owen St., Huskisson, NSW 2540. ☎ **02/4441 5001.** 7 units, none with bathroom. A$60 (U.S.$42) double; A$80 (U.S.$56) family room. Additional person A$20 (U.S.$14) extra. AE, BC, DC, MC, V.

Safety Warning

Jervis Bay is notorious for its **car break-ins,** a situation that the local police force has been unable to bring under control. If you park your car anywhere in the national park, remove all valuable items, including things in the trunk.

Rooms at the "Huskie Pub," as it's known, are clean and simple, with not much more than a double bed and tea- and coffee-making facilities. One family room has two small rooms, with a double in one and a set of bunks in the other. Rooms share bathrooms down the hall. There's also a little common room and ironing facilities. The pub below is popular with locals and the odd tourist, who come to eat fairly reasonable bistro food, play pool, and listen to bands on the weekends. The bar closes around 10pm during the week and no later than 11:45pm on Friday and Saturday nights. The Thai restaurant across the road is pretty good.

Huskisson Beach Tourist Resort. Beach St., Huskisson, Jervis Bay 2540. ☎ and fax **02/ 4441 5142.** TV. Cabins A$48–$75 (U.S.$33.60–$52.50) midweek, A$60–$80 (U.S.$42–$56) Fri–Sat. BC, DC, MC, V.

This resort is the very pinnacle of cabin accommodations on this part of the east coast. Cabins vary in price depending on size, but even the smallest has room enough for a double bed and triple bunks, and a small kitchen with microwave and cooktop. Larger cabins have two separate bedrooms. There's a swimming pool, a game room with videos, a full-size tennis court, and barbecue facilities on the grounds.

BATEMANS BAY
275km (165 miles) S of Sydney

This laid-back holiday town offers good surfing beaches, arts and crafts galleries, boat trips up the Clyde River into wilderness areas, good game fishing, and bushwalks in both the huge Morton and the smaller Deua national parks.

GETTING THERE   Batemans Bay is about a 5½- to 6-hour drive from Sydney. **Premier Motor Service** (☎ **1300/368 100** in Australia, or 02/4423 5233) runs coaches to Batemans Bay from Sydney's Central Station, Monday to Friday at 7:30am (arriving at 1pm), 9:30am (arriving at 3:05pm), and 4:15pm (arriving at 9:45pm. The fare is A$30 for adults and A$22 for children, one-way.

VISITOR INFORMATION   **Batemans Bay Visitor Information Centre,** at the corner of Princes Highway and Beach Road (☎ **1800/802 528** in Australia, or 02/ 4472 6800), offers maps of the area and will make bookings. It's open daily from 9am to 5pm.

GAME FISHING & A RIVER CRUISE
If you fancy some serious fishing, contact **OB1 Charters, Marina,** Beach Rd., Batemans Bay (☎ **1800 641 065** in Australia, or ☎/fax 02/4472 3944). The company runs full-day game fishing trips and morning snapper-fishing trips (as well as afternoon snapper trips in summer). Expect to encounter black Marlin, blue Marlin, giant king fish, mako sharks, albacore tuna, yellow-fin tuna, and blue tuna in winter. The trip includes all tackle and bait, afternoon and morning teas, and lunch. It costs A$120 (U.S.$84) per person. Snapper trips for A$65 (U.S.$45.50) include all gear and bait, and morning or afternoon tea.

A river cruise on the **MV *Merinda,*** Innes Boatshed, Orient St., Batemans Bay (☎ **02/4472 4052;** fax 02/4472 4754), is a pleasant experience. The 3-hour cruise leaves at 11:30am daily and travels inland past townships, forests, and farmland. It costs just A$14 (U.S.$9.80) for adults, and A$7 (U.S.$4.90) for children; a fish-and-chips lunch is A$6 (U.S.$4.20) extra.

A NICE PLACE TO STAY

The Esplanade. 23 Beach Rd. (P.O. Box 202), Batemans Bay, NSW 2536. ☎ **1800/659 884** in Australia, or 02/4472 0200. Fax 02/4472 0277. 23 units. A/C TV TEL. A$90 (U.S.$63) double; A$140–$300 (U.S.$98–$210) suites. Additional person A$15 (U.S.$10.50) extra. Children under 18 free in parents' room. AE, BC, DC, MC, V.

This four-star hotel is right on the Batemans Bay river estuary and close to the town center. Rooms are light and well-furnished, and all have kitchenettes and balconies (some with good water views). Some doubles and suites have spas; they cost the same as rooms without spas, so when booking specify whether you want one. Eat at the hotel's à la carte restaurant, or at the Batemans Bay Soldiers' Club just opposite, which has a restaurant, a bistro, cheap drinks, and a free evening kids club.

NAROOMA
345km (207 miles) from Sydney

Narooma is a pleasant seaside town with beautiful deserted beaches, an interesting golf course right on a headland, a natural rock formation in the shape of Australia (popular with camera-wielding tourists), and excellent fishing. However, its major attraction is ✪ **Montague Island,** the breeding colony for thousands of shearwaters (or mutton birds, as they're also called) and a hangout for juvenile seals.

Just 18 kilometers (11 miles) farther south is Central Tilba, one of the prettiest towns in Australia and the headquarters of the boutique ABC Cheese Factory. You'll kick yourself if you miss this charming historical township (pop. 35; one million visitors annually).

GETTING THERE   Narooma is a 7-hour drive from Sydney down the Princes Highway. **Premier Motor Service** (☎ 1300/368 100 in Australia, or 02/4423 5233) runs coaches to Narooma from Sydney's Central Station Monday to Friday at 7:30am (arriving at 2:05pm), 9:30am (arriving at 4:45pm), and 4:15pm (arriving at 10:45pm). The one-way fare is A$40 (U.S.$28) for adults and A$26 U.S.$18.20) for children.

VISITOR INFORMATION   The **Narooma Visitors Centre,** Princes Highway, Narooma (☎ **02/4476 2881;** fax 02/4476 1690; www.acr.net.au/eta), has good information on the area and can book accommodations and tours.

WHAT TO SEE & DO: WHALES, GOLF, ABORIGINAL CULTURE & MORE

A must if you're visiting the area is a boat tour with ✪ **Narooma Charters** (☎ and fax **02/4476 2111**), which offers spectacular tours of the coast on the lookout for dolphins, seal colonies, and little penguins, and also includes a tour of Montague Island. Morning and afternoon tours take 3½ hours and cost A$50 (U.S.$35) for adults and A$35 (U.S.$24.50) for children. A 4½-hour tour includes some of the world's best whale watching (between mid-September and early December) and costs A$60 (U.S.$42) for adults and A$45 (U.S.$31.50) for children. The last time I went on this trip, we saw no fewer than eight humpback whales—some of them mothers with calves—right by the side of the boat. The company also offers game fishing from February to the end of June, and scuba diving in the seal colonies from August to the end of December. Dives cost A$60 (U.S.$42); gear rental is approximately A$30 (U.S.$21) extra.

Narooma Golf Club (☎ **02/4476 2522**) has one of the most interesting and challenging coastal courses in Australia. A round of golf costs A$20 (U.S.$ 14).

While in the area, I recommend stopping off at the ✪ **Umbarra Aboriginal Cultural Centre,** Wallaga Lake, just off the Princes Highway on the Bermagui road (three-quarters of the way between Narooma and Bermagui; ☎ **02/4473 7232;** fax 02/4473 7169). The center offers activities such as boomerang and spear throwing, and painting with natural ochres for A$6.50 (U.S.$4.55) per person, or A$20 (U.S.$14) for a family of four. There are also discussions, Aboriginal archival displays, and a retail store. It's open Monday to Friday from 9am to 5pm, and Saturday and Sunday from 9am to 4pm (closed Sundays in winter). The center's Aboriginal guides also offer 2-hour four-wheel-drive/walking trips of nearby Mt. Dromedary and Mumbulla Mountain, taking in sacred sites. The tours cost A$45 (U.S.$31.50) per person. Reservations are essential.

If you want to attempt **Mt. Dromedary** without a guide, ask for directions in Narooma. The hike takes around 3 hours to the top, and passes through stands of forest pealing with bell birds.

AN AFFORDABLE PLACE TO STAY

Whale Motor Inn. Princes Hwy., Narooma 2546. ☎ **02/4476 2411.** Fax 02/4476 1995. 17 units. A/C TV TEL. A$65 (U.S.$45.50) double; A$70–$100 (U.S.$49–$70) suite. Additional person A$10 (U.S.$7) extra. AE, BC, DC, MC, V.

This quiet motor inn has the best panoramic ocean views on the south coast and the largest rooms in town. Standard rooms have a queen-size and a single-person sofa bed. Standard suites have a separate bedroom, two extra sofa beds, and a kitchenette. Executive and spa suites are very spacious, better furnished, and have a kitchenette and a large balcony or patio. The restaurant, Harpoons, specializes in local seafood. There's also a swimming pool.

MERIMBULA

480km (288 miles) S of Sydney, 580km (348 miles) NE of Melbourne

This seaside resort (pop. around 7,000) is the focal point of the coastal country between Bega and Eden, and is the last place of interest before the Princes Highway.

GETTING THERE   The drive from Sydney takes about 7 hours, from Melbourne about 7½ hours. Both Kendell Airlines and Hazelton Airlines operate flights to Merimbula. The Greyhound-Pioneer bus trip from Sydney takes more than 8 hours.

VISITOR INFORMATION   The **Merimbula Tourist Information Centre,** at Beach Street, Merimbula (☎ **1800/150 457** in Australia, or 02/6495 1129; fax 02/6495 1250), can book tours and accommodations. It's open from 9am to 5pm daily (10am to 4pm in winter).

SPECIAL EVENTS   Jazz fans should head for the **Merimbula Jazz Festival** held on the Queen's Birthday long weekend in June. A country music festival takes place the last weekend in October.

EXPLORING THE AREA

Merimbula is a good center from which to discover the surrounding Ben Boyd National Park and Mimosa Rocks National Park, which both offer bushwalking. Another park, Bournda National Park, is situated around a lake and encompasses good walking trails and a surf beach.

Golf is the game of choice in Merimbula itself, and the area's most popular venue is the **Pambula-Merimbula Golf Club** (☎ **02/6495 6154**), where you can spot kangaroos grazing on the fairways of the 27-hole course. Another favorite is **Tura Beach Country Club** (☎ **02/6495 9002**), which is known for its excellent coastal views.

Eden, 20 kilometers (12 miles) south of Merimbula, was once a major sealing port. (Its activities now are largely restricted to chopping down trees—take a walk in any of the native forests around here, and the stumps tell their own story.) The rather gruesome **Eden Killer Whale Museum,** on Imlay Street in Eden (☎ 02/6496 2094), is the only reason to stop off here. It has a dubious array of relics, including boats, axes, and remnants of one of the area's last killer whales, called Old Tom. Old Tom led a pack of killer whales that herded a group of baleen whales into Two Fold Bay to be killed by whalers. He was eventually found washed up and dead after his own pod had been gradually whittled away by the whalers when they ran out of other prey. The museum is open Monday through Saturday from 9:15am to 3:45pm and Sunday from 11:15am to 3:45pm. In January, the museum is open daily from 9:15am to 4:45pm. Admission is A$4 (U.S.$2.80) for adults and A$1 (U.S.70¢) for children. Thankfully you can still see a scattering of whales off the coast in October and November.

WHERE TO STAY

Ocean View Motor Inn. Merimbula Dr. at View St., Merimbula, NSW 2548. ☎ 02/6495 2300. Fax 02/6495 3443. 20 units. A/C TEL TV. A$55–$100 double (depending on season). Additional person A$10 (U.S.$7) extra. BC, MC, V.

This pleasant motel has good water views from 12 of its rooms (the best are rooms 9, 10, and 11). The rooms are spacious and modern, with plain brick walls, busy patterned carpets, and one long balcony serving the top six rooms. Fourteen rooms have kitchenettes. All have showers. It's a friendly place, and serves sausage, bacon, and egg breakfasts to your room for A$7 (U.S.$4.90). A Laundromat and a medium-size outdoor saltwater pool are on the premises.

6 The Snowy Mountains: Skiing & More

Thredbo: 519km (312 miles) SW of Sydney, 208km (131 miles) SW of Canberra, 543km (325 miles) NE of Melbourne.

Made famous by Banjo Patterson's 1890 poem the "Man from Snowy River," the Snowy Mountains are most commonly used for what you'd least expect to happen in Australia—skiing. It starts to snow around June and carries on until September. During this time hundreds of thousands of people from all over the country flock here to ski at the major ski resorts—Thredbo and Perisher Blue, and to a lesser extent Charlotte Pass and Mount Selwyn. It's certainly different skiing here, with ghostly white gums as the obstacles instead of pine trees.

The whole region is part of the **Kosciusko** (pronounced "ko-zi-*os*-co") **National Park,** the largest alpine area in Australia. During the summer months the park is a beautiful place for walking, and in spring the profusion of wildflowers is exquisite. A series of lakes in the area, including the one in the resort town of Jindabyne, are favorites with trout fishermen.

Visitors either stay at Jindabyne, 62 kilometers (37 miles) south of Cooma, or Thredbo Village, 36 kilometers (21½ miles) southwest of Jindabyne. Jindabyne is a pretty bleak-looking resort town on the banks of the man-made Lake Jindabyne, which came into existence when the Snowy River was damned to provide hydroelectric power.

Thredbo Village is set in a valley of Mt. Crackenback and resembles a European-style resort. From here, the Crackenback chairlift provides easy access to the top of Mt. Kosciusko, which at 2,228 meters (7,352 ft.) is Australia's highest peak. The mountain has stunning views of the alpine region, and some good walks.

Ski Condition Updates

For up-to-date ski field information call: **Perisher Blue,** ☎ 02/6459 4485; **Thredbo,** ☎ 02/6459 4100; **Charlotte Pass,** ☎ 02/6457 5247; or **Mount Selwyn,** ☎ 02/6454 9488.

SNOWY MOUNTAIN ESSENTIALS

GETTING THERE From Sydney, the Parramatta Road runs into the Hume Highway. Follow the Hume Highway south to Goulburn, where you turn onto the Federal Highway toward Canberra. From there take the Monaro Highway to Cooma, then follow the Alpine Way through Jindabyne and on to Thredbo. Chains may have to be used on the slopes in winter and can be rented from local service stations. The trip takes around seven hours from Sydney, with short breaks.

Impulse Airways, a subsidiary of Ansett, has daily flights from Sydney to Cooma. Flights cost around A$180 (U.S.$126) round-trip. A connecting bus to the ski fields takes about 1 hour and is available from June to October. It's run by **Snowy Mountain Hire Cars** (☎ **02/6456 2957**) and costs A$36 (U.S.$25.20) one-way.

In winter only (from around June 19 to October 5), Greyhound-Pioneer operates daily buses to and from Sydney, via Canberra, to Cooma. The journey takes around 7 hours from Sydney, and three from Canberra. A one-way ticket costs A$47 (U.S.$32.90).

VISITOR INFORMATION Pick up information about the ski fields and accommodations at either the **Cooma Visitors Centre,** 119 Sharp St., Cooma, NSW 2630 (☎ **02/6450 1740;** fax 02/6450 1798), or the **Snowy Region Visitor Centre,** Kosciuszko Road, Jindabyne, NSW 2627 (☎ **02/6450 5600;** fax 64561 249).

HITTING THE SLOPES & OTHER ADVENTURES

Obviously, skiing is the most popular activity around here. More than 50 ski lifts serve the combined fields of Perisher Valley, Mount Blue Cow, Smiggins Holes, and Guthega. Perisher Valley offers the best overall ski slopes; Mount Blue Cow is generally very crowded; Smiggins Holes offers good slopes for beginners; and Guthega has nice light, powdery snow and less-crowded conditions. Thredbo has some very challenging runs and the longest downhill runs. A day's ski pass costs around A$62 (U.S.$43.40) for children, and A$36 (U.S.$25.20) for adults.

A skitube train midway between Jindabyne and Thredbo on the Alpine Way travels through the mountains to Perisher Valley and then to Blue Cow. It costs A$10 (U.S.$7) a day for adult skiers and A$6 (U.S.$4.20) for child skiers; A$22 (U.S.$15.40) for nonskiing adults and A$11 (U.S.$7.70) for nonskiing children. Prices are cheaper in summer. Ski gear can be rented at numerous places in Jindabyne and Thredbo.

WHERE TO STAY

You'll have to book months ahead to find a place to stay during the ski season (especially on weekends). And don't expect to find many bargains. The **Kosciusko Accommodation Centre,** Nuggets Crossing, Jindabyne, NSW 2627 (☎ **1800/026 354** in Australia, or 02/6456 2022; fax 02/6456 2945), can help find and book accommodations in the area. Other private agents that can help find you a spot for the night include **The Snowy Mountains Reservation Centre** (☎ **02/6456 2633**) and the **Thredbo Resort Centre** (☎ **1800/020 589** in Australia).

Summertime Fun

Instead of forking over major cash for a hotel room during the ski season, when even a bed at the YHA goes for A$93/U.S.$65.10 for 2 days (see below), consider visiting the Snowy Mountains in summer, when the region is popular for hiking, canoeing, fishing, and golf. Thredbo Village has tennis courts, a nine-hole golf course, and mountain-bike trails. Accommodations in summer cost about one-third of winter rates.

Riverside Cabins. Thredbo, NSW 2625. ☎ **1800/026 333** in Australia, or 02/6459 4299. Fax 02/6459 4195. 36 units. TV TEL. Winter A$310–$450 (U.S.$217–$315) double. Summer A$110–$150 (U.S.$77–$105) double. Ask about weekly rates. AE, BC, DC, MC, V.

These studio and one-bedroom cabins (which sleep 2 and 4, respectively) are above the Thredbo River and overlook the Crackenback Range. They are also a short walk from the Thredbo Alpine Hotel and local shops. Each room is fully self-contained and most have balconies.

Thredbo Alpine Apartments. Thredbo, NSW 2628. ☎ **1800/026 333** in Australia, or 02/6459 4299. Fax 02/6459 4195. 35 units. TV TEL. Winter A$165–$390 (U.S.$115.50–$273) 1-bedroom, A$275–$555 (U.S.$192.50–$388.50) 2-bedroom, A$375–$680 (U.S.$262.50–$476) 3-bedroom; highest rates apply weekends and July 30–Sept 1. Summer A$120 (U.S.$84) 1-bedroom, A$150 (U.S.$105) 2-bedroom, A$170 (U.S.$119) 3-bedroom. Ask about weekly rates. AE, BC, DC, MC, V. Underground parking.

These apartments are very similar in standard to the Riverside Cabins (above) and are managed by the same people. All are fully self-contained and have balconies with mountain views. Some have queen-size beds. There's limited daily maid service and in-house movies.

Thredbo Alpine Hotel. P.O. Box 80, Thredbo, NSW 2625. ☎ **02/6459 4200.** Fax 02/6459 4201. E-mail: thredbo.com.au. 65 units. MINIBAR TV TEL. Winter A$320–$390 (U.S.$224–$273) double. Summer A$140–$170 (U.S.$98–$119) double. Ask about weekly rates and packages. Rates include breakfast. AE, BC, DC, MC, V.

The center of activity in Thredbo after the skiing is finished for the day is this large resort-style lodge. Rooms vary; those on the top floor of the three-story hotel were refurbished in 1998 and have a king-size bed instead of a standard queen. The rooms are all wood paneled. Thredbo's only nightclub is here. There's also a swimming pool, a sauna, and a spa.

SUPER-CHEAP SLEEPS

Thredbo YHA Lodge. P.O. Box 100, Thredbo, NSW 2625. ☎ **02/6457 6376.** Fax 02/6457 6043. 50 beds and 3 rooms with 2 single beds. Winter A$93 (U.S.$65.10) 2 days, A$190 (U.S.$133) 5 days, $283 (U.S.$198.10) 7 days. Summer room with single bed A$16 (U.S.$11.20) YHA members, A$19 (U.S.$13.30) non-YHA members. Rates are per person. AE, BC, MC, V.

If you want to stay here over the ski season, you'll have to enter a ballot for a bed by the end of April (most people end up getting what they put in for, and some people cancel, so it's always worth checking). Dorms usually sleep four, but there is one with six beds. There's a TV room in summer, and a laundry and kitchen. The Lodge has good mountain views.

Following in the Path of the Man from Snowy River

Horseback riding is a popular activity for all those who want to ride like the "Man from Snowy River." **Reynella Kosciusko Rides,** located in Adamanaby, 44 kilometers (26½ miles) northwest of Cooma (☎ **02/6454 2386;** fax 02/ 6454 2530), offers 3-day/4-night and 5-day/6-night treks through the Kosciusko National Park for A$560 (U.S.$392) and A$995 (U.S.$696.50) respectively, from October to the end of April. The trips work out to be about U.S.$100 a night per person, but they are all-inclusive and include camping and homestead accommodations.

Shorter, and cheaper, rides are offered by **Jindabyne Trail Rides** (☎ **02/ 6456 2421;** fax 02/6456 1254). Gentle, half-hour rides on the slopes above Jindabyne cost about A$20 (U.S.$14) per person.

7 North of Sydney: Australia's Holiday Coast

The Pacific Highway leads over the Sydney Harbour Bridge and merges into the Sydney-Newcastle Freeway. It travels on into Newcastle, an industrial seaside town, and skirts the recreational areas of Tuggerah Lake and Lake Macquarie (neither of great interest compared to what's beyond). From here on, the Pacific Highway stays close to the coast until it reaches Brisbane, some 1,000 kilometers (620 miles) from Sydney.

Along the coast, you'll find excellent fishing and some superb beaches, most of them virtually deserted. Inland, the Great Dividing Range, which separates the wetter eastern plains from the dry interior, offers up rain forests, extinct volcanoes, and tropical-fruit farms as you head even farther north toward the Queensland border. Along the way, too, are a series of national parks. Those you shouldn't miss include the Dorrigo and Mount Warning National Parks, both of which offer some of the country's best and most accessible rain forests.

The farther north you travel the more obviously tropical the landscape gets. By the time visitors reach the coastal resort town of Coffs Harbour, temperatures have noticeably increased and banana palms and sugarcane plantations start to appear.

PORT MACQUARIE
423km (254 miles) N of Sydney

Port Macquarie (pop. 28,000) is roughly halfway between Sydney and the Queensland border. The main attractions here are some wonderful ocean beaches, including **Flynn's,** which can offer exceptional surfing. Boating and fishing are other popular pastimes.

GETTING THERE   From Sydney, motorists follow the Pacific Highway and then

Travel Tip

The **Pacific Highway** is gradually being upgraded, its conditions vary, and the distances are long. Travelers should be aware that the route is renowned for its accidents. Although you could make it from Sydney to Brisbane in a couple of days, you could also easily spend more than a week stopping off at attractions along the way.

the Sydney-Newcastle freeway (F3). Eastern Australia Airways flies between Sydney and Port Macquarie. The coach trip from Sydney takes about 7 hours.

VISITOR INFORMATION   The **Port Macquarie Visitor Information Centre,** at the corner of Clarence and Hay streets, under the Civic Centre (☎ **1800/025 935** in Australia, or 02/6581 8000; e-mail: vicpm@midcoast.com.au; Web site: www. holidaycoast.net.au), is open Monday through Friday from 8:30am to 5pm and Saturday and Sunday from 9am to 4pm.

EXPLORING THE AREA

The **Billabong Koala and Wildlife Park,** 61 Billabong Drive, Port Macquarie (☎ **02/6585 1060**), is a family-owned nature park where you can get close to hand-raised koalas, kangaroos, emus, wombats, many types of birds, and fish in the lily ponds. You can pat the koalas, which have been bred on the property, at 10:30am, 1:30pm, and 3:30pm. There are also barbecue facilities, picnic grounds, and a restaurant. Allow 2 hours to fully experience this recommended wildlife park. It's open daily from 9am to 4:30pm; admission is A$7.50 (U.S.$5.25) for adults and A$4 (U.S.$2.80) for children.

The 257-passenger vessel *Port Venture* (☎ **02/6583 3058;** fax 02/6584 2866) leaves from the wharf at the end of Clarence Street Monday, Tuesday, Thursday, Saturday, and Sunday at 10am and 2pm for a 2-hour scenic cruise on the Hastings River. (There's a boom net affixed to the side so you can cool off in the river while the boat's moving.) It costs A$17 (U.S.$11.90) for adults, A$7 (U.S.$4.90) for children under 14, and A$42 (U.S.$29.40) for a family. Reservations are essential. The boat also travels up the river on a 5-hour barbecue cruise every Wednesday morning, leaving at 10am. It docks at a private bush park along the way and passengers can tuck into a traditional Aussie barbecue of steaks, fish, and salad. There are opportunities for fishing, bushwalking, swimming, and a 20-minute four-wheel-drive trip for an extra A$5 (U.S.$3.50). The cruise costs A$32 (U.S.$22.40) for adults, A$5 (U.S.$3.50) for children, and A$80 (U.S.$56) for a family. A 4-hour barbecue cruise leaves on Friday at 10:15am. It costs A$30 for adults, A$13 for children, and A$75 for a family.

WHERE TO STAY

El Paso Motor Inn. 29 Clarence St., Port Macquarie, NSW 2444. ☎ **1800/027 965** in Australia, or 02/6583 1944. Fax 02/6584 1021). 55 units. A/C MINIBAR TV TEL. A$85 (U.S.$59.50) standard double; A$95 (U.S.$66.50) deluxe double; A$115 (U.S.$80.50) spa rooms; A$140 (U.S.$98) suite. Additional person A$10 (U.S.$7.50) extra. A$30 (U.S.$21) surcharge per room Easter, Christmas, and some long weekends. BC, DC, MC, V.

Located right on the waterfront, this motel offers standard motel-type rooms; the more expensive deluxe doubles are a little larger and have newer furniture and a fresher coat of paint, having been refurbished in 1998. Two rooms come with spas, and some come with kitchenettes. The 3-room suite is on the third floor; it has good ocean views and a kitchenette. The motel also has a heated pool, a sauna, a spa, a recreation room, a licensed restaurant overlooking the sea, and a cocktail bar.

COFFS HARBOUR: BANANA CAPITAL OF OZ

150km (90 miles) N of Port Macquarie, 572km (343 miles) N of Sydney, 427km (256 miles) S of Brisbane

The relaxed capital of Australia's Holiday Coast is bounded by rain forests, beaches, and sand. The state's "banana republic" headquarters—the area produces more bananas than anywhere else in Australia—is bordered by hillsides furrowed with neat rows of banana palms. Farther inland, the rolling hills plateau into the mystical Dorrigo National Park, one of the best examples of accessible rain forests anywhere in the world. Inland too is the Nymboida River, known for its excellent white-water rafting.

Coffs Harbour itself is a rather disjointed place, with an old town center retail area; the Jetty Strip (with its restaurants and fishing boats) near the best swimming spot, Park Beach; and a new retail area called The Plaza. Wide sweeps of suburbia separate all three of these areas, making it a difficult town to negotiate if you don't have a car.

GETTING THERE   It takes around 7 hours to drive from Sydney to Coffs Harbour without stops; from Brisbane it takes around 5 hours. The Pacific Highway in this region is notoriously dangerous, and there have been many serious accidents in recent years involving drivers who've endured long hours behind the wheel. Ongoing road-widening projects should hopefully improve things. Ansett, Qantas, and Eastern Australian Airlines fly nonstop to Coffs Harbour from Sydney. Several coach companies, including Greyhound-Pioneer and McCafferty's, make the trip from Sydney in about 9 hours. A Countrylink train from Sydney (see chapter 4) costs A$67 (U.S.$46.90).

GETTING AROUND   If you don't have a car, you can get around on the **Coffs Explorer** (☎ **02/6653 7115**), a red double-decker bus. Every Wednesday the bus takes visitors on a tour of the town's major tourist sights, including the zoo and the Big Banana. The tour is free, but you pay for entrance to attractions. A better city tour, one that includes a short rain forest walk, departs every Thursday and costs A$30 (U.S.$21), including morning tea and lunch. On Tuesdays the bus heads via Bellingen to Dorrigo National Park; this tour costs A$30 (U.S.$21) and includes morning tea and a barbecue lunch.

VISITOR INFORMATION   Find the **Coffs Harbour Visitors Information Centre** (☎ **1800/025 650** in Australia, or 02/6652 1522) just off the Pacific Highway, at the corner of Rose Avenue and Marcia Street, 2 blocks north of the city center. It's open from 9am to 5pm daily and can book accommodations and tours.

CHECKING OUT THE BIG BANANA & OTHER FUN THINGS TO DO

You can't miss the 10-meter (33-ft.) reinforced concrete banana alongside the highway at the **Big Banana Theme Park** (☎ **02/6652 4355**), 3 kilometers (2 miles) north of town. The park includes an air-conditioned, diesel-powered train that takes visitors on a 1-hour trip of a 45-acre banana plantation containing some 18,000 banana trees. Along the route the train passes various off-the-wall exhibits related to farming, Aborigines, and local history. There are three stops along the way: a short stroll through the banana plantation; a look at the property's hydroponic glasshouses; and a stop at the viewing platform and cafeteria, which serves up banana bread, banana cake, banana splits, banana shakes—you get the idea. Chocolate-covered bananas are a big hit. Other shops here sell ice cream, tacky souvenirs, crafts, opals, clothing, and candy. The park is open daily from 9am to 4pm (3pm in winter). Admission is free, but the train tour costs A$10 (U.S.$7) for adults, A$6 (U.S.$4.20) for children, and A$25 (U.S.$17.50) for a family. I had my doubts about the place before I went, but I must admit I ended up enthusiastic about it—even if only about the wackiness of the place.

The **Coffs Harbour Zoo** (☎ **02/6656 1330**), 10 minutes north of town on the Pacific Highway, has plenty of breeding koalas (you can pet them), as well as wombats, kangaroos, dingoes, Tasmanian Devils, water birds, and aviaries. The award-winning native gardens are full of wild birds expecting a feed. The zoo is open daily from 8:30am to 4pm. Admission is A$12 (U.S.$8.40) for adults, A$6 (U.S.$4.20) for children, and A$30 (U.S.$21) for a family.

A free natural attraction in the area is **Mutton Bird Island,** which you can get to via the Coffs Harbour jetty. A steep path leads up the side of the island, but the

A Deep-Sea Fishing Bargain

The *Pamela Star* (☎ 02/6658 4379) offers good-value deep-sea fishing trips for A$50 (U.S.$35), including lunch and all tackle and bait. The boat leaves Coffs Harbour jetty at 6:30am and returns at 12:30pm daily.

views from the top are worth it. From September through April the island is home to thousands of shearwaters (or mutton birds), which make their nests in burrows in the ground. If you prefer fish, try diving with gray nurse sharks, manta rays, and moray eels with **Island Snorkle and Dive** (☎ 02/6654 2860) or **Dive Quest** (☎ 02/6654 1930).

You may also be interested in **Georges Gold Mine**, 40 kilometers (24 miles) west of Coffs Harbour on Bushman's Range Road (☎ 02/6654 5355 or 02/6654 5273). You get to go into a typical old-timer gold mine, see the "stamper battery" crushing the ore, and pan for gold yourself. The mine is open Wednesday through Sunday (daily during school and public holidays) from 10am to 4pm. Admission is A$8.50 (U.S.$5.95) for adults, A$4 (U.S.$2.80) for children, and A$25 (U.S.$17.50) for a family.

SHOPPING FOR ARTS & CRAFTS

There are several recognized craft drives in the area, where tourists can go in search of quality souvenirs. Pick up a free copy of *Discover the Coffs Harbour Region* from the tourist information center for more details on the dozens of craft shops you could visit. One of the best is the **Australian Wild Flower Gallery** (☎ 02/6651 5763), just off West High Street and Bennetts Road. Wolfgang Shultze carves intricate designs out of pewter, silver, and gold, to make detailed native animal– and plant–influenced jewelry, charms, and spoons. Pieces cost between A$5 to $36 (U.S.$3.50 to $25.20). The gallery is open daily from 9am to 5pm.

On the way to or from the Dorrigo rain forest, stop off at the township of **Bellingen,** 20 minutes south of Coffs Harbour on Waterfall Way. It's a pleasant place with several interesting craft shops. Among the best is **The Old Church** (☎ 02/6655 0438), 8 Church St. (just off the main road), surrounded by courtyards of garden plants and fruit trees. It's open daily from 8:30am to 5:30pm.

EXPLORING THE RAIN FORESTS & OTHER OUTDOOR ADVENTURES

Coffs Harbour's main tourist attraction is its location as a good base for exploring the surrounding countryside. You must see the World Heritage–listed **Dorrigo National Park,** 68 kilometers (41 miles) west of Coffs Harbour, via Bellingen (see above). Perched on the Great Dividing Range that separates the lush eastern seaboard from the more arid interior, the rain forest here is the best I've seen in Australia (it's a desperate pity that so much of it fell to the axes of early settlers). Entry to the rain forest is free.

The **Dorrigo Rainforest Centre** (☎ 02/6657 2309) is the gateway to the park and has extensive information on the local rain forest. Just outside is the 21-meter-high **Skywalk,** which offers a bird's-eye view of the forest canopy. Several rain-forest walks leave from the Rainforest Centre, the Glade Picnic Area (about one km away), and the Never-Never Picnic Area (a 10-km drive along Dome Rd.). Most tracks are suitable for wheelchairs. Bring a raincoat or an umbrella—it's called a rain forest for good reason. You'll find the **Dorrigo Tourist Information** office (☎ 02/6657 2486) in the center of Dorrigo township.

One of the best tour operators in the area is the award-winning **Mountain Trails 4WD Tours,** (☎ 02/6658 3333; fax 02/6658 3299). Full-day tours that include visits to two rain forest areas and a good lunch cost A$80 (U.S.$56) for adults and A$60 (U.S.$42) for children under 16. Half-day tours of one rain forest cost A$56 (U.S.$39.20) for adults and A$40 (U.S.$28) for children.

For a bit more personal action, try horseback riding through the rain forest 23 kilometers (14 miles) southwest of Coffs Harbour with **Valery Trails** (☎ **02/6653 4301**). Two-hour rides leave at 10am and 2pm daily and cost just A$30 (U.S.$21) per person.

More hectic are ✪ **white-water rafting trips** through the wilderness on the furious Nymboida River with ✪ **Wow Rafting,** 1448 Coramba Rd., Coramba via Coffs Harbour, NSW 2450 (☎ **1800 640 330** in Australia, or 02/6654 4066). Full-day trips, with a barbecue lunch, cost A$135 (U.S.$94.50). Trips operate year-round, depending on water levels. A 2-day trip costs A$295 (U.S.$206.50), including all meals and overnight camping. If the water level in the Nymboida is low, then you raft on the Goolang Creek, which offers a shorter run that is still very exciting. Most of the rapids are graded 3 out of 6 on the rapid scale (to give some sort of comparison, 1 is a trickle and 6 is Niagara Falls). Needless to say, some of them can be pretty hairy. The rafting guides are real characters, and although they're safety conscious, they are likely to make sure you're dunked a few times.

Looking for yet another adrenaline rush? Then head to the **Raleigh International Raceway** (☎ **02/6655 4017**), where you can zip around the track behind the wheel of your very own . . . go-kart. It's located 23 kilometers (14 miles) south of Coffs Harbour and 3 kilometers (2 miles) along Valery Road off the Pacific Highway, north of Nambucca Heads. Five high-speed laps cost A$12 (U.S.$8.40), 10 cost A$20 (U.S.$14), and 16 cost A$30 (U.S.$21). It's open daily from 9am to 5pm (6pm in summer).

Out to sea, the *Pacific Explorer* catamaran (☎ **0418/663 815** mobile phone, or 02/6652 7225 after working hours) operates whale-watching trips between June and October. The 2½-hour cruise costs A$35 (U.S.$24.50). Between November and May, there's a 3-hour dolphin-watching cruise that also costs A$35 (U.S.$24.50).

WHERE TO STAY

Coffs Harbour is a popular beachside holiday spot with plenty of motels along the Pacific Highway offering standard roadside rooms for A$35 (U.S.$24.50) to A$49 (U.S.$34.30) per night. Coffs Harbour fills up during school holidays and the Christmas and Easter periods, but at other times you'll see plenty of vacancy signs. Nicer, better positioned (and more expensive) options include the **Caribbean Motel,** 353 High St., Coffs Harbour, NSW 2450 (☎ **02/6652 1500;** fax 02/6651 4158), where doubles go for A$55 to $85 (U.S.$38.50 to $59.50) in low season and A$85 to $120 (U.S.$59.50 to $84) in peak season; and the **Coffs Harbour Motor Inn,** 22 Elizabeth St., Coffs Harbour, NSW 2450 (☎ **02/6652 6388;** fax 02/6652 6493), which has rooms from A$72 to $78 (U.S.$50.40 to $54.60) in low season and A$102 to $108 (U.S.$71.40 to $75.60) in peak season.

A real budget option is the **Park Beach Caravan Park,** Ocean Beach, Coffs Harbour, NSW 2450(☎ **02/6648 4888;** fax 02/6651 2465). This place offers on-site, two-berth caravans for A$26 (U.S.$18.20), two-person cabins with TV for A$32 (U.S.$22.40), and cabins with attached bathrooms from A$40 (U.S.$28).

✪ **Pelican Beach Centra Resort.** Pacific Hwy., Coffs Harbour, NSW 2450. ☎ **1800/ 02 8882** in Australia, 800/835 7742 in the U.S. and Canada, or 02/6653 7000. Fax 02/ 6653 7066. 112 units. A/C MINIBAR TV TEL. A$98–$170 (U.S.$98–$105) standard (1 or 2 people); A$205–$265 (U.S.$143.50–$185.50) family room (up to 4 people); A$265–$420 (U.S.$185.50–$294) suite (1 or 2 people). Additional person A$25 (U.S.$17.50) extra. Ask about usually available good-value deals. The higher rates are for Dec 26–Jan 18.

Something Fruity

A more placid activity is a visit to **Kiwi Down Under Farm** (☎ 02/6653 4449), a fascinating organic farm growing kiwi fruit and macadamia nuts, among other things. No nasty sprays are used here. Free 30- to 45-minute guided tours of the property leave at 2, 3, and 4pm on weekends and school holidays. The tea shop on the premises serves amazing scones and jam for A$4.50 (U.S.$3.15), as well as good-value and excellent vegetarian lunches for A$8.50 (U.S.$5.95). The farm is 14 kilometers (8½ miles) south of Coffs Harbour (turn off onto Gleniffer Road, just south of Bonville; it's another 4km/2½ miles, following the signs).

For a little extra money, try this Bali-style resort complex situated 7 kilometers (4 miles) north of Coffs Harbour beside a long stretch of creamy sand (the beach is dangerous for swimming). Terraced over six levels, the resort's rooms all have balconies and many have ocean views. Standard rooms are light and modern, with either twin or queen beds. Family rooms have a kitchenette and dining area, and one queen and two single beds divided by a half wall. Suites have a separate bedroom, kitchenette, lounge area, and spa bath. Two rooms are equipped for travelers with disabilities. Outside in the landscaped gardens are three tennis courts, a minigolf course, a volleyball court, and a lagoon-like heated pool. There are also indoor and outdoor spas, a sauna, a gym, and a barbecue area. A game room and a kids club that operates on weekends and school holidays keeps children out of your hair. The pricey (but award-winning) Shores Restaurant offers indoor and terrace dining. Taxis operate from the resort to the town center for A$3 (U.S.$2.10) each way.

Sanctuary Resort. Pacific Hwy., Coffs Harbour, NSW 2450. ☎ **02/6652 2111**. Fax 02/6652 4725. 37 units. A/C TV TEL. A$75 (U.S.$52.50) standard double; A$85 (U.S.$59.50) superior double; A$150 (U.S.$105) executive double. Additional person A$12 (U.S.$8.40) extra. Holiday surcharges. Ask about lower rates through Aussie auto clubs. AE, BC, DC, MC, V.

If you like animals you'll love this animal sanctuary/guest house complex situated about 2 kilometers (1¼ miles) south of town. Wandering around the grounds are wallabies, kangaroos, peacocks, and several species of native birds. The rooms are comfortable, with the more expensive rooms being larger and more recently renovated. The executive room comes with a spa.

In Nearby Nambucca Heads

Much smaller than Coffs Harbour (it virtually closes down after 6pm), Nambucca (pronounced "nam-*buck*-a") Heads—44 kilometers (26½ miles) south—is another coastal option, though it's hardly an exciting place for younger visitors. The **Nambucca Valley Visitor Information Centre** (☎ 02/6568 6954; fax 02/6568 5004; e-mail:nambuct@midcoast.com.au), is on the Pacific Highway on the southern entrance to town. It's open daily from 9am to 5pm.

Scotts Guesthouse. 4 Wellington Dr., Nambucca Heads, NSW 2448. ☎ **02/6568 6386**. Fax 02/6569 4169. 8 units (all with shower only). TV. A$70–$100 (U.S.$49–$70) double (depending on season). Additional adult A$20 (U.S$14) extra; additional child A$15 (U.S.$10.50) extra. Rates include continental breakfast. AE, BC, DC, MC, V. Free parking.

Scotts, a friendly B&B run by an Irish couple, offers good motel-style rooms in a modernized 1887 house not far from the beach. All rooms are spacious and very modern, and have a good-size balcony with a good view. They come with a queen-size bed, a shower, and a fridge. Family rooms have an extra double sofa bed and a single. Try to get room no. 1 for the best views. There's a coin-op laundry on the premises.

Beilby's Beach House. 1 Ocean St., Nambucca Heads 2448 ☎ and fax **02/6568 6466**. E-mail: beilbys@midcoast.com.au. 5 units, 3 with bathroom (shower only). TV. A$40–$50 (U.S.$28–$35) double without bathroom; A$60–$75 (U.S.$42–$52.50) double with bathroom; A$80–$100 (U.S.$56–$70) family room. BC, MC, V.

If you're looking for a peaceful place to stay, then come to Beilby's (named after the beach opposite). The standard rooms are basic but comfortable enough and have either a queen or a double bed. Three come with an attached shower. The family room is basically two small rooms with an adjoining door. All rooms have a verandah overlooking a bush garden. There's a large swimming pool in the garden, a guest kitchen, a large covered barbecue area, a guest laundry, Internet facilities, and computer games for the kids. It's a short walk through the bird-filled bush to the beach. While a few backpackers stay here, the guests range from young couples to families to senior citizens.

WHERE TO DINE

Seafood Mama's. Pacific Hwy. ☎ **02/6653 6733.** Reservations recommended. Main courses A$12.50–$25 (U.S.$8.75–$17.50). AE, BC, DC, MC, V. Wed–Fri noon–2pm; daily 6–10pm. ITALIAN/SEAFOOD.

Seafood Mama's is right on the ocean, near the Pelican Beach and the older Nautilus resorts, 7 kilometers (4¼ miles) north of Coffs Harbour. This award-winning restaurant packs a mean barbecue seafood dish of octopus, prawns, fish, calamari, and mussels. Also on the menu in this rustic, bottles-hanging-from-the-ceiling type of Italian joint are some well-regarded veal and steak dishes, and plenty of pastas, It's cheerful, friendly, and informal, and does take-out and hotel deliveries.

For similar fare at cheaper prices try **Maria's Italian Restaurant,** 368 High St., Coffs Harbour Jetty (☎ **02/6651 3000**), where great pastas cost A$9.50 to $13.50 (U.S.$6.65 to 9.45) and pizzas are A$8 to $11.50 (U.S.$5.60 to $8.05); other mains cost between A$14 and $17.50 (U.S. $9.80 and $12.25).

BYRON BAY: A BEACHSIDE BOHEMIA

78km (47 miles) SE of Murwillumbah

The sun's rays hit Byron, the most easterly point on the Australian mainland, before they land anywhere else. This geographical position is good for two things: You can **spot ✪ whales** close to shore as they migrate north in June and July, and it's holistically attractive to the town's alternative community. Byron Bay is at the forefront of the "creative edge of culture." Painters, craftspeople, glassblowers, and poets are so plentiful they almost fall from the macadamia nut trees. The place is loaded with float tanks, "pure body products," beauty therapists, and massage centers. Although Byron Bay attracts squadrons of roving backpackers each summer to its party scene and discos, many of the locals simply stay at home, sipping their herbal tea and preparing for the healing light of the coming dawn.

Families love Byron Bay for the beautiful beaches, and surfers flock here for some of the best surfing in the world. Wategos Beach and an area off the tip of Cape Byron called The Pass are particularly good, but since all of Byron Bay's main beaches face in different directions, you are bound to find the surf is up on at least one. Main Beach, which stretches along the front of the town (it's actually some 50km/30 miles long), is good for swimming. West of Main Beach is Belongil Beach, which acts as an unofficial nudist beach when the authorities aren't cracking down on covering up. Clarke's Beach, which offers good surfing, curves away to the east of Main Beach toward Cape Byron. The Cape Byron Lighthouse on Cape Byron is one of Australia's most powerful. It's eerie to come up here at night to watch the stars and see the light reach some

40 kilometers (24 miles) out to sea. A nice walk just south of the main town center goes through the rain forest of the Broken Heads Nature Reserve.

Behind Byron you'll find hills that could make an Irishman weep, as well as rain forests, waterfalls, and small farms burgeoning with tropical fruits. A good operator taking trips inland is **Forgotten Country Ecotours** (☎ **02/6687 7843**). **Byron Bay to Bush Tours** (☎ **02/6685 6889,** or 0418/662 684 mobile phone; e-mail: bush@mullum.com.au) operates day trips to the hippy hangout of Nimbin and up into the rain forest, visiting a macadamia nut farm on the way and having a barbecue on the company's own organic farm. The trip leaves at 9:30am Monday to Saturday and costs A$30 (U.S.$21). This company also operates trips to the Sunday market at Channon on the second Sunday of each month and to the market at Bangalow on the fourth Sunday. These trips cost A$15 (U.S.$10.50).

GETTING THERE   If you're driving up the north coast, leave the Pacific Highway at Ballina and take the scenic coast road via Lennox Head. Byron Bay is around 10 hours by car from Sydney and 2 hours (200km/120 miles) from Brisbane. Ansett flies from Sydney to Ballina, 20 kilometers (12 miles) south of Byron Bay. The Coolangatta airport is just north of the Queensland border, 112 kilometers (67 miles) away. Countrylink runs daily trains from Sydney to Byron Bay for A$85 (U.S.$59.50) one-way for adults and A$42.50 (U.S.$29.75) for children. Greyhound Pioneer buses from Sydney take around 13½ hours and cost A$69 (U.S.$48.30) one-way; the trip from Coffs Harbour costs around A$35 (U.S.$24.50).

VISITOR INFORMATION   Stop at the **Byron Visitors Centre,** 80 Jonson St., Byron Bay, NSW 2481 (☎ **02/6685 8050;** fax 02/6685 8533 or 02/6685 8463). It's open daily from 9am to 5pm. Another option, half an hour farther south, is the **Ballina Tourist Information Centre,** on the corner of Las Balsas Plaza and River Street, Ballina (☎ **02/6686 3484;** fax 02/6686 0136). It's also open from 9am to 5pm daily. A couple of good Web sites to check out before you leave home are www.byronbay.net.au and www.byrontobush.com.au.

SPECIAL EVENTS   Byron really goes to town during its Easter weekend **Blues Festival.** On the first Sunday of every month an extraordinary local **crafts market** brings hippies and funky performers out from the hinterland.

ENJOYING THE AREA: SURFING, DIVING & MORE

Most of the budget accommodations in Byron Bay offer free surfboards for guests. Alternatively, try the **Byron Bay Surf Shop** on Lawson Street (☎ **02/6680 9250**). It rents surfboards for A$12 (U.S.$8.40) for 4 hours or A$20 (U.S.$14) per day (you'll need to leave a A$400/U.S.$280 credit-card or cash deposit). The shop can also arrange surf lessons for around A$25 (U.S.$17.50) per hour.

The best place to **dive** around Byron Bay is at **Julian Rocks,** about 3 kilometers (2 miles) off shore. Cold currents from the south and warmer ones from the north meet here, which makes it a good spot to find a large variety of sea life. **Byron Bay Dive Centre,** 111 Jonson St. (☎ **02/6685 7149**), charges A$70 (U.S.$49) for the first dive and A$40 (U.S.$28) for each subsequent dive. **Sundive,** in the Byron Hostel complex on Middleton Street (☎ **02/6685 7755**), also charges A$70 (U.S.$49) for the first dive, but only A$35 (U.S.$24.50) for subsequent dives.

An unusual option for thrill seekers is to learn to use a trapeze with **Flying Trapeze** (☎ **02/6685 8000**), located 3 kilometers (2 miles) west of town at the Byron Bay Beach Club. A fun hour-long class costs A$15 (U.S.$10.50); a more thorough 2-hour class costs A$20 (U.S.$14) and includes chances to swing through the air and let go (hopefully your partner catches you). Classes run twice daily during NSW school holidays and generally in the afternoon from Tuesday to Sunday at other times.

For the Adventurous . . .

An unusual way to get to Byron Bay is on a 5-day surf safari from Sydney with **Aussie Surf Adventures,** P.O. Box 614, Toukley, NSW 2263 (☎ **1800/113 044** in Australia, or 0414 863 787 mobile phone; fax 02/4396 1797; e-mail: surfadventures @hotmail.com). The trips leave at 8:30am every Monday from Sydney's Circular Quay and stop off for surfing, body boarding, fishing, and nature walks along the way. Beginners to experienced surfers are all welcome. The trip costs A$365 (U.S.$255.50), including all meals, surfing lessons, and surfing and camping equipment.

A highly recommended 3-day tour is with the very likable Ivan from **The Pioneering Spirit** (☎ **1800/672 422** in Australia, or 0412/048 333 mobile phone; www.users.omcs.com.au/pioneering). Suitable for young (or young at heart) adventurous travelers, the trip by minicoach leaves Sydney every Friday en route to Byron. Along the way you stop off for swimming, native animal spotting, a tour of the Hunter Valley and Dorrigo National Park, and bushwalking. Overnight accommodations are in basic but interesting buildings. The trips costs A$175 (U.S.$122.50) including transport, all meals, accommodations, and entry fees.

WHERE TO STAY

A major stop on the well-worn backpacking trail to the Gold Coast and Cairns in Queensland, Byron Bay has plenty of lodges, resorts, and hostels chasing the budget travelers' buck. Real estate agents **Elders R Gordon & Sons** (☎ **02/6685 6222;** e-mail: eldersbb@omcs.com.au) can book rooms and cottages in Byron Bay and in the hinterland.

Aquarius Backpackers Resort. 16 Lawson St. (P.O. Box 136), Byron Bay, NSW 2481. ☎ **1800 028 909** in Australia, or 02/6685 7663; fax 02/6685 7439. 31 units, 4 with bathroom. A$45 (U.S.$31.50) backpacker double without bathroom; A$75–$150 (U.S.$52.50–$105) motel double with bathroom. A$20 (U.S.$14) dorm bed. Motel rooms are A$30 (U.S.$21) more on weekends. AE, BC, MC, V.

One of the friendliest places in Byron, this resort is aimed at budget travelers from all over the world who want to hang out and meet other people. Rooms are very clean and simply furnished. Dorms sleep between six and eight; all have a refrigerator as well as an attached bathroom. Double rooms are equally basic. The motel rooms come with a double bed, a sofa bed, a TV, and a kitchenette. The more expensive ones have a spa. The resort has a very nice swimming pool, cheap bicycle rental, a laundry, a game room, a TV room, Internet and fax machines, and a sociable barbecue area. An excellent cafe sells cheap meals.

✪ **Holiday Village Backpackers.** 116 Jonson St., Byron Bay, NSW 2481. ☎ **02/ 6685 8888.** Fax 02/6685 8777. 42 units, 12 with bathroom. A$35–$50 (U.S.$24.50– $35) single or double in hostel; A$37–$52 (U.S.$25.90–$36.40) self-contained double. A$18 (U.S.$12.60) dorm bed. BC, DC, MC, V.

Byron Bay's original hostel is still one of the best. It's located in the center of town next door to Woolworth's supermarket and is only a few minutes walk from the bus and train stops and the main beach. It's classified as a five-star backpackers' hostel, which is as good as it gets. Dorm rooms are clean, and doubles in the hostel are above average and come with a double bed, a fan, and a wardrobe. For a couple of dollars more you can stay in a fully self-contained unit with a separate bedroom, lounge, and kitchen area. On the premises you'll find a volleyball court; a spa and pool; a TV and video lounge (there's a video library); barbecues; a basketball hoop; Internet and e-mail access; and free surfboards, body boards, and bicycles.

J's Bay Hostel. 7 Carlyle St., Byron Bay, NSW 2481. ☎ **1800/678 195** in Australia, or 02/6685 8853. Fax 02/6685 6788. 30 units, 2 with bathroom. A$42 (U.S.$29.40) single or double without bathroom; A$48 (U.S.$33.60) single or double with bathroom. A$16–$20 (U.S.$11.20–$14) dorm bed. YHA discount A$2 (U.S.$1.40). Inquire about weekly rates. BC, MC, V.

This huge hostel, located 400 meters (433 yards) from the beach and 200 meters (around 215 yards) from the town center, has spotlessly clean four-share and ten-share dorms that come with ceiling fans, bunks, and cubbyholes for personal belongings. The double and single rooms are in a separate wing and are pretty standard for this type of budget accommodation. There's a good-size communal kitchen, a verandah, a laundry, a large heated pool, and a barbecue in the hostel's central courtyard. The hostel offers free bikes and body boards and can arrange tours. It's wheelchair accessible.

Byron Central Apartments. Byron St., Byron Bay, NSW 2481. ☎ **02/6685 8800.** Fax 02/6685 8802. 26 units. TV TEL. A$90–$180 (U.S.$63–$126) apt. Rates vary depending on season; low season is Apr–Sept. Rates higher over Christmas/New Year period. Ask about discounts for multinight stays. AE, BC, DC, MC, V.

Although these apartments are a bit pricey in peak season, they are certainly worth considering if you're in Byron at other times of the year (especially if you decide to stay more than one night, because prices drop after the first night to A$75/U.S.$52.50 per night). You can also save money by cooking your own meals. The units have ceiling fans, full kitchens, a queen-size bed and a queen-size sofa bed, and free in-house movies. Those on the first floor have balconies. There are also a few loft-style apartments with separate dining, lounge, and sleeping areas. Units for people with disabilities are available. The landscaped, mostly concrete surrounds contain a saltwater pool and a barbecue. There's also a laundry. The apartments are a 2-minute walk from the main beach and town.

Worth a Splurge

The Byron Bay Waves Motel (The Waves). Corner of Lawson and Middleton sts. (P.O. Box 647), Byron Bay, NSW 2481. ☎ **02/6685 5966.** Fax 02/6685 5977. E-mail: info@ byronwaves.com. Web site: www.byronwaves.com. A/C TV TEL. 19 units. A$140–$235 (U.S.$98–$164.50) double; A$225–$375 (U.S.$157.50–$262.50) suite; A$350–$490 (U.S.$245–$343) penthouse. Rates vary depending on season. Additional adult A$40 (U.S.$28) extra; additional child under 16 A$20 (U.S.$14) extra. AE, BC, DC, MC, V.

This exceptional motel is just 60 meters from Main Beach and just around the corner from the town center. The rooms are very nice, and all come with a queen-size bed, a marble bathroom with shower and king-size tub, a safe, a refrigerator, an iron and ironing board, a hair dryer, and tea- and coffee-making facilities. Four rooms on the ground floor have a courtyard; one room is suitable for travelers with disabilities. The suites have a king-size bed and a large balcony. The penthouse is a plush, fully self-contained one-bedroom apartment. The six family rooms sleep three adults, or two adults and two children.

WHERE TO DINE

Beach Hotel Barbecue. In the Beach Hotel, at Bay and Johnson sts. ☎ **02/6685 6402.** Main courses A$3.90–$13.50 (U.S.$2.75–$9.45). No credit cards. Daily noon–3pm. PUB/BARBECUE.

The outdoor meals served at this pub near the beach make it popular with visitors and locals alike. About the cheapest thing on the menu is the burger, and the most expensive a steak. The Beach Hotel Bistro here is open from 10am to 9pm daily and serves coffee, cakes, and snacks throughout the day; a full lunch menu is served from noon to 3pm and dinner from 6pm to 9pm.

Earth 'n' Sea. 11 Lawson St. ☎ **02/6685 6029.** Reservations recommended. Main courses A$11–$21 (U.S.$7.70–$14.70). AE, BC, MC, V. Daily from noon. PIZZA/PASTA.

This popular eating spot has been around for years and offers a fairly extensive menu of pastas and pizzas, including such unusual combinations as prawns, banana, and pineapple. Pizzas come in three sizes; the small is just enough to satisfy the average appetite.

The Pass Café. At the end of Brooke Drive, on Cape Byron Walking Track, Palm Valley. ☎ **02/6685 6074.** Main courses A$7–$12 (U.S.$4.90–$8.40). BC, MC, V. Daily 8am–11:30am and noon–3pm. MEDITERRANEAN.

Though not as well positioned as Rae's Restaurant and Bar (see below), The Pass Café rivals Rae's for breakfasts and lunches, and if you happen to be heading to or from the local rain forest on the Cape Byron Walking Track, you'll find this a great place to stop off. Breakfast choices range from simple fresh fruit and muffins to gourmet chicken sausages. Lunch specials include Cajun chicken, octopus and calamari salad, as well as fresh fish, meat dishes, and plenty of good vegetarian options.

✪ **Raving Prawn.** Feros Arcade (between Jonson and Lawson sts.). ☎ **02/6685 6737.** Reservations recommended. Main courses A$15–$24 (U.S.$10.50–$16.80). AE, BC, DC, MC, V. Tues–Sat 6–10pm (winter to around 9pm); open daily during school holidays. SEAFOOD.

There are fish all over the walls at this excellent eatery, but there's more than fish on the menu. You can tuck into veal, chicken, or vegetarian dishes if you want, but I wouldn't miss out on the fabulous signature dish, the Jewfish in a herb-mustard crust. The forest-berry tart is the best desert on the menu.

Worth a Splurge

Rae's Restaurant and Bar. Watago's Beach, Byron Bay. ☎ **02/6685 5366.** Reservations recommended. Dinner main course A$18–$28 (U.S.$12.60–$19.60); lunch A$14–$26 (U.S.$9.80–$18.20). AE, BC, DC, MC, V. Wed–Sun noon–3pm, daily 7–10pm. MODERN AUSTRALIAN/SEAFOOD.

You can't beat Rae's for either its location or its food. It's right on the beach, about a 2-minute drive from the town center, and has a nice secluded, privileged air about it. Inside it's all Mediterranean blue and white. The menu changes daily, but you may find the likes of grilled Atlantic salmon, red curry of roast beef fillet, braised lamb shanks, and yellow fin tuna ready for your plate. Tell the chef if you have any special dietary requirements, and he will go out of his way to please you. Next door to the restaurant, but part of the same establishment, is Rae's on Watago's, an exclusive guest house offering luxury beachside suites.

MURWILLUMBAH

321km (192½ miles) N of Coffs Harbour, 893km (535½ miles) N of Sydney, 30km (18 miles) S of Queensland border.

The focal point of the Tweed Valley, Murwillumbah (pop. 8,000) is a good base for touring the surrounding area, which includes the forested slopes of Mt. Warning, picturesque country towns, and a countryside dominated by sugarcane, banana, dairy and beef, and timber industries.

GETTING THERE   Murwillumbah is inland from the Pacific Highway. The nearest airport is at Coolangatta, 34 kilometers (20½ miles) away just over the Queensland border. Countrylink trains link Murwillumbah with Sydney (trip time is 12 hours and 40 minutes); a one-way ticket costs around A$88 (U.S.$61.60). Greyhound Pioneer buses from Sydney to Murwillumbah cost A$69 (U.S.$48.30) one-way (trip time is 14½ hours).

VISITOR INFORMATION   The **Murwillumbah Visitors Centre,** at the corner of the Pacific Highway and Alma Street, Murwillumbah, NSW 2484 (☎ 02/ 6672 1340), is worth visiting before you head out to see more of the Tweed Valley or the beaches to the east. Another option is the **Tweed Heads Visitors Centre,** at the corner of Bay and Wharf streets, Tweed Heads, NSW 2485 (☎ 07/5536 4244).

SEEING THE AREA

If you're looking for a Big Avocado to go with your Coffs Harbour Big Banana, then head for the Tweed Valley's top attraction, **Tropical Fruit World,** on the Pacific Highway (☎ 02/6677 7222), 15 kilometers (9 miles) north of Murwillumbah and 15 kilometers south of Coolangatta. Some 400 varieties of tropical fruit are grown here; you can explore the 200-acre plantation on an interesting 1½-hour tractor-train tour. Four-wheel-drive rain-forest adventures and riverboat rides also are offered. It's open daily from 10am to 6pm (to 5pm in winter). Also on the property are a restaurant, kiosk, fruit market, and gift shop. Admission to food and shopping areas is free. Guided tours cost A$20 (U.S.$14) for adults, A$10 (U.S.$7) for children 3 to 12, and A$50 (U.S.$35) for a family of five.

The 1,154-meter (3,815 ft.) **Mt. Warning** is part of the rim of an extinct volcano formed from volcanic action some 20 to 23 million years ago. Many good bushwalks through the Mt. Warning World Heritage Park circle the mountain and lead to its summit.

WHERE TO STAY & DINE

Budget-conscious travelers will appreciate the **Mt. Warning/Murwillumbah Backpackers YHA,** 1 Tumbulgum Rd., Murwillumbah, NSW 2484 (☎ 02/6672 3763). It has two eight-bed dorms and four double rooms. The hostel is right on the banks of the Tweed River, and you can rent canoes and rowboats here. Rates are A$14 (U.S.$9.80) for YHA members and A$16 (U.S.$11.20) for nonmembers in a dorm, and A$16 (U.S.$11.20) for members and A$17 (U.S.$11.90) for nonmembers in a double.

✪ **Crystal Creek Rainforest Retreat.** Brookers Rd., Upper Crystal Creek, Murwillumbah, NSW 2484. ☎ **02/6679 1591.** Fax 02/6679 1596. 7 cabins. TV. A$165 (U.S.$115.50) double without spa; A$165–$195 (U.S.$115.50–$136.50) double with spa. Ask about lower midweek rates and weekly specials. BC, MC, V. Not suitable for children. Pick-up service from the airport is available.

Crystal Creek is tucked away in a little valley of grazing cows just 25 minutes by car from the Pacific Highway. Self-contained cabins nestle on the edge of a rain forest bordering the Border Ranges National Park. There are plenty of native birds, possums, echidnas, wallabies, and bandicoots around and about. The water is always cold, and guests can swim in the natural pools and laze around on hammocks strung up in the bush. Cabins have two comfortable rooms, a balcony, a kitchen, a barbecue, and plenty of privacy. To live up to the ecolodge's image, everything inside is green, even the sheets. Two new glass-terrace cabins overlook the rain forest and mountain and have a king-size bed and a double spa. Several tours are offered, including four-wheel-drive rain-forest tours and visits to local country markets and arts and crafts galleries. Bird watching and canoeing are popular on the nearby lake. Guests cook their own food or eat at the casual restaurant. Smoking is not permitted on the property.

AFTER DARK

The clubs up here near the Queensland border are huge, and offer cheap bistro meals (as well as pricier ones in the more upscale restaurants), inexpensive drinks, entertainment, and hundreds of poker machines. The biggest service club in New South Wales is the **Twin Towns Services Club,** Wharf Street, Tweed Heads (☎ **07/5536 2277**), open Sunday to Thursday from 9:30am to 1am, and Friday and Saturday from 9:30am to 2am. Another worth checking out is **Seagulls Rugby League Club,** Collan Drive, Tweed Heads (☎ **07/5536 3433**). It's open 24 hours.

To gain admittance to these "private" clubs, you must sign the registration book just inside the door.

8 Outback New South Wales

The Outback is a powerful Australian image. Although it's hot, dusty, and prone to flies, it can also be a romantic place where wedge-tailed eagles float in the shimmering heat and where you can spin around in a circle and follow the unbroken horizon. If you drive out here, you have to be constantly on the lookout for emus, large flightless birds that dart across roads open-beaked and wide-eyed, staring for a moment through your windshield, before sprinting away into the salt bush savanna. When you turn off the engine, it's so quiet you can hear the scales of a sleepy lizard, as long as your forearm, scraping the rumpled track as it turns to taste the air with its long, blue tongue.

The scenery out here is like a huge canvas with a restricted palette of paint: blood red for the dirt, straw-yellow for the blotches of Mitchell grass, a searing blue for the surreally large sky. Out here you can see the stars in the puddles at night after rain, and walk over land barely touched by human feet since The Dreamtime. There is room to be yourself in the Outback, and you'll soon find out that personalities can easily roam freely toward the eccentric side. It's a hard-working place, too, where miners, sheep and cattle farmers, and assorted other types try to eke out a living in Australia's hard center.

BROKEN HILL

1,157km (694 miles) W of Sydney, 508km (311 miles) NE of Adelaide

At heart, Broken Hill—or "Silver City," as it's been nicknamed—is still very much a hard-working, hard-drinking mining town. Its beginnings can be traced to 1883, when the trained eye of a boundary rider named Charles Rasp noticed something odd about the craggy rock outcrops at a place called the Broken Hill. Today, the city's main drag, Argent Street, bristles with finely crafted colonial mansions, heritage homes, hotels, and public buildings. Look deeper and you see its quirkiness. Around one corner you'll find the radio station built to resemble a giant wireless set with round knobs for windows, and around another the headquarters of the Housewives Association, which ruled the town with an iron apron for generations. Then there's the Palace Hotel, made famous in the movie *The Adventures of Priscilla, Queen of the Desert,* with its high painted walls and a mural of Botticelli's *Birth of Venus* on the ceiling two flights up.

Traditionally a hard-drinking but religious town, Broken Hill has 23 pubs (down from 73 in its heyday around the turn of the last century) and plenty of churches, as well as a Catholic cathedral, a synagogue, and a mosque to serve its 24,500 inhabitants.

GETTING THERE　From Sydney, take the Great Western Highway to Dubbo, then the Mitchell Highway to the Barrier Highway, which will take you to Broken Hill. From Adelaide, take the Barrier Highway to Broken Hill.

Driving Safety Tips

The options in this section are all generally accessible by two-wheel-drive cars, although you should never attempt to travel on dirt tracks after rain. Distances are huge out here, so always make sure you have plenty of water and fuel. Take a good map, and always tell someone exactly where you're heading. Never wander off the main tracks unless you have a detailed local map of the area and have told someone when to expect to hear from you.

There are regular **flights** on Kendell Airlines from Adelaide and Hazelton Airlines from Sydney. Standard one-way fares run around A$175 (U.S.$122.50) from Adelaide and A$354 (U.S.$247.80) from Sydney. Southern Australian Airlines also connects Broken Hill to Adelaide, Melbourne, and Mildura.

The *Indian Pacific* **train** stops here on its way to Perth. It departs Sydney for Broken Hill at 2:55pm on Monday and Thursday, and arrives in Broken Hill the next day at 9am; the fare is A$100 (U.S.$70) one-way for an adult and A$50 (U.S.$35) for a child in an economy seat. The train leaves Broken Hill for Adelaide at 9am on Tuesday and Thursday and arrives at 4:25pm the same day; the fare is A$52 (U.S.$36.40) for adults and A$26 (U.S.$18.20) for children.

Greyhound-Pioneer **buses** run from Adelaide (trip time: 7 hours) for A$56 (U.S.$39.20) and from Sydney (trip time: 16 hours) for A$99 (U.S.$69.30).

VISITOR INFORMATION   The **Broken Hill Tourist and Travelers Centre,** at Blende and Bromide streets, Broken Hill, NSW 2880 (☎ **08/8087 6077;** fax 08/ 8088 5209; E-mail: tourist@pcpro.net.au; Web site: www.murrayoutback.org.au), has a good selection of information and souvenirs as well as a cafe. It's open daily from 8:30am to 5pm.

The **National Parks & Wildlife Service (NPWS)** office is at 5 Oxide St. (☎ **08/ 8088 5933**), and the **Royal Automobile Association of South Australia** (which offers reciprocal services to other national and international auto-club members) is at 261 Argent St. (☎ **08/8088 4999**). You can buy National Park entry tickets here.

GETTING AROUND   **Silver City Tours,** 380 Argent St. (☎ **08/8087 3144**), conducts tours of the city and surrounding Outback. City tours take around 4 hours and cost A$26 (U.S.$18.20) for adults and A$8 (U.S.$5.60) for children.

Hertz (☎ **08/8087 2719;** fax 08/8087 4838), rents four-wheel-drive vehicles suitable for exploring the area.

EXPLORING THE TOWN: ART GALLERIES, A MINE TOUR & THE WORLD'S LARGEST SCHOOLROOM

With the largest regional public gallery in New South Wales and 22 private galleries, Broken Hill has more places per capita to see art than anywhere else in Australia. The **Broken Hill City Art Gallery,** Chloride Street, between Blende and Beryl streets (☎ **08/8088 5491**), houses an extensive collection of Australian colonial and impres-

What Time Is It, Anyway?

Broken Hill runs its clocks on central standard time, to correspond with South Australia. The surrounding country, however, runs half an hour faster on eastern standard time. Also, the phone code here is 08, the same as the South Australia code, despite being in New South Wales.

sionist works. Of particular interest is the *Silver Tree,* a sculpture wrought from pure silver mined from beneath Broken Hill and dedicated to the discoverer of the first mineral deposits, Charles Rasp. This is also a good place to see works by the "Brushmen of the Bush," a well-known group of artists, including Pro Hart, Jack Absalom, Eric Minchin, and Hugh Schultz, who spend many days sitting around campfires in the bush trying to capture its essence in paint. The gallery is open Monday through Friday from 10am to 5pm, and Saturday and Sunday from 1 to 5pm. Admission is A$3 (U.S.$2.10) for adults, A$2 (U.S.$1.40) for children, and A$6 (U.S.$4.20) for a family.

Other galleries worth visiting around town include the **Hugh Schultz Gallery,** 51 Morgan St. (☎ **08/8087 6624**), **Absalom's Gallery,** 638 Chapple St. (☎ **08/ 8087 5881**), and the **Pro Hart Gallery,** 108 Wyman St. (☎ **08/8087 2441**). All are open daily.

To get a real taste of mining in Broken Hill, tour underground at **Delprat's Mine** (☎ **08/8088 1604**). Visitors go 120 meters (396 ft.) below the surface. Children under 6 aren't allowed. Tours run Monday through Friday at 10:30am and Saturday at 2pm. The 2-hour tour costs A$23 (U.S.$16.10) for adults and A$18 (U.S.$12.60) for children.

One thing not to be missed is a visit to the School of the Air and the Royal Flying Doctor Service base. Both places help show the enormity of the Australian interior. The **School of the Air**—the largest schoolroom in the world, with students scattered over 800,000 square kilometers (312,000 sq. miles)—conducts lessons via two-way radios. Visitors can listen in on part of the day's first teaching session Monday through Friday at 8:30am (except public holidays). Bookings are essential and must be made through the Tourist and Travelers Centre (see "Visitor Information," above). The cost is A$2 (U.S.$1.40) per person.

The **Royal Flying Doctor Service** base is at the Broken Hill Airport (☎ **08/ 8088 0777**). The service maintains communication with more than 400 outback stations, ready to fly at once in case of an emergency. The base at Broken Hill covers 25 percent of New South Wales, as well as parts of Queensland and South Australia. Continuous explanatory lessons are held at the base Monday through Friday from 9am to noon and 3 to 5pm; Saturday and Sunday from 9am to noon. Admission is A$2 (U.S.$1.40) for adults; free for children.

WHAT TO SEE & DO NEARBY

CHECKING OUT A GHOST TOWN Silverton (pop. 50), 23 kilometers (14 miles) northwest of Broken Hill, is a popular location for moviemakers—at least 44 movies have been filmed here, including *A Town Like Alice* and *Mad Max.* It has a Wild West feel about it, with camels instead of horses sometimes placed in front of the Silverton Pub, which is well worth a visit for its kitschy Australian appeal. Silverton was once the home of 3,000 people, following the discovery of silver here in 1882, but within 7 years almost everyone had left. There are some good art galleries here, as well as a restored jail and hotel.

DISCOVERING ABORIGINAL HAND PRINTS Mootwingee National Park, 130 kilometers (78 miles) northeast of Broken Hill, was one of the most important spiritual meeting places for Aborigines on the continent. Groups came from all over the country to peck out abstract engravings on the rocks with sharpened quartz tools and to sign their hand prints to show they belonged to the place. The ancient, weathered fireplaces are still here, laid out like a giant map to show where each visiting group came from. Hundreds of ochre outlines of hands and animal paws, some up to 30,000 years old, are stenciled on rock overhangs. The fabulous 2-hour Outback trip from

A Fabulous Place to Enjoy the Sunset

Just outside town in the **Living Desert Nature Park** is the best collection of sculptures this side of Stonehenge. Twelve sandstone obelisks, up to 3 meters (10 ft.) high and carved totem-like by artists from as far away as Georgia, Syria, Mexico, and the Tiwi Islands, make up the Sculpture Symposium. Surrounding them on all sides is brooding mulga scrub. It's fantastic at sunset.

Broken Hill to Mootwingee is along red-dirt tracks not really suitable for two-wheel drives, and should not be attempted after heavy rain. Mootwingee National Park (☎ 08/8088 5933) organizes inspections of the historical sites every Wednesday and Saturday morning at 10:30am Broken Hill time (11am Mootwingee, or Eastern Standard time). The tours may be canceled in very hot weather. The NPWS office in Broken Hill (☎ 08/8088 5933) also has details. You can camp at the Homestead Creek campground for A$10 (U.S.$7) a night. It has its own water supply.

EXPLORING WHITE CLIFFS   White Cliffs, 290 kilometers (174 miles) east of Broken Hill, is an opal-mining town that's bigger than it looks. To escape the summer heat, most houses are built underground in mine shafts, where the temperature is a constant 23°C (73°F). Prospecting started here in 1889, when kangaroo shooters found the colorful stones scattered on the ground. A year later the rush was on, and by the turn of the century about 4,000 people were digging and sifting in a lawless, waterless hell of a place.

Today, the country looks like an inverted moonscape, pimpled with bone-white heaps of gritty clay dug from the 50,000 mine shafts that surround the town. These days, White Cliffs is renowned for its eccentricity. Take **Jock's Place,** for instance, an old underground museum filled to the beams with junk pulled from old mine shafts used as rubbish tips in the olden days. Then there's a house made of beer flagons, and a nine-hole ✪ **dirt golf course** where the locals play at night with fluorescent green golf balls.

WHERE TO STAY: ABOVE GROUND & BELOW

If it's cool outside, you could spend the night in a caravan park. The **Broken Hill Caravan Park** (☎ 08/8087 3841) is about 3 kilometers (2 miles) west of the city center on Rakow Street (the Barrier Highway). It has on-site vans from A$23 (U.S.$16.10) and cabins from A$30 (U.S.$21). The **Tourist Lodge,** at 100 Argent Street (☎ 08/8088 2086), is associated with the YHA and has dorm beds for A$16 (U.S.$ 11.20) and doubles for A$40 (U.S.$28) with air-conditioning (and a little cheaper without).

Another option is to rent a local cottage through **Broken Hill Historic Cottages** ☎ 08/8087 5305) or **Sue Spicer's Holiday Cottages** (☎ 08/8087 8488). Fully equipped cottages cost from A$65 (U.S.$45.50) per night and can often sleep up to six.

Broken Hill Overlander Motor Inn. 142 Iodide St., Broken Hill, NSW 2880. ☎ 08/8088 2566. Fax 08/8088 4377. Reservations can be made through Best Western (☎ 800/780-7234 in the U.S. and Canada, 0800/39 3130 in the U.K., 0800/237 893 in New Zealand, 13 17 79 in Australia). 15 units. A/C TV TEL. A$76–92 (U.S.$53.20–$64.40) double. Additional person A$10 (U.S.$7) extra. AE, BC, DC, MC, V.

This is my favorite place to stay in Broken Hill, although admittedly that's not really saying much in this Outback town. It's set way back from the road, has nice green areas with a pool and barbecue facilities, and is very quiet. There is also a spa and sauna on the premises. The more expensive four-star rated rooms are much nicer than the

---

A Little Night Putting

If you fancy an after-hours round of golf in the dirt (and who doesn't?), contact the secretary of the **White Cliffs Golf Club,** John Painter (☎ **08/8091 6715** after hours). He'll be happy to supply you with a golf club or two and a couple of balls for A$2 (U.S.$1.40). Otherwise, put A$2 (U.S.$1.40) in the black box at the first tee if you have your own clubs—but be warned, bush playing can damage your clubs, and crows often make off with the balls. Visitors can play daily, day or night, but if you want some company, then turn up on Sunday when club members shoot it out.

---

cheaper variants, and considerably larger. Two family rooms sleep up to six in a combination of single and queen-size beds.

✪ **Underground Motel.** Smiths Hill, (P.O. Box 427), White Cliffs, NSW 2836. ☎ **1800/ 02 1154** in Australia, or 08/8091 6677. Fax 08/8091 6654. 30 units, none with bathroom. A$70 (U.S.$49) double. Additional person A$16 (U.S.$11.20) extra. BC, MC, V.

I love this place. It's worth making the scenic trip out to White Cliffs just to stay here for the night. All but two of the rooms are underground; they're reached by a maze of spacious tunnels dug out of the rock and sealed with epoxy-resin to keep out the damp and the dust. The temperature below ground is a constant 22°C (71°F), which is decidedly cooler than a summer day outside. Rooms are comfortable but fairly basic, and toilets and showers are shared. Turn off the light and it's as dark as a cave. Upstairs is a bar and dining room, where every night guests sit around large round tables and dig into the roast of the day (vegetarians are catered for, too). It's a good way to meet people. There's also a pool on the premises. Two rooms above ground are good for claustrophobics.

WHERE TO DINE

The best place for a cheap meal is at one of the local clubs. You'll find one of the best bistros at the **Barrier Social & Democratic Club,** at 218 Argent St. (☎ **08/ 8088 4477**); it serves breakfast, lunch, and dinner. There's also a host of Chinese restaurants around town, including the **Oceania Chinese Restaurant** on Argent Street (☎ **08/8087 3695**), which has a A$7 (U.S.$4.90) lunch special and offers main courses for around A$9.50 (U.S.$8.65). You can get a late night snack at the **International Deli** (☎ **08/8087 3427**), on Oxide Street (near Beryl Street); it's open until midnight.

LIGHTNING RIDGE: OPALS GALORE
765km (459 miles) NW of Sydney, 572km (343 miles) SW of Brisbane

Lightning Ridge, or "The Ridge," as it's known to the locals, is perhaps the most fascinating place to visit in all of New South Wales. Essentially, it's a hard-working opal-mining town stuck out in the arid far-northern reaches of New South Wales—where summer temperatures regularly hover around 45°C (113°F). Lightning Ridge thrives off the largest deposit of black opal in the world. Good quality opals from here can fetch a miner around A$8,000 (U.S.$5,600) per carat, and stones worth upward of A$500,000 (U.S.$350,000) each are not unheard of. Tourists come here to get a taste of life in Australia's "Wild West." A popular tourist activity in the opal fields is to pick over the old white heaps of mine tailings. Stories (perhaps tall tales) abound of tourists finding overlooked opals worth thousands of dollars.

I strongly recommend that you try to get out to the **Grawin** and **Glengarry** opal fields, each about an hour or so from Lightning Ridge on a dirt track just suitable for 2-wheel-drive cars (but check with locals before you go). These full-on frontier townships are bristling with drills and hoists pulling out bucket loads of dirt and buzzing with news of the latest opal rush.

GETTING THERE   From Sydney it takes about 9 hours to drive to Lightning Ridge, via Bathurst, Dubbo, and the fascinating town of Walgett (note the large Aboriginal community and the siege mentality of many local shop owners). **Countrylink Holidays** (☎ **13 28 29** in Australia) offers a 4-night, 3-day Lightning Ridge tour from Sydney for A$328 (U.S.$229.60) for adults, and A$163 (U.S.$114.10) for children, including train fare, accommodations, some meals, and entrance fees. Hazelton Airlines also flies to Lightning Ridge.

VISITOR INFORMATION   Information is available from the **Lightning Ridge Tourist Information Centre,** Morilla Street, (P.O. Box 1779), Lightning Ridge, NSW 2834 (☎ **02/6829 0565;** fax 02/6829 0565). It's open Monday to Friday from 8:30am to 4pm.

Soaking Up the Wild West Scene

Any visit to Lightning Ridge should start with an orientation trip with **Black Opal Tours** (☎ **02/6829 0368;** fax 02/6829 1206). The company offers two slightly different 5-hour tours of the opal fields for A$65 (U.S.$45.50) and A$70 (U.S.$49) per person. A 1-day tour is less of a value at A$100 (U.S.$70). Also ask about their shorter tours, as well as their 2- and 3-day tours of the area.

Among the many points of interest is the 15-meter-tall (50 ft.) homemade **Amigo's Castle,** which dominates the old, worked-out opal fields immediately surrounding the modern township of Lightning Ridge. Complete with turrets, battlements, dungeons, and a wishing well, the castle has been rising out of these arid lands for the past 17 years, with every rock scavenged from the surrounding area and lugged in a wheelbarrow or in a rucksack on Amigo's back. Amigo hasn't taken out insurance on the property, so there are no official tours, but if he feels like a bit of company, he'll show you around.

The ✪ **Artesian Bore Baths,** 2 kilometers (1 mile) from the post office on Pandora Street, are free of charge, open 24-hours a day, and said to have therapeutic value. The water temperature hovers between 40°C and 50°C (104°F to 122°F). It's an amazing place to visit at night with the stars out.

The underground **Bush Moozeum** (☎ **02/6829 0016**), has an extraordinary collection of everything from old bottles to the pickled leg of a miner, who lost (and later donated) the leg following a fall down a mine shaft. Admission is A$8 (U.S.$5.60), and for that you might get a couple of free drinks at the well-stocked underground bar from the museum's true-blue Aussie owner.

The **Bevans' Black Opal & Cactus Nursery** (☎ **02/6829 0429**), contains more than 2,000 species of cactus and succulent plants, including many rare specimens. Betty Bevan cuts her own opals, and many are on display. It costs A$2 (U.S.$1.40) to look around.

Something Special

If you're in Australia around Easter, make sure you come to Lightning Ridge for the **Great Goat Race** and the rodeo.

There are plenty of opal shops, galleries, walk-in opal mines, and other unique things to see in Lightning Ridge. You might want to take a look at **Gemopal Pottery** (☎ 02/6829 0375), on the road to the Bore Baths. The resident potter makes some nice pots out of clay mine tailings, and lives in one of his five old Sydney railway carriages.

WHERE TO STAY & DINE

The Wallangulla Motel. Morilla St. (corner of Morilla and Agate sts.), Lightning Ridge, NSW 2834. ☎ **02/6829 0542.** Fax 02/6829 0070. 43 units. A/C TV TEL. A$60–$72 (U.S.$42–$50.40) double; A$75 (U.S.$52.50) family room; A$100 (U.S.$70) family room with spa. AE, BC, DC, MC, V.

The best motel in town offers two standards of rooms, the cheaper being in an older section of the property. Newer rooms are better furnished and generally nicer, and worth the extra money. There are two large family rooms, both with two bedrooms and a living room, and one with a spa bath. Guests can use the barbecue facilities, and there is a special arrangement with the bowling club across the road for meals there to be charged back to your room. The Bowling Club has a restaurant with pretty good food and a very cheap bistro.

Brisbane 7

by Natalie Kruger

Queensland's capital is just the way you want a subtropical capital to be. Set in a curve of the stately Brisbane River, Brisbane's streets are lined with palms, gardens are full of mango and banana trees, and the weather forecast always seems to be "fine and warm." Folk here are so laid-back that smart shorts and deck shoes will get you in most places.

Is there much to see? Well, not touristy stuff. The city's only major visitor attraction is the country's largest koala sanctuary, where you can cuddle one of these cutie-pies for free.

What you *will* encounter is a pleasant outdoorsy city full of history, charming architecture, and bursting foliage. Brisbane (pronounce it "*Briz*-bun" if you want to fit in) is renowned for its cute timber Queenslander cottages and houses, set up high on stilts to catch the breeze and create underneath a dim, dark, cool retreat from the worst of the midday sun. Many houses have been converted to rainbow-colored cafes and shops selling antiques, pretty clothes, and nice housewares.

Stroll the city streets and admire the gracious colonial sandstone civic buildings, in-line skate or bike along the river, have a beer in the courtyard of a pub, or wend your way downriver on the CityCats (one of the cheapest tours in town). If it's a weekend, browse one of the colorful handcrafts markets. There's even a man-made beach in the city center. Thanks to a public-spirited city council that sponsors frequent free entertainment, chances are a free movie or concert will be showing when you visit. Getting around is cheap, good food is inexpensive, and accommodations are affordable, especially in the city's lovely bed-and-breakfasts.

The city is located on the southern coast of the state, less than 2 hours' drive south from the Sunshine Coast and an hour north of the Gold Coast.

1 Orientation

ARRIVING

BY PLANE   Major international airlines flying into **Brisbane International Airport** from Europe, Asia, and New Zealand include Qantas, Air New Zealand, British Airways, and Cathay Pacific. From North America you will most likely fly to Sydney and connect on one of several daily direct flights made by Qantas and Ansett, or fly direct from Auckland, in New Zealand. Ansett and Qantas operate flights throughout the day from state capitals, Cairns, and several other regional towns.

Brisbane International Airport is 16 kilometers (10 miles) from the city, and the domestic terminal is 2 kilometers (1¼ miles) farther away. The Arrivals Floor, on Level 2, has an information desk open to meet all flights, help you with flight inquiries, dispense tourist information, and make your hotel bookings. It also has lockers that cost A$4 to $10 (U.S.$2.80 to $7) for 24 hours, and a check-in counter for passengers transferring to domestic flights. Travelex currency-exchange bureaus are located on both the departures and arrivals floors. **Avis** (☎ **07/3860 4200**), **Budget** (☎ **07/ 3860 4466**), **Hertz** (☎ **07/3860 4522**), and **Thrifty** (☎ **07/3860 4588**) have desks on Level 2; in the airport there is also a free-call board connecting you to smaller local car-rental companies that sometimes offer better rates. Showers and baby change rooms are located on levels 2, 3, and 4; Level 4 has an ATM.

The domestic terminal has lockers (A$2/U.S.$1.40 for 24 hours), a Travelex currency-exchange bureau, showers, and the big four car rental desks (call the telephone numbers above). An interterminal shuttle runs every 15 minutes and costs A$2.50 (U.S.$1.75).

Skytrans (☎ **07/3236 1000**) runs a shuttle to city hotels (every 45 minutes from 5am to 10:45pm) for A$7.50 (U.S.$5.25) to the Roma Street Transit Centre, or A$9.50 (U.S.$6.65) to hotels. Kids ages 4 to 14 pay less than half price, and there are family discounts. Round-trip fares are cheaper. The trip takes about 30 minutes, and bookings are not needed. No public buses serve the airport. A taxi to the city costs around A$20 (U.S.$14) from the international terminal and around A$24 (U.S.$16.80) from the domestic terminal.

BY TRAIN **Queensland Rail** (☎ **13 22 32** in Queensland, or 07/3235 1122) operates several long-distance trains most days of the week to Brisbane from Cairns. The 32-hour trip from Cairns costs A$135 (U.S.$94.50) for a sitting berth, and A$165 (U.S.$115.50) for an economy-class sleeper. **Countrylink** (☎ **13 22 32** in New South Wales, or 02/9379 1298) runs daily train service to Brisbane from Sydney. The 13½-hour trip from Sydney costs A$96 to $134 (U.S.$67.20 to $93.80) in a sitting berth, and A$229 (U.S.$160.30) for a sleeper. Make sure you book the through-service; some services transfer to coach in Murwillumbah, just south of the border, tacking an extra 2¼ hours to the trip. This train/coach service has no sleepers.

All intercity and interstate trains pull into **Brisbane Transit Centre at Roma Street** (in the city center), often called the Roma Street Transit Centre. From here, most city and Spring Hill hotels are a few blocks' walk or a quick cab ride away. The Transit Centre has food outlets, showers, tourist information, and lockers.

Queensland Rail CityTrain (☎ **07/3235 5555**) provides a daily train service from the Sunshine Coast, and plentiful services from the Gold Coast.

BY BUS All intercity and interstate coaches pull into the Brisbane Transit Centre (see "By Train" above). **McCafferty's** and **Greyhound Pioneer** serve the city several times daily. A one-way Cairns–Brisbane ticket costs around A$144 (U.S.$100.80), and the trip takes 28½ hours. The Sydney–Brisbane trip takes 17 hours and costs A$71 (U.S.$49.70) one-way. **Coachtrans** (☎ **07/5588 8777**) provides plentiful daily services from the Gold Coast.

BY CAR The Bruce Highway from Cairns enters the city from the north. The Pacific Highway enters Brisbane from Sydney in the south.

VISITOR INFORMATION

Brisbane Tourism, P.O. Box 12260, Elizabeth St., Brisbane, QLD 4002 (☎ **07/ 3221 8411,** fax 07/3229 5126), has its prime information outlet in the Queen Street Mall at Albert Street (☎ 07/3229 5918). It's open from 9am to 5:30pm Monday through Thursday, to 7pm or later Friday, and to 4pm Saturday; Sunday it's open from

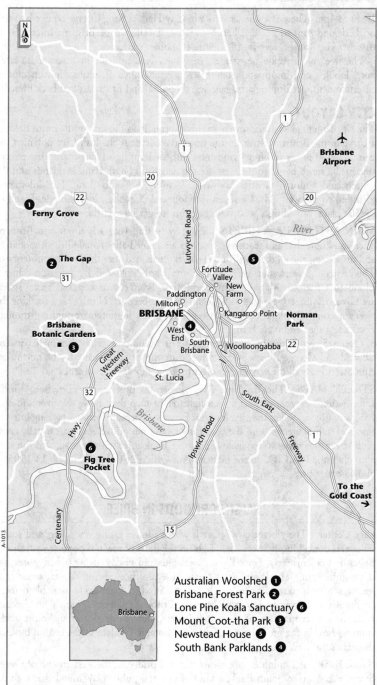

Australian Woolshed ①
Brisbane Forest Park ②
Lone Pine Koala Sanctuary ⑥
Mount Coot-tha Park ③
Newstead House ⑤
South Bank Parklands ④

10am to 4pm. There is a smaller outlet in City Hall, at King George Square between Adelaide and Ann streets at Albert Street, and another at the Brisbane International Airport. The Roma Street Transit Centre is another source.

The free color weekly newspaper, *Brisbane News,* available in newsstands, cafes, hotel lobbies, and information booths, is a great source of information on dining, entertainment, performing arts, galleries, shopping, and Brisbane's laid-back lifestyle.

CITY LAYOUT

The city center's glass office towers shimmer proudly in the sun on the north bank of a curve of the Brisbane River. In the tip of the curve are the lush City Botanic Gardens. The 30-meter (98-foot) sandstone cliffs of Kangaroo Point rise on the eastern side of the south bank; to the west are the delightful South Bank Parklands and the Queensland Cultural Centre, known collectively as South Bank. Five kilometers (3 miles) to the west, Mt. Coot-tha (pronounced "Cewtha") looms modestly out of the flat plain, providing a great vantage point for gazing over the city.

MAIN ARTERIES & STREETS   It is easy to find your way around in Brisbane once you know that all the east-west streets are named after female British monarchs and princesses, and all the north-south streets are named after their male counterparts. The "female" streets start with Ann in the north, followed by Adelaide, Queen, Elizabeth, Charlotte, Mary, Margaret, and Alice. From east to west, the "male" streets are Edward, Albert, George, and William. William becomes North Quay, flanking the river's northeast bank. Brunswick Street is the main thoroughfare running through Fortitude Valley and New Farm.

Queen Street is the main thoroughfare; it becomes a pedestrian mall between Edward and George streets. Roma Street exits the city diagonally to the northwest. Ann Street leads all the way east into Fortitude Valley and New Farm.

STREET MAPS   **The Brisbane Map,** free from Brisbane Tourism (see "Visitor Information") or your concierge, is a lightweight map that shows the river and outlying suburbs, as well as the city. It's great for drivers because it shows parking lots and one-way traffic directions on the confusing city-center grid. Rental cars usually come with street directories. Newsagents and some bookstores sell this map, and the state auto club, the **R.A.C.Q.,** in the General Post Office, 261 Queen St. (☎ **13 1905**) is also a good source.

NEIGHBORHOODS IN BRIEF

City Center   The vibrant city center is where a lot of eating, shopping, and socializing gets done. Queen Street Mall, right in the heart of town, is popular with shopaholics and cinemagoers, especially on weekends and Friday nights (when stores stay open until 9pm). The Eagle Street financial/legal office precinct houses some great restaurants with river views to match, and on Sundays there are fashionable markets by the Riverside office tower here. Much of Brisbane's gorgeous colonial architecture is in the city center, too. Strollers, bike riders, and in-line skaters shake the sticky summer heat in the green haven of the City Botanic Gardens at the central business district's southern end.

South Bank   A 7-minute walk across Victoria Bridge, at the western end of Queen Street, takes you to South Bank, a kind of peaceful public playground that includes the Queensland Cultural Centre and the parks, rain-forest walks, bars, and restaurants of South Bank Parklands. This is where people come to see a play, meet for dinner, shop in weekend markets, or just chill out on the riverbank.

Fortitude Valley   Ten years ago, this suburb of derelict warehouses just east of the city center was a no-go zone. Today it's a stomping-ground for street-smart young folk who meet in restored pubs and eat in cool cafes. The lanterns, food stores, and shopping mall of Chinatown are here, too. Take Turbot Street from the city to the Valley's main drag, Brunswick Street.

New Farm   Always a nice residential suburb, New Farm is fast becoming the city's "in" destination for cafe-hopping, shopping, and cinema-going. Merthyr Street is where the action is, especially on Friday and Saturday nights. It's embryonic, but getting bigger all the time. From the intersection of Wickham and Brunswick streets, follow Brunswick southeast for 13 blocks to Merthyr.

Paddington   If you think this hilltop suburb a couple of miles northwest of the city is the prettiest in Brisbane, you have lots of company. Cute, brightly painted Queenslander cottages line the main street, Latrobe Terrace, as it winds west along a ridge top. Many of the houses have been turned into adorable shops and cafes, and the street is never empty of people browsing for antiques, enjoying coffee and cake, or just moseying around to admire the charming architecture.

Park Road   A street rather than a neighborhood, this unlikely commercial-district avenue in Milton, a few miles from town, buzzes with white-collar office workers who down cappuccinos at alfresco restaurants, scout interior design stores for a new *objet* to grace the living room, and stock up on European designer rags.

West End   This small inner-city enclave is alive with ethnic restaurants, cute cafes, and the odd interesting houseware or fashion store. Most action is at the intersection of Vulture and Boundary streets.

2 Getting Around

BY PUBLIC TRANSPORTATION

Bus, train, and ferry service is coordinated by **Brisbane Transport.** For timetable and route inquiries, call Transinfo ☎ **13 12 30.** The most convenient places to buy the passes described below and to pick up timetables and route maps are the Brisbane Transport outlets on the Elizabeth Street–level of the Myer Centre, which fronts Queen Street Mall; at Brisbane Transport's Brisbane Administration Centre, 69 Ann Street; at the Roma Street Transit Centre; or at Brisbane Tourism's information kiosk in Queen Street Mall. You can also buy passes on the bus, at the train station (passes containing a train component, that is), or on the ferry. Any news agency displaying a yellow-and-white Bus & Ferry Tickets Sold Here banner sells bus/ferry passes, but not train passes, special tour tickets, or family passes.

A single sector or zone on the bus, train, or ferry costs A$1.40 (U.S.$1). Whether they buy a single ticket or a pass, kids under age 5 travel free, kids ages 5 to 15 pay half fare; all seniors except Queensland residents and all students pay full fare. If you plan on doing lots of bussing and ferrying around, **weekly passes** and **Ten Trip Saver** tickets are available from the outlets described above.

MONEY-SAVING PASSES   The **Rover Link pass** is good for one day of travel on most trains, ferries, and buses. The pass cannot be used on weekday trains before 9am,

A Money-Saving Tip

Due to some incomprehensible decision by a bureaucrat somewhere, it's at least A$2 (U.S.$1.40) cheaper to buy transit passes on a bus or at a newsagent than on a ferry.

Brisbane

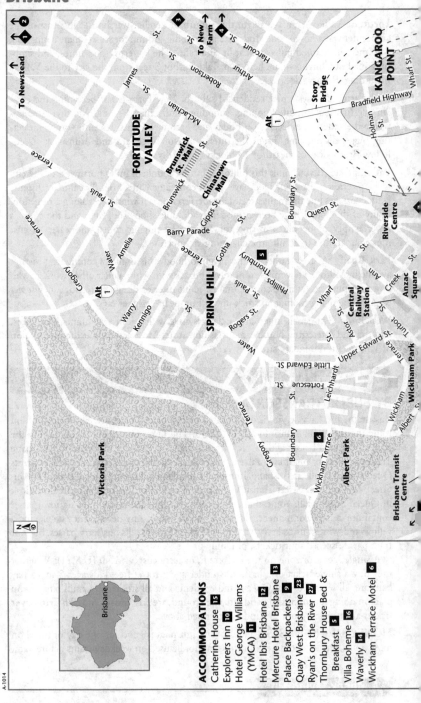

ACCOMMODATIONS

Catherine House **15**
Explorers Inn **10**
Hotel George Williams (YMCA) **11**
Hotel Ibis Brisbane **12**
Mercure Hotel Brisbane **13**
Palace Backpackers **9**
Quay West Brisbane **23**
Ryan's on the River **27**
Thornbury House Bed & Breakfast **5**
Villa Boheme **16**
Waverly **14**
Wickham Terrace Motel **6**

A-1014

242

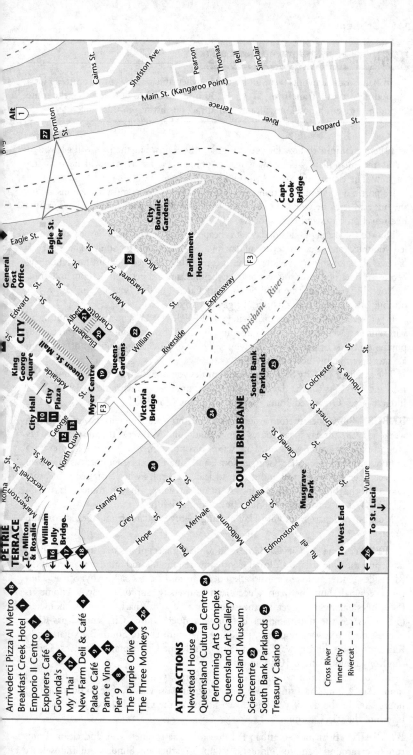

Arrivederci Pizza Al Metro 18
Breakfast Creek Hotel 1
Emporio Il Centro 7
Explorers Café 10
Govinda's 20
My Thai 17
New Farm Deli & Café 4
Palace Café 9
Pane e Vino 21
Pier 9 8
The Purple Olive 3
The Three Monkeys 26

ATTRACTIONS
Newstead House 2
Queensland Cultural Centre 24
Performing Arts Complex
Queensland Art Gallery
Queensland Museum
Sciencentre 22
South Bank Parklands 25
Treasury Casino 19

Cross River ――――
Inner City ― ― ―
Rivercat ‑ ‑ ‑ ‑

Brisbane Bus Service is Changing

Brisbane's bus networks were under review when this book went to print, so it's a good idea to call **TransInfo** (☎ **13 12 30** in Australia) to double-check the route numbers given in hotel, restaurant, and attractions listings in this book.

and there are limits to how far you can go on the trains, but the pass will get you as far as the Australian Woolshed, which is probably as far as you will be traveling anyhow. The Rover Link costs A$8 (U.S.$5.60).

It's possible you won't use trains to get around Brisbane, as most attractions are on the bus and ferry networks. In that case, get a **Day Rover pass,** which allows unlimited travel on buses and ferries for A$7 (U.S.$4.90).

On weekends and public holidays, it's cheaper to buy an **Off-Peak Saver pass,** which lets you travel on buses and ferries all day for A$4 (U.S.$2.80) for adults. The Off-Peak Saver is also available on weekdays, but it is probably too inconvenient for sightseeing because it does not cover the cost of travel before 9am and between 3:30pm and 7pm.

Note that passes can't be used on the City Circle bus line (see "By Bus" below) or on tour buses like City Sights (see "Organized Tours").

If you see peak-hour buses displaying a FULL FARE ONLY sign, that does not mean you cannot travel on them with a discounted ticket or pass. It just means you cannot purchase a ticket or pass on the bus; you will have to purchase your ticket or pass from a ticket agent before boarding the bus.

The excellent ✪ **City Sights bus tour** entitles you to unlimited travel on buses, ferries, and CityCats for the day, and at the same time gets you around to 19 points of interest—see "Organized Tours" later in this chapter for details.

BY BUS   Buses operate from around 5am to 11pm weekdays, with fewer services on weekends. On Sunday many routes stop around 5pm. Midweek, the smart way to get around the city center is aboard City Circle bus no. 333, which does a loop every 5 minutes around Eagle, Alice, George, Roma, and Albert streets as far north as Wickham Terrace, then up Ann Street and down Adelaide Street. It's wheelchair-accessible, too. Look for the blue-and-white stops. A ticket anywhere on the route costs A70¢ (U.S.50¢). It runs Monday to Friday from 7am to 5:40pm.

Most buses depart from City Hall at King George Square, from Adelaide or Ann streets.

BY FERRY   The fast **CityCat** ferries run to many places of interest, including South Bank and the Queensland Cultural Centre; the restaurants and Sunday markets at the Riverside Centre; and New Farm Park, not far from the cafes of Merthyr Street. They run every half hour between Queensland University, approximately 9 kilometers (5½ miles) along the river to the south, and Brett's Wharf, about 9 kilometers (5½ miles) to the north. Slower but more frequent **Inner City** and **Cross-River** ferries stop at a few more points, including the south end of South Bank Parklands, Kangaroo Point, and Edward Street right outside the City Botanic Gardens. Ferries run from around 6am to 10:30pm daily.

To stop people from camping out on the ferries, you cannot travel on ferries for more than 2 hours at a time, even with a transit pass; you are free to do another 2 hours later in the day if you wish. Two hours on the CityCat takes you the entire length of the CityCat run.

BY TRAIN   Brisbane's suburban rail network is fast, quiet, safe, and clean. Trains run from around 5am to midnight, stopping earlier on Sunday. All trains leave Central Station, between Turbot and Ann streets at Edward Street.

BY TAXI   Call **Yellow Cabs** (☎ **13 19 24** in Australia) and **Black and White Taxis** (☎ **13 10 08** in Australia). There is a major taxi rank on Edward Street at Queen Street.

BY CAR   Brisbane's grid of one-way streets is a real test, even for locals, so plan every step of your route before you set off. You probably won't need a car unless you want to go to Brisbane Forest Park. Parking rates are much less exorbitant than in Sydney. At **King George Square Car Park** (☎ **07/3403 4420**), a parking lot under City Hall, the most you will be charged during the day (to 6pm) is A$14 (U.S.$9.80), and the maximum charge from 6pm to 6:30am the next morning is A$4 (U.S.$2.80). It's a flat A$5 (U.S.$3.50) on weekends. Enter from Roma Street just before it intersects with Ann Street. You can also enter from Adelaide Street at nights and on weekends. Most hotels and motels have free parking.

   Avis (☎ 07/3221 2900), **Budget** (☎ 07/3220 0699), and **Hertz** (☎ 07/3221 6166) all have outlets in the city center. **Thrifty** (☎ 07/3252 5994) is on the edge of the city center at 325 Wickham St., Fortitude Valley. Local company **Shoe Strings Car Rental** (☎ 07/3268 3334), located near the airport, seems to have good rates and delivers cars to the airport for free.

FAST FACTS: Brisbane

American Express   The office at 131 Elizabeth St. (☎ **07/3229 2729**) cashes traveler's checks, exchanges foreign currency, and refunds lost traveler's checks.

Business Hours   Banks are open Monday through Thursday from 9:30am to 4pm, and until 5pm on Fridays. See "Shopping" for store hours. Some restaurants close Monday and/or Tuesday nights, and bars are generally open from 10am or 11am until midnight.

Car Rentals   See "Getting Around," earlier in this chapter.

Climate   See "When to Go" in chapter 3.

Currency Exchange   Travelex, Lennons Plaza, Queen Street Mall between Albert and George streets (☎ **07/3229 8610**), is open Monday through Thursday from 9am to 6pm, Friday from 9am to 8pm, Saturday from 9:30am to 5pm, and Sunday from 10:30am to 4pm.

Dentist   The **Adelaide and Albert Street Dental Centre,** located at **City Mall 24 Hour Medical Service** (see "Doctor" below) is open Monday through Friday from 8am to 6pm and Saturday from 9am to 1pm; the dental surgery is on call 24 hours. Call ☎ **07/3229 4121.**

Doctor   **City Mall 24 Hour Medical Service** is located on the second floor, 245 Albert St. at Adelaide Street, diagonally opposite City Hall (☎ **07/ 3211 3611**). It's open Monday through Friday from 7:30am to 7pm, Saturday from 8:30am to 5pm, and Sunday from 10am to 4pm; doctors are on call for home visits 24 hours.

Drugstores (Chemist Shops)   The **T&G Corner Day & Night Pharmacy,** 141 Queen Street Mall (☎ **07/3221 4585**) is open Monday through Thursday from 7:30am to 9pm, Friday from 7:30am to 9:30pm, Saturday from 8am to 9pm, and Sunday from 8:30am to 5:30pm. There is also a pharmacy under the **City Mall 24 Hour Medical Service** (see "Doctor" above).

Embassies/Consulates   The United States and Canada have no representation in Brisbane; see chapter 4, "Settling into Sydney," for those countries' nearest offices. The **British Consul General** is at Level 26, Waterfront Place, 1 Eagle St. (☎ **07/3236 2575**), and the **New Zealand Consulate General** is at 288 Edward St. (☎ **07/3221 9933**).

Emergencies   Dial ☎ **000** for fire, ambulance, or police help in an emergency. This is a free call from a private or public telephone.

Eyeglass Repair   OPSM in the Wintergarden, 171–209 Queen Street Mall (☎ **07/3221 1158**), and in the Myer Centre, 91 Queen Street Mall (☎ **07/ 3229 2913**), is a reputable chain retailer and repairer of eyeglasses.

Hospitals   The nearest public casualty ward is at **Royal Brisbane Hospital,** about a 15-minute drive from the city at Herston Road, Herston (☎ **07/ 3253 8111**).

Hot lines   Lifeline (☎ **13 11 14**) is a 24-hour emotional crisis counseling service.

Information   See "Visitor Information," earlier in this chapter.

Liquor Laws   See "Fast Facts" in chapter 3.

Lost Property   For lost property on **trains,** call ☎ **07/3235 1859;** on **ferries and buses,** call the Brisbane City Council (☎ **07/3403 8888**). Call police head-quarters (☎ 07/3364 6464) for the telephone number of the station closest to where the item was lost.

Luggage Storage/Lockers   Lockers big enough for a suitcase are located on Level A (use the Albert Street entrance) in the **Myer Centre,** 91 Queen Street Mall (☎ **07/3221 4199**). The **Brisbane Transit Centre** on Roma Street also has baggage lockers.

Maps   See "City Layout," earlier in this chapter.

Newspapers/Magazines   The *Courier-Mail* (Monday through Saturday) and the *Sunday-Mail* are Brisbane's daily newspapers. The free color weekly *Brisbane News* provides a good guide to dining, entertainment, and shopping.

Police   Dial ☎ **000** in an emergency, or ☎ **07/3364 6464** for police head-quarters. Police are stationed 24 hours a day beside the Brisbane Tourism information booth on Queen Street Mall at Albert Street (☎ **07/3220 0752**).

Safety   Brisbane is relatively crime free, but groups of kids have been known to attempt muggings in lonely areas late at night. Stick to well-lit streets and busy precincts.

Taxis   See "Getting Around," earlier in this chapter.

Time Zone   Brisbane is GMT plus 10 hours. It does not observe daylight saving time, which means it's on the same time as Sydney and Melbourne in winter, and 1 hour behind those cities from October to March, when they go to daylight saving. For the exact local time, call ☎ **1194.**

Weather   Call ☎ **1196** for the southeast Queensland weather forecast.

3 Accommodations You Can Afford

Accommodations in Brisbane are generally cheaper than in Sydney. Brisbane has many clean motels, some nifty little budget places, and charming B&Bs in stylish homes close to the city or right smack in the heart of town. Spring Hill is just a few blocks (uphill) from the city center, so it almost counts as downtown. To stay at Kan-garoo Point you will need to drive or bus over the Story Bridge, or take one of the cross-river ferries (trip time: 3 minutes) that depart every 10 minutes from 5:30am to almost midnight.

✪ **Catherine House.** 151 Kelvin Grove Rd., Kelvin Grove, Brisbane, QLD 4059. ☎ and fax **07/3839 6988.** 5 units, 3 with bathroom (1 with tub). A/C. A$65 (U.S.$45.50) single; A$95–$110 (U.S.$66.50–$77) double. Children 7–10 A$15 (U.S.$10.50) extra. Rates include full breakfast. Ask about packages. AE, BC, DC, MC, V. Free parking. Free pickup from Roma St. Transit Centre or airport. Bus: 370. Small children not permitted.

Hostess Joy Harman used to be the chef at one of Brisbane's leading restaurants, so be prepared for gastronomic treats at her large, pretty two-story 1881 house. It's a long walk or a bus ride to the city. The rooms are all done up differently in a picturesque Victorian style; one room has two extra beds for kids. Joy lends hair dryers, and guests may use her phone on an honor system. The guest TV lounge is cozy, but on a hot Queensland evening most guests retreat to the cool rear deck looking onto the pool and palm-filled gardens. Joy cooks and serves dinner out here on request for A$35 (U.S.$24.50) per person with wine—an offer you would be wise to take! There is also a laundry. No smoking indoors.

✪ **Explorers Inn** (YWCA). 63 Turbot St. (near George St.), Brisbane, QLD 4000. ☎ **1800/ 62 3288** in Australia, or 07/3211 3488. Fax 07/3211 3499. E-mail: explorer@powerup. com.au. 58 units (all with shower only). A/C TV TEL. A$64–$84 (U.S.$44.80–$58.80) double. No charge for third person. AE, BC, DC, MC, V. No parking; Carlton Crest Hotel parking lot charges max. A$10 (U.S.$7) per 24 hrs. (located on same block, on Roma St. at Ann St.). Train: Roma St. Bus: City Circle 333.

You will be knocked over when you see such pert style and terrific value in one place— and in the heart of town, too! The tiny, ship-shape rooms at this YWCA were designed by the architect/owners to fill all your needs. Each has a narrow, curving slip of desk; a minifridge; a clock-radio; individually controlled air-conditioning (even some five-star hotels don't give you that); and a tiny private bathroom only minutely bigger than the shower cubicle it holds (the front desk lends hair dryers). The friendly staff is on hand to help with tour bookings. The river is a block away, and it's 2 blocks to the Roma Street Transit Centre. Downstairs is the equally good-value Explorers Café restaurant and bar (see "Great Deals on Dining" below).

✪ **Hotel George Williams** (YMCA). 317–325 George St. (between Turbot and Ann sts.), Brisbane, QLD 4000. ☎ **1800/064 858** or 07/3308 0700. Fax 07/3308 0733. 42 units (some with shower only). A/C TV TEL. A$85 (U.S.$59.50) double. Additional person A$15 (U.S.$10.50) extra. Children 3 and under free. Ask about packages. AE, BC, DC, MC, V. Limited free parking. Train: Roma St. Bus: City Circle 333.

It's hard to believe this groovy joint is a Y. Your room looks like it belongs in an interior design magazine, with its colorful bedcovers, chrome chairs, and artsy bedside lamps on curly chrome stands. The *very* small rooms can accommodate up to four adults. Each has a miniscule private bathroom, a wardrobe, a full-length mirror, self-serve tea and coffee, a minifrige, and individually controlled air-conditioning. Three rooms are set up for guests with disabilities. Among the useful facilities and services are 24-hour reception, laundry and dry cleaning services, safe deposit boxes, free baby baths if you're with an infant, hair dryers, and free access to the YMCA gym downstairs. The hip BYO cafe serves breakfast and pastas inside or out on the sunny terrace. The Y is close to the river and Roma Street Transit Centre.

Hotel Ibis Brisbane. 27–35 Turbot St. (between North Quay and George St.), Brisbane, QLD 4000. ☎ **1300/65 6565** in Australia, 1800/221 4542 in the U.S. and Canada, 0181/ 283 4500 in the U.K., 0800/44 4422 in New Zealand, or 07/3237 2333. Fax 07/3237 2444. 218 units. A/C TV TEL. A$150 (U.S.$105) double. Additional person A$20 (U.S.$14) extra. Children under 16 free in parents' room if they use existing bedding. Ask about weekend packages. AE, BC, DC, JCB, MC, V. Discounted parking approx. A$8.50 (U.S.$5.95) in nearby parking lots. Train: Roma St. Bus: City Circle 333.

Rooms at this sister property to the Mercure just around the corner (see below) are bigger than the Mercure's, and so are good value if you don't mind doing without a few of the facilities of its slightly ritzier sibling—no river views, no in-room iron and ironing board, no minibar, no pool. The hotel was rebuilt inside a gutted building in 1998, so the rooms are brand new. They are simply and smartly furnished with bright red bedcovers, and small but smart bathrooms with hair dryers. Three rooms are designed for guests with disabilities. There is 11am to 11pm room service, laundry and dry cleaning service, and a tour desk. The Ibis shares the Mercure's restaurant and bar.

Mercure Hotel Brisbane. 85–87 North Quay, Brisbane, QLD 4000. ☎ **1300/65 6565** in Australia, 1800/221 4542 in the U.S. and Canada, 0181/283 4500 in the U.K., 0800/44 4422 in New Zealand, or 07/3236 3300. Fax 07/3236 1035. 191 units. A/C MINIBAR TV TEL. A$150 (U.S.$105) double; A$184 (U.S.$128.80) studio suite; A$230 (U.S.$161) executive suite. Additional person A$20 (U.S.$14) extra. Children 16 and under free in parents' room if they use existing bedding. Ask about weekend packages. AE, BC, DC, JCB, MC, V. Discounted parking A$8.50 (U.S.$5.95) in adjacent parking lot. Train: Roma St. Bus: City Circle 333.

You'll get champagne views at a six-pack price in the riverside rooms at this bright little 14-story hotel across the water from South Bank. Renovated in 1998, the compact rooms have comfortable but unassuming furniture and a small, modern bathroom with hair dryer. Business travelers like it here, so look forward to corporate-class treats such as complimentary newspapers, 24-hour room service, and a cocktail bar. There's a pool, sauna, and Jacuzzi, and the YMCA gym is just behind. The rooms are a little fuddy-duddy compared to the ultrasleek art deco lobby and restaurant, but with that river panorama before you, who cares! Half the rooms have water views; the others have city outlooks.

✪ **Ryan's on the River.** 269 Main St. (at Scott St.), Kangaroo Point, Brisbane, QLD 4169. ☎ **07/3391 1011.** Fax 07/3391 1824. E-mail: reservations@ryans.com.au. 23 units (all with shower only). A/C TV TEL. A$99–$129 (U.S.$69.30–$90.30) double. Additional person A$10 (U.S.$7) extra. Ask about packages. AE, BC, DC, MC, V. Free parking. Ferry: Thornton St. from Edward St. or Eagle St. Pier (Cross River Ferry).

River and city views from every room, friendly staff, and large, airy rooms make this one of Brisbane's best moderately priced hotels. The city ferry stop is right below, across a strip of parkland, where a riverside walk/bike path leads to a playground, the Kangaroo Point cliffs, and all the way to South Bank. Out under a marquee by the small saltwater pool and lounge chairs by the river, you can cook up a nightly barbecue dinner provided by the hotel for just A$6 (U.S.$4.20). Breakfast is served out here, too. Renovated in late 1998, the rooms all have irons and boards, hair dryers, and balconies. Rooms on the south side have partial views of the river, those on the north are quieter and have great city and Story Bridge views (the bridge lights up at night), and rooms on the western side get the Full Monty, a superb river-and-city vista that's the envy of every five-star hotel in Brisbane.

✪ **Thornbury House Bed & Breakfast.** 1 Thornbury St., Spring Hill, Brisbane, QLD 4000. ☎ **07/3832 5985.** Fax 07/3832 7255. 10 units, 2 with bathroom (1 with shower only). TV. A$55 (U.S.$38.50) single; A$90–$100 (U.S.$63–$70) double. Rates include full breakfast. AE, BC, MC, V. Free parking in vacant lot across street; metered on-street parking. Bus: 23. Airport shuttle.

Michelle Bugler has turned her charming 1886 cottage into a restful retreat from the city. Every room is individually decked out with Oriental rugs, comfy beds, high-quality bathrobes, and old furniture and knickknacks. The three pretty bathrooms are impeccably clean; by the time you arrive, two more rooms may have their own attached bathrooms. Downstairs is also a self-contained apartment with modern decor. Michelle serves a scrumptious breakfast downstairs in the ferny courtyard, where you can help yourself to tea, coffee, cookies, and the newspaper all day. A 10-minute walk from this quiet street brings you to the city center. Guests may use Michelle's microwave and laundry, and there's a pay phone in the hall. Hair dryers are available. No smoking indoors.

Villa Boheme. 19 Sheehan St., Milton, Brisbane, QLD 4064. ☎ **07/3876 2360.** Fax 07/3876 2359. 15 units (all with shower only). A/C TV TEL. A$70 (U.S.$49) studio double; A$100 (U.S.$70) family apt. to sleep 4. Additional person A$10 (U.S.$7) extra. Weekly rates available. AE, BC, MC, V. Free parking. Train: Milton. Bus: 410.

A couple of train stops from town, and just around the corner from the buzzing restaurant strip of Park Road, this almost new two-story Tuscan-style complex has studio and two-bedroom apartments. It's just a stroll to the river; in fact, a half-hour walk along the riverside bike path takes you to the city center. The apartments are contemporary, light, and compact but well designed, with a kitchenette hidden behind a neat roller shutter, a sleeping nook hidden by a Roman blind, a rather tiny bathroom (bring your own hair dryer) that doubles as the laundry, and a balcony. They are serviced three times a week. There's a pool, too. No smoking indoors.

✪ **Waverley.** 5 Latrobe Terrace at Cochrane St., Paddington, Brisbane, QLD 4064. ☎ **07/3369 8973,** or 0419/741 282 mobile phone. Fax 07/3876 6655. 4 units (all with shower only). TV. A$60–$70 (U.S.$42–$49) single; A$90–$100 (U.S.$63–$70) double. Additional person A$20 (U.S.$14) extra. Rates include full breakfast. AE, BC, DC, MC, V. Free parking. Bus: 144, 374.

Right on the main shopping strip in trendy Paddington, this lovely three-story 1888 residence retains most of its original features such as tongue-in-groove walls, soaring ceilings, and polished timber floors. The two delightful, air-conditioned front rooms, renovated in 1995, are spacious and individually furnished with chiropractic mattresses, comfy sofas, and attractive bathrooms. You can also stay in two self-contained apartments downstairs. Your hostess, Annette Henry, cooks a hearty breakfast in the homey kitchen (ask for her bacon and corn muffins). There's also a cozy lounge and fireplace, and a lofty rear deck. Facilities include a laundry, pay phone, and hair dryers. No smoking indoors.

Wickham Terrace Motel. 491 Wickham Terrace, Spring Hill, Brisbane, QLD 4000. ☎ **1800/773 069** in Australia, or 07/3839 9611. Fax 07/3832 5348. 47 units (some with shower only). A/C TV TEL. A$88–$93 (U.S.$61.60–$65.10) single; A$94–99 (U.S.$65.80–$69.30) double. Additional person A$10 (U.S.$7) extra; child under 15 A$5 (U.S.$3.50). Discounts apply for direct bookings. AE, BC, DC, JCB, MC, V. Free parking. Train: Roma St. Bus: City Circle 333.

It's a 10-minute walk to the city from this modest but respectable Best Western motel overlooking leafy Albert Park. Someone forgot to tell the decorators that the public area's exposed brick, Spanish archways, and leather sofas went out with the '70s, but the rooms are only a little dated and in pristine condition. Most are a good size and are neat and airy with firm mattresses, desk space, and iron and board. Some have furnished balconies. There's a small pool, Jacuzzi, sundeck, and barbecue out back, and a cocktail bar on the third floor. The restaurant serves breakfast and dinner.

SUPER-CHEAP SLEEPS

Palace Backpackers. Corner of Ann and Edward sts., Brisbane, QLD 4000. ☎ **1800/676 340** in Australia, or 07/3211 2433. Fax 07/3211 2466. 120 rooms (350 beds), none with bathroom. A$28 (U.S.$19.60) single; A$38 (U.S.$22.60) double. A$15–$18 (U.S.$10.50–$12.60) dorm bed. BC, MC, V. Train: Central. Bus: City Circle 333. Courtesy shuttle to and from Roma St. Transit Centre 7:45am–7pm.

Once a temperance hall, this lovely Heritage-listed five-story building in the heart of town with wrought-iron lace verandahs now plays host to less than temperate backpackers. Don't think it isn't for you on that account; the place is well run, and a beautiful restoration has provided simple but very pleasant private rooms with iron beds, proper mattresses and crisp linen, lockers, and either air-conditioning or fans. Only someone literally carrying a backpack is entitled to a dorm bed. The spick-and-span renovated bathrooms are cleaned twice a day. There are rooms and bathrooms for travelers with disabilities. There's a neat rooftop sundeck with a barbecue, TV lounges with Internet access, a tour desk, a communal kitchen, and an excellent cafe (see "Great Deals on Dining"). No smoking in rooms.

WORTH A SPLURGE FOR A WEEKEND

✪ **Quay West Brisbane.** 132 Alice St. (between Albert and George sts.), Brisbane, QLD 4000. ☎ **1800/672 726** in Australia, or 07/3853 6000. Fax 07/3853 6060. 134 apts. A/C MINIBAR TV TEL. A$290–$310 (U.S.$203–$217) 1-bedroom apt; A$340–$450 (U.S.$238–$315) 2-bedroom apt. Additional person A$30 (U.S.$21) extra. Bed & Breakfast weekend pkg., including breakfast, A$195 (U.S.$136.50) 1-bedroom apt. Ask about other special packages. AE, BC, DC, JCB, MC, V. Valet and self-parking A$8 (U.S.$5.60). Bus: City Circle 333. Ferry: Edward St. (Inner City and Cross River Ferry); or Riverside (CityCat), then a 10-minute stroll.

When the business folk desert on the weekends, it's time for you to move into these glamorous serviced apartments just 4 blocks from Queen Street Mall. There's no need to splurge for a two-bedroom, since a one-bedroom apartment will sleep four with the sofa bed. The apartments have all the amenities of a five-star hotel—daily servicing, 24-hour room service, concierge, a bar and restaurant with a lovely outdoor terrace—but with the bonus of their own laundry, dining area, separate bedroom, and fully equipped kitchen. Pamper yourself in the plunge pool or Jacuzzi; then, back in your room, gaze over the Botanic Gardens, flip through the free newspaper, turn up your stereo, or watch TV (both of them).

4 Great Deals on Dining

Eating well in Brizzie won't cost all that much, especially if you bring your own beer and wine and if you like ethnic nosh. For cheap meals, head to the stylish Merthyr Street bistro strip in New Farm, the cafes of Given Terrace and Latrobe Terrace in Paddington, the Asian ethnic houses around the intersection of Vulture Street and Boundary Street in West End, and the cheap and cheerful cafes nudged shoulder to shoulder in Brunswick Street Mall in Fortitude Valley. Fortitude Valley is also where you'll find Brisbane's Chinatown. There are also loads of moderately priced restaurants on Park Road in Milton, though few of these are BYO. In the city center you'll find cheap, lively sidewalk cafes along Albert Street.

A surprise cluster of fabulously affordable and darn good restaurants has mushroomed in recent years in the unlikely location of Baroona Road and Nash Street in Rosalie, an otherwise sleepy suburb next to Paddington. Rosalie is about an A$8 (U.S.$5.60) cab ride from the city. After dinner here, stop for an ice cream at **Cold Rock,** 13 Nash St. (☎ **07/3368 1900**), or for *yummy* desserts at gallery-cum-cafe **Freestyle Tout,** 19 Nash St. (☎ **07/3876 2288**).

IN THE CITY CENTER

✪ **Emporio Il Centro.** Eagle St. Pier. ☎ **07/3229 9915.** Reservations not accepted. Main courses A$6.90–$9.80 (U.S.$4.85–$6.85). AE, BC, DC, MC, V. Mon–Fri 7am–6:30pm, Sun 8am–3pm. Bus: City Circle 333. Ferry: Riverside (CityCat and Inner City Ferry) or Eagle St. Pier (Cross River Ferry). CAFE FARE.

This swank little cafe overlooking the Brisbane River has the water views and European style of Il Centro, its sibling restaurant next door, without the high prices. Smartly suited office workers descend on its high circular tables and bar stools for breakfast or lunch—simple but hip fare like panini and Turkish bread sandwiches with Mediterranean vegetables and prosciutto; tomato and basil soup; and good coffee.

✪ **Explorers Café.** 63 Turbot St. (near corner of George St.) ☎ **07/3211 3488**. Reservations recommended at lunch. Main courses A$9–$15.90 (U.S.$6.30–$11.15) dinner, A$5.50–$13.90 (U.S.$3.85–$9.75) lunch, A$1.40–$9.90 (U.S.$1–$6.95) breakfast. AE, BC, DC, MC, V. Daily 7–9:30am, noon–2pm, 6–8:30pm; open for coffee all day. Happy hour Mon–Fri 5–6pm. Train: Roma St. Bus: City Circle 333. INTERNATIONAL.

What a find, you think, as you stumble on this pleasant basement restaurant under the Explorers Inn (see "Accommodations You Can Afford" above). Decent-sized lunches like chicken satay on rice cost a reasonable A$8.50 (U.S.$5.95), a seafood salad is A$6 (U.S.$4.20), and a small pizza supreme with sun-dried tomatoes, olives, and meats is a fabulous A$4.90 (U.S.$3.45). City office workers think the place is a find, too, so you'll have to reserve a table in the morning to get ahead of them for lunch. The ambience is warm and dignified for such an inexpensive joint, with exposed brick walls, potted palms, trendy sisal matting, and a cool corrugated iron bar. At night the crowd switches to guests from the hotel above and the meals get a bit beefier—lamb curry, rib fillet, and so on. A small pasta makes a generous dinner for A$9 (U.S.$6.30).

Pane e Vino. Albert St. at Charlotte St. ☎ **07/3220 0044**. Main courses A$18.90–$19.90 (U.S.$13.25–$13.95); pastas and risottos A$11–$15 (U.S.$7.70–$10.50); light meals, foccacias, and panini A$5–$10 (U.S.$3.50–$7). AE, BC, DC, MC, V. Sun–Thurs 7:30am–10pm, Fri–Sat 7:30am–11:30pm. Bus: City Circle 333. ITALIAN/CAFE FARE.

The relaxed mood at this contemporary open-sided cafe on a busy street corner is too relaxed for the high-powered corporate lunch crowd, which is why it's a haven for you. Fetch the day's papers from the corner and enjoy a cup of java amid the modish decor of polished concrete floors and sleek timber furniture, or come for a simple but sophisticated meal. The main courses, such as seared eye fillet with silky mashed potatoes, might tip the budget scales too far, but the lighter stuff—such as chicken spaghetti with olive paste, artichokes, and cream—should be just right. Even cheaper are the paninis and huge foccacias. The groovy stainless steel bar serves a full range of beers, spirits, and wines.

SUPER-CHEAP EATS
Govinda's. 2nd fl., 199 Elizabeth St. (opposite Myer Centre). ☎ **07/3210 0255**. A$6 (U.S.$4.20) all-you-can-eat; A$5 (U.S.$3.50) students and seniors. No credit cards. Mon–Sat 11:30am–2:30pm, Fri 5:30–8:30pm. Sunday Feast 5:30–8:30pm A$3 (U.S.$2.10) all-you-can-eat, with lectures and dancing. Bus: City Circle 333. VEGETARIAN.

If you're a seasoned vegetarian traveler in Oz, you already know to seek out the Hare Krishnas' chain of Govinda restaurants. This one serves vegetable casserole, dahl, samosas, deep-fried kofta balls, and other tasty stuff. The atmosphere is pretty spartan, but who cares when the food is so satisfying? This is a stimulant-free zone, so don't come expecting alcohol, tea, or coffee. They do take-out.

Palace Café. In the Palace Backpackers, corner of Ann and Edward sts. ☎ **07/3211 2433**. Main courses A$2.90–$8 (U.S.$2.05–$5.60). No credit cards. Mon–Fri 7:30am–8pm, Sat–Sun 7:30am–4:30pm. Train: Central. Bus: City Circle 333. CAFE FARE.

It's designed for the backpackers staying upstairs (see "Accommodations You Can Afford" above), but you don't have to sleep here to dine at this airy, colorful cafe. Just A$3 (U.S.$2.10) gets you beans on toast for *brekkie*, and even less buys you a three-filling sandwich for lunch. Fortifying roast beef or chicken is on the dinner menu, and there are burgers, minipizzas, and even a seafood plate for lunch at a grand A$8 (U.S.$5.60). A TV, mags, and two computers with Internet access make the place feel homey.

WORTH A SPLURGE

Pier 9. Eagle St. Pier, 1 Eagle St. ☎ **07/3229 2194.** Reservations recommended. Main courses A$17.95–$32.50 (U.S.$12.60–$22.75). AE, BC, DC, JCB, MC, V. Daily 11:30am–10pm; supper to 11pm. Bus: City Circle 333. Ferry: Riverside (CityCat and Inner City Ferry) or Eagle St. Pier (Cross River Ferry). MOD OZ SEAFOOD.

This light, bright contemporary restaurant, decked out with blond timber furniture, cream tongue-in-groove timber walls, and plate-glass windows overlooking the Brisbane River, is the city's favorite spot for seafood. Start with a half dozen oysters done any of six ways, including steamed with sweet miso and black bean dressing or served with smoked salmon, crème fraîche, and Sevruga caviar. Proceed to shellfish, such as local ocean king prawns, or go for Gulf of Carpentaria brown-bellied mudcrab. The fish menu leans towards light, crisp Asian finishes, such as baked Atlantic salmon steak with Bombay potatoes, sesame fried eggplant, chili, and clam and lime dressing. The place is busy all the time, so be prepared to take a seat at the bar by the open kitchen if you turn up without a reservation.

IN NEW FARM

New Farm Deli & Café. Merthyr St. at Brunswick St. ☎ **07/3358 2634.** Reservations recommended at dinner. Main courses A$3.50–$12.50 (U.S.$2.45–$8.75). AE, BC, DC, MC, V. Mon–Sat 7am–6pm, Fri–Sat 6pm–late, Sun 7am–5pm. Closed public holidays. Bus: 167, 168, 178. CAFE FARE.

Well-heeled local residents and the corporate crowd pack this cheery deli located at the rear of a small shopping complex. Try to get a seat outside. Loads of inventive pastas, filling toasted foccacia sandwiches, and gourmet burgers stack the menu, and there are blackboard specials such as hot pancetta, and tomato and mushroom risotto. Service is fast and pleasant.

✪ **The Purple Olive.** 79 James St. (between Arthur and Harcourt sts., New Farm. ☎ **07/3254 0097.** Reservations recommended. Main courses A$12.90–$22.50 (U.S.$9.05–$15.75); lunch specials Mon–Fri A$9.90 (U.S.$6.95). AE, BC, DC, MC, V. Tues–Fri noon–2:30pm; Mon–Fri 6pm–late; Sat–Sun noon–late. Bus: 168, 178. MOD OZ.

IN ROSALIE

My Thai. 141 Baroona Rd., Rosalie. ☎ **07/3368 2744.** Reservations recommended. Main courses A$7–$15 (U.S.$4.90–$10.50); average A$11 (U.S.$7.70). AE, BC, DC, MC, V. Daily 5:30–9:30pm. Bus: 475. THAI.

There's better Thai in the world, but all Thai food is good food, and the friendly service and well-lit courtyard seating beneath a big tree make this place a pleasant spot for dinner. The sweet, comfy interior is cozy in winter. We had a perfectly decent *neua pad bai krapow,* a spicy dish of beef with sweet basil, garlic, and chili, and a plate of stir-fried veggies that were fresh and crisp. Seafood lovers will find plenty to tempt them—prawns, calamari, and perch fillets get the full Thai treatment with lemon grass, coconut milk, and herbs. BYO.

IN MILTON

Arrivederci Pizza Al Metro. 1 Park Rd. ☎ **07/3369 8500.** Reservations recommended Fri and Sat dinner. Pizzas for two A$9.50–14.50 (U.S.$6.65–$10.15); pizzas for four A$9.50–$26 (U.S.$6.65–$18.20). AE, BC, DC, MC, V. Daily 10am–late. Train: Milton. Bus: 410. PIZZA.

ⓕ Family-Friendly Restaurants

Explorers Club (see p. 251). How nice to eat someplace where the kids can have what they want—burgers, fries, and yummy ice cream—and you can have what you want—flash-fried calamari, chicken medallions with lemon couscous, and a macadamia tart—and still be solvent on the way out! And you get to sit in grown-up surrounds while you do it.

My Thai (see p. 252). If your kids will eat Asian food, bring 'em to this pretty courtyard restaurant. The beauty of Thai meals is that everyone shares the dish, so you do not have to fork out for separate meals for every family member. Grown-ups spill Thai food on the tablecloths all the time, so management won't care if your kids do.

Arrivederci Pizza Al Metro (see p. 252). A pizza for a family of four, with plentiful toppings, will cost you around A$5 (U.S.$3.50) each at this cheerful family-run joint.

Cheapest of the bunch along the happening Park Road restaurant strip is this big pizzeria with airy indoor seating and some alfresco tables. They offer 21 toppings, mostly the basic but tasty kinds like salami, peppers, cheese, and mushrooms. It's just a humble joint, but it's a nice night out if you bring a bottle of red, dine outside, and then stroll up the street to people-watch and window-shop.

IN WEST END

The Three Monkeys. 58 Mollison St. (just off Boundary St.) ☎ **07/3844 6045**. Main courses A$4.50–$7.90 (U.S.$3.15–$5.55). AE, BC, MC, V. Mon–Thurs 9am–midnight, Fri–Sat 9am–1am, Sun 10am–late. Bus: 167, 177. CAFE FARE.

Locals make a beeline for this cute, hippy-chic cafe after a show at the Queensland Performing Arts Complex a few blocks away. What draws them? Huge plates of hearty homemade stuff like lasagna, moussaka, and vegetarian courgette bake, with very fresh side salads, at absurdly low prices. The dark winding rooms are bedecked with so many striped Moroccan fabrics, Asian wooden gewgaws, and wind chimes you fear you might never emerge; but keep going and you come to a palmy courtyard out back. The sinful cakes are a must.

IN ALBION

Breakfast Creek Hotel. 2 Kingsford Smith Drive (at Breakfast Creek Rd.), Albion. ☎ **07/3262 5988**. Main courses A$13.50–$19.90 (U.S.$9.45–$13.95). AE, BC, DC, MC, V. Meals: daily noon–2:30pm, Mon–Fri 5:30–9:30pm, Sat 5–9:30pm, Sun 5–8:30pm. Pub: Sun–Thurs 10am–10pm, Fri–Sat 10am–11pm. Bus: 300, 322. Wickham St. becomes Breakfast Creek Rd; the hotel is just off the route to the airport. STEAK.

Steak, footy, and beer are the three favorite eatin', talkin', and drinkin' pursuits at this ornate gabled historic pub overlooking the Brisbane River. It's fondly known to its fans as the Brekkie Creek. Thongs (flip-flops) are the minimum footwear—in fact, if you don't have any you'd better go out and buy some or you won't fit in. Order a XXXX (Fourex) beer, sit yourself down in the beer garden on plastic seats under umbrellas, and peruse the blackboard menu. You don't have to like steak to eat here—there are fish and chicken dishes—but most red-blooded patrons wouldn't dream of eating anything else. There are all kinds of meat cuts, and every meal is uniformly served with an Idaho potato with yummy bacon sauce, coleslaw, and tomato. On footy nights (Aussie Rules Football, Rugby League, or Rugby Union) be prepared for big crowds. There's a band on Sunday afternoons.

5 Exploring Brisbane

WHERE TO CUDDLE A KOALA & OTHER TOP ATTRACTIONS

Lone Pine Koala Sanctuary. Jesmond Rd., Fig Tree Pocket. ☎ **07/3378 1366.** Admission A$12.50 (U.S.$8.75) adults, A$6.50 (U.S.$4.55) children 3–13, family pass A$29 (U.S.$20.30). Admission with BBQ lunch A$27.50 (U.S.$19.25) per person; admission with breakfast A$21 (U.S.$14.70) per person. Daily including Christmas 7:30am–4:45pm; 1–4:45pm on ANZAC Day (Apr 25).

This is *the* place in Australia to cuddle a koala. Lone Pine was Australia's first koala sanctuary, and with 130 of these adorable "bears" that are not really bears, it's still the biggest. I was unexcited about cuddling one, but when that gray fur ball grips you with its little paws, you never want to put it down. Koala-cuddling is outlawed in New South Wales and Victoria, because it is thought to stress the animals, but the ones working the photo rounds at Lone Pine seemed well cared for and perfectly relaxed to me. You can cuddle them any time of the day for free, and have your photo taken holding one for A$8 (U.S.$5.60); once you have purchased one photograph, your companions can take as many photos of you as they like with their own cameras. Koalas sleep about 18 hours a day, which has led to a myth that they get "stoned" on the eucalyptus oil in the leaves they eat. That's just a vicious rumor—their sleepy behavior is just an adaptation to the leaves' low-energy content.

Lone Pine is not just about koalas—you can also hand-feed kangaroos, wallabies, and emus, and see parrots, wombats, Tasmanian devils, skinks, lace monitors, frogs, bats, turtles, possums, and other Aussie wildlife. There is a restaurant and cafe, and you are free to bring a picnic to eat overlooking the river. There are also currency-exchange facilities and a gift shop.

Getting There: Undoubtedly the nicest way to get to Lone Pine is a cruise down the Brisbane River aboard the *M.V. Miramar* (☎ **07/3221 0300**). The boat departs North Quay at the top end of Queen Street Mall, beside the casino next to Victoria Bridge, at 10am and makes the 19-kilometer (12-mile) trip upriver to Lone Pine, past Queenslander homes and native bush, all with a commentary from the captain. You have 2 hours to explore Lone Pine before returning downstream and arriving back in the city at 2:45pm. The fare is A$15 (U.S.$10.50) for adults and A$8 (U.S.$5.60) for children ages 3 to 13, including a map, transfers from city hotels when available, and discounted entry to Lone Pine (A$9/U.S.$6.30 for adults, and A$5/U.S.$3.50 for kids). Cruises are every day except Christmas and ANZAC Day.

If you want to drive, take Milton Road to the roundabout at Toowong cemetery, and then take the Great Western Freeway toward Ipswich. Signs will direct you to Fig Tree Pocket and Lone Pine. The sanctuary is 20 minutes from the city center by car. Bus 445 goes directly to the Sanctuary from the Green Stop at Adelaide Street near Albert Street.

Chow Time!

A good time to visit Lone Pine is around 3pm on weekdays and 9am on weekends, when the koalas are given fresh eucalyptus leaves. The normally lethargic critters are more active around mealtime.

South Bank Parklands. At South Bank across Victoria Bridge at western end of Queen St. ☎ **07/3867 2051** for Visitor Information Centre or 07/3867 2020 for recorded entertainment information. Free admission. Wildlife Sanctuary A$8 (U.S.$5.60) adults, $7 (U.S.$4.90) seniors and students, $6 (U.S.$4.20) children under 14. Park: daily 24 hours; Visitor Information Centre: Sun–Thurs 8am–6pm, Fri 8am–10pm, Sat 8am–8pm. Train: South Brisbane. Ferry: South Bank (CityCat) and Old South Bank (Inner City Ferry). Bus: Countless bus routes depart Adelaide St. near Albert St., cross the Victoria Bridge, and stop at the Queensland Cultural Centre; walk through the Centre to South Bank Parklands. Plentiful underground parking in Queensland Cultural Centre. The Parklands are a 7-minute walk from town.

When you don't feel like spending lots of money, do what the locals do—come to this delightful 16-hectare (40-acre) complex of parks, restaurants, souvenir shops, playgrounds, street theater, weekend markets, and even an artificial palm-lined beach with real waves and sand, where you can swim, stroll, and cycle the meandering pathways; meet friends over a *caffe latte* in one of the cafes; enjoy the city views; and maybe take in a 3D movie at the IMAX cinema. Kids will like the snakes, butterflies, flying foxes, and tarantulas in the Wildlife Sanctuary. From the parklands it's an easy wander to the museum, art gallery, and other buildings of the adjacent Queensland Cultural Centre (see below).

Queensland Cultural Centre. At South Bank across Victoria Bridge at western end of Queen St. ☎ **07/3840 7595.** Train: South Brisbane. Ferry: South Bank (CityCat) and Old South Bank (Inner City Ferry). Bus: Countless bus routes depart Adelaide St. near Albert St., cross the Victoria Bridge, and stop outside. Plentiful underground parking. The Centre is a 7-minute walk from town.

Adjacent to South Bank Parklands (see above), this low-rise, modernistic complex stretching along the south bank of the Brisbane River houses many of the city's performing arts venues as well as the state art gallery, museum, and library in a series of interlinked buildings. Thanks to plenty of open plazas and fountains inserted by thoughtful architects, it is a pleasing place to wander or to just sit and watch the river and the city skyline.

The **Queensland Performing Arts Complex** (☎ **07/3840 7444** administration or 07/3840 7482 tours) houses the 2,000-seat Lyric Theatre for musicals, ballet, and opera; the 1,800-seat Concert Hall for orchestral performances; the 850-seat Optus Playhouse Theatre for plays; and the 315-seat Cremorne Theatre for theater-in-the-round, cabaret, and experimental works. The complex has a restaurant and a cafe. Free 40-minute front-of-house tours leave from the ticket sales foyer at noon Monday through Friday; no bookings are needed. Backstage tours must be booked and cost A$5 (U.S.$3.50).

The **Queensland Art Gallery** (☎ **07/3840 7350**) does a good job not only of attracting blockbuster exhibitions, such as Renoir and Van Gogh, that often in the past would make it only to Sydney and Melbourne, but also of showcasing diverse modern Australian painters, sculptors, and other artists. Indoor/outdoor light-filled spaces and water features give the place an uplifting feel. Admission is free. Free guided tours run Monday through Friday at 11am, 1pm, and 2pm and on weekends at 11am, 2pm, and 3pm. There is a gift shop and bistro. The gallery is open daily from 10am to 5pm; closed Good Friday, Christmas, and until noon on ANZAC Day (April 25).

The **Queensland Museum** on the corner of Grey and Melbourne streets (☎ **07/3840 7635**) displays an eclectic assortment ranging from natural history specimens and fossils to a World War I German tank. Kids will like the blue whale model suspended from the entrance. The museum has a cafe and gift shop. Admission is free, except to traveling exhibitions, and it is open daily from 9:30am to 5pm; closed Christmas and Good Friday.

Cheap Thrills: What to See & Do for Free (or Almost) in Brisbane

- **Enjoy free entertainment at South Bank Parklands.** On weekends and school holidays, there is almost always some kind of free entertainment at South Bank Parklands, such as street theater, live bands, movies under the stars, or concerts. Even when there's nothing going on, it's a great place to hang out, picnic by the river, and people-watch. Call the entertainment line (☎ **07/ 3867 2020**) to see what's on.

- **Attend a free lecture, film, or gallery talk at the Queensland Art Gallery.** Free lectures and gallery talks on a topical artist or issue take place on the first and third Wednesday of the month. A free "Sunday at the Gallery" public program at 2pm features a gallery talk, film, or musical performance and kids' activities. One or two Fridays a month, a free short film on an artistic subject is screened at 12:30pm. It's a good idea to book a seat for the Wednesday and Friday activities; just show up on Sundays. Call ☎ **07/3840 7255** for details.

- **Drop in on a lecture or film in the Queensland Museum Theatre.** Topics range from the plight of the endangered golden-shouldered parrot to peace in Northern Ireland. These events take place most Wednesdays and some Saturdays at lunchtime, and are mostly free or cost just A$2 (U.S.$1.40).

- **Watch the Queensland Parliament in action.** If Parliament is sitting, the best show in town can sometimes be in the Green Chamber at Parliament House (See "More Attractions," below). Aussie politicians drop decorum in Parliament for no-holds-barred trading of taunts and insults that are sometimes banal, sometimes shocking, often funny. The free 10:30am tour at Question Time is the juiciest, when each side of politics tries to expose the other.

- **Having a Coke in the Premier's Lounge in the Treasury Casino.** If you stick to sipping a soft drink, it won't cost you much to enjoy the gentlemen's club atmosphere and river views here. Live piano plays Monday to Saturday from 9pm.

- **"Walking the walk" on the Mangrove Boardwalk.** The free Mangrove Boardwalk extends 400 meters (¼ mile) right out over the Brisbane River in the City Botanic Gardens, located along Alice Street. It's open and lit up until midnight.

MORE ATTRACTIONS

Australian Woolshed. 148 Samford Rd., Ferny Hills. ☎ **07/3351 5366**. Admission to ram show A$12 (U.S.$8.40) adults, A$8 (U.S.$5.60) seniors and students, A$5.50 (U.S.$3.85) children 3–14. Waterslide A$6 (U.S.$4.20) for 4 hours. Minigolf A$4 (U.S.$2.80) 9 holes, A$5.50 (U.S.$3.85) 18 holes. Daily 7am–5pm (Ram show 8am, 9:30am, 11am, 1pm, and 2:30pm). Train: Ferny Grove (station is 800m (½ mile) from the Woolshed). Kelvin Grove Rd. from the city becomes Enoggera Rd., then Samford Rd.; the trip is 14 kilometers (8½ miles).

A trip to this fun Australian sheep farm theme park is the next best thing to actually visiting a fair dinkum sheep station. Remember in the movie *Babe* how that piglet got apparently dumb sheep to make some smart moves in the show arena? That's just what happens in the Woolshed's ram show—eight well-behaved rams from the major Australian breeds walk calmly through the audience when their names are called and each takes his place on a dais with his name on it. Amazing! After the sheep-shearing, spinning, and sheepdog demonstrations that follow in the entertaining 1-hour show, you will be classing wool and whistling in the flock like a true bushie. You can also milk a cow, bottle-feed baby farm animals, feed kangaroos, see wombats and emus, and have your photo taken cuddling a koala for A$8.50 (U.S.$5.95). The gift shop has won awards for its quality souvenirs, a cut above the touristy merchandise usually sold in theme parks. A rustic restaurant serves Aussie specialties, and billy tea and damper is served up at 9am, 10:30am, and 12:30pm. On some Friday and Saturday nights the Woolshed hosts a traditional bush dance and dinner, featuring country dancing, spoon-playing, sing-a-longs, a live bush band, and a two-course barbecue dinner. Tickets cost A$35 (U.S.$24.50) per person at the door, or A$30 (U.S.$21) if you pay in advance. The fun starts at 7pm and goes until midnight. You must book to attend the dance; the minimum entry age for the bush dance and dinner is 18.

Brisbane Botanic Gardens at Mt. Coot-tha. Mt. Coot-tha Rd., Toowong, 7km (4 miles) from the city. ☎ **07/3403 2533.** Admission to Botanic Gardens is free. Planetarium Sky Theatre $9 adults, A$7.50 (U.S.$5.25) for seniors and students, A$5.50 (U.S.$3.85) children under 15 (not recommended for children under 6). Gardens open daily 8am–5pm (5:30pm in summer). Planetarium Sky Theatre Wed–Fri 3:30 and 7:30pm; Sat 1:30, 3:30, and 7:30pm; Sun 1:30 and 3:30pm. Reservations not necessary but advisable; call ☎ 07/3403 2578 Wed–Sun noon–7pm. Bus: 471; also 410. See "Organized Tours" for details on Brisbane Transport's daily bus tour.

A 15-minute drive or bus ride from the city takes you to these 52-hectare (130-acre) gardens at the base of Mt. Coot-tha. They feature diverse Aussie natives and exotics you probably won't see at home, including an arid zone, a glass Tropical Dome conservatory housing lush rain-forest plants, a cactus house, fragrant plants, a Japanese garden, African and American plants, wetlands, pine forests, and a bamboo grove. There are lakes and walking trails, usually a horticultural show or arts-and-crafts display in the auditorium on weekends, and a cafe. Free 1-hour guided tours leave the kiosk at 11am and 1pm Monday through Saturday (except public holidays).

While you're here, don't miss the Sir Thomas Brisbane Planetarium, where a fascinating 45-minute astronomical show re-creates the Brisbane night sky. Kids over 6 will like this.

Newstead House. Newstead Park, Breakfast Creek Rd., Newstead. ☎ **07/3216 1846.** Admission A$4 (U.S.$2.80) adults, A$3 (U.S.$2.10) seniors and students, A$2 (U.S.$1.40) children 6–16, and $10 (U.S.$7) for a family pass. Mon–Fri 10am–4pm, Sun and most public holidays 2–5pm. Closed Christmas, Good Friday, and ANZAC Day (April 25). Bus: 300, 306, 322.

Brisbane's oldest surviving home has been restored to its late Victorian splendor in a peaceful park overlooking the Brisbane River. Wander the rooms, admire the gracious exterior dating from 1846, and on Sundays and public holidays between March and November, take Devonshire tea. The U.S. Army occupied the house during World War II, and the first American war memorial built in Australia stands on Newstead Point on the grounds.

Parliament House. George St. at Alice St. ☎ **07/3406 7562.** Free admission and tours. Tours Mon–Fri at 9am, 10am, 11:15am, 2:30pm, 3:15pm, and 4:15pm; Sun 10am–2pm when Parliament is not in session. Mon–Fri 10:30am and 2:30pm when Parliament is in session. Bus: City Circle 333. Ferry: Queensland University of Technology (QUT) Gardens Point (CityCat and Inner City Ferry).

Queensland's seat of government was built in 1868 in an odd but happy mix of French Renaissance and tropical colonial styles. It's impressive from the outside, and guided 20-minute tours show off its ornate interior of Waterford chandeliers, Colebrookdale balustrades, and the gold-leaf coffered ceilings in the Council Chamber. When Parliament is in session the tour is restricted, but it finishes with a visit to the Parliamentary action. The House is a stop on Brisbane's Heritage Trail (see "City Strolls" below) and the City Sights tour bus.

✪ **Sciencentre.** 110 George St. between Mary and Charlotte sts. ☎ **07/3220 0166.**
Admission A$7 (U.S.$4.90) adults, A$5 (U.S.$3.50) seniors, students, and children 5–15, A$2
(U.S.$1.40) children 3–4, and A$24 (U.S.$16.80) for a family pass. Open daily 10am–5pm.
Closed Good Friday and Christmas, and until 1pm ANZAC Day (April 25). Bus: City Circle 333.
Ferry: Queensland University of Technology (QUT) Gardens Point (CityCat and Inner City
Ferry).

Adults love this hands-on science museum as much as the kids 12 and younger for
whom it was designed. Become part of a battery, see walls expand before your eyes,
watch shadows float in space, carry a briefcase with a mind of its own—these and
other amazing feats demonstrating the principles of science cover three fascinating
floors. Twenty-minute interactive shows run throughout the day.

CITY STROLLS
Because Brisbane is flat, leafy, warm, and full of colonial-era Queenslander architecture,
it is a great city for strolling. Pick up one of the free **Heritage Trail Maps** from the Brisbane Tourism information booths (see "Visitor Information" above) and set off to
explore on your own. The guides have a history of the area you are about to walk, and
excellent detailed information and illustrations of historic buildings and other sights
along the way. Free guided walks of the **City Botanic Gardens** (☎ 07/3403 7913) at
Alice Street leave from the rotunda at the Albert Street entrance Tuesday to Sunday at
11am and 1pm (except public holidays). Rain forest, camelias, lily ponds, palm groves,
and formal flower beds offer a blissfully cool reprieve on a summer's day. The Gardens
are free and open 24 hours.

A 30-minute uphill stroll from the Brisbane Botanic Gardens at Mt. Coot-tha (see
"More Attractions," above) brings you to the summit, where you discover sweeping
views of the city right out to Moreton Bay. Reward yourself with an inexpensive lunch
in the cafe next to the lookout.

For organized walking tours, see below.

6 River Cruises & Other Organized Tours

RIVER CRUISES Cruises along the Brisbane River aboard the *Club Crocodile
River Queen* paddle wheeler (☎ 07/3221 1300) are a good way to take in the
Queenslander homes, historic buildings, and tropical foliage—especially in October
and November when big jacaranda trees burst into mauve flowers all over the city. The
boat departs from the Eagle Street Pier throughout the day. Cheapest are the
90-minute morning and afternoon tea cruises, which board at 9:45am and 3:15pm
and cost A$20 (U.S.$14). Children ages 4 to 14 pay half price, and seniors receive a
15% discount.

BUS TOURS Brisbane Transport (☎ 13 12 30 in Australia) runs three bus tours
that are a much better value than commercial tours, especially as tour tickets entitle
you to unlimited access to buses, ferries, and CityCats for the day. The ✪ **City Sights**
bus tour stops at 19 points of interest in a continuous loop around the city center,
South Bank, and Fortitude Valley, including Chinatown, South Bank Parklands, the
Queensland Cultural Centre, Sciencentre, the Riverside Centre (where markets are
held Sundays), the City Botanic Gardens, the casino, and various historical buildings.
The driver of the old-fashioned open tram-style bus gives a commentary, and you can
hop on and off at any stop you like, and do the loop any number of times. The bus
departs every 40 minutes from 9am to 12:20pm and 1:40 to 4:20pm. The whole trip,
without stopping, takes 80 minutes. Tickets cost A$15 (U.S.$10.50) for adults, A$10
(U.S.$7) for children ages 5 to 15, and A$30 (U.S.$21) for a family pass. Your ticket
comes with discounted admission to some attractions along the way. Buy your ticket

River Cruises on the Cheap

One of the cheapest tours in town is cruising the river aboard the fast ✪ **CityCat ferries.** Board at North Quay, QUT Gardens Point, or Riverside and head downstream under the Story Bridge to New Farm Park, past Newstead House to the restaurant row at Brett's Wharves; or glide upriver past the city and South Bank to the University of Queensland's lovely campus (take a peek at its impressive Great Court while you're there). This trip in either direction will set you back a whopping A$3.20 (U.S.$2.25).

on board. You can join anywhere along the route, but the most central stop is City Hall, Stop 2 on Adelaide Street at Albert Street.

The 2-hour **City Heights** tour whisks you to the top of Mt. Coot-tha for a great city view, and then on to Mt. Coot-tha Botanic Gardens. It departs City Hall, Stop 2 on Adelaide Street, daily at 2pm and costs A$7 (U.S.$4.90) for adults, A$5 (U.S.$3.50) for children ages 5 to 15, and A$15 (U.S.$10.50) for families.

The **City Nights** tour shows you the city lights from Mt. Coot-tha, the Brisbane River at South Bank, the illuminated cliffs at Kangaroo Point, New Farm Park, and Fortitude Valley. It departs City Hall, Stop 2 on Adelaide Street, at 6pm daily and returns at 8:30pm. Tickets are A$15 (U.S.$10.50) for adults, A$10 (U.S.$7) for kids ages 5 to 15, and A$30 (U.S.$21) for a family.

WALKING TOURS   The Brisbane City Council has a wonderful program called **Walking for Pleasure** (☎ **07/3403 8888**): Most days a free guided walk departs from somewhere in the city or suburbs, exploring all kinds of territory from bushland to heritage buildings to riverscapes to cemeteries. The beauty of the walks is that they are aimed at locals, not tourists, so you get to explore Brisbane side-by-side with the townsfolk. Every walk has a flexible short-/medium-/long-distance option and usually lasts about 2 hours. Most are easy, but some are more demanding. Most start and finish near public transport and end near a food outlet of some kind.

7 Enjoying the Great Outdoors or Catching an Aussie Rules Football Match

OUTDOOR ACTIVITIES

ABSEILING & ROCK CLIMBING   The **Kangaroo Point** cliffs just south of the Story Bridge are a breeze for first-time abseilers to scale—I know because I've done it and survived. **Outdoor Pursuits** (☎ **07/3391 8766**) stages rock climbs up the cliffs every second Sunday from 8:30am. The experience lasts 3 hours and costs A$30 (U.S.$21) per person. At 1pm you can abseil back during a 4-hour session for A$35 (U.S.$24.50) per person. You will fit in four or five abseils in the course of the afternoon. If you want to climb in the morning and abseil in the afternoon, you can buy both experiences as a package for A$55 (U.S.$38.50).

BIKING   Bike tracks unspoiled by pesky roads stretch for 350 kilometers (210 miles) over Brisbane's level terrain. You often share them with pedestrians and in-line skaters. One great scenic route starts just west of the Story Bridge, sweeps through the City Botanic Gardens, and follows the river all the way out to the sprawling parklands of the University of Queensland; it's about 9 kilometers (5½ miles), all up. **Brisbane Bicycle Sales and Hire,** 87 Albert St. (☎ **07/3229 2433**), will rent you a bike and furnish you with the Brisbane City Council's free detailed bike maps. Rentals start at A$9 (U.S.$6.30) for 1 hour and go up to A$20 (U.S.$14) for the day; overnight and weekly rentals are available. The price includes helmets, which are compulsory in Australia. The **Brisbane City Council** at City Hall (☎ **07/3403 8888**) and Brisbane Tourism's information booths (see "Visitor Information" above) also give out bike maps.

BUSHWALKING   Brisbane Forest Park, a 28,500-hectare (71,250-acre) expanse of bush land, waterfalls, and rain forest a 20-minute drive north of the city, has hiking trails ranging in length from just a few hundred meters up to 8 kilometers (5 miles). Some tracks have themes—one highlights the native mammals that live in the park, for example, and another, the 1.8-kilometer (just over 1-mile) Mt. Coot-tha Aboriginal Art Trail, showcases contemporary Aboriginal art with tree carvings, rock paintings, etchings, and a dance pit. Because the park is so big, most walks depart from seven regional centers that are up to a 20-minute drive from headquarters, so you will need a car. Make a day of it and pack a picnic. **Park Headquarters** (☎ **07/3300 4855**) is at 60 Mt. Nebo Rd., The Gap. Here you will find a wildlife display, a restaurant, a crafts shop, and an information center.

IN-LINE SKATING   In-line skaters can use the network of bike/pedestrian paths. See "Biking" for locations of where to find a map, or just head down to the City Botanic Gardens at Alice Street and find your own way out along the river. **SkateBiz,** 101 Albert St. (☎ **07/3220 0157**), rents blades and protective gear for A$10 (U.S.$7) (the price goes up to A$12/U.S.$8.40 on Sunday) for 2 hours. All-day rental is A$25 (U.S.$17.50). The shop closes at 5:30pm, so if you turn up to rent gear after 3:30pm, you need to take an overnight rental for A$15 (U.S.$10.50). Take photo ID. The store is open daily.

JOGGING   Take to any dual-use pedestrian/bike path (see "Biking" for information about where to find a bike map) or head to the City Botanic Gardens and out along the river.

SPECTATOR SPORTS

Aussie Rules and cricket are played at "The Gabba," as Aussies fondly dub the **Woolloongabba Cricket Ground,** 411 Vulture St. at Stanley Street, Woolloongabba, a 5-minute drive south of the city. Among the many buses to the Gabba are 165, 169, 185, 189, and 195.

AUSTRALIAN RULES FOOTBALL (AFL)   If you want to see what this uniquely Aussie game is all about, get along to see the Brisbane Lions. Tickets are about A$25 (U.S.$17.50); book through **TicketMaster** (☎ **13 61 00** in Australia). The season kicks off in late March and ends in late August, and most games are played on Saturday night.

CRICKET   Boring to some, fascinating to others, cricket is big business in Australia, and some of the most important national and international matches are played in Brisbane in the season from October to late February. Most matches are played midweek and weekends during the day; a few are played at night. Most tickets cost between A$20 (U.S.$14) and A$40 (U.S.$28). Book through **Ticketek** (☎ **13 19 31** in Queensland, 07/3404 6644 outside the state).

9 The Shopping Scene

Brisbane's best shopping is centered on **Queen Street Mall.** Fronting the mall at 171–209 Queen Street, under the Hilton, is the three-level **Wintergarden** shopping complex (☎ **07/3229 9755**), housing upscale jewelers and Aussie fashion designers. Farther up the mall at 91 Queen St. at Albert Street is the **Myer Centre** (☎ **07/ 3221 4199**), which has Brisbane's biggest department store and five levels of moderately priced stores, mostly fashion. The historical **Brisbane Arcade,** 160 Queen Street Mall, is lined with the boutiques of highly regarded local Queensland designers. Just down the mall from it you will find the **Broadway on the Mall** arcade (☎ 07/3229 5233), which stocks affordable fashion, gifts, and accessories on two levels.

The trendy suburb of ✪ **Paddington,** just a couple of miles from the city by cab (or take the no. 144 bus to Bardon), is the place to go for antiques, books, art, handicrafts, one-of-a-kind clothing designs, and unusual gifts. The shops—cute, colorfully painted Queenslander cottages—line the main street, **Given Terrace,** which becomes Latrobe Terrace. Don't miss the second wave of shops around the bend from the first lot.

You will find a handful of elegant houseware and fashion boutiques, art galleries, one or two antique shops, and buzzing cafes and restaurants on **Park Road,** linking Coronation Drive and Milton Road in Milton. Parking is difficult, so take an A$8 (U.S.$5.60) taxi or the Ipswich train from Central or Roma Street station to Milton station.

SHOPPING HOURS Brisbane shops are open from 8:30am to 5:30pm Monday through Friday, 8:30am to 5pm on Saturday, and 10:30am to 4pm on Sunday. They stay open until 9pm Friday in the city, when the Queen Street Mall is abuzz with cinema-goers and revelers, and Thursday in Paddington. In the suburbs stores often close Sundays.

MARKETS Authentic retro '50s and '60s fashion, off-beat stuff like old LPs (vinyl lives), second-hand crafts, and all kinds of junk and treasure are all up for sale at Brisbane's only alternative markets, **Brunswick Street Markets,** Brunswick Street next to Chinatown Mall, in Fortitude Valley (☎ **0418/886 400** mobile phone). Hang around in one of the many coffee shops and listen to live folk bands. It's held Saturday from 7am to 4pm.

Friday night is a fun time to visit the **South Bank Craft and Lantern Markets,** Stanley Street Plaza, South Bank Parklands (☎ 07/3870 2807), because the buzzing outdoor handcrafts market is lit by lanterns. The market is held Friday from 5pm to 10pm, Saturday from 11am to 5pm, and Sunday from 9am to 5pm.

Brisbane's glamour set likes trawling the **Riverside Markets** at the Riverside Centre, 123 Eagle St. (☎ **07/3289 7077,** or 0414/888 041 mobile phone), to buy attractive housewares, colorful pottery, wooden blanket chests, handmade toys, painted flower pots, and other stylish wares. It's held Sunday from 8am to 4pm.

10 Brisbane After Dark

You can find out about other festivals, concerts, and performing arts events, and book tickets, through **Ticketek** (☎ **13 19 31** in Queensland, 07/3404 6700 outside Queensland; ☎ 1900/93 9277 for recorded events information service, which is charged at A40¢/U.S.28¢ per minute, more from a pay phone). You can book in person at Ticketek agencies, the most convenient of which are on Level E at the Myer Centre at 91 Queen Street Mall, in the Roma Street Transit Centre, and in the Visitor Information Centre at South Bank Parklands. There is usually a A$2.20 (U.S.$1.55) fee per ticket. The telephone company Telstra runs a "what's on" guide to all kinds of entertainment; call ☎ **13 16 20** for the cost of a local call.

Dial 'n' Charge (☎ **13 62 46** in Australia) is another major booking agent for performing arts and classical music, including all events at the Performing Arts Complex (PAC). There is a A$6 (U.S.$4.20) fee per booking, not per ticket. You can also inquire and book in person at the Dial 'n' Charge box office at the PAC between 9am and 9pm Monday through Saturday, and at its outlet at the South Bank Parklands Visitor Information Centre.

The free, color weekly newspaper *Brisbane News* lists performing arts; jazz and classical music performances; art exhibitions; rock concerts; and public events. The free weekly *TimeOff,* which comes out Wednesdays and can be found in bars and cafes, is a good guide to live music, as is the *Courier-Mail* newspaper on Thursday.

THE PERFORMING ARTS

Most of Brisbane's performing arts happen at the Performing Arts Complex (PAC) in the Queensland Cultural Centre (see "Exploring Brisbane," earlier in this chapter). To find out what's playing and to book tickets, call Dial 'n' Charge (see above).

THEATER

La Boite Theatre. Performing at La Boite Theatre, 57 Hale St., Petrie Terrace. ☎ **07/ 3369 1622**. Tickets A$27 (U.S.$18.90); previews A$15 (U.S.$10.50).

This innovative company performs contemporary all-Australian plays in a tiny theater-in-the-round on the edge of the city center.

qtc (Queensland Theatre Company). Performing at Optus Playhouse and Cremorne Theatres at the Performing Arts Complex (PAC), South Bank. ☎ **07/3840 7000** administration. Tickets A$27–$45 (U.S.$18.90–$31.50); student rush tickets available 1 hour before performance $18 (U.S.$12.60).

Queensland's state theater company's seven or so productions a year run the gamut from Shakespeare to premiere Australian works. *Shine* star Geoffrey Rush guest-starred with them recently.

TN Theatre Company. Performing at the Twelfth Night Theatre, 4 Cintra Rd., Bowen Hills. ☎ **07/3252 5122**. Tickets A$40 (U.S.$28) Mon–Thurs, A$47 (U.S.$32.90) Fri–Sat.

Popular hits and comedies, such as Alan Ayckbourne's *Bedroom Farce,* featuring actors with faces well known to Australians, run at this venue just north of the city center.

BALLET & OPERA

Opera Queensland. Performing in the Lyric Theatre at the Performing Arts Complex (PAC). ☎ **07/3875 3030** for administration. Tickets A$30–$105 (U.S.$21–$73.50).

This state company performs a lively repertoire of three annual works, such as *Fledermaus, Faust,* and *Julius Caesar,* as well as musicals and choral concerts. Free talks on the opera you are about to see start in the foyer 45 minutes before every performance, and free close-up tours of the set are held after every performance (except the final night).

The Queensland Ballet. Performing at Cremorne Theatre, Optus Playhouse Theatre at the Performing Arts Complex (PAC); studio performances at the company's offices, Drake St. at Montague Rd., West End, and other venues. ☎ **07/3846 5266** administration. Tickets A$40–$50 (U.S.$28–$35), studio performances A$15 (U.S.$10.50).

Mostly classical works come from the state ballet company, although they do perform some modern works, too. Recent performances included *Peer Gynt,* a gala show at the Lyric Theatre with international guest dancers, and a small tightrope work at the intimate Cremorne Theatre.

CLASSICAL MUSIC

The **Brisbane City Council** (☎ **07/3403 8888**) sponsors free lunchtime concerts in City Hall most Thursdays, and sometimes on other days, too, usually from 12:30 to 1:30pm. Performers range from classical to percussion/folk fusion to military bands.

Queensland Philharmonic. Performing at the Performing Arts Complex (PAC) and City Hall. ☎ **07/3844 5599** for administration. Tickets A$35–$45 (U.S.$24.50–$31.50); student rush tickets available 1 hour before performance A$10–$15 (U.S.$7–$10.50).

In addition to its traditional and Baroque repertoire, the 31-strong Philharmonic steps into jazz, blues, and percussion territory with an occasional Treble Clef Café series in City Hall, featuring food, drink, and cabaret-style seating.

Queensland Symphony Orchestra. Performing at the Concert Hall in the Performing Arts Complex (PAC), City Hall, and intimate works at its studios at 53 Ferry Rd., West End. ☎ **07/ 3377 5000** for administration. Tickets A$32–$42 (U.S.$22.40–$29.40); student rush tickets available 30 min. before start of performance A$10 (U.S.$7).

The state's leading orchestra plays a diverse mix of classical and contemporary orchestral and chamber music. They also make the odd foray into fun material, such as Cole Porter hits and gospel music. Free talks are given in the foyer 1 hour before all major performances. Their occasional "Tea and Symphony" concerts at City Hall include tea and coffee.

THE CLUB & MUSIC SCENE
NIGHTCLUBS

Fridays. Upstairs in Riverside Centre, 123 Eagle St. ☎ **07/3832 2122.** Cover A$7 (U.S.$4.90) from 9pm; no cover Wednesday.

This indoor/outdoor bar, restaurant, and nightclub complex overlooking the Brisbane River is a haunt for professionals in their 20s and for university students. Every night sees some kind of unbeatable happy-hour deal, cocktail club, or drinks special, and the dance action starts pumping around 11pm. Every second Wednesday from 6pm the Wine Club welcomes over-30s with all the wine, champagne, spirits, beer, food, and live bands they can take for A$25 (U.S.$17.50). Live music plays on the impressive riverfront terrace from 3:30pm or so on Sunday. As the name implies, Friday is the big night.

Margaux's. 5th fl. of the Brisbane Hilton, 190 Elizabeth St. ☎ **07/3234 2000.** Happy hour 9:30–10:30pm. Cover A$5 (U.S.$3.50), includes free drink with entry before 10pm.

A smart mid-30s to mid-40s crowd gathers to dance and chat over cocktails and supper at this clubby joint. It's open Friday and Saturday from 9:30pm to 3am.

Super Deluxe. Upstairs in the Empire Hotel, 339 Brunswick St. at Ann St., New Farm. ☎ **07/ 3852 1216.** Cover Fri–Sat A$6 (U.S.$4.20).

Super-cool young groovers dance to an all-night beat at this nightclub upstairs in one of Brisbane's most historic hotels. It's open Friday and Saturday from 9pm to 5am.

COOL SPOTS FOR JAZZ & BLUES

Brisbane City Travelodge Jazz & Blues Bar. Ground fl. of the Brisbane City Travelodge, next to Roma Street Transit Centre, Roma St. ☎ **07/3238 2222**. Cover A$5 (U.S.$3.50), and varying cover charges for major visiting acts. No cover Tues.

One of Brisbane's leading live jazz venues is in the unlikely setting of this busy railway hotel. A mixed crowd in their 20s to 40s listens to jazz on Tuesday, a lucky dip of styles on Wednesday, blues on Thursday, and funk on Friday and Saturday.

PUBS & BARS

City Rowers Tavern. Eagle St. Pier, 1 Eagle St. ☎ **07/3221 2888.** Cover varies.

Downstairs is a modernistic tavern with great river views from the terrace, pool tables, a big sports screen, and sometimes live bands; upstairs is a nightclub playing the latest disco hits. Waterfront workers (the kind that wear Italian suits, not the sort that shift cargo) drink up big at the daily 5 to 9pm happy hour.

Empire Hotel. 339 Brunswick St. at Ann St., New Farm. ☎ **07/3852 1216.**

Friday and Saturday nights find this heritage-listed pub packed with the Hip, the Young, and the Beautiful. Don't come here in a suit, and forget about it if you're over 35—you're not welcome. Most nights a DJ plays in the downstairs Art Nouveau bar. Upstairs is the Super Deluxe club on Friday and Saturday (see "Nightclubs" above). By day, the place is more like a friendly country pub where people drop in and relax around the pool tables.

Jameson's Restaurant & Bar. 475 Adelaide St. ☎ **07/3831 7633.**

This downstairs wine bar leads a chameleon-like existence—it might host a literary night with a famous Aussie novelist one night, comedy cabaret the next, a Great Debate on a topic like "Better? Sex or Horseracing?" the following evening, live jazz bands the night after, and '80s dance tunes at the end of the week. No matter what's going on, the mood is always friendly and stylish.

Plough Inn. South Bank Parklands. ☎ **07/3844 7777.**

Kick back on the wide wooden verandah or lounge in the beer garden at this authentic re-creation of an Aussie country pub. There are live bands Friday and Saturday nights and Sunday afternoon. The steak bar is open for lunch and dinner daily.

The Wickham. 308 Wickham St., Fortitude Valley. ☎ **07/3852 1301.** No cover.

Drag shows entertain a mixed girl/guy crowd every night here at the city's premier gay venue. By day it's an Aussie pub, by night it's a club with lasers and DJs. Tuesday is boys' night, Wednesday is karaoke night. When the action gets too much, chill out at the pool tables, in the video poker lounge, or in the cafe.

THE CASINO

Treasury Casino. On Queen St. between George and William sts. ☎ **07/3306 8888.** Must be 18 years old to enter; neat casual attire required (no beachwear, but jeans or shorts are OK). Open 24 hours. Closed Christmas, Good Friday, and until 1pm ANZAC Day (April 25).

A modern casino is housed in this gorgeous heritage building that was built in 1886 as, ironically enough, the state's Treasury offices. Three levels of 100 gaming tables offer roulette, blackjack, baccarat, craps, sic-bo, and traditional Aussie two-up. There are more than 1,000 slot machines. Of the several eateries, go for lunch or dinner at Pastano, where nothing is over A$10 (U.S.$7). Free live bands appear nightly in the Livewire Bar. Ask about Ride and Dine deals where your bus, train, ferry, or taxi fare entitles you to buy a package of cheap gaming chips and a meal.

Queensland & the Great Barrier Reef

by Natalie Kruger

Queensland is where Aussies go for their holidays. "Beautiful one day, perfect the next" is the state tourism authority's marketing slogan, and that's not a bad way to sum up the state's embarrassment of riches—great beaches, great warm weather, and of course, the Great Barrier Reef. A necklace of white sandy beaches graces almost the entire Queensland coastline, off which a string of the world's most beautiful islands and coral atolls dangle. In the southern end of the state, just above the New South Wales border, the Gold Coast beaches and theme parks pull tourists by the bucket-load. In the northern reaches of the state, from Townsville on up, is another drawing card— a tangled 110-million-year-old rain forest full of rare plants and animals.

Queensland is a big producer of bananas and pineapples and is one of the world's biggest sugar producers. Most of this stuff is grown on the warm wet coastline, and that's where you will spend most of your time, too. Much of the state's inland is vast, dry grassland of little interest to anyone but beef cattle farmers and mining conglomerates. Queenslanders, or "banana benders," are the occasional butt of jokes by "southerners" (anyone not from Queensland) for their habit of taking things just a bit slower than folk do elsewhere. But strangely enough, those same southerners bolt for the Queensland beaches the moment the first chill of winter hits in the south.

Brisbane is the state's relaxed capital. It has a nice tropical feel, but most people base themselves on the Gold Coast or the Sunshine Coast and take side trips to Brisbane. Farther north of Brisbane, the world's largest sand island, Fraser Island, attracts hard-drinkin' four-wheel-drivin' fishermen and ecotourists.

Beyond that lies a tiny, little-visited coral cay, Lady Elliot Island. The island's gateway, Bundaberg, is home to a wonderful marine turtle rookery on the beach. Keep going north, and you reach Gladstone, the gateway to the Great Barrier Reef's most spectacular island, coral-wreathed Heron Island. As you carry on up the coast, you begin to bump into one tropical island after another until you hit 74 of them in the beautiful Whitsunday area.

North of the Whitsundays is popular Dunk Island and the lovely rain-forest settlement of Mission Beach. Then you come to Cairns, with rain forest hills and villages to explore and a harbor full of cruise and dive boats waiting to take you to the Reef. Cairns is fine as a base, but savvy folks these days head an hour north to the trendy village of

Queensland

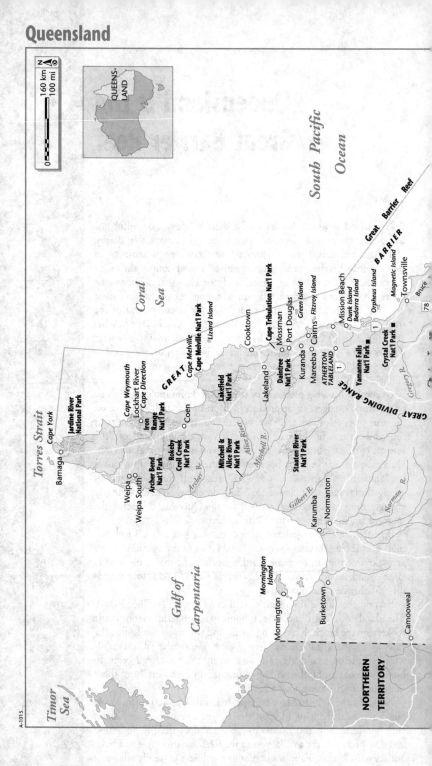

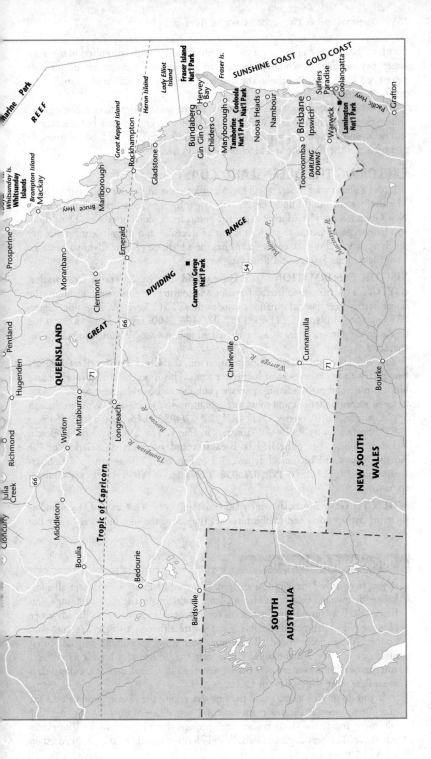

Port Douglas, where country sugar farmers rub shoulders with city golfers in the main street. Beyond that, the countryside starts to get wild and remote. Few people have penetrated Cape York Peninsula, the forested roadless northern tip of Australia that juts up toward New Guinea.

It's possible to spend a fortune on water sports, sailing trips, Reef cruises, game-fishing excursions, rain-forest 4WD tours and the like in Queensland, but this chapter will help you scout out the best deals. Cheap accommodations and food are generally plentiful, and the sunshine and beaches are always free.

EXPLORING THE QUEENSLAND COAST

Without a doubt your itinerary will include at least one trip to the Great Barrier Reef. The Reef starts around Bundaberg and runs right up the Queensland coast almost to New Guinea, so you have lots of departure points from which to explore. Don't think you have to go to Cairns to see it; it is just as accessible and magnificent from pretty much anywhere along the coast. Cairns has the advantage of good flight connections from Melbourne, Sydney, and Brisbane.

VISITOR INFORMATION   The **Queensland Tourist & Travel Corporation (QTTC)** is a bountiful resource on traveling and touring the entire state, including the Great Barrier Reef. For information, write to the QTTC, Level 36, Riverside Centre, 123 Eagle St., Brisbane, QLD 4000 (☎ **07/3406 5400;** fax 07/3406 5329). It has offices in the United States and the United Kingdom—see "Visitor Information" in chapter 3.

You will also find excellent information on the **Great Barrier Reef Visitors Bureau's** Web site at www.great-barrier-reef.com. This is not an official tourist office but a private company offering itinerary planning and booking services for a wide range of accommodations and tours throughout north Queensland. Write to them at 5/12 Grant St., Port Douglas, QLD 4871 (☎ **07/4099 4644;** fax 07/4099 4645).

For information on B&Bs and farmstays in Cairns, Port Douglas, Mission Beach, and Townsville, contact the **Bed & Breakfast and Farmstay Association of Far North Queensland Inc.,** c/o Lilybank Bed & Breakfast, 75 Kamerunga Rd., Stratford, Cairns, QLD 4870 (☎ **07/4058 1227;** fax 07/4058 1990; www.bnbnq. com.au).

WHEN TO GO   Australia's winter (June to Aug) is high season in Queensland as shivering Sydneysiders and Melburnites head north to the sun. Summer is very hot

---

Queensland in Three Days

If you have only 3 days in Queensland, you could happily spend them all snorkeling, diving, and fishing on Heron Island, undoubtedly the most stunning Great Barrier Reef cay surrounded by acres of coral gardens. Heron also has the advantage of being one of the more affordable island resorts, although it will still eat into your budget. Alternatively, spend all your time snorkeling, swimming and rain-forest hiking on a 3-day, 2-night sailing trip around the Whitsunday Islands. From here, you can head to the outer Great Barrier Reef for a day. You'll probably enjoy 3 days spent here more than 3 days in Cairns.

If you do go to Cairns, spend the first day taking the Skyrail gondola over the rain forest canopy to the mountain-top rain forest village of Kuranda. The next day take a day trip to the Great Barrier Reef, perhaps aboard Quicksilver's *Wavepiercer* catamaran. The next day explore the World Heritage–listed Daintree Rain Forest on a 4WD day safari.

Cheap Thrills: What to See & Do for Free (or Almost) in Queensland

- **Breathing in the sea air on a stroll along The Esplanade in Cairns.** Watch the ocean (if the tide's in) or the seabirds pecking at the mud flats (if it's out), watch the cruise boats pull in in the late afternoon, and at night join the throngs of people enjoying a cheap feed at the hordes of fish-and-chips shops, hamburger joints, and pizzerias lining the strip.

- **Strolling the Flecker Botanic Gardens, 3 kilometers northwest of Cairns.** The walking tracks, gardens, ferns, wetlands, and orchids are blissful in the summer heat and relaxing anytime.

- **Exploring the Wet Tropics rain forests at Mission Beach**. The Daintree Rain Forest north of Cairns is best explored on a 4WD safari, which costs money, but the even denser Wet Tropics rain forests at Mission Beach, a 90-minute drive south of Cairns, can be explored on foot for nothing. A bonus is that you may easily spot a cassowary, a giant ostrich-like bird with blue horny head like a dinosaur. The kids will love 'em.

- **Hitting the beach!** Beaches are always free in Oz, and Queensland has hundreds of them. Park your towel on any of Cairns' pretty palm-lined crescents, such as Palm Cove or Trinity Beach, or head south to the almost deserted, incandescently beautiful Mission Beach, which is bordered by thick jungle and has magical views across to Dunk Island.

- **Joining a free ranger-guided walk at Kingfisher Bay Resort on Fraser Island.** Learn how Aboriginals used native plants for food, spot dolphins and dugongs (manatees) from the headland, or look for native dingoes. The walks take place every day.

- **Soaking up the scene at Cavill Mall in Surfers Paradise on the Gold Coast.** Buy an ice cream cone from one of the numerous takeouts nearby and watch the surfies and Aussie families soaking up some sun. Marina Mirage on Sea World Drive at Main Beach is another good people-watching spot.

- **Checking out a koala colony.** You don't have to pay admission to a wildlife park to see koalas. A colony of these normally shy creatures has set up camp in the trees near the parking lot at the entrance to the Noosa National Park, which is just a stroll from the main strip on Hastings Street in Noosa Heads. Say hello to the koalas, then carry on around the headland along the park's network of trails. Park entry is free.

- **Feeding the birds at O'Reilly's Rainforest Guesthouse in the Gold Coast hinterland.** Not just any birds, mind you, but brilliant black-and-gold Regent bowerbirds, crimson-and-cobalt rosellas, and a flurry of other wild rain forest birds wait to be fed every morning. You will gasp with delight when they land on your hands to eat. If you're quick, the photos will be great.

and sticky across most of the state and in Brizzie, as the locals call Brisbane. From the Whitsundays northward, winter almost doesn't exist. See "When to Go" in chapter 3 for maximum and minimum temperatures and days of rainfall in Brisbane and Cairns. North Queensland, from around Cairns northward, gets a monsoonal Wet Season from December to March or April, which brings heavy rains and cyclones. You can visit the Great Barrier Reef during the Wet without a problem, but parts of the

---

Life's a Beach

Which Queensland beach is right for you? If it's surf you're after, head to the Gold Coast or Sunshine Coast close to Brisbane, for the Great Barrier Reef puts a stop to the swell north of Hervey Bay. North of Gladstone, deadly box jellyfish, known as "stingers," are a real wet blanket, putting a stop to all swimming on the mainland (but not the islands) from October to May. Never swim in unprotected seas at that time. Most popular beaches have small net enclosures for safe swimming, but it can be a drag having to stay within those. If you love swimming and you're visiting in stinger season, head to an island or choose a hotel with a good pool!

Daintree Rain Forest are often cut off by swollen creeks and floodwaters. If you want to visit north Queensland between January and April, try heading a little farther south to the beautiful Whitsundays, which are generally beyond the reach of the rains (although not beyond the reach of cyclones).

GETTING AROUND   By Car   The Bruce Highway travels along the coast from Brisbane all the way to Cairns. Its condition varies, but it is mostly a narrow two-lane highway. It is not an interesting drive, as the scenery most of the way is monotonous eucalyptus bush land, and unfortunately the highway is not right by the sea.

The QTTC publishes regional motoring guides. All you are likely to need, however, is a state map from the **Royal Automobile Club of Queensland (RACQ),** 300 St. Pauls Terrace, Fortitude Valley, Brisbane, QLD 4006 (☎ **13 19 05** in Australia, or 07/3361 2444). If you are already in Brisbane, you can get maps and motoring advice from the more centrally located RACQ office in the General Post Office (GPO) building at 261 Queen Street. For road condition reports, call ☎ 07/3219 0900. The state's Department of Natural Resources (☎ **07/3896 3216**) publishes an excellent range of "Sunmap" maps that highlight tourist attractions, national parks, and the like, although they are of limited use as road maps. You can pick these up at newsagents and gas stations throughout the state.

By Bus   McCafferty's (☎ **13 14 99** in Australia) and Greyhound Pioneer (☎ 13 20 30 in Australia) make the trip from Brisbane to Cairns in about 28 hours, stopping at all or most towns along the route. Both have good-value passes. Another option is the cheap, fun "alternative" buses, beloved of students and backpackers, that ply the Queensland coast. See chapter 3 for more details on getting around by bus.

By Train   Queensland Rail (☎ **13 22 32** in Queensland, or 07/3235 1122) operates several long-distance trains of varying degrees of luxury along the Brisbane– Cairns route, a 32-hour trip. See the "Getting Around" section in chapter 3 for more details.

By Plane   It ain't the cheapest but it sure is the fastest way to eat miles in such a big state. Beware the "milk run" flights that stop at every tin-pot town en route, as these can eat valuable vacation time. **Ansett** and **Qantas** and their respective subsidiaries, Flight West Airlines and Sunstate Airlines (book through the parent airlines) serve most coastal towns from Brisbane, but only a few from Cairns.

---

1 Exploring the Great Barrier Reef

It's the only living structure on Earth visible from the moon; at 348,700 square km (238,899 sq. miles), it's bigger than the United Kingdom; it's over 2,000 kilometers (1,200 miles) long, stretching from Lady Elliot Island off Bundaberg to just south of Papua New Guinea; it's home to 1,500 kinds of fish, 400 species of corals, 4,000 kinds of clams and snails, and who knows how many sponges, worms, starfish, and sea urchins; in short, the Great Barrier Reef is the Eighth Wonder of the World. Today, the Great Barrier Reef is listed as a World Heritage Site and is the biggest Marine Park in the world.

INTRODUCING THE GREAT BARRIER REEF

The Reef is not a plant, but one big conglomeration of tiny animals called coral polyps. They like to coat themselves in limestone to keep safe, and as they die, their limestone bodies cement into a reef on which more living coral grows. And so it goes on, slowly constructing a megametropolis of coral polyp skyscrapers just under the surface of the water.

You will see three kinds of reef on the Great Barrier Reef—fringing, ribbon, and platform. *Fringe reef* is the stuff you will see just off the shore of islands and along the mainland. *Ribbon reefs* create "streamers" of thin long reef along the outer edge of the Reef, and are only found north of Cairns. *Platform*, or *patch* reefs, are splotches of coral emerging up off the continental shelf all the way along the Queensland coast. Platform reefs are the most common kind, and are what most people are thinking of when they refer to the Great Barrier Reef. Island resorts in the Great Barrier Reef Marine Park are either "continental," meaning they are essentially part of the Australian landmass, or "cays," crushed dead coral and sand amassed over time by water action. Cays are surrounded by dazzling coral and fish life. Continental islands may have terrific coral, some coral, or none at all.

Apart from the dazzling fish life around the corals, the Reef is home to large numbers of green and loggerhead turtles, one of the biggest dugong (manatee) populations in the world, sharks, giant manta rays, and sea snakes. In winter (July to September) humpback whales gather in the warm waters around the Whitsunday Islands to give birth to calves.

To see the Reef you can snorkel it, fish it (recreational fishing is permitted in most zones of the Reef), fly over it, and dive it. When most people say Great Barrier Reef they mean the "Outer Reef," the network of platform and ribbon reefs that lies an average of 65 kilometers (41 miles) off the coast (about 1 hr. to 90 minutes by boat from the mainland). You should definitely get out and see that, but there is plenty of fringing reef to explore around the islands closer to the mainland.

Learning about the Reef before you visit enhances the already beautiful marvels you are going to see. ✪ **Reef Teach** (☎ **07/4051 6882**) is an evening slide show presentation by Paddy Colwell, an enthusiastic marine biologist and scuba diver. He tells you everything you need to know about the Reef, from how it was formed to how coral grows, from what dangerous critters to avoid to how to take successful underwater photos. It takes place throughout the year at 14 Spence St., Cairns, Monday through Saturday at 6:15pm, and costs A$10 (U.S.$7) per person.

Townsville is the headquarters of the Great Barrier Reef Marine Park Authority, and a visit to its showcase, ✪ **Great Barrier Reef Aquarium** (see "The North Coast:

When to Visit the Reef

April to November is the best time to visit. There's nothing wrong with December to March, but it can be uncomfortably hot and humid then, particularly as far north as the Whitsundays, Cairns, and Port Douglas. In the winter months of June to August, the water can be a touch chilly (heat-loving Aussies think so, anyway), but it rarely drops below 22° C (72° F).

Reef Tax

Every passenger over 4 years old must pay a A$4 (U.S.$2.80) Environmental Management Charge (EMC), commonly called "reef tax," every time they visit the Great Barrier Reef. This money goes towards the management and conservation of the Reef. Your tour operator will collect it from you when you pay for your trip. On visits of less than 3 hours, the tax is A$2 (U.S. $1.40).

Mission Beach, Townsville & the Islands," below) is a superb introduction to this underwater fairyland. Star of the Aquarium is a re-created living reef ecosystem in a massive viewing tank. If you want to learn more about the Reef, write to the Great Barrier Reef Marine Park Authority, P.O. Box 1379, Townsville, QLD 4810 (☎ 07/4750 0700; fax 07/4772 6093; www.gbrmpa.gov.au).

EXPLORING THE REEF

✪ **Snorkeling** the Reef is one of the most wondrous experiences you will have on your Aussie vacation. Green and purple clams, pink sponges, red starfish and purple sea urchins, and fish from electric blue to neon yellow to lime are a truly magical sight. Don't think snorkeling is the poor cousin to diving. Coral's rich colors only survive with lots of light, so the nearer the surface the brighter and richer the marine life. That means snorkelers bobbing about on top of the Reef are in a plum position to see it at its best.

If your Reef cruise offers a **guided snorkel tour,** often called a "snorkel safari," take it. They are worth the extra cost of A$20 (U.S.$14) or so. On such a safari I saw a family of teensy-tiny scarlet and turquoise clown fish hiding in an anemone, discovered giant clams, held a coral that oozed a natural sunscreen gel, and felt a sea cucumber "dissolve" through my fingers. These weird creatures "digest" themselves when attacked or picked up and re-form when you put them down. Most safaris, which are suitable for both beginners and advanced snorkelers, are led by marine biologists who tell you heaps about the fascinating sea creatures before you. Snorkeling is an easy skill to master, and the crew on cruise boats are always happy to tutor you if you are unsure.

A day trip to the Reef also offers you a great opportunity to go **diving**—even if you have never dived before. Every major cruise boat listed in "Day Trips to the Reef," and many dedicated dive boats listed in "Diving the Reef" (below) offer introductory dives that allow you to dive without certification to a depth of 6 meters (20 ft.) in the company of an instructor. You will need to complete a medical questionnaire on board and

Reef Safety Warnings

Coral is very sharp and coral cuts get infected quickly and badly. Ask your cruise boat for antiseptic cream and apply it to grazes as soon as you come out of the water.

The sun and reflected sunlight off the water can burn you fast. Remember, you're facing down when you snorkel, so put sunscreen on your back and the back of your legs, especially around your knees and the back of your neck, even behind your ears, all places that rarely get exposed to the sun. Apply more when you leave the water.

And another word on safety, this time the Reef's—the Great Barrier Reef is a Marine Park and removing coral (living or dead), shells, or any other natural item is an offense. If everyone who has ever visited the Reef took a piece, it would not be worth your coming to see what's left.

The Great Barrier Reef

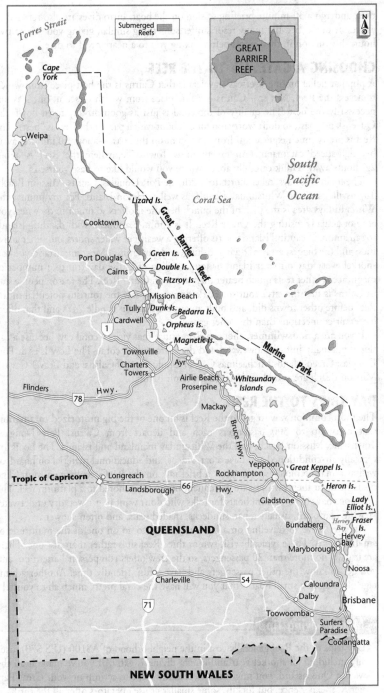

Torres Strait

Submerged Reefs

N

GREAT BARRIER REEF

Weipa

Cape York

Lizard Is.

Coral Sea

South Pacific Ocean

Cooktown

Green Is.
Port Douglas
Double Is.
Cairns
Fitzroy Is.

Great Barrier Reef

Mission Beach
Tully   Dunk Is.
Cardwell   Bedarra Is.
Orpheus Is.
Magnetic Is.

Marine Park

Townsville
Charters Towers   Ayr
Airlie Beach   Whitsunday
Proserpine   Islands

Flinders   Hwy.
78

Mackay

Bruce Hwy.

Yeppoon   Great Keppel Is.

Tropic of Capricorn   Longreach   Rockhampton   Heron Is.
Landsborough   66   Hwy.

Lady Elliot Is.
Gladstone

QUEENSLAND   Bundaberg   Hervey Bay   Fraser Is.
Hervey Bay
Maryborough

Noosa

Charleville   54   Caloundra
Dalby
Toowoomba   Brisbane

71

Surfers Paradise
Coolangatta

NEW SOUTH WALES

then undergo a 30-minute briefing session on the boat. Intro dives are also referred to as "resort dives" because many resorts offer something similar, giving you one or two hours' instruction in their pools before taking you to a nearby reef to dive.

CHOOSING A GATEWAY TO THE REEF

A popular belief among overseas travelers is that Cairns is the best place from which to access the Reef. Not so—Cairns is a fine place from which to see it, but it is not necessarily the best. The quality of the coral is just as good off any town down the Queensland coast, so don't worry too much about which part of the Reef is "best." The Reef is pretty much equidistant from any point on the coast—about 90 minutes away by high-speed catamaran. An exception is Townsville, where the Reef is about 2½ hours away. Think carefully about where you would like to base yourself.

The main gateways, taken north to south, are Port Douglas, Cairns, Mission Beach, Townsville, and the Whitsunday Islands, as well as Heron Island. For my money, the **Whitsundays** area is the pick of the bunch because it offers so much to do when you are not actually visiting the Outer Reef. It is a mini-Caribbean with dazzling islands to sail among; beautiful island resorts offering a wealth of water sports and other activities; and the biggest array of diving, fishing, and day cruises. Most important, you can snorkel every day off your island or join a sailing or cruise day trip to a number of magnificent inner reefs much nearer than the main Outer Reef. The reason people stay in Cairns is that the city's tourism marketing people saw the tourism potential in the Reef before other towns did, and built an airport that can handle 747s and that offers better air connections than the other gateways.

If you are a **nonswimmer,** choose a Reef cruise that visits a coral cay, because a cay slopes gradually into shallow water and the surrounding coral. The Low Isles at Port Douglas; Green Island, Michaelmas Cay, or Upolu Cay off Cairns; and Beaver Cay off Mission Beach are good locations. So is Heron Island.

DAY TRIPS TO THE REEF

The most common way to get to the Reef is on one of the big **motorized catamarans** that carry up to 300 passengers each and depart from Cairns, Port Douglas, Townsville, Mission Beach, and the Whitsunday mainland and islands. The boats are typically air-conditioned and have a bar, videos, and educational material on board, as well as a marine biologist who gives a brief talk on the Reef's ecology en route. The boats tie up at their own private permanent pontoon anchored to a platform reef. The pontoons have glass-bottom boats for folks who don't want to get wet, dry underwater viewing platforms, usually a bar, sundecks, shaded seats, and often showers.

An alternative to traveling on a big tour boat is to go on one of the multitude of **smaller boats.** These typically visit two or three Reef sites rather than just one. There are usually no more than 20 passengers, so the crew offers you personal attention, and you get to know the other passengers and have a fun, friendly time. Another advantage of going in a small boat is that you will have the coral pretty much all to yourself.

Money-Saving Tip

Day trips to the Reef generally cost in the neighborhood of A$100 (U.S.$70), usually including all snorkel gear and lunch; diving is extra. If you've made it all the way to Queensland, you might not necessarily want to scrimp on your Great Barrier Reef experience, but luckily, some smaller cruise operators offer all the thrills at a fraction of the price. Be sure to check out the "Budget Snorkeling & Diving" box in this chapter.

The drawbacks of a small boat are that you have only the cramped deck to sit on when you get out of the water, and your traveling time to the Reef may be a half hour or so longer. If you're a nervous snorkeler, you may feel safer going in a big boat where you are surrounded by 300 other passengers in the water.

Most day-trip fares include your snorkel gear—fins, mask, and snorkel, and wet suits in winter, although you rarely need them—free use of the underwater viewing chambers and glass-bottom boat rides, a plentiful buffet or barbecue lunch, and morning and afternoon refreshments. Most of the big boat operators and many of the smaller dive boats offer introductory dives for people who have never dived before, as well as regular dives for certified divers. Diving is an optional activity for which you pay extra. The big boats post snorkeling scouts to keep a lookout for anyone in trouble and to count heads periodically. If you wear glasses, check whether your boat offers prescription masks as this could make a big difference to the quality of your experience! Don't forget, you can travel as a snorkel-only passenger on most dive boats, too.

The major launching points for day trips to the Reef follow, listed from north to south.

FROM PORT DOUGLAS

Without a doubt the most glamorous large vessels visiting the Outer Reef are the ✪ **Quicksilver** *Wavepiercers* (☎ 07/4099 5500) based in Port Douglas. These ultra-sleek high-speed, air-conditioned 37-meter (121-ft.) and 45.5-meter (149-ft.) catamarans carry 300 or 440 passengers to Agincourt Reef, a ribbon reef 39 nautical miles (72 km/43 miles) from shore on the very outer edge of the Reef. After the 90-minute trip to the Reef you tie up at a two-story pontoon, where you spend 3½ hours on the Reef.

Quicksilver departs Marina Mirage at 10am daily except Christmas Day. The cost for the day is A$135 (U.S.$94.50) for adults and half price for kids ages 4 to 14. There are no family passes as such, but if two adults and two children pay to travel together, a third child travels free. Coach transfers from your Port Douglas hotel are an extra A$5 (U.S.$3.50). Cairns and northern beaches passengers can join the boat, too (see "From Cairns," below). Guided snorkel safaris cost A$28 (U.S.$19.60) per person, and introductory dives cost A$94 (U.S.$65.80) per person. Qualified divers take a dive-tender boat to make one dive for A$61 (U.S.$42.70) or two dives for A$94 (U.S.$65.80) per person, all gear included. Because Quicksilver carries so many passengers, it is a good idea to book snorkel safaris and dives in advance.

If you want to snorkel intensively in a small group of no more than 20 passengers, *Wavelength* (☎ **07/4099 5031**, or 07/4099 3295 after hours) is a good choice. Its modern 15.2-meter (50-ft.) vessels visit three sites on the Outer Reef each day (most other operators just visit one site). The sites vary each day, depending on the weather. The trip also includes talks about the Reef and its marine life. The boat departs from the Port Douglas Slipway at 8:30am daily and gets to the Reef in about 90 minutes, which gives you 5 hours on the coral. The cost, including lunch and transfers from your Port Douglas hotel, is A$103 (U.S.$72.10) for adults and A$65 (U.S.$45.50) for children ages 2 to 12.

The dive boat *Poseidon* (see "Diving the Reef," below) welcomes snorkelers. It presents a Reef ecology talk en route and takes you on a free guided snorkel safari. Lunch and transfers from Port Douglas hotels are included in Poseidon's price of A$110 (U.S.$77) for adults and A$80 (U.S.$56) for children ages 3 to 14. Round-trip transfers from Cairns and the northern beaches are A$12 (U.S.$8.40) adults, half price for kids.

In addition to its proximity to the Outer Reef, Port Douglas offers easy day-trip access to the Low Isles, two pretty coral-wrapped cays close to shore on the Inner Reef. See the "Port Douglas, Daintree & the Cape Tribulation Area" section in this chapter.

Feeling Green?

If you are inclined to be **seasick,** come prepared with medication. Some boats sell a ginger-based natural antiseasickness pill, but it doesn't always work!

FROM CAIRNS

Cairns passengers can board the most luxurious vessel visiting the Reef, the **Quick-silver *Wavepiercer*** (listed above under "From Port Douglas") in Cairns at the Marlin Marina at 8am and at Palm Cove Jetty on Cairns' northern beaches at 8:30am. It arrives at Port Douglas at 9:30am and leaves for the Reef at 10am. All of these trips run daily except Christmas. The fare for the whole day for Cairns and Palm Cove passengers is A$145 (U.S.$101.50) for adults, half price for kids ages 4 to 14. A free pickup from your hotel is included in the price.

If you prefer to visit the Reef straight from Cairns, large-scale operator **Great Adventures** (☎ **1800/079 080** in Australia, or 07/4051 0455) does daily cruises in fast, air-conditioned catamarans to a three-level pontoon on the Outer Reef. The pontoon has a children's swimming area, a semisubmersible, and an underwater observatory. You get about 4 hours total on the Reef. The cost for the day is A$130 (U.S.$91) for adults, A$65 (U.S.$45.50) for children ages 4 to 14, and A$325 (U.S.$227.50) for a family of two adults and two kids. Hotel transfers are A$6 (U.S.$4.20) per adult, A$3 (U.S.$2.10) per child, and A$15 (U.S.$10.50) per family extra from Cairns and the northern beaches, and A$12 (U.S.$8.40) per adult, A$6 (U.S.$4.20) per child, and A$25 (U.S.$17.50) per family extra from Port Douglas. The boat departs the Great Adventures terminal at Trinity Wharf near the Hilton at 10:30am.

Guided snorkel tours are A$15 (U.S.$10.50) per person extra. Introductory dives cost A$80 (U.S.$56) per person extra, while certified divers pay A$55 (U.S.$38.50) for one dive, A$80 (U.S.$56) for two dives, or A$175 (U.S.$122.50) for the whole day—cruise, lunch, snorkeling, and two dives with all gear.

You have an option to depart Cairns with Great Adventures at 8:30am and spend 2 hours on Green Island en route. This gives you time to walk nature trails, rent snorkel gear and water sports equipment, or laze on the beach before continuing to the Outer Reef. This cruise costs A$10 (U.S.$7) more per adult and A$5 (U.S.$3.50) more per child than the Reef-only cruise above. Guests staying on Green Island can join the cruise for A$104 (U.S.$72.80) adults, half price for kids.

Sunlover Cruises (☎ **1800/810 512** in Australia, or 07/4050 1333) has a choice of two Outer Reef trips aboard its large, fast catamarans. The first trip stops at Fitzroy Island for a guided rain-forest walk before heading on to Moore Reef on the Outer Reef. Transfers from city and northern beaches hotels are free. The day costs A$130 (U.S.$91) for adults, A$65 (U.S.$45.50) for children ages 4 to 14, and A$325 (U.S.$227.50) for a family of four. This trip consists of 1 hour on Fitzroy and about 3 on the Reef. Note that a free guided snorkel safari is included in the price—that's good value.

Sunlover's second trip departs Cairns and picks up passengers at Palm Cove before heading to Arlington Reef. In addition to the free snorkel tour, this cruise includes an optional tour of the Arlington Reef Pearl Farm for an extra A$10 (U.S.$7) per adult, A$5 (U.S.$3.50) per child. In total, you spend about 4 hours on the Reef. The price is A$116 (U.S.$81.20) for adults, A$58 (U.S.$40.60) for kids, and A$290 (U.S.$203) for a family.

Introductory dives on either trip cost A$85 (U.S.$59.50) per person for one dive or A$125 (U.S.$87.50) for two, while qualified dives are A$75 (U.S.$52.50) for one dive or A$95 (U.S.$66.50) for two, including all gear. Both cruises include lunch and free transfers from Cairns and northern beaches hotels. Both boats depart Trinity Wharf in Cairns at 9:30am daily.

A gorgeous alternative to motoring to the Reef is to sail to it. **Ocean Spirit Cruises** (☎ **1800/644 227** in Australia, or 07/4031 2920) operates two sailing cats that take no more than or 100 or 150 passengers to Michaelmas Cay or Upolu Cay, lovely white sand islands on the Outer Reef surrounded by rich reefs. This trip is a good value, since it includes a pleasant 2 hours sailing to either cay, a free guided snorkeling safari, and a free glass of bubbly and live musical entertainment on the way home—in addition to the usual reef ecology talks, semisubmersible rides, lunch, and transfers from your Cairns or northern beaches hotel. Another plus is that you spend your out-of-water time on a beautiful beach, not on a pontoon or boat deck. You get about 4 hours on the Reef.

The day trip to Michaelmas Cay is A$140 (U.S.$98) for adults, A$70 (U.S.$49) for children ages 4 to 14, and A$390 (U.S.$273) for a family of two adults and two kids. The day trip to Upolu Cay costs A$109 (U.S.$76.30) for adults, A$54.50 (U.S.$38.15) for kids, and A$300 (U.S.$210) for a family. Transfers from Port Douglas are A$35 (U.S.$24.50) adults, half price for kids. Introductory dives cost A$80 (U.S.$56) for one dive or A$125 (U.S.$87.50) for two, and certified dives cost A$50 (U.S.$35) for one or A$80 (U.S.$56) for two, all gear included. An introductory dive/sail package to Upolu costs A$169 (U.S.$118.30) per person, a savings of A$20 (U.S.$14). The boats depart Marlin Marina at 8:30am daily.

FROM MISSION BEACH

Mission Beach is the closest point on the mainland to the Reef, just 1 hour by the high-speed *Quick Cat* catamaran (☎ **1800/654 242** in Australia, or 07/4068 7289). The trip starts with an hour at Dunk Island 20 minutes offshore, where you can walk rainforest trails, play on the beach, or parasail or jet ski for an extra fee. Then it's a 55-minute trip to sandy Beaver Cay on the Outer Reef, where you have 3 hours to snorkel or to check out the coral from a semisubmersible or glass-bottom boat. There's no shade on the cay, so come prepared with a hat and sunscreen. The trip departs Clump Point Jetty at 10am; it departs daily in high season between July 1 and October 31, and every day except Sunday the rest of the year. It costs A$122 (U.S.$85.40) for adults, A$100 (U.S.$70) for seniors, A$61 (U.S.$42.70) for children ages 4 to 14, and A$305 (U.S.$213.50) for a family of four. Free pickups from Mission Beach are included. An introductory scuba dive costs A$70 (U.S.$49) for the first dive and A$30 (U.S.$21) for the second. You should prebook your introductory scuba dive to ensure a place. Qualified divers pay A$50 (U.S.$35) for the first dive, A$30 (U.S.$21) for the second, all gear included. You can join this trip from Cairns; coach connections from your Cairns hotel cost an extra A$13 (U.S.$9.10) for adults and A$6.50 (U.S.$4.55) for children.

FROM TOWNSVILLE

The only Reef cruise operator to offer fishing as well as snorkeling and diving is **Pure Pleasure Cruises** (☎ **07/4721 3555**), which operates the large *Wavepiercer 2001* catamaran to a pontoon on Kelso Reef, where you will find 350 types of hard and soft corals and 1,500 fish species. A marine biologist gives talks en route. The cruise costs A$120 (U.S.$84) for adults, A$110 (U.S.$77) for seniors and students, and A$60 (U.S.$42) for children ages 5 to 15. The family price is A$300 (U.S.$210) for two adults and two children (the family package includes reef tax). Glass-bottom boat trips are free, and optional ecology snorkeling tours are A$15 (U.S.$10.50). Introductory dives are an extra A$60 (U.S.$42), and qualified divers can make two dives for just

Budget Snorkeling & Diving

As well as all the "big guys" listed here, countless smaller operators run cruises to the Reef from Cairns that are more affordable as a rule. **Down Under Dive** (☎ **1800/079 099** in Australia, or 07/4031 1288) offers excellent, affordable trips aboard its fast catamaran, *Supercat*. Although surveyed for 200 passengers, the boat carries a maximum of 80. The day trip is just A$65 (U.S.$45.50) for snorkelers or A$110 (U.S.$77) for certified divers (which covers two dives and all gear) including a free guided snorkel safari and visits to two sites. Introductory dives cost an extra A$49 (U.S.$34.30) for the first one and A$25 (U.S.$17.50) for a second. A family pass for two adults and two children up to age 14 is A$220 (U.S.$154). Pickups from your hotel are A$5 (U.S.$3.50) from the city or A$10 (U.S.$7) from the northern beaches. Divers are left to explore on their own; a guided dive to the best spots is A$15 (U.S.$10.50) extra. There's also live musical entertainment on board. The boat departs Marlin Marina at 8:30am daily.

The following two boats come recommended by Pat and Mike Woolford of Lilybank Bed & Breakfast, in Cairns. *Seahorse* (☎ **07/4041 1919**), a 20-passenger 15.2-meter (50-ft.) sailing schooner, visits Upolu Cay daily for just A$60 (U.S.$42) per adult and A$35 (U.S.$24.50) children ages 2 to 13. Like the big guys, it has an onboard marine naturalist; unlike the big guys, its guided snorkel safari is free. You can even lend a hand sailing if you like. Introductory dives are optional at A$49 (U.S.$34.30), and a certified dive is just A$25 (U.S.$17.50) with all gear supplied. Wet suits, which you will need only in winter (and probably not even then) are A$5 (U.S.$3.50). Transfers from the city are A$5 (U.S.$3.50), and from the northern beaches A$10 (U.S.$7). The boat departs Marlin Marina daily at 8:55am.

Reef Magic (☎ **07/4031 1588**) is a fast 22-meter (72-ft.) air-conditioned catamaran that runs daily to 1 of 10 Outer Reef locations, where the Reef is yours for 5 hours. The boat is surveyed for 140 people but usually carries between 50 and 80. The price of A$89 (U.S.$62.30) for adults, A$49 (U.S.$34.30) for children ages 4 to 14, and A$249 (U.S.$174.30) for a family of four includes a free glass-bottom boat trip and free transfers from Cairns and northern beaches hotels. A guided snorkel tour is A$20 (U.S.$14). Introductory divers pay just A$50 (U.S.$35) for the first dive and A$25 (U.S.$17.50) if they want a second, while certified divers pay A$35 (U.S.$24.50) for one, A$25 (U.S.$17.50) for the second. Wet suits are A$5 (U.S.$3.50) for snorkelers. The boat leaves Marlin Marina daily at 9am.

Don't overlook ✪ **Green Island,** a stunning coral cay on the Inner Reef 50 minutes east of Cairns, as a Great Barrier Reef destination. It's closer to the mainland, and the snorkeling and diving are every bit as good as on the Outer Reef. Unlike the Outer Reef, where you will most likely be stuck on a pontoon or a boat when you are not in the water, Green Island has beautiful white coral sand beaches to lie on and lush rain forest to stroll in. A half-day trip costs just A$45 (U.S.$31.50). See the "Cairns" section in this chapter.

A$50 (U.S.$35). If you would rather catch fish than look at them, you and other keen fisherfolk can head off to deeper water to cast a line for sweetlip, coral trout, and other reef beauties. The staff will clean and wrap your catch, and your hotel chef should be happy to cook it for you. Fishing is complimentary. Cruises depart from the Great Barrier Reef Aquarium every day except Monday and Thursday at 9am and from

---

Money-Saving Tip

Pure Pleasure Cruises (☎ 07/4721 3555), which operates the large *Wavepiercer 2001,* has money-saving packages with all the Townsville accommodations recommended in this guide.

Picnic Bay Jetty on Magnetic Island at 9:20am. A courtesy shuttle picks up from most hotels. The boat takes 186 passengers, is air-conditioned, and has a video and bar. The trip takes 2½ hours each way, which gives you 3½ to 4 hours on the Reef.

FROM THE WHITSUNDAYS

FantaSea Cruises (☎ 07/4946 5111) makes a daily trip to Hardy Reef from Shute Harbour, near Airlie Beach, in a high-speed, air-conditioned catamaran. The boat has a bar, and a biologist gives a marine ecology talk en route. You anchor at the FantaSea Reefworld pontoon, and spend up to 4 hours on the Reef. The day trip costs A$129 (U.S.$90.30) for adults, A$97 (U.S.$67.90) for seniors and students, A$65 (U.S.$45.50) for children ages 4 to 14, and A$299 (U.S.$209.30) for a family of four. Guided snorkel safaris cost A$20 (U.S.$14) extra. Introductory dives are A$75 (U.S.$52.50) extra; certified dives are A$65 (U.S.$45.50) for the first dive and A$25 (U.S.$17.50) for the second. Ask about dive packages. The cruise departs at 8:30am and picks up passengers at South Molle, Hamilton, and Daydream island resorts. Guests at Club Crocodile Long Island transfer to Shute Harbour by water taxi to join the boat. If you're staying at Airlie Beach, the company provides free coach transfers to Shute Harbour.

A fun alternative to this day trip is FantaSea's 2-day, 1-night **ReefSleep,** in which you spend the night on the pontoon. This gives you a fabulous chance to snorkel at night when the coral is luminescent in the moonlight and nocturnal sea creatures get busy. The trip costs A$298 (U.S.$208.60) per person and includes a marine biologist's slide presentation, two scuba dives, plenty of night snorkeling, two buffet lunches, dinner under the stars with wine, and breakfast and more snorkeling on the second day. The accommodations are clean, comfortable bunkhouses. There's a limit of eight guests per night, so you have the Reef all to yourself.

MULTIDAY CRUISES ALONG THE REEF

Down Under Dive (☎ 1800/079 099 in Australia, or 07/4031 1288; fax 07/4031 1373) in Cairns offers an affordable chance to "sleep on the Reef" aboard a glamorous 42.6-meter (140-ft.) 1890s-style brigantine, the S.V. *Atlantic Clipper.* She's a sleek, romantic sailing ship with towering masts, a roomy Jacuzzi on the foredeck, a cocktail bar, a comfortable dining room, and single, double, triple or quad-share air-conditioned cabins. A motorized launch takes you from Cairns to the ship's reef mooring; from there you sail to up to the four popular reef complexes of Norman, Hastings, and Saxon reefs, and Michaelmas Cay. The emphasis is on fun and relaxation, with lots of snorkeling and diving. Trips range from a 2-day, 1-night stay in a triple or quad cabin for A$180 (U.S.$126) for snorkelers or A$255 (U.S.$178.50) for divers, to a 4-day, 3-night journey for A$380 (U.S.$266) for snorkelers or A$495 (U.S.$346.50) for divers. Single, triple, and quad-share cabins do not have private showers; doubles do. Add A$15 (U.S.$10.50) per person per night to the above prices for a single cabin, A$25 (U.S.$17.50) per person per night for a double. Snorkelers can make introductory dives for A$49 (U.S.$34.30) for the first dive and A$25 (U.S.$17.50) for each subsequent dive. Certified divers can make up to four dives a day. The all-inclusive prices include all dive and snorkel gear, meals, and pickups from your Cairns city accommodation.

DIVING THE REEF

Divers have a big choice of dive boats that make 1-day runs to the Outer Reef and live-aboard dive boats making excursions that last up to a week. As a general rule, on a typical 5-hour day trip to the Reef, you will fit in about two dives.

The companies listed next give you an idea of what kinds of diving trips are available and how much they cost. This is by no means an exhaustive list of the dive operators up and down the Reef, for there are far too many to include here. The section on "The Active-Vacation Planner" in chapter 3 has more pointers for locating a dive operator. The prices quoted here include full gear rental; knock off about A$20 (U.S.$14) if you have your own gear.

FROM CAIRNS Tusa Dive (☎ 07/4031 1248) runs two 20-meter (65-ft.) dive boats daily to two dive sites from a choice of 21 locations on the Outer Reef. A day's diving costs A$155 (U.S.$108.50) with wet suits, guided snorkel tours, lunch, and transfers from your Cairns or northern beaches hotel. For an extra fee you can get a video done of the day's dive. If you want to be shown the best spots under the water, you can take a guided dive with the dive team for an extra A$15 (U.S.$10.50). Day trips for introductory divers cost A$165 (U.S.$115.50) for one dive or A$190 (U.S.$133) for two. The groups are kept to a maximum of 25 people, so you get personal attention. The company is the Nitrox and Rebreather facility for north Queensland, and certified divers can take two introductory dives on Nitrox/Safe Air in one day for A$195 (U.S.$136.50).

Deep Sea Divers Den (☎ 07/4031 5622) does day trips to the Outer Reef with small groups in a fast, modern boat. The cost is A$140 (U.S.$69.30), which covers two dives, all dive gear, reef tax, snorkel gear, and lunch, or A$170 (U.S.$119) with an underwater guide. The cost of the day if you take an introductory dive is just A$135 (U.S.$94.50), or A$160 (U.S.$112) with two intro dives. Pickups from hotels are free in Cairns and A$10 (U.S.$7) per person from the northern beaches. The boat departs daily.

TAKA II (☎ 07/4051 8722; fax 07/4031 2739) is a solid 22-meter (72-ft.) live-aboard vessel that makes a 3-night trip to the ribbon reefs, Cod Hole, Clam Garden, Agincourt Reef, and Opal Reefs. The boat carries a maximum of 26 people in air-conditioned deluxe double or single cabins, standard double cabins, or quad-share cabins. The trip costs from A$675 to $875 (U.S.$472.50 to $612.50) from January to June, depending on your choice of cabin, and includes 10 or 11 dives, hotel pickups, and all meals. Dive gear rental is A$60 (U.S.$42) extra. From July to December add about A$145 (U.S.$101.50) per person to the price. An alternative 4-night journey to the Coral Sea is A$775 to $975 (U.S.$542.50 to $682.50) per person, including 14 or 15 dives. Add about A$150 (U.S.$105) per person to the price from July to December. Gear rental is A$80 (U.S.$56) extra on this trip. TAKA runs underwater photography courses in conjunction with its trips for A$150 (U.S.$105) for beginners or A$100 (U.S.$70) for advanced photographers.

FROM PORT DOUGLAS The waters off Port Douglas are home to dramatic coral spires and swim-throughs at the Cathedrals; giant clams and pelagics at Barracuda Pass; a village of parrot fish, anemone fish, unicorn fish, and two Moray eels at the

Diving Tips

Don't forget to bring your "C" certification card, and it's a good idea to bring along your dive log also. Remember not to fly for 24 hours after diving.

Pressed for Time?

If you don't have time for a full day on the Outer Reef, don't forget that you can dive the coral cay of Green Island, just 27 kilometers (16 miles) off Cairns, in half a day (see "Exploring the Islands & Beaches" in the Cairns section in this chapter).

soaring pinnacle of Nursery Bommie; fan corals at Split-Bommie; and many other wonderful sites.

Poseidon (☎ 07/4099 4772) is a fast 18-meter (58-ft.) vessel that visits three Outer Reef sites. The day-trip price of A$105 (U.S.$73.50) for adults, A$71 (U.S.$49.70) for kids ages 3 to 14 includes snorkel gear, a marine biology talk, free snorkel safaris, lunch, and pick-ups from Port Douglas hotels. Certified divers pay A$20 (U.S.$14) extra per dive, plus A$25 (U.S.$17.50) gear rental. Guides will accompany you under the water, free of charge, to show you great locations. Introductory divers pay A$60 (U.S.$42) for one dive, and A$35 (U.S.$24.50) each for the second and third. The vessel carries no more than 48 passengers, one-third its capacity, and gets you to the Reef in just over an hour, which gives you 5 hours on the coral. The boat departs Marina Mirage daily at 8:30am.

The **Quicksilver** *Wavepiercers* (see "Day Trips to the Reef" earlier in this section) runs dive-tender boats from their pontoon.

FROM MISSION BEACH Quick Cat Dive Adventures (see "Day Trips to the Reef," above) takes divers on its day cruises to the Reef.

FROM TOWNSVILLE Off Townsville, you can dive not only the Reef but also a wreck, the ✪ **Yongala,** which lies off the coast in 30 meters (98 ft.) of water with good visibility. A cyclone sent the Yongala with 49 passengers and 72 crew members to the bottom of the sea in a cyclone in 1911. Today it's surrounded by a mass of coral and rich marine life, including barracuda, grouper, rays, and turtles. **Mike Ball Dive Expeditions** (☎ 07/4772 3022; fax 07/4721 2152) runs 3-day, 2-night trips to the Yongala aboard a large, purpose-built live-aboard dive boat for around A$430 (U.S.$301), depending on your cabin choice. The trip includes six dives at the wreck. It departs once a week.

FROM THE WHITSUNDAYS In and around the Whitsunday Islands, you can visit the Outer Reef and explore the many excellent Reef dive sites close to shore. Two of the more established companies are **Reef Dive** (☎ 1800/075 120 in Australia, or 07/4946 6508) and **Kelly Dive** (☎ 1800/063 454 in Australia, or 07/4946 6122). A day trip with scuba and snorkel gear, two dives, lunch, and a pickup from your Airlie Beach accommodations costs around A$135 (U.S.$94.50) per person.

DIVE COURSES Loads of dive companies in Queensland offer dive courses, from initial open-water certification right up to dive master, rescue diver, and instructor level. To take a course, you will need to have a medical exam done by a Queensland doctor (your dive school will arrange it). Expect to pay around A$35 (U.S.$24.50) for the exam. You will also need two passport photos for your certificate, and you must be able to swim! Some courses take as little as 3 days, but 5 days is generally regarded as the best. Open-water certification usually requires 2 days of theory in a pool, followed by 2 or 3 days out on the Reef, where you make between four and nine dives.

Friends of mine who took a course with **Deep Sea Divers Den** (☎ 07/4031 2223; fax 07/4031 1210) in 1998 recommend their professionalism. The company has been in operation since 1974 and claims to have certified 55,000 divers. Their 5-day

---

Money-Saving Tip

Dive-course prices drop if you travel to the Reef each day for your practical sessions, instead of living aboard the company's boat. Of course, then you have to pay for your meals and accommodations on land, so tally up the cost for both ways before you commit to either.

---

open-water course involves 2 days of theory in the pool in Cairns, and 3 days and 2 nights on a live-aboard boat. The course costs A$495 (U.S.$346.50) per person, including all meals on the boat, nine dives (including a guided night dive), all your gear and a wet suit, and transfers from your city hotel. The same course over 4 nights, with 1 night on the boat and four dives instead of nine, costs A$395 (U.S.$276.50). New courses begin every day of the week.

If you are pressed for time, a **PADI referral course** might suit you. It allows you to do your pool and theory work at home and spend just 2 or 3 days on the Reef doing your qualifying dives. **Pro Dive** (☎ 07/4031 5255; fax 07/4051 9955) has a 3-day, 2-night referral course featuring nine dives and a "Reef Teach" marine biology session for A$480 (U.S.$336) per person. A 2-day referral course with the minimum four dives required is A$400 (U.S.$280) per person.

Other dive-course operators in Cairns include **Down Under Dive** (see above), **Rum Runner** (☎ 07/4052 1388; fax 07/4052 1488), **TAKA Dive** (see above), and **Tusa Dive** (☎ 07/4031 1248; fax 07/4031 5221). **Great Adventures** (☎ 07/4051 0455; fax 07/4051 7556) runs courses on Fitzroy Island off Cairns. In Port Douglas, **Quicksilver Dive** (☎ 07/4099 5050; fax 07/4099 4065), operated by the same company that operates the Quicksilver catamaran to the Reef, offers reasonably priced courses. In Townsville, **Mike Ball Dive Expeditions** (see above; fax 07/4721 2152) conducts a 5-day course every week that concludes with a dive on the *Yongala* wreck. In the Whitsundays, contact **Reef Dive** (☎ 07/4946 6508; fax 07/4946 5007) or **Kelly Dive** (☎ 07/4946 6122; fax 07/4946 4368). In Bundaberg, contact **Salty's Dive Centre** (☎ 07/4151 6422).

2 Cairns

346km (207½ miles) N of Townsville; 1,807km (1,084 miles) N of Brisbane

When international tourism to the Great Barrier Reef boomed a decade or two ago, Cairns (pronounced "cans") boomed with it. The result is a small sugar-farming town on the north Queensland coast with five-star hotels, island resorts off shore, big Reef-cruise catamarans in the harbor, and souvenir shops proliferating where the corner store used to be.

Not everyone realizes that Cairns is close to not one, but two, great natural wonders. The Great Barrier Reef is nearby, of course, but a couple of hours north lies a precious 110-million-year-old rain forest, the Daintree, where plants that are fossils elsewhere in the world exist in living color. The Daintree is part of the Wet Tropics, a World Heritage–listed area that stretches from north of Townsville to south of Cooktown, beyond Cairns, and houses half of Australia's animal and plant species. From Cairns you can glide over this Wet Tropics rain forest canopy in a gondola to the mountain village of Kuranda, where hiking trails, gorges, and towering waterfalls are the only things that interrupt the bush.

Cairns itself has little to recommend it. There are no beaches in town, the shopping is lackluster, and there are only a handful of really good restaurants. It's the Reef and the rain forest that will hold your attention here. If you are spending more than a day or two in the area, consider basing yourself on the city's pretty northern beaches, in Kuranda, or in Port Douglas (see "Port Douglas, Daintree & the Cape Tribulation Area" later in this chapter). Although prices will be higher in the peak season, which is the Australian winter and early spring from July to October, the town has affordable accommodations year-round.

ESSENTIALS

GETTING THERE   By Plane   Qantas (☎ **13 13 13** in Australia) and **Ansett** (☎ **13 13 00** in Australia) have multiple direct flights throughout the day to Cairns from Sydney and Brisbane, and between them at least one flight a day from Alice Springs and Darwin. Qantas also flies direct from Ayers Rock once or twice a day. From Melbourne you can fly direct on weekends only, regardless of which airline you fly; midweek you must connect through Sydney or Brisbane. From other state capitals you connect in Melbourne, Sydney, or Brisbane, or in Alice Springs in Perth's case. **Flightwest Airlines** (book through Ansett) and **Sunstate Airlines** (book through Qantas) both fly several times a day from Townsville. Ansett and Qantas both fly direct from Hamilton Island in the Whitsundays. Several carriers fly to Cairns from various Asian cities, and from Auckland.

An **airport tax** of A$3.50 (U.S.$2.45) per adult, A$1.75 (U.S.$1.25) per child for domestic passengers; and A$8 (U.S.$5.60) per adults, A$4 (U.S.$2.80) per child for international passengers is included in your airline ticket every time you land at or depart Cairns Airport. The airport has lockers, showers, parents' rooms, ATMs and currency exchange outlets in both terminals.

Cairns Airport is 8 kilometers (5 miles) north of downtown, and a 5-minute walk or a A$2 (U.S.$1.40) shuttle ride separates the domestic and international terminals. The cheapest transportation to your hotel is the **Australia Coach** (☎ **07/4031 3555**) shuttle, which costs A$4.50 (U.S.$3.15). It meets major flights, but may not meet you if you're coming on a small plane from an out-of-the-way destination. Bookings are not needed, just go to their counters in every terminal. Seniors and students get no discounts; the first two children under age 11 travel free, and all remaining children pay A$2 (U.S.$1.40). **Coral Coaches** (☎ **07/4098 2600**) meets most flights and does frequent drop-offs and pickups at all city and northern beaches accommodations. Only some trips require reservations; others are on a first-come, first-served basis, but booking is a good idea. The adult one-way fare is A$6 (U.S.$4.20) to the city, A$10 (U.S.$7) to Trinity Beach, A$12 (U.S.$8.40) to Clifton Beach, and A$13 (U.S.$9.10) to Palm Cove. Round-trip fares are double. Children ages 4 to 14 pay half price, seniors play half price plus A$1 (U.S.70¢), and students pay adult fare.

A **taxi** from the airport costs around $10.50 (U.S.$7.35) to the city, A$22 (U.S.$15.40) to Trinity Beach, A$26.60 (U.S.$18.65) to Clifton Beach, and A$29.50 (U.S.$20.65) to Palm Cove. Call **Black & White Taxis** (☎ **13 10 08** in Cairns).

Avis, Budget, Hertz, and Thrifty all have **car rental** offices at the domestic and international terminals (see "Getting Around," below).

By Train   Long-distance trains operate from Brisbane several times a week, calling at most towns and cities along the way on a route that is loosely parallel to the Bruce Highway. Trains pull into the **Cairns Central terminal** (☎ **13 22 32** in Australia for reservations or inquiries 24 hours a day, or 07/4052 6297 for the terminal from 8am to 6pm, 07/4052 6203 after hours) on McLeod Street at Shields Street in the center of town. It has no showers, lockers, or currency exchange booths, but you will find 24-hour ATMs outside the Cairns Central shopping mall, right above the terminal.

Staying Connected

You can check your e-mail and set up a temporary e-mail address at **Travellers' Contact Point,** 2nd floor, 13 Shields St. (☎ **07/4041 4677**) for A$5 (U.S.$3.50) for 30 minutes. You can also send and receive faxes, and have mail sent there. It's open daily from 8am to 8pm.

The trip from Brisbane takes around 30 hours. An upright seat on the *Sunlander* or *Spirit of the Tropics* costs A$129 (U.S.$90.30). Sleeping berths, available only on the *Sunlander,* cost A$159 (U.S.$111.30) for a shared three-berth cabin and $243 (U.S.$170.10) for a private cabin.

For more details on Queensland's long-haul trains, see chapter 3.

By Bus McCafferty's (☎ **07/4051 5899** for Cairns terminal) and **Greyhound Pioneer** (☎ **07/4051 3388** for Cairns terminal) buses pull into **Trinity Wharf Centre** on Wharf Street in the center of town. Buses travel from the south via all towns and cities on the Bruce Highway, and from the west from Darwin via Tennant Creek on the Stuart Highway and the Outback mining town of Mt. Isa to Townsville, where they join the Bruce Highway and head north.

The 46-hour Sydney-Cairns trip costs A$200 (U.S.$140), the 28½-hour trip from Brisbane is A$144 (U.S.$100.80), and from Darwin, the journey takes 39 hours and costs A$260 (U.S.$182).

By Car From Brisbane and all major towns in the south, you'll enter Cairns on the Bruce Highway. To reach the northern beaches or Port Douglas from Cairns, take Sheridan Street in the city center, which becomes the Captain Cook Highway.

VISITOR INFORMATION **Tourism Tropical North Queensland** is located at 51 The Esplanade, Cairns, QLD 4870 (☎ **07/4051 3588;** fax 07/4051 0127; www.tnq.org.au). Its Visitor Information Centre has information not just on Cairns and its environs but also on Mission Beach, Port Douglas and the Daintree rain forest, Cape York, and Outback Queensland. It's open daily from 8:30am to 5:30pm (closed Christmas and New Year's Day).

CITY LAYOUT Cairns' downtown precinct is laid out on a grid five blocks deep bounded in the east by the **Esplanade** on the water, and in the west by **McLeod Street,** where the train station and the Cairns Central shopping mall are located. In between are shops, offices, and restaurants. Cruises to the Great Barrier Reef and other tour boats leave from the edge of this 5-block area, either from **Trinity Wharf** on Wharf Street, beside the Hilton, or from the adjacent **Marlin Marina** beside the Pier Mall.

Twenty minutes out of the city along the **Captain Cook Highway** are the **northern beaches** of the Marlin Coast. The beaches are really suburbs of Cairns, each with its own identity. Heading north from Cairns, the beaches are Holloway's Beach, Yorkey's Knob, Trinity Beach, Kewarra Beach, Clifton Beach, Palm Cove, and Ellis Beach, in that order.

GETTING AROUND **By Bus** Local company **Sunbus** (☎ **07/4057 7411**) operates services in Cairns and to the northern beaches, departing City Place at the

Croc Alert!

Dangerous crocodiles inhabit Cairns waterways. Do not swim in, or stand on the bank of, any river or stream.

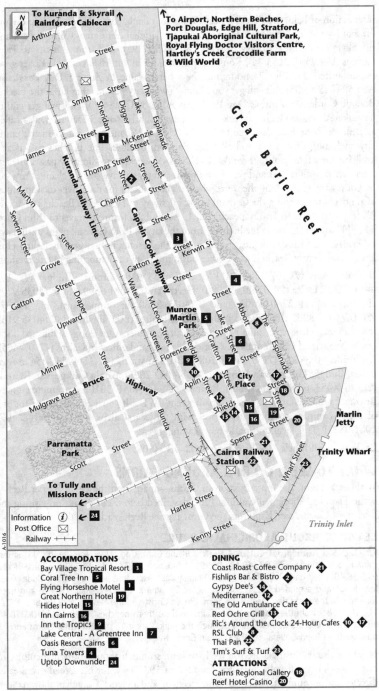

To Kuranda & Skyrail
Rainforest Cablecar

To Airport, Northern Beaches,
Port Douglas, Edge Hill, Stratford,
Tjapukai Aboriginal Cultural Park,
Royal Flying Doctor Visitors Centre,
Hartley's Creek Crocodile Farm
& Wild World

Great Barrier Reef

Arthur
Lily
Street
Smith
Street
Digger
Street
Sheridan
Street
The Esplanade
Lake Street
McKenzie Street
James
Thomas Street
Street
Charles
Street
Kuranda Railway Line
Captain Cook Highway
Street
Kerwin St.
Street
Gatton
Street
Street
Grove
Street
Gatton
Street
Draper
Street
Upward
Water
Street
McLeod
Street
Florence
Street
Sheridan
Grafton
Street
Abbott
Street
The Esplanade
Minnie
Munroe Martin Park
Lake Street
Street
Bruce
Highway
Mulgrave Road
Aplin Street
City Place
Street
Shields
Street
Spence
Street
Parramatta Park
Street
Scott
Bunda
Street
Wharf Street
Marlin Jetty
Trinity Wharf
To Tully and
Mission Beach
Cairns Railway Station
Hartley Street
Kenny Street
Trinity Inlet

Information
Post Office
Railway

A-1016

ACCOMMODATIONS
Bay Village Tropical Resort **3**
Coral Tree Inn **5**
Flying Horseshoe Motel **1**
Great Northern Hotel **19**
Hides Hotel **15**
Inn Cairns **16**
Inn the Tropics **9**
Lake Central - A Greentree Inn **7**
Oasis Resort Cairns **6**
Tuna Towers **4**
Uptop Downunder **24**

DINING
Coast Roast Coffee Company **21**
Fishlips Bar & Bistro **2**
Gypsy Dee's **14**
Mediterraneo **12**
The Old Ambulance Café **11**
Red Ochre Grill **13**
Ric's Around the Clock 24-Hour Cafes **10** **17**
RSL Club **8**
Thai Pan **22**
Tim's Surf & Turf **23**

ATTRACTIONS
Cairns Regional Gallery **18**
Reef Hotel Casino **20**

intersection of Lake and Shields streets. Fares are calculated by where you hop on and off, not by zones; a single fare from the city to Tjapukai Aboriginal Cultural Park and the Skyrail Rainforest Cableway is A$2.80 (U.S.$1.95), and from the city to Palm Cove is A$4.95 (U.S.$3.45). Round-trip tickets are about 10% cheaper. Passes good for unlimited travel for 24 hours may be a better value. A **Zone 1 Day Pass** costs A$5.50 (U.S.$3.85) and will get you around a wide city perimeter as far as the Flecker Botanic Gardens; a **Zone 2 Day Pass** costs A$6.75 (U.S.$4.70) and will get you to Tjapukai Aboriginal Cultural Park and the Skyrail; and a **Zone 3 Day Pass,** also called a "Beaches Zone-Free Pass," costs A$8.95 (U.S.$6.25) and lets you roam the entire city, including Palm Cove and all other northern beaches. The Beaches pass is also available for a family of four for A$20 (U.S.$14). Weekly and monthly passes are also available. Buy all tickets and passes on board, and try to have correct change. You can hail buses anywhere along the route where it's convenient for the driver to stop. Buses 1C and 1H travel along the Captain Cook Highway to Holloway's Beach; 1, 1A, and 3X (express) travel to Trinity Beach; and 1, 1A, and 2X (express) travel to Palm Cove. The "N" route runs along the highway from the city to Palm Cove all night until dawn on Friday and Saturday nights, stopping at all the beaches in between, including Holloways and Trinity Beaches. Most other buses run from early morning to late evening.

By Car   Avis (☎ 07/4051 5911 city, 07/4035 9100 airport), **Budget** (☎ 07/4051 9222), **Delta** (☎ 07/4032 2000), **Hertz** (☎ 07/4051 6399 city, 07/4035 9299 airport, 07/4031 2260 4WDs, and 07/4031 2260 for campervans), and **Thrifty** (☎ 07/4051 8099 city, 07/4035 9033 domestic airport terminal, and 07/4035 9132 international airport terminal) all have Cairns offices. One long-established local outfit, **Sugarland Car Rentals,** has reasonable rates and offices in Cairns (☎ 07/4052 1300) and Palm Cove (☎ 07/4059 1087). **Britz Australia** (☎ 1800/33 1454 in Australia), **Budget Campervan Rentals** (☎ 07/4032 2065), **Koala Campervan Rentals** (☎ 07/4053 6740), and **Maui Rentals** (☎ 07/4051 3010) rent motorhomes. Britz and most major rental car companies rent 4WDs. If you're in the market for one of these, compare the big guys' prices with those at **Cairns 4WD Hire** (☎ 07/4051 0822). This local outfit also rents camping gear.

By Taxi   Call **Black & White Taxis** at ☎ **13 10 08.**

WHAT TO SEE & DO IN & AROUND CAIRNS

Without a doubt, the top attraction in Cairns—apart from the Great Barrier Reef—is the Tjapukai Aboriginal Cultural Park, described below. For details on visiting the Reef from Cairns, see "Exploring the Great Barrier Reef," earlier in this chapter.

LEARNING ABOUT ABORIGINAL CULTURE

✪ **Tjapukai Aboriginal Cultural Park.** Off the Capt. Cook Hwy. (beside the Skyrail terminal), Smithfield. ☎ **07/4042 9999.** Admission A$24 (U.S.$16.80) adults, A$12 (U.S.$8.40) children 4–14, A$60 (U.S.$42) family pass. Ask about packages that include transfers, lunch and a guided Magic Space tour, or Skyrail and/or Scenic Rail travel to and from Kuranda on the same day. Daily 9am–5pm. Closed Christmas and New Year's Day. Bus: 1, 1A, 1C, 1F, N. Book shuttle transfers from Cairns and northern beaches hotels (A$12/U.S.$8.40 adults and A$6/U.S.$4.20 children) through the park. Park is 15 min. north of Cairns and 15 min. south of Palm Cove along the Captain Cook Hwy.

Nowhere else in Australia are you likely to learn so much about Aboriginal culture in one place. This cultural center was founded in 1987 by a former Broadway theater director and accountant, American Don Freeman, and a French Canadian show dancer, Judy Freeman. After working in street theater in Guatemala and India for some years, they went to Sydney, packed their stuff and their two young kids in a secondhand ambulance, and drove north until it got warm. They came to a stop in Kuranda, where

Travel Tip

If you're staying in Cairns, be sure to check out also what there is to see and do in and around Port Douglas (see "Port Douglas, Daintree & Cape Tribulation," later in this chapter). Many tour operators in Port Douglas offer free or inexpensive transfers from Cairns.

they founded an Aboriginal play that stands in the 1997 *Guinness Book of Records* as the longest-running show in Australia. The play eventually closed and evolved into the wonderful cultural park you see today. Although Don and Judy are still heavily involved, the park is 51 percent owned by the Aboriginal people who work in it.

Housed in striking premises incorporating Aboriginal themes and colors, the park is based around three performances: first, a stirring film on how the white man's arrival in Cairns 120 years ago impacted the Tjapukai. Next you move to the Creation Theatre for a fabulous dramatic reenactment of the Dreamtime creation. Third is an energetic dance by Aboriginal men incorporating ancient and new steps, performed in the open-sided Dance Theatre. Each show takes 20 minutes and is designed to flow into the next one. It's a good idea to do the shows in the order listed here, although you can wander through the premises at your own pace and do them in any order you like. The shows commence hourly, so there is always something on or about to start; only the dance troupe breaks for lunch.

Throughout the day there are also ongoing didgeridoo demonstrations, spear- and boomerang-throwing lessons, and a short talk on "bush tucker."

Allow at least 2½ hours to see everything, plus time to study the ancient artifacts and Dreamtime murals in the Magic Space museum, known as the "Wow!" room because of everyone's reactions when they walk in. The gallery and gift shop is the best place in town to buy authentic Aboriginal art, didgeridoos, boomerangs, and quality gifts and souvenirs.

MORE ATTRACTIONS

Three kilometers northwest of Cairns in Edge Hill, are the **Flecker Botanic Gardens,** 94 Collins Ave., (☎ **07/4044 3398**). The park is full of walking trails, ferns, wetlands, orchids, and gardens illustrating Aboriginal plant use. Recently added is Australia's Gondwana Inheritance garden, which is devoted to the history of plant evolution. Free guided walks take place at 1pm Monday to Friday. There is a licensed cafe and a nice book/gift shop. The gardens are open Monday to Friday 7:30am to 5:30pm, and from 8:30am weekends. The gardens are a 10-minute drive from the city, or take bus 1B.

In Cairns

Cairns Regional Gallery. Shields St. at Abbott St. ☎ **07/4031 6865.** Admission A$6 (U.S.$4.20) adults, A$3 (U.S.$2.10) seniors, students, and children 10–17; free admission on Fri. Daily 10am–6pm. Closed Good Friday and Christmas.

Modern paintings, sculpture, computer installations, and other kinds of works by a changing array of Australian and international artists are on show at Cairns' premier gallery, including pieces by Aboriginals and Torres Strait Islanders from Australia's far north. Make time to enjoy a cup of coffee on the alfresco terrace cafe.

Royal Flying Doctor Visitors Centre. 1 Junction St., Edge Hill. ☎ **07/4053 5687.** Admission A$5 (U.S.$3.50) adults, A$2.50 (U.S.$1.75) children, A$15 (U.S.$10.50) family pass for 2 adults and unlimited kids. Mon–Fri 8:30am–5pm, Sat–Sun 9am–4:30pm. Closed Good Friday and Christmas. Bus: 1B.

The Royal Flying Doctor Service (RFDS), the free aeromedical service that provides a "mantle of safety" for all Outback Australians, has a base in Cairns. You can watch a film and attend a talk on how the service began, browse through memorabilia, and board a former RFDS plane.

On the Northern Beaches

Hartley's Creek Crocodile Farm. Capt. Cook Hwy. (40km/24 miles north of Cairns, 25km/15 miles south of Port Douglas). ☎ **07/4055 3576.** Admission A$14.50 (U.S.$10.15) adults, A$7 (U.S.$4.90) children 4–14, A$40 (U.S.$28) family pass for 2 adults and unlimited kids. Daily 8:30am–5pm. Closed Christmas. Transfers available through Coral Coaches (☎ 07/4098 2600) from Cairns A$20 (U.S.$14) and Port Douglas A$18 (U.S.$12.60) round-trip, including park admission.

This working crocodile farm may be only a humble attraction tucked away in the rain forest, but many visitors find the sinister fascination of its huge captive crocs makes up for the modest scale. At 11am you can see these monsters get hand-fed or hear an eye-opening talk on the less aggressive freshwater crocodiles. At 3pm watch the brave keepers demonstrate the infamous saltwater crocodile "death roll" during the 45-minute croc attack show. Kids will enjoy patting koalas and learning about dingoes and other Aussie animals at the 30-minute mammal talk at 1pm; at 2pm there is a snake show about Australia's venomous reptiles; and at 4pm it's koala-feeding time. This attraction makes a good stop en route to Port Douglas. Crocodiles never move much except when they eat, so go at show time to see them in action. The same advice applies to visiting Wild World, described next.

Wild World. Captain Cook Hwy. (22km/13 miles north of the city center), Palm Cove ☎ **07/4055 3669.** Admission A$18 (U.S.$12.60) adults, A$9 (U.S.$6.30) children 4–15, A$16.20 (U.S.$11.35) students. Daily 8:30am–5pm. Closed Christmas. Bus: 1, 1A, N. Transfers available through Coral Coaches (☎ 07/4098 2600) from Cairns for A$30 (U.S.$21) and Port Douglas for A$38 (U.S.$26.60), round-trip, including admission.

Get a dose of all your favorite Aussie wildlife here—some kind of talk or show takes place just about every 15 or 30 minutes throughout the day, including koala cuddling and talks (have your photo taken cuddling one for an extra A$8/U.S.$5.60), saltwater crocodile feeding and talks, lorikeet feeding, cane toad racing, and snake talks. Lots of other critters are on show, too, like kangaroos (which you can hand-feed), emus, cassowaries, dingoes, and native birds in a walk-through aviary. An Aboriginal culture show runs several times during the day.

EXPLORING THE ISLANDS & BEACHES

You do not have to go all the way to the Outer Great Barrier Reef to snorkel and get a taste of island living off Cairns. Green and Fitzroy Islands offer reef, rain-forest walks, beaches, and water sports less than an hour from the city wharf. See "Where to Stay" later in this section for details of the resort on Fitzroy Island.

✪ **GREEN ISLAND** Fifty minutes and 27 kilometers (16 miles) east of Cairns by motorized catamaran is 15-hectare (37-acre) Green Island, an absolutely beautiful Great Barrier Reef coral cay surrounded by dazzling reefs and marine life. The island is home to an extremely expensive ecoresort, but anyone can visit as a day guest. You can snorkel over wide-ranging reefs or glide over the coral in a glass-bottom boat, rent water-sports equipment, go parasailing, take an introductory or certified dive, walk through lush rain and vine forest, swim in the day guests' pool, or laze on the white coral sand beach under a rented umbrella. If you don't snorkel, make sure you do not miss the incredible display of clown fish, potato cod, anemones, and other fishy things at the little underwater observatory on the jetty. It's very old, so the viewing windows are getting cloudy, but it's worth the few dollars' entry price to see such magical scenes.

The island has a small private attraction called **Marineland Melanesia,** where you can see old nautical artifacts; primitive art; a turtle and reef aquarium; and live crocodiles, including Cassius, at 5.5 meters (18 feet) claimed to be the biggest saltwater croc in captivity. Admission is A$7 (U.S.$4.90) with croc shows at 10:45am and 1:45pm.

Great Adventures (☎ **1800/079 080** in Australia, or 07/4051 0455) makes half- and full-day trips to Green Island from Cairns. Half-day trips depart Cairns at 8:30am and get back at 12:30pm (which gives you a little over 2 hours on the island) or depart Cairns at 12:30pm and get back at 5:30pm (which gives you over 3 hours). Half-day trips are A$45 (U.S.$31.50) for adults, A$22.50 (U.S.$15.75) for children ages 4 to 14, or A$112.50 (U.S.$78.75) for a family of four. This includes a guided rain-forest walk with a naturalist and a choice of snorkel equipment or a glass-bottom boat ride. Full-day trip departs at 10:30am and returns at 5:30pm, and includes both snorkel gear and a glass-bottom boat ride, the guided rain-forest walk, and a hot lunch. It costs A$90 (U.S.$63) for adults, A$45 (U.S.$31.50) for kids, and A$225 (U.S.$157.50) for a family of four. If you need to be picked up from your Cairns city or northern beaches hotel, add A$6 (U.S.$4.20) for adults, A$3 (U.S.$2.10) for kids, and A$15 (U.S.$10.50) for a family. If you're staying in Port Douglas, you can join the 10:30am departure for an extra A$12 (U.S.$8.40 for adults, A$6 (U.S.$4.20) for kids and $30 (U.S.$21) for a family. The boats depart the Great Adventures terminal at Trinity Wharf, next to the Hilton.

Once you arrive on the island, activities are extra: A$10 (U.S. $7) for a glass-bottom boat ride or snorkel gear; A$10 (U.S.$7) for a half-hour canoe or paddle-ski rental; A$15 (U.S.$10.50) for a guided snorkeling tour; A$20 (U.S. $14) for deck chairs and a beach umbrella; A$25 (U.S. $17.50) per hour for a windsurfer; A$30 (U.S.$21) for a catamaran (U.S.$21), A$75 (U.S.$52.50) for adults or A$40 (U.S.$28) for kids ages 10 to 14 for parasailing; A$55 (U.S.$38.50) for one dive if you are certified; and A$85 (U.S.$59.50) for one introductory scuba dive, or two dives if you are certified.

If all that is looking a bit heavy on the wallet, there is a cheaper way to enjoy the island for the day. Pack your own lunch, buy a straight round-trip Great Adventures transfer to the island from Cairns at A$40 (U.S.$28) adults and A$20 (U.S.$14) kids, rent snorkel gear when you get there at A$10 (U.S.$7) per person, forget about forking out for water sports—and glory in the beach, rain-forest trails, and coral for free. Hotel transfers will cost you A$5 (U.S.$3.50) for adults from Cairns, A$8 (U.S.$5.60) for adults from the northern beaches, and A$20 (U.S.$14) for adults from Port Douglas. There is an inexpensive outdoor grill/snack bar, an ice-cream parlor, and a small store on the island.

FITZROY ISLAND   Great Adventures (see above) also runs day trips to less much glamorous but equally scenic Fitzroy Island, a hilly national park–island 45 minutes offshore with some good diving. Here you can hire windsurfers, catamarans and canoes; hike through dense forest to the mountain-top lighthouse; view coral from a glass-bottom boat; take a beginners' or certified dive, and swim in the modest pool. Water sports prices are on a par with, or slightly less than, those on Green Island. The coral is not as much in evidence—to see some you will need to take a snorkeling trip in the dive boat to the other side of the island for A$25 (U.S.$17.50), including snorkel gear. A 20-minute walk through the forest around the island brings you to a small sand beach. One introductory dive, or two certified dives, cost A$80 (U.S.$56), all gear included. Great Adventures runs a half-day trip at A$49 (U.S.$34.30) for adults, A$23 (U.S.$16.10) for kids ages 4 to 14, and A$115 (U.S.$80.50) for a family of four. It includes 3 hours on the island, lunch, and a glass-bottom boat trip; snorkel gear is A$10 (U.S.$7) extra. The boat departs Cairns at 10:30am and gets back at 3:30pm. A full-day trip, including snorkel gear, a glass-bottom boat tour, and lunch, costs A$70 (U.S.$49) for adults, A$35 (U.S.$24.50) for kids, and A$175 (U.S.$122.50) for a family of four. Full-day trips depart Cairns at 8:30am and get back at 3:30pm, or depart at 10:30am and get back at 5:30pm. Add A$6 (U.S.$4.20) for adults, A$3 (U.S.$2.10) for kids, and A$15 (U.S.$10.50) for a family for pick-ups at your Cairns city or northern beaches hotel. Transfers from Port Douglas are available for the 10:30am day trip for A$12 (U.S.$8.40) for adults, A$6 (U.S.$4.20) for kids, and A$30 (U.S.$21) for a family.

It may work out to be cheaper, especially if you want to go for the whole day, to buy a straight Great Adventures round-trip transfer from Cairns for A$30 (U.S.$21) adults and A$15 (U.S.$10.50) for kids. On the island, you can then pay A$25 (U.S.$17.50) for the snorkel trip, buy a cheap lunch from the pool bar, forego the water sports, and enjoy the rain forest and beach for free. The boats leave Cairns at 8:30am and 10:30am.

Raging Thunder Adventures (☎ 07/4030 7990) takes guided sea kayak expeditions around Fitzroy Island. The trip departs at 8am from the Great Adventures terminal in Wharf Street and includes transfers from your hotel, catamaran transfers to the island, 3 hours of kayaking, snorkeling gear, lunch on a private beach, and a guided rain-forest walk to the island's hilltop lighthouse. The full-day trip costs A$98 (U.S.$68.60); A$135 (U.S.$94.50) with an overnight stay in bunkhouse accommodation.

A SIDE TRIP TO KURANDA

Few travelers visit Cairns without making at least a day trip to the pretty mountain village of **Kuranda,** 34 kilometers (20½ miles) west of Cairns near the Barron Gorge National Park. Although it's undeniably touristy, the cool mountain air and mist-wrapped rain forest refuse to be spoiled, no matter how many tourists clutter the streets. The shopping in Kuranda—for leather goods, Australian-wool sweaters, opals, crafts, and more—is a little more individual and unusual than in Cairns, and the handful of cafes and restaurants are much more atmospheric. The town is easily negotiated on foot, so pick up a visitors' guide and map at the Skyrail gondola station or train station (see below for how to get there) when you arrive.

GETTING THERE   Getting to Kuranda is part of the fun. Some people drive up the winding 25-kilometer (15-mile) mountain road, but undoubtedly the most popular routes are to chuff up the mountainside in a scenic train, or to glide silently over the rain-forest canopy in the world's longest gondola cableway, the ✪ **Skyrail Rainforest Cableway.**

The most popular way to get there is to go one way on the Skyrail (mornings are best for photography from the Skyrail) and the other way on the train.

By Skyrail   The **Skyrail Rainforest Cableway** (☎ 07/4038 1555) is a magnificent feat of engineering and one of Australia's best tourism attractions. More than 100 six-person gondolas leave every few seconds from the terminal in the northern

---

Travel Tip

Unless you are sure which tours you want to take, it often pays to wait until you get to Cairns to book them. Cases of unknowledgeable travel agents booking energetic teenagers on a coach-trip full of knitting old ladies are not uncommon. Local travel agents, your hotel or B&B host, and other travelers in Cairns are good sources of advice. Cairns has some 600 tour operators, so even in peak season, it is rare for a tour to be booked up more than 24 hours in advance.

Cairns suburb of Smithfield for the 7.5 kilometer (4½ mile) journey. The view of the coast as you ascend is wonderful. You can make two optional stops, one at Red Peak station to explore the forest on a raised boardwalk (hang around for the free guided walks that depart every 20 minutes) and another to view the spectacular 280-meter Barron Falls and visit the Rainforest Interpretative Center. A one-way ticket is A$27 (U.S.$18.90) for adults and A$13.50 (U.S.$9.45) for children ages 4 to 14 (hotel transfers are not available); a round-trip ticket, including transfers from your Cairns or northern beaches hotel, is A$56 (U.S.$39.20) for adults and A$28 (U.S.$19.60) for children, or A$67 (U.S.$46.90) for adults and A$33.50 (U.S.$23.45) for children from Port Douglas. You must make a reservation to travel within a 15-minute segment. The journey takes about 40 minutes one-way, or 90 minutes if you make the two stops. The cableway operates from 8am to 5pm, with last boarding at the Cairns end at 3:30pm. The Skyrail terminal is on the Captain Cook Highway at Kamerunga Road, 15 kilometers (9 miles) north of Cairns.

By Scenic Railway   The 34-kilometer (20½-mile) **Kuranda Scenic Railway** (☎ **1800/620 324** in Australia, or 07/4031 3636) hugs a fern-covered mountainside past gorges and waterfalls on the 90-minute trip from Cairns to Kuranda. It rises 328 meters (1,076 feet) and goes through 15 tunnels before emerging at the pretty Kuranda station, which is smothered in ferns. The train itself is an old historic locomotive. It departs Cairns Central at 8:30am and 9:30am Sunday through Friday every day except Christmas and leaves Kuranda at 2pm and 3:30pm Sunday through Friday. (Saturday departure from Cairns Central is at 8:30am only, with return trip at 3:30pm only.) The fare is A$25 (U.S.$17.50) one-way for adults, A$15 (U.S.$10.50) for Australian seniors and students (no discounts for international visitors), and A$13 (U.S.$9.10) for children ages 4 to 14. A pass for a family of four (only available Monday and Thursday to Saturday) is A$63 (U.S.$44.10) one-way.

Skyrail/Train Combination Tickets   In most cases, these packages represent convenience rather than savings. A package combining one-way travel on the Skyrail and a trip back on the Scenic Railway is A$52 (U.S.$36.40) for adults and A$26.50 (U.S.$18.55) for children; A$66 (U.S.$46.20) for adults and A$33.50 (U.S.$23.45) for kids with round-trip transfers from Cairns or the northern beaches; and A$77 (U.S.$53.90) for adults and A$39 (U.S.$27.30) for kids with round-trip transfers from Port Douglas. A shuttle bus operates between the Skyrail terminal and the nearest train station at Freshwater, 7 kilometers (4 miles) away, for A$4 (U.S.$2.80) adults, A$2 (U.S.$1.40) kids one-way. A three-way package including the Skyrail, the Scenic Railway, and entry to the Tjapukai Aboriginal Cultural Park (see above) is A$76 (U.S.$53.20) for adults and A$38.50 (U.S.$26.95) for kids, or A$90 (U.S.$63) for adults and A$45.50 (U.S.$31.85) for kids including transfers from Cairns/ northern beaches, or A$101 (U.S.$70.70) for adults and A$51 (U.S.$35.70) for kids with transfers from Port Douglas. Also available are four-way packages that include

Coming Down the Mountain

The Adventure Company (☎ **07/4051 4777**) offers a novel way to get back down from Kuranda—on foot, along a path once used by the Aboriginal Djabugay (Tjapukai) people. Your guide points out the local trees, plants, birds, and butter-flies, and you get to cool off in Stoney Creek's rock pools along the way. The descent leaves Kuranda at 12:45pm and gets back to Cairns around 6pm. The price, including afternoon tea and a transfer home to your hotel, is A$58 (U.S.$40.60).

entry to the Rainforestation Nature Park (see below). Book packages through Skyrail, Queensland Rail, or the Tjapukai Aboriginal Cultural Park.

By Bus   The cheapest way to reach Kuranda is by bus. **White Car Coaches** (☎ 07/ **4091 1855**) operates several daily bus services to Kuranda departing from outside the Tropical Paradise travel agency at 44 Spence St., Cairns. The fare is A$7 (U.S.$4.90) for adults (half price for Queensland-resident seniors), A$4.65 (U.S.$ 3.25) for high school students, and A$3.50 (U.S.$2.45) for kids ages 4 to 12.

Browsing Kuranda's Markets

Kuranda is known for its markets that sell locally made arts and crafts, fresh produce, boomerangs, T-shirts, and jewelry. There are actually two markets—the small "original" markets behind Kuranda Market Arcade, which mainly seem to sell cheap imports these days; and the 90-stall Heritage markets, which offer better quality and a wider variety of goods. Try to visit Kuranda Wednesday through Friday or Sunday when both markets are open.

Even the Heritage markets are getting "diluted" by commercial imported products, however. In response, a breakaway group of about 100 artisans sell their genuine locally made work in the ✪ **Kuranda Arts Co-operative,** 20 Coondoo St. (☎ 07/ 4093 9026**),** open from 10am to 4pm daily. You will find quality furniture crafted from recycled Australian hardwoods, jewelry, handcrafts, and all kinds of stuff here.

Soaking up the Rain-Forest Scenery

You can explore the rain forest, the river esplanade, or Barron Falls along a number of easy walking tracks. If you want to learn about the rain forest, explore it with Brian Clarke of ✪ **Kuranda Rainforest Tours** (☎ 07/4093 7476) who runs informative 45-minute river cruises. The cruises depart regularly from 10:15am to 2:30pm from the riverside landing across the railway footbridge near the train station. He also runs a daily 400-meter walk through the rain forest, leaving at 11:45am and returning at 12:35pm. Brian is a former professional crocodile hunter and has lived in the rain forest for 30 years. The cruise or the walk costs A$10 (U.S.$7) for adults, A$5 (U.S.$3.50) for children, and A$25 (U.S.$17.50) for families. Buy your tickets on board.

Kuranda's Nature Parks & Other Attractions

Of Kuranda's two walk-through aviaries, ✪ **Birdworld** (☎ 07/4093 9188), behind the Heritage Markets off Rob Veivers Drive, is probably the most interesting, as it has eye-catching macaws and a cassowary. The ✪ **Aviary, 8 Thongon St. (☎ 07/ 4093 7411**), is good if you want to see a bigger range of Australian species. Birdworld is open daily from 9am to 4pm; admission is A$8 (U.S.$5.60) for adults, A$7 (U.S.$4.90) for seniors, and A$3 (U.S.$2.10) for school-age children. The Aviary is open 10am to 3:30pm; admission is A$9 (U.S.$6.30) for adults, A$8.10 (U.S.$5.70) for seniors and students, A$4.50 (U.S.$3.15) for kids ages 4 to 16, and A$23 (U.S.$16.10) for a family of four. Both aviaries are closed Christmas.

Australian nocturnal creatures are on show at the **Wildlife Noctarium,** Coondoo Street at Therwine Street (☎ 07/4093 7334), open 10am to 3pm daily (closed Christmas). Feeding times are 10:30am, 11:30am, 1:30pm, and 2:30pm. Admission is A$9 (U.S.$6.30) for adults, $4 (U.S.$2.80) for children ages 4 to 14, and A$20 (U.S.$14) for a family of four.

Travel Tip

If you visit Kuranda, don't forget to bring some warm clothing in winter. It never gets to freezing, but it does get nippy up in the mountains.

Rainforestation Nature Park. On the Kennedy Hwy., a 5-min. drive from the center of Kuranda. ☎ **07/4093 9033.** Daily 9am–4pm. Closed Christmas. Shuttle throughout the day from outside Skyrail/train terminal 9:45–11am and the Australian Butterfly Sanctuary 10am–2:45pm; A$4 (U.S.$2.80) adults, A$2 (U.S.$1.40) children, and A$10 (U.S.$7) family, round-trip.

At this 40-hectare (100-acre) nature and cultural complex, you can take a 45-minute ride into the rain forest in a World War II amphibious Army Duck. You'll hear commentary on orchids and other rain-forest wildlife along the way. You can also see a performance by Aboriginal dancers; learn about Aboriginal legends and throw a boomerang on the Dreamtime Walk; or have your photo taken cuddling a koala in the wildlife park. You can do any of these activities separately, or do them all (except cuddle a koala) in a package that costs A$29 (U.S.$20.30) for adults, A$14.50 (U.S.$10.15) for kids ages 4 to 14, or A$78 (U.S.$54.60) for a family of five. Koala photos are A$8 (U.S.$5.60). The Army Duck runs on the hour beginning at 10am; the Aboriginal dancers perform at 11:30am and 2pm; and the 30-minute Dreamtime Walk leaves at 11am, noon, 1:30pm, and 2:30pm.

✪ **Australian Butterfly Sanctuary.** 8 Rob Veivers Dr. ☎ **07/4093 7575.** Admission A$10.50 (U.S.$7.35) adults, A$9.50 (U.S.$6.65) seniors and students, A$5 (U.S.$3.50) children 5–16; family discount A$1 (U.S.70¢) per person. Daily 9:45am–4pm. Free guided tours every 15 min.; last tour departs 3:15pm. Closed Christmas.

A rainbow-hued array of 1,500 tropical butterflies—including the electrifyingly beautiful "Ulysses blue" and Australia's largest species, the Cairns birdwing—is housed in a lush walk-through enclosure here. Take the free guided tour and learn about the butterfly's fascinating life cycle. The creatures land on you if you wear pink, red, and other bright colors.

EXPLORING THE WET TROPICS

The 110-million-year-old World Heritage–listed **Daintree Rain Forest,** 2 hours north of Cairns, gets most of the attention (see the "Port Douglas, Daintree & the Cape Tribulation Area" section later in this chapter), but tracts of rain forest closer to Cairns are just as pristine. These rain forests and the Daintree are part of the **Wet Tropics,** a World Heritage area that stretches from Cape Tribulation to Townsville. This dense, lush environment has remained unchanged by Ice Ages and other blips on the geological timeline, and today the plants and animals here retain primitive characteristics. Within the tract's mangroves, eucalyptus woodlands, and tropical rain forest are 65% of Australia's bird species, 60% of its butterfly species, and many of its frogs, reptiles, bats, marsupials, and orchids.

Because so much rain-forest wildlife is nocturnal and often difficult to spot, consider joining **Wait-A-While Environmental Tours** (☎ **07/4033 1153**). Wait-A-While's naturalist guides take you into restricted parts of the forest to spot a range of wildlife: musky-rat kangaroos, platypus, ringtail possums, cassowaries, amethystine pythons, birds, and tree frogs. They use only low-wattage bulbs and quiet 4WD or off-road vehicles to minimize their impact on the animals. Tours, which go to either the Atherton Tableland or the Daintree wilderness, depart Cairns daily at 2pm and return around midnight or 1am. The cost, A$120 (U.S.$84) for adults and A$90 (U.S.$63) for children under 15, includes binoculars, torches (flashlights), reference books, National Park permits, dinner either in a country restaurant or a picnic dinner, and candlelit supper in the rain forest. Tour groups include no more than eight people. The Atherton Tableland trip is best for viewing wildlife; the Daintree trip is more about getting back to a true wilderness.

Wildlife-Viewing Tip

If you want to spot wildlife, be careful which rain-forest tour you pick. To avoid contact with humans on the coast, rain-forest animals are increasingly retreating to higher altitudes; however, most tour operators to the Daintree and Cape Tribulation National Parks customarily stick to the lowlands. Many people on those day tours end up saying "But where are all the animals?" The afternoon-into-night trips offered by **Wait-a-While Environmental Tours** offer the most wildlife-viewing-for-your-buck.

Just over 50 kilometers (30 miles) southwest of Cairns in the **Wooroonooran National Park** are the rain-forested slopes of **Mt. Bartle Frere,** at 1,622 meters (5,320 feet) the highest peak in Queensland. The **Adventure Company** (☎ 07/ 4051 4777) runs 2-day hikes on the mountain, camping out in hammocks. The rugged Tuesday trip goes all the way to the summit for views of Great Barrier Reef islands. On the Thursday itinerary, you stay lower and swim in mountain streams. The price is A$198 (U.S.$138.60) per person, including all meals and camping. Four-day hikes are available.

WHITE-WATER RAFTING & OTHER OUTDOOR ACTIVITIES

The **Adventure Company** (☎ 07/4501 4777; or contact Great Expeditions, 440 Main St., 2nd floor, Lyons, CO 80540 ☎ 888/388 7333 or 303/823 6653 in the United States; www.adventures.com.au) offers a wide range of outdoor adventures, from hiking or biking through the rain forest to sea kayaking in the Great Barrier Reef Marine Park. It also offers white-water rafting, bungee jumping, hot-air ballooning, four-wheel driving, sky diving, and other high-octane thrills.

BIKING   Cairns hosted the 1996 World Mountain Bike Championships. Bike trails crisscross the wild hills behind the city. **Dan's Mountain Biking** (☎ 07/4033 0128) runs a wide range of guided tours in small groups. Most cost A$59 (U.S.$41.30) per person.

BUNGEE JUMPING   Contact **A. J. Hackett Bungy** (☎ 07/4057 7188). The cost is A$95 (U.S.$66.50) per person. Free transport is provided to the site, which is 20 minutes north of town on McGregor Road. Documentation of your adventure will cost you another A$25 (U.S.$17.50) for photos or A$39 (U.S.$27.30) for a video.

FISHING   Cairns is the world's giant black marlin capital. Catches over 1,000 pounds hardly raise an eyebrow in this neck of the woods. The game-fishing season is September to December, with November the biggest month. Book early, as game boats are reserved months in advance. Game fishers can also battle Pacific sailfish, dogtooth and yellowfin tuna, Spanish mackerel, wahoo, dolphinfish, barracuda, and tiger shark. Reef anglers can expect to land coral trout, red emperor (sea perch), and sweetlip. Mangrove jack, barramundi, and tarpon lurk in the estuaries. Call **Cairns Reservations Centre,** Shop 5 in the Hilton Hotel complex, Wharf Street (☎ 1800/807 730 in Australia, or 07/4051 4107), to book a charter. Expect to pay around A$400 (U.S.$280) per person per day for heavy-tackle game fishing, A$200 to $270

Travel Tip

Mosquitoes love the rain forest even more than people do, especially in summer. Don't head into the jungle without a mighty strong insect repellent.

The Secret of the Seasons

High season in Cairns includes the period from early July to early October; 2-week school vacations around Easter, mid-July, and late September; the Christmas holiday through January. Hotel occupancy is high in those periods, so book ahead. During the **low season,** from November to June, always ask about discounted rates. Many hotels will be willing to negotiate. Standby rates are usually easy to come by then, too.

(U.S.$140 to $189) for light tackle stuff, A$100 to $140 (U.S.$70 to $98) for reef fishing, and A$120 (U.S.$84) for a day or A$70 (U.S.$49) for a half day in the Cairns Inlet estuary.

GOLF   Greens fees at the lush 9-hole course at **Novotel Palm Cove Resort,** Coral Coast Drive, Palm Cove (☎ **07/4059 1234**) are just A$15 (U.S.$10.50); clubs are an additional A$15 (U.S.$10.50) and a cart is A$15 (U.S.$10.50).

WATER SPORTS   Cairns Parasail & Watersport Adventures (☎ **07/4031 7888**) offers single and tandem parasail trips, hair-raising 100-kilometer-per-hour (60 MPH) jet-boat rides, jet-ski rental, and "chariot" rides (you ride in an inflatable two-seat contraption that's pulled by a speedboat) in Trinity Harbour at Marlin Marina. The chariot ride costs A$25 (U.S.$17.50) and each of the other activities costs A$60 (U.S.$42); prices include free pick-up from your Cairns city hotel. Check out also the packages combining these thrills with bungee jumping, white-water rafting, fishing, sky diving, 4WD safaris, horseback riding, and trips to Green Island or the Great Barrier Reef. The company is located on the ground floor, marina-side, in The Pier Marketplace.

WHITE-WATER RAFTING   Several companies offer exciting white-water rafting trips from Cairns on the Grade 3 to 4 ✪ **Tully River,** 90 minutes south of Cairns near Mission Beach; the Grade 3 Barron River in the hills behind the city; and the Grade four to five rapids of the inland Johnstone River. One of the best outfitters is ✪ **RnR Rafting** (☎ **07/4051 7777**), or book through The Adventure Company, above.

One-day trips on the Tully are suitable for all ages and abilities and are the most popular (see the description in "The North Coast: Mission Beach, Townsville & the Islands" section later in this chapter). The trip costs A$128 (U.S.$89.60) from Cairns, or A$138 (U.S.$96.60) from Port Douglas, including transfers.

Closer to Cairns, the gentler Barron River is good choice for the timid. The half-day trip costs A$70 (U.S.$49) from Cairns or A$80 (U.S.$56) from Port Douglas, including pickup from your accommodations and two hours' rafting.

WHERE TO STAY

Cairns has a good supply of affordable accommodations, both in the heart of the city and along the northern beaches. Or you can choose to stay in the peaceful village of Kuranda, or get away from it all at an island resort.

IN CAIRNS

Unless noted otherwise, shops, restaurants, cinemas, the casino, bus terminals, the train station, and the Marlin Marina and Trinity Wharf departure terminals for Great Barrier Reef cruises are all within walking distance of the following accommodations.

✪ **Bay Village Tropical Retreat.** Corner Lake and Gatton sts., Cairns, QLD 4870. ☎ **07/ 4051 4622.** Fax 07/4051 4057. www.bayvillage.com.au. E-mail: reservations@ bayvillage. com.au. 64 units (most with shower only). A/C TV TEL. A$120 (U.S.$84) double; A$140 (U.S.$98) studio; A$195–$225 (U.S.$136.50–$157.50) 2-bedroom apt. Additional person

Where's the Beach?

One major drawback of staying in Cairns city: there's no beach, just mud flats with no swimming. To reach the white sands, you'll have to drive at least 15 minutes north of the city center.

A$20 (U.S.$14) extra. Children 3 and under stay free in parents' room. AE, BC, DC, JCB, MC, V. Limited free parking; ample on-street parking. Free city center and airport shuttle.

This recently renovated place has tile floors, freshly painted yellow or cream walls, and bright tropical bedcovers. An inviting swimming pool tucked away in a lush, private garden courtyard adds to the charm at this two-story hotel a half-mile from the city center. All the accommodations are smartly decorated and a decent size, but the studio apartments with kitchenettes are especially roomy; a few even come with decadent double showers. The bathrooms are compact but smartly done; all have hair dryers. There's always a helpful staff member around. Facilities include a free guest barbecue; room service; and a rustic, European-style restaurant.

Cairns Bed & Breakfast. 48 Russell St., Edge Hill, Cairns, QLD 4870. ☎ **1800/802 566** in Australia, or 07/4032 4121. Fax 07/4053 6557. www.cairns.aust.com/cairnsbnb. E-mail: cairnsb&b@internetnorth.com.au. 3 units (all with shower only). A/C TV. A$65 (U.S.$45.50) single; A$85 (U.S.$59.50) double; A$105 (U.S.$73.50) triple. Rates include full breakfast. No credit cards. Free on-street parking. Bus: 1B, N. Free transfers from airport, trains and coach terminals (arrange when booking).

Norah and Bernie Hollis's purpose-built B&B is 5 kilometers (3 miles) away from the airport or city, in a simple, pleasant suburb close to good restaurants, the bus route, and on the edge of a conservation wetlands area popular with bird-watchers. Guests share the house with Bill the Dog, Martin the cat, and dozens of Norah's teddy bears. Each cool, tile-floor room has its own entrance; all are furnished in Laura Ashley, with throw rugs, embroidered towels, and framed prints. The bathrooms are small but sweet and tidy. Hair dryers are available. Breakfast is served by the pool. Your hosts are a good source for down-to-earth advice on tours (Bernie is a tour guide), which mostly pick up from the door. They also provide dinner for A$20 (U.S.$14) per person. No smoking.

✪ **Coral Tree Inn.** 166–172 Grafton St., Cairns, QLD 4870. ☎ **07/4031 3744.** Fax 07/4031 3064. 58 units (some with shower only). A/C TV TEL. A$88 (U.S.$61.60) double; $120 (U.S.$84) suite. Additional person A$10 (U.S.$7) extra. Children 12 and under free in parents' room if they use existing bedding. AE, BC, DC, MC, V. Limited free parking; ample on-street parking. Airport shuttle.

The focal point of this airy, modern resort-style motel just a 5-minute walk from the city center is the clean, friendly communal kitchen that overlooks the small palm-lined pool and newly paved sundeck. It's a great spot to cook up a steak or reef fish fillet on the free barbie and join other guests at the big communal tables. Local restaurants deliver, free fresh-roasted coffee is on the boil all day, and a vending machine sells wine and beer, so you don't even have to go down to the pub for supplies! The smallish, basic but neat motel rooms were spruced up in 1998. They have white painted brick walls, terra-cotta tile or freshly carpeted floors, and clean new bathrooms sporting marble-look laminate countertops (ask for a hair dryer at reception). In contrast, the suites on the top (third) floor are huge and stylish enough to do any corporate traveler proud. They are some of the best-value accommodations in town. All rooms have a private balcony or patio; some look out onto the drab commercial buildings next door, but most look out over the pool. A tour desk takes care of your tour and rental car bookings. A lovely continental breakfast is just A$6 (U.S.$4.20) per person.

Flying Horseshoe Motel. 281–289 Sheridan St., Cairns, QLD 4870. ☎ **1800/814 171** in Australia, or 07/4051 3022. Fax 07/4031 2761. www.cairns.net.au/~rhino/flying_horseshoe/ horseshoe.html. E-mail: rhino@cairns.net.au. 51 units (shower only). A/C MINIBAR TV TEL. A$79–$89 (U.S.$55.30–$62.30) single; A$89–A$99 (U.S.$62.30–$69.30) double; A$99 (U.S.$69.30) single studio apt., A$109 (U.S.$76.30) double studio apt. Additional person A$10 (U.S.$7) extra; children under 15 A$5 (U.S.$3.50). AE, BC, DC, JCB, MC, V. Free parking. Bus: 1, 1A, 1C, 1D, 4, N. Call motel's toll-free number for free pickup at airport, train station, or bus terminal.

You will find clean rooms and a warm welcome from your hosts at this pleasant spot about 10 blocks from the city center. Unlike most motels, where you're stuck watching TV in your room at night, here you can breathe in the balmy evening air from your balcony, gather round the pool for a hearty buffet, or soak in the Jacuzzi in the garden courtyard. Every room is freshly decorated and spacious enough, with hair dryer in the bathroom; business rooms are slightly bigger. The apartments are by the highway, so expect some traffic noise. The helpful staff run a tour- and car-rental desk and can arrange dry cleaning, free newspaper delivery, in-room massages, baby-sitting, and secretarial services. The bus to the city stops just across the road.

Great Northern Hotel. 69 Abbott St., Cairns, QLD 4870. ☎ **1800/804 910** in Australia, or 07/4051 5151. Fax 07/4051 3090. www.gnh.iu.com.au. E-mail: gnh@iu.com.au. 33 units (30 with shower only). A/C MINIBAR TV TEL. A$69 (U.S.$48.30) single; A$79 (U.S.$55.30) double; A$99 (U.S.$69.30) triple or family room. Children under 5 free. Rates include continental breakfast. AE, BC, DC, MC, V. No parking. Airport shuttle.

This modest old hotel is smack bang in the middle of town, a block from the jetty and right opposite the casino. It's tucked in between shops on one of Cairns' busiest streets. All the major restaurants and shopping arcades are just a block or 2 away. Although the place is far from spiffy and new, the rooms are well maintained, quiet, and spacious, if viewless and a bit dark. Most received a lick of paint and new bedcovers and curtains in 1998. Hair dryers are available at reception. There are several extra-large rooms almost twice the size of a standard room, perfect for families. The friendly management runs a small tour desk, and there's a quiet cocktail bar on the second floor.

Hides Hotel. 87 Lake St., Cairns, QLD 4870. ☎ **1800/079 266** in Australia, or 07/4051 1266. Fax 07/4031 2276. 107 units, 70 with bathroom (68 with shower only). AC TV TEL. A$70 (U.S.$49) double without bathroom; A$90–$110 (U.S.$63–$77) double with bathroom. Additional person A$20 (U.S.$14) extra; children 4–17 A$10 (U.S.$7). Rates include continental breakfast. Ask about packages. AE, BC, DC, MC, V. Free parking. Airport shuttle.

Time has left this colonial three-story hotel overlooking a pedestrian plaza in the center of town a little the worse for wear, but the place does have redeeming features, such as the high ceilings bearing ornate plasterwork, the new carpets, and fresh paint in all the rooms. Choose from smallish rooms in the original 1885 building, or smarter, larger, lighter tile-floor rooms in the 1960s wing. The spanking-new white bathrooms in the new wing are a vivid contrast to the badly dated shower units in the old building. Hair dryers are available at the front desk. Most rooms have no views, but a few open onto a huge old verandah that overlooks the busy streets. This is a great

Travel Tip

Don't think you must stay in Cairns city just to be closer to the tour operators— almost all tour companies and Great Barrier Reef cruise operators will pick you up and drop you off whether you're staying in Cairns, on the northern beaches, or even as far afield as Port Douglas (see "Port Douglas, Daintree & the Cape Tribulation" section later in this chapter).

spot to eat your basic breakfast, but it gets *very* noisy on Friday and Saturday nights when the public bar below starts to roar. The hotel belongs to the Flag chain.

Lake Central—A Greentree Inn. 137–139 Lake St., Cairns, QLD 4870. ☎ **1800/226 466** in Australia, or 07/4051 4933. Fax 07/4051 9716. 57 units (all with shower only). A/C MINIBAR TV TEL. A$115 (U.S.$80.50) studio and double; A$135 (U.S.$94.50) family room. Additional person A$25 (U.S.$17.50) extra; children under 12 free in parents' room if they use existing bedding. AE, BC, DC, MC, V. Free parking. Airport shuttle.

Smartly refurbished in 1997 with terra-cotta floors and quality rattan furniture, these accommodations will save money on meals because all have a microwave and a toaster. All but the studio rooms have a large separate bedroom, and the family rooms have an additional area partitioned off for the kids. The pretty white bathrooms are roomy; hair dryers are available at the reception desk. To the side of the building is a rather small saltwater pool with only a couple of lounge chairs. Downstairs is a nice Italian wine bar and restaurant. The hotel is a member of the Rydges chain, popular with business travelers for its decent standards. You're two blocks from the Esplanade and another block or two to the Great Barrier Reef cruise jetties.

⭐ **Lilybank Bed & Breakfast.** 75 Kamerunga Rd., Stratford, Cairns, QLD 4870. ☎ **07/4055 1123.** Fax 07/4058 1990. www.lilybank.com.au. E-mail: bbnetwork@internetnorth.com.au. 6 units (4 with shower only). A/C. A$55 (U.S.$38.50) single; A$65–$85 (U.S.$45.50–$59.50) double. Additional person A$25 (U.S.$17.50) extra. Rates include full breakfast. AE, BC, MC, V. Free parking. Bus: 1E, 1F. Taxi from airport approx. A$11 (U.S.$7.70). Children not permitted.

This lovely 1890s Queenslander homestead, originally the mayor's residence, is located in a leafy suburb 6 kilometers (3¾ miles) from the airport and a 10-minute drive from the city. Guests sleep in large, attractive rooms, all individually decorated with such features as wrought-iron beds and patchwork quilts. Each bathroom is different, too, although all are comfortable and a good size (hair dryers are available). The largest room has French doors opening onto a "sleep-out," an enclosed verandah with two extra beds. You can also stay in the gardener's cottage, renovated with slate floors, stained-glass windows, a king-size bed, and a bar. The house is set in gardens with a picturesque rock-lined saltwater pool. The yummy breakfast is served in the relaxed conservatory by the fishpond. Your engaging hosts are Mike and Pat Woolford, and you share the house with four dogs, an irrepressible talking parrot, and a giant green tree frog. There's a guest TV lounge, a guest kitchen, and phone and e-mail access. Many tours pick up at the door, and several good restaurants are a stroll away, so you don't need a car to stay here. No smoking indoors.

Pyne Cottage Bed & Breakfast. 7 Pyne St., Edge Hill, Cairns, QLD 4870. ☎ **07/4053 7773.** Fax 07/4053 4477. www.bnbnq.com.au/pynecottage. E-mail: pynecottage@iig.com.au. 3 units (all with shower only). A/C. A$45–$60 (U.S.$31.50–$42) single; A$60–$75 (U.S.$42–$52.50) double. Additional person A$10 (U.S.$7) extra. Rates include continental breakfast. No credit cards. Free on-street parking. Bus: 1B, N.

Marilyn and Terry Foreman have done a great job of filling their pleasant suburban home with lovely antiques. Each warm and inviting guest room is individually decorated with such features as old timber wardrobes, throw rugs, calico curtains, or pretty pine-paneled period bathrooms. Marilyn lends hair dryers. By the time you arrive, you may be able to stay in the cottage that is being built in the garden. Eventually all rooms will have TV; for now guests use the one in the living room. Rooms don't have phones, but you can use the public telephones at the nearby post office. Your helpful hosts will take you to and from the airport when possible; most tours pick up at the door, and your hosts will drop you into town for any that don't. Restaurants and take-outs, the Flecker Botanic Gardens, and the bus to the city are all a short walk away. No smoking indoors.

Super-Cheap Sleeps

✪ Inn the Tropics. 141 Sheridan St., Cairns, QLD 4870. ☎ **1800/807 055** in Australia, or 07/4031 1088. Fax 07/4051 7110. www.cairns.net.au/~innthetropics. E-mail: innthetropics@ cairns.net.au. 51 units, 6 with bathroom (shower only). A$30 (U.S.$21) single without bathroom, A$40 (U.S.$28) single with bathroom; A$40 (U.S.$28) double without bathroom, A$50 (U.S.$35) double with bathroom. AE, BC, DC, JCB, MC, V. Limited free parking. Airport shuttle.

A cut above a backpacker hostel, this cheerful, well-run YWCA lodge four blocks from the city center has small, simple but appealing private rooms with a minifridge and sink, tea- and coffee-making facilities, well-lit clean private bathrooms with plenty of counter space, brick tile floors, and freshly painted concrete brick walls. Some even have TVs. Homey touches abound, from the framed Monet prints to the ornamental seahorses on the doors. The shared bathrooms are very clean. Air-conditioning is A$1 (U.S.70¢) for 3 hours. Out in the welcoming courtyard is a pretty shady pool and a barbecue where guests can cook up their own dinner. The management rents bikes, runs an extensive tour desk, and provides currency exchange. Ric's Around the Clock 24-Hour Café (see "Where to Dine" below) is just around the corner.

Uptop Downunder. 164 Spence St., Cairns, QLD 4870. ☎ **1800/243 944** in Australia, or 07/4051 3636. Fax 07/4052 1211. Email: uptop@castaway.com.au. 45 units, none with bathroom. A$28 (U.S.$19.60) single; A$32 (U.S.$22.40) double. A$15 (U.S.$10.50) dorm bed. YHA/Hostelling International members discount A$1 (U.S.70¢). AE, BC, MC, V. Free parking for 15 cars. Free transfer from airport, train, or coach terminal (book in advance, or call when you arrive). Lodge runs free shuttle to town throughout the day.

After a hard day's sightseeing, it's a pleasure to return to the lounge chairs scattered around the palm-lined pool at this cheerful backpacker lodge set amid an acre of tropical gardens. The dorm rooms are clean; the private rooms are very simple but airy and clean, with a double and a single bed, a minifridge, and pretty bedcovers. Some are air-conditioned (a must Nov to Mar), others have fans. Don't fuss about sharing the showers—the communal bath block and laundry are superclean. The staff is friendly; amenities include a big communal kitchen and dining area, a barbecue, free tea and coffee, a basic grocery store and snack bar, a TV lounge, bikes for rent, telephones, e-mail access, safes, and a tour desk.

Worth a Splurge

Inn Cairns. 71 Lake St., Cairns, QLD 4870. ☎ **07/4041 2350.** Fax 07/4041 2420. www. inncairns.com.au. E-mail: bookings@inncairns.com.au. 38 units. A/C TV TEL. A$144 (U.S.$100.80) double. Additional person A$10 (U.S.$7) extra. Children under 5 free. AE, BC, DC, MC, V. Free parking. Airport shuttle.

If you like stylish surroundings, you'll like these spacious new one-bedroom apartments in the town center. They feature terra cotta floors, wrought-iron and rattan furniture, and timber louvered blinds. The roomy bathrooms are equally smart, with thick white towels. Guests can enjoy the sun on the rooftop deck, which has palms and views to the sea, or around the small but elegant pool and barbecue gazebo. Each apartment has a VCR, security intercom, and laundry; hair dryers are available at reception. You can stock up on supplies at the Woolworth's supermarket across the road, or dine at the bistro downstairs. You're three blocks from where the Great Barrier Reef cruises depart.

Oasis Resort Cairns. 122 Lake St., Cairns, QLD 4870. ☎ **1800/64 2244** in Australia, 800/221-4542 in the U.S. and Canada, 0181/283 4500 in the U.K., 0800/44 4422 in New Zealand, or 07/4080 1888. Fax 07/4080 1889. www.oasis-cairns.com.au. E-mail: oasis@internetnorth.com.au. 314 units. A/C MINIBAR TV TEL. A$180–$195 (U.S.$126–$136.50) double; A$270 (U.S.$189) suite. Additional person A$30 (U.S.$21) extra. Up to 2 children under 16 free in parents' room if they use existing bedding; free cribs. Ask about special packages. AE, BC, DC, MC, V. Free parking. Airport shuttle.

So what if downtown Cairns doesn't have a beach? You've got a neat little sandy one right here—and a swim-up bar to boot—at the big swimming pool in the expansive courtyard at this attractive six-story resort in the heart of town. The rooms are not the biggest you've ever seen in an upscale hotel, but they are neat and colorful. All have balconies, views into tropical gardens or over the pool/sundeck/bar area, and good bathrooms with hair dryers. The roomy suites have a TV in the bedroom and a large Jacuzzi bath; they are arguably the best-value suites in town. The hotel's buffet is a steep A$25.50 (U.S.$17.85); however, the kids' menu is only A$6 (U.S.$4.20). Other amenities include a gym, a separate kiddy pool, a concierge and tour desk, room service, and a free newspaper delivered to your door.

Tuna Towers. 145 The Esplanade at Minnie St., Cairns, QLD 4870. ☎ **07/4051 4688.** Fax 07/4051 8129. www.ozemail.com.au/~tunatowr. E-mail: tunatowr@ozemail.com.au. 60 units. A/C MINIBAR TV TEL. A$120 (U.S.$84) single; A$125 (U.S.$87.50) double; A$130 (U.S.$91) studio apt. single; A$135 (U.S.$94.50) studio apt. double; A$150 (U.S.$105) suite. Additional person A$10 (U.S.$7) extra. AE, BC, DC, JCB, MC, V. Free parking. Airport shuttle.

You get wonderful views of Trinity Bay or nice views of the city and mountains from the balcony of every room at this Flag-member multistory motel and apartment complex. From the outside the building is attractive and modern; on the inside, the accommodations are light, spacious, and airy with up-to-date decor. Every bathroom is modern and is equipped with a hair dryer. There's a small pool and Jacuzzi out front, and a pleasant restaurant and cocktail bar. It's just a couple of blocks to the center of town.

ON THE NORTHERN BEACHES

Cairns has a string of white sandy beaches, starting 15 minutes north of the city center. All are low-key, relaxed, and, as yet, blissfully noncommercial. Most have just two or three casual restaurants and a handful of shops, maybe a tour desk and a rental-car outlet. **Holloways Beach** is the closest to the city, 10 minutes from the airport, and has a relaxed atmosphere. **Trinity Beach,** 15 minutes from the airport, is secluded, quiet, and scenic. The prettiest and most upscale of all the northern beaches is **Palm Cove,** 20 minutes from the airport; its handful of cute, rainbow-hued shops and tasteful apartment blocks overlook a postcard-perfect beach. Palm Cove also has the greatest number of restaurants and cafes, about a dozen or so. Add 5 minutes to the traveling times above to reach the city. Regular local bus service runs to and from the city.

✪ **Absolute Beachfront B&B.** 6–10 Peacock Lane, Trinity Beach, Cairns, QLD 4879. ☎ **07/4055 6664.** Fax 07/4057 8996. www.absolutebeach.com.au. E-mail: kay@absolutebeach.com.au. 3 units (2 with shower only, 1 with Jacuzzi). A/C TV. A$65 (U.S.$45.50) single; A$80–$100 (U.S.$56–$70) double. Additional person A$20 (U.S.$14) extra. Rates include continental breakfast. BC, MC, V. Free parking. Bus: 1, 1A, 3X, N. Airport shuttle. Free airport transfers for guests staying 3 nights or more. Children not permitted.

"Absolute Luxury" would be another good name for this new, architecturally stunning home built right on the beach. Set tightly between a rain forest–covered hill and the beach, the house is built around a soaring timber atrium, completely open at the front to catch the breeze. The only obstacle between you and the sand is the pool set in palm-studded lawns. The sleek contemporary rooms, each a little different, have such

Safe Swimming

All the northern beaches have small, netted enclosures for safe swimming from October to May, when deadly **box jellyfish** (stingers) render all mainland north Queensland beaches off limits.

features as Balinese four-poster beds, polished limestone or timber floors, and Oriental rugs. The bathrooms have hair dryers and are equally hip; all have stone floors and plush towels. All rooms have views to the sea and tropical gardens. Owners Kay and John Lane leave you to your own devices as much as you want, so this is a good retreat for those who like privacy. No smoking indoors.

Beaches at Holloways. 2 Marietta St., Holloways Beach, Cairns, QLD 4870. ☎ **07/ 4055 9972.** Fax 07/4055 9886. www.beaches-at-holloways.com.au. E-mail: ozidave@ cairns.net.au. 3 units (2 with shower only). A/C. A$50–$75 (U.S.$35–$52.50) single; A$70– $80 (U.S.$49–$56) double. Additional person A$20 (U.S.$14) extra. Rates include full breakfast. BC, MC, V. Free on-street parking. Bus: 1C, 1H, N. Airport shuttle.

Relaxed and gregarious owners David and Josephine Hopkins have given over the upstairs of their expansive, light-filled home opposite Holloways Beach to guests. Guest rooms are fresh and comfortable; bathrooms are pretty, practical, and come with hair dryers and bathrobes. The two front rooms open onto a lovely bougainvillea-clad verandah overlooking the sea. There's a pool in the garden, and a guest TV and VCR lounge. Several inexpensive restaurants, including a good alfresco Italian BYO, are just down the road. No smoking indoors.

Coconut Lodge Resort. 95–97 Williams Esplanade, Palm Cove, QLD 4879. ☎ **1800/ 623 171,** or 07/4055 3734. Fax 07/4059 1022. 26 units (8 with Jacuzzis, some with shower only). A/C TV TEL. A$89–$99 (U.S.$62.30–$69.30) double; A$175 (U.S. $122.50) suite. Additional person A$15 (U.S.$10.50) extra; children under 11 A$10 (U.S.$7). Weekly rates available. AE, BC, MC. V. Limited free parking; ample free on-street parking. Bus: 1, 1A, 2X, N. Airport shuttle.

This modest motel in the heart of Palm Cove was rebuilt from the ground up in 1998 and now features elegant white columns outside, cool tile floors inside, and big new rooms. Suites have ocean views, some rooms come with Jacuzzis, and hair dryers are provided. Out back a handful of old rooms remain, with severely dated furniture and scant natural light—pay the extra A$10 (U.S.$7) for a room in the new wing. There's a tour and car-rental desk on the premises, but for now the rooftop swimming pool is a mere blueprint, so you will have to cool off at the beautiful beach just across the road. This place is a great value.

✪ **The Reef Retreat.** 10–14 Harpa St., Palm Cove, Cairns, QLD 4879. ☎ **07/4059 1744.** Fax 07/4059 1745. www.reefretreat.com.au. E-mail: reefr@ozemail.com.au. 30 units (18 with shower only, 6 with shower and Jacuzzi). A/C TV TEL. A$110–$130 (U.S.$77–$91) studio double; A$130 (U.S.$91) suite; A$225 (U.S.$157.50) 2-bedroom apt. Ocean view or Jacuzzi supplement A$10 (U.S.$7) in suites. Additional person A$20 (U.S.$14) extra. Children under 3 free in parents' room if they use existing bedding; crib A$10 (U.S.$7). AE, BC, DC, MC, V. Free parking. Bus: 1, 1A, 2X, N. Airport shuttle.

Tucked back one row of buildings from the beach is this little gem—a low-rise collection of contemporary studios and suites built around a swimming pool in an almost mystically peaceful grove of palms and silver paperbarks. All the rooms in the newer or extensively renovated wings have cool tile floors and smart teak and cane furniture. The studios are a terrific value and much larger than the average hotel room. In some of the studios, you can even lie in bed and see the sea. The extra-private honeymoon suites have a Jacuzzi and a kitchenette outside on the balcony, where you can hide behind timber blinds. Every room has a kitchenette; the apartment and one suite have a full kitchen. There's a free barbecue on the grounds, and a Jacuzzi. If you can live without having your room cleaned daily, you can deduct the A$15 (U.S.$10.50) per day cleaning charge from your room rate and pick up free fresh towels from the front desk each day. There is an iron and ironing board in the laundry, and hair dryers are free from reception. There's no elevator.

Tropical Holiday Units. 63–73 Moore St. (at Trinity Beach Rd.), Trinity Beach, Cairns, QLD 4879. ☎ **1800/079 022** in Australia, or 07/4057 6699. Fax 07/4057 6565. www. ozemail.com.au/~trophol/. E-mail: trophol@ozemail.com.au. 52 units (all with shower only). A/C TV TEL. A$75–$105 (U.S.$52.50–$73.50) 1-bedroom apt., A$94–$125 (U.S.$65.80–$87.50) 2-bedroom apt. Additional person A$16 (U.S.$11.20) extra. Children under 4 stay free. Weekly rates available. AE, BC, DC, MC, V. Free parking. Bus: 1, 1A, 3X, N. Airport shuttle. Free airport transfers for guests staying 5 nights or more.

You're a block from Trinity Beach at these roomy, clean, well-equipped apartments. The furnishings are rather dated, but each has everything a family or couple could want for a penny-wise vacation—a basic kitchen, a comfy living and dining area, large bedrooms, an internal laundry, a balcony, and the luxury of space. Servicing is weekly. There are three saltwater pools and Jacuzzis and a barbecue. The friendly managers book your rental cars and tours. A small general store, a pub, and a couple of inexpensive eateries are just down the road.

IN KURANDA

A 30-minute winding mountain drive, a 90-minute train trip, or a 40-minute Skyrail gondola ride over the treetops brings you to this pretty village in the hills behind Cairns. A local bus travels from two to five times a day from Cairns city for A$7 (U.S.$4.90) one-way. Kuranda is cool, rain-foresty, and blissfully peaceful, despite the daily influx of tourists from the city. There is a handful of good restaurants and quite a lot to see and do. One drawback is that not many tours pick up here. Guests at Kuranda Rainforest Resort can take a free shuttle into Cairns to meet most tours.

Kuranda Rainforest Resort. Kennedy Hwy. at Greenhills Rd., Kuranda, QLD 4872. ☎ **1800/806 996** in Australia, or 07/4093 7555. Fax 07/4093 7567. www.ozemail. com.au/ ~kuresort. E-mail: kuresort@ozemail.com.au. 70 units (all with shower only). TV TEL. A$125 (U.S.$87.50) double; A$175 (U.S.$122.50) split-level pole cabin. Rates include continental breakfast. AE, BC, DC, MC, V. Airport transfers A$5 (U.S.$3.50) per person.

A 2-minute drive from the center of Kuranda village, this retreat consists of rustic slab-wood cabins nestled into 3.5 hectares (9 acres) of dense rain forest. Whether you opt for a diminutive standard cabin, or the larger split-level pole variety with minibar, cooking facilities, a bed downstairs, and three or four single beds or bunks on the mezzanine level (reached by a ladder), you will feel snug as a bug in a rug in the cozy interiors. The bathrooms are small but neatly tiled; the pole cabins have hair dryers, and an iron and ironing board are located in the communal laundry. Every visitor comments on the delightful rain-forest-wrapped swimming pool, Jacuzzi, and child's wading pool that look as though they were crafted from the natural rock (check out the honeymoon cave behind the pool's waterfall), and the open-air poolside restaurant where bandicoots and birds are regular visitors. The staff at the Envirocare Information Centre and Wet Tropics display in the lobby can tell you all you need to know about rain forest animals, plants, and nearby nature walks. Reception runs a tour desk and rents mountain bikes; there's also a tennis court, a gym, and a library. You can even hand-feed wallabies in the on-site sanctuary. A free shuttle runs into the center of Kuranda twice a day and into Cairns three times a day.

✪ **TENTative Nests.** 26 Barron Falls Rd., Kuranda, QLD 4872. ☎ **07/4093 9555.** Fax 07/ 4093 9053. www.cairns.aust.com/tentnests/. E-mail: tentnest@internetnorth.com.au. 6 permanent tents, none with bathroom. A$55 (U.S.$38.50) single; A$110 (U.S.$77) double without meals; A$60 (U.S.$42) single, A$120 (U.S.$84) double with continental breakfast; A$88 (U.S.$61.60) single, A$176 (U.S.$123.20) double with breakfast and dinner. Children 4–11 half price. AE, BC, DC, MC, V. City or airport transfers A$5 (U.S.$3.50) per person.

The owners describe this as an "eco-educational overnight rain forest experience" where you can have a "Treeincarnation" in Mother Nature's rain forest. That's just another way of saying you get to sleep out in fun tent "nests" in the rain forest! This is not exactly camping the hard way—your "nest" is a timber-floored tent, and there's a gourmet bush tucker dinner waiting for you at night (cooked by the Red Ochre Grill, no less—see "Where to Dine" below). The kooky Queenslander reception cottage and amazing guest lounge are hung with wacky artworks. To reach your nest you tiptoe past creepy-crawlies up a rain-forest path; you're given a strong torch (flashlight), and there are some fairy lights to show the way at night. Every tent has a mattress on the floor, tables and chairs, towels, insect screens, a lantern—and best of all, a hammock on the balcony. Everyone eats breakfast and dinner together in a wonderful open-sided pole house in the trees. The emphasis is on things ecofriendly, from the biodegradabale soaps and shampoos to the composting toilets, which are located—along with hot showers and a laundry—under the lounge (they also have a hair dryer). During the day and at night on guided spotlight walks, you will see lots of wildlife—and there's no chance you will miss Roosky, the pet kangaroo. Owners Teena and Joell are happy to advise on tours and direct you to nearby walking tracks; Barron Falls Gorge and Kuranda are within walking distance.

ON AN ISLAND

Of several island resorts off Cairns, the modest Fitzroy Island Resort is the only one even remotely affordable. Pros: Idyllic surrounds and an array of water sports are right outside your door. Deadly stingers don't make it to the islands, so you're safe in the water year-round. Cons: Your dining options are limited to what the island offers—in Fitzroy's case, burger-style take-outs or an à la carte restaurant. You fork out for transfers (Fitzroy's are A$30/U.S.$21 round trip) every time you want to go to the mainland to shop, join a tour, or visit the Great Barrier Reef.

Fitzroy Island Resort. 24km (15 miles) southeast of Cairns (P.O. Box 898, Cairns, QLD 4870). ☎ **1800/079 080** in Australia (the number for Great Adventures, which takes reservations for the resort), or 07/4051 9588. Fax 07/4052 1335. www.fitzroyislandresort.com.au. E-mail: res@fitzroyislandresort.com.au. 8 cabins (all with shower only); 128 quad-share bunkhouses, none with bathroom. Cabins A$340 (U.S.$238) double, including all meals and nonmotorized beach equipment. Additional child 4–14 A$79 (U.S.$55.30) extra. Bunkhouses A$28 (U.S.$19.60) per person per bed (sharing with up to 3 strangers) or A$16 (U.S.$11.20) for YHA/Hostelling International members; A$95 (U.S.$66.50) double/triple sole use, plus A$5 (U.S.$3.50) per person towel charge for duration of stay; beach equipment costs extra for bunkhouse guests. AE, BC, DC, MC, V. Round-trip launch transfers A$30 (U.S.$21) adults, A$15 (U.S.$10.50) children 4–14. Coach transfers to Trinity Wharf in Cairns from Cairns/northern beaches hotels A$6 (U.S.$4.20), from Port Douglas hotels A$12 (U.S.$8.40); half price children 4–14.

This unpretentious getaway, a 45-minute boat ride from Trinity Wharf, is one of the few affordable island resorts off the Queensland coast, and then only if you stay in the bunkhouses. It's no glamour-puss resort, but rather a leftover from the first wave of resorts built years ago when tourism was just taking off in north Queensland. The public areas look very old, and the facilities are not extensive; what you do get is a low-key friendly atmosphere and lots of natural beauty. It has catamarans, canoes and surf skis (all free for cabin, but not bunkhouse, guests), hiking trails through dense National Park forest, and, for a fee, dive lessons from introductory to instructor level. Divers can make drift dives over the reefs dotted around the island to see manta rays, reef sharks, turtles, and plenty of coral. There is good snorkeling at two points around the island that you can reach twice a day on the dive boat. This will set you back A$15 (U.S.$10.50) for the trip, plus A$10 (U.S.$7) for snorkeling gear. The beach in front of the resort is bare and uninteresting, but a 20-minute walk through the bush gets you to a nice white sandy point. By the time you arrive, the cabins should be air-conditioned; if you stay in the bunkhouses, the heat will be tough to bear between

November and March. The comfortable beach cabins have timber floors, a bed in front and two bunks out back, fans, TV, in-room irons and hair dryers, and a large balcony with views through the trees to the sea. The regular bunkhouse accommodations are basic carpeted rooms with four bunks; family bunkhouses have a double bed plus four bunks in an adjacent room. All meals are included in the tariff for cabin guests; bunkhouse guests can self-cater in the communal kitchen or pay for meals in the restaurant. Apart from a good tour desk, the only other facility is a shop selling clothes and sundries. To catch a cruise to the Great Barrier Reef from here, you must return to Cairns.

WHERE TO DINE
IN CAIRNS

Being a tourist town, Cairns is overloaded with mediocre restaurants with a high turnover. The places below offer good food at good prices. Many are popular local hangouts.

Gypsy Dee's. 41A Shields St., Cairns. ☎ **07/4051 5530.** Reservations recommended. Main courses A$12.50–$18.50 (U.S.$8.75–$12.95). 10% discount before 7pm. Daily 5:30pm–2am. Happy hour Mon–Fri 5:30–6:30pm, Wed–Sun 9:30–10:30pm. AE, BC, DC, MC, V. MULTI-ETHNIC.

Part restaurant, part bar, part disco—no one seems to know just what Gypsy Dee's is, but everyone loves coming here. You can sit outside or in the dark cavernous interior where foil stars hang from the ceiling and candles glow on the tables. The menu has six appealing choices for vegetarians, some pastas, and a range of main courses, such as kangaroo fillet on warm Asian greens with coriander-peanut pesto. After 9 or 10 every night, a live band strikes up anything from soft melodies to top 40, depending on the mood of the crowd. The tables get pushed back if everyone feels like dancing, which they do most of the time. There's a bar and a late-night supper menu. Licensed and BYO wine only (no BYO beer or spirits).

✪ **Mediterraneo.** 74 Shields St. ☎ **07/4051 4335.** Reservations recommended on weekends. Main courses A$16.80–$21.80 (U.S.$11.75–$15.25); pasta A$10.80–$13.80 (U.S.$7.55–$9.65). AE, BC, DC, MC, V. Mon–Sat 6pm–late. ITALIAN.

Every time I come to Cairns I head straight to this place, where the friendly, professional service and talented chefs keep locals-in-the-know coming back for more. Many of the menu's classic dishes come with a modern twist, such as the fettucine portofino with prawns, shallots, cream, and an untraditional hint of curry. And don't overlook the traditional favorites, such as like a mixed seafood casserole; beef with white wine and mushrooms; and veal topped with Parma ham, provolone, and tomato sauce. Such dishes might raise a yawn from trendy diners, but here they are cooked with aplomb. The gnocchi with four cheeses is the best I've ever had—plump, moist, and packed with flavor. The decor is trendy but not showy, just a polished concrete floor, framed sketches on the wall, and timber tables. There's also a courtyard out back. BYO.

Red Ochre Grill. 43 Shields St. ☎ **07/4051 0100.** Reservations recommended. Main courses A$8–$17 (U.S.$5.60–$11.90) at lunch, A$17–$24 (U.S.$11.90–$16.80) at dinner. Australian game platter A$32 (U.S.$22.40) per person, seafood platter A$40 (U.S.$28) per person. AE, BC, DC, JCB, MC, V. Mon–Fri 12 noon–3pm, daily 6pm–late. GOURMET BUSH TUCKER.

You could accuse this restaurant/bar of using weird and wonderful Aussie ingredients as a gimmick to pull in crowds, but the folks who flock here are anything but gullible—they know good food when they taste it. Daily specials are big on fresh local seafood, such as tempura bugs (a delectable crustacean) on lemongrass skewers. On the regular menu is emu pate with bush tomato chili jam and fresh damper, and wallaby topside done over a mallee-fired grill (*mallee* is a timber) with sweet potato mash. You can even eat the Aussie coat of arms by ordering a game platter of kangaroo and emu served with native warrigal spinach and yam gratin. Although the place is slick enough for a night out, it is also informal enough for a casual meal. Check out the rundown of bush tucker ingredients on the menu—that way you will know when you're eating a fat slimy witchetty grub! Just kidding.

R.S.L. (Returned Services League) Club. 115 The Esplanade at Florence St. ☎ **07/ 4051 5804**. Reservations recommended. Main courses A$12–$15 (U.S.$8.40–$10.50). BC, MC, V. Mon–Thurs 6–8:30pm, Fri 6–9pm, Sat 6–8:30pm, Sun 6–8pm. MOSTLY AUSSIE.

R.S.L. war veterans' clubs are renowned across Australia for good, no-nonsense food served at prices to match. Here they do old faves like veal schnitzel, chicken Kiev, and garlic King prawns, as well as pastas. Meals are served in a modest but pleasant dining room and a palm-filled garden bistro that catches the sea breeze. Just ignore the Keno results blaring away silently from the closed-circuit monitor in the corner—R.S.L. clubs are also renowned for gambling. This is a club, so you will need to sign in before you enter. Entry gives you access to the club's slot machines, too.

Thai Pan. 43–45 Grafton St. ☎ **07/4052 1708**. Reservations recommended. Main courses A$9.50–$18.90 (U.S.$6.65–$13.25). AE, BC, DC, MC, V. Daily 6pm–late. LAO/THAI.

Delicately fragrant curries and carefully prepared stir-fries and soups are served up in this humble brick restaurant. Thai food is always a sure bet in Australia, and this place is no exception. Try the *pad gratium* (tender beef fried in a complex garlic sauce with crisp vegetables); one of the many seafood dishes, such as the mixed seafood cooked in basil and a hint of chili; or one of the plentiful vegetarian choices. As with many Asian restaurants, the wine list is unremarkable, so bring your own. Licensed and BYO (BYO corkage A$1.50/U.S.$1.05 per person).

✪ **Tim's Surf & Turf.** Trinity Wharf (end of Abbott St.). ☎ **07/4031 6866**. Reservations accepted only for groups of 8 more. Main courses A$5.90–$13.90 (U.S.$4.15–$9.75); many dishes under A$10 (U.S.$7). No credit cards. Daily noon–2:30pm, 5:30–9:30pm. STEAK/SEAFOOD.

For huge hearty meals at unbeatable prices, you can't go wrong at this cheerful chain outlet overlooking Trinity Inlet. Most restaurateurs given a waterfront location in a big tourist town would open a rip-off joint charging outrageous prices, but not Tim, bless 'im! The seafood platters, oysters, thick grain-fed steaks, pastas, roasts, quiche, and other simple fare are all cooked with skill.

More Cheap Eats

The **Esplanade** along the seafront is always good for a cost-conscious feed, as it's packed with cheap cafes, pizzerias, fish-and-chips places, and ice-cream parlors. The **Pier Marketplace** on the waterfront beside Marlin Marina has a cheap food court with water views, but you will find better quality at the food court in the **Cairns Central Mall** (☎ 07/4041 4111) over the railway station on McLeod Street. All but a few food outlets in the mall close at night, however. The **Reef Hotel Casino,** 35 Wharf St. (☎ 07/4030 8897) does a nightly Asian buffet for A$15 (U.S.$10.50) per person in the Hot Wok Kitchen on the ground floor; it's open from 6pm. Fans of the **Johnny Rockets** chain will find a franchise in the Pier Marketplace, serving its trademark burgers (around A$6/U.S.$4.20); it's open from 8am to 10pm daily.

Super-Cheap Eats

Coast Roast Coffee Company. 21 Lake St. ☎ **07/4041 1028.** Main courses A$4–$6.95 (U.S.$2.80–$4.85). AE, BC, MC, V. Tues–Sat 7:30am–10:30pm, Sun 7:30am–6pm, Mon 7:30am–7pm. SANDWICHES/CAFE FARE.

This elegant timber-and-brass coffee bar serves muffins and Danish pastries; salad rolls; and inexpensive gourmet foccacia, bagel, and panini sandwiches. It's also a good pit stop for a hot breakfast of poached eggs on toast before boarding your Great Barrier Reef cruise.

Ric's Around the Clock 24-Hour Café. Tropical Arcade, Abbott St. at Shields St. ☎ **07/ 4051 5150;** and 40 Aplin St. at Sheridan St. ☎ **07/4041 4848.** Main courses A$1–$12.50 (U.S.70¢–$8.75); most meals less than A$10 (U.S.$7). AE, BC, DC, JCB, MC, V. Open 24 hours. BURGERS/CAFE FARE.

Famous for his "cook your own breakfast" barbecue packs, Ric's humble laid-back outlets are popular with backpackers, teenagers, and locals looking for a cheap, filling feed. Menu items include a range of steak, chicken, and fish burgers; meat dishes like beef casserole or roast chicken; seafood; pizzas; and sandwiches. Breakfast items are available all day. A bottomless tea or coffee is A$1.50 (U.S.$1.05) with a meal, A$2 (U.S.$1.40) on its own. They do kids' menus, too. They deliver to city hotels.

The Old Ambulance Café Bistro. 135 Grafton St., Cairns. ☎ **07/4051 0511.** Main courses A$4.80–$10.50 (U.S.$3.35–$7.35). Mon–Sat 7am–late, Sun 10am–5pm. No credit cards. LIGHT FARE.

Drop in for a coffee, a slice of cake, a toasted foccacia sandwich, a baked potato with special toppings, or a light but filling meal of eggplant parmigiana, prawn and chicken risotto, or chicken breast with Heike's famous curry vinaigrette. The small menu is supplemented by blackboard specials each day, and the food is nicely prepared. This trendy little place used to be an ambulance station, but the wailing sirens have been replaced by young corporate types and moms with prams. BYO.

Worth a Splurge

✪ **Fishlips Bar & Bistro.** 228 Sheridan St. (between Charles and McKenzie sts.) ☎ **07/ 4041 1700.** Reservations recommended. Main courses A$9.50–$24 (U.S.$6.65–$16.80); most dishes A$18.50 (U.S.$12.95); crayfish market price. AE, BC, DC, JCB, MC, V. Fri noon–2:30pm; daily 5:30pm–late. MOD OZ SEAFOOD.

Ask locals where they go for seafood—as opposed to where they send tourists—and they direct you to this cute bluebird-blue shack about 2 kilometers (1¼ miles) from town on a nondescript section of Sheridan Street. The building is so 1920s, you feel as though you should be sitting at the table in a red-and-white-striped neck-to-knee bathing suit. Chef Ian Candy is renowned for thinking up new ways to present seafood and cooking it with flair. Appetizers might be a salad of reef fish, squid, mussels, and prawns wok-tossed on greens with cracked *bugs* (a kind of lobster, not an insect). The extremely popular local barramundi, or "barra," usually shows up in two incarnations, maybe simply beer-battered with rough-cut chips (fries) and fresh tartar sauce, or dressed up tandoori-style with cucumber, yogurt, and tomato risotto. There are plenty of nonseafood options as well, such as wok-tossed crocodile with pumpkin-seed salsa. There's a vegetarian choice on every menu, too. How nice to see that 30-odd wines on the wine list come by the glass. Dine in the pretty blue-and-yellow interior, complete with portholes, or on the deck out front decorated with bright blue pots and palm trees. Licensed and BYO wine only (no BYO beer or spirits).

ON THE NORTHERN BEACHES

Colonies. Upstairs in Paradise Village shopping center, Williams Esplanade, Palm Cove. ☎ **07/4055 3058.** Reservations recommended at dinner. Average breakfast A$8.50

(U.S.$5.95), main courses A$6–$12.50 (U.S.$4.20–$8.75) at lunch, A$12.50–$24.50 (U.S.$8.75–$17.15) at dinner. Daily 7:30am–10:30pm. AE, BC, DC, MC, V. Bus: 1, 1A, 2X, N. MOD OZ.

It may not have the ocean frontage of the grander restaurants along Williams Esplanade, but you are still within earshot of the waves from the verandah of this cheery little aerie upstairs behind a seafront building. The atmosphere is simple enough for a morning coffee, and special enough at night for a full-fledged dinner banquet of mussels sautéed in white wine, followed by peppered lamb fillet in red wine and herbs with a port mint glaze. The long menu includes loads of inexpensive choices at both lunch and dinner, such as pastas, vegetable soups, green chicken curry, and hot savory *scones* (biscuits) with bacon and melted cheese. The extra-yummy desserts include banana splits and "spacacamino," vanilla ice cream dressed with Scotch whisky and freshly ground coffee beans. Licensed and BYO (corkage A$1.50/U.S.$1.05).

Pizza Trinity. On the Esplanade, Trinity Beach. ☎ **07/4055 6958** or 07/4057 6677. Main courses A$7–$17 (U.S.$4.90–$11.90). No credit cards. Daily 6–10pm. Closed Mon in low season. PIZZA.

Recently, Brisbane's *Courier-Mail* voted this the best pizza joint in Queensland. It's just a few humble tables huddled under an awning on the sidewalk across the road from the beach, but you'll forget the meager surrounds when you tuck into the pizza. Try the Normandy (chicken, marinated artichokes, and onion topped with Camembert) or the Queenslander (mango base, mozzarella, bell pepper, pineapple, nuts, and King prawns). There are also more traditional toppings, as well as lasagna and spaghetti. They deliver and do take-out. BYO.

Worth a Splurge

Far Horizons. At the Allamanda resort, 1 Veivers Rd. (southern end of Williams Esplanade), Palm Cove. ☎ **07/4055 3000.** Reservations recommended. Main courses A$20.50–$26 (U.S.$14.35–$18.20). AE, BC, DC, JCB, MC, V. Daily 6:30–10:30am, noon–2:30pm, and 6:30–9:30pm. Bus: 1, 1A, 2X, N. MOD OZ.

You can't quite twiddle your toes in the sand, but you are just yards from the beach at this pleasant restaurant within the Allamanda resort. The laid-back fine-dining fare includes plenty of fresh seafood. My generous main-course serving of orecchiette pasta shells with pumpkin, avocado, olives, garlic, and parmesan was firm and tasty. I could also have ordered King Island beef in a choice of sauces, or one of the favorites, bug-tails panfried with steamed bok choy and sweet soya beurre blanc. Lime and coconut pudding is a typical dessert; the frozen mocha mousse is also popular. The restaurant sometimes sets up dining on the lawn among the palm trees beside the beach. The service is relaxed and friendly and the crowd is a mix of hotel guests from this and other nearby resorts. On Friday and Saturday nights a saxophonist plays in the cocktail bar.

3 Port Douglas, Daintree & the Cape Tribulation Area

Port Douglas 67km (40 miles) N of Cairns; Mossman 19km (11½ miles) N of Port Douglas; Daintree 49km (29½ miles) N of Port Douglas; Cape Tribulation 34km (20½ miles) N of Daintree

The tiny fishing village of ✪ **Port Douglas** has the distinction of being the only place in the world where two World Heritage areas—the Daintree Rain Forest and the Great Barrier Reef—lie side by side. Just over an hour's drive from Cairns, through rain forest and along the sea, Port Douglas may be a one-horse town, but it's got a cute main street with stylish shops and seriously trendy restaurants, and a beautiful 4-mile long beach called, well, ✪ **Four Mile Beach.**

Folks often base themselves in "Port," as the locals call it, rather than in Cairns, because they like the peaceful rural surroundings, the uncrowded beach, and the charmed absence of tacky development (so far, anyway). Don't think you will be isolated if you stay here—many reef and rain-forest tours originate in Port Douglas and many of the tours discussed in the Cairns section earlier in this chapter pick up from Port Douglas.

Daintree National Park lies just north of Port Douglas; and just north of that is Cape Tribulation National Park, another wild tract of rain forest and hilly headlands sweeping down to the sea. Exploring these two national parks is easy on a 4WD day safari from Port Douglas.

ESSENTIALS

GETTING THERE   Port Douglas is a scenic 65-minute drive from Cairns, in part along a narrow winding road that skirts the coast. Take Sheridan Street out of the city as it becomes the Captain Cook Highway; stay on the highway and follow the signs to Mossman and Mareeba until you reach the Port Douglas turnoff on your right.

The cheapest way to get to Port Douglas is also the most glamorous, by taking one of the giant **Quicksilver *Wavepiercer*** (☎ 07/4099 5500) catamarans along the green hilly coastline. They depart Marlin Marina in Cairns at 8am, Palm Cove jetty at 8:30am, and arrive in Port Douglas at 9:30am. You can stay onboard and go straight to the Great Barrier Reef for the day if you like. Transfers from Cairns are A$20 (U.S.$14) one-way, A$30 (U.S.$21) round-trip, half price for kids ages 4 to 14.

A round-trip ticket aboard **Coral Coaches** (☎ 07/4099 5351) to Port Douglas hotels is A$30 (U.S.$21) from Cairns city hotels, or A$44 (U.S.$30.80) from the Cairns airport. Fares for children 14 and under are half price. The coaches meet all major flights between 6am and 8:30pm. It's not strictly necessary, but it's a good idea to book; five buses per day are reservations only.

VISITOR INFORMATION   Write for information to the **Port Douglas Daintree Tourism Association,** Reef Anchor House, Office 5, 40 Macrossan St., Port Douglas, QLD 4871 (☎ 07/4099 4588; fax 07/4099 4994; www.ozemail.com.au/~dsta/). The association has no visitor information office in Port Douglas. Instead, visitors should visit one of several private tour information and booking centers in town. One of the biggest and most centrally located is the **Port Douglas Tourist Information Centre,** 23 Macrossan St. (☎ 07/4099 5599), open from 7:30am to 6pm or later daily.

GETTING AROUND   Of the big-four rental car companies, only **Budget** (☎ 07/4099 4690) and **Avis** (☎ 07/4099 4331) have offices in Port Douglas. Check out the good deals from the local companies, including **Port Douglas Car Rental** (☎ 07/4098 5898) and **Crocodile Car Rentals** (☎ 07/4099 5555). All rent 4WDs as well as regular vehicles.

Local bus company **Coral Coaches** (☎ 07/4099 5351) makes a circuit of town that stops at most of the places you probably want to visit, such as the Rainforest Habitat, Four Mile Beach, and Marina Mirage. Fares range from A$1.30 to $3.20 (U.S91¢ to $2.25). The bus starts at 7:30am and runs hourly until 10am, then half hourly until 9:30pm, then hourly again until midnight.

Safety Tips

The **tap water** is *not* safe for drinking in Port Douglas. Most hotels provide free bottled water. Deadly marine stingers (jellyfish) infest the water from October to May; swim only in areas partitioned off by stinger nets during those months.

Port Douglas, Daintree & Cape Tribulation

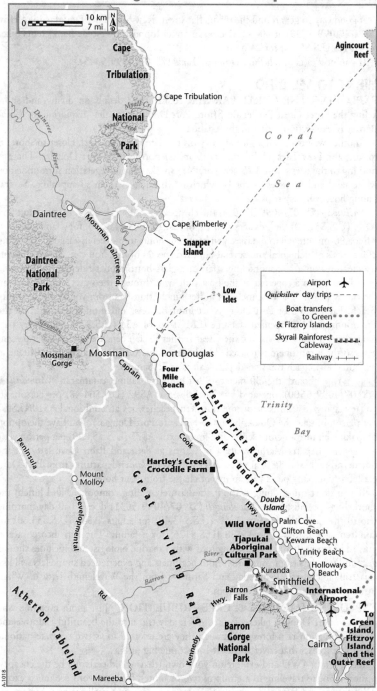

0   10 km
     7 mi

Cape
Tribulation
National
Park

Cape Tribulation

Myall Cr.

Noah Creek

Daintree

Daintree
National
Park

Mossman
Gorge

Mossman

Cape Kimberley

Snapper
Island

Low
Isles

Port Douglas

Four
Mile
Beach

Mossman

Peninsula

Mount
Molloy

Great Dividing Range

Developmental

Rd.

Kennedy

Atherton Tableland

Mareeba

Hartley's Creek
Crocodile Farm

Cook

Hwy.

Double
Island

Wild World

Tjapukai
Aboriginal
Cultural Park

Barron River

Kuranda

Barron
Falls

Barron
Gorge
National
Park

Hwy.

Palm Cove

Clifton Beach

Kewarra Beach

Trinity Beach

Holloways
Beach

Smithfield

International
Airport

Cairns

To
Green
Island,
Fitzroy
Island,
and the
Outer Reef

Agincourt
Reef

Coral

Sea

Great Barrier Reef

Marine Park Boundary

Trinity

Bay

Legend

Airport ✈

Quicksilver day trips -----

Boat transfers
to Green ••••••
& Fitzroy Islands

Skyrail Rainforest ■-■-■-■
Cableway

Railway +++++

A-1018

A good way to get around the town's flat streets is by bike. **Port Douglas Bike Hire** (☎ **07/4099 5799**) at 40–42 Macrossan Street (opposite Westpac Bank) rents bikes for A$12 (U.S.$8.40) for 24 hours.

If you need a taxi, call **Port Douglas Taxis** (☎ **07/4099 5345**).

WHAT TO SEE & DO

EXPLORING THE GREAT BARRIER REEF   For details on diving and snorkeling the outer Great Barrier Reef from Port Douglas, see the "Exploring the Great Barrier Reef" section earlier in this chapter.

Another way to spend a pleasant day on the Great Barrier Reef, closer to shore, is to visit the **Low Isles** 15 kilometers (9 miles) northeast of Port Douglas. There is nothing to the isles—just 3.75-acre coral-cay specks of lush vegetation surrounded by white sand and 55 acres of coral—which is what makes them so appealing. Several sailing boats run day trips.

Sailaway (☎ **07/4099 5599**) is the cheapest at A$85 (U.S.$59.50) per adult and A$45 (U.S.$31.50) for kids ages 3 to 14, or A$215 (U.S.$150.50) for a family of four. After a 90-minute sail to the isles, you have four hours to snorkel in a lagoon sheltering 200 species of rich coral and several hundred species of fish. You can also learn about sea creatures on a free snorkeling safari or a glass-bottom boat ride, go *boom-netting* (you hang on to a rope net as the boat pulls you through the water), or just laze on the pretty beach. The cost includes buffet lunch, transfers from your Cairns, Trinity Beach, Palm Cove, or Port Douglas accommodations, and snorkel gear; add on the Environmental Management Charge (EMC) tax of A$4 (U.S.$2.80) for every passenger over 4 years old visiting the Great Barrier Reef. There are just 26 other passengers, so the atmosphere is relaxed. The boat departs C17 berth at Marina Mirage at 9:30am daily; coach transfers depart Cairns at 7:15am.

The trip aboard the 30-meter (98-ft.) luxury sailing catamaran *Wavedancer* (☎ **07/4099 5500**), operated by Quicksilver, is A$92 (U.S.$64.40) per person. (If you're staying in Cairns or on the northern beaches, it's an additional A$10/U.S.$7 per person to take the Quicksilver *Wavepiercer* to Port Douglas). You have the option of making an introductory scuba dive for an extra A$77 (U.S.$53.90) per person. The *Wavepiercer* departs Marlin Marina in Cairns at 8am and Palm Cove Jetty on the northern beaches at 8:30am to connect with *Wavedancer* departures from Port Douglas. The company picks you up free of charge from your hotel.

If you don't mind doing without the leisurely sailing component and lunch, the snorkeling-specialist boat *Wavelength* (☎ **07/4099 5031**) does a half-day morning trip to the Low Isles for just A$62 (U.S.$43.40) for adults, A$48 (U.S.$33.60) for children ages 2 to 12, or A$180 (U.S.$126) for a family. The trip incorporates a guided beach walk and a snorkeling tour with a marine biologist and includes snorkel gear and transfers from your hotel. Both beginners and experienced snorkelers will like this trip. It departs Wednesday and Saturday from the Wavelength jetty in Wharf Street at 8:30am and returns at 1pm.

EXPLORING DAINTREE & CAPE TRIBULATION   Just about everyone who comes to Port Douglas takes a guided 4WD day trip into the beautiful Daintree and Cape Tribulation rain forests. Although they are referred to as two separate national parks, the forests that cover them are in fact one big jungle.

You can rent a 4WD and explore on your own (that would certainly be the cheapest option if you're traveling in a group of two or more), but you won't see much except palm fronds and ferns unless you have a guide to interpret it all for you. Most companies basically cover the same territory and sights, including a one-hour Daintree River cruise to spot crocs, a visit to the lovely Marrdja Botanical Walk, a stroll along

The Land that Time Forgot

While Ice Ages rose and fell and Noah bobbed about on the briny, the World Heritage–listed Daintree Rain Forest did not evolve over the last 110 million years the way other rain forests did. Instead, it stayed primitive, and is now home to rare plants that are key links in the evolution story. In the 56,000-hectare (140,000-acre) **Daintree National Park** you will find cycads, dinosaur trees, fan palms, giant strangler figs, and epiphytes like the basket fern, staghorn, and elkhorn. Nighttime croc-spotting tours on the Daintree River vie for popularity with early morning cruises to see the rich bird life. Pythons, lizards, frogs, and electric blue Ulysses butterflies attract photographers, and sport fishermen come here for a fight with big barramundi.

an isolated beach, lunch at a pretty spot somewhere in the forest, and a visit to Mossman Gorge. Some tours also go to the picturesque Bloomfield Falls in Cape Tribulation National Park. Expect to pay about A$100 (U.S.$70) per adult and about A$70 (U.S.$49) per child, give or take A$10 (U.S.$7). Trips that include Bloomfield Falls are about A$30 (U.S.$21) more. A plethora of tour operators offers such trips. Among the more respected are **Trek North Safaris** (☎ 07/4051 4328), **BTS Tours** (☎ 07/4099 5665), and **De Luxe Safaris** (☎ 07/4098 2097). As is the case in most tourist hot spots, some tour operators battle each other fiercely to pay tour desks the highest commission to recommend their tours, even though those tours may not necessarily be the best ones for your needs. Take tour desks' recommendations with a grain of salt, and if possible, get a word-of-mouth recommendation from other travelers. You may not see too much wildlife, as rain-forest animals are either shy, camouflaged, nocturnal, or all three! Most 4WD tours will pick you up in Port Douglas at no charge (from Cairns and the northern beaches you usually have to pay a small fee). Floods and swollen creeks can quash your plans to explore the Daintree in the Wet Season (from Dec to Mar or Apr), so keep your plans flexible then.

Hazel Douglas of ✪ **Native Guide Safari Tours** (☎ 07/4098 2206; www. internetnorth.com.au/native) runs an excellent 4WD tour of the rain forest from an Aboriginal perspective. Hazel is a full-blood Aboriginal who grew up in a tribal lifestyle in the Daintree. She imparts her traditional knowledge of the plants, animals, Dreamtime myths, and Aboriginal history on a full-day tour departing at 9:15am from your Port Douglas hotel. Passengers from Cairns transfer up on the Quicksilver catamaran and return either by coach (northern beaches) or catamaran (Cairns city). The trip costs A$105 (U.S.$73.50) for adults and A$70 (U.S.$49) for children ages 3 to 14 from Port Douglas, and A$115 (U.S.$80.50) for adults and A$80 (U.S.$56) for children from Cairns.

If your chosen safari does not visit **Mossman Gorge,** 21 kilometers (12½ miles) northwest of Port Douglas near the sugar town of Mossman, try to get there under your own steam. The gushing river tumbling over boulders, and the network of short forest walks are magical. (Don't climb on the rocks or enter the river, as strong

Drat Those Aussie Mozzies!

Mozzies, as Aussies call mosquitoes, love the rain forest as much as people do, so throw some insect repellent in your day pack when touring the Daintree and Cape Tribulation.

currents have claimed the life of at least one tourist recently). **Coral Coaches** (☎ 07/4099 5351) makes daily runs to the gorge from Port Douglas at 8:15am, 11am, and 12:45pm, returning at 1:15pm, 3:15pm, and 4:30pm, for A$18 (U.S.$12.60) round-trip. Pack a picnic and make a pleasant couple of hours of it, or maybe splurge on afternoon tea or lunch at Silky Oaks Lodge (see "Worth a Splurge: Dining in the Rain Forest," below).

Most 4WD Daintree tours include a 1-hour cruise on the ✪ **Daintree River,** but if yours does not, or you want to spend more time on the river, cruises are available on a variety of boats, ranging from open-sided "river trains" to small fishing boats. One of the best cruises is offered by Dan Irby's Mangrove Adventures (☎ 07/4090 7017), whose small open boat can get up side creeks the bigger boats can't. Dan is a wildlife artist and photographer; he takes no more than 10 people at a time on 2-, 3- and 4-hour cruises. Chances are you will spot lots of fascinating wildlife on his 2-hour night cruise. A 2-hour trip costs A$35 (U.S.$24.50), while a 4-hour cruise is A$60 (U.S.$42). Night trips depart from the Daintree Eco Lodge, 20 Mossman Daintree Rd., 4 kilometers (2½ miles) south of Daintree village; day trips leave from the Daintree River ferry crossing. Take the Captain Cook Highway north to Mossman, where it becomes the Mossman Daintree Road, and follow it for 24 kilometers (15½ miles) to the signposted turnoff for the ferry on your right. The ferry is 5 kilometers (3 miles) from the turnoff. You will need a car to get there.

Bird-watchers love the Wet Tropics rain forests of which the Daintree and Cape Tribulation national parks are part. Over half of Australia's bird species have been recorded within 200 kilometers (120 miles) of this area. **Fine Feather Tours** (☎ 07/4098 3103) offers a full-day bird-watching safari through the Wet Tropics to the edge of the Outback for A$130 (U.S.$91), and a morning cruise on the Daintree River for A$98 (U.S.$68.60). The tours depart Port Douglas at 6:30am in summer and 7am in winter. Binoculars and reference books are included.

OK, so it's not in the rain forest, but the ✪ **Rainforest Habitat wildlife sanctuary** (☎ 07/4099 3235) is not just as good as the real thing, it's better. That's because you don't see much wildlife in the real rain forest (the animals are too shy and well hidden), but here 150 animal species from the Wet Tropics are gathered in one place for you to see up close. You can see saltwater and freshwater crocodiles, hand-feed kangaroos, and have your photo taken beside (but not holding) a koala (from 10 to 11am and 3 to 4pm for A$7/U.S.$4.90). The highlight is the walk-through aviary, which houses 70 Wet Tropics bird species so tame you can almost touch them. You'll get the most out of your visit if you take one of the excellent free guided tours that leave every hour on the hour. Rainforest Habitat is located on Port Douglas Road at the turnoff from the Captain Cook Highway. It's open daily from 8am to 5:30pm (last entry at 4:30pm); admission is A$16 (U.S.$11.20) for adults, A$8 (U.S.$5.60) for kids ages 4 to 14. Between 8am and 11am, the park serves a great buffet breakfast for A$30 (U.S.$21) for adults and A$15 (U.S.$10.50) for kids, including admission. Allow 2 hours here.

One company that does show you plenty of rain-forest critters in the wild is **Wait-A-While Environmental Tours** (☎ 07/4033 1153) whose rain-forest wildlife-spotting walks are described in "Exploring the Wet Tropics," under "What to See & Do in & Around Cairns" earlier in this chapter. Port Douglas visitors can join the company's Daintree tour, which departs at 3pm Monday, Wednesday, and Thursday, and gets back around midnight or 1am; the tour costs A$110 (U.S.$77) for adults, A$80 (U.S.$56) for kids under 14.

DISCOVERING ABORIGINAL CULTURE   In addition to Native Guide Safari Tours (see "Exploring the Daintree & Cape Tribulation," above), the native KuKu-Yalanji tribe will teach you about bush medicines and foods, Dreamtime legends, and the sacred sites their families have called home for tens of thousands of years. ✪ **KuKu-Yalanji Dreamtime Tours** (☎ **07/4098 1305**) offers a 1-hour guided walk through the rain forest to see cave paintings and visit "special sites"; the tour is followed by a Dreamtime story over billy tea and damper in a bark *warun* (a kind of shelter). You can buy artifacts from the tribe's information center, gift shop, and art gallery. The tours depart Monday through Friday at 10am, 11:30am, 1pm, and 2:30pm from the Kuku-Yalangi community on the road to Mossman Gorge (1 km/½ mile before you reach the Gorge parking lot). Tours cost A$15 (U.S.$10.50) for adults and A$7.50 (U.S.$5.25) for children under 16. A tour with a transfer from Port Douglas is A$37 (U.S.$25.90) for adults and A$18 (U.S.$12.60) for kids, and runs Monday to Friday at 9:15am.

OUTDOOR ACTIVITIES

Some companies in Cairns that offer outdoor activities will provide inexpensive or free pick-ups from Port Douglas hotels. See "White-Water Rafting & Other Outdoor Activities" in the Cairns section above for details.

The cheapest and best outdoor activity in Port Douglas, however, is to do absolutely nothing but laze on spectacular ✪ **Four Mile Beach.** From May to September the water is stinger-free. From October to April, swim in the stinger safety net. **Get High Parafly** (☎ 07/4099 6366) offers parasailing, jet skiing, inflatable tube rides, waterskiing, and other water sports on the beach. Expect to pay around A$25 (U.S.$17.50) to A$55 (U.S.$38.50) for each activity. Take the hourly boat from the booking office at Berth C4 at Marina Mirage to get to the company's beach location.

Visitor greens fees at the championship **Sheraton Mirage golf course** on Port Douglas Road are a steep A$135 (U.S.$94.50) for 18 holes. Whacking a ball on the hotel's aquatic driving range is a more manageable A$6 (U.S.$4.20) for a small bucket of balls, A$12 (U.S.$8.40) for a big one, plus A$2 (U.S.$1.40) for club rental. Contact the Pro Shop (☎ **07/4099 5537**). An 18-hole round on the humbler but equally picturesque course at the **Mossman Golf Club,** Newell Beach Road, Mossman (☎ **07/ 4098 2089**) is A$20 (U.S.$14), or A$12 (U.S.$8.40) for nine holes, plus A$15 (U.S.$10.50) for clubs.

Mowbray Valley Trail Rides (☎ **07/4099 3268**), located 13 kilometers (8 miles) inland from Port Douglas, offers half-day rides through rain forest and sugarcane fields to Collards Falls, or to a swimming hole in the Hidden Valley, for A$60 (U.S.$42). It also runs full-day trips along the mountainous Bump Track, followed by a dip in a rain-forest pool and barbecue lunch at Mowbray Falls, for A$90 (U.S.$63). Transfers from your Port Douglas accommodations are included. Transfers from Cairns are A$15 (U.S.$10.50) per person. **Wonga Beach Trail Rides** (☎ 07/4098 7583) does 3-hour rides through the rain forest and along Wonga Beach, 35 minutes north of Port Douglas, for A$55 (U.S.$38.50), including transfers from Port Douglas.

Bike 'n' Hike (☎ 07/4099 4650 for the booking agent) takes folks biking, hiking, and swimming in natural lagoons in the Hidden Valley in the rain forest near Port Douglas. You don't need to be a strong cyclist to take part. Only seven people are allowed per trip. Half-day tours depart Monday, Wednesday, and Friday and cost A$55 (U.S.$38.50). Full-day tours depart Sunday, Tuesday, Thursday, and Saturday and cost A$79 (U.S.$55.30). Pickups from your Port Douglas hotel, a 21-speed mountain bike, a snack, drinks (and lunch on the full-day trip) are included. Transfers from Cairns and Palm Cove are A$15 (U.S.$10.50) extra. Experienced mountain bikers can descend the steep 14-kilometer (8½-mile) Bump Track through dense rain forest from the top of the Great Dividing Range. This half-day trip for a maximum of four riders leaves Monday, Wednesday, and Friday and costs A$65 (U.S.$45.50).

The Secret of the Seasons

High season in Port Douglas is generally from June 1 through October 31.

WHERE TO STAY

Although there are plenty of ritzy hotels and resorts in Port Douglas, you will find a small supply of good, inexpensive places to stay. Many of the value-for-money choices are holiday apartments with kitchens (so you can save money on meals). Booking agent **Port Douglas Accommodation** (☎ **1800/645 566** in Australia, or 07/4099 4488; fax 07/4099 4455; www.portdouglasaccom.com.au) represents several affordable apartments.

Another money-saving option is camping. You will find both campsites and air-conditioned self-contained park cabins at **Glengarry Caravan Park** (☎ **07/ 4098 5922;** fax 07/4099 3158), located in pleasant grounds 8 kilometers (5 miles) from town on Mowbray River Road. It has powered campsites for A$18 (U.S.$12.60), tent sites for A$14 (U.S.$9.80). Cabins go for A$60 (U.S.$42) double.

✪ **Archipelago Studio Apartments.** 72 Macrossan St., Port Douglas, QLD 4871. ☎ **07/ 4099 5387.** Fax 07/4099 4847. www.archipelago.com.au. E-mail: archipelago@portdouglas. tnq.com.au. 21 units (all with shower only). A/C TV TEL. High season A$99–$149 (U.S.$69.30– $104.30) double; low season A$79–$119 (U.S.$55.30–$83.30) double. Additional person A$20 (U.S.$14) extra. AE, BC, MC, V.

You won't find a friendlier or more convenient place to stay in Port Douglas than these sweet and homey apartments 10 seconds from the beach and a 5-minute walk from town. The apartments are on the small side (most suit only three people, max), but all are well cared for with neatly painted walls, cane furniture, and bright bedcovers. All have a little kitchenette and compact, newly tiled bathrooms. You can opt for a tiny Garden apartment with a patio; or upgrade to a Balcony or Seaview apartment, both a bit larger and with private balconies. Seaview apartments are actually quite roomy and have nice side-on views along Four Mile Beach. Towels are changed daily and linen weekly, but general servicing will cost you A$20 (U.S.$14) extra. There's a nice saltwater pool with a Jacuzzi, sundeck, and barbecue; a guest laundry with iron and ironing board; and hair dryers at the front desk. The wonderfully hospitable proprietor, Wolfgang Klein, will advise you on the best tours and make your bookings for you.

Pelican Inn. 123 Davidson St., Port Douglas, QLD 4871. ☎ **07/4099 5266.** Fax 07/ 4099 5821. www.pelican-inn.com.au. E-mail: reservations@pelican-inn.com.au. 17 units. A/C MINIBAR TV TEL. High season A$99 (U.S.$69.30) double; low season A$89 (U.S.$62.30) double. Additional person A$15 (U.S.$10.50) extra; children 3–12 A$5 (U.S.$3.50). Free cribs. AE, BC, DC, MC, V.

This neatly maintained little Flag motel is just a 10-minute stroll from town. Each good-sized, spick-and-span room has freshly painted walls, a microwave, a toaster, and a sink. The bathrooms are a little old but have plenty of counter space and nice thick towels. Hair dryers are available from the front desk, and an iron and ironing board are in the laundry. The motel's surprisingly spacious and hip Mediterranean restaurant is popular with locals. I wouldn't get excited about the pretty pool—it's located right in front and is not very private—but Four Mile Beach just a short stroll away (in stinger season, it's about a 20-minute walk to the stinger net).

Port Douglas Terrace. 17 The Esplanade, Port Douglas, QLD 4871. ☎ **1800/621 195** in Australia, or 07/4099 5397. Fax 07/4099 5206. www.portdouglasbeachfront.com.au. E-mail:

beaches@internetnorth.com.au. 17 units (some with shower only). A/C TV TEL. High season A$160 (U.S.$112) 1-bedroom beachfront apt.; A$130–$190 (U.S.$91–$133) 2-bedroom garden or beachfront apt.; A$198 (U.S.$138.60) 2-bedroom penthouse. Low season A$120 (U.S.$84) 1-bedroom beachfront apt.; A$98–$135 (U.S.$68.60–$94.50) 2-bedroom garden or beachfront apt.; A$145 (U.S.$101.50) 2-bedroom penthouse. Additional person A$15 (U.S.$10.50) extra. A$5 (U.S.$3.50) crib. AE, BC, DC, JCB, MC, V. Free parking. Free transfers from Cairns airport (48-hours notice requested).

The best-value beachfront accommodations in town, especially in low season, are these clean, quiet units in this low-rise complex on Four Mile Beach, a 5-minute walk from town. Although the paint is peeling here and there, the apartments are airy and respectably furnished with an open-plan kitchen (dishwashers in the two-bedroom beachfront units only), tiny but up-to-date bathrooms with hair dryers, laundry facilities, cool tile floors, latticed balconies, and VCRs. All are serviced weekly. Room 4 has a small garden patio as well as sea views. The roomier penthouses (rooms 11 and 14) have nifty rooftop living areas overlooking the sea and larger bathrooms. If you don't mind missing out on a view, the two-bedroom units in the gardens at the rear are a little darker but also cheaper and still nice enough with cane furniture and a furnished garden patio. A lovely saltwater pool is tucked among the palms, and there's a full-size tennis court.

✪ **Port O'Call Lodge.** Port St. at Craven Close, Port Douglas, QLD 4871. ☎ **07/ 4099 5422.** Fax 07/4099 5495. 28 units (all with shower only). High season A$68–$84 (U.S.$47.60–$58.80) double; low season A$55–$65 (U.S.$38.50–$45.50) double. Additional person A$10 (U.S.$7) extra. A$19 (U.S.$13.30) dorm bed (A$18/U.S.$12.60 for YHA/Hostelling International members). Children under 3 free. BC, MC, V. Free minibus to and from Cairns Mon, Wed, and Sat.

There's a nice communal feeling to this modest motel, located on a suburban street a 10-minute walk from town. Backpackers, families, and anyone on a budget seems to treat it like a second home, swapping travel stories as they cook up a meal in the communal kitchen and dining room. The rooms are light, cool, and fresh with tile floors, loads of luggage and bench space, air-conditioning, and small patios. The compact bathrooms are efficiently laid out with old but neat fixtures (BYO hair dryer). It's probably worth upgrading the extra A$5 to $8 (U.S.$3.50 to $5.60) for the deluxe rooms, which have a TV, clock radio, self-serve tea and coffee facilities, and a mini-refrigerator. The dormitories are really motel rooms, complete with private bathrooms and no more than five beds and/or bunks to a room. Air-conditioning is an extra A$5 (U.S.$3.50) per night or A$10 (U.S.$7) for 24 hours in the dorms. An iron and ironing board are in the laundry. At night the lively poolside bistro is the place to be (see "Where to Dine," below). Other facilities include bikes for hire, free board games, a pay phone, and a small general store. The friendly front desk staff is happy to make tour recommendations and bookings.

The White House. 19 Garrick St., Port Douglas, QLD 4871. ☎ **07/4099 5600.** Fax 07/ 4099 5600. E-mail: whitehouse@internetnorth.com.au. 9 units (all with shower only). A/C TV TEL. High season (usually Jun 1–Oct 31) A$150–$170 (U.S.$105–$119) 1-bedroom apt.; A$180 (U.S.$126) 2-bedroom apt.; A$215 (U.S.$150.50) 3-bedroom penthouse. Low season (usually Nov 1–May 31) A$110–$145 (U.S.$77–$101.50) 1-bedroom apt.; A$155 (U.S.$108.50) 2-bedroom apt.; A$180 (U.S.$126) 3-bedroom penthouse. Additional person A$15 (U.S.$10.50) extra. Minimum stay 3 nights. AE, BC, DC, MC, V.

On a quiet street 1 block from Four Mile Beach are these spacious, attractive apartments housed in a lovely white three-story building in the Queenslander style. Although the upper-floor units are the most expensive, the one ground-floor apartment is one of the nicest, sporting a sleek modern kitchen and a garden patio. All the accommodations have good-quality furniture, full kitchens and laundries, VCRs, and hair dryers. The penthouses have their own rooftop terraces. There is a small pool and Jacuzzi with not much lounging space, and a barbecue. Town is a five-minute stroll away.

A LUXURY B&B HIDEAWAY IN THE COUNTRY

✪ **Marae.** Lot 1, Ponzo Rd., Shannonvale (P.O. Box 133, Port Douglas, QLD 4871). ☎ **07/ 4098 4900.** Fax 07/4098 4099. www.internetnorth.com.au/marae. E-mail: marae@ internetnorth.com.au. 3 bedrooms (two with shower only). TV. A$70 (U.S.$49) single; A$100 (U.S.$70) double. Minimum 2-night stay. Rates include full breakfast. BC, MC, V. From Port Douglas take Captain Cook Hwy. toward Mossman for 10km (6 miles), turn left onto Mt. Molloy turnoff for 1km (½ mile), then turn right onto Ponzo Rd. for 2km (1¼ miles); Marae's driveway is on your left. Transfers from Cairns and Port Douglas can be arranged at extra cost, but having your own transport is advisable. No children allowed.

Your hostess Andy Morris has turned her architecturally stunning timber home, on a rural hillside 15 kilometers (9miles) from Port Douglas, into a glamorous and soothing retreat. The rustic-meets-sleek contemporary bedrooms have white mosquito nets and smart linens on timber beds, and elegant bathrooms with hair dryers. Two are air-conditioned. The downstairs room opens onto a plunge pool overlooking the valley. Wallabies and bandicoots (a kind of small marsupial) feed in the garden, king-fishers and honey eaters use the pool, and butterflies are everywhere. You can laze on the two decks, or wander the rain-forest trails of Mossman Gorge just a few miles away.

WHERE TO DINE IN PORT DOUGLAS

A good place to chill out by the water over an inexpensive meal is the **Port Douglas & District Combined Club,** 7 Ashford St. (☎ **07/4099 5553**). It's just a humble corrugated iron shed with pool tables and slot machines, but the food is remarkably good, and it's got the same water views of Dickson Inlet as the pricier On the Inlet down the road (see below). It's open 10am to 10pm daily; for meals 12:30 to 2pm and 5:30 to 8:30pm.

Court House Hotel. Macrossan St. at Wharf St. ☎ **07/4099 5181.** Menu items A$4–$11 (U.S.$2.80–$7.70). No credit cards. Daily 11:30am–2pm and 5:30–9pm. PUB GRUB.

You won't find a cooler or more relaxing spot to enjoy a meal than out under the giant mango tree in the courtyard of this 120-year old pub. You order at the counter, buy your drinks inside at the bar, and collect your meal when your number is called. Toasted sandwiches, porterhouse steaks with red wine butter, fish burgers, and Thai red chicken curry is what you can expect, cooked well and in big servings, too. They do kids' meals for around A$4.50 (U.S.$3.15). Don't expect anything fancy—the ambience is about as unpretentious as you can get.

On the Inlet. 3 Inlet St. ☎ **07/4099 5255.** Reservations recommended in high season. Main courses A$11.50–$35 (U.S.$8.05–$24.50). AE, BC, DC, JCB, MC, V. Daily noon–9:30pm. SEAFOOD.

No-nonsense seafood and a no-fuss atmosphere make this waterside venue popular with the locals. It's nothing flashy—just white plastic chairs on a shady deck with nice views. Kick back over a long lunch, which might include fried calamari with tartar sauce to start, followed by a stack of chilled Moreton Bay bugs. Or you could try the sizzling garlic prawns for an appetizer and a seafood plate of fried fish, calamari, prawns, scallops, and fries for a main course. From the Sunset Bar you can watch sting rays and groupers feed in the depths below. A take-out section up front serves fish-and-chips for under A$10 (U.S.$7). The restaurant doubles as a seafood wholesaler, so you know it's fresh.

Worth A Splurge: Dining in the Rain Forest

Enjoying a meal in the rain forest, surrounded by green ferns, burbling brooks, and birdsong, is a great experience. At **Baaru House** restaurant, at the luxury Daintree Eco Lodge, 20 Mossman Daintree Rd. (☎ **07/4098 6100**), 4 kilometers (2½ miles) south of Daintree village, which is 49 kilometers (30 miles) north of Port Douglas, you dine in an airy insect-screened timber pole house surrounded by the sounds of crickets, frogs, birds, and rushing water. Hearty and delicious rather than grand, main courses cost up to A$25 (U.S.$17.50), but the menu also includes pastas and pizzas from A$12 (U.S.$8.40). It's open daily 7 to 10am, noon to 2pm, and 6:30 to 9pm.

At the ♻ **Tree House Restaurant** at Silky Oaks Lodge (☎ **07/4098 1666**), 7 kilometers (4 miles) west of Mossman, which is 19 kilometers (11½ miles) north of Port Douglas, you dine on upscale modern Australian fare at polished timber tables on a large verandah above the Mossman River. It's open all day, serving meals from 7 to 10am, noon to 2:30pm, and 6 to 9pm. Main courses are A$12 to $23 (U.S.$8.40 to $16.10) at lunch, A$19.50 to $24 (U.S.$13.65 to $16.80) at dinner. Morning or afternoon tea, served from 10am and 2:30pm, is less than A$10 (U.S.$7) per person. Bring your swimsuit and take a dip in the picturesque river beforehand. Take the Captain Cook Highway approximately 3 kilometers (2 miles) past Mossman and turn left into Finlayvale Road at the small white-on-blue SILKY OAKS LODGE sign. Take care, as the road is a narrow, rough country lane.

You don't have to leave Port Douglas to eat in the trees, however. **Treetops** restaurant at the Radisson Treetops Resort, Port Douglas Road (☎ **07/4030 4333**), has five open-sided tree houses set high up in the rain-forest canopy overlooking the pool. Each has about four tables. The atmosphere at night is truly magical as the sophisticated dishes, including a fair nod to seafood, are cooked in front of your eyes over an open flame. Expect to pay about A$60 (U.S.$42) per person for a three-course table d'hôte menu. Hours are seasonal, so check ahead. It is usually open for dinner only.

Port O' Call Bistro. Port St. at Craven Close. ☎ **07/4099 5422.** Main courses A$7.50–$10.50 (U.S.$5.25–$7.35). Open 5–9pm. Happy hour 5–7pm. BC, MC, V. Daily.

Locals patronize this casual poolside bistro and bar at the Port O' Call Lodge (see "Where to Stay" above) almost as often as guests do, because it offers good, honest food in hearty portions at painless prices. In the glow of the tiki flares around the pool, the atmosphere is fun and friendly. Barbecue your own steak or fish for around A$8 (U.S.$5.60) with salad and fries, or place an order at the bar for things like reef fish in white wine, fettucine carbonara, or a homemade steak pie with baked potato and salad. Tuesday night is the extra-popular A$8 (U.S.$5.60) curry night with live bands, Friday night is pasta night with a choice of three pastas with salad and garlic bread for just A$7 (U.S.$4.90), and Sunday is roast night (A$9.50/U.S.$6.65 with veggies and potatoes).

✪ **Salsa Bar & Grill.** 38 Macrossan St. ☎ **07/4099 4922.** Reservations recommended at dinner. Main courses A$8.50–$12.50 (U.S.$5.95–$8.75) at lunch, A$18–$21.50 (U.S.$12.60–$15.05) at dinner. AE, BC, DC, JCB, MC, V. Daily noon–3pm, 3–5:45pm (happy hour snacks), and 6–10pm. MOD OZ/CALIFORNIAN.

First the buzzing crowds dining on the street catch your eye. Then the prices grab you. Then you taste the terrific food, and you know why locals dig this groovy trendsetter.

Port Douglas After Dark

Dyed-in-the-wool locals meet at the 120-year-old **Court House Hotel** (☎ 07/ **4099 5181**) at the western end of Macrossan Street at Wharf Street. It's a bit rough around the edges, but you will find the natives friendly. Live bands play Monday, Friday, and Saturday nights and Sunday afternoon. The pub is open daily 10am until midnight (until 9pm Sunday).

My vegetable and goat cheese burrito with black bean corn salsa was out of this world. Or you could chow down on the bacon and beef burger with tomato chili jam, or the grilled barramundi with citrus beurre blanc. I would have had the Mississippi Mud Pie for dessert— layers of coffee ice cream and chocolate fudge sauce—but the waitress said it took 3 hours to eat, and I didn't have that long. By day the tablecloths are brown paper; at night the white cloths come out. There's always lounge music playing, and the ultracontemporary bar next door is a good place for a pre- or post-dinner cocktail.

WORTH A SPLURGE

✪ **Nautilus.** 17 Murphy St. (entry also from Macrossan St.), Port Douglas. ☎ 07/ **4099 5330.** Reservations recommended. Main courses A$25.90–$36 (U.S.$18.15–$25.20). AE, BC, DC, JCB, MC, V. Daily 6:30pm–late. TROPICAL/SEAFOOD.

If it's good enough for Bill and Hillary, it might be good enough for you. President Clinton and the First Lady dined here in November 1996 during a visit Down Under and by all accounts loved it. The restaurant is extremely popular, with an appealing setting outdoors under the palm trees and stars and a reputation for cleverly cooked seafood. A typical starter is grilled roasted tomato and watermelon soup with fresh crab meat and yogurt sorbet. For mains, go for a seafood dish like the mud crab caught daily, or grilled yellowfin tuna on a salad of roasted peppers, pink papaw, and avocado with black sesame dressing. There are plenty of choices for nonseafood eaters, too. If you want a meal fit for a president, you can order what he ordered—a fresh seafood tapas plate, followed by deep-fried coral trout with sweet chili sauce and Asian spices, and rounded off with a hot mango soufflé.

4 The North Coast: Mission Beach, Townsville & the Islands

For years the lovely town of ✪ **Mission Beach** was something of a well-kept secret. Farmers retired here; then those who liked to drop out and chill out discovered it; today, it's a petite, prosperous, and stunningly pretty rain-forest town. The beach here is one of the most gorgeous in Australia, a long white strip fringed with dense tangled vine forests, the only surviving lowlands rain forest in the Australian tropics. It is also one of the least crowded and least spoiled, so clever has Mission Beach been at staying out of sight, out of mind, and off the tourist trail.

The nearby Tully River is the white-water rafting capital of Australia (although the folks on the Nymboida River in New South Wales might argue about that). Thrill-seekers can also bungee jump and tandem skydive when they're not rushing down the rapids between lush rain-forest banks.

From Mission Beach it's just a matter of minutes in a ferry to Dunk Island, a large resort island that welcomes day-trippers. You can even sea kayak there from the mainland. Mission Beach is closer to the Great Barrier Reef than any other point along the coast—just an hour—and cruise boats depart daily from the jetty, stopping en route at Dunk Island.

A few hours' drive south brings you to the city of Townsville, also a gateway to the Great Barrier Reef, but more important to visitors as a gateway to Magnetic Island, a picturesque, laid-back haven for flip-flops wearers and water-sports enthusiasts.

MISSION BEACH: THE CASSOWARY COAST
140km (84 miles) S of Cairns; 240km (144 miles) N of Townsville

Tucked away off the Bruce Highway, the exquisitely pretty township of Mission Beach has somehow managed to duck the tourist hordes. It's actually a conglomeration of four beachfront towns: South Mission Beach, Wongaling Beach, Mission Beach proper, and Bingil Bay. Most commercial activity centers around the small nucleus of shops and businesses at Mission Beach proper. It's so isolated that signs on the way into town warn you to watch out for ultra-shy cassowaries emerging from the jungle to cross the road. Dense rain forest hides the town from view until you come around the corner to Mission Beach proper and discover tidy villages of appealing hotels, neat shops, and smart little restaurants. Just through the trees is the fabulous beach. A mile or so north of the main settlement of Mission Beach is Clump Point Jetty.

ESSENTIALS
GETTING THERE   From Cairns, follow the Bruce Highway south. The Mission Beach turn-off is at the tiny town of El Arish, about 15 kilometers (9 miles) north of Tully. Mission Beach is 25 kilometers (15 miles) off the highway. It's a 90-minute trip from Cairns. If you're coming from Townsville, there is an earlier turnoff just north of Tully that leads 18 kilometers (11 miles) to South Mission Beach.

Coral Coaches (☎ 07/4031 7577) operates four or five door-to-door shuttles a day between Port Douglas, the northern beaches, Cairns city, Cairns airport, and Mission Beach. A one-way fare is A$40 (U.S.$28) from Port Douglas, A$30 (U.S.$21) from the northern beaches and Cairns airport, and A$25 (U.S.$17.50) from Cairns city. Children's fares are about two-thirds of adult prices. If you're prepared to do without a door-to-door drop-off, the regular **McCaffertys** and **Greyhound Pioneer** coaches are much cheaper at A$12 (U.S.$8.40) one-way. Both companies call two or three times a day at Mission Beach proper. Trip time from Cairns is just over 2 hours. Trip time from Brisbane is over 26 hours, and the fare is A$139 (U.S.$97.30).

The nearest train station is in Tully; **Queensland Rail** (☎ 13 22 32 in Queensland, or 07/3235 1122) operates several long-distance trains a week on its Cairns–Brisbane route. The one-way fare is A$21 (U.S.$14.70) from Cairns; from Brisbane it's A$131 (U.S.$91.70), or A$161 (U.S.$112.70) in an economy-class sleeper. A bus transfer to Mission Beach with **Mission Beach Bus & Coach** (☎ 07/ 4068 7400) is A$5 (U.S.$3.50).

Wildlife Safety Tips

Endangered **cassowaries** (ostrich-like birds with a blue boney crown on their head) can kill with their enormous claws, so never approach one. If you disturb one, back off slowly and hide behind a tree.

Dangerous **crocodiles** inhabit the local waterways. Do not swim in, or stand on the bank of, any river or stream.

You will no doubt spend plenty of time lazing and strolling the area's 14 kilometers (8½ miles) of gorgeous beaches, but be careful about where you swim. Deadly **marine stingers** inhabit the sea from October through April; in these times swim only in the stinger nets erected at the north and south ends of Mission Beach.

Travel Tip

There is no bank or ATM in Mission Beach, so come with enough cash, traveler's checks, and/or a credit card. You can get a cash advance on your MasterCard or Visa at the post office in Mission Beach proper.

VISITOR INFORMATION   The **Mission Beach Visitor Centre,** Porters Promenade, Mission Beach, QLD 4852 (☎ **07/4068 7099;** fax 07/4068 7066), is located at the northern end of town. It's open Monday through Saturday 9am to 5pm, and Sunday 10am to 2pm.

GETTING AROUND   The local **bus** (☎ **07/4068 7400,** or call the bus driver while he's driving at 0419/745 875 mobile phone) travels day and night between all four beach communities, stopping outside all the accommodation houses listed below, at Clump Point Jetty, and at Wongaling Beach near the water taxi to Dunk Island. **Sugarland Car Rentals** (☎ **07/4068 8272**) offers free pickup and delivery of *minimokes* (low-speed cars good for putt-putting around), regular cars, and 4WDs.

WHAT TO SEE & DO IN THE AREA

EXPLORING THE REEF   The *Quick Cat* runs snorkel and dive trips from Mission Beach to Beaver Cay on the outer Great Barrier Reef. See "Exploring the Great Barrier Reef" section earlier in this chapter for details.

WHITE-WATER RAFTING ON THE TULLY   A day's rafting through the rain forest on the Grade 3 to 4 Tully River is an adventure you won't soon forget. In raftspeak, Grade 4 means "exciting rafting on moderate rapids with a continuous need to maneuver rafts." On the Tully, that translates to regular hair-raising but manageable rapids punctuated by calming stretches that let you just float downstream. You don't need experience, just a decent level of agility and an enthusiastic attitude. I highly recommend ✪ **RnR Rafting** (☎ **07/4051 7777**), whose trip includes 5 hours on the river with fun-loving and expert guides, a barbecue lunch in the rain forest, and an early dinner back in the town of Tully while you watch a video of your trip. With transfers, the day costs A$118 (U.S.$82.60) from Mission Beach, A$128 (U.S.$89.60) from Cairns or Townsville, and A$138 (U.S.$96.60) from Port Douglas. The trip runs daily (Townsville pick-ups are only available Tuesday, Thursday, and Sunday).

EXPLORING THE RAIN FOREST & COAST   Walking, wildlife spotting, canoeing in the forest, and kayaking along the pristine coast are all well worth doing in these parts. Hiking trails through national-park rain forest, fan palm groves, and along the beach abound. The 8-kilometer (5-mile) **Licuala Fan Palm track** starts at the parking lot on the Mission Beach–Tully Road about 1.5 kilometers (1 mile) west of the turnoff to South Mission Beach. The track leads through dense forest, over creeks, and comes out on the El Arish–Mission Beach Road about 7 kilometers (4 miles) north of the post office. When you come out, you can cross the road and keep going on the 1.2-kilometer (less than 1-mile) **Lacey Creek loop** in the **Tam O'Shanter State Forest.** A shorter **Rainforest Circuit** option leads from the parking lot at the start of the Licuala Fan Palm track and makes a 1.2-kilometer (less than a mile) loop incorporating a fan palm boardwalk. There's also a 10-minute "follow the cassowary footprints to the nest" children's walk leading from the parking lot.

If you would rather see the sea than rain forest, take the 7-kilometer (4-mile) **Edmund Kennedy track,** which starts below the Horizon resort at the southern end of the Kennedy Esplanade in South Mission Beach. You get alternating views of the ocean and the rain forest on this trail. The Mission Beach Visitor Centre has free trail maps.

Ingrid Marker of **Sunbird Adventures** (☎ 07/4068 8229) offers a range of sea-kayaking and trekking expeditions that interpret the rich environment around you. No more than eight people are allowed on each trip, so you get personal attention and time to ask questions. Her morning sea kayak expedition (A$40/U.S.$28 per person) journeys around Bingil Bay. Her full-day rain-forest trek visits the Liverpool/Nyleta Creek area, and includes a dip in a natural swimming hole (A$59/U.S.$41.30 per person). Her night walks are held on Bicton Hill and are great for kids because they spot glow-in-the-dark fungi, and frogs and shrimps in the streams (A$20/U.S.$14 per person). The sea kayaks and full-day treks depart at 8am; the night walks depart at 7pm, returning around 9:30pm. Ingrid picks you up from your accommodation for free. All food on the trip is locally grown organic produce. Not all tours depart every day, so check her schedule.

Several other companies run half- or full-day expeditions into the rain forest. Contact **Mission Beach Rainforest Treks** (☎ 07/4068 7137) and **Nature Tours** (☎ 07/4068 8582). The latter offers trips by inflatable canoe down the calm waters of Liverpool Creek.

HITTING THE BEACH   Of course, lazing on the uncrowded beach is what everyone comes to Mission Beach to do. From June to September you can swim anywhere, and the water is still warm; from October to May stick to the stinger safety nets at Mission Beach proper (behind Castaways resort) and South Mission Beach.

A DAY TRIP TO DUNK ISLAND   Dunk is one of the prettiest islands off the Queensland coast, just 5 kilometers (3 miles) offshore from Mission Beach. Thick bush land and rain forest cover much of its 12 square kilometers (5 square miles), most of which is a national park. The island is renowned for its myriad birds and electric-blue Ulysses butterflies.

Staying at the upscale Dunk Island Resort is a budget-busting experience, but you can still pop over for the day to snorkel, hike in the forest, or do all sorts of water sports. **Dunk Island Ferry & Cruises** (☎ 07/4068 7211; or 07/4065 6333 after hours) runs round-trip cruises for A$22 (U.S.$15.40) for adults and A$11 (U.S.$7.70) for kids ages 10 to 14 (free for younger kids). This cruise costs the same as the regular water taxi fare (see below) and includes free snorkeling gear (with a A$20/U.S.$14 refundable deposit). The ferry company will pick you up from your hotel to meet the 8:45am and 10:30am daily departures from Clump Point Jetty. If you would like a barbecue lunch on the boat, it's an extra A$9 (U.S.$6.30) for adults and A$4 (U.S.$2.80) for kids. In the afternoon, you can go boom-netting on an optional 90-minute cruise around Bedarra Island that departs Dunk Island at 1:45pm. This cruise is free for kids under 14, and A$24 (U.S.$16.80) for adults. A package deal that includes the trip to Dunk Island, trip around Bedarra Island, and lunch is A$49 (U.S.$34.30) for adults; a savings of A$6 (U.S.$4.20). You can also get to Dunk by the **water taxi** (☎ 07/4068 8310), which runs six times a day from Wongaling Beach. The round-trip fare is A$22 (U.S.$15.40) for adults and A$11 (U.S.$7.70) for kids ages 4 to 14, but does not include snorkel gear, which costs A$10 (U.S.$7) extra per person. A free bus picks up from hotels between Clump Point and South Mission Beach (which includes all accommodations recommended below except the Bingil Bay Resort Motel).

Once on Dunk, you pay as you go for activities and equipment rental on the island. Everything from waterskiing to catamaran sailing is available, but Dunk has such nice beaches and rain-forest walking trails (half a dozen, ranging in duration from 15 minutes to 4 hours), that you won't need to shell out a chunk of change for water sports to enjoy the day. On Monday and Thursday mornings, you can visit an artist's gallery reached via a 40-minute trail through the rain forest; admission is A$4 (U.S.$2.80).

Ingrid Marker of **Sunbird Adventures** (see above) runs unusual full-day guided ☸ **sea-kayak expeditions to Dunk Island.** Ingrid says if you can pedal a bike for an hour, you can sea kayak for the hour it takes to get to the island. You glide over reefs, looking for sea turtles; spend the morning snorkeling in Coconut Bay; have a picnic lunch of oysters, mussels, and fresh produce (all organic) in Hidden Palm Valley; then hike the rain forest. At morning and afternoon tea you get a choice of no less than nine organic teas and coffees. The trip costs A$80 (U.S.$56) per person.

WHERE TO STAY

☸ **Beachcomber Coconut Caravan Village.** Kennedy Esplanade, South Mission Beach, QLD 4854. ☎ **07/4068 8129.** Fax 07/4068 8671. 43 cabins, 24 with bathroom (shower only); 2 permanent tents, 48 powered sites, approx. 40 tent sites. Unpowered campsite A$13.50 (U.S.$9.45) single, A$15.50 (U.S.$10.85) double; powered campsite A$17.50 (U.S.$12.25) double; permanent tent A$20 (U.S.$14) single, A$24 (U.S.$16.80) double. Cabin A$43–$85 (U.S.$30.10–$59.50) double. Additional person A$4 (U.S.$2.80) extra in campsite, children 2–14 A$2 (U.S.$1.40); additional person A$10 (U.S.$7) in cabin, children A$5 (U.S.$3.50). Linens A$5 (U.S.$3.50) sheet set, A$2 (U.S.$1.40) towel set, A$4 (U.S.$2.80) blanket in regular cabins (free in deluxe cabins). BC, MC, V.

It's no surprise to learn that this delightful little caravan park, located across the road from the beach (and, more important in summer, the stinger net), wins the local garden award every year. Its neat lawns and abundant palms are lovely, as are the new, smartly painted deluxe cabins, which are almost as roomy and as well appointed as an apartment. Deluxe cabins have an en suite bathroom with a hair dryer and fluffy white towels, a separate living and dining area, a good-size kitchen, a master bedroom, a bunkroom for the kids, and a corner Jacuzzi! The regular cabins have much older decor and less room, but they're fine enough. Campers have a communal kitchen, a fridge, and barbecues. Pitch your tent at the jungle's edge, and keep an eye out for the wild cassowaries that stroll in now and then. Sometimes they even walk into the office! There's a lovely pool with lounge chairs, free Ping-Pong, half-court tennis, a TV and game room, a playground, a basketball hoop, a take-out shop, and a tour desk.

Bingil Bay Resort Motel. Cutten St. (off Alexander Dr.), Bingil Bay, QLD 4852. ☎ **07/ 4068 4852.** Fax 07/4068 7226. 6 units (all with shower only). TV. A$55–$75 (U.S.$38.50–$52.50) single; A$60–$80 (U.S.$42–$52.50) double. Additional person A$10 (U.S.$7) extra. Crib $5 (U.S.$3.50). Ask about family discounts. BC, MC, V.

Developers of posh resorts would kill for the site of this motel, which has a pool set among tropical gardens. The accommodations can't quite match all this natural splendor, though. They are a good size, mostly freshly painted, and very clean, but they sport humble fittings and a disappointing, very un-sea-like brown carpet. Pay the extra A$10 (U.S.$7) for an upstairs room with sea views. All but the cheapest rooms have air-conditioning. You won't want to sit in the licensed restaurant and bar because both have absolutely no sea views (what was *wrong* with architects in those days?), but the staff will cheerfully serve you meals out by the pool. The front desk runs a tour desk, and lends hair dryers; iron and ironing board are in the laundry. There are no stinger safety nets here, so to swim in the ocean from October to May you will have to drive or take the bus to Mission Beach.

Mackays. 7 Porter Promenade, Mission Beach, QLD 4852. ☎ **07/4068 7212.** Fax 07/ 4068 7095. 22 units (some with shower only). TV. A$65–$85 (U.S.$45.50–$59.50) single; A$70–$90 (U.S.$49–$63) double; A$85 (U.S.$59.50) single 1-bedroom apt., A$90 (U.S.$63) double 1-bedroom apt. Higher rates apply at Easter. Additional person A$15 (U.S.$10.50) extra; children under 14 A$6 (U.S.$4.20). Crib A$6 (U.S.$4.20). Ask about special packages. BC, MC, V.

This delightfully well-kept motel is one of the best-value places to stay in town. It's just 80 meters (260 feet) from the beach and 400 meters (¼ mile) from the heart of Mission Beach. The friendly Mackay family repaints the rooms annually, so the place always looks brand new. All the rooms are pleasant and spacious with white tiled floors, cane sofas, colorful bedcovers, and very clean bathrooms (BYO hair dryer). Those in the newer section are air-conditioned, and some have views of the attractive granite-lined pool and gardens. Rooms in the older painted-brick wing have garden views from a communal patio and no air-conditioning. Be sure to ask about the special packages offered; they can be extremely good deals. When I last visited a 2-night package in a deluxe room with a full-day white-water rafting trip for two and light breakfast each day was A$376 (U.S.$263.20) double, a savings of A$72 (U.S.$50.40) per couple.

Mission Beach Eco Village. Clump Point Rd., Mission Beach. QLD 4852. ☎ **07/4068 7534.** Fax 07/4068 7538. E-mail: ecovilla@znet.net.au. 17 bungalows (all with shower only). A/C TV TEL. A$130 (U.S.$91) double; A$141 (U.S.$98.70) family or spa bungalow. Lower rates for singles in Feb, Mar (except Easter), and Nov. Minimum 2-night stay. Additional person A$10 (U.S.$7) extra. AE, BC, DC, MC, V.

This lodge occupies a magical site in the rain forest on Clump Point, surrounded on three sides by water. You don't see the sea from your room (except for glimpses through dense trees from a few of them), but it's a mere step away to the sandy beach where you can swim and snorkel in a picture-perfect lagoon. The owner is planning to provide stinger suits so guests can participate in water activities year-round. You stay in simply furnished, roomy little bungalows under the trees. Each has pine paneling, a tile floor, a very clean bathroom, and a deck. Some have a kitchenette and a dining area, some have Jacuzzis; family bungalows have an extra three bunks for the kids. An iron and ironing board and a hair dryer are either in your room or available at the front desk or in the laundry. Breakfast and dinner are served among the trees in an open-sided Malaysian longhouse-style restaurant and bar. The natural-looking pool is lined with rocks and trees, and there's a Jacuzzi and barbecue area.

Worth a Splurge

✪ **The Horizon.** Explorer Dr., South Mission Beach, QLD 4852. ☎ **1800/079 090** in Australia, or 07/4068 8154. Fax 07/4068 8596. www.thehorizon.com.au. Email: info@ thehorizon.com.au. 55 units, all with bathroom. A/C MINIBAR TV TEL. A$215 (U.S.$150.50) double; A$265–$380 (U.S.$185.50–$266) suite. Additional person A$30 (U.S.$21) extra; children 3–12 A$20 (U.S.$14). Children stay free in parents' room if they use existing bedding. Crib A$10 (U.S.$7). AE, BC, DC, MC, V.

With its beguiling views across the pool to Dunk Island, its rain-forest setting, and its impressive rooms, this resort perched on a steep hillside is one of the most comfortable and beautiful you will find Down Under. Even the least expensive rooms are spacious and have luxurious bathrooms fitted with hair dryers. All but a handful of rooms have some kind of sea view; a half dozen retain the older-style bathrooms from a previous resort development, but the sea views from these rooms are the best. It's just a minute or two down the rain-forest track to the beach, there is a day/night tennis court, and the tour desk will book you on day trips if you do decide to ever leave the sundeck.

WHERE TO DINE

Having a picnic on the beach or in one of the many small rain-forest parks and barbecue areas that dot the beachfront is the obvious way to enjoy a meal in Mission Beach's beautiful surrounds. The **Mission Beach Gourmet Delicatessen,** (☎ 07/ **4068 7660**) is the place to stock up for cheap but tasty outdoor fare. Most restaurants and cafes are clustered in Mission Beach proper, but you will find a couple more in South Mission Beach. For dirt-cheap tummy-filling meals that are short on ceremony but long on taste, try **That'll Do** (☎ 07/4068 7300); it's next to the supermarket on

Porter's Promenade in Mission Beach. The burgers, fish-and-chips, chili, and ice cream rarely cost more than A$4 (U.S.$2.80). Take your food to go, or eat at one of the plastic tables. You can even BYO. It's open 11am to 8pm; closed Thursday.

Butterflies. In the Promenade Shopping Centre, Porter's Promenade, Mission Beach. ☎ **07/ 4068 7397.** Reservations recommended. Main courses A$9.95–$14.95 (U.S.$6.95–$10.45). BC, MC, V. Thurs–Tues 6–9pm or later. Closed during the Wet Season (usually Jan–Mar). CONTEMPORARY MEXICAN.

When it took 55 minutes to get our meals at this alfresco garden joint, we were not happy. And when the waitress did not even offer a menu to neighboring customers who sat down 10 minutes earlier, our opinions dived. But when the excellent food arrived, things brightened up. My Mexican beef pizza came in an angel-thin crispy crust "bowl" topped with salad drizzled with an enticing honey and lemon dressing with guacamole. My food-fussy partner reported his fish in a brie parcel, one of a number of less Mexican blackboard specials, as "seriously good." Portions were a decent size, too. The waitress can't last long in her job at the rate she was going, so give the service here the benefit of the doubt and try it out. BYO.

TOWNSVILLE & MAGNETIC ISLAND
346km (207½ miles) S of Cairns; 1,371km (822½ miles) N of Brisbane

Townsville is a bit like Cairns without the crowds, the palms, or the touristy ambience. Unglamorous but friendly, it's mainly an industrial and army-base town nestled by the sea below the pink face of Castle Rock, which looms 300 meters (about 1,000 feet) directly above. It's unlikely you will visit here if you're flying around the country, unless you're a diver visiting the *Yongala* wreck or the other excellent reef sites off the coast. If you're traveling the Queensland coast by bus or train, however, you may find yourself passing through. In that case, you will find the town has a few attractive features.

One such feature is the headquarters of the Great Barrier Reef Marine Park Authority, where you can visit the Great Barrier Reef Aquarium, which houses a marvelous man-made living reef in a huge tank. Cruises depart to the real thing most days from the harbor, although the Reef is farther from shore here than elsewhere along the coast, about 2½ hours away. Another attraction worth visiting is the Museum of Tropical Queensland. It's closed for rebuilding until June 2000, but when it opens it will house maritime archaeological exhibits and a great dinosaur fossil display. You'll also want to explore the lovely old Australian pubs with wrought-iron verandahs that abound in the city. Just five miles offshore is "Maggie," or Magnetic Island, a popular place for water sports, hiking, and spotting koalas in the wild.

ESSENTIALS
GETTING THERE Townsville is on the Bruce Highway, a 3-hour drive north of Airlie Beach and 4½ hours south of Cairns. The Bruce Highway breaks temporarily in Townsville. From the south, there is a signposted "Bruce Highway Alt 1" alternate route into the city. From the north, the highway leads into the city as Ingham Road.

Ansett, Qantas, and their respective intrastate subsidiaries **Flight West Airlines** and **Sunstate Airlines** (book through the parent airlines) each have many direct flights a day from Cairns (trip time: 50 minutes), several direct flights a day from Brisbane (trip time: just under 2 hours), and one or two direct flights a day from Mackay, a coastal town 1-hour south by road from the Whitsundays (trip time: about 1 hour, 10 minutes). Qantas has direct flights from Sydney on weekends (trip time: 2 hours, 35 minutes).

Several **Queensland Rail** (☎ **13 22 32** in Queensland, or 07/3235 1122) long-distance trains stop at Townsville each week. The trip from Cairns is 5½ hours and costs A$41 (U.S.$28.70). From Brisbane the journey takes just over 20 hours; fares range from A$118 (U.S.$82.60) for a sitting berth to A$148 (U.S.$103.60) for an economy-class sleeper.

Greyhound Pioneer and McCafferty's buses stop at Townsville many times a day on their Cairns–Brisbane routes.

VISITOR INFORMATION   The best source is the Information Center (☎ 07/ 4721 3660), in the heart of town on Flinders Mall; it's open Monday through Saturday 9am to 5pm, and Sunday 9am to 1pm. There's another outlet, the Highway Information Center (☎ 07/4778 3555) on the Bruce Highway about 10 kilometers (6 miles) south of the city; it's open daily 9am to 5pm. For an information packet, write to Townsville Enterprise, Enterprise House, The Strand, Townsville, QLD 4810 (☎ 07/4771 3061; fax 07/4771 4361).

GETTING AROUND   Acacia Luxury Transport (☎ 07/4775 5544) runs a door-to-door airport shuttle. It only meets flights from Brisbane, not from Cairns or elsewhere. A single trip into town is A$5 (U.S.$3.50) per person, A$8 (U.S.$5.60) if there are two of you, or A$12 (U.S.$8.40) for a family of two adults and two kids. Reservations are not necessary but are a good idea. Sunbus (☎ 07/4725 8482) is the local bus company. Most buses depart Flinders Street Mall; you can also hail a bus anywhere en route where the driver can easily pull over. A 24-hour pass for all routes is A$9 (U.S.$6.30), or A$20 (U.S.$14) for a family. Car rental chains in Townsville include Avis (☎ 07/4721 2688 town, 07/4725 6522 airport), Budget (☎ 07/4725 2344 town and airport), Hertz (☎ 07/4775 5950 town, 07/4775 4821 airport), and Thrifty (☎ 07/4772 4600 town, 07/4725 4655 airport). Local company Townsville Car Rentals (☎ 07/4772 1093) has cheap rates and also rents scooters. The park garage on Ogden Street is free for the first two hours.

Detours Coaches (☎ 07/4721 5977) runs tours to most attractions in and around Townsville.

THE TOP ATTRACTIONS

For details on visiting the Great Barrier Reef from Townsville, see "Exploring the Great Barrier Reef" earlier in this chapter.

✪ Great Barrier Reef Aquarium. 2/68 Flinders St. ☎ 07/4750 0800. Admission A$14.80 (U.S.$10.35) adults, A$12.80 (U.S.$8.95) seniors and students, A$6.50 (U.S.$4.55) children 4–14, A$35 (U.S.$24.50) family pass. Daily 9am–5pm. Closed Christmas.

The highlight of this outstanding attraction is a 2.5 million liter (650,000 gallon) aquarium that houses a complete living reef ecosystem. Gazing into the enormous tank brimming with colorful fish, anemones, starfish, corals, and sea cucumbers is a truly magical experience. There's also a vast range of smaller live tanks, static educational displays about the Reef and many of the animals that live on it, and a touch pool. On the daily program may be shark feeding, baby-turtle feeding for kids, and— thanks to a two-way underwater microphone—the chance to ask questions of divers in the aquarium as you sit in the theatrette and watch them. There are guided tours at 11am and 2pm, a film on the hour, and kids' activities on weekends. It's worth visiting this wonderful attraction just as much after you have visited the Reef as before you go.

Museum of Tropical Queensland. 70–84 Flinders St. ☎ 07/4721 1662. Admission not set at press-time. Daily 9am–5pm from June 2000. Closed Christmas and Good Friday.

This attraction is closed until June 2000, when it will reopen at impressive new A$20 million (U.S. $14 million) premises. It will house a fascinating display of relics from The Pandora, a 24-gun frigate that was carrying 14 recaptured mutineers from the infamous Bounty when it struck the reef off Townsville in 1791 and went down with

31 crew and 4 prisoners. The museum also has Australia's biggest collection of dinosaur fossils; Aboriginal artifacts; and great displays of Australia's weird, wonderful, and just plain deadly wildlife. You will also be able to watch *Pandora* conservators and taxidermists at work. (Don't watch the animal-stuffers before lunch!)

Omnimax. 2/80 Flinders St. (next to Great Barrier Reef Aquarium). ☎ **07/4721 1481.** Admission A$10 (U.S.$7) adults, A$8 (U.S.$5.60) seniors and students, A$5 (U.S.$3.50) children 5–15, A$25 (U.S.$17.50) family. Open daily. Movies shown hourly from 10:30am; last screening 4:30pm.

The films shown on the 18-meter (59-ft.) dome-shaped screen here are generally about topics like whales, the *Titanic,* the Great Barrier Reef (naturally), and outer space.

OTHER THINGS TO SEE & DO

You can **swim** year-round in the stinger-free enclosure at the narrow strip of beach at the far (western) end of The Strand, a scenic waterfront drive; you can walk there or take the no. 7 bus. Also at the far end is a lovely man-made rock pool for swimming. By the time you read this, The Strand should be redeveloped with parklands, aquatic sculptures, and three more stinger nets closer to town. The whole strip makes for a lovely stroll, especially in late afternoon. And don't miss the views of Cleveland Bay and Magnetic Island from **Castle Hill;** it's a 2.5-kilometer (1½ mile) drive or a shorter, but steep, walk up from town. To drive to the top, follow Stanley Street west from Flinders Mall to Castle Hill Drive; the walking trails up are posted en route.

   Cotters Market, held every Sunday in Flinders Mall from 8:30am to 12:30pm, has 200 stalls of arts and crafts, foodstuffs like homemade jams and chocolates, and seasonal fruit and veggies.

   At the **Billabong Sanctuary** (☎ 07/4778 8344) on the Bruce Highway 17 kilometers (11 miles) south of town, you can see a range of Aussie wildlife in a natural setting, take a free photo with (but not hold) a koala, hug a wombat, hand-feed 'roos, or hold a fruit bat. There are daily talks and shows; one of the most popular is the saltwater crocodile feeding at noon and 2:30pm. Admission is A$18 (U.S.$12.60) for adults, A$14 (U.S.$9.80) for students, A$13 (U.S.$9.10) for seniors, A$9 (U.S.$6.30) for kids ages 3 to 16, and A$43 (U.S.$30.10) for a family of five. The sanctuary is open every day except Christmas from 8am to 5pm. Take your swimsuit as there is a pool. To save money on cafe food, pack a picnic or barbecue supplies and eat in the pleasant grounds.

WHERE TO STAY

Aquarius on the Beach. 75 The Strand, Townsville, QLD 4810. ☎ **1800/62 2474** in Australia; or 07/4772 4255. Fax 07/4721 1316. 100 units. A/C TV TEL. A$110–$120 (U.S.$77–$84) double. Additional person A$20 (U.S.$14) extra; children under 15 A$10 (U.S.$7). AE, BC, DC, MC, V. Airport shuttle. Bus: 7.

You get nice views of the bay and Magnetic Island from every room at this slightly older-style 14-story waterfront hotel. It's popular with business executives who like the location and the practical facilities, such as room service, a car rental desk, an excellent top-floor restaurant (see "Where to Dine," below), a palm-lined swimming pool and

Money-Saving Tip

All the Townsville accommodations listed here offer **packages** incorporating a day trip to the Great Barrier Reef with Pure Pleasure Cruises (see "Exploring the Great Barrier Reef" earlier in this chapter). Be sure to inquire.

children's pool, free in-room movies, and a free taxi phone in the lobby. With a kitch-enette, sofa, desk, and a small dining table with two chairs squeezed into every room, there's not much space left over, but the accommodations are comfortable. If space is important to you, ask for a corner room, as they are slightly larger. The nice bathrooms come with hair dryers. Parts of the decor are a little faded and worse for wear, but the views and facilities here make this a good value. The Strand beach is across the road; the center of town and the island ferry terminals are a 15-minute walk away.

Coral Lodge Bed & Breakfast Inn. 32 Hale St. (off Stokes St.), Townsville, QLD 4810. ☎ **07/4771 5512.** Fax 07/4721 6461. 10 units, two with bathroom (shower only). A/C TV TEL. A$45–$55 (U.S.$31.50–$38.50) single; A$50–$60 (U.S.$35–$42) double. Additional person A$5 (U.S.$3.50) extra. Rates include continental breakfast. BC, MC, V. Airport shuttle.

On a quiet hill on the outskirts of town, owners Di and John have created welcoming and extremely well-priced lodgings out of this 100-year-old Queenslander guest house. The fittings are quite old—pre-1960s, I'd venture in some cases—so don't expect anything flashy. However, the mattresses are high-quality, the Sheridan bed linen is fresh, and the whole place very clean. Most rooms face tropical gardens or have lofty views over the city. Eight share bathrooms and a communal kitchen, but the two self-contained units upstairs have their own bathroom (BYO hair dryer) and full kitchen. At prices like these, go for these units as they are airier and bigger than the slightly dark rooms downstairs, and have curtained-off bunks for the kids. There is a guest laundry downstairs. Breakfast, delivered to your room the night before, is a neat tray of boxed cereals, toast, and fruit juice. John feeds wild possums every night in the peaceful garden and barbecue area, which is a nice cool spot to sit anytime. Flinders Malls is 200 meters away.

Seagulls Resort. 74 The Esplanade, Belgian Gardens, QLD 4810. ☎ **1800/079 929** in Aus-tralia, or 07/4721 3111. Fax 07/4721 3133. E-mail: resort@seagulls.com.au. 70 units (all with shower only). A/C TV TEL. A$93 (U.S.$65.10) double; A$103 (U.S.$72.10) suite; A$129 (U.S.$90.30) 2-bedroom apt. Additional person A$14 (U.S.$9.80) extra; children under 15 A$8 (U.S.$5.60). AE, BC, DC, JCB, MC, V. Airport shuttle. Bus: 4, 5, 7.

This popular low-key resort a 5-minute drive from the city is built around an inviting freeform saltwater pool in 1.2 hectares (3 acres) of dense tropical gardens. Despite its Esplanade location, the rooms do not boast waterfront views, but they are comfortable and a good size. The larger Reef suites have painted brick walls, a sofa, dining furni-ture, and a kitchen sink. Apartments have a main bedroom and a bunk bedroom, a kitchenette, dining furniture, and a roomy balcony. Last refurbished in late 1997, the fittings are modest but in good condition. Every room has a hair dryer. The whole resort is wheelchair-friendly, with bath facilities for people with disabilities. The accommodation wings are centered around the pool and its pretty open-sided restau-rant, which is popular with locals. There's a tour desk, gift shop, room service at dinner, a pool bar (daily happy hour from 5 to 6pm), free in-room movies, a small tennis court, a barbecue, and a playground for the kids. It's not within walking distance of town, but the resort makes free transfers to the city and Magnetic Island ferry terminals at 9am, noon, and 5pm. There's a bus stop right outside, and most tour companies pick up at the door.

A B&B with Victorian Charm
○ **The Rocks.** 20 Cleveland Terrace, Townsville, QLD 4810. ☎ **07/4771 5700,** or 0416/044 409 mobile phone. Fax 07/4771 5711. E-mail: therocks@ultra.net.au. 8 units, 2 with a single shared bathroom (shower only). A$78 (U.S.$54.60) single; A$88–$98 (U.S.$61.60–$68.60) double. Rates include continental breakfast. BC, MC, V. Airport shuttle.

If you have a weakness for Victoriana, you will sigh with delight when you enter this exquisitely renovated old Queenslander home. The owners have fitted it with genuine

19th-century antiques, from the crimson velvet settee to the grandfather clock in the drawing room. Even your meals are served on collectible dinnerware. Every room is decorated with lovely linens, old trunks, and in a few, even original washbasins tastefully wrapped in muslin "gowns"—my favorite was the lavender pitch-ceilinged room that served as an operating theater when U.S. forces occupied the house during World War II. Three rooms are air-conditioned. Two rooms share an en suite bathroom located between them; the others share a historically decorated bathroom with a cast-iron claw-foot bath. Breakfast is served on a big old wooden dining table, and complimentary sherry is served at 6pm on the wide verandah, where you find nice views of Magnetic Island and Cleveland Bay. Despite the old-world ambience, the house has telephone, fax, Internet, and e-mail access for guests (although not in your room). Free tea and coffee are available, and your hostess Jenny Ginger cooks up Sri Lankan feasts for dinner at extra cost, on request. There's also an outdoor Jacuzzi, a billiards table (antique, of course) and a guest laundry. The house has wheelchair access throughout and shower bathroom facilities suited for travelers with disabilities. The Strand is a minute's stroll away, and you are a 15-minute walk from town and the Magnetic Island ferries.

WHERE TO DINE

Apart from the suggestions below, you will find more restaurants and cafes on Palmer Street, an easy stroll across the river from Flinders Mall.

Michel's Cafe and Bar. 7 Palmer St. ☎ **07/4724 1460.** Reservations recommended. Main courses A$10.90–$17.90 (U.S.$7.65–$12.55). AE, BC, DC, MC, V. Tues–Fri 11:30am–2:30pm, Tues–Sun 5:30pm–midnight. MOD OZ.

This big contemporary space has been packed with Townsville's "in" crowd every time I have visited. Owner/chef Michel Flores works in the open kitchen where he can keep an eye on the excellent service. A nice starter is the refreshing lovely pumpkin and paw-paw soup. On my last visit, the lamb filled with sundried tomatoes, pesto, and pine nuts was well cooked, but a little lacking in flavor; the ricotta ravioli in creamy basil sauce was better. You might choose a Louisiana blackened rib fillet, or kangaroo. There are also plenty of casual choices like the stylish pizzas or warm salads. Kids are welcome. Many of the wines come by the glass, averaging A$5.50 (U.S.$3.85).

Palmer's Bistro. In the Australian Hotel, 11 Palmer St. ☎ **07/4771 4339.** Reservations recommended at dinner. Main courses A$13–$18.50 (U.S.$9.10–$12.95). AE, BC, DC, MC, V. Daily noon–2pm, Mon–Thurs 6:30–9pm (until 9:30pm Fri–Sat). MOD OZ.

Out behind this beautifully restored old pub is a cool, quiet courtyard restaurant, with a smart black-and-white tile floor, hanging potted ferns, and a white pagoda in one corner. The food is good, and the meals are huge. After being warned by the waitress not to over-order, I had a Cajun chicken salad which came warm in a light irresistible batter with a yummy honey and chili sauce. It was so filling I couldn't find room for dessert, such as bread-and-butter pudding or Swiss chocolate crepe. There's heftier fare such as a Cowboy Grill of steak, sausages, bacon, and rissoles; or veal topped with prawns and avocado in filo.

✪ **The Thai Exchange.** Exchange Hotel, 151 Flinders St. E., Townsville. ☎ **07/4771 3335.** Main courses A$8.50–$14.50 (U.S.$5.95–$10.15). AE, BC, DC, MC, V. Tues–Sat 6pm–late. THAI.

On the upstairs verandah of this wonderful old pub you can feast on fabulous Thai food for well under A$10 (U.S.$7) if you share one meal. I made the mistake of ordering two dishes—rich and tasty chicken and green beans in ginger, and a vegetarian stir-fry—and could only manage half the chicken and none of the stir-fry. The menu has a wide offering of meat and seafood dishes curried, roasted, stir-fried, or steamed, plus noodle and rice dishes, omelets, traditional Thai salads, and soups. The ingredients are fresh and the chili factor is mild—ask for more heat if you want it.

Worth a Splurge

✪ **Zouí Alto.** On 14th fl. at Aquarius on the Beach, 75 The Strand. ☎ **07/4721 4700.** Reservations recommended. Main courses A$17.50–$22 (U.S.$12.25–$15.40), breakfast buffet A$15.50 (U.S.$10.85) full, A$10.50 (U.S.$7.35) continental. AE, BC, DC, MC, V. Daily 7–9:30am; Fri noon–3pm; Mon–Sat 6:30–9:30pm. Bus: 1B. MOD OZ.

This is not just one of the best restaurants in Townsville, it's one of the best in the country. Chef Mark Edwards, who's cooked for the King of Norway, turns out terrific food, while his effusive wife Eleni runs the front of the house, which is idiosyncratically decked out in primary splashes and Greek urns. My baked tomato, bocconcini, and red onion tart with fresh thyme, olives, rocket, and red capsicum almost melted in my mouth. Main courses include ravioli with choice of filling—pumpkin and blue vein cheese, sweet potato and ginger, or sun-dried tomato and goat's cheese, when I visited—and blue eye cod coated in chili and tomato jam on a mound of champ with coriander and peanut pesto. For dessert, I went for a perfectly caramelized lime tart with ice cream. Go for breakfast, or arrive before sunset, to make the most of the spectacular views of Castle Hill on one side and the bay on the other.

TOWNSVILLE AFTER DARK

Not much happens until Friday and Saturday night in Townsville. The Bank nightclub, 169 Flinders St. East (☎ **07/4771 6148** or 07/4721 1916) gets a young crowd who like to party, dance, and pick each other up. Less frenetic social animals prefer to gather at one of the city's lovely historical pubs edged with wrought-iron lace verandahs. The most popular is the ✪ **Exchange,** 151 Flinders St. East (☎ 07/ 4771 3335)—choose your poison from the hip wine bar downstairs or the Western bourbon and cigar saloon upstairs; ask the bar staff to tell you about the resident ghost. Film star Errol Flynn used to like staying at the Australian, 11 Palmer St. (☎ 07/ 4771 4339); no doubt he knocked back a beer or two on the wide upstairs verandah, and you can, too.

   The Quarterdeck (☎ 07/4722 2333), which is down by the water and belongs to the Sheraton at the Breakwater marina on Sir Leslie Thiess Drive, has dinner music Thursday evening, live bands Friday and Saturday night from 9pm, and live jazz on Sunday winter afternoons and summer evenings. A grill is open for steaks, seafood, and light meals from 11:30am to 9pm daily. You may want to combine a meal here with a visit to the laid-back casino off the Sheraton's lobby. Shorts are de rigeur on the main floor; the Gallery gaming room off the side is a tad dressier (all that means is no denim or sportswear).

A SIDE TRIP TO MAGNETIC ISLAND

8km (5 miles) E of Townsville

More a suburb than a side trip, "Maggie" is a delightful 51-square-kilometer (20-square-mile) national park island 20 minutes from Townsville by ferry. A population of 2,500 locals live here, but it's also popular with Aussies from the mainland who love its holiday atmosphere. If you want an island interlude during your Aussie vacation but don't want to pay through the nose for water sports, accommodations, and food at the ritzy island resorts farther north, Maggie is your ideal alternative. It is quite a busy little place as visitors and locals zip about between the small settlements dotted around its coast, but peace-seeking visitors will find plenty of unspoiled nature to restore their souls. Most folks come for the 20 or so pristine (and amazingly uncrowded) bays and white beaches that rim the island, but hikers, botanists, and bird watchers may want to explore the eucalyptus woods, patches of gully rain forest, and granite tors. (The island got its name when Captain Cook thought the "magnetic" rocks were throwing off his compass.) The place is famous for **wild koalas** that are easily spotted up in the gum trees by the side of the road; ask a local to point you to the nearest colony. Rock wallabies are often spotted in the early morning. Maggie is off the international tourist trail by and large, and it's definitely a flip-flops kind of place, so leave your Prada stilettos in your suitcase.

GETTING THERE & GETTING AROUND   You can take your own car across on the ferry, but most people get around by renting a fun minimoke from the oodles of moke rental outfits on the island. Minimokes are cute baby cars unlikely to send your speedometer much over 60 kilometers per hour (36 m.p.h.). **Holiday Moke Hire** (☎ 07/4778 5703) right near the jetty rents them for around A$35 (U.S.$24.50) a day, plus A30¢ (U.S.21¢) per kilometer. Even cheaper is the frequent **bus** service (that comes with a free commentary from the driver, no less). You can purchase a single fare, but the all-day pass costing A$9 (U.S.$6.30) for adults, A$4.50 (U.S.$3.15) for kids, or A$22.50 (U.S.$15.75) for a family of four can be a good value. A bus for travelers with disabilities can be arranged on request.

Sunferries (☎ 07/4771 3855 Flinders Street terminal, or 07/4721 4798 Breakwater terminal) runs services from the 168–192 Flinders Street terminal and the Breakwater terminal on Sir Leslie Thiess Drive throughout the day. The company has a courtesy coach that runs from bus stop **A** on Flinders Street Mall, or you can arrange a free pick-up at your hotel. Round-trip tickets are A$13 (U.S.$9.10) for adults, A$11 (U.S.$7.70) for seniors and students, A$6.50 (U.S.$4.55) for children ages 5 to 15, and A$27 (U.S.$18.90) for a family of five. Combination tickets combining the ferry with an all-day Magnetic Island bus pass or minimoke rental can save you a couple of dollars.

Out & About on the Island

There is no end to the things you can do on Maggie—snorkeling, swimming in one of a dozen or more bays, catamaran sailing, waterskiing, paraflying, horseback riding on the beach, biking, tennis or golf, scuba diving, sea kayaking, sailing or cruising around the island, taking a Harley Davidson tour, fishing, and more. Equipment for all these activities is for rent on the island at reasonably moderate prices.

Most activities are spread out around **Picnic Bay** (where the ferry pulls in) and the island's three settlements: Arcadia, Nelly Bay, Arcadia and Horseshoe Bay.

The island is not on the Great Barrier Reef, but surrounding waters are part of the Great Barrier Reef Marine Park. There is good **reef snorkeling** at Florence Bay on the southern edge, Arthur Bay on the northern edge, and Geoffrey Bay, where you can

---

Magnetic Island Travel Tips

If you're going over to Magnetic Island for the day, pick up a copy of the free *Magnetic Island Guide* from any tourist information center or hotel lobby or at the ferry terminal in Townsville before you go. Because there are so many choices of activities and tours, it will help if you plan your day before you arrive. Also, there is no bank on the island, so carry cash (not every business will cash traveler's checks) and a credit card.

Be warned: Deadly **marine stingers** make swimming and snorkeling a bad idea from October to May except at the safe swimming enclosure at Picnic Bay. You can still do water sports on top of the water, if your rental outlet provides a protective lycra stinger-suit, but you won't want to pour yourself into one of those in the intensely sticky summer heat from November to March.

even reef-walk at low tide (wear sturdy shoes and do not walk directly on coral to avoid damaging it). First-time snorkelers will have an easy time of it in Maggie's weak currents and softly sloping beaches. Outside stinger season there is good **swimming** at any number of secluded bays found all around the island. Alma Bay is a good choice for families as it is reef free and has shady lawns and a playground; Rocky Bay is a petite, secluded cove.

One of the best, and therefore the most popular, of the island's 20 kilometers (12 miles) of **hiking trails** is the Nelly Bay to Arcadia trail, a one-way journey of 5 kilometers (3 miles) that takes 2½ hours. The first 45 minutes, starting in rain forest and climbing gradually to a saddle between Nelly Bay and Horseshoe, are the most interesting. Another excellent walk is the 2-kilometer (1¼-mile) trail to the **Forts,** remnants of World War II defenses, which, not surprisingly, have great 360° sea views. The best **koala spotting** is on the track up to the Forts off Horseshoe Bay Road. Carry water wherever you go on the island, as some bays and hiking trails are not near shops.

If you feel like splurging, consider the jet-ski circumnavigation of the island offered by **Adrenalin Jet Ski Tours & Hire** (☎ 07/4778 5533). The half-day tour is conducted on two-seat jet skis and costs A$99 (U.S.$69.30), which includes your wet suit and lunch. Tours depart at 9:45am from Horseshoe Bay. Keep your eyes peeled for dolphins, dugongs (manatees), and sea turtles.

Where to Stay & Dine

Magnetic Island has plenty of affordable accommodations, from motels and apartments to A-frame chalets and permanent tents; to book a room, call **Magnetic Island Holidays** (☎ 1800/678 478 in Australia, or 07/4778 5155; fax 07/4778 5158). In the peak season (June to Sept), some apartments are available on a weekly basis only. Maggie is littered with inexpensive restaurants, laid-back cafes, and take-out joints. Popular with the locals is **Andy's Chinese Restaurant** in Picnic Bay (☎ 07/ 4778 5706), where you can get a decent meal for under A$15 (U.S.$10.50) per person. It's BYOB.

Dandaloo Gardens. 40–42 Hayles Ave., Arcadia, Magnetic Island, QLD 4819. ☎ 07/ 4778 5174. Fax 07/4778 5185. 8 units (all with shower only). TV. A$65–$75 (U.S.$45.50–$52.50) apt. (sleeps 5 or 6). Weekly and standby rates available. AE, BC, DC, MC, V. Local bus.

Tucked under towering rain-forest trees and crimson bougainvillea, these spacious and airy free-standing cabin-style apartments are ideal for families. Each has a roomy living area and a kitchen, and there's lots of playground equipment on the grounds. The interiors are simple but appealing, with polished timber floors and framed prints on the freshly painted walls. The four cabins in the back are a little older. Four units have VCRs, and each has a deck or patio. Six are air-conditioned; by the time you read this, all of them should be. The bathrooms are short on space for families, but they are smart looking and clean. The grounds are really lovely and quiet (except for the voluble birds); there's a nice pool with a waterslide (for the kids), lounge chairs (for you), and a barbecue.

Marshall's Bed & Breakfast. 3–5 Endeavour Rd., Arcadia, Magnetic Island, QLD 4819. ☎ 07/4778 4112. 4 units, none with bathroom. A$38 (U.S.$26.60) single; A$55 (U.S.$38.50) double. Additional person A$20 (U.S.$14) extra. "Third night free" standby deal Oct–June, excluding school vacations. Rates include continental breakfast. BC, MC, V (no credit cards on standby rate). Free pickup from ferry terminal on the island. No children under 12.

Stella and Paul Marshall welcome guests to their comfortable, unpretentious home in peaceful Arcadia, a 10-minute drive from the Picnic Bay ferry terminal. The homey rooms have appliqué bedcovers and other nice touches, and Stella gives guests the run of her book-stocked living room. Out back the indoor/outdoor house opens to a rain-forest garden where some of the island's 160 species of birds congregate. You share one of two super-clean bathrooms right near your room, one with a tub (BYO hair dryer). Once or twice a week, Paul leads guests on free evening koala-spotting walks to the Forts. Both hosts are happy to spend time with you, and you will find them rich sources of advice on the best bays, hiking trails, and wildlife hot spots all over the island.

5 The Whitsunday Coast & Islands

A day's drive or a 1-hour flight south of Cairns brings you to the dazzling collection of 74 islands known as the Whitsundays. No more than three nautical miles separates most of the islands, and altogether they represent countless bays, beaches, dazzling coral reefs, and fishing spots that comprise one fabulous Great Barrier Reef play-ground. Sharing the same latitude as Rio de Janeiro and Hawaii, the water is at least 22°C (72°F) year-round, the sun shines most of the year, and winter requires only a light jacket at night.

All the islands are composed of densely rain-forested national-park land, mostly uninhabited, and the surrounding waters belong to the Great Barrier Reef Marine Park. Don't expect palm trees and coconuts—these islands are covered with dry-looking pine and eucalyptus forests full of dense undergrowth, and rocky coral coves far outnumber the few sandy beaches. More than half a dozen islands have resorts that offer just about all the activities you could ever want—snorkeling, scuba diving, sailing trips, reef fishing, waterskiing, jet skiing, parasailing, sea kayaking, hiking, rides over the coral in semisubmersibles, fish feeding, putt-putting around in dinghies to secluded beaches, tennis, squash, and aqua-aerobics classes. Accommodations range from small, low-key wilderness retreats to midrange family havens to Australia's most luxurious resort, Hayman. Day-trippers are welcome to play a round at one of the country's most impressive golf resorts, Laguna Quays, 45 minutes down the coast.

The village of **Airlie Beach** is the center of the action on the mainland. The Whit-sundays are just as good a stepping stone to the outer Great Barrier Reef as Cairns—in my opinion, the Whitsundays are better because you don't have to make the 90-minute trip to the Reef before you hit coral. Just about any Whitsunday island has fringing reef around its shores, and there are good snorkeling reefs between the islands, a quick boat ride away from your island or mainland accommodations.

ESSENTIALS

GETTING THERE   By Car   The Bruce Highway from Cairns in the north or Brisbane in the south leads to Proserpine, 26 kilometers (15½ miles) inland from Airlie Beach. At Proserpine, take the turnoff that says "Whitsunday"—there are almost no signs to Airlie Beach, but you will come to it on this road around the bend from Abel Point Marina. The trip takes around 3½ hours from Townsville and 2½ from Mackay. Sandra and Roger Boynton of **Whitsunday Car Security** (☎ **07/4946 9955,** or

Money-Saving Tips

Does all this fun in the Whitsunday Islands come cheap? If you stay in a hotel on the mainland, yes. If you stay on an island, no. On any trip to the Whitsundays, you'll usually end up spending money on water sports, sailing trips, diving expeditions, and the like, all potential budget-busters. But don't despair—standby and package deals on activities and accommodations abound most of the year, even at the most luxurious resorts.

The Whitsunday Region

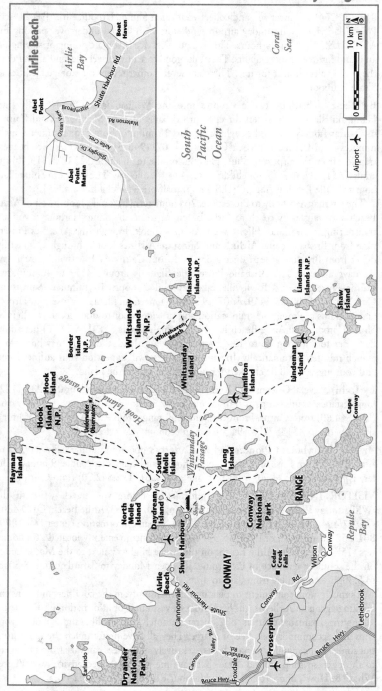

Airlie Beach

Airlie Bay

Boat Haven

Abel Point

Broadwater

Shute Harbour Rd

Waterson Rd

Ocean View

Airlie Cres

Shingley Dr.

Abel Point Marina

Coral Sea

South Pacific Ocean

N

10 km
7 mi

Airport ✈

Hasiewood Island N.P.

Whitsunday Islands N.P.

Lindeman Islands N.P.

Shaw Island

Border Island N.P.

Whitehaven Beach

Hook Island

Hook Island N.P.

Hook Island Passage

Underwater Observatory

Whitsunday Island

Hamilton Island

Lindeman Island

Hayman Island

South Molle Island

Whitsunday Passage

Long Island

Cape Conway

North Molle Island

Daydream Island

Shute Bay

Repulse Bay

Shute Harbour

RANGE

Airlie Beach

Cannonvale

Conway National Park

CONWAY

Cedar Creek Falls

Wilson

Conway

Letherbrook

Shute Harbour Rd

Conway Rd.

Dryander National Park

Earlando

Cannon Valley Rd.

Strathdickie Rd.

Proserpine

Foxdale

Bruce Hwy

Bruce Hwy.

1

018/186 264) will meet you and collect your car at Shute Harbour, Airlie Beach, Abel Point Marina, or Whitsunday airport, and store it in locked undercover parking for A$12 (U.S.$8.40) for 24 hours. This is a great service if you are sailing or staying on an island for one or more nights. They take good care of your vehicle, and after 4 days they even valet-clean it for free. There are several other secure car-storage facilities at Shute Harbour.

By Plane   There are two air routes into the Whitsundays. One is to fly into Hamilton Island with **Ansett** direct from Brisbane, Sydney, Melbourne, and Cairns, or **Qantas** from Sydney. The flight is 2 hours 10 minutes from Sydney and 1 hour 5 minutes from Cairns. **FantaSea Cruises** (☎ 07/4946 5111) provides the cheapest transfers from the airport to Shute Harbour on the mainland: A$22 (U.S.$15.40) for adults, A$12 (U.S.$8.40) for children ages 4 to 14, one-way. The bus from Shute Harbour to Airlie Beach is A$6.50 (U.S.$4.55), half price for children under 12.

The alternative is to fly to Proserpine, 26 kilometers (15½ miles) southwest of Airlie Beach and transfer by coach to Airlie Beach, or to nearby Shute Harbour if you are transferring to an island. **Flight West Airlines** (book through Ansett) serves Proserpine from Brisbane daily; **Airlink** and **Sunstate Airlines** (book through Qantas) fly direct from Brisbane at least once a day, and from Cairns via Townsville once a day, six days a week. The Brisbane–Proserpine flight is around 1 hour 40 minutes; Cairns–Proserpine via Townsville takes around 2 hours 10 minutes. **Sampsons Coaches** (☎ 1300/65 5449, or 07/4945 4011) meets all flights at Proserpine airport and all trains at Proserpine train station and provides door-to-door coach transfers to Shute Harbour and Airlie Beach hotels. The single fare is $11 (U.S.$7.70) per adult, half price for children up to 12. If you stay on an island, the resort may book your launch transfers automatically. In some cases these will appear on your airline ticket, and your luggage will be checked through all the way to the island.

By Train   Several **Queensland Rail** (☎ 13 22 32 in Queensland, or 07/3235 1122) long-distance trains stop at Proserpine every week. The one-way fare is A$64 (U.S.$44.80) from Cairns. From Brisbane fares range from A$105 (U.S.$73.50) for a sitting berth to A$135 (U.S.$94.50) for an economy-class sleeper.

By Bus   **Greyhound Pioneer** and **McCafferty's** operate multiple daily services to Airlie Beach from Brisbane (trip time: 18 hours) and Cairns (trip time: 9 hours). The fare is A$107 (U.S.$74.90) from Brisbane and A$61 (U.S.$42.70) from Cairns.

VISITOR INFORMATION   For information before you travel, write to the **Whitsunday Visitors & Convention Bureau,** P.O. Box 83, Airlie Beach, QLD 4802 (☎ 07/4946 6673; fax 07/4946 7387). The bureau's information center (☎ 1800/ 801 252 in Australia, or 07/4945 3711) is rather inconveniently located 26 kilometers (15½ miles) from Airlie Beach, on the Bruce Highway next to the Motor Lodge on the southern entrance to Proserpine. It's open Monday to Saturday from 8:30am to 5:30pm and Sunday from 9am to 4pm.

It's much more convenient to pick up information from the countless independent booking agents in Airlie Beach. Each stocks a vast range of information on Reef trips, sailing trips, bareboat charters, dive operators, hotels, and the like, and will book your trips and accommodations free of charge. They all have pretty much the same stuff, but some agents manifest certain boats exclusively, and prices can vary from one agent to the next, so shop around. One that gave me good unbiased advice was **Where? What? & How?,** Shop 1, 283 Shute Harbour Rd. (☎ 07/4946 5255).

GETTING AROUND   Avis (☎ 07/4946 6318), Hertz (☎ 07/4946 7401) and **Thrifty** (☎ 07/4946 7727) have outlets in Airlie Beach and at Proserpine Airport (telephone numbers serve both locations). **Tropic Car Hire** (☎ 07/4946 5216) and

Safety Tips

Although they have not been sighted at Airlie Beach for 5 years, deadly **marine stingers** may inhabit the shoreline from October to April. Swim at your own risk during these months. The deadly stingers do not make it to the islands, so swimming in the islands is safe year-round.

The rivers in these parts are home to dangerous **saltwater crocodiles** (which mostly live in fresh water, contrary to their name), so no swimming in streams, rivers, and water holes.

Airlie Beach Car & Scooter Rentals (☎ **07/4946 6110**) are local companies offering good deals.

Sampsons Coaches' (☎ **1300/65 5449** or 07/4945 4011) airport run (see above) doubles as the local bus service between Airlie Beach and Shute Harbour. It runs mostly on the half hour from outside the ANZ and Westpac Banks and Whitsunday Wanderers Resort.

Whitsunday All Over (☎ **07/4946 6900**), Seatrek Cruises (☎ 07/4946 5255), and **FantaSea Cruises** (☎ **07/4946 5111**) provide launch transfers from Shute Harbour to the resort islands throughout the day as well as interisland transfers. One-way transfers range from A$8 to $22 (U.S.$5.60 to $15.40). Whitsunday All Over services Daydream Island, South Molle Island, Long Island, and Hamilton Island airport. Seatrek serves Daydream Island, South Molle Island, and Hook Island. FantaSea's Blue Ferry services Hamilton Island airport, South Molle Island, and Daydream Island. See the island resort listings in "Where to Stay" for prices. You can pick up timetables at all tour-booking agencies in Airlie Beach or Shute Harbour, at tour desks, and on island resorts. It is not usually necessary to reserve a spot, but it is a good idea to prebook your arrival and departure, so you don't miss your connections. Don't assume there is a boat leaving every 10 minutes; most islands only receive a boat every 1 or 2 hours, some only once or twice a day.

Don't forget to add a A$4 (U.S.$2.80) per person **Environmental Management Charge** to the price of all cruises in and around the Great Barrier Reef. This tax goes toward Reef upkeep. Shute Harbour levies a A$2 (U.S.$1.40) adult, A$1 (U.S.70¢) child jetty tax.

CHOOSING A BASE

Many people like to combine a couple of days at Airlie Beach with a few days on an island.

The advantages of staying on the mainland are cheaper accommodations, a choice of restaurants, and freedom to visit a different island each day. What the mainland does not have is great swimming, snorkeling, or extensive water sports.

The main advantage of staying on an island is that swimming, snorkeling, bushwalking, and a huge range of water sports, many of them free, are right outside your door. The deadly stingers that can infest Airlie's shores do not make it to the islands, so swimming in the islands is safe year-round. You won't be isolated if you stay on an island, as most Great Barrier Reef cruise boats, "sail & snorkel" yacht excursions, Whitehaven Beach cruises, dive boats, fishing tour vessels, and so on stop at the island resorts every day or on a frequent basis. Be warned, however, that once you're "captive" on an island, you may be slugged with high food and drink prices. Bear in mind, too, that although most island resorts offer nonmotorized water sports, such as windsurfers and catamarans, free of charge, you will pay for activities that use fuel, such as parasailing, waterskiing, and dinghy rental.

Come Sail with Me

What! Me sail my own yacht? Yes, you! One of the absolute delights of a Whitsundays vacation is sailing yourself around the islands on a ✪ **"bareboat,"** or self-skippered, chartered yacht. Most of the many bareboat yacht charter companies in the islands will want one person on the boat to have a little experience at the helm of a vessel, but don't worry if you don't know one end of a boat from another. You do not need a license, and sailing is surprisingly easy in these uncrowded waters, where the channels are deep and hazard-free and the seas are protected from big swells by the Great Barrier Reef farther out to sea. The 74 islands are so close to each other that one is always in sight, and safe anchorages are everywhere. If you have absolutely no boating experience, the company may require you to take a skipper along for the first day at a typical extra cost of A$150 (U.S.$105) a day. If you think you know what you're doing but you wouldn't like to bet on it, you can choose to have a skipper accompany you for an extra fee for the first couple of hours, or even overnight, to help you get the hang of things. In any case, most companies mail you a preparation kit before you leave home, and you receive a thorough 2- to 3-hour briefing before departure and are given easy-to-read maps marking channels, anchorage points, and the very few dangerous reefs. Your charter company will radio in once or twice a day to check that you're still afloat, and you can contact them any time for advice.

Most yachts are fitted for two to eight passengers. Try to get a boat with two berths more than you need if your budget will bear it, as space is always tight. The boats usually have a galley kitchen, a barbecue mounted to the stern, hot showers, toilet, linen, a radio and/or stereo, a motorized dinghy, and snorkeling equipment. Sleeping quarters are usually not all that luxurious and include a mix of single galley berths and one or two very compact private cabins. You can purchase your own provisions or have the charter company stock the boat for you at an extra cost of about A$30 (U.S.$21) per person per day. Most operators will load a windsurfer, fishing tackle, and scuba diving equipment on request for an extra fee, if they are not already standard.

In peak season (see below) you may have to charter the boat for a week. At other times, most companies stipulate a minimum of 5 days, but many will in fact rent for 3 nights if you ask, rather than let a vessel sit idle in the marina. Five nights is a good length of time as it allows you to get familiar enough with the boat to relax and enjoy yourself.

Everywhere in the Whitsundays, extreme low tides may reveal rocky mud flats below the sand line, so expect some unsightliness then. Water sports can be limited at low tide because of the low water level.

EXPLORING THE ISLANDS

SAILING & SNORKELING TRIPS   A cheaper alternative to skippering your own yacht—also called "bareboating"—around the Whitsundays (see box) is to join one of the numerous yachts offering three-day, two-night sailing adventures around the islands. You can get involved with sailing the boat as much or as little as you want, snorkel to your heart's content over one dazzling reef after another, beach-comb, explore national-park trails, learn to sail if you want, call into secluded bays, swim, sunbathe, and generally have a laid-back good time. A few companies offer introduc-

For a 5-night rental in peak season, expect to pay around A$280 (U.S.$196) to A$410 (U.S.$287) for a four- to six-berth yacht, per boat, per night. For a standard six- to eight-berth yacht in peak season, expect to pay around A$360 to $660 (U.S.$252 to $462). Rates in the off-season, and even in the Whitsundays' busiest time from June to August, will be anywhere from A$25 (U.S.$17.50) to A$70 (U.S.$49) less. If you are prepared to book within 14 days of when you want to sail, the deals can be even better; you should usually be able to find a boat at such late notice in the off-season. You will be asked to lodge a credit card bond of around A$750 (U.S.$525). Mooring fees of A$10 to $50 (U.S.$7 to $35) per boat per night apply if you want to call into one of the half-dozen island resorts.

A number of bareboat charter companies offer **"sail 'n stay"** packages that combine a few days sailing with a few days at an island resort. A typical package offered by Whitsunday Rent-A-Yacht (see below) includes 4 nights on the boat and 3 nights on Daydream Island Resort for A$890 (U.S.$623) per person on a twin-share basis.

Most bareboat charter companies will make complete holiday arrangements for you in the islands, including accommodations, transfers, tours, and sporting activities. Most companies operate out of Airlie Beach or Hamilton Island, or both. Some of the better-known bareboat charter companies include **Australian Bareboat Charters** (☎ **1800/075 000** in Australia, or 07/4946 9381; fax 07/4946 9220; www.ozemail.com.au/~bareboat), **Queensland Yacht Charters** (☎ **1800/075 013** in Australia, or 07/4946 7400; fax 07/4946 7698; www.whitsunday.net.au/qyc/qyc.htm), **Sail Whitsunday** (☎ **1800/075 045** in Australia, or 07/4946 7070; fax 07/4946 7044; www.whitsunday.net.au/bareboat/sailwhit.htm), **The Moorings** (☎ **800/535 7289** in the U.S. and Canada; www.moorings.com; in Australia contact the company's booking agents **Club Seafarer** ☎ **1300/656 484,** or 02/9389 5856; fax 02/9389 9341), and **Whitsunday Rent-A-Yacht** (☎ **1800/075 111** in Australia, or 07/4946 9232; fax 07/4946 9512; www. rentayacht.com.au). The Whitsunday Visitors & Convention Bureau (see "Visitor Information," above) can furnish you with a complete list of operators.

If you don't want to sail yourself, there are countless skippered sailing trips through the islands (see the "Sailing & Snorkeling Trips" section for details).

tory and qualified scuba diving for an extra cost per dive. Most boats carry a maximum of 12 passengers, so the atmosphere is always friendly and fun. The food is generally good, the showers are usually hot, and you sleep in comfortable but small berths off the galley. Some have petite private twin or double cabins.

In peak season, expect to pay A$275 to $305 (U.S.$192.50 to $213.50) per person. Prices usually include all meals, any Marine Park entrance fees, snorkel gear, and courtesy transfers to the departure point (Abel Point Marina or Shute Harbour). In the off-season, the boats compete fiercely for passengers; you'll see signboards on the main street in Airlie Beach advertising standby deals for A$250 (U.S.$175) or even as low as A$200 (U.S.$140). A few better-known operators are *Ragamuffin II* (☎ **1800/67 7119** in Australia, or 07/4946 5299), a 55-foot ocean-going yacht; the famous Australian racing maxiyacht *Condor* (☎ **1800/635 334** in Australia, or 07/4946 7172),

The Secret of the Seasons & How to Get the Best Deal

High season in the Whitsundays is school vacations, which occur mid-April, late June to early July, late September to early October, late December, and all of January. The Aussie winter from June to August is popular, too. You have to book months ahead to secure high-season accommodations, but at any other time you can get some very good deals indeed. Specials on accommodations, sailing trips, day cruises, and diving excursions fairly leap off the blackboards outside the tour-booking agents in Airlie Beach.

---

which incorporates a trip to the outer Great Barrier Reef; and **Prosail** (☎ 07/ 4946 5433), which runs trips on a fleet of yachts. Contact the Whitsunday Visitors & Convention Bureau (see "Visitor Information" above) for details on other charters.

If you just want to get out on the water for a day, there are myriad yachts that will pick you up from Airlie Beach or the islands. They anchor at great snorkeling spots (free snorkel gear is included), and many have free water sports, such as windsurfing. Most offer novice and certified scuba dives for an extra fee. You eat a buffet lunch on the beach or on the boat, sunbathe, swim, and meet other travelers. Among the best are Australia's first America's Cup challenger, *Gretel* (☎ 1800/675 790 in Australia, or 07/4948 0999), and the 80-foot Sydney-to-Hobart race winner *Maxi Ragamuffin* (☎ 07/4946 7777). To give you an idea of the cost, a day on *Gretel* is A$68 (U.S.$47.60) for adults, A$32.50 (U.S.$22.75) for the first child over age 5 and no charge for the second, plus an optional A$45 to $55 (U.S.$31.50 to $38.50) if you want to scuba dive. These prices include the A$4 (U.S.$2.80) reef tax.

Ecoadventurers can zip over the water in a 65-kilometer-per-hour (41 m.p.h.) motorized raft with **Ocean Rafting** (☎ 07/4946 6848). Because the rafts are fast, you see and do a lot in a day. There's an onboard naturalist, and the emphasis is on enjoying and appreciating the Reef and National Park ecosystems. Snorkeling lessons are offered, too. The rafts are small, and there's not much sun protection, so the trips are not for those who prefer air-conditioning (or for kids under age 7 because they bounce out). The tours cost A$65 (U.S.$45.50) plus A$5 (U.S.$3.50) Marine Park fees and A$8 (U.S.$5.60) for lunch; they depart Abel Point Marina daily at 10am.

ISLAND HOPPING   Day-trippers can visit most of the island resorts, where they can use the resorts' water sports equipment, laze on their beaches, and eat at their restaurants. Use of a resort's pool, beaches, and hiking trails is always free, but you will have to pay for just about every other activity. As a rough guide, expect to pay around A$50 (U.S.$35) for a parasail, A$35 (U.S.$24.50) for 15 minutes of jet skiing or waterskiing, A$50 (U.S.$35) to rent a dinghy for half a day, A$10 (U.S.$7) per day for snorkel gear, and from A$10 (U.S.$7) to A$20 (U.S.$14) for a catamaran or windsurfer for 30 minutes. Prices vary from island to island. Be aware that some activities are only available at scheduled times—parasailing was only done at 2pm at South Molle Island when I visited, for example—so check ahead if you have your heart set on a certain activity. Low tides turns some island beaches into rocky mud flats, which can limit water sports, and high tide can cover the coral so you can't snorkel; check how the tides will affect your chosen activities before booking a trip. It's also a good idea to call the island the day before just to see what guided hikes, paddle-ski races, and other events they will have going when you visit.

Hamilton Island, 16 kilometers (9½ miles) southeast of Shute Harbour, is the least attractive of the islands, but its resort has by far the widest range of activities, including

Hitting the Sand at Whitehaven Beach

The 6-kilometer (3¾-mile) stretch of pure white silica sand on ✪ **Whitehaven Beach** will leave you in rapture. The beach, located on uninhabited Whitsunday Island, does not boast a lot of coral, but the swimming is good, and the densely forested shore is beautiful for strolling. Take a book and chill out. Some sailboat day trips visit it, as do several motorized vessel operators, including the *Lindeman Pacific* (☎ 07/4946 6922, or 07/4946 5580 after hours) and **Fantasea Cruises** (☎ 07/4946 5111). Expect to pay around A$60 (U.S.$42) per person for the day, with lunch, or A$44 (U.S.$30.80) for a half day without lunch.

coral snorkeling (at low tide), parasailing, waterskiing, windsurfing, speedboat rides, sailing and fishing trips to nearby islets, tennis and squash, sky diving, go-karts, a shooting range, minigolf, and an aquatic driving range. There are also hiking trails, including a challenging trek up Passage Peak for panoramic views; a 1-hour island bus tour that includes a stop at the island's small fauna park, where you see koalas and other Aussie wildlife; and a lovely freeform pool with loads of lounge chairs. Because the resort is spread out and divided by a steep hill, you will probably to take the shuttle, which costs A$5 (U.S.$3.50) a day, or use the inexpensive minibus taxi service. Renting an electric golf cart is a rather steep A$15 (U.S.$10.50) per hour or A$55 (U.S.$38.50) per day. You will find a bakery, a deli, and some cheap pizza/cafe/burger-style options among the resort's 10 restaurants, plus a couple of pleasant bars.

South Molle Island, (see "Where to Stay"), 7 kilometers (4¼ miles) from Shute Harbour, is an unpretentious but very pretty island covered with rain forests and open grassland. Visitors can play a round on the 9-hole golf course; use the catamarans, windsurfers, and paddle skis; go parasailing, waterskiing, or jet skiing; laze on the palm-lined white sand beach or by the pool and Jacuzzi; or hike 16 kilometers (9½ miles) of national park walking trails, including a steep climb to Spion Kop peak for fabulous 360° views of the Whitsundays. Free fish-feeding takes place on the jetty at 10am and rainbow lorikeet–feeding is at 3pm. You can also take a speedboat to nearby reefs for a guided snorkel safari for A$25 (U.S.$17.50), or rent a dinghy to putt-putt around the shore to a secluded snorkeling or fishing spot. The coffee shop serves inexpensive meals, and there's a bar.

Daydream Island, 8 kilometers (5 miles) from Shute Harbour, is a popular day-trip choice because it has a good patch of coral reef just offshore. It has windsurfers, catamarans, and paddle skis for rent, and a large shady pool for lounging. Be aware that day-trippers are allowed only on the barer, cramped southern end of the island, not the greener, prettier northern end, which has most of the resort facilities and the island's only real beach. The southern end has inexpensive food outlets, a bar, and a couple of shops.

Day-trippers to Club Crocodile Long Island Resort on **Long Island** (see "Where to Stay"), 10 kilometers (6 miles) from Shute Harbour, can rent water-sports equipment and use the resort's beach, Jacuzzi, gym and sauna, volleyball court, basketball court, Ping-Pong tables, and tennis courts. You can hike 20 kilometers (12 miles) of rain-forest trails, swim in two pools, and snorkel among the modest coral in the bay. A cafe serves gigantic meals for A$8.50 (U.S.$5.95) and less. A 20-minute walk from Club Crocodile takes you to quiet little Palm Bay Hideaway, where you can swim, order meals, and chill out on a tiny pretty bay.

Hook Island (see "Where to Stay"), 40 kilometers (24 miles) from Shute Harbour, is the best day-trip destination for avid snorkelers. Snorkel gear costs A$5 (U.S.$3.50) per person per day to rent; you can also rent canoes, visit the underwater observatory for A$7 (U.S.$4.90) adults and A$4 (U.S.$2.80) kids, go diving, and walk bushland trails. The cafe and licensed bar sell meals.

Getting There   You can get to the islands under your own steam by taking one of the scheduled boats (see "Getting Around," above), or join one of the many organized day trips that visit one, two, or even three islands in one day. The major day-trip operators are **FantaSea Cruises** (☎ 07/4946 5111), **Whitsunday All Over** (☎ **1300/366 494** or 07/4946 6900) and **Seatrek Cruises** (☎ **07/4946 5255** for the booking agent). Several yachts offer day trips also. Prices for day trips vary from as little as A$15 (U.S.$10.50) to a single island, up to A$59 (U.S.$41.30) for a full day visiting three islands. Lunch is sometimes extra. Kids generally pay half price. Check whether snorkel gear is included if you want to explore the coral. Look into any discounts your chosen operator may offer, too—recently, Seatrek Cruise offered customers a 75 percent discount on wind-powered water sports on South Molle Island.

MORE OUTDOOR ACTIVITIES

FISHING   Reef fishing is superb throughout the islands; red emperor, coral trout, sweetlip, and snapper are common catches. One of the most popular charter vessels is the 54-foot timber cruiser *Moruya* (☎ **07/4946 6665**, or 07/4946 7127 after hours). Day trips depart Shute Harbour daily at 10am and return around 6pm; they include lunch, hotel pickup, bait, and tackle. The crew cleans your catch for you. Adults pay A$68 (U.S.$47.60), seniors A$60 (U.S.$42), and children ages 4 to 14 A$34 (U.S.$23.80).

The 40-ft *Marlin Blue* (☎ **07/4946 5044,** 07/4948 0999 after hours, or 018/774 020 for the boat itself) takes reef and game anglers out from Abel Point Marina and South Molle Island Resort for A$185 (U.S.$129.50) per person for a full day, based on a shared charter. That includes lunch, bait, and tackle; drinks are extra. The boat departs the mainland at 7am.

If you want to undertake your own fishing expedition, several outfitters rent boats. **Cruise Away Whitsunday** (☎ **07/4946 9330**) in Shute Harbour rents motorized dinghies for A$40 (U.S.$28) for a half day and half-cabin cruisers for A$60 (U.S.$42) for a half day, plus tackle and bait.

GOLF   It ain't cheap, but golf fanatics may think it's worth every penny to play a round on the championship ✪ **Turtle Point golf course** at the Laguna Quays Resort, 45 minutes south of Airlie Beach. This stunning woodland and oceanside course is one of Australia's best. An A$99 (U.S.$69.30) day trip from Airlie Beach includes 18 holes, cart rental, club and shoe rental, round-trip coach transfers, and lunch. Golfers are free to use the resort's pool, bars, and facilities. Book through the resort ☎ **1800/812 626** in Australia, or 07/4947 7777.

HIKING & 4WD SAFARIS   The hills behind Airlie Beach stretch into the nearby Conway State Forest and are rich in giant strangler figs, ferns, and palms. If you're

Whale Watching in the Whitsundays

Humpback whales migrate to the Whitsundays every July to September to give birth to their calves. These curious and fearless leviathans of the deep come right up to the boat. **Fantasea Cruises** (☎ **07/4946 5111**) runs half-day whale-watching cruises in season; trips feature an onboard whale talk and educational videos.

lucky you'll spot a giant blue Ulysses butterfly. Several companies run half-day 4WD safaris. A trip with **Whitsunday 4WD Tours** (☎ **07/4946 1190**), incorporating a walk along a 2-kilometer (1¼-mile) rain-forest trail and a drive to Cedar Creek Falls, costs A$30 (U.S.$21) for adults and A$15 (U.S.$10.50) for kids.

Hiking trails ranging in length from 1 kilometer (just over half a mile) to 5.4 kilometers (3¼ miles) lead through open forest or down to the beach in Conway National Park, which spans Shute Harbour Road between Airlie Beach and Shute Harbour. One trail has signboards explaining the Aboriginal uses of the plants you are passing; several trails offer impressive views of the islands. The trails depart from one of three parking lots along Shute Harbour Road. The **Department of Environment information center** (☎ **07/4946 7022**) on Shute Harbour Road at Mandalay Road, 2.5 kilometers (1½ miles) northeast of Airlie Beach has maps and self-guiding brochures; it's open Monday through Friday from 8am to 5pm and most, but not all, Saturdays from 9am to 1pm.

SEA KAYAKING   If you have strong arms, sea kayaking is a wonderful way to enjoy the islands. Daydream Island and the beaches and bays of the North, Mid, and South Molle group of islands are all within paddling distance of the mainland. It's common to see dolphins, turtles, and sharks along the way. One of the area's most established operators is **Salty Dog Sea Kayaking** (☎ **07/4946 4848** or 018/067 913), which takes escorted day trips through the islands on Monday, Thursday, and Friday, departing at 7am and returning at 5pm. The trips usually depart from Shute Harbour, but also run from the island resorts on request. Two-day expeditions depart Tuesday and Saturday. A day trip is A$65 (U.S.$45.50) per person, 2-day trips are A$195 (U.S.$136.50); rates include snorkel gear, meals, hotel pickup, and, on overnight trips, camping gear. They also deliver sea kayaks to you anywhere in the Whitsundays. A full day's rental is A$35 (U.S.$24.50) for a single kayak, A$65 (U.S.$45.50) for a double.

WATER SPORTS   Airlie Beach is not great for swimming or snorkeling, but you can rent jet skis, WaveRunners, windsurfers, aquabikes, pedal cats, catamarans, and paddle skis to use on the bay. Take your pick from the several rental outfits along the beach.

AIRLIE BEACH
640km (384 miles) S of Cairns; 1,146km (687½ miles) N of Brisbane

The little town of Airlie Beach is the focal point of activity on the Whitsunday mainland. The town is only a few blocks long, but you will find an adequate choice of decent accommodations, a small selection of good restaurants and bars, a nice boutique or two, and facilities such as banks and a supermarket. Cruises and yachts depart from either Shute Harbour, a 10-minute drive south on Shute Harbour Road, or Abel Point Marina, a 10-minute walk west along the foreshore or a quick drive over the hill on Shute Harbour Road. Despite its name, Airlie Beach has no real beach, just a narrow strip of sand around a curving bay that is unsightly at low tide when the water recedes. The beach is made for sunbathing rather than swimming, and the gentle bay is good for water sports.

WHERE TO STAY

Airlie Beach Hotel Motel. 16 The Esplanade (foot entrance on Shute Harbour Rd.), Airlie Beach, QLD 4802. ☎ **07/4946 6233.** Fax 07/4946 7476. 30 units (all with shower only). A/C TV TEL. A$45–$60 (U.S.$31.50–$42) single; A$55–$70 (U.S.$38.50–$49) double. Additional person A$15 (U.S.$10.50) extra. 63 new units (due to open in Nov 1999) will cost approx. A$120 (U.S.$84) double. AE, BC, DC, MC, V. Limited free parking.

This two-story motel is smack-dab in the middle of town, next to the bay. Renovations throughout 1999 progressively spruced up the rooms here. The refurbishing is impressive and total, from new carpet and fresh paint to all-new bathrooms with smart stone-look floors and fluffy towels. All rooms have a toaster, but bring your own hair dryer. Although the place backs onto its own pub-cum-restaurant, Mangrove Jack's, it was remarkably quiet on a busy midweek night, even in the room closest to the action. That may change temporarily through 1999, as the owners plan to add a four-story collection of 63 larger and slightly grander hotel rooms, suites, and apartments right along the beachfront next to this motel. The existing 30 motel units will be reduced to 20. Expect some construction noise until November 1999. By that time, too, the motel's less-than-lovely parking lot should be transformed into a spiffy new pool area. Although pricier than the existing motel rooms, the new beachfront units look as though they'll be a good value.

✪ **Boathaven Lodge.** 440 Shute Harbour Rd., Airlie Beach, QLD 4802. ☎ **07/4946 6421.** Fax 07/4946 4808. 12 units (all with shower only). A/C TV. A$70–$80 (U.S.$49–$56) double. Additional person A$20 (U.S.$14) extra. Children 14 and under A$10 (U.S.$7). AE, BC, DC, MC, V. Free parking.

The guest book at this friendly place is full of comments from people all over the world writing that the lodge felt "just like home," and they're right. They could have added "terrific value." These studio and one- and two-bedroom apartments, situated a 400-meter (¼ mile) stroll from town among tropical gardens, all have wonderful views over tranquil Boathaven Bay. The simple but attractive one-bedroom apartments are quite new and have an expansive living areas with terra-cotta floors, a modern bathroom (borrow a hair dryer at reception), indoor palms, a nice kitchenette, and a big timber deck. Studios are smaller and older but still nice with solid timber furniture, a more modest-looking bathroom, and a kitchenette, but no deck or indoor living area. Studios get some road noise, especially noticeable when the windows are open. The grounds have a barbecue and there's a laundry with iron and ironing board. The extra-pleasant hosts, Peter and Jan Cox, will go out of their way to help you choose and book cruises, yacht charter, and tours. In 1999 the pool is being moved to a perch overlooking the bay; in 2000 more apartments may be added.

✪ **Whitsunday Terraces Resort.** Golden Orchid Dr. (off Shute Harbour Rd.), Airlie Beach, QLD 4802. ☎ **1800/075 062** in Australia, or 07/4946 6788. Fax 07/4946 7128. www. whitsunday.net.au/terraces.htm. 70 units (some with shower only). A/C TV TEL. A$125 (U.S.$87.50) studio; A$135 (U.S.$94.50) 1-bedroom apt. Additional person A$15 (U.S.$10.50) extra. Rates lower for stays of 4 nights or more. AE, BC, DC, MC, V. Free parking.

These studio and one-bedroom apartments terraced on a hillside above Airlie Beach win the "value with a view" prize hands-down. The apartments are furnished differently but all to a high standard in a contemporary style—mine had a white-tiled floor, cane furniture, and light green walls and curtains. Every one has a big balcony and a kitchenette. Guests like to gather around the main swimming pool/sundeck/barbecue area, which, like the rooms, has sweeping views over the town to the bay and Twin Cone Island. The one-bedroom apartments are especially spacious, with a roomy living area. All are serviced daily. An upscale restaurant and cocktail bar adjoin the pool, and there are two Jacuzzis, plus a few extra services you don't always get in apartment complexes, such as dry cleaning and a tour desk. Irons and ironing boards are in the guest laundry, and the front desk loans hair dryers.

Whitsunday Wanderers Resort. Shute Harbour Rd., Airlie Beach, QLD 4802. ☎ **1800/ 075 069** in Australia, or 07/4946 6446. Fax 07/4946 6761. 124 units (all with shower only). A/C TV TEL. A$109 (U.S.$76.30) double. Additional person A$16 (U.S.$11.20) extra; children

4–14 A$10 (U.S.$7). Ask about off-season discounts, overnight and honeymoon packages, and packages that include meals. AE, BC, DC, MC, V. Free parking.

Set in seven hectares (18 acres) of tropical gardens on the main street of Airlie Beach, this humble resort fits right in with the laid-back Airlie lifestyle. Accommodations are scattered around the grounds in blocks of four- to eight-rooms with open-air parking under the trees. The room decor is old-fashioned, but you get plenty of space, a kitchenette, a decent-sized bathroom, and a big balcony or patio for your money. Hair dryers are on loan at reception, and irons and ironing boards are in the communal laundry. This is a good choice for families as there is plenty of room in the grounds for the kids to run around, as well as five half- and full-size tennis courts, an 18-hole minigolf course, archery, Ping-Pong, volleyball, several pools, a Jacuzzi, a gym, and a kids' playground. All except the tennis courts are free of charge. There's also a free kids club during school vacations. There's a nice restaurant, a bar, barbecues, and a comprehensive tour desk. In the off-season, rooms can be as low as A$75 (U.S.$52.50) double.

WHERE TO DINE

⭐ **Mangrove Jack's.** In the Airlie Beach Hotel Motel, 16 The Esplanade (enter via Shute Harbour Rd.). ☎ **07/4946 6233.** Reservations recommended. Main courses A$6.90–$15.95 (U.S.$4.85–$11.15). AE, BC, DC, MC, V. Daily 11:30–2:30pm; Sun–Fri 5:30–9:30pm (until 10pm Fri); Sat 11:30am–10pm. WOOD-FIRED PIZZA/CAFE FARE.

Bareboat sailors, local sugar farmers, Sydney yuppies, and European backpackers all flock to this big open-fronted sports bar/restaurant. The mood is upbeat but pleasantly casual, the surrounds are spick-and-span, and the food passes muster. Wood-fired pizza with trendy toppings is the specialty. Our chicken burger came on a gigantic foccacia bun in a field of fries, and our lamb stack with roasted eggplant, provolone cheese, and baked peanut-rosemary pesto was tasty, although I could have done with more pesto. There is no table service; just place your order at the bar and collect your food when your number is called. The more than 50 wines come by the (big) glass.

Mamma's Boys International Food Court & the Boardwalk Bar. In and next to Magnum's Backpacker's & Bar, Shute Harbour Rd. ☎ **07/4946 6266.** Menu items A$2.50–$15 (U.S.$1.75–$10.50); many meals under A$10 (U.S.$7). AE, BC, DC, MC, V. Daily 11am–late. STEAK/INTERNATIONAL FOOD COURT.

Eating in Airlie is all about being casual, and you won't find a nicer place to chill out than under the big old tree in this atmospheric street-side courtyard. Fetch a big, tasty meal from the food court next door, and eat it at one of the timber tables under the tree. Go for Thai, Chinese, or Malaysian noodles; huge barbecued prime ribs from Butcher Bob's Grill; a beef kabob with spicy peanut sauce from Ahmed's Kebabs; a chargrilled seafood pizza from Mamma's Boys; catch of the day battered or crumbed from Old Salty's—you get the idea. Sandwiches for around A$2.50 (U.S.$1.75) are a good choice for the kids. A live band plays most nights. The food court also does takeout.

THE WHITSUNDAY ISLAND RESORTS

Almost no island resort in the Whitsundays comes cheap. There are about 10 resorts of varying degrees of splendor; accommodations range from positively glitzy to comfortably midrange to quite old-fashioned. But even the most run-down assortment of decades-old cabins can charge a small fortune.

Of the full-service resorts, Club Crocodile Long Island and South Molle Island Resort represent the best bang for your buck, as the rates at each resort include all meals. Both islands' rates also include a lot of activities. As a general rule, nonmotorized activities and water sports such as catamarans, windsurfers, and paddle skis are free, while you pay extra for activities that use fuel, such as parasailing or waterskiing. Of the two resorts, South Molle is prettier and a tad more upscale than Club Crocodile Long Island. It also has faster and more frequent connections to the mainland and other islands.

An alternative to these "big" island resorts are the quiet, low-key affairs tucked away under the palms, often with few facilities to speak of. Hook Island Wilderness Resort and Whitsunday Wilderness Lodge fall into this category. Unlike South Molle Island Resort and Crocodile Club, these resorts usually don't offer day trips to the Great Barrier Reef, fishing expeditions, dive excursions, and sail-and-snorkel trips, but that suits their quiet, nature-loving guests just fine.

Club Crocodile Long Island. Long Island, Whitsunday Islands (Private Mail Bag 26, Mackay, QLD 4740). ☎ **1800/075 125** in Australia, or 07/4946 9400 (or book through Flag International). Fax 07/4946 9555. E-mail: clubcroc@powerup.com.au. 156 units, 140 with bathroom (shower only). Beachfront & Garden units A$221–$251 (U.S.$154.70–$175.70) single, A$290–$330 (U.S.$203–$231) double. Additional person A$145–$165 (U.S.$101.50–$115.50) extra; children 3–17 A$45 (U.S.$31.50). Lodge rooms A$105 (U.S.$73.50) single, A$175 (U.S.$122.50) double. Rates include all meals. Lower rates in off-season. Ask about standby, honeymoon, overnight, and longer-stay packages. AE, BC, DC, JCB, MC, V. Whitsunday All Over (☎ **07/4946 6900**) provides 30-minute launch transfers from Shute Harbour for A$24 (U.S.$16.80) adults, A$14 (U.S.$9.80) children 4–14, round-trip.

Club Croc is probably the most unpretentious of all the Whitsunday resorts, and its cheap package deals make it popular with families and young couples. It faces a wide, curving bay that has moderately good reef snorkeling. Lots of beachfront water sports await you: catamaran sailing, windsurfing, surf skiing, jet skiing, waterskiing, scuba diving, and more. You can join organized activities, like jet-ski races, or just do your own thing. Nightly entertainment can be anything from a raging disco to casino games, live bands, karaoke, talent quests, or cane toad races. Other free activities include aerobics, beach and pool volleyball, basketball, Ping-Pong, and daytime tennis ($5 at night). There are also 20 kilometers (12 miles) of national park trails, where you often see wallabies; two swimming pools; a gym, Jacuzzi, and sauna; and a kids' playground. A free Kids' Club takes 4- to 12-year-olds off their parents' hands every day, and baby-sitting can be arranged for a fee. The resort has a beauty salon and boutique.

The recently renovated Beachfront rooms have a stylish Mediterranean look, with glass-louver windows and a view of the sea through the trees. Garden rooms, located behind the beachfront rooms, are a little older and darker with painted brick walls and carpeted floors. Both types have air-conditioning, minifridges, TVs, telephones, and patios or balconies. Your best value, however, are the appealing, recently decorated Lodge rooms, which have polished timber floors, freshly painted walls, and a fan (but no bathroom, telephone, or view). They're compact but nice if you just want a bed and don't mind shared bathroom facilities. They have no air-conditioning, so take them only from April to October. Hair dryers are available at the reception desk, and there

---

Money-Saving Tips

It's likely you will have to pay the "rack" rates quoted below during school vacations only. At other times, you can usually get a package deal that's a much better value than the rack rate. Ansett and Qantas both offer airfare-inclusive packages from most Australian state–capital cities and Cairns. If you show up in the Whitsundays in the off-season without a reservation, you can sometimes snare an excellent standby deal. It never hurts to ask.

is a guest laundromat. There's nothing fancy about the food served in the seafront buffet restaurant, so you might want to buy a barbecue-it-yourself meat pack from the little cafe. Casual is the byword here; pack your old surf shorts, not your Ralph Lauren chinos.

Hook Island Wilderness Resort. Whitsunday Islands (Private Mail Bag 23, Mackay, QLD 4741). ☎ **07/4946 9380.** Fax 07/4946 9470. A/C. 16 tent sites; 2 10-bed dorms; 10 cabins, 4 with bathroom (shower only). A$60 (U.S.$42) cabin without bathroom double; additional person A$20 (U.S.$14) extra, children 4–14 A$15 (U.S.$10.50). $95 (U.S.$66.50) cabin with bathroom double; additional person A$25 (U.S.$17.50) extra, children A$20 (U.S.$14). Tent site A$13 (U.S.$9.10) adults, A$7 (U.S.$4.90) children 4–14. Dorm bed A$20 (U.S.$14) adults, A$15 (U.S.$10.50) children. Ask about standby rates and packages. BC, MC, V. Seatrek Cruises (☎ **07/4946 5255** for the booking agent) provides transfers from Shute Harbour for A$25 (U.S.$17.50) adults, A$20 (U.S.$14) children ages 4–14, round-trip. Transfers take 1 to 1½ hours, depending on the vessel.

Although this humble little place is just a tiny collection of cabins and campsites on the beach, it boasts the loveliest fringing coral of all the island resorts. To stay here you need to be able to get along without room service, in-room telephones, and smart accommodations, so this place attracts folk who want to snorkel, dive, and chill out. Great snorkeling is just footsteps from shore, and the resort's dive center can get you to good dive sites with ease. The cabins are just basic huts with beds or bunks that sleep six or eight. All come with fresh bed linen (BYO bath towels), tea- and coffee-making facilities, and a minifridge. You can rustle up meals yourself in the communal kitchen by the beach, or buy cooked meals from the casual cafe and bar. There is a pool and Jacuzzi, a volleyball net, canoes and paddle boards to rent, and an underwater observatory. Snorkel gear costs A$10 (U.S.$7) to rent for the duration of your stay. The staff will drop you off at a deserted beach for A$10 (U.S.$7) per person, or take you to coral gardens for A$20 (U.S.$14) per person. Hook is the second largest of all the Whitsunday islands. The resort takes up just 5% of the area—the other 95% is unblemished natural scenery. You probably won't want to leave the island, but if you do, day trips to Whitehaven Beach are offered twice a week.

✪ **South Molle Island Resort.** South Molle Island, Whitsunday Islands (Private Mail Bag 21, Mackay, QLD 4741). ☎ **1800/075 080** in Australia, or 07/4946 9433. Fax 07/4946 9580. 200 units (all with shower only, some also with Jacuzzis). AC MINIBAR TV TEL. A$205–$245 (U.S.$143.50–$171.50) single; A$310–$390 (U.S.$217–$273) double. Additional person A$170–$195 (U.S.$119–$136.50) extra; children 3–14 A$50 (U.S.$35). Rates include all meals. Lower rates in off-season. Ask about standby rates, honeymoon, and longer-stay packages. AE, BC, DC, MC, V. Whitsunday All Over (☎ 07/4946 6900) runs 25-min. transfers from Shute Harbour for A$24 (U.S.$16.80) adults, A$14 (U.S.$9.80) children 4–14, round-trip. FantaSea Cruises (☎ 07/4946 5111) runs 25-min. transfers from Shute Harbour for A$16 (U.S.$11.20) adults, A$8 (U.S.$5.60) children 4–14, round-trip; and 25-min. transfers from Hamilton Island for A$38 (U.S.$26.60) adults, A$19 (U.S.$13.30) children, round-trip.

A calm, peaceful air pervades this isle, despite the catamarans, windsurfers, and paddle skis lined up along the beach and the guests whizzing around on jet skis, waterskis, and hair-raising donut rides in the bay. A curving, white-sand beach, lined with palm trees, greets you as you dock at the jetty. The island attracts all kinds—young singles and couples, families who like the free daily kids' club (for tykes ages 5 and under), and seniors who have been coming here for new years. The resort is getting on in years, so expect a nicely maintained but modest collection of timber and brick buildings set among tropical gardens, not a chrome palace. A refurbishing in 1998 and 1999 really brightened the accommodations, though. Some rooms are free-standing, others are built in wings; all are more or less spacious and have comfortable furnishings and irons and ironing boards, but no hair dryer. The 405-hectare (1,012-acre) island is hilly and covered in grasslands and forests with 16 kilometers (10 miles) of national-park walking trails, including a steep climb to the top of the island for fabulous 360° views. Little bays and inlets rim the shore, and you can hike to them or rent a dinghy to pop around to a private spot for sunbathing. The snorkeling is not the best here, but you will find some pockets of coral and fish life; snorkeling safaris to better reefs nearby run most days for A$25 (U.S.$17.50). A packed daily activities program offers everything from sailing lessons to beach cricket to coconut-throwing competitions, and the dive shop makes daily dive trips and runs courses. There is a gym, a Jacuzzi, a sauna, archery, Ping-Pong, a toddlers' pool, volleyball net, and day/night tennis courts (all free). The swimming pool is a big, rather cheerless rectangle, but it does have shady lounge chairs under the palms. There's also a 9-hole golf course; it's not exactly something Greg Norman is ever likely to play on, but guests and day-trippers enjoy it. During Aussie school vacations a free Kids' Club operates for 6 to 12 year olds.

Although the outdated dining room lacks atmosphere, the Mediterranean, seafood, Asian, and other theme buffets are fine; very good à-la-carte meals are available at extra cost in Coral's restaurant. Some kind of live entertainment plays every night. The "Flames of Polynesia" dinner show on Friday nights attracts yachtsfolk from every direction, as well as day-trippers from the mainland and other islands.

✪ **Whitsunday Wilderness Lodge.** South Long Island, Whitsunday Islands (P.O. Box 842, Airlie Beach, QLD 4802). ☎ and fax **07/4946 9777.** www.whitsundaywilderness.com.au. 10 units (all with shower only). A$1,668 (U.S.$1,167.60) single; A$2,780 (U.S.$1,946) double. Rates include 6 nights' accommodation, all meals, helicopter transfers from Hamilton Island Airport, and all daily excursions, including equipment and wet suit. BC, MC, V. Payments can also be made by direct bank transfer. 10-min. helicopter transfers depart Hamilton Island at 3:30pm Mon, returning at 9:45am the following Sun. No children under 15.

The all-inclusive meals, activities, and transfers make this one of the best-value vacation experiences in Australia. The Whitsunday Wilderness Lodge shows off the country's au naturel luxury. Tucked away in a secluded sandy cove under towering pines and palm trees, this environmentally sensitive lodge is for people who want to explore the wilderness by land, sea, and air in basic comfort, but without the crowds, noisy water sports, or man-made atmosphere of a resort. No more than 20 guests stay at the lodge at a time, and you all arrive and depart on the same day. It's such a friendly and intimate group experience that, according to proprietor David Macfarlane, some people cry when it's time to go home!

Guests sleep in clean, simple rooms with hot showers and views to the sea. The lodge is solar powered, so electricity-sucking devices like hair dryers and irons are discouraged. By the time you read this, new cabins will dot the exquisitely pretty foreshore. Every one has a refrigerator, tea- and coffee-making facilities, a double and single bed, and a balcony. There is no TV or radio, and only one public phone. Cool breezes replace air-conditioning. Your social life centers on an open-sided gazebo by the beach where hearty meals are served buffet-style. The food is terrific.

A typical week's itinerary might include sailing across the Whitsunday Passage to a well-known snorkel spot; exploring the rich mainland mangroves by sea kayak; bushwalking through dense forest; and sailing to the rarely visited sandy beaches of Genesta Bay in Conway National Park. The schedule is organized, but you don't have to participate in everything. You'll have plenty of time to just relax in a hammock or go swimming with Myrtle, the gregarious pet kangaroo.

CAMPING ON THE ISLANDS

Despite the fact that camping facilities are almost nonexistent, camping on uninhabited islands in the Whitsundays is delightful. There are no showers, and few spots have toilets or even shelters, so be prepared to really rough it. Campfires are not permitted on the islands, so you will need a gas stove. **Island Camping Connection** (☎ 07/ **4946 5255**) arranges camping on several deserted islands. The company provides transfers to any island for A$35 (U.S.$24.50) per person (two-person minimum) round-trip (price includes water containers). They also rent camping kits with tents, bedroll, gas stoves, and all other necessities for A$30 (U.S.$21) for two people for the first day, A$10 (U.S.$7) every day thereafter (plus a A$250/U.S.$175 deposit). They also rent snorkel gear for A$5 (U.S.$3.50) per person for the duration of your camp. You bring your own food, a sense of adventure, and a permit from the Department of Environment. Permits are A$3.50 (U.S.$2.45) per person, per night for anyone over 5 years old; you can pick them up from the Department's office on Shute Harbour Road at Mandalay Road, in Airlie Beach (☎ **07/4946 7022**). The office is open Monday through Friday from 8am to 5pm, and most but not all Saturdays from 9am to 1pm. You must organize your boat transport before you go for your permit—consider a sea kayak! Although there are loads of sites, book ahead to secure a spot during school vacations.

6 En Route from North Queensland to Brisbane: The Capricorn Coast & the Southern Reef Islands

Once you get south of the Whitsundays, you're looking at a long drive through uninspiring rural scenery until you hit the beaches of the Sunshine Coast just north of Brisbane. The not particularly charming rural towns and dearth of resorts in this region suggest there is nothing to see or do. That isn't entirely so, however. For a start, the most spectacular Great Barrier Reef island of them all, Heron Island, is off the coast from Gladstone. Heron's shallow reefs are a nonstop source of enchantment for snorkelers, and its waters boast 21 fabulous dive sites. In summer giant turtles nest on its beaches and in winter humpback whales are a common sight.

North of Gladstone is Rockhampton and the pretty Capricorn Coast, named after the Tropic of Capricorn that runs through it. Most likely you will use Rockhampton as a stepping stone to Great Keppel Island, a friendly resort island popular with happy-go-lucky travelers and young Aussies on holiday. To the south, off the small town of Bundaberg, lies another tiny coral cay, Lady Elliot Island. There is nothing tropical or pretty about the island—it's mostly treeless, windswept, and used as a nesting site by tens of thousands of sea birds—but the fringing reef is first rate. Two little-known attractions in Bundaberg are its good shore scuba diving and an awe-inspiring loggerhead turtle rookery that operates in summer on the beach. Farther south lies the world's largest sand island, Fraser Island, which can be negotiated only by 4WD.

ROCKHAMPTON: GATEWAY TO GREAT KEPPEL ISLAND
1,055km (633 miles) S of Cairns; 638km (383 miles) N of Brisbane

"Rocky" is the unofficial capital of the sprawling beef-cattle country inland, and the gateway to pleasant Great Keppel Island, which boasts some of the few inexpensive island retreats in Queensland.

ESSENTIALS
GETTING THERE   Rockhampton is on the Bruce Highway 3½ hours south of Mackay, and almost 2 hours north of Gladstone. If you are not fed up with driving, the **Capricorn Coast scenic route "10"** leaves the Bruce Highway just north of the city, passes a 16-kilometer (9½-mile) stretch of pretty coastline from Yeppoon to Emu Park, and returns to town from the east. The whole detour is 96 kilometers (57½ miles).

Sunstate Airlines and **Airlink** (book through Qantas) and **Flight West Airlines** (book through Ansett) have several direct flights a day from Brisbane, and from Cairns via Townsville and Mackay.

Several **Queensland Rail** (☎ **13 22 32** in Queensland, or 07/3235 1122) trains call into Rockhampton weekly or daily on the Brisbane–Cairns route. The trip from Brisbane takes just 7 hours on the high-speed Tilt train; the fare is A$67 (U.S.$46.90). From Cairns the train takes 19½ hours and costs A$105 (U.S.$73.50) for a sitting berth, A$135 (U.S.$94.50) for an economy-class sleeper.

McCafferty's and **Greyhound Pioneer** call many times a day at Rockhampton on their daily coach services between Brisbane and Cairns. The fare is A$63 (U.S.$44.10) from Brisbane and A$95 (U.S.$66.50) from Cairns.

VISITOR INFORMATION Rockhampton's tourism bureau is **Capricorn Tourism,** whose information center is at the southern entrance to the city on Gladstone Road (at the Capricorn Spire), Rockhampton, QLD 4700 (☎ **07/4927 2055;** fax 07/4922 2605). It's open daily 9am to 5pm. The **Capricorn Coast Information Center** (☎ **1800/675 785** in Queensland, or 07/4939 4888) has more comprehensive information on exploring the pretty coastal region east of Rockhampton; it's located in Yeppoon, on the scenic route at Ross Creek roundabout, and is open daily 9am to 5pm.

GETTING AROUND   **Avis** (☎ 07/4927 3344), **Budget** (☎ 07/4926 4888), **Hertz** (☎ 07/4922 2721), and **Thrifty** (☎ 07/4927 8755) have offices in Rockhampton. Check local company **Rockhampton Car Rentals** (☎ 07/4722 7802) for cheaper rates.

EXPLORING THE AREA: CAVERNS, ABORIGINAL CULTURE & MORE

You will see few stalactites and stalagmites at ✪ **Olsen's Capricorn Caverns** (☎ **07/4934 2883**) 23 kilometers (13 miles) north of Rockhampton at Olsen's Caves Road, off the Bruce Highway, but you will see tiny insectivorous bats, and will be treated to a nifty underground musical presentation in the "Cathedral." A 1-hour tour is A$11 (U.S.$7.70) for adults, A$10 (U.S.$7) for seniors and students, and A$5.50 (U.S.$3.85) for children ages 5 to 15; it departs daily on the hour from 9am to 4pm (closing time is 5pm). Spelunkers can squeeze through tunnels and chimneys and rock-climb on a 4-hour adventure tour that costs A$40 (U.S.$28); book 24 hours ahead for this. Plan enough time here to walk the 30-minute dry rain-forest trail, watch the video on bats in the interpretive center, and feed the wild kangaroos. You can buy sandwiches from the kiosk to eat on the pleasant grounds, take a dip in the pool, and even camp if you like for A$10 (U.S.$7) double for a tent site or A$16 (U.S.$11.20) for a powered site. Rothery's Coaches (☎ **07/4922 4320**) provide transfers from town.

Also on Olsen's Caves Road, 2 kilometers (1¼ miles) off the highway, are the **Cammoo Caves** (☎ **07/4934 2774**), where you can guide yourself on a 40-minute walk. Admission is A$7 (U.S.$4.90) for adults, A$6 (U.S.$4.20) for students and seniors, and A$3 (U.S.$2.10) for children ages 5 to 15; the caves are open daily from 8:30am to 4:30pm. Closed Christmas and Good Friday.

The **Dreamtime Cultural Centre** (☎ **07/4936 1655**), located on the Bruce Highway opposite the Yeppoon turnoff, 6 kilometers (3¾ miles) north of town, showcases Aboriginal culture. Ninety-minute tours of burial sites and rock art, with didgeridoo demonstrations and boomerang-throwing classes, run daily at 10:30am and 1pm. There's also a sandstone cave replica, a display on the dugong (manatee) culture of the Torres Strait Islanders, and an Aboriginal crafts shop. The center is open daily 10am to 3:30pm. Closed ANZAC Day, Christmas, and New Year's Day. Admission, including the tour, is

A$11 (U.S.$7.70) for adults, A$9.50 (U.S.$6.65) for students, A$7.50 (U.S.$5.25) for seniors, and A$5 (U.S.$3.50) for kids ages 5 to 17. Ask about family deals.

Rockhampton has two free public **botanic gardens,** both nice for a stroll and a barbecue picnic. The **Kershaw Gardens,** which display Aussie rain forest, wetland, and fragrant plants from north of the 30th parallel, also have a monorail and a pioneer-style slab hut where Devonshire teas are served. Enter off Charles Street. Admission is free to the **Zoo in the Rockhampton Botanic Gardens** (☎ 07/4922 1654), which features chimps, crocs, 'roos, koalas, monkeys, flying foxes, lorikeets, and a range of other creatures. It is open 6am to 6pm daily. Enter off Ann Street or Spencer Street.

WHERE TO STAY

Southside Holiday Village. Lower Dawson Rd. (south side of town), Rockhampton, QLD 4700. ☎ **1800/075 911** in Australia, or 07/4927 3013. Fax 07/4927 7750. 20 tent sites; 37 powered campsites, 6 with bathroom (shower only); 26 cabins and villas, 20 with bathroom (shower only). Tent site A$11 (U.S.$7.70) single, A$13 (U.S.$9.10) double; additional person A$3 (U.S.$2.10) extra, children A$2 (U.S.$1.40) extra. Powered campsite A$16–$22 (U.S.$11.20–$15.40) double. Caravan A$28 (U.S.$19.60) single, A$31 (U.S.$21.70) double; additional person A$4 (U.S.$2.80) extra. Cabins and villas A$44–$52 (U.S.$30.80–$36.40) single, A$47–$55 (U.S.$32.90–$38.50) double; additional person A$7 (U.S.$4.90) extra. Linen in caravans and cabins A$5 (U.S.$3.50) per set for duration of stay. A$5 (U.S.$3.50) surcharge per unit on long weekends and school holidays. BC, MC, V.

Set in pretty landscaped grounds a few hundred meters from the tourist bureau, this well-run park of villas, cabins, and campgrounds is as pleasant a place to stay as you could ask for. The kids will like the playground, the half tennis court, and the water slide in the pool, you will like the spick-and-span deluxe air-conditioned villas with separate bedrooms, bunk beds, tiny but neat bathrooms with fresh new towels and hair dryers, cooking facilities, iron and board, TV, and cute latticed patios. Ask for a villa away from the main road. Three times a day, Monday to Saturday, the park runs a courtesy coach into town and the Botanic Gardens.

WHERE TO DINE

Rockhampton R.S.L. Club. Cambridge St. ☎ **07/4927 1737.** Reservations recommended on weekends. Smart dress required. Main courses A$6.95–$11.95 (U.S.$4.90–$8.40). No credit cards. Mon–Sat noon–2pm, 6–8pm. Club open 10am–midnight. Courtesy bus picks up from hotels. TRADITIONAL AUSTRALIAN.

How can you beat A$6.95 (U.S.$4.90) for roast of the day when it includes three huge slices of pork with generous servings of hot vegetables, and potatoes smothered in hot gravy? By ordering the half-serve for A$3.95 (U.S.$2.80), that's how, for that should be enough to fill you up. Australia's Returned Services League (R.S.L.) clubs are renowned for good big meals at small prices. The wine is a great value, too, at A$8 (U.S.$5.60) a bottle. You'll need to sign in at the door.

GREAT KEPPEL ISLAND

15km (9 miles) E off Rockhampton

This 1,454-hectare (3,635-acre) island is home to **Great! Keppel Island Resort** (☎ 07/4939 5044), renowned among Australians ages 18 to 35—and older folk, too—for its fab array of water sports and activities. Room rates at the resort are a budget-buster, but anyone can take a day trip from the mainland. Day-trippers can pay to use much of the resort's water sports equipment, swim for free in one of its pools, patronize the store, eat at the inexpensive cafe or moderately priced Anchorage Char Grill, and drink at the Wreck Bar. Windsurfing and catamarans (A$15/U.S.$10.50 an hour), parasailing (A$40/U.S.$28), tube rides (A$10/U.S.$7), waterskiing (A$20/U.S.$14 for 10 minutes), snorkeling (A$10/U.S.$7 for gear all day), jet skiing (A$30/U.S.$21 for 15 minutes) and fishing handlines (A$5/U.S.$3.50 day) are all available to day visitors. Seventeen beaches on the island are accessible by walking trails or dinghy (which you can rent). Stop by the information center near the Wreck Bar to book activities and pick up walking trail maps.

Although Great Keppel isn't as pretty and palm-filled as the Whitsunday Islands or the isles off Cairns, it's a pleasant, peaceful destination nonetheless. It has only modest to good coral, not the superb underwater gardens you will find elsewhere. For the best snorkeling take a boat trip (A$15/U.S.$10.50) from the island to nearby reefs. The shallow waters and fringing reef make the island a good choice for beginner divers; experienced divers will see corals, sea snakes, turtles, and rays. Book diving at the Beach Hut at Keppel Haven (see "Where to Stay"). If you stay overnight, bring your camera—the island is justly famous for psychedelic sunsets.

Keppel Tourist Services (see below) runs several day excursions from Rosslyn Bay Harbour. The cheapest way to visit the island is to go across on the ferry and plan your own day. This will set you back A$27 (U.S.$18.90) for adults, A$25 (U.S.$17.50) for seniors and students, A$14 (U.S.$9.80) for children ages 5 to 14, and A$65 (U.S.$45.50) for a family, round-trip. Your second choice is to book a day-trip package that includes lunch at Keppel Haven (see below) and a 10% discount on non-motorized water sports. This costs A$39 (U.S.$27.30) for adults, A$34 (U.S.$23.80) for seniors and students, A$21 (U.S.$14.70) for children ages 5 to 14, and A$104 (U.S.$72.80) for families.

A third alternative is to join the company's cruise to the Big Peninsular, a 644-square-meter (7,000-sq.ft.) pontoon moored on a reef off the island's north shore. Here you can snorkel, boom-net, take a glass-bottom boat ride, view coral from an underwater chamber, swim, and rest at tables and chairs under umbrellas. The cost, with lunch, is A$70 (U.S.$49) adults, A$40 (U.S.$28) kids, A$55 (U.S.$38.50) for seniors and students, and A$175 (U.S.$122.50) for a family. Trips run Tuesday to Sunday at 9:15am; daily during school vacations. Dives for beginners and certified divers can be arranged on request.

Keppel Tourist Services also runs daily trips at 12:15pm from the island to **Middle Island Underwater Observatory,** a few hundred yards offshore. Keep an eye out for whales from June to September. Tickets are A$10 (U.S.$7) adults, A$5 (U.S.$3.50) kids ages 5 to 14. For the same price, boom-netting trips from the island run at 2:30pm Tuesday to Sunday; daily during school vacations.

GETTING THERE   The ferry operated by **Keppel Tourist Services** (☎ 07/4933 6744) makes the 35-minute crossing from Rosslyn Bay Harbour, approximately 55 kilometers (33 miles) east of Rockhampton, daily at 7:30am, 9:15am, 11:30am, and 3:30pm. It leaves the island at 8:15am, 2pm, and 4:30pm. An extra 6pm service runs Fridays. From Rockhampton, take the Capricorn Coast scenic drive route "10" to Emu Park and follow the signs to Rosslyn Bay Harbour. If you're coming to Rockhampton from the north, the scenic drive turnoff is just north of the city, and from there it's 46 kilometers (27½ miles) to the harbor. You can leave your car in undercover storage at **Great Keppel Island Security Car Park** (☎ 07/4933 6670) at 422 Scenic Highway, near the harbor.

Rothery's Coaches (☎ 07/4922 4320) runs a daily service from Kern Arcade on Bolsover Street in Rockhampton to Rosslyn Bay Harbour and back, three times a day. You can request a free pickup from the airport, train station, or your hotel. Round-trip fares from town are A$14 (U.S.$9.80) for adults, A$10.50 (U.S.$7.35) for seniors and students, and A$7 (U.S.$4.90) for children ages 4 to 14. The round-trip fare to/from the airport is A$24 (U.S.$16.80) for adults, A$18 (U.S.$12.60) for seniors and students, and A$12 (U.S.$8.40) for children.

VISITOR INFORMATION   The **Great Keppel Island Information Centre** at the ferry terminal at Rosslyn Bay Harbour (☎ **1800/77 4488** in Australia) dispenses information about the island's activities and accommodations.

WHERE TO STAY

In addition to the two options described below, you can stay in cute new permanent tents at the **Great Keppel Island YHA Backpackers Village** (☎ **07/4927 5288,** or book through Hostelling International). A bed in a twin, double, or triple shared tent is A$16 (U.S.$11.20) for YHA/Hostelling International members, A$19 (U.S.$13.30) for nonmembers.

No matter where you stay on the island, you can eat at the casual but fine bistro at Keppel Haven (such a good value it attracts guests from the big resort), at the island's pizza joint, and at the cafe or Anchorage Grill at Great! Keppel Island Resort.

Keppel Haven. Great Keppel Island via Rockhampton, QLD 4700. ☎ **1800/35 6744** in Australia, or 07/4933 6744. Fax 07/4933 6429. A/C. 40 permanent tents, none with bathroom; 12 cabins, all with bathroom (shower only). Tent A$13 (U.S.$9.10) per person triple or quad-share, A$16 (U.S.$11.20) per person twin/double. Cabin A$95 (U.S.$66.50) double; additional person A$20 (U.S.$14) extra. Children under 5 free. A$5 (U.S.$3.50) per person linen for duration of stay. Ask about 3-day, 2-night packages with Keppel Tourist Services that include ferry transfers and 10% discount on water sports. BC, MC, V.

Not far from the ferry drop-off point at the beach is this campground-style enclave of humble but pretty cabins and tents. Renovated in 1998, the cabins have terra-cotta–look floors, bright new kitchenettes, a small double bedroom, four bunks in the living/dining area for the kids, fans, and a little porch. By the time you arrive, all will have air-conditioning. The permanent tents are bigger than those at Keppel Kampout (see below) and come with twin or double beds, four bunks separated by a canvas partition, and electricity. Catamarans, windsurfers, fishing tackle, snorkel gear, and dinghies are available on a pay-as-you-go basis. There's a pretty restaurant, a general store selling basic groceries, and a communal kitchen and barbecues. The front desk has hair dryers; BYO towels.

Keppel Kampout. Great Keppel Island via Rockhampton, QLD 4700. ☎ **1800/35 6744** in Australia, or 07/4933 6744. Fax 07/4933 6429. 23 permanent tents, none with bathroom. A$60 (U.S.$42) per person, shared accommodation. Standby rate A$54 (U.S.$37.80) per person. Rates include three meals a day, water sports, and snorkeling and boom-netting tours. BC, MC, V.

The permanent tents here have raised floors, little verandahs, twin beds, cupboards and linen, and are equipped with electricity. They're situated on a landscaped patch next door to Keppel Haven and a short walk from Great! Keppel Island Resort and the beach. Catamarans, windsurfers, fishing tackle, snorkeling trips, and boom-netting cruises are all free (they're usually A$10/U.S.$7 or A$15/U.S.$10.50 each), and all your meals (even wine at dinner) are included in the one low price! Guests are encouraged to mingle in the pleasant, open-air dining area and TV lounge; all that's asked of you is that you wash your own dishes. BYO towels; they provide hair dryers.

Money-Saving Tip

Keppel Tourist Services provides discounted round-trip transfers from the mainland for A$25 (U.S.$17.50) per adult for guests of YHA Backpackers Village, Keppel Kampout, and Keppel Haven.

GLADSTONE: GATEWAY TO HERON ISLAND

550km (330 miles) N of Brisbane; 1,162 (697½ miles) S of Cairns

The industrial port town of Gladstone is the departure point for the breathtakingly beautiful coralscapes of Heron Island.

ESSENTIALS

GETTING THERE & GETTING AROUND   Gladstone is on the coast 21 kilometers (12½ miles) off the Bruce Highway. **Sunstate Airlines** (book through Qantas) and **Flight West Airlines** (book through Ansett) have many flights a day from Brisbane (trip time: 85 minutes) and one direct flight a day from Rockhampton. From Cairns both airlines operate a "milk run" via Townsville, Mackay, and Rockhampton.

   Queensland Rail (☎ 13 22 32 in Queensland, or 07/3235 1122) operates trains most days to Gladstone from Brisbane and Cairns. The fare from Brisbane (trip time: 6 hours on the high-speed Tilt train) is A$60 (U.S.$42); fares from Cairns (trip time: 20 hours) range from A$109 (U.S.$76.30) for a sitting berth to A$139 (U.S.$97.30) for an economy-class sleeper.

   McCafferty's and **Greyhound Pioneer** operate many daily coaches to Gladstone on their Brisbane–Cairns runs. The fare is A$57 (U.S.$39.90) from Brisbane (trip time: 10½ hours) and A$105 (U.S.$73.50) from Cairns (trip time: 17½ hours).

   Avis (☎ 07/4978 2633), **Budget** (☎ 07/4972 8488), **Hertz** (☎ 07/4978 6899) and **Thrifty** (☎ 07/4972 5999) all have offices in Gladstone.

VISITOR INFORMATION   The **Gladstone Area Promotion & Development Bureau's Information Centre** is located in the ferry terminal at Gladstone Marina, Bryan Jordan Drive, Gladstone, QLD 4680 (☎ **07/4972 9922;** fax 07/4972 5006). It's open 8:30am to 5pm Monday through Friday, and 9am to 5pm Saturday and Sunday.

WHERE TO STAY

Country Plaza International. 100 Goondoon St., Gladstone, QLD 4680. ☎ **07/ 4972 4499.** Fax 07/ 4972 4921. 72 units. A/C MINIBAR TV TEL. A$105 (U.S.$73.50) double. Additional person A$10 (U.S.$7) extra; A$7 (U.S.$4.90) children under 12. A$115 (U.S.$80.50) double, A$135 (U.S.$94.50) triple Heron Island stopover package, including full breakfast and transfers to Gladstone Marina. AE, BC, DC, MC, V. Free parking. Free shuttle from airport, coach terminal, marina, and train station.

This four-level hotel in the center of town runs a free shuttle to the wharf for guests bound for Heron Island. It also happens to be Gladstone's best hotel. It caters primarily to business travelers, so it has ample facilities—spacious rooms with a sofa, modern bathrooms with hair dryers, in-room irons and ironing boards, fax/modem outlets, an upscale seafood restaurant, room service, complimentary tea and coffee in the lobby, and an outdoor swimming pool and sundeck. Most rooms have a nice, if rather industrial, view over the port or the city.

HERON ISLAND: CORAL, TURTLES, WHALES & MORE

72km (43¼ miles) NE of Gladstone

When I asked a friend of mine, a longtime travel writer who's been to many enviable spots all over the globe, to name her favorite place, she replied without hesitation, "Heron Island." When you see Heron, it's not difficult to understand her answer. This coral cay speck, a National Park in its own right, is right on the Great Barrier Reef. Step off the beach, and you enter magnificent fields of coral that seem to stretch for miles. Needless to say, snorkeling and reef-walking are major occupations for visitors—if they're not diving, that is, for the island is home to 21 of the world's most stunning dive sites.

Heron is also a rookery for giant green and loggerhead turtles. Resort guests gather on the beach from late November to February to watch the female turtles lay eggs, and from February to mid-April to see the hatched babies scuttle down the sand to the water. Humpback whales pass through from June to September.

GETTING THERE   A courtesy coach meets flights at 10:30am to take guests to Gladstone Marina for the 2-hour launch transfer to the island; it departs 11am daily (except Christmas). Round-trip boat transfer costs A$156 (U.S.$109.20) for adults, half price for kids ages 3 to 14.

WHERE TO STAY & DINE: WORTH A SPLURGE

✪ **Heron Island.** Via Gladstone, QLD 4680 (P&O Australian Resorts, GPO Box 5287, Sydney, NSW 2001). ☎ **13 24 69** in Australia, 800/225 9849 in the U.S. and Canada, 0171/265 3052 in the U.K., 0800/441 766 in New Zealand, 02/9364 8800 (Sydney reservations office), or 07/4972 9055 (the island). Fax 02/9299 2477 (Sydney reservations office). www.poresorts. com.au. E-mail: resorts_reservations@poaustralia.com in Australia; poresorts@ aol.com in the United States; alison.kent@potravel.co.uk in the United Kingdom. 117 units, 87 with bathroom (86 with shower only). Cabins A$170 (U.S.$119) per person, or A$140 (U.S.$98) per person quad-share. A$245 (U.S.$171.50) per person Reef suite, A$278 (U.S.$194.60) per person Heron suite; A$435 (U.S.$304.50) single or A$360 (U.S.$252) per person double Beach House or Point Suite. Children 3–14 50% of adult rate if they use existing bedding (no discount for children in cabins). Free crib. Rates include 3 meals a day. Ask about special packages. AE, BC, DC, JCB, MC, V.

There probably hasn't been a guest yet to Heron who didn't immediately dump the suitcase on the bed the moment they arrived, grab some snorkel gear for A$10 (U.S.$7) per day, and head straight for the water. So beautiful and endless is the coral it's hard to know where to start. If you are unsure how to snorkel, the staff will teach you. At low tide the staff take guided reef-walks among the thousands of coral outcrops. For A$10 (U.S.$7) you can join a guided snorkel safari from the beach, and for A$14 (U.S.$9.80) you can take a 5-minute boat trip to snorkel the reef edge. If you do not want to snorkel, you can still see the coral from the windows of a semi-submersible vessel. Other guest activities make the most of the island's natural attractions—turtle walks during the nesting season, whale-spotting walks in whale season, island ecology and bird-life walks, stargazing, and evening wildlife slide presentations—all free. (Speaking of birds, sea birds abound, so pack a big cheap straw hat for protection from their calling cards). A national parks interpretive center is stocked with reference material on the plants and animals you'll see. In the unlikely event you get bored with snorkeling, there are barbecue cruises to nearby Wilson Island (where there is more snorkeling, actually) and sunset cruises, as well as a beach-side pool and lovely beaches.

The resort runs two dive trips a day to a choice of 21 sites, plus adventure and night dives. For A$125 (U.S.$87.50), first-time divers can learn the basics in the pool in the morning before heading out to the reef for a shallow dive in the company of an instructor. Weekly 4-day open water dive-certification courses cost A$495 (U.S.$346.50) per person. A single dive costs A$44 (U.S.$30.80); packages of four

Money-Saving Tip

Heron Island's only resort isn't cheap, but it appears in this book because it's worth every cent. Day-trippers are not allowed, so you need to stay at least 1 night. All meals, as well as many activities, are included in the tariff, so it's a better value than it looks at first glance.

dives over 2 days are A$144 (U.S.$100.80) if you buy them before you arrive. Dive packages for up to 10 days are available.

With such natural magnificence outside the door, it's not surprising that the resort itself is comfortable rather than glamorous. The Reef Suites are standard motel-style rooms that lack sea views; Heron Suites near the beach have screened-off sleeping quarters; and Point Suites, which have great views, are actually one big room with a king-size bed and a sitting area. There's also one beach house, which has a separate bedroom. All are pleasant and come with hair dryers. Your cheapest option is to stay in one of the 30 clean Turtle Cabins, which come with double and/or single bunks and shared bath facilities. You may end up sharing the cabin with a stranger, but some folks think that's half the fun. None of the accommodations is air-conditioned; all rooms have fans. If you want to stay in touch with the world you will have to use the public telephone and TV.

Dining/Diversions: The maitre d' assigns your table in the restaurant on the first night, similar to the way a ship operates. Breakfast and lunch are fabulous buffets, and dinner is usually an excellent four-course menu. Coffee and snacks are available between meals at the Pandanus Lounge bar overlooking the reef. There is some kind of live entertainment nightly, be it a band, a bush dance, games, dancing, or movies.

Amenities: Swimming pool, free day/night tennis court, game room, boutique/shop, free child care for 5- to 10-year-olds during school vacations, baby-sitting (must be prebooked), conference facilities.

BUNDABERG: GATEWAY TO LADY ELLIOT ISLAND
384km (230½ miles) N of Brisbane; 1,439km (863½ miles) S of Cairns

The small sugar town of Bundaberg is the last point south (or the first point north) from which you can explore the Great Barrier Reef. If you visit the area between November and March, allow an evening to visit the wonderful Mon Repos turtle rookery (see the "Up Close and Personal with a Turtle" story in this section). Divers may want to take in some of Australia's best shore diving right off Bundaberg's beaches.

GETTING THERE & GETTING AROUND   Bundaberg is on the Isis Highway, 52 kilometers (31¼ miles) off the Bruce Highway from Gin Gin in the north and 55 kilometers (33 miles) off the Bruce Highway from just north of Childers in the south. Ansett subsidiary **Flight West Airlines** and Qantas subsidiary **Sunstate Airlines** fly to Bundaberg daily from Brisbane and Rockhampton. From Cairns it's a "milk run" via Townsville, Mackay, and Rockhampton. Sunstate flies from Gladstone twice a week.

Queensland Rail (☎ **13 22 32** in Queensland, or 07/3235 1122) trains stop in Bundaberg most days en route between Brisbane and Cairns. The fare is A$43 (U.S.$30.10) from Brisbane; fares range from A$118 (U.S.$82.60) for a sitting berth to A$226 (U.S.$158.20) for a first-class berth from Cairns. **McCafferty's** and **Greyhound Pioneer** operate many daily coach services from Brisbane and Cairns. The trip from Brisbane takes 6½ hours, and the fare is A$43 (U.S.$30.10). From Cairns it is a 23-hour trip, and the fare is A$115 (U.S.$110.60).

All the big car rental companies are in Bundaberg: **Avis** (☎ 07/4152 1877), **Budget** (☎ 07/4153 1600), **Hertz** (☎ 07/4155 2755) and **Thrifty** (☎ 07/4151 6222).

VISITOR INFORMATION   The **Bundaberg District Tourism and Development Board Information Center** is at 271 Bourbong St. at Mulgrave Street, Bundaberg (☎ **1800/060 499** in Australia, or 07/4152 2333; fax 07/4153 1444). It's open daily from 9am to 5pm, 10am to 3pm on public holidays.

Up Close & Personal with a Turtle

It was just after 7pm when we got the call. "We've got hatchers, repeat hatchers!" came the crackly message over the radio, and two minutes later I was stumbling along the beach in the dark with 69 other excited people.

Our mission? To stare awestruck as baby turtles emerged from their sandy nest. Every night from mid-November to early February, folks flock to Mon Repos Beach in Bundaberg to see giant female loggerheads inch their way up past the high-tide mark, laboriously dig a hole in the sand, and lay their eggs. Then every evening from January to mid-March, you get to watch the youngsters hatch.

By the time we reached a hole in the sand that was being guarded by state Department of Environment rangers, tiny turtles petite enough to fit in a matchbox were streaming out, little flippers waving. They moved fast because even under cover of night, seabirds, crabs, and dingoes can pounce on them before they reach the water. Out of a thousand babies, only one survives.

We handed one infant around to inspect it, as it peeked at us with the cutest, beadiest eyes and flapped its flippers like mad. When every last turtle was out, the rangers got us to form two lines down the beach like a guard of honor, and the turtles raced down the corridor to the water. Within 15 minutes, all 100 or so were safely in the waves. Next the rangers "processed" the nest to count the number of dead and unhatched babies. We found one little fella still alive, caught up in grass roots, and set him free.

Mon Repos Conservation Park is one of the two largest loggerhead turtle rookeries in the South Pacific. The visitor center by the beach has a great educational display on the turtle life cycle and shows films at approximately 7:30pm each night in summer. Visitors can turn up anytime from 7pm on; the action goes on through the night, sometimes as late as 6am. You may have to wait around for quite a while. Nesting happens around high tide; hatching usually occurs between 8pm and midnight. Try to get there early to join the first group of 70 people, the maximum allowed at one laying or hatching. Crowds can be up to 500 strong in mid-December and January. Take a flashlight if you can.

The ✪ **Mon Repos Turtle Rookery** (☎ **07/4159 1652** for the visitor center) is 14 kilometers (8½ miles) east of Bundaberg's town center. Follow Bourbong Street out of town toward Burnett Heads as it becomes Bundaberg–Bargara Road. Take the Port Road to the left and look for the MON REPOS signs to the right. Admission is A$4 (U.S.$2.80) for adults, A$2 (U.S.$1.40) for seniors and children ages 5 to 15, and A$10 (U.S.$7) for a family.

WHAT TO SEE & DO

The best shore diving in Queensland is in Bundaberg's **Woongarra Marine Park.** It has soft and hard corals, urchins, rays, sea snakes, and 60 fish species, plus a World War II Beaufort bomber wreck. There are several scuba operators. **Salty's** (☎ **1800/ 625 476** in Australia, or 07/4151 6422; fax 07/4151 4938) rents dive gear for A$30 (U.S.$21) and most mornings will give you a lift down to the beach and point out some good spots. If you want a dive master to accompany you, take one of their boat trips, which cost A$55 (U.S.$38.50) for one dive or A$75 (U.S.$52.50) for two, including gear. They also run four-day learn-to-dive courses priced from a very affordable A$149 (U.S.$104.30) per person. The courses are cheap because there's no need to rent a boat to get students to the shore coral.

WHERE TO STAY

Acacia Motor Inn. 248 Bourbong St., Bundaberg, QLD 4670. ☎ **1800/35 1375** in Australia, or 07/4152 3411. Fax 07/4152 2387. 26 units. A/C TV TEL. A$60 (U.S.$42) single; A$70 (U.S.$49) double. Additional person A$10 (U.S.$7) adults, A$6 (U.S.$4.20) children under 12. A$5 (U.S.$3.50) crib. AE, BC, DC, MC, V.

This tidy Flag motel is a short stroll from the town center. It offers slightly dated but clean, well-kept rooms and extra-large family rooms at a decent price. Some rooms have hair dryers. Local restaurants provide room service, and many are within walking distance. There's a pool.

LADY ELLIOT ISLAND
80km (48 miles) NE of Bundaberg

The southernmost Great Barrier Reef island, Lady Elliot is a 42-hectare (105-acre) coral cay ringed by a wide shallow lagoon filled with dazzling coral life.

Reef walking, snorkeling, and diving are the main reasons people come to this coral cay that's so small you can walk across it in 15 minutes. You may snorkel and reef-walk during only the 2 to 3 hours before and after high tide, so plan your schedule accordingly. You will see dazzling corals and brilliantly colored fish, clams, sponges, urchins, and anemones. Divers will see a good range of marine life, including green and loggerhead turtles (which nest on the beach from November to March). Whales pass by from June to September.

Lady Elliot is a sparse, grassy island rookery, not a lush tropical paradise, so don't expect white sand and palm trees. Some folks will find it too spartan; others will relish chilling out in a beautiful, peaceful location with reef all around. Just be prepared for the musty smell and constant noise of those birds.

GETTING THERE   You reach the island via a 25-minute flight from Bundaberg. Connections are available from Hervey Bay. Book your air travel along with your accommodation. Round-trip fares are A$145 (U.S.$101.50) for adults and A$73 (U.S.$51.10) for children ages 3 to 14. Day trips from Bundaberg or Hervey Bay are A$185 (U.S.$129.50) for adults and A$98 (U.S.$68.60) for children, including snorkel gear, a guided reef walk, and lunch.

WHERE TO STAY

Lady Elliot Island Resort. Great Barrier Reef via Bundaberg. (P.O. Box 206, Torquay, QLD 4655). ☎ **1800/072 200** in Australia, or 07/4125 5344. Fax 07/4125 5778. 40 units, 20 with bathroom (shower only). A$135–$170 (U.S.$94.50–$119) single; A$150–$260 (U.S.$105–$182) double or triple; A$236–$440 (U.S.$165.20–$308) quad. Children A$38–$65 (U.S.$26.60–45.50). Meal packages available. Ask about 2-, 4-, 5-, and 7-night packages, and dive packages. AE, BC, DC, MC, V.

You could say Lady Elliot is the least glamorous of all the Great Barrier Reef islands. If the wildlife reminds you of *The Birds*, the accommodations may make you think you're on the set of *M*A*S*H**. Rooms are basic. Reef units have a double bed (some also have two bunks), a chair or two, wardrobe space, and a deck with views through the trees to the sea. Island suites are more luxurious and have a tiny kitchenette, a

---

Travel Tip

When you land on the grass airstrip at Lady Elliot Island, you'll think you're on the set of Hitchcock's *The Birds*. The air is thick with tens of thousands of swirling noddy terns and bridal terns that nest in every available branch and leave their mark on every available surface, including you (so bring a big cheap straw hat for protection).

diminutive living/dining area, one or two separate bedrooms, and great sea views from the deck. Both room types have modern bathrooms, a fridge, and tea and coffee. The lodge rooms contain simply a bed or bunks and a small wardrobe. The 14 permanent tents, which have electric lighting and a wooden floor, are actually more spacious and cooler than the lodges. Lodges and tents share the public toilets and showers. All accommodations have fans. There are few resort facilities, other than a boutique, a swimming pool, a casual bar and snack area, and an education center. There is no air-conditioning, no keys (secure storage is at front desk), no TVs, no radio, and only one public telephone. The food is basic. The low-key activities program includes things like bush-tucker tours, fish feeding, guided snorkeling, badminton, and movie screenings, most of which are free. Snorkel gear costs A$5 (U.S.$3.50) a day for mask and snorkel, A$5 (U.S.$3.50) for fins, and A$10 (U.S.$7) for a half wet suit. Dives cost A$67.50 (U.S.$47.25) for certified divers and A$110 (U.S.$77) non-divers who want to take an introductory dive. The island accommodates no more than 140 guests at any one time, so you pretty much get the reef to yourself.

7 Fraser Island: Eco-Adventures & 4WD Fun

1,547 (928¼ miles) S of Cairns; 260km (156 miles) N of Brisbane; 15km (9 miles) E of Hervey Bay

The biggest sand island in the world, this 162,000-hectare (405,000-acre) World Heritage–listed island off the central Queensland coast attracts a curious but happy mix of sensitive ecotourists and Aussie "blokes" who like fishing. Fraser is a pristine vista of eucalyptus woodlands, soaring dunes, gin-clear creeks, ancient rain forest, postcard-blue lakes, ochre-colored sand cliffs, and a stunning 75-mile-long beach. For 4WD fans though, Fraser's true beauty lies in its complete absence of paved roads. On weekends when the fish are running, it's nothing to see 100 4WDs lining 75-Mile Beach. The heady mix of a big catch, too much liquid amber (beer), and a powerful 4WD leads to so much wild driving up and down the beach that the police do random blood-alcohol breath tests on the sand on Friday and Saturday nights!

Fraser is not a well-known hitching post on the international tourist trail. Some folk think it's boring, but if you like your nature natural, it might be your kind of place.

ESSENTIALS

GETTING THERE   **Hervey** (pronounced "Harvey") **Bay** is the key gateway to the island, which is approximately 15 kilometers (9 miles) across the Great Sandy Straits. Take the Bruce Highway to Maryborough, and follow the 34-kilometer (20½-mile) road to Hervey Bay. From the north turn off the highway at Torbanlea, north of Maryborough, and cut across to Hervey Bay. Allow 5 hours from Brisbane and 3 from the Sunshine Coast. **Fraser Coast Secure Vehicle Storage** (☎ 07/4125 2783) at 629 The Esplanade, in Hervey Bay, will store your car for A$3 (U.S.$2.10) to A$8 (U.S.$5.60) per 24 hours.

Guests at Kingfisher Bay Resort (see "Where to Stay & Dine: Worth a Splurge," below) can get to the island aboard the **Kingfisher Bay Fastcat,** which departs the **Urangan Boat Harbour** at Hervey Bay six times a day from 8:30am to 6:30pm, or 7pm some days. Round-trip fare for the 40-minute trip is A$30 (U.S.$21) for adults and A$15 (U.S.$10.50) for children ages 4 to 14. The resort runs a courtesy shuttle from the Hervey Bay airport and coach terminal to the harbor.

Four-wheel-drive vehicles have to be transferred by **Fraser Venture barge** (☎ 07/4125 4444) from River Heads, 17 kilometers (10¼ miles) south of Hervey Bay. The round-trip fare for vehicle and driver is A$65 (U.S.$45.50), plus A$4 (U.S.$2.80) for each extra passenger. The barge leaves several times a day.

Flight West Airlines (book through Ansett) and **Sunstate Airlines** (book through Qantas) have direct flights from Brisbane to Hervey Bay. From Cairns and other northern cities, you must fly to Brisbane first.

Both **Greyhound Pioneer** and **McCafferty's** coaches stop in Hervey Bay on their Brisbane–Cairns routes. The 5-hour trip from Brisbane costs A$32 (U.S.$22.40). From Cairns it's A$132 (U.S.$92.40) for the 24-hour trip.

The nearest train station is in Maryborough West, 34 kilometers (20¼ miles) from Hervey Bay. Passengers on the high-speed Tilt train (Sunday to Friday) and the *Spirit of Capricorn* (Saturday) can book a connecting bus service to Urangan Boat Harbour via **Queensland Rail** (☎ **13 22 32** in Queensland, or 07/3235 1122). The fare from Brisbane for the 2½-hour Tilt train trip or the 4½-hour *Spirit of Capricorn* trip is A$37 (U.S.$25.90), plus A$4.30 (U.S.$3) for the bus. Fares are A$126 (U.S.$88.20) in a sitting berth and A$156 (U.S.$109.20) in an economy-class sleeper from Cairns (trip time: just under 27 hours). Train passengers from the north must take a courtesy shuttle to Maryborough Central, then take the next available local bus to Urangan Boat Harbour.

VISITOR INFORMATION   Write for information to **Hervey Bay Tourism & Development Bureau,** 10 Bideford St., Torquay, Hervey Bay, QLD 4655 (☎ **1800/ 811 728** in Australia, or 07/4124 9609; fax 07/4125 4341). The **Marina Kiosk** at Urangan Boat Harbour has information and maps. There are several National Parks & Wildlife Service information offices on the island.

There are no towns and very few facilities, food stores, or services on the island, so if you're camping, bring supplies with you.

GETTING AROUND   4WD is the only permissible mode of transport on the island. **Kingfisher Bay Resort 4WD Hire** (☎ **07/4120 3366**) rents 4WDs for A$175 (U.S.$122.50) a day, sometimes less in low season (plus an A$500/U.S.$350 bond). The staff will give you a thorough briefing on 4WD techniques and a report on day-to-day conditions on the island. Book well ahead as they do not have a lot of vehicles. You'll pay about A$150 (U.S.$105) a day if you rent a 4WD in Hervey Bay, but then you'll have to pay the vehicle ferry fee; contact **Bay 4WD Centre** (☎ **07/ 4128 2981**) or **Island Explorers** (☎ **07/4124 3770**). In Noosa on the Sunshine Coast, contact **Sunshine 4WD Hire** (☎ **07/5447 3702**). You must purchase a Vehicle Access Permit for your 4WD; the permit costs A$30 (U.S.$21) if you get it from your rental car company or at Urangan Boat Harbour, or A$40 (U.S.$28) if you purchase it at one of the Queensland Parks & Wildlife Service offices on the island. Your rental company will usually arrange barge transfers and secure car storage.

Fraser Island Taxi Service (☎ **07/4127 9188**) will take you anywhere on the island—in a 4WD, of course. It's based at Eurong on the eastern side of the island. A typical fare, say from Kingfisher Bay Resort to Lake McKenzie, is A$50 (U.S.$35) one-way.

ECO-EXPLORING THE ISLAND

Fraser's gem-like turquoise lakes and tea-colored "perched" lakes in the dunes are among the island's biggest attractions. ۞ **Lake McKenzie** is the blue kind and is absolutely beautiful; a swim here may be the highlight of your visit. **Lake Birrabeen** is another popular swimming spot. A giant sand dune is gradually engulfing peaceful **Lake Wabby**—that's bad for the lake but good for your photo album as you'll be able to snap some stunning shots! Don't miss a refreshing swim in the fast-flowing clear shallows of ۞ **Eli Creek.** Wade up the creek for a mile or two and let the current carry you back down. You should also take the boardwalk through a verdant forest of palms and ferns along the banks of **Wanggoolba Creek.**

4WD Fundamentals

Driving a 4WD is great fun and not hard for a beginner to learn, but if you've never driven one before you should get a good briefing from your rental company before you head out. Fraser's loose sand tracks can be tricky, and getting bogged is common. The beach can be dangerous for the novice—if you travel too high up on the beach, you can get trapped in soft sand; if you travel too low, a surprise wave can bog your vehicle in treacherously soft sand under the water (and rust your car). Car rental companies don't like that, and they can smell salt on an axle a mile away! Stick to the firmest tracks, know the tides, and don't be afraid to ask for advice. You'll have to drive a lot slower on a 4WD trail than you would on a conventional road; take that into account when you plan your day. For example, it takes a full day to get to Indian Head and back, and then only when the tide is favorable. Look out for planes landing on the beach.

Unfortunately, you can't swim at ✪ **75 Mile Beach,** which hugs the eastern edge of the island, because of strong currents and a healthy shark population. Instead, swim in the ✪ **Champagne Pools** (also called the Aquarium)—pockets of soft sand protected from the worst of the waves by rocks. The bubbling seawater turns the pools into miniature spas. The pools are just north of **Indian Head,** a 60-meter (197-foot) rocky outcrop at the northern end of the beach.

When I was a kid, it was popular to bring back as souvenirs from Fraser bottles of striped red, ochre, gold, and black sand. These days, people prefer to view the island's famous colored sand in its natural setting—the 70-meter (230-foot) cliffs called the **Cathedrals,** which stretch for miles north of the settlement of Happy Valley on the eastern side of the Island.

Some of Queensland's best **fishing** is on Fraser Island. Anglers can throw a line in the surf gutters off the beach (freshwater fishing is not allowed). Bream, whiting, flathead, and swallowtail are the beach catches. Indian Head is good for rock species and tailor; and the waters east off Waddy Point yield northern and southern reef fish. Kingfisher Bay Resort (see "Where to Stay & Dine: Worth a Splurge") offers free fish clinics, rents tackle, and organizes half-day fishing jaunts.

From August through October, tour boats crowd the straits to see humpback whales returning to Antarctica with calves in tow. Kingfisher Bay Resort runs a ✪ **whale-watching cruise** from Urangan Harbour. **Mimi Macpherson** (☎ **07/4124 7247**), sister of supermodel Elle, runs a cruise from Hervey Bay.

WHERE TO STAY & DINE: WORTH A SPLURGE

✪ **Kingfisher Bay Resort.** Fraser Island (PMB 1, Urangan, QLD 4655). ☎ **1800/072 555** in Australia, or 07/4120 3333. Fax 07/4120 3326. www.kingfisherbay.com. E-mail: Reservations@kingfisherbay.com. 261 units, 252 with bathroom. TV TEL. A$220 (U.S.$154) double or triple. A$750 (U.S.$525) 3 nights in 2-bedroom villa (sleeps 5), A$960–$1,260 (U.S.$672–$882) 3 nights in 3-bedroom villa (sleeps 8); minimum 3-night stay in villas. Additional person A$20 (U.S.$14) extra. Free crib. Ask about package deals. AE, BC, DC, MC, V.

This sleek, environment-friendly ecoresort lies low along Fraser's west coast. The air-conditioned guest rooms are smart and contemporary, with a Japanese screen opening onto a balcony looking into the bush. The 2- and 3-bedroom villas have kitchens. Travelers on one of the resort's organized package tours (see "Organized Tours & Package Deals on Fraser Island" below) stay in the pleasantly rustic Wilderness Lodge, which is actually eight lodges, each with four double, twin, or four-bunk rooms; simple but atmospheric shared living quarters; shared bathrooms; and a deck. They are not air-conditioned but do have fans. Lodge guests have access only to the Sandbar

Organized Tours & Package Deals on Fraser Island

If staying at the Kingfisher Bay Resort seems beyond your budget, consider taking an action-packed day trip or booking a package deal. Kingfisher Bay Resort itself offers a range of packages. Its 3-day, 2-night package, including Fastcat transfers from Hervey Bay, tours of the island, and quad-share accommodations in the Wilderness Lodge (see "Where to Stay & Dine: Worth a Splurge" above), is just A$225 (U.S.$157.50) per person, and that includes most meals. The resort also offers a day trip from Hervey Bay with touring and lunch for A$75 (U.S.$52.50) per person.

restaurant and pool, but heck, that's the most fun place to be anyhow, and you are still free to join in all the daily activities.

The resort's impressive lineup of ecoeducational activities includes daily 4WD tours with a ranger to points of interest around the island, free guided ranger walks daily, and an excellent free Junior Eco-Ranger program on weekends and school vacations. You can also join bird-watching tours, fly- and reef fishing trips, guided canoe trips, sunset champagne sails, and dugong- (manatee) spotting cruises. Wildlife videos play continuously in the lobby, and the on-site ranger office lists the animals and plants you are most likely to spot.

Other facilities include two swimming pools, Jacuzzi, sundeck, water sports equipment and fishing tackle for rent, day/night tennis courts, volleyball, game room, tour desk, baby-sitting, and (for a fee) a kids' club.

CAMPING

Fraser has eight camping areas, most with showers and toilets. Camping permits, which you can buy at the various Queensland Parks & Wildlife Service offices on the island (☎ 07/4127 9128), are A$3.50 (U.S.$2.45) per person per night.

8 The Sunshine Coast

If not many international visitors make it to the Sunshine Coast, that's probably because they can't elbow their way in past all the upper-crust Sydneysiders and Melburnites filling the hotel rooms and hogging the restaurant tables. The warm sunshine and miles of pleasant beaches on this stretch of coastline an hour and a half north of Brisbane attract Aussie southerners like flies to a honey pot. Whereas the Gold Coast (see section 9 later in this chapter) is like a mini-Florida, all built-up and tacky, the Sunshine Coast is like Hawaii, all pineapple plantations and sugarcane. Despite the unsightly commercial shop development that has sprung up in recent years, the Sunshine Coast is still a great spot if you like chilling out on white beaches and enjoying a good meal.

The Sunshine Coast commences at Caloundra, 83 kilometers (50 miles) north of Brisbane and runs all the way to Rainbow Beach, 40 kilometers (24 miles) north of the village of **Noosa Heads,** where the fashionable action is. There are plenty of inexpensive motels and holiday apartments to rent. Noosa's restaurants are great, and although none are outrageously expensive, few are cheap—so be prepared to spend up a little if you want to eat out.

Most of the Sunshine Coast's sunbathing, dining, shopping, and socializing takes place on trendy Hastings Street, the main strip of Noosa Heads, and on the adjacent Main Beach. The commercial strip of **Noosa Junction** is a 1-minute drive away; a 3-minute drive west along the river takes you to the low-key town of **Noosaville,** where the mass of ordinary Aussie families rent holiday apartments.

SUNSHINE COAST ESSENTIALS

GETTING THERE   If you're driving from Brisbane, take the Bruce Highway north to Aussie World theme park at Palmview, then exit onto the Sunshine Motorway to Noosa Heads. The trip takes about 2 hours.

Sunstate Airlines (book through Qantas) has many flights daily (trip time: 30 minutes) from Brisbane to the **Sunshine Coast Airport** in Maroochydore, 42 kilometers (25¼ miles) south of Noosa Heads. **Qantas** and **Ansett** both fly from Sydney about once a day and have direct flights from Melbourne on weekends. From Cairns, you will need to fly to Brisbane and back to Maroochydore. **Henry's Airport Bus Service** (☎ **07/5474 0199**) meets all flights; door-to-door transfers to Noosa Heads are A$12 (U.S.$8.40) for adults and A$6 (U.S.$4.20) for kids ages 4 to 14, one-way. Bookings are not necessary.

The nearest train station to Noosa Heads is in Cooroy, 25 kilometers (15 miles) away, to which **Queensland Rail** (☎ **13 22 32** in Queensland, or ☎ 07/3235 1122) operates two daily services from Brisbane on its suburban **CityTrain** (☎ **07/3235 5555**) network. The trip takes about 2 hours and 20 minutes and the fare is A$13 (U.S.$9.10). Queensland Rail's long-distance trains departing Brisbane pick up but do not drop off passengers in Cooroy, with the exception of the high-speed Tilt train (which runs Sunday to Friday) and the *Spirit of Capricorn* (which runs Saturday). The fare on both trains is A$21 (U.S.$14.70). Several Queensland Rail trains make the 29½-hour trip from Cairns each week; the fare is A$131 (U.S.$91.70) for a sitting berth, A$161 (U.S.$112.70) for an economy-class sleeper. Local bus company **Sunbus** (☎ **07/5492 8700**) meets most trains at Cooroy station and travels to Noosa Heads; take bus no. 12.

Several coach companies have service to Noosa Heads from Brisbane and elsewhere on the Gold Coast, including **Sun-Air** (☎ **1800/804 340** in Australia, or 07/5478 2811) and **Suncoast Pacific** (☎ **07/5443 1011** on the Sunshine Coast, 07/3236 1901 in Brisbane) which also runs from Hervey Bay. **McCafferty's** and **Greyhound Pioneer** have many daily services from all major towns along the Bruce Highway between Brisbane and Cairns. Trip time to Noosa Heads is 2 hours and 20 minutes from Brisbane, and just under 26 hours from Cairns. The single fare is A$15 (U.S.$10.50) from Brisbane and A$139 (U.S.$97.30) from Cairns.

VISITOR INFORMATION   Write for information to **Tourism Sunshine Coast Ltd,** P.O. Box 264, Mooloolaba, QLD 4557 (☎ **07/5477 7311,** fax 07/5477 7322). In Noosa, drop into the **Tourism Noosa Information Centre** (☎ **07/5447 4988,** fax 07/5474 9494) at the eastern roundabout on Hastings Street where it intersects Noosa Drive. It's open daily from 9am to 5pm.

GETTING AROUND   Major car rental companies on the Sunshine Coast are **Avis** (☎ 07/5443 5055 Sunshine Coast Airport, 07/5447 4933 Noosa Heads), **Budget** (☎ 07/5448 7455 airport, 07/5447 4588 Noosa Heads), **Hertz** (07/5443 6755 airport, 07/5447 2253 Noosa Heads), and **Thrifty** (☎ 07/5443 1733 airport, 07/5447 2299 Noosa Heads). Myriad local outfits rent cars and 4WDs, including **Trusty** (☎ 07/5447 4777) and **Sunshine Coast Car Hire** (☎ 07/5447 2859).

The local bus company is **Sunbus** (☎ **07/5492 8700**).

EXPLORING THE AREA

HITTING THE BEACH & OTHER OUTDOOR FUN   **Main Beach** is the place to swim, surf, and sunbathe. If the crowd of bikini-clad supermodel look-alikes is too much of a scene for you, hop in a cab or take bus no. 10 to **Sunshine Beach,** just behind Noosa Junction off the David Low Way, about 2 kilometers (1¼ miles) from Noosa Heads. It's less fussy and just as beautiful. Both beaches are patrolled 365 days a year. Two-time Australian and World Pro-Am champ **Merrick Davis** (☎ **0418/**

The Sunshine Coast

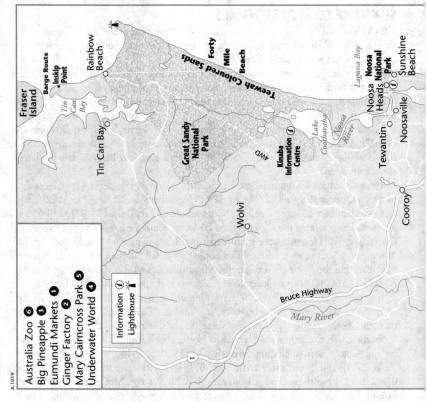

Fraser Island
Barge Route
Inskip Point
Rainbow Beach
Tin Can Bay
Tin Can Bay
Forty Mile Beach
Teewah Coloured Sands
Great Sandy National Park
4WD
Kinaba Information Centre
Lake Cootharaba
Noosa River
Laguna Bay
Noosa Noosa National Park
Noosa Heads
Tewantin
Noosaville
Sunshine Beach
Wolvi
Cooroy
Bruce Highway
Mary River

Information
Lighthouse

Australia Zoo ⑥
Big Pineapple ③
Eumundi Markets ①
Ginger Factory ②
Mary Cairncross Park ⑤
Underwater World ④

A-1019

---

787 577 mobile phone) gives 90-minute surf lessons on Main Beach daily to beginners and experts for A$30 (U.S.$21) per person. He will pick you up from your Noosa accommodations gratis. Merrick also rents surfboards and body boards.

If you want to rent a windsurfer, canoe, kayak, surf ski, catamaran, jet ski, or canopied fishing boat—that you can play with on the Noosa River, or take upriver into Great Sandy National Park (see below)—check out the dozens of outfits along Gympie Terrace between James Street and Robert Street in Noosaville. One of the biggest is **Pelican Boat Hire** (☎ **07/5449 7239**), beside the Big Pelican. Expect to pay about A$8 (U.S.$5.60) an hour for a canoe and A$25 (U.S.$17.50) for a catamaran, and A$25 (U.S.$17.50) for a canopied fishing boat for 2 hours. If you would rather have someone show you where the fish are biting, there is no end of guided fishing charters. **River Fishing Safaris** (☎ **07/5447 1121,** or 0412/630 731 mobile phone) runs escorted estuary and river trips for experts and beginners. A half-day outing is A$55 (U.S.$38.50) for adults and A$25 (U.S.$17.50) for kids.

EXPLORING NOOSA NATIONAL PARK A 10-minute stroll northeast from Hastings Street brings you to the delightful 432-hectare (1,080-acre) Noosa National Park. Proving that nature and humankind can live in harmony, a koala colony has set up house in the parking lot (or more likely, the parking lot set up house around them). A network of well sign-posted, not-too-difficult walking trails leads through the bush. The most scenic is the 2.7 kilometer (1½ mile) coastal trail. The shortest trail is the 1 kilometer (just over ½ mile) Palm Grove circuit; the longest is the 4.7 kilometer (3 mile) Tanglewood trail inland to Hell's Gates.

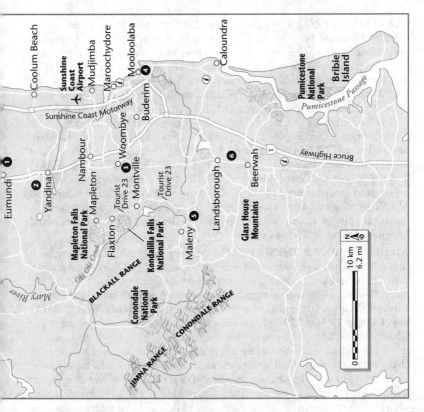

NORTH OF NOOSA: GREAT SANDY NATIONAL PARK   Stretching north of Noosa along the coast is the 56,000-hectare (140,000-acre) Great Sandy National Park (often called **Cooloola National Park**), home to forests, beach, and freshwater lakes, including the state's largest, **Lake Cootharaba.** The popular thing to do here is to cruise the silent Everglades formed by the Noosa River and tributary creeks. The park's information office, the **Kinaba Information Center** (☎ **07/5449 7364**), is on the western shore of Lake Cootharaba, about 30 kilometers (18 miles) from Noosaville. It has a display on the area's geography and a mangrove boardwalk to explore; it's accessible only by boat, which you can easily rent from the numerous boat-rental outfits in Noosaville (see above). Several operators run half-day cruises into the Everglades, and guided kayak tours explore the park's lower reaches (the Everglades are in the northern end of the Park, too far to kayak to).

The other way to see the park is to travel in a 4WD along **40-Mile Beach,** a designated highway with traffic laws, for a close-up view of the **Teewah colored sand cliffs.** We think the sands are a bit over-rated, but this is a great place to get away from the crowds and enjoy magnificent "in the wild" swimming in turquoise surf. Lifeguards do not patrol the beach, so swim with others for safety. Some days the beach is so busy it looks like a 4WD convention. Tours are available, or you can rent a 4WD and explore on your own. To reach the beach, cross Noosa River on the ferry at Tewantin, then take Maximilian Drive for 4 kilometers (2½ miles) to the beach. Stock up on water, food, and gas in Tewantin. The ferry (☎ **07/5449 8013**) costs A$8 (U.S.$5.60) per vehicle round-trip; it operates from 6am to 10pm Sunday through Thursday, and 6am to midnight Friday and Saturday.

DAY TRIPS TO FRASER ISLAND   Fraser Island (see the "Fraser Island" section earlier in this chapter) is accessible on a long 4WD-only day trip—11 or 12 hours— from Noosa. You won't see everything in 1 day or even 2, and tides can limit your routes, so plan ahead. Several car-rental companies in Noosa, including Thrifty (see "Getting Around" earlier in this section) and **Sunshine 4WD Hire** (☎ 07/ **5447 3702**), offer 2-day Fraser packages including 4WD rental, maps, tips on where to drive and what to see, and even camping gear. Expect to pay about A$110 (U.S.$77) per day for a little Suzuki Sierra soft-top, plus about A$85 (U.S.$59.50) for a complete two-person camping kit. You'll have to cross to the island on the **Rainbow Venture barge** (☎ **07/5486 3154**), which makes the 15-minute trip to Hook Point on the island's southern tip daily from 7am to 4:30pm. The round-trip fare is A$55 (U.S.$38.50) per vehicle and driver plus A$1 (U.S.70¢) per passenger; you will also have to purchase a National Parks & Wildlife Service Vehicle Access Permit for A$30 (U.S.$21) per vehicle. Several companies in Noosa Heads offer organized one- and two-day camping or accommodated 4WD tours to the island. Contact **Fraser Island Adventure Tours** (☎ **07/5444 6957**).

WILDLIFE PARKS & THEME PARKS   Maybe it's something in the fertile volcanic soil, but small-scale theme parks centered around Aussie wildlife or local produce thrive on the Sunshine Coast. Here are some of the most interesting.

An 80-meter (256-foot) moving walkway through a tank filled with sharks, stingrays, groupers, eels, and coral is the highlight at **Underwater World** (☎ 07/ **5444 8488**, or 07/5444 2255 for recorded information), an aquarium complex at The Wharf at Mooloolaba, 31 kilometers (18½ miles) south of Noosa Heads. Kids can pick up starfish and sea cucumbers in the touch pool. There are also static displays on whales and sharks, shark-breeding and freshwater crocodile talks, a subsonic adventure ride, and an educational 30-minute seal show. It's open daily from 9am to 6pm (last entry at 5pm). Closed Christmas. Admission is A$18.90 (U.S.$13.25) for adults, A$12 (U.S.$8.40) for seniors and students, A$9.90 (U.S.$6.95) for children ages 3 to 15, and A$49.90 (U.S.$34.95) for a family pass. Allow 2 hours to see everything, more if you want to attend all the talks. Take bus route no. 1.

At the small but charming **Ginger Factory,** Pioneer Road, Yandina (☎ 07/ **5446 7100**), you can watch the works of a ginger-processing plant that supplies most of the world's sugar-cured ginger. You can also shop for ginger plants and a huge range of ginger products, and browse a handful of gift shops. Skip the short and uninteresting train trip. Entry is free. The park is open from 9am to 5pm daily; closed Christmas. (The factory closes some weekends and for a couple of weeks around Christmas; call first, to make sure factory is open before you head out.) Within the park grounds is a tiny wildlife sanctuary housing koalas (you can get yourself photographed cuddling one at 12:30pm for an extra A$6/U.S.$4.20), freshwater crocodiles, wombats, birds, and other native animals. It's really too small to be worth the admission price, but your kids may like it. Admission is A$6 (U.S.$4.20) for adults, A$5 (U.S.$3.50) for seniors, A$4 (U.S.$2.80) for students, A$3 (U.S.$2.10) for kids up to age 16, and A$15.50 (U.S.$10.85) for families. Allow 90 minutes for both the factory and the wildlife park.

At the **Big Pineapple** (☎ **07/5442 1333**), 6 kilometers (3½ miles) south of Nambour on the Nambour Connection Road in Woombye—don't worry, you can't miss the 16-meter- (52½-ft.) tall yellow fruit—you can take a train ride through a working pineapple plantation, ride through a rain forest and a macadamia farm in a macadamia-shaped carriage (April to Nov), and take a boat ride through a hydroponics greenhouse. The park also has a baby animal farm, kangaroos, koalas, a rain-forest walk, and a gift shop. It's open 365 days a year from 9am to 5pm; (opens later on Christmas and ANZAC Day; call for exact time). Entry is free; the train, macadamia tour, and boat ride each cost A$6 (U.S.$4.20) to A$8 (U.S.$5.60) per person. A family pass to all tours is A$47 (U.S.$32.90). Allow half a day if you do everything.

Farther south on the Glass House Mountains Tourist Drive 24 at Beerwah, off the Bruce Highway, is **Australia Zoo** (☎ **07/5494 1134**), which showcases Australian animals in interactive demonstrations with their keepers. The zoo's owners, Steve and Terri Irwin, are renowned in Australia for manhandling dangerous saltwater crocs. There's otter feeding at 10:30am; a snake show at 11am; Galapagos tortoise feeding at 11:30am; an American alligator show at noon; otter feeding again at 1pm; a free photo opportunity of you patting (not cuddling) a koala at 2:30pm; another photo op at 2:45pm, this time of you with a python, for an extra A$8 (U.S.$5.60); a birds-of-prey demonstration at 3pm; and otters again at 3:30pm. The highlight is the saltwater croc show at 1:30pm. You can also hand-feed 'roos, watch venomous snakes and pythons, and see wild birds on the grounds. Admission is A$13 (U.S.$9.10) for adults, A$10 (U.S.$7) for seniors and students, A$6.50 (U.S.$4.55) for kids ages 3 to 14, and A$37 (U.S.$25.90) for a family. The park is open daily 8:30am to 4pm. Closed Christmas.

A SCENIC MOUNTAINTOP DRIVE THROUGH THE SUNSHINE COAST HINTERLAND

A leisurely drive along the lush green ridge-top of the ✪ **Blackall Ranges** behind Noosa is a popular half- or full-day excursion. Cute mountain villages, full of crafts shops and cafes, and terrific views of the coast are the main attractions. Macadamia nuts, peaches, and other home-grown produce is often for sale by the road at dirt-cheap prices.

If it's Saturday, start at the colorful outdoor ✪ **Eumundi Markets** in the historical village of Eumundi, 13 kilometers (8 miles) west of Noosa along the Eumundi Road. It's a real scene, as trendy locals and visitors wander among dozens of stalls selling locally grown organic lemonade, fruit, groovy hats, teddy bears, antique linen, home-made soaps, handcrafted hardwood furniture—even live emu chicks! When shopping's done, everyone pops into the trendy cafes on Eumundi's main street. The market runs from 6:30am to 2pm.

From Eumundi, take the Bruce Highway down to **Nambour** and turn right onto the Nambour–Mapleton road. (The turn-off is just before you enter Nambour, so if you find yourself in town, you have gone too far.) A winding 12-kilometer (7¼-mile) climb up the range between rolling farmland and forest brings you to **Mapleton,** a neat village with a good pub that does lunch. From here, detour almost 4 kilometers (2½ miles) to see the 120-meter (393½-ft.) falls in **Mapleton Falls National Park.** A pretty 200-meter (656-ft.) bushwalk departs from the lovely picnic grounds and ends with great views over the Obi Obi Valley. There is also a 1.3 kilometer (¾ mile) circuit.

Get back on the main Mapleton–Maleny Road and head south 3.5 kilometers (2 miles) through lush forest and farms to **Flaxton Gardens.** Perched on the cliff with breathtaking coast views is a wine cellar offering tastings and sales, a pottery, a cafe, and a gift shop. A bit farther south you can detour right and walk the 4.6 kilometers (2¾ miles) round-trip trail to the base of the 80-meter (262-ft.) **Kondalilla Falls.** You can swim here, too. It's a slippery downhill walk, and the climb back up can be tough. Keep a sharp lookout in quiet spots and you may see a platypus in the river.

Back on the main road, travel south for 5.5 kilometers (3½ miles) to **Montville.** This cutesy English-style village has become such a tourist stop that it has lost what-ever authentic character it had. Lots of people decry its touristy facade, but everyone still ends up strolling the tree-lined streets and browsing the gift shops and galleries.

The next stop, 13 kilometers (8 miles) down the road, is **Maleny,** which is more modern but less tacky than Montville. Antiques and handcrafts are the things to buy here. Be sure to follow the signs around to Mary Cairncross Park for spectacular views of the ✪ **Glass House Mountains,** 11 volcanic plugs protruding out of the plains. The park has a kiosk, a playground, free wood barbecues, and a rain-forest information center; a nice 1.7 kilometer (1 mile) walking trail loops through the rain forest past some giant strangler figs.

You can either backtrack to Noosa the way you came or, if you're in a hurry, drive down to Landsborough and then rejoin the Bruce Highway.

WHERE TO STAY
IN NOOSA HEADS

✪ **Halse Lodge.** 2 Halse Lane, off Noosa Dr. at Noosa Parade, Noosa Heads, QLD 4567. ☎ **1800/242 567** in Australia, or 07/5447 3377. Fax 07/5447 2929. 7 units, none with bathroom. A$45 (U.S.$31.50) double. A$17–$18 (U.S.$11.90–$12.60) dorm bed. Discounts for YHA/Hostelling International members. Linen A$2 (U.S.$1.40) per person per stay. BC, MC, V.

It's a backpackers' hostel, but don't let that put you off staying here. The gracious National Trust–listed Queenslander house is set in two acres of rain forest on a hill overlooking the town and the sea. It's almost as cozy and welcoming as a B&B, and it's kept extra-clean by on-the-ball managers. There's a kitchen, but smart guests order one of the healthy cooked breakfasts for under A$5 (U.S.$3.50) and dinners for around A$6.50 (U.S.$4.55). Smoking is not permitted.

Jacaranda. 12 Hastings St. ☎ **07/5447 4011** via Holiday Noosa. Fax 07/5447 3410. 28 units (24 with shower only). A/C TV TEL. High season A$105–$120 (U.S.$73.50–$84) studio, A$150–$160 (U.S.$105–$112) suite. Low season A$70–$75 (U.S.$49–$52.50) studio, A$90–$95 (U.S.$63–$66.50) suite. Only weekly rates available in high season. BC, MC, V.

These units are not as fancy as the swank apartment blocks up on the hill, but if you don't mind views of the river instead of the ocean, this neat block set back off the road in the thick of the Hastings Street action will do just fine. Most of the one-bedroom apartments face the Noosa River; a few look onto the parking lot and the small, shady swimming pool. The decor is fine—stone-look tile floors, painted brick walls, and lime-washed furniture—although the kitchens are a little old. The studios are small, dark, and lack views, and have only a toaster and crockery, not a kitchen. Bring your own hair dryer. *Note:* you cannot make international calls on the in-room phones, and you can receive calls during office hours only. The beach is just down the alleyway across the road.

✪ **Noosa Village Motel.** 10 Hastings St., Noosa Heads, QLD 4567. ☎ **07/5447 5800.** Fax 07/5474 9282. 11 (all with shower only). TV. High season A$130 (U.S.$91) double, A$180 (U.S.$126) family room, A$220 (U.S.$154) apt. (sleeps 6). Low season A$80 (U.S.$56) double, A$120 (U.S.$84) family room, A$150 (U.S.$105) apt. Additional person A$10 (U.S.$7) extra. BC, MC, V.

All the nice letters from satisfied guests pinned up on the wall here convinced us that this clean, bright little motel in the heart of Hastings Street was worth recommending—and that's before we saw the pleasant rooms. Each one is spacious and freshly painted with a toaster and crockery, a refrigerator, a small but spotless shower,

---

Travel Tips

Room rates on the Sunshine Coast are mostly moderate, but they jump sharply in the Christmas period from December 26 to January 26, during school holidays, and in the week following Easter. Book well ahead at these times. Weekends are often busy, too.

and a ceiling fan. Better than the rooms, though, is the cheerful atmosphere. Proprietors John and Mary Skelton are continually sprucing up the place.

IN THE HINTERLAND

✪ **Avocado Grove Bed & Breakfast.** 10 Carramar Ct., Flaxton, QLD 4560. ☎ and fax **07/5445 7585.** 4 units, 3 with bathroom (shower only), 1 with private adjacent bathroom. A$80 (U.S.$56) double; A$100 (U.S.$70) suite. Rates include full breakfast. Ask about 2-night weekend and 3-night midweek packages. BC, MC, V. Turn right off ridge-top road onto Ensbey Rd.; Carramar Ct. is the first left.

Noela and Ray Troyahn's modern Queenslander home is in a peaceful rural setting in the middle of an avocado grove just off the ridge-top road. The cozy, comfortable rooms have country-style furniture, full-length windows opening onto private verandahs, fans, and oil heaters for cool mountain nights. Hair dryers are supplied. The big suite downstairs has a TV and a fridge. Colorful parrots and other birds are a common sight. Guests are welcome to picnic on the peaceful sloping lawns that have wonderful views west to Obi Obi Gorge in the Connondale Ranges. Noela prepares a big country-style breakfast, and provides tea and coffee any time. No smoking indoors.

WHERE TO DINE

Hastings Street comes alive at night with vacationers wining and dining at restaurants as sophisticated as those in Sydney and Melbourne. Good inexpensive restaurants are harder to find, and precious few are BYO. Noosa Junction is a better, if less atmospheric, bet for cheap nosh. Noosa National Park has barbecues and tables at the entrance and many quiet spots with great ocean views, so if it's lunchtime, why not picnic?

Café Sulago. 2 Hastings St. ☎ **07/5447 4650.** Reservations recommended. Main courses A$2–$11.90 (U.S.$1.40–$8.35) lunch, A$10.90–$16.50 (U.S.$7.65–$11.55) dinner. BC, MC, V. Daily 8am–3pm; Wed–Mon 6–9pm. CAFE FARE.

Streetside chairs and tables under umbrellas create an atmosphere good enough for a night out at this modest eatery, one of the few in town that's BYO. Lunch might be a seafood platter or Thai fish cakes with salad and sweet chili dipping sauce. You can order cheaper fare from the blackboard menu, which offers sandwiches, hot dogs, burgers, and the like. Choices at dinner include pastas, steak burgers, and seafood, such as the fish of the day in lemon butter, lemon pepper, or crusted with mango and lime mayo for a reasonable A$12.90 (U.S.$9.05). Between 6pm and 7pm, all main courses are A$10.90 (U.S.$7.65). Locals take full advantage of this great deal, so be sure to make a reservation.

✪ **Season.** 30 Hastings St. ☎ **07/5447 3747.** Reservations not accepted. Light meals and main courses A$13–$23 (U.S.$9.10–$16.10). AE, BC, DC, MC, V. Daily 5:30–10pm. MOD OZ.

Ever since chef Gary Skelton opened this casual place, it has been full of vacationing Sydneysiders who used to patronize his groovy Sydney pizza joint. There's a tiny indoor eating room, but most folks line up for a seat at one of the terrazzo tables on the casual verandah. Choose from a sliding scale of dish sizes, ranging from the salmon fish cakes with an avocado, asparagus, and rocket salad, to the chargrilled beef with blue cheese soufflé. The menu varies seasonally, but seafood always seems to get a good run. BYO. Smoking is not permitted.

Wok In Noosa. At the roundabout on Noosa Dr. at Sunshine Beach Rd. ☎ **07/5448 0372.** Main courses A$7.50–$13 (U.S.$5.25–$9.10). No credit cards. Tues–Sun noon–3pm, 5pm–9pm. ASIAN NOODLES.

Locals flock to this clean, cheery joint for fresh, tasty meals that are usually under A$10 (U.S.$7). Most take their food to go, but some stay to eat in the colorful dining room, where you help yourself to cutlery, a bottle opener, and wine glasses. Don't overlook the big range of *laksas*, a satisfying tummy-filler that comes in a bowl the size of a baby's bathtub. They deliver—minimum order is A$15 (U.S.$10.50), plus A$2.50 (U.S.$1.75) delivery charge. Kids' meals are A$5.50 (U.S.$3.85), plus a free popsicle. BYO.

WORTH A SPLURGE

✪ **Artis.** 8 Noosa Dr. ☎ **07/5447 2300.** Reservations recommended. Main courses A$23–$25 (U.S.$16.10–$17.50). AE, BC, DC, MC, V. Daily 6:30pm–late. MOD OZ.

Only uninformed tourists turn up at this elegant A-frame restaurant without a reservation. Everyone else knows to book in advance, so their entree of roasted salmon with molasses-baked ham, Roma tomatoes, and gnocchi doesn't end up going to someone else. The food is not only stylish, it's also hearty and darn good. Desserts are tropical treats such as glazed mango with black sticky rice, and kaffir lime ice cream. The sleek modern interior manages to be warm and intimate, but on a warm night, ask to sit outside on the terrace under the stars and just ignore the noisy traffic. Live jazz plays Friday evening.

9 The Gold Coast

You will either love or hate the Gold Coast. Its fans praise its white-sand beaches that stretch uninterrupted for a glorious 30 kilometers (18 miles), its glitzy shops, its pulsing energy. Its detractors—and there are plenty of 'em—lament its endless strips of neon-lit motels, cheap souvenir shops, soulless apartment towers, and over-exposed sunburned flesh in bikinis and stilettos. In the '50s this strip of coastline was little more than a huddle of holiday shacks, but 40 years of unabashed development has seen touristy tack elevated to new heights Down Under. Build it big and build it fast was the credo, with the result that skyscrapers cast a spoilsport shadow on Surfers Paradise beaches in the afternoon.

Theme parks also draw big crowds to the Gold Coast. The parks are not as large or as sophisticated as Disneyland, but they're exciting enough to get folks from Sydney and Melbourne to hop on a plane. Apart from the three major parks—Dreamworld, Warner Bros. Movie World, and Sea World—there are of plenty of smaller-scale ones. Also attracting crowds are the 40 golf courses, dinner cruises, and loads of adrenaline-based outdoor activities, from bungee jumping to jet skiing. The best activity on the Gold Coast, though, is the natural kind, and it doesn't cost a cent—hitting that surf and lazing on the beach.

GOLD COAST ESSENTIALS

GETTING THERE   By Car   Access to the Gold Coast Highway, which runs the length of the Coast, is off the Pacific Highway from Sydney or Brisbane. The drive takes about 80 minutes from Brisbane. From Sydney it's an 11-hour trip, sometimes longer, on the crowded, rundown Pacific Highway.

By Plane   Domestic flights land at the **Coolangatta Airport** (renamed Gold Coast Airport), 25 kilometers (15 miles) south of Surfers Paradise. **Ansett** and **Qantas** operate plenty of direct flights from Sydney, Melbourne, and Brisbane. **Coachtrans airport shuttles** (☎ **13 12 30** in Queensland, or 07/5588 8777) meet every flight; the fare to Surfers Paradise is A$9 (U.S.$6.30) one-way and A$14 (U.S.$9.80) round-trip. A taxi from the airport to Surfers Paradise is about A$30 (U.S.$21), depending on the traffic, which can be heavy.

The nearest international gateway is Brisbane International Airport. The **Coachtrans Airporter bus** meets most flights between 5:50am and 7:30pm and makes about 20 trips a day from the domestic and international terminals at Brisbane Airport to Gold Coast accommodations for A$29 (U.S.$20.30) adults, A$15 (U.S.$10.50) children ages 4 to 14, one-way; or A$50 (U.S.$35) adults, A$25 (U.S.$17.50) kids, round-trip. The trip takes about 1 hour 20 minutes to Surfers Paradise. You do not need to book in advance.

By Bus   Coachtrans (☎ **13 12 30** in Queensland, or 07/5588 8777) also runs 23 regular public buses daily between Brisbane and the Gold Coast; buses depart from the Brisbane Transit Centre on Roma Street. Every second service on average is express, which takes 1 hour 20 minutes to Surfers Paradise. The fare is A$13 (U.S.$9.10) one-way. Bookings are not necessary.

McCafferty's and **Greyhound Pioneer** make daily stops at the Gold Coast from Sydney and Brisbane; buses pull into the centrally located Surfers Paradise Transit Centre on Beach Road. The trip from Sydney takes 15 to 16 hours, and the fare is A$71 (U.S.$49.70). Trip time from Brisbane is 90 minutes, and the fare is $13 (U.S.$9.10).

By Train   Suburban trains (call **Queensland Rail Citytrain** at ☎ **07/3235 5555**) depart Brisbane Central and Roma Street stations every 30 minutes for the 80-minute trip to the Gold Coast suburb of Robina. The fare is A$8.30 (U.S.$5.85) adults, A$4.20 (U.S.$2.95) children ages 5 to 15. Numerous local buses meet the trains to take passengers to Surfers Paradise.

If you come by train to Surfers Paradise from Sydney or other southern cities (call **Countrylink** at ☎ **13 22 32** in Australia, or 07/9379 1298), you will need to transfer to a connecting coach in Casino or Murwillumbah, which are just south of the Queensland border. The trip from Sydney takes 14 to 15 hours and the fare is A$91 to $125 (U.S.$63.70 to $87.50) for a sitting berth, and A$217 (U.S.$151.90) for a sleeper.

VISITOR INFORMATION   The **Gold Coast Tourism Bureau** has an information kiosk on Cavill Avenue in Surfers Paradise (☎ **07/5538 4419**). It is stacked with loads of brochures on things to see and do, and they will make book tours and arrange accommodations for you. The kiosk is open Monday through Friday from 8am to 5pm, Saturday from 9am to 5pm, and Sunday from 9am to 3:30pm. To obtain material in advance, write to the bureau at P.O. Box 7091, Gold Coast Mail Centre, QLD 9726 (☎ 07/5592 2699, fax 07/5570 3144).

ORIENTATION   The heart of the Gold Coast is ✪ **Surfers Paradise**—"Surfers" to the locals, with an unvoiced "s" on the end—a high-rise forest of apartment towers, shops, dirt-cheap eateries, taverns, and amusement parlors. The pedestrians-only Cavill Mall in the center of town connects the Gold Coast Highway to The Esplanade, which runs along the beach.

The Gold Coast Highway is the main artery that connects the endless beachside suburbs lining the coast. Just north of Surfers is ✪ **Main Beach,** where you'll find the

Money-Saving Tips

Discount coupons and **special deals** are advertised in the countless free weekly pocket guides—to tours, cruises, car rental, restaurants, nightclubs, etc.—available in hotel lobbies and shops everywhere. Grab as many as you can and make the most of them!

The Secret of the Seasons

School holidays, especially the Christmas vacation through the end of January, are peak season on the Gold Coast. Accommodations are booked months in advance at these times. The rest of the year, occupancy levels plummet and so do rates! Packages and deals abound in the off-season, and perfectly adequate motel rooms can go for as little as A$50 (U.S.$35) double on standby.

Gold Coast's first up-and-coming pocket of cool, especially on Tedder Avenue, lined with shops, restaurants, and cafes. Heading south of Surfers, the biggest suburbs are **Broadbeach,** where retail complexes and restaurants are mushrooming; family-oriented **Burleigh Heads;** and the twin towns of **Coolangatta** in Queensland and **Tweed Heads** just over the border in New South Wales. Because Coolangatta only hopped onto the development bandwagon in the last few years, it has a sleepy small-town feel ideal for small kids (and burnt-out adults!). The airport is Coolangatta.

Immediately west of Surfers Paradise and Broadbeach lie affluent suburbs such as **Ashmore** and **Nerang,** and luxury residential estates. This is where you will find many of the city's championship golf courses.

GETTING AROUND   It's not necessary to have a car to get around. The hotels listed below are within walking distance of the beach, shops, and restaurants, and many tour companies pick up at hotels. You can reach the theme parks by bus. A car is handy for a day trip to Mt. Tamborine, however, and to get around to restaurants and golf courses. Parking is cheap and plentiful in numerous parking lots and on the side streets between the Gold Coast Highway and The Esplanade.

Avis (☎ 07/5539 9388), **Budget** (☎ 97/5538 1344), **Hertz** (☎ 07/5538 5366), and **Thrifty** (☎ 07/5538 6511) have outlets in Surfers Paradise and at Coolangatta Airport. Endless local outfits rent cars at cheap rates—one well-established company is **Letz Rent-A-Car** (☎ 07/5538 2622); it's next to the Trickett Gardens Holiday Inn.

The **Gold Coast Tourist Shuttle** (☎ **1300/655 655** in Australia, or 07/5574 5111) makes a continuous loop of the area's popular precincts: Marina Mirage, Sea World, Main Beach, the center of Surfers Paradise, Broadbeach, Pacific Fair Shopping Centre, the casino, Warner Bros. Movie World, Wet 'n' Wild, and Dreamworld. The shuttle will pick you up and drop you off anywhere along the route. It runs from 9am to midnight and passes by each stop about every 30 minutes to every hour. An all-day pass is A$12 (U.S.$8.40) adults, A$6 (U.S.$4.20) for kids ages 4 to 14. You must book a seat an hour ahead for the local service, a day ahead for the theme parks.

Surfside Buslines (☎ **13 12 30** in Queensland) is the local bus company. Time-tables cost A20¢ (U.S.15¢) from the Gold Coast Tourism Bureau information booth in Cavill Mall. A single-zone fare is A$1.20 (U.S.85¢). A typical fare—say, from Surfers Paradise to Currumbin Bird Sanctuary—is four zones, which is A$3.30 (U.S.$2.30). You can hop on and off the bus network as often as you like with a Gold Pass that costs A$10 (U.S.$7) for 24 hours and A$16 (U.S.$11.20) for 3 days; 5- and 7-day passes are available. Routes 1 and 1A run the length of the Gold Coast Highway 24 hours a day.

WHAT TO SEE & DO ON THE COAST
HITTING THE BEACHES

Needless to say, the wide white sandy beaches are the number one attraction on the Gold Coast—and best of all, they're free! No fewer than 35 patrolled beaches stretch almost uninterrupted for 30 kilometers (18 miles) from the Spit north of Surfers

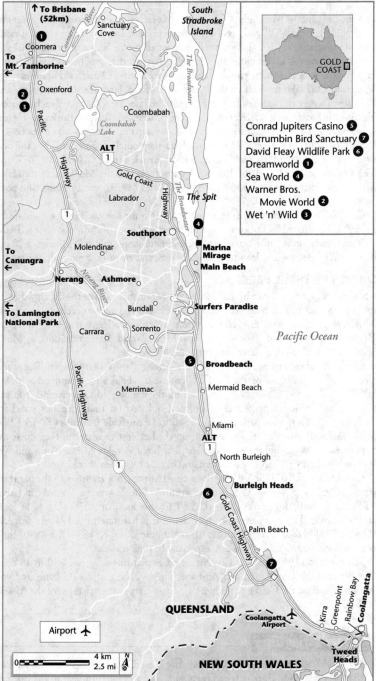

The Gold Coast

South Stradbroke Island

↑ To Brisbane (52km)

Coomera ①

Sanctuary Cove

← To Mt. Tamborine

Oxenford ②
③

Coombabah

Coombabah Lake

The Broadwater

ALT 1

Gold Coast Highway

Labrador

The Spit

Southport

④

Marina Mirage

Main Beach

Molendinar

← To Canungra

Nerang

Ashmore

Surfers Paradise

Bundall

← To Lamington National Park

Carrara

Sorrento

Pacific Ocean

⑤ Broadbeach

Merrimac

Mermaid Beach

Miami

ALT 1

North Burleigh

1

⑥ Burleigh Heads

Gold Coast Highway

Palm Beach

⑦

Kirra
Greenpoint
Rainbow Bay
Coolangatta

QUEENSLAND

Coolangatta Airport

Airport ✈

Tweed Heads

0 — 4 km / 2.5 mi   N↓

NEW SOUTH WALES

GOLD COAST

Conrad Jupiters Casino ⑤
Currumbin Bird Sanctuary ⑦
David Fleay Wildlife Park ⑥
Dreamworld ①
Sea World ④
Warner Bros. Movie World ②
Wet 'n' Wild ③

371

Paradise to Rainbow Bay south of Coolangatta. In fact, the Gold Coast is really just one long fabulous beach—all you need do is step onto it at any point and you will easily spot the nearest set of red and yellow flags, planted by the lifeguards, that signal safe swimming. There is no division into "trendy," "gay," "surfie," or "family" beaches, but in general, singles and young couples tend to cluster around ☉ **Surfers Paradise,** while Mum and Dad take the kids to the quieter surf of **Coolangatta, Greenmount,** and **Rainbow Bay** in the south. The most popular beaches are ☉ **Main Beach, Surfers North, Elkhorn Avenue, Surfers Paradise, Mermaid Beach, Burleigh Heads, Coolangatta,** and **Greenmount.** All these beaches are patrolled 365 days a year.

Surfers will find a decent wave most places they put in their board, but the best breaks are at Burleigh Heads and Kirra. **Surfers Beach Club** (☎ **07/5526 7077**), on The Esplanade in front of the Paradise Centre (opposite the McDonald's on Cavill Mall), rents surfboards for A$20 to $25 (U.S.$14 to $17.50) per 24 hours, and body boards for A$20 (U.S.$14).

Cavill Mall is a good place to hang out and watch the crowds. Here you will find a Ripley's Believe It or Not museum, souvenir stores, and loads of cheap restaurants. In the Paradise Centre on the mall's southern side are more shops, shooting galleries, a 10-pin bowling alley, electronic video games, bumper cars, and an 18-hole minigolf course.

DOING THE THEME PARKS

Theme parks seem to thrive in the Gold Coast's nourishing soil of tourist crowds with money to spend and nothing to do once they've overdosed on the beach and shopping. There are parks devoted to everything from avocados to ice, but the big three are Dreamworld, Sea World, and Warner Bros. Movie World. Right next door to Movie World is Wet 'n' Wild, a water-slide fun park.

Of all the parks, only Sea World is handily located in the center of town. The others are in northern bushland on the Pacific Highway; it's about a 15-minute drive to Wet 'n' Wild and Movie World, and 5 minutes up the highway to Dreamworld. You can ride free to the theme parks and get a free Gold Pass for unlimited bus travel for 24 hours if you buy your park entry ticket aboard a **Surfside Buslines** (☎ **13 12 30** in Queensland) bus. Park tickets bought on the bus cost the same as they do at the park gates, but you avoid the entry queues. Take bus 1A or 3 to Movie World and Wet 'n' Wild; bus 1A or 10 to Dreamworld; and bus 2 or 9 to Sea World.

Coachtrans (☎ **07/5588 8788**) does daily door-to-door transfers to the big three parks, as well as to Wet 'n' Wild, and Currumbin Bird Sanctuary. Round-trip fare is A$12 (U.S.$8.40) for adults, A$6 (U.S.$4.20) for kids, or A$30 (U.S.$21) for a family of four. The company also does round-trip transfers to Sea World for A$6 (U.S.$4.20) for adults, A$3 (U.S.$2.10) for children, and A$15 (U.S.$10.50) for a family. Book a day ahead if you can, especially in peak season.

You can also hail the regular Coachtrans buses that run daily every 30 to 45 minutes between the Gold Coast and Brisbane. They will be marked Brisbane, and you will find them on the Gold Coast Highway. Try to have correct change for the A$4.30 (U.S.$3) fare.

Money-Saving Tip

Sea World, Warner Bros. Movie World, and Wet 'n' Wild sell a **3 Park Super Pass** that gets you a full-day's entry to each park plus a free return visit to the one you like best. It costs A$105 (U.S.$73.50) for adults and A$68 (U.S.$47.60) and kids ages 4 to 13. You can't buy the pass at the theme parks; it's available from any travel agent.

Dreamworld. Pacific Hwy. (25km/15 miles north of Surfers Paradise), Coomera. ☎ **1800/ 073 300** in Australia, 07/5588 1111, or 07/5588 1122 (24-hr info line). Admission (all-inclusive except skill games, souvenir photos, and helicopter rides) A$44 (U.S.$30.80) adults, A$26 (U.S.$18.20) children 6–13. Daily 10am–5pm; Main St., Plaza Restaurant, and Koala Country open at 9am. Closed Christmas and until 1:30pm ANZAC Day.

Adrenaline-crazed thrill-seekers will love the action rides here, such as the Tower of Terror, in which you drop 38 stories at 160kmph (96 m.p.h.). They'll also get a kick out of Thunderbolt, Australia's fastest double-loop roller coaster; Wipeout, which spins, twists, and tumbles you upside down in a random sequence (but only exerts a sissy 2.5 G units of pressure); and Enterprise, which loops a loop at 60 kilometers per hour (36 m.p.h.). These high-octane offerings make the park's other offerings look tame. Rides apart, Dreamworld is actually more of a family fun park laid out Disney-style—except that here giant koalas roam the streets instead of Mickey Mouse. The other eclectic offerings include an IMAX theater, a native Aussie wildlife park where you can cuddle a koala and hand-feed kangaroos, river cruises livened up by a bushranger shoot-out on the banks, a magic and illusion show, skills games, and a carousel and other rides for young kids. A big highlight is to watch trainers swim, wrestle, and play with three gold and two snowy-white Bengal tigers on Tiger Island. Naturally, souvenir stores, restaurants, cafes, and ice-cream shops abound. There's a water-slide fun park, too, so bring your swimsuit. If this is your idea of fun, give your-self a full day here.

Sea World. Sea World Dr. (3km/2 miles north of Surfers Paradise), The Spit, Main Beach. ☎ **07/5588 2222,** or 07/5588 2205 for recorded show times. Admission (all-inclusive except dolphin experiences, helicopter rides, and powered water sports) A$41 (U.S.$28.70) adults, A$26 (U.S.$18.20) seniors and children 4–13. Daily 9:30am–5pm; ANZAC Day 1:30pm–6:30pm. Closed Christmas.

It's not as sophisticated as similar parks in the United States, but folks still flock here to see performing dolphins and sea lions, ski shows, an aquarium, shark feeding, and an array of rides. A monorail gets you around the grounds. There's a free water-slide playground. Waterskiing, parasailing, WaveRunners, and banana rides are available for an extra fee. A special experience you might want to try is to snorkel with dolphins. The experience, in which you get to touch a dolphin, costs A$75 (U.S.$52.50) and is for adults only. If you don't care whether you actually touch a dolphin, you can snorkel freely with them in a sandy lagoon for A$50 (U.S.$35). Kids can attend a 30-minute dolphin talk, pat one, and have their photo taken with it for a rather steep A$25 (U.S.$17.50). You could spend a full day here, but a long half-day oughta do it.

Warner Bros. Movie World. Pacific Hwy. (21km/12½ miles north of Surfers Paradise), Oxenford. ☎ **07/5573 3999,** or 07/5573 8485 for recorded information. Admission (all-inclusive) A$39 (U.S.$28.70) adults, A$24 (U.S.$16.80) seniors and children 4–13. Daily 9:30am–5:30pm; rides and attractions operate 10am–5pm. Closed Christmas.

Australia's answer to Universal Studios just about matches its U.S. counterpart for thrills and spills. The park has a Wild West theme, and is based around working studios where *The Phantom,* starring Billy Zane; *20,000 Leagues Under the Sea,* with Michael Caine; and *Streetfighter,* with Jean-Claude Van Damme were filmed. The big must-see attraction is the heart-stopping and hilarious Police Academy Stunt Show with Commandant Lassard. If you already know how Superman flies across sky-scrapers and you've heard a Foley sound studio in action before, the train ride around the sets might bore you, but it's a great introduction to cinema tricks for first-timers. It features a stage show in the original Riddler's Lair set from *Batman Forever.* Not to be outdone by Dreamworld, Movie World has a couple of tummy-turning rides as well, including the Lethal Weapon roller coaster and Batman—The Ride, a simulated high-speed chase in the Batmobile. Other attractions include an illusion show, a bloopers cinema, and a Wild West flume ride. Young kids can take rides and see stage shows by Yosemite Sam and Porky Pig in the Looney Tunes Village, and there's a Looney Tunes Parade through the streets each day. If you can stomach Daffy Duck and Wonder Woman first thing in the morning, join them and other characters for "Breakfast with the Stars," and a song-and-dance show at 9:30am. You won't need a whole day here; most parades and shows take place between 11am and 4pm.

Wet 'n' Wild. Pacific Hwy. (next to Warner Bros. Movie World), Oxenford. ☎ **07/ 5573 6233,** or 07/5573 2255 for recorded information. Admission A$23 (U.S.$16.10) adults, A$16 (U.S.$11.20) children 4–13. Daily Jan 10am–9pm, Feb 10am–5pm, Mar–Apr 10am–4:30pm, May–Aug 10am–4pm, Sep–Oct 10am–4:30pm, Nov–Dec 10am–5pm. Open to 9pm on Dive-In Movie nights. Closed Christmas and ANZAC Day.

Hurtling down a seven-story piece of fiberglass at 70kmph (44 m.p.h.) is just one of many water-slide options at this aquatic fun park. If that's not for you, try corkscrewing seven times inside an enclosed slide, aptly dubbed Twister, before you're spit out into the pool, or racing head-first down an eight-lane speedslide. Terror Canyon has you hurtling in the dark through a fiber-optic light show before splashdown far below. A flume of water takes you bobsledding around a mountain on the River Rapids slide. Scaredy-cats can stick to the four regular white-water flumes, float gently past palm-studded "islands" in the Calypso Beach section, or swim in the artificial breakers in the Wave Pool or in the regular pool. There's also a water playground for young kids. Every night in January, and Saturday night from September to April, is Dive-In Movie night, during which film fans can recline on a rubber tube in the pool while watching the flick. A stunt show plays at 2:30pm (5pm on movie nights). The water is heated to 26°C (79°F) for year-round swimming.

EXPLORING THE WILDLIFE & AUSTRALIAN PARKS

✪ **Currumbin Bird Sanctuary.** Gold Coast Hwy. (18km/11 miles south of Surfers Paradise), Currumbin. ☎ **07/5534 1266.** Admission A$16 (U.S.$11.20) adults, A$9 (U.S.$6.30) seniors and children 4–15, A$40 (U.S.$28) family of four. Daily 8am–5:30pm. Closed Christmas and until 1pm ANZAC Day. Bus: 1, 1A, or Coachtrans.

There's hardly a Queenslander alive who can't show you childhood snapshots of himor herself draped in rainbow lorikeets. The birds flock to this park in the thousands every morning and afternoon to be fed by delighted visitors. These impossibly beautiful birds have a green back, blue head, and red and yellow chest, and they love sitting on you, especially if you're holding a tin pan full of the bread, milk, and honey mix the park staff doles out to visitors. Lorikeet feeding is at 8am and 4pm. While you're here, you can also have your photo taken cuddling a koala at 8:30am and noon (for A$9.95/U.S.$7), hand-feed kangaroos, stroll or take a free miniature train ride through parkland, and attend animal talks and feeding demonstrations. An Aboriginal song and dance show takes place at 3:30pm. Lots of native birds are drawn to the wetlands within the grounds. Allow 2 to 3 hours to see everything.

✪ **David Fleay Wildlife Park.** West Burleigh Rd.(17km/10¼ miles south of Surfers Paradise), West Burleigh. ☎ **07/5576 2411.** Admission A$9.50 (U.S.$6.65) adults, A$6.50 (U.S.$4.55) seniors and A$4.50 (U.S.$3.15) children 4–17, or A$27 (U.S.$18.90) for a family. Free reentry if rained out. Daily 9am–5pm. Closed Christmas Day and until 1pm ANZAC Day. Bus: 4.

This is one of Australia's premier wildlife parks. You'll see a platypus, saltwater and freshwater crocodiles, wallabies, kangaroos, glider possums, dingoes, wombats, the rare Lumholtz's tree kangaroo, and a big range of Australian birds, including emus, wedge-tail eagles, black swans, and lorikeets. You walk on a series of raised boardwalks through picturesque mangrove, rain-forest, and eucalyptus habitats, where most of the animals roam free. There's also a darkened nocturnal house. A program of Creature Feature talks and feeding demonstrations throughout the day includes a reptile show and saltwater croc feeding—when the crocs are hungry that is; they only feed from October to April. If you're interested in Aboriginal culture, you'll want to hear Bernie, the park's Aboriginal Interpretation Officer, talk about weaponry and bush medicine. Knowledgeable volunteers give free guided tours throughout the day. The Department of Environment took over the park when its renowned founder, zoologist Dr. David Fleay, died in 1993. Because the department frowns on the public handling animals, you can't cuddle a koala or hand-feed kangaroos here, but you can take photos of yourself beside koalas in the trees for A$9 (U.S.$6.30). There's a cafe, a gift shop, and picnic tables. You can see everything here in about 90 minutes, but you'll probably want to spend longer enjoying the restful setting and intriguing wildlife.

CRUISING THE COAST

The Gold Coast is overrun with all kinds of cruise boats and sailing vessels clamoring to take you out for a morning or a day on **The Broadwater,** a calm strip of water between the mainland and The Spit, north of Surfers Paradise and Main Beach. Wander down to Marina Mirage, off Sea World Drive, in Main Beach, and take your pick from the many boats based there.

Two of the biggest companies are **Shangri-La Cruises** (☎ 07/5557 8888) and **Island Queen Showboat Cruises** (☎ 07/5557 8800). Both companies run a similar range of cruises, including morning shopping forays to Sanctuary Cove Marine Village, seafood buffet luncheon trips, canal cruises to spy on the luxury homes in the residential waterway estates, Polynesian or Vegas-theme dinner cruises, and even transfers to the theme parks. The boats have air-conditioned covered spaces, bars, and an open-top deck. Expect to pay A$26 (U.S.$18.20) for a 2-hour shopping jaunt, and A$55 (U.S.$38.50) for a dinner cruise. Prices include a pickup from your hotel.

GETTING ACTIVE

Surfers Beach Club (☎ 07/5526 7077), on The Esplanade in front of the Paradise Centre (opposite the McDonald's on Cavill Mall), rents surfboards and other sporting equipment, including in-line skates for A$15 (U.S.$10.50) for 3 hours. For high-powered water sports, contact one of the many operators on The Broadwater at Sea World Drive, such as **Aussie Bob's** (☎ 07/5591 7577), located at Berth 14D at Marina Mirage. Bob's does parasailing (A$50/U.S.$35 per person) and speedboat rides (A$40/U.S.$28 per person), and rents tandem jet skis for A$60 (U.S.$42) per boat. Powered sports equipment is not permitted within 400 meters (¼ mile) from shore anywhere along the Coast.

Bungee Downunder (☎ 07/5531 1103), on The Broadwater at Sea World Drive (just south of Sea World), does 45.7-meter (150-ft.) jumps over water from a floating barge for A$70 (U.S.$49). Two photos of you looking exhilarated or terrified midair are A$20 (U.S.$14). It is open daily 10am to 5pm. Hotel pick-ups for you and your scaredy cat nonjumping friends are free.

You can chase black marlin and many other fish in the Gold Coast waters on a day trip with numerous **fishing** charter boats, most based at Marina Mirage. Tony Smith, skipper of **Black Bass Fishing Charters** (☎ 07/5531 0755, or 014/44 8071) takes you 64.4 to 80.5 kilometers (40 to 50 miles) out to sea for black marlin, dolphinfish, wahoo, and Spanish mackerel in summer, snapper and pearl perch in winter. The price of A$120 (U.S.$84) per person for the day includes all gear and lunch—that's a good value for game fishing.

Golf on the Cheap

Hitting the links on the Gold Coast doesn't have to cost you an arm and a leg. Sure, the Coast has a lot of glamorous courses, but at the cheap and cheerful end of the spectrum is **Emerald Lakes Golf Course** on Nerang–Broadbeach Road at Alabaster Drive, Carrara (☎ **07/5594 4400**). The course welcomes all comers for just A$16 (U.S.$11.20) for nine championship holes on a par-68 course. After 2:30pm, "Happy Golf" kicks in, during which you can play as many holes as you can fit in until the end of the day for just A$15 (U.S.$10.50). The course is 10 minutes inland from Surfers Paradise.

The Gold Coast boasts more than 40 **golf courses.** Nine holes generally cost A$35 (U.S.$24.50), including a cart, with additional charges of around A$12.50 (U.S.$8.75) for clubs and A$10 (U.S.$7) for shoes. Grandest is the Scottish links–style ✪ **Hope Island Golf Club,** Oxenford–Southport Road, Hope Island, 25 minutes north of Surfers Paradise (☎ **07/5530 8988**), designed by the Thomson-Wolveridge team. A 9-hole round is A$45 (U.S.$31.50), but few golfers can resist going the whole 18 for A$90 (U.S.$63), including cart rental. Other championship fairways can be found at **The Palms at the Hyatt Regency Sanctuary Cove Resort,** Casey Road, Sanctuary Cove on Hope Island (☎ **07/5577 6151**); Lakelands, Gooding Drive, Merrimac (☎ 07/5579 8700), designed by Jack Nicklaus; and the two 18-hole courses at **Royal Pines Resort,** Ross Street, Ashmore (☎ **07/5592 9170**).

WHERE TO STAY

✪ **Mercure Resort Surfers Paradise.** 122 Ferny Ave., Surfers Paradise, QLD 4217. ☎ **1800/ 64 2244** in Australia, 1800/221-4542 in the U.S. and Canada, 0181/283 4500 in the U.K., 0800/44 4422 in New Zealand, or 07/5579 4444. Fax 07/5579 4492. 402 units. A/C MINIBAR TV TEL. A$145–$160 (U.S.$101.50–$112) double; A$175–$190 (U.S.$122.50–$133) family room. Additional person A$20 (U.S.$14) extra. Children under 16 free in parents' room if they use existing bedding. Free crib. Ask about special packages. AE, BC, DC, JCB, MC, V.

If you're a parent and your idea of a holiday is to not even see your kids for most of the day, this place is for you. The resort has a licensed childcare center for little ones as young as 6 weeks up to 4 years old. For 5- to 12-year-olds, there's the Gecko Club, complete with powered minicars, the Leonardo de Gecko painting room, and an underwater pirate adventure world. You can sip cocktails around the pleasant leafy pool complex and watch the kids play on the water slide. The child-care center charges a moderate fee, but the Gecko Club is free; both operate daily year-round. The low-rise building is comfortable, not grand; rooms have views of either the pool or the tropical gardens. All have hair dryers, irons, and ironing boards. Family quarters sleep up to five in two separate rooms, and some have kitchenettes. Features like a packed daily activity program, two restaurants and a bar, karaoke nights, room service, a gym, a sauna, Jacuzzis, tennis courts, a basketball court, and a tour desk make this hotel a good value for the money. The center of Surfers Paradise and the patrolled beach are a few blocks across the highway. Some rooms are near the highway, so ask for a quiet spot.

Pink Poodle. 2903 Gold Coast Hwy. (at Fern St.), Surfers Paradise, QLD 4217. ☎ **07/ 5539 9211.** Fax 07/5539 9136. 20 units (all with shower only, 1 with Jacuzzi). A/C TV TEL. A$60 (U.S.$42) single; A$70 (U.S.$49) double. A$30 (U.S.$21) surcharge from Christmas Day to mid-Jan. Additional person A$10 (U.S.$7) extra, A$8 (U.S.$5.60) children under 13. Crib A$5 (U.S.$3.50). A, BC, DC, MC, V.

You can't miss the pink neon poodle marking this Best Western motel an easy 1.2-kilometer (¾-mile) walk south of town. It was an institution with honeymooners in

Accommodations Tip

Most accommodations will require a 1-week minimum stay during school holiday periods, and a 4-day minimum stay at Easter and during the Indy car race carnival in October; book well ahead for those times.

decades gone by, but these days it's just a well-kept motel with very large, recently renovated rooms with fluffy towels and good mattresses. Most have balconies or patios. The front desk lends hair dryers. Even in the room closest to the highway, the traffic noise is muted; it's the rainbow lorikeets in the trees outside that will wake you up. A nice garden pool and a Jacuzzi face a suburban street. The restaurant does a room service breakfast for A$6 (U.S.$4.20). The front desk runs a tour desk. The patrolled beach is at the end of the street.

GOOD-VALUE VACATION APARTMENTS

Apartments make good sense for families and for any traveler who is prepared to self-cater to save money. Because the Gold Coast has a dramatic over-supply of apartments that stand empty outside school vacations, you can get a spacious modern unit with ocean views for the cost of a low-priced midrange hotel. The three complexes listed below are particularly good values. Apartment block developers got in quick to snag the best beachfront spots when the Gold Coast boomed in the 1970s, so it's apartment complexes, not hotels, that have the best ocean views.

✪ **Bahia Beachfront Apartments.** 154 The Esplanade, Surfers Paradise, QLD 4217. ☎ **07/5538 3322.** Fax 07/5592 0318. 30 units. TV TEL. High season A$115 (U.S.$80.50) double 1-bedroom apt., A$155 (U.S.$108.50) double 2-bedroom apt. Low season A$89 (U.S.$62.30) 1-bedroom apt., A$122 (U.S.$85.40) 2-bedroom apt. Additional person A$15 (U.S.$10.50) extra. Weekly rates available. AE, BC, DC, MC, V.

You get champagne views at a beer price at this 14-story apartment complex 800 meters (½ mile) north of the town center. Units are big and airy, and simply but neatly furnished with linoleum tiles, a big modern kitchen, and combined bathroom/laundry. Front-facing apartments have a mirrored rear wall to reflect the ocean. Like many apartments on the Gold Coast, these are not air-conditioned, but the sea breeze is a good substitute on all but the hottest days. Corner apartments have two balconies, and only units in the southwest corner of the building and on the first two floors miss out on the sea view. Unlike most Coast apartments, these are serviced daily. There's a tour desk, a heated pool, a child's pool, gym equipment, a sauna, and Jacuzzi. A patrolled beach is across the road.

Shangri-La. 28 Northcliffe Terrace, Surfers Paradise, QLD 4217. ☎ **07/5570 2366.** Fax 07/5592 3929. E-mail: shangrila@one.net.au. 109 units. A/C TV TEL. High season A$150 (U.S.$105) 1-bedroom apt., A$192 (U.S.$134.40) 2-bedroom apt. (up to 4 people), A$240 (U.S.$168) 3-bedroom apt. (up to 6 people). Low season A$114 (U.S.$79.80) 1-bedroom apt., A$150 (U.S.$105) 2-bedroom apt., A$180 (U.S.$126) 3-bedroom apt. Weekly rates available. Additional person A$20 (U.S.$14) extra. AE, BC, DC, JCB, MC, V. Free parking.

Indy Madness!

When the **Gold Coast Indy car race** takes over the town for 4 days in October, hotel rates skyrocket and most hostelries demand a minimum stay of 3 or 4 nights. Don't leave accommodation bookings to the last minute! Contact the Gold Coast Tourism Bureau (☎ **07/5538 4419,** fax 07/5570 3259) to find out the exact dates.

Every apartment in this 24-story tower has ocean or ocean/hinterland views from a big balcony. The empty lot across the street on the beachfront is ominously ripe for a tower to rise and block the view, but since it's been vacant 8 years, the owners cross their fingers that it will stay that way. This is the kind of place the locals like to stay because you get a big living room, a dining area, a full kitchen, separate sleeping quarters, and loads of space. The furnishings are modern, neat, and clean. You do your own servicing, or pay A$20 to $30 (U.S.$14 to $21) per day extra for it. You usually don't get much in the way of services and facilities with a holiday apartment, but this block has a lot: dry cleaning, a tour desk, in-house movies, a cocktail bar and bistro that even does room service at dinner, a smallish outdoor pool and a heated indoor pool with a sauna and Jacuzzi, a game room, and a tennis court. The front desk lends hair dryers. The heart of Surfers Paradise shopping and dining is a 4-block walk along The Esplanade.

✪ **Trickett Gardens Holiday Inn.** 24–30 Trickett St., Surfers Paradise, QLD 4217. ☎ **1800/ 074 290** in Australia, or 07/5539 0988. Fax 07/5592 0791. www.about-australia.com/ trickett/index.htm. E-mail: bobmille@fan.net.au. 33 units (all with shower only). A/C TV TEL. High season (Dec 26 to mid-Jan) A$116 (U.S.$81.20) double 1-bedroom apt., A$144 (U.S.$100.80) double 2-bedroom apt. Low season A$92 (U.S.$64.40) double 1-bedroom apt., A$100 (U.S.$70) double 2-bedroom apt. Additional person A$16 (U.S.$11.20) extra. A$6 (U.S.$4.20) for children under 3 with extra bedding. AE, BC, DC, JCB, MC, V. Free parking.

This super-clean, well-maintained three-story apartment block 100 meters (a few hundred feet) from the beach and 2 blocks from Cavill Mall is not a member of the Holiday Inn chain, but rather a family-run concern. It's hard to beat for location, price, and comfort. The one- and two-bedroom painted brick apartments have modest but neat furnishings, a spacious airy living area, a kitchen, safes, and a small combined bathroom and laundry with a hair dryer. Each has a balcony overlooking the pool (which is heated in winter), Jacuzzi, and barbecue under the bougainvillea and palms. There's room service at breakfast and dinner, a tour desk, and free newspaper delivery daily. No smoking indoors.

WHERE TO DINE

The Gold Coast is full to the rafters with cheap restaurants, especially in and around Cavill Mall. Look for discount and "special offer" coupons in the many free tourist guides available in hotel lobbies and information booths. Many stylish new restaurants and cafes, most reasonably priced, are springing up around Surf Parade and Victoria Avenue at Broadbeach, as well as in the nearby Oasis shopping mall. A coffee and an Italian-style gourmet sandwich by the water won't cost the earth at the stylish Marina Mirage shopping center opposite the Sheraton on Sea World Drive at Main Beach, nor at one of the hip Tedder Avenue cafes in Main Beach. Royal Pines Resort's Parkview restaurant does lunchtime main courses for less than A$10 (U.S.$7) Monday to Saturday, a good option if you're golfing there.

Billy T. Bones On the Beachfront Café Bar Grill. Under the Iluka Beach Resort Hotel, The Esplanade at Hanlan St., Surfers Paradise. ☎ **07/5526 7913.** Main courses A$9.95–$14.95 (U.S.$7–$10.50). Sunday full buffet breakfast A$9.90 (U.S.$6.95) adults, A$5.90 (U.S.$4.15) children under 13. AE, BC, DC, MC, V. Daily 6:30am–10pm. STEAK/PASTA/SEAFOOD.

Write down your order at one of the timber dining tables, hand it to the waitress, and sit back to make the most of the sea views from this pleasantly casual spot across the road from the beach. They do big cooked breakfasts for A$6.90 (U.S.$4.85), with thick toast and decent coffee (and with good lean bacon—hard to find in Australia, my English husband tells me). The long list of lunch and dinner options includes such fare as pastas, burgers, honey tempura prawns on rice, or southern fried chicken.

Grain-fed steaks, also hard to find Down Under, come with an Idaho baked potato with bacon bits and sour cream, coleslaw, and a choice of mushroom, pepper, or chili sauce. Look for the good-value blackboard specials.

✪ **Eazy Peazy Thai and Japanezy.** Tedder Ave. at Peak Ave., Main Beach. ☎ **07/ 5591 9000.** Main courses A$9.90–$19.90 (U.S.$6.95–$13.95); average A$14.90 (U.S.$10.45). AE, BC, DC, MC, V. Mon 6–9:30pm, Tues–Fri noon–3pm and 6–10pm, Sat–Sun noon–10pm. THAI AND JAPANESE.

You can have a quick feed of tempura at the noodle bar or make a night of it at the relaxed tables and chairs set up alfresco on the corner of happening Tedder Avenue. Everything on the lengthy menu is light and tasty, from the sushi to the Thai chili beef salad to the marinated fried chicken on light Japanese veggies. My chicken and vegetables with satay came out as a huge plate of crisp steamed greens with plenty of meat and fresh satay. The soups are good tummy-fillers for around A$8 (U.S.$5.60). Some heavy French stuff, like bread and butter pudding with toffee sauce and ice cream, slips onto the dessert menu. Licensed and BYO. The proprietors have opened a new Indian restaurant, **Get It India** (☎ **07/5527 0027**) at 14–16 Tedder Ave., open the same hours and taking the same credit cards as this place. Main courses average A$12.90 (U.S.$9.05).

✪ **La Porchetta.** In The Mark Centre, 3 Orchid Ave. (just off Cavill Mall), Surfers Paradise. ☎ **07/5527 5273.** Reservations recommended. Main courses A$4.40–$13.50 (U.S.$30.80– $9.45); most meals under A$10 (U.S.$7). AE, BC, DC, MC, V. Daily 11am–late. PIZZA/ITALIAN.

Pizza for A$4.40 (U.S.$3.10)? That must be for a slice, we thought. But nope, six bucks at this bustling alfresco joint buys you the whole shebang, a small pizza—about 25 centimeters (5 inches) across—with olives, anchovies, tomato, cheese, and oregano. Two of us pigged out on a medium, easily big enough for three, which had a yummy crispy crust topped with good-quality Italian sausage and basil. Traditional pastas, steaks, chicken, and seafood dishes all come with salad or vegetables. Be prepared to wait for a table, as it's no surprise the place is popular. They do takeout, too.

The Times Café. Imperial Plaza, Gold Coast Hwy. at Elkhorn Ave., Surfers Paradise. ☎ **07/ 5538 3211.** Lunch specials around A$7.50 (U.S.$5.25); main courses A$9.90–$21 (U.S.$6.95–$14.70). AE, BC, DC, MC, V. Daily 8:30am–late. CAFE FARE.

Smartly dressed shoppers and office workers come into this mock-Deco haven to escape the welter of cheap hamburger joints and chicken takeouts outside. The place feels a bit like a cardboard movie set, with green walls, purple striped upholstery, rococo gilt picture frames, and mirrored ceiling, but the food is tasty. At lunch, skip the main courses like spiced snapper fillet on rice with roasted vegetables and citrus butter, and go straight for a filling hot foccacia sandwich with veal, olives, sun-dried tomatoes, mesclun, and basil dressing. It's A$7.50 (U.S.$5.25) with a free cappuccino, and the foccacia is bigger than the dinner plate it comes on. Maple syrup pancakes are on the breakfast menu.

WORTH A SPLURGE

✪ **RPR's.** 21st fl., Royal Pines Resort, Ross St., Ashmore. ☎ **07/5597 1111.** Reservations recommended. Main courses all A$28.50 (U.S.$19.95); Sunset Dining special A$40 (U.S.$28) for 2 courses and glass of champagne if you leave before 7pm. AE, BC, CB, DC, JCB, MC, V. Mon–Sat 5:30pm–9:30pm. MOD OZ.

Husband-and-wife team chef David Fryer and restaurant manager Karen Fryer turn out arguably the slickest dishes on the Gold Coast in this atmospheric aerie with views of the city lights from every table. Meat dishes like grain-fed Mandalong lamb with braised red peppers and rocket pesto sit alongside a big range of fish dishes, David's favorite food to work with. Fresh reef fish fillet in a brioche herb crust with buttered asparagus and lemon beurre blanc is typical. His accidental signature dish, though, is his pumpkin and ricotta pot stickers with Asian greens and curry oil—customers like them so much they won't let him take them off the menu. Save room for dessert.

THE GOLD COAST AFTER DARK

The jeans and T-shirt set love the laid-back **Billy's Beach House,** on The Esplanade at Hanlan Street, Surfers Paradise (☎ 07/5592 4419) for its drinks promotions. There's always a live band Sunday nights. Cover is A$3 to $6 (U.S.$2.10 to $4.20). At night a dress code of long pants and enclosed shoes (that is, no thongs or sandals) applies. An impressive light show and nonstop dance music attract an upscale crowd of 20- to 40-somethings at **Fortunes** on the top floor of Conrad Jupiters Casino (see below). The club is open Tuesday to Saturday; the cover is A$5 (U.S.$3.50) after 10pm Friday and $8 (U.S.$5.60) after 9:30pm Saturday. All ages and types frequent **Melba's,** 46 Cavill Ave., Surfers Paradise (☎ 07/5538 7411), a perennially popular neon-lit dance club. Tuesday and Thursday are ladies' nights (male strippers do their stuff on Thursdays), and cocktails are A$4 (U.S.$2.80) all night. Cover is A$8 (U.S.$5.60).

There's a genuine Rolls Royce parked in the corner at **Rolls** nightclub at the Sheraton Mirage, Sea World Drive, Main Beach (☎ 07/5591 1488)—you can reserve it as your booth for the night. A mixed-age crowd of sophisticated locals rubs shoulders with hotel guests. There is no cover; the club opens Friday and Saturday night. At 10:30pm they push back the tables at **Saks,** Marina Mirage, Sea World Drive, Main Beach (☎ 07/5591 2755) and this elegant cafe/wine bar turns into a dance floor for fashionable 20- and 30-somethings. Friday, Saturday, and Sunday are the coolest nights to turn up, and there's a live band Sundays; no cover.

Revelers 20 to 35 years old go to **Shooters Saloon Bar,** in the Mark shopping complex, Orchid Avenue, Surfers Paradise (☎ 07/5592 1144) for a fun, hip, but not slavishly trendy night of dancing. There's usually some kind of competition going on, from Bachelor of the Year awards to swimwear parades. Cover is A$5 (U.S.$3.50) after 10pm. It's open daily from 11am to 5am.

It's not as big some Vegas casinos, but **Conrad Jupiters Casino,** Gold Coast Highway, Broadbeach (☎ 07/5592 1133), has plenty to keep the gambler amused— 88 gaming tables and 1,100-plus slot machines with roulette, blackjack, Caribbean stud poker, baccarat and minibaccarat, craps, Pai Gow and Sic Bo, as well as the classic Aussie two-up. Downstairs the 1,000-seat Jupiter's Casino stages floor shows and live song performances; and there are nine bars, including an English-style pub. Of the six restaurants, the good-value Food Fantasy buffet is outrageously popular, so be prepared to wait. The casino is open 24 hours. You must be 18 to enter, and smart, casual attire (no swimsuits) is required.

Many go to the **Twin Towns Services Club,** Pacific Highway at Marine Parade, Tweed Heads (☎ 1800/014 014 in Australia, or 07/5536 1977 for bookings, and 07/5536 2277 for administration office) for the 275 slot machines, Keno, and sports betting, but you can also catch big-name acts—like Glenn Campbell, Don McLean, or Eartha Kitt—in the Auditorium (tickets for performances A$10/$U.S.$7 to A$25/$17.50). Live music plays every afternoon and evening. On Monday nights they show free recently released movies at 6:30pm and 8:45pm. Just to make sure nothing comes between you and the one-armed bandits (slot machines), there's free child care every night and from lunchtime Friday through Sunday. There's also a free bus that runs from the Dolphin Arcade on the Gold Coast Highway in Surfers Paradise. The club is over the state border by a matter of meters (yards) so don't forget it runs on New South Wales time, one hour ahead of the Gold Coast in summer. Admission is free.

10 The Gold Coast Hinterland: Back to Nature

The cool, green, hilly Gold Coast hinterland—the "green behind the gold," as the tourism spin doctors are fond of putting it—is only a half-hour drive from the Coast, but it is a world away from the neon lights, glaring sun, and those darn theme parks. Up here, at an altitude of 500 to 1,000 meters (approximately 1,500 to 3,500 feet), the tree ferns drip moisture, the air is crisp, and the architecture is all cottage charm, not skyscraper brash.

Two places should spark your interest—the villages of Mt. Tamborine, and the Lamington National Park. **Mt. Tamborine** shelters a little conglomeration of villages known for their craft shops, galleries, oh-so-cute cafes, and lovely B&Bs. Easy walking trails wander from the streets through rain forest and eucalyptus woodland, and as you drive you constantly come across magnificent views from a new vantage point.

Even more impressive is the 20,200-hectare (50,500-acre) ✪ **Lamington National Park** that lies to the south of Mt. Tamborine. The park, at around 1,000 meters (3,328 feet) above sea level, is a refreshing eucalyptus and rain-forest wilderness riddled with walking trails. It's famous for its rich, colorful bird life (much of it tame), wallabies, possums, and other wildlife. It is reached by a tightly turning road, and as you wind higher and higher, gnarled tangled vines and dense brooding eucalyptus and ferns make a cavern over your car that's so dark you need to turn on your headlights. The park is about 90 minutes from the Coast—but once you're ensconced up in the ridges in one of its two rather special mountain retreats, the world will seem remote indeed.

The hinterland is close enough to the Gold Coast and even to Brisbane to make a pleasant day trip, but you will almost certainly want to stay overnight, or longer, once you breathe in the soul-restoring powers of the forest.

MT. TAMBORINE

40km (24 miles) NW of Surfers Paradise; 70km (42 miles) S of Brisbane

Cute craft shops, pretty tea-houses, and idyllic mountain roads twisting among ferns and farmland are what visitors come to Mt. Tamborine to explore. The mountaintop is really more of a plateau than a peak, and it's home to a string of villages, all a mile or 2 apart—Eagle Heights, North Tamborine, and Mt. Tamborine proper—which together are what folks usually mean when they say they are off to Mt. Tamborine for the day. Many of the shops and cafes are only open Thursday, Friday, and weekends.

ESSENTIALS

GETTING THERE   From the Gold Coast, head to Nerang and follow the signs that say Beaudesert. The Mt. Tamborine turnoff is off this road. Alternatively, head up the Pacific Highway to Oxenford and take the Mt. Tamborine turn-off, the first exit after Warner Bros. Movie World. Many tour operators run minibus and 4WD day trips from the Gold Coast, and some also run tours from Brisbane.

VISITOR INFORMATION   Head to the **Gold Coast Tourism Bureau** (see "Visitor Information" in the "Gold Coast" section above) to stock up on information and tourist maps before you head out. **Brisbane Tourism** outlets (See "Visitor Information" in chapter 7) also have a little information. Once you arrive, the **Tamborine Mountain Information Centre** is in Doughety Park, where Geissmann Drive becomes Main Western Road in North Tamborine (☎ **07/5545 3200**). It's open daily from 10:30am to 3:30pm.

EXPLORING THE MOUNTAIN

With a map in hand, you are well equipped to drive around Mt. Tamborine's twisty-turny roads to admire the wonderful views over the valleys and to poke around in the shops. New Age candles, homemade soaps, maple pecan fudge, framed tropical watercolors, German cuckoo clocks, and Aussie antiques are some of the things you can buy in the mountain's cute stores. The best place to shop is the quaint strip of galleries, cafes, and shops known as **Gallery Walk** on Long Road, between North Tamborine and Eagle Heights. Eagle Heights has few shops but great views back toward the coast. North Tamborine is mainly a commercial center where you still find the odd nice gallery or two. Mt. Tamborine itself is mainly residential.

Queensland is not exactly the wine capital of the universe, but up here in the cool air, the **Mount Tamborine Vineyard and Winery,** 32 Hartley Rd. (☎ 07/5545 3506), northwest of North Tamborine off the Main Western Road, turns out an agreeable drop. Shiraz, merlot, grenache merlot, sauvignon blanc, chardonnay, and muscat are some of the offerings. The cellar door is open for free tastings from 10am to 4pm daily. The Bush Turkey Port makes a nice gift.

Allow time to walk some of the **trails** that wind through forest throughout the villages. Most are reasonably short (a kilometer/mile or two or less) and easy. The Mt. Tamborine Information Centre can give you a map marking them.

WHERE TO STAY: A RAIN FOREST B&B

✪ **Tamborine Mountain Bed & Breakfast.** 19–23 Witherby Crescent, Eagle Heights, QLD 4721. ☎ **07/5545 3595.** Fax 07/5545 3322. 4 units (all with shower only). A/C TV. Single, Fri and Sat A$107 (U.S.$74.90) per night for 2-night stay, A$137 (U.S.$95.90) for Sat-only stay, Sun–Thurs A$90 (U.S.$63). Double, Fri–Sat A$127 (U.S.$88.90) per night for 2-night stay, A$157 (U.S.$109.90) for Sat-only stay, Sun–Thurs A$110 (U.S.$77). Additional person A$30–$50 (U.S.$21–$35) extra. Rates include full breakfast. BC, MC, V. Children under 11 not permitted.

Proprietors Carolyn Rose and Michael Perrin give you a genuinely warm welcome to their restful timber home that has stunning views to the Gold Coast skyline from the breakfast balcony. Laze by the open fire in the timber-lined living room, or out on the lovely verandah where rainbow lorikeets, kookaburras, and crimson rosellas flit about over the bird feeders (and even flit right through your hair). The day I visited a 6-foot goanna had been sunning himself on the verandah all morning. The ferny gardens have four purpose-built rustic timber rooms. Each is individually decorated in a charming Edwardian/cottage style with four-poster beds, mosquito nets, or heritage-tile bathrooms. Special treats are the purified rainwater in the bathroom and the handmade avocado soap and shampoo. Carolyn lends hair dryers. The rooms are heated in winter. With notice, Carolyn will provide dinner. The Queensland automobile association, the RACQ, awards the place five stars. No smoking indoors.

LAMINGTON NATIONAL PARK

70km (42 miles) W of Gold Coast; 115km (69 miles) S of Brisbane

Subtropical rain forest, 2,000-year-old, moss-covered Antarctic beech trees, giant strangler figs, and misty mountain air characterize Lamington's high narrow ridges and plunging valleys. Its great stretches of dense rain forest make it one of the most important subtropical parks in southeast Queensland, and one of the loveliest. The park is crisscrossed with 160 kilometers (96 miles) of walking trails that track through thick forest, past ferny waterfalls, and along mountain ridges with soaring views across green valleys. Happily, the trails vary in difficulty and length, from 1-kilometer (½-mile) strolls up to 23-kilometer (14-mile) treks. The park is a haven for bird lovers who come to see and photograph the gorgeously hued rosellas, bowerbirds, rare lyrebirds, and other species that live here, but that's not the only wildlife you will see. Groups of small, pretty wallabies, called *pademelons*, graze outside your room. In summer you may well see giant carpet pythons curled up in a tree or large goannas sunning themselves on rock ledges. Near streams you may be stopped by a hissing Lamington Spiny Crayfish, an aggressive little monster 6 inches long, patterned in royal blue and white like a Wedgwood dinner plate. The park comes alive with owls, possums, and sugar-gliders at night, when the dingoes howl.

Most visitors are fascinated by the park's **Antarctic beech trees,** which begin to appear above the 1,000-meter (3,330-ft.) line. Looking for all the world like something out a medieval fairy tale, these mossy monarchs of the forest stand 20 meters (66 ft.) tall and measure up to 8 meters (26 ft.) around the base. They are survivors of a time when Australia and Antarctica belonged to the supercontinent, Gondwana, when it was covered by wet, tropical rain forest. The species survived the last Ice Age, and the trees you see here are about 2,000 years old, suckering off root systems about 8,000 years old. The trees are a 2½ hour walk from O'Reilly's Rainforest Guesthouse (see below).

ESSENTIALS

GETTING THERE By Car O'Reilly's is 37 kilometers (22¼ miles) from the town of Canungra. Because the road is very twisty and winding, take it slow, allow yourself an hour from Canungra to reach O'Reilly's, and plan to arrive before dark. **Binnaburra** is 35 kilometers (21 miles) from Nerang via Beechmont, or 26 kilometers (15½ miles) from Canungra, on a similarly winding mountain road. From the Gold Coast go west to Nerang, where you can turn off to Binnaburra via Beechmont, or go on to Canungra where you will see the O'Reilly's and Binnaburra turn-offs. From Brisbane, follow the Pacific Highway south and take the Beenleigh/Mt. Tamborine exit to Mt. Tamborine. From there follow the signs to Canungra. Allow a good 2½ hours to get to either resort from Brisbane, and 90 minutes from the Gold Coast. Binnaburra sells unleaded fuel; O'Reilly's has emergency supplies only.

Tips for Exploring Lamington National Park

The easiest way to explore the park is to base yourself at **O'Reilly's Rainforest Guesthouse** in the Green Mountains section of the park, or at **Binnaburra Mountain Lodge** in the Binnaburra section (see "Where to Stay & Dine: Worth a Splurge" below). Most of the trails lead from one or the other of these resorts, and a 23-kilometer (14-mile) Border Trail connects them; it follows the New South Wales–Queensland border for much of the way, and can be walked by most reasonably fit folk in a day. Guided walks and activities at both resorts are for houseguests only; however, both properties welcome day visitors who just want to walk the trails for free. Both have inexpensive cafes for day-trippers.

If you can be bothered to carry them, it is a good idea to bring a torch (flashlight) and maybe binoculars for wildlife spotting. The temperature is often 4°C to 5°C (10°F to 20°F) cooler than on the Gold Coast, so bring a sweater in summer and bundle up in winter when nights get close to freezing. September to October is orchid season, and the frogs come out in noisy abundance in February and March.

By Coach   The **Mountain Coach Company** (☎ 07/5524 4249) does daily transfers to O'Reilly's from all Gold Coast hotels and Coolangatta Airport. The fare is A$35 (U.S.$24.50) adults, A$17 (U.S.$11.90) children round-trip and includes a commentary and a cafe stop at Mt. Tamborine en route. **Allstate Scenic Tours** (☎ 07/3285 1777) makes a coach run from outside the Roma Street Transit Centre in Brisbane every day except Saturday at 9:30am, arriving at O'Reilly's at 12:45pm. It costs A$35 (U.S.$24.50) adults, A$25 (U.S.$17.50) kids ages 4 to 16, round-trip.

The Binnaburra resort runs a daily shuttle from the Surfers Paradise Transit Centre on Beach Road that costs A$16 (U.S.$11.20) per adult, half price for kids ages 5 to 14, each way. It departs at 1:15pm and arrives at 2:15pm. The same Allstate Scenic Tours coach that takes visitors to O'Reilly's (see above) takes passengers to Canungra, where Binnaburra Mountain Lodge sends a bus down to collect you. The Brisbane–Canungra leg is A$25 (U.S.$17.50) adults, A$15 (U.S.$10.50) kids ages 4 to 16, round-trip. The coach from Canungra up the mountain is free for lodge guests, and there's a small fee for campers and day-trippers.

DAY TRIPS   Companies running day tours from both Brisbane and the Gold Coast include **Coachtrans** (☎ 1300/36 1788, or 07/3236 4165), and **Backtracks 4WD Safaris** (☎ 1800/356 693 in Australia, or 07/5573 5693). The Gold Coast Tourism Bureau can get you in touch with other day tour operators; see "Visitor Information" in the "Gold Coast" section.

VISITOR INFORMATION   The best sources of information on hiking are **O'Reilly's Rainforest Guesthouse** and **Binnaburra Mountain Lodge** (see "Where to Stay" below for both); ask them to send you copies of their walking maps. There is a national parks information office at both properties. For detailed information on hiking and camping in the park, contact the ranger at **Lamington National Park,** Green Mountains section (which is at O'Reilly's), via Canungra, QLD 4211 (☎ 07/5544 0634).

WHERE TO STAY & DINE: WORTH A SPLURGE

The rates at these two delightful mountaintop retreats include all activities, morning and afternoon tea, and supper; those at Binnaburra include three meals a day. There is little to choose between them. The rooms are cozier and cuter at Binnaburra, and its lounge and dining room are more modern and attractive; the family-owned O'Reilly's is a little homier and more welcoming. Both properties offer ample walking trails of a similar type and distance; guided walks, including nighttime wildlife-spotting trips; nice food; and a restful, enjoyable experience. Look into the special-interest workshops both properties run throughout the year, which can be anything from gourmet weekends to mountain-jogging programs.

✪ **Binnaburra Mountain Lodge.** Beechmont via Canungra, QLD 4211. ☎ **1800/074 260** in Australia, or 07/5533 3622. Fax 07/5533 3647. www.binnaburralodge.com.au. E-mail: binnabur@fan.net.au. 41 cabins, 22 with bathroom (shower only). MINIBAR. A$145–$185 (U.S.$101.50–$129.50) single; A$250–$330 (U.S.$175–$231) double. Additional person A$125–$165 (U.S.$87.50–$115.50) adults, A$39 (U.S.$27.30) children 5–16. Rates decrease with every night you stay. Rates include all meals and activities. Ask about 2-night packages. Minimum 2-night stay weekends, 3-night stay public holidays. AE, BC, DC, JCB, MC, V.

Binnaburra is every bit the postcard-perfect mountain lodge: cute chalets nestled in the forest, a fire roaring in the lounge, and birds twittering in the lofty trees. The original cabins, built in 1935, are still in use today; they've been outfitted with modern comforts, but not 20th-century "inconveniences," such as telephones, radios, or clocks. Of the 21 trails leading from the lodge, 9 are short walks of less than 6 kilometers (3½ miles). The 12 longer trails range from a 9-kilometer (5½-mile) walk through "dry" rain forest to the 23-kilometer (14-mile) Border Trail to O'Reilly's. On Tuesday the resort buses hikers to O'Reilly's so they can spend the day walking back to Binnaburra. The lodge also conducts abseiling at least twice a week for anyone from beginners to advanced adventurers. Because there are no TVs, your evening fun might consist of parlor games, a weekly bush dance, or evening slide presentations on the local natural history. Kids can entertain themselves in the excellent playground; special activities for kids are offered during school holidays.

While none of the accommodations is grandly decorated, all are prettily decorated with pine-paneled walls and floral bedcovers, and equipped with heaters and electric blankets. The cutest and most spacious are the mud-brick and weatherboard Acacia cabins, which have private bathrooms and the best views over the Numinbah Valley. There are two kinds of less-expensive Casuarina cabins—the nicest are the small and very cozy huts with a pitched ceiling, a washbasin, and a nice aspect into the forest and over the valley. Less atmospheric are the bunkroom-style rooms that sleep four to six people—good for families and groups of friends. Guests in Casuarina cabins share bath facilities, which include a Jacuzzi. Meals are served in the lovely stone-and-timber dining room. Seating is communal, so you get to meet other travelers. Free tea and coffee is on the boil all day. There is also a craft shop, a natural history library, a Laundromat, and conference rooms.

✪ **O'Reilly's Rainforest Guesthouse.** Via Canungra, Lamington National Park Rd., Lamington National Park, QLD 4275. ☎ **1800/688 722** in Australia, or 07/5544 0644. Fax 07/5544 0638. www.oreillys.com.au. E-mail: reservations@oreillys.com.au. 49 units, 43 with bathroom (shower only). A$90–$200 (U.S.$63–$140) single; A$150–$240 (U.S.$105–$168) double. Additional person A$20 (U.S.$14) extra; children 17 and under free in parents' room if they use existing bedding. Free crib. Rates include all activities. Rates decrease with every night you stay. Minimum 2-night stay weekends, 3-night stay long weekends, 4-night stay Easter and Christmas. Ask about packages for stays of 2 nights or more. Meal plans A$59 (U.S.$41.30) adults, A$30 (U.S.$21) children 10–17, A$15 (U.S.$10.50) children 4–9 for 3 meals per day; 2-meal package available. AE, BC, DC, MC, V.

A highlight of your stay at this cozy retreat will surely be the chance to hand-feed brilliantly colored rain-forest birds every morning. Nestled high on a cleared plateau, the buildings are closed in on three sides by dense tangled rain forest and open to picturesque mountain views to the west. The rain forest begins right at the parking lot, from which 19 trails fan out through the bush. One of the nicest is the 7.6-kilometer (4½-mile) round-trip trail to Elabana Falls, which takes about half a day. The staff run half-day and full-day guided walks, and half-day 4WD bus trips. Once a week they will take guests to Binnaburra so guests can hike back to O'Reilly's on the all-day Border Trail; let them know when you book if you want to do this. Every night there is a slide show on the area's wildlife or history, or spot-lighting walks to see possums, glowworms, and, in season, luminous fungi. Sometimes in summer there are cliff-top campfire nights with steaks cooked over the fire. On weekends and school holidays there is a "Scrub Club" for kids over age 5.

The timber resort complex is inviting rather than grand. The guest lounge has an open fire and is scattered with old-fashioned sofas, chairs, and an upright piano. The modestly furnished rooms are not particularly atmospheric, but they are pleasant enough. Each has a small fridge (except for rooms in the Tooloona block), a heater, and electric blankets. The six rooms in the Tooloona block, which dates from the 1930s and was renovated in 1998, have communal bathrooms and basic furniture. The largest rooms are the six motel-style Elabana rooms, also renovated in 1998; they have en suite bathrooms. The 37 Bithongabel rooms have the best views; they're also the most expensive and have en suite bathrooms. Two rooms have wheelchair access. Reception lends hair dryers. The maitre d' assigns you to a table in the dining room, so you get to meet other guests over wonderful food. If you do not buy a meal package, buffet breakfast and lunch cost A$22 (U.S.$15.40) per meal, and a three-course dinner is A$30 (U.S.$21). After dinner, guests head to the hexagonal timber bar, perched up high for great sunset views. Among the services and facilities are a pleasant cafe and gift shop, a day/night tennis court, a basketball court, a game room, a Laundromat, baby-sitting, and free tea, coffee, and cookies all day.

CAMPING

✪ **Binnaburra Campsite.** Beechmont via Canungra, QLD 4211. ☎ 1800/074 260 in Australia, or 07/5533 3758. Fax 07/5533 3658. 7 powered campsites, 18 unpowered tent sites; 13 permanent tents, none with bathroom. Tent sites A$9 (U.S.$6.30) adult, A$6 (U.S.$4.20) seniors and students, A$27 (U.S.$18.90) family of five; powered site A$3 (U.S.$21) extra per night. Permanent tents A$36 (U.S.$25.20) for a 2-bed tent, A$54 (U.S.$37.80) for a 4-bed tent. Children 5–15 half price. Linen A$2 (U.S.$1.40) per bed. Ask about weekly discounts and midweek specials. AE, BC, DC, JCB, MC, V.

Binnaburra Mountain Lodge's neat little campsite is perched on the hill a few hundred meters/yards from the main building. Cute permanent tents are equipped with carpeted floors, screened windows, pine beds and mattresses, and electric lighting. They have great valley views from a private verandah. Campers may pay to take part in the lodge activities and take meals in the dining room. Possum's Kitchen sells basic take-out food and grocery supplies that you can cook on the coin-operated gas barbecues (bring your own cutlery and crockery). You share shower blocks, and there's a coin-op Laundromat. If you want to light a campfire, buy wood before you arrive; roadside homesteads en route usually sell it.

The Red Centre   9

by Natalie Kruger

The Red Centre is the landscape many think of when they think of Australia—vast horizons, fiery red sand as far as the eye can see, mysterious monoliths, cloudless blue sky, harsh sunlight, and the rhythmic twang of the didgeridoo. It's home to ancient mountain ranges; "living fossil" palm trees that survived the Ice Age; the powerful Finke River, thought to be the world's first-ever watercourse; and of course, Ayers Rock, which the Aborigines call Uluru. Aboriginal people have lived here for tens of thousands of years, long before the Pyramids were a twinkle in a Pharaoh's eye. The Centre is still largely unexplored by white Australians. A single highway cuts through it from Adelaide in the south to Darwin in the north; a few 4WD tracks make a lonely spiderweb across it; but there are many, many areas where non-Aborigines have never set foot.

Alice Springs is the unofficial capital of Central Australia. First off, let's get one thing straight—Alice Springs and Uluru are not side by side. Never a day goes by that a tourist does not wander into the Alice Springs visitor center after lunch and say he or she wants to "go and see the Rock this afternoon." The Rock is 462 kilometers (272 miles) away. You can see it in a day from Alice, but it takes a Herculean effort.

The Red Centre is more than just a Rock, however. Allow yourself a few days to experience all there is to see and do in this iconic heart of Australia—such as visiting the impressive Olgas monoliths near Ayers Rock, stark Kings Canyon, or the School of the Air in Alice Springs; taking an Aboriginal bush tucker walk; or staying at an Outback homestead where you can hike, ride horses, or learn to throw a boomerang. If you base yourself at Alice Springs, it's easy to radiate out to lesser-known but beautiful attractions like Palm Valley, Glen Helen Gorge, and Standley Chasm. Too many international visitors (and Australians, too) fly in, snap a photo of the Rock, and head home, only to miss the real essence of the desert.

Is the Centre expensive? If you camp, join a safari, or stay in bunkhouse accommodations with shared bathrooms, no. You will have no trouble finding a perfectly nice hotel room, cabin, or the like with a private bathroom in Alice Springs for less than A$100 (U.S.$70). However, Kings Canyon Resort and Ayers Rock Resort, which are the other two main accommodation centers, can be pricey if you do not select your accommodations and tours carefully. This chapter's "Kings Canyon" and "Uluru–Kata Tjuta National Park" sections contain advice on how to enjoy these places and preserve your budget.

EXPLORING THE RED CENTRE

VISITOR INFORMATION   The **Northern Territory Tourist Commission (NTTC)** is located at Tourism House, 43 Mitchell St., Darwin, NT 0800 (☎ **08/8999 3900;** fax 08/8999 3888; www.nttc.com.au). The Commission publishes an excellent full-color *Central Australia Holiday Guide,* which details hotels, tour operators, car-rental companies, airlines, and attractions, and gives a good overview of all there is to see and do. The Commission also publishes a 52-page *Motoring Guide.* It is less informative than the holiday guide, and the maps are only rudimentary, but it does contain good details on campsites and campervan parks throughout the Northern Territory. The Commission operates a **Holiday Centre** (☎ **1800/621 336** in Australia; fax 08/8951 8582), which assists you in planning your itinerary, provides tips and advice, and makes hotel, car-rental, and tour reservations.

Add 5% tax to all accommodations tariffs in the Northern Territory. If you are taking a holiday package, the tax is payable on the accommodations component of the package. The tax is not payable on camping.

GETTING AROUND BY CAR   The **Automobile Association of the Northern Territory (AANT),** 79–81 Smith St., Darwin, NT 0800 (☎ **08/8981 3837;** fax 08/8941 2965) offers reciprocal emergency breakdown service to members of overseas automobile associations, as well as motoring maps, accommodation guides, and advice.

The rough and rugged Northern Territory is a four-wheel-driver's paradise, as the pavement tends to be limited to major highways and arterial roads. You will be able to get to 95% of everything you'll want to see driving a conventional 2WD car, but some of the most stunning scenery and best attractions are in remote locations accessible only by 4WD. Many more attractions are on good *unsealed* (unpaved) roads suitable for a 2WD car, but your car-rental company will probably not insure you for driving on them. If you want to have access to everything, you're left with two choices—join a 4WD tour (see below) or drive a 4WD vehicle yourself. Anyone can drive a 4WD, but if you've never driven one, make sure your car-rental company gives you a thorough briefing on how to do it before you head off. For details on safe driving, see "Getting Around" in chapter 3.

If you're exploring the area on your own, always remember to check road conditions with local authorities before you set off. The **Northern Territory Department of Transport and Works** has a 24-hour recorded report on road conditions in the Red Centre (☎ **1800/246 199** in the Northern Territory). You can call the AANT in Darwin during office hours for road conditions, and tune in to radio FM88 for up-to-date road reports as you are driving. Local tour companies, the Central Australian Tourism Industry Association (see "Visitor Information" in the Alice Springs section below), and police stations in remote areas should also be able to help.

Red Centre Travel Tips

Uluru is notorious for its plagues of flies in summer. Don't be embarrassed to cover your hat and head with the fly-nets sold in resort stores—you'll look like the Dreamtime Beekeeper from Outer Space, but there will be "no flies on you, mate"—an Aussie way of saying you are doing the right thing. In the winter, temperatures drop below freezing at night in the Alice and Uluru, and the wind can be sharp, so bring plenty of warm clothing. For more tips on when to visit, see "When to Go" in chapter 3.

The Red Centre

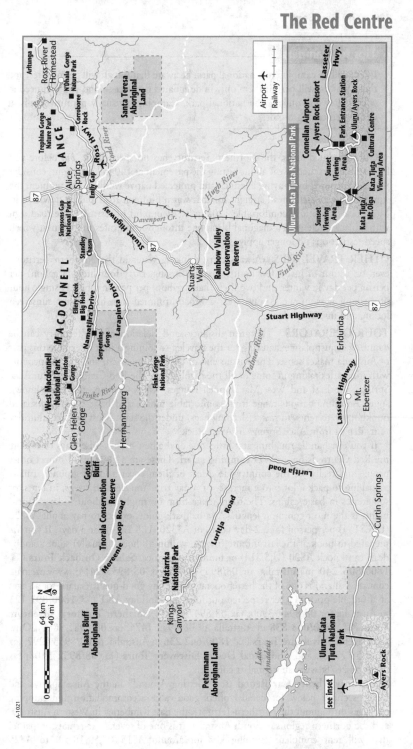

Tips for Campers

If you will be camping in a national park, be aware that not all will permit fires, and those that do will permit them only in designated fireplaces—and you will need to collect firewood outside the national park. Camping is usually permitted only at designated campgrounds.

Outside settled areas, the Northern Territory has no speed limit, *but* before you break into an excited sweat about hitting the pavement at 140 miles an hour, consider the dangers posed by straying livestock and protected native wildlife. The moment the sun goes down, cattle head straight for that warm bitumen road and lie down on it. Most locals stick to a comfortable 120kmph (72 m.p.h.) or less. A white road sign with a black circle with a diagonal black line through it indicates the point at which speed restrictions no longer apply.

OTHER TRAVEL TIPS   Always carry drinking water in the Northern Territory, even on a tour of just a few hours. If you're hiking, carry four liters (a gallon) per person per day in winter, and two liters (half a gallon) per person for every single hour of walking in summer. Always wear a broad-brimmed hat, high-factor sunscreen lotion, and insect repellent.

TOUR OPERATORS   The great distances and isolation of the Territory can be daunting or just plain exhausting for the traveler, so joining a tour to explore this part of Australia makes sense. There is no end of coach, minicoach, and 4WD operators with itineraries taking in some or all the highlights of the Red Centre—Uluru, Alice Springs, the East and West MacDonnell Ranges, Kings Canyon, and lesser-known spots. Accommodations range from comfortable motels and basic cabins, to shared bunkhouses, to tents, to *swags* (sleeping bags) under the stars. Most of these multiday tours depart from Alice Springs or Ayers Rock.

If you can handle roughing it a little, one of the best money-wise ways to explore the Red Centre is on a **4WD camping safari.** These are a great way to meet other people and really see the countryside. Most of them cover a lot of ground, usually managing to pack a lot into a mere 2- or 3-day trip. You sleep in swags, in tents, or sometimes in basic cabins. The tours range from overnight to about 5 days; 2 or 3 nights is the most common length. As a ballpark guide, expect to pay about A$220 (U.S.$154) per person for a 2-day safari, or A$320 (U.S.$224) for 3 days. If you are prepared to book at the last minute (that is, within 48 hours, usually) some standby deals can knock A$20 (U.S.$14) or more off the price. **Sahara Outback Tours** (☎ **1800/806 240** in Australia, or 08/8953 0881; fax 08/8953 2414; www.ozemail. com.au/~sahara) is one of the better operators offering good-quality safaris for all ages at affordable prices. Other respected outfitters are **Holiday AKT** (☎ **1800/891 121** in Australia, or 08/8947 3900; fax 08/8947 3988), **Northern Territory Adventure Tours** (☎ **1800/063 838** in Australia, or 08/8952 1474; fax 08/8981 9058), **Outback Scenic Adventure Tours** (☎ **1800/642 236** in Australia, or 08/8953 5292; fax 08/8953 2758), and **Aboriginal Desert Discovery Tours** (☎ **08/8952 3408;** fax 08/8953 2678; www.aboriginalart.com.au).

Territory Thrifty Car Rental (see "Getting Around" in the Alice Springs and Uluru sections below for details) offers good-value accommodation and camping packages throughout the Northern Territory, the East Kimberley in Western Australia, and the northern regions of South Australia. It is one of several car-rental companies that will rent complete camping kits for around A$15 (U.S.$10.50) to A$25 (U.S.$17.50) a day.

462km (277 miles) NE of Ayers Rock; 1,491km (894½ miles) S of Darwin; 1,544km (932½ miles) N of Adelaide; 2,954km (1,772½ miles) NW of Sydney

No matter what direction they come from, anyone who flies to Alice Springs must soar for hours over a vast and numbingly flat, unchanging landscape. That's why folks are so surprised when they reach Alice Springs and see low but dramatic mountain ranges, rich red and rippling in the sunshine. Many people excitedly mistake them for Ayers Rock, but that baby is close to 483 kilometers (300 miles) down the road. These hills, jutting their weathered cliff faces up against the town's streets, are the MacDonnell Ranges.

In the early 1870s, a handful of telegraph-station workers struggled nearly one thousand miles north from Adelaide through uncompromising desert to settle by a small spring in what must truly have seemed like the end of the earth. Alice Springs, as the little settlement was called, was nothing but a few huts built around a repeater station on the ambitious telegraph line that was to link Adelaide with Darwin and the rest of the world. Today, "the Alice," as Australians fondly dub her, has all the paraphernalia a city of 25,000 people should have, like shops, banks, radio stations, and nightclubs. Many tourists really only come to Alice to get to Ayers Rock, a few hundred miles down the road, but the town has plenty of charms all her own. The striking red folds of the ✪ **MacDonnell Ranges** hide shady gorges with nice picnic grounds, picturesque (and cold!) spring-fed swimming holes, a planned 200-kilometer (125-mile) hiking trail partly ready for your boots now, old gold-rush towns, museums, and an Aussie cattle station that welcomes visitors. One of the world's top 10 desert golf courses abuts the ranges.

This is the heart of the Aboriginal "Arrernte" tribe's country, and Alice is a rich source of tours, shops, and galleries for anyone with an interest in Aboriginal culture, art, or simple souvenirs. There is a sad side to the town's Aboriginal riches. Not every Aboriginal succeeds in splicing his or her ancient civilization with the 20th century, and the result is dislocated communities living in the river bed with only alcohol for company.

Despite the isolation, Alice Springs is not an expensive town to visit. Accommodations, restaurants, and attractions are all, for the most part, modestly priced.

ESSENTIALS

GETTING THERE   By Plane   Ansett, Qantas and/or their respective subsidiary regional airlines fly to Alice Springs once or twice a day from most state capitals, Cairns, and Ayers Rock. Both airlines also operate one or two direct services from Broome in Western Australia on weekends. **Airnorth** (☎ **1800/627 474** in Australia, or 08/8945 2866) does a "Centre Run" from Darwin via Katherine and Tennant Creek every day except Sunday. Flight time to Alice is 3½ hours from Sydney and Perth, and 2½ hours from Cairns. The **Alice Springs Airport Shuttle** (☎ **1800/ 621 188** in the Northern Territory, or 08/8953 0310) meets all the big interstate flights, but not flights from smaller regional areas like Tennant Creek, and costs A$9 (U.S.$6.30) one way or A$15 (U.S.$10.50) round-trip per person. A taxi from the airport to town, a distance of about 15 kilometers (9 miles), costs about A$20 (U.S.$14).

By Train   The *Ghan* train, named after Afghani camel-train drivers who carried supplies inland in the 19th century, travels from Melbourne to Adelaide and across the harsh Simpson Desert to Alice Springs. This scenery is both fascinatingly empty and extremely monotonous all the way from Adelaide to Alice, so don't be concerned that you miss a lot of it by overnighting on the train. It departs Melbourne at 10:35pm every Wednesday and arrives in Alice 36 hours later at 10am Friday. From Adelaide it leaves Monday and Thursday at 2pm, arriving in Alice at 10am the next day. The one-way journey costs A$170 (U.S.$119) from Adelaide and A$250 (U.S.$175) from Melbourne in a sitting berth coach class car equipped with a VCR, and A$351 (U.S.$245.70) from Adelaide, A$525 (U.S.$367.50) from Melbourne, in a private holiday class sleeper with shared facilities at the end of each car. Children ages 4 to 15 pay half the coach fare and just over half the holiday class fare. Only Australian seniors and students are entitled to discounted fares. Meals in both classes cost extra. See "Getting Around" in chapter 3, for more details on the train's facilities, and its booking agents overseas. By the time you read this, plans may be in place for a Melbourne-to-Sydney leg to be added to the *Ghan* route, thus enabling a seamless, if very long, Sydney–Alice Springs rail journey. Contact **Great Southern Railway** (☎ **1800/ 888 480** or 13 21 47 in Australia, or 08/8213 4696; fax 08/8213 4490; www.gsr. com.au).

By Bus   **Greyhound Pioneer** (☎ **13 20 30** in Australia) serves Alice Springs twice daily from Adelaide and daily from Darwin. **McCafferty's** (☎ **13 14 99** in Australia) serves Alice four times a week from Adelaide and daily from Darwin. It's a 19-hour trip from Adelaide, and the fare is A$135 (U.S.$94.50) one-way. The trip takes around 20 hours from Darwin and costs A$145 (U.S.$101.50) one-way.

By Car   Alice Springs is on the **Stuart Highway** linking Adelaide and Darwin. If you are driving, allow three days to make the trip from Adelaide, and a solid two, or a more comfortable three, days from Darwin. From Sydney you will need to connect to the Stuart Highway via Broken Hill and Port Augusta north of Adelaide; from Cairns you will need to join it via Mt. Isa and Tennant Creek. Both routes are extremely long, dull, and best avoided. From Perth it is an even longer, duller drive across the Nullarbor Plain to Port Augusta to connect with the Stuart Highway.

VISITOR INFORMATION   The **Central Australian Tourism Industry Association (CATIA) Visitor Information Centre** is on Gregory Terrace at the southern end of Todd Mall, Alice Springs, NT 0870 (☎ **08/8952 5800;** fax 08/8953 0295). It is an excellent one-stop shop for information on touring, not just in and around Alice but also to Kings Canyon and the Uluru–Kata Tjuta National Park (Ayers Rock). It has loads of brochures, touch-screen displays, motoring advice and road-condition reports, and National Park notes; it will also make bookings for you. It is open Monday to Friday from 8:30am to 5:30pm, and from 9am to 4pm weekends and public holidays.

SPECIAL EVENTS   The town is host to a couple of bizarre events you may want to catch. The **Camel Cup** (yep, it's a camel race) is held usually on the second weekend in July. On the first Saturday in October, everyone from hundreds of miles around turns out for a day of much mirth-making and beer-drinking at the **Henley-on-Todd Regatta.** At this one-of-a-kind event crowds cheer as the proud owners of gaudily decorated, homemade bottomless "boats" race them on foot or on 4WD chassis down the dry bed of the Todd River, which runs through the center of town. Well, what else do you do on a river that only flows three days a year?

GETTING AROUND   **Avis** (☎ 08/8953 5533), **Budget** (☎ 08/8952 8899), **Hertz** (☎ 1800/89 1112 in the Northern Territory, or 08/8952 2644), and **Territory Thrifty Car Rental** (☎ **1800/89 1125** outside the Northern Territory, or 08/ 8952 9999) all rent conventional and 4WD vehicles. Local company **Outback Auto Rentals** (☎ **1800/652 133** in Australia, or 08/8953 5333) had terrific deals on my visit—A$49 (U.S.$34.30) a day for a small manual Starlet with 100 kilometers (60 miles) free and A20¢ (U.S.12¢) per kilometer after that; compared with A$75

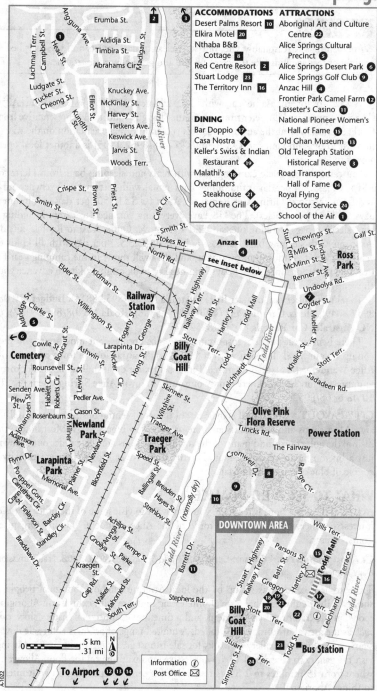

Safety Tip

Alice Springs is reasonably safe, but steer clear of dark streets and the river bed at night as teenage kids like to accost people and generally cause trouble.

(U.S.$52.50) for the same car with 100 kilometers (60 miles) free and A25¢ (U.S.12¢) per extra kilometer from one of the "big guy" outfits. A representative from Outback meets you at the airport and gives you an informal orientation on the way in to town to pick up your car. **CC Rentals** (☎ **08/8952 1405**) is another local operator with low rates.

You can rent complete camping kits with tents and sleeping bags from Hertz for A$14 (U.S.$9.80) per day (minimum 7 days' rental, with certain 4WD vehicles only) and from Territory Thrifty Car Rental for A$25 (U.S.$17.50) per day (minimum 5 days, all kinds of vehicles). The kits have everything you need to camp, including a tent, sleeping bags, cooking utensils, and a gas stove. Outback Auto Rentals' kits do not come with sleeping bags but cost only A$10 (U.S.$7) per day with all kinds of vehicles, even if you just rent overnight, and they will throw in the camping gear for free if you rent for more than 4 days. You need to book camping kits in advance with all companies.

To rent a **campervan,** contact **Brits Australia** (☎ 08/8952 8814), **Budget** (☎ 08/8952 8049), **Hertz Campervans** (☎ 08/8953 5333), **Koala** (☎ 08/8952 9177), or **NQ Australia Car Rentals** (☎ 08/8952 2777).

There is no local public transportation in Alice Springs, but most tours will pick you up at your hotel. The best way get around to the attractions in town is aboard the **Alice Wanderer bus** (see "Organized Tours, below, for details). **Taxi** fares are exorbitant, presumably because there is only one outfit in town, **Alice Springs Taxis** (☎ **13 10 08** or 08/8952 1877).

CITY LAYOUT　　**Todd Mall** is the heart of the small central business district (CBD) area. Most shops and restaurants are here or just a few blocks away. Most hotels, the casino, the golf course, and many of the town's attractions are a few miles out of town, just a bit too far to get to on foot. The dry Todd River "flows" through the city a couple of blocks east of Todd Mall.

WHAT TO SEE & DO IN ALICE

As well as the attractions listed here, you may want to visit some of the other places of interest in Alice, described in the route of the Alice Wanderer bus in "Organized Tours," below.

✪ **Aboriginal Art and Culture Centre.** 86 Todd St. ☎ **08/8952 3408.** Free admission. Daily 8am–6pm.

This excellent center was set up by the local Arrernte tribe of Aboriginal people to showcase their culture. It has a small, interesting museum with exhibits on Aboriginal foods, music traditional and modern, and a timeline of Aboriginal history since *contact,* as the arrival of Europeans is called. A limited range of artifacts is for sale downstairs, and a huge art gallery of works for sale is upstairs. Even if you are not buying, visit the gallery to take a peek at the impressive sand painting on the floor. Allow anywhere from 15 minutes to 2 hours to explore the center, depending on your interest in things Aboriginal.

Alice Springs Cultural Precinct. Larapinta Dr. at Memorial Ave., 2km (1¼ miles) south of town. Incorporating the Museum of Central Australia (☎ **08/8952 5022**); Araluen Centre

A Degree from Didgeridoo University

Fancy yourself as a Ray Charles of the desert? Think with a bit of practice you could be the Louis Armstrong of central Australia? Then there's only one place for you to hone your talents—Didgeridoo University, at the Aboriginal Art and Culture Centre (see above).

Paul Ah Chee-Ngala has set up the "campus" to satisfy an ever-growing demand from world travelers to master the apparently simple but evocative rhythms of the didgeridoo. In truth, the university is an alcove in the culture center, and the degree takes just one hour. Classes begin every day at 1 and 5pm and cost A$10 (U.S.$7) adults, A$5 (U.S.$3.50) kids. (The class is included free as part of the Centre's half-day tour described in "Organized Tours," below.) Paul guarantees you will be able to make kangaroo-hopping sounds on the darn thing by the end of the hour—unless you are one of 1 in 30 people who cannot blow through their lips! The trick to didgeridoo playing is to breathe in and blow out at the same time, a technique known as circular breathing.

No one is sure how long didgeridoos have been around, but everyone agrees it's a long time. The instrument originated in Arnhemland, a remote area in the Top End of the Northern Territory. You can make your own didgeridoo (first you need to find a tree that has been hollowed by termites), or you can buy one from the souvenir stores in the Alice Springs mall.

There is no such thing as a good or bad didgeridoo. Look for one that is resonant and that you like the sound of. The diameter, the wood used, and the unique surface of the wood inside the instrument are what make each didgeridoo unique. Didgeridoos were never traditionally painted, so don't worry about selecting an authentic design on yours. The range of the instrument can vary from a high wail on G to a deep and somber A that was mostly used only in ceremonies. The shorter the didgeridoo, the higher the pitch.

If you can't take a "degree" at the Aboriginal Art and Culture Centre, you can learn to play the thing in your own living room via an audio lesson on the center's Web site, www.aboriginalart.com.au. The site sells didgeridoos, too.

for Arts & Entertainment (☎ **08/8953 3111**); Aviation Museum (☎ **08/8952 1411**); and the Pioneer Memorial Cemetery. Admission to Museum of Central Australia: A$6 (U.S.$4.20) adults; A$4 (U.S.$2.80) children under 16, seniors, and students; A$15 (U.S.$10.50) family. Free admission to aviation museum, arts and entertainment center, and cemetery. Daily 10am–5pm. Closed Christmas and Good Friday. Take a cab or the Alice Wanderer bus (see "Organized Tours," below).

Several attractions are clustered within walking distance of one another in this precinct. Along with fossils, natural history displays, and meteorites, the newly relocated Museum of Central Australia hopes to incorporate the Strehlow Exhibition, an absorbing display of research into Aboriginal language and customs made by T.G.H. Strehlow, a Lutheran missionary's son who grew up among the Aranda tribe in nearby Hermannsburg. The Araluen Centre for Arts & Entertainment has two art galleries of Aboriginal and contemporary Aussie artists and is worth a visit just for the impressive "Honey Ant Dreaming" and other stained-glass windows in the foyer. This is the place to catch any visual and performing arts events visiting town. The Aviation Museum preserves Northern Territory aerial history with old radios, engines, and aircraft housed in the original hangar on the site of Alice's first airstrip. The cemetery contains the graves of the aviator Connellan family, famous Aussie artist Albert Namitjira, and a number of "Afghani" (Pakistani) camel herders buried facing Mecca.

✪ **Alice Springs Desert Park.** Larapinta Dr., 6km (3½ miles) north of town. ☎ **08/ 8951 8788.** Admission A$12 (U.S.$8.40) adults; A$6 (U.S.$4.20) seniors, students, and children 5–16; A$30 (U.S.$21) family of 6. Daily 7:30am–6pm (last entry 5pm). Closed Christmas.

This wildlife and flora park condenses 1,000 square kilometers (386 square miles) of three different central Australian desert habitats into a 1.6-kilometer (1-mile) trail. Here you can see 120 of the animal species that live in and around Alice but that you won't necessarily be able to spot easily in the wild. These include a collection of 25-centimeter (10-inch) giant stick insects that a tourist found hanging in a tree and that the park suspects is a new species, speedy bush mice called dunnarts, an adorable endangered hopping marsupial called the bilby, and striped raccoon-like numbats. Don't miss the exciting Birds of Prey show or the 20-minute film on Australia's 4,500-million-year history, which has a surprise shot at the end—see it for yourself! Dining options at the park include Madigan's, which serves sophisticated bush tucker, and a cafe. Allow 3 hours to see the lot.

It is easy to explore the Desert Park on your own, but you can take a guided tour such as the one run by the Aboriginal Art and Culture Centre (see "Organized Tours," below), which will help you learn a bit more about the plants, landscapes, and wildlife. **Desert Park Transfers** (☎ 08/8952 4667) will get you to the park from your hotel for A$20 (U.S.$14) for adults, A$14 (U.S.$9.80) for seniors, students, and children ages 5 to 14, and A$60 (U.S.$42) for a family of six. (Price includes park admission.)

Frontier Camel Farm. Lot 5129 Ross Hwy. (4km/2½ miles from town). ☎ **1800/806 499** in Australia, or 08/8953 0444. Admission to farm, museum, and reptile house A$5 (U.S.$3.50) adults, A$2.50 (U.S.$1.75) children 5–12, A$10 (U.S.$7) family. Admission plus guided tour of farm and reptile house and short camel ride A$10 (U.S.$7) adults, A$8 (U.S.$5.60) seniors and students, A$5 (U.S.$3.50) children, A$25 (U.S.$17.50) family. Daily 9am–5pm; guided tours 10:30am daily, also 2pm April–Oct. Closed Christmas, New Year's Day, and Camel Cup Day. Take a cab or the Alice Wanderer bus (see "Organized Tours," below).

Camels might not be the first animal that comes to mind when you think of Australia, but their ability to get by without water was key to opening up the arid inland parts of the country to European settlement in the 1800s. One early explorer traveled 354 kilometers (220 miles) in 8 days on camels without giving them a drink. The first camel was imported to Australia from the Canary Islands in the 1840s. With the advent of cars, they were released into the wilds of central Australia, and today there are 200,000 of them roaming the desert. You can drop into this camel farm at any time to take a short ride on a camel, browse the interesting black-and-white photos in the camel museum, or inspect a fearsome collection of arid-zone snakes, but it's worth timing your visit so you can take one of the guided tours. The best way to enjoy the farm, though, is to get on the back of a camel and take the three-hour Todd River Ramble (see "Camel Safaris and Other Outdoor Activities," below, for details).

National Pioneer Women's Hall of Fame. The Old Courthouse, 27 Hartley St. ☎ **08/ 8952 9006.** Admission A$1 (U.S.70¢) or A$2 (U.S.$1.40) donation. Daily 10am–2pm or by appointment. Closed mid-Dec to early Feb.

With a collection of photographs, domestic artifacts, and other memorabilia, this museum remembers over 100 ordinary Aussie women who were pioneers in their fields, be they farmers, governesses, or pilots.

✪ **Old Telegraph Station Historical Reserve.** On the Stuart Hwy. 4km (2½ miles) north of town. ☎ **08/8952 3993.** Admission A$4 (U.S.$2.80) adults, A$3 (U.S.$2.10) seniors, A$2 (U.S.$1.40) children 16 and under, A$10 (U.S.$7) family (2 adults and 2 children). Daily

8am–5pm; picnic grounds open to 7pm May–Sep, to 9pm Oct–Apr. Grounds open but no tours available Christmas and Good Friday. Take a cab or the Alice Wanderer bus (see "Organized Tours," below), or the riverside walking/bike track that starts at the northern end of Todd Mall at Wills Terrace.

Alice Springs began life as this charming telegraph repeater station in 1871. Situated by a pretty, permanent water hole fed by the very springs that gave the town its name, this is a truly peaceful spot amid red hills, towering gums, and green lawns. Aided by a map and a detailed brochure you pick up free from the entrance to the reserve, you can wander through the cute old station master's residence, now restored with displays of old furniture and cooking implements of the time; the telegraph office, with its Morse code tap-tapping away; the shoeing yard packed to the rafters with blacksmith's equipment; and the stables, which house two vintage buggies and lots of old saddlery. The atmosphere turns even more authentic when you order *scones* (biscuits) and tea from a "kitchen-maid" in period dress in the wonderful historic kitchen. The scones come straight from the enormous original wood-fired stove (they're only served from April to October). Allow a good hour to see everything.

Royal Flying Doctor Service (RFDS). 8–10 Stuart Terrace, at the end of Hartley St. ☎ **08/ 8952 1129.** Admission A$5 (U.S.$3.50) adults, A$2 (U.S.$1.40) children 12 and under. Mon–Sat 9am–4pm, Sunday and public holidays 1–4pm. Closed Christmas and New Year's Day.

Alice Springs is a major base for this airborne medical service that treats people who live in remote Outback areas. You can see the radio operations in action handling the odd emergency and, more commonly, routine clinic and diagnosis calls. Half-hour tours of the base and museum begin every 30 minutes and include an interesting short video.

School of the Air. 80 Head St. ☎ **08/8951 6834.** Admission A$3 (U.S.$2.10) adults, A$2 (U.S.$1.40) seniors and children 5–16. Mon–Sat and public holidays 8:30am–4:30pm, Sun 1:30–4:30pm. Closed Christmas, Boxing Day (Dec 26), New Year's Day, and Good Friday.

Sitting in on school lessons may not be your idea of a vacation, but this school is different—it broadcasts by radio to a 1,300,000-square-kilometer (501,800-square-mile) "schoolroom" of children on remote Outback stations. The classroom covers an area the size of Germany, Great Britain, Ireland, New Zealand, and Japan. You can sit in on class between 8:30am and 2:30pm Monday to Friday when school's in session. Outside those hours you can still hear taped radio classes, watch a video, learn more from the interactive CD-ROM, and fiddle with the old radios and other memorabilia.

ORGANIZED TOURS
AROUND TOWN & OUT IN THE DESERT

By far the best-value way to see the town's attractions is on the ✪ **Alice Wanderer** bus (☎ **1800/669 111** in Australia, or 08/8952 2111). It makes a running loop of town attractions every 70 minutes; you hop on and off as you please and get a nice commentary from the bus owner/driver, Bruce Cotterill. It picks up from accommodations for no charge, and departs from the southern end of Todd Mall daily at 9am, 10:10am, 11:20am, 12:30pm, 1:40pm, 2:50pm, and 4pm. The fare is A$20 (U.S.$14) for adults, A$18 (U.S.$12.60) for seniors, and A$10 (U.S.$7) for students and kids ages 5 to 15. Entry to attractions is extra; many of them are free. You buy tickets onboard.

    The bus goes to most major attractions, including the Old Telegraph Station, the Frontier Camel Farm, the School of the Air, the Royal Flying Doctor Service, ANZAC Hill for a two-minute photo stop, the Aboriginal Art and Culture Centre, and the Alice Springs Cultural Precinct. It also drops in on a few lesser-known spots, like the **Road Transport Hall of Fame,** Norris Bell Avenue off the Stuart Highway, 8 kilometers (5 miles) south of town (☎ **08/8952 7161**), home to a B-Model Mack truck and other vintage and veteran trucks and cars. It's open daily from 9am to 5pm, admission is A$4 (U.S.$2.80) for adults, A$3 (U.S.$2.10) for seniors, A$2.50 (U.S.$1.75) for kids, and A$9 (U.S.$6.30) for a family. Next door to the Road Transport Hall of Fame, the Wanderer calls at the **Old *Ghan* Museum** (☎ **08/8955 5047**), which holds the original *Ghan* train that plied the Adelaide– Alice Springs line from 1929 to 1980. The train makes runs of 10 kilometers (6 miles) and 25 kilometers (15 miles) along the track on certain days each week if enough people are interested; call to see whether it's running. The museum and train are open from 9am to 5pm daily in the peak winter season (shorter hours in summer). Admission is A$4 (U.S.$2.80) adults, A$3 (U.S.$2.10) for seniors and students, A$2.50 (U.S.$1.75) for kids, and A$11 (U.S.$7.70) for a family. The Wanderer also calls at **Panorama Guth,** 65 Hartley St. (☎ **08/8952 2013**), an art gallery housing a delightful 360° painting by artist Henk Guth of central Australian landscapes. It's open Monday to Saturday from 9am to 5pm and Sunday from noon to 5pm (closed Sunday December to February).

They are not quite as good a value as the Wanderer, but guided coach tours are also available. Contact **AAT Kings** (☎ **08/8952 1700**). Expect to pay A$45 (U.S.$31.50) for a half-day tour. **Alice Springs Tour Professionals** (☎ **08/8953 0666**) does a variety of 1- and 2-day tours combining the top attractions with such popular activities as hot-air balloon trips, didgeridoo lessons, and camel rides. A day tour costs around A$100 (U.S.$70).

ABORIGINAL TOURS

The half-day ✪ **Aboriginal Desert Discovery Tour** offered by the Aboriginal Art and Culture Center (see "What to See and Do in Alice," above) won the Australian Tourism Award for Aboriginal and Torres Strait Islander Tourism in its first year of operation. This fascinating tour starts at the Culture Centre with an explanation of *the Dreamtime,* the undefined period of time when the world was created, according to Aboriginal beliefs. Next, the tour heads out into the bush, where you get to taste bush coconuts, bush bananas, and mistletoe seeds on a 1.5-kilometer (1-mile) bush tucker walk; visit a mock-up of a traditional Aboriginal camp; test your skill at boomerang and spear throwing; and hear about Aboriginal culture, beliefs, and family relationships over billy tea and damper. The tour ends with a 1-hour didgeridoo lesson back at the Cultural Centre. The tour costs A$60 (U.S.$42) for adults and A$33 (U.S.$23.10) for children under age 14 (including hotel pickup) and departs daily between 8am and 8:30am. It can be combined with a half-day **Desert Park** tour, which alone costs A$40 (U.S.$28) for adults and A$20 (U.S.$14) for children, to make a full-day tour costing A$95 (U.S.$66.50) for adults and A$55 (U.S.$38.50) for children.

Rod Steinert Tours (☎ **08/8558 8377**) also offers Aboriginal Dreamtime and Bushtucker tours. You'll visit an Aboriginal Walpiri community where you'll learn about Aboriginal lifestyles, get boomerang- and spear-throwing lessons, see a mock performance of a traditional male Aboriginal dance ceremony (called a "corroboree"), and have an opportunity to buy crafts and Dreamtime artwork the folk paint in front of you. This tour is also your big chance to eat *witchetty grubs* (fat, white, curly grubs about 2 inches long—they are slimy and have a pleasantly mild and nutty flavor)! The tour departs daily at 8:30am and returns at 11:30am. The price, which includes hotel pick-up, is A$69 (U.S.$48.30) for adults and A$34.50 (U.S.$24.15) for children ages 3 to 14. The tour will also drop you off at the airport at no charge if you are catching a plane straight afterward.

CAMEL SAFARIS & OTHER OUTDOOR ACTIVITIES

CAMEL SAFARIS   Riding a camel down the dry Todd River is one of the nicest ways to get a feel for Alice Springs. **Frontier Camel Farm** (☎ **1800/806 499** in Australia, or 08/8953 0444) runs a ✪ **Todd River Ramble** that includes a one-hour camel ride down the river bed, a browse through the museum at the farm, an interesting talk by the snake-keeper at the farm's reptile house, a peek at the farm's kangaroo pen, and transfers from your hotel. The ramble costs A$45 (U.S.$31.50) for adults and A$25 (U.S.$17.50) for kids ages 6 to 12; kids under six who can ride, ride for for free. Rides depart daily at 8:30am and 1:30pm April through October, and 8:30am and 3pm November through March.

HOT-AIR BALLOON FLIGHTS   A very popular way to appreciate the true vastness of the central Australian desert is to take a hot-air balloon flight over it. The stony desert floor stretches to the horizon, the MacDonnell Ranges ripple over the landscape, and sometimes wild horses and kangaroos bound away beneath you. **Spinifex Ballooning** (☎ **1800/677 893** in Australia, or 08/8953 4800) and **Ballooning Downunder** (☎ **1800/801 601** in Australia, or 08/8952 8816) are the two most reasonably priced operators. A 30-minute flight with Ballooning Downunder costs A$110 (U.S.$77) without breakfast or A$120 (U.S.$84) with it, and A$55 (U.S.$38.50) for children ages 6 to 12; a 60-minute flight will set you back A$170 (U.S.$119) per adult and A$80 (U.S.$56) per child ages 6 to 12 (children under 6 not permitted), with breakfast. *Brekkie*, as Aussies call it, is a champagne affair outside in the bush. Add A$8 (U.S.$5.60) per person for mandatory insurance. There is another price to pay for such scenic splendor, though, apart from your fee—you have to get up 90 minutes before dawn. The jaunt takes most of the morning, by the time you take your flight, have breakfast, and get back to town.

BUSHWALKING   The rugged country around Alice Springs is made for hiking, as long as you carry plenty of water, tell someone where you are going, and avoid walking in the heat of the day. One of Australia's newest long-distance hiking trails, the ✪ **Larapinta Trail** through the striking West MacDonnell Ranges, starts at the Old Telegraph Station 4 kilometers (2½ miles) from Alice. When it's completed, the trail will finish on Mt. Razorback, some 220 kilometers (132 miles) away. Hikes on the trail range in difficulty from easy to hard, but all have been designed with ordinary people in mind who are fit enough to trek with a backpack. Eight of the trail's 13 sections are completed. Sections vary in distance from an 8-kilometer (5-mile) section to several 23- to 29-kilometer (14- to 17½-mile) sections that take at least two days each. The trail winds through spectacular red gorges (see the "West MacDonnell Ranges" section later in this chapter), along ridges, past spring-fed swimming holes, and through desert country and bushland, with some great views along the way. The very first section from Alice to Simpson's Gap, a 24-kilometer (14½-mile), 2-day overnight walk, is ideal for inexperienced walkers. It has nice views and good birdlife. There's a basic campground halfway. The Parks & Wildlife Commission desk at the CATIA Visitor Information Centre in Alice Springs (see "Visitor Information" above) sells trail maps for A$3 (U.S.$2.10) per section, maintains a voluntary walker-registration system, and provides information on trail conditions and campsites. Camping facilities will be simple at best on the popular routes; nonexistent on less-traveled sections, so in that case you pitch your tent wherever looks good. **Centre Sightseeing Tours** (☎ **08/8952 2111**) runs transfers to various road- and 4WD-access points along the trail, from most of which you can choose a 1-, 2-, or 3-day hike. *Note:* Don't try to hike from November to March as the heat is too extreme.

BIKING A paved 17-kilometer (11-mile) bike trail leads from John Flynn's Grave on Larapinta Drive 7 kilometers (4 miles) from town through gently undulating bushland and desert to Simpson's Gap (see "West MacDonnell National Park," below. Eighteen signboards along the way tell you about local points of interest. A town bike path covers the 7 kilometers (4 miles) from Alice to the start of the trail. **Centre Cycles** (☎ **08/8953 2966**) on Lindsay Avenue at Undoolya Road, just across the Todd River footbridge at the northern end of Todd Mall, rents bikes for A$15 (U.S.$10.50) per day. *Note:* Carry water, as there is only one tap en route. Recommended in cooler months only.

GOLF The **Alice Springs Golf Club** (☎ **08/8952 5440**) boasts a Thomson-Wolveridge golf course rated one of the top 10 desert courses in the world by touring pros. Located 1 kilometer (½ mile) from town on Cromwell Drive, the par-72 course winds through the red rocky rough of the MacDonnell Ranges. It's open daily from 7am to 6pm in winter, from 6am to 6:30pm in summer. Nine holes are A$17.50 (U.S.$12.25), 18 holes are A$30 (U.S.$21), clubs are A$9 (U.S.$6.30) for 9 holes and A$15 (U.S.$10.50) for 18, and a cart, which many locals do not bother with, is A$15 (U.S.$10.50) for 9 holes or A$25 (U.S.$17.50) for 18.

SHOPPING AT THE SOURCE FOR ABORIGINAL ART

At the top of the shopping list for most travelers to Alice are Aboriginal arts and crafts. You will find no shortage of things to buy: linen and canvas paintings, didgeridoos, spears, clapping sticks, coolamons (a dish used by women to carry anything from water to babies), animal carvings, baskets, and bead jewelry. Aboriginal art can be heart-stopping expensive for large canvases or works by world-renowned painters, but you will find plenty of small works by lesser-known artists for under A$200 (U.S.$140).

A good place to start is the ✪ **Aboriginal Art and Culture Centre** (see "What to See & Do in Alice," above), which is owned by Aborigines from the local Southern Arrernte tribe. The calm atmosphere in the large upstairs gallery encourages you to browse, and the staff downstairs is always happy to advise you. The Centre is open daily from 8am to 6pm; you can also buy art, didgeridoos, souvenirs, and books over the Internet at www.aboriginalart.com.au.

The **CAAMA (Central Australian Aboriginal Media Association)** store at 101 Todd St. (☎ **08/8952 9207**) stocks a good range of locally made carvings, boomerangs, didgeridoos, and souvenirs. It's open Monday to Friday from 9am to 5pm, sometimes Saturday from 9am to 3pm. The **Jukurrpa** gallery on Stott Terrace between Gap Road and Leichhardt Terrace (☎ **08/8953 1052**) is an Aboriginal women's co-operative selling carvings, craft items, weapons, tools, and seed jewelry. It's open Monday to Friday from 9am to 5pm. At the Aboriginal-owned and operated didgeridoo specialist, **Slippery Didja's,** 45 Gap Rd. (☎ **08/8952 2739**), you can make your own didgeridoo if you have four hours up your sleeve. The shop also custom-designs them and sells them straight off the shelf, along with clapping sticks, paintings, and other items.

Aboriginal-owned **Warumpi Arts,** Shop 7, 105 Gregory Terrace (☎ **08/8952 9066**), next to the Diplomat Motor Inn, sells paintings in the bold, dramatic, earth-hued designs of the Papunya people, who were the first tribe to put Aboriginal art on the world map. It is open Monday to Friday from 9am to 5pm, Saturday from 10am to 2pm. **Papunya Tula Artists,** 78 Todd St. (☎ **08/8952 4731**), is another source of this people's work, selling mostly unmounted paintings on linen and a select range of carvings, weapons, and seed jewelry. It's open Monday to Friday from 9am to 5pm, Saturday from 10am to 2pm, and Sunday from 1pm to 5pm.

You will find several large stores on Todd Mall selling affordable Aboriginal art and souvenirs. **The Original Dreamtime Art Gallery,** 63 Todd Mall (☎ **08/8952 8861**) stocks a wide selection, including didgeridoos, boomerangs, carvings of native animals, woven baskets, Aboriginal print scarves, fire sticks, and CDs. It's open Monday to Friday from 9am to 6pm, Saturday from 9am to 4pm (sometimes later), and Sunday from 10am to 4pm. **Arunta Art Gallery & Bookshop,** 72 Todd St. (☎ **08/8952 1544**) stocks not only Aboriginal and European artworks, but also a good range of books on Aboriginal art, language, and archaeology, as well as Australian history, geology, wildlife, and biographies. It's open Monday to Friday from 9am to 5:30pm, Saturday from 10am to 5:30pm.

If you are interested in investing in serious artwork, speak to Roslyn Premont, proprietor of **Gallery Gondwana,** 43 Todd Mall (☎ **08/8953 1577**) or her manager, Bryce Ponsford. Both are knowledgeable authorities on Aboriginal art, and Roslyn has written a book on desert art. Her gallery sells only top-notch works. Roslyn's second gallery, **Gondwana II,** 11 Todd Mall (☎ **08/8953 5511**), stocks elegant and unusual crafts and design pieces by noted Australian artists. Both galleries are open Monday to Friday from 9:30am to 6pm, Saturday and Sunday from 10am to 5pm, or by appointment. These hours are extended in July, August, and September.

WHERE TO STAY

Note: There's a 5% tax on all accommodations in the Northern Territory. Some hotels include the tax in the room rates; these are noted below.

✪ **Desert Palms Resort.** 74 Barrett Dr. (1km/½ mile from town), Alice Springs, NT 0871. ☎ **1800/678 037** in Australia, or 08/8952 5977. Fax 08/8953 4176. 80 units (all with shower only). A/C TV TEL. A$85 (U.S.$59.50) double including 5% tax. Additional person A$10 (U.S.$7) extra. AE, BC, DC, MC, V. Free coach/train station/airport shuttle.

This little park has a cheerful ambience, thanks to the cute individual cabins among green manicured lawns and the very friendly service from the front-desk staff. From the outside, the cabins seem small; inside, they are surprisingly large and well-kept, with a pine pitched ceiling, a minikitchen, a narrow sliver of a bathroom with new white tiles, and a furnished front deck. Out back is a handy barbecue area and the Alice Springs Golf Club, to which guests here enjoy honorary social membership. A pretty pool with its own little island is out front. There's also a tennis court, laundry with iron and board, hair dryers on loan at reception, film processing, basic grocery and liquor supplies, and a tour desk. Lasseter's Casino is a 3-minute walk away.

Elkira Motel. 65 Bath St., Alice Springs, NT 0870. ☎ **1800/809 252** in Australia, or 08/8952 1222. Fax 08/8953 1370. 58 units (some with shower only). A/C TV TEL. A$75–$85 (U.S.$52.50–$59.50) single, A$60–$95 (U.S.$42–$66.50) double. Rates include 5% tax. Additional person A$12 (U.S.$8.40) extra. Children under 3 free in parents' room if they use existing bedding. Lower rates in off-season. AE, BC, DC, MC, V.

If you want an inexpensive room in the heart of the central business district but the standard rooms at The Territory Inn (see below) are a little too small for you, you may settle for one of the deluxe rooms at this unpretentious Best Western motel. The standard rooms here are a little on the cramped side, too, but they're very clean and have recently renovated bathrooms with hair dryers, carpets, floor tiles, and wall paneling (eight have kitchenettes). Deluxe rooms are the same but a bit larger. Ask for a room away from the road, as the traffic can be noisy. The penny-wise budget rooms are extremely tiny and the dated fittings are pretty knocked around, but you get a bed, a TV, a phone, and a minirefrigerator for A$60 (U.S.$42). There's a modest pool with a nice barbecue area under lovely big trees, and a vine-covered terrace restaurant doing a steak or fish main course for around A$15 (U.S.$10.50).

✪ **Nthaba B&B Cottage.** 3 Cromwell Dr., Alice Springs, NT 0870. ☎ **08/8952 9003.** Fax 08/8953 3295. E-mail: nthaba@ozemail.com.au. 1 free-standing cottage (shower only). A/C TV. A$90 (U.S.$63) single, A$120 (U.S.$84) double. Weekly rates available. Rates include full breakfast. BC, MC, V.

Your hostess Anne Cormack has created a delightful oasis of green-terraced lawns and garden blooms in the unlikely red dust of central Australia at her home, about 1.5 kilometers (1 mile) from the town center. You stay in a charming slate-floored brick cottage with its own entrance, a petite sitting room, separate twin or double bedroom (the twin beds zip together to form a comfortable king size), and your own bathroom with a hair dryer. You can even prepare light meals in the kitchenette. The cottage is beautifully furnished with classic and antique pieces. There is no private phone, but you are welcome to use Anne's. The Alice Springs Golf Club is a short walk away. No smoking.

Red Centre Resort. Stuart Hwy. (north of town), Alice Springs, NT 0870. ☎ **1800/ 089 616** in Australia, or 08/8950 5555. Fax 08/8952 8300. 127 units, 99 with bathroom (shower only). A$79 (U.S.$55.30) double motel room; A$89 (U.S.$62.30) double apartment. Additional person A$15 (U.S.$10.50) extra. A$15 (U.S. $10.50) per person in quad-share bunkhouse (supply your own linen). All rates include 5% tax. Children 14 and under free in parents' room if they use existing bedding. AE, BC, DC, MC, V. Free airport shuttle.

Although it's 4.5 kilometers (3 miles) from the center of town, this laid-back 7-hectare (18-acre) complex of motel rooms, studio apartments with kitchenettes, and bunkhouse rooms has such a friendly ambience you won't mind making the trip. A free shuttle runs into town throughout the day, anyhow, so you won't be stranded. The heart of the place is the welcoming pool and the poolside bistro, where everyone gathers to swap tour notes or enjoy the live entertainment that plays most nights in the cooler months. You get lots for your money here—a tour desk, an à la carte restaurant and casual bistro, a day/night tennis court, a volleyball court, a game room with pool tables and Ping-Pong, a pool for the kids, baby-sitting, dry cleaning, room service, Internet access, and a free temporary e-mail address. Management will supply free utensils if you want to cook up a storm on the barbecue. The spick-and-span motel rooms and apartments are air-conditioned and have exposed brick walls, fashionable whitewashed furniture, TV, telephone, and ample space. Iron and boards and hair dryers are available at reception. The motel rooms are serviced daily, and the apartments weekly.

The Territory Inn. Leichhardt Terrace (backing onto Todd Mall), Alice Springs, NT 0870. ☎ **1800/089 644** in Australia, or 08/8952 2066. Fax 08/8952 7829. 108 units (all with shower only, 1 suite with Jacuzzi). A/C MINIBAR TV TEL. A$95–$130 (U.S.$66.50–$91) double; A$190 (U.S.$133) suite. Additional person A$15 (U.S.$10.50) extra. Rates include 5% tax. Children under 14 free in parents' room if they use existing bedding. AE, BC, DC, MC, V. Free airport shuttle.

This pleasant hotel is smack-bang in the center of town on Todd Mall. Rooms in the new wing are your standard modern motel variety; all of them are clean, comfortable, large, and decorated nicely enough. The rooms in the original wing are small and a little dark, but sport a pretty heritage theme with floral bedcovers and lace curtains. Most of the rooms center around a courtyard that has a barbecue for guests and a dining area under a pergola. The helpful staff runs a tour desk; other amenities include a Laundromat, in-room iron and boards in deluxe rooms, hair dryers for loan, and a postcheckout shower room. The tiny heated pool and Jacuzzi are tucked away in a utilitarian corner, so this is not the place for chilling out by the pool. The advantage of staying here is that you're within walking distance of shops and restaurants. A big bonus is that room service is from the marvelous Red Ochre Grill (see "Where to Dine"), which is in the hotel complex.

SUPER-CHEAP SLEEPS

Stuart Lodge. Stuart Terrace (between Hartley and Todd sts.), Alice Springs, NT 0870. ☎ **1800/249 124** in Australia (YWCA central reservations), or 08/8952 1894. Fax 08/ 8952 2449. E-mail: stuart.lodge@ywca.org.au. 31 units, 1 with bathroom (tub/shower). A/C. A$25–$35 (U.S.$17.50–$24.50) single; A$35–$45 (U.S.$24.50–$31.50) double; A$50 (U.S.$35) triple. 10% discount YWCA members. Free crib. Weekly rates available. BC, MC, V.

Two blocks from Todd Mall and close to the long-distance coach terminals, this YWCA-owned hostel is quieter and less rowdy than the average backpacker lodge, so it is popular with solo travelers, seniors, and anyone wanting party-free privacy. It offers diminutive but neatly painted single, double, and triple rooms that are serviced daily; a robe, a writing desk, and self-serve tea and coffee are standard. By the time you read this, all rooms should have minifridges, too. Every two rooms share one (old but clean) bathroom; the front desk lends hair dryers. The furnishings are pretty humble, but there's a small pool, a communal kitchen, and free barbecues, a tour desk, a pay phone, TV lounges, and a laundry. The continental breakfast is a bargain at A$3.70 (U.S.$2.60). The friendly managers are very helpful. No smoking.

WHERE TO DINE

Alice Springs doesn't exactly overflow with restaurants, but it does have a few worth checking out, and most of them are affordable. Don't confine your dining to indoor restaurants, though, especially in summer. See the "Dinner in the Desert" box for where to find ripper Aussie bush dinners, Outback-style.

✪ **Bar Doppio.** 2–3 Fan Arcade (off the southern end of Todd Mall). ☎ **08/8952 6525.** Main courses A$3.80–$9 (U.S.$2.65–$6.30) at lunch, A$6–$14 (U.S.$4.20–$9.80) at dinner. No credit cards. Mon–Sat 7:30am–9pm, Sun 10am–8pm. VEGETARIAN/CAFE FARE.

If you're in need of a dose of cool—style, that is, not air-conditioning—this laid-back cafe is the place in Alice to drink good coffee; eat cheap, wholesome food; and chill out. Bags of coffee beans are stacked all over, gypsy music plays, and no table or chair matches. There are world magazines to read, and the staff doesn't care if you sit here all day. And boy, is it cheap! At dinner, lamb cutlets on creamy polenta with fried green tomatoes are A$9 (U.S.$6.30). At lunch, try the gourmet sandwiches, spuds with hot toppings, or hot lentil dahl with jasmine rice. Hot and cold breakfast choices stay on the menu until 11am. Sit inside or outside in the shade on the arcade, or take out. It's BYO.

✪ **Casa Nostra.** Corner of Undoolya Rd. and Stuart Terrace. ☎ **08/8952 6749.** Reservations recommended. Main courses A$6.80–$16 (U.S.$4.75–$11.20). BC, MC, V. Mon–Sat 5pm–late. Closed Christmas to end of Jan. ITALIAN.

The only difference between this cheery homespun Italian family eatery and every other Italian restaurant in the world is that this one has autographed photos of Tom Selleck pinned to the wall. Judging by his scrawled praise, Tom loved eating here when on location in Alice filming *Quigley Down Under.* You have seen the red-checked table-cloths and the basket-clad chianti bottles before; the food may surprise you for being so darn good. A long list of pastas like the masterful carbonara (served without the bucketloads of cream less-knowledgeable restaurants tip on it), traditional pizzas, and chicken and veal dishes are the main offerings. BYO (corkage A$1/U.S.70¢ per person).

Keller's Swiss & Indian Restaurant. In the Diplomat Hotel, Gregory Terrace. ☎ **08/ 8952 3188.** Reservations recommended at dinner. Main courses A$10.80–$21 (U.S.$7.55–$14.70). AE, BC, MC, V. Thurs–Fri 11am–2pm, daily 5:30pm–late. SWISS/ INDIAN.

Dinner in the Desert

Why eat outside in the dust when you can sit in a perfectly good restaurant? Because the Outback is a beautiful place to be outdoors, that's why, especially at night. Alice Springs and Ayers Rock have several "restaurants" under the stars where you might get your feet dirty, but your tastebuds, eyes, and ears will appreciate the experience.

Ayers Rock Resort's ✪ **"Sounds of Silence"** dinner is a must-do, even if it won't be your cheapest meal this vacation. You dine in a clearing in the sand dunes, where you are welcomed by smartly aproned waitstaff bearing champagne and canapés. You watch the sun set over the Olgas to the music of a lone didgeridoo. Then everyone sits down at white-clothed, candle-lit tables and feasts on a gourmet barbecue of kangaroo, barramundi, and emu; salads and sauces conjured up with native vegetables, berries, and nuts; and Aussie wines. After everyone has eaten, the lanterns are extinguished, the didgeridoo falls silent, and you are left with nothing but the stillness of the bush at night. It is the first time some guests have ever heard complete silence. From out of the dark, an astronomer steps forward to point out the constellations of the southern hemisphere and the gloriously brilliant Milky Way. In winter, everyone gathers around a campfire with port afterward.

"Sounds of Silence" is held nightly, weather permitting, and costs A$95 (U.S.$63) for adults and A$47.50 (U.S.$31.50) for children under age 15, including transfers from your Ayers Rock Resort accommodations. You can book through the reception desk or tour desk at any Ayers Rock Resort accommodation. It's mighty popular, so book three months ahead in peak season. (See "Where to Stay" under "Uluru–Kata Tjuta National Park [Ayers Rock/The Olgas]," below.)

Anyone can turn up to dinner in a limousine, but your friends will have no comeback when you say you rolled up on a camel. A 1-hour sunset saunter on

This is the only place in town (heck, probably in the world) where you can have fondue and *vindaloo* (a fiery curry dish) at the same meal. You call it weird, and the restaurant calls it successful, since this cheerful place is always full of local office workers, tourists, or U.S. staff from the nearby Pine Gap satellite-tracking station. You might start with the wonderfully crisp spiky Indian *pakoras* (fritters) of onion, potato, and carrot with a yummy mint sauce, followed by schweinsteak Dijon (pork with mustard and wine sauce). Or do the cuisines the other way around, and start with a Swiss sausage and cheese salad followed by Indian fish curry. There are vegetarian choices as well as some uniquely Swiss takes on Aussie dishes, such as the kangaroo stroganoff. The unpretentious decor has a split personality, too, with an Alpine mural on the wall and toy camels lurking in the potted plants. Take-out meals are available from the corner shop front. No smoking before 9pm.

Malathi's. 51 Bath St. ☎ **08/8952 1858.** Main courses A$11–$22 (U.S.$6.95–$13.65). AE, BC, DC, MC, V. Restaurant: Fri noon–2pm, Tues–Sat 5:30pm–late (Mon from 5:30pm, take-out only). Bar: daily noon–late. ASIAN/WESTERN.

Located in an unprepossessing building a couple of blocks from Todd Mall, this place serves up an eclectic assortment of Oriental dishes from all over Asia, plus a few true-blue Aussie choices, such as flavorsome King Island steak. Don't be put off by the pink walls, old carpet, and Asian print tablecloths, because the food here is outstanding.

camelback down the dry Todd River is part of the ✪ **Take a Camel Out to Dinner** nights offered by **Frontier Camel Tours** (☎ **1800/806 499** in Australia, or 08/8953 0444) in Alice Springs. It's one pretty journey past river red gums as black cockatoos and rainbow lorikeets whirl overhead. At the end of the ride at the Frontier Camel Farm, there is time for an informal talk about camels and a look at the Camel Farm's museum and reptile house. Afterward, you dine on a tasty three-course bush tucker meal of barramundi or steak and yummy wattle-seed bread. This meal is served inside, not out in the sand. The cost of A$80 (U.S.$56) for adults and A$60 (U.S.$42) for children ages 6 to 12 includes pick-up from your hotel. The rides run nightly year-round, departing at 4pm and fin-ishing up around 8:30pm from April through October, and departing at 5pm and finishing up at 9:30pm from November through March. There is also a "Take a Camel Out to Breakfast" option that departs at 6:30am and returns at 9:30am on Monday, Wednesday, and Saturday. It costs A$55 (U.S.$38.50) for adults and A$35 (U.S.$24.50) for children.

An Australiana campfire night is the theme behind **Camp Oven Kitchen's** nightly outdoor bush dinners. At white-clothed slab tables lit with oil lamps, you sit down to soup and damper straight off the campfire, kangaroo kebabs, roast beef and veggies, and golden syrup dumplings with fresh cream, a favorite of Aussie swagmen in days gone by. All the food is cooked in a camp oven, Australian stock-camp style. The evening kicks off at 5:30pm with stock-whip cracking and boomerang throwing and includes a stroll to learn about the Aboriginal history of the site, a star talk, and, most nights, guitar music and bush ballads. The meal, including transfers from your hotel but not including drinks, costs A$69 (U.S.$48.30) for adults and A$55 (U.S.$38.50) for kids under age 12. Tours depart 5:30pm in winter, 6pm in summer. Call ☎ **08/8952 2922.**

My lamb korma was the best I've ever had, spicy, tender, but not swimming in oil like so many kormas I have known. You might want to try the vegetarian *laksa* (a nour-ishing broth) followed by spicy Thai seafood noodles, or *barra Devi*, barramundi pieces \in onion and ginger sauce. They do take-out, too. The restaurant also houses Sean's Bar, a small Irish pub. You can buy wine at the restaurant or BYO (but don't BYO beer or spirits).

Red Ochre Grill. Todd Mall. ☎ **08/8952 9614.** Reservations recommended at dinner. Main courses A$18–$22 (U.S.$12.60–$15.40); buffet breakfast A$8.50 (U.S.$5.95) conti-nental, A$15 (U.S.$10.50) full. AE, BC, DC, MC, V. Daily 6:30am–late. GOURMET BUSH TUCKER.

If you have never tried kangaroo fillet with *quandong* (bush peach) chili glaze, croco-dile confit on pawpaw (papaya) with native plum coulis, or camel fillet with onion relish, now's your chance. The chef fuses Australian bush ingredients with dishes from around the world, and although the results might sound a bit strange, this is mouth-watering food cooked well. Even the side orders embrace bush tucker, such as the seasonal vegetables baked in paper bark, and the fries with *warrigal* (native spinach) pesto. The hot and cold buffet and à la carte breakfast menu serves more the kind of food you would expect, but if you're feeling adventurous first thing in the morning there are some bush choices, such as native *yabbies* (small crayfish) with your scrambled eggs. Opt for the contemporary interior, or sit outside in the attractive courtyard.

WORTH A SPLURGE

Overlanders Steakhouse. 72 Hartley St. ☎ **08/8952 2159.** Reservations essential in peak season. Main courses A$16.50–$25 (U.S.$11.55–$17.50). AE, BC, DC, MC, V. Daily 6pm–late. AUSSIE OUTBACK.

This perennially popular restaurant is famous for its "Drover's Blowout" menu, which assaults the mega-hungry with soup and damper; then a platter of crocodile vol-au-vents, camel Scotch fillet, kangaroo fillet, and emu medallions—those are just the appetizers—followed by a choice of barramundi or Scotch fillet steak in red wine and mushroom sauce, followed by dessert. The regular menu will satisfy hearty appetites, too, with dishes such as aged beef and kangaroo steaks from the grill; barramundi with prawns, or Tasmanian salmon; and less "steaky" choices like lamb Wellington, honey and chili chicken shashliks (kabobs), and ricotta and spinach crepes. The decor in the barn-like interior shouts Outback, from the rustic wooden tables to the saddlebags hanging from the roof beams.

THE ALICE AFTER DARK

In his one-of-a-kind ✪ **Sounds of Starlight** performance (☎ **08/8953 0826**), musician Andrew Langford combines some evocative Outback landscape photos projected on a screen with the sounds of the didgeridoo and other world instruments, like Aztec hum drums and African rattles. The result is a cleverly spun image of Australia's ancient land, animals, and Aboriginal people. The 90-minute performance runs from Tuesday to Saturday between March and November at 7pm at his theater at 40 Todd Mall. Tickets are A$15 (U.S.$10.50) for adults, A$12 (U.S.$8.40) for seniors, and A$10 (U.S.$7) for children ages 5 to 13. You can make bookings through any tour desk or at the **Original Dreamtime Gallery** at 63 Todd Mall (☎ **08/8952 8861**).

True-blue Aussie **folksinger Ted Egan** does a mean concert, putting some clever words to "music" played on that uniquely Australian instrument, an empty Fosters beer carton. If that's not proof of Aussie resourcefulness, what is? The shows run Monday through Thursday, April through October in the **Settlers Function Room,** Palm Circuit (☎ **08/8952 9952**). Tickets are A$15 (U.S.$10.50) for adults, A$10 (U.S.$7) for children and students under age 18, and free for kids under age 10. Dinner is available from 6pm, with main courses around A$10 (U.S.$7). Book ahead, as Ted is a popular guy.

The **Araluen Centre for Arts and Entertainment** (☎ **08/8952 5022**) on Larapinta Drive is the town's venue for theater, dance, musical performances, and visual arts exhibitions.

Lasseter's Casino, 93 Barrett Drive (☎ **08/8950 7777**), is open daily from 10am for slot machines and from midday for blackjack, roulette, baccarat, keno, money wheel, and the famous Aussie game of two-up. It closes at 3am weekdays and 4am Friday and Saturday. Meals at its one restaurant, Kings, go for less than A$15 (U.S.$10.50), and buffet dinners are A$18 (U.S.$12.60). Live bands play most nights in Limerick's, an Irish-theme pub.

2 Road Trips from Alice Springs

Before you leave Alice Springs on one of the side trips described below, drop in or call the **Parks & Wildlife Commission desk** (☎ **08/8951 5210**) at the **CATIA Visitor Centre** (see "Visitor Information," above). It's the official source of maps and information on the national parks and conservation/heritage reserves in the West and East

MacDonnell Ranges. The desk can fill you in on the free daily program of ranger campfire talks, guided walks, and slide shows scheduled at many of the points of interest mentioned below, and in Alice, from April to October.

THE WEST MACDONNELL RANGES

West Macdonnell National Park   the drive west from Alice Springs into West Macdonnell National Park is a stark but picturesque wonderland rived with striking gorges and dotted with idyllic water holes. Meal facilities are limited, so pack a picnic lunch. Wear sensible shoes so you can explore a walking trail or two. Campers should bring their own food supplies. The tourism authorities discourage swimming at the water holes, because the spring-fed water is freezing and can cause cramps, but it is permitted at most holes (if there's enough water, that is); just be careful of underwater snags. You may not want to stop at every gorge en route, as they all start to look alike after a while; most folks call at two or three and enjoy lunch at one.

From Alice, follow Larapinta Drive west for 18 kilometers (11 miles) to the 8-kilometer (5-mile) turn-off to **Simpson's Gap,** a shady water hole situated between steep red ridges lined with massive ghost gums. It's a peaceful place to sit by the water, especially in the afternoon when little gray rock wallabies hop out on the cliffs (so maybe time a visit here on your way back to Alice). You can also wander one of the two 500-meter (547-yard) walking trails. A 17-kilometer (10¼-mile) round-trip trail leads to nearby Bond Gap. Swimming is not permitted.

Another 23 kilometers (13 miles) along the main road and 9 kilometers (5½ miles) down a turnoff is **Standley Chasm** (☎ **08/8956 7440**). This towering cleft in the rock is only a few meters wide but 80 meters (262 feet) high. You get to it along a lush 1.5-kilometer (1-mile) trail beside the creek. Midday is the popular time to be here, when the chasm's orange walls burn bright in the overhead sun. You may spot dingoes nearby, and wildflowers bloom along the creek. A kiosk sells snacks and drinks. Admission is A$4 (U.S.$2.80) for adults and A$3.50 (U.S.$2.45) seniors and children ages 5 to 14. The Chasm is open from 7:30am to 6pm daily (closed Christmas).

Not far past Standley Chasm, branch right onto Namatjira Drive and head 42 kilometers (25 miles) to **Ellery Creek Big Hole.** This is a beautiful permanent spring-fed water hole, but take a dip only if you're game to brave freezing temperatures! The water is so cold the Tourism Authority actually warns people to take a flotation device. There's a 3-kilometer (2-mile) marked walking trail here that tells you about the area's geological history.

Eleven kilometers (6½ miles) farther along Namatjira Drive is **Serpentine Gorge.** Take the path up to the lookout for a good view of the ranges through the gorge walls. Another 12 kilometers (7 miles) on are ochre pits, where signboards tell you how the Aboriginal people quarried the colors for body paint and for decorating objects used in ceremonial performances. Twenty-six kilometers (15½ miles) farther west of the ochre pits are the red walls of **Ormiston Gorge** (☎ **08/8956 7799** for the ranger station/visitor center). This is a good spot to picnic, swim in the (very cold) 14-meter-(45½-feet-) deep pool surrounded by red cliffs, and walk a choice of trails, such as the 30-minute Ghost Gum Lookout Trail or the 7-kilometer (4-mile) gorge loop. You can camp here for A$5 (U.S.$3.50) per adult and A$2 (U.S.$1.40) per child, or A$12 (U.S.$8.40) for a family of six. The campground has hot showers and free gas grills (fires are not allowed).

A few kilometers farther on is the permanent swimming hole of **Glen Helen Gorge,** where the mighty Finke River cuts through the ranges. This is a lovely spot for a picnic. Near the gorge is **Glen Helen Homestead** (☎ **08/8956 7489,** fax 08/8956 7489), which sells snacks from 8am to 5pm and has campsites with hot showers

---

Tips for Driving the Mereenie Loop Road

Some maps and guides will tell you that you can travel Mereenie Loop Road in a conventional 2WD car, but it is really too rough for that, and anyhow, rental companies will not rent you a 2WD car for this road. The road crosses Aboriginal land, for which you will need an A$2- (U.S.$1.40-) per-vehicle permit from the CATIA Visitor Information Centre in Alice Springs. If you join the Mereenie Loop Road in Hermannsburg, you can get a permit at the Kata-Anga Tearooms there. You can also get the permit at Kings Canyon Resort, if you do the drive from the other direction.

Camping is not permitted anywhere along the road. Take food supplies, carry plenty of water, and keep the tank full.

---

for A$5 (U.S.$3.50) per person, A$10 (U.S.$7) for a family of four, and A$15 (U.S.$10.50) for a powered site. By the time you read this the homestead's 25 motel rooms and restaurant may have reopened after renovations.

TRAVELING THE MEREENIE LOOP ROAD   If you have a 4WD, you can carry on past Glen Helen Gorge, and link back south to Hermannsburg, described below, and then on to Kings Canyon (see below) on the rough, unsealed (unpaved) Mereenie Loop Road. This 320-kilometer (192-mile) trip is a more scenic route through Outback countryside than taking the highway to Kings Canyon. En route, about 55 kilometers (33 miles) from either Glen Helen or Hermannsburg, you can visit **Tnorala (Gosse Bluff) Conservation Reserve,** a 5-kilometer (3-mile) crater left by a meteorite that smashed to earth 142 million years ago. The crater is a sacred Aboriginal site, so visitors may not enter certain significant sites within the reserve.

HERMANNSBURG HISTORICAL PRECINCT   An alternative to visiting the gorges described above is to take Larapinta Drive 128 kilometers (77 miles) from Alice Springs to the Lutheran Mission at the **Hermannsburg Historical Precinct** (☎ 08/8956 7402). Some maps will show this route as an unsealed road, but the route was sealed in 1997. Settled by German missionaries in the 1870s, the town was given back to its Aboriginal owners in 1982. The pretty farmhouse-style mission buildings have been restored, and there is a museum, a gallery housing works by famous artist Albert Namatjira, and tearooms serving a fabulous apple strudel from a recipe imported from Germany in 1898. The Mission is open daily from 9am to 4pm March through November, and from 10am to 4pm November through April. Admission with tea or coffee is A$4 (U.S.$2.80) for adults and A$2.50 (U.S.$1.75) for kids under age 16, plus A$3 (U.S.$2.10) per person for a guided tour of the gallery (tours depart every hour). A family pass is A$10 (U.S.$7), or A$20 (U.S.$14) including the gallery tour. The precinct is closed Christmas, New Year's Day, and Good Friday, and may be closed for the week between Christmas and New Year's—call ahead to check.

At Hermannsburg is the turnoff to the 46,000-hectare (115,000-acre) ✪ **Finke Gorge National Park,** 15 kilometers (9 miles) to the south. The park is most famous for Palm Valley, home to groves of rare *Livistona mariae* cabbage palms that have survived since the days when central Australia was a steamy jungle. The Finke River is thought to be the world's oldest waterway (350 million years at last count); it served as a trade route to bring pearl shell from the coast to Arrernte Aboriginals living out here. You will need a 4WD to explore this park; south of Palm Valley (which is the most interesting bit, anyhow), the road gets too sandy for all but experienced four-wheel drivers. Four walking trails ranging in length from 1.5 kilometers (1 mile) to 5 kilometers (3 miles) take you up rocky cliffs or among palms. There is a campsite about 4 kilometers (2½ miles) from the palms; it has showers, toilets, and free gas grills. (Get in quick if you like your showers hot.) Fires are permitted, but you must collect your firewood outside the park. Camping is A$5 (U.S.$3.50) for adults, A$2 (U.S.$1.40) for kids ages 5 to 14, and $12 (U.S.$8.40) for a family of six. For information on the park, stop in the CATIA Visitor Centre in Alice Springs before you leave, as there is no visitor center here. The ranger station (☎ **08/8956 7401**) is for emergencies only. Several companies run tours from Alice Springs. **AAT Kings** (☎ **08/8951 1700**) does a 1-day Palm Valley trip for A$89 (U.S.$62.30) per adult. **Central Oz 4WD Tours** (☎ **08/8953 4755**) runs overnight camping safaris in the park.

From Hermannsburg you can join up with the Mereenie Loop Road (see above) to Kings Canyon.

ORGANIZED TOURS   Among the many companies that run half- and full-day coach tours to the West MacDonnells are **AAT Kings** (☎ 08/8952 1700), **Centre Sightseeing Tours** (☎ 08/8952 2111), and **Centremen Tours** (☎ 08/8953 2623). **Alice Springs Holidays** (☎ 1800/801 401 in Australia, or 08/8953 1411) and **Central Oz 4WD Tours** (☎ 1800/240 230 in Australia, or 08/8953 4755) are 4WD specialists that limit the number of tour participants, so the tours are more personal. Expect to pay about A$40 (U.S.$28) for a half-day tour and A$80 (U.S.$56) for a full day. A half-day trip typically takes in Simpsons Gap and Standley Chasm only, with lunch at Standley Chasm. If you want to visit Standley Chasm at midday, your half-day tour will leave around 10am and return around 2pm.

THE EAST MACDONNELL RANGES

Not as many tourists tread the path into the ranges east from Alice as they do into the more spectacular West MacDonnells. If you do venture east, however, you'll be rewarded with some lovely scenery, fewer crowds, swimming holes, and traces of Aboriginal history. We even spotted wild camels on our visit. You'll almost certainly want to visit the *dinky-di* (that's Australian for "authentic"—as in "fair dinkum") **Ross River Homestead** (☎ 08/8956 9711), an easy 83 kilometers (50 miles) from Alice at the end of the Ross Highway. At the homestead you can throw boomerangs, learn how to crack a stock whip, ride horses, and generally do the stuff Aussies do on an Outback farm. Day visitors are welcome between 8am and 10pm daily year-round, or you can stay overnight (see "Where to Stay," below). As the whip-cracking and billy tea experience at Ross River Homestead goes from 10am to noon, you may want to head there first, then drop in on the attractions listed below on your way back. The Ross Highway is sealed (paved) all the way to the Ross River Homestead. A further 36 kilometers (23 miles) off the highway past the homestead is the gold-rush ghost town of **Arltunga Historical Reserve** (☎ 08/8956 9770 for the visitor center and ranger station).

The first points of interest along the way are **Emily and Jessie Gaps,** 10 kilometers (6 miles) east of Alice. Just simple gaps in the range, Emily is the most interesting, whereas Jessie is the prettiest picnic spot. You can cool off in the Emily Gap swimming hole if there is any water, but even if there is not, don't miss the Caterpillar Dreaming Aboriginal art on the wall on your right as you walk through the gap. No one knows how old it is. Because the rock painting is archaeologically important, and this is a registered Aboriginal sacred site, visitors are asked not to touch it.

At the outcrop called **Corroboree Rock,** 33 kilometers (20 miles) on, you can make a short climb up this rocky outcrop that was highly important to local Aborigines. They probably did not perform corroborees here, but may have kept objects of ceremonial importance among the rocks.

Another 33 kilometers (20 miles) on is the turnoff to **Trephina Gorge Nature Park,** a peaceful 18-square-kilometer (7-square-mile) beauty spot with many birds and several walking trails, ranging in duration from 45 minutes to 4½ hours. An easy amble between the brick-red walls of the gorge to a water hole takes only a few minutes. Small, uncrowded campsites among the trees have basic toilets and barbecues and no showers. The camping fee is A$2.50 (U.S.$1.75) for adults and A$1 (U.S.70¢) for kids. The last 5 kilometers (3 miles) of the 9-kilometer (5½-mile) access road into Trephina are unsealed, but you can make it in a conventional car.

Those interested in Aboriginal culture should definitely call in at **N'Dhala Gorge Nature Park,** another 17 kilometers (11 miles) on, past the Ross River Homestead turn-off, to see the open air art gallery of rock carvings, or petroglyphs, made by the Eastern Arrernte tribe. It's thought there might be up to 6,000 rock carvings, hundreds or thousands of years old, in this gorge, along with rock paintings. A 1.5-kilometer (1 mile) trail leads you through this quiet gorge to the carvings; signposts explain the complex Dreamtime meaning of the carvings. Camping here is a bit rough—with pit toilets and barbecues, but no showers or drinking water. The camping fee is A$2.50 (U.S.$1.75) for adults and A$1 (U.S.70¢) for kids. To reach the park, you need a 4WD vehicle to traverse the 11-kilometer (6½-mile) access road, and you must ford the mostly dry Ross River bed, which is impassable after heavy rain. Entry to the park is free.

Access from the highway to the gold-rush ghost town of **Arltunga Historical Reserve** is on the good-quality, unsealed Arltunga Road. You can wander through the ruins of camps and huts, explore the underground mines (take a flashlight), and visit the restored police station and jail. The visitor center is open daily from 8am to 5pm and has a good slide show on the difficulties early settlers faced in the Outback. Entry to the Reserve is free. Right beside the Reserve is the **Arltunga Bush Hotel** (☎ 08/ 8956 9797), a pub with cold beer, hot meals, and campsites with hot showers for A$5 (U.S.$3.50) per person.

ORGANIZED TOURS   Among the tour companies running half- or full-day tours to the East MacDonnells are **AAT Kings** and **Centre Sightseeing Tours** (see "Organized Tours" in the "West MacDonnells" section, above). Expect to pay about A$90 (U.S.$63) for a full-day tour; Centre Sightseeing runs one at A$60 (U.S.$42). If you prefer small groups of no more than four passengers, go with **Central Oz 4WD Tours** (☎ 1800/240 230 in Australia, or 08/8953 4755).

WHERE TO STAY

Ross River Homestead. Ross Hwy, 83km (50 miles) east of Alice Springs (P.O. Box 3271, Alice Springs, NT 0871). ☎ **1800/241 711** in Australia, or 08/8956 9711. Fax 08/ 8956 9823. E-mail: rrhca@ozemail.com.au. Web site: www.ozemail.com.au/~rrhca. 48 units, 30 with bathroom (shower only). A/C. Cabin A$78 (U.S.$54.60) double. Additional person A$17 (U.S.$11.90) extra. Bunkhouse quad-share A$15 (U.S.$10.50) per person; linen A$5 (U.S.$3.50) extra per person. Unpowered campsite A$7.50 (U.S.$5.25) per adult, A$3.75 (U.S.$2.65) per child; powered campsite A$9.50 (U.S.$6.65) per adult, A$4.75 (U.S.$3.35) per child. AE, BC, DC, MC, V. Air and road transfers from Alice Springs are available.

This *fair dinkum* (genuine) 100-year-old Aussie station offers day visitors and overnight guests a condensed taste of Outback life. Entry to the homestead, the eight bushwalking trails, and the kangaroo enclosure is free; you pay for any other activities and meals you choose. A 1-hour horse or camel ride is A$28 (U.S.$19.60) for adults and A$23 (U.S.$16.10) for kids, a wagon ride is A$10 (U.S.$7) for adults and A$5 (U.S.$3.50) for kids, and whip-cracking and boomerang-throwing lessons over billy tea and damper, offered from 10am to noon, cost A$5 (U.S.$3.50) per person (free to cabin guests). Overnight accommodations are rustic, roomy log cabins with private bathrooms; there are also more-basic bunkhouse accommodations with shared sleeping quarters and shared facilities, as well as shady campgrounds. All guests, including campers, may use the restaurant and bar, but the pool is for cabin guests only. Life ain't all tough in the Outback—the cabins are heated to ward off Alice's frosty winter nights, and there's a swimming pool and Jacuzzi. Reasonably priced meals for day visitors and guests are served in the wonderfully atmospheric original homestead. If enough people are interested, the homestead arranges three-course cookouts under the stars, sometimes combined with overnight horse and camel safaris.

3 Kings Canyon

Anyone who saw the Australian movie *The Adventures of Priscilla, Queen of the Desert* will remember the soaring stony plateau the transvestites climb to look over the majestic plain below. You can stand on that very same spot (wearing sequined underpants is optional) at ✪ **Kings Canyon** in **Watarrka National Park** (☎ 08/8956 7488 for park headquarters), 320 kilometers (192 miles) southwest of Alice Springs as the crow flies. The sheer red sandstone walls of the canyon drop 100 meters (about 330 ft) to a forested floor with crystal-clear rock pools and centuries-old gum trees. The park contains the western point of the George Gill Range and is an important conservation refuge for native plants and animals.

The most popular way to see the canyon is to do the steep 6-kilometer (3½-mile) walk up the side and around the rim. Even for the fit and healthy, it's a strenuous 3- to 4-hour hike, but well worth the effort. The walk starts with a steep climb, followed by a more level track around the rim through a maze of rounded sandstone formations called the Lost City. Across a bridge you come to the blissful Garden of Eden, a fern-fringed pocket of palms around a permanent water hole. The trail returns along the other side of the rim through more weathered sandstone rocks to the starting point. There are lookout points along the way. If you are lucky enough to visit after rain, the canyon walls will teem with waterfalls.

If you are not up to the rim walk, you can still experience the canyon by hiking along the shady bed of Kings Creek at the bottom. The trail wanders along the mostly dry creek bed to a lookout point and comes back the same way. Wear your walking boots, as the ground can be very rocky. This walk is good for young kids and travelers in wheelchairs for the first 700 meters (½ mile). It is only 1.3 kilometers (¾ mile) long and takes about an hour.

Most people who visit Watarrka National Park stay at Kings Canyon Resort (see below). A hotel room is not cheap here, so even if you normally take a room with private bath, consider taking a bunkhouse with shared bath for the night. The canyon walks are free, but if you do not have a car, budget A$20 (U.S.$14) per person, round-trip, for the resort shuttle bus to take you to and from the start of the canyon.

Apart from walking the canyon, you can explore the park from an Aboriginal viewpoint with ✪ **Lilla Aboriginal Tours** (☎ 08/8956 7909; book through Kings Canyon Resort). The company's Aboriginal guides take you on an easy 1-kilometer (a bit more than half a mile) walk to sacred caves and rock-painting sites in the Lilla community. You learn about the significance of the artworks and the Dreamtime events that created the land in this area. You also find out how the plants around you are in fact medicines and food, and you can have a go at throwing a spear and a boomerang. The tour lasts 1½ to 2 hours and departs at 9am, 11am, and 4pm daily from the company's offices, 14 kilometers (9 miles) from Kings Canyon Resort. The resort provides transfers for A$15 (U.S.$10.50) per person, round-trip, with a minimum of two passengers. *Note:* the tour does not run from mid-December to mid-January. It costs

A$25 (U.S.$17.50) for adults, A$20 (U.S.$14) for seniors and students, and is free for kids under age 15.

ESSENTIALS

GETTING THERE Keen 4WD fans can drive themselves to Kings Canyon from Alice Springs on the unsealed Mereenie Loop Road (see "Road Trips from Alice Springs," above).

The regular route to the canyon is the 480-kilometer (288-mile) trip from Alice Springs south via the Stuart Highway, then west onto the Lasseter Highway, then north and west on the Luritja Road. All three roads are sealed all the way. Uluru (Ayers Rock) is 306 kilometers (183½ miles) to the south of the canyon on a sealed road; to get to the Rock from Kings Canyon, you need to backtrack along Luritja Road for 168 kilometers (89 miles) to the Lasseter Highway, then take the Lasseter Highway west for 125 kilometers (75 miles) to Ayers Rock Resort. Ayers Rock itself is 18 kilometers (11 miles) farther on.

Greyhound Pioneer (☎ **13 20 30** in Australia) makes a daily trip from Ayers Rock to Kings Canyon for A$21 (U.S.$14.70), and a 2-day Alice–Ayers Rock–Kings Canyon–Alice loop tour for A$139 (U.S.$97.30) (the trip does not operate in the reverse direction).

ORGANIZED TOURS Loads of companies offer tours from Alice Springs and Ayers Rock. Many of them are one-way, 1½-day trips between Alice and Ayers Rock that include a stop at Kings Canyon. You usually spend the night in the campground or bunkhouses at Kings Canyon Resort, and take a canyon-rim walk in the afternoon or first thing in the morning, before traveling on to your next destination. Among the companies offering this itinerary are **Sahara Outback Tours** (☎ **1800/806 240** in Australia, or 08/8953 0881) and **Holiday AKT** (☎ **1800/89 1121** in Australia, or 08/8947 3900). The Sahara Outback Tours trip costs A$120 (U.S.$84), including meals and hotel pickup in Alice or Uluru (Ayers Rock); you sleep on a camp bed in a permanent tent. That's not a bad value considering that renting a car for 2 days will cost around A$75 (U.S.$52.50) per day, and a night in the bunkhouse will cost A$80 (U.S.$56) double. One-way or return day trips are available from Alice Springs with **Austour** (☎ **1800/335 009** in Australia, or 08/8953 0666), among others, and from Ayers Rock with **AAT Kings** (☎ **08/8956 2171**). Expect to pay between A$116 (U.S.$81.20) and A$160 (U.S.$112). If you don't mind missing out on a guided walk of the canyon, Austour also has a one-way Alice Springs–Kings Canyon journey that costs just A$90 (U.S.$63).

WHERE TO STAY

Kings Canyon Resort. Luritja Rd., Watarrka National Park, NT 0872. ☎ **1800/089 622** in Australia, 02/9360 9099 Sydney reservations office, or 08/8956 7442 resort. Fax 02/ 9332 4555 Sydney reservations office, or 08/8956 7410 resort. 132 units, 90 with bathroom; 66 powered campsites and tent sites. A/C TV. July–Nov A$266–$322 (U.S.$186.20–$225.40) double motel room. Dec–June A$231-$285 (U.S.$161.70-$199.50) double motel room. Additional person A$23 (U.S.$16.10) extra in motel room. A$80 (U.S.$56) double bunkhouse; A$135 (U.S.$94.50) family bunkhouse (sleeps 4); or A$36 (U.S.$25.20) per bed in quad-share bunkhouse. No children permitted in bunkhouses unless room is booked for sole use. Tent sites A$11 (U.S.$7) per person; powered sites A$26 (U.S.$18.20) double. Additional person A$10 (U.S.$7) extra; A$5 (U.S.$3.50) children 6–15 in powered campsite. Rates may be higher Dec 30 1999–Jan 2 2000. Ask about packages in conjunction with Ayers Rock Resort and Alice Springs Resort. AE, BC, DC, JCB, MC, V.

This attractive, low-slung complex 7 kilometers (4 miles) from Kings Canyon is designed to blend unobtrusively into the landscape. The cheapest way to stay here is to opt for the double, twin, quad, or family bunkhouses if you can tolerate using communal bathrooms for the night. The bunkhouses are actually pretty spiffy, with neatly painted concrete brick walls, tiled floors, smart bedcovers, bedside tables, a minifridge, dining furniture, air-conditioning, TV, and lockers (should you opt to share with a stranger). The nicely decorated standard motel rooms have extras like a hair dryer, an iron and board, and nice views from the balcony, but they aren't really worth the money. You can cut meal costs by cooking up a steak at the friendly barbecue area where everyone gathers to chat, or by eating in the cafe instead of in the posher restaurant. There are two bars, two swimming pools, a well-stocked general store, a tour desk, a laundry, a tennis court, and a sunset-viewing platform.

4 Uluru–Kata Tjuta National Park (Ayers Rock/The Olgas)

462km (277 miles) SW of Alice Springs; 1,934km (1,160½ miles) S of Darwin; 1,571km (942½ miles) N of Adelaide; 2,841km (1,704½ miles) NW of Sydney.

✪ **Ayers Rock** is the Australia tourism industry's pin-up icon, a glamorous red stone that has probably been splashed on more posters than Cindy Crawford has been on magazine covers. Just why people trek from all over the world to gawk at it is a bit of a mystery. Is it its size? Hardly, for nearby Mt. Connor is three times as big. Is it its shape? How so, when most folk agree that the neighboring Olgas are prettier? You can only put its popularity down to the faint shiver up the spine and the indescribable sense of place it evokes in anyone who looks at it. Even taciturn Aussie bushmen reckon it's "got somethin' spiritual about it."

Ayers Rock is commonly known by its Aboriginal name, Uluru. In 1985 the Uluru–Kata Tjuta National Park was returned to its Aboriginal owners, the Pitjant-jatjara and Yankunytjatjara people, together known as the Anangu, who continue to manage the property jointly with the Australian Nature Conservation Agency. Uluru is not the only monolith in the 1,325-square-kilometer (511-square-mile) national park. The round red heads of the Olgas, or Kata Tjuta, are here and so is flat-topped Mt. Connor. People used to speculate that the three rocks were meteorites, but we now know they were formed by conglomerate sediments laid down 600 to 700 million years ago in an ancient inland sea, and thrust up above ground (348 meters/1,141 feet in Ayers Rock's case) by geological forces. With a circumference of 9.4 kilometers (5½ miles) the Rock is no pebble, especially as two-thirds of it is thought to be underground. In photos it looks like a big smooth blob. In the flesh, it's actually more interesting—it's dappled with holes and overhangs, and its sides are edged with draped curtains of stone, creating little coves and gorges.

JUST THE FACTS

GETTING THERE   By Plane   Ansett flies to **Ayers Rock (Connellan) Airport** direct from Sydney daily, from Alice Springs once or twice a day, and from Perth four times a week. **Qantas** flies direct from Sydney, Perth, and Cairns daily; **Airlink** (book

Between a Rock & a Hard Place

You will find no towns for hundreds of miles near Ayers Rock/Uluru, which only adds to its rare beauty. Many visitors stay at **Ayers Rock Resort,** which makes up the "township" of Yulara, 18 kilometers (11 miles) away. It's the only place to stay, and that means it's expensive, right? Yep. But don't worry—there are affordable, comfortable rooms and some good-value dining options among the high-priced hotels and restaurants there, and we show you where to find them.

through Qantas) flies from Alice Springs twice a day. Ansett and Qantas flights from most other ports around Australia go via Alice Springs. As a general rule, the flight is around 3 hours from Sydney, 2 hours and 40 minutes from Perth, 4 hours from Cairns, and 55 minutes from Alice. The airport is 6 kilometers (3¾ miles) from Ayers Rock Resort.

By Bus   Greyhound Pioneer makes daily trips to Ayers Rock from Alice Springs. **McCafferty's** serves the Rock from Alice on Sunday, Tuesday, Thursday, and Friday. It's a 5½-hour trip, and the one-way fare is A$59 (U.S.$38.50).

By Organized Tour   Several companies offer day tours to Ayers Rock and the Olgas from Alice Springs. These tours cost A$150 (U.S.$105) per person on average and are a good way to see a lot in a day if your time is short, but it's one long day. The tours start around 5:30am in winter or 6am in summer, and you will not get back until late. Contact **Alice Springs Tour Professionals** (☎ **08/8953 0666**) or **Day Tours Alice Springs** (☎ **08/8953 4664**). Several tour companies offer one-way coach tours from Alice Springs; expect to pay around A$120 (U.S.$84). **Austour** (☎ **1800/335 009** in Australia, or 08/8953 0666) is one of the biggest tour operators.

By Car   Take the Stuart Highway south from Alice Springs for 199 kilometers (119½ miles), then turn onto the Lasseter Highway for 244 kilometers (146½ miles) to Yulara.

VISITOR INFORMATION   For information before you leave home, write to the **Central Australian Tourism Industry Association (CATIA)** in Alice Springs (see "Visitor Information" in Alice Springs section, above). To learn more about Ayers Rock/Uluru and the Olgas/Kata Tjuta, drop in at the **Ayers Rock Resort Visitor Centre,** near the Desert Gardens Hotel on Yulara Drive, Yulara, NT 0872 (☎ **08/ 8957 7377;** fax 08/8956 2222). The Visitor Centre has excellent displays on the area's geology, wildlife, and Aboriginal heritage, plus a souvenir store selling books and videos. It's open daily from 8:30am to 7:30pm.

Every hostelry at Ayers Rock has its own tour desk, but you can also book tours at the **Ayers Rock Tour & Information Centre** (☎ **08/8956 2240**) at the Yulara Town Square within the resort complex. It has little information on the national park, but it does sell books, maps, souvenirs, and a self-guided tape tour of Uluru for A$14.95 (U.S.$10.45). It's open daily from 8:30am to 8:30pm.

At the Rock itself, the ✪ **Uluru–Kata Tjuta Cultural Centre** (☎ **08/8956 3138**), 1 kilometer (½ mile) from the base of Uluru, is owned and run by the Anangu, the Aboriginal owners of Uluru. At the center you can learn all about Aboriginal legends and laws. It's worth spending some time here to understand the area's significance to Aboriginal people. It has information on tours and ranger activities; park notes; and animal, plant, and bird-watching checklists; as well as a booking desk for Anangu Tours, a souvenir store, an art gallery, and a cafe. It also houses the **Maruku Arts and Crafts** center. Open daily from 7am to 5:30pm April through October, and from 7am to 6pm November through March.

Uluru Travel Tip

Don't think a visit to Uluru is just about snapping a few photos and going home. You can walk around the Rock, climb it (although the owners prefer that you don't), fly over it, ride a camel to it, motorcycle around it on a Harley Davidson, trek through the Olgas, eat in an outdoor restaurant, tour the night sky, and join Aboriginal people on some rather special walks. Give yourself at least a couple of days in this area.

PARK ENTRANCE FEES   Entry to the Uluru–Kata Tjuta National Park is A$15 (U.S.$10.50) per adult; free for children under age 16. The entry pass is valid for 5 days.

RULES & REGULATIONS   You wouldn't like folk photographing your face or backyard without permission, and for the same reason the Anangu people ask you not to photograph sacred sites or Aboriginal people themselves without the subject's permission. They also ask you to approach sacred sites quietly and respectfully.

GETTING AROUND

It costs an arm and a leg every time you want to get from point A to point B at Ayers Rock. Ayers Rock Resort runs a great free shuttle around the resort complex every 15 minutes or so between 10:30am and 2:30pm, and again between 6:30pm and 12:30am, but to get to the Rock itself or to the Olgas, you will need to take transfers or a join tour. Tours are an easy way to take in everything, but you are crammed in with lots of tourists, so you can miss out on the area's special qualities. Although taking a tour is a good way to learn about the area's history and the indigenous culture, you can pick up all the information you need at the Ayers Rock Resort Visitor Centre or the Uluru–Kata Tjuta Cultural Centre (see "Visitor Information" above for both). Both have plenty of comprehensive park notes and walking guides.

GETTING AROUND BY SHUTTLE   If you want to explore on your own but don't want to rent a car, the easiest and cheapest way to get around is with **Sunworth Shuttles** (☎ **08/8956 2152**). They provide minibus transport anywhere around the Rock and the Olgas throughout the day. The company makes a sunrise run from the Ayers Rock Resort to Ayers Rock for A$25 (U.S.17.50); after that, it runs from the resort to the Rock every 45 minutes for A$20 (U.S.$14). It stops at several places around the Rock, so you can walk a section of the base and catch the next bus whenever you get tired. Sunset trips cost just A$15 (U.S.$10.50). Sunworth makes four trips daily to the Olgas for A$35 (U.S.$24.50) in the morning and A$40 (U.S.$28) in the afternoon. The afternoon trip includes sunset viewing at Ayers Rock. All fares are round-trip.

GETTING AROUND BY CAR   If two or more are traveling together, and you want to visit the Rock and the Olgas in one day, it might be cheaper to rent a car than pay for transfers. Roads to all the places you want to see are sealed, so you will not need a 4WD. You can rent a car at the airport or the resort. Expect to pay a little more for a car here than in Alice—around A$70 to $100 (U.S.$49 to $70) per day. Most car-rental companies will give you the first 100 kilometers (60 miles) free, then charge A25¢ (U.S.18¢) per kilometer after that. Consider this per-kilometer charge when budgeting, because the round-trip to the Olgas is more than 100 kilometers (60 miles) alone, without driving to the Rock.

  Avis (☎ 08/8956 2266), **Hertz** (☎ 08/8956 2244) and **Territory Thrifty Car Rental** (☎ 08/8956 2030) rent regular cars and 4WDs. With notice, Territory Thrifty rents camping kits if you take the car for 3 days or more. You will be charged a substantial fee, ranging from approximately A$80 (U.S.$56) to A$200 (U.S.$140), if you pick up your rental car in Alice Springs and return it at Ayers Rock.

GETTING AROUND BY ORGANIZED TOUR   Virtually every tour company picks you up at your hotel, lodge, or campground, no matter where in the resort you stay. Two of the biggest companies are **Uluru Experience** (☎ **1800/803 174** in Australia, or 08/8956 2563), which specializes in ecotours for small groups; and large-coach operator **AAT Kings** (☎ **08/8956 2171**).

ABORIGINAL TOURS If you do just one tour at Ayers Rock, make it with ☮ **Anangu Tours** (☎ **08/8956 2123**). Because this company is owned and run by the Aboriginal owners of the region, you will get a meaningful perspective on Uluru that is completely different from the geology and natural science slant you will pick up from most other tours. Their most popular tour is the **Liru Walk,** named after the ancestral army of poisonous snake-men whose battles left scars on the face of Uluru. The walk is a 2-kilometer (1¼-mile) trail leading from the Uluru–Kata Tjuta Cultural Centre to the Rock. You will hear the stories of how the landscape around you was shaped, discover bush tucker along the way, and try your hand at throwing a spear. The tour departs daily at 8:30am from the Cultural Centre and costs A$39 (U.S.$27.30) for adults and A$20 (U.S.$14) for kids ages 5 to 15. This tour doesn't include hotel pickup; if you want a hotel pickup, you will have to join the **Uluru Breakfast Tour,** which includes hotel pickup, a continental breakfast at the Cultural Centre cafe overlooking Uluru, and the Liru Walk for a rather hefty A$78 (U.S.$54.60) for adults and A$63 (U.S.$44.10) for children. The Uluru Breakfast Tour departs at 6:45am.

The company's other main tour is the **Kuniya sunset tour,** which departs at 3pm April through September, 4pm October through March, and costs A$65 (U.S.$45.50) for adults and A$49 (U.S.$34.30) for children with hotel pick-up, or A$39 (U.S.$27.30) for adults and A$20 (U.S.$14) for kids if you get there yourself.

DISCOVERING AYERS ROCK

SUNRISE, SUNSET Sunset is undoubtedly the most magnificent time to catch the Rock's beauty, although some days it's more colorful than others. On a good day, fiery oranges, peaches, pinks, reds, and then indigo and deep violet creep across its face almost as if it were a giant opal. A sunset tour with **AAT Kings** (☎ **08/8956 2171**) departs one hour before sunset and returns 20 minutes after sundown; the cost is A$24 (U.S.$16.80) for adults and A$12 (U.S.$8.40) for children under age 15, including hotel pick-up.

At sunrise the colors are less dramatic, but the spectacle of the Rock being unveiled by the dawn is quite moving. You'll have to get an early start—most tours leave about 75 minutes before the sun comes up. AAT Kings' sunrise tour costs A$34 (U.S.$23.80) for adults and A$17 (U.S.$11.90) for kids.

CLIMBING IT Aborigines refer to tourists as *minga* (little ants), because that's just what we look like as we crawl all over Uluru. Climbing this megalith is no picnic—there's sometimes a ferociously strong wind that can easily blow you right off, the walls are almost vertical in places so you have to hold on to a chain, and it can be freezing cold or insanely hot. Coming down is no piece of cake, either. Quite a few people climbing the rock have died from heart attacks, heat stress, exposure, or simply falling off, so if you are unfit, have breathing difficulties or heart trouble, high or low blood pressure, or are just plain scared of heights, don't do it. The Rock is closed to climbers during high winds, wet weather, and when temperatures exceed 36°Celsius (97°F). Bring drinking water with you from the resort.

If you are not put off by all that, however, you will be rewarded when you reach the top with 360° views of the plain far below, the Olgas, and Mt. Connor. The Rock's surface is rutted with ravines about 2.5 meters (8 feet) deep, so be prepared for some scrambling. The climb up takes about one hour for the fit, and the climb down takes about the same. Less-sure-footed climbers should allow 3 to 4 hours all told.

The Anangu really do not like people climbing Uluru, because the climb follows the trail their ancestral Dreamtime Mala men took when they first came to Uluru. They allow people to climb, but prefer that they don't do it.

WALKING, DRIVING, OR BUSING AROUND IT The 9.4-kilometer (5½-mile) Base Walk circumnavigating Uluru is a fairly easy trail. It takes about two hours with no stops, but allow yourself 3 to 4 hours to stop and get a feel for the water holes, folds, and overhangs that make up its walls. A shorter walk is an easy 1-kilometer (½-mile) round-trip trail from the Mutitjulu parking lot to the pretty water hole near the Rock's base that's home to Wanampi, an ancestral sea snake. There's some rock art in a cave here. The Liru Track is another easy trail; it runs 2 kilometers (1¼ miles) from the Uluru–Kata Tjuta Cultural Centre to Uluru, where it links with the Base Walk.

Whatever walk you decide to take, you should make time for the free daily stroll with the park ranger along the ✪ **Mala Walk.** On this trail the ranger, who is often an Aborigine, explains the Dreamtime myths behind Uluru, talks about local Aboriginal lifestyles and hunting techniques in days gone by, and about the significance of the rock art and other sites you see along the way. The walk leaves the Mala Walk sign at the base of Uluru at 10am May through September, and at a cooler 8am October through April. It takes between 1 and 2 hours to walk the 2-kilometer (1¼-mile) trail.

You can easily do all these walks on your own. Before setting off, arm yourself with the excellent self-guided walking notes available for a small charge from the Uluru–Kata Tjuta Cultural Centre (see "Visitor Information," above).

An alternative to walking around the base is to drive around it yourself or take a coach tour around it. **AAT Kings** (☎ **08/8956 2171**) offers a tour that incorporates a leisurely drive around Uluru, a short walk to the Mutitjulu water hole, and your choice of a walk into the peaceful water hole at Kantju Gorge or a visit to the Uluru–Kata Tjuta Cultural Centre. The tour costs A$37 (U.S.$25.90) for adults and A$19 (U.S.$13.30) for children under age 15. **Uluru Experience** (☎ **08/8956 2563**) conducts a 5-hour morning tour that includes short walks into the base to see Aboriginal art and hear about the Dreamtime. The tour also includes breakfast and a stop at the Uluru–Kata Tjuta Cultural Centre. It costs A$69 (U.S.$48.30) for adults, and A$54 (U.S.$37.80) for children ages 6 to 15; free for children under 6.

FLYING OVER IT Flights are not cheap, but they will give you some spectacular photos. A 30-minute scenic flight over the Rock and the Olgas with **Rockayer** (☎ **08/8956 2345**) costs A$67 (U.S.$46.90) per adult, A$55 (U.S.$38.50) per child ages 4 to 14. **Ayers Rock Helicopters** (☎ **08/8956 2077**) offers 15-minute flights over Uluru for A$75 (U.S.$52.50) per person, and 30-minute trips over the Rock and the Olgas for A$145 (U.S.$101.50) per person, although when I visited this flight was going for just A$100 (U.S.$70)—and in peak season. All rates include transfers to Ayers Rock (Connellan) Airport.

MOTORCYCLING AROUND IT This is your big chance to fulfill your *Easy Rider* dreams as you burn into the desert on the back of a Harley. A 50-kilometer (30-mile) blast around the Rock with **Uluru Motorcycle Tours** (☎ **08/8956 2019**) will set you back A$90 (U.S.$63), or A$105 (U.S.$73.50) at sunset with a glass of champagne or a beer. They drive the bike, you sit behind the driver, hang on, and admire the view.

VIEWING IT ON CAMELBACK **Frontier Camel Tours** (☎ **08/8956 2444**) makes forays to view Uluru at sunrise and sunset. Amble through red sand dunes to a viewing area, dismount to watch the sun rise or sink, and remount to return to the depot for billy tea and yummy beer bread in the morning or champagne in the evening. The 2-hour tours depart from the camel depot at Ayers Rock Resort, and cost A$65 (U.S.$45.50) per person, including transfers from your hotel. You can link the sunrise tour to an AAT Kings Base Tour (see above) for A$100 (U.S.$70) per adult and A$83 (U.S.$58.10) per child ages 5 to 14, a saving of A$2 (U.S.$1.40) per adult and A$1 (U.S.70¢) per child. The sunset tour can be combined with a cook-it-yourself barbecue dinner at the Outback Pioneer Hotel and Lodge (see "Where to Stay," below) and a tour of the heavens at the Ayers Rock Observatory, for A$100 (U.S.$70) per adult and A$95 (U.S.$66.50) per child. Each day between 10:30am and 2:30pm you can tour the depot and take a short camel ride for A$9 (U.S.$6.30) for adults, A$5 (U.S.$3.50) for children, or A$25 (U.S.$17.50) for a family.

EXPLORING THE OLGAS

Massive ✪ **Mt. Olga,** known to the Aborigines as Kata Tjuta, or "many heads," is a lesser-known sister monolith to Uluru. Fifty kilometers (30 miles) west of Uluru, the Olgas' 36 momentous red domes bulge out of the earth like turned clay on a potter's wheel. The tallest dome is actually 200 meters (656 feet) higher than Ayers Rock. The Olgas are even more important in Aboriginal Dreamtime legend than Uluru, and many visitors find them even more awe inspiring than the Rock.

Two trails take you in among the domes, the 7.4-kilometer (4½-mile) **Valley of the Winds walk,** which is fairly challenging and takes 3 to 5 hours, and the 2.6-kilometer (1½-mile) **Gorge walk,** which is easy and takes about an hour. Both walks have lookout points and shady stretches. The Valley of the Winds trail is closed when temperatures rise above 36°Celsius (97°F).

WHERE TO STAY

Ayers Rock Resort is not only in the township of Yulara, it *is* the township. This is the only place to stay at or near Uluru. To protect the precious plants and wildlife in the area, the resort was set about 16 kilometers (10 miles) from Uluru, outside the boundary of the national park. Because everyone either is a tourist or lives and works here, the resort has a village atmosphere, right down to the town square. There's a supermarket, an ANZ bank, a post office, a police station, a Royal Flying Doctor Service base, a hair and beauty salon, and even a primary school on the grounds.

You have a choice of five separate hotels, apartment buildings, or lodges, along with campsites—and none of them is all that cheap. The cheapest way to do your whole stay at Ayers Rock may be to rent a car and camping kit from Territory Thrifty Car Rental (see "Getting Around," above) and stay in the campground.

You can book accommodations through the resort's central reservations office in Sydney, Suite 101, Level 1, 80 William St., East Sydney, NW 2011 (☎ **1800/ 089 622** in Australia, or 02/9360 9099; fax 02/9332 4555; www.ayersrock.aust.com on the Web). You can also book Kings Canyon Resort accommodations through this office.

High season is usually July 1 to November 30. Book well ahead in this period. Note that rates may also be higher during the New Year's period, from December 30 to January 2.

Travel Tip

Most tourists visit Uluru in the mornings and the Olgas in the afternoon. If you want to beat the crowds, reverse the order and do the Valley of the Winds walk in the morning, then visit Uluru in the afternoon. That way you will find both places a little more silent and spiritual. Bring drinking water with you from the resort, as there is no kiosk and only one emergency tank on the Valley of the Winds trail.

Money-Saving Tip

Ayers Rock Resort, Alice Springs Resort, and Kings Canyon Resort are owned by the same company, and packages for stays at two or all three resorts are sometimes available. Ask when you are making your reservation.

Ayers Rock Campground. Within Ayers Rock Resort, Yulara Dr., Yulara, NT 0872. ☎ **08/ 8956 2055.** Fax 08/8956 2260. 220 tent sites, 198 powered sites, 14 cabins. A$114 (U.S.$79.80) cabin (sleeps up to 6); A$11 (U.S.$7.70) per person tent site; A$26 (U.S. $18.20) double powered site. Additional person A$10 (U.S.$7) extra; A$5 (U.S.$3.50) children 6–15 in powered site. Minimum 2 nights in cabins during school vacations. AE, BC, DC, JCB, MC, V. Free airport shuttle.

Pitch your tent on green lawns instead of red dust at this friendly landscaped campsite, and look for the Southern Cross from your sleeping bag. The campground has its own pool, volleyball court and playground, free barbecues, clean communal bathrooms, public long-distance and international pay phones, Laundromat, and tour desk so you don't have to hightail it over to the Ayers Rock Tour & Information Centre to make bookings. If you don't want to camp, but you do want to travel cheap, consider one of the air-conditioned cabins. They're clean, modern, and a great value with a kitchenette, petite dining furniture, one double bed, and four bunks. You share bath facilities. Remember, campers can use all the other resort facilities, too.

Outback Pioneer Hotel and Lodge. Yulara Dr., Yulara, NT 0872. ☎ **1800/089 622** in Australia, or 08/8956 2170. Fax 08/8956 2320. 125 units; 12 cabins, none with bathroom; 36 quad-share bunk rooms; 4 20-bed dorms. A/C. High season A$288 (U.S.$201.60) double, $128 (U.S.$89.60) cabin. Low season A$274 (U.S.$191.80) double, A$124 (U.S.$86.80) cabin. Additional person A$20 (U.S.$14) extra. A$31 (U.S. $21.70) bunk-room bed, A$25 (U.S.$17.50) dorm bed year-round. No children in bunkhouses/dorms unless room is booked for sole use. AE, BC, DC, JCB, MC, V. Free airport shuttle.

A fun, happy, all-ages crowd congregates at this midrange collection of hotel rooms, cabins, and dorms. The decent-sized hotel rooms got a smart refurb in early 1999; each has an uncramped bathroom, a minibar, a TV, pay-per-view movies, a telephone, and a hair dryer. Twelve rooms also have a sink and a microwave. The cabins have a double bed and a bunk, shared bath facilities, and a shared kitchen but are still comfortably decked out with a TV, self-serve tea and coffee, and a minirefrigerator. The bunkhouse and dorms are basic but air-conditioned, which is the main thing in summer! Out by the nice pool there are plenty of lounge chairs and shady tables and chairs.

Spinifex Lodge. Yulara Dr., Yulara, NT 0872. ☎ **08/8956 2131.** Fax 08/8956 2163. 34 rooms, 34 quad-share bunkhouses, none with bathroom. A/C. High season A$126 (U.S.$88.20) double or bunkhouse. Low season A$122 (U.S.$85.40) double or bunkhouse. Additional person A$20 (U.S.$14) extra. AE, BC, DC, JCB, MC, V. Free airport shuttle.

If you don't want to camp, the clean, cool, comfortably furnished rooms here are your best bet. All rooms have a kitchenette and pay-per-view movies, although bathroom facilities are shared. There's no pool, but you can walk a few hundred meters and use the one at Desert Gardens. There's no restaurant either, but Gecko's Café, the bakery, and the supermarket are just next door, as is the Ayers Rock Tour & Information Centre.

WHERE TO DINE
Note: See the "Dining in the Desert" box earlier in the chapter for details on Ayers Rock Resort's excellent "Sounds of Silence" dining experience.

When You See the Southern Cross for the First Time

At the **Ayers Rock Observatory,** located near the Uluru lookout within the Ayers Rock Resort complex, you can take a 1-hour tour of the southern hemisphere heavens (the stars are different from those in the northern hemisphere). Check out your zodiac constellation, the Southern Cross, the planets, the moon, and the marvelous Milky Way. To visit the observatory, you must join a tour with **Uluru Experience** (☎ **1800/803 174** in Australia, or 08/8956 2563), who provide hotel pick-up and a tour at 8:30pm or 10:15pm. The tour costs A$25 (U.S.$17.50) for adults, A$18 (U.S.$12.60) for children ages 6 to 15, and A$63 (U.S.$44.10) for a family of four or five.

Of all the in-hotel restaurants, the do-it-yourself ✪ **Pioneer Barbeque and Bar** at the **Outback Pioneer Hotel and Lodge** is the best value and the most fun. Join the throngs of guests throwing a steak on the communal barbie. You dine in a rustic shed with big tables, lots of beer, and live music. Buy your meat at the bar and cook it yourself, then help yourself to the all-you-can-eat salad, a baked potato, and bread. A tasty, juicy beef pattie costs A$10 (U.S.$7), while sizable steaks and barramundi cost around A$15 (U.S.$10.50). The place is open nightly for dinner. If that's still too pricey, just down the side from the barbecue is a kiosk doing burgers for around A$5 (U.S.$3.50) and sandwiches for A$3.50 (U.S.$2.45). You can buy your food here and still eat it at the noisy tables in the Pioneer Barbeque and Bar.

Your other cheap(ish) option is **Gecko's Café** on the Town Square, which does wood-fired pizzas and à la carte main course for A$13.50 (U.S.$9.45) to A$25.50 (U.S.$17.85). It's open all day from breakfast until late. Also on the Town Square you will find a take-out joint doing burgers for A$6 (U.S.$4.20), sandwiches, and the like; an ice-cream shop; a bakery where a Danish and an instant coffee will cost you less than A$4 (U.S.$2.80); and cheapest of all, the supermarket.

5 En Route to Darwin from Alice Springs

Alice Springs–Darwin: 1,489km (893½ miles)

If you're driving or coaching it along the Stuart Highway from Alice Springs to Darwin, or vice versa, settle in for a long trip, because there's not a lot to see, apart from great sunsets. From **Elliott** north, war buffs can stop at numerous **World War II sites** along the way, mostly modest things like stores depots, sometimes more haunting spots like U.S. airfields. Look for the white-on-brown tourist road signs marking their locations. The terrain from the Red Centre to the Top End is flat, stony, and monotonous most of the way. Allow at least two long days to reach Darwin; if you have the time, spend three days, overnighting at Tennant Creek and Katherine. We found fuel was cheapest at those towns. *Note:* If you're making this trip on your own, be sure to review the driving precautions discussed at the beginning of this chapter.

The first sight from Alice Springs worth stopping for is the **Devil's Marbles Conservation Reserve** by the highway, 393 kilometers (236 miles) north of Alice, just beyond Wauchope. To you and me, they are hundreds of massive granite boulders, some the size of houses, that have balanced perilously on top of one another for thousands of years. To the Aborigines, they are Karlu Karlu, the eggs of the Rainbow Serpent, the Dreamtime Creator. Visit at dawn or sunset for the most spectacular photos. Entry is free. Don't confuse these with the much less impressive Devil's Pebbles, a low mound of boulders on the left side of the highway near Tennant Creek.

For a map of the route from Alice Springs to Darwin, refer to the Northern Territory map at the beginning of chapter 10.

You will probably spend the night in the gold-mining town of **Tennant Creek** (pop. 4,000), 114 kilometers (68½ miles) north of the Devil's Marbles. You can pan or fossick for gold here, go underground into a modern gold mine, and tour the historical gold battery stamp to see the precious yellow stuff extracted from ore. The mine and the battery stamp, as well as a mining museum, various mining machinery relics, and the Tennant Creek Regional Tourist Association information center are all housed in the **Battery Hill Regional Centre,** 1.5 kilometers (1 mile) east of the town center on Peko Road, Tennant Creek, NT 0860 (☎ **08/8962 3388;** fax 08/8962 2509). You can book all local tours here. The gold stamp battery and the underground mine tour are each A$12 (U.S.$8.40) for adults, and A$6 (U.S.$4.20) for kids ages 5 to 14. They are open Monday to Friday from 9am to 5pm and Saturday from 9am to noon. The **Bluestone Motor Inn,** Paterson Street (which is the same thing as the Stuart Highway), Tennant Creek, NT 0861 (☎ **08/8962 2617;** fax 08/8962 2883) and the **Eldorado Motor Lodge,** Paterson Street/Stuart Highway, Tennant Creek, NT 0861 (☎ **08/8962 2402;** fax 08/8962 3034) are the best motels in town. In addition to the gold mining tours, there are half-day horseback cattle drives through the bush, and campfire and bush tucker tours, so you may want to slot in a full day in Tennant Creek.

At the roadhouse of **Renner Springs,** 161 kilometers (96½ miles) up the road, stop for a "coldie" (a cold beer) with the "truckies" (truck drivers) at the rough-and-ready **Desert Hotel.** When you reach **Elliott** (pop. 600), another 91 kilometers (54½ miles) on, you're halfway to Darwin. Just north of Elliott, the turn-off for **Newcastle Waters** marks the end of the Outback and the start of the Top End. The land gets a bit greener from here. Make the detour of a few miles west off the highway for a beer at the wonderful Outback pub at **Daly Waters** (☎ **08/8975 9927**); the pub walls are festooned with rusty tools, old harnesses, antique bottles, and every memento imaginable from the hordes of visitors who have stopped by since it opened in 1938. It sells meals and fuel and has campgrounds. Next to the pub is an old World War II aerodrome with the wreckage of a B-25 Mitchell bomber. The airstrip was a refueling stop for Qantas in the 1930s and is, in fact, Australia's first international airport. There is a B-25 fuselage and wing on display at the **Larrimah Roadhouse,** 90 kilometers (54 miles) up the highway.

A dip in the crystal-clear thermal pools, always a steady 34°C, at ✪ **Mataranka,** 159 kilometers (95½ miles) up the highway from Daly Waters, is a wonderfully soothing antidote to driving. What looks like the world's entire population of flying foxes lives around these pools. Admission is free. Mataranka is the first major stop since Tennant Creek, and boasts a couple of restaurants, a bar, and a couple of low-key motels and campgrounds. While you're here, inspect some Aboriginal *humpies* (bark shelters) and the convincing replica of the slab-hut Elsey Homestead, the famous setting in the classic Aussie book *We of the Never Never.* From April to September a free homestead tour operates daily at 11am.

Katherine and **Katherine Gorge National Park** (see "Katherine" in chapter 10) are 105 kilometers (63 miles) farther on. Another 91 kilometers (54½ miles) past Katherine brings you to **Pine Creek,** whose architecture harks back to the 1870s gold rush. You can see a steam engine and gold stamp battery in action, and pan for gold (and be sure of finding some!) at **Gun Alley Gold Mining** (☎ **08/8976 1221**), open daily from April to October from 8:30am to 3pm. Admission is A$5 (U.S.$3.50) per person. Just north of Pine Creek you can swing right onto the sealed (paved) **Kakadu Highway** and head to Darwin via Kakadu National Park. It's 455 kilometers (273 miles) to Darwin by this route, or 225 kilometers (135 miles) if you stick to the Stuart Highway. At the very end of the Stuart Highway in Darwin, the road becomes a closed roundabout and turns back on itself—all the way to Adelaide!

ORGANIZED TOURS BETWEEN ALICE & DARWIN **Territory Link Tours** (☎ **1800/642 224** in Australia, or phone/fax 08/8388 5905) provides guided, door-to-door, 2½-day minibus transfers and tours operating once a week in both directions between Alice Springs and Darwin. The trip makes numerous stops at points of interest, and owner/driver Bill Goudie shares his ample knowledge of wildlife, history, and Aboriginal culture along the way. The trip overnights at Wauchope and Mataranka in basic but comfortable accommodations. You can add to the tour a 2- or 4-hour cruise of Katherine Gorge or a half-day canoe trip of the gorge. The one-way trip is A$209 (U.S.$146.30) per person with shared bath facilities or A$295 (U.S.$206.50) with a private bathroom. Meals are extra—A$10 (U.S.$7) for two breakfasts and two lunches. Bill also offers either journey as an extended 6-day itinerary that takes in a 3-day loop around Ayers Rock and Kings Canyon. Some camping is involved on this tour. It costs A$570 (U.S.$399) per person in accommodations with shared facilities or A$690 (U.S.$483) per person in motel rooms with private bath. The 6-day tour prices include some meals.

Northern Territory Adventure Tours runs a 6-day safari between Alice and Darwin in a 23-seat bus. The tour is aimed at having fun, partying, and seeing lots of sights along the way. The Alice–Darwin tour takes 3 days to get from Alice to Darwin and then does a 3-day loop around Kakadu National Park. The Darwin–Alice trip takes 3 days to get to Alice and then does a 3-day loop around Ayers Rock and the Olgas. There's plenty of time for swimming in natural water holes, canoeing down rivers, hiking, and seeing Aboriginal rock art. You camp every night except for one spent in a dorm bed. The one-way trip is A$540 (U.S.$378) per person, which covers most meals, camping fees, and all park entrance fees except the Uluru–Kata Tjuta National Park fee of A$15 (U.S.$10.50). The bus departs three times a week in both directions year-round.

The Top End 10

by Natalie Kruger

The northernmost section of Australia, from Broome on the west coast of Western Australia to Arnhemland in the Northern Territory, is what Aussies refer to as the "Top End." It is a genuine last frontier, a place of hardship and wild beauty, where folk come to remember what a true wilderness feels like.

The rugged northwest portion of Western Australia is known as the Kimberley; there beef-cattle farming, pearl farming, and tourism thrive in a rocky moonscape of red cliffs, waterfalls, mighty rivers, sparse gums, and lagoons. Visit a million-acre cattle station rich in ancient Aboriginal rock art sites, tour the world's largest diamond mine, or cruise the lush Ord River. In the cute town of Broome, ride a camel on the beach, tour ancient gorges, and visit a working pearl farm.

The Top End of the Northern Territory is slightly more populated. Darwin, the capital, is a smallish city, but rich, modern, and tropical. Katherine, to its south, is a small farming town famous for its beautiful river gorge. Here you can visit an Aboriginal community, explore vast cattle stations, and soak in natural thermal pools. To the east of Darwin and Katherine is Kakadu National Park, home to wetlands, crocodiles, and millions of birds—one-third of the country's bird species, in fact. Farther east still is Arnhemland, an endless stretch of rocky ridges and flooding rivers owned by Aboriginal people.

Life in the Top End, especially in the Northern Territory, is a bit different than elsewhere in Australia. It has a slightly lawless image that I suspect Territorians enjoy cultivating among tenderfoot Aussies from south of the border. The isolation, the intense humidity in the summer Wet Season, monsoonal floods, crocodiles, and other dangers breed a tough kind of guy and girl. This is Crocodile "Mick" Dundee territory, and although he may only be a movie character, the scriptwriters didn't have to exaggerate all that much when they invented him.

EXPLORING THE TOP END

VISITOR INFORMATION   For information on Darwin, Kakadu National Park, and Katherine, contact the **Northern Territory Tourist Commission (NTTC)** at Tourism House, 43 Mitchell St., Darwin, NT 0800 (☎ **08/8999 3900,** fax 08/8999 3888; www.nttc.com.au). See "Visitor Information" in chapter 3 for the commission's offices in the United States, the United Kingdom, and New Zealand. The Commission publishes an excellent 64-page color touring guide, *Holidaying in the Top End*. If you plan to drive yourself, you may want to ask the

Commission for its free 52-page *Motoring Guide;* it's not as informative as the Top End holiday guide, and its maps are only rudimentary, but it does contain good details on campsites and campervan parks throughout the Territory. If you are interested in staying at bed-and-breakfasts or taking a farmstay holiday, the Commission produces on behalf of the Northern Territory Bed & Breakfast Council a pamphlet that lists a dozen or so of this kind of place, mostly around Darwin. You can view the properties and make bookings online at www.ozemail.com.au/~orangewo/nt/dir_ind.htm. The Commission operates a **Holiday Centre** (☎ **1800/621 336** in Australia; fax 08/ 8951 8582), which will assist you in planning your itinerary and making reservations.

Add 5% tax to all accommodation tariffs in the Northern Territory. If you are taking a holiday package, the tax is payable on the accommodation component of the package. The tax is not payable on camping.

For information on the Kimberley region, contact the **Western Australian Tourism Commission,** 16 St. Georges Terrace, Perth, WA 6000 (☎ **08/9220 1700;** fax 08/9220 1702; www.wa.gov.au/watc). You can call the Western Australian Tourist Centre from within Australia (☎ **1300/361 351**) to ask for information and make bookings.

WHEN TO GO   The sanest time to visit is during the winter **Dry Season** (or "the Dry," as it's called). This is roughly from late April to the end of October. Not a cloud will grace the sky, and temperatures will be warm and comfortable, even hot in the middle of the day. Winter is high season, so book every tour, hotel, or campsite well in advance.

The Top End's **Wet Season** (or "the Wet") runs from November (sometimes as early as October) to March or April, sometimes a few weeks longer in the Kimberley. During the Wet it doesn't rain all the time, but when it does, it comes down in buckets, usually for an hour or two each day, mainly in the late afternoon or overnight. The land floods as far as the eye can see, and roads are cut off for hours, days, or even months at a time. Flash floods in particular pose a danger to unwary motorists. Many attractions are inaccessible because of the floodwaters, and some tour companies shut up shop for the season. And then there's the murderous humidity, not to mention the high temperatures you will experience at this time. Many people find the buildup to the Wet, in October and November—when clouds gather but do not break—the toughest time to be in the Top End.

Having said all that, the Wet is a wonderful time to travel. Waterfalls become massive torrents, lightning storms crackle against the sky, the land turns green, swimming holes overflow, and cloud cover keeps the worst of the sun off you. You can travel in the Wet if you keep your plans flexible, do not overexert yourself, avoid being outside in the middle of the day, and carry lots of drinking water. Even if you normally camp, you should sleep in air-conditioned accommodations at this time of year. If your heart is set on a particular organized tour, book it ahead, as some tours will operate not at all or else on a reduced schedule.

For more details on when to visit the Top End, see "When to Go" in chapter 3.

GETTING AROUND   The **Automobile Association of the Northern Territory (AANT),** 79–81 Smith St., Darwin, NT 0800 (☎ **08/8981 3837;** fax 08/8941 2965),

---

Money-Saving Tip

Tour prices often drop by as much as A$20 to $30 (U.S.$14 to 21) per person in the Wet Season because of the low numbers of travelers visiting the Top End then. Keep an eye out for special deals.

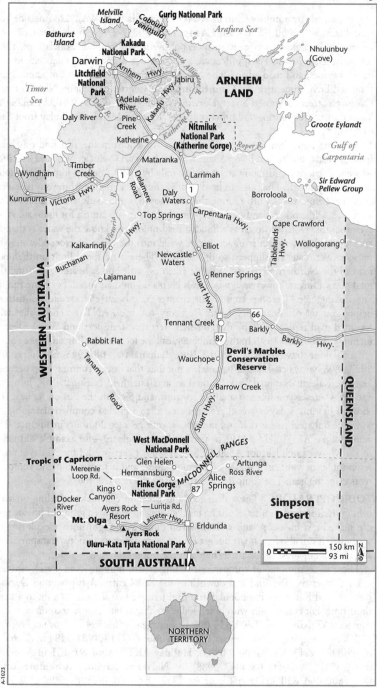

Melville Island

Bathurst Island

Cobourg Peninsula

Gurig National Park

Arafura Sea

Nhulunbuy (Gove)

Kakadu National Park

Darwin

Litchfield National Park

Arnhem Hwy.

Jabiru

South Alligator R.

ARNHEM LAND

Groote Eylandt

Timor Sea

Adelaide River

Daly R.

Pine Creek

Kakadu Hwy.

Daly River

Katherine

Katherine R.

Nitmiluk National Park (Katherine Gorge)

Roper R.

Gulf of Carpentaria

Mataranka

Sir Edward Pellew Group

Wyndham

Timber Creek

1

Larrimah

Borroloola

Kununurra

Victoria Hwy.

Delamere Road

Daly Waters

1

Carpentaria Hwy.

Cape Crawford

Top Springs

Victoria R.

Elliot

Wollogorang

WESTERN AUSTRALIA

Kalkarindji

Buchanan Hwy.

Newcastle Waters

Renner Springs

Tablelands Hwy.

Lajamanu

Rabbit Flat

Stuart Hwy.

Tennant Creek

66

Barkly

Barkly Hwy.

QUEENSLAND

Tanami Road

87

Wauchope

Devil's Marbles Conservation Reserve

Barrow Creek

Stuart Hwy.

West MacDonnell National Park

MACDONNELL RANGES

Tropic of Capricorn

Glen Helen

Arltunga

Mereenie Loop Rd.

Hermannsburg

Ross River

Kings Canyon

Finke Gorge National Park

Alice Springs

Simpson Desert

Docker River

Ayers Rock Resort

Luritja Rd.

87

Mt. Olga

Lasseter Hwy.

Erldunda

Ayers Rock

Uluru-Kata Tjuta National Park

0   150 km

93 mi

N

SOUTH AUSTRALIA

NORTHERN TERRITORY

A-1023

and the **Royal Automobile Club of Western Australia (RACWA),** 228 Adelaide Terrace, Perth, WA 6000 (☎ **08/9421 4444;** fax 08/9221 2708), both offer reciprocal emergency breakdown service to members of overseas automobile associations. Their respective Darwin and Perth offices are a good source of motoring maps, accommodations guides, and road advice. The Northern Territory Department of Land, Planning and Environment runs a **Land Information Centre,** First Floor, Nichol's Place, Cavenagh Street at Bennett Street, Darwin, NT 0800 (☎ **08/8999 7032**), selling all kinds of maps for touring and other purposes. It's open Monday to Friday from 8am to 4pm.

As in the Red Centre, you can reach most attractions in the Top End on sealed (paved) roads, but to reach some you will need a 4WD vehicle. We have specified which attractions in this book are accessible only by 4WD. You can join a 4WD tour, or rent one yourself. They are not hard to drive, but get a briefing from your rental car company before you set off. During the Wet Season, some roads will be under water all season, while others can flood unexpectedly, leaving you cut off for hours, days, or even months. Don't try to cross a flooded road unless you know the water is shallow and the road underneath is intact. Never wade into the water, as crocodiles may be present. Wet roads are slippery, so drive slowly. There is no speed limit on the open road in the Northern Territory. Wildlife (such as cattle and kangaroos) crossing the road poses a threat, however, so wise locals keep a lid on their speed. For more tips on safe driving, see "Getting Around" in chapter 3,. Always check **road conditions** before you set off. In the Northern Territory call the **AANT,** or check the daily recorded road report made by the Northern Territory Transport and Works Department (☎ **1800/246 199**). In the Kimberley, call the local tourist bureau or the police.

Go-it-alone travelers will like the **Blue Banana** (☎ **08/8945 6800;** fax 08/8927 5808; www.octa4.net.au/banana), a minibus that does a running loop between Darwin, Kakadu National Park, Katherine, and Litchfield National Park. Jump on and off wherever you like at the 20 or so stops, and pick up the bus on its next trip through (it runs 4 days a week). You get treated to a guided commentary along the way. The only real rule is that you must book your next leg 24 hours in advance. The whole loop is A$170 (U.S.$119), or you can buy a single leg—for example Katherine to Darwin via Litchfield for A$90 (U.S.$63). Your ticket is valid for 90 days. You're responsible for your own meals, accommodations, and activities, but the company rents camping gear. The company also runs inexpensive 4-day tours.

TOUR OPERATORS   Great distances and isolation can make traveling on your own in the Top End a rather daunting task. Joining an organized group or private tour can make life a bit easier, and will show you things you might not see exploring on your own. It can also be a smart budget choice, since accommodations, transportation, and often all or most meals are included in the price.

There is no shortage of companies running coach, minibus, and 4WD camping tours all over the Top End and down into the Red Centre. A trip around Darwin, Kakadu, and Katherine is a popular Top End triangle that shows you a lot in a fairly short time. For coach tours with hotel, lodge, or shared bunkhouse accommodations, contact **AAT Kings** (☎ **1800/334 009** in Australia, or 08/8941 3844; fax 08/8941 3386). For camping safaris, contact **Billy Can Tours** (☎ **1800/81 3484** in Australia, or 08/8981 9813; fax 08/8941 0803), **Holiday AKT** (**1800/891 121** in Australia, or 08/8947 3900; fax 08/8947 3988), or **Northern Territory Adventure Tours** (☎ **1800/063 838** in Australia, or 08/8952 1474; fax 08/8981 9058). A 3-day Kakadu National Park and Katherine Gorge trip with AAT Kings from Darwin costs from A$445/U.S.$311.50 (shared bunkhouse) to A$599/U.S.$419.30 (deluxe hotel).

Croc Alert! (& Other Safety Tips)

Saltwater crocodiles are a serious threat in the sea, estuaries, lakes, wetlands, and rivers of the Top End—even hundreds of kilometers inland. They may be called "saltwater" crocs, but they live in fresh water. Never jump in the water or stand on the bank unless you want to be lunch.

Always carry 4 liters (a gallon) of drinking water per person a day when walking (2 liters/half a gallon per person per hour in summer). Wear a broad-brimmed hat, high-factor sunscreen lotion, and insect repellent containing DEET (Aerogard and RID brands both contain it).

Deadly marine stingers put a stop to ocean swimming in the Top End from October to April.

A 3-day 4WD camping safari into Kakadu National Park from Darwin with **Billycan Tours** is A$580 (U.S.$406).

Katherine-based ✪ **Far Out Adventures**(☎ **08/8972 2552;** fax 08/8972 2228) has a wide range of 1- to 12-day camping and accommodated tours into Kakadu, Darwin, Arnhemland, Litchfield National Park, the Kimberley, and beyond.

Territory Thrifty Car Rental (see "Getting Around" in each section below) offers good-value accommodation and camping packages throughout the Northern Territory and the East Kimberley. Like several other rental car companies, it rents complete camping kits.

SUGGESTED ITINERARIES   The vast distances, seasonal floods, and isolation all need to be considered when you're planning a trip to the Top End. Don't try to do too much, because just getting from place to place takes some time. If you have time for only one day trip from Darwin, I'd go to Litchfield National Park. It's closer, smaller, and prettier than Kakadu. If you have only 3 days, spend 2 in Kakadu National Park and 1 in Darwin. Tack on some time in Katherine if you have 4 or 5 days. If you have a week, consider a camping safari combining Kakadu, Katherine Gorge, and Litchfield National Park. If you have 10 days up your sleeve, and a sense of adventure, take a safari across the Gibb River Road from Kununurra to Broome.

1 Darwin

1,489km (893½ miles) N of Alice Springs

Named after the founder of evolution himself, Australia's northernmost capital has always had a touch of Asian exoticism about it. With its proud white civic buildings, pink bougainvillea rambling over fences, and real estate prices second only to Sydney, Darwin is no poor-cousin outpost. It's a modern tropical city—extremely modern, actually, as most of it was rebuilt after Cyclone Tracy wiped out the city on Christmas Eve 1974. Don't fuss about unpacking your jacket and tie here. Shorts and rubber thongs will get you most places—even the swankest official state invitations stipulate dress as "Territory Rig," which means long pants and a short-sleeved open-necked shirt for men.

Darwin is most commonly used as a stepping-off point to Kakadu National Park, Katherine Gorge, and the Kimberley, but give yourself at least a day to wander the pleasant streets and parklands. The barramundi fishing is excellent, and the city's World War II history is worth exploring (the harbor contains an official U.S. war grave).

ESSENTIALS

GETTING THERE   By Plane   Qantas and **Ansett** serve Darwin daily from most state capitals; flights are either direct or connect in Alice Springs. Qantas flies direct from Cairns daily. Ansett flies daily from Broome via Kununurra. **Airlink** (book through Qantas) makes a direct Broome–Darwin flight on Sunday and late (flight arrives at 2:40am) Friday night. **Air North** (☎ **1800/627 474** in Australia, or 08/8945 2866, or book through Ansett) flies to Darwin 6 days a week from Alice Springs via Tennant Creek and Katherine; it also operates an extra daily service from Katherine. Flying time is about 5½ hours from Sydney; just under 4½ hours from Perth; 4 hours from Cairns; and about 2 hours from Alice Springs, or 4 hours with Air North. There are also direct flights to Darwin from Asia.

The **airport shuttle bus** (☎ **1800/358 945** in the Northern Territory, or 08/8981 5066) meets every flight and delivers to the city for A$6 (U.S.$4.20) one way or A$10 (U.S.$7) round-trip. Up to two children travel free. You don't need to book a seat. A **cab** to the city is around A$13 (U.S.$9.10), or A$15 (U.S.$10.50) at night and on weekends.

By Bus   Greyhound Pioneer runs two buses daily to Darwin from Alice Springs, and **McCafferty's** has one daily run. The trip takes 19½ hours, and the fare is A$145 (U.S.$101.50). Greyhound has daily service also from Broome via Katherine; this trip takes 25 hours and costs A$202 (U.S.$141.40).

By Car   Darwin is at the end of the Stuart Highway. Allow at least 2 full days to drive from Alice Springs (see "En Route to Darwin from Alice Springs" in chapter 9.

There is no train service to Darwin.

VISITOR INFORMATION   The Darwin Region Tourist Association at Beagle House, Knuckey Street at Mitchell Street, Darwin, NT 0800 (☎ **08/8981 4300;** fax 08/8981 0653; e-mail: drtainfo@ozemail.com.au), is the place to go for maps and information. It's open Monday through Friday from 8:30am to 5:45pm, Saturday from 9am to 2:45pm, and Sunday and public holidays from 10am to 2pm.

CITY LAYOUT   The heart of the city is the Smith Street pedestrian mall. One street over you will find the lively **Mitchell Street Tourist Precinct,** full of backpacker lodges, cheap eateries, and souvenir stores. This is where Greyhound and McCafferty's coaches pull in. Two streets past Mitchell Street is **the Esplanade,** where lush walkways follow the harbor. In the **Wharf** precinct, near town, are some upscale restaurants, a few tourist attractions, a jetty popular with local fishermen, and a working dock. **Cullen Bay Marina** is a "millionaire's row" of restaurants, cafes, and expensive boats; it's a 25-minute walk from town. A couple of miles from the town center is **Fannie Bay,** where you'll find the beach, Botanic Gardens, sailing club, golf course, and casino.

GETTING AROUND   For car and 4WD rentals, call Avis (☎ 08/8981 9922), **Budget** (☎ 08/8981 9800), **Hertz** (☎ 08/8941 0944), or **Territory Thrifty Car Rental** (☎ 08/8924 0000). **Nifty Rent-A-Car** (☎ 08/8981 2999) and **Delta** (☎ 08/8941 0300) are two local companies with good rates. For campervan rentals, call **Brits Australia** (☎ 08/8981 2081), **Budget Campervans** (☎ 1800/643 985 in Australia), **Hertz** (☎ 08/8981 0188), and **Maui** (☎ 08/8981 0911). Hertz and Territory Thrifty Car Rental rent camping kits.

Darwinbus (☎ **08/8924 7666**) is the local bus company. The city terminus is on Harry Chan Avenue. A typical fare is A$1.60 (U.S.$1.15). Kids ages 5 to 14 pay half price; there are no discounts for seniors or students. The Darwin Region Tourist Association (see "Visitor Information") has timetables.

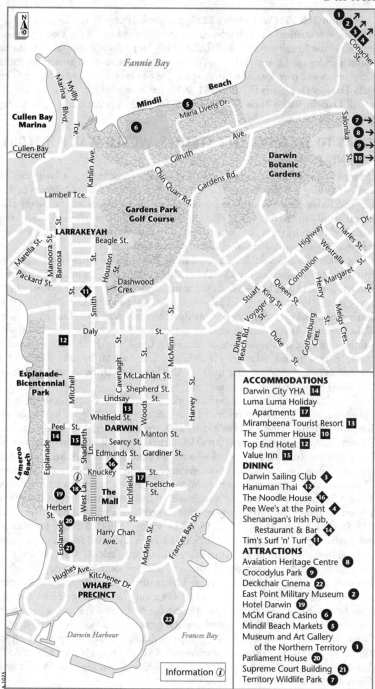

Darwin

N

Fannie Bay

Cullen Bay
Marina

Myilly Marina Blvd.
Marina Tce.

Cullen Bay
Crescent

Mindil **Beach**

Maria Liveris Dr.

Ave.

Gilruth

Chin Quan Rd.

Gardens Rd.

**Darwin
Botanic
Gardens**

Salonika St.

Kahlin Ave.

Lambell Tce.

**Gardens Park
Golf Course**

LARRAKEYAH

Beagle St.

Marella St.
Manoora St.
Baroosa

Packard St.

Houston St.
Smith St.

Dashwood
Cres.

Daly St.

St.

McMinn St.

Highway
Coronation Dr.
Westralia
Charles St.

Stuart
King St.
Queen St.
Henry St.
Margaret St.

Voyager St.
Duke St.
Gottenburg Cres.
Meigs Cres.

Dinah Beach Rd.

**Esplanade–
Bicentennial
Park**

Cavenagh St.
McLachlan St.
Shepherd St.
Lindsay St.
Whitfield St.

Mitchell St.

DARWIN

Woods St.
Manton St.

Harvey St.

Searcy St.
Peel St.
Shadforth Ln.
Edmunds St.
Gardiner St.

Knuckey St.
Itchfield St.
Foelsche St.

The Mall
West La.
Bennett St.

Herbert St.

Esplanade

Lameroo Beach

Harry Chan
Ave.

Hughes Ave.
Kitchener Dr.

**WHARF
PRECINCT**

Darwin Harbour

Frances Bay

Frances Bay Dr.

McMinn St.

ℹ Information

ACCOMMODATIONS
Darwin City YHA **14**
Luma Luma Holiday
  Apartments **17**
Mirambeena Tourist Resort **13**
The Summer House **10**
Top End Hotel **12**
Value Inn **15**

DINING
Darwin Sailing Club **3**
Hanuman Thai **12**
The Noodle House **16**
Pee Wee's at the Point **4**
Shenanigan's Irish Pub,
  Restaurant & Bar **14**
Tim's Surf 'n' Turf **11**

ATTRACTIONS
Avaiation Heritage Centre **8**
Crocodylus Park **9**
Deckchair Cinema **22**
East Point Military Museum **2**
Hotel Darwin **19**
MGM Grand Casino **6**
Mindil Beach Markets **5**
Museum and Art Gallery
  of the Northern Territory **1**
Parliament House **20**
Supreme Court Building **21**
Territory Wildlife Park **7**

A-1025

The **Tour Tub bus** (☎ 1800/63 2225 in Australia, or 08/8981 5233) does a loop of most city attractions and major hotels between 9am and 4pm daily. Hop on and off as often as you like all day for A$18 (U.S.$12.60) for adults and A$9 (U.S.$6.30) for children under age 12. Your ticket also entitles you to discounts on attractions, tours, and purchases all over town. The Tub departs the Knuckey Street end of Smith Street Mall. **Darwin Day Tours** (☎ 08/8981 8696) has a range of sightseeing tours.

Call **Darwin Radio Taxis** (☎ 13 10 08) for a cab. The rank is at the Knuckey Street end of Smith Street Mall.

WHAT TO SEE & DO: CITY STROLLS, WORLD WAR II HISTORY, FISHING & MORE

Darwin's ample parks, stunning harbor, and tropical clime make it a lovely city for strolling (during the Dry Season, that is). Pick up a copy of the free "Darwin & The Top End Today" visitor guide from any hotel lobby or the airport, and follow the **Historical Stroll,** which takes you to 17 points of interest. The free "Darwin: Discovering Our City" brochure from the Darwin Region Tourist Association (see "Visitor Information") maps a marked historical trail along the Esplanade.

The 5-kilometer (3-mile) walk along **Fannie Bay** from the MGM Darwin Grand casino at Mindil Beach to the East Point Military Museum is a pleasant, level trail through parkland and bushland, dotted along the way with seafront barbecues and picnic spots. The beachfront walk joins East Point Road about 3 kilometers (less than 2 miles) north of the casino; East Point Road becomes Alec Fong Lim Drive closer to the museum. As you near the military museum, look out for the some 2,000 wild wallabies that live on the east side of Alec Fong Lim Drive. If it's a hot day (and it usually is in Darwin), take along a swimsuit, and cool off in Lake Alexander, a croc-free saltwater pond on your right off Alec Fong Lim Drive, about 2 kilometers (1¼ miles) before you reach the museum.

All kinds of native Northern Territory wildlife, including dingoes, camels, birds, and snakes, are on display in re-created rain-forest, bush, and lagoon habitats at the **Territory Wildlife Park** (☎ 08/8988 7200), 60 kilometers (36 miles) south of Darwin. Take the Stuart Highway for 50 kilometers (30 miles) and turn right onto the Cox Peninsula Road for another 10 kilometers (6 miles). The park has a nocturnal mammal house, a reptile house, a walk-through aquarium with turtles and stingrays, 12 aviaries, and an enclosure where you can mingle with kangaroos and wallabies. Allow 4 hours too see everything, plus traveling time. The park is open daily from 8:30am to 6pm (last entry at 4pm), and closed Christmas. Admission is A$12 (U.S.$8.40) for adults, A$8.50 (U.S.$5.95) for seniors, A$6 (U.S.$4.20) for students and children ages 5 to 16, and A$30 (U.S.$21) for a family of two adults and four kids.

If you have a fascination with crocodiles, **Crocodylus Park** (☎ 08/8947 2510), a 15-minute drive from town on McMillan's Road (opposite the police station) in Berrimah, is for you. In addition to being a fascinating crocodile museum and education center, this wildlife research facility offers exciting croc-feeding sessions and free guided tours at 10am, noon, and 2pm. You can have your photo taken holding a baby croc. You'll also see hawksbill sea turtles, green iguanas, some very cute black-capped Capuchin monkeys, and four kinds of flightless birds. The park is open daily from 9am to 5pm (closed Christmas). Admission is A$15 (U.S.$10.50) for adults, A$12 (U.S.$8.40) for seniors, and A$7.50 (U.S.$5.25) for children ages 4 to 15. The park is 5 minutes from Darwin Airport; take bus no. 5 or 9.

The **Museum and Art Gallery of the Northern Territory,** Conacher Street, Fannie Bay (☎ 08/8999 8201), also holds an attraction for crocodile fans—the preserved body of Sweetheart, a 5.1-meter (17-ft.) saltwater croc. Sweetheart terrorized dinghies in Kakadu National Park, and her number came up when she went too far and ate someone. The museum and gallery have terrific sections on Aboriginal art and culture, as well as displays on South East Asian and Pacific art, a small but good natural history section, a gallery of recent maritime archaeology, and a photographic display of the aftermath of Cyclone Tracy. Both the museum and the gallery are open Monday through Friday from 9am to 5pm and weekends and public holidays from 10am to 5pm (closed Christmas and Good Friday). Admission is free to permanent exhibits. Take bus no. 4 or 6.

Darwin had an active military history as an Allied supply base in World War II, and was the only Australian city bombed by the Japanese. Many American airmen based here died fighting in the Pacific theater. Eighty-eight lives were lost when the destroyer U.S.S. *Robert E. Peary* went down in Darwin Harbour; today, a monument to the ship stands on the Esplanade. Those with an interest in things military should visit the **East Point Military Museum,** East Point Road, East Point (☎ **08/8981 9702**), housed in a World War II gun command post. The museum is open daily from 9:30am to 5pm (closed Christmas and Good Friday). Admission is A$8 (U.S.$5.60) for adults, A$6 (U.S.$4.20) for seniors, A$3 (U.S.$2.10) for children under age 15, and A$20 (U.S.$14) for a family. No buses run here; take the Tour Tub or a cab.

Military or aircraft buffs should not miss the excellent ✪ **Australian Aviation Heritage Centre**, 557 Stuart Hwy., Winnellie (☎ 08/8947 2145). A B-52 bomber on loan from the United States is the prized exhibit, but the center also boasts a B-25 Mitchell bomber, Mirage and Sabre jet fighters, a rare Japanese Zero fighter captured in the Tiwi Islands, and displays on World War II and Vietnam. Friendly guides are on hand to give you a free tour. The center is 10 minutes from town; take the no. 5 or no. 8 bus (the no. 8 is the most direct), and ask the driver to drop you off at the gate. The center is open daily from 9am to 5pm; hours are sometimes shorter in the Wet Season. Admission is A$8 (U.S.$5.60) for adults, A$5 (U.S.$3.50) for seniors and students, A$4 (U.S.$2.80) for children under age 12, and A$20 (U.S.$14) for a family.

In the **Wharf precinct,** on Kitchener Drive, World War II naval oil-storage **tunnels** are open to the public. A guide tells you the history of the tunnels at the entrance, and photos inside tell you more about war-era Darwin as you guide yourself through. Admission is A$4 (U.S.$2.80) for adults and $2 (U.S.$1.40) for children. U.S. servicemen based in Darwin during the War will be glad to know that the **Hotel Darwin,** 10 Herbert St. (☎ 08/8981 9211) is still here. It has not changed much, and the Green Room and dance floor still play host to live music.

The harbor, wetlands, and rivers of the Top End are close to **fishing** heaven. The big prey is barramundi, but other catches include tarpon, salmon, and marlin. Loads of charter boats offer half- and 1-day jaunts on the harbor and rivers near town, as well as safaris of up to 10 days into Kakadu National Park, the Tiwi Islands, and remote Arnhemland. If you just want to cast a line in Darwin Harbour, **Tour Tub Fishing Charters** (☎ **08/8981 5233**) will pick you up from Stokes Hill Wharf and take you out in a canopied boat for A$65 (U.S.$45.50) for a half day, or A$115 (U.S.$80.50) for a full day, including lunch and a pickup from your city hotel or the airport. Expect to pay about A$200 (U.S.$140) per person, including hotel pickup and lunch, for a full-day jaunt in the inland wetlands, and upwards of A$250 (U.S.$175) for game fishing in the harbor. In most cases, the more passengers join the boat, the less you pay.

On Thursday nights, head to the ✪ **Mindil Beach Markets** for great arts and crafts. You may also find a cheap didgeridoo, unusual jewelry, or artworks at the small Night Markets held in the Mitchell Street Tourist Precinct opposite Shenanigans Irish pub.

The Darwin Shopping Scene

Darwin's best buys are Aboriginal arts and crafts. The Aboriginal-owned **Raintree Aboriginal Art Gallery,** 20 Knuckey St. (☎ **08/8941 9933**), sells a great range of authentic Aboriginal artworks and artifacts from northern and central Australia at reasonable prices. **Indigenous Creations,** with locations at 31 Smith Street Mall (☎ **08/8941 0424**), Smith Street Mall at Knuckey Street (☎ **08/8941 2858**), and a classier outlet called **Cultural Images** in the Mitchell Street Transit Centre (☎ **08/8941 2515**), stocks a mix of affordable Aboriginal-made artifacts and Western-style souvenirs. **Framed: The Darwin Gallery,** 55 Stuart Hwy. (☎ **08/8981 2994**), 5 minutes by car outside town, stocks Aboriginal and non-Aboriginal contemporary artworks.

WHERE TO STAY

Cheap sleeps are hard to find in Darwin, especially from April to October, the peak travel season (the Dry Season). From November to March, the Wet Season, hotels may drop rates by as much as A$40 (U.S.$28) double. Remember to add the 5% Northern Territory accommodation tax to the rates below.

Primavera All Suite Hotel, 81 Cavenagh St., Darwin, NT 0801 (☎ **1800/357 760** in Australia, or 08/8981 7771), a member of the Best Western chain, has full kitchens and separate bedrooms in all its quarters; the double rate is A$130 (U.S.$91). In addition to the Mirambeena Tourist Resort listed below, other Flag hotels in Darwin include the **Metro Inn,** 38 Gardens Rd., Darwin, NT 0800 (☎ **1800/022 523** in Australia, or 08/8981 1544), where doubles go for A$115 to $130 (U.S.$80.50 to $91) in the Dry Season, and A$99 to $110 (U.S.$69.30 to $77) double in the Wet; and **Poinciana Inn,** Mitchell Street at McLachlan Street, Darwin, NT 0800 (☎ **1800/355 114** in Australia, or 08/8981 8111), where doubles are A$120 (U.S.$84) in the Dry and A$90 (U.S.$63) in the Wet.

Luma Luma Holiday Apartments. Knuckey St. at Woods St., Darwin, NT 0800. ☎ **1800/656 988** in Australia, or 08/8981 1899. Fax 08/8981 1882. 64 units (all with shower only). A/C TV TEL. Dry Season A$109 (U.S.$76.30) studio; A$136 (U.S.$95.20) 1-bedroom apt. (sleeps four); A$198 (U.S.$138.60) 2-bedroom apt. (sleeps 6). Wet Season A$92 (U.S.$64.40) studio; A$121 (U.S.$84.70) 1-bedroom apt.; A$162 (U.S.$113.40) 2-bedroom apt. Additional person A$15 (U.S.$10.50) extra. Free crib. AE, BC, DC, JCB, MC, V. Free parking. Bus: 4, 5, 6, 8, 10.

These nicely decorated, good-sized serviced apartments built in the city center in 1997 are perfect for families. Even the one-bedroom apartment sleeps four comfortably; take a two-bedroom apartment and the kids get their own en suite bathroom and their own TV in the bedroom. The studios have a kitchenette, whereas apartments come with full kitchens. Bathrooms are big enough for everyone to spread out all their gear; the front desk lends hair dryers. The complex has a nice big swimming pool, an important consideration in Darwin's heat. Apartments from the third to the top (seventh) floor have views over the city. Smith Street Mall is just 2 blocks away. No smoking.

Mirambeena Tourist Resort. 64 Cavenagh St., Darwin, NT 0800. ☎ **1800/891 100** in Australia, or 08/8946 0111. Fax 08/8981 5116. www.mirambeena.com.au. E-mail: email@mirambeena.com.au. 225 units (all with shower only). A/C TV TEL. A$130–$163 (U.S.$91–$114.10) double; A$199 (U.S.$139.30) town house (sleeps 4). Additional person A$22 (U.S.$15.40) extra. Free crib. Ask about lower rates Oct–May. AE, BC, DC, JCB, MC, V. Free parking. Bus: 4, 5, 6, or 10.

You're just a stone's throw from the city center at this modern Flag hotel complex, but the tempting saltwater swimming pools, Jacuzzis, and the treetop restaurant, all shaded by the leaves of a sprawling strangler fig, let you pretend you're on a remote jungle island. All rooms were refurbished in 1998; each is a decent size and has a hair dryer, iron and board, and some kind of garden or pool view. Town houses are good for families if you can handle sharing the compact en suite bathroom with your kids. The place also has a pool bar and cafe, minibar on request, dry cleaning service and laundry, room service at meal times, a gym, a game room, minigolf, a children's pool, a tour desk, secretarial service, and a lobby shop.

Top End Hotel. Mitchell St. at Daly St., Darwin, NT 0801. ☎ **1800/626 151** in Australia, or 08/8981 6511. Fax 08/8941 1253. 40 units (all with shower only). A/C TV TEL. Dry Season A$110 (U.S.$77) single; A$120 (U.S.$84) double; A$136 (U.S.$95.20) triple. Wet Season A$85 (U.S.$59.50) single; A$95 (U.S.$66.50) double; A$105 (U.S.$73.50) triple. Children 3–12 A$20 (U.S.$14) extra during Dry, A$15 (U.S.$10.50) extra during Wet. AE, BC, DC, JCB, MC, V. Free parking. Bus: 4, 5, 6, 8, or 10.

This two-story Best Western hotel has succeeded in creating a quiet, family atmosphere, despite the trendy new complex of bars, restaurants, sports betting outlets, slot machines, and a liquor store on one side of the premises. Most of the accommodations face a lovely saltwater swimming pool surrounded by lawn, palms, and barbecues rather than the bar complex. Rooms were renovated at the end of 1998, and each is a good size with quality fittings, fresh paint, new bedcovers, and smart new bathroom tiles and countertops. Each has a nice little furnished patio or balcony. You're close to Cullen Bay Marina, just across the road from the Esplanade, and 1 kilometer from Smith Street Mall.

Value Inn. 50 Mitchell St., Darwin, NT 0800. ☎ **08/8981 4733.** Fax 08/8981 4730. 93 units (all with shower only). A/C TV. A$64 (U.S.$44.80) single, double, or triple. AE, BC, MC, V. Free parking for approx. 40 cars. Bus: 4 or 5

Value it's called, and value it is. The cheerful rooms at this neat little hotel just across the road from the Darwin City YHA (see below) are very compact but tidy with modern fittings. Each room is just big enough to hold a queen-size and a single bed, a minirefrigerator, en suite bathroom, and a small writing table. Two rooms are set up for guests with disabilities. The views aren't much, but you'll probably spend your time in the cafes along the street anyhow. Smith Street Mall is 1 block away, and the Esplanade walking path is 2 blocks away. There's a public pay phone and a coffee vending machine on each floor, and a small garden swimming pool off the parking lot. Breakfast is just A$5.50 (U.S.$3.85).

SUPER-CHEAP SLEEPS

Darwin City YHA. 69 Mitchell St., Darwin, NT 0800. ☎ **08/8981 3995.** Fax 08/ 8981 6674. E-mail: yhant@ozemail.com.au. 130 units, 2 with bathroom (shower only). A/C. A$39 (U.S.$27.30) single; A$42 (U.S.$29.40) double without bathroom; A$56 (U.S.$39.20) double with bathroom. A$18 (U.S.$12.60) dorm bed. A$3 (U.S.$2.10) discount per person for YHA/Hostelling International members. Linen A$2 (U.S.$1.40) for length of stay. BC, MC, V. Ample on-street parking. Bus: 4 or 5 (6 or 10 citybound only). Free airport shuttle.

The single and double rooms at this upbeat backpacker hostel in the Mitchell Street Tourist Precinct are pretty basic, but the mattresses are firm, and the communal bathrooms are clean. Well-behaved guests laze elbow-to-elbow around the pool; a second lofty sundeck and an open-air kitchen and dining area overlook the pool. The hostel also has TV rooms, and bikes for rent. A major tour desk in the lobby offers an array of sensibly priced trips and activities. Reception is open 24 hours and has safes. Shenanigan's Irish pub (see "Where to Dine" below) is in the complex, and coach terminals, cheap cafes, the Smith Street Mall, and the Esplanade are steps away. The air-conditioning is noisy and is turned on only between 7pm and 9am, so think twice about staying here in Darwin's horrifically hot summer.

A TOP END B&B

✪ **The Summer House.** 3 Quarry Crescent, Stuart Park (P.O. Box 104, Parap, NT 0820). ☎ **08/8981 9992.** Fax 08/8981 0009. E-mail: summerhouseb&b@octa4.net.au. 3 units (all with shower only). A/C TV TEL. A$65 (U.S.$45.50) single without breakfast, A$75 (U.S.$52.50) single with breakfast; A$75 (U.S.$52.50) double without breakfast, A$90 (U.S.$63) double with breakfast. Additional person A$20 (U.S.$14) extra plus A$7.50–$9 (U.S.$5.25–6.30) for breakfast. AE, BC, MC, V. Free parking. Bus: 6. From the airport, take the Stuart Hwy. 1.5km (1 mile) to Stuart Park; turn left onto Woolner Rd., immediately right onto Iliffe St., right onto Armidale St., and immediately left onto Quarry Crescent.

In the rough-and-ready Northern Territory, accommodation choices are all too often limited to impersonal motels, which makes a stay at this cool, contemporary home all the more delightful. In a leafy suburb 3 kilometers (2 miles) from town and 5 kilometers (3 miles) from the airport, Jill Farrand has converted her block of four residential apartments into hip, elegant units for guests. Each unit has a separate bedroom, a spacious living area, a kitchenette, and a petite bathroom (with hair dryer). Louver blinds on all sides encourage a breeze, and on hot Top End nights you can relax in the Jacuzzi in the back garden and listen to the fruit bats in the trees. It's a short stroll to a shopping center and the bus stop. Jill also rents two town houses and a house for stays of a week or more for A$550 (U.S.$385) per week.

WHERE TO DINE

Cullen Bay Marina is packed with cool restaurants and cafes, and while you won't find any dirt-cheap meals on the menu, it's a shame not to sit down here over a simple pasta and a glass of wine during your visit—the clinking masts and smart shops give it such a nice buzz. It's a 25-minute walk from town or a short cab ride. As well as the recommendations below, you will find cheap fare at the **Mitchell Street Tourist Precinct,** which has an Asian food arcade, a crêperie, and a couple of casual cafes. If it's Thursday, don't even think about eating anywhere other than the **Mindil Beach Markets. Salvatore's,** under the All Seasons hotel at the Knuckey Street end of Smith Street Mall (☎ **08/8491 9823**) serves up good, light meals, most for less than A$10 ((U.S.$7), from 7am until midnight. The cool crowd hangs at **Roma Bar,** 30 Cavenagh St. (☎ **08/8981 6729**) for good coffee and cheap nosh; it's open from 7am to 5pm Monday to Friday, from 8am to 2pm weekends.

Darwin Sailing Club. Atkins Dr., Fannie Bay. ☎ **08/8981 1700.** Lunch specials A$5–$7.80 (U.S.$3.50–$5.50); main courses A$8–$28.50 (U.S.$5.60–$19.95). BC, MC, V. Daily noon–2pm, 6–9pm. Bar: Sun–Thurs 10am–midnight, Fri–Sat 10am–2am. Bus: 4 or 6. STEAK/SEAFOOD/CHINESE.

█ Cheap Eats & More!

If it's Thursday, join the entire city (well, 8,000 locals, anyhow) at the ✪ **Mindil Beach Sunset Market** to feast at the 60 terrific (and cheap!) Asian food stalls, listen to live bands, wander among 200 arts and crafts stalls, and mix and mingle with the masseurs, tarot card readers, and street performers. The action runs from 5 to 10pm in the Dry (May to October). The beach is a A$5 (U.S.$3.50) cab ride from town, and the Tour Tub does A$4 (U.S.$2.80) transfers (A$3/U.S.$2.10 for Tub passengers) on Thursday nights from major city hotels and the Knuckey Street end of Smith Street Mall.

It's hard to imagine a more unpretentious spot to eat than this outdoor terrace over-looking Fannie Bay, or a more scenic one. The tables and chairs are just rough timber or plastic under palm trees; the service is the do-it-yourself kind (place your order at the bar, take a number, and go get your meal when your number is called); and the company is reptilian—a family of large goannas lurking around your ankles waiting for meaty scraps. Frankly, I've eaten better beef satay, but with views like this, who cares? The huge menu sticks to variations on basics, like steaks with a choice of sauces, Chinese stir-fries, and loads of seafood choices. The club is members-only, but over-seas visitors are welcome; just see management when you arrive and they will sign you in for free.

Hanuman Thai. 28 Mitchell St. ☎ **08/8941 3500.** Reservations recommended. Main courses A$8.50–$19.50 (U.S.$5.95–$13.65). AE, BC, DC, JCB, MC, V. Mon–Fri noon–2:30pm, daily 6:30pm–late. Bus: 4 or 5 (6 or 10 citybound only). CONTEMPORARY THAI.

This elegant city restaurant works hard as a business-lunch venue by day and as a pop-ular rendezvous for couples, families, and more business folk by night. Painted black inside from top to toe, it serves up sophisticated dishes, such as marinated chicken wrapped in pandan leaves with a mild chili and malt sugar sauce, and grilled mari-nated local Gulf prawns with a sauce of crushed coriander and coconut milk sprinkled with kaffir lime leaf julienne. My single serving of Masuman beef with roasted spices, tamarind, peanuts, palm sugar, and coconut cream was almost big enough for two. It was rich, tender, and not too oily. The spicy seafood, chicken, or beef salads make a satisfying light meal for A$10 (U.S.$7) or less. Desserts are a Thai take on French clas-sics, such as black rice brulée and lychee bavarois.

The Noodle House. 33 Knuckey St. ☎ **08/8941 1742.** Main courses A$6–$15 (U.S.$4.20–$10.50). AE, BC, MC, V. Mon–Fri 11am–2pm, daily 6–10pm. Bus: 4, 5, 6, 8, 10. CHINESE.

Most meals do not top A$8 (U.S.$5.60) at this unpretentious eatery just around the corner from Smith Street Mall. Tummy-fillers like pineapple and chicken fried rice or shredded beef fried rice are just A$6.50 (U.S.$4.55). The long menu includes many meat dishes, such as Szechuan beef or chicken and roast duck, and there are the usual Chinese soup suspects. The brown tiled floor, pink vinyl tablecloths, and plastic flowers are not exactly the stuff romantic dinners for two are made of, but the place has a friendly atmosphere. BYO.

Shenanigan's Irish Pub, Restaurant & Bar. 69 Mitchell St. at Peel St. ☎ **08/8981 2100.** Daily specials approx. A$9.50–$14 (U.S.$6.65–$9.80); main courses A$6.50–$17.50 (U.S.$4.55–$12.25). AE, BC, DC, MC, V. Meals daily noon–9pm; pub open daily 11am–2am. Bus: 4 or 5 (6 or 10 citybound only). IRISH PUB FARE.

Hearty Irish stews, braised beef and Guinness pies, and "Gaelic" steaks in mushroom, bacon, and Jameson whiskey sauce (plus the odd pint of Guinness itself) gets everyone in the mood for eating, talking, and dancing at this convivial bar/restaurant. Like Irish pubs all over the world, this one draws a friendly mix of solo travelers, families, seniors, and backpackers to eat in atmospheric wooden booths, standing up at bar tables, or by the fire. The snack menu does lighter stuff like toasted sandwiches, but your best bet is the list of nightly specials, such as chicken and chili pasta or poached barramundi in white wine sauce with fries and salad—most come in around A$10 (U.S.$7).

✪ **Tim's Surf 'n' Turf.** In the Asti Motel, Smith St. at Packard Place ☎ **08/8981 9979.** Main courses A$6–$15 (U.S.$4.20–$10.50). BC, MC, V. Mon–Fri noon–2pm, daily 5:30–9:30pm. Bus: 4, 5, 6, 8, 10. STEAK/SEAFOOD.

Locals fairly bash the door down to get into this unpretentious restaurant housed under a cheap motel on the city fringe. The modest surrounds are not the attraction, so what is? Hearty, no-nonsense food, cooked well, in portions big enough to feed an army. No namby-pamby 300-gram (10½-oz.) steaks here, no sir—Tim's steaks are 700-gram (24½-oz.) monsters over an inch thick and grain-fed, a boon in Australia where the beef is mostly grass-fed and hence a little chewy. Garlic prawns, seafood platters, crocodile schnitzel, lasagna, oysters at A$7 (U.S.$4.90) a dozen, and roast of the day (at a senseless A$7/U.S.$4.90!) are typical menu items. Kids' meals are just A$3.50 (U.S.$2.45) and *free* before 6:30pm.

WORTH A SPLURGE

✪ **Pee Wee's at the Point.** Alec Fong Lim Dr., East Point Reserve. ☎ **08/8981 6868.** Reservations recommended. Main courses A$20.50–$24.50 (U.S.$14.35–$17.15). AE, BC, DC, MC, V. Daily 6pm–late, Sun 11am–3pm. MOD OZ CREOLE.

Surrounded on three sides by junglelike forest, and fronting beautiful Fanny Bay, this modern steel-and-glass venue affords views of the harbor from every table, inside or out on the deck. Some of the dishes don't have much to do with Creole cuisine—the warm kangaroo salad with hazelnut dressing and roast veggies doesn't, for example, but some most definitely do, such as the Hot Flushes—whole chilies stuffed with Mexican cheese sauce, rolled in crumbs, and fried (wash 'em down with an icy beer). Seafood lovers will find plenty to tempt them. For such a glam place, the wine list shows admirable restraint with its prices.

DARWIN AFTER DARK

Pick up the free fortnightly street mag, *Pulse,* for a guide to live bands, performing arts shows, nightlife, and public festivals. If it's Thursday, you are mad to be anywhere except the **Mindil Beach Markets.** Ditto if it's Sunday and you're not at the free ✪ **Sunset Jazz** at the MGM Grand Casino, Gilruth Avenue, Mindil Beach (☎ 08/8943 8888), every Sunday from 4:30 to 8:30pm from April to November.

Lie back in a deck chair at the **Deckchair Cinema** (☎ **08/8981 0700**) to watch Aussie hits, foreign films, and cult classics under the stars. Movies are screened Wednesday through Sunday in the Dry (usually Apr to Nov) with late sessions Friday and Saturday nights. The cinema is off Mavie Street behind Old Stokes Hill Power Station near the Wharf (a 20-minute walk from the center of town). Tickets are A$10 (U.S.$7) for adults, A$8 (U.S.$5.60) for seniors and students, and A$5 (U.S.$3.50) for kids ages 5 to 15. Check the daily newspaper, *NT News,* for schedules, or pick up a schedule at the Darwin Region Tourist Association (see "Visitor Information," above).

Darwin Entertainment Centre, 93 Mitchell St. (☎ 08/8981 9022 administration, 08/8981 1222 box office) is the city's main performing arts venue.

The slot machines at the **MGM Grand Casino,** Gilruth Avenue, Mindil Beach (☎ **08/8943 8888**), are in play 24 hours a day; Keno and gaming tables close at 6am Saturday and Sunday and at 4am all other nights. The dress regulation is neat but casual.

PUBS, CLUBS & LIVE MUSIC

By law, most Darwin nightclubs must charge a A$5 (U.S.$3.50) cover after midnight Friday and Saturday.

Shenanigan's Irish Pub, 69 Mitchell St. at Peel Street (☎ **08/8981 2100**), most nights has that wonderful mix of live Irish music, dancing, blarney, and laughter called "craik," oiled by lots of Harp lager, Kilkenny beer, and Guinness on tap. The drinking ain't quite as atmospheric, but it's just as enthusiastic at another Irish pub down the road, **Kitty O'Shea's,** Mitchell Street at Herbert Street (☎ **08/8941 7947**). When the U.S. Marines are in town, they head to **Rorke's Drift,** 46 Mitchell St.(☎ **08/ 8941 7171**), a cozy English-style pub and restaurant. **Sweetheart's** in the MGM Grand Casino (see above) is one of the most popular nightclubs for 18s to 45s, and is open Tuesday to Sunday from 8pm to 4am. Wednesday is jazz night 'til 1am. Live jazz, blues, and classic and "soulful" rock play nightly at **Nirvana Restaurant & Wine Bar,** 130 Smith St. (☎ **08/8981 2025**), a 1970s relic renowned for good food. It does oysters, cheese platters, light meals, and wine by the glass.

Rattle 'n Hum, 12 Cavenagh St. (☎ **08/8981 2678**), is a megapopular backpacker nightclub with party games, cheap meals, even cheaper drinks, best belly competitions, and dancing on tables. If this is your kind of scene, it's open nightly from 9pm to 4am. **Tracy's Bar** in the Central Darwin Hotel, 122 The Esplanade (☎ **08/ 8981 5388**), is a popular after-work watering hole. The **Jabiru Bar** in the Novotel Atrium, 100 The Esplanade (☎ **08/8941 0755**) has a uniquely Territorian form of entertainment—hermit crab–racing—every Friday at 6:30pm. Catch live bands over a beer and steak at **Lizard's Outdoors Bar & Grill,** shoot some pool over a pizza and have a dance at **Bar Blah Blah,** or place a bet at the **Sportie's Bar,** all located in the Top End Hotel complex, Mitchell Street at Daly Street (☎ **08/8981 6511**).

A SIDE TRIP TO LITCHFIELD NATIONAL PARK
120km (72 miles) S of Darwin

An easy 90-minute drive south of Darwin is a miniature Garden of Eden full of monsoonal forests, waterfalls, rocky sandstone escarpments, glorious natural swimming holes, and prehistoric cycads that look like they walked off the set of *Jurassic Park.* ✪ **Litchfield National Park** is much smaller (a mere 146,000 hectares/365,000 acres) and much less famous than its big sister, Kakadu, yet most folks would say it is prettier.

Its main attractions are the **swimming holes,** like the magical plunge pool at Florence Falls, 27 kilometers (16¼ miles) from the eastern park entrance. The pool is surrounded by towering sandstone cliffs and monsoon rain forest and fed by the double torrents of the falls. The view from the lookout at the top takes in the whole valley. It's quite a hike down to the water, so the easily accessible pool at Wangi Falls, 49 kilometers (29½ miles) from the eastern entrance, actually gets more crowds. Surrounded by cliffs and forests, it has beauty enough of its own. There are a number of manageably short **walking trails** through the park, too, like the one up to the lookout above Wangi Falls and the one that connects Florence Falls with more idyllic swimming grottos a couple of miles away at **Buley Rockhole,** a series of cute birdbath-like rock holes and waterfalls. If you have a 4WD vehicle, you can swim at **Sandy Creek Falls,** just under 50 kilometers (30 miles) from the eastern entrance. The water holes above are generally regarded as crocodile-free; the same is not true of the Finiss and Reynolds rivers in the park, so no leaping into those! The park is also home to thousands of "magnetic" termite mounds, up to 2 meters (6.5 feet) high.

ESSENTIALS
GETTING THERE   From Darwin, head south for just over 86 kilometers (51½ miles) on the Stuart Highway and follow the park turnoff on the right through the town of Batchelor for 34 kilometers (20½ miles).

VISITOR INFORMATION   The **Parks & Wildlife Commission** district office in Batchelor, on the corner of Nurdina Street and Pinaroo Crescent (☎ **08/8976 0282**), has maps and information; most locations of interest in the park have signboards. Entry to the park is free.

GETTING AROUND   The roads to most water holes in the park are paved, although a few areas, like Sandy Creek Falls and the odd complex of sandstone pillars known as the Lost City, are only accessible by 4WD. In the Wet Season (approximately November to March), some roads in the park—usually the 4WD ones—may be closed, and Wangi water hole may be off-limits due to turbulence and strong currents. Check with the Parks & Wildlife Commission office before you leave Darwin during this time.

ORGANIZED TOURS   Litchfield is relatively small, so it is easy to see most of it on a day trip from Darwin. Several companies run day trips, including **Nature Territory Tag-Alongs** (☎ **08/8981 6473**) and **Northern Territory Adventure Tours** (☎ **1800/063 838** in Australia, or 08/8952 1474). Expect to pay between A$80 (U.S.$56) and A$100 (U.S.$70) per person.

CAMPING   There are basic campsites with toilets, showers, and wood-fired barbecues at Florence Falls and Wangi Falls, plus several more sites throughout the park. You may collect firewood in the park, but do so as you are driving, as there is none around the campgrounds. The camping fee is A$5 (U.S.$3.50) for adults, A$2 (U.S.$1.40) for kids ages 5 to 15, and A$12 (U.S.$8.40) for families. A kiosk at Wangi Falls sells BBQ packs. *Note:* There is no fuel or alcohol, so if you need either item, stock up in Batchelor.

2 Kakadu National Park

257km (154¼ miles) E of Darwin

✪ **Kakadu National Park,** a World Heritage area, is Australia's largest national park—at a mere 1,755,200 hectares (4,388,000 acres)—and its pride and joy.

Cruising the lily-clad wetlands to spot fearsome crocodiles, swimming in exquisite natural water holes, hiking through spear grass and cycads, fishing for prized barramundi, soaring in a light aircraft over torrential waterfalls in the Wet Season, photographing the millions of birds and thousands of deadly saltwater crocodiles that live here, flying over the eerie red escarpment that juts 200 meters (656 ft.) above the floodplain, and admiring superb Aboriginal rock art sites are the activities that draw people here.

The name "Kakadu" comes from "Gagudju," the group of languages spoken in the northern part of the park at the turn of the century. No one knows for sure, but it is thought that Aboriginal people have lived in this part of the world for 40,000 years. Today, Aborigines manage the park as its owners in conjunction with the Australian Nature Conservation Agency. This is one of the few places in Australia where some Aborigines stick to a fairly traditional lifestyle of hunting and living off the land. You won't see them, as they keep away from prying eyes, but their culture is on display at a purpose-built cultural center and at rock art sites. Kakadu and the vast wilds of Arnhemland to the east are the birthplace of the x-ray style of art for which Aboriginal artists are famous.

JUST THE FACTS

VISITOR INFORMATION   You can find information on Kakadu and book tours to it at the **Darwin Region Tourist Association visitor centre** (see "Visitor Information" in the Darwin section, above). For information before you leave home, write to the **Bowali Visitor Centre,** Kakadu National Park, P.O. Box 71, Jabiru, NT 0886 (☎ **08/8938 1120;** fax 08/8938 1123).

There are two main park **entry stations**—the northern station on the Arnhem Highway, used by visitors from Darwin, and the southern station on the Kakadu

Highway for visitors from Katherine. Both stations hand out free visitor guides with maps, and in the Dry Season they issue a timetable of free guided ranger walks, talks, and slide shows taking place in the park that week. The main place to go for information in the park, however, is the park headquarters at the **Bowali Visitor Centre** (☎ **08/8938 1120**) on the Kakadu Highway, 5 kilometers (3 miles) from Jabiru, approximately 100 kilometers (60 miles) from the northern entry station and 131 kilometers (78½ miles) from the southern entry station. It's well worth visiting the center, as it is housed in an Outback-style environmentally friendly building and has a video theatrette showing some excellent films on the park's natural history and Aboriginal culture; there's also a gift shop selling Aboriginal arts and crafts, and a cafe. The center also stocks maps and free park notes, and information officers are on hand to help you plan your visit. The center is open daily from 8am to 5pm.

You can also book tours and get information at the **Jabiru Travel Centre,** Shop 6, Tasman Plaza, Jabiru, NT 0886 (☎ **08/8979 2548,** fax 08/8979 2482).

GETTING THERE   Follow the Stuart Highway 34 kilometers (20½ miles) south of Darwin, and turn left onto the Arnhem Highway, all the way to Kakadu. The trip takes 2½ to 3 hours. If you're coming from the south, turn off the Stuart Highway at Pine Creek onto the Kakadu Highway and follow the Kakadu Highway for 79 kilometers (47½ miles) to the park entrance station. **Greyhound Pioneer** (☎ **13 20 30**) makes a daily run from Darwin for A$29 (U.S.$20.30) one-way, and one-, two-, and three-day tours for A$60 (U.S.$42) to A$186 (U.S.$130.20); meals and accommodations are not included.

FEES & REGULATIONS   The park entry fee of A$15 (U.S.$10.50) per adult is valid for 14 days. Children age 15 and under are free.

TIPS FOR EXPLORING   Nearly every visitor makes the mistake of not allowing enough time to see Kakadu. This is a big place—about 200 kilometers (120 miles) long by 100 kilometers (60 miles) wide, and the attractions are spread out over big distances. Plan to spend a couple of nights here.

Major attractions (except Jim Jim Falls) are accessible in a conventional vehicle on sealed (paved) roads, but a 4WD vehicle allows you to see more. Within the park, **Territory Thrifty Car Rental** rents 4WDs and regular cars at the **Gagudju Crocodile Hotel** (☎ **1800/891 125,** or call the hotel at 08/8979 2800). In Darwin, most of the rental car companies listed in "Getting Around" in the Darwin section rent 4WD vehicles. Always check the conditions of unsealed (unpaved) roads by calling the information desk at park headquarters (☎ 08/8938 1120); in the Wet Season (late November to March or April), call daily to check floodwater levels on all roads, paved and unpaved. The Bowali Visitor Centre, main attractions such as Nourlangie and Yellow Waters Billabong, and the towns of Jabiru and Cooinda are above the Wet Season floodwaters and are accessible year-round.

Facilities are limited in Kakadu. The only town is Jabiru, a small mining community where you can find a bank, a pharmacy, a police station, a doctor, and a travel agent. The only other real settlements are the three resorts (see "Where to Stay," below).

ORGANIZED TOURS   If you do not have your own wheels, there are any number of commercial tours running to Kakadu from Darwin. Tours are a good idea because much of the park's geological, ecological, and Aboriginal attractions really only come to life with a knowledgeable guide to help you understand what you are looking at. The prettiest water holes, best sunset lookouts, and most prolific wildlife spots can change from day to day or month to month with the seasons, so it helps to be with someone with good local knowledge.

Kakadu is really too far and too big to do in a day trip from Darwin. Many people find the park gets better the more time they spend here. If you have only one day, however, consider **Triple RRR Tours** (☎ **08/8985 1599**) and **AAT Kings** (☎ **08/8941 3844**), who pack a lot of attractions into their day tours from Darwin. You will pay around A$130 (U.S.$91) per person on a day trip. Plenty of companies, including AAT Kings, offer 2- and 3-day accommodated coach tours from Darwin, often combining Kakadu with Katherine or Litchfield National Park. Expect to pay between A$300 to $650 (U.S.$210 to $455) per person for a coach trip, depending on the standard of accommodation you choose.

If you love the outdoors, a **4WD camping safari** is the most satisfying way to see Kakadu because you can hike, swim, and really soak up the atmosphere off the beaten track in a small group. From Darwin, some one-night adventures are available, but most trips take 2 nights and 3 days. **Billy Can Tours, Northern Territory Adventure Tours, Australian Outback Expeditions,** and many other operators offer such trips from Darwin. **Far Out Adventures** runs safaris from Katherine. A 3-day 4WD camping trip to Kakadu will cost between A$375 to $580 (U.S.$262.50 to $406) per person as a rule, including camping gear, park fees, and meals.

See "Exploring the Top End" earlier in this chapter for contact details for tour operators. This is a popular destination with backpackers and retirees, so many operators offer discounts for students and seniors. Prices will be lower in the Wet Season.

Once you are in the park, tours can be booked at your hotel tour desk or at Jabiru Travel Centre (see "Visitor Information," above).

WHEN TO GO The **Dry Season,** from May to October, is overwhelmingly the most popular season, thanks to equable temperatures and sunny days. Many tours, park hotels, and even campsites are booked out a year in advance, so don't travel without reservations at this time. In the **Wet Season,** from approximately November to March, floodwaters cover much of the park, some attractions are cut off all season or unexpectedly for days, and the heat and humidity are extreme. Some tour companies do not run during the Wet, and ranger talks, walks, and slide shows are not offered. The upside of visiting during the Wet Season is that there are no crowds, the park is green, waterfalls swell from a trickle to a roar. Lightning storms are spectacular, especially in the very hot "buildup" to the Wet in November. Plan to travel at an easy pace at this time and don't even think about camping in this heat—stay in air-conditioned accommodations.

SEEING THE HIGHLIGHTS
EN ROUTE TO KAKADU

En route to the park, stop in at the **Fogg Dam Conservation Reserve,** approximately 60 kilometers (36 miles) from Darwin, off the Arnhem Highway. Here you'll get a close-up look at beautiful geese, egrets, ibis, brolgas, and other wetland birds from bird hides and boardwalks leading through monsoon forests to raised lookouts. Stick to the path, as this is crocodile country. Entry is free every day of the year.

Just down the road at Beatrice Hill, you may want to call in on the **Window on the Wetlands Visitor Centre,** a hilltop center with sweeping views across the floodplain and interesting touch-screen information on the ecology of the Adelaide River wetlands. It's free and open daily from 7:30am to 7:30pm.

Just past Beatrice Hill on the highway at the Adelaide River (you can't miss the statue of a grinning croc), you can join the **Famous Jumping Crocodiles cruise** (☎ **08/8988 8144**) to watch wild saltwater crocodiles leap out of the water for hunks of meat the captain dangles over the side of the boat. The 90-minute cruise departs at

Never Smile at a You-Know-What

The Aboriginal Gagudju tribe of the Top End have long worshipped a giant croc-odile called Ginga, but the way white Australians go on about these reptilian relics of a primeval age, you'd think they worshipped 'em, too. There is scarcely a soul in the Northern Territory who will not earbash you with his or her own particular croc story, and each one you hear will be taller, weirder, and more unbelievable than the last.

Aussies are good at pulling your leg with tall tales, but when they warn you not to swim in crocodile country, believe them. After all, crocodiles are good at pulling your leg, too—literally. To be sure you don't end up as lunch, take note of these tips:

1. There are two kinds of crocs in Australia: the highly dangerous and enor-mously powerful saltwater (or estuarine) kind, and the "harmless" fresh-water kind, which will attack only if threatened or accidentally stood on. Saltwater crocs can and do swim in the ocean but they live in fresh water.

2. Don't swim in any waterway, swimming hole, or waterfall unless you have been specifically told that it is safe. Make sure that advice comes from someone authoritative, such as a recognized tour operator or a park ranger. One local old-timer told a friend of mine it was "OK to swim on the west side of the bridge, luv, but there's some big crocs on the east side." Some advice! As if crocodiles can't swim 10 yards under a bridge! Besides, you can never be sure exactly where these critters lurk from year to year. Every Wet Season, crocs head upriver to breed and spread out over a wide flooded area. As the floodwaters subside in the Dry Season, they are trapped in whatever waterway they happen to be in at the time—so what was a safe swimming hole last Dry Season might not be so croc-free this year.

3. Never stand on or walk along a riverbank, and stand well back when fishing. A 22-foot croc can be one inch beneath the surface of that muddy water and utterly invisible. You won't see him until you're in his jaws.

4. Plant your campsite and clean fish at least 25 meters (82 ft.) back from the bank.

And if you come face to face with a crocodile? Everyone has different advice on what to do in this unappealing situation, but it all boils down to one thing: Run!

9am, 11am, 1pm, and 3pm from May to August, and at 9am, 11am, and 2:30pm from September to April (closed December 24th and 25th). It costs A$26 (U.S.$18.20) for adults, A$20 (U.S.$14) for seniors, and A$15 (U.S.$10.50) for chil-dren ages 5 to 15. Farther down the track, stop for a drink at the **Bark Hut Inn** on your left (☎ **08/8978 8988**). Well, pretend you want a drink; you're actually here for an eyeful of the colorfully tough Territory truckies and station hands propping up the bar, looking for all the world like extras from *Crocodile Dundee*.

TOP PARK ATTRACTIONS

CRUISES   Undoubtedly the biggest attraction in the park is ✪ **Yellow Waters Bill-abong,** a lush lake 50 kilometers (30 miles) south of the Bowali Visitor Centre. It's rich with freshwater mangroves, paperbarks, pandanus palms, and often water lilies. In the Dry, you will see marvelous bands of thousands of birds gathering here to drink—sea eagles, honking magpie geese, kites, china-blue kingfishers, and jacanas,

---
Bird-Watching Tip

Early morning and late afternoon are the best times for bird watching, when the birds flock to water holes to drink.

---

called "Jesus birds" because they seem to walk on water as they step nimbly across the lily pads. This is also one of the best places in the park to spot saltwater crocs. Cruises in canopied boats with a running commentary depart near Gagudju Lodge Cooinda six times a day from 6:45am in the Dry and 7am in the Wet. A 90-minute cruise costs A\$23.50 (U.S.\$16.45) for adults and A\$12.50 (U.S.\$8.75) for children ages 2 to 14. A 2-hour cruise (available in the Dry only) costs A\$27 (U.S.\$18.90) for adults and A\$13.50 (U.S.\$9.45) for children. Book through Gagudju Lodge Cooinda (see "Where to Stay," below). The short cruise is enough for you to see everything, but wildlife fans should take the 2-hour trip. Even though it means spending the night in the park and getting up before dawn, the sunrise cruise is especially good because the birds are most active and noisy then. In the Wet, when the billabong floods to join up with Jim Jim Creek and the South Alligator River, the bird life spreads far and wide over the park and the crocs head upriver to breed, so wildlife viewing is not as good. It is still an interesting cruise, as you drift through the eerily flooded tops of the paperbarks—you will just need sharper eyes to spot birds and you probably won't see crocodiles.

Another excellent cruise is the **Guluyambi Aboriginal Culture Tour** (☎ **1800/089 113** in Australia or 08/8979 2411 for booking agent, Kakadu Tours) on the East Alligator River, which forms the border between Kakadu and isolated Arnhemland. Unlike the Yellow Waters journey, which focuses on crocs, birds, and plants, this cruise tells you about Aboriginal myths, bush tucker, and hunting techniques. The cruise is limited to 25 passengers. Cruises last 1 hour and 45 minutes and leave at 9am, 11am, 1pm, and 3pm daily from May to October; in the Wet Season the schedule shifts to two half-day cruises on the Magela Creek system, with a climb of Ubirr Rock thrown in. Transportation to the boat is not included, so you will need to get yourself to the departure point at the Upstream Boat Ramp, 44 kilometers (28½ miles) east of the Bowali Visitor Centre. A free bus runs to the ramp from Merl campground or the Border Store. The cruise costs A\$25 (U.S.\$17.50) for adults and A\$11 (U.S.\$7.70) for children ages 4 to 14.

ABORIGINAL ART & CULTURE　Aboriginal art and culture are prime attractions for many who visit Kakadu. The two most superb sites for viewing Aboriginal rock art are Nourlangie Rock and Ubirr Rock. Nourlangie is 31 kilometers (18½ miles) southeast of the Bowali Visitor Centre. It features x-ray-style paintings of animals and a vivid striped Dreamtime figure of Namarrgon, the "Lightning Man," alongside modern depictions of a white man in cowboy boots, a rifle, and a sailing ship. Rangers have told me that Nourlangie is a "tourist" art site and that there is "much better" stuff hidden elsewhere in the park, but this site is impressive notwithstanding. There are as many as 5,000 art sites throughout the park, of which the Aboriginal owners make a few accessible to visitors. You'll also find rock paintings at Nanguluwur, near Nourlangie, and at Ubirr Rock, which is worth the 250-meter (820-ft.) steep climb for the great views of the floodplain at sunset. Access to Ubirr can be limited in the Wet, but the views of fork lightning storms up here at that time are breathtaking. Unlike most sites in Kakadu, Ubirr is not open 24 hours—it opens at 8:30am from May to November and at 2pm from December to April, and closes every day at sunset. There is a 1.5-kilometer (1-mile) signposted trail around

Nourlangie's paintings, a 3.4-kilometer (2-mile) trail at Nanguluwur, and a 1-kilometer (½-mile) track at Ubirr. Access to all these sites is free. You can walk the trails yourself or join a guided ranger by booking at the Bowali Visitor Centre.

The unique culture, history, and lifestyles of the local Aboriginal tribes are on show at the **Warradjan Aboriginal Cultural Centre** (☎ **08/8979 0051**) at Cooinda. This circular building was built in the shape of a pig-nose turtle at the direction of the Aboriginal owners. The displays on bush tucker and the Dreamtime creation myths of the local Bininj people are worth a visit. A video shows regularly in the theatrette, and there's a quality gift shop. The center is open from 9am to 5pm daily, and admission is free. It is connected to Gagudju Lodge Cooinda and the Yellow Waters Billabong by a 1-kilometer (½-mile) trail.

SCENIC FLIGHTS   Scenic flights over the rugged escarpment are well worth doing, especially in the Wet Season when Jim Jim Falls and Twin Falls are in full flood. The plane makes figure-eight patterns over the falls in the Wet, so you get a good view; make sure your flight includes this. From the air is also the best way to appreciate the Gagadju Crocodile Hotel, which is cleverly built in the shape of a crocodile. **Kakadu Air** (☎ **1800/089 113** in Australia, or 08/8979 2411) does 30-minute flights from Jabiru for A$65 (U.S.$45.50) per person and 1-hour flights from Cooinda for A$110 (U.S.$77) per person.

MORE ATTRACTIONS

Not all of Kakadu's attractions are natural. Tours of the **Ranger Uranium Mine,** 13 kilometers (8 miles) east of the Bowali Visitor Centre, reveal how this controversial material is extracted from a large open-cut mine and turned into yellowcake to fire nuclear power plants around the world. Ninety-minute tours depart daily from May through October at 10:30am and 1:30pm and cost A$15 (U.S.$10.50) per person. The tours depart by bus from Jabiru Airport, which is near the mine. Book through **Kakadu Tours** (☎ **1800/089 113** in Australia, or 08/8979 2411).

SWIMMING, FISHING & BUSHWALKING

In the eastern section of the park rises a massive red sandstone escarpment that sets the stage for two magnificent waterfalls, **Jim Jim Falls** and **Twin Falls.** In the Dry, a 1-kilometer (½-mile) walk through rain forest leads to a gorgeous plunge pool at Jim Jim Falls, 103 kilometers (62 miles) from the Bowali Visitor Centre. Taking a swim in this deep green rock pool, surrounded by 150-meter (490-ft.) cliffs, is a magical experience.

Paddling yourself on an air mattress past the odd "harmless" freshwater crocodiles at nearby Twin Falls is great, too. From November to April, and sometimes even as late as May, both falls are inaccessible but are magnificent when viewed from a scenic flight. If you don't have an air mattress handy, John and Bronwen Malligan of ✪ **Kakadu Gorge and Waterfall Tours** (☎ **08/8979 2025**) run an excellent small-group day trip for active people. You get to bushwalk into Jim Jim Falls for morning tea, four-wheel drive through the bush, then paddle in a tandem canoe to Twin Falls for lunch on the beach. Tours depart Jabiru and Cooinda from May to November and cost A$120 (U.S.$84) for adults, A$100 (U.S.$70) for kids ages 4 to 14 (no kids

---

Croc Alert!

Although lots of folk swim at these and other water holes, such as Gubara, Maguk, and Koolpin Gorge, you do so at your own risk. Saltwater crocodiles have been known to slip through the traps rangers set for them alongside popular swimming holes. The only place rangers recommend you swim is the hotel pool.

under age 4 allowed). The trip is definitely worth the expense—it will be one of your most memorable experiences in Australia. Book in advance in July, the busiest month.

Another idyllic swimming spot is **Gunlom Falls,** about 170 kilometers (102 miles) south of the Bowali Visitor Centre. This is the pool that Paul Hogan and Linda Koslowski plunged into in the movie *Crocodile Dundee*. A climb to the top of the falls rewards you with great views of southern Kakadu. Access can be cut off in the Wet, so check with park rangers before heading out.

Kakadu's wetlands are brimful of barramundi, and there is nothing Territorians like more than to hop into a tin dinghy barely big enough to resist a croc attack and go looking for them. John and Bronwen Malligan, mentioned above, also run **Kakadu Fishing Tours** (☎ **08/8979 2025**) and are two of the most experienced fishing operators in the Top End. Their guided fishing trips depart from Jabiru, 5 kilometers (3 miles) east of the Bowali Visitor Centre, and cost A$110 (U.S.$77) per person for a half day (A$180/U.S.$126 if there is only one of you) and A$220 (U.S.$154) per person for a full day (minimum two people). They also do fly-fishing.

An interesting collection of bush and wetlands **trails** are marked throughout the park, including many short strolls and six half- to full-day treks. Typical trails include a 600-meter (less than ½-mile) amble through the Manngarre Monsoon Forest near Ubirr Rock; an easy 3.8-kilometer (2¼-mile) circular walk through a floodplain and beside a billabong at the Iligadjar Wetlands near the Bowali Visitor Centre; or a tough 12-kilometer (7¼-mile) walk through rugged sandstone country at Nourlangie Rock. One of the best wetlands walks is at **Mamukala,** about 10 kilometers (6 miles) from All Seasons Frontier Kakadu Village (see "Where to Stay," below). Countless thousands of magpie geese feed here, especially in the late Dry Season around October. An observation platform gives you a good view of them, and a sign explains the dramatic seasonal changes the wetlands undergo. Choose from a 1-kilometer (½-mile) or 3-kilometer (2-mile) meander. The Bowali Visitor Centre has a complete range of hiking-trail maps and a booklet titled **"Bushwalking"** in Kakadu. There are also some challenging unmarked trails along creeks and gorges, for which you will need good navigational skills.

CAMPING

There are plenty of campgrounds in the park, mostly near popular billabongs and wetlands. If you want to camp in the wild rather than at a designated campground, you will need a permit from the Bowali Visitor Centre. These can take a week to process, so plan ahead. It is wise to bring a mosquito net, as mosquitoes here carry the potentially dangerous Ross River virus.

The best-equipped campgrounds are at the **All Seasons Frontier Kakadu Lodge and Caravan Park, All Seasons Frontier Kakadu Village,** and **Gagudju Lodge Cooinda** (see "Where to Stay & Dine," below). Campers are free to use all the facilities at the lodges, although in extremely busy times, the pool at Gagudju Lodge Cooinda may be available only to bungalow guests.

Tent site–only campgrounds with hot showers and toilets are found at Gunlom, Mardugal Billabong, Muirella Park near Nourlangie Rock, and Merl in the northeast. A ranger visits most campgrounds daily in the Dry to collect a nightly fee of A$5

Bushwalking Tips

Try to plan your walk in the early morning or late afternoon, especially in the Wet, as the heat can dehydrate you quickly. If you want to make an overnight walk and you want to camp at an undesignated campsite, you will need a camping permit from the rangers at the Bowali Visitor Centre, which can take a week to arrange.

(U.S.$3.50) per person. In the Wet, you may be asked to pay at the Bowali Visitor Centre.

Fewer crowds, no camping fees, and the peace of the bush are the payoffs for going without showers and having only basic toilets at the free "bush camps" located throughout the park. Inquire at the park entry stations or at the Bowali Visitor Centre for a map marking them.

You will need a 4WD to access Jim Jim and Gunlom, as well as many of the free bush camps. Jim Jim Falls is open in the Dry only; Gunlom, Mardugal, Muirella Park, and Merl may be closed in the Wet.

WHERE TO STAY & DINE

The three establishments listed below are the only places to stay in Kakadu, except for the upscale **Gagudju Crocodile Hotel,** Flinders Street, Jabiru, NT 0886 (☎ **1800/ 808 123** in Australia, 800/835-7742 in the U.S. and Canada, 0345/58 1666 in the U.K., or 181/335 1304 in London, 0800/801 111 in New Zealand, or 08/8979 2800; fax 08/8979 2707; e-mail executivesec@crocodile.sphc.com.au). Built in the shape of a crocodile, it has very comfortable rooms and is connected to the Bowali Visitor Centre by a 2-kilometer (1¼-mile) walking track. Rates are A$180 to $210 (U.S.$126 to $147) double in the Dry and A$150 to $210 (U.S.$105 to $147) in the Wet. Ask about packages in the Wet.

Add 5% tax to the accommodation rates below. High season is usually from April 1 to November 30.

All Seasons Frontier Kakadu Lodge & Caravan Park. Jabiru Dr., Kakadu National Park, NT 0886. ☎ **1800/811 154** in Australia, or 08/8979 2422. Fax 08/8979 2254. www. allseasons.com.au. E-mail: flodge@allseasons.com.au. 24 triple- or quad-share bunk rooms, none with bathroom, 186 powered and 100 unpowered campsites. High season A$110 (U.S.$77) bunk room (sleeps up to 4 people). Low season A$75 (U.S.$52.50) bunk room. A$18 (U.S.$12.60) double, unpowered campsite; A$22 (U.S.$15.40) double, powered campsite. AE, BC, DC, MC, V.

Located within walking distance of Jabiru and 2 kilometers (1¼ mile) from the Bowali Visitor Centre, this humble van park offers very simple air-conditioned bunk rooms with one double bed and a single bed, or four bunks, plus a minifridge and self-serve tea and coffee. Bunk room guests use communal bath and kitchen facilities. The nice gardens are home to a swimming pool, Jacuzzi, and barbecues; and there's a bar, bistro, and laundry. No smoking in bunk rooms.

All Seasons Frontier Kakadu Village. Arnhem Hwy. (41km/24½ miles west of Bowali Visitor Centre), Kakadu National Park, NT 0886. ☎ **1800/818 845** in Australia, or 08/ 8979 0166. Fax 08/8979 0147. www.allseasons.com.au. E-mail: fvillage@allseasons.com.au. 137 units, 20 powered and approx. 60 unpowered campsites. A/C MINIBAR TV TEL. High season A$168 (U.S.$117.60) double; low season A$132 (U.S.$92.40) double. Additional person A$30 (U.S.$21) extra. Children 13 and under free in parents' room if they use existing bedding. A$10 (U.S.$7) double, unpowered campsite; A$14 (U.S.$9.80) powered campsite. Additional person in campsite A$5 (U.S.$3.50) extra. AE, BC, DC, MC, V.

This property is not far beyond the northern entrance to the park. The downside is that it is the farthest accommodation from major attractions like Yellow Waters and Nourlangie, although many tour operators do pick up here. The upside is that the resort's soothing green lawns and tropical gardens adorned with wandering peacocks and chattering native birds are a wonderfully restful haven from the harsh surrounds of Kakadu outside. All but the end rooms of the neatly decorated motel-style accommodations have pitched timber ceilings, and all have restful green views from a balcony or patio. Hair dryers are free at reception. There's a buffet restaurant, a cafe and bar, a day/night tennis court, a shady swimming pool, a Jacuzzi, and a good tour desk.

Don't yield to the temptation to dive into the lily-filled lagoon down the back—like every other waterway in Kakadu, it is home to saltwater crocs! A 3.6-kilometer (2-mile) nature trail winds from the hotel through monsoon forest and past a billabong. Keep an eye out for standby specials—when I visited at the start of the Wet in late October a double room and breakfast, booked within 72 hours, was going for A$90 (U.S.$63).

Gagudju Lodge Cooinda. Kakadu Hwy. (50km/30 miles south of Bowali Visitor Centre), Jim Jim, NT 0886. ☎ **1800/500 401** in Australia, 800/835-7742 in the U.S. and Canada, 0345/58 1666 in the U.K., or 181/335 1304 in London, 0800/801 111 in New Zealand, or 08/8979 0145. Fax 08/8979 0148. A/C. 48 cabins, 34 budget rooms, 57 powered and 300 unpowered campsites. High season cabin A$140 (U.S.$98) double. Low season cabin A$110 (U.S.$77) double. Additional person A$25 (U.S.$17.50) extra; children 12 and under free. Budget rooms A$25 (U.S.$17.50) per bed; A$18/U.S.$12.60 per bed YHA/Hostelling International members. A$10 (U.S.$7) per adult, powered campsite; A$8 (U.S.$5.60) per adult, unpowered campsite. Children 2 to 12 in campsite A$2 (U.S.$1.40) extra. AE, BC, DC, MC, V. Free parking.

This modest lodge is situated at the departure point for Yellow Waters Billabong cruises. The air-conditioned cabins, or "bungalows," are simply furnished, but each one is big and comfortable with a telephone, a minirefrigerator, and self-serve tea and coffee. The budget rooms are just two beds in a corrugated-iron demountable building with shared bathrooms and a communal fridge. They are rented on a per-bed basis, so if you are traveling alone you may find yourself sharing a room with a stranger. Tropical gardens keep the place feeling cool, and there is a small shady pool. The lodge is something of a town center, so there is a general store, a gift shop, a tour desk, currency exchange, a post office, fuel, and other useful facilities. The very casual indoor/outdoor Barra Bar & Bistro has live entertainment 5 nights a week in the Dry and a nightly cook-your-own barbecue with crocodile, water buffalo, and kangaroo steaks. Mimi's serves great meals in a "bush sophisticated" atmosphere. Scenic flights depart from the lodge's airstrip, and the Warradjan Aboriginal Cultural Centre is a 15-minute bushwalk away.

3 Katherine

314km (188½ miles) S of Darwin; 512km (307 miles) E of Kununurra; 1,177km (706 miles) N of Alice Springs

The townsfolk in Katherine are understandably proud that more people cruise Katherine Gorge, where dramatic sheer orange walls drop into the tranquil blue-green river, every year than visit Ayers Rock. The gorge and its surrounding river ecosystem are located in **Nitmiluk National Park.** In the Dry, the gorge is a haven not just for cruisers but also for canoeists, who must dodge the odd freshwater crocodile (the "friendly" kind) as they paddle. In the Wet, the gorge can become a foaming torrent at times, and jet boating is the only way to tackle it. Hikers will find nice trails any time of year throughout the park. Farther afield from Katherine are ✪ **hot springs** to soak in, uncrowded rivers to canoe, and Aboriginal communities who welcome visitors with guided tours.

ESSENTIALS

GETTING THERE   Air North (☎ **1800/627 474** in Australia, or 08/8945 2866) flies once or twice a day from Darwin, and a similar schedule from Alice Springs via Tennant Creek. The trip from Darwin takes 50 minutes and costs A$144 (U.S.$100.80) one-way. From Alice, it's a 3-hour flight, and the one-way fare is A$369 (U.S.$258.30). Air North flights can be booked and ticketed through Ansett.

McCafferty's and **Greyhound Pioneer** both stop in Katherine once or twice a day from Darwin and Alice Springs. Greyhound also makes a daily run from Broome via Kununurra. It's a 4-hour trip from Darwin, and the fare is A$39 (U.S.$27.30) one-way. From Alice, it's a 14½-hour journey and costs A$133 (U.S.$93.10) one-way. From Broome the trip takes 22 hours and costs A$180 (U.S.$126).

Katherine is on the **Stuart Highway,** which links Darwin and Alice Springs. From Alice Springs, allow a good 2 days to make the drive—see "En Route to Darwin from Alice Springs" in chapter 9. The **Victoria Highway** begins in Katherine and heads west to Kununurra.

VISITOR INFORMATION   The **Katherine Region Tourist Association,** Stuart Highway at Lindsay Street, Katherine, NT 0851 (☎ **08/8972 2650,** fax 08/8972 2969), has information on things to see all around Katherine and makes tour bookings. In the Dry Season, it's open Monday through Friday from 8am to 6pm, and weekends from 10am to 3pm (closed Sunday in April). In the Wet, it's open Monday through Friday from 8:30am to 5pm, and is closed weekends.

The **Nitmiluk Visitor Centre** (☎ **08/8972 1886**), located at the end of the Gorge Road, 32 kilometers (19 miles) from town, dispenses information on Nitmiluk National Park. It has maps; displays on the park's plant life, geology, and Aboriginal history; a gift shop; and a cafe. Gorge cruises depart right outside, and you can buy tickets here for the cruises. It's open daily from 7am to 7pm or later, April through September; October through March hours vary, depending on the crowds, but usually run from 7am to 6pm (although it sometimes closes as early as 4pm).

GETTING AROUND   **Hertz** (☎ **08/8971 1111**) and **Territory Thrifty Car Rental** (☎ **1800/891 125** in Australia, or 08/8972 3183) have outlets in Katherine.

Travel North (☎ **1800/089 103** in Australia, or 08/8972 1044)(provides transfers from Katherine to the cruise, canoe, and helicopter departure points at the Nitmiluk Visitor Centre. Round-trip fares are A$16 (U.S.$11.20) for adults and A$7.50 (U.S.$5.25) for children ages 5 to 15. Travel North also runs a wide range of local tours.

EXPLORING KATHERINE GORGE (NITMILUK NATIONAL PARK)

Cruising the gorge in an open-sided flat-bottom boat is the most popular way to appreciate its beauty. Katherine Gorge is actually a series of 13 gorges, but most cruises operate only on the first two, as the second gorge is the most photogenic. All cruises are operated by **Travel North** (☎ **1800/089 103** in Australia, or 08/8972 1044). You will see plenty on a 2-hour cruise, which costs A$28 (U.S.$19.60) for adults and A$12 (U.S.$8.40) for children ages 5 to 15. Cruises depart at 9am, 11am, 1pm, and 3pm daily. There is also a 4-hour cruise to the third gorge at 9am (and 11am and 1pm in busy periods); this trip costs A$41 (U.S.$28.70) for adults and A$19 (U.S.$13.30) for kids. If you want to spend the whole day outdoors, take the 8-hour safari to the fifth gorge (available April to October only). In addition to cruising, you get to swim, hike, and have a barbecue lunch. All-day trips cost A$71 (U.S.$49.70) per person, adult or child. Because each gorge is cut off from the next by shallow rocks, all the cruises involve some walking along the bank to transfer to a boat in the next gorge, so wear sturdy shoes.

In the Wet Season, when the river can become a swirling torrent of floodwater (especially around January and February), Travel North runs a jet boat several times a day as far as the third gorge. This 45-minute adventure costs A$34 (U.S.$23.80) for adults and A$25 (U.S.$17.50) for kids ages 5 to 15. Departure times vary from day to day.

Cruising is nice, but in a **canoe** you can discover sandy banks and waterfalls along the way and get up close to the gorge walls, the birds, and those crocs (don't worry, they're the freshwater kind who usually won't hurt you if you don't hurt them). The gorges are separated by rocks, so be prepared to carry your canoe quite often. You can go it alone in a rented canoe, or join a guided paddle. Half-day canoe rental from Travel North is A$24 (U.S.$16.80) for a single canoe and A$37 (U.S.$25.90) for a double; full-day rental is A$34 (U.S.$23.80) for a single canoe and A$50 (U.S.$35) for a double. There is a A$20 (U.S.$14) deposit. The fee includes a life jacket and dry-bag for storage. Once the river gets too high for go-it-alone canoeing, Travel North runs guided canoeing adventures instead. These last 5½ hours and cost A$37 (U.S.$25.90) per person.

In fact, guided paddles are a good idea any time of year as you will learn and see more. The most knowledgeable company is ✪ **Gecko Canoeing** (☎ **1800/634 319** in Australia, or 08/8972 2224), whose tours are accredited for their ecotourism content. They will pick you up from your accommodations for an all-day escorted canoe safari at a cost of A$95 (U.S.$66.50) per person. In the Dry Season, the company also runs multinight trips that venture farther afield on the Katherine, Flora, and Daly river systems.

Approximately 100 kilometers (60 miles) of **hiking trails** criss-cross Nitmiluk National Park. Trails—through rocky sandstone-conglomerate terrain and dry forests, past water holes, and along the gorge—range in duration from 1 hour to 5 days. Ask at the Nitmiluk National Park ranger station, located in the Nitmiluk Visitor Centre, for trail maps. Overnight walks and the 5-day **Edith Falls trail** require a deposit of A$20 to $50 (U.S.$14 to $35) per person.

WHAT TO SEE & DO AROUND KATHERINE

ABORIGINAL CULTURE TOUR   The ✪ **Manyallaluk Aboriginal community,** a 90-minute drive from Katherine, welcomes visitors who want to meet Aboriginal people and learn more about Aboriginal culture. You are greeted with billy tea and damper when you arrive, and then you can sit down and have a chat with Aboriginal people about how they splice traditional ways with 20th-century living. You can then take a gentle 90-minute guided bushwalk to look for bush medicine and bush tucker. A terrific barbecue lunch of stuff like high-grade kangaroo fillet, kangaroo tail, Scotch fillet steak, or barramundi is served. After lunch try lighting a fire with two sticks, weaving baskets, throwing spears, painting on bark, and playing a didgeridoo. You will have plenty of time to take a dip in a natural water hole, too. You can also buy locally made Aboriginal art and artifacts at better prices than you will find in town. A one-day tour costs A$110 (U.S.$77) for adults with a pickup from Katherine, or A$75 (U.S.$52.50) if you drive yourself out there. Children under age 16 pay A$50 (U.S.$35) for the tour with transfer, or A$40 (U.S.$28) without transfer. On a 2-day tour you spend the first day doing the activities described above, camp overnight near a rock pool, and spend the next day leisurely exploring superb ancient rock art sites by 4WD. The 2-day tours cost A$250 (U.S.$175) for adults and A$100 (U.S.$70) for children. Some tour participants expect the community to be a kind of Aboriginal Culture World theme park, with a new attraction every 10 minutes, but that's not how it is. It's an unstructured experience, so it's up to you to take part. Aboriginal people can seem shy or disorganized to Westerners, but this is not necessarily the case. Just be patient, communicate, and slide into "Outback" time, and you will be rewarded with a rich day. Both tours run Monday, Wednesday, and Saturday; check to see whether tours are running in the Wet Season. You can camp overnight for A$5 (U.S.$3.50) adults, A$3 (U.S.$2.10) kids. Call **Manyallaluk: The Dreaming Place** (☎ 08/8975 4727).

MORE ORGANIZED TOURS   Mike Keighley of ✪ Far **Out Adventures** (☎ 08/ 8972 2552) runs a wide range of 4WD tours around Katherine and farther afield to the Pine Creek gold fields, Litchfield National Park (see "Side Trips from Darwin," above), Kakadu National Park (see above), and into the little-explored Gregory, Keep River, and Flora National Parks. If you want to meet some Aboriginal people and get off the beaten track, take the all-day **Never Never tour.** This takes you to the 5,000 square kilometer (1,930 square mile) ✪ **Elsey Station,** made famous in the Australian book and film *We of the Never-Never,* where you will meet children of the Mangarrayi Aboriginal tribe, sample bush tucker, and swim in pristine rivers. A visit to the Cutta Cutta caves and a dip in the lush natural Jacuzzi of the Mataranka Thermal Pools are included in this tour. It costs A$140 (U.S.$98) per person, or A$280 (U.S.$196) per person if only two people travel in the group that day. Mike has been accepted as an honorary family member of the Mangarrayi tribe and is a mine of information about Aboriginal culture and the bush.

On Mike's Katherine River **sunset dinner cruises,** you look for crocs and other wildlife before gathering around the campfire to eat barramundi steaks and play guitar. This experience is A$39 (U.S.$27.30) for adults and A$18 (U.S.$12.60) for children ages 4 to 15, including transfers. Dinner cruises depart at 6pm Monday, Wednesday, and Friday through Sunday from April to November. BYO wine or beer.

OTHER ATTRACTIONS & ADVENTURES   At the **School of the Air,** Giles Street (☎ 08/8972 1833), you can sit in on an 800,000 square kilometer (262,400 square mile) "classroom" as children from the Outback do their lessons by radio. One-hour tours begin on the hour from 9am to 11am and again at 1pm and 2pm (there's no tour at noon). You see a video and displays and hear on-air lessons; the tours also run during school holidays, without the on-air classes. The school is open Monday through Friday from 9am to 3pm from April until the end of the school year, around mid-December. Admission is A$4 (U.S.$2.80) for adults and A$2 (U.S.$1.40) for kids ages 6 to 12.

WHERE TO STAY

The shady campsites at the **Nitmuluk Gorge Caravan Park,** a short walk from where cruises depart, cost A$7 (U.S.$4.90) for adults and A$3.50 (U.S.$2.45) for kids ages 5 to 15. Powered sites are A$18 (U.S.$12.60) double (additional person A$7/ U.S.$4.90 extra). The campground has a licensed bistro, a tour desk, and barbecues. Kangaroos and wallabies often graze right on the grounds.

The **Nitmiluk National Park ranger station** in the Nitmiluk Visitor Centre (see above) has maps of bush campsites located throughout the park. These are very basic sites—no showers, no soaps, or shampoos allowed because they pollute the river system, and with simple pit toilets. Most are beside natural swimming holes. The bush camping fee is A$3 (U.S.$2.10) per person per night.

Knotts Crossing Resort. Corner Giles and Cameron sts., Katherine, NT 0850. ☎ **08/ 8972 2511.** Fax 08/8972 2628. 126 units, 41 campsites. A/C TV. A$100 (U.S.$70) motel single; A$110–$130 (U.S.$77–$91) motel double; A$75 (U.S.$52.50) village double; A$65 (U.S.$45.50) cabin double. A$7.50 (U.S.$5.25) per person, unpowered campsite; A$18 (U.S.$12.60) double, powered campsite. Additional person A$10 (U.S.$7) per person extra in motel; A$10 (U.S.$7) adults and A$5 (U.S.$3.50) children 5–12 in cabin or village room; A$7.50 (U.S.$5.25) adults or A$5 (U.S.$3.50) children 15 and under in powered campsite. AE, BC, DC, MC, V.

This tropically landscaped collection of motel rooms and cabins is the nicest place to stay in Katherine. Best budget choices are the dapper little "village" rooms, built in 1998 and smartly furnished with a double bed and bunks, private bathroom, kitchenette, TV, telephone, and a joint verandah facing a small private garden pool with a barbecue. Individual cabins behind the village have no telephone but offer a little more privacy, each with a kitchenette, TV, and its own private bathroom just outside the door. The motel rooms of exposed brick are huge, clean, and modern. Locals like to meet at the informal bar beside the large pool and Jacuzzi, surrounded by palms, and Katie's Bistro is one of the smartest places to eat in town. A small sundries store doubles as a tour and car-rental desk.

4 The Kimberley: Adventure Travel off the Beaten Path

Most Aussies would be hard put to name a single settlement, river, or mountain within the vast wilds of the Kimberley, so rarely visited and sparsely inhabited are its red, rocky plateaus, junglelike ravines, and lonely coastline. In the winter Dry Season the area's biggest river, the Fitzroy, is bone dry but in the Wet, its swollen banks are second only to the Amazon in the volume of water that surges to the sea.

The unofficial capital of the East Kimberley is **Kununurra,** a small agricultural town that serves as the gateway to wildlife river cruises; the Bungle Bungles, a massive labyrinth of beehive-shaped rock formations; and a million-acre cattle station where you can hike, fish, and cruise gorges by day and sleep in comfy permanent safari tents by night. The main town in the West Kimberley is the Outback port of ✪ **Broome,** whose waters give up the world's biggest and best South Sea pearls. Linking Kununurra and Derby, near Broome, is the **Gibb River Road,** an isolated 4WD track through cattle-station country that is becoming popular with adventure travelers.

EXPLORING THE KIMBERLEY

Enormous distances, high petrol costs (often A$1 or more per liter, equivalent to U.S.$2.65 per gallon), and limited roads and other facilities can push up the cost of traveling in the Kimberley, despite reasonably priced accommodations and food. The Kimberley has lots of attractions so remote that they can only be reached by aerial tours or charter boats, which are just too expensive for most of us. Many more sights are accessible only on unpaved roads, for which your rental car is not insured, so you will need to budget for renting a 4WD. Depending on the size of the vehicle and the mileage you cover, you can expect to pay about A$120 (U.S.$84) per day, plus fuel. Your 4WD rental company should provide all the auto tools and spares you will need and provide self-drive itineraries and safe driving tips. You can often rent complete camping gear.

If you rent a 4WD yourself, allow for an average speed of 60kph (36 m.p.h.) on the area's rough, unsealed roads. Never exceed 80kph (48 m.p.h.), as unexpected dips and smooth patches can take drivers by surprise. *Always carry spare fuel, food, and water!*

You can also explore by joining a guided **4WD safari.** Because fuel, food shops, and fresh water are scarce and the country is rough and remote, taking a guided tour is a safe, easy option, and also a lot of fun because you meet like-minded travelers and get a running commentary from the driver. Guided tours are also the best value because all of your travel, accommodations, and meals are usually included. Plenty of tours, ranging from a couple of days to 2 weeks, depart from Broome, Kununurra, Darwin, and even Perth. Many incorporate all of the Kimberley destinations listed in this book. *Note:* Most tours run only in the Dry Season, from April or May to October or November.

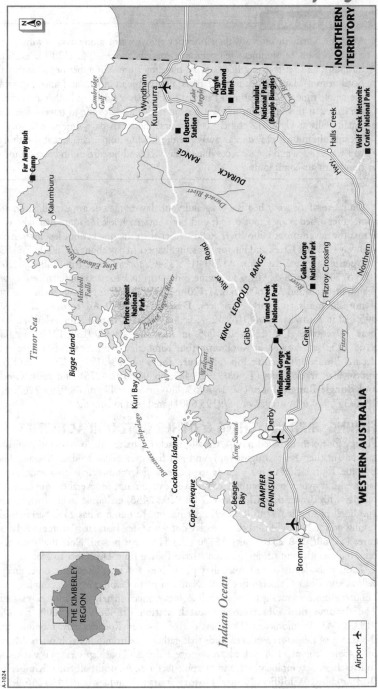

The Kimberley Region

NORTHERN TERRITORY

WESTERN AUSTRALIA

Timor Sea

Indian Ocean

Cambridge Gulf

Wyndham
Kununurra
Lake Argyle
Argyle Diamond Mine
Purnululu National Park (Bungle Bungles)
Ord River
Halls Creek
Wolf Creek Meteorite Crater National Park
El Questro Station
DURACK RANGE
Durack River
Far Away Bush Camp
Kalumburu
King Edward River
Mitchell Falls
Prince Regent National Park
Prince Regent River
Bigge Island
Buccaneer Archipelago
Kuri Bay
Walcott Inlet
KING LEOPOLD RANGE
Gibb River Road
Geikie Gorge National Park
Fitzroy Crossing
Tunnel Creek National Park
Windjana Gorge National Park
Great Northern Hwy
Fitzroy River
Cockatoo Island
Derby
Cape Leveque
C. Beagle Bay
DAMPIER PENINSULA
King Sound
Broome

THE KIMBERLEY REGION

Airport ✈

A-1024

451

Wise in the Wet

As in the Northern Territory, the Kimberley enjoys warm sunny days in winter and a Wet Season in summer. Temperatures soaring above 50°C (120°F), extreme humidity, and far-reaching floods make traveling from November or December to April or mid-May difficult in some parts, impossible in others, and uncomfortable the whole time. Many National Parks, the Gibb River Road, and other attractions are closed at this time. But the Wet Season is also a great time to travel—the rain usually falls at night, the scenery is lush, and the locals have time to talk to you because the tourist crowds stay away! Before leaving home, check that the things you want to see and do are accessible in the Wet, and be sure to find accommodations with air-conditioning!

On most safaris, your bed is a swag and your shower may be a waterfall, although some offer a bed with a roof over it and hot showers. Look for tours that take you across the adventurous Gibb River Road, rather than the quicker but less interesting highway via Halls Creek and Fitzroy Crossing. Expect to pay about A$260 (U.S.$182) per person for a 2-day trip, A$780 (U.S.$546) for a 6-day trip, and A$1,100 (U.S.$770) for an 8-day trip. The same 8-day trip in basic accommodations rather than tents is around A$1,600 (U.S.$1,120) per person. Safaris typically include most, if not all, meals and park entry fees. **Desert Inn 4WD Adventure** (☎ 1800/805 010 in Australia, or 08/9169 1257; fax 08/9168 2271) and **Kimberley Wilderness Adventures** (☎ 1800/804 005 in Australia, or 08/9168 1711; fax 08/9168 1253) are located in Kununurra (but Kimberley Wilderness Adventures also departs Broome). **Over the Top Adventure Tours** (☎ 08/9192 3977; fax 08/9193 7496), **Flat Track Tours** (☎ 08/9192 1487; fax 08/9192 1275), and **Halls Creek and Bungle Bungle Tours** (☎ 1800/636 802 in Australia, or 08/9193 7267; fax 1800/357 979 in Australia, or 08/9193 6801) are based in Broome.

FISHING, BIRD WATCHING & OTHER OUTDOOR ACTIVITIES

Fishing for northern blue-fin tuna, trevally, mackerel, barracuda, barramundi, sailfish, salmon (in the May to August run), and reef fish is excellent around Broome. The Broome Tourist Bureau has a guide to species and locations. It is cheapest to rent tackle and try your luck from the jetty, or you can join one of several charter boats. A full day with **Broomtime Charters** (☎ 08/9192 2458) including tackle, bait, lunch, and hotel pickup is A$130 (U.S.$91) per person. Kununurra has good barramundi fishing on the beautiful Ord River. A day out with Greg Harman's **Ultimate Adventures** (☎ 08/9168 2310) costs A$170 (U.S.$119) per person. Note that cyclones, rain, high winds, and strong tides can restrict fishing from December to March.

The Kimberley is one of Australia's prime bird-watching sites. The blue, green, yellow, and violet Gouldian finch, the Nankeen night heron, tawny frogmouth, and hundreds more species get "twitchers," as locals affectionately dub birders, excited. The **Broome Bird Observatory research station** (☎ 08/9193 5600, fax 08/9192 3364), 25 kilometers (15 miles) out of town on Roebuck Bay, monitors the thousands of migratory wetlands birds that gather here from Siberia. It offers 2-hour tours from Broome of shore birds, mangrove and inland bush species, plus weeklong courses, basic accommodations, and camping facilities. An ornithologist at **Kimberley Birdwatching, Wildlife & Natural History Tours** (☎ and fax 08/9192 1246) leads trips throughout the Kimberley.

In the cooler Dry Season, bushwalking is a great way to enjoy the unspoiled natural environment. **East Kimberley Tours** (☎ 08/9168 2213; fax 08/9168 2544), will

Travel Tip

When calling or faxing remote Kimberley tour operators and cattle stations, keep trying if you don't get through the first time. Some stations have only radio satellite connections, and all hands may be out on the farm when you call, especially during the Wet Season.

tailor walking tours through the Carr–Boyd and Cockburn Ranges, the Bungles Bungles, and Keep River National Park. **Kimberley Bushwalks** (☎ and fax **08/ 9191 7017**) has hit on the clever idea of using pack-camels so you do not have to carry your gear. Its trips visit country inaccessible by car or boat, such as little-known forested parts of the Fitzroy River, into the Great Sandy Desert sandhills, through ancient springs and billabongs, and to the Jarlmadanga Aboriginal community in the purple Mt. Anderson ranges. A 1-day walk costs A$120 (U.S.$84) per person; a 5-day trek is A$800 (U.S.$560) per person.

If you want to camp out under the stars, **Kimberley Caravan & Outback Supplies,** Shop 3, Frederick Street, Broome (☎ **1800/645 909** in Australia, or 08/ 9193 5354) sells and rents everything you need, from primus stoves to tents. A basic kit with tent, mosquito nets, a cooler, a stove, utensils, and a 20-liter (53-gal.) water container is A$29 (U.S.$20.30) per day, less by the week. Kununurra has no camping outfitter, but you might be able to get a car rental company to rent you a kit.

KUNUNURRA
827km (496 miles) SW of Darwin; 1,032km (619 miles) E of Broome

Given the arid conditions in the Kimberley, it's quite a surprise to swoop over a field of sugarcane as you come in to land at Kununurra. This smart little town (pop. 6,000) is a booming agricultural center that was created by the damming of the mighty Ord River to form Lake Argyle. Ninety-five percent of Australia's melons and even some of its bananas come from this unlikely patch of the country.

Kununurra is the gateway to several big attractions. A cruise down the dammed Ord River to see birds, dramatic cliffs, and crocs is a must. So is a flight over or a hike into the Bungle Bungles, monumental domes of rock that look like giant beetles. The world's biggest diamond mine, the Argyle Diamond Mine, is not in South Africa but near Kununurra, and can be visited by coach tour. The town is also a gateway to El Questro Station, where you can hike to magnificent gorges, fish, cruise rivers, horse-back ride, and see wonderful Aboriginal art.

GETTING THERE   **Ansett** flies from Darwin and Broome once a day. It's a 1-hour flight from Darwin, and the fare is A$181 (U.S.$126.70) one-way. From Broome the trip takes an hour and 20 minutes, and the fare is A$266 (U.S.$186.20). Add A$10 (U.S.$7) tax every time you land and depart Kununurra airport.

There is no train to Kununurra. **Greyhound Pioneer** serves the town daily from Broome and also from Darwin, via Katherine. From Broome the trip takes just over 14 hours, and the one-way fare is A$137 (U.S.$95.90); from Darwin, trip time is 8 hours and 20 minutes, and the one-way fare is A$102 (U.S.$71.40).

Kununurra is 512 kilometers (307 miles) west of Katherine on the Victoria Highway. Forty-five kilometers (27 miles) west of Kununurra, the Victoria Highway joins the Great Northern Highway, which leads to Broome. The Gibb River Road is an alternative 4WD scenic route from Derby near Broome (see later in this chapter); it connects with the Great Northern Highway 53 kilometers (32 miles) west of town.

VISITOR INFORMATION   The **Kununurra Tourist Bureau** is at Coolibah Drive, Kununurra, WA 6743 (☎ **08/9168 1177;** fax 08/9168 2598). It's open Monday through Saturday from 7:30am to 5pm, and Sunday from 8am to 5pm. Wet Season hours may be restricted to half days on weekends and an 8am opening time weekdays.

GETTING AROUND   **Avis** (☎ 08/9169 1258), **Budget** (☎ 08/9168 2033), **Handy Rentals** (☎ 08/9169 1188), **Hertz** (☎ 08/9169 1424), and **Territory Thrifty Car Rental** (☎ 08/9169 1911) all rent 4WD vehicles.

WHAT TO SEE & DO

RIVER CRUISES   The **Ord River** is one of the most picturesque waterways in Australia; it's lined by massive red cliffs and teeming with birds and freshwater crocodiles. Jeff Hayley of ✪ **Triple J Tours** (☎ **1800/242 682** in Australia, or 08/9168 2682) runs excellent daily cruises during which he entertains passengers with a humorous medley of tidbits—ecological, geological, and nonsensical. There are several different itineraries. My cruise started with a 70-kilometer (42-mile) coach ride (with commentary) to Lake Argyle, which was formed when the river was dammed. We took a self-guided tour through a historic homestead before boarding the boat. The cruise is 55 kilometers (33 miles), and the boat travels fast and is a bit noisy, but Jeff pulls in at numerous tranquil spots. We had afternoon tea at a lovely bush camp. This costs A\$85 (U.S.\$59.50) for adults and A\$45 (U.S.\$31.50) for children ages 2 to 12, including pickup from your Kununurra hotel. You will spot lots of crocs and nocturnal animals if you take Jeff's great 2-hour sunset cruise, on which he catches a young croc and brings it on board for you to touch. Expect to pay about A\$30 (U.S.\$21) for adults, half price for kids. You will need to book cruises in advance in the Wet.

✪ **Kimberley Canoeing** (☎ **1800/805 010** in Australia, or 08/9169 1257) offers 1-, 2- and 3-day self-guided canoeing safaris down the Grade 1 (that means "gentle") Ord River. You paddle in two-person Canadian canoes and camp at riverside bush kitchens with raised sleeping platforms. The company provides transfers from Kununurra to the headwaters at Lake Argyle, camping and cooking gear, watertight barrels, and plastic foam coolers; you provide the sleeping bag, the food, and the sense of adventure (1-day trips include BBQ lunch). Prices range from A\$105 to \$160 (U.S. \$42 to \$73.50) per person. If your love of the outdoors does not extend to 3 days alone in the wilderness, **Big Waters Kimberley Canoe Safaris** (☎ **1800/641 998** in Western Australia and the Northern Territory, or 08/9169 1998) runs an afternoon guided canoe trip from Kununurra that shows you crocs, bird life, and wetlands scenery. It costs A\$40 (U.S.\$28) per person.

DIAMONDS IN THE ROUGH   Turning out an impressive 35 million carats a year—that's about 8 tons of pure diamond—the **Argyle Diamond Mine** is famed as the only mine in the world to produce the rare pink diamonds in commercial quantities, as well as champagne, cognac, yellow, green, and the more common white rocks. For security reasons, to see the mine you must join an organized tour with either **Belray Diamond Tours** (☎ **1800/632 533** in Australia, or 08/9168 1014) or **Slingair Heliwork** (☎ **1800/095 500** in Australia, or 08/9169 1300). Most are aerial tours costing A\$200 (U.S.\$140) or more, but on Thursdays between June and September Belair offers a coach tour from Kununurra, which takes 2½ hours each way, plus your time at the mine. The tour is still no bargain at A\$155 (U.S.\$108.50) per person. During 3½ hours at the mine, you will see rough and polished gems in the viewing room, drive into the open pit to see diamonds extracted from the earth—as

long as safety conditions permit it that day—and, if you have a[...]
tour, buy diamonds!

SPENDING THE DAY AT EL QUESTRO STATION   You do n[...]
✪ **El Questro Station** (see "Where to Stay," below) to enjoy the wond[...]
When aristocratic Englishman Will Burrell bought this 1-million-acre catt[...]
1991, he turned it into a kind of Outback holiday camp where anyone from t[...]
bers of the international jet set to humble 4WD enthusiasts could revel in its [...]
beauty. Although it's a working cattle station, guests do not really get involved in [...]
cow side of things. Instead, they go barramundi fishing in wetlands and rivers, soa[...]
under palm trees in the thermal waters of Zebedee Springs, hike past towering rocky
red ranges and desolate saltpans, cruise through tranquil Chamberlain Gorge, ride
horses across stony plains, join rangers on bird-watching tours, ride mountain bikes,
or view Aboriginal rock paintings.

Day-trippers are welcome for a fee of A$10 (U.S.$7), or A$5 (U.S.$3.50) if you
only go as far as Emma Gorge, plus the regular fees charged for all activities. Children
under 12 are free. El Questro's office in Kununurra, on Banksia Street just around the
corner from the tourist bureau, can provide maps and directions. Pay at the station
store near the campground (see "Where to Stay" below), where you can buy basic supplies and fuel. You do not need reservations. The staff will give you a map and point
out all there is to see and do, and you will find the rangers friendly and knowledgeable. Most activities depart the station store near the Bungalows (see "Where to Stay"
below). The station offers organized day trips from Kununurra for A$115
(U.S.$80.50) per person. Ask the staff to identify which swimming spots are croc-free,
and don't swim anywhere else!

Once you arrive at the station store, you will pay for transfers to other locations.
For example, a transfer to fishing spots is A$5 (U.S.$3.50) per person, and A$30
(U.S.$21) per person between the station and Emma Gorge. If you plan on doing a
lot of zipping around, consider renting a 4WD vehicle in Kununurra. The station
store also rents them.

WHERE TO STAY

At El Questro Station

✪ **El Questro Station.** Gibb River Rd., 100km (60 miles) southwest of Kununurra (P.O.
Box 909, Kununurra, WA 6743). ☎ **08/9169 1777.** Fax 08/9169 1383. www.
elquestro.com.au. E-mail: sales@elquestro.com.au. See below for lodging options. AE, BC, DC,
MC, V. 4WD transfers from Kununurra A$80–$90 (U.S.$56–$63) per adult round-trip; children
under 12 half price. Take the Great Northern Highway 58km (35 miles) towards Wyndham,
then the unsealed Gibb River Road.

Apart from a stratospherically expensive up-scale homestead, the station has several
somewhat more democratic types of accommodations to suit modest tastes and purse
sizes. All have laundry facilities.

✪ **Emma Gorge Resort.** 27 tent cabins, none with bathroom. A$70 (U.S.$49) single;
A$103 (U.S.$72.10) double. Children 3–12 A$30 (U.S.$21) extra. A$155 (U.S.$108.50) family
tent with 1 double and 2 single beds. Emma Gorge is 1 hr. by road from Kununurra.

This neatly kept oasis of permanent tents nestled around lush lawns under soaring red
cliffs is a great solution for those who want to camp in the wilderness without sacri-
ficing comfort. Although they are only tents, the accommodations here are terrifically
comfortable for they have a wooden floor, electric lights, a standing fan, insect screens,
nice firm twin beds, a bedside table, and a torch (flashlight) for getting around at
night. Clean and modern shower/toilet facilities are shared. Reception stocks sundries
and souvenirs and even lends hair dryers. The bush verandah restaurant serves up

et bush tucker meals that would put many big-city restaurants to shame. There's
n-made swimming pool, but most folks walk the 1.6-kilometer (1-mile) trail
g lush Emma Gorge to the natural Jacuzzi created by a waterfall and swimming
e enclosed by 46-meter (150-ft.) cliffs.

Questro Bungalows. 4 bungalows, all with bathroom (shower only). A/C. A$105
U.S.$73.50) single; A$140 (U.S.$98) double. Additional person A$30 (U.S.$21) extra. Bungalows are 90 min. by road from Kununurra.

These basic but comfortable rooms located at the heart of the station operations are
good for families or large groups. Each bungalow has a double bed and twin bunks,
and en suite bathrooms. The Steakhouse restaurant, overlooking the Pentecost River,
serves steak and "barra burgers."

Black Cockatoo Riverside Camping Riverside camp locations near the station
store are available for a nightly charge of A$10 (U.S.$7) per adult, free for children
under 12. Campers share shower facilities and use the bungalows' restaurant. Secluded
riverside campsites are a 10-minute drive away.

In Kununurra

The Country Club Hotel. 76 Coolibah Dr., Kununurra, WA 6743. ☎ **08/9168 1024.** Fax
08/9168 1189. 90 units, all with bathroom (20 with tub). A/C TV TEL. Dry season A$140
(U.S.$98) double, A$185 (U.S.$129.50) apt. Wet Season A$115 (U.S.$80.50) double, A$150
(U.S.$105) apt. No charge for additional person in room. AE, BC, DC, MC, V.

Located just across the road from the tourist bureau, this low-rise motel has clean new
rooms, tropical gardens, and a lovely shaded pool and pool bar. There is a Chinese
restaurant and a casual garden bar and grill, and an Italian poolside menu. The rooms
have tiled floors and plenty of space. The two two-bedroom apartments lack living
space, so families may be better off getting connecting motel rooms. The hotel has free
in-house movies, a tour desk, a laundry, and hair dryers for loan at the front desk.

PURNULULU (BUNGLE BUNGLES) NATIONAL PARK

Rising out of the landscape 250 kilometers (150 miles) south of Kununurra are thousands of enormous beehive sandstone domes 200 to 300 meters (656 to 984 ft.) high,
called the Bungle Bungles. Thought to be named after the bungle beetle (though who
knows where the beetle got a name like that), the Bungle Bungles get their distinctive
orange and gray stripes from algae found in the permeable layers, and mineral graining
in nonpermeable layers. The formations are 360 million years old.

The domes look spectacular from the air—and that's the only way to see them in
the Wet. As the Wet subsides in early June until late October, the soaring gorges and
forested creeks at the base of the Bungle Bungles are accessible on foot. Highlights are
the beehive walls of **Cathedral Gorge,** the wonderful natural rock pool of **Frog Hole
Gorge,** and palm-filled **Echidna Chasm,** where there are boulders 680 million years
old. You may see rainbow bee-eaters and flocks of budgerigars. Keep an eye peeled for
nailtail wallabies and euros, a kind of kangaroo.

GETTING THERE & GETTING AROUND If you're exploring by car, allow at
least one overnight to explore the 3,000 square kilometer (1,158 square mile) park;
entry is A$8 (U.S.$5.60) per vehicle. Take the Victoria Highway 45 kilometers
(27 miles) west of Kununurra, then turn left onto the Great Northern Highway for
201 kilometers (120½ miles) to the park turnoff; allow 2 hours to cover the tough 53
kilometers (32 miles) from the highway to the park entrance. Turkey Creek, 53 kilometers (32 miles) north of the turnoff, is the nearest place for supplies. There are no
accommodations in the park, but several basic campgrounds with toilets and water but
no showers are open between April and September. The camping fee is A$7

(U.S.\$4.90) for adults, A\$1 (U.S.70¢) for kids under 16. Bring all food with you. For information call the state **Department of Conservation and Land Management (CALM)** (☎ **08/9168 0200**) in Kununurra; a ranger station in the park is manned during the Dry Season.

ORGANIZED TOURS   Aerial tours are not cheap; they cost about A\$160 (U.S.\$112) for a 2-hour flight from Kununurra. Contact **Slingair Heliwork** (☎ **1800/095 500** in Australia, or 08/9169 1300) and **Alligator Airways** (☎ **1800/ 632 533** in Australia, or 08/9168 1333).

In the Dry Season, several companies offer 2- to 4-day 4WD hiking/camping safaris. An excellent affordable choice is the 2-day trip run by **Bungle Bungle Adventure Tours** (☎ **1800/641 998** in Western Australia and the Northern Territory, or 08/9169 1998; fax 08/9168 3998). It costs A\$260 (U.S.\$182) per person.

DRIVING THE GIBB RIVER ROAD

Traversing this sandy, rocky, unpaved 660-kilometer (396-mile) road that links the east and west Kimberley regions is becoming a must-do experience for seasoned adventure travelers. You're in the real Outback here, mate, populated only by stark ranges, rivers that flood to the horizon in the Wet and vanish in dust bowls in the Dry, spooky-looking boab trees, and huge cattle stations. In addition to admiring the natural scenery, you can visit many homesteads along the way that offer activities such as horseback riding, fishing, and hiking. Some have basic accommodations, ranging from campsites with hot showers to rooms at the homestead. They ain't the lap of luxury, but neither is the road. Expect ribbed "corrugation" on the gravel, soft patches, and bumpy rocks along the road that will limit your speed to 60 kmph (36 m.p.h.) or slower for much of the way. This trip is for self-reliant adventure seekers who know how to change a tire, not for sightseers who like their comforts. It is possible to drive the road in 3 or even 2 days, but give yourself at least 4 or 5 days to do some sightseeing. *Note:* The road is open only from May to October; it is underwater in the Wet Season.

The road starts on the **Great Northern Highway,** 53 kilometer (32 miles) west of Kununurra. **El Questro Station** (see "Where to Stay" in the Kununurra section, above) is the first stop, 33 kilometers (20 miles) along the road (and 16km/10 miles off it). The next stop is **Ellenbrae Station** (☎ 08/9161 4325), 136 kilometers (81½ miles) down the road. Here you can have a room with dinner and breakfast in the homestead for A\$80 (U.S.\$56) for adults and A\$40 (U.S.\$28) for children under 12. The unique bathroom is built onto the side of the boab tree in the yard. Camping is A\$7 (U.S.\$4.90) for adults, A\$2 (U.S.\$1.40) for children. A craft shop sells locally made goods, and as this book went to press the station was planning to introduce a kiosk selling coffee and light refreshments. They also do vehicle repairs.

Mt. Elizabeth Station (☎ 08/9191 4644), 139 kilometers (83½ miles) on and 25 kilometers (15 miles) off the road, operates aerial tours from May to September to remote Prince Regent Nature Reserve, King's Cascade, Mitchell Falls, the Horizontal Waterfall, and other spots on the north Kimberley Coast. It also runs guided tours to nearby gorges. A room with dinner and breakfast is A\$105 (U.S.\$73.50) for adults and A\$60 (U.S.\$42) for children under age 15. Camping is A\$7 (U.S.\$4.90) for adults, A\$1 (U.S.70¢) for children.

Another 90 kilometers (54 miles) farther west, the **Beverley Springs Station** homestead (☎ 08/9191 4646) lies 42 kilometers (25 miles) off the road in a pretty strip of rain forest. It offers short walks, a 90-meter (300-ft.) waterfall, guided tours to gorges on the property, and fishing. You can stop for a hot meal here any time for A\$15 (U.S.\$10.50) at lunch, A\$20 (U.S.\$14) at dinner. Dinner, bed, and breakfast is

A$89 (U.S.$62.30) per person in the homestead with shared bath, or A$95 (U.S.$66.50) in a native-style huts with en suite bathroom.

Thirty-eight kilometers (23 miles) on you can camp at **Silent Grove,** 19 kilometers (11½ miles) off the road, or **Bell Gorge,** in King Leopold Range National Park (☎ **08/9192 1036** is the ranger station) for A$7 (U.S.$4.90) for adults, A$1 (U.S.70¢) for children. Bell Gorge is 9 kilometers (5½ miles) down the track from Silent Gorge, and has pretty, private riverside campsites. A 1-kilometer (½-mile) walking track from Bell Gorge leads to a lookout over the falls.

Mt. Hart Station (☎ **08/9191 4645**), 30 kilometers (18 miles) on and 50 kilometers (30 miles) off the road in the King Leopold Ranges, has lovely grounds, hiking trails, gorges, and a croc-free swimming hole. You must book ahead to stay here; it has no facilities for day visitors. Accommodations in the homestead with shared bathroom cost A$105 (U.S.$73.50) per person, including dinner and breakfast.

Windjana Gorge National Park (see below) lies 65 kilometers (39 miles) farther along and 20 kilometers (12 miles) off the road. From the turnoff to Windjana, it's another 126 kilometers (75½ miles) into Derby, the last 60 kilometers (36 miles) of which are sealed. **Derby** (☎ **08/9191 1426** is the Derby Tourist Bureau) is a small coastal town 221 kilometers (132½ miles) northeast of Broome. It's famous in these parts for its jail cell inside a boab tree. The Great Northern Highway leads from Derby to Broome.

If you want to stay in rooms along the road, rather than in the campground, it's best to book ahead.

ORGANIZED TOURS   Many tour operators do guided Gibb River Road 4WD safaris that take 5 to 10 days. **Flat Track Tours** and **Halls Creek and Bungle Bungle Tours** have itineraries from Broome and Kununurra; **Kimberley Wilderness Adventures** does safaris from Broome (see "Exploring the Kimberley," above, for contact details). **Northern Territory Adventure Tours** (see "Exploring the Top End," earlier in this chapter) does trips from Broome and Darwin via Katherine.

DRIVING THE ROAD ON YOUR OWN   To drive the Gibb River Road in a rented 4WD, you will need written permission from your rental car company. Only robust high-clearance 4WD vehicles can manage the track, so do not rent a light 4WD runabout. Carry cash (there are no ATMs, and traveler's checks are not always accepted), spare fuel, enough drinking water and food to last 3 or 4 days longer than you think you'll need, a tool kit, a tire puncture repair kit and a high lift jack, a spare tire, radiator hoses, a spare fan belt, and a first aid kit. Your rental car company should provide all of this. The **Derby Tourist Bureau** (☎ **08/9191 1426;** fax 08/9191 1609) publishes a good A$2 (U.S.$1.40) guide that lists fuel stops (very important, as what few fuel locations there are can close down at short notice), accommodations, and other facilities along the way. The tourist bureaus in Kununurra and Broome usually have copies.

TUNNEL CREEK & WINDJANA GORGE NATIONAL PARKS

Windjana Gorge National Park is 21 kilometers (12½ miles) off the Gibb River Road and about 240 kilometers (144 miles) east of Broome. The massive 350 million-year-old walls of the gorge, which shoot straight up as high as 100 meters (328 feet) above the sandy desert floor, are actually an old limestone barrier reef. A picturesque 7-kilometer (4-mile) round-trip trail winds through the gorge, revealing fossilized marine creatures laid down in the Devonian period. This reef is actually part of a much larger barrier reef—comprising hundreds of coral patches, some a couple of miles across, other hundreds of miles wide—built when this part of Australia was an ocean floor. As the ocean floor subsided, those little coral-building creatures kept on building their reefs higher and higher. When the ocean floor pushed up above sea level, the reefs were left high and dry and became the **Napier Ranges.** The **Lennard River,** which carved Windjana gorge, only flows in the Wet, but freshwater crocodiles, fruit bats, and birds are common year-round in and around the residual pools.

Thirty kilometers (18 miles) from Windjana Gorge is **Tunnel Creek National Park,** where you can explore a cave that is part of the same ancient reef system that includes Windjana Gorge. To reach the cave, you must wade through the creek for 750 meters (about half a mile) in the dark. Before you leave Broome, ask your hotel to lend you a torch (flashlight) to reveal the tunnel's stalactites, small fish, five bat species (including rare ghost bats), and even the odd freshwater croc (the friendly sort!). Wear sneakers that you can get wet, and expect the water to be cold! When you emerge, you can see a sampling of the Wandjina Aboriginal rock art that is unique to the area.

GETTING THERE & GETTING AROUND   You can include Windjana and Tunnel Creek on a Gibb River Road safari, or visit from Broome. *Note:* Both parks are usually closed in the Wet from November to March. To get to Windjana, take the Great Northern Highway east for 187 kilometers (110 miles), take a left onto the Derby Highway for 43 kilometers (25 miles) to Derby, then head east along the Gibb River Road. The last 70 kilometers (42 miles) to Windjana, and from there to Tunnel Creek, are graded but unpaved, so a 4WD is best. Camping at Windjana Gorge costs A\$7 (U.S.\$4.90) for adults, A\$1 (U.S.70¢) for kids. The campground has cold showers, toilets, barbecues and wood, and a public telephone. There is no camping in Tunnel Creek National Park. Neither park has an entry fee.

Broome Day Tours (☎ **1800/801 068** in Australia, or 08/9192 1068) and **Over The Top Adventure Tours** (☎ **08/9192 3977**) offer coach and 4WD tours, respectively, from Broome. Expect to pay about A\$150 (U.S.\$105) per person.

For information on the park, and to check accessibility and road conditions outside June to September, call the state **Department of Conservation and Land Management (CALM)** in Broome (☎ **08/9192 1036**).

GEIKIE GORGE NATIONAL PARK

Freshwater versions of saltwater beasties such as sharks, sawfish, and stingrays lurk in the Fitzroy River, which flows through Geikie Gorge (pronounced "Geekie"). The gold and grey 30-meter (98-ft.) walls of the gorge cliffs were laid down in the Devonian period and were carved out by the mighty Fitzroy River. Although strictly speaking the gorge is part of a reef, like Windjana Gorge and Tunnel Creek, Geikie's walls were built not by coral but by algae. Like Windjana Gorge, these walls show primitive life forms that lived in a time before reptiles and mammals were around. Today, pandanus palms, wild passion fruit, mangroves, and river gums line the banks, and freshwater crocodiles and all kinds of birds can be seen. If you spot a stream of water arching out of the river, that's an archer fish targeting an insect by spitting at it. The local shire is making moves to dam the mighty Fitzroy, which makes sense to some farmers but will wreak havoc on the ecology of fishes and rare birds and will flood Aboriginal cultural sites.

The most popular way to experience the park is on a wildlife and geology cruise with the park rangers. They conduct several 90-minute cruises each day, fewer in the seasonal cusp around April/May and September/October. Cruises cost A\$17.50 (U.S.\$12.25) for adults, and just A\$2.50 (U.S.\$1.75) for school-age kids. Bookings are not needed, but check the schedule with the ranger (☎ **08/9191 5121**). There are also two walking trails to explore, a 1-hour round-trip "reef" trail along the base of the gorge wall, and a 20-minute walk along the river bank to a fishing and swimming hole.

GETTING THERE & GETTING AROUND   The gorge is 418 km (251 miles) east of Broome, so be prepared for a long day. The road is paved all the way. Take care you can handle the water level on the several concrete fords. There is no camping in the park. The nearest town is **Fitzroy Crossing,** 18 kilometers (11 miles) before the entrance (☎ **08/9191 5355** is the Fitzroy Crossing Tourist Bureau). During the Wet, access to the park depends on the state of floodwaters; no rangers are based in the park at that time. Call the **Department of Conservation and Land Management** office in Broome (☎ **08/9192 1036**) to check accessibility. The same companies that offer tours to Windjana Gorge and Tunnel Creek (see above) run tours to Geikie Gorge from May to November. Over the Top Adventure Tours' 2-day itinerary combines all three parks.

BROOME

2,250km (1,350 miles) N of Perth; 1,859km (1,115½ miles) SW of Darwin

Part rough Outback town, part glam seaside resort, the pearling port of ✪ **Broome** (pop. 10,000) is a fascinating mixture of Australia and Asia you won't see anywhere else. Chinese and Japanese pearl divers used to work the pearling luggers in the old days, and as the Chinese settled here, they affixed their distinctive architecture to typical Australian buildings. The result is a main street so cute it could be a movie set, with neat rows of very Australian corrugated iron stores wrapped by verandahs and trimmed with Chinese peaked roofs. The people are a unique mixture, too, as the Chinese divers often married Aboriginal women. The Japanese usually returned home rather than settle here, but not all of them made it. Cyclones, the bends, sharks, and crocodiles all took their toll. The Japanese legacy in the town is a rather eerie divers' cemetery with Asian inscriptions on the 900 rough-hewn headstones, incongruously surrounded by the Aussie bush.

For such a small and remote place, Broome is surprisingly sophisticated. Walk the streets of Chinatown and you will rub shoulders with Aussie tourists, itinerant workers, Asian food-store proprietors, tough-as-nails cattle hands from the local stations, and well-heeled visitors from Europe and America drinking good coffee at a couple of trendy cafes. Broome's world-best South Sea pearls are still its bread and butter, although the old timber pearling luggers have been replaced with gleaming high-tech vessels equipped with stainless-steel security doors.

The rich can shop for pearls here, of course, but most people come to laze by the green tropical sea on the 26 kilometers (15½ miles) of ✪ **Cable Beach,** ride camels at sunset, tour the nearby ancient Windjana and Geikie gorges, visit Aboriginal communities, and fish the unplundered seas.

GETTING THERE   Ansett has the best service to Broome, with daily direct flights from Perth and from Darwin via Kununurra, and a weekly service from Alice Springs. Qantas subsidiary **Airlink** (book through Qantas) flies from Perth several times a week, and has two flights a week from Alice Springs and a couple from Darwin. From Sydney and other state capitals you will need to connect via Alice Springs or Darwin. Perth–Broome is a 2¾-hour flight and costs A$537 (U.S.$375.90) one-way. Darwin–Broome is a 2-hour flight, sometimes longer depending on the aircraft, and the fare is A$392 (U.S.$274.40) one-way. Add A$10 (U.S.$7) tax when you land at and depart from Broome Airport.

Greyhound Pioneer has a daily service from Perth that takes 32 hours. The fare is A$234 (U.S.$163.80). Greyhound's daily service from Darwin takes just under 24 hours; the one-way fare is A$202 (U.S.$141.40).

There is no train service to Broome.

Broome is 34 kilometers (20½ miles) off the **Great Northern Highway.** The **Gibb River Road** is an alternate 4WD scenic route from Kununurra (see "Driving the Gibb River Road," above).

VISITOR INFORMATION   The **Broome Tourist Bureau** is on the Great Northern Highway at Bagot Street, Broome, WA 6725 (☎ **08/9192 2222;** fax 08/9192 2063). In the Dry Season, it's open Monday through Friday from 8am to 5pm, and Saturday and Sunday from 9am to 4pm; in the Wet, it's open Monday to Friday from 9am to 5pm, Saturday from 9am to 1pm, and Sunday from 9am to noon.

Book accommodation and tours well ahead in the peak season, June to August.

GETTING AROUND   ATC Rent-A-Car (☎ 08/9193 7788), **Avis** (☎ 08/ 9193 5980), **Broome Broome Car Rentals** (☎ 1800/676 725 in Australia, or 08/ 9192 2210), **Budget** (☎ 08/9193 5355), **Hertz** (☎ 08/9192 1428), and **Thrifty** (☎ 08/9192 2210) all rent conventional cars and 4WDs. For campervans, call **Kimberley Caravan & Outback Supplies** (☎ 1800/645 909 in Australia, or 08/ 9193 5354) who are agents for Britz Australia, Budget, and Koala campervans.

The **Town Bus** (☎ **08/9193 6000**) runs Broome's only bus route. It does an hourly loop of most attractions from 7am to 6:30pm daily. A single fare is A$2.50 (U.S.$1.75), and a day pass is A$8 (U.S.$5.60).

Broome Taxis (☎ **08/9192 1133**) operates the airport shuttle and regular cabs. The airport to town run is about A$5 (U.S.$3.50) per person, depending on your drop-off point.

WHAT TO SEE & DO: PEARLS, CAMEL RIDES, OUTDOOR MOVIES & MORE

Head to **Chinatown** on Carnarvon Street and Dampier Terrace when you arrive, to get a feel for the town. Most shops, cafes, and services are here.

If you do not have a car, the 3-hour **Broome Explorer** coach tour run each morning by **Broome Day Tours** (☎ **1800/801 068** in Australia, or 08/9192 1068) is a good introduction to the town's pearling history. Highlights are the Japanese pearl divers' cemetery, and dinosaur footprints at Gantheaume Point. Tours cost A$39 (U.S.$27.30) for adults, A$35 (U.S.$24.50) for seniors, and A$20 (U.S.$14) for children ages 6 to 16. The tour departs daily during the Dry from May to October, less often during the Wet.

During a tour of the **Willie Creek Pearl Farm** (☎ **08/9193 6000**), 38 kilometers (23 miles) north of town, you will see the intricate process of an oyster getting "seeded" with a nucleus to form a pearl, and learn about pearl farming firsthand from the managers. The tour costs A$17.50 (U.S.$12.25).

When he is not away on tour, Aboriginal actor Stephen "Baamba" Albert presents the seamier side of Broome's history on fun walking tours of Chinatown. A 90-minute morning tour costs A$25 (U.S.$17.50). The tours meet outside Sun Pictures at 8am in the Wet, 9am in the Dry. He also does 2-hour evening tours with a sing-along, departing at 4:30pm, for A$30 (U.S.$21). Call ✪ **Baamba** (☎ **0417/988 328** mobile phone).

Probably the most popular Dry season pastime in Broome is lazing on the 26 glorious sandy kilometers (15½ miles) of ✪ **Cable Beach.** The beach is about 6 kilometers (3½ miles) out of town; the town bus runs there regularly. A beach hut near Cable Beach Inter-Continental Resort rents catamarans and windsurfers in the Dry; from April to November the water is off-limits because of deadly marine stingers. A novel way to experience the beach is on camelback, especially at sunset. **Broome Camel Safaris** does half-hour morning rides between around 7:15 and 9:15am for A$15

Stairway to the Moon

You've heard of a stairway to heaven? Well, Broome has a stairway to the moon. Broome's tides rise and fall by as much as 10 meters (33 ft.) every 12 hours, leaving vast expanses of beach and mud flats exposed in ripples. On the happy coincidence of a full moon and a low tide for several nights every 2 weeks, nature treats the town to a special show as the light of the rising moon falls on the rippled sand and mud, creating a magical "stairway to the moon" effect. A great place to see this is from the clifftop bar at the Mangrove Hotel (see "Where to Stay"), which is on the highest point in town facing east. The locals sometimes hold markets at Town Beach on stairway nights. The Broome Tourist Bureau can tell you the dates the next stairway is due.

(U.S.$10.50) per person. **Ships of the Desert** (no phone) does one-hour afternoon and sunset rides for A$25 (U.S.$17.50) per person. Book through the Tourist Bureau. Reigning four-time state surf champ Josh Parmateer (☎ **0418/958 264** mobile phone) gives surf lessons on the beach from July to September. A 2-hour lesson is A$70 (U.S.$49) per person, or A$30 (U.S.$21) per person if there are two of you. Josh supplies the boards and wet suits.

Broome has several good art galleries selling vivid oil and watercolor landscapes and a small range of Aboriginal art. Even if you're not buying, it's interesting to browse the paintings, sculpture, pottery, and carvings at **Matso's,** 60 Hamersley St. (☎ **08/9193 5811**) open daily from 10am to 5pm. Have lunch, coffee, or one of the gallery's own brewed beers on the cafe verandah.

Don't leave town without taking in a recent-release Hollywood movie at the adorable **Sun Pictures cinema,** Carnarvon Street near Short Street (☎ **08/9192 1077**). Built in 1916, it's the oldest "picture gardens" in the world. The audience sits in canvas deck chairs under the stars to watch films screened through a 1950s projector. In the Wet, everyone takes cover at the back and the show goes on through the rain. One or two movies screen nightly. Tickets are A$10 (U.S.$7) for adults, A$8 (U.S.$5.60) for students or seniors, and A$6 (U.S.$4.20) for children ages 3 to 16.

The swish **Cable Beach Inter-Continental Resort,** Cable Beach Road (☎ **08/9192 0400**) is beyond most budgets, but anyone can enjoy a beer and a free sunset at the resort's casual Sunset Bar. It's popular, so get there early! It has live entertainment Sundays.

WHERE TO STAY & DINE

As well as in-hotel dining options below, head on over to the **Cable Beach Inter-Continental Resort,** Cable Beach Road (☎ **08/9192 0400**) for Broome's greatest range of menus. There's Pandanus for a ritzy splash-out, the Kimberley Grill for modern bush tucker and steaks, Sketches pasta bar, the Walking Wok for stir-fries, and the casual colonial-style Lord Mac's for breakfast, lunch, and buffet dinner inside or on the terrace.

✪ **The Kimberley Club.** 62 Frederick St., Broome, WA 6725. ☎ **08/9192 3233.** Fax 08/9192 3530. 50 quad-share dorm beds, 24 private rooms. A$15–$17 (U.S.$10.50–$11.90) dorm bed; A$55 (U.S.$38.50) double. AE, BC, DC, MC, V. Free pickup from Greyhound Pioneer terminal.

This stylish new Outback-style lodge within walking distance of town might be aimed at the backpacker market, but travelers of all persuasions will like its clean private rooms furnished simply with a double or twin beds and two bunks. You share the clean new shower/toilet facilities, and can rent towels for A$2 (U.S.$1.40) for the duration of your stay. The air-conditioning is coin-operated at A$1 (U.S.70¢) for 4 hours, although you are unlikely to need it in the Dry, thanks to some clever air-flow work by the architects. The rooms are spartan (no TV, no tea and coffee, no fridge, no sink), but you will spend most of your time around the rock-lined pool and the large, rustic open-sided dining area. The crowd is always friendly, so this is a great spot to socialize and meet other travelers. There's a TV lounge, Internet access, a small volleyball court, pool tables, Ping-Pong, a communal kitchen, and a tour desk with an emphasis on fun, cheap, and exciting activities. The Fat Time Bar serves hearty meals like Thai green chicken curry or lasagna for A$8 (U.S.$5.60). You need to like loud music to stay here, but it's lights-out at 11pm, so everyone gets some sleep. Excellent value for the money.

Mangrove Hotel. 120 Carnarvon St., Broome, WA 6725. ☎ **1800/094 818** in Australia, or 08/9192 1303. Fax 08/9193 5169. E-mail: mangrovehotel@bigpond.com. 68 units, all with bathroom (2 with Jacuzzi, one with tub). A/C TV TEL. High season A$120–$140 (U.S.$84–$98) double; A$185 (U.S.$168) suite; A$220 (U.S.$154) 2-bedroom apt. Low season A$110–$130 (U.S.$77–$91) double; A$180 (U.S.$126) suite; $220 (U.S.$54) 2-bedroom apt. Additional person A$25 (U.S.$17.50) extra. Free crib. AE, BC, DC, MC, V. Free airport shuttle.

The best views in Broome are across Roebuck Bay from this pleasant clifftop hotel, a 5-minute walk from town. It's worth hightailing it back from sightseeing just to watch from the tables and chairs lining the cliff edge as dusk falls over the bay. By the time you get here the new Tides Garden cafe/bar will be open for lunch and dinner over-looking the bay; Charter's restaurant, one of Broome's best, is open nightly from 6pm. There's no faulting the clean well-kept standard rooms, the ultra-roomy deluxe rooms with a balcony, the two suites that sleep four and have a Jacuzzi, and the two-bedroom apartment. All rooms have hair dryers, irons, and boards. Two swimming pools and two Jacuzzis in the gardens overlooking the bay, limited room service, and a tour desk are among the services and facilities. The bus to town stops across the road.

11 Perth & Western Australia

by Natalie Kruger

Many international visitors—heck, many east coast Australians!—never make the trek over to Western Australia. It's too far away, too expensive to fly to, too big when you get there, they say. All these things are true, actually—but don't dismiss a trip here out of hand. Getting to the capital, Perth, need not be expensive, and there's plenty to see and do in and around the city, like snorkeling on coral reefs, wine tasting, and exploring historic towns. Your reward for going the extra mile, or the extra thousand miles in Western Australia's case, is the opportunity to experience some of Australia's most dazzling natural attractions.

The Southwest "hook" of the state, below Perth, is far and away the prettiest place to visit. Massive stands of karri and jarrah trees stretch to the sky, the surf is fantastic, and the coastline wave-smashed and rugged. But if you think trees, surf, and cliffs are all boring, you'll just have to content yourself with visiting the 45 wineries in the Southwest's Margaret River region responsible for turning out some of Australia's most desirable reds and whites.

Head east around 666 kilometers (400 miles) inland from Perth and you strike what, in the 1890s, was the richest square mile of gold-bearing earth ever found in the world. The mining town of Kalgoorlie fuses lovely 19th-century gold-rush architecture with a zeal for pumping out almost 6 kilos (2,000 oz.) of gold a day at the close of the 20th century. This is an iconic Australian town, Australia's answer to the Wild West.

Once you drive north of Perth past Geraldton on the Midwest coast, you know you're in the Outback. Orange sand, scrubby trees, and spiky grass are all you see for hundreds of miles. About 850 kilometers (510 miles) north of Perth is a special phenomenon, daily visits by wild dolphins to the shores of Monkey Mia. Another 872 kilometers (523 miles) on one of Australia's best-kept secrets, a 260-kilometer (156-mile) coral reef stretching along the isolated Outback shore. It's a second Great Barrier Reef, barely discovered by world travelers or Aussies themselves. The reef is making a name for itself as a whale shark habitat, where you can swim with these mysterious 12-meter (40-ft.) fish-monsters every Aussie fall.

EXPLORING THE STATE

VISITOR INFORMATION The **Western Australian Tourism Commission (WATC),** 16 St. Georges Terrace, Perth, WA 6000 (☎ **08/9220 1700,** fax 08/9220 1702), is the state's official tourism

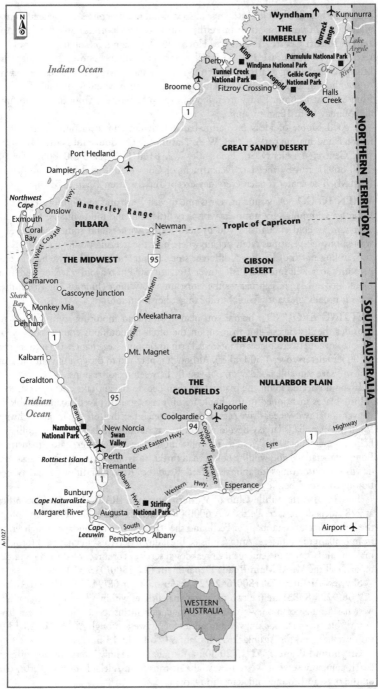

N

Indian Ocean

Wyndham ↑ ✈ Kununurra

THE KIMBERLEY

Durrack Range

Lake Argyle

Derby King

Windjana National Park Purnululu National Park

Tunnel Creek National Park ✈ Leopold Geikie Gorge National Park

Broome Fitzroy Crossing Halls Creek

Ord River

Range

GREAT SANDY DESERT

NORTHERN TERRITORY

Port Hedland ✈

Dampier

Northwest Cape Hamersley Range

Onslow North West Coastal Hwy.

Exmouth PILBARA Newman Tropic of Capricorn

Coral Bay

THE MIDWEST 95 GIBSON DESERT

SOUTH AUSTRALIA

Carnarvon

Gascoyne Junction Northern

Shark Bay Meekatharra

Monkey Mia GREAT VICTORIA DESERT

Denham Great

Mt. Magnet

Kalbarri NULLARBOR PLAIN

Geraldton THE GOLDFIELDS

Indian Ocean 95 Kalgoorlie ✈

Coolgardie 94

Brand Hwy. Coolgardie Hwy.

Nambung National Park New Norcia Esperance Hwy. Highway

Swan Valley Great Eastern Hwy. Eyre 1

✈ Perth

Rottnest Island Fremantle Albany Hwy. Western Hwy. Esperance

1

Bunbury Stirling National Park

Cape Naturaliste

Margaret River Augusta

Cape Leeuwin South Albany

Pemberton

Airport ✈

A-1027

WESTERN AUSTRALIA

marketing board. It publishes a range of special-interest brochures and general touring guides. When you first arrive in Perth, drop into the **Commission's Western Australian Tourist Centre,** Albert Facey House, 469 Wellington St., on the corner of Forrest Place (☎ **1300/361 351** in Australia, or call the number above). It has maps and brochures pertaining to attractions throughout the state, gives personal advice on what to see and do, and has a free booking service. It's open Monday through Thursday from 8:30am to 6pm, Friday from 8:30am to 7pm, Saturday from 8:30am to 5pm, and Sunday from 10am to 5pm.

A good source of ideas on nature-based activities and attractions in the state's national and marine parks is the **"W. A. Naturally" Outdoor and Nature Information Centre,** 47 Henry St., Fremantle, WA 6160 (☎ **08/ 9430 8600,** fax 08/ 9430 8699), run by the state Department of Conservation and Land Management (CALM). The center is open every day except Tuesday from 10am to 5:30pm.

WHEN TO GO   Any time of year is fine to visit Perth and the Southwest. The city is blessed with long, dry summers with very little rain, and mild winters. The Southwest can get cold enough for you to need warm sweaters and sometimes gloves in winter, but temperatures rarely get anywhere near the freezing point.

Traveling north of Perth is a different story. Summer can be absolute hell, as temperatures soar well into the 40s°C (over 104° to 120°F), so avoid traveling here from December to March. February is the worst month. Winter (June to August) in these parts is usually pleasantly cool, but it can get hot then, too.

GETTING AROUND   Before you plan a whirlwind motoring tour of the state, consider the distances—not to mention the often monotonous countryside—you'll have to cover between places of interest. Perth to Broome (see chapter 10) is more than 2,500 kilometers (over 1,500 miles). Although it may add to the cost of your vacation, you will save valuable holiday time if you fly between major regions.

If you do decide to hit the road rather than take to the air, take a few precautions. All the places mentioned in this book are on major sealed (paved) roads suitable for conventional two-wheel-drive cars. However, remember that off the major highways, Western Australia is largely devoid of people, gas stations (so keep the tank full), and help in emergencies. In Western Australia more than most other states, road trains (long semi-trailers) and wildlife pose a road threat, so avoid driving at night, dusk, and dawn—all prime times for animals to feed. Read the "Road Conditions & Safety" section in chapter 3 before you set off.

The **Royal Automobile Club of Western Australia (RACWA),** which has offices at 228 Adelaide Terrace, Perth, WA 6000 (☎ **08/9421 4444;** fax 08/9221 2708), is the best source of road maps of Perth and the state. It's open Monday through Friday from 8:30am to 5pm. See "Auto Clubs & Breakdown Services" in chapter 3 for information on its statewide emergency breakdown service. For a recorded road-condition report, call the **W. A. Main Roads Department** (☎ **1800/013 314**).

Skywest Airlines (☎ **1800/642 225** in Australia, or 08/9478 9999) and **Airlink** (☎ **08/9225 8383**) are the two main regional airlines within Western Australia. Skywest has a range of money-saving, accommodation-inclusive vacation packages from Perth. You can make bookings and inquiries for Skywest through Ansett (☎ **13 13 00** in Australia), and for Airlink through Qantas (☎ **13 13 13** in Australia).

Greyhound Pioneer (☎ **13 20 30** in Australia) is the only interstate long-distance coach company serving Western Australia. It runs from Adelaide over to Perth, then up the coast to Broome and across to Darwin.

Apart from the east-west train line from Adelaide via Kalgoorlie, operated by **Great Southern Railway** (see "Getting Around" in chapter 3), the only intrastate long-distance trains are operated by **Westrail** (☎ **13 10 53** in Western Australia, or

Tiptoeing through the Wildflowers

Every year from August to November, Mother Nature blesses just about the entire state of Western Australia with a bountiful carpet of white, yellow, mauve, pink, red, and blue ✪ **wildflowers.** Some 8,000 species in all stretch for miles across fields and along highway shoulders.

This annual burgeoning is matched by an explosion of wildflower shows and festivals in country towns throughout the state. Coach and rail tour companies go into overdrive ferrying flower enthusiasts from all around Australia and the globe. The blossoms cluster conveniently in the cooler southern half of Western Australia, where you can easily explore them on day trips from Perth, or on longer jaunts of up to 5 days or so.

Probably the most popular route is what the tourism authority calls the **Everlasting Trail,** north of Perth. Everlastings spread a riot of color over a wide area— but they only show after rain, so you need to time your visit to see their display at its max. There are several routes to take in this district, but the best follows the Great Northern Highway to Wubin, 272 kilometers (163 miles) north of Perth, and on to Mullewa, another 222 kilometers (133 miles) north. Mullewa's Wildflower Show every August is one of the state's best. From here, head back to Perth down the Brand Highway. You could do the trip in a day if you put your foot down, but give yourself 2 or 3 days to, you know, smell the roses.

If time is short, don't despair. You can see lots of blossoms without leaving Perth. Kings Park, right in town, proudly conducts free guided walks through its annual displays of 2,000 species, and assorted national parks on the city's outskirts, such as the John Forrest park in the Mundaring Hills, have plenty of blooms to enjoy.

Because Australian flora is adapted to desert conditions, it tends to sprout on dry, sunny days following a rain shower. The **Western Australia Tourist Centre** (see "Visitor Information," in "Exploring the State") runs a **Wildflower Desk** during the season to keep you up-to-date on whatever hot spot is blooming brightest that week, and can book you on one of the many appropriate tours. The center publishes a free 32-page *Wildflower Holiday Guide* that details which species you can see where on the main self-drive wildflower routes throughout the state, as well as accommodations and attractions en route. Interstate buses and trains and regional hotels fill up fast in wildflower season, so book ahead.

08/9326 2244; fax 08/9326 2619) from Perth to the Southwest and the southern coast, Northam in the Avon Valley, and Kalgoorlie. Westrail also runs coach services to the Southwest and as far north as Kalbarri on the Midwest coast north of Perth.

TOUR OPERATORS   These three large coach tour companies offer tours around Perth and throughout the state: **Australian Pacific Tours** (☎ **1800/675 222** in Australia, or call its Western Australian booking agent at 08/9221 4000; fax 08/9221 5477), **Australian Pinnacle Tours** (☎ **1800/999 304** in Australia, or 08/9221 5411; fax 08/9221 5477) and **Feature Tours** (☎ **1800/999 819** in Australia, or 08/9479 4131; fax 08/9479 4130). **Overland 4WD Safaris** (☎ **08/9358 3588;** fax 08/9350 5060) runs extended 4WD safaris from Perth all over the state.

A wonderful option for nature lovers is the ✪ **Landscope Expeditions** tour program run by the state Conservation and Land Management Department (CALM) (☎ **08/9380 2433,** or fax 08/9380 1066 for a free schedule, or check it out at www.calm.wa.gov.au). On these exciting trips you assist CALM scientists on research projects, such as reintroducing endangered species to the Shark Bay World Heritage region, observing solar eclipses from a boat in the Houtman Abrolhos Islands, or learning about 17th-century Dutch shipwrecks on the dramatic Zuytdorp Cliffs. Accommodations vary, but you will usually be camping or sharing basic bunkhouses or cabins.

The largest tall ship in Australia, the three-masted square rigger barquentine **STS Leeuwin II,** operated by **Leeuwin Ocean Adventure** ☎ **08/9430 4105;** fax 08/ 9430 4494) runs ecovoyages along the dramatic and isolated Western Australian coastline. Voyages, which can last up to 11 days, depart from the ship's base in Fremantle and from other ports around the coast. Trips cost about A$89 (U.S.$62.30) a day for students and A$100 (U.S.$70) a day for adults—not a bad value for an adventure, including accommodations and meals.

SUGGESTED ITINERARIES   If you have only 2 or 3 days to spare, spend a day in bustling Fremantle in Perth, and then do some serious wine-tasting, hiking, or surfing in the Margaret River area in the Southwest. If you have 5 days or more, consider a 4WD safari roving through the Southwest karri forests or taking in the weird limestone peaks of the Pinnacles in Nambung National Park north of Perth, the Midwest sheep stations, and the Monkey Mia dolphins. If you are coming by train from Adelaide, stop off for a day or so in Kalgoorlie before continuing on to Perth; it's a shame to pass through this vibrant town without seeing it. Diving and snorkeling freaks with 5 days or a week to spare could spend 2 days in Perth (make one of them a visit to the coral and dive sites of Rottnest Island), and then fly (or drive) to Exmouth on the Northwest Cape to spend the remaining time diving and snorkeling Ningaloo Reef.

1 Perth

4,405km (2,643 miles) W of Sydney; 2,557km (1,534 miles) S of Broome

Australians often refer to Sydney as their "Emerald City," but really, Perth has a better claim to that tag. The city's silver skyscrapers glint in the sun as they rise like spires into a very blue sky, and the Indian Ocean sparkles with a kind of magic on the shore. The city and the port town of Fremantle are probably best known to visitors as the site of Australia's spirited defense of the America's Cup yacht race in 1987. On that occasion the Cup returned to American shores, where it had lived for so long, but the enthusiasm whipped up in the city in those heady times lives on. Perth has an energetic vibrancy that only Sydney can match—in fact, Perth residents delight in telling you their city gets more sunny days (more than 300) than any other Australian capital, Sydney included. The city is the fourth largest in Australia after Sydney, Melbourne, and Brisbane.

It is unlikely you will come all the way to Perth without visiting the wine regions of the Southwest a few hours away, the dolphins at Monkey Mia on the state's Midwest coast, or the marvels of Ningaloo Reef farther north. You will not regret spending a day to two in the city en route, however, for Perth is not one of those drab, anonymous capitals that exist only to serve the needs of its economy. There's lots for the visitor here. Wander through the historic warehouses, museums, and working docks of ✪ **Fremantle;** stock up at the plentiful Aboriginal art and souvenir stores; eat at some of Australia's best restaurants; ride a bike through a 405-hectare (1,000-acre) park in the middle of the city; and snorkel over the coral on picturesque Rottnest Island, Perth's very own miniature reef resort. Many of the city's attractions are outdoorsy, and that means they are often cheap or, even better, free.

Perth

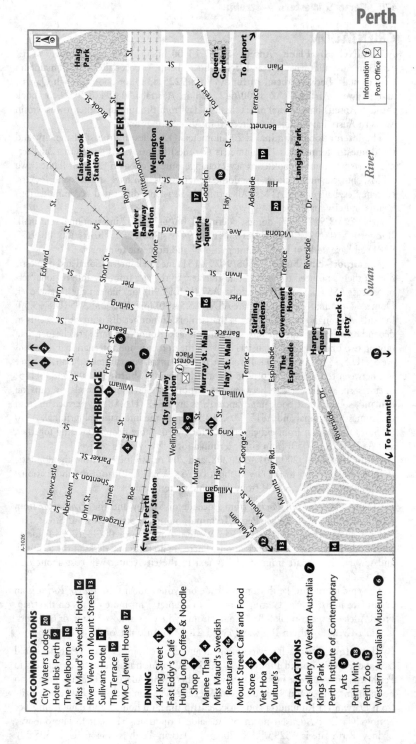

N↗

Haig Park

Brook St.

Claisebrook Railway Station

EAST PERTH

Wellington Square

McIver Railway Station

Queen's Gardens

To Airport

Edward St.

Parry St.

Short St.

Stirling

Pier

Moore

Royal

Wittenoom St.

Goderich

Victoria Square

Hay

17

18

Bennett

Terrace

Langley Park

19

Adelaide

Ave.

20

Hill

Rd.

Newcastle

Aberdeen

Shenton St.

John St.

James

Fitzgerald

Roe

West Perth Railway Station

Parker St.

Lake St.

4

NORTHBRIDGE

Beaufort St.

6

Francis St.

5

William St.

3

7

Forrest Place

City Railway Station

Wellington St.

Murray St.

8 **9**

King St.

11

Milligan

Hay

St. George's

Murray St. Mall

Hay St. Mall

William St.

Barrack St.

Irwin St.

Pier St.

16

Stirling Gardens

Government House

Riverside Terrace

Victoria

Riverside Dr.

10

Mounts Bay Rd.

Mount St.

Malcolm St.

12

13

14

Terrace

The Esplanade

Esplanade

Harper Square

Barrack St. Jetty

15→

↓ To Fremantle

Swan River

← **1** **2**

Information ⓘ
Post Office ⊠

A-1026

ACCOMMODATIONS
City Waters Lodge **20**
Hotel Ibis Perth **9**
The Melbourne **10**
Miss Maud's Swedish Hotel **16**
River View on Mount Street **13**
Sullivans Hotel **14**
The Terrace **19**
YMCA Jewell House **17**

DINING
44 King Street ◆ **1**
Fast Eddy's Café ◆ **8**
Hung Long Coffee & Noodle Shop ◆ **4**
Manee Thai ◆ **4**
Miss Maud's Swedish Restaurant ◆ **6**
Mount Street Café and Food Store ◆ **3**
Viet Hoa ◆ **2**
Vulture's ◆ **3**

ATTRACTIONS
Art Gallery of Western Australia ● **7**
Kings Park ● **12**
Perth Institute of Contemporary Arts ● **5**
Perth Mint ● **18**
Perth Zoo ● **15**
Western Australian Museum ● **6**

469

ORIENTATION

ARRIVING   By Plane   Ansett (☎ **13 13 00** in Australia) and **Qantas** (☎ **13 13 13** in Australia) have several direct flights to Perth Airport daily from all mainland state capitals. Between them, **Airlink** (☎ **08/9225 8383,** or book through Qantas) and **Skywest Airlines** (☎ **1800/642 225** in Australia, 08/9478 9999, or book through Ansett) have several direct flights a day from Broome and other towns within Western Australia; Airlink flies direct from Alice Springs daily.

The **international terminal** is 20 kilometers (12 miles) northeast of the city, and the **domestic terminal** is 12 kilometers (7 miles) from town. The international terminal has a Thomas Cook currency-exchange bureau open to meet all flights, two ATMs, showers, and lockers. The domestic terminals also have showers and lockers, currency exchange, and ATMs. All terminals also have direct-dial accommodations boards and city maps.

Avis (☎ 08/9277 1177 domestic terminal, 08/9477 1302 international terminal), **Budget** (☎ 08/9277 9277), **Hertz** (☎ 08/9479 4788), and **Thrifty** (☎ 08/9277 9281) all have desks at both the international and domestic terminals.

The **airport–city shuttle** (☎ **08/9479 4131**) meets all international and domestic flights; there's no need to book a seat. Transfers to the city from the international terminal cost A$9 (U.S.$6.30) for adults, A$7 (U.S.$4.90) for children age 12 and over. Domestic terminal–city transfers are A$7 (U.S.$4.90) for adults and A$5 (U.S.$3.50) for kids. Although the official line is that seniors do not get discounts, that seems to depend on who's driving the bus, so be sure to ask. Round-trip fares are cheaper than buying two one-way fares. Transfers between the domestic and international terminals are $5 (U.S.$3.50) per person. If you are flying Qantas, you can take the airline's free bus between terminals. The private **Fremantle Airport Shuttle** (☎ **08/9383 4115**) operates six services a day between the airport and Fremantle hotels. It runs on demand, so you must book in advance. Fares are A$12 (U.S.$8.40) per person from the domestic terminal and A$15 (U.S.$10.50) from the international terminal, A$10 (U.S.$7) per person from either terminal for two or more people traveling together, and A$25 (U.S.$17.50) from either terminal for a family of up to five.

Public buses nos. 200, 201, 202, 208, and 209 run to the city from the domestic terminal only. A **taxi** to the city is about A$25 (U.S.$17.50) from the international terminal and A$20 (U.S.$14) from the domestic terminal.

By Train   The *Indian Pacific* from Adelaide or Sydney and the *Prospector* from Kalgoorlie pull into the **East Perth Terminal,** Summers Street off Lord Street, East Perth. Call **Westrail** ☎ **13 10 53** in Western Australia, or 08/9326 2244) for all information, schedules, and reservations. There are no car rental desks at the terminal, and few facilities apart from a cafe. A taxi to the city center will cost about A$8 (U.S.$5.60).

The epic journey to Perth from Adelaide or Sydney aboard the *Indian Pacific* is an experience in itself. See "Getting Around" in chapter 3 for more details on the train. From Adelaide the trip takes 38½ hours; from Sydney it's almost 3 days, or 66 hours. Contact **Great Southern Railway** (☎ **13 21 47** in Australia, or 08/8213 4696).

By Bus   Interstate coach services arrive at and depart from the **East Perth Terminal** (see above). **Greyhound Pioneer** (☎ **13 20 30** in Australia) runs coach services to Perth five times a week from Sydney via Canberra and Adelaide. The trip time is 56 hours from Sydney and 34 hours from Adelaide. The company also has service daily from Darwin via Kununurra and Broome (trip time: 60 hours); and daily from Alice Springs via Port Augusta, north of Adelaide (trip time: 51 hours). The one-way Sydney–Perth fare is A$295 (U.S.$206.50); Darwin–Perth is A$436 (U.S.$305.20).

The state rail service, **Westrail** (see above), also runs coaches from Kalbarri in the north, and Esperance, Albany, and Bunbury in the south.

By Car   If you're coming from the east, the **Great Eastern Highway** becomes Guildford Road, which becomes Lord Street, leading into the city center. The cleanest route from the north is the **Mitchell Freeway,** which becomes Riverside Drive, forming the southern boundary of the city-center grid. From the south, the **Albany Highway** leads into Riverside Drive.

VISITOR INFORMATION   The **Western Australian Tourist Centre (WATC),** Albert Facey House, 469 Wellington St. on the corner of Forrest Place (☎ **1300/ 361 351** in Australia), is the official visitor information source for Perth. It's open Monday through Thursday from 8:30am to 6pm, Friday from 8:30am to 7pm, Saturday from 8:30am to 5pm, and Sunday from 10am to 5pm. Because the WATC covers the whole state, however, I found its information on Perth somewhat restricted and the queues for assistance long. You will probably find a greater supply of information at the **Perth Tourist Lounge,** Level 2, Carillon Arcade off 680 Hay St. Mall (☎ **08/9481 8303**). It's open Monday through Saturday from 10am to 5pm and Sunday from noon to 4pm.

There are half a dozen free pocket guides to Perth available at the airport, in hotel foyers, and at the Western Australian Tourist Centre or the Perth Tourist Lounge. They are all shamelessly "touristy," though. Much more informative is in the local magazine *Scoop* (A$6.95/U.S.$4.90 from newsagents), a great guide to the city's hip restaurants, cultural life, shops, bars, festivals, and the latest things to see and do. For the low-down on free public events, theater, and classical/jazz music performances, art exhibitions, restaurant reviews, and shops, pick up a copy of the free *Perth Weekly.*

CITY LAYOUT   The city center is 19 kilometers (11½ miles) upriver from the Indian Ocean and stretches north from a broad scenic reach of the Swan River. **Hay Street** and **Murray Street** are the two major city streets, 1 block apart; both are bisected by pedestrian malls between William and Barrack streets. The traffic runs west on Hay and east on Murray. This, and the medley of other one-way streets in the city center, can make driving confusing. It helps all newcomers, drivers or not, to know that Adelaide Terrace and St. Georges Terrace are one and the same street. The name change occurs at Victoria Avenue.

Of the many free pocket guides to Perth, *Your Guide to Perth & Fremantle* has the best street map because it shows one-way streets, public toilets and telephones, taxi stands, and street numbers as well as most attractions and hotels.

NEIGHBORHOODS IN BRIEF

City Center   The center of town is home to a few attractions and is where you'll fine many shops and department stores, connected by a honeycomb of shopping arcades. A good introduction to Perth's charms is to take in the great views from the pedestrian and bike path that skirts the river along Riverside Drive. Within walking distance on the western edge of the central business district are Mt. Eliza and Kings Park.

Northbridge   Just about all of Perth's nightclubs, trendy restaurants, and cool bars and cafes are in this 5-block precinct just north of the railway line, within easy walking distance of the city center. It's roughly bounded by James, Beaufort, Aberdeen, and Lake streets. What locals call the Cultural Centre—an umbrella term that refers to the Western Australian Museum, the Art Gallery of Western Australia, the state library, and the Perth Institute of Contemporary Art—is in the heart of Northbridge. The Blue and Weekend free CAT buses deliver you right into this part of town.

Subiaco On the other side of Kings Park from the city is the well-heeled suburb of Subiaco. Saturday morning just wouldn't be Saturday morning for Perth's see-and-be-seen crowd without a stroll through Subiaco's villagelike collection of cafes, markets, upscale boutiques, antique shops, and art galleries. Intersecting Hay Street and Rokeby (pronounced "Rockerby") Road are the main promenades. Take the train to Subiaco station.

Fremantle Not only is this Perth's working port, Fremantle is also Perth's second city heart, and the city's favorite weekend spot to relax, eat, shop, and sail. A careful 1987 restoration of its long-neglected Victorian warehouses saw "Freo" emerge as a wonderful living example of a 19th-century seaport. It has all the charm that San Francisco's Fisherman's Wharf is supposed to have, without that development's stale commercial taint. Fremantle is 19 kilometers (11½ miles) down river on the mouth of the Swan River. See "A Day Out in Fremantle" later in this chapter for details on how to get there.

Scarborough Beach This is one of Perth's prize beaches 12 kilometers (7¼ miles) north of the city center. The district is a little tatty with that oversupply of cheap take-out food outlets that seem to plague Aussie city beaches, but if you like sun, sand, and surf, this is the most convenient place to be. Of all the beachside suburbs it has the most facilities, such as supermarkets, bars, restaurants, shops, surf-gear rental stores, and the like. It takes about 15 to 20 minutes to reach by car, about 35 minutes on the bus.

GETTING AROUND

BY PUBLIC TRANSPORTATION **Transperth** runs Perth's buses, trains, and ferries. For route and timetable information, call ☎ **13 62 13** in Western Australia, or drop into the Transperth information offices at the Plaza Arcade off Hay Street Mall, the Perth Railway Station, the Wellington Street Bus Station, or the City Bus Port on Mounts Bay Road. You can transfer from bus to ferry to train on one ticket. You pay onboard for buses, and buy train and ferry tickets at coin-only vending machines at train stations and ferry terminals. Travel costs A$1.70 (U.S.$1.20) in one zone, and A$2.40 (U.S.$1.70) in two, which gets you most places. Children ages 5 to 14 travel for around half-price, but seniors and students not living in Western Australia pay full fare.

If you're sightseeing, a **FastCard** pass allowing multiple rides may be a better option than purchasing individual tickets. There are quite a few types: a **MultiRider** pass gives you 10 trips at a savings of 15%. A **DayRider** pass allows one day's unlimited travel after 9am on weekdays and all day on weekends and public holidays, and costs A$6.50 (U.S.$4.55), less for children. Validate your FastCard in the validation machine on the bus or ferry or on the train platform every time you board. You can buy FastCards from Newspower newsagents and at Transperth information offices.

Buses and trains run from about 5:30am until about 11:30pm.

A Free Ride

A welcome freebie in Perth is the **Free Transit Zone (FTZ)** in the city center. You can travel free on trains and buses within this zone at any hour, day and night. It is bounded by Kings Park Road, Thomas Street in the west, Newcastle Street in the north, the Causeway, and Barrack Street Jetty. Basically, this means you can travel to Kings Park, Northbridge, east to major sporting grounds, and anywhere in the city center for free. Signs mark the FTZ boundaries; just ask the driver if you're unsure.

By Bus   Most people using public transport to get around Perth take the bus. The **Wellington Street Bus Station,** located next to Perth Railway Station at Forrest Place, and the **City Bus Port** on the western edge of the city on Mounts Bay Road, are the two main depots. The vast majority of buses travel east or west along St. Georges Terrace. Hail the bus from your stop, as drivers do not always stop unless they know it's their bus you want.

By far the best way to get around in the city and Northbridge is on the distinctive silver, free **CAT (Central Area Transit)** buses that run a continual loop of the city and Northbridge. The Red CAT runs east–west from East Perth as far as Subiaco in the west every 5 minutes, Monday through Friday from 7am to 6pm. The Blue CAT runs north–south as far north as Northbridge and south to Riverside Drive every 7½ minutes, Monday through Friday from 7am to 6pm. The Weekend CAT follows a similar north–south route to the Blue Cat. It runs every 10 minutes on Friday from 6pm to 1am, Saturday from 8:30am to 1am, and Sunday from 10am to 5pm. Look for the silver CAT bus stops. Transperth information offices give out free route maps.

By Train   Trains are a fast, clean, safe way to travel. Not all major attractions are on the train line, although Fremantle is, and so are Cottesloe Beach and Subiaco. Most trains run every 15 minutes during the day, and every half hour at night. All trains leave from **Perth Railway Station** at the end of Forrest Place on Wellington Street.

By Ferry   You will probably only use the ferries to visit Perth Zoo. Ferries run every half hour from the **Barrack Street Jetty** to Mends Street in South Perth. Ferries run Monday through Friday from 6:50am to 7:15pm (to 9:15pm on Friday, from September to April), with extra services in morning and evening peak hours. On Saturday, they run from 7:50am to 9:15pm, and on Sunday from 7:50am to 7:15pm.

BY TAXI   Cabs are easily hailed, and there are plenty of ranks in the city. Perth's two taxi companies are **Swan Taxis** (☎ **08/9444 4444**) and **Black & White Taxis** (☎ **08/ 9333 3333**). The initial fare is A$2.60 (U.S.$1.80) on weekdays and A$3.60 (U.S.$2.50) on weeknights and weekends, plus A$1 (U.S.70¢) per kilometer (½ mile) traveled.

BY CAR   You would think that with a population of less than 1.3 million spread out over 5,369 square kilometers (2,072½ square miles), Perth would be an easy place to navigate by car. Not so. The roads are fine, but Perth's signposting is notorious for telling you where you have been, not where you are going. Some interstate highways are announced with insignificant signs more suited to a side street. If your car rental company supplies a free street directory, take it!

Parking garages are plentiful in Perth. One of the best and cheapest is **KC Park Safe,** 152–158 St. Georges Terrace between William Street and King Street (☎ **08/ 9321 0667**).

A 1.8% state tax applies to car rentals. Of the big chains, Budget seems to have good rates. The major car-rental companies are **ATC Rent-A-Car** (☎ 1800/999 888 in Australia but outside Western Australia, or 08/9325 1833); **Avis** (☎ 08/9325 7677); **Budget** (☎ 08/9322 1100); **Delta** (☎ 08/9226 0026); **Hertz** (☎ 08/9321 7777); and **Thrifty** (☎ 08/9481 1999). ATC Rent-A-Car, Avis, Budget, Delta, and Thrifty have Fremantle outlets, also.

You may get a better rate from one of the local companies, such as **Bayswater Car Rental** (☎ 08/9325 1000 in Perth, or 08/9430 5300 in Fremantle), **Hawk Rent A Car** (☎ 08/9221 9688), and new guys Perth Rent-A-Car (☎ 08/9225 5855, and 08/9430 4322 in Fremantle). Perth Rent-A-Car delivers cars to the airport and your hotel free of charge, and Hawk delivers free to city hotels during business hours.

FAST FACTS: Perth

American Express   The bureau is located at 645 Hay St. Mall (☎ **08/ 9261 2711**) and is open Monday through Friday from 8:30am to 5:30pm and Saturday from 9am to noon. To get refunds on lost or stolen checks, first call 1800/251 902 to report them; the 645 Hay St. office will then refund them. Call 1800/230 100 to report lost or stolen credit cards.

Business Hours   Banks are open Monday through Thursday from 9:30am to 4pm and until 5pm on Friday. City shops are usually open Monday through Friday from 9am to 5:30pm (Thursday to 9pm in the suburbs, including Fremantle, and Friday to 9pm in the city), and Saturday from 9am to 5pm. Most (but not all) major stores are open Sunday from noon to 4pm or later in the city, and from 10am to 6pm in Fremantle.

Currency Exchange   In the city, go to the American Express office (see above) or **Interforex,** Shop 24, London Court off Hay St. Mall (☎ **08/9325 7418**), open daily from 9am to 6pm, and Friday to 9pm. Interforex has a Fremantle bureau at the corner of William and Adelaide streets (☎ **08/9431 7022**); it's open daily from 8am to 8pm.

Dentist/Doctor   Perth Dental Emergencies and Doctors at Forrest Chase are located together on the Upper Walkway Level, Forrest Chase shopping complex, 425 Wellington St. opposite Perth Railway Station. Call the dental surgery on ☎ 08/9221 4749 and the doctors' surgery on ☎ 08/9221 4757. Both services can be reached after hours on ☎ 08/9383 1620). The surgeries are open daily from 8am to 8pm. In case of poisoning, call Poisons Information (☎ 13 11 26).

Drugstores   Forrest Chase Pharmacy, located in the dental and medical surgery listed in "Dentist/Doctor" above (☎ 08/9221 1691) is open Monday to Thursday and Saturday from 8am to 7pm, Friday from 8am to 9pm, and Sunday from 10am to 6pm. Shenton Pharmacy, 214 Nicholson Rd., Subiaco (☎ 08/ 9381 1358 business and after hours) will deliver across Perth.

Embassies/Consulates   The **United States Consulate** is on the 13th floor, 16 St. Georges Terrace (☎ **08/9231 9400**). The **Canadian Consulate** is on the 3rd floor, 267 St. Georges Terrace (☎ **08/9322 7930**). The **British Consulate-General** is at Level 26, Allendale Square, 77 St. Georges Terrace (☎ **08/9221 5400**).

Emergencies   Dial ☎ **000** for fire, ambulance, or police in an emergency. This is a free call, and no coins are needed from a public phone.

Hospitals   Royal Perth Hospital on Wellington Street in the city center has a public casualty ward (☎ 08/9224 2244).

Lost Property   For lost property on public transport, call Transperth on ☎ 08/ 9322 3502 for items left on buses and ferries and ☎ 08/9326 2660 for things left on trains. Check with the local police station closest to where the item was lost (call central police operations ☎ 13 14 44 to find out the nearest station's telephone number).

Luggage Storage/Lockers   The Perth Tourist Lounge, Level 2, Carillon Arcade, 680 Hay St. Mall (☎ 08/9481 8303) rents lockers and stores baggage. There are baggage lockers at the international and domestic terminals at the airport.

Police   Dial ☎ **000** in an emergency. City Police Station, 60 Beaufort St. (☎ 08/ 9223 3305), and Fremantle Police Station, 45 Henderson St. (☎ 08/ 9430 5244), are open 24 hours. For general police inquiries call ☎ 13 14 44.

Post Office   The General Post Office on Forrest Place (☎ 13 18 18) is open Monday through Friday from 8am to 5:30pm, Saturday from 9am to 12:30pm, and Sunday from noon to 4pm. Some newsagents sell stamps.

Safety   Steer clear of the back streets of Northbridge at night, even if you are not alone, as groups of teenage boys like to pick fights around here.

Time Zone   Western Australian time is GMT + 8 hours, and has no daylight saving. This means it is normally 2 hours behind Sydney and Melbourne, 3 in daylight saving time (from Oct to March). Call ☎ 1194 for the exact time (this is charged as a local call).

Weather   Call ☎ 1196 for the cost of a local call.

ACCOMMODATIONS YOU CAN AFFORD

Perth has plenty of inexpensive accommodations right in the city center. Rates can be a good deal lower than those quoted below whenever business is slow throughout the year, so don't be afraid to ask for the lowest rate going. While accommodations near the beaches are often at a premium during school vacations and on weekends, city hotels that rely on business travelers often need all the business they can get at these times. That can mean great special rates on weekends.

IN THE CITY CENTER

City Waters Lodge. 118 Terrace Rd. (between Victoria Ave. and Hill St.), Perth, WA 6000. ☎ **1800/999 030** in Australia, or 08/9325 1566. Fax 08/9221 2794. www.citywaters. com.au. E-mail: perth@citywaters.com.au. 72 units. A/C TV TEL. A$73 (U.S.$51.10) single; A$78 (U.S.$54.60) double; A$83 (U.S.$58.10) triple or family apt. to sleep 4; A$98 (U.S.$68.60) 2-bedroom apt. to sleep 5. BC, JCB, MC, V. Free parking. Blue and Weekend CAT Stop 19 "Barrack Square." Airport shuttle.

Try to get one of the apartments on the end of this older-style three-story block down by the river, as they have lovely views. The apartments' fixtures are old, especially in the kitchen and bathroom, but you get plenty of living space, daily maid servicing, and the same brand of mattresses used by the city's top five-star hotels. By the time you get here the interiors will have been nicely spruced up with new paint, carpets, and soft furnishings. Owners Hazel and Brian are about to put in a landscaped barbecue area. There is a guest Laundromat, and a deli next door. As there is no elevator, Brian helps you with your luggage. City buses run along St. Georges Terrace a block away, and you're a 5-block walk from Hay Street Mall.

Hotel Ibis Perth. 334 Murray St. (near Queen St.), Perth, WA 6000. ☎ **1800/64 2244** in Australia, 1-800/221-4542 in the U.S. and Canada, 0181/283 4500 in the U.K., 0800/44 4422 in New Zealand, or 08/9322 2844. Fax 08/9321 6314. www.hotelweb.fr. 172 units (all with shower only). A/C MINIBAR TV TEL. A$124 (U.S.$86.80) double; A$184 (U.S.$128.80) family room or suite. Additional person A$25 (U.S.$17.50) extra. Children 12 and under free in parents' room if they use existing bedding. Ask about weekend packages. AE, BC, DC, JCB, MC, V. Discounted self-parking A$7 (U.S.$4.90) at nearby Queen Street Carpark. Bus: Red and Weekend CAT Stop 28 "King St." Airport shuttle.

Ibis is one of those reputable chain brands offering the "four-star facilities at a three-star price." Vacationers may find the modern, neat, and comfortable rooms a bit on the small side, but they are ideal for business travelers. Family rooms have a separate bedroom for Mum and Dad. Hair dryers and iron and boards are in your room. You get lots of services and facilities for the price, including 24-hour reception and room service, two bars, safety deposit boxes, dry cleaning service, a tour desk, and discounted access to a nearby health club. There is a formal grill but most guests join Perth locals in the convivial Valentine's streetfront bistro and bar. You're right in the heart of town here, with shops, cinemas, and Murray Street Mall just a block or 2 away.

✪ **Miss Maud's Swedish Hotel.** 97 Murray St. (at Pier St.), Perth, WA 6000. ☎ **1800/ 998 022** in Australia, or 08/9325 3900. Fax 08/9221 3225. www.missmaud.com.au. 51 units. A/C MINIBAR TV TEL. A$99–$119 (U.S.$69.30–$83.30) single; $116–$136 (U.S.$81.20– $95.20) double. Additional person A$10 (U.S.$7) extra. All rates include full smorgasbord breakfast. AE, BC, DC, JCB, MC, V. Discounted parking A$7.50 (U.S.$5.25) at the Kings Hotel parking lot 1 block away on Hay sts. between Pier and Irwin sts. Bus: Red CAT Stop 1 "Pier St."; Blue and Weekend CAT Stop 5 "Murray St. Mall East." Airport shuttle.

Never mind that the bedspread clashes with the carpet and the paint's peeling off the door. That disregard for fashionable appearances is what makes this adorable hotel just like staying at grandma's. My cute and cozy Nordic room featured pine pelmets and a mural of a Swedish autumn forest covering one wall. Larger Scandinavian rooms have a sitting area. Rooms 105, 205, 133, and 233 have balconies overlooking the street. There's limited room service, laundry and dry cleaning service, hair dryers in the bathroom, a laundromat, safe deposit boxes, a private sundeck tucked away as a little surprise up among the rooftops, and a guest TV lounge. The real Miss Maud, Maud Edmiston wants guests to feel they are in a European family hotel, and she certainly succeeds. A fabulous full buffet breakfast is included at Miss Maud's Swedish Restaurant downstairs (see "Great Deals on Dining," below).

✪ **River View on Mount Street.** 42 Mount St., Perth, WA 6000. ☎ **08/9321 8963.** Fax 08/9322 5956. 48 units (all with shower only). A/C TV TEL. A$75–$85 (U.S.$52.50–$59.50) apt (sleeps three). AE, BC, DC, MC, V. Free parking. Bus: Red CAT Stop 18 "QVI" (located over the freeway footbridge accessed from the corner of St. Georges Terrace and Milligan St.). Airport shuttle.

Situated in a quiet leafy street of apartments just a walk from the center of town and Kings Park, these roomy studio apartments in an older-style redbrick block should all be refurbished by the time you arrive, with trendy new kitchens (no dishwasher), attractive contemporary-style bathrooms, air-conditioning, and fresh carpets, curtains, and fittings. Some have views of the river a few blocks away. Every room has a fax outlet and data jack for laptops. Servicing is done weekly. The helpful on-site managers run a tour desk and provide a dry cleaning and laundry service. There's also a guest laundromat, and the excellent Mount Street Café and Food Store downstairs (see "Great Deals on Dining," below) sells prepared curries and deli items. An elevator is planned, but until then be prepared to hike the stairs if you stay on the third floor.

Sullivans Hotel. 166 Mounts Bay Rd., Perth, WA 6000. ☎ **1800/999 294** in Australia, or 08/9321 8022. Fax 08/9481 6762. www.sullivans.com.au. E-mail: perth@sullivans.com.au. 70 units (all with shower only). A/C TV TEL. A$98–$120 (U.S.$68.60–$84) double; A$175 (U.S.$122.50) 2-bedroom apt. No charge for up to 4 people in a room. Weekly rates available. AE, BC, DC, MC, V. Free parking. Bus: 201 and all 7 series buses stop outside hotel (within Free Transit Zone). Airport shuttle.

This four-story family-owned hotel about 1.5 kilometers (1 mile) from the center of town is popular with Europeans and South Africans for its small-scale private ambience. Despite being on the main road into the city, none of its accommodations seem to be noisy. The rooms are furnished with simple laminate fittings, not glamorous but clean, large, and comfortable. Deluxe rooms are a bit larger still, and come with balconies and a safe. Bathrooms have hair dryers; irons are in the Laundromat. Out back is a private swimming pool, a sundeck, and a barbecue area nestled against a grassy hill. Room service operates from 10am to 10pm, and the bar sends drinks up at no extra charge. Most meals in the conservatory-style restaurant are less than A$15 (U.S.$10.50).

The Terrace. 195 Adelaide Terrace, Perth, WA 6000. ☎ **1800/098 863** in Australia, or 08/9492 7777. Fax 08/9221 1956. www.terracehotel.com.au. E-mail: terrace@omen.net.au. 182 units (some with shower only). A/C TV TEL. A$110 (U.S.$77) single; A$139 (U.S.$97.30) double; A$187–$195 (U.S.$130.90–$136.50) family room or 1- or 2-bedroom apt. Additional person A$20 (U.S.$14) extra. Children 12 and under free of charge. Ask about bed & breakfast packages and low-season specials. AE, BC, DC, MC, V. Free parking. Bus: Red CAT Stop No. 9 "Carlton." Airport shuttle.

Don't be put off by the "rack" rates listed above, for this well-kept city hotel often has better deals going. There's a variety of room types here, and all are a good size and very clean and neat. Most have kitchens or kitchenettes. The accommodations on the third and fourth floors have been refurbished, and rooms on the fifth to seventh (top) floors have balconies, some with views of the Swan River. Amenities include dry cleaning service, fax and photocopying, and a late-departures shower room. Front desk loans hair dryers if your room does not have one; irons and boards are in the laundry. The Terrace is 5 blocks from Murray Street Mall and the Perth train station, and 2 blocks from the jogging track and bike path along the river. The hotel is a member of the Flag chain.

Super-Cheap Sleeps

YMCA Jewell House. 180 Goderich St., Perth, WA 6000. ☎ **1800/998 212** in Australia, or 08/9325 8488. Fax 08/9221 4694. 207 units, none with bathroom. A$32–$36 (U.S.$22.40–$25.20) single; A$38–$42 (U.S.$26.60–$29.40) double; A$48 (U.S.$33.60) triple; A$58 (U.S.$40.60) family room. Weekly rates available. AE, BC, DC, JCB, MC, V. Free off-street parking for limited number of cars. Bus: Red CAT Stop 4 "Bennett St." Airport shuttle.

You may not like the dingy carpets and pre-loved furniture here, but you will love the price and the views. The river panorama from the south rooms in this 11-story one-time nurses' quarters must be the envy of many smarter city hotels. Bathrooms are communal but clean, and actually have a tub as well as showers. Some rooms just contain beds, but heck, splash out the extra two to four bucks on a deluxe room with a TV, minifridge, self-serve tea and coffee, a fan (important in summer), and daily housemaid service, with linen and towels supplied. BYO hair dryer. There is 24-hour reception, a laundry, dry cleaning service, public telephones, currency-exchange service, a tour desk, several TV lounges, and a helpful staff. The dining room serves hearty favorites like roast beef for A$7.50 (U.S.$5.25). The Perth Mint is a block away, and Hay Street Mall is a 5-block stroll in the other direction.

Worth a Splurge

✪ **The Melbourne.** Corner of Hay and Milligan sts., Perth, WA 6000. ☎ **1800/685 671** in Australia, or 08/9320 3333. Fax 08/9320 3344. 35 units (all with shower only). A/C MINIBAR TV TEL. A$170 (U.S.$119) double; A$200 (U.S.$140) suite. Additional person A$25 (U.S.$17.50) extra. Children 6 and under free in parents' room if they use existing bedding. Ask about overnight, weekend, and theater packages. AE, BC, DC, MC, V. Valet parking A$8 (U.S.$5.60); no self-parking. Bus: Red CAT Stop 18 "QVI." Airport shuttle.

It's a bit odd to find a New Orleans–style decor in a gold rush–era Aussie pub built in 1897, but it works here. A thorough 1997 renovation restored this long-derelict hotel in Perth's posh West End into the gracious four-star establishment it is today. Original trappings in the public areas include pressed metal ceilings, floral carpets, and a polished timber staircase. Guest rooms drop the Southern splendor in favor of the "business traveler" look, but they nod to the plantation style in the wooden blinds and brass-trimmed fans. Rooms have hair dryers, irons, and boards. First floor outside rooms open onto the verandah; second floor rooms lack a verandah but have lovely high ceilings. The clubby Café at the Melbourne is open all day for meals and drinks, while the exquisitely decorated Louisiana's steak and seafood grill is open for lunch during the week. The street-front bar, ornately restored with paneled walls, etched glass windows, and black-and-white photos of Mississippi steamers, is a happening place to be on Friday nights.

ON THE BEACH

West Beach Lagoon. 251 West Coast Hwy., Scarborough, WA 6109. ☎ **1800/999 339** in Australia, or 08/9341 6122. Fax 08/9341 5944. 68 units (some with shower only, some with Jacuzzi and shower). A/C TV TEL. A$100–$135 (U.S.$70–$94.50) apt. sleeping up to 4. Additional person A$10 (U.S.$7) extra. Free crib. Ask about off-season specials. AE, BC, DC, MC, V. Free parking. Bus: 400. Airport transfers by arrangement (not 24 hours) A$9–$12 (U.S.$6.30–$8.40) adults, A$4.50–$6 (U.S.$3.15–$4.20) children, and A$22–$24 (U.S.$15.40–$16.80) families.

You don't get sea views from this rather old low-rise Flag apartment complex set back 1 block from the beach, but the sand and surf are just a minute away. The one- and two-bedroom apartments are a little dated but are big enough for a family, with full kitchens (no dishwasher), combined bathroom and laundry, VCRs, and decent mattresses. Ask for a hair dryer, iron, and board when you arrive. The rooms center around a nice private shady pool and sundeck, with a barbecue and dining tables under thatched shelters scattered about. A beauty salon, a tour desk, and two restaurants, as well as a Jacuzzi and sauna, are also on site.

IN FREMANTLE

There's a perpetual holiday atmosphere in this picturesque port city. Although you are 19 kilometers (11½ miles) from Perth's city center, public transport connections are good, so you could happily explore all of Perth from this pleasant base, although most top attractions are here in Freo. There are good restaurants and a happening nightlife, too.

✪ **Danum House.** 6 Fothergill St. (at Bellevue Terrace, behind Fremantle Prison), Fremantle, WA 6160. ☎ **08/9336 3735.** Fax 08/9335 3414. Danum@nettrek.com.au. 2 units (both with shower only). A$95–$105 (U.S.$66.50–$73.50) single; A$100–$110 (U.S.$70–$77) double. Minimum 2-night stay. Rates include full breakfast. BC, MC, V. No off-street parking. Train: Fremantle. Fremantle airport shuttle. Children not permitted.

Kind and cheerful hostess Christine Sherwin has created a truly welcoming haven in her beautifully decorated Federation (ca. 1909) home within walking distance of town. The front room is done up in grand, rich colors; it even has its own Victorian full-length sash window opening onto a patio in a tropical cottage garden. The other very large room has an ornate mantle, floral wallpaper, long drapes, and that most colonial of furnishings, a daybed, as well as a real bed for sleeping. Both rooms sport antique furniture, ornate ceilings roses, fireplaces, very high ceilings, and ceiling fans. Even the bathrooms share the colonial decor. You can borrow a hair dryer from Christine and use her laundry. She serves a hearty breakfast in the dining room however early you like, and you can wind down after a hard day's sightseeing in the guests' comfy TV/CD/reading room over complimentary tea and coffee. Help yourself to the complimentary sherry and chocolates on the sideboard. No smoking.

Fremantle Colonial Accommodation. 215 High St., Fremantle, WA 6160. ☎ **08/ 9430 6568**. Fax 08/9430 6405. 6 units in guest house, 2 with bathroom (shower only). 3 cottages, all with bathroom (1 with shower only). TV. Guest house A$70–$90 (U.S.$49–$63) single; A$75–$100 (U.S.$52.50–$70) double. Additional person A$10–$15 (U.S.$7–$10.50) extra. Rates in guest house include continental breakfast. Cottages A$130 (U.S.$91) double. Additional person A$20 (U.S.$14) extra (maximum total A$170/U.S.$119 for 5 people). BC, MC, V. Free parking. Train: Fremantle. Fremantle airport shuttle.

A stroll in any direction from this historical terrace house on Freo's main street brings you to a museum, a harbor, shops, or other attractions. All the rooms are prettily decorated in colonial style—one has a blue-and-yellow liberty-print quilt and an ornate plaster ceiling rose, another has lace curtains and a fireplace. The very clean bathrooms are tiled in dark green or maroon and white. All rooms are air-conditioned. They vary in size but all have a table stocked with cereals, tea and coffee, a kettle, a toaster, and a minirefrigerator. Your hostess, Val Wieland, delivers juice, milk, yogurt, fruit, and bread for toasting to your room by 6pm the night before, so you eat when you like. Every room is supplied with bathrobes. This is more a guest house where people come and go, than a personal B&B where you get to know your host. The in-room dining tables are quite small, as are the TVs, so this place is more for folks who just want somewhere to lay their heads at night, rather than a comfortable establishment in which to hang around for half the day.

A better value, in my book, are Val's three limestone cottages. Perched on a grassy hill overlooking the town, 1 block behind the guest house, They were built in 1857 and the 1880s as prison guards' and prison nurses' quarters. Val has restored the interiors to their original handsome colors. Each has two pretty bedrooms with patchwork quilts, complimentary toiletries, fireplaces, antique furniture, and rag dolls or teddy bears in the corner. Each also has a large eat-in kitchen with a modern stove alongside the original wood-fired one, a sunroom, laundry facilities, a cute wooden porch out front, and a lovely stone courtyard out back with outdoor dining furniture. They have fans, and may be air-conditioned by the time you stay. One is fitted for travelers with disabilities.

GREAT DEALS ON DINING

Perth's restaurant scene bubbles over with terrific ethnic places that are kind to your wallet and a treat for your tastebuds. If you can't find the kind of cuisine you want in Northbridge, it probably doesn't exist, for this restaurant Mecca has Thai, Greek, Vietnamese, Malaysian, Italian, Chinese, and just about every other kind of food you can think of. Don't forget that going BYO (Bring Your Own wine or beer) lessens the pain in your wallet. Some restaurants charge corkage fees on BYO wine, usually A$1 or $2 (U.S.70¢ or $1.40) per person, but sometimes as much as A$4 (U.S.$2.80) per person.

For an inexpensive pasta, a Turkish bread sandwich, or excellent coffee and cake anytime, the ✪ **DOME** chain of cafes can't be beat. You will find them at Trinity Arcade off Hay Street Mall (☎ **08/9226 0210**); on the corner of Lake and James streets, Northbridge (☎ **08/9328 8094**); 13 South Terrace, Fremantle (☎ **08/9336 3040**); 19 Napoleon St., Cottesloe (☎ **08/9383 1071**); 26 Rokeby Rd., Subiaco (☎ **08/ 9381 5664**); and on Rottnest Island (☎ **08/9292 5026**).

IN THE CITY CENTER

Fast Eddy's Café. 454 Murray St. (at Milligan St.). ☎ **08/9321 2552**. Reservations recommended Fri and Sat night. Main courses A$2.90–$16.75 (U.S.$2.05–$11.75); average A$10 (U.S.$7). BC, MC, V. Daily 24 hours. Bus: Red CAT Stop 27 "Milligan St."; Weekend CAT Stop 2 "Entertainment Centre." FAST FOOD.

Steaks, burgers, sandwiches, and soup are served up 24 hours a day at this popular local chain decked out with 1930's soap powder posters and Coca-Cola advertisements. One side is table service; the same food will cost you about a third of the price at the Victorian-era-meets-1950s diner on the other side, which boasts marble counters and iron stools. The food ain't fancy, but neither is the price. A$7.85 (U.S.$5.50) will get you a Fast Eddyburger (you pay only A$3.35/U.S.$2.35 in the diner), A$9.65 (U.S.$6.75) buys lasagne, and spare ribs marinated and charcoal grilled will set you back A$13.95 (U.S.$9.75). For dessert try the pancakes, fudge sundaes, or hot apple pie, and for breakfast choose from cornflakes, eggs Benedict, or the full fry-up.

Great Take-Out

It's a take-out joint, not a restaurant, but you will find the most scrumptious gourmet dishes in Perth at ✪ **Lamont's Wine & Food, 123 St. Georges Terrace** (☎ **08/9321 9907**). Grab some veal ravioli with goat's cheese, roast capsicum, and eggplant; or chicken with chermoula, couscous, pumpkin, and parsley, and find a shady tree to eat under. Main courses cost A$7 to $13 (U.S.$4.90 to $9.10), while sandwiches costs between A$5 to $6.50 (U.S.$3.50 to $4.55). Desserts, such as macadamia tarts, chocolate truffle cake, and blueberry trifle, are all under A$5 (U.S.$3.50). They also sell deli items and wine.

44 King Street. 44 King St. ☎ **08/9321 4476.** Reservations not accepted. Main courses A$3–$11.50 (U.S.$2.10–$8.05) breakfast, A$7.50–$23.50 (U.S.$5.25–$16.45) lunch and dinner. AE, BC, DC, MC, V. Daily 7am–late; Sun brunch 7am–4pm. Bus: Red and Weekend CAT Stop 28 "King Street"; Blue CAT Stop 1 "Cloisters." MOD OZ.

Trendy socialites and corporate types may come here to see and be seen, but there's no doubt they stay for the food. The interior is a mix of industrial design and European cafe style, with dark timber tables, exposed air ducts, and large windows opening to the street. This place is renowned for a sophisticated grazing menu at good prices. Zucchini blossom and lemon risotto is typical for lunch or dinner; toasted macadamia nut muesli with cardamom poached pear is on the breakfast menu. Not only does the menu helpfully suggest a wine for each dish (many of them boutique or hard-to-get labels), it also offers taster-size glasses for around A$3 to $6 (U.S.$2.10 to $4.20). Lots of people drop in just for coffee and the famous cakes. They also do take-out.

✪ **Mount Street Café and Food Store.** Under the River View apts, 42 Mount St. ☎ **08/9485 1411.** Reservations recommended at lunch and dinner. Main courses A$5.50–$24.50 (U.S.$3.85–$17.15); many meals under A$10 (U.S.$7) at breakfast and lunch. BC, MC, V. Sun–Tues 7:30am–5pm; Wed–Sat 7:30am–9pm. Bus: Red CAT Stop 18 "QVI" (located over freeway footbridge accessed from corner of St. Georges Terrace and Milligan St.). MOD OZ.

Chef Toby Uhlrich was to be executive chef at the Hilton before he decided to make the move to this small, charming al fresco cafe on the edge of the central business district. Although dinner main courses are all over A$20 (U.S.$14), lunch is cheap— lemon pepper chicken breast with bacon, salad, and mayo on dark rye with julienne vegetables is just A$9 (U.S.$6.30). Other gourmet sandwiches are even cheaper. For breakfast, the eggs Benedict come in huge portions, elegantly presented on dark rye with the freshest asparagus you have ever tasted. The surrounds are just as uplifting as the food: a shaded stone terrace with contemporary timber tables and magazine stands. Drop by any time for cakes, muffins, and good coffee, but be prepared to fight the regulars for a table. BYO.

A Swedish Smorgasbord

Miss Maud's Swedish Restaurant. 97 Murray St. at Pier St. (under Miss Maud Swedish Hotel). ☎ **08/9325 3900.** Reservations recommended. Smorgasbord breakfast A$14.50 (U.S.$10.15) Mon–Sat, A$15.50 (U.S.$10.85) Sun; lunch A$21.50 (U.S.$15.05); dinner A$26.95 (U.S.$18.85) Sun–Thurs, A$29.95 (U.S.$20.95) Fri–Sat. À la carte main courses, sandwiches, and light meals A$3.95–$19.50 (U.S.$2.75–$13.65). AE, BC, DC, MC, V. Open all day for coffee & cake. Meals: Mon–Sat 6:45am–10am, noon–2:30pm, and 5:30–10pm (Fri and Sat to 11pm); Sun 6:45–10:30am, noon–3pm, and 5:30–10pm. INTERNATIONAL.

"Good food and plenty of it" is the tack here, and the constant crowds packing the place prove the formula works, even if the food is not all that sophisticated. There is an extensive à la carte menu, but everyone bypasses that and goes straight for the smorgasbord. At breakfast, that means 50 dishes like fresh-cooked pancakes or pikelets (a smaller, sweeter pancake), fresh fruit and melons, and the usual breakfast suspects. At lunch and dinner you can tuck into 2 kinds of soup, 10 salads, a big range of seafood, cold meats, 3 roasts, hot vegetables, pasta, cheeses, half a dozen tortes, mousse, fruit, and ice cream—65 dishes in all. Miss Maud (Edmiston) runs the restaurant along the same friendly lines as her hotel upstairs (see "Accommodations You Can Afford," above). Service is fast and polite. Eat dinner and leave by 7:15pm Monday to Saturday and you get a A$5 (U.S.$3.50) discount.

Worth a Splurge

✪ **Fraser's.** Fraser Ave. (next to the Visitor Information Centre), Kings Park. ☎ **08/9481 7100.** Reservations essential. Main courses A$19–$29 (U.S.$13.30–$20.30). AE, BC, DC, MC, V. Mon–Fri 7–10:30am, Sat–Sun 7:30–11am; daily for lunch from noon on, dinner from 6pm–late. Closed Good Friday. Bus: 33 westbound from St. Georges Terrace. MOD OZ/SEAFOOD.

Not every restaurant could turn out food to match the dazzling views this restaurant enjoys over the city and Swan River, but this one does. Fraser's superb way with seafood (and duck, chicken, beef, and kangaroo) has made it a finalist in a national "restaurant of the year" award. Don't skip eating here just because you don't care for seafood—the spiced beef chunks with eggplant *pahie* (curry) and lentil dahl, accompanied by chutney and yogurt salsa, is possibly the most heavenly meal on earth. To make the most of the view, dine outside on the terrace under the peppermint tree.

IN NORTHBRIDGE

Hung Long Coffee & Noodle House. 344 William St. ☎ **08/9227 9541.** Main courses A$5.50–$7.50 (U.S.$3.85–$5.25). AE, BC, MC, V. Thurs–Tues 10am–3pm, 5–10:30pm. Train: Perth. Bus: Blue and Weekend CAT Stop 10 "Aberdeen Street." VIETNAMESE.

You wouldn't know to walk a couple of extra blocks up William Street to this ultra-clean, ultra-humble diner unless locals, or *Frommer's*, whispered in your ear. The place consists of laminate tables in a bare room, but who cares when the ingredients are fresh, the service friendly, and the food cheap. The most expensive thing on the long menu is "Vietnamese beef stew egg noodle soup cooked slowly with Chinese herbs, cinnamon, lemon grass, ginger, and tomato and served with French bread." How's that for A$7.50 (U.S.$5.25)? BYO.

Manee Thai. 19 Lake St. ☎ **08/9228 1991.** Reservations recommended Fri and Sat night. Main courses A$11.80–$15.50 (U.S.$8.25–$10.85) ; buffet A$19.95 (U.S.$13.95). AE, BC, DC, MC, V. Tues–Sun 6:30–10:30pm. Train: Perth. Bus: Blue and Weekend CAT Stop 14 "James Street." THAI.

Gold-framed mirrors, rosewood chairs, and a hushed ambience make this a good choice for a not-too-expensive night out. This is upscale, authentic Thai, focused almost entirely on chicken, duck, and fish. Unusually for a Thai menu, there is little for vegetarians. I couldn't complain about the tasty *toong tong,* wrapped parcels of pork with chili dipping sauce, nor about the hearty chicken mussaman curry. If you want to try a little of everything, always fun with Thai food, opt for the buffet. Service is

Super-Cheap Eats in Northbridge

God bless the Hare Krishnas for their wonderfully cheap restaurants dispensing delicious vegetarian nourishment. Their **"Food for Life"** restaurant at 200 William St., Northbridge (☎ **08/9227 1684**) serves an all-you-can-eat buffet for just A$5 (U.S.$3.50) (A$4/U.S.$2.80 for seniors and students) Monday to Friday from noon to 2:30pm.

attentive. The wine list prices are OK, but beware the BYO corkage fee of A$4 (U.S.$2.80) per person! Licensed and BYO.

Viet Hoa. 349 William St. ☎ **08/9328 2127.** Reservations recommended on Fri and Sat night. Most main courses A$5–$14 (U.S.$3.50–$9.80). AE, BC, MC, V. Daily 10am–10pm. Train: Perth. Bus: Blue and Weekend CAT Stop 10 "Aberdeen Street." VIETNAMESE.

With its tablecloths, fake plants, and airy dimensions, the Viet Hoa is a little more upscale than the Hung Long Coffee & Noodle House (see above) across the road, but the prices are just a few dollars higher. The cold Vietnamese spring rolls remind you what fresh food is supposed to taste like. The stir-fries, satays, and sweet-and-sour dishes are huge, so don't over-order! BYO.

Vultures. Francis St. at William St., Northbridge. (☎ **08/9227 9087**). Reservations recommended for dinner Fri–Sat. Main courses A$9.50–$24.50 (U.S.$6.65–$17.15); dine-in or take-out sandwiches at lunch A$4.50–$6.50 (U.S.$3.15–$4.55). AE, BC, DC, MC, V. Daily 11am–1am, or later if there is demand; Fri–Sat until 4am. Open 365 days a year. Bus: Blue and Weekend CAT Stop 9 "TAFE." MOD OZ.

Come in, sit down, relax—you can even plop yourself right down in the Balinese four-poster beds that have cushions to sit on and a low coffee table inside. The groovy, relaxed ambience here attracts all types, from couples doing dinner à deux in the streetside courtyard, to cool teenage nightclubbers hanging out after a big night. The food is smart and simple—sashimi, roast chicken nachos, a divine fresh vegetable filo infused with saffron, Moreton Bay bugs (a sought-after crustacean) with garlic-lime butter and salted chili cabbage, and beef fillet with zucchini and red pepper mousse on a rich beef jus. It's nice to see a good range of wines by the glass.

ON THE BEACH

The Blue Duck. 151 Marine Parade, North Cottesloe. ☎ **08/9385 2499.** Reservations recommended. Main courses A$8.50–$24.50 (U.S.$5.95–$17.15). Kids' menu A$6.50 (U.S.$4.55). AE, BC, DC, MC, V. Mon–Sat 6am–midnight; Sun 6am–10:30pm (kitchen closes 8:30pm). Train: Grant Street, then a walk of approx. 6 blks. Bus: 70, 71, 72, 73. MOD OZ.

For ocean views it's hard to beat this casual cafe-cum-restaurant perched right over the sand. Although the interior doesn't have quite the panoramic position as the outside balcony, it has a nice seaside ambience and is just as packed with locals as the balcony. The food is tasty and spicy with Asian touches. Try the crispy teriyaki chicken breast with pickled ginger and coriander, or the quesadilla with prawns, mozzarella, and English spinach. There are plenty of lighter, less expensive dishes, such as Thai-spiced fettucine. Licensed and BYO.

✪ **North Cott Express Café.** 149 Marine Parade, North Cottesloe. ☎ **08/9385 0338.** Reservations recommended on weekends. Main courses A$5–$12.50 (U.S.$3.50–$8.75). No credit cards. Daily 6:30am–5pm. Train: Grant Street, then a walk of approx. 6 blks. Bus: 70, 71, 72, 73. CAFE FARE.

It's just a humble beach shack with plastic furniture, but this laid-back cafe next to the trendier Blue Duck has the same sea views (from the front three tables, anyhow; try to snare one) and the same breezy ambience. It also has terrific food. Go for the toasted flatbreads with fillings like tandoori chicken, roasted pumpkin, cucumber, and chutney for A$8 (U.S.$5.60). Burgers, Thai salads, and pastas are on the lunch menu. In the morning, grab a newspaper from the stand and settle in for a lazy breakfast. BYO.

✪ **Indiana Tea House.** 99 Marine Parade (on Cottesloe Beach opposite Forrest St.), Cottesloe. ☎ **08/9385 5005.** Reservations recommended. Grazing menu A$10–$27.50 (U.S.$7–$19.25). AE, BC, DC, MC, V. Daily 7am–late. Train: Cottesloe. Bus: 70, 71, 72, 73. MOD OZ.

You'll think you're Somerset Maugham at Raffles Hotel at this delightful turn-of-the-century bathhouse-turned-restaurant overlooking Cottesloe Beach. All the colonial Asian trappings—the bamboo birdcages, plaster lions, and palms—will make you want to head straight for the timber bar and order a Singapore Sling. Actually, this tasteful stucco building with bay windows and wooden floors is new—it just looks old. The Spice Islands-meets-Down Under food is up to date, though: a grazing menu of light to full-on dishes such as beef loin with Shahjira crust, garlic-scented potato, and shiraz-braised sweet onions. You don't have to go whole hog; just drop by for mid-morning coffee over the newspapers if you like. Go in the daytime to make the most of those ocean views.

IN FREMANTLE
You can get casual dine-in or take-out seafood meals for about A$6 (U.S.$4.20) at **Kailis' Fish Market Café** (☎ 08/9335 7755) on Fishing Boat Harbour off Mews Road. There's a Fremantle branch of **Fast Eddy's** (see above) at 13 Essex St. (☎ 08/9336 1671) and another **Miss Maud's Swedish Restaurant** (see above) at 33 South Terrace (☎ 08/9336 1599).

Gino's Pizzeria and Ristorante. 95 Market St. (behind Gino's Trattoria & Café on South Terrace). ☎ **08/9430 6126**. Reservations recommended on weekends; some tables always kept unreserved. Pizzas A$7.50–$14. (U.S.$5.25–$9.80). Main courses A$7.90–$15.50 (U.S.$5.55–$10.85). AE, BC, DC, JCB, MC, V. Daily 5pm–late, Fri–Sun from noon. Train: Fremantle. WOOD-FIRED PIZZA/ITALIAN.

All the traditional favorites get served up alongside the tastiest wood-fired pizzas in Perth at this big, friendly Italian restaurant. Servings are huge—one pizza is easily enough for two. The pizza base is high, airy, and crispy, and the toppings are innovative but not spoiled by too many ingredients. Traditional main courses, such as pasta and veal parmigiana, share the menu with trendier offerings, such as chargrilled swordfish in a balsamic vinaigrette. The decor is upbeat with terrazzo tables, a groovy concrete and timber floor, and a stainless steel bar. Licensed and BYO.

Roma. 9–13 High St. ☎ **08/9335 3664**. Reservations not accepted. Main courses A$6–$13 (U.S.$4.20–$9.10); oysters/crayfish A$16–$21 (U.S.$11.20–$14.70). No credit cards. Mon–Sat 12–2pm, 5–10pm; closed public holidays. Train: Fremantle. ITALIAN.

It may be sparsely furnished with laminate tables and tile floors, but this classic family-run Italian joint has been pulling in the crowds for years—since 1954, in fact. Ravioli and lasagna are A$10 (U.S.$7) or under, or you can upgrade to a mix-and-match menu of roast chicken, scaloppini, and filet mignon with spaghetti, salad, mushrooms, or asparagus. BYO.

EXPLORING PERTH
Art Gallery of Western Australia. Perth Cultural Centre, 47 James St. at Beaufort St., Northbridge. ☎ **08/9492 6600** administration, 08/9492 6622 recorded information line. Free admission, donation requested. Entry fee may apply to special exhibitions. Daily

Java Joints
Don't leave Freo (Freemantle) without a *short black* (espresso) or a *flat white* (coffee with milk) at the port's "cappuccino strip" on South Terrace. On weekends this street bursts at the seams with locals flocking to al fresco Italian-style cafes that serve good java and excellent foccacia, pasta, and pizza at piffling prices. DOME, Old Papa's, and Gino's Trattoria & Café are the ones to look for.

10am–5pm; from 1pm ANZAC Day. Closed Christmas and Good Friday. Train: Perth. Bus: Blue CAT Stop 8 "Museum" and Weekend CAT Stop 7 "Culture Centre."

This is the state's leading gallery. Most outstanding among its international and Australian paintings, prints, sculpture, craft, and drawings is the Aboriginal art collection, regarded as the finest in Australia.

Cohunu Koala Park. Off Mills Road E., Gosnells (or located in the suburb of Martin on some maps). ☎ **08/9390 6090.** Admission A$14 (U.S.$9.80) adults, A$12.60 (U.S.$8.80) seniors, A$6 (U.S.$4.20) children 3–14. Daily 10am–5pm; koala cuddling 10am–4:30pm. Closed Christmas. Train: Gosnells on Armadale Hwy., plus A$10 (U.S.$7) cab. By car: Take Riverside Dr. across Swan River onto Albany Hwy., follow for approx. 25km (15 miles) to Gosnells, turn left onto Tonkin Hwy. and right half a mile later onto Mills Rd. E. Cab from the city is approx. A$30 (U.S.$21).

Here's your chance to have your photo taken cuddling a koala (for A$15/U.S.$10.50). You can also feed 300 kangaroos and emus wandering in natural enclosures, see wombats asleep in their burrows in an underground observing tunnel, and walk through the aviary that houses Australian native birds. Wild water birds also collect on the ponds in this 16-hectare (40-acre) park. Allow 4 hours to see it all, including travel time.

Kings Park & Botanic Garden. Fraser Ave. off Kings Park Rd. ☎ **08/9480 3600.** Free admission. 24 hours, 365 days. The Visitor Information Centre on Fraser Ave. inside the park is open daily 9:30am–4pm (closed Christmas and Good Friday). Bus: 33 from St. Georges Terrace stops outside Visitor Centre; 102, 103, 104, 200, 202, 208, and 209 stop outside the gates.

This 400-hectare (988-acre) hilltop park of botanic gardens and uncultivated remnant bushland on the edge of the city center is Perth's pride and joy. This is where to come to inspect weird and wonderful Western Australian flora, get to know the solitude of the Australian bush (especially if you are not visiting much bushland elsewhere on your trip), and bike, hike, or drive an extensive network of roads and trails. Bikes can be rented at **Koala Bike Hire** (☎ **08/9321 3061**) behind the restaurant complex. Visiting the park's colorful display of wildflowers from August to October is a highlight of many Perth residents' calendars. An Aboriginal artist is always at work in the **Artists in Residence gallery** under the lookout on Fraser Avenue. There are barbecue and picnic facilities, several playgrounds, kiosks, tearooms, and the incomparable Fraser's (see "Great Deals on Dining," above). The park is not small, so it's best to pick up a map from the Visitor Information Centre before exploring. The **Perth Tram Co.** (☎ **08/9367 9404**) runs 1-hour tours of the park and neighboring University of Western Australia in replica 1899 wooden trams. Tours depart daily from outside the Visitor Information Centre on Fraser Avenue at 11am, 12:15pm, 1:15pm, and 2:15pm (and occasionally at 3:15pm on Sunday, subject to demand; check with the driver). Tickets cost A$10 (U.S.$7) for adults, A$8 (U.S.$5.60) for seniors, A$5 (U.S.$3.50) for children ages 4 to 14, and A$25 (U.S.$17.50) families.

Perth Institute of Contemporary Arts (PICA). 51 James St., Northbridge. ☎ **08/ 9227 9339.** Free admission; charges may apply to some performances. Tues–Sun 11am–8pm. Closed Christmas to mid-Jan, and Good Friday. Train: Perth. Bus: Blue and Weekend CAT Stop 15 "Alexander Library."

Picture Perfect

For the only photo of Perth you'll need, snap the view over the city and river from the War Memorial in Kings Park—it's superb day or night.

Cutting-edge experimental works in all kinds of media—including video, sculpture, photography, film, writing, performance art, and painting—can be found in what was once the Perth Boys' School.

Perth Mint. 310 Hay St. at Hill St., East Perth. ☎ **08/9421 7425.** Admission A$5 (U.S.$3.50) adults, A$4 (U.S.$2.80) seniors and students, A$3 (U.S.$2.10) children age 17 and under, A$15 (U.S.$10.50) families; free admission to the shop. Mon–Fri 9am–4pm, Sat–Sun 9am–1pm. Closed Christmas, New Year's Day, and Good Friday.

If you have always wanted to handle a A$200,000 (U.S.$140,000) gold bar, this is your chance. During the 1890s gold rush, a monthly escort brought gold from Kalgoorlie to this infant mint, to be made into coins for Great Britain, Australia, and other countries. Bullion is still traded here today, so if you stumble across a gold nugget on your travels through Western Australia, this is where to bring it. You can mint your own medallion, ogle a sizable collection of natural nuggets, and watch a gold-pour demonstration, which take place on the hour from 10am weekdays, and from 10am to noon weekends. The shop in the wonderful old former Bullion Receiving Room sells gold coins, nugget jewelry, and souvenirs, as well as Sydney 2000 Olympic Games commemorative gold coins, which are minted here. Allow an hour to tour the mint.

Perth Zoo. 20 Labouchere Rd., South Perth. ☎ **08/9474 3551** for recorded information, 08/9367 7988 administration. Admission A$10 (U.S.$7) adults, A$5 (U.S.$3.50) children 4–15, A$27.50 (U.S.$19.25) family of 4. Daily 9am–5pm. Ferry: Barrack St. Jetty to Mends St. Jetty, South Perth. Ask about ferry/zoo entry passes. Bus: 110 weekdays, 108 weekends and public holidays from City Bus Port.

This is a good place to see numbats, wombats, Tasmanian devils, dingoes, kangaroos, koalas, crocodiles, black swans, and just about every other kind of Aussie wildlife, in natural habitats. Notable exotic species include Nepalese red pandas, Rothschild's giraffes, Cambodian sun bears, and Sumatran tigers. All up, there are some 230 species. Feeding demonstrations and talks run throughout the day, and for kids, there's a zoo train and a carousel. Allow 4 or 5 hours here, including ferry travel.

Underwater World. Sorrento Quay at Hillarys Boat Harbour, 91 Southside Dr., Hillarys. ☎ **08/9447 7500.** Admission A$16 (U.S.$11.20) adults, A$8 (U.S.$5.60) children 3–14, A$12.50 (U.S.$8.75) seniors and students, A$40 (U.S.$28) family of 4, with additional child A$5 (U.S.$3.50) extra. Daily 9am–5pm. Closed Christmas. Train and bus: Take Joondalup train line to Warwick, transfer to bus no. 423. By car: take Mitchell Hwy. approx. 30km (18 miles) north, turn left into Hepburn Ave., turn left at the T junction of Hepburn Ave. and West Coast Dr., and follow signs.

You won't catch performing dolphins and seals à la Sea World, but there's plenty for the kids to see here, including a moving walkway through an underwater tunnel of sharks, rays, turtles, and all kinds of fish; a touch pool where kids can handle sea urchins, sea stars, and even small Port Jackson sharks; and lots of aquarium exhibits, including leafy sea dragons, sea mammals, and dangerous sea critters. Throughout the day you can watch sharks and three Indian Ocean bottle-nosed dolphins who live in a seminatural harbor pen being fed. Children age 10 and over (and grown-ups, too) can swim with the dolphins for A$75 (U.S.$52.50) per person on Saturday and Sunday. You must bring your own snorkeling gear and wet suit, though, and book weeks—if not months—in advance. If you're a certified diver with your own gear, you can take a 30-minute dip in the shark tank for A$65 (U.S.$45.50). If you are under age 18, you will need a letter of permission from your parents. Allow 4 to 5 hours, including travel time, to see everything.

⭐ **Western Australian Museum.** Francis St. at Beaufort St., Northbridge. ☎ **08/ 9427 2700.** Free admission (donation requested). Admission fee may apply to special exhibitions. Sun–Fri and public holidays 10:30am–5pm; Sat, Anzac Day, and Boxing Day 1–5pm. Closed Christmas and Good Friday. Train: Perth. Bus: Blue and Weekend CAT Stop 8 "Museum."

Kids will like the drawers full of insects and the genuine termite mound in the lobby, the mammal and blue whale skeletons, the butterfly gallery, and the bizarre megamouth shark preserved in a tank set in the ground in the courtyard. The main attraction for grown-ups is one of the best collections of Aboriginal artifacts in Australia. Stay 2 hours for a good smattering of everything, longer if you want to study the Aboriginal collection in detail.

HITTING THE BEACH

Perth shares Sydney's good luck in having beaches in the metropolitan area—19 of them, in fact, laid end to end along the 35-kilometer (21-mile) Sunset Coast from Cottesloe in the south to Quinns Rocks in the north. Crowds are rarely a problem; in fact, on weekdays you can get a whole beach to yourself. Mornings are best as a strong afternoon wind off the Indian Ocean, known as the "Fremantle Doctor," can be unpleasant, especially in summer. *Rips* (strong currents) are a hazard at most beaches, so never swim alone at an unpatrolled beach. On summer weekends and public holidays, most beaches are patrolled by volunteer surf lifesaving clubs, who assess where the rips are and mark a safe swimming area with red and yellow flags. You are expected to swim between these flags at all times.

A walk and cycle path runs alongside nine beaches from Sorrento Beach in the north to City Beach, and picks up again at Swanbourne Beach to Cottesloe Beach.

On weekends and public holidays, from the last Saturday in September to the last Sunday in April, and every day during summer school holidays, the Sunset Coaster bus no. 928 stops hourly at most beaches on its way from Fremantle to Hillarys. A quick way to connect to it is to take the train to Cottesloe and walk a few blocks west to the bus route on Marine Parade, or save the walk by taking the train to Fremantle, where you can pick up the bus right outside the train station. Alternatively, take the train to Glendalough station to connect with Sunset Coaster bus no. 929, which travels to Scarborough, Trigg, and other beaches on the way north to Hillarys. It operates the same days and months as no. 928. Surfboards and body boards of 2 meters (6½ ft.) or less can be carried on the bus and train, as long as the fins are covered.

These are four of the most popular beaches:

⭐ **COTTESLOE**   This pretty crescent, graced by the delightful Edwardian-style Indiana Tea House restaurant (see "Dining," above), is Perth's most fashionable beach. It has good, safe swimming, a small surf break, a kiosk, changing rooms, and plentiful parking. A couple of good cafes are nearby, including The Blue Duck and North Cott Café at North Cottesloe, a few blocks up the road (see "Dining"). The beach is patrolled on weekends in summer, and a beach ranger pops in periodically midweek. Train: Cottesloe. Bus: 70, 71, 72, 73.

SCARBOROUGH   Biggest of all the beaches, Scarborough's white sands stretch for miles from the base of the Rendezvous Observation City Hotel. Swimming is generally safe, and surfers are always guaranteed a wave, although inexperienced swimmers should take a rain check when the surf is rough. The busy shopping precinct across the road means there's always somewhere to buy snacks and drinks, or take a leisurely lunch. Lifeguards patrol daily in summer, and there are changing rooms and ample parking. Bus: 400.

SWANBOURNE   Perth's only nude beach is at Swanbourne North; people keep their swimmers on at Swanbourne Main. Swimming is safe at "Swannie," with few rips. Surfers tend to leave the beach alone until bigger swells arrive in winter. Lifeguards patrol on weekends, and the roaming beach inspector keeps an eye on swimmers midweek. There's a kiosk, ample parking, and changing rooms. Bus: 36.

TRIGG   Surfers like this beach best because of its consistent swells. There are changing rooms, a kiosk, and plenty of parking. Lifeguards patrol daily in summer; the beach inspector calls in periodically in winter. Bus: 400 to Scarborough, then a 10-minute walk north; also, Sunset Coasters 928 or 929 weekends, school vacations, and public holidays.

A DAY OUT IN FREMANTLE

The heritage port precinct of Fremantle, 19 kilometers (11½ miles) from downtown Perth on the mouth of the Swan River, is probably best known outside Australia as the site of the 1987 America's Cup challenge. Just before that event, the city fathers embarked on a major restoration of its gracious but rundown warehouses and derelict Victorian public buildings. The Cup may be gone, but today "Freo" is a bustling district of al fresco cafes, museums, galleries, pubs, markets, and shops in a masterfully preserved historical atmosphere. It's still a working port, so you will see lots of fishing boats unloading and gleaming yachts riding in and out of the harbor. In fact, the ambience is so authentic that locals make a beeline for the place every weekend, which results in a wonderful hubbub of buzzing shoppers, market-stall holders, java drinkers, yachties, tourists, and fishermen. A visit here is one of the nicest ways to spend a day in Perth. Allow a full day to take in even half the sights—and don't forget to knock back an ale or two on the verandahs of one of the gorgeous old pubs.

ESSENTIALS

GETTING THERE   Parking is plentiful on side streets, but driving is frustrating in the maze of one-way traffic. Most attractions are within walking distance, so take the train to Fremantle station and explore on foot.

A nice way to get to the port and see Perth's river suburbs at the same time is on a cruise. Of the several companies running cruises from Barrack Street Jetty, **Oceanic Cruises** (☎ **08/9325 1191** Perth, and 08/9430 5127 Fremantle) had the best prices when this book went to press: A$8 (U.S.$5.60) adults, A$5 (U.S.$3.50) children ages 6 to 14, one-way. It's cheaper to take the train back than return on the boat. The trip takes about 75 minutes and includes commentary.

GETTING AROUND   The best and easiest way to immerse yourself in the whole precinct is to explore on foot. Although I recommend tackling the town on your own, **Elaine Berry,** of the Maritime Museum (see below), offers a 90-minute walking tour for A$7.50 (U.S.$5.25) for adults and A$2 (U.S.$1.40) for school-age kids; call ☎ **08/9336 1906.** The **Fremantle Tram** (☎ **08/9339 8719,** or 018/094 361) departs hourly from Fremantle Town Hall from 10am to 5pm. There are various routes. Tickets cost A$8 to $10 (U.S.$5.60 to $7) adults, A$6 to $8 (U.S.$4.20 to $5.60) seniors, A$3 to $5 (U.S.$2.10 to $3.50) for children age 15 and under, and A$15 to $20 (U.S.$10.50 to $14) for families. Buy tickets onboard.

VISITOR INFORMATION   The **Fremantle Tourist Bureau** is located in Town Hall, Kings Square, William St. at Adelaide St., Fremantle, WA 6160 (☎ **08/9431 7878;** fax 08/9431 7755). It's open Monday through Saturday from 9am to 5pm and Sunday from 10:30am to 4:30pm. You may get more personal attention at the Fremantle Tourist Centre in Esplanade Park, opposite the Esplanade Hotel,

Marine Terrace at Essex Street (☎ **08/9339 8719;** fax 08/9339 3616), a private booking center that specializes in Fremantle tours and attractions; it's open daily from 9am to 4:30pm.

SEEING THE SIGHTS IN FREMANTLE

As soon as you arrive, wander down to the docks—either Victoria Quay, where sailing craft come and go, or Fishing Boat Harbour off Mews Road, where the fishing boats bring in their catches—to get a breath of salt air and a view of the sea. The tallest Tall Ship in Australia, the **STS** *Leeuwin II* (☎ **08/9430 4105**), is moored at B Shed on Victoria Quay and is open to the public (see "Outdoor Activities & Spectator Sports" for details on sailing excursions).

You will want to explore some of Freo's excellent museums and other attractions, described below, but take time to stroll the streets and admire the gracious 19th-century offices and warehouses, many now painted in rich, historically accurate colors.

Freo's best shopping is arts and crafts, from handblown glass to Aboriginal art to alpaca wool clothing. There are plenty of outlets all over town, but worth a look are the assorted art, craft, and souvenir stores on High Street, west of the mall; the A Shed and E Shed markets on Victoria Quay (open Friday to Sunday only); and Bannister Street CraftWorks, an arts co-operative (closed Monday).

The most popular watering holes are the **Sail & Anchor,** 64 South Terrace (☎ **08/9335 8433**), which brews its own Brass Monkey Stout; the **Norfolk,** 47 South Terrace at Norfolk St. (☎ **08/9335 5405**); and the beautifully restored front bar and garden courtyard at **Phillimore's** at His Majesty's Hotel on Phillimore Street at Mouat Street (☎ **08/9336 4681**), which often has live jazz and funk.

Fremantle Arts Centre. 1 Finnerty St. at Ord St. ☎ **08/9335 8244**. Free admission. Daily 10am–5pm. Closed Christmas and Good Friday.

This striking neo-Gothic 1860s building, built by convicts, houses one of Western Australia's best contemporary arts and crafts galleries with a constantly changing array of works. The shop sells some high-quality Western Australian crafts, a bookshop sells Australian literature and art books, and there is a leafy courtyard cafe.

Fremantle History Museum. 1 Finnerty St. at Ord St. (part of the Fremantle Arts Centre, see above). ☎ **08/9430 7966**. Free admission; donation requested. Sun–Fri 10:30am–4:30pm, Sat and public holidays 1–5pm. Closed Christmas, Boxing Day (Dec 26), and Good Friday.

Housed in a convict-built former lunatic asylum next to the Fremantle Arts Centre, this small but densely packed museum uses lots of old photographs and personal possessions to paint a realistic picture of what life was like for Fremantle's first settlers, the Aboriginal people they displaced, and later generations up to the present day.

Fremantle Prison. 1 The Terrace. ☎ **08/9430 7177**. Free admission to courtyard. Tours A$10 (U.S.$7) adults, A$4 (U.S.$2.80) children 6–15; candlelight tours Wed and Fri A$12 (U.S.$8.40) adults, A$6 (U.S.$4.20) children. Daily 10am–6pm (last tour at 5pm); Wed and Fri from 7:30pm. Closed Christmas and Good Friday.

Even jails sported attractive architecture back in the 1850s. This limestone jail, ironically built by convicts who no doubt ended up inside it, was a maximum-security prison until 1991. You can enter the courtyard and watch a video free of charge, but to see bushranger Joe Moondyne's cell, the gallows, and cell walls featuring some wonderful artwork by the prison inhabitants, you need to take the 75-minute tour, which runs regularly throughout the day. It is followed by a 45-minute tour of the women's cells. For the candlelight tours at 7:30pm Wednesday and Friday, you must book ahead.

Historic Boats Museum. B Shed, Victoria Quay. ☎ **08/9430 4680**. Admission by dona-tion. Mon–Fri 10am–3pm, Sat–Sun and public holidays 11am–4pm. Closed Christmas and Good Friday.

If you like messin' about in boats, you will like messin' about here. The historic boats on show here are mostly small, from the state's first pilot vessel to racing skiffs and fishing dinghies. The pattern of the winged keel that won Australia the 1983 America's Cup is on display, too. Serious boatheads can watch Australia's biggest collection of marine engines in operation on Thursday and Friday from 12:30 to 3pm and on week-ends from 1 to 4pm.

The Roundhouse. Arthur Head (entry over the railway line from High St.). ☎ **08/ 9336 1077**. Free admission; donation requested. Daily 9am–5pm. Closed Christmas and Good Friday.

A peep at this 12-sided jail, the state's oldest public building—built around 1830—takes only a minute. There are no displays or memorabilia, but it's worth a look for history's sake, and for the sea views on the other side. Whaling took place from the beach below the jail last century, and the time cannon just to its west, a replica of a gun salvaged from an 1878 wreck, is fired daily at 1pm, just as it used to be in the 1800s.

✪ **Western Australian Maritime Museum.** Cliff St. ☎ **08/9431 8444**. Free admission; donation requested. Daily 10:30am–5pm; Anzac Day and Boxing Day (Dec 26) 1–5pm. Free guided tours 11am and 2pm. Closed Christmas and Good Friday.

Fascinating archaeological displays of shipwrecks and treasure recovered off the treach-erous Western Australian coast make this museum well worth a visit. Displays date from the 1600s, when Dutch explorers became the first Europeans to encounter Australia.

WHALE-WATCHING & OTHER CRUISES

Golden Sun (☎ 08/9325 1616), **Boat Torque 2000** (☎ 08/9221 5844 Perth and 08/9430 5844 Fremantle), **Captain Cook Cruises** (☎ 08/9325 3341), and **Oceanic Cruises** (☎ 08/9325 1191 Perth and 08/9430 5127 Fremantle) run an assortment of half- and full-day cruises to historic homes up the Swan River, the vineyards of the Swan Valley, Rottnest Island, and other small islands. They also run sunset, luncheon, and dinner cruises on the Swan River. All cruises depart the Barrack Street Jetty. They can be pricey, from A$25 (U.S.$17.50) for a scenic afternoon cruise upriver, up to A$60 (U.S.$42) for a dinner cruise. One of the cheaper options is a 90-minute twi-light cruise offered by Captain Cook Cruises. It departs at 5:30pm from September to April and costs A$12 (U.S.$8.40) per person, adult or child.

From September through December, Perth's waters are alive with **southern right whales** and **humpback whales** returning from the north with their calves. Hump-backs are the most playful of whales and will often come right up to your boat. From Fremantle, **Boat Torque's** 2-hour whale-watching cruises cost A$20 (U.S.$14) for adults, A$14 (U.S.$9.80) for seniors and students, and A$9 (U.S.$6.30) for children ages 4 to 12. The boat departs Northport at Rous Head, and a courtesy coach will col-lect you from Fremantle train station 45 minutes before departure. Boat Torque also has cruises departing from Hillarys, but they are more expensive—A$37 (U.S.$25.90) for adults with a coach pickup from Perth, A$27 (U.S.$18.90) direct from Hillarys. **Oceanic Cruises** operates whale-watching trips in a 30.5-meter (100-ft.) sailing schooner from Fremantle. The trips costs A$25 (U.S.$17.50) for adults, $20 (U.S.$14) for seniors and students, and $12 (U.S.$8.40) for children ages 4 to 12. (Expect these prices to rise in a season or two.) The company also operates whale-watching cruises in an ocean-going catamaran for A$18 (U.S.$12.60) for adults,

A$8 (U.S.$5.60) for kids. The Rottnest Island ferry, *Sea Eagle III* (☎ **08/9335 6406**), does whale-watching trips Thursday through Monday between ferry runs. Cruises depart C Shed at Fremantle's Victoria Quay at 1pm and return at 3pm. Tickets are A$18 (U.S.$12.60) for adults, A$16 (U.S.$11.20) for students, and $9 (U.S.$6.30) for children ages 4 to 12. **Captain Cook Cruises** runs whale-watching cruises from Perth. Departure days and times vary from year to year with every cruise operator, so check ahead.

OUTDOOR ACTIVITIES & SPECTATOR SPORTS
OUTDOOR ACTIVITIES

The **Activity Booking Centre** at Kiosk 3, Old Perth Port, Barrack St. Jetty, Perth (☎ **08/9221 1828**), is a booking agent for a huge range of outdoor activities. If your favorite activity is not listed below, the Centre can probably organize it for you.

BIKING   Bike tracks stretching for miles along the Swan River, through Kings Park, around Fremantle, and all the way down the beaches make Perth Australia's most spectacular city for cyclists. There is a superb 9.5-kilometer (5¾-mile) track around Perth Water, the broad expanse of river in front of the central business district; it starts at the Swan River on Riverside Drive in the city and goes over the Causeway bridge, back along the other bank, and over the bridge at the Narrows, back to the city.

The Activity Booking Centre, mentioned above, and **Koala Bike Hire** near the Visitor Information Centre in Kings Park (☎ **08/9321 3061**) are two of the biggest bike-rental outfits. It is illegal to ride without a helmet in W.A., and your rental company will include a helmet free of charge. You can take your bike on ferries without paying extra. On trains, believe it or not, you need to buy your bike a one-zone adult fare, which is good all day. To travel on weekdays from 6 to 9am and 3 to 6pm, you are supposed to ring the Passenger Service Manager at the end of the line on which you are traveling—Fremantle (☎ 08/9335 0300), Armadale (☎ 08/9326 2367), Midland (☎ 08/9274 9728) or Joondalup (☎ 08/9326 2165)—to obtain a free 3-month permit over the telephone. Sounds like Aussie bureaucracy is alive and well.

CANOEING, KAYAKING & WHITE-WATER RAFTING   **Rivergods** (☎ **08/ 9259 0749**) runs canoeing, kayaking, and rafting adventures on the Swan and other rivers near Perth.

One of the best ecoitineraries in Perth is Rivergods' ✪ **1-day sea kayak trip to Seal and Penguin Islands** in the Shoalwater Islands Marine Park just south of Perth, where you snorkel with sea lions. You also paddle into limestone caves, and see penguins being fed on Penguin Island. On the return journey you tie your kayaks together, raise a kite and kayak-sail home! The cost for the day is A$95 (U.S.$66.50), including lunch and snorkel gear. Pickup from your hotel costs an extra A$10 (U.S.$7). This trip runs daily from October to June. In the rainier winter months, from June to October, the company also runs white-water rafting trips on the Grade 3 to 4 Murray River, south of Perth. A day trip with pickup from your hotel, wet suits, and lunch is A$130 (U.S.$91) per person.

FISHING   Dhufish, pink snapper, and cod are running in the ocean off Perth. **Mill's Charters,** opposite Underwater World at Hillary's Boat Harbour (☎ **08/9246 5334,** or 08/9401 0833 after hours) runs fishing trips aboard 18.3- and 21.3-meter (60- and 70-ft.) cruisers. A full-day excursion costs A$75 (U.S.$52.50) weekdays, and A$85 (U.S.$59.50) on weekends and public holidays, including tackle and bait; BYO lunch and drinks. One of the best fishing spots in Perth is Rottnest Island (see "Side Trips From Perth," below). **Rottnest Malibu Diving** (☎ **08/9292 5111**) rents tackle by the hour for beach and jetty fishing.

GOLF   Golfers are spoiled for choice among Perth's many public and private courses. Pick up a free copy of Golf Maps Australia's "Complete Guide to Golf WA" at the Western Australian Tourist Centre, for reviews and maps of some of the state's best courses. An 18-hole round on a public course costs around A$20 to $40 (U.S.$14 to $28) midweek, more on weekends. Most convenient to the city is **Burswood Park Public Golf Course,** part of the Burswood International Resort Casino Complex just across the Swan River from town on the Great Eastern Highway, Burswood (☎ **08/ 9362 7576** for the pro shop). An 18-hole round on the par-70 course is A$15 (U.S.$10.50) weekdays and A$25 (U.S.$17.50) weekends. A cart for 9 holes is A$20 (U.S.$14), and club rental is A$10 (U.S.$7) for a half set. Among the most scenic courses are the **Araluen Country Club,** Country Club Avenue, Roleystone, a 45-minute drive from Perth (☎ **08/9397 9000**), and the 27 championship holes designed by Robert Trent Jones, Jr., at **Joondalup Resort Hotel,** Country Club Boulevard, Joondalup, a 25-minute drive north of Perth (☎ **08/9400 8888**). The **Novotel Vines Resort,** Verdelho Drive in the Swan Valley (☎ **08/9297 0222 3000**), a 40-minute drive from Perth, has a 36-hole bushland course recently ranked the country's 11th best championship course by *Golf Australia* magazine. Kangaroos often come onto the course at the Joondalup and Novotel Vines resorts.

HORSEBACK RIDING   You may spot kangaroos and emus when you ride at **The Stables,** Yanchep Beach Road, Yanchep (☎ **08/9561 1606**), in semirural country about 50 kilometers (30 miles) north of Perth. As well as rides ranging from 2 hours (A$30/ U.S.$21) to a full day (A$80/U.S.$56), there are evening Ride 'n' Dine trips to a local restaurant (A$45/U.S.$31.50, including your meal), Ride 'n' Swim visits to the beach (A$40/U.S.$28), and overnight camping treks (A$70/U.S.$49—bring your own dinner and breakfast to cook on the fire). The stable will pick you up from Joondalup train station; if there are enough customers coming from Perth that day, it will send a courtesy bus to collect you from your Perth hotel. You can stay overnight in The Stables' B&B accommodations for A$100 (U.S.$70) double with shared bath.

SAILING   The tallest Tall Ship in Australia, the **STS *Leeuwin II*** (☎ **08/9430 4105**), sails from B Shed at Victoria Quay, Fremantle, when she is not out on charter. Half-day twilight or breakfast trips cost A$50 (U.S.$35) for adults, A$30 (U.S.$21) for children under age 12. Full-day trips, including lunch, are A$80 (U.S.$56) for adults and A$50 (U.S.$35) for children.

SCUBA DIVING & SNORKELING   Rottnest Island's corals, reef fish, and limestone caverns, in 18- to 35-meter (59- to 115-ft.) visibility, are a gift from heaven to Perth divers and snorkelers. **Rottnest Malibu Diving** (☎ **08/9292 5111**) on Rottnest Island (see "Side Trips From Perth," below) and **Diving Ventures,** at 37 Barrack St. in Perth (☎ **08/9421 1052**) and 384 South Terrace in South Fremantle (☎ **9430 5130**), offer organized Rottnest Island dive day trips and scuba gear rental. Diving Ventures charges $120 (U.S.$77) for a day trip with two dives, including lunch and all gear rental.

SURFING   You will find good surfing at many city beaches, Scarborough and Trigg in particular (see the "Hitting the Beach" section earlier in this chapter). Rottnest Island (see "Side Trips from Perth," below) also has good breaks. **Murray Smith Surf Centre,** Shop 14, Luna Maxi Mart, Scarborough (☎ **08/9245 2988**), rents body boards for A$15 (U.S.$10.50) a day and Mach T boards for A$30 (U.S.$21) a day. Surfing tuition from **Surfing WA Surf Schools** (☎ **08/9448 0004**) costs A$40 (U.S.$28) per person per hour for one person, or A$35 (U.S.$24.50) per person per hour for two people. Boards and wet suits are provided. Lessons run daily at a number of beaches but are usually at Trigg Beach, sometimes at Scarborough Beach.

SPECTATOR SPORTS

AUSTRALIAN RULES FOOTBALL (AFL) Perth's highly successful Aussie Rules team, the **West Coast Eagles,** is based at **Subiaco Oval,** 171 Subiaco Rd., Subiaco (☎ 08/9381 1111, or 1900/997 374, a pay-per-minute recorded-information line). Call **Red Tickets** (☎ 08/9484 1222) to book seats. The Eagles sometimes play also at the WACA cricket ground (see below). Games are played in winter, usually on Friday nights and Sunday afternoons.

CRICKET The **Western Australia Cricket Association,** Nelson Crescent, East Perth (☎ 08/9265 7222), whose acronym WACA is pronounced "Whacker" by loving fans, is host to major national and international matches over the summer season. Big matches sell out fast. Various promoters sell tickets to different match series, so to find out where to get tickets for whatever game is playing when you are in town, call the WACA.

THE SHOPPING SCENE

Perth's city center is a major retail precinct. Most shops are located on the parallel Hay Street and Murray Street Malls, located one block apart, and in the network of arcades running off them, such as the Plaza, City, and Carillon arcades, and the upscale Trinity Arcade. London Court off Hay Street Mall is a convincing re-creation of a Tudor street, lined with a unique range of fashion, gift, and jewelry shops. The **Perth Tourist Lounge,** Level 2, Carillon Arcade (☎ **08/9481 8303**), gives away discount vouchers for shops in the Carillon Arcade; you don't need to book a tour with them to qualify for it. Opening off Murray Street Mall on Forrest Place is the Forrest Chase shopping center, which houses the Myer department store and boutiques on two gallery levels.

If time is short and you want to avoid most of the chains, skip the city center and spend half a day in fashionable Subiaco. Hay Street and Rokeby Road in "Subi" are lined with smart boutiques, home accessories shops, art galleries, cafes, and antiques shops. Fremantle's shopping is mostly limited to a good selection of crafts, some not too exciting markets, and Aboriginal souvenirs (see "A Day Out in Fremantle," above).

Shops are open to 9pm on Friday in the city, and to 9pm on Thursday in Subiaco, Claremont, and Fremantle.

ABORIGINAL ART & CRAFTS Low prices are usually ensured at **Bellamy's Aboriginal Art Gallery and Bookshop,** 43 High St., Fremantle (☎ **08/9430 7439**) because it's a wholesaler to other Aboriginal craft shops in Perth. It stocks original paintings on fabric, didgeridoos, spears, boomerangs, wooden jewelry and carvings, umbrellas, backpacks, T-shirts, jars, plates, and the like.

If you can't find what you are looking for at **Creative Native,** 32 King St. (☎ **08/9322 3398**), then it probably doesn't exist, because this store stocks Perth's

Desert Designs

Aboriginal artist Jimmy Pike grew up in Western Australia's Sandy Desert and began transferring his Dreamtime art and designs to fabrics in 1981. Today his highly successful range of merchandise includes clothing, rugs, and jewelry. The children's clothes are especially cute. The **Desert Designs Japingka Gallery,** 47 High St., Fremantle (☎ **08/9335 8265**) stocks original paintings and limited edition prints by Jimmy and his artistic partner, Doris Gingingara, plus changing exhibitions by other leading Aboriginal artists. It also stocks high-quality hand-tufted woolen floor rugs in Aboriginal designs. There's another branch of **Desert Designs** at 114 High Street Mall, Fremantle (☎ **08/9430 4101**).

widest range of Aboriginal arts and crafts. Downstairs is a retail Emporium. Upstairs is the King Street Fine Art Gallery, which sells original works by Aboriginal artists. There's another branch in Freemantle at 65 High St. (☎ 08/9335 6995).

FASHION   Popular Aussie artist Ken Done (pronounced like "phone") has made a name for himself by coming up with colorful designs of things like Australian fish, flowers, surfers, and sailboats, and then sticking them on everything from handbags to swimwear. You can find his designs at **Done Art and Design,** Shop 16, Forrest Chase (☎ **08/9221 4432**).

If it's more traditional Aussie attire you are after, head to **R. M. Williams,** Shop 38, Carillon Arcade (☎ **08/9321 7786**), for the store's trademark Australian clothing for rugged Outback types, including Akubra hats, Driza-bone raincoats, and the extremely popular—and durable—classic riding boot.

JEWELRY   Western Australia is renowned for having the best South Sea pearls in the world, farmed off Broome, and for Argyle diamonds mined in the Kimberley. The **Perth Mint** (see "Exploring Perth," earlier in this chapter) is a good source of gold-nugget and coin jewelry. You will also find a big range of opals in Perth. Most shops will deduct tax of around 15 to 30% from their prices for international travelers who show their passport and airline ticket. The discount varies from store to store, and according to how much of the item was manufactured in Western Australia. Many imported items, like watches, are also duty-exempt to international travelers.

Artisans of the Sea, corner of Marine Terrace and Collie Street, Fremantle (☎ **08/ 9336 3633**), is owned by the Kailis family, which runs one of Western Australia's biggest pearling operations, in Broome. This store sells elegant South Sea pearl strands and gold jewelry.

Tasteful and understated are the bywords at **Costello's,** Shop 5–6, London Court (☎ **08/9325 8588**), and **Swan Diamonds,** Shop 4, London Court (☎ **08/ 9325 8166**). These family-owned sister stores sell designs using opals, Argyle diamonds, and Broome pearls.

The particularly innovative designers at **Linney's,** 37 Rokeby Rd., Subiaco (☎ **08/ 9382 4077**), have won the Australian Jewelry Design award for their artistic one-of-a-kind pieces, often inspired by the Australian landscape.

You'll find a wide range of opals and designs to suit all budgets at **Quilpie Opals & Gems,** Shop 6, Piccadilly Arcade off Hay Street Mall (☎ **08/9321 8687**). The company owns an opal mine in Quilpie, Queensland, and employs a professional and knowledgeable staff.

PERTH AFTER DARK

The *West Australian* and *Sunday Times* newspapers list cinema screening times and details of some concert and theater performances and public events. Your best guide to hip dance clubs, concerts, gig listings, art-house cinemas, and art galleries is the *X-press* newspaper, free every Thursday at 520 pubs, boutiques, cafes, and live-music venues across town. *Scoop* and the *Perth Weekly* (see "Visitor Information," earlier in this chapter) are also good sources.

PERFORMING ARTS   To find out what's being staged by the West Australian Opera Company, West Australian Ballet, and the Black Swan Theatre Company, as well as other performing arts groups around town, call booking agent **BOCS** (☎ **08/ 9484 1133**). The opera and ballet perform usually perform at **His Majesty's Theatre,** a restored "grand-dame" venue. The Black Swan Theatre Company mostly play at the **Subiaco Theatre Centre** in Subiaco. The West Australian Symphony Orchestra (☎ **08/9326 0000** for inquiries and bookings) performs at the **Perth Concert Hall,** 5 St. Georges Terrace next to the Duxton Hotel. Blessed with the best acoustics in

Australia, it has housed performances by the London Philharmonic and Chicago Symphony Orchestras. Although it's a classical music venue, other performers who rely on good sound —comedians Billy Connolly and Rowen Atkinson and musicians such as B. B. King and Wynton Marsalis—have also used it.

The month-long **Festival of Perth** (☎ 08/9386 7977) showcases classic and contemporary performing arts, film, and literature every February to March. In summer, look for outdoor concerts at Perth Zoo (☎ 08/9474 3551) and in Kings Park (☎ 08/9480 3600).

PUBS & BARS   For a trendy take on the traditional corner pub, head to **The Brass Monkey,** 209 William St. at James St., Northbridge (☎ **08/9227 9596**), where a youngish crowd meets. Downstairs are two bars and a beer garden; upstairs are a cocktail bar (open Friday and Saturday nights) and a good brasserie with seating on the verandah, open for lunch and dinner daily. Stand-up comedy plays Wednesday night in the cocktail bar.

Bright young things get into serious pickup mode at **Brooklyn,** 161 James St., Northbridge (☎ **08/9328 7200**), a cavernous bar and beer garden dominated by two fairy-lit palm trees. The music is loud, and there's a DJ out back Friday and Saturday. On Saturday nights it's absolutely packed, so prepare to queue!

Apart from being a nice place for a drink, **Greenwich,** located under His Majesty's Theatre, 825 Hay St. (☎ **08/9321 5324**), is a venue for all kinds of events—short jazz and fusion Tuesday, films every second Wednesday, an underground dance club Thursday, music from original indie bands Wednesday, touring bands Friday and Saturday, and a backroom DJ on weekends.

Head to **Rosie O'Grady's,** 205 James St., Northbridge (☎ **08/9328 1488**), for rollicking good company, Celtic music, and Guinness on tap. There's another Rosie O'Grady's at 23 William St., Fremantle (☎ 08/9335 1645).

In Subiaco, "suits" flock to the "Subi," also known as the **Subiaco Hotel,** 465 Hay St. at Rokeby Road, Subiaco (☎ **08/9381 1028**), a popular restored heritage pub. It's big on Friday night.

THE CASINO   Blackjack, baccarat, roulette, craps, pai gow, Super Pan Caribbean Stud Poker, and Two-Up (the Aussie contribution to the gambling world), are all played on Burswood Casino's 98 public gaming tables and 1,141 video gaming machines. Except for Christmas Day, Good Friday, and ANZAC Day, the casino is open 24 hours and is part of the **Burswood International Resort Casino** complex, Great Eastern Highway, just over the river from the city (☎ 08/9362 7777). It has a showroom, free floor shows, and nine restaurants and six bars within the resort and casino complex. It's about a A$10 (U.S.$7) cab ride to Burswood from the city, less in off-peak traffic, or take a train to Burswood station. Bus 980 is an express service to the casino; it departs the City Bus Port on Mounts Bay Road Monday through Friday at 9:15 and 10:15am, and the Wellington Street Bus Terminal at 9:25 and 10:25am. The A$12 (U.S.$8.40) round-trip fare includes gaming vouchers, a free drink, and a free snack. The bus returns at 2:30pm and 3:30pm.

2 Side Trips from Perth

ROTTNEST ISLAND: GETTING FACE TO FACE WITH THE FISHES

This wildlife reserve just off the Perth coast is the most popular day trip from the city. Rottnest's blue waters, rocky coves, and many sheltered beaches harbor coral reefs and 97 kinds of tropical fish that make for ✪ **fabulous snorkeling.** You may spot humpback whales from September to December, and dolphins surfing the waves anytime. The island is also home to 10,000 *quokkas,* cute otter-like marsupials that reach up to your knees. A wonderful thing about Rottnest is that it's car-free. Everyone gets around by bike (or bus, if you tire of pedaling).

ESSENTIALS

GETTING THERE   The only way to get to the island is by ferry, either from Perth (trip time: 1 hour, 45 minutes) or Fremantle (trip time: 25 minutes). It's cheaper to take the train to Fremantle for A$2.40 (U.S.$1.70) and catch the boat from there than to take the boat from Perth. **Boat Torque 2000** (☎ **08/9221 5844** in Perth and 08/9430 5844 in Fremantle), **Captain Cook Cruises** (☎ **08/9325 3341**), and **Oceanic Cruises** (☎ **08/9325 1191** in Perth and 08/9430 5127 in Fremantle) operate daily services from Perth and Fremantle. Typical fares are A$45 (U.S.$31.50) for adults, A$40 (U.S.$8) for seniors and students, and A$14 (U.S.$9.80) for children ages 4 to 12 from Perth; or A$32 (U.S.$22.40) for adults, A$27 (U.S.$18.90) for seniors and students, and A$10 (U.S.$7) for children from Fremantle. This includes a free coach pickup from your Perth hotel or the Fremantle train station.

An even cheaper option is to take the train to Fremantle and walk from the station to the Rottnest Express ferry, *Sea Eagle III* (☎ **08/9335 6406**), which runs daily from Fremantle only. The fare is A$27 (U.S.$18.90) for adults, A$20 to $22 (U.S.$14–$15.40) for seniors and students, and A$10 (U.S.$7) for children ages 4 to 12.

All fares quoted here are round-trip, returning the same day. You pay about A$5 (U.S.$3.50) more if you return another day. Ask your boat operator about money-saving diving and accommodations packages.

VISITOR INFORMATION   For information before you arrive, write to the **Rottnest Island Authority,** E Shed, Victoria Quay, Fremantle, WA 6160 (☎ **08/ 9432 9300;** fax 08/9432 9339; www.rottnest.wa.gov.au). When you arrive, call at the **Rottnest Island Visitor Centre** (☎ **08/9372 9752**), located right at the end of the jetty. A short walk from the jetty is the **Environment Office (08/9372 9771)**, which has information on fishing and boating regulations, and on snorkeling trails.

GETTING AROUND   Ferries pull into the jetty in the main town, called "Settlement," at Thomson Bay. **Bell-A-Bike Rottnest** (☎ **08/9292 5105**), next to the Rottnest Hotel, near the jetty, rents bikes. Daily rates are A$13 to $23 (U.S.$9.10–$16.10) for adult bikes, including helmet (compulsory in Oz) and lock.

The yellow **Bayseeker** bus does regular trips around the island, calling at all the best bays. An all-day ticket costs A$5 (U.S.$3.50) for adults, A$3 (U.S.$2.10) for seniors and students, A$2 (U.S.$1.40) for children ages 4 to 12, and A$12 (U.S.$8.40) for families.

SNORKELING & SURFING

Most people come to Rottnest to snorkel, swim, surf, dive, or fish. As soon as you arrive, rent a bike and your preferred aquatic gear, and pedal around the coast until you come to a beach that suits you. **The Basin, Little Parakeet Bay,** and **Little**

Island Orientation Tours

Many first-time visitors take the 2-hour **Island Bus Tour** because it is a good introduction to the bays and the island's cultural and natural history—and because it includes a stop to pat the quokkas. It costs A$12 (U.S.$8.40) for adults, A$9 (U.S.$6.30) for seniors and students, A$6 (U.S.$4.20) for kids ages 4 to 12, and A$32 (U.S.$22.40) for families. Tours depart twice a day, usually at 11am and 1:30pm. Buy tickets from the Visitor Centre.

Salmon Bay are good snorkel spots (ask at the Environment Office for a laminated map of the snorkelers' trails at Parker Point). Surfers should try **Cathedral Rocks** or **Strickland Bay** for some of the best breaks in the state. Fishermen will catch squid, salmon, and tailor as well as all kinds of reef fish. **Rottnest Malibu Diving** (☎ 08/ 9292 5111), near the jetty, rents snorkel gear, dive gear, wet suits, surf boards, boogie boards, sea kayaks, and fishing tackle. The company conducts trips to some of the 100-plus dive sites around Rottnest. Some dives feature limestone caverns and some of the island's 14 shipwrecks. A shore or boat dive with all gear included is A$55 (U.S.$38.50). If you have never dived before but want to try, a 3-hour theory lesson followed by a boat dive is A$115 (U.S.$80.50).

FOR HISTORY BUFFS

Rottnest has quite a bit to offer history buffs, who may want to walk (45-minute trip), cycle, or take the train to the **Oliver Hill World War II gun emplacements,** with still-intact 28-millimeter (9-in.) guns and battery tunnels housing an engine room, plotting room, and observation posts. You can explore on your own, or take a guided tour on the hour between 10am and 2pm. Tours cost A$2 (U.S.$1.40) for adults, A50¢ (U.S.35¢) for kids. The train fare, which includes the tour (except for the last trip of the day), costs A$9 (U.S.$6.30) for adults, A$6 (U.S.$4.20) for seniors and students, A$4.50 (U.S.$3.15) for children ages 4 to 12, and A$24 (U.S.$16.80) for families. It departs from the station near the Visitor Centre several times a day.

The island was once a **penal colony,** notably for Aboriginal prisoners whose labor built some of the old structures on the island during the last century, and for World War I prisoners of war. Volunteer guides run free 1-hour historical walking tours of the island to architectural points of interest around **Thomson Bay,** like the Governor's residence, the chapel, 19th-century boat sheds, the small museum (open daily from 11am to 4pm), and the former Boys' Reformatory. Tours depart from the Environment Office at 11:30am and 2:30pm. You can guide yourself around Thomson Bay, using a heritage-trail map sold at the Visitor Centre.

WHERE TO STAY & DINE

Call the **Rottnest Island Authority's accommodation booking service** (☎ 08/ 9432 9111; fax 08/9432 9315) to book the campgrounds described below, or one of the more than 250 holiday homes, apartments, cabins, and historic cottages under its control. Its phone lines are often busy in summer, so try faxing, or call its office in E Shed on Victoria Quay, Fremantle (☎ 08/9372 9752), open Monday to Friday from 8:30am to 4:45pm. Summer rates range from A$67 (U.S.$46.90) for a four-bed bungalow to A$299 (U.S.$209.30) for an eight-bed cottage. Winter rates are lower. These rates are for a 1-night stay; rates generally drop considerably, even at the campground cabins, if you stay 2 nights or more. There is a minimum 2-night stay on weekends. Look for money-saving packages in winter. Accommodations are located in four small settlements around the island, all within a 20-minute walk from Thomson Bay and connected by a free bus. Because of water and electricity restrictions, no island accommodation is air-conditioned. Linen is not included, so allow about A$12 (U.S.$8.40) extra per person per week for that; the Rottnest Island Authority also has TVs, heaters, fans, and much more equipment for rent at reasonable rates. In the very oldest and cheapest units you may also need to rent cutlery and crockery. Avoid school vacations if you can; so popular is the island during these periods that the Authority allocates bookings by a ballot system. Book well in advance all through summer.

Apart from a general store, a bakery, and a chicken-and-chips outlet, the island's eateries are limited to two rather expensive hotel restaurants, and a DOME cafe.

Allison Camping Area and Caroline Thomson Camping Area. C/o Rottnest Island Authority, E Shed, Victoria Quay, Fremantle, WA 6160. ☎ **08/9432 9111**. Fax 08/9372 9715. www.rottnest.wa.gov.au. E-mail: enquiries@rottnest.wa.gov.au. 52 cabins, 30 with bathroom. 50 tent sites. Summer A$28–$43 (U.S.$19.60–$30.10) cabin without bathroom; A$73 (U.S.$51.10) cabin with bathroom. Winter A$23–$33 (U.S.$16.10–$23.10) cabin without bathroom; A$67 (U.S.$46.90) cabin with bathroom. Tent site A$5 (U.S.$3.50) adults, A$2.50 (U.S.$1.75) children under 12, year-round. Minimum 2-night stay weekends. BC, MC, V.

Of the island's two camping areas, both located at Thomson Bay, the Allison Camping Area is the larger, with tent sites and two-, four- and six-berth cabins with a fridge and cooktop but no running water or bathroom. The Caroline Thomson Camping Area has canvas cabins with private bathrooms and kitchenettes. Both campgrounds have a shower and toilet block, and gas barbecues. Alcohol is not permitted, and a quiet time rule applies between 11pm and 7am.

Rottnest Hotel. C/o Post Office, Rottnest Island, WA 6161. ☎ **08/9292 5011**. Fax 08/9292 5188. 18 units. TV. Summer A$155–$175 (U.S.$108.50–$122.50) double. Winter A$110–$130 (U.S.$77–$91) double. Rates include continental breakfast. AE, BC, DC, MC, V.

This 1864 building near the jetty, once the state governor's summer residence, is now the local pub where day-trippers gather in the beer garden to admire the ocean views over an ale or two. The building contains pleasant, modern motel-style rooms. Bay-side rooms have private courtyards with sea views.

Rottnest Youth Hostel. Kingstown Barracks, C/o Post Office, Rottnest Island, WA 6161. ☎ **08/9372 9780**. Fax 08/9292 5141. 9 units, none with bathroom. A$44 (U.S.$30.80) double, or A$38 (U.S.$26.60) double for YHA/Hostelling International members. Additional person A$19 (U.S.$13.30) adults; A$10 (U.S.$7) children 12 and under. A$19 (U.S.$13.30) dorm bed, or A$16 (U.S.$11.20) for YHA/Hostelling International members. BC, MC, V.

As well as dorm rooms, this YHA/Hostelling International–property has private family rooms furnished simply with a double bed and double bunks. Located in Kingstown, 1.2 kilometers (less than a mile) from Thomson Bay, it is housed in 1936 barracks that were used by the Australian Army until 1984. It serves cheap meals, provides a barbecue, and has a TV room.

IN PURSUIT OF THE GRAPE IN THE SWAN VALLEY
20km (12 miles) NE of Perth

Twenty minutes from the Perth central business district is the Swan Valley, home to two of Australia's best wine labels. In all, there are 21 wineries as well as wildlife parks, antiques and craft shops, and restaurants. Some restaurants and wineries close Monday and Tuesday.

Lord Street from the Perth city center becomes Guildford Road and takes you to Guildford, at the start of the Swan Valley. The Swan Valley Visitor Information Centre is the place to arm yourself with a map of the wineries and other attractions. You will find it in the **Guildford Village** Potters Studio at 22 Meadow St., Guildford (☎ **08/9279 9859**). It's open Monday through Friday from 9:30am to 3pm, and Saturday and Sunday from 9:30am to 4pm. Several companies (see "Whale-Watching & Other Cruises," earlier in this chapter) run day cruises from Perth.

TOURING THE WINERIES & OTHER THINGS TO DO

If you see only one winery, make it **Houghton's,** Dale Road, Middle Swan (☎ **08/9274 5100**). This is Western Australia's biggest winery and one of its oldest. The big-beamed timber cellar has old wine-making machinery on show, there are beautiful picnic grounds under huge spreading jacaranda trees, and next to the cellar is a lovely cafe and art gallery selling local artists' works. The other big-name winery is **Sandalford,** 3210 West Swan Rd., Caversham (☎ 08/ 9274 5922), which sells lunch platters to eat under trellised vines. Its gift store sells nifty versions of wine apparatus, such as bottle openers and glasses. Both wineries' cellar doors are open daily for tastings from 10am to 5pm.

If you have kids, call at the **Caversham Wildlife Park,** Arthur Street, West Swan (☎ 08/9274 2202). You can stroke koalas (but not hold them, as the owner believes it stresses them), feed kangaroos, pat farm animals, take a camel ride for A$3.50 (U.S.$2.45), and gawk at a wide range of Western Australian wildlife. It's open daily 9am to 5pm. Admission is A$8 (U.S.$5.60) for adults, A$7 (U.S.$4.90) for seniors and students, and A$3 (U.S.$2.10) for children ages 2 to 14.

Lovers of old stuff should browse the **junk-shop strip** on James Street in Guildford (most shops are open daily), or visit **Woodbridge,** a beautifully restored and furnished 1883 manor house at Ford Street in West Midland (☎ 08/9274 2432). The house is open to the public Monday and Tuesday and Thursday through Saturday from 1 to 4pm, and Sunday and public holidays from 11am to 5pm. Admission is A$3.50 (U.S.$2.45) for adults, A$1.50 (U.S.$1.05) for seniors and school-age children, and A$8 (U.S.$5.60) for a family.

WHERE TO STAY

The Swan is too close to Perth to require an overnight stay. You probably won't regret splashing out on a night at Hansons, however.

Worth a Splurge

✪ **Hansons Swan Valley.** 60 Forest Rd., Henley Brook, WA 6055. ☎ **08/9296 3366.** Fax 08/9296 3332. 10 units, all with bathroom (some with Jacuzzis and shower, some with shower only). A/C MINIBAR TEL TV. A$130–$180 (U.S.$91–$126) double. Ask about single rates in slow midweek periods. AE, BC, DC, MC, V. Rates include full breakfast. Take West Swan Rd. to the Middle Swan, turn right at Little River Winery into Forrest St. Hansons is on the left at the end of the road. Children under 15 not permitted on weekends and other peak periods.

"At last," some of you will cry as you step into the sleek entry hall, "a B&B that's not down-on-the-farm hokey or drowning in chintz." Instead, these rooms have stark white walls and groovy furniture à la Philippe Starck. All rooms have bathrobes, VCRs, and minibars stocked with cheeses, chocolates, and other goodies. Hair dryers and ironing boards are sent to your room on request. Former advertising executives Jon and Selina Hanson set out to create a slick B&B of the kind they would like to stay in themselves, and it works. The house is set on a 10-hectare (25-acre) farm and has a swimming pool. Selina cooks up a gourmet storm for breakfast (fresh mushrooms on toasted brioche with grilled veal, for example) and serves equally fab fare for dinner, when you should expect to pay around A$22 (U.S.$15.40) for a main course. If you like, she will serve dinner on your balcony, knocked back with the bottles you snared during the day's successful wine-hunting expedition, naturally. Smoking is prohibited indoors.

WHERE TO DINE

✪ **Lamont's.** 85 Bisdee Rd., Millendon near the Upper Swan ☎ **08/9296 4485.** Reservations recommended, especially for dinner. Main courses A$19.50–$23 (U.S.$13.65–$16.10). AE, BC, DC, MC, V. Wed–Sun 10am–5pm, and for dinner the 1st Sat of each month. Take the Great Northern Hwy. to Baskerville in the Upper Swan, turn right into Haddrill Rd. for 1.6km (1 mile), right into Moore Rd. for 1km (just over ½ mile), and right into Bisdee Rd. MOD OZ.

This highly regarded restaurant is housed in a rustic timber building at Lamont Winery. Chef Kate Lamont serves full-flavored main courses using the best of the season's local produce, such as marron, or grilled venison with a rich reduced-stock sauce, and gutsy desserts such as chocolate oblivion with rich cream. Lots of regulars make the drive from Perth just to eat here. A gallery on the grounds shows Western Australian art and crafts.

YORK: TAKING A STEP BACK IN HISTORY

The state's first inland settlement, this peaceful National Trust–classified village on the Avon River 99 kilometers (59½ miles) east of Perth oozes charm from an unspoiled Victorian and Federation (ca. 1901) streetscape. There are several great B&Bs, historic buildings of stone wrapped by wrought-iron lace verandahs, art galleries, a rose garden, a medley of small museums—including one housing a A$30 million (U.S.$21 million) display of vintage cars—and one of the state's finest jarrah furniture shops.

To get to York from Perth, take Lord Street from the city center and follow it as it becomes Guildford Road to Guildford, where it becomes the Great Eastern Highway. Follow this for 15 to 20 minutes to The Lakes, then take the York turnoff on the Great Southern Highway. The whole drive takes about 75 minutes. **Westrail** (☎ **13 10 53** in Australia, or 08/9326 2244) runs a coach service 5 days a week from Perth for a good-value A$9.70 (U.S.$6.80).

The **York Tourist Bureau** is at the Town Hall, Avon Terrace at Joaquina Street, York, WA 6302 (☎ **08/9641 1301;** fax 08/9641 1787). It's open Monday through Friday from 9:30am to 5pm, and weekends from 10am to 5pm in winter; summer hours are a little shorter.

EXPLORING THE TOWN

Just wandering the streets is the best way to soak up the period charm of York's old buildings, like the faithfully restored railway station (open only on weekends), the impressive Town Hall built in 1911, the library, the convent, old pubs like the York and the Castle, St. Patrick's church, the Uniting Church, Holy Trinity Church with its lovely stained glass windows, the fire station, and the old hospital. Among the sights worth seeing is the **Old Gaol and Courthouse,** 132 Avon Terrace (☎ **08/9641 2072**) housing a colonial-era courthouse that's still in use, cells, stables, and a simple trooper's cottage. It's open daily from 9am to 4pm, although these times can vary as the staff are volunteers; closed Christmas and Good Friday. Admission is A$3 (U.S.$2.10) for adults, A$1.50 (U.S.$1.05) for children and seniors, and A$7.50 (U.S.$5.25) for families.

The short walk out of town to the excellent **Residency Museum,** on Brook Street (☎ **08/9641 1751**), is well worth it for its displays of everything from prayer books, children's toys, needlework, and old kitchenware, to antique furniture, farm tools, and other memorabilia of life in York in days gone by. It's open Tuesday to Thursday and public holidays from 1 to 3pm, Saturday and Sunday from 1 to 5pm, and daily during school vacations (as with the Gaol, these times vary as the staff are volunteers); closed Christmas and Good Friday). Admission is A$2 (U.S.$1.40) for adults and A$1 (U.S.70¢) for children ages 8 to 15 or so.

If you are in the area on a Friday, Saturday, Sunday, or Monday between 10am and 4:30pm in spring (September to Christmas) or autumn (mid-March to mid-June), you can explore the evolution of the rose from ancient times to the modern day at the **Avon Valley Historical Rose Garden** (☎ **08/9641 1469**), 2 kilometers (1¼ miles) out of town on Osnaburg Road. Admission is A$3 (U.S.$2.10) for adults; free for children.

Of the several special-interest museums in York, the ✪ **York Motor Museum,** 116–124 Avon Terrace (☎ **08/9641 1288**), is the most spectacular. Among the more than 70 veteran, vintage, classic, and racing vehicles and motorcycles on display are the world's first car (an 1886 Benz), a 1906 Cadillac, and a 1964 Ferrari 250. The museum is open daily from 9am to 4pm in summer, until 5pm in winter. Admission is A$7 (U.S.$4.90) for adults, A$6 (U.S.$4.20) for students and seniors, and A$2 (U.S.$1.40) for children under age 12.

WHERE TO STAY & DINE

You can eat cheaply at several inexpensive cafes, but even nicer is a picnic on the lawns under shady trees beside the Avon, near the suspension bridge.

✪ **Hillside Country Retreat.** Forrest St. ☎ **08/9641 1065.** Fax 08/9641 2417. E-mail: hillside@avon.net.au. 6 units (all with shower only). A/C TV. A$85 (U.S.$59.50) single; A$120 (U.S.$84) double. Rates include full breakfast. No credit cards.

When a U.S. diplomat stayed at this adorable homestead a few years ago, he said he'd never seen so much stuff in one place. He was referring to the old pogo sticks, farm machinery, wooden ice skates, original radios, old road signs, the 1910 washing machine, and countless other relics of a bygone era that grace every spare inch of wall and floor space. Forget sightseeing; you won't want to stop gazing at all the old trash and treasure in your room! Each individually furnished room has a potbelly stove, en suite bathroom, VCR, and minifridge, and you get treated to fresh flowers in your room, complimentary port, sherry, chocolates, plunger coffee, and a daily newspaper. Whether you stay in the colonial homestead or in the rustic mud-brick servants' quarters, your room has pretty antique furnishings. Hair dryers are provided. Breakfast is served in the garden from the quaint pagoda-style Morris Edwards Tea and Ginger Beer House. Smoking is prohibited indoors.

NEW NORCIA: A TOUCH OF EUROPE IN AUSTRALIA

It's the last thing you expect to see in the Australian bush—a Benedictine monastery town with elegant European architecture, a fine museum, and a collection of Renaissance art—but New Norcia, 132 kilometers (79 miles) north of Perth, is no mirage. Boasting a population of 55 (when everyone's at home, that is), this pretty town and the surrounding 8,000-hectare (20,000-acre) farm were established in 1846 by Spanish Benedictine missionaries. Visitors can tour beautifully frescoed chapels, marvel at one of the finest religious art collections in Australia, stock up on famous New Norcia gourmet breads and nutcake straight from the monastery's 120-year-old wood-fired ovens, and attend prayers with the 18 monks who live here.

New Norcia is an easy 2-hour drive from Perth. From the city center take Lord Street, which becomes Guildford Road, to Midland. Here, join the Great Northern Highway, which takes you through the Swan Valley to New Norcia. **Westrail** and **Greyhound Pioneer** run coach services from Perth several times a week.

Conference groups can book the town solid, so reserve accommodations and tours in advance, especially in wildflower season from August to October. Write for information and book town tours at the **New Norcia Tourist Information Centre,** New Norcia, WA 6509 (☎ **08/9654 8056;** fax 08/9654 8124) in the Museum and Art Gallery, just off the highway behind St. Josephs, beside the Trading Post and Roadhouse. Its hours are those of the museum and gallery (see below). You can also check out the monastery's Web site at www.newnorcia.wa.edu.au.

EXPLORING THE TOWN & MONASTERY

The Information Centre's intriguing two-hour ✪ **walking tours** are a must. Tickets cost A$10 (U.S.$7) for adults and A$5 (U.S.$3.50) for children ages 12 to 17; free for younger children. Tours depart daily except Christmas at 11am and 1:30pm, and allow time for you to attend prayers with the monks if you wish. The guide strolls you around some of the town's 27 National Trust–classified buildings and gives an insight into the monks' lifestyle. You will also see the delightful frescoes in the old monastery chapel and in St. Ildephonsus' and St. Gertrude's colleges. Much of the monastery is closed to visitors, but the tour does show you the fruit gardens and a glimpse of the men-only courtyard. Heritage walking-trail maps sold for A$3 (U.S.$2.10) at the Information Centre include buildings not visited on the tour, such as the octagonal apiary.

For many people, the highlight of a trip to **New Norcia** is the ✪ **museum and art gallery** full of relics from the monks' past—old mechanical and musical instruments, artifacts from the days when New Norcia was an Aboriginal mission, gifts to the monks from the Queen of Spain, and an astounding collection of paintings by Spanish and Italian artists forming one of Australia's most valuable religious art collections. The oldest I saw was dated 1492. Give yourself at least an hour here. The museum and gallery are open daily from 9:30am to 5pm August through October, and from 10am to 4:30pm November through July (closed Christmas). Admission is A$4 (U.S.$2.80) for adults, A$3 (U.S.$2.10) for seniors and students, and A$1 (U.S.70¢) for children ages 6 to 12.

Apart from joining the monks for prayers, you can join them for Mass in the **Holy Trinity Abbey Church** Monday through Saturday at 7:30am and on Sunday at 9am.

WHERE TO STAY

New Norcia Hotel. Great Northern Hwy., New Norcia, WA 6509. ☎ **08/9654 8034.** Fax 08/9654 8011. 17 units, 1 with bathroom. A$40 single (U.S.$28) without bathroom, A$60 (U.S.$42) double without bathroom, A$75 (U.S.$52.50) family room without bathroom; A$80 (U.S.$56) double with bathroom, A$95 (U.S.$66.50) triple with bathroom. AE, BC, DC, MC, V.

When they thought a Spanish Royal visit to New Norcia was imminent in 1926, the monks built this grandiose white hotel fit for, well, a king. Sadly, the Royals never materialized, and the building has fallen into disrepair. Until recently, guests could only look forward to depressing rooms with dusty lace curtains and old cheap furniture, not the Iberian splendor promised by the imposing facade. Only the high ceilings, grand central staircase, and ornate pressed-metal ceilings hinted at what used to be. The good news is that the monks plan to revitalize the property with antiques, ornate gold-framed paintings, fresh carpets, and other innovations with the help of knowledgeable new management. Let's hope they achieve their wishes, for the place has the potential to be spectacular. None of this is to say it doesn't already have a faded charm, however. The gracious front verandah is a peaceful place for a drink overlooking the fields (it's big enough to hold a football game on), and the bar sure gets jumping on Friday and Saturday nights when local farmers come to town. Inexpensive meals are served in the bar all day and the Wildflower dining room opens weekend nights. This is the only place to stay in New Norcia.

3 Margaret River & the Southwest: Wine Tasting in Australia's Prettiest Corner

290km (174 miles) S of Perth

Say "Margaret River" to Australians and they think "great wine!" The 45 wineries nestled among the region's statuesque karri forests contribute only around 1% to Australia's total wine output, yet are responsible for 10% of the country's premium wines. But not even most Australians know about the Southwest's other attractions—like the spectacular surf breaks on the 130-kilometer (78-mile) stretch of coast from Cape Naturaliste in the north to Cape Leeuwin on the very southwest tip of Australia; the magnificent coastal cliffs tailor-made for abseiling and rock climbing; and the network of limestone caves. There's whale watching June through December, and wildflowers line the roads August through October. If you like hiking, pack your boots, because there are plenty of hiking trails to tackle, from a 15-minute town stroll around Margaret River to the 6-day Cape-to-Cape trek along the sea cliffs. This is one of the world's last unspoiled wildernesses.

And more good news—it's affordable. Cute B&Bs and lodges are inexpensive, tastings at top-class wineries are usually free, and the beaches and hiking trails will not cost you a cent.

ESSENTIALS

GETTING THERE   It's a 3½-hour drive to Margaret River from Perth; take the inland **South Western Highway** (the quickest route) or the slightly more scenic **Old Coast Road** to Bunbury, where you pick up the Bussell Highway to Margaret River.

Maroomba Airlines (☎ 08/9478 3850) flies to Busselton from Perth Monday, Wednesday, and Friday. The fare is A$180 (U.S.$126) round-trip, plus A$20 (U.S.$14) Busselton airport tax. Ask about 3-day advance-purchase fares and packages.

Westrail runs the *Australind* train twice daily between Perth and Bunbury, with coach connections to Margaret River (A$26.10/U.S.$18.25 one way) every day except Saturday. It also runs an all-bus service from Perth to Margaret River every day except Saturday (A$24.50/U.S.$17.15 one way). **Southwest Coachlines** (☎ 08/9324 2333) runs daily services to Margaret River, departing Perth City Bus Port at 1:30pm weekdays and 9am weekends, public holidays, and daily during school vacations. The fare is A$23 (U.S.$16.10).

VISITOR INFORMATION   You will pass many wineries on the way, but it's worth heading first to the **Augusta-Margaret River Tourism Association,** on the Bussell Highway at Tunbridge Street, Margaret River, WA 6285 (☎ **08/9757 2911;** fax 08/9757 3287;www.netserv.net.au/amrta/welcome.html). It has comprehensive information on wineries, attractions, tour operators, hiking trails, restaurants, and accommodations throughout the Southwest. Plan to fork out A$2.95 (U.S.$2.05) for a brief but useful winery guide listing cellar-door hours, or A$5.95 (U.S.$4.15) for a spiffier color version. The office is open daily from 9am to 5pm.

GETTING AROUND   **Busselton,** which boasts the longest jetty in the southern hemisphere, marks the start of the Southwest. Nine kilometers (5½ miles) past the town, the **Bussell Highway** makes a sharp left and heads south among the wineries through Vasse, the tiny village of Cowaramup, the township of Margaret River, the tiny fishing port of Augusta, and on to windswept Cape Leeuwin. An alternate route is along **Caves Road,** which runs parallel to the Bussell Highway through the wineries and forests before rejoining the highway 3 kilometers (2 miles) north of Augusta.

The wineries, beaches, restaurants, and forests are quite spread out, so you will miss out on a lot without a car. Although the region is only 10 kilometers (6 miles) wide, east to west, in most places, it is 99 kilometers (59½ miles) from Busselton in the north to Augusta in the south. **Avis** (☎ 1800/679 880 in Australia, or 08/9721 7873) has offices in Bunbury, Busselton, and Margaret River. Rent a car for 2 days or more and you can drive it back to Perth without paying the A$50 (U.S.$35) "one-way" charge. The quality of road signposting in the Southwest is dismal, so arm yourself with the Augusta-Margaret River Tourism Association's A$3.95 (U.S.$2.75) regional map of the Southwest; it marks wineries and other attractions.

Margaret River Tour Company (☎ 0419/91 7166 mobile phone) and **Mile-saway Tours** (☎ 1800/818 102 in Australia, or 08/9754 2929) run sightseeing, adventure, and winery tours from Margaret River. A half-day wine-tasting jaunt with either company costs A$40 (U.S.$28).

Special Events in the Southwest

Every February or March, the **Leeuwin Estate winery** (☎ 08/9757 6253) stages a spectacular outdoor concert starring some leading showbiz star (the likes of Shirley Bassey, Julio Iglesias, or Diana Ross). Some 6,500 guests gather on the grounds to picnic during the performance and sip Leeuwin Estate wine. Tickets are A$90 (U.S.$63). This is a *big* local event, so book months ahead.

The **Margaret River Region Wine Festival** takes place over 3 days in late November.

TOURING THE WINERIES

Fans of premium wines (and who isn't?) will have a field day in the Margaret River region. Cabernet sauvignon is the star red variety, while chardonnay, semillon, and sauvignon blanc are the pick of the bunch among whites. Viticulture only began here in 1965, and more wineries are opening all the time, so expect to see some bare, unlandscaped new cellars alongside the prettier established ones. Most wineries offer ✪ **free tastings** from 10am to 4:30pm daily.

The "big three" wineries are **Cape Mentelle,** 4 kilometers (2½ miles) west of Margaret River on Wallcliffe Road (☎ 08/9757 3266); **Leeuwin Estate,** Stevens Road, Margaret River (☎ 08/9757 6253); and **Vasse Felix,** Caves Road at Harman's Road South, Willyabrup (☎ 08/9755 5242). Leeuwin Estate in particular has a towering reputation, especially for its chardonnay. A relative newcomer on the scene, **Hay Shed Hill,** Harman's Mill Road, Willyabrup (☎ 08/9755 6234), seems to be forever picking up the trophy for Western Australia's "Best Pinot Noir." Another newcomer, **Voyager Estate,** Stevens Road, Margaret River (☎ 08/9385 3133), boasts exquisite rose gardens around an imposing South African Cape Dutch–style cellar. It does a highly drinkable shiraz grenache. Other good labels to look for are Arlewood Estate, Evans & Tate, Fermoy Estate, Lenton Brae Estate, and Sandalford.

WHAT TO SEE & DO BETWEEN THE WINERIES

The Southwest's limestone ridges are riddled with 350 or so caves, five of which are open to the public every day except Christmas. Before or after you visit a cave, call at the excellent **CaveWorks** ecointerpretive center at Lake Cave, Caves Road, 15 kilometers (9 miles) south of Wallcliffe Rd. (☎ 08/9757 7411), open daily from 9am to 5pm. Entry is A$5 (U.S.$3.50) for adults and A$3 (U.S.$2.10) for children ages 4 to 16, or free if you tour Lake, Jewel, Mammoth, or Moondyne caves. **Lake Cave,** right outside CaveWorks, 300 steps down an ancient sinkhole, contains an underground stream. Just a few minutes north along Caves Road is **Mammoth Cave,** where you can see the fossilized jaw of a baby *zygotaurus trilobus,* an extinct giant wombat. ✪ **Jewel Cave,** 8 kilometers (5 miles) north of Augusta on Caves Road, is the prettiest, with

Wine-Buying Tip

The place to buy wine if you want to take it out of Australia is the **Margaret River Regional Wine Centre,** 9 Bussell Hwy., Cowaramup (☎ 08/9755 5501), as most wineries don't deliver internationally. It stocks every local wine and does daily tastings of select vintages. It is open Monday through Saturday from 10am to 8pm, and Sunday from noon to 6pm. You can order off its Web site at www.mrwines.com.

delicate stalactite formations. Tours of Lake and Jewel caves and self-guided tours of Mammoth cave cost A$12 (U.S.$8.40) each for adults, A$5 (U.S.$3.50) for children ages 4 to 16, or A$34 (U.S.$23.80) for a family. A 7-day Grand Pass for entry into Lake, Jewel, and Mammoth caves plus CaveWorks costs A$30 (U.S.$21) for adults, A$12 (U.S.$8.40) for children, and A$84 (U.S.$58.80) for a family. Tour hours vary, but you can usually rely on a tour departing every hour or half hour from 9am or 9:30am to 3:30pm or 4pm, sometimes later during school vacations. Book tours through CaveWorks.

Just next to Jewel Cave is **Moondyne Cave,** an "adventure cave" where you get down-and-dirty crawling on your hands and knees. The 2-hour experience costs A$25 (U.S.$17.50) for adults and A$18 (U.S.$12.60) for kids ages 10 to 16 (kids under 10 are not permitted). Tours depart daily at 2pm. Book through CaveWorks. A similar 3-hour adventure tour is offered at **Ngilgi Cave,** Caves Road, Yallingup (☎ **08/ 9755 2152)** for A$30 (U.S.$21) for anyone over 14. It departs daily at 9:30am. You need to book both adventure tours 24 hours ahead. Ngilgi also has a semiguided tour where you walk yourself through and ask the guides questions; this tour costs A$9 (U.S.$6.30) for adults and A$4 (U.S.$2.80) for children ages 5 to 17. Ngilgi Cave is open daily from 9:30am, with the last tour at 4pm (5pm during school vacations).

You can pick your own kiwifruit, raspberries, and other fruit at **The Berry Farm,** 222 Bessell Rd. outside Margaret River (☎ **08/9757 5054),** or buy them ready-made as attractively packaged sparkling, dessert, and port wines; jams; and vinegars. The farm is open daily from 10am to 4:30pm.

Like most charming rural regions, **Margaret River** has its share of craft galleries. The **Melting Pot Glass Studio,** Lot 158 Boodjidup Rd., Margaret River (☎ **08/ 9757 2252)** does glassblowing demonstrations daily. Margaret River Art Galleries, **83–85** Bussell Hwy., Margaret River (☎ 08/9757 2729) sells art, sculpture, pottery, and woodwork pieces by Western Australian artists. One of the best—and most expensive—galleries is the **Gunyulgup Galleries,** Gunyulgup Valley Drive near Yallingup (☎ **08/9755 2177),** which sells top-of-the-line jewelry, glass, silverware, and artworks.

ENJOYING THE GREAT OUTDOORS

Nature fans will love the Southwest's rugged scenery and fresh air. Greg Miller of ✪ **Adventure Plus** (☎ **08/9758 1913,** or 0419/961 716 mobile phone) arranges all kinds of outdoor adventures—abseiling and rock climbing coastal cliffs, caving, mountain biking, surfing, canoeing, and camping. He welcomes beginners. Prices vary according to the activity you select, but a day's action usually costs around A$70 (U.S.$49), or A$50 (U.S.$35) for half a day. Hiking, of course, is always free (well,

---

A Scenic Drive & a Spectacular View

If you're exploring the area by car, make the picturesque drive down **Caves Road** to Augusta, 43 kilometers (25 miles) south of Margaret River. **Boranup Drive,** a scenic side route off Caves Road, goes through towering karris and is particularly magical—but be warned, your rental car is not insured on its unpaved surface! The Boranup Drive departs Caves Road 6 kilometers (3½ miles) south of Mammoth Cave and rejoins it after a 14-kilometer (8½-mile) meander. Near Augusta, a dazzling view over the Indian and Southern oceans rewards you if you climb to the top of **Cape Leeuwin** lighthouse. It is open daily from 9am to 4pm. Entry is A$3.50 (U.S.$2.45) for adults and A$1.50 (U.S.$1.05) for children ages 6 to 14. *Note:* kids under age 6 are not permitted up the stairs.

almost—the tourism association sells hiking maps for a dollar or so). For guided hikes with meals, camping gear supplied, 4WD support, and someone to put up your tent each night, contact **Walk the Edge** (☎ **08/9757 2821**). Expect to pay about A$100 (U.S.$70) per day.

Helen Lee of ✪ **Cave & Canoe Bush Tucker Tours** (☎ **08/9757 9084**) takes you on a fun excursion canoeing up the river, exploring a cave, and eating a bush tucker lunch. The tour runs from Prevelly Park beach near Margaret River, usually from 10am to 2pm daily in summer, and several times a week in winter. Book at the tourism association in Margaret River (see "Visitor Information"). It costs A$25 (U.S.$17.50) for adults and A$15 (U.S.$10.50) for kids under age 15. Highly recommended.

Surfing lessons from four-time Western Australian professional surfing champion ✪ **Josh Parmateer** ☎ **08/9757 3850,** or 0418/958 264 mobile phone), are a must— take it from this surf virgin! Two-hour lessons in the gentle waist-deep surf at **Prevelly Park beach,** 9 kilometers (5½ miles) west of Margaret River, run daily and cost A$70 (U.S.$49) per person, or A$30 (U.S.$21) per person if there are two of you. Josh supplies the boards and wet suits. Lessons run from October to June. If you are already a Master of the Surf Universe, try the legendary **Smiths Beach** or the **Three Bears** (Mama, Papa, and Baby) break at Yallingup, the double-barreled North Point at Gracetown, or the plentiful breaks at **Prevelly Park. Beach Life,** 117 Bussell Hwy., Margaret River (☎ **08/9757 2888**) rents boards and wet suits for around A$30 (U.S.$21) a day.

From June to December whales play right offshore all along the coast. There is a whale lookout near the Cape Naturaliste lighthouse. Daily 3-hour whale-watching cruises with ✪ **Naturaliste Charters** (☎ **08/9755 2276**) depart Augusta from June to September. From September to December, cruise departures switch to Dunsborough, where humpbacks rest their calves. Cruises cost A$35 (U.S.$24.50) for adults and A$15 (U.S.$10.50) for children ages 4 to 14; children under age 4 are free.

WHERE TO STAY

While not the prettiest village in the Southwest, Margaret River has the advantage of a bank, a supermarket, and a few restaurants and shops. The hamlet of Cowaramup is closer to more wineries, and has a general store, a restaurant, and one or two interesting craft shops.

IN MARGARET RIVER

Rosewood Cottage. 54 Wallcliffe Rd., Margaret River, WA 6285. ☎ **08/9757 2845.** Fax 08/9757 3509. 4 units (3 with shower only). A$75 (U.S.$52.50) double with continental breakfast; A$85 (U.S.$59.50) double with full breakfast; A$85 (U.S.$59.50) double apt. with continental breakfast. Additional person A$20 (U.S.$14) extra in apt. AE, BC, MC, V.

Jenny and Kevin Towers-Hammond have turned their home into a cozy B&B accommodating guests in English-style rooms with exposed roof beams, soft floral decor, ceiling fans, and hair dryers. By the time you arrive there will be a new two-bedroom apartment, with living area and kitchenette, set up for travelers with disabilities. Guests can rest up in winter by the fire in the cozy sitting room equipped with CDs, a TV, and books, or out on the verandah overlooking the lovely garden in summer. Jenny is famous for her homemade waffles and jams at breakfast, served in the country-style dining room. It is an easy stroll to the Margaret River main street from the house. No smoking indoors.

IN COWARAMUP

✪ **The Noble Grape.** Lot 18, Bussell Hwy., Cowaramup, WA 6284. ☎ and fax **08/9755 5538.** E-mail: noblegrape@netserv.net.au. 6 units (all with shower only). TV. A$60

(U.S.$42) single; A$75 (U.S.$52.50) double. Additional person A$20 (U.S.$14) extra; children 3–12 A$15 (U.S.$10.50) extra. Rates include continental breakfast. AE, BC, DC, MC, V.

Spacious, pretty rooms surrounded by blooming English-cottage gardens await you at Louise and Chris Stokes' colonial-style B&B in the heart of Cowaramup. Each smartly maintained room is adorned with antiques and has a roomy modern bathroom, a minirefrigerator, ceiling fans and heating, plenty of luggage space, a comfy sitting area with reading material, and a small rear patio opening onto the trees. One room caters to travelers with disabilities. Louise arranges a delicious breakfast buffet of homemade muffins, jams, muesli, yogurts, and freshly made tea and plunger coffee every morning. A cooked breakfast is available for an extra A$6 (U.S.$4.20). When you don't want to go out to dinner, especially after a hard day's wine tasting and sight-seeing, the inexpensive room service menu is a welcome sight. Hair dryers are free at reception, and guests are welcome to use their hosts' laundry. No smoking indoors.

✪ **Sandyknowe Farmhouse Bed & Breakfast.** Miamup Rd., Cowaramup, WA 6284. ☎ **08/9755 5336,** or 08/9755 5092 after hours. Fax 08/9755 5336 (same as tel.). 5 units, 4 with bathroom (1 with tub, 3 with shower only). A$60–$70 (U.S.$42–49) single; A$80–$90 (U.S.$56–63) double. Additional person A$20 (U.S.$14) extra; children under 12 A$10 (U.S.$7) extra. Rates include full breakfast. Minimum 2-night stay required. BC, MC, V.

Judy Dunbar grew up on this idyllic farm 3 kilometers (2 miles) from Cowaramup. Now she and husband Bob share with guests their sprawling country home and their 138 working acres populated by cows, ducks, guinea fowl, a pony, Carey the dog, and a baby *galah* (a kind of native parrot) called Jack. The rooms are big and comfortable, furnished in a fresh homespun style, each with outside access. You tuck into a hearty hot and cold buffet breakfast at the family dining table each morning, and Judy packs you off for the day with a free basket of homemade biscuits and cake, a flask of hot water, and herbal teas. You have the run of the house and the farm, including the two comfy sitting rooms with fireplaces and TVs, the kitchen to prepare dinner, and the wood-fired barbecue in the yard. Kids will love the animals and the chance to spot kangaroos, while you will appreciate the peace and the bird-filled gardens. No smoking inside.

In Vasse

✪ **Newtown House.** 737 Bussell Hwy. (8km/5 miles past Busselton), Vasse, WA 6280. ☎ **08/9755 4485,** or 0417/172 048 (mobile phone). Fax 08/9755 4485 (same as tel). 4 units (all with shower only). MINIBAR TV. A$125 (U.S.$87.50) double. Rates include continental break-fast. AE, BC, DC, MC, V.

The rooms in this converted National Trust–listed 1851 homestead at the northern end of the Margaret River region are as delightful as you'll find anywhere in the South-west, but many people come here for the fabulous food turned out by proprietor Stephen Reagan, who happens to be one of Western Australia's most renowned chefs (see "Where to Dine"). Every room has a contemporary country decor, with wrought-iron table and chairs and pine furniture. Hair dryers and irons are available on request. The fixings for a gourmet continental breakfast are sent up to your room the night before, so breakfast is any time you want it. When you're not out exploring the area, you can play croquet in the gorgeous rose and lavender gardens, or wander into the barn-cum-studio and chat with the friendly resident painter. Smoking is prohibited.

WHERE TO DINE

Many wineries serve inexpensive light lunches during tasting hours. You can also stock up for a picnic at the supermarket in Margaret River, and enjoy it in the wineries' grounds; **Cape Mentelle** and **Vasse Felix** both have green shady picnic areas beside a brook. The **Berry Farm** serves moderately priced lunches and morning and afternoon teas in an old timber cottage. **Goodfella's,** 97 Bussell Hwy., Margaret River (☎ **08/ 9757 3184**) specializes in gourmet wood-fired pizzas for under A\$15 (U.S.\$10.50).

✪ **Arc of Iris.** 151 Bussell Hwy., Margaret River. ☎ **08/9757 3112.** Reservations recommended. Main courses A\$10–\$18 (U.S.\$7–\$12.60). No credit cards. Wed–Mon 6:30pm–late. ASIAN/MOD OZ.

Don't be deceived by the humble brick interior, the mismatched laminate tables, the lime green vinyl chairs, or the old Vegemite jars that pass for wine glasses—in-the-know locals love this one-of-a-kind joint for its good food, alternative atmosphere, and friendly service. You might go for the braised venison to complement the velvety shiraz you picked up at the winery that day, the vegetarian Hokkien noodles to suit your chardonnay, or the mussels in white wine for your new-found favorite sauvignon blanc. BYO.

The Valley Café. Carters Rd. (near Caves Rd.), Margaret River. ☎ **08/9757 3225.** Reservations recommended. Main courses A\$10–\$15.50 (U.S.\$7–\$10.85) lunch, A\$14–\$18 (U.S.\$9.80–\$12.60) dinner. Seafood, market price. AE, BC, DC, MC, V. Fri–Wed 10am–5pm, Fri–Sat 6–10pm. MOD OZ.

Voted Most Popular Southwest Café in 1998, this new establishment serves up casual but stylish meals, along with views over the surrounding countryside. Typical lunch dishes include the homemade pasta of the day, or perhaps risotto with Augusta smoked chicken, sun-dried capsicum (bell pepper), and shaved Parmesan. Dinner might include a mixed grill of venison, lamb, and veal or a seafood special. BYO.

WORTH A SPLURGE

✪ **Newtown House.** 737 Bussell Hwy. (8km/5 miles past Busselton), Vasse. ☎ **08/ 9755 4485,** or 0417/172 048 mobile phone. Reservations recommended. Main courses A\$9.50–\$16.50 (U.S.\$6.65–\$11.55) at lunch, A\$22.50–\$24.50 (U.S.\$15.75–\$17.15) at dinner. AE, BC, DC, MC, V. Tues–Sat 10am–late. MODERN FRENCH/AUSTRALIAN.

If you're going to splurge on a good restaurant, this is one of the best places to do it in the Southwest. Folks come from far and wide to savor chef Stephen Reagan's skill in preparing such dishes as breast of duckling with star anise, ginger, soy, and oyster sauce on egg noodles. Desserts are no letdown, either—caramel soufflé with lavender ice cream and hot caramel sauce is a typical offering. Located in a historic homestead, the restaurant consists of two simple, intimate rooms with sisal matting and boldly colored walls. See "Where to Stay" above for details on accommodations here. BYO.

4 The Goldfields

595km (357 miles) E of Perth

After Paddy Hannan struck gold in 1893, the wheat-belt town of **Kalgoorlie** found itself in the happy position of having the richest square mile of gold-bearing earth in the world. That patch of land soon earned the moniker of the "Golden Mile." Today Kalgoorlie (pop. 33,000) is an Outback gold-rush boomtown, a mixture of yesteryear charm and late 20th-century corporate gold fever. The town is perched literally on the edge of the Superpit, a giant open-cut mine currently 4.5 kilometers (2¾ miles) long, 1.5 kilometers (1 mile) wide, and 300 meters (984 ft.) deep that yields around 26,562.5 kilos (850,000 oz.) of the precious yellow stuff every year—a mere 72.7 kilos (2,328 oz.) a day.

Kalgoorlie's isolation, kangaroos, and wide dusty streets lined with lovely old wrought-iron lace verandahs are about as "real Australian" as a town can get. Walking through town is almost like walking onto a Western movie set. Countless bars still do the roaring trade they notched up in the 1890s, but they now serve gold-mining

Fun Fact

In Kalgoorlie's young days, its streets were paved with a blackish spoil from the mining process, called "tellurides." It took a while before someone realized that tellurides contain up to 40% gold and 10% silver, but when they did, those streets were ripped up in one big hurry. The city fathers had paved the streets with gold and didn't even know it!

executives from Adelaide and Perth. In fact, the abundance of pubs, the ratio of males to females, and the thirst resulting from working in the mine all day add up to a notoriously raucous nightlife scene. Wet T-shirt competitions are not unheard of, and the beer flows in torrents.

Come to Kalgoorlie to pan for gold, shop for gold jewelry, roam ghost towns with an Aussie bushman, admire the architecture, gamble with miners at a two-up den in the eucalypts, learn how to track emus with Aboriginals, and prop up the bar for an ale or two (after all, "when in Rome"!).

Life on the Golden Mile is not so lively for everyone, however. Just down the road 39 kilometers (23½ miles) in Coolgardie, another 1890s gold-rush boomtown, the gold ran out in 1963. The town's semiabandoned air is a sad foil to Kalgoorlie's brash energy, but much of the lovely architecture remains, and wandering the streets signposted with historical markerboards gives you a pleasant tingle of nostalgia.

ESSENTIALS

GETTING THERE   **Skywest Airlines** (☎ **1800/642 225** in Australia, 08/9478 9999, or book through Ansett) flies to Kalgoorlie from Perth several times a day. The flight takes 1 hour and 5 minutes.

Greyhound Pioneer makes the 8-hour trip daily from Perth. The fare is A$89 (U.S.$62.30). It also has a daily service from Adelaide, which takes 27 hours and costs A$199 (U.S.$139.30).

Kalgoorlie is a stop on the *Indian Pacific* train service that runs in both directions between Sydney and Perth through Adelaide twice a week. Contact **Great Southern Railway** (☎ **13 21 47** in Australia, or 08/8213 4696). The *Prospector* train makes about one or two trips daily from Perth to Kalgoorlie. The one-way fare is A$49.30 (U.S.$34.50). Call **Westrail** (☎ **13 10 53** in Western Australia, or 08/9326 2244).

By road, Kalgoorlie is 595 kilometers (357 miles) east of Perth on the Great Eastern Highway. The 2,182-kilometer (1,309-mile) journey west from Adelaide features the longest straight stretch of highway in the world, the mind-numbingly flat and treeless Nullarbor Plain. If you want to drive from Adelaide, get advice from the **RACWA** (☎ **08/9421 4444**) in Perth or the **Royal Automobile Association of South Australia (RAA)** in Adelaide (☎ **08/8202 5400**).

VISITOR INFORMATION   The **Kalgoorlie-Boulder Tourist Centre,** 250 Hannan St., Kalgoorlie, WA 6430 (☎ **08/9021 1966;** fax 08/9021 2180), dispenses information on Kalgoorlie and outlying regions. The Hannan Street Heritage Trail map to the town's architecture, which the center sells for a few dollars, is worth buying. The center is open Monday through Saturday from 8:30am to 5pm, and Sunday and public holidays from 9am to 5pm. The **Coolgardie Tourist Bureau,** 62 Bayley St., Coolgardie, WA 6429 (☎ **08/9026 6090;** fax 08/9026 6008) is open daily from 9am to 5pm.

GETTING AROUND   **Avis** (☎ 08/9021 1722), **Budget** (☎ 08/9093 2300), **Hertz** (☎ 08/9093 2211), and **Thrifty** (☎ 08/9021 4722) have offices in Kalgoorlie.

Halfpenny Rentals (☎ 08/9021 1804, or 0419/211 804 mobile phone) is a local company that offers good rates.

The local bus service does not visit most attractions, so you will need to drive, take a cab, or join a tour. **Goldrush Tours** (☎ 1800/620 440 in Australia, or 08/9021 2954) does half-day tours of Kalgoorlie and Coolgardie.

TOURING A GOLD MINE & OTHER ADVENTURES IN KALGOORLIE

Gold is the theme of many attractions in Kalgoorlie. The best is ✪ **Hannan's North Tourist Mine,** Broad Arrow Road, about 6 kilometers (3¾ miles) north of the Tourist Centre on the Goldfields Highway (☎ 08/9091 4074), where you can don a hard hat and go underground to see how a real mine works today. Back on top you can pan for gold, watch a gold pour, watch a video in a re-created miner's tent, and pore over an impressive collection of mining memorabilia, old shaft heads, machinery, and huts in a re-created miners' village. The admission fee, which includes all activities, is A$15 (U.S.$10.50) for adults, A$11 (U.S.$7.70) for seniors and students, A$7.50 (U.S.$5.25) for school-age children, and A$38 (U.S.$26.60) for a family. It's a few dollars cheaper if you don't want to go underground. Underground tours, gold panning, and gold pouring are each staged four or five times throughout the day. The attraction is open daily from 9am to 5pm (closed Christmas and Boxing Day). Wear enclosed shoes, and allow 3 to 4 hours to see it all.

The **Museum of the Goldfields,** 17 Hannan St. (☎ 08/9021 8533), contains the first 12-kilo (400-oz.) gold bar minted in town, the Western Australian State Gold Collection, and some interesting historical displays on the town. Ride the free elevator up the mining head at the entrance for 360° views. The museum is open daily from 10am to 4:30pm, closed Christmas and Good Friday. Admission is free, with a donation requested.

Don't leave town without ogling the awesome Superpit, the gigantic open-cut mine from which most of the town's gold-bearing ore is extracted. Some 70 million tons of ore are removed each year. A lookout platform at Outram Street in Boulder, off the Eastern Bypass Road, is open daily from 6am to 6pm except when blasting closes it temporarily. Entry is free.

When they're not digging money out of the ground, the locals gamble for it at the **Bush Two-Up School,** 7 kilometers (4 miles) north of town on the Goldfields Highway past Hannan's North Tourist Mine. You can play this time-honored game of heads or tails in the school's authentic two-up ring out in the gum trees, with rusted corrugated-iron walls and no roof. The ring is open daily from 4:30pm to dusk, or later if the crowds are big (closed Christmas and Good Friday), and admission is free. Kids under age 18 are not permitted.

The **Royal Flying Doctor Service (RFDS)** (☎ 08/9093 1500) has a base at Kalgoorlie-Boulder Airport where visitors can browse a large display of memorabilia on this Outback aero-medical service, and watch a 20-minute video. Most communication is done through Perth these days, so it unlikely you will witness the radio operations, but you can look over the aircraft if one is in town. It is open Monday to Friday from 11am to 3pm. Admission is by donation.

Geoffrey Stokes of ✪ **Yamatji Bitja Aboriginal Bush Tours** (☎ 08/9093 3745, or 015/378 602) grew up the Aboriginal way in the bush. On his full-day 4WD tours you do stuff like forage for bush tucker, eat witchetty grubs (if you're game!), cook kangaroo and damper over a fire, track emus, and learn Aboriginal bushcraft. Tours cost A$70 (U.S.$49) per person. On twilight tours that cost A$30 (U.S.$21) per person, you listen to Dreamtime legends with billy tea and damper around a campfire. On overnight and longer tours into the bush you learn how to throw a boomerang, hunt kangaroos or goanna for dinner (with a gun, unless you're a really good shot with a boomerang), and sleep under the stars. The experience costs A$150 (U.S.$105) per person for the first night and A$80 (U.S.$56) for every night thereafter. Kids ages 4 to 12 are half price on all tours. All prices include hotel pickups.

EXPLORING COOLGARDIE

A few hours spent wandering Coolgardie's quiet streets graced with charming historical facades is a pleasant stroll back in time. The 150 signboards erected around the place, many with photos, detail what each site was like in the town's heyday at the turn of the century. The **Goldfields Exhibition,** 62 Bayley St.(☎ **08/9026 6090**), tells the town's history in a lovely 1898 building once used as the mining warden's courthouse (the Tourist Bureau is also here). Admission is A$3 (U.S.$2.10) for adults, A$2.50 (U.S.$1.75) for seniors, A$1 (U.S.70¢) for children under age 16, or A$7 (U.S.$4.90) for a family. It's open daily from 9am to 5pm. The **Railway Station Museum** (☎ **08/ 9026 6388**) in Woodward Street, 1 block south of Bayley Street, houses gold-rush memorabilia in the original 1896 station building, and a nicely preserved steam train. It's open daily from 9am to 4pm (closed Christmas and Good Friday). Admission is by donation.

If you like period architecture and interiors, browse through the National Trust–owned **Warden Finnerty's Residence** (☎ **08/9026 6028**) on McKenzie Street off Hunt Street. Built in 1895 for the mining warden, it has been restored with elegant period furniture. It is open daily from 9am to 4pm; admission is A$2 (U.S.$1.40), for adults A$1 (U.S.70¢) for kids.

WHERE TO STAY

Railway Motel. 51 Forrest St., Kalgoorlie, WA 6430. ☎ **1800/355 209** in Australia, or 08/9088 0000. Fax 08/9088 0290. 73 units (some with Jacuzzis). A/C MINIBAR TV TEL. A$140–$160 (U.S.$98–$112) double. Additional person A$30 (U.S.$21) extra. Children under 12 free. Free crib. Ask about weekend packages. AE, BC, DC, MC, V.

Although it's not the cheapest place in town, this colonial-style motel opposite the railway station, 4 blocks from the center of town, is the most conveniently located for the price. Its recently refitted rooms are popular with corporate travelers. All rooms come with hair dryers and in-room iron and boards, and some have kitchenettes. There is also a restaurant, a bar, room service, a heated swimming pool, and a Jacuzzi.

WHERE TO DINE

Akudjura. 418 Hannan St. (next to Hannan's View Motel). ☎ **08/9091 3311.** Reservations recommended. Main courses A$12.50–$22 (U.S.$8.75–$15.40). AE, BC, DC, MC, V. Mon 6pm–late, Tues–Sun 10:30am–late. MOD OZ.

The Italianate outdoor terrace under sailcloth, and the polished wood floors, curved silver bar, and blond wood furniture make this Kalgoorlie's first groovy restaurant. Bright young servers provide snappy service as you watch the traffic go by from the air-conditioned interior, or listen to the lion's head fountain burbling out on the patio. The menu ranges from all-day light meals like baguettes with roast vegetables and basil pesto to stylish main courses like chargrilled kangaroo with *kumara* (sweet potato) chips and spicy native plum sauce. The wine list carries the kind of labels you want to drink—good rather than extravagant—at prices you don't mind paying.

5 The Midwest & the Northwest: Where the Outback Meets the Sea

The Midwest and Northwest coasts of Western Australia are treeless, riverless semi-desert, occupied by vast sheep stations and only a handful of people. Temperatures soar into the 40s°C (over 115°F) in summer, and the sand burns bright orange in the blazing sun. But it's not the land you come here for—it's what's in the sea that you're interested in. Since the 1960s, a pod of **bottle-nosed dolphins** has been coming in to shallow water at **Monkey Mia** in the Shark Bay World Heritage region to greet delighted humans on the shore. Their magical presence has generated worldwide publicity and drawn people from every corner of the globe. So popular are the dolphins that a resort has been built on the lonely shore just to accommodate the crowds.

Another 872 kilometers (523 miles) north on the Northwest Cape, adventure-seekers from around the world come to snorkel with awesome ✪ **whale sharks**—measuring up to 18 meters (59 feet) long—every fall (March to early June). The Cape's parched shore and green waters hide an even more dazzling secret, though—a second barrier reef 260 kilometers (156 miles) long and 2 kilometers (1¼ miles) wide. ✪ **Ningaloo Reef Marine Park** protects 250 species of coral and 450 kinds of fish, dolphins, mantas, whales, and turtles in its 5,000 square kilometers (1,640 square miles). What is so amazing about the reef is not that it is here, but that so few people know about it. A mere 8,000 tourists a year make their way here. To you, that means beaches pretty much to yourself and a genuine sense of the frontier. And even the Great Barrier Reef can't beat Ningaloo Reef's proximity to shore, for a step or two off the beach is all it takes to enter a magical underwater garden.

The Midwest and Northwest are really too hot to visit between November and March, when some tour operators close down because of the heat. The best time to visit is April to October, when it will still be warm enough to swim.

SHARK BAY (MONKEY MIA)
853km (512 miles) N of Perth; 1,867km (1,120 miles) S of Broome

There is no guarantee the dolphins will show on time or at all, but they rarely miss a visit. Apart from these delightful sea-mammals, Shark Bay's waters teem with fish, turtles, the world's biggest population of dugongs (10,000 at last count), manta rays, sea snakes, and from June through October, whales. The area's only town is Denham (pop. 500) 129 kilometers (77½ miles) from the highway, which has a hotel or two, a restaurant, a couple of shops, and several fishing charter operators. There is no settlement, only a resort (see below), at Monkey Mia.

ESSENTIALS
GETTING THERE   **Skywest Airlines** (☎ **1800/642 225** in Australia, or 08/9478 9999, or book through Ansett) and **Western Airlines** (☎ 08/9277 4022) both fly three times a week from Perth to Shark Bay Airport (also called Monkey Mia Airport), 18 kilometers (11 miles) from Monkey Mia Dolphin Resort. At press time, there were no flights from Broome or Exmouth (although you can fly from Shark Bay to Exmouth). The one-way fare is A$249 (U.S.$174.30), plus A$13 (U.S.$9.10) Shark Bay airport tax. The Shark Bay Airport Bus (☎ 08/9948 1358) meets every flight and transfers you to Monkey Mia Dolphin Resort (see "Where to Stay & Dine") for A$7 (U.S.$4.90) per person one way. You do not need to book a seat.

There is no train to Shark Bay. **Greyhound Pioneer** travels several times daily from Perth and daily from Broome to the Overlander Roadhouse at the Shark Bay turnoff on the North West Coastal Highway. These services connect with the Overlander-Monkey Mia Dolphin Resort coach service, which only runs Monday, Thursday, and Saturday. The trip from Perth takes around 9 hours and the single fare is A$133 (U.S.$93.10). From Broome, it's about a 22-hour trip, and the fare is A$235 (U.S.$164.50) one way.

Driving time from Perth is about 9 hours on a two-lane highway. Beware of wildlife on the road and keep the gas tank full. Take the Great Northern Highway, then the Brand Highway to Geraldton, 424 kilometers (254½ miles) north of Perth, then the North West Coastal Highway for 280 kilometers (168 miles) north. Turn onto the Denham–Hamelin Road at the Overlander Roadhouse. Monkey Mia is 152 kilometers (91 miles) from the turnoff, 23 kilometers (14 miles) past Denham. If you want to break the journey, the Mercure Inn Geraldton, Brand Highway, Geraldton, WA 6530 (☎ 08/9921 2455, fax 08/9921 5830) has smart, clean motel rooms. Rates are A$105 (U.S.$73.50) double. In spring, you might want to take the Everlasting Trail wildflower route to Geraldton, described in "Tiptoeing through the Wildflowers" earlier in this chapter.

Many companies offer coach, 4WD, and aerial tours to Monkey Mia from Perth. Most road tours take up to 5 days, but **Feature Tours** (☎ **08/9479 4131**) runs overnight 24-hour express coach tours from Perth.

VISITOR INFORMATION   You will find excellent and wide-ranging information on Shark Bay's unique natural history and all local tours at the **Dolphin Information Centre** (☎ **08/9948 1366**), conveniently located at Monkey Mia Dolphin Resort (see "Where to Stay & Dine"). The official visitor information outlet is the **Shark Bay Tourist Centre** at 71 Knight Terrace, Denham, WA 6537 (☎ **08/9948 1253;** fax 08/9948 1065), open daily from 7:30am to 6:30pm.

Entry to the Monkey Mia Reserve is A$5 (U.S.$3.50) per adult, A$2 (U.S.$1.40) per child ages 6 to 16, and A$10 (U.S.$7) for a family. If you stay 2 days or up to 2 weeks, it is A$8 (U.S.$5.60) for adults and A$20 (U.S.$14) for a family for the duration of your stay.

GETTING AROUND   ATC Rent-A-Car (☎ **1800/999 888** in Australia but outside Western Australia, or 08/9948 1658) rents cars and 4WDs from its Denham office at 83 Knight Terrace. It will deliver to the airport 8 kilometers (5 miles) away for A$5 (U.S.$3.50), or to the resort for A$8 (U.S.$5.60).

SEEING THE DOLPHINS

At 7am guests at Monkey Mia Dolphin Resort are already gathering on the beach in quiet anticipation of the dolphins' arrival. By 8am three or more dolphins usually show, and they come and go until the early afternoon. Because of the crowds the dolphins attract (about 40 people a session in low season, coachloads in high season), a park ranger instructs everyone to line up knee-deep in the water as these playful swimsters cruise by your legs. You are not supposed to approach them, but if they come up to you, it's okay to pat them. Sometimes the dolphins even offer you a fish as a present! Feeding times are different each day to keep them from depending on the food. Once the crowd disperses, smart folk dive into the water just up the beach outside the

Money-Saving Tip

Monkey Mia Dolphin Resort sells airfare-inclusive, self-drive, and fly-drive accommodations packages that can be a good value. See "Where to Stay & Dine" below for contact information.

no-swimmers-allowed Dolphin Interaction Area because the dolphins often head there after the show. Apart from the Monkey Mia Reserve entry fee, there is no charge to see the dolphins.

A GREAT WILDLIFE CRUISE

Don't do what so many visitors do—come to Monkey Mia, see the dolphins, and then head back to Perth without seeing the rest of Shark Bay's incredible marine life. During a 2½-hour dugong (manatee) cruise aboard the sailing catamaran ✪ *Shotover* (☎ **08/9948 1481**), we saw a hammerhead shark, a baby great white, two very large sea snakes that we hauled out of the water for a closer look, three turtles, plenty of dolphins that came up to the boat, and a baby dugong riding on its mum's back. Dugongs leave the area from mid-May to August, so if you come then you may be "limited" to spotting dolphins, turtles, and other creatures. The dugong cruise departs at 1pm daily from the front of Monkey Mia Dolphin Resort and costs A$34 (U.S.$23.80). The boat also does a daily 2-hour dolphin cruise at 10:30am (A$29/U.S.$20.30). Children ages 5 to 14 are half price on both cruises.

WHERE TO STAY & DINE

Monkey Mia Dolphin Resort. Monkey Mia Rd., Shark Bay (P.O. Box 119, Denham, WA 6537). ☎ **1800/653 611** in Australia, 08/9385 3611 Perth reservations office, or 08/9948 1320 resort. Fax 08/9385 3486 Perth reservations office, or 08/9948 1034 resort. www.monkeymia.com.au. E-mail: sales@monkeymia.com.au. Tent sites; 90 powered sites; 10 on-site caravans; 6 canvas condo permanent tents, all with bathroom (shower only); 13 park homes, none with bathroom; 46 motel rooms, all with bathroom (shower only). A$140–$160 (U.S.$98–$112) motel room double or triple. A$70 (U.S.$49) up to 4 people in canvas condo; A$80 (U.S.$56) up to 4 people in park home. A$16–$20 (U.S.$11.20–$14) double, caravan site (with your own caravan) plus A$2 (U.S.$1.40) per night for power hookup; A$35–$50 (U.S.$24.50–$35) up to 4 people sharing caravan rented from resort, plus A$2 (U.S.$1.40) per night for power hookup. A$7 (U.S.$4.90) per person tent site; A$14 (U.S.$9.80) per bed for backpackers. Additional person A$4–$10 (U.S.$2.80–$7) extra. Linen A$10 (U.S.$7) per person in park homes, canvas condos, caravans, and for backpackers. Lower rates Nov 1–Mar 31 and May 1–Jun 30 .Weekly rates available. AE, BC, DC, MC, V.

"Set right on the very beach the dolphins visit daily, this pretty resort of green lawns and palms is such an oasis in the harsh surrounds, you think it's a cruel mirage. Most comfortable of the room types are the spacious air-conditioned motel rooms with a sink, a fridge, and a telephone. The Deluxe kind look right onto the beach and have their own barbecues. Your best budget choice is the permanent safari-tent canvas condos, which sleep up to six and have carpeted floors, electricity, a separate kitchen/living/dining area from the bedroom. They are not air-conditioned, so think twice about them in summer. Air-conditioned park homes sleep six and come with cooking facilities. The resort is equipped with a well-stocked supermarket, free tennis courts, a volleyball court, a tour desk, a pool and Jacuzzi fed by naturally warm underground water, a cafe, barbecues, and the airy Bough Shed Restaurant and cocktail bar overlooking the sea. A tour desk books you on 4WD tours, fishing trips, and other activities throughout the region, and rangers give free talks and slide shows some nights at the Dolphin Information Centre.

THE NORTHWEST CAPE

1,272km (763 miles) N of Perth; 1,567km (940 miles) S of Broome

Driving along the only road on the ✪ **Northwest Cape,** which sticks out into the Indian Ocean, is like driving on the moon. Hundreds of red anthills taller than you march away to the horizon, sheep and 'roos threaten to get under the wheels, and the sun beats down from a harsh blue sky. On the Cape's western shore is coral-filled Coral

Bay, a tiny cluster of dive shops, backpacker lodges, a low-key resort, and charter boats nestled on sand so white, water so blue, and ochre dust so orange you think the town-folk computer-enhanced it. Stretching north of town are deserted sandy beaches edged by coral. On the Cape's east coast is Exmouth (pop. 2,400), born in 1967 as a support town to the nearby Harold E. Holt Naval Communications Station, a joint Australian–United States center. Apart from whale shark diving, scuba diving and snorkeling are the big activities on the Cape, along with 4WD trips over the Cape Range and sur-rounding sheep stations.

ESSENTIALS

GETTING THERE   **Skywest Airlines** (☎ **1800/642 225** in Australia, or 08/9478 9999, or book through Ansett) flies 5 times a week from Perth, and on Saturday from Monkey Mia, to **Learmonth Airport** near Exmouth. A shuttle bus meets every flight and takes you the 35 kilometers (21 miles) to your Exmouth hotel for A$15 (U.S.$10.50) one way. It does not take bookings. **Coral Bay Adventures** (☎ **08/9942 5955**) makes transfers from Learmonth to Coral Bay, approximately 120 kilo-meters (72 miles) away for A$75 (U.S.$52.50) per person one-way, A$150 (U.S.$105) per person if you are the only person on the bus! Bookings are required.

Greyhound Pioneer operates three services a week from Perth to Coral Bay and Exmouth. The trip takes close to 17 hours and costs A$159 (U.S.$111.30) to Coral Bay and A$176 (U.S.$123.20) to Exmouth. You can also take the daily Greyhound coaches north from Perth or south from Broome (also about 17 hours) to the Giralia turnoff on the highway, where you join a thrice-weekly service in the wee morning hours to Exmouth (not Coral Bay). The Broome–Exmouth fare is A$218 (U.S.$152.60); to get to Coral Bay from Broome, you will need to rent a car in Exmouth, or hop off the Greyhound bus at Learmonth Airport and join the Coral Bay Adventures shuttle.

There is no train to the Northwest Cape.

The drive from Perth is through lonely country on a good two-lane highway. Beware of wildlife on the road, and keep the gas tank full. From Perth, take the Great Northern Highway, then the Brand Highway to Geraldton, then the North West Coastal Highway to Minilya; the Exmouth turnoff is 7 kilometers (4 miles) north of Minilya. Exmouth is 225 kilometers (135 miles) from the turnoff. Overnight at the **Mercure Inn Geraldton,** Brand Highway, Geraldton, WA 6530 (☎ **08/9921 2455,** fax 08/9921 5830), a decent motel. Rates are A$105 (U.S.$73.50) double.

VISITOR INFORMATION   The **Exmouth Tourist Bureau,** Payne Street, Exmouth, WA 6707 (☎ **08/9949 1176;** fax 08/9949 1441; e-mail: exmouth-tour@nwc.net.au) is open daily from 8:30am to 5pm. It also handles inquiries and bookings for activities and tours in Coral Bay. The **Coral Bay Tourist Association** is in the Coral Bay Supermarket, Coral Bay Arcade, Robinson Street, Coral Bay, WA 6701 (☎ and fax **08/9942 5988**).

GETTING AROUND   Many tours and dive operators pick up from either Exmouth or Coral Bay accommodations, but not usually both. The roads to Exmouth and Coral Bay are sealed (paved) but most of the western side of the Cape is not. Your 2WD rental car will not be insured for travel on unpaved roads.

Avis (☎ 08/9949 2492) and **Budget** (☎ 08/9949 1534) rent 4WDs as well as regular cars from their Exmouth offices. Exmouth company **Allens Car Hire** (☎ 08/9949 2403) rents conventional 2WD vehicles at good rates. **Exmouth Cape Tourist Village** rents 12 Suzuki Sierra 4WDs (to guests only) at an excel-lent A$66 (U.S.$46.20) a day, plus an extra A$45 (U.S.$31.50) per day fitted out for camping with two swags, an "esky" (plastic-foam cooler), and a cooker. Rental drops to A$30 (U.S.$21) a day, plus camping gear, for three days or longer. There is no local bus service.

DIVING WITH WHALE SHARKS

"Diving" is not really a correct term for this activity, because it's by snorkeling that you get close to these leviathans of the deep. Whale sharks are sharks, not whales, and they are the world's biggest fish, reaching an alarming 12 to 18 meters (39 to 59 ft.) in length. Terrified? Don't be. Their gigantic size belies a gentle nature (whew), and they cruise along unconcerned by the humans swarming around them like flies. Despite having a mouth big enough to swallow a boatload of snorkelers in one go, they eat plankton (whew again). Several boat operators take eager snorkelers out to swim with the fish when they appear from March through early June. One of the best is **Exmouth Diving Centre** (☎ **1800/655 156** in Australia, or 08/9949 1201) **and its Coral Bay sister company, Ningaloo** Reef Diving Centre (☎ **08/9942 5824**). Expect to pay around A$220 (U.S.$154) for the trip, which takes a day. Gear and wet suit are included. Shark protection regulations limit your boat to a maximum of 90 minutes with the fish.

DIVING, SNORKELING & FOUR-WHEEL DRIVING

Scuba dive the unspoiled waters of the Cape and you will see grouper, nudibranchs, manta rays, angel fish, octopus, morays, potato cod (which you can hand-feed), and loads of other underwater marvels. It's not uncommon for divers to see humpback and false killer whales, large sharks, dolphins, and turtles. The companies listed above run daily dives from either Exmouth or Coral Bay, as well as learn-to-dive courses. For a 2-dive day trip you will pay around A$110 (U.S.$77), with all gear supplied. Ningaloo's snorkeling is as brilliant as the Great Barrier Reef's, and you can even snorkel with humpback whales and manta rays with a "wingspan" up to 7 meters (23 ft.) off Coral Bay. Snorkel gear from the numerous dive operators rents for about A$12 (U.S.$8.40) per day. Exmouth Diving Centre and Ningaloo Reef Diving Centre run a variety of snorkel tours, including afternoon trips to the great coral at Bundegi Beach near Exmouth.

Because the Cape has few roads, touring is best done on a "Top of the Range" off-road 4WD trip with ✪ **Neil McLeod's Ningaloo Safari Tours** (☎ **08/9949 1550**). Neil takes you on a 240-kilometer (144-mile) escapade over the Cape Range National Park ridges and down to the reef. I climbed an old lighthouse, cruised Yardie Creek Gorge to spot rock wallabies, saw loads of 'roos, and scoffed Neil's mum's fruit cake for morning tea. The highlight was snorkeling in dazzling Turquoise Bay. This highly recommended full-day trip departs Exmouth, costs A$110 (U.S.$77) for adults and A$80 (U.S.$56) for children under age 12, and picks up from your hotel at 7:30am. On weekends you can extend this safari into an overnight campout on Neil's sister's 250,000-acre sheep station and spend the next day snorkeling at Coral Bay. All meals are included in the cost of A$250 (U.S.$175) for adults and A$180 (U.S.$126) for kids under age 12.

WHERE TO STAY & DINE

Exmouth and Coral Bay are 150 kilometers (90 miles) apart. Coral Bay is a good few degrees cooler than Exmouth and has divine diving, swimming, and snorkeling right outside the door; a restaurant and bar; a small supermarket; and little else. Exmouth is hot, dusty, and not particularly pretty but has more facilities, including a super-market and a cinema. Most tours not having to do with the reef, such as 4WD safaris, leave from Exmouth. Both places have loads of dive and snorkel companies. Wherever you stay, book ahead in whale shark season (Mar through early Jun).

In Exmouth

Apart from Exmouth Cape Tourist Village described below, the only place to stay in town—and the poshest—is the **Potshot Hotel Resort,** Murat Road, Exmouth, WA 6707 (☎ **08/9949 1200;** fax 08/9949 1486). Motel rooms and apartments cost A$99 to $165 (U.S.$69.30 to $115.50) double. Its poolside bar is the town's most popular watering hole, and its restaurant is fine, too.

Exmouth Cape Tourist Village. Truscott Crescent at Murat Rd., Exmouth, WA 6707. ☎ **08/9949 1101.** Fax 08/9949 1402. 200 tent sites and unpowered/powered campsites; 30 private dorm rooms; 100 dorm beds; 5 cabins, none with bathroom; 10 park homes, none with bathroom; 8 park homes with private bathroom just outside the door (shower only); 4 park home chalets, all with bathroom (shower only). A$7 (U.S.$4.90) per person tent site; A$15 (U.S.$10.50) dorm bed; A$17 (U.S.$11.90) unpowered site; A$19 (U.S.$13.30) powered site; A$18 (U.S.$12.60) single, A$36 (U.S.$25.20) double, private dorm room; A$60 (U.S.$42) park homes with shared facilities or cabin, A$65 (U.S.$45.50) park home with private bathroom outside, A$75 (U.S.$52.50) chalet. Discounts of A$1–$2 (U.S.70¢–$1.40) for YHA/Hostelling International members. BC, MC, V.

The park home suites and chalets nestled among the gardens at this amiable tourist village all have a clean kitchen/dining/living area with a linoleum floor, plastic dining suite, three or four bunks in the living area, and a separate double bedroom. The homes are air-conditioned. Chalets have an internal bathroom and a TV; homes share bathroom facilities, or have a clean, modern private shower room just outside. The cabins, some of which are new, have a kitchen and two bedrooms. A saltwater pool, a dive shop, and a good range of inexpensive action-oriented tours are among the services and facilities. On-site you will also find a minimart, public telephones, e-mail and Internet access, and mountain bikes for rent (they're free for backpackers).

In Coral Bay

Ningaloo Reef Resort. At the end of Robinson St., Coral Bay (postal: Maud Landing, Coral Bay, WA 6701). ☎ **08/9942 5934.** Fax 08/9942 5953. www.williams.com.au/resort.htm. E-mail: WHALESHARK@Bigpond.com. 33 units, all with bathroom (shower only), plus 6 dorm beds. A$15 (U.S.$10.50) per dorm bed; A$90–$110 (U.S.$63–$77) single; A$105–$110 (U.S.$73.50–$77) double; A$130 (U.S.$91) apt. Additional person A$10 (U.S.$7) extra; children under 12 A$5 (U.S.$3.50) extra. Ask about weekly rates. BC, MC, V.

This low-rise complex of motel rooms, studios, and apartments stands out as the best place to stay among Coral Bay's profusion of backpacker hostels. Centered around a blissfully green lawn overlooking the bay, the rooms are not fancy, but all are clean, neatly furnished, air-conditioned, and have TVs (fans only and no TVs in the dorms). Bring a hair dryer. Some bathrooms were overdue for a paint job; the motel bathrooms are newer than the studios. Studios have kitchenettes. The place has the only real restaurant in town, and a nice communal air, thanks to the bar doubling as the local pub.

Adelaide & South Australia

by Marc Llewellyn

Adelaide has the advantage over the other Australian state capitals in that it boasts Outback, vineyards, major wetlands, animal sanctuaries, a major river, and mountain ranges practically at its doorstep. Cost-conscious travelers will appreciate the city's inexpensive restaurants and accommodations (cheaper than in Sydney or Melbourne) and its small-town appeal.

If you plan to travel outside the city, a trip to one of the area's wine-producing regions should be at the top of your itinerary, seeing as how Australian wines have been taking home many of the most important international wine prizes for the past few years. Of all the wine areas, the Barossa is the closest to Adelaide and the most interesting. Centered around the town of Gawler, the oldest country town in South Australia, the Barossa is well known for its German architecture, including its 19th-century Lutheran churches, as well as its dozens of pretty hamlets, fine restaurants, and vineyards offering cellar-door tastings.

If you want to see animals instead of, or in addition to, grapes, you're in luck. You're likely to come across the odd kangaroo or wallaby near the main settlements, especially at dusk, or you could visit one of the area's many wildlife reserves. Otherwise, head out into the Outback where animals abound, or over to Kangaroo Island, which is without a doubt the best place in Australia to see many types of native animals in the wild without having to travel enormous distances.

Other places well worth visiting are the craggy Flinders Ranges. Although the scenery along the way from Adelaide is mostly unattractive grazing properties devoid of trees, the Flinders Ranges offer an incredible landscape of multicolored rocks, rough-and-ready characters, and even camel treks though the semidesert. On the other side of the mountain ranges the real Outback begins.

The South Australian Outback is serenely beautiful, with giant skies, red earth, and wildflowers after the rains. Out here you'll find bizarre opal-mining towns, such as Coober Pedy, where summer temperatures can reach 50°C (122°F) and where most people live underground to escape the heat.

If you prefer your landscape with a little more moisture, then head to the Coorong, a water-bird sanctuary rivaled only by Kakadu National Park in the Northern Territory (see chapter 10).

EXPLORING THE STATE

VISITOR INFORMATION   The **Tourism South Australia Travel Centre,** in the AMP Building, 1 King William St., Adelaide, SA 5000 (☎ **08/8303 2033,** or 1300/366 779 in Australia; fax 08/8303 2231; e-mail: sthaustour@tourism.sa.gov.au; www.visit-southaustralia.com.au), is the best place to collect information on Adelaide and traveling in the state.

For general information about South Australia's national parks, contact the **Department of Environment & Natural Resources Information Centre,** Australis House, 77 Grenfell St., Adelaide, SA 5000 (☎ **08/8204 1910,** fax 08/8204 1919). It's open Monday to Friday from 9am to 5pm.

GETTING AROUND   South Australia, at four times the size of the United Kingdom, has a lot of empty space between places of interest. The best way to see it is by car, although a limited rail service connects Adelaide with some areas. As for roads, the **Stuart Highway** bisects the state from south to north; it runs from Adelaide through the industrial center of Port Augusta (gateway to the Flinders Ranges), and onward through Coober Pedy to Alice Springs in the Red Centre. The **Eyre Highway** travels westward along the coastline and into Western Australia, whereas the **Barrier Highway** enters New South Wales just before the mining city of Broken Hill. The **Princes Highway** takes you east to Melbourne. You should seek travel advice from the **Royal Automobile Association of South Australia (RAA),** 41 Hindmarsh Square, Adelaide, SA 5000 (☎ **08/8202 4500;** fax 08/8202 4520), if you are planning to drive into the Outback.

1 Adelaide

"The City of Churches" has a reputation as a sleepy place, full of parkland and surrounded by vineyards. It's a throwback to the comfortable lifestyle of 1950s Australia that the more-progressive state capitals have left behind. The city attracts fewer visitors than, say, Sydney and Melbourne. Yet what Adelaide lacks in overall pulling power, it makes up for in charm—and the fact that it remains largely undiscovered by mass tourism.

Adelaide is a quiet and relatively uncrowded city, with wide tree-lined streets, numerous parks and gardens, sidewalk cafes, colonial architecture, and the River Torrens running through its center. It's a pleasant, open city, perfect for strolling or bicycling.

Although the city's immigrant population has added a cosmopolitan feeling that's evident in its diverse restaurants and complements its Mediterranean climate, Adelaide still has a feeling of old England about it. That's not surprising when you learn that Adelaide was the only Australian capital settled entirely by English free settlers rather than convicts, and that it attracted plenty more Brits after World War II, when they flocked here to work in the city's car parts and domestic appliance industries.

But it was earlier immigrants, from Germany, who gave Adelaide and the surrounding area a romantic twist. Arriving as refugees from their religious-torn country in the 1830s, German immigrants brought with them their wine-making skills, and established the wineries of the Barossa, the Clare Valley, the Coonawarra, and the Southern Vales. Today, more than one-third of all Australian wine—including some of the world's very best—comes from areas mostly within an hour's drive of Adelaide. As a result, Adelaidians of all socioeconomic groups are more versed in wine than even the French are, and regularly compare vintages, wine-growing regions, and wine-making trends.

South Australia

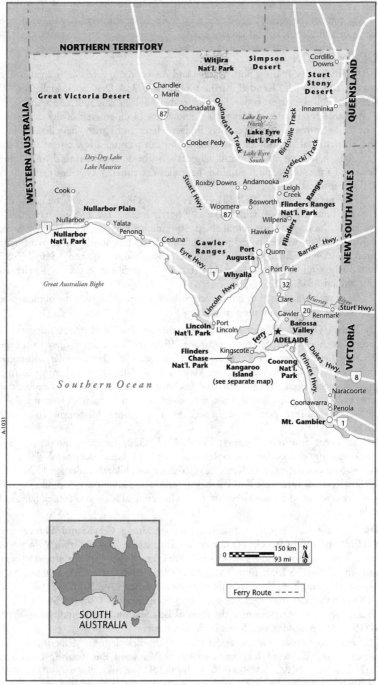

NORTHERN TERRITORY

WESTERN AUSTRALIA

QUEENSLAND

NEW SOUTH WALES

VICTORIA

Witjira Nat'l. Park

Simpson Desert

Cordillo Downs

Sturt Stony Desert

Chandler
Marla

Great Victoria Desert

Oodnadatta

87

Oodnadatta Track

Innaminka

Coober Pedy

Lake Eyre North

Lake Eyre Nat'l. Park

Birdsville Track

Strzelecki Track

Dey-Dey Lake
Lake Maurice

Lake Eyre South

Cook

Roxby Downs

Andamooka

Leigh Creek

Stuart Hwy.

Bosworth

Flinders Ranges

Nullarbor

Yalata
Penong

Woomera

87

Wilpena

Flinders Ranges Nat'l. Park

Nullarbor Plain

Nullarbor Nat'l. Park

Ceduna

Hawker

Gawler Ranges

Port Augusta

Quorn

Flinders Ranges

Barrier Hwy.

Eyre Hwy.

1

Whyalla

Port Pirie

Great Australian Bight

Lincoln Hwy.

32

Clare

Murray River

Sturt Hwy.

Gawler

20

Renmark

Lincoln Nat'l. Park

Port Lincoln

Barossa Valley

★ ADELAIDE

Ferry

Dukes Hwy.

Flinders Chase Nat'l. Park

Kingscote

Kangaroo Island
(see separate map)

Coorong Nat'l. Park

Princes Hwy.

Southern Ocean

Naracoorte

Coonawarra

Penola

Mt. Gambier

1

8

A-1031

SOUTH AUSTRALIA

0   150 km
     93 mi

N

Ferry Route - - - -

519

Any time of the year is a good time to visit Adelaide, although May to August can be chilly and December and January hot.

ORIENTATION

ARRIVING   By Plane   Both **Qantas** and **Ansett** fly to Adelaide from the other major state capitals. **Kendell Airlines** (☎ **1800/338 894** in Australia, or 08/ 8231 9567) is the largest regional airline serving Adelaide and South Australia.

Adelaide International Airport is 5 kilometers (3 miles) west of the city center. The major car-rental companies (Avis, Budget, Hertz, and Thrifty) have desks in both the international and domestic terminals. You can pick up a few tourist brochures here, but there is no official tourist help desk. In the domestic terminal you'll find a bank and a post office. Both terminals have showers, currency-exchange desks, shops, and places to eat.

The **Transit Bus** (☎ **08/8381 5311;** fax 08/8387 1678; www.transitregency. com.au) links the airport with major city hotels and the rail and bus stations. On weekdays, buses leave the terminals at 30-minute intervals between 6:30am and 9:30pm, and on weekends and public holidays buses run hourly (on the half hour) from the airport. Adult tickets are A$6 (U.S.$4.20) one way, and A$10 (U.S.$7) round-trip. Children's tickets cost A$3 (U.S.$2.10) each way. A **taxi** to the city will cost around A$15 (U.S.$10.50).

Check with your hostel or hotel when making a reservation, as some of them offer free pick-up services from the airport.

By Train   One of the great trains of Australia, the *Indian Pacific*, transports passengers to Adelaide from Perth (trip time: 36 hours) and from Sydney (trip time: 28 hours) twice a week, on Tuesday and Thursday. The other legendary Australian train is the *Ghan*, which runs from Melbourne to Adelaide and then up to Alice Springs weekly from November to April, and twice a week from May to October; trip time is 20 hours. The *Ghan* also runs a new service from Adelaide to Darwin.

The *Overlander* provides daily service to and from Melbourne (trip time: 12 hours).

Call **Great Southern Railways** (☎08/8213 4530) for more information and bookings, or check out timetables and fares on Great Southern's Web site (www.gsr.com.au/fares.htm). Rates are discounted for children under age 15.

The **Keswick Interstate Rail Passenger Terminal**, 2 kilometers (1¼ miles) west of the city center, is the main railway station. The terminal has a small snack bar and a cafe.

By Bus   Several major national operators, including **Greyhound Pioneer** and **McCafferty's,** run coaches to and from South Australia. The fare from Sydney (trip time: 22 hours) is around A$99 (U.S.$69.30); from Melbourne (trip time: 11 hours) around A$50 (U.S.$35); from Alice Springs (trip time: 20 hours), around A$150 (U.S.$105); and from Perth (trip time: 34 hours), around A$220 (U.S.$154).

Within the state the largest bus operator is **Stateliner** (☎ **08/8415 5555**).

Intercity coaches terminate at the **Central Bus Station,** 101 Franklin St. (☎ **08/ 8415 5533**), near Morphett Street in the city center.

Adventurous types should consider traveling to Adelaide from Melbourne (or vice versa) on the **Wayward Bus,** operated by the **Wayward Bus Touring Company,** 237 Hutt St., Adelaide, SA 5000 (☎ **1800/882 823** in Australia, or 08/8232 6646; fax 08/8232 1455). These 21-seat buses make the trip in three days via the Great Ocean Road; the fare is A$170 (U.S.$119) for adults and A$119 (U.S.$83.30) for children under age 15. You spend around four hours a day on the bus, and the driver acts as your guide. A picnic lunch each day and entry to national parks are included

The Adelaide Festival & Other Special Events

Adelaide is home to Australia's largest performing arts festival, the **Adelaide Festival,** which takes place over three weeks in March during even-numbered years. The festival includes literary and visual arts as well as dance, opera, classical music, jazz, cabaret, and comedy. The festival encompasses Writers' Week and a fringe comedy festival.

In February and March of odd-numbered years the three-day **Womadelaide Festival** of world music takes place, with concerts held in the Botanic Gardens. Crowds of 60,000 or more turn up to watch Australian and International artists.

Contact **Adelaide Festival,** 105 Hindley St., Adelaide, SA 5000 (☎ **08/ 8216 4444;** fax 08/8216 4455; www.festivals.on.net/adelaide.html), for more information.

in the fare. You must arrange your own accommodations in Port Fairy and Beachport. You can leave the trip and rejoin another later. Reservations are essential.

VISITOR INFORMATION   Head to the **Tourism South Australia Travel Centre,** in the AMP Building, 1 King William St., Adelaide, SA 5000 (☎ **1300/366 779** in Australia, or 08/8303 2033; fax 08/8303 2231; e-mail: sthaustour@tourism.sa.gov.au; www.visit-southaustralia.com.au), for maps and travel advice. It's open weekdays from 8:45am to 5pm, and weekends from 9am to 2pm. There's also an information booth in Rundle Mall, open daily from 10am to 5pm.

CITY LAYOUT   Adelaide is a simple city to find your way around in because of its grid-like pattern, which was planned down to each wide street and airy square by Colonel William Light in 1836. The city's official center is **Victoria Square,** where Town Hall is located. Bisecting the city from south to north is the city's main thoroughfare, **King William Street.** Streets running perpendicular to King William Street change names when they cross King William Street—Franklin Street changes to Flinders Street, for example. The most interesting cross streets for visitors are the restaurant strips of Gouger Street and Rundle Road; the latter runs into the pedestrian-only shopping precinct of Rundle Mall. Also important is Hindley Street, with its inexpensive restaurants and nightlife. On the riverbanks just north of the city center you'll find Adelaide Plaza, the home of the Festival Centre, the Convention Centre, and the Adelaide Casino. Bordering the city center on the north and south are **North Terrace,** which is lined with galleries and museums and leads to the Botanic Gardens, and **South Terrace.**

Follow King William Street south and you'll be chasing the tram to the beachside suburb of **Glenelg.** Follow King William Street north and it crosses the River Torrens and flows into sophisticated **North Adelaide,** an area crammed with Victorian and Edwardian architecture. North Adelaide's two main thoroughfares, O'Connell Street and Melbourne Street, are lined with multicultural restaurants, cafes, and bistros. To the northwest of the city is **Port Adelaide,** the historic maritime heart of South Australia and the home of some of the finest colonial buildings in the state, as well as good pubs and restaurants.

GETTING AROUND
BY PUBLIC TRANSPORTATION

By Bus   Adelaide's public bus network is divided into three zones, and fares are calculated according to the number of zones traveled. The city center is classed as

Money-Saving Tip

If you plan to get around the city via public transportation, it's a good idea to purchase a **Daytrip ticket,** which covers unlimited travel on buses, trams, and city trains within the metropolitan area, and costs A$5.40 (U.S.$3.80) for adults and A$2.50 (U.S.$1.75) for children ages 5 to 15. Tickets are available from most train stations, newsagencies, and from the Passenger Transport Board Information Centre.

Zone 1. Fares are A$1.60 (U.S.$1.10) in this zone from 9am to 3pm on weekdays and A$2.80 (U.S.$1.95) most other times. You can buy tickets on board the bus or at newsagencies around the city. You can pick up a free metro information and timetable booklet at the **Passenger Transport Board Information Centre** (☎ **08/8210 1000**), on the corner of Currie and King William streets; it's open Monday to Saturday from 8am to 6pm, and Sunday from 10:30am to 5:30pm. For timetable information over the phone, call the **Passenger Transport Infoline** (☎ **08/8210 1000**).

The **City Loop** bus provides free bus service around the city center along North Terrace, East Terrace, Grenfell Street, Pulteney Street, Wakefield Street, Grote Street, Morphett Street, Light Square, Hindley Street, and West Terrace.

The **Adelaide Explorer** bus stops at 10 sights around town and costs A$23 (U.S.$16.10) for adults, A$15 (U.S.$10.50) for children, and A$55 (U.S.$38.50) for a family of four. The bus stops at each destination every 1½ hours in summer and every 3 hours in winter. The full loop takes a leisurely 2¾ hours, with commentary. Call ☎ **08/8364 1933** for details. Buy tickets on the bus.

By Tram   The Glenelg Tram runs between Victoria Square and the beachside suburb of Glenelg. Tickets are valid for two hours and cost A$1.60 (U.S.$1.10) for adults and A80¢ (U.S.55¢) for children ages 5 to 14 between 9am and 3pm, and A$2.80 (U.S.$1.95) for adults and A$1 (U.S. 70¢) for children during peak time. The journey takes 29 minutes.

BY TAXI & CAR   The major cab companies are **Yellow Cabs** (☎ **13 22 27**), **Suburban** (☎ **08/8211 8888**), and **Amalgamated** (☎ **08/8223 3333**). **Access Cabs** (☎ **1300/360 940** in South Australia only) offers wheelchair taxis.

The big four car-rental companies have offices in the area: **Avis,** 136 North Terrace (☎ 08/8410 5727); **Budget,** 274 North Terrace (☎ 08/8223 1400); **Hertz,** 233 Morphett St. (☎ 08/8231 2856); and **Thrifty,** 100 Franklin St. (☎ 08/8211 8788).

FAST FACTS: Adelaide

American Express   The **AMEX office,** at 13 Grenfell St. (☎ **08/8202 1400**), is open during normal business hours.

Business Hours   Generally, **banks** are open Monday through Thursday from 9:30am to 4pm and Friday from 9:30am to 5pm. **Stores** are generally open Monday through Thursday from 9am to 5:30pm, Friday from 9am to 9pm, Saturday from 9am to 5pm, and Sunday from 11am to 5pm.

Currency Exchange   Banks and hotels, the casino, and the Myer department store in Rundle Mall all cash traveler's checks. The **Thomas Cook** office is at 45 Grenfell St. (☎ **08/8212 3354**).

Dentist   Contact the Australian Dental Association Emergency Information Service (☎ 08/8272 8111), open nightly from 5pm to 9pm, and Saturday and Sunday from 9am to 9pm. The service will put you in touch with a dentist.

Doctor   Contact the **Royal Adelaide Hospital,** on North Terrace (☎ **08/ 8223 0230**), or Emergency Medical Service (☎ **08/8223 0230**). The Travellers' Medical & Vaccination Centre, 29 Gilbert Place (☎ **08/8212 7522**), offers vaccinations and other travel-related medicines.

Drugstores (Chemists)   Burden Chemists, Shop 11, Southern Cross Arcade, King William St., (☎ **08/8231 4701**), is open Monday through Thursday from 8am to 6pm, Friday from 8am to 8pm, and Saturday from 9am to 1pm.

E-mail   Ngapartji Multimedia Centre, 211 Rundle St., (☎ **08/8232 0839**), offers e-mail and Internet access Monday to Thursday from 8:30am to 7pm, Friday from 8:30am to 10pm, Saturday from 10am to 10pm, and Sunday from noon to 7pm.

Emergencies   Dial ☎ **000** to call an ambulance, the fire department, or the police in a emergency.

Hospitals   The Royal Adelaide Hospital, North Terrace (☎ **08/8222 4000**) is located in the city center.

Lost Property   If you've lost something on the street, contact the nearest police station. For items left on public transport, contact the Lost Property Office on the main concourse of the Adelaide Railway Station on North Terrace (☎ **08/ 8218 2552**); it's open Monday through Friday from 9am to 5pm.

Luggage Storage/Lockers   Luggage lockers at Adelaide Airport in the domestic terminal cost A$1 (U.S.70¢) per hour to a maximum of A$7 (U.S.$4.90) for 24 hours. You need exact change. At the Central Bus Station on Franklin Street (☎ **08/8415 5533**) luggage lockers cost A$2 (U.S.$1.40) for 24 hours.

Post Office   The General Post Office (GPO) is at 141 King William St., Adelaide, SA 5000 (☎ **08/8216 2222**). It's open Monday through Friday from 8am to 6pm and Saturday from 8:30am to noon. General delivery mail (*poste restante*) can be collected Monday through Friday from 7am to 5:30pm and Sunday from 9am to 1pm.

Safety   Adelaide is a very safe city, although it's wise to avoid walking along the River Torrens at night, and through side streets near Hindley Street after dark.

ACCOMMODATIONS YOU CAN AFFORD
IN THE CITY CENTER

Barron Townhouse. 164 Hindley St., Adelaide, SA 5000. ☎ **1800/888 241** in Australia, 800/624-3524 in the U.S. and Canada, 0800/892 407 in the U.K., 0800/803 524 in New Zealand, or 08/8211 8255. Fax 08/8231 1179. www.flag.co.au/hotels/townadel.htm. 68 units. A/C MINIBAR TV TEL. A$114 (U.S.$79.80) standard double; A$152 (U.S.$106.40) deluxe double; A$162 (U.S.$113.40) executive room. Additional person A$16 (U.S.$11.20) extra. Rates include snack-pack breakfast. Children under 12 free in parents' room. Lower rates in off-season and weekends. Ask about package deals. AE, BC, DC, JCB, MC, V. Free parking.

Friendly staff and garish china flamingos welcome you to this uninspiring-looking four-star concrete block. It's a 10- to 15-minute walk from the center of town, 5 minutes from the casino, and not far from the nightclub and "red light" district. Rooms are spacious and comfortable enough, and there's a very good rooftop pool and sauna. Downstairs is the informal Flamingos bistro, due to be renovated in mid-1999, and the cocktail lounge.

City Park Motel. 471 Pultney St., Adelaide, SA 5000. ☎ **08/8223 1444.** Fax 08/8223 1133. 18 units, 14 with bathroom (shower only). A/C TV TEL. A$50 (U.S.$35) double without bathroom; A$69 (U.S.$48.30) double with bathroom. Additional person A$10 (U.S.$7) extra. AE, BC, DC, MC, V. Free parking. The tram to Glenelg stops just around the corner, and 3 streets up is a bus stop for the free City Loop bus.

The rooms in this first-floor motel just outside the city center have modern furnishings and nice bathrooms with a shower. Some rooms have private balconies. Also on the premises is a separate bathroom with a tub. The best room is no. 45. The building underwent an A$1 million (U.S.$700 thousand) upgrade in 1998, and downstairs there's a new cocktail bar, nightclub, and bistro.

Moore's Brecknock Hotel. 401 King William St., Adelaide, SA 5000. ☎ **08/8231 5467.** Fax 08/8410 1968. 10 units, none with bathroom. A/C A$50 (U.S.$35) double; A$65 (U.S.$45.50) triple. Rates include continental breakfast. AE, BC, DC, MC, V. Free parking. The tram to Glenelg stops in front of the hotel.

Adelaide's original Irish pub, built in 1851, still attracts a lot of Irish who come here for the great selection of beer and reasonably priced home-style cooking—it reputedly serves Adelaide's best hamburgers. The pub is also very popular with American guests who use the hotel accommodations upstairs as a base from which to discover Kangaroo Island and other parts of the state. The Brecknock is about 4 blocks from Victoria Square. Live bands perform downstairs Friday, Saturday, and Sunday evenings, but the music finishes at 1am on Friday and Saturday, and at 10pm on Sunday, so you shouldn't have too much trouble sleeping. Rooms are large and pleasantly decorated in old-world style. They were last refurbished in 1988. Each has a double bed, a single bed, and a sink; bathrooms are down the hall. A laundry and a luggage lock-up room are on the premises. At the time this book went to press, plans were in the works for a 56-bed backpackers' accommodation to be opened adjacent to the property; it should be ready by mid-1999.

Super-Cheap Sleeps

✪ **Adelaide City Backpackers.** 239 Franklin St., Adelaide, SA 5000. ☎ **08/8212 2668.** Fax 08/8212 7974. 13 units, none with bathroom. A$35 (U.S.$24.50) double. A$13 (U.S.$9.10) dorm bed. Additional person A$10 (U.S.$7) extra; children A$5 (U.S.$3.50) extra. BC, DC, MC, V. Free parking. 5-minute walk from city center, or take City Loop bus to Morphett St.

Specialized private backpacker hostels are such an exceptional value in Australia that you sometimes wonder whether they make any money at all. This busy, family-owned place is set up in a two-story 19th-century building in a nice area of town just 2 minutes from the bus station. In all, there are five dorm rooms, each of which sleeps 4 to 10 people, and simple-style doubles, all of which share bathrooms. There are also a garden/courtyard, two TV lounges (one nonsmoking), a bar, a kitchen, and a laundry. Home-cooked meals (included free for your first night's stay) are available every evening for just A$4 (U.S.$2.80). At the weekly Sunday evening barbecue, you can meet other travelers. The hostel arranges free pickups from the airport and the bus and train stations.

Travel Tip

If you plan to be in town during the biennial **Adelaide Festival** (the next one will be held in early March 2000), make sure you book your accommodations well in advance. Accommodations can also get pretty scarce during the Christmas and New Year's period, so it's wise to book well in advance if you intend to be here during this time.

Adelaide Accommodations & Dining

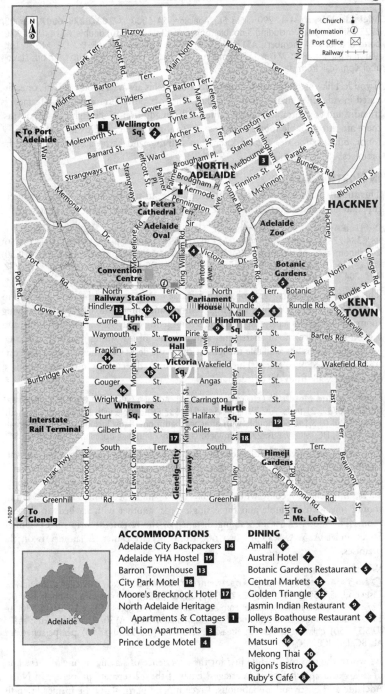

ACCOMMODATIONS
- Adelaide City Backpackers **14**
- Adelaide YHA Hostel **19**
- Barron Townhouse **13**
- City Park Motel **18**
- Moore's Brecknock Hotel **17**
- North Adelaide Heritage Apartments & Cottages **1**
- Old Lion Apartments **3**
- Prince Lodge Motel **4**

DINING
- Amalfi **6**
- Austral Hotel **7**
- Botanic Gardens Restaurant **5**
- Central Markets **15**
- Golden Triangle **12**
- Jasmin Indian Restaurant **9**
- Jolleys Boathouse Restaurant **5**
- The Manse **2**
- Matsuri **16**
- Mekong Thai **10**
- Rigoni's Bistro **11**
- Ruby's Café **8**

Adelaide YHA Hostel. 290 Gilles St., Adelaide, SA 5000. ☎ **08/8223 6007.** Fax 08/ 8223 2888. 58 beds, including 3 double rooms. A$42 (U.S.$29.40) double. A$14 (U.S.$9.80) dorm bed for YHA members, A$17 (U.S.$11.90) for nonmembers. AE, BC, DC, MC, V. Limited free parking. Bus: 171 or 172 from King William St.; there's free pickup from bus station after 4pm (call from station).

If you feel like meeting people, then a youth hostel is always a good bet. This one, situated in Adelaide's main square near the corner of South Terrace and East Terrace, is friendly and comfortable, though quite small. In addition to the eight-person dorms, there are three double rooms that sleep up to three people. There's no lounge or TV room, but a barbecue, a good kitchen, a laundry, and a travel agency are on the premises.

IN NORTH ADELAIDE

This suburb across the river is an interesting place to stay because of its nice architecture and good restaurants. It's about a 10-minute bus ride from the city center.

Old Lion Apartments. 9 Jerningham St., North Adelaide, SA 5006. ☎ **08/8334 7799.** Fax 08/8334 7788. 57 units. A/C TV TEL. A$130 (U.S.$91) 1-bedroom apt.; A$145 (U.S.$101.50) 2-bedroom apt.; A$180 (U.S.$126) 3-bedroom apt. Additional person A$15 (U.S.$10.50) extra, A$5 (U.S.$3.50) children 3–12. AE, BC, CB, DC, MC, V. Free parking. Bus: 272, 273, 204.

These nice apartments were constructed inside a renovated old brewery building in 1997. The units are spacious, with high ceilings, and come with a kitchenette, a living room, French doors separating bedrooms from living quarters, a shower and tub, and a good-sized balcony. All apartments also have use of a washing machine and drier. VCRs and videos are available for rent at the front desk. Continental breakfast costs A$8.50 (U.S.$5.95) extra. The complex is on a direct bus route and about a 15-minute walk from the city center.

Princes Lodge Motel. 73 Lefevre Terrace, North Adelaide 5006. ☎ **08/8267 5566.** Fax 08/8239 0787. 21 units. A/C TV TEL. A$48 (U.S.$33.60) double with separate private bathroom; A$58 (U.S.$40.60) double with attached bathroom. Rates include continental breakfast. AE, BC, DC, MC, V. Bus: 222 from Victoria Square (with pick-ups along King William St.).

One of the best motels in Adelaide, the Princes Lodge looks more like a large private home than your typical simple brick roadside structure. Rooms are nicely decorated and were upgraded in 1997 and 1998 with new beds. All have the usual motel appliances, and generally come with a double and a single bed. There are three family rooms: one with a double and three single beds, another with six beds in the one room. The motel is within walking distance of the restaurant strip on O'Connell Street and a A$5 (U.S.$3.50) taxi ride from the city center. A laundry is on the premises.

Worth a Splurge

✪ **North Adelaide Heritage Apartments & Cottages.** Office: 109 Glen Osmond Rd., Eastwood, SA 5063. ☎ **08/8272 1355,** or 0418/289 494 (mobile phone). Fax 08/ 8272 1355. E mail: heritage@senet.com.au. 12 units. TV TEL. Rates A$115–$170 (U.S.$80.50– $119), depending on accommodation. Additional person A$50 (U.S.$35) extra; A$25 (U.S.$17.50) children under 12. Breakfast A$6–$12 (U.S.$4.20–$8.40) per person extra. AE, BC, DC, JCB, MC, V.

It's worth the trip to Adelaide just for the experience of staying in one of these out-of-this-world apartments and cottages. Each of the 12 separate properties in North Adelaide and Eastwood are fabulous. I recommend particularly the former Friendly Meeting Chaple Hall, a small, simple gabled hall of blue-stone rubble trimmed with brick. Built in 1878, it's stocked with period pieces and antiques and rounded off with a modern, fully stocked kitchen, a huge spa bath, a queen-size bed, and CD player and TV.

Another standout is the George Lowe Esq. This huge 19th-century apartment is also stocked with antiques, has a huge four-poster bed in the bedroom, a separate bathroom, a lounge, and a full kitchen. Guests also have use of nice gardens. All properties are within easy walking distance of the main attractions in the area. The company has just bought the old North Adelaide Fire Station and has renovated it into three separate apartments.

IN GLENELG

I'd recommend anyone, without hesitation, to stay in Glenelg rather than in the city center. The journey to the city center by car or tram takes less than 30 minutes, and the airport is less than 10 minutes away. Add to this the sea, the lovely beach, the fun fair, the great shops, the good pub, and the nice accommodations and you have a perfect place to ease up on your holiday.

Atlantic Tower Motor Inn. 760 Anzac Hwy., Glenelg, SA 5045. ☎ **08/8294 1011.** Fax 08/8376 0964. 27 units (20 with shower only). A/C TV TEL. A$68 (U.S.$47.60) double; A$88 (U.S.$61.60) deluxe double; A$115–$130 (U.S.$80.50–$91) suite. Additional person A$10 (U.S.$7) extra; children under 15 free in parents' room. Free parking. Hotel is 1 block from the tram stop.

I've stayed here several times and highly recommend it if you're looking for somewhat inexpensive accommodations near the beach. You can't miss this tubular building not far from the sea, with its slowly revolving restaurant on the 12th floor. Rooms are simple, but very bright, and have nice park views through large windows; each room has a double and a single bed, and even comes with a toaster. The deluxe rooms are a bit nicer and come with baths rather than just showers. Suites have two rooms and excellent views; the most expensive have a spa. The gently turning Rock Lobster Cafe upstairs was voted the American Express best seafood restaurant in South Australia in 1997.

GREAT DEALS ON DINING

With more than 600 restaurants, pubs, and cafes, Adelaide boasts more dining spots per capita than anywhere else in Australia. Many of them are clustered in particular areas, such as on Rundle and Gouger streets in the city and in North Adelaide, where you'll find almost every style of cuisine imaginable. For cheap noodles, laksas, and sushi, as well as plenty of cakes, head to Adelaide's **Central Markets** (☎ 08/8203 7494), behind the Adelaide Hilton Hotel between Gouger and Grote streets.

Because of South Australia's healthy wine industry, you'll find that many restaurants have extensive wine lists—though with spicier foods it's probably wiser to stick with beer, or a fruity white in a pinch. Many Adelaide restaurants allow diners to bring their own wine (BYO), but most charge a steep corkage fee to open your bottle—A$6 (U.S.$4.20) or so is not uncommon.

IN THE CITY CENTER

Amalfi. 29 Frome St. (just off Rundle St.). ☎ **08/8223 1948.** Reservations recommended. Main courses A$12.50–$16.50 (U.S.$8.80–$11.55). AE, BC, DC, MC, V. Mon–Thurs 11:30am–3pm, and 5:30–11pm, Fri 11:30am–3pm and 5:30pm–midnight, Sat 5:30pm–midnight. ITALIAN.

Come here for good Italian cooking at reasonable prices, served up in a lively atmosphere. The pizzas are the best in Adelaide—though a little expensive—and consistently good veal and pasta dishes are always on the menu. Be sure to check out the daily specials board, where you can pick out a very good fish dish or two.

Something Different—Dining Tours

If you like good food and wine, but can't decide on just one restaurant, try one of **Graeme Anderson's** (☎ 08/8336 8333; fax 08/8336 4075) three interesting dining tours: Grazing on Gouger, Asia on a Plate Tours, and East East East Tours. **Grazing on Gouger** is a progressive luncheon in Gouger Street, taking in five courses at five restaurants, with Barossa wines included. The tour runs every Friday and Saturday and costs A$70 (U.S.$49) per person; meet at noon in the lobby of the Adelaide Hilton. The **Asia on a Plate Tour** is a progressive lunch at three top Asian restaurants on Gouger Street. The tour runs every Friday at noon and costs A$70 (U.S.$49), including wine; meet upstairs in Matsuri restaurant, 167 Gouger St. The **East East East Tour** is a progressive lunch through Adelaide's progressive east end, in which you enjoy fine dishes and good wines. It runs every Saturday at noon and costs A$80 (U.S.$56), including wine. Private tours are also available on request.

Austral Hotel. 205 Rundle St. ☎ **08/8223 4660.** Main courses A$7.50–$9 (U.S.$5.25–$6.30) in bistro, A$15–$16 (U.S.$10.50–$11.20) in restaurant. AE, BC, MC, V. Daily noon–3pm, and 6–10:30pm. MODERN AUSTRALIAN.

This large pub, with dark timber and forest-colored wallpaper, is a pleasant place for a good-value pub meal. You can dine at the bar, outside on the sidewalk, or in the dining room. The bistro serves burgers, fish-and-chips, pastas, laksas, and Thai curries. The restaurant is a bit more posh, and serves up risotto, handmade crab ravioli, beef fillets, chicken dishes, venison, paella, and baby octopus.

Botanic Gardens Restaurant. 309 North Terrace. ☎ **08/8232 3266.** Reservations recommended. Main courses A$18–$25 (U.S.$12.60–$17.50). AE, BC, DC, MC, V. Fri noon–3pm (Thai only); Tues–Sat 6pm–late. THAI/MODERN AUSTRALIAN.

You'll find two of Adelaide's best chefs at this snappy restaurant. The food is heavily Asian-influenced, especially Thai, and is beautifully presented by thoughtful waiters who really know their job. On the menu you might find a tartlet of oysters and leeks with a lemon butter sauce, Thai curries, and braised goose. Desserts often include old-timers such as steamed pudding and blancmange with stewed prunes, as well as more Asian-influenced items such as sago with jackfruit and coconut ice cream.

Golden Triangle. 106a Hindley St. ☎ **08/8211 8222.** Reservations recommended. Main courses A$9.50–$15 (U.S.$6.65–$10.50). AE, BC, DC, MC, V. Daily noon–2:30pm, and 5pm until last customer. THAI/LAOS/BURMESE.

From Thai chicken laksa and Burmese beef curry to tom-yum soup and Indonesian Nasee Goreng, the Golden Triangle covers a lot of ground. The restaurant is small and narrow, with sea-green walls, a buddha in the corner, and just 10 tables. This grotto-like joint is dark, cramped, and badly furnished, but all this only serves to emphasize the wonderfully authentic food that will blow your socks off. Pop in for lunch for around A$5 (U.S.$3.50), or a dinner special that includes a starter and main course (except seafood), a glass of wine, fruit juice or coffee, and a cinema ticket thrown in for the nearby movie complex—all for just A$22.50 (U.S.$15.75).

Jasmin Indian Restaurant. 31 Hindmarsh Square. ☎ **08/8223 7837.** Reservations recommended. Main courses A$14.50–$16.50 (U.S.$10.15–$11.55). Lunch banquet A$18 (U.S.$12.60), dinner banquet A$27 (U.S.$18.90). AE, BC, DC, JCB, MC, V. Tues–Fri noon–2:30pm; Tues–Sat 5:30–9:30pm. NORTH INDIAN.

Prices have crept up as this place has gotten more popular, but this family-run Adelaide institution a block south of Rundle Mall is still a good value. Indian artifacts and signed cricket bats from visiting Indian teams decorate the walls. The atmosphere is comfortable yet busy, and the service is professional. The house special is the very hot beef vindaloo, but all the old favorites, such as tandoori chicken, butter chicken (a big seller here), lamb korma, and malabari beef with coconut cream, ginger, and garlic, are on the menu, too. Mop it all up with naan bread, and cool your palate with a side dish of raita. The suji halwa, a semolina pudding with nuts, is the best I've tasted.

✪ **Matsuri.** 167 Gouger St. ☎ **08/8231 3494.** Reservations recommended. Main courses A$9.50–$1680 (U.S.$6.65–$11.80). AE, BC, DC, MC, V. Fri noon–2pm, Wed–Mon 5:30–11pm. JAPANESE.

I really like the atmosphere in this very good Japanese restaurant on the popular Gouger Street restaurant strip. The food is prepared by world-famous ice sculptor and sushi master Takaomi Kitamura and is very nicely presented. The sushi and sashimi dishes are some of the best in Australia. Diners on a budget will be happy to know that every Monday is "sushi festival night," when sushi is 50% off. Sushi is discounted 30% during happy hour Wednesday through Sunday if your order is placed before 7pm (you can order over the phone and eat later). Other popular dishes include vegetarian and seafood tempura, *yose nobe* (a hot pot of vegetables, seafood, and chicken), and *chawan mushi* (a steamed savory custard dish). The service is friendly and considerate. BYO; corkage is A$4.50 (U.S.$3.15) a bottle.

Mekong Thai. 68 Hindley St. ☎ **08/8231 2914.** Reservations recommended. Main courses A$9.60–$10.90 (U.S.$6.75–$7.65). AE, BC, MC, V. Daily 5:15pm–late. THAI/MALAYSIAN/CAMBODIAN.

Although this place is not much to look at—with simple tables and chairs, some outside in a portico—it has a fiery reputation for good food among in-the-know locals. The food is spicy and authentic and the portions are filling. It's also a vegetarian's paradise, with at least 16 meat-free mains on the ethnically varied menu.

Rigoni's Bistro. 27 Leigh St. ☎ **08/8231 5160.** Reservations recommended. Main courses A$10.90–$16 (U.S.$7.65–$11.20); antipasto bar (lunch only) A$9.90–$11.90 (U.S.$6.95–$8.35). AE, BC, DC, JCB, MC, V. Mon–Fri noon–2:30pm and 6–10pm. ITALIAN.

Located on a narrow lane west of King William Street, this traditional Italian trattoria is often packed at lunch, though less frantic in the evening. It's big and bright, with high ceilings and russet quarry tiles. Window seats are at a premium. A long central bar through the middle of the dining room has brass plates marking the stools of regular diners. The food is good and very traditional. The chalkboard menu changes often, but you are quite likely to find lasagna, veal in white wine, marinated fish, and various pasta dishes. In addition, there's an extensive salad bar with a variety of antipasto. An outside dining area should be completed by the time you read this.

Ruby's Café. 255b Rundle St. ☎ **08/8224 0365.** Main courses A$7.70–$15.20 (U.S.$5.40–$10.65). AE, BC, MC, V. Sun 9am–5pm; daily 6:30–11:30pm. MODERN AUSTRALIAN.

Situated in suitably unpretentious surroundings for a former market cafe catering to local workers, Ruby's is an Adelaide institution. It still has its laminated tables and the NO SPITTING, NO COARSE LANGUAGE sign behind the bar, despite being far more upmarket than that. Basically, you get a very good restaurant meal in an old cafe atmosphere at good prices. Main courses include filling curries and upscale pasta dishes, hearty meals such as lamb shanks, and quite a few vegetarian options. The toffee pudding with toffee sauce is a favorite. The menu changes every six weeks.

Worth a Splurge

✪ **Jolleys Boathouse Restaurant.** Jolleys Lane. ☎ **08/8223 2891.** Reservations recommended. Main courses A$16–$19.50 (U.S.$11.20–$13.65). Lunch A$19.50 (U.S.$13.65) for 1 course, A$29.50 (U.S.$20.65) for 2 courses, and A$38.50 (U.S.$26.95) for 3 courses. AE, BC, DC, MC, V. Daily noon–2:30pm; Wed–Sat 6:30–9pm. MODERN AUSTRALIAN.

Jolleys is nicely situated on the banks of the River Torrens, with views of boats, ducks, and black swans. Business people and ladies-who-lunch rush for the three outside tables for a bit of al fresco dining, but if you miss out you won't be too let down by the bright and airy interior, with its cream-colored tablecloths and director's chairs. You might start with the intriguing goat's curd ravioli with red pesto and chives. Moving on, you could tuck into the roasted duck with hazelnut risotto (close your eyes to the peaceful quacking out on the river if you can). The banana and cardamon soufflé for dessert is wicked.

IN NORTH ADELAIDE

✪ **The Manse.** 142 Tynte St., North Adelaide. ☎ **08/8267 4636.** Reservations recommended. A$17.50–$21.50 (U.S.$12.25–$15.05). Fri noon–3pm; Mon–Sat 6–10pm. AE, BC, DC, MC, V. Bus: 182, 224, 226, 228, or 229. SEAFOOD.

Swiss chef Bernhard Oehrli has a fine touch when it comes to seafood, and I recommend this place wholeheartedly. The surroundings are neat and gracious, with a log fire inside to keep you warm in winter, and room to dine outside on the sidewalk on sunnier days. As for the food, the scallops are almost fresh enough to waddle off your plate and head for the sea, whereas the rare tuna in Japanese-style tempura is so delicate it melts in your mouth. If you want something other than seafood, you can't go wrong with one of the duck or veal dishes. For desert try the warm chocolate gâteau or the rhubarb gratin with ice cream.

SEEING THE SIGHTS
THE TOP ATTRACTIONS

Art Gallery of South Australia. North Terrace. ☎ **08/8207 7000.** Daily 10am–5pm. Guided tours Mon–Fri at 11am and 2pm; Sat and Sun at 11am and 3pm. Closed Christmas.

Adelaide's premier public art gallery has a pretty good range of local and international works and a fine Asian ceramics collection. The bookshop has an extensive collection of art publications.

✪ **The Migration Museum.** 82 Kintore Ave. ☎ **08/8207 7580.** Free admission. Mon–Fri 10am–5pm, Sat–Sun and public holidays 1–5pm. Closed Good Friday and Christmas Day.

This museum dedicated to immigration is one of the most important and fascinating in Australia. With touching, personal displays, it tells the story of the waves of immigrants who have helped shape this multicultural society, from the boatloads of convicts who came here in 1788 to the ethnic groups who have been trickling in over the past two centuries. It's a hands-on museum, so don't expect anything stuffy.

South Australian Maritime Museum. 126 Lipson St., Port Adelaide. ☎ **08/8207 6255.** Admission A$8 (U.S.$5.60) adults, A$3 (U.S.$2.10) children, A$20 (U.S.$14) family. Daily 10am–5pm. Closed Christmas Day. Bus: 153 or 157 from North Terrace in the city to Stop 40 (Port Adelaide). Train: From the city station, North Terrace to Port Adelaide.

Over 150 years of maritime history are commemorated in this Port Adelaide museum. Most of the exhibits can be found in an 1850s Bond Store, but the museum also incorporates an 1863 lighthouse and three vessels moored alongside Wharf No.1, just a short walk away. The fully rigged replica of the 16.45-meter (54-ft.) ketch *Active II* is very impressive.

Adelaide Attractions

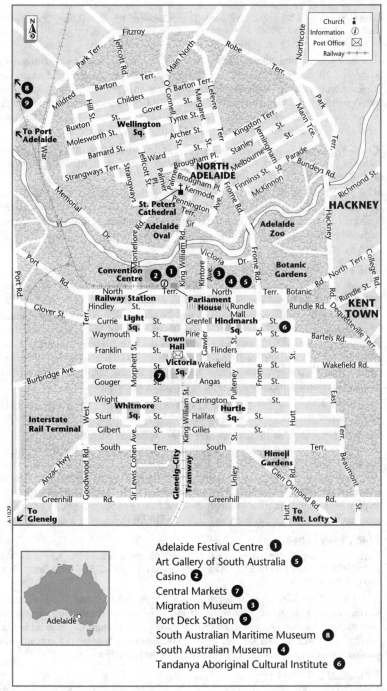

Legend:
- Church †
- Information *i*
- Post Office ✉
- Railway ┼┼┼

Attractions:

Adelaide Festival Centre ❶
Art Gallery of South Australia ❺
Casino ❷
Central Markets ❼
Migration Museum ❸
Port Deck Station ❾
South Australian Maritime Museum ❽
South Australian Museum ❹
Tandanya Aboriginal Cultural Institute ❻

South Australian Museum. On North Terrace between the State Library and the Art Gallery. ☎ **08/8207 7500.** Free admission. Daily 10am–5pm. Closed Good Friday and Christmas Day.

The state's natural and cultural history are the focus here, including a well-known collection of Aboriginal artifacts. A new permanent exhibition on the great Australian explorer and scientist Sir Douglas Mawson opens in 1999, and a new Australian Aboriginal Cultures Gallery is due to open in 2000. If you're interested in learning even more about the exhibits, take one of the Behind-the-Scenes tours. The tours are conducted after museum hours and cost A\$12 (U.S.\$8.40) for adults.

✪ **Tandanya Aboriginal Cultural Institute.** 253 Grenfell St. ☎ **08/8223 2467.** Admission A\$4 (U.S.\$2.80) adults, A\$3 (U.S.\$2.10) children 13 and under, A\$10 (U.S.\$7) family. Daily 10am–5pm.

This place offers a great opportunity to experience Aboriginal life through Aboriginal eyes. Exhibits change regularly, but all give insight into Aboriginal art and cultural activities. At noon every day there's a didgeridoo performance. A shop sells Aboriginal art and books on Aboriginal culture, and a cafe on the premises serves up several bush tucker items.

THE FLORA & THE FAUNA

Botanic Gardens. North Terrace. ☎ **08/8228 2311.** Free admission. Mon–Fri 7am–sunset; Sat–Sun 9am–sunset.

You'll feel like you're at the true heart of the city when you stroll among the huddles of office workers having a picnic lunch on the lawns here. Park highlights include duck ponds, giant water lilies, an Italianate garden, a palm house, a broad avenue of shady Moreton Bay figs, and the Bicentennial Conservatory—a large glass dome full of rainforest species. You might want to have lunch in the Botanic Gardens Restaurant (see "Great Deals on Dining," above), right in the center of the park.

Adelaide Zoo. Frome Rd. ☎ **08/8267 3255.** Admission A\$10 (U.S.\$7) for adults, and A\$5 (U.S.\$3.50) for children. Daily 9:30am–5pm.

To be honest, if you've already experienced the wonderful Melbourne Zoo, or even Taronga Zoo in Sydney, this zoo is probably not worth your while. But if you haven't yet seen a kangaroo in captivity, then plan a visit here. Of course, other Australian animals have a home at the zoo, too, and the nicely landscaped gardens and lack of crowds make it a pleasant place for an entertaining stroll. The zoo houses the only Pygmy blue-tongue lizard in captivity in Australia, a species thought to be extinct since the 1940s, until a specimen was discovered inside the belly of a dead snake.

FOR TRAIN BUFFS

Port Dock Station. Lipton St., Port Adelaide. ☎ **08/8341 1690.** Admission A\$8 (U.S.\$5.60) for adults, A\$3 (U.S.\$2.10) for children, and A\$19 (U.S.\$13.30) for a family. Daily 10am–5pm.

This former Port Adelaide railway yard houses Australia's largest and finest collection of engines and rolling stock. There are around 104 items on display, including some 30 engines. Among the most impressive trains are the gigantic Mountain-class engines, and so-called "Tea and Sugar" trains that once ran between railway camps in remote parts of the desert country. Admission fee includes a train ride.

ORGANIZED TOURS

Festival Tours (☎ **08/8374 1270**), operates a morning city-sights tour costing A\$29 (U.S.\$20.30) for adults and A\$20 (U.S.\$14) for children. Tours run between 9:30am and noon every day except Sunday.

A Trip to the Seaside

If you need a beach fix while in Adelaide, head to the lovely suburb of **Glenelg,** just a 30-minute tram ride from the city center. Glenelg has much more to offer than just the beach, the ocean, and a classic pier, however, as if those weren't enough. It's also where you catch the ferry to Kangaroo Island and is home to some interesting attractions.

Try to visit the **HMS** *Buffalo,* Adelphi Terrace, Patawalonga Boat Haven, Glenelg (☎ **08/8294 7000**), a full-scale replica of the ship that brought the first settlers to South Australia. Admission is A$2.50 (U.S.$1.75) for adults and A$1.50 (U.S.$1.05) for children. It's open daily from 10am to 5pm. There's a seafood restaurant inside with main courses around A$19 (U.S.$13.30). At the time this book went to press, the management here was changing, and the future of the ship and the museum was unknown. If you plan to visit, call first.

The carousel and giant gray hillock you can see from the seafront is **Magic Mountain,** Colley Reserve, Glenelg (☎ **08/8294 8199**). You can keep the kiddies happy for hours here with the water slides, bumper boats, minigolf, shooting galleries, and video games. Water slides cost A$10 (U.S.$7) for an hour and A$6 (U.S.$4.20) for 30 minutes. A 3-hour lock-in on Saturday mornings and school holidays from 9am to noon, with unlimited use of supervised water slides and most other attractions, costs A$12 (U.S.$8.40).

Want to get face-to-face with one of South Australia's famous Great White sharks (and live to tell the story)? At the **Shark Museum,** 14 August Street, Glenelg (☎ **08/8376 3373**), you'll find full-size models of the terrors of the sea, as well as filming cages, shark jaws, photos, and fossils. Admission is A$3.50 (U.S.$2.45) for adults and A$2.50 (U.S.$1.75) for children.

History buffs will want to visit the **Old Gum Tree,** under which Governor Hindmarsh read the 1836 proclamation making Australia a colony; it's on Mac-Farlane Street.

For maps and brochures on the area, as well as on other parts of the state, head to the **Glenelg Tourist Information Centre** (☎ **08/8294 5833**), in the Foreshore Building near the seafront. It's open daily from 9am to 5pm.

The **Adelaide Explorer** (☎ **08/8364 1933**) is a replica tram that circles the city, stopping at a number of attractions, including Glenelg. The route takes 2¾ hours to complete, and you can get on or off anywhere along the route and rejoin another tram later on. Trams depart from 38 King William St. daily at 9am, 10:20am, 12:10pm, 1:30pm, and 3pm; tickets are A$23 (U.S.$16.10) for adults, A$15 (U.S.$10.50) for children ages 6 to 14, and A$55 (U.S.$38.50) for a family of four.

ENJOYING THE GREAT OUTDOORS

BICYCLING   Adelaide's parks and river banks are very popular with cyclists. Rent your bicycle from **Linear Park Hire** (☎ **018/844 588,** a mobile phone). The going rate is A$20 (U.S.$14) for 24 hours, with a helmet, lock, and baby-seat (if needed). **Recreation SA** (☎ **08/8226 7301**) publishes a brochure showing Adelaide's cycling routes. Pick one up at the Tourism South Australia Travel Centre (see "Visitor Information," above). The **Map Shop,** 16A Peel St. (☎ **08/8231 2033**), is also a good source for maps.

HIKING & JOGGING   The banks of the River Torrens are a good place for a jog. The truly fit or adventurous types might want to tackle the **Heysen Trail,** a spectacular 1,600-kilometer (960-mile) walk through bush, farmland, and rugged countryside that starts 80 kilometers (48 miles) south of Adelaide. The trail goes all the way to the Flinders Ranges by way of the Adelaide Hills and the Barossa Valley. Believe it or not, many people attempt it. A few even finish. For more information on the trail, visit the Tourism South Australia Travel Centre (see "Visitor Information," above).

GOLF   The **City of Adelaide Golf Course** (☎ **08/8267 2171**) is quite close to town and has two short 18-hole courses and a full-size championship course. Greens fees are a modest A$12.50 to $15 (U.S.$8.70–$10.50), depending on the course, Monday through Friday; A$3 (U.S.$2.10) extra on weekends. Clubs are available to rent.

TENNIS   At the **Memorial Drive Tennis Courts** (☎ **08/8231 4371**), just across the River Torrens from the city on War Memorial Drive, in North Adelaide, courts cost A$12 (U.S.$8.40) per hour until 5pm, and A$18 (U.S.$12.60) per hour until 10pm.

TAKING IN AN AUSSIE RULES GAME & OTHER SPECTATOR SPORTS

CRICKET   The **Adelaide Oval** (☎ **08/8300 3800**), on the corner of War Memorial Drive and King William Street, is the venue for international matches during the summer season.

FOOTBALL   Unlike in New South Wales, where Rugby League is the most popular winter sport, here in Adelaide you'll find plenty of Australian Rules fanatics. Games are usually played on a Saturday either at the **Adelaide Oval** (see above) or at **Football Park** (☎ **08/8268 2088**), on Turner Drive, West Lakes. The home teams are the Adelaide Crows and the Port Adelaide Power. Games are played February to October, with the finals held in September and October. Tickets must be purchased well in advance from **BASS** (☎ **13 12 46** in South Australia, or 08/8400 2205).

THE SHOPPING SCENE

Rundle Mall (between King William and Pulteney sts.) is Adelaide's main shopping street. This pedestrian-only thoroughfare is home to all the big names in fashion as well as good bookshops and plenty of take-out places.

Adelaide's **Central Markets** (☎ **08/8203 7494**), behind the Adelaide Hilton Hotel between Gouger and Grote streets, is the largest produce market in the southern hemisphere and a good place to shop for vegetables, fruit, meat, and fish. The colorful markets are worth popping into even if you're not looking for picnic fixings. The markets, held in a huge warehouse-like structure, are open Tuesday from 7am to 5:30pm, Thursday from 11am to 5:30pm, Friday from 7am to 9pm, and Saturday from 7am to 3pm. **Market Adventures** (☎ **08/8336 8333,** or mobile 018/842 242; fax 08/8336 4075) runs behind-the-scenes tours of the markets every Tuesday and Thursday at 10:30am and 1:30pm, Friday at 10am and noon, and Saturday at 8:30am. The tours cost A$22 (U.S.$15.40) for adults, and A$12 (U.S.$8.40) for children ages 3 to 11. Phone for directions.

Elsewhere, the renowned **Jam Factory Craft and Design Centre,** in the Lions Art Centre, 19 Morphett St. (☎ **08/8410 0727**), sells an excellent range of locally made ceramics, glass, furniture, and metal items. You can also watch the craftspeople at work here.

Shopping for Opals

South Australia is home to the world's largest sources of white opals (the more expensive black opals generally come from Lightning Ridge in northern New South Wales). There are plenty of places to buy around town, but **Opal Field Gems,** 3rd floor, 29 King William St. (☎ **08/8212 5300**) is one of the best. As a rule, you're not going to find any bargains, so just buy what you like (and can afford— good opals cost many thousands of dollars).

For the best boots you're ever likely to find, as well as other Aussie fashion icons, including Akubra hats, moleskin pants, and Driza-bone coats, head to the **R.M. Williams** shop on Gawler Place (☎ **08/8232 3611**).

ADELAIDE AFTER DARK

The local newspaper, the *Adelaide Advertiser,* lists all performances and exhibitions in its entertainment pages. The free tourist guide *Today in Adelaide,* available in most hotels, also has information. Tickets for theater and other entertainment events in Adelaide can be bought from **BASS** outlets at the Festival Theatre, Adelaide Festival Centre, King William Road; Centre Pharmacy, 19 Central Market Arcade; Verandah Music, 182 Rundle St.; and on the 5th floor of the Myer department store, Rundle Mall. Call BASS at ☎ **08/8400 2205,** or 13 12 46 in South Australia.

THE PERFORMING ARTS

The major concert hall in town is the **Adelaide Festival Centre,** King William Road (☎ **08/8216 8600** for general inquiries, and 08/8400 2205 for the box office). The Festival Centre encompasses three auditoriums: the 1,978-seat Festival Theatre, the 612-seat Playhouse, and the 350-seat Space Centre. This is the place in Adelaide to see opera, ballet, drama, orchestral concerts, the Adelaide Symphony Orchestra, plays, and experimental drama.

There is also an outdoor amphitheater used for jazz, rock and roll, and country music concerts; an art gallery; a bistro; a piano bar; and the Silver Jubilee Organ, the world's largest transportable concert-hall organ (built in Austria and paid for by public subscription to commemorate Elizabeth II's Silver Jubilee).

The **Adelaide Repertory Festival** presents a season of five productions a year, ranging from drama to comedy, at its base, the **Arts Theatre,** 53 Angus St. (☎ **08/ 8221 5644**). The theatre, which is just a short walk from many hotels and restaurants, is also the home of the **Metropolitan Musical Theatre Company,** which presents two musical-comedy productions a year. Tickets for performances are around A$15 (U.S.$10.50) for adults, and A$6 (U.S.$4.20) for children.

Her Majesty's Theatre, 58 Grote St. (☎ **08/8216 8600**), is a 1,000-seat venue opposite Central Markets that presents drama, comedy, smaller musicals, dance, opera, and recitals. Tickets are generally A$30 to $55 (U.S.$21 to $38.50).

THE BAR & CLUB SCENE

Adelaide's nightlife ranges from twiddling your thumbs to nude lap-dancers. For adult entertainment (clubs with the word "strip" in the name) head to Hindley Street— there are a few pubs, too, but I wouldn't recommend them. For information on gay and lesbian options, pick up a copy of the *Adelaide Gay Times.*

For the younger set, **Synagogue** nightclub on Rundle Street (☎ **08/8223 4233**) is the one of the latest places to hang out, especially on Friday and Saturday nights. Cover is A$4 (U.S.$2.80) during the week and A$8 (U.S.$5.60) Friday and Saturday nights.

If you're looking for an all-ages pub, the locals will point you toward **The Austral,** 205 Rundle Mall (☎ **08/8223 4660**); **The Lion,** at the corner of Melbourne and Jerningham streets (☎ **08/8367 0222**); and the **British Hotel,** 58 Finniss St. (☎ **08/ 8267 2188**), in North Adelaide, where you can cook your own steak on the courtyard barbecue. Also popular with tourists and locals alike is the **Earl of Aberdeen,** 316 Pulteney St., at Carrington Street, (☎ **08/8223 6433**), a colonial-style pub popular for after-work drinks. The **Port Dock,** 10 Todd St., Port Adelaide (☎ **08/8240 0187**), was licensed as a pub in 1864 and has kept up with tradition ever since. It even brews four of its own beers and pumps them directly to its three bars with old English beer engines. Most pubs are open from 11am to midnight.

THE CASINO

Dwarfed by the old railway station it's situated in, the **Adelaide Casino,** North Terrace (☎ **1800/888 711** in Australia, or 08/8212 2811), still manages to pack in two floors of gaming tables and slot machines. There are also four bars and several dining options, including a fast-food station and the Pullman buffet restaurant—where the food is excellent, by the way, ranging from smoked meats and hot roasts to jellyfish, Asian salads, and bean curd sushi. The early-bird special (from 5:30 to 7:30pm Wednesday through Friday, and Sunday) offers the full buffet, including wine, for A$29 (U.S.$20.30) per person—including a A$10 (U.S.$7) refund on valet parking. The casino, which is right next to the Adelaide Hilton, is open Sunday through Thursday from 10am to 4am and Friday and Saturday from 10am to 6am.

2 Side Trips from Adelaide

THE BAROSSA: ON THE TRAIL OF THE GRAPE

More than one-fourth of Australia's wines, and a disproportionate number of top labels, originate in the Barossa and Eden valleys—collectively known as the Barossa. Beginning just 45 kilometers (27 miles) northeast of Adelaide and easily accessible from the city, the area has had an enormous influence on the city's culture. In fact, Adelaidians of all socioeconomic levels talk more about wine than even the French do.

The area was first settled by German immigrants from Silesia, who came here to escape religious persecution. They brought with them their particular brand of culture, their food, and their vines. They also built the Lutheran churches that dominate the Barossa skyline. With the help of wealthy English aristocrats, the wine industry went from strength to strength. Today, more than 50 wineries can be found in an area that still retains its German flavor.

Travel Tips

If you have the choice of exploring either the Barossa or the Hunter Valley in New South Wales (see chapter 6), I recommend the Barossa, which despite being a little more touristy, has more to offer in terms of history and architecture.

Another famous wine-producing region is the **Coonawarra,** 381 kilometers (228½ miles) southeast of the capital and near the Victoria border; it's particularly convenient if you're driving from Melbourne. The area is just 12 kilometers (7 miles) long and 2 kilometers (just over 1 mile wide), but the scenic countryside is crammed with historical villages and 16 wineries. The **Clare Valley,** 135 kilometers (81 miles) north of Adelaide, is another pretty area; it produces some outstanding examples of cool-climate wine.

Drinking & Driving—Don't Do It!

Australia's drunk-driving laws are strict and rigidly enforced. If you'll be chasing the grape around the Barossa, choose a designated driver or take a guided tour.

The main towns in the area are **Angaston,** the farthest away from Adelaide; **Nuriootpa,** the center of the rural services industry; and **Tanunda,** the nearest town to the city. Each has interesting architecture, craft and antiques shops, and specialty food outlets. Adventurous types may want to rent a bike in Adelaide, take it on the train to Gawler, and then cycle through the Barossa. Other options are to explore the area by hot-air balloon, Harley-Davidson, or limousine.

ESSENTIALS

WHEN TO GO   The best time to visit the Barossa is in the **spring** (September and October), when it's not too hot, and there are plenty of flowering trees and shrubs, and **autumn** (April and May), when the leaves turn red. The main wine harvest is late summer and early autumn (February and March). The least crowded time is winter (December, January, and February), when you can spend a cozy evening around the fireplace.

GETTING THERE   If you have a car (by far the most flexible way to visit the Barossa), I recommend taking the **scenic route** from Adelaide (the route doesn't have a specific name, but it's obvious on any map). It takes about half an hour longer than the Main North Road through Gawler, but the trip past magnificent stands of river gums, pine plantations, and even alpaca farms is worthwhile. Follow the signs to Birdwood, Springton, Mount Pleasant, and Angaston.

Various companies run limited **sightseeing tours** from Adelaide. One of the best, **Festival Tours** (☎ **08/8374 1270**), offers a day trip that visits three wineries and other attractions. It costs A$59 (U.S.$41.30) for adults and A$46 (U.S.$32.20) for children, including a restaurant lunch. Public buses run infrequently to the major centers from Adelaide. There are no buses between wineries.

VISITOR INFORMATION   The excellent **Barossa Wine & Visitor Centre,** on the main road at 66–68 Murray Street, Tanunda, SA 5352 (☎ **08/8563 0600;** www.dove.net.au/~bwta; e-mail bwta@dove.net.au) has plenty of detailed maps, brochures on accommodations and wineries, and touring information. It's open Monday through Friday from 9am to 5pm and weekends from 10am to 4pm. It's worth popping into the center's small audiovisual display section for an introduction to the world of wine. Admission is A$2 (U.S.$1.40) for adults; children are free. You'll need a least an hour to look around.

TOURING THE WINERIES

With 48 wineries offering free cellar-door tastings and/or daily tours charting the wine-making process, you won't be stuck for places to visit. All wineries are well signposted. Below are just a few of my favorites, but don't be shy about just stopping whenever you come across a winery that takes your fancy.

Penfolds. Nuriootpa. ☎ **08/8560 9389.** Tastings and sales, Mon–Fri 10am–5pm, Sat 9am–5pm, Sun 1–5pm.

Australia's largest wine producer churns out some 22.5 million liters (5.8 million U.S. gallons) from this one winery every year. Penfolds also owns other wineries all over the country. It all started when Dr. Christopher Rawson planted a few vines in 1844 to make wine for his patients. The winery now houses the largest oak-barrel maturation cellars in the southern hemisphere.

Wolf Blass. Stuart Hwy., Nuriootpa. ☎ **08/8562 1955.** Mon–Fri 9:15am–4:30pm, Sat–Sun 10am–4:30pm.

This winery's Germanic-style black-label vintages have an excellent international reputation, while its cheaper yellow-label vintages are the toast of many a Sydney dinner party. The small Wolf Blass museum is worth a peek.

Seppelts. Seppeltsfield. ☎ **08/8562 8028.** Tastings Mon–Fri 10am–5pm, Sat 10:30am–4:30pm, Sunday 11am–4pm. Tours hourly Mon–Fri 11am–3pm, Sat–Sun 11:30am–2:30pm; adults A$4 (U.S.$2.80), children A$1 (U.S.70¢).

This National Trust–listed property was founded in 1857 by Joseph Seppelt, an immigrant from Silesia. The wine tour around the gardens and blue-stone buildings is considered one of the best in the world. Check out the family's giant Romanesque mausoleum on a nearby slope, skirted by roadside palms planted during the 1930s recession to keep winery workers employed.

Yalumba. Eden Valley Rd., Angaston. ☎ **08/8561 3200.** Tastings Mon–Sat 10am–5pm, Sun noon–5pm.

This winery was built in 1849, making it the oldest family-owned wine-making business in Australia. It's also huge. Look out for the sad-looking Himalayan bear in the corner of the large tasting room—following a run-in with a hunting rifle, it's been Yalumba's advertising gimmick. The winery's Signature Red Cabernet-Shiraz is among the best you'll ever taste.

Rockford. Krondorf Rd., Tanunda. ☎ **08/8563 2720.** Tastings Mon–Sat 11am–5pm. Closed Sun.

Most of the buildings here were constructed in 1984 out of recycled local materials, but you'd never know it. The wine is pressed between mid-March and the end of April, in the traditional way with turn-of-the-century machinery; it's a fascinating sight. Demand for Rockford wines, especially the Basket Pressed Shiraz, far exceeds supply.

Orlando. Barossa Hwy., Rowland Flat. ☎ **08/8521 3140.** Tastings Mon–Fri 10am–5pm, weekends and public holidays 10am–4pm.

This large winery was established in 1847 and is today the home of many award-winning brands. Its big seller is the well-known Jacobs Creek brand, now sold worldwide. Premium wines include the Lawson Shiraz and its Jacaranda Ridge Cabernet; new vintages of either will set you back at least A$45 (U.S.$31.50) a bottle. There is an opal shop and craft shop here, too.

WHERE TO STAY

There are plenty of standard motels and lots of interesting B&Bs throughout the Barossa, some with rooms for as little as A$60 (U.S.$42). Rooms are often booked solid on the weekends, so don't expect to find any bargains then. Always ask about

A Wine Tip

As you are out and about tasting wine, try a **sparkling red.** It may turn up noses elsewhere, and it does take some getting used to, but considering that the world's wine industry now hangs on Australia's every wine offering, it may well be the great tipple of the future.

The Barossa

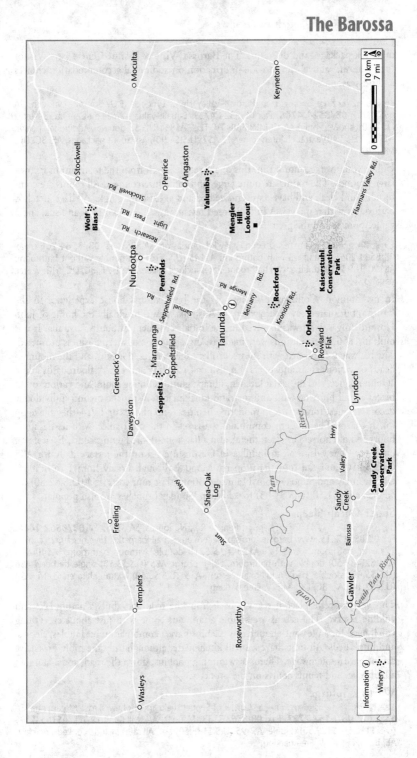

midweek packages and discounts. The **Barossa Wine & Visitor Centre** (see "Visitor Information," above) can provide information on additional accommodation choices and off-season deals.

Chateau Yaldara Motor Inn. Barossa Valley Hwy., Lyndoch (P.O. Box 62, Lyndoch, SA 5351). ☎ **08/8524 4268.** Fax 08/8524 4725. E-mail: yaldara@mail.mdt.net.au. 34 units (all with shower only). A/C MINIBAR TV TEL. A$83 (U.S.$) double. Additional person A$12 (U.S.$8.40) extra; children under 12 A$7 (U.S.$4.90). Ask about packages. AE, BC, DC, MC, V.

Unlike your average motor inn, this one is set well back from the road within its own large grounds. The rooms are quite large, and some interconnect. All rooms are comfortable and clean and have a queen-size bed and at least one single. All have attached bathrooms with a shower. A fully licensed restaurant, an outdoor pool and spa, and a game room are on the premises.

✪ **Collingrove Homestead.** Eden Valley Rd., Angaston, SA 5351. ☎ **08/8564 2061.** Fax 08/8564 2061. 5 units, 3 with bathroom. A$145 (U.S.$101.50) double without bathroom; A$170 (U.S.$119) double with bathroom. Rates include full breakfast. AE, BC, DC, MC, V. Free parking.

In my opinion, Collingrove is not just the best country-house experience in the Barossa, but, dare I say it, anywhere in Australia. It was originally the home of John Howard Angas, who was involved in the initial settlement of South Australia. It was built in 1856, and additions were made as Angas's successful sheep business prospered. The hallway is festooned with spears, artillery shells, rifles, portraits, and the mounted heads of various stags and tigers. English oak paneling and creaky floorboards add a certain nuance, and the cedar kitchen, library, glorious dining room, and various other places are all bursting with antiques and knickknacks. What the quaint, individually decorated guest rooms lack in modern amenities—no phones or TVs—they make up for in charm. The modern communal spa is set in the old stables, with its flagstone floors and old horse harnesses; there's also a flagstone-floored tennis court. Even if you don't stay here, visitors can indulge in Devonshire tea on the terrace daily for A$5 (U.S.$3.50) and can tour the property Monday through Friday from 1 to 4:30pm and Saturday and Sunday from 11am to 4:30pm. The tour costs A$4 (U.S.$2.80) for adults and A$1.50 (U.S.$1.05) for children. Sunday brunches are also popular.

Super-Cheap Sleeps

Barossa Valley (SA) Tourist Park. Penrice Rd., Nuriootpa, SA 5355. ☎ **08/8562 1404.** Fax 08/8562 2615. www.barossa.touristpark.com.au. E-mail: barpark@dove.net.au. 25 cabins, 17 with bathroom. A/C TV. A$30 (U.S.$21) double without bathroom; A$40–$55 (U.S.$28–38.50) double with bathroom. Linen charge A$5 (U.S.$3.50) single bed and A$8 (U.S.$5.60) double bed. Additional person A$5 (U.S.$3.50) extra; children 3–15 A$3 (U.S.$2.10). AE, BC, DC, MC, V. Free parking.

This very peaceful place is set way back from the road and abuts a nature lake and wildlife reserve. The cabins are simple affairs but come with just about everything you'll need for a pleasant-enough stay. Cabins have a combination of doubles, singles, and bunk beds. All units have a small kitchenette, although only the more expensive cabins have a microwave. There's a swimming pool just down the road, and a laundry, a barbecue, and tennis courts on the property.

Worth a Splurge

The Hermitage of Marananga. Corner of Seppeltsfield and Stonewell rds., Marananga, SA 5351. ☎ **08/8562 2722.** Fax: 08/8562 3133. 11 units. A/C MINIBAR TV TEL. A$165–$185 (U.S.$115.50–$129.50) double; A$195 (U.S.$136.50) apt. All rates include cooked breakfast. AE, BC, DC, MC, V. Free parking.

This is by far the best of the area's motels—but you certainly pay for it. The rooms are awkwardly shaped but have been recently renovated. They include a small balcony, a fridge, and tea- and coffee-making facilities. The main building is old-fashioned and bursting with character. It is also cool in the heat of summer. Outside are a swimming pool and spa, and fantastic views over the valley to the ranges beyond. A four-course, country-style dinner in the restaurant costs around A$30 (U.S.$21). There are good walks around the property and at dusk plenty of kangaroos in the surrounding fields. The new apartment is fully self-contained, with its own private balcony overlooking the vineyards, a separate bedroom, a double fold-out divan in the lounge room, and a tub.

✪ **Marble Lodge.** 21 Dean St., Angaston, SA 5351. ☎ **08/8564 2478.** Fax 08/8564 2941. www.marble.mtx.net/. Reservations recommended. 2 units. A/C TV TEL. A$165 (U.S.$115.50). Rate includes breakfast, bottle of champagne, and minibar drinks. AE, BC, DC, MC, V.

Wake up and smell the roses—there are plenty of them in the beautiful gardens surrounding this romantic historic property. Away from the main house is a lodge, made of local marble with a tile roof, that's been divided into two suites. The larger of the two has two rooms and an open fire. The other suite is basically a large combination bedroom/sitting room, also with an open fire. Both suites have access to a shared spa bath and are tastefully furnished in antiques. There's always fresh fruit, homemade biscuits, and chocolates in the room, and it's a 5-minute walk to three local restaurants. Ask about another double room (with a shared bathroom) in the homestead that's sometimes available. There's also a tennis court on the grounds.

WHERE TO DINE

The Barossa prides itself on its cuisine as well as its wine, so you'll find plenty of places of note to eat; many of them serve up traditional German foods in line with the area's heritage. Put the **1918 Bistro & Grill,** 94 Murray St., Tanunda (☎ **08/8563 0405**) at the top of your list. Appetizers, ranging in price from A$8.90 (U.S.$6.25) to A$13 (U.S.$9.10), are enough to fill you up. I recommend the baked mushrooms. Another hot spot, for lunch or dinner, is **Vintner's Bar & Grill,** Nuriootpa Road, Angaston (☎ **08/ 8564 2488**); the wine list here is six pages long! Main courses cost A$14 to $18 (U.S.$9.80–$12.60). Both restaurants serve essentially Modern Australian cuisine. You'll find perhaps the valley's best German-style bakery in Lyndoch—the **Lyndock Bakery and Restaurant.** In Angaston, you must stop off at the **Angas Park Hotel,** which serves up incredible value home-cooked meals, including steaks, for around A$6 to $8 (U.S.$4.20–$5.60).

THE ADELAIDE HILLS

Only a 25-minute drive from Adelaide, and visible even from the main shopping street, are the tree-lined slopes, pretty valleys, winding roads, and historic townships of the Adelaide Hills. You might want to walk part of the **Heysen Trail** (see "Enjoying the Great Outdoors" in the Adelaide section, earlier in this chapter), browse through

---

Devonshire Tea

Even if you're not staying at the **Collingrove Homestead,** Eden Valley Road, Angaston (☎ **08/8564 2061**), stop in for Devonshire tea served on the terrace daily for A$5 (U.S.$3.50). Sunday brunches are also popular. You can also tour the historic property (see "Where to Stay").

the shops in Hahndorf, stop in Melba's Chocolate Factory in Woodside, or visit Cleland Wildlife Park or Warrawong Sanctuary. Otherwise, it's a nice outing just to hit the road and drive. Should you decide to stay overnight, the area offers lots of cozy B&Bs.

ESSENTIALS

GETTING THERE   The Adelaide Hills are just a 25-minute drive from Adelaide via Greenhill and Glen Osmond roads. **Adelaide Sightseeing** (☎ **08/8231 4144**) runs outings to the gorgeous little town of Hahndorf (see below) as well as to Cleland Wildlife Park. An afternoon excursion to Hahndorf costs A$28 (U.S.$19.60) for adults and A$19 (U.S.$13.30) for children; the tour to Cleland costs A$26 (U.S.$18.20) for adults and A$20 (U.S.$14) for children, including park entry.

VISITOR INFORMATION   Visitor information and bookings are available through the **Adelaide Hills Tourist Information Centre,** 41 Main St., Hahndorf (☎ **08/8388 1185**). It's open Monday to Friday from 9am to 5pm, and Saturday and Sunday from 10am to 4pm. Detailed maps are available also at the Tourism South Australia Travel Centre in Adelaide (see "Visitor Information" in the Adelaide section, earlier in this chapter).

BIRDWOOD: FOR VINTAGE-CAR FANS

Birdwood, located 46 kilometers (27½ miles) east and slightly north of Adelaide, is best known for the restored 1852 flour mill that now contains the **National Motor Museum** (☎ **08/8568 5006**). Here you'll find the best collection of vintage cars anywhere in Australia, including the first vehicle to cross Australia (in 1908). The complex also includes tearooms and a gift shop, and you can picnic along the banks of the upper reaches of the River Torrens. The museum is open daily from 9am to 5pm (closed Christmas). Admission is A$8.50 (U.S.$5.95) for adults, A$3.50 (U.S.$2.45) for children ages 5 to 15, and A$22 (U.S.$15.40) for a family of four.

WOODSIDE: CHOCOLATE LOVERS UNITE!

Visitors come here for **Melba's Chocolate Factory,** Henry Street (☎ **08/8389 7926**), where chocoholics will find a huge range of handmade chocolates to tempt the taste-buds. Melba's is part of **Heritage Park,** a complex that includes a woodturner, a cheese maker, a ceramics studio, and a leather maker. It's open Monday through Friday from 10am to 4pm; and Saturday, Sunday, and public holidays from noon to 5pm.

MYLOR: GETTING BACK TO NATURE

Mylor is located 25 kilometers (15 miles) southeast of Adelaide, and 10 kilometers (6 miles) south of Mt. Lofty via the town of Crafters. Here you'll find the **Warraong Sanctuary,** Stock Road, Mylor (P.O. Box 35, Stirling, SA 5152; ☎ **08/8370 9422**). Unlike many other wildlife parks, the animals here are not kept in enclosed runs. Instead, park founder Dr. John Wamsley took a 35-acre tract of former farming land, replanted it with natural bush, fenced it off, and went around shooting the introduced rabbits, cats, dogs, and foxes that plague much of Australia. Then the good doctor took to reintroducing animals native to the site—such as kangaroos, various types of wallabies, bandicoots, beetongs, platypuses, possums, frogs, birds, and reptiles. They are all thriving, not only because he eliminated their unnatural predators, but also because he re-created waterways, rain forests, and black-water ponds. The animals roam free, and you're guided through on 1½ -hour dawn or sunset walks (A$15/ U.S.$10.50 per person). There's a restaurant on the premises, and overnight accommodations are available in large cabins with bathrooms, wall-to-wall carpeting, and

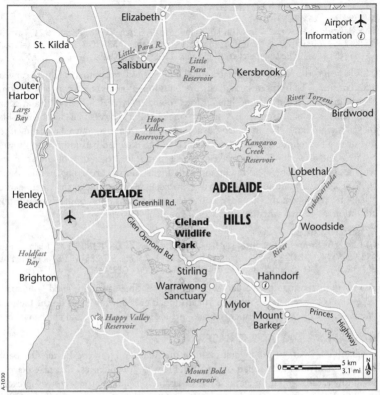

air-conditioning. The cabins cost A$99 (U.S.$69.30) per person, including a one-course dinner, breakfast, a dusk tour, and a dawn tour. The cabin alone costs A$80 (U.S.$56).

Compared to Cleland Wildlife Park (see below), there are fewer varieties of animals here (you won't find any koalas, for example), but it's more educational and you get the feeling that you're in the wild rather than in a zoo.

HAHNDORF: GERMAN HERITAGE, CRAFTS & MORE

This ✪ **historic German-style village** is one of South Australia's most popular tourist destinations. The town, located 29 kilometers (17½ miles) southeast of Adelaide, was founded in 1839 by Lutherans fleeing religious persecution in their homeland of eastern Prussia. They brought with them their wine-making skills, foods, and architectural inheritance and put it all together here. Hahndorf still resembles a small German town in appearance and atmosphere, and is included on the World Heritage List as a Historical German Settlement. Walking around you'll notice **St. Paul's Lutheran Church,** erected in 1890. The **Wool Factory, L'Unique Fine Arts & Crafts,** and **Bamfurlong Fine Crafts** are all worth checking out; all are within walking distance of Main Street.

Busway Travel (☎ **08/8262 6900**) operates half-day tours daily to Hahndorf, including a German lunch, and a visit to Mt. Lofty Summit (see below). Tours cost A$28 (U.S.$19.60) for adults and A$19 (U.S.$13.30) for children. Tours leave from the Busway Travel offices on Bank Street, off North Terrace, in Adelaide.

Where to Stay

The Hahndorf Resort. 145A Main Rd., Hahndorf, SA 5245. ☎ **08/8388 7921.** Fax 08/ 8388 7282. 60 units. A/C TV TEL. A$46 (U.S.$32.20) cabin; A$89 (U.S.$62.30) motel room; A$105 (U.S.$73.50) Bavarian chalet; A$155 (U.S.$108.50) spa chalet. AE, BC, DC, MC, V.

This large resort has a variety of accommodations, as well as approximately 80 caravan and tent sites. The fully self-contained, air-conditioned cabins come with a bathroom, a small kitchen area, a TV, and linen. Motel rooms are typical of their type and come with queen-size beds (some have an extra single) and a shower. The chalets look like they're straight out of Bavaria; each can accommodate from two to five people in either one or two bedrooms. All have a full kitchen and an attached bathroom with shower. Some of them overlook a small lake. The spa rooms are larger and, of course, come with a spa bath. There's a restaurant with main courses averaging around A$15 (U.S.$10.50), a swimming pool, a small gym, a couple of putting greens, a canoe lake, a half-size tennis court, a laundry, and a few emus, kangaroos, and horses running around in an animal sanctuary. Bicycles are available for rent.

Where to Dine

✪ **Karl's German Coffee Shop.** 17 Main St., Hahndorf. ☎ **08/8388 7171.** Main courses A$3.90–$10.50 (U.S.$2.75–$7.35) at lunch; A$8.90–$13.90 (U.S.$6.25–$9.75) at dinner. AE, BC, DC, MC, V. Wed–Sun and public holidays 11am–10pm. GERMAN.

Pop into this Bavarian beer-cellar-style eatery at any time of day for good homemade cakes and coffee. At lunch, the ploughman's lunch goes down well, as do the German sausages with sauerkraut. Dinner favorites include seafood, steaks, and chicken dishes.

OAKBANK: A DAY AT THE RACES

Oakbank is the site of the biggest event in the Adelaide Hills, the **Easter Oakbank Racing Carnival,** which is part of the Australia-wide "picnic races" that take place in small towns throughout the nation. The Oakbank horse races attract crowds in excess of 70,000 a day over the long Easter weekend. General admission is A$9 (U.S.$6.30), plus another A$5 (U.S.$3.50) to get into the grandstand. It's an institution you really shouldn't miss if you're in the area at Easter. Call the **Oakbank Racing Club** (☎ **08/ 8212 6279**) for details. You can't miss the racetrack; it's right off the main road.

Where to Stay

Adelaide Hills Country Cottages. P.O. Box 100, Oakbank, SA 5243. ☎ **08/8388 4193.** Fax 08/8388 4733. 3 units. A/C TV. A$160– $200 (U.S.$112–$140) double. Additional person A$50 (U.S.$35) extra. Two-night minimum stay required. Rates include provisions for full-cooked breakfast. MC, V. Free parking. Oakbank is 35 minutes from Adelaide, 7 minutes from Hahndorf, and less than an hr. from the Barossa Valley.

These three self-contained cottages have won several tourism awards, including the 1998 Australian Tourist Commission award for best hosted accommodation in Australia. The cottages are 1 kilometer (half a mile) apart and are surrounded by 150 acres of scenic countryside. The Apple Tree cottage, circa 1860, sleeps up to five, has a spa bath and antiques, and overlooks an orchard and a lake; the Gum Tree Cottage sleeps four and has wonderful country views from its windows; and the Lavender Fields Cottage, which also sleeps up to four, overlooks a lily-fringed duck pond. All the cottages have open fireplaces and fully equipped kitchens. This is a great place to relax and a good base for exploring the area. You'll get a couple of free drinks and a fruit basket on your arrival.

MT. LOFTY: VIEWS & 'ROOS

Visitors make the pilgrimage to the top of the 701-meter (2,300-ft.) Mt. Lofty, 16 kilometers (10 miles) southeast of Adelaide, for the panoramic views over Adelaide, the surrounding Adelaide plains, and the Mt. Lofty Range. There are several nice bushwalks from the top. You can find the **Summit Restaurant** (☎ **08/8339 2600**) up here, too; it's open for lunch daily and dinner Wednesday through Sunday. Main courses include such dishes as roasted field mushrooms on polenta, roast duck breast with black rice, and veal porterhouse, and range from A$11.50 to $18.90 (U.S.$8.05 to $13.25). In the same building is the **Summit Cafe,** selling good sandwiches and cakes, and Devonshire tea for A$3.50 (U.S.$2.45). The restaurant runs a car service to Adelaide and back for up to four people for A$10 (U.S.$7) per person round-trip.

Almost at the top of Mt. Lofty, off Summit Road, you'll find the **Cleland Wildlife Park** (☎ **08/8339 2444**). Here you'll find all the usual Australian animals on offer—including the largest male red kangaroo I've ever seen. Although the park is not as good as similar wildlife parks elsewhere in Australia, it does have a very good wetlands aviary. One of the drawbacks of Cleland is that it's got some unimaginative enclosures, most notably the one for the Tasmanian Devils. The park is open daily from 9:30am to 4:30pm. Visitors can meet at the Tasmanian Devil enclosure at 2pm and join the animal-feed run (you follow a tractor around the park as it drops off food).

Admission to **Cleland** is A$7.50 (U.S.$5.25) for adults and A$4.50 (U.S.$3.15) for children ages 3 to 14. Koala holding and photo sessions are allowed daily from 2 to 4pm (but not on very hot summer days); on Sunday there's an additional session from 10am to noon. The privilege will cost you A$8 (U.S.$5.60) per photo. A kiosk and restaurant are on the premises.

3 Kangaroo Island

110km (66 miles) South of Adelaide

✪ **Kangaroo Island** is the best place to see Australian marsupials in the wild. Period. Spend a couple of days on the island with the right guide and you might find yourself stroking semitame kangaroos, creeping through the bush on the trail of wallabies, or walking along a beach past a colony of sea lions. You might spot sea eagles, black swans, fairy penguins, the rare glossy cockatoo, the island's lone emu, or a bunch of koalas hanging sleepily in the trees.

The secrets to Kangaroo Island's success are the near perfect conditions found here, the most important of which is that there are no introduced foxes or rabbits to take their toll on the native inhabitants or their environment. About one-third of the island is unspoiled national park, and there are plenty of wildlife corridors to give the animals a chance to move about the island, thus lessening the problems of inbreeding.

While the animals are what most people come to see, no one goes away without also being impressed by the scenery—low mallee scrubland; dense eucalyptus forests; rugged coastal scenery; gorgeous beaches, caves, lagoons, and black-water swamps.

The island's history is a tumultuous one. Soon after its discovery, sealers arrived and took a heavy toll on the local seal and sea lion population—in just one year, 1803–04, they managed to kill more than 20,000. Between 1802 and 1836, Aboriginal women from both the mainland and Tasmania were kidnapped, brought to Kangaroo Island, and forced to work catching and skinning seals, kangaroos, and wallabies, and lugging salt from the salt mines.

In 1836 Kangaroo Island became the first place in South Australia to be officially settled. The state's capital was Kingscote, until it was abandoned a couple of years later in favor of Adelaide. In spite of its early settlement, Kangaroo Island had very few residents until after World War II, when returned soldiers set up farms here. Today, more than a million sheep are raised on the island.

Kangaroo Island

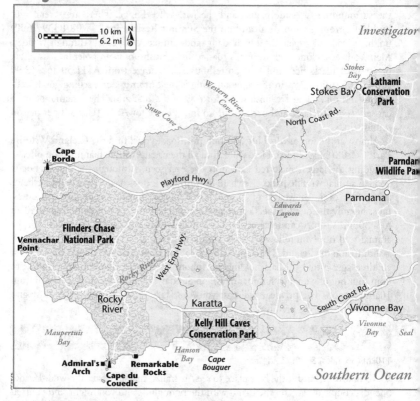

ISLAND ESSENTIALS

WHEN TO GO   The best time to visit Kangaroo Island is between November and March (although you'll have difficulty finding accommodations over the Christmas school-holiday period). July and August tend to be rainy, and winter can be cold (but often milder on mainland South Australia around Adelaide). Many companies offer day trips from Adelaide, but I strongly advise spending at least 2 days here—3 or even 5 days would be even better. There really is a lot to see, and you won't regret spending the extra time.

GETTING THERE   **Kendell Airlines** (☎ **08/8231 9567**) flies Kingscote from the Ansett terminal at Adelaide Airport. The round-trip fare is about A$174 (U.S.$121.80); 14-day advance-purchase fares are around A$116 (U.S.$81.20). The flight takes about 25 minutes. *Note:* You are restricted to 10 kilograms (2¼ lbs.) of luggage on these aircraft.

 If you prefer to go by sea, **Kangaroo Island SeaLink** (☎ **13 13 01** in Australia, or 08/8553 1122), operates two vehicle and passenger ferries four times daily (sometimes five times in peak periods) from Cape Jervis on the tip of the mainland to Penneshaw on Kangaroo Island. The trip takes 40 minutes; the round-trip fare is A$60 (U.S.$42) for adults, A$30 (U.S.$21) for children, and A$130 (U.S.$91) for cars. Connecting bus service (round-trip) from Adelaide to Cape Jervis is provided for an extra A$28 (U.S.$19.60) for adults and A$14 (U.S.$9.80) for children. **Kangaroo Island Fast Ferries** (☎ **08/8376 8300**; fax 08/8376 8333) operates the fast *Enigma III*

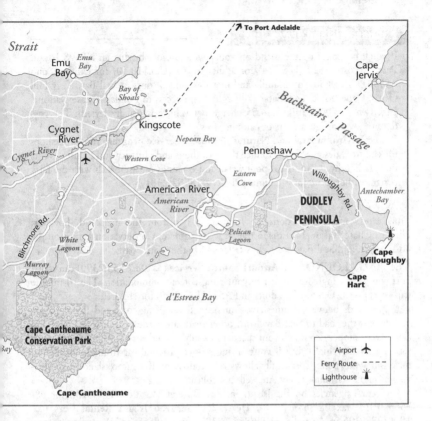

Wednesday, and Friday through Monday between Glenelg and Kingscote (no cars). The ferry leaves Glenelg at 8am and arrives at Kingscote at 10:30am. The return ferry leaves Kingscote at 4pm. The round-trip fare is A$86 (U.S.$60.20) for adults and A$50 (U.S.$35) for children. The *Enigma III* runs year-round, but is often canceled in the off-season due to bad weather or lack of passengers, so call first. Both ferry companies can arrange accommodations, tours, and car rental on the island.

VISITOR INFORMATION   **Tourism Kangaroo Island,** The Gateway Information Centre, Howard Drive, Penneshaw (P.O. Box 336, Penneshaw, Kangaroo Island, SA 5222) (☎ **08/8553 1185;** fax 08/8553 1255; www.tourkangarooisland.com.au; e-mail: tourki@kin.on.net), has plenty of maps and information and can book accommodations and island tours. For more information on the island's national parks, contact the **National Parks and Wildlife Service (NPWS)** office, 37 Dauncey St. (P.O. Box 39, Kingscote, SA 5223) (☎ **08/8553 2381;** fax 08/8553 2531). It's open Monday through Friday from 9am to 5pm.

   In addition, hotel and motel staff generally carry a stack of tourist brochures and can point you in the right direction as far as where to go and what to see.

ISLAND LAYOUT   Kangaroo Island is Australia's third-largest island, at 156 kilometers (93½ miles) long and 57 kilometers (21 miles) wide at its widest point. The distance across the narrowest point is only 2 kilometers (1¼ miles). Approximately 3,900 people live on the island—over half on the northeast coast in one of the three main towns: **Kingscote** (pop. 1,800), **Penneshaw** (pop. 250), and **American River** (pop. 200).

Kangaroo Island Travel Tips

If you'll be exploring the island on your own, consider buying an **NPWS Island Pass.** It costs A$20 (U.S.$14) for adults, A$15 (U.S.$10.50) for children, and A$55 (U.S.$38.50) for a family and includes guided tours of Seal Bay, Kelly Hill Caves, Cape Borda, and Cape Willoughby and access to Flinders Chase National Park (where a A$6.50/U.S.$4.55 charge per vehicle is usually levied). The pass doesn't cover penguin tours or camping fees.

The **Environmental and Natural Resources Service program** runs workshops for children, designed to introduce them to the island's history and nature. Events include lighthouse and tidal-pool walks and evenings on the beach with the fairy penguins. For more information, call ☎ **08/8552 2381.**

The island's major attractions are located farther from the mainland, however; Flinders Chase National Park is in the far west, Lathami Conservation Park is on the north coast, and Seal Bay and Kelly's caves are on the south coast.

GETTING AROUND   An **Airport Shuttle Service** (☎ **08/8553 2390**) can transport you from Kingscote Airport to your Kingscote accommodation. The 10-minute trip costs A$10 (U.S.$7) for adults and A$5 (U.S.$3.50) for children.

Major roads between Penneshaw, American River, Kingscote, and Parndana are paved, as is the road to Seal Bay. Most other roads are made of ironstone gravel and can be very slippery, so watch your speed, especially around curves. All roads are accessible by 2WD vehicles, but if you're bringing over a rental car from the mainland, make sure your policy specifically allows you to drive on Kangaroo Island. Avoid driving at night—animals rarely fare well in a collision with a car.

Car-rental agencies on the island include **Budget** (☎ **08/8553 3133,** or 08/8553 1034; fax 08/8553 2888), **Hertz & Kangaroo Island Rental Cars** (☎ **1800/088 296** in Australia, or 08/8553 2390; fax 08/8553 2878), or **Boomerang Rent-a-Car** (☎ and fax **08/8553 9006**). You can pick up cars at the airport or ferry terminals.

ORGANIZED TOURS   Although their trips are hardly aimed at the budget-conscious traveler, the itineraries offered by highly recommended ✪ **Kangaroo Island Wilderness Tours** (☎ **08/8559 2220;** fax 08/8559 2288) are definitely worth the splurge. The company operates several small 4WDs (maximum: six people) and takes visitors around the islands on very informative 1-day trips that cost A$205 (U.S.$143.50) per person, including transfers, an excellent lunch with wine, and park entry fees. 2-, 3-, and 4-day trips, with all meals and accommodations included, cost A$513 (U.S.$359.10), A$821 (U.S.$574.70), and A$1,129 (U.S.$790.30), respectively.

Another good operator is ✪ **Adventure Charters of Kangaroo Island,** Kingscote, SA 5223 (☎ **08/8553 9119;** fax 08/8553 9122), with the knowledgeable and gregarious Craig Wickham at the helm. Day trips cost A$215 (U.S.$150.50) per person with a big lunch, or A$380 (U.S.$266), including round-trip airfare from Adelaide. **Kangaroo Island Odysseys,** P.O. Box 494, Penneshaw, SA 5222 (☎ and fax **08/8553 1294**) offers a similar day trip in small vehicles for A$205 (U.S.$143.50) with lunch. **Kangaroo Island Adventures,** P.O. Box 570, Penneshaw, SA 5222 (☎ **13 13 01** in Australia), operates a 1-night, 2-day trip in conjunction with the Sealink ferry service from Cape Jervis; rates start at A$195 (U.S.$136.50) per person. This trip includes coach travel from Adelaide to Cape Jervis, ferry travel, transfers, park entry fee, guided coach tours, and accommodations.

The best options for travelers on a budget, though, are the trips with **Kangaroo Island Ferry Connection** (☎ **08/8553 1233;** fax 08/8553 1190; e-mail: kifc@kin.on.net). You get round-trip bus and ferry transportation from Adelaide, an evening stroll to check out the penguins, a night in a hostel dorm (you can pay a little extra to upgrade to a double), and a full-day tour of the major south coast attractions, including morning tea and lunch—all for just A$168 (U.S.$117.60). You could spend most of the first day touring the island, too, for a total cost of A$205 (U.S.$143.50).

EXPLORING THE ISLAND

The island is much bigger than you might think, and you can spend a fair bit of time just getting from one place of interest to the next. Of the many, many places to see, ✪ **Flinders Chase National Park** is one of the most important. It took 30 years of lobbying until reluctant politicians finally agreed to preserve this unique western region of the island in 1919. Today, the park makes up around 17% of the island and is home to plenty of animals, some beautiful coastal scenery, and two old lighthouses. Bird-watchers have recorded at least 243 species of birds here. Koalas are so common in parts that they're almost falling out of the trees. Platypus can be spotted, but you'll probably need to make a special effort and sit next to a stream in the dark for a few hours to have any chance of seeing one. Kangaroos, wallabies, and brush-tailed possums are so tame and numerous that the authorities were forced to erect a barrier around the Rocky River Campground to stop them from bounding up and carrying away picnickers' sandwiches!

The most impressive coastal scenery can be found at **Cape du Couedic** at the southern tip of the park, where millions of years of crashing ocean have created curious structures—like the hollowed-out limestone promontory called **Admiral's Arch** and the aptly named **Remarkable Rocks,** where you'll see huge boulders balancing atop a massive granite dome. At Admiral's Arch, a colony of some 4,000 New Zealand fur seals play in the rock pools and snooze on the rocks. This place can be spectacular during rough weather.

Elsewhere on the island, you shouldn't miss the unforgettable experience of walking through a colony of Australian sea lions at **Seal Bay.** The Seal Bay Conservation Park was declared in 1972, and these days some 100,000 people visit it each year. Boardwalks have been built through the dunes to the beach to reduce the impact of so many feet. The colony consists of about 500 animals, but at any one time you might see up to 100 basking with their pups here. The rangers who supervise the area lead guided trips throughout the day, from 9am to 4:15pm. If you come here without a coach group, you must join a tour. Tours cost A$7.50 (U.S.$5.25) for adults, A$5 (U.S.$3.50) for children, and A$15 (U.S.$10.50) for a family.

Lathami Conservation Park, just to the east of Stokes Bay, is a wonderful place to see wallabies in the wild. Just dip in under the low canopy of casuarina pines and walk silently, keeping your eyes peeled, and you're almost certain to spot them. If you're fortunate, you may even come across a very rare glossy cockatoo—it's big and black and feeds mainly on casuarina nuts.

Another interesting spot, especially for bird-watchers, is **Murray Lagoon,** on the northern edge of **Cape Gantheaume Conservation Park.** It's the largest lagoon on

Don't Feed the Animals, Please

Don't feed any native animals on Kangaroo Island. Kangaroos and wallabies might beg for food, but they are lactose-intolerant and can go blind, or catch disease, from being fed human food.

the island and an important habitat for thousands of waterbirds. Contact the NPWS (see "Visitor Information," above) for information on a ranger-guided Wetland Wade.

If you're into caving, then head to the **Kelly Hill Caves Conservation Park** on the south coast, not far from the southern edge of Flinders Chase National Park. The largest of the caves is open for tours throughout the day with NPWS rangers. Entry costs A$5 (U.S.$3.50) for adults, A$3.50 (U.S.$2.45) for children, and A$13.50 (U.S.$8.45) for a family.

If you want to see **fairy penguins**—tiny 1-kilogram (2¼-lb.) animals that stand just 33 centimeters (13 in.) tall—forget the touristy show at Phillip Island near Melbourne. On Kangaroo Island you get to see them in a totally natural environment. Tours are conducted nightly by the NPWS (see "Visitor Information," above) and cost A$5 (U.S.$3.50) for adults, A$3.50 (U.S.$2.45) for children, and A$13.50 (U.S.$9.45) for families. Times of tours change seasonally, so call to confirm. Tours of a colony near **Penneshaw** gather at the Interpretive Centre adjacent to the penguins, and tours of the **Kingscote** colony meet at the reception desk of the Ozone Hotel.

WHERE TO STAY

There are more than 40 accommodations options to choose from on the island, from cozy B&Bs and beach cottages, to farms and campgrounds. If you're on a super-tight budget, head to the **Penneshaw Youth Hostel,** 43 North Terrace, Penneshaw, Kangaroo Island, SA 5222 (☎ **08/8553 1284;** fax 08/8553 1295), with dorm beds for A$14 (U.S.$) and doubles for A$16 (U.S.$) per person (A$2/U.S.$1.40; less for YHA members).

If you feel like sleeping out in one of 40 self-contained cottages or coastal lodgings, then contact **Kangaroo Island Remote and Coastal Farm Accommodation** (☎ **08/8553 1233;** fax 08/8553 1190). Standards vary, and prices range from A$40 to $100 (U.S.$28 to $70). The staff can also arrange lodgings in local farms, homes, and B&Bs for A$60 to $110 (U.S. $42 to $77) for a double with breakfast.

The **NPWS** (see "Visitor Information," above) also offers basic lodgings for rent, including relatively isolated lighthouse cottages, from A$20 (U.S.$14) per adult per night.

Camping is allowed only at designated sites for a minimal fee, the main place being at Rocky River in Flinders Chase National Park.

In & Near Kingscote

Graydon Holiday Lodge. 16 Buller St., Kingscote, Kangaroo Island, SA 5223. ☎ **08/8553 2713.** Fax 08/8553 3289. 7 self-contained units. TV. A$74 (U.S.$51.80) double. Additional person A$10 (U.S.$7) extra; children A$8 (U.S.$5.60) extra. A$10 (U.S.$7) surcharge for 1-night stays. Lower rates during off-season. BC, MC, V.

A cheaper alternative to the motels listed below, and perfect if you want to cook your own food, the Graydon offers large, spartan two-bedroom units (sleeping up to six) with plain brick walls and office-style carpets. The property is just 1 minute from the waterfront, and a 5-minute walk from the center of Kingscote and the shops. There are barbecue and laundry facilities on the premises, and all rooms are supplied with linen and towels. Rooms are cooled by a ceiling fan and the sea breeze.

Ozone Hotel. The Foreshore (P.O. Box 145), Kingscote, SA 5223. ☎ **08/8553 2011.** Fax 08/8553 2249. 37 units. A/C TV TEL. A$80–$100 (U.S.$56–$70) double; A$105 (U.S.$73.50) triple. Additional person A$5 (U.S.$3.50) extra. AE, BC, DC, JCB, MC, V.

The best known of Kangaroo Island's tourist lodgings, the Ozone was renovated in 1997, so the shine still hasn't quite rubbed off. The property gets its name from the aroma from the sea—which virtually laps at its door. It's a nice, centrally located

---

Money-Saving Tip

The **Ozone Hotel** often offers special 1-night accommodation packages in conjunction with **Kendell Airlines** (☎ **1800/338 8894** in Australia, or 08/ 8231 9567), including 2-day car rental. Call the hotel or the airline for details.

---

choice, with an à la carte restaurant, a casual bistro serving good meals, a couple of bars, a game room, a pool and sauna, and a laundry. Rooms are comfortable with plenty of space; most of the more expensive ones have water views of Nepean Bay. Family rooms have a double bed and two singles.

✪ **Wisteria Lodge.** 7 Cygnet Rd., Kingscote., Kangaroo Island, SA 5223. ☎ **08/ 8553 2707.** Fax 08/8553 2200. Reservations can be made through Flag Inns (☎ **800/ 624-3524** in the U.S. and Canada, 0800/892 407 in the U.K., 0800/803 524 in New Zealand, 13 24 00 in Australia). 20 units. A/C MINIBAR TV TEL. A$120 (U.S.$84) double; A$136 (U.S. $95.20) triple; spa room A$153 double (U.S.$107.10); A$173 triple (U.S.$121.10); A$220 (U.S.$154) family room. Additional person A$16–$20 (U.S.$11.20–$14) extra; children 3–12 A$13–$17 (U.S.$9.10–$11.90) extra. Breakfast A$8 (U.S.$5.60) extra. Ask about money-saving packages (including transport to the island, transfers, meals, and day tours). AE, BC, DC, MC, V.

All rooms at the modern, and definitely unglamorous looking, Wisteria Lodge are standard motel-type, boosted by ocean views over Nepean Bay. Deluxe rooms offer a spa and queen-size beds. There's a pool, a spa, a playground, and half-size tennis court. Simple meals, such as pastas, steak, apricot chicken, and fish, are served in the Beachcomber restaurant.

IN AMERICAN RIVER

Popular with fishermen and located 37 kilometers (22¼ miles) from Kingscote, American River lacks a beach, but offers black swans on Pelican Lagoon instead. Wild wallabies abound, and egrets, magpies, and cockatoos offer early-morning wake-up calls.

Casuarina Holiday Units. 9 Ryberg Rd., American River, SA 5221. ☎ and fax **08/ 8553 7020.** 6 units (all with shower only). TV. A$50 (U.S.$35) double. AE, BC, DC, MC, V.

These simple, country-style units are a good value. Each comes with a double bed, two singles, a fan, a heater, a TV, and an attached shower. There's a laundry, a barbecue, a children's' playground, and fish-cleaning facilities if you manage to catch anything.

Worth a Splurge

✪ **Wanderers Rest.** Bayview Road (P.O. Box 34), American River, SA 5221. ☎ **08/ 8553 7140.** Fax 08/8553 7282. 9 units (all with shower only). MINIBAR TV. A$150 (U.S.$105) double; A$195 (U.S.$136.50) triple. Rates include full breakfast. Ask about package deals. AE, BC, DC, MC, V. Children under 12 not accepted.

This highly recommended guest house is set on a hillside with panoramic views across the sea to the mainland. It offers large, comfortably furnished rooms with balconies and king-size beds that convert to twins. There's a pool and spa in the garden and a game room. Breakfasts are hearty, and packed lunches are available. Dinnertime can be a hoot, with guests sipping beer and wine around the dining room table and tucking into King George whiting caught that day (or steak, lamb chops, or a vegetarian stir-fry); main courses cost A$17 (U.S.$11.90). Smoking is not permitted.

IN PARNDANA

Developed by soldier-settlers after World War II, Parndana today is a rural service center situated a 25-minute drive from Seal Bay and Stokes Bay, and just around the corner from **Parndana Wildlife Park,** which has more than 50 aviaries with collections of native and other birds, some of them rare and protected.

✪ **The Open House.** 70 Smith St., Parndana, SA 5221. ☎ **08/8559 6113.** Fax 08/8559 6088. 4 units (all with shower only). A$69 (U.S.$48.30) per adult, including breakfast, A$45 (U.S.$31.50) children under 14, including breakfast; A$90 (U.S.$63) per adult, including dinner and breakfast; A$65 (U.S.$45.50) children under 14, including dinner and breakfast. BC, MC, V.

The best thing about The Open House is mealtime, when the guests sit around a communal table, tuck into delicious home-cooked meals, and imbibe plenty of wine. The rooms—two with double beds, one with a queen-size bed, one with two singles, and a family room sleeping up to four—are comfortable and homey and come with a private bathroom with shower. The very friendly owner, Sarah Wall, took over the house in June 1998, soon after she moved here; but she can already offer excellent advice on what to do around the island, and whips up a mean packed lunch.

WHERE TO DINE

You'll find a few cheap take-out booths scattered around the island at the most popular tourist spots. For lunch you could get sandwiches at the deli on Dauncey Street, behind the Ozone Hotel, in Kingscote.

IN CYGNET RIVER

The Café. Playford Hwy., Cygnet River. ☎ **08/8553 9187.** Main courses A$6.50–$16.50 (U.S.$4.55–$11.55). AE, BC, DC, MC, V. Daily 10am–10pm Jan to early Feb; Wed–Sat 10am–10pm, Sun noon–2:30pm other times. CAFE FARE

It's nice to eat outside here in the courtyard on a warm day, and the sandwiches, pizzas, and milk shakes are good any time. The big seller at lunch is the tandoori chicken burger, while at dinner the King George whiting and the Cygnet River haloumi cheese with olive bread and semidried tomatoes are the most popular dishes.

IN PENNESHAW

Dolphin Rock Café by the Sea. 43 North Terrace (next to the YHA). ☎ **08/8553 1284.** Main courses A$2.75–$9 (U.S.$1.95–$6.30). AE, BC, MC, V (with A$15/U.S.$10.50 minimum). Winter 7:30am–7:30pm; summer 7am–8:30pm. TAKE-OUT/BURGERS.

Plastic tables and chairs and budget meals are what you'll find at this favorite of the backpacker crowd. Popular dishes include the individual pizzas and French fries with gravy. Also on offer are fish-and-chips, hamburgers, and roasted chicken. Across the road, the fairy penguins come in at dusk.

4 Flinders Ranges National Park

460km (246 miles) north of Adelaide

The dramatic craggy peaks and ridges that make up the Flinders Ranges rise out of the South Australian desert country. The colors of the rock vary from deep red to orange, with sedimentary lines easily visible as they run down the sides of cliffs. Much of the greenery around here is stunted arid land vegetation. The most remarkable attraction is **Wilpena Pound,** a natural circle of cliff faces that form a gigantic depression on top of a mountainous ledge. The wind whipping over the cliff edges can produce some exhilarating white-knuckle turbulence if you fly over it in a light aircraft. Kangaroos and emus can sometimes be seen wandering around the park, but outside the park kangaroos are heavily culled.

ESSENTIALS

GETTING THERE   By car, take Highway 1 out of Adelaide to Port Augusta (3½ hours), then head east on Route 47 via Quorn and Hawker (another 45 minutes). It's another hour to Wilpena Pound. Alternatively, take the **scenic route** (it doesn't have a specific name) through the Clare Valley (around 5 hours): From Adelaide head to Gawler and then through the Clare Valley; follow signs to Gladstone, Melrose, Wilmington, and Quorn.

Several companies run organized trips to the national park from Adelaide. **Wallaby Tracks Adventure Tours** (☎ **08/8648 6655;** fax 08/8648 6655; http://headbush. mtx.net; e-mail: headbush@dove.net.au) depart Adelaide every Tuesday for a 3-day camping trip for A$279 (U.S.$195.30), all-inclusive. The company also offers a 2-day, 2-night Weekend Escape package departing Adelaide every Friday afternoon and returning Sunday night for A$199 (U.S.$139.30). It also runs a 10-day true Australian bush expedition, from Adelaide to Alice Springs, called Bush and Four Wheel–Drive Adventures. You get to visit desert, Aboriginal communities, see Uluru, the Olgas, and Kings Canyon (see chapter 9). It costs A$695 (U.S.$486.50), including bush camping.

VISITOR INFORMATION   Before setting off, contact the **Flinders Ranges & Outback of South Australia Regional Tourism Association (FROSATA)** at 56b Glen Osmond Rd., Adelaide (☎ **08/8373 3430**). I strongly recommend a visit to the **Wadlata Outback Centre** at 41 Flinders Terrace, Port Augusta (☎ **08/8642 4511**), an excellent, award-winning interactive museum and information center that gives you a good idea of life in the region. The museum costs A$7 (U.S.$4.90) for adults, A$4.50 (U.S.$3.15) for children. It's open Monday to Friday from 9am to 5:30pm, and Saturday and Sunday from 10am to 4pm.

In Hawker, both the Mobil service station and the post office act as information outlets.

Park entrance is A$5 (U.S.$3.50) per vehicle, payable at the National Parks & Wildlife Service office near the Wilpena Pound Resort, or by exchanging cash for a ticket at unmanned ticket booths around the park.

GETTING AROUND   You can creep up on wildlife among the gorges with **Kev's Kamel Kapers** (☎ 0419/839 288 mobile phone) in Hawker. Remarkable 2-hour sunset trips cost A$20 (U.S.$14) half-day excursions are A$50 (U.S.$35) and full-day safaris, including a champagne lunch, cost A$80 (U.S.$56) for adults and A$60 (U.S.$42) for children under age 16. Overnight camel treks are available, and on weekends and public holidays 15-minute camel rides cost just A$5 (U.S.$3.50). The tours run only from March to the end of October.

WHERE TO STAY

The **Flinders Ranges Caravan Park** (☎ **08/8648 4266;** fax 08/8648 4366) and the **Hawker Caravan Park** (☎ **08/8648 4006;** fax 08/8648 4139), both in Hawker, offer on-site caravans from A$30 (U.S.$21). Most large landholders in the area also lease former shearer, overseer, and jackaroo cottages and old School of the Air buildings. Contact FROSATA (see "Visitor Information," above) for details.

✪ **Andu Lodge.** 12 First St., Quorn, SA 5043. ☎ **1800/639 933** in Australia, or 08/ 8648 6655. Fax 08/8648 6655. E-mail: headbush@dove.net.au. 64 beds. A$25 (U.S.$17.50) single; A$38 (U.S.$26.60) double; A$48 (U.S.$33.60) family room (sleeps 4). A$14 (U.S.$9.80) dorm bed. AE, BC, DC, MC, V.

This fabulous backpackers' lodge is one of the best in Australia. Situated in Quorn, in the central Flinders Ranges (42km/25 miles from Port Augusta), this upscale former hotel is air-conditioned in summer, heated in winter, and has nice clean rooms (dorms sleep six). There's also a nice TV room, laundry, a computer for e-mailing, and a kitchen area. The hostel offers transfers from Port Augusta for A$6 (U.S.$4.20) each way, and runs a range of trips with an emphasis on Aboriginal culture and ecotourism. Included among them are a day trip to Wilpena Pound for A$79 (U.S.$55.30)(the tour plus a 2-night stay at the hostel costs just A$99/ U.S.$69.30). On Sunday there's a Southern Flinders Tour costing A$65 (U.S.$45.50), which takes in a couple of impressive gorges on the lookout for flora and fauna, including the yellow-footed rock wallaby. Guests can also rent mountain bikes for A$12 (U.S.$8.40) for half a day and A$20 (U.S.$14) for a full day. Quorn, by the way, was where the old *Ghan* railway used to start and finish, and where part of the movie *Gallipoli* was filmed. The population is just 1,300, and four friendly pubs all serve A$5 (U.S.$3.50) meals.

Wilpena Pound Resort. Wilpena Pound, SA 5434. ☎ **1800/805 802** in Australia, or 08/8648 0004. Fax 08/8648 0028. 60 units. A/C TV TEL. A$98–$115 (U.S.$68.60–$80.50) double; A$130 (U.S.$91) self-contained unit. Additional person A$10 (U.S.$7) extra; children 2–14 A$5 (U.S.$3.50) extra. AE, BC, DC, MC, V.

The nearest place to Wilpena Pound itself, this partly refurbished resort almost monopolizes the overnight tourist market around here. Standard rooms are adequate and offer respite from the summer heat. The self-contained units come with a stovetop, a microwave, a sink, and cooking utensils. There's also a rather tacky dining room and bar, a general store, and a swimming pool. The resort also operates a campground; powered camp sites cost A$17 (U.S.$11.90) a night for two people and unpowered sites go for A$10.50 (U.S.$7.35) for two people (additional person A$2/U.S.$1.40 extra). There are some good walks around the area. The resort also offers half-hour scenic flights over the ranges for A$120 (U.S.$84) for one person, A$65 (U.S.$45.50) each for two, or A$55 (U.S.$38.50) each for three or more. They also operate good 4WD tours with lunch for A$75 (U.S.$52.50) for a full day and A$55 (U.S.$38.50) for a half day.

✪ **Prairie Hotel.** Corner of High St. and West Terrace, Parachilna, SA 5730. ☎ **08/ 8648 4895.** Fax 08/8648 4606. 12 units (some with shower only). A/C TV. A$90–$135 (U.S.$63–$94.50) double; A$200 (U.S.$140) double with spa. Additional person A$20–$30 (U.S.$14–$21) extra. Rates include light breakfast. AE, BC, DC, MC, V.

If you are going to stay anywhere in the Flinders Ranges, stay here. This tiny, tin-roofed, stone-walled pub offers a memorable experience and is well worth the dusty 89-kilometer (53½-mile) drive over the Ranges from Hawker. A new addition to the pub contains nice rooms, each with a queen-size bed and a shower. The older-style rooms are smaller and quaint. Three units have tubs. The bar out front is a great place to meet the locals and other travelers (who all shake their heads in wonder that this magnificent place is still so undiscovered).✪**Meals** here, prepared by young chef Darren (Bart) Brooks, are top-notch—very nearly the best I've had in Australia. Among his specialties are so-called feral foods, such as kangaroo-tail soup to start, and a mixed grill of emu sausages, camel steak, and kangaroo as a main course. I hope he's still there when you visit because with such a talent he's sure to be poached. The owner's brother runs remarkable scenic flights over Wilpena Pound and out to the salt lakes.

WHERE TO DINE

The **Old Ghan Restaurant** on Leigh Creek Road, Hawker (☎ 08/8648 4176), is open for lunch and dinner Wednesday through Sunday and is interesting for its historic connection with the Outback. It used to be a railway station on the Ghan railway line to Alice Springs, before flooding shifted the line sideways. The food here is unexciting, but the homemade pies have a following. If you find yourself in Port Augusta, the main town in the area, head to the **Standpipe Motor Inn** (☎ **08/8642 4033**) for excellent Indian food. The rooms here are nice enough, and quiet, and cost A$80 (U.S.$56).

5 Outback South Australia

South Australia is the driest state in the nation. This is well borne out once you leave behind the parklands of Adelaide and head into the interior. The Outback is as harsh as it is beautiful. Much of it is stony deserts, salt pans, and sand hills, roamed by kangaroos and wild goats—but after spring rains it can burst alive with wildflowers.

It was always difficult to travel through these parts, and even today there are only four main routes. One of them, the **Birdsville Track,** is famed in Outback history as the trail along which stockmen once drove their herds of cattle south from Queensland. Another, the **Strzelecki Track,** runs through remote sand dune country to Innamincka and on to Coopers Creek. Both tracks cut through the "dog fence"—a 5,600-kilometer- (3,360-mile-) long barrier designed to keep dingoes out of the pastoral lands to the south.

If you follow the Stuart Highway, or the **Oodnadatta Track,** you'll pass the mining towns of ✪ **Coober Pedy,** Andamooka, and Mintabie, where people from all over the world have been turned loose in the maddening search for opal. Out here, too, are national parks, such as the daunting **Simpson Desert Conservation Park,** with its seemingly endless blood-red sand dunes and spinifex plains; and **Lake Eyre National Park,** with its dried-up salt pan that during the rare event of a flood is a temporary home to thousands of water birds.

COOBER PEDY
854km (512½ miles) NW of Adelaide, 689 km (413½ miles) S of Alice Springs

Tourists come to this Outback opal-mining town for one thing: the people. More than 3,500 people, from 44 nations, work and sleep here—mainly underground. The majority of townsfolk suffer from the so-called opal fever, which keeps you digging and digging on the trail of the elusive shimmering rocks. Though some are secretive and like to keep to themselves, many others are colorful characters all too ready to stop for a chat and spin a few yarns.

Historically, Coober Pedy was a rough place, and it still has a certain Wild West air about it. The first opal was found here in 1915, but it wasn't until 1917, when the Trans Continental Railway was completed, that people began seriously digging for opal. Since then, minors have mainly lived underground—you'll understand why when you encounter the heat, the dust, and the flies for yourself.

The town got its name from the Aboriginal words *kupa piti,* commonly thought to mean "white man in a hole." Remnants of the holes left by early miners are every-

Travel Warning

Be careful out here if you intend to drive. Distances between points of interest can be huge, and water supplies, petrol, food, and accommodations are far apart. Always travel with a good map and plenty of expert advice. If you plan to travel off-road, a 4WD is a must.

where, mostly in the form of bleached-white hills of waste called mullock heaps. It's a popular tourist activity to *noodle,* or search through, these heaps in hopes of finding overlooked slivers of color.

As for the town itself, there isn't much to look at, except for a couple of underground churches, some casual restaurants, and a handful of opal stores. These places are all within walking distance of each other on the main highway. The only other roads lead off to camps and mounds and holes in the ground.

ESSENTIALS

GETTING THERE   **Kendell Airlines** has daily flights to Coober Pedy from Adelaide. **Greyhound-Pioneer** runs services from Adelaide to Coober Pedy for A$76 (U.S.$53.20) one-way for adults, and A$61 (U.S.$42.70) for children. The trip takes about 12 hours. The bus from Alice Springs to Coober Pedy costs A$75 (U.S.$52.50) for adults and A$60 (U.S.$42) for children. Passengers bound for Ayres Rock transfer at Erldunda. If you drive from Adelaide it will take you about 9 hours to reach Coober Pedy along the Stuart Highway. It will take you another 7 hours to drive the 700 kilometers (420 miles) to Alice Springs.

VISITOR INFORMATION   The **Coober Pedy Tourist Information Centre,** Hutchinson Street, (☎ **1800/637 076** in Australia, or 08/8672 5298) is open Monday through Friday from 9am to 5pm (closed public holidays).

SEEING THE TOWN

Coober Pedy Scenic Tours (☎ **08/8672 5688**), run tours of the opal fields and township, including visits to an underground mine, home, and potteries, as well as a tour of the underground Serbian Church. You also get to witness an opal-cutting demonstration and noodle through the mullock heaps. The tour takes 4 hours and costs A$36 (U.S.$25.20) for adults, A$18 (U.S.$12.60) for children, and A$90 (U.S.$63) for families.

The tours of the town organized by Radeka's (below) cost A$25 (U.S.$17.50) and are popular with budget travelers.

A very enjoyable option is to take part in the **Mail Run,** a 12-hour journey out into the bush to see part of Australia that most Australians never see. Tours leave every Monday and Thursday from **Underground Books** (☎ **08/8672 5558**) in Coober Pedy and travel along 600 kilometers (360 miles) of dirt roads to Oodnatta and William Creek cattle station, stopping off at five different stations along the route. It can get pretty hot and dusty outside, but it's relatively comfortable inside the air-conditioned 4WD. Bring your own lunch, or buy it at one of the major stop-offs. The tour costs A$70 (U.S.$42) for adults and A$35 (U.S.$24.50) for children, although children might find the long trip difficult. This could easily be one of the most memorable experiences you'll have in Australia.

WHERE TO STAY

✪ **The Backpacker's Inn at Radeka's Downunder Motel.** 1 Oliver St., Coober Pedy, SA 5723. ☎ **08/8672 5223.** Fax 08/8672 5821. 105 dorm beds, 9 motel rooms. A$70 (U.S.$42) double; additional person A$19 (U.S.$13.30) extra. A$14 (U.S.$9.80) dorm bed (A$13/U.S.$9.10 with all discount cards, including YHA). AE, BC, MC, V.

Whereas all other underground motel rooms in Coober Pedy are actually built into the side of a hill, the hostel accommodations at this centrally located motel are truly underground—some 6.5 meters (21¼ ft.) underground, that is. This makes for comfortable year-round temperatures. Dorms generally contain just four beds, although there are two large dorms that sleep up to 20 people. The twin rooms are simply furnished in typical hostel style (of course, there are no windows). Guests have the use of a TV and video room, a pool table, free coffee and tea, a new kitchen and dining room, and a bar. The motel rooms are quite comfortable, and come with attached bathrooms with a shower. Some have a kitchenette.

Desert View Underground Apartments. Shore Place, Catacombe Rd. (P.O. Box 272, Coober Pedy, SA 5723). ☎ **08/8672 3330.** Fax 08/8672 3331. 11 units. TV. A$80 (U.S.$56) double. Additional person A$20 (U.S.$14) extra; children 5–12 A$12 (U.S.$8.40) extra. AE, BC, DC, MC, V.

This place offers good-value rooms dug into the side of a hill. Units have a separate lounge and kitchen area, an attached bathroom with shower, a master bedroom with a double bed, and a separate bedroom with two single beds. A family room comes with a double bed and four bunks. Outside you'll find a laundry, a small pool, and a barbecue area. You can save a lot of money by buying your groceries at the local supermarket and cooking them up here instead of eating out. Half-day tours of the township can be arranged for A$20 (U.S.$14).

Worth a Splurge

Desert Cave Hotel. Hutchison St., Coober Pedy (P.O. Box 223, Coober Pedy, SA 5723). ☎ **08/8672 5688.** Fax 08/8672 5198. 50 units (19 underground). A/C MINIBAR TV TEL. A$152 (U.S.$81.40) double; A$160 (U.S.$112) family room (sleeps 5). Additional person A$15 (U.S.$10.50) extra. AE, BC, DC, MC, V.

Although not the only underground hotel in town, this is the most luxurious. It was dug out using tunneling machines brought in from the opal fields, which ground up the hard desert sandstone to make tunnels 3 meters (10 ft.) high and 2 meters (6½ ft.) wide The walls were then sealed to block out dust and moisture. Staying underground is an amazing experience, but for those who feel a little uneasy about the idea, there are identically laid-out rooms above ground. Umbertos restaurant is reached from below ground by a winding staircase, which is well worth clambering up for the specialty chargrilled dishes. Also on the premises is a cafe serving lighter meals for lunch, a game room, a pool, and a spa. A 3-day accommodation package (all inclusive, including tours) from Adelaide costs A$340 (U.S.$238) per person, including round-trip airfare.

WHERE TO DINE

The Opal Inn (☎ **08/8672 5430**) offers good-value counter meals of the typical pub-grub variety. Head to **Traces** (☎ **08/8672 5147**), the township's favorite Greek restaurant, for something a bit different.

6 The Coorong

Few places in the world attract as much wildfowl as the Coorong, one of Australia's most precious sanctuaries. Basically, the Coorong is made up of an area that includes the mouth of the Murray River the huge Lake Alexandrina the smaller Lake Albert and a long, thin sand spit called the Younghusband Peninsula. The Coorong National Park encompasses a small, and by far the most scenic, part of this area. Although the area is under constant environmental threat because of pollutants coming south via the Murray River from the farmlands to the north, it still manages to host large colonies of native and visiting birds, such as the Australian pelican, black swans, royal spoonbills, greenshank, and the extremely rare hooded plover. The national park, which stands out starkly against the degraded farming land surrounding it, is also home to several species of marsupials, including wombats.

ESSENTIALS

GETTING THERE   The best way to visit the Coorong is by car, although a guided tour of the area is highly recommended once you reach either the main settlement of Goolwa, on the western fringe of the waterways, or more preferably Meninge, on the eastern boundary. From Adelaide, follow the Princes Highway along the coast.

VISITOR INFORMATION   **Goolwa Tourist Information Centre,** Old Library Building, Cadell Street, Goolwa (☎ **08/855 1144**), has information on the area and can book accommodations. The best time to visit the Coorong is in December and January, when the lakes are full of migratory birds from overseas. Plenty of birds can be spotted year-round, however. *Note:* Remember to bring binoculars.

GETTING AROUND   The best tour operator in the area is ✪ **Coorong Nature Tours** (☎ **08/8574 0037,** or 015/714 793 mobile phone), based in Narrung. Tours are run by David Dadd, a delightful, unassuming Cockney who fell in love with the Coorong when he arrived at the age of 11. He offers memorable half-day, full-day, and 2- and 3-day tours of the area, with pickup either from Meningie or Adelaide. Half-day tours cost A$60 (U.S.$42) per person from Meningie, and full-day tours cost A$110 (U.S.$77) per person, or A$160 (U.S.$105) with pickup from Adelaide. Bookings are essential.

WHERE TO STAY

There are plenty of hotels, B&Bs, campgrounds, and caravan parks in Goolwa and along the main road running parallel to the national park. One of the ones I prefer is the **Goolwa Camping and Tourist Park,** 40 Castle Road, Goolwa, SA 5214 (☎ **08/ 8555 2144**). It has 70 caravans and a large area for tents. A two-berth van costs A$25 (U.S.$17.50) a night, and a six-berth costs A$35 (U.S.$24.50) for the first two people, A$5 (U.S.$3.50) for each additional adult, and A$3 (U.S.$2.10) for each additional child. Bring your own bedding.

Grahams Castle Resort. Corner of Castle and Bradford sts., Goolwa, SA 5214. ☎ **1800 243 303** in Australia, or 08/8555 3300. Fax 08/8555 3828. 22 units, none with bathroom. A$15 (U.S.$10.50) per person. AE, BC, DC, MC, V.

This former conference center is classified as a three-star backpackers accommodation and has a swimming pool, tennis court, cafe, and laundry. Rooms are very basic with two single beds, heating, and a shower shared between two rooms. It's very popular with budget groups, so it could get noisy.

✪ **Portalloch.** P.M.B. 3, Narrung via Tailem Bend, SA 5260. ☎ **08/8574 0088.** Fax 08/8574 0065. 4 cottages. TV. A$85–$150 (U.S.$59.50–$105) per cottage. Additional person A$14–$20 (U.S.$9.80–$14) extra. BC, MC, V.

Located smack dab in the middle of nowhere on the eastern edge of the Coorong, Portalloch is a working farm property—with plenty of cows, ducks, chickens, and dogs wandering about. The whole place is classified by the National Trust of South Australia, and history is evident everywhere, from the cottages once used by farm hands to the giant wooden shearing shed and other outbuildings crammed with relics from the past. You can stay in a choice of four cottages scattered across the property. The Shearer's Hut is a stone cottage that sleeps up to nine people; the Overseers stone cottage sleeps up to 8 people; the Boundary Rider's Cottage is built of timber, iron, and stone, and sleeps 5; and the Station Hand's Cottage, once the home of Aboriginal workers, sleeps 4. (One additional unit, the Shearer's Quarters, is mainly for large groups and sleeps 12.) All of the units are modern and comfortable inside, and have their own kitchen facilities and barbecue. There's a private beach on the property if you want to swim in the lake, and guests have the use of a dinghy, a canoe, a tennis court, and a Ping-Pong table. Fascinating historical tours of the property cost A$10 (U.S.$7) per person for the first two people, and A$6 (U.S.$4.20) per person thereafter. Coorong Nature Tours will pick you up from here for no extra charge. There's plenty of bird life on and around the property.

13 Melbourne

by Marc Llewellyn

Melbourne, the capital of Victoria and Australia's second-largest city, with a population well over 3 million, is a melting pot of cultures. For a start, there are more people of Greek descent living here than in any other city in the world, except Athens. Then there are the Chinese, the Italians, the Vietnamese, and the Lebanese—they've all added something to Melbourne. In fact, almost one-third of Melburnites were born overseas or have parents who were born overseas. With such a diverse population, and with trams rattling through the streets and a host of stately European architecture surrounding you, you could easily forget you're in Australia at all. Melbourne (pronounced *Mel*-bun) feels like a cosmopolitan mix of Rome, Lisbon, and Hong Kong, with a dash of London thrown in. It's a restless, image-conscious city that's always exciting and always changing, depending what street you're on.

Throughout Australia, Melbourne has a reputation of being at the head of the pack when it comes to shopping, restaurants, fashion, music, and cafe culture. Time after time, it's beat out other state capitals in bids for major international concerts, plays, exhibitions, and sporting events, such as the Formula One Grand Prix.

The city also revels in its healthy rivalry with its northern neighbor, Sydney—but when Sydney won the 2000 Olympic Games and was in the throes of mass delirium, you could have heard a pin drop in Melbourne.

Melbourne's roots go back to the 1850s, when gold was found in the surrounding hills. British settlers flocked here and took up residence and have since prided themselves on coming freely to their city, rather than having been forced here in convict chains. The city grew wealthy and remained largely a conservative bastion until World War II, when another wave of immigration, this time mainly from southern Europe, made it a more relaxed place. As further waves of migrants arrived, Melbourne evolved into the exciting, cosmopolitan city it is today.

Frugal travelers will be happy to hear that the public transport system is an effective and cheap way to explore the city and that, in general, hotel prices are slightly lower than in Sydney. You can save a lot of money on food if you stick to the cheap-eat zones, such as Chinatown, and pick up lunchtime snacks around the city in places like the Queen Victoria Market.

1 Orientation

ARRIVING

BY PLANE   Melbourne is served by two airports: Essendon Airport and Melbourne Tullamarine Airport. Major international and domestic airlines fly into the latter. Airlines serving Melbourne include Ansett Australia, Qantas, British Airways, United, and Air New Zealand. **Tullamarine Airport** is 22 kilometers (13 miles) northwest of the city center. There's an information desk at the international terminal, open from 7am to 7pm daily, but surprisingly there isn't one in the domestic terminal. The international terminal also has snack bars, a restaurant, currency-exchange facilities, and duty-free shops. Showers are also available on the first floor of the international area. Baggage trolleys are free in the international baggage claim hall, but cost A$2 (U.S.$1.40) if hired in the parking lot, departure lounge, or the domestic terminal. Baggage lockers cost A$4 (U.S.$2.80) per day.

Thrifty, Budget, Avis, and **Hertz** all have rental desks at the airport (see "Getting Around," later in the chapter).

Getting into Town: Skybus (☎ **03/9662 9275**) picks up passengers in front of the baggage claim area every 30 minutes from 5:30am to 11pm. The trip into the city center takes around 35 minutes and costs A$10 (U.S$7) one-way and A$18 (U.S.$12.60) round-trip. There are no discounts for children or seniors. The service travels direct to the Skybus terminal, at Station Bay 30 on Spencer Street, then continues to Spencer Street Railway Station. Most travelers disembark at the Skybus terminal and take a free shuttle bus to their hotel. If you're staying outside the city center, you can catch either a taxi or a tram to your hotel. For return service to the airport, call Skybus at least 1 hour in advance and allow at least 40 minutes for traveling time.

Skybus also has a service connecting the city to the *Spirit of Tasmania* (the ferry to Tasmania). It departs from the Melbourne Transit Centre, 58 Franklin St., at 3:45pm, and from Spencer Street Rail Station (Bay 45) at 4pm, every Monday, Wednesday, and Friday. The bus also takes ferry passengers into the city. It costs A$4 (U.S.$2.80) one-way, and A$7 (U.S.$4.90) round-trip.

A **taxi** to the city center takes about 30 minutes and costs between A$25 to $30 (U.S.$17.50 to $21), so it's probably worth taking one if two or more of you are traveling together.

BY TRAIN   Interstate trains arrive at **Spencer Street Train Station,** at Spencer and Little Collins streets (5 blocks from Swanston Street in the city center). Taxis and buses connect with the city. The **Sydney–Melbourne XPT** travels between Australia's two largest cities daily (trip time: around 10½ hrs.). The fare is A$96 (U.S.$67.20) in economy, A$134 (U.S.$93.80) in first class, and A$229 (U.S.$160.30) for a first-class sleeper. If you book well in advance, you can receive discounts of up to 10% to 40% off these fares.

The *Overlander* provides daily service between Adelaide and Melbourne (trip time: 12 hours). Fares are A$58 (U.S.$40.60) in economy, A$116 (U.S.$81.20) in first class, and A$182 (U.S.$127.40) for a first-class sleeper. You can transport your car on the *Overlander* for A$100 (U.S.$70).

Daylink services also connect Melbourne with Adelaide. The trip is by train from Adelaide to Bendigo and by bus from Bendigo to Melbourne. The total trip time is 11 hours, and the fare is A$51 (U.S.$35.70) in economy and A$59.40 (U.S.$41.60) in first class.

The **Canberra Link** connects Melbourne with the nation's capital. The journey takes around 11 hours and costs A$49 (U.S.$34.30) in economy and A$64.50

(U.S.$45.15) in first class. For information and reservations for all trains, call **V/Line** (☎ **13 22 32** in Australia, or 03/9619 5000) Monday to Saturday from 8am to 8pm, and Sunday from 10am to 6pm.

BY BUS   Several bus companies connect Melbourne with other state capitals and regional areas of Victoria. Among the biggest operators are **Greyhound-Pioneer** (☎ **13 20 30** in Australia, or 03/9600 1687) and **McCafferty's** (☎ 13 14 99 in Australia, or 03/9670 2533). Trip time to or from Sydney is 12 hours; to or from Adelaide, 10 hours; and to or from Canberra, 8 hours. McCafferty's prices are generally a few dollars cheaper. Greyhound-Pioneer buses arrive at and depart from **Melbourne's Transit Centre,** at 58 Franklin St. McCafferty's coaches arrive at and depart from the **Spencer Street Coach Station,** at 205 Spencer St. Take a tram or taxi from either station to your hotel. **V/Line buses** (☎ **13 22 32**), which travel all over Victoria, also depart from the Spencer Street Coach Station.

BY CAR   You can drive from Sydney to Melbourne along the **Hume Highway,** although a much nicer route is via the coastal **Princes Highway,** for which you should allow a minimum of 2 days, with stops. For information on all aspects of road travel in Victoria, contact the Royal Automotive Club of Victoria (☎ 03/9790 3333).

VISITOR INFORMATION

The first stop on any visitor's itinerary should be the **Victorian Visitors Information Center,** Melbourne Town Hall, Swanston Street, at the corner of Little Collins Street (☎ **13 28 42** in Australia, or 03/9658 9955; fax 03/9790 2955; www.tourism.vic. gov.au). You'll find everything you need here, and the staff can make reservations for accommodations and tours. The **Melbourne Greeter Service** operates from the Town Hall, too. This service connects visitors to enthusiastic local volunteers who offer free one-on-one orientation tours of the city. Bookings for this service are essential—make sure you state your interests. The center is open Monday to Friday from 9am to 6pm, and on Saturday and Sunday from 9am to 5pm.

You'll find some information services at **The National Trust Shop,** Shop 21, Block Arcade, 282 Collins St. (☎ **03/9654 7448**), and at **Information Victoria,** 356 Collins St. (☎ **1300/366 356**). Staffed information booths are also in Bourke Street Mall, Flinders Street Station (on the corner of Flinders Street and Swanston Walk), and at Queen Victoria Market (on the corner of Therry and Queen streets).

For information and brochures on touring Victoria, you can call **Victorian Tourist Information Service** (☎ **13 28 42** in Australia).

Good **Web sites** include CitySearch Melbourne (melbourne.citysearch.com.au); and Melbourne, Australia (www.melbourne.org).

CITY LAYOUT

Melbourne is situated on the Yarra River and stretches inland from Port Philip Bay, which lies to its south. Look at a map, and you'll see a distinct central oblong area surrounded by Flinders Street to the south, Latrobe Street to the north, Spring Street to the east, and Spencer Street to the west. Cutting north-to-south through its center are the two main shopping thoroughfares, **Swanston Street** and **Elizabeth Street.** A series of cross streets, including the pedestrian-only **Bourke Street Mall,** run between the major thoroughfares. If you continue south along Swanston Street it turns into **St. Kilda Road,** which runs to the coast. If you've visited Sydney, you'll find Melbourne's city center to be much smaller, and far less congested with people and cars.

The city center is surrounded by various urban villages, such as South Yarra, Richmond, Carlton, and Fitzroy. The seaside suburb of St. Kilda has a rather scruffy city beach, which as a Sydneysider I'd think twice about swimming off of.

NEIGHBORHOODS IN BRIEF

Melbourne is huge. At more than 6,110 square kilometers (92,359 sq. miles), it's one of the biggest cities in the world (compare this to greater New York, which covers 3,950 square kilometers/1,525 square miles). This is pretty amazing sprawl for a city that was only born in the 1850s. Brief descriptions of the areas of most interest to visitors follow:

City Center   Made up of a grid of streets north of the Yarra River, the city center is bordered to the south by Flinders Street and to the north by Latrobe Street. The eastern and western borders are Spring Street and Spencer Street, respectively.

Chinatown   This colorful section of the city center is centered on Little Bourke Street between Swanston and Exhibition streets. It's a colorful area, with plenty of ✪ **cheap restaurants.** Tram: Any to the city.

Carlton   North of the city center, Carlton is a tourist mecca, famous for the Italian restaurants strung along Lygon Street. It has a distinct Mediterranean flair. It's also the home of the University of Melbourne, so there's a healthy student scene. Tram: 1 or 22 from Swanston Street (trip time from city center: 15 minutes).

Fitzroy   A ruggedly bohemian place filled with students and artists and popular for people watching, Fitzroy revolves around Brunswick Street, with its cheap restaurants, busy cafes, art galleries, and pubs. Around the corner, on Johnston Street, are tapas bars and Spanish clubs. Tram: 11 from Collins Street; 86 from Bourke Street (trip time from city center: 15 minutes).

Richmond   One of Melbourne's earliest settlements, Richmond, east of the city center, is now a multicultural quarter based around historic streets and back lanes. Victoria Street is reminiscent of Ho Chi Minh City, with Vietnamese sights, sounds, aromas, and restaurants everywhere. Bridge Road is a bustling fashion precinct. Tram: 48 or 75 from Flinders Street to Bridge Road; 70 from Batmans Avenue at Princes Bridge to Swan Street; 109 from Bourke Street to Victoria Street (trip time from city center: 10 minutes).

St. Kilda   Very hip and bohemian in a shabby sort of way, this seaside suburb south of the city center has Melbourne's highest concentration of dining spots, ranging from glitzy to cheap, and some superb cake shops and delis. Brush up on your in-line skating skills and wear your Ray-Bans. Tram: 12 from Collins Street; 16 from Swanston Street; 94 or 96 from Bourke Street (trip time from city center: 20 minutes).

South Yarra/Prahan   This posh part of town southeast of the city center is crammed with chic boutiques, cinemas, nightclubs, and galleries. Chapel Street is famous for its sidewalk restaurants and designer fashion houses. Commercial Road is popular with the gay community. Tram: 6, 8, or 72 from Swanston Street (trip time from city center: 20 minutes).

South Melbourne   One of the oldest working-class districts of the city, South Melbourne is known for its historic buildings, old-fashioned pubs and hotels, and its markets. Tram: 12 from Collins Street; 1 from Swanston Street (trip time from city center: 15 minutes).

WIilliamstown   A lack of extensive development has left this outer waterfront suburb with a rich architectural heritage centered on Ferguson Street and Nelson Place—both reminiscent of old England. On the Strand, overlooking the sea, are a line of bistros and restaurants, and a World War II warship museum. Ferry: from Southgate, the World Trade Center, or St. Kilda Pier.

2 Getting Around

BY PUBLIC TRANSPORTATION

Trams, trains, and buses are operated by **The Met.** Tram travel within the city costs A$1.50 (U.S.$1.05) for adults, A$80¢ (U.S.56¢) for children, for a single journey. Or you could buy a **2-Hour Metcard ticket** for unlimited transport on bus, train, or ferry within the central zone for up to 2 hours. The Metcard ticket costs A$2.30 (U.S.$1.60) for adults, A$1.30 (U.S.90¢) for children. Many visitors find that the best deal is the **Zone 1 Metcard Daily ticket,** which allows travel on all transport within the city center from 5:30am to midnight (when transportation stops). This ticket costs A$4.40 (U.S.$3.10) for adults, A$2.30 (U.S.$1.60) for children. If you're staying in town for a few days, you might consider a **Metcard Weekly ticket,** which costs A$19.10 (U.S.$13.40) for adults, A$9.50 (U.S.$6.65) for children, and is good for travel in one zone.

Buy single-trip and 2-hour tram tickets at ticket machines, special ticket offices (such as at the tram terminal on Elizabeth Street, near the corner of Flinders Street), at most newsagents, and at Metcard vending machines at many railway stations and on trams. You'll need to validate your Metcard at the Metcard Validator machine found on station platforms, buses, and trams, before each journey; the only exception to this is a ticket purchased from a vending machine on a tram, which is automatically validated for that journey only. Vending machines on trams only accept coins, whereas larger vending machines at train stations give change up to A$10 (U.S.$7).

You can pick up a free route map from the Victorian Visitors Information Center, in the Town Hall on Swanston Street, or at the **Met Information Centre,** 103 Elizabeth St., at the corner of Collins Street (☎ **13 16 38,** or 03/9617 0900). It's open Monday to Friday from 8:30am to 4:30pm, and Saturday from 9am to 1pm.

BY TRAM   Melbourne has the oldest tram network in the world. Trams are still an essential part of the city, as well as being a major cultural icon. There are some 700 mostly green-and-yellow trams running over 325 kilometers (195 miles) of track. Instead of phasing out this nonsmoggy method of transport, Melbourne is busily expanding the network.

The **City Circle Tram** is the best way to get around the very center of Melbourne—and it's free. These burgundy-and-cream trams travel a circular route between all the major central attractions and past shopping malls and arcades. The trams run in both directions every 10 minutes between 10am and 6pm, except Good Friday and Christmas Day. City Circle Tram stops are marked with a burgundy sign.

Popular tram routes from the city include numbers 94, 96, and 16 to St. Kilda Beach; numbers 48, 75, and 70 to East Melbourne; number 57 to North Melbourne; and number 8 to South Yarra. Trams can be hailed at numbered green-and-gold tram-stop signs. To get off the tram, press one of the red buttons located near handrails, or pull the cord running above your head.

Money-Saving Transit Pass

Available at newsagents, the **Getabout Travelcard,** which two adults and up to four children can use for 1 day on weekends only, is worth knowing about. It costs between A$9.10 (U.S.$6.40) and A$15.60 (U.S.$10.95), depending on how far you want to go.

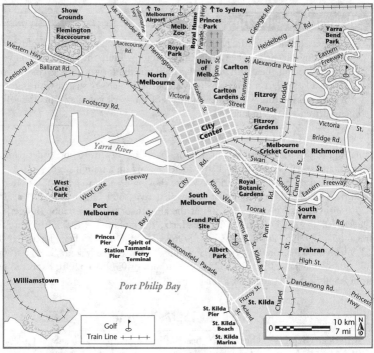

BY EXPLORER BUS

City Explorer (☎ **03/9563 9788**) operates double-decker London-style buses that pick up and drop off at 16 stops around the city, including Queen Victoria Market, Crown Casino, Captain Cook's Cottage, the Melbourne Cricket Ground (MCG), Chinatown, Melbourne Zoo, the Botanic Gardens, and Melbourne Central, among others. There is full commentary onboard. Get on and off as often as you want during the day. A bus returns to each stop hourly. The first bus leaves Town Hall on Swanston Street at 10am and the last leaves at 4pm. Tickets cost A$22 (U.S.$15.40) for adults, A$10 (U.S.$7) for children, and A$50 (U.S.$35) for a family of five.

The **City Wanderer** is owned by the same company and travels a similar route, but it makes trips to historic Williamstown and the Scienceworks Museum instead of to Melbourne Zoo and Carlton.

BY TAXI

Cabs are plentiful in the city, but it may be difficult to hail one in the city center late Friday and Saturday nights. Base fares are A$2.60 (U.S.$1.80) from 6am to midnight, and A$3.60 (U.S.$2.50) from midnight until 6am. On top of the base fare, you'll be charged A96¢ (U.S.67¢) per kilometer. There is an extra charge of A$1 (U.S.70¢) if you call ahead for pickup. Taxi companies include **Silver Top** (☎ **13 10 08,** or 03/9345 3455), **Embassy** (☎ **13 17 55,** or 03/9277 3444), and **Black Cabs** (☎ **13 22 27**).

BY CAR

Driving in Melbourne is not fun. Roads can be confusing, there are trams and aggressive drivers everywhere, and there is a strange rule about turning right from the left

Melbourne Driving Tips

Some intersections in central Melbourne have a *Hook turn* rule, which confuses drivers from anywhere else. The rule requires you to pull into the left lane if you want to turn right. You then turn across the traffic in the forward-facing lane to your right. Also keep alert for *fairways* in Melbourne, which are shared with trams. A road sign will indicate what times and days of the week you may cross the yellow line to drive in the tram lane.

lane. Add to this the general lack of parking spaces and expensive hotel valet-parking charges, and you'll know why it's better to get around on a tram instead.

If you plan on taking a day trip or you're shoving off to travel around the rest of Victoria, here are the major rental companies: **Avis,** 400 Elizabeth St. (☎ 1800/225 533 in Australia, 03/9338 1800 at the airport, or 03/9663 6366) **Budget,** 11 Queens Rd. (☎ 13 27 27 in Australia); **Hertz,** 97 Franklin St. (☎ 13 30 39 in Australia, 03/9379 9955 at the airport, or 03/9698 2555); **Delta,** 85 Franklin St. (☎ 13 13 90 in Australia, or 03/9662 2399); and **Thrifty,** 390 Elizabeth St. (☎ 1800/652 008 in Australia, 03/9330 1522 at the airport, or 03/9663 5200). Expect to pay from A$30 (U.S.$21) a day for a small car.

FAST FACTS: Melbourne

American Express   The AMEX head office is at 233 Collins St. (☎ 03/9633 6333). It's open Monday to Friday from 8:30am to 5:30pm, and Saturday from 9am to noon.

Baby-sitters   Call Dial-an-Angel (☎ 03/9525 9261). Minimum 3 hours.

Business Hours   In general, **stores** are open Monday to Thursday and Saturday from 9am to 5:30pm, Friday from 9am to 9pm, and Sunday from 10am to 5pm. The larger department stores stay open Thursday evening until 9pm. **Banks** are open Monday to Thursday from 9:30am to 4pm and Friday from 9:30am to 5pm.

Camera Repair   **Vintech Camera Repairs,** 5th Floor, 358 Lonsdale St. (☎ 03/9602 1820), is well regarded.

Dentist   Call the **Dental Emergency Service** (☎ 03/9341 0222) for emergency referral to a local dentist.

Doctor   The casualty department at the **Royal Melbourne Hospital,** Grattan Street, Parkville (☎ 03/9342 7000) responds to emergencies. The **Traveller's Medical & Vaccination Centre,** 2nd Floor, 393 Little Bourke St., (☎ 03/9602 5788), offers a full vaccination and travel medical service.

Consulates   The following English-speaking countries have consulates in Melbourne: **United States,** 553 St. Kilda Rd. (☎ 03/9526 5900); **United Kingdom,** Level 17, 90 Collins St. (☎ 03/9650 4155); **New Zealand,** 60 Albert Rd., South Melbourne (☎ 03/9696 0399); and **Canada,** 1st Floor, 123 Camberwell Rd., Hawthorn (☎ 03/9811 9999).

Drugstores/Chemists   The **24-hour Pharmacy** (☎ 02/9686 6522) can be found at the Crown Casino, on the lower promenade near the hotel entrance. Despite its name, it's open Sunday to Tuesday from 9am to 9pm, Wednesday and Thursday from 9am to 10pm, and Friday and Saturday from 9am to midnight.

The **McGibbony & Beaumont Pharmacy** is in the Grand Hyatt hotel complex, 123 Collins St. (☎ **03/9650 1823**). It's open Monday to Friday from 8am to 6:30pm, Saturday from 9:30am to 2:30pm, and Sunday from 9:30am to noon.

E-mail   Melbourne Central Internet, Level 2, Melbourne Central, corner of Elizabeth and Latrobe streets (☎ **03/9663 8410**), is open Monday through Friday from 11am to 6pm, Saturday and Sunday from 11am to 5pm. The **Internet Kennel,** 123 Acland St., St. Kilda (☎ **03/9534 7655**), is open Monday to Saturday from noon to 6pm. A newcomer into the e-mail scene is **Global Gossip,** 440 Elizabeth St., Melbourne(☎ **03/9663 0511**), open daily from 8am to midnight.

Emergencies   In an emergency, call ☎ **000** for police, ambulance, or the fire department.

Eyeglasses   OPSM has several stores in Melbourne, including ones at 376 Bourke St. (☎ **03/9670 9885**) and 82 Collins St. (☎ **03/9650 4822**). They often have good deals on contact lenses, but you'll need to bring a prescription with you.

Hot Lines   If you need a helping hand, try the **Poisons Information Service** (☎ 13 11 26); **Crisis Line** (☎ 03/9329 0300); **Lifeline** (☎ 13 11 14); **Alcoholics Anonymous** (☎ 03/9416 1818); **Alcohol and Drug Counselling Service** (☎ 03/9416 1818); **Traveller's Aid,** which offers help for travelers, 169 Swanston St. (☎ 03/9654 2600); or the **Gay & Lesbian Switchboard** (☎03/9510 5488), which offers counseling nightly from 6 to 10pm (Wednesday from 2 to 10pm).

Laundry/Dry Cleaning   Take your best suits to the **Brown Gouge Dry Cleaners** in the Myer Department Store (☎ **03/9661 2639**). **A City Edge** has do-it-yourself laundry machines at 39 Errol St., North Melbourne (☎ **03/ 9326 7006**); it's open daily from 6am to 11pm. The **South Yarra "8 to 8" Laundromat,** 326 Toorak Rd., South Yarra (☎ **03/9827 4892**), is open daily from 8am to 8pm.

Lost Property   Contact the nearest police station, or call in at the **Melbourne Town Hall,** Swanston Street (☎ **03/9658 9774**).

Newspapers   Melbourne relies on two morning newspapers: *The Age* and the *Herald-Sun.* Both have a Sunday edition.

Post Office   The General Post Office (GPO) is at the corner of Bourke Street Mall and Elizabeth Street (☎ **03/9203 3042**). It's open Monday to Friday from 8:15am to 5:30pm, and Saturday from 10am to 1pm. Poste Restante hours are the same.

Safety   St. Kilda might be coming up in the world, but it's still not wise to walk around here late at night. Parks and gardens can also be risky, as can the area around the King Street nightclubs.

Taxes   Sales tax, where it exists, is included in the price. There is no hotel tax as yet in Melbourne.

Telephones   The number for Melbourne's Directory Assistance is **1223,** and international Directory Assistance is **1225.** There's also the Telephone Interpreting Service, offering 24-hour free communication assistance at **13 14 50.**

Weather   Call ☎ **1196** for recorded weather information.

3 Accommodations You Can Afford

Getting a room is generally easy enough on weekends, when business travelers are back at home with the kids. You need to book well in advance, however, during the city's hallmark events (say, the weekend before the Melbourne Cup, and during the Grand Prix and the Ford Australia Open). Accommodations are often cheaper in Melbourne than in Sydney, but you'll still be paying big-city prices for most properties.

Once considered dead after offices closed for the day, the city center has been rejuvenated in recent years, and you'll feel right in the heart of the action if you stay here. Otherwise, the various suburbs are all exciting satellites, with good street life, restaurants, and pubs—all just a quick tram ride from the city center. (Transportation from the airport to the suburbs is a little more expensive and complicated than to the city center, however.)

IN THE CITY CENTER

✪ **Ibis Melbourne.** 15–21 Therry St., Melbourne, VIC 3000. ☎ **1800/642 244** in Australia, 800/221-4542 in the U.S. and Canada, 0800/44 4422 in New Zealand, or 03/9639 2399. Fax 03/9639 1988. 250 units (some with shower only). AC TV TEL. A$155 (U.S.$108.50) double; A$185 (U.S.$129.50) 1-bedroom apt.; A$235–$265 (U.S.$164.50–$185.50) 2-bedroom apt. Additional person A$25 (U.S.$17.50) extra. Children under 18 free in parents' room. Ask about package deals. AE, BC, DC, MC, V. Parking A$6 (U.S.$4.20).

Don't balk when you read the rack rates here. This is a very good-value hotel, especially when you consider that money-saving deals—such as a double room with breakfast for just A$110 (U.S.$77)—are available almost year-round. The Ibis is right next door to the bus station and a short walk from the central shopping areas. The four-star rooms are spacious, immaculate, and bright, and have an attached shower. Apartments come with kitchenettes and a tub. All guests have free use of the swimming pool, sauna, and spa just up the road at the Melbourne City Baths. There's a restaurant, a bar, and a business center on the premises.

Hotel Y. YWCA Melbourne, 489 Elizabeth St., Melbourne, VIC 3000. ☎ **03/9329 5188.** Fax 03/9329 1469. E-mail: melb@ywca.org.au. 59 units. A$89–$110 (U.S.$62.30–$77) double; A$99–A$120 (U.S.$69.30–$84) triple; A$155 (U.S.$108.50) apt. (sleeps 4). Additional person A$25 (U.S.$17.50) extra. A$30 (U.S.$21) dorm bed. No parking. AE, BC, DC, MC, V.

This place won the 1996 and 1997 Australian Tourism Awards as the best budget accommodation in both Melbourne and all of Australia. Unfortunately, the price of success has affected its room rates. The Y welcomes both women and men. All rooms are sparsely furnished and not overly large. The most expensive rooms have been refurbished recently and have a TV, a refrigerator, and air-conditioning. There used to be a gym here, and at the time this book went to press, a swimming pool, too, but there were moves by the management to get rid of it. So, the Y is no longer the best budget accommodation in Melbourne, in my opinion. The hotel is situated right near the Queen Victoria Market and is a short tram ride down Elizabeth Street or a 10-minute walk from the city center.

Kingsgate Budget Hotel. 131 King St., Melbourne, VIC 3000. ☎ **03/9629 4171** Fax 02/9629 7110. www.kingsgatehotel.com.au. 225 units (75 with bathroom). A$50–$80 (U.S.$35–$56) double; A$65–$95 (U.S.$45.50–$66.50) triple; A$110 (U.S.$77) deluxe quad. Additional person A$15 (U.S.$10.50) extra. AE, BC, DC, MC, V. Parking A$5 (U.S.$3.50) a day at Crown Casino, a 5-minute walk away.

A 10-minute walk from the city center brings you to this interesting hotel, which feels like a very basic B&B. From the outside, the hotel looks like a terrace building, but inside it's a maze of corridors and rooms. The staff is very friendly. The

Melbourne Accommodations

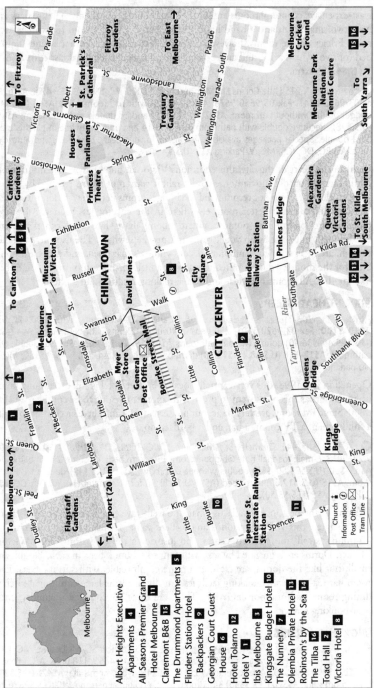

Map labels:

To Fitzroy
To Carlton
To Melbourne Zoo
To Airport (20 km)
To East Melbourne
To St. Kilda, South Melbourne
To South Yarra

Parade
Fitzroy Gardens
St. Patrick's Cathedral
Albert St.
Gisborne St.
Houses of Parliament
Princess Theatre
Carlton Gardens
Museum of Victoria
Exhibition St.
Russell St.
CHINATOWN
David Jones
Melbourne Central
Swanston St.
Lonsdale St.
Myer Store
General Post Office
Bourke Street Mall
Elizabeth St.
Queen St.
Latrobe St.
William St.
Bourke St.
King St.
Little Bourke St.
Spencer St. Interstate Railway Station
Spencer St.
Market St.
Flinders St.
Collins St.
Little Collins St.
City Square
Walk
CITY CENTER
Flinders Lane
Flinders St. Railway Station
Batman Ave.
Princes Bridge
Queens Bridge
Kings Bridge
Queensbridge St.
Yarra River
Southgate
Southbank Blvd.
St. Kilda Rd.
City Rd.
Alexandra Gardens
Queen Victoria Gardens
Melbourne Cricket Ground
Melbourne Park National Tennis Centre
Treasury Gardens
Wellington Parade
Wellington Parade South
Landsdowne St.
Spring St.
Nicholson St.
Macarthur St.
Victoria St.
Franklin St.
A'Beckett St.
Peel St.
Dudley St.
Queen St.
Flagstaff Gardens
Lonsdale St.

Legend:
† Church
ⓘ Information
⊠ Post Office
-- Tram Line

Melbourne (inset location map)

Accommodations list:

Albert Heights Executive Apartments **4**
All Seasons Premier Grand Hotel Melbourne **11**
Claremont B&B **15**
The Drummond Apartments **5**
Flinders Station Hotel Backpackers **9**
Georgian Court Guest House **6**
Hotel Tolarno **12**
Hotel Y **1**
Ibis Melbourne **3**
Kingsgate Budget Hotel **10**
The Nunnery **7**
Olembia Private Hotel **13**
Robinson's by the Sea **14**
The Tilba **16**
Toad Hall **2**
Victoria Hotel **8**

least-expensive economy rooms are for the backpacking crowd only. They're dark and have two single beds and a hand basin; there's barely enough room to swing a backpack. Pricier deluxe rooms, however, are light, spacious, and have a bouncy double bed (or two twins), a TV, and an en suite bathroom. A cooked breakfast costs A$6.50 (U.S.$4.55) extra.

Victoria Hotel. 215 Little Collins St., Melbourne, VIC 3000. ☎ **1800/331 147** in Australia, or 03/9653 0441. Fax 03/9650 9678. 468 units (29 with bathroom). TEL. A$60 (U.S.$42) budget double without bathroom; A$120 (U.S.$84) standard double with bathroom; A$140 (U.S.$98) executive double with bathroom. Children 14 and under stay free in parents' standard double. Special packages available. Ask about lower weekly, corporate, and auto club rates. AE, BC, DC, JCB, MC, V. Parking A$7 (U.S.$4.90).

Right in the heart of the city, this enormous Victorian hotel has a huge musty lobby reminiscent of an old movie house, and a rabbit warren of rooms reached by rickety wooden elevators. I do not recommend the budget rooms here; they're hot, for starters. You can find a much better room elsewhere in the city for less money. All budget rooms share bathrooms. Some standard rooms have fans and others are air-conditioned, but once again you'll get better deals elsewhere. The executive doubles, though, are nice, with contemporary decor, windows that open, and nice bathrooms. Still, for the money, I'd be tempted to stay just a little farther out of town, somewhere like the Ibis. All rooms have tea- and coffee-making facilities and a phone.

SUPER-CHEAP SLEEPS

Flinders Station Hotel Backpackers. 35 Elizabeth St., Melbourne, VIC 3000. ☎ **03/9620 5100.** Fax 03/9620 5101. 250 beds in 40 units, 2 units with bathrooms. A$42–$52 (U.S.$29.40–$36.40) double without bathroom; A$69–$89 (U.S.$48.30–$61.30) double with bathroom. A$12–$18 (U.S.$8.40–$12.60) dorm bed. Higher rates Dec 15–Apr 15. BC, MC, V. No parking.

Opened in late 1998, this very centrally located budget hotel is still expanding, taking up two floors as this book went to press, with another five due to be completed before 2000. Standard rooms are very basic, but modern and clean. There's a coin-op laundry, a full kitchen, a TV room, a bar, and a bottle shop.

✪ **Toad Hall.** 441 Elizabeth St., Melbourne, VIC 3000. ☎ 03/9600 9010. Fax 03/9600 9013. E-mail: toadhall.hotel@bigpond.com. 130 dorm beds, 4 rooms, 2 with bathroom. A$45–$50 (U.S.$31.50–$35) double without bathroom; A$70 (U.S.$49) double with bathroom. A$18 (U.S.$12.60) dorm bed (A$17/U.S.$11.90 for YHA members). AE, BC, DC, MC, V. Parking A$5 (U.S.$3.50).

"It's one of the best in Australia" is what one well-traveled guest said of Toad Hall. I have to agree; this 1858 mansion is an excellent value. It's just a short tram ride or a 10-minute stroll from the city center, and just down the road from Queen Victoria Market. Dorms are segregated by sex, with four to six bunk beds in each. Doubles are small, but like the dorms, are clean and quite comfortable, with springy beds. Each room has tea- and coffee-making facilities. I really liked the large communal kitchen, dining room, and outdoor courtyard. There are three TV lounges, a laundry, and a tour-booking service.

WORTH A SPLURGE

✪ **All Seasons Premier Grand Hotel Melbourne.** 33 Spencer St., Melbourne, VIC 3000. ☎ 1300/361 455 in Australia, or 03/9611 4567. Fax 03/9611 4655. 118 units. A/C MINIBAR TV TEL. A$290 (U.S.$203) studio suite; A$350 (U.S.$245) 1-bedroom suite; A$420 (U.S.$294) 2-bedroom suite; A$520 (U.S.$350) 3-bedroom suite. Additional person A$40 (U.S.$28) extra. Children under 16 free in parents' room. Ask about weekend and seasonal packages. AE, BC, DC, MC, V. Parking A$12 (U.S.$8.40). Tram: 48 or 75 from Flinders St.

I've included this place because it often offers rates of A$175 (U.S.$122.50) per night, which is no bargain but is a pretty good deal considering what you get. Don't be shy about asking for the best price available, as room rates here, as at other major hotels in Melbourne, are very fluid.

This majestic building, the former railway department headquarters, is striking for its remarkable scale and imposing Italianate facade. Building started on the six-story site in 1887, and additions were still being made in 1958. It finally became a hotel in late 1997. Rooms come with plush red Pullman carpets, a full kitchen with dishwasher, a CD player, a second TV in the bedroom, and great views over the railway tracks. All rooms are decorated similarly but vary in size; some have balconies. Suites are mostly split level, with bedrooms on the second floor. Guests have use of a free laundry, gym, sauna, Jacuzzi, indoor pool, and BBQs.

IN CARLTON

✪ **Albert Heights Executive Apartments.** 83 Albert St., East Melbourne, VIC 3002. ☎ 1800/800 117 in Australia, or 03/9419 0955. Fax 03/9419 9517. 34 units. A/C TV TEL. A$135 (U.S.$94.50) double; A$108 (U.S.$75.60) for members of any international auto club with identification. Additional person A$20 (U.S.$14) adults; A$15 (U.S.$10.50) children. Rates include light breakfast on first morning. Ask about special deals. AE, BC, DC, MC, V. Free parking. Tram: 42 or 109; or a 10-minute walk to city.

For good, moderately priced accommodations with cooking facilities, so you can cut down on meal costs, you can't go wrong with the Albert Heights, a favorite of American travelers. It's in a very nice area of Melbourne, a few minutes walk from the city center. There are parks at each end of the street. Each unit in this neat brick building is large, clean, and attractive. If you want your own space, or are traveling with your family, you can use the sofa bed in the living room. Each unit comes with a full kitchen with a microwave (no conventional oven), a dining area, a large bathroom, a VCR, and two phones. A very popular Jacuzzi and a laundry are on the premises.

The Drummond Apartments. 371 Drummond St., Carlton, VIC 3053. ☎ **03/9345 3888.** Fax 03/9349 1250. 10 units. TV TEL. A$95 (U.S.$66.50) studio apt.; A$108 (U.S.$75.60) 1-bedroom apt. AE, BC, DC, MC, V. Off-street parking. Tram: 1 or 22 from Swanston St.

Very nice and functional rooms at a decent price are what you'll find at this good, semibudget option. Plus, you can cook your own meals. All rooms are modern and clean, and come with a full kitchen. One-bedroom apartments also have a sofa bed. All rooms have a hair dryer and an iron and ironing board. There's a communal laundry, and breakfast packs are available on request. It's within walking distance of the city center.

Georgian Court Guest House. 21 George St., East Melbourne, VIC 3002. ☎ **03/9419 6353.** Fax 03/9416 0895. 31 units, 21 with bathroom. A/C TV. A$77 (U.S.$53.90) double without bathroom; A$97 (U.S.$67.90) double with bathroom. A$10–$20 (U.S.$7–$14) surcharge during busy periods, such as the Melbourne Grande Prix and other major sporting events. Additional person A$20 (U.S.$14) extra; children under 15 A$10 (U.S.$7) extra. Rates include buffet breakfast. AE, BC, DC, MC, V. Free parking. Tram: 78 or 45. Georgian Court is behind the Hilton, a 15-minute walk from the city center.

The Georgian Court's appearance hasn't changed much since it was built in 1910. The sitting and dining rooms both have high ceilings, and offer a bit of old-world atmosphere. The bedrooms are nice, though furnished with little more than plain pine furniture and a double bed. Most rooms have air-conditioning, though you might find that some doubles without bathroom still have a fan. Home-style cooking is on the menu at dinner: a one-course meal costs A$13.50 (U.S.$9.45); two courses, A$17.50 (U.S.$12.25); and three courses, A$19.50 (U.S.$13.65).

IN FITZROY

✪ **The Nunnery.** 116 Nicholson St., Fitzroy, Melbourne, VIC 3065. ☎ 03/9419 8637. Fax 03/9417 7736. www.bakpak.com/nunnery.com.au. 24 units, none with bathroom. A$40 (U.S.$28) single; A$50–$60 (U.S.$35–42) double; A$75 (U.S.$52.50) triple. A$18–$22 (U.S.$12.60–$15.40) dorm bed. BC, DC, MC, V. Off-street parking. Tram: 96 from the city to East Brunswick (stop 13).

This former convent is an exceptional budget accommodation. Set in a terrace on the city's edge, the Nunnery is perfectly situated near the restaurant and nightlife scenes on Lygon Street and Brunswick Street, in nearby Carlton. Rooms vary in size from six-bed dorms to former nuns' cells. Twin rooms come with either two singles or a set of bunks. All have basic furnishings and share bathrooms. Some second-floor rooms have good views over the neighboring Royal Exhibition Buildings and the city skyline. There's a large guest kitchen, a small courtyard where you can eat breakfast, and a large sitting room filled with couches, a fireplace, and a TV. The staff is very friendly.

IN ST. KILDA

✪ **Hotel Tolarno.** 42 Fitzroy St., St. Kilda, Melbourne, VIC 3182. ☎ 03/9537 0200. Fax 03/9534 7800. E-mail: htolarno.com.au. Web site: www.htolarno.com.au. 36 units (some with shower only). TV TEL. A$100 (U.S.$70) standard double; A$115 (U.S.$80.50) balcony double; A$165–$235 (U.S.$115.50–$164.50) suite (sleeps up to 4). Additional person A$15 (U.S.$10.50) extra. AE, BC, DC, MC, V. On-street parking. Tram: 16 from Swanston St.; 96 from Flinders St. (about a 15-minute ride).

The Hotel Tolarno is a right in the middle of St. Kilda's cafe and restaurant strip, and a long stone's throw away from the beach. The whole place was renovated and expanded in 1998 and has a new foyer and breakfast room and lounge. Rich red carpets bedeck the corridors throughout this 1950s–60s retro-style building. Rooms vary, but all are modern and nice. Some of the most popular rooms are in the front of the building and have balconies overlooking the main street. All rooms have showers, and some newer rooms in newer additions have Jacuzzi tubs. Breakfast is A$8 (U.S.$5.60) per person extra. There's a restaurant and bar on the property.

Olembia Private Hotel. 96 Barkly St., St. Kilda, Melbourne, VIC 3182. ☎ **03/9537 1412.** Fax 03/9537 1600. 23 units, none with bathroom. A$40 (U.S.$28) single; A$54 (U.S.$37.80) double. A$18 (U.S.$12.60) dorm bed. AE, BC, MC, V. Free parking. Tram: 12 from Collins St., 16 from Swanston St., 94 or 96 from Bourke St.

This sprawling Edwardian house, built in 1922, is set back from a busy St. Kilda street behind a leafy courtyard. It's popular with tourists, business travelers, and young families; and everyone gets together for the frequent video nights, wine and cheese parties, and barbecues. The clean bedrooms are simply furnished, with little more than a double bed, or two singles, a desk, a hand basin, and a wardrobe. Rooms have been recently repainted and upgraded. Guests share six bathrooms. There's a guest kitchen, a dining room, a very comfortable sitting room, and a courtyard area with barbecues. The Olembia is near St. Kilda beach and the host of restaurants lining Acland Street.

✪ **Robinson's by the Sea.** 335 Beaconsfield Parade, St. Kilda, Melbourne, VIC 3182. ☎ 03/9534 2683. Fax 03/9534 2683. 5 units, none with bathroom. A$120–$160 (U.S.$84–$112) double. Rates include cooked breakfast. AE, BC, DC, MC, V. Free parking. Tram: 12 to Cowderoy St., St. Kilda.

If you want something very special, Robinson's by the Sea fits the bill. The management (and pet dog) at this 1870s heritage B&B just across the road from the beach are incredibly friendly. They encourage an evening social scene, and downstairs you'll find a comfortable, antiques-filled living room and a dining room. Four of the five bedrooms are located upstairs. Each unit is unique. For example, the Eastern Room has a four-poster queen-size bed and Indian and Chinese furniture, whereas the Rose Room is decorated with patterned flowers and pastel colors. The units all share three communal bathrooms, one with a tub and shower, a second with a shower, and the third with a Jacuzzi tub and shower. There are wood floorboards and fireplaces throughout.

IN SOUTH YARRA

Claremont B&B. 189 Toorak Rd., South Yarra, VIC 3141. ☎ **03/9826 8000,** or 03/9286 8222. Fax 03/9827 8652. 80 units, none with bathroom. TV. A$58 (U.S.$40.60) double. Additional person A$10 (U.S.$7) extra. Children stay free in parents' room. Rates include continental breakfast. AE, BC, DC, MC, V.

The high ceilings and the mosaic tiles in the lobby welcome visitors into the interior of this old-world hotel, which reopened in 1995 after a complete overhaul. It's an attractive place with sparsely furnished but comfortable rooms, each with either a double or a single bed, a TV, and a refrigerator. On the premises you'll find a coin-op laundry and 24-hour tea and coffee. There is no elevator in this three-story building, so it could be a bad choice for travelers with disabilities.

WORTH A SPLURGE

The Tilba. 30 W. Toorak Rd. (at Domain St.), South Yarra, VIC 3141. ☎ **03/9867 8844.** Fax 03/9867 6567. 15 units, 1 cottage. TV TEL. A$140–$195 (U.S.$98–$136.50) double. Rates include breakfast. AE, BC, DC, MC, V. Closed the first week of Jan, Easter week, and the last week of Dec. Free parking. Tram: 6, 8, or 72 from Swanston St. No children under 12.

With its turreted facade, antique furniture, and leaded windows, the Tilba is the city's most elegant and romantic small hotel. The 1907 building started life as a private mansion and was used as an army hostel during World War II; it has been an exclusive hotel since the early '90s. The tranquil Tilba, which overlooks Faulkner Park, attracts mostly business travelers, who appreciate the home-like atmosphere. The bedrooms, some of which were former stables or lofts, are all unique in size, design, and color. The sitting and breakfast rooms are richly decorated with antiques and have open fireplaces.

4 Great Deals on Dining

Melbourne's ethnically diverse population ensures a healthy selection of international cooking styles. Chinatown, in the city center, is a fabulous hunting ground for authentic Chinese, Malaysian, Thai, Indonesian, Japanese, and Vietnamese fare, often at bargain prices. Carlton has plenty of Italian cuisine; Richmond is crammed with Greek and Vietnamese restaurants; and Fitzroy has cheap Asian, Turkish, Mediterranean, and vegetarian food. To see and be seen, head to Chapel Street or Toorak Road in South Yarra, or to St. Kilda to take in the sea breeze and join the throng of Melburnites dining out along Fitzroy and Ackland streets. Most of the cheaper places in Melbourne are strictly BYO (bring-your-own wine or beer).

IN THE CITY CENTER

Bamboo House. 47 Little Burke St. ☎ **03/9662 1565.** Reservations recommended. Main courses A$17–$24 (U.S.$11.90–$16.80). AE, BC, DC, MC, V. Mon–Fri noon–3pm; Mon–Sat 5:30–11pm, Sun 5:30–10pm. NORTHERN REGIONAL CHINESE/CANTONESE.

If Flower Drum (see "Worth a Splurge," below) is full (or breaks your budget), try this place, which is esteemed by both the Chinese community and local business big shots. The service here really is a pleasure, and the food (especially the delicious chicken with shallot sauce) is worth writing home about. The waiters are all eager to help you construct a feast from the myriad Cantonese and northern Chinese dishes. (Don't leave without a taste of the duck in plum sauce!) Other popular dishes include pan-fried dumplings, spring onion pancakes, and the signature dish, Sichuan smoked duck.

☺ **Café Segovia.** 33 Block Arcade. ☎ **03/9650 2373.** Main courses A$8–$13 (U.S.$5.60–$9.10). Mon–Fri 7:30am–11pm, Saturday 8am–6pm, Sunday 9am–5pm. AE, BC, DC, MC, V. CAFE.

Café Segovia is one of the most atmospheric cafes in Australia, with a smoky, sensual interior reminiscent of Spain. Seating is also available outside in the arcade itself, but you'll have to come early at lunchtime to nab a chair. Typical cafe food is on offer, such as focaccias, cakes, and light meals.

Hard Rock Cafe. 1 Bourke St. (next to The Windsor Hotel). ☎ **03/9633 6193.** Reservations recommended. Main course A$9.75–$19.95 (U.S.$6.85–$13.95). AE, BC, DC, MC, V. Daily noon–midnight. AMERICAN.

You know the drill here. The ubiquitous Hard Rock serves up large portions of typical theme-restaurant fare—nachos, T-bone steaks, chicken, salads, and burgers—in a rock and roll atmosphere. Bottomless soft drinks are served, but there are no free refills for coffee.

Hopetoun Tearooms. Shops 1 and 2, Block Arcade. ☎ **03/9650 2777.** Main courses A$4.50–$8.50 (U.S.$3.15–$5.95) (minimum charge A$5/U.S.$3.50 per person noon–2pm). Mon–Thurs 8:30am–5pm, Fri 8:30am–6pm, Sat 10am–3:30pm. Closed Sunday. AE, BC, DC, MC, V. CAFE.

The first cup of coffee served in this Melbourne institution left the pot in 1891. It's all very civilized here, with green-and-white Regency wallpaper and marble tables. The cakes are very good; the sandwiches go for A$4.50 to $6.50 (U.S.$3.15–$4.55) and the focaccias for A$7 to 8.50 (U.S.$4.90 to 5.95). Scones, croissants, and grilled food are also available.

Il Solito Posto. Basement of 113 Collins St. (enter via George Parade). ☎ **03/9654 4466.** Reservations recommended. Main courses A$8.50–$13 (U.S.$5.95–$9.10) in bistro, A$17.50–$23.50 (U.S.$12.25–$18.45) in trattoria. AE, BC, DC, MC, V. Mon–Sat 7:30am–1am. NORTHERN ITALIAN.

This sunken restaurant is split into two parts. The bistro is quite casual, with a blackboard menu offering good pastas, soups, and salads. Then there's the sharper and more upmarket trattoria, with its à la carte menu offering the likes of steak, fish, and veal dishes. The coffee is good, too.

Little Reata. 68 Little Collins St. ☎ **03/9654 5917.** Reservations recommended. Main courses A$10.50–$16 (U.S.$8.05–$11.20). AE, BC, DC, MC, V. Daily 5:30pm–7am (limited menu 11pm–5am); Tues–Fri noon–2:30pm. TEX-MEX.

Typical Tex-Mex cooking is served up inside the blood-red walls of this dimly lit restaurant. The house specialty is the chicken fajitas (chicken marinated in tequila and lime with tortillas, salad, salsa, and sour cream). There's an interesting cocktail selection available for A$6 to $8.50 (U.S.$4.20 to $5.95).

Supper Inn. 15 Celestial Ave. ☎ **03/9663 4759.** Reservations recommended. Main courses A$9–$12 (U.S.$6.30–$8.40). AE, BC, DC, MC, V. Daily 5:30pm–2:30am. CANTONESE.

Head here if you get the Chinese-food munchies late at night. It's a friendly place with a mixed crowd of locals and tourists chowing down on such dishes as steaming bowls of congee (a rice-based porridge), barbecued suckling pig, mud crab, or stuffed scallops. Everything's authentic, not like some of the Westernized slop you often get served.

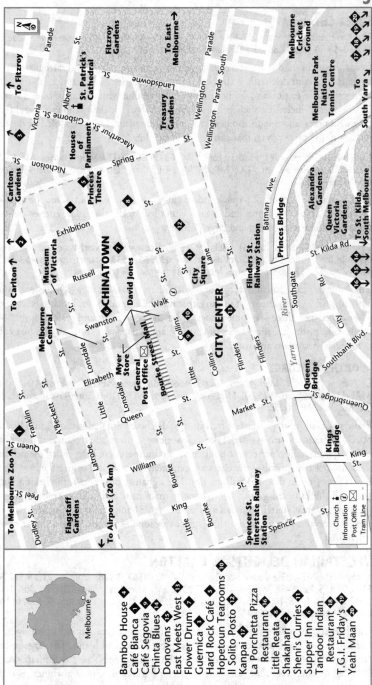

Bamboo House 4
Café Bianca 1
Café Segovia 9
Chinta Blues 14
Donovans 15
East Meets West 7
Flower Drum 3
Guernica 3
Hard Rock Café 5
Hopetoun Tearooms 12
Il Solito Posto 16
Kanpai 17
La Porchetta Pizza Restaurant 10
Little Reata 8
Shakahari 2
Sheni's Curries 11
Supper Inn 6
Tandoor Indian Restaurant 18
T.G.I. Friday's 19
Yeah Maan 20

SUPER-CHEAP EATS

✪ **Café Bianca.** Store 97–98, Queen Victoria Market. No phone. Main courses A$2.60–$3.80 (U.S.$1.85–$2.65). Market hours. No credit cards. PIZZA.

Inside the main market building, past the meat and fish sellers, and farther on past a range of cake and deli stalls is the best little pizza take-out in Australia. It's tiny, and there's nowhere to sit, but who has time to hang around with so much to see anyway? All the pizzas, including such gourmet concoctions as chicken tandoori pizza, fresh asparagus pizza, and potato and herb pizza, are homemade. Don't be fooled by the pretenders to the pizza crown that can be found nearby.

East Meets West. 271 Flinders Lane. ☎ **03/9650 8877.** Main courses A$5.50–$7 (U.S.$3.50–$4.90). AE, BC, DC, MC, V. Mon–Fri 10am–6:30pm, Sat 10:30am–2:30pm. ASIAN/FAST FOOD.

This little place is great for a quick Indian curry, a plate of noodles, some spring rolls, or fish-and-chips. It's simple and cheap, with a few small tables. The curries are delicious and come in medium and large portions.

Sheni's Curries. Shop 16, 161 Collins St. (on the corner of Flinders Lane and Russell St., opposite the entrance to the Grand Hyatt). ☎ **03/9654 3535.** Lunch specials A$4–$6.50 (U.S.$2.80–$4.55). No credit cards. Mon–Fri 11am–4pm. SRI LANKAN.

This tiny (it seats 30) and very busy place offers a small range of excellent-value, authentic Sri Lankan curries. You can either dine here or take your lunch special to go. Choose between three vegetable dishes and a choice of meat and seafood dishes. All meals come with rice, three types of chutney, and a papadam. You can also buy extra items such as samosas and roti.

WORTH A SPLURGE

✪ **Flower Drum.** 17 Market Lane. ☎ **03/9662 3655.** Reservations required. Main courses A$21–$36 (U.S.$14.70–$25.20). Mon–Sat noon–3pm and 6–11pm, Sun 6–10:30pm. AE, BC, DC, MC, V. CANTONESE.

Praise pours in from all quarters for this upscale choice situated just off Little Bourke Street, Chinatown's main drag. Take a slow elevator up to the restaurant, which has widely spaced tables (perfect for politicians and business people to clinch their deals). Take note of the specials—the chefs are extremely creative and utilize the best ingredients they find in the markets each day. The signature dish here is the Peking duck, although the buttered garfish is my favorite main course. The king crab dumplings in soup is a great starter. You can also prearrange a banquet for two or more diners; you'll be served more unusual dishes (such as abalone). One- or 2-day advance notice is required.

VEGETARIAN DELIGHTS IN CARLTON

Shakahari. 201–203 Faraday St., Carlton. ☎ **03/9347 3848.** Main courses A$11.50–$12.50 (U.S.$8.05–$8.75). AE, BC, DC, MC, V. Mon–Sat noon–3:30pm, Sun–Thurs 6–9:30pm, Fri–Sat 6–10:30pm. Tram: Any tram going north along Swanston St. toward Melbourne University. VEGETARIAN.

Good vegetarian food isn't just a meal without meat; it's a creation in its own right. At Shakahari you are assured of a creative meal that's not at all bland. The large restaurant is quite low key, but the service can be a bit inconsistent. The Sate Samsara (skewered, lightly fried vegetables and tofu pieces with a peanut dip) is a winner, as is the couscous, served in a vast earthenware pot. Also served up are curries, croquets, tempura avocado, and veggie burgers (on a plate with salad, not in a bun).

A Special Meal on Wheels

Talk about eating on the move! A fully refurbished 1927 tram featuring the **Colonial Tramcar Restaurant** trundles through the streets of Melbourne while all aboard tuck into a silver-service feast and sip champagne. It's very romantic, with velvet seats, lots of polished brass, and fresh flowers on the tables. Stabilizers have been fitted to ensure you won't spill your drink, and one-way windows mean you can enjoy the passing scenery knowing you're not on display. The limited menu might begin with foie gras, a choice of appetizer (perhaps Tasmanian salmon or pepper-crusted kangaroo), and either steak mignon or chicken breast for the main course. A cheese platter, desserts, coffee, and liqueurs top it all off.

Reservations are recommended well in advance; call ☎ **03/9696 4000,** or fax 03/9696 3787. The early three-course dinner (at 5:45pm) is A$55 (U.S.$38.50) per person; a later five-course dinner (at 8:35pm) costs A$80 (U.S.$56) Sunday to Thursday, A$90 (U.S.$63) Friday and Saturday, with all drinks included. The tram departs from and returns to Stop 125 on Normandy Road (on the corner of Clarendon Street), opposite the Crown Casino.

WORTH A SPLURGE IN FITZROY

✪ **Guernica.** 257 Brunswick St., Fitzroy. ☎ **03/9416 0969.** Reservations recommended. Main courses A$17.90–$22.90 (U.S.$12.55–$16). AE, BC, DC, MC, V. Sun–Fri noon–3pm; daily 6–10:30pm. Tram: 11 from Collins St., or 86 from Bourke St. MODERN AUSTRALIAN.

Dimly lit and featuring a giant print of Picasso's famous 1936 painting, this restaurant serves up some exciting dishes, many jazzed up with a healthy tingle of spice or pepper. Choices range from the coconut-fried garfish with Vietnamese fried noodles to the spiced lamb cutlets with creamed feta cheese, roasted eggplant, and lemon and pomegranate molasses. The desserts are some of the best in town and include the marvelous palm-sugar caramelized rice pudding with toasted coconut ice cream. Check out the blackboard selections of good Australian wines by the glass. The restaurant is non-smoking in the evenings until 10pm.

SEASIDE DINING IN ST. KILDA

La Porchetta Pizza Restaurant. 80 Acland St., St. Kilda. ☎ **03/9534 1888.** Main courses A$5–$13.50 (U.S.$3.50–$9.45). Sun–Thurs 11am–midnight, Fri–Sat 11am–2am. Tram: 16 from Swanston St. or 96 from Bourke St. PIZZA.

This very busy, quite large, and very noisy pizza joint is a very good value. There are some 22 different pizzas to choose from, with the largest (ranging in price from A$6 to $7.80 (U.S.$4.20–$4.50) being just large enough to fill two. A range of pasta dishes cost from A$6 to $9 (U.S.$4.20–$6.30). Chicken, seafood, veal, and steaks are also on the menu. The heart-pounding pace here means it's not for the faint-hearted.

Chinta Blues. 6 Ackland St., St. Kilda. ☎ **03/9534 9233.** Reservations recommended. Main courses A$7.50–$16 (U.S.$5.25–$11.20). AE, BC, MC, V. Mon–Wed noon–2:30pm and 6–10pm; Thurs–Sat noon–2:30pm and 6–10:45pm; Sun noon–9:45pm. Tram: 16 from Swanston St. or 96 from Bourke St. MALAYSIAN.

Head to this very popular eatery if you're looking for simple, satisfying food with a healthy touch of spice. The big sellers are the Laksa, the Mei Goreng, the chicken curry, the sambal spinach, and a chicken dish called ayam blues. It's very busy, especially at lunch.

WORTH A SPLURGE

✪ **Donovans.** 40 Jacka Blvd., St. Kilda. ☎ **03/9534 8221.** Reservations recommended. Main courses A$20–$25 (U.S.$14–$17.50). Daily noon–10:30pm. AE, BC, DC, MC, V. Tram: 12 from Collins St., 16 from Swanston St., 94 or 96 from Bourke St. MODERN MEDITERRANEAN.

Donovans is so near the sea that you expect the fish to jump through the door and onto the plate—and indeed, you do get extremely fresh seafood. The restaurant is all higgledy-piggledy and charming, with lots of cushions, a log fire, and the sound of jazz and breakers on the beach. The menu includes a mind-boggling 53 dishes, so you are sure to find something to suit your fancy. Favorites include the swordfish fillet with warm onion relish, or the home-style fish stew, big enough for two, with generous amounts of prawns, clams, mussels, and fish. If you're not a big fish-eater, then choose from several pasta and meat dishes.

MORE ETHNIC EATS IN SOUTH YARRA

Kanpai. 569 Chapel St., South Yarra. ☎ **03/9827 4379.** Reservations recommended. Main courses A$12–$34 (U.S.$8.40–$23.80). (average price A$12.50/U.S.$8.75). AE, BC, DC, MC, V. Daily noon–11pm. Tram: 6, 8, or 72 from Swanston St. JAPANESE.

You have to book early in the day to get a seat at this very popular restaurant on the Chapel Street restaurant strip. The sushi and sashimi dishes are very fresh, and the miso soup is well worth plundering with your chopsticks. There's a good vegetarian selection, too.

Tandoor Indian Restaurant. 517 Chapel St., South Yarra. ☎ **03/9827 8247.** Reservations recommended Fri and Sat night. Main courses A$9–$14 (U.S.$6.30–$9.80). AE, BC, DC, MC, V. Tues–Fri noon–2:30pm; daily 6–11pm. Tram: 6, 8, or 72 from Swanston St. INDIAN.

This basic Indian restaurant was far less crowded than many of the others on the Chapel Street strip when I last visited—all I can say is that the "in" crowd didn't know what they were missing. The curries here are rich and spicy, with the vegetarian paneer butter masala and the cheese kofta being some of the best I've tasted in Australia. Some dishes, such as the crab masala curry, are truly inspirational. The main courses are quite large, so you'll probably not need a first course, but I highly recommend side dishes of naan bread (one per person) and a cucumber raita to cool the palate.

T.G.I Friday's. 500 Chapel St., South Yarra. ☎ **03/9826 5044.** Main courses A$7.95–$17.95 (U.S.$5.55–$12.55). AE, BC, DC, MC, V. Sun–Thurs noon–11pm, Fri–Sat noon–1am. Tram: 6, 8, or 72 from Swanston St. AMERICAN BISTRO.

This huge 350-seat bistro, part of the U.S.–based chain, is very American (which I guess could be considered ethnic cuisine in Australia), with ketchup on the tables, red-and-white striped tablecloths, and lots of paraphernalia screwed to the walls and loitering on shelves. Treat yourself to nachos, steaks, wings, salads, pastas, hamburgers, ribs, and Cajun chicken. There's a kids' menu featuring hamburgers, chicken, hot dogs, pizza, and macaroni-and-cheese for A$3.95 to $4.50 (U.S.$2.75 to $3.15).

✪ **Yeah Maan.** 340 Punt Rd. (at Fawkner St.), South Yarra. ☎ **03/9820 2707.** Reservations not accepted. Main courses A$8.60–$13 (U.S.$6–$9.10). AE, BC, DC, MC, V. Tues–Sat 6–10:30pm, Sun 5–9:30pm. Tram: 6, 8, or 72 from Swanston St. Caribbean.

Is this the coolest restaurant in Australia or what? Calypso music wafts amid the home-made triangle-backed chairs, diners wait in the lounge for a table to become free, palm trees sway—and the food! Wow! The whole place is rockin', mon, with the 75 seats almost continually occupied. The authentic Trinidadian goat curry is a must, as is the Barbados burrito. The Jamaican KFC (chicken marinated for two days in approximately 30 spices and then smoked), and the Jumbo-Jumbie cassava shoestring fries (cassava is similar to a potato), are very, very popular. The staff is ultra-friendly.

5 Seeing the Sights

Melbourne may not have as many major attractions as Sydney, but visitors come here to experience the contrasts of old-world architecture and the exciting feel of a truly multicultural city.

If you'd like to see the city aboard a leisurely cruise, call **Melbourne River Cruises** (☎ **03/9614 1215** Mon to Fri or 03/9650 2055 on weekends). This company offers three cruises, one up the Yarra River, one down the Yarra River (both take between 1 and 1¼ hours), and a 2- to 2½-hour round-trip cruise on the Yarra. Cruises run at various times throughout the morning and afternoon; call ahead to check the schedule. The shorter cruises cost A$13 (U.S.$9.10) for adults, A$6.50 (U.S.$4.55) for children ages 3 to 12, and A$35 (U.S.$24.50) for a family. The longer cruise costs A$25 (U.S.$17.50) for adults, A$20 (U.S.$14) for children, and A$65 (U.S.$45.50) for a family.

SIGHTSEEING SUGGESTIONS FOR FIRST-TIME VISITORS

If you have time to see only one major attraction in Melbourne, then by all means make it the **Melbourne Zoo.** If you have the luxury to follow a more leisurely itinerary, here are my suggestions:

If You Have 1 Day   Take a trip up to the top of the **Rialto Towers Observation Deck** to get your bearings, then visit the **National Gallery of Victoria,** walk through the **Botanic Gardens,** and stroll around the city streets. If you have time, head to **Phillip Island** to see the fairy penguins.

If You Have 2 Days   Visit the **Queen Victoria Market** and take a tram to the **Melbourne Zoo.** Head out to **St. Kilda** in the evening for a great choice of restaurants.

If You Have 3 Days   Rent a car or take a bus trip to explore the environs of Melbourne. I'd suggest either touring the **Yarra Valley wineries** and the **Healesville Sanctuary,** or going to the **Mornington Peninsula** and staying overnight in Portsea. Another option is a two-day excursion down the **Great Ocean Road** (see chapter 14).

If You Have 4 Days   Head out to the **Dandenong Ranges** or the gold-field town of **Ballarat** (see chapter 14).

THE TOP ATTRACTIONS

✪ **Melbourne Zoo.** Elliot Ave., Parkville. ☎ **03/9285 9300,** or 03/9347 9530. Admission A$14 (U.S.$9.80) adults, A$7 (U.S.$4.90) children 4–15. Daily 9am–5pm (open later Thurs–Sun in Jan–Feb). Free guided tours Mon–Fri 10am–3pm, Sat–Sun 11am–4pm (go to the main office and arrange tours there). Tram: 55 or 56 going north on William St. to Stop 25; nos. 18, 19, 20 from Elizabeth St. to Stop 16 (then it's a short walk to your left, following the signs). Train: Royal Park Station. Bus: City Explorer.

This place is a must-see. Built in 1862, it's the oldest zoo in the world, and still among the best. There are some 3,000 animals here, including the ever-popular kangaroos, wallabies, echidnas, koalas, wombats, and platypus. Rather than being locked up in tiny cages, most animals are kept in almost natural surroundings or well-tended gardens. Don't miss the wonderful butterfly house, with its thousands of colorful Australian butterflies flying around; the enormous free-flight aviary; the lowland gorilla exhibit; and the tree-top monkey displays. Allow at least 1 hour if you just want to see the Australian natives, or around 2½ hours to tour the whole zoo.

A Sightseeing Tip

If you're a student or a senior over age 60, you can sometimes receive hefty discounts on entrance fees to attractions in Australia. Just carry some relevant identification, and always remember to ask!

Rialto Towers Observation Desk. Rialto Building, 55th Floor, Collins St. (between William and King sts.). ☎ **03/9629 8222.** Admission A$7.50 (U.S.$5.25) adults, A$5 (U.S.$3.50) children, A$22 (U.S.$15.40) family. Sun–Thurs 10am–10pm, Fri–Sat 10am–11pm. Tram: Any tram on Collins St.

From this observation deck, near the top of the tallest building in the southern hemisphere, you get a magnificent 360° view of the whole of Melbourne and beyond. Look for the Melbourne Cricket Ground (MCG) and the new Crown Casino. For A$2 (U.S.$1.40) you can watch a 20-minute film that tells you what you're looking at, but you might as well just take a map up with you and figure it out for yourself. Of interest are the displays telling about life in Melbourne, past and present. You'll find a licensed cafe here, too.

Rippon Lea House Museum & Historic Garden. 192 Hotham St., Elsternwick. ☎ **03/9523 6095.** Admission A$9 (U.S.$6.30) adults, A$5 (U.S.$3.50) children 5–16, A$20 (U.S.$14) family of up to six. Tues–Sun and public holidays 10am–5pm (house closes at 4:45pm). Guided tours of house every half hour 10:30am–4pm; guided tour of estate at 2pm. Closed Good Friday and Christmas Day. Tram: 67 to Stop 40, then walk up Hotham St. Bus: 216/219 from Bourke and Queen sts. in the city to Stop 4. Train: Sandringham Line from Flinders Street Station to Rippon Lea Station.

This grand Victorian house, 8 kilometers (5 miles) from the city center, is worth a visit to get a feel for old-money Melbourne. Boasting dozens of rooms, Rippon Lea House was built by socialite Sir Frederick Thomas Sargood between 1868 and 1903; a pool and ballroom were added in the 1930s. Although the Romanesque architecture is interesting (note the stained glass and polychrome brickwork), the real attraction is the surrounding 5.3 hectares (13 acres) of gorgeous landscaped gardens, which include a conservatory, a lake, a lookout tower, an orchard, extensive flower beds, and ornate shrubbery. If you're here during school vacations, on a weekend, or on a public holiday, you might like to drop into the tearoom, which is open from 11am to 4pm.

✪ **Queen Victoria Market.** Between Peel, Victoria, Elizabeth, and Therry sts. on the northern edge of the city center. ☎ **03/9269 5822.** Tues and Thurs 6am–2pm, Fri 6am–6pm, Sat 6am–3pm, Sun 9am–4pm. Tram: any tram traveling north along William St. or Elizabeth St.

The Queen Vic is a Melbourne institution covering several blocks. It should be on everybody's itinerary if they are in Melbourne for a couple of days or more. At the hundreds of stalls, both indoors and out, you can find virtually anything from live rabbits to bargain-basement clothes. It can get cramped, and there's a lot of junk to sort through, but you'll get a real taste of Melbourne and its ethnic mix. Look out for the interesting delicatessen section and the ✪ **cheap eateries.** Allow at least an hour to take it all in.

Two organized 2-hour tours of the market take in its food and heritage. **The Foodies Dream Tour** departs every Tuesday, Thursday, Friday, and Saturday at 10am and costs A$18 (U.S.$12.60) for adults and A$15 (U.S.$10.50) for children under age 15, including sampling. The Heritage Market Tour departs at 10:30am on the same days and includes morning tea. It costs A$12 (U.S.$8.40) for adults and "would most likely bore children to death," according to the guide. Call ☎ **03/9320 5822** for reservations.

Melbourne Attractions

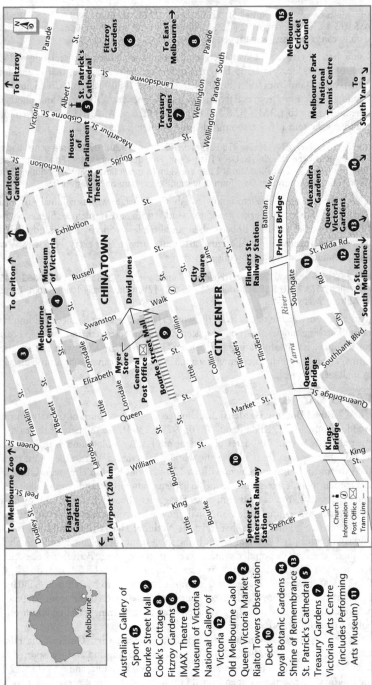

Australian Gallery of Sport **15**
Bourke Street Mall **9**
Cook's Cottage **8**
Fitzroy Gardens **6**
IMAX Theatre **1**
Museum of Victoria **4**
National Gallery of Victoria **12**
Old Melbourne Gaol **3**
Queen Victoria Market **2**
Rialto Towers Observation Deck **10**
Royal Botanic Gardens **14**
Shrine of Remembrance **13**
St. Patrick's Cathedral **5**
Treasury Gardens **7**
Victorian Arts Centre (includes Performing Arts Museum) **11**

Old Melbourne Gaol. Russell St. ☎ **03/9663 7228.** Admission A$8 (U.S.$5.60) adults, A$5 (U.S.$3.50) children, A$22 (U.S.$15.40) family. Daily 9:30am–4:30pm. Tram: City circle tram to corner of Russell and Latrobe sts.

Come here to view a spooky collection of death masks and artifacts relating to 19th-century prison life. Some 135 hangings took place here, including that of the notorious bandit (and Australian hero) Ned Kelly, in 1880. The jail closed in 1929. Chilling night tours run every Sunday and Wednesday (call ahead and check the schedule); they cost A$18 (U.S.$12.60) for adults and A$10 (U.S.$7) for children (although the tour is not recommended for children under age 12).

National Gallery of Victoria. 180 St. Kilda Rd. ☎ **03/9208 0222.** Free general admission; call about special exhibits. Daily 10am–5pm. Free guided tours Mon–Fri at 11am, noon, 2pm, and 3pm; Sat 2pm; and Sun at 11am and 2pm (summer times may vary slightly). Closed Good Friday and Christmas Day. Tram: Any southbound tram on Swanston St.

This is the best place in Victoria to view Aboriginal art, as well as colonial Australian, Asian, and European works. Look for works from artists such as Sidney Nolan, Russell Drysdale, and Tom Roberts; there are also a few works by Rembrandt, Picasso, Manet, and Turner. A free Aboriginal arts tour starts at 2pm every Thursday. A cafe and a restaurant are on the premises.

IMAX Theatre. Royal Exhibition Building, Rathdowne St., Carlton. ☎ **03/9663 5454.** Admission A$13.95 (U.S.$9.80) adults, A$9.95 (U.S.$7) children. Daily 10am–10pm. Tram: 1, or 22 from Swanston St.

This eight-story movie screen rivals the world's largest screen at Sydney's Darling Harbour. Watching movies about outer space, the African Serengeti, and the deep oceans, for example, is an exhilarating experience: The movies are shot with special giant-format cameras and complemented by amazing sound. It can also be a little dizzying, as it all seems so real.

PARKS & GARDENS

The ✪ **Royal Botanic Gardens,** 2 kilometers (1¼ miles) south of the city on Birdwood Avenue, off St. Kilda Road (☎ **03/9252 2300),** are the best of their type in Australia. More than 100 acres of gardens are lush and blooming with more than 12,000 plant species from all over the world. Don't miss a visit to the oldest part of the garden, the Tennyson Lawn, with its 120-year-old English elm trees. Other special corners include a fern gully, camellia gardens, rain forests, and ponds full of ducks and black swans. You can either discover the gardens by wandering at your own pace (most plant species are labeled, so you'll know what you're seeing), or you can take one of the free guided walks that leave the **National Herbarium Building,** F Gate, Sunday to Friday at 11am and noon. Bring snacks and your picnic blanket to Shakespeare in the Park, a popular summer event in the gardens. Performances occur in January and February, and tickets cost around A$30 (U.S.$21). Call ☎ **03/9252 2300** for details. The gardens are open November to March from 7:30am to 8:30pm, in April from 7:30am to 7pm, and May to October from 7:30am to 5:30pm. Admission is free. To get there, catch a no. 8 tram traveling south on St. Kilda Road and get off at Stop 21.

Nearby, in **King's Domain,** take a look at Victoria's first Government House, Latrobe's Cottage (☎ **03/9654 5528**). It was built in England and transported out, brick by brick, in 1836. Admission is A$4 (U.S.$2.80) for adults and A$3 (U.S.$2.10) for children. The cottage is open from 11am to 4:30pm every day except Friday. On the other side of Birdwood Avenue is the Shrine of Remembrance, a memorial to the servicemen lost in Australia's wars. It's designed so that at 11am on Remembrance Day (the 11th of November), a beam of sunlight hits the Stone of Remembrance in the

Inner Shrine. Note the eternal flame in the forecourt. To reach King's Domain, take a no. 15 tram traveling south down St. Kilda Road and get off at Stop 12

In **Fitzroy Gardens,** off Wellington Parade, is **Cook's Cottage** (☎ **03/ 9419 4677**), which was moved to Melbourne from Great Ayton, in Yorkshire, England, in 1934 to mark Victoria's centenary. It's claimed (with some debate) that Captain Cook lived here between his long voyages. The interior is spartan and cramped, not unlike a ship's cabin. Admission is A$3 (U.S.$2.10) for adults, A$1.50 (U.S.$1.05) for children ages 5 to 15, and A$7.50 (U.S.$5.25) for a family of up to six. It's open daily from 9am to 5pm.

You can find the **Treasury Gardens** east of the central business district: Look out for the Memorial to **John F. Kennedy** near the lake. Treasury Gardens and Fitzroy Gardens can be reached by tram no. 75 traveling east along Flinders Street. Get off at Stop 14 for Treasury Gardens and at Stop 14A for Fitzroy Gardens.

6 Enjoying the Great Outdoors or Catching an Aussie Rules Football Match

OUTDOOR ACTIVITIES

BICYCLING   Extensive bicycle paths wind through the city and suburbs. For details on the 20 most popular routes, pick up a copy of *Melbourne Bike Tours,* published by Bicycle Victoria (☎ **03/9328 3000;** fax 03/9328 2288; www.bv.com.au), available at most bookshops. Bicycle Victoria also runs several major cycling tours throughout the state every year.

Cycle Science, 320 Toorak Rd., South Yarra (☎ **03/9826 6870**), rents bicycles for A$15 (U.S.$10.50) for 2 hours, A$20 (U.S.$14) 4 hours, A$30 (U.S.$21) for a full day, and A$70 (U.S.$49) for a week. The shop is open Monday to Thursday from 9am to 7pm, Friday from 9am to 8pm, Saturday from 9am to 5pm, and Sunday from 11am to 5pm. Take tram no. 8 to Toorak Road.

You can also rent a bike from **Hire a Bike** at St. Kilda Pier (☎ **03/9531 7403,** or 014/401 348 mobile phone). Non-Australians must show their passports.

GOLF   One of the best public golf courses in Australia is **Yarra Bend,** Yarra Bend Road, Fairfield (☎ **03/9481 3729**). Greens fees are about A$15 (U.S.$10.50), and club rental is an extra A$10 (U.S.$7) for a half set and A$25 (U.S.$17.50) for a full set.

The **Royal Melbourne Golf Club,** in the suburb of Black Rock, 24 kilometers (14½ miles) from the city center, is rated as one of the world's 10 best golf courses. It's very exclusive and open to members only, but if you belong to a top-notch golf club at home, you might be able to wheedle your way in.

IN-LINE SKATING   The promenade in St. Kilda is the most popular place to strap on a pair of skates. You can rent all you need at **Rock'n'n'Roll'n,** 11a Fitzroy St., St. Kilda (☎ **03/9525 3434**). The first hour costs A$8 (U.S.$5.60). Successive hours are less expensive.

TENNIS   The venue for the Australian Open, **Melbourne Park National Tennis Centre** (☎ **03/9286 1244**), on Batman Avenue in the city center, is a great place to play tennis. When tournaments are not scheduled, its 22 outdoor courts and 4 indoor courts are open to the public. You can rent courts Monday to Friday from 7am to 11pm, and Saturday and Sunday from 9am to 6pm. Charges range from A$14 to $30 (U.S.$9.80 to $21) per hour, depending on the time of day (outdoor courts are cheaper, with A$20 (U.S.$14) per hour the most charged). Show courts 1, 2, and 3 are also for hire at the same prices. Racquets are available for A$3 (U.S.$2.10).

SPECTATOR SPORTS

AUSTRALIAN RULES FOOTBALL   Melbourne's number one sport is Australian Rules Football, a skillful—but often violent—ball game the likes of which you've never seen: This game has rules that most Australians don't understand! It's is played either at the Melbourne Cricket Ground (MCG), Brunton Avenue, Yarra Park, Jolimont; or at Waverley Park, Wellington Road, Mulgrave. The season runs from the third weekend in March to the last Saturday in September. For game information, call **AFL Headquarters** at ☎ **03/9643 1999.** Buy tickets through **TicketMaster** (☎ **13 61 22** in Australia).

CAR RACING   Melburnites' opinions are still split over the annual **Australian Formula One Grand Prix,** whose development resulted in mass demonstrations against the destruction of thousands of trees in the city's beloved Albert Park. The race takes place in early March. Call **TicketMaster** (☎ **13 61 22** in Australia), or the **Grand Prix Hotline** (☎ **13 16 41** in Australia, or 03/9258 7100) for information and tickets (including accommodation bookings and airfares). Also check out the Grand Prix's Web site at www.grandprix.com.au.

CRICKET   From October to March, cricket's the name of the game in Melbourne. The **Melbourne Cricket Ground (MCG),** Brunton Avenue, Yarra Park, Jolimont (☎ **03/9657 8879**), once the main stadium for the 1956 Melbourne Olympic Games, is perhaps Australia's most hallowed cricket field. The stadium can accommodate 97,500 people. For the uninitiated, 1-day games are the ones to look out for; test games take several days to complete. Buy tickets at the gate, or in advance through **Ticketmaster** (☎ **13 61 22** in Australia).

Tours of the MCG, including the free museum with signed cricket bats, memorabilia, and so on, leave on the hour daily from 10am to 3pm. The **Australian Gallery of Sport and the Olympic Museum** are also at the MCG. The museum traces the development of the modern Olympics.

HORSE RACING   Australia's top thoroughbreds (and a few from overseas) have been competing for the **Melbourne Cup,** run on the first Tuesday in November, since 1861. Melbourne society types put on a show when they all dress up for the occasion, and it seems that the entire nation stops in its tracks to at least tune in on TV.

The city has four race tracks: **Flemington** (which holds the Melbourne Cup), on Epson Road in Flemington (☎ **03/9371 7171**); **Moonee Valley,** on McPherson Street in Mooney Ponds (☎ **03/9373 2222**); **Caulfield,** on Station Street in Caulfield (☎ **03/9257 7200**); and **Sandown,** on Racecourse Drive in Springvale (☎ **03/9518 1300**). If you're staying in the city center, Flemington and Moonee Valley tracks are the easiest to get to; either way, the trip only takes about 10 minutes. Take tram no. 57 from Flinders Street to reach the Flemington racetrack, and catch tram no. 59 from Elizabeth Street to travel to Moonee Valley.

TENNIS   The **Australian Open,** one of the world's four Grand Slam events, is played during the last 2 weeks of January every year at **Flinders Park National Tennis Center,** on Batman Avenue (☎ **03/9286 1234**). Tickets for the Australian Open go on sale in mid-October and are available through **Ticketek** (☎ **03/9299-9079**). Also check the Australian Open Web site: www.ausopen.org. Guided tours of the center are offered Wednesday to Friday from April to October, subject to availability. They cost A$5 (U.S.$3.50) for adults and A$3 (U.S.$2.10) for children. To get to Flinders Park National Tennis Center, take a train from the Flinders Street Station to Richmond Station, and take the special Tennis Center tram from there.

7 The Shopping Scene

THE SHOPPING SCENE

Ask almost any Melburnite to help you plan your time in the city, and they'll advise you to shop 'til you drop. All of Australia regards Melbourne as a shopping mecca—it's got everything, from famous fashion houses to major department stores and unusual souvenir shops. If you're coming from Sydney, I say, "Save your money until you get to Melbourne, and then indulge!"

Start at the magnificent city arcades, such as the **Block Arcade** (running between Collins and Little Collins streets), which has more than 30 shops, including the historic Hopetoun Tea Rooms, and the **Royal Arcade** (stretching from Little Collins Street to the Bourke Street Mall). Then hit the courts and lanes around **Swanston Street,** and the huge **Melbourne Central** shopping complex between Latrobe and Lonsdale streets (where you'll find Daimaru, an international department store).

Next, take your wallet with you as you fan out across the city, taking in **Chapel Street** in South Yarra, for its Australian fashions, and **The Jam Factory,** 500 Chapel St., South Yarra (☎ 03/9826 0537—a series of buildings with a range of shops and food outlets, including U.S.–based Borders Books, as well as 16 cinema screens. Get there on tram no. 8, or take no. 72 from Swanston Street.

There's also **Toorak Road** in Toorak, for Gucci and other high-priced, high-fashion names; **Bridge Road** in Richmond for budget fashions; **Lygon Street** in Carlton for Italian fashion, footwear, and accessories; and **Brunswick Street** in Fitzroy for a more alternative scene.

Serious shoppers might like to contact **Shopping Spree Tours** (☎ 03/9596 6600), a company that takes you to all those exclusive and alternative shopping venues, manufacturers, and importers you wouldn't be likely to find by yourself. Tours depart Monday to Saturday at 8:30am. They cost A$50 (U.S.$35) per person, including lunch and a visit the Rialto Observation Deck. The shops visited are elected by general consensus on the day, but they usually include clothing and shoe shops.

See "Fast Facts: Melbourne," earlier in the chapter for normal shopping hours.

MELBOURNE SHOPPING A TO Z

ABORIGINAL CRAFTS

The Aboriginal Gallery of the Dreaming. 73–77 Bourke St., City. ☎ **03/9650 3277.**

This place stocks an extensive range of acrylic dot paintings and represents more than 120 artists. Boomerangs, didgeridoos, pottery, jewelry, bark paintings, prints, books, and music are also available. The gallery's open Monday to Friday from 10am to 5:30pm (to 6:30pm on Friday), and Sunday from noon to 5pm.

Aboriginal Handcrafts. 125–133 Swanston St. (9th fl.). ☎ **03/9650 4717**.

Didgeridoos, bark paintings, boomerangs, and so forth are sold here, with the profits going to Aboriginal colleges. The shop is open Monday to Thursday from 10am to 4:30pm, and Friday from 10am to 5pm.

BOOKS

The Hill of Content Bookshop. 86 Bourke St., City ☎ **03/9662 9472.**

You can find a wide selection of books here, including some titles on Melbourne. It's open Monday to Thursday from 9am to 5:30pm, Friday from 9am to 9pm, Saturday from 9am to 5pm, and Sunday from noon to 5pm; closed public holidays.

Borders. In The Jam Factory, 500 Chapel St., South Yarra. ☎ **03/9824 2299.**

Specialists in Australian, U.K., and U.S. books, music, and videos, Borders is a massive establishment where you could browse for hours. The CD section beats many music shops. It's open daily from 9am to midnight.

CRAFTS

An interesting **Arts & Crafts Market** is held on The Esplanade, St. Kilda, on Sunday from 9am to 4pm. Take tram no. 16 from Swanston Street, or no. 96 from Bourke Street.

The Australian Geographic Shop. Shop 130, Level 2, Melbourne Central shopping complex. ☎ **03/9639 2478.**

Head here for high-quality Australiana, including crafts, books, and various gadgets. Open Monday to Thursday from 10am to 5pm, Friday from 10am to 9pm, Saturday from 10am to 6pm, and Sunday from 11am to 6pm.

The Meat Market Craft Center. 42 Courtney St., North Melbourne. ☎ **03/9329 9966.**

A wide range of craft works by leading local artists, woodworkers, printers, potters, and jewelers is on sale here. Open Tuesday to Sunday from 10am to 5pm.

DEPARTMENT STORES

Daimaru. In the Central Melbourne shopping complex. ☎ **03/9660 6666.**

With six floors of interesting merchandise, including Asian foodstuffs and top-label fashions, this Japanese department store is giving the established chain stores a real run for shoppers' money. Open Monday to Thursday from 10am to 6pm, Friday from 10am to 9pm, Saturday from 10am to 6pm, and Sunday from 11am to 6pm.

David Jones. 310 Bourke St. Mall, City. ☎ **03/9643 2222.**

Like its major competitor, Myer (see below), DJ's, as it's affectionately known, spans 2 city blocks and offers similar goods. Open Monday to Thursday from 9:30am to 6pm, Friday from 9am to 9pm, Saturday and Sunday from 9am to 6pm.

Georges. 162 Collins St., City. ☎ **03/9929 9999.**

Melbourne's glitziest out-of-the-ordinary department store offers very exclusive men's and women's fashions, top-of-the-range stationery and pens, unusual stylish knickknacks, perfumes, hats, and the like. There's a cafe and cheap eatery here, too. Open Monday to Wednesday and Saturday from 10am to 6pm, Thursday from 10am to 7pm, Friday from 10am to 8pm, and Sunday from 11am to 5pm.

✪ **Myer. 314 Bourke St. Mall, City.** ☎ 03/9661 1111.

The grand dame of Melbourne's department stores has 12 floors of household goods, perfume, jewelry, and fashions stretching over 2 blocks (it claims to be the fifth largest store in the world). A good food section on the ground floor offers, among other things, good sushi. Open Saturday to Wednesday from 10am to 6pm, Thursday from 10am to 7pm, and Friday from 10am to 9pm.

FASHION

Of course, you can always head to the major department stores (see above) if you're looking for fashions. High-fashion boutiques line the eastern stretch of Collins Street between the Grand Hyatt Melbourne and the Hotel Sofitel, and also are along Chapel Street, in South Yarra.

In addition, many thousands of retail shops and factory outlets dot the city, many of them concentrated on Bridge Road near Punt Road and Swan Street near Church

Street in Richmond. You'll be able to find designer clothes, many just last season's fashions, at a fraction of the original price.

Country Road. 252 Toorak Rd., and other locations, including Chapel St., South Yarra. (☎ **1800/801 911** in Australia, or 03/9824 0133).

Country Road is one of Australia's best-known names for men's and women's fashion (it also sells designer cooking equipment and housewares). It isn't cheap, but you get what you pay for in terms of quality.

High and Mighty, Big and Tall. 270 Little Collins St., City. ☎ **03/9654 1288.**

The name pretty much says it all. This store specializes in clothes for "large—even hugely built" men and has some very fashionable clothes on two floors, from casual wear to business suits. (I was disappointed that nothing fit me.) Open Monday to Thursday from 9:30am to 5:30pm, Friday from 9:30am to 9pm, Saturday from 9am to 5pm, and Sunday from noon to 5pm.

Mortisha's. Shop 8–10, Royal Arcade, City. ☎ **03/9654 1586.**

Head to this Gothic, satin-lined, coffin-like store for everything from Victorian gowns and vampy velvet dresses to original bridal wear. There's also some very unusual jewelry and accessories for fans of the Addams Family. Open Monday to Thursday from 10am to 5:30pm, Friday from 10am to 8:30pm, Saturday from 10am to 5pm, and Sunday from noon to 4pm.

Paddington Coat Factory. 461–463 Chapel St., South Yarra. ☎ **03/9429 9491.**

Exquisite, high-fashion clothes made by hot, young Australian designers—such as Andrea Yasmin, Susie Mooratoff, and Lara Agnew—go for between A$39 and $500 (U.S.$27.30–$350) at this Melbourne sister store of the one in Paddington, Sydney.

R.M. Williams. In the Melbourne Central shopping complex. ☎ **03/9663 7126.**

Stock up here on genuine Aussie gear: great boots, Driza-bone coats, Akubra hats, and more. Open Monday to Thursday and Saturday from 10am to 6pm, Friday from 10am to 9pm, and Sunday from 11am to 6pm.

Sam Bear. 225 Russell St. ☎ **03/9663 2191.**

Come here for a good solid range of camping equipment, Driza-bone coats, Akubra bush hats, R.M. Williams boots and clothing, Blundstone boots (my favorites), and army clothing. Open Monday to Thursday from 9am to 5:30, Friday from 9am to 8pm, and Saturday from 9am to 5pm.

Surf, Dive 'N Ski Australia. The Jam Factory, Chapel St., South Yarra. ☎ **03/9826 4071.**

In addition to surfboards, boogie boards, and sunglasses, this store has a very wide range of hip and happening beach and cruise wear at reasonable prices. Australian clothing icons here include Ripcurl, Quicksilver, and Billabong. Open Monday to Thursday from 9:30am to 7pm, Friday from 9am to 9pm, Saturday from 10am to 6pm, Sunday from noon to 6pm.

Vegan Wares. 78 Smith St., Collingwood. ☎ **03/9417 0230.**

Instead of leather, Vegan Wares uses microfibre to create tough, stylish shoes, handbags, and belts. Open Monday to Friday from 11am to 6:30pm and Saturday from 11am to 5pm.

Discount Fashion
Overseas Designer Warehouse. 18 Ellis St., South Yarra (off Chapel St., between Toorak Rd. and Commercial Rd.). ☎ **03/9828 0399.**

End-of-run and last season's high fashions can still be expensive here, but you can also find a few bargains if you really search. Open daily from 10am to 6pm.

Samples & Seconds Shop. 399 Elizabeth St., City. ☎ **03/9329 9382.**

Just like the name says, head here for discounted women's clothing, including last-year's fashions and clothes with slight faults. Open Monday to Friday from 9:30am to 5:30pm, Saturday from 9am to 2pm, and Sunday from 10am to 2pm.

FOOD

Ackland Street in St. Kilda has quite superb cake shops and delis. The Melbourne Central shopping complex has some surprisingly good take-out stores, too. I especially recommend **Saint Cinnamon,** on the ground floor opposite the information booth, which makes delicious cinnamon rolls while you wait. They cost A$2.40 (U.S.$1.70) each.

Haigh's Chocolates. 26 Collins St., City. ☎ **03/9650 2114,** and Shop 26, The Block Arcade, 182 Collins St., City ☎ 03/9654 7673.

Indulge in some 50 manifestations of Australia's best chocolate, from milk to dark, fruit flavored, and shaped. I recommend the Sparkling Shiraz truffle if you need a serious treat. Open Monday to Thursday from 8:30am to 6pm, Friday from 8:30am to 7pm, and Saturday from 9am to 5pm.

Suga—Melbourne Candy Kitchen. Shop 20, Royal Arcade, City. ☎ **03/9663 5654.**

If you have a sweet tooth, you'll spend a fortune at this little traditional candy shop that makes its produce before your very eyes. Rock candy is a specialty, and you can even get your name (or the name of someone back home) spelled out in its center. Open Monday to Thursday and Saturday from 10am to 6pm, Friday from 10am to 8pm, and Sunday from noon to 8pm.

tea too tea. 89 Fitzroy St., St. Kilda (☎ **03/95 34 6266**), and 340 Brunswick St., Fitzroy (☎ 03/9417 3722).

These interesting little shops sell very fine-quality and unusual teas from Australia, India, Sri Lanka, New Guinea, South America, China, Japan, South Africa, Turkey, and Japan. They are open Monday to Thursday from 10am to 7pm, Friday from 10am to 8pm, Saturday from 10am to 7pm, and Sunday from 10am to 6pm.

Death by Chocolate

If you love chocolate, sign up now for the **Chocolate Indulgence Walk** or the **Chocolates & Other Desserts Walk** by calling ☎ **03/9815 1228,** or 0412/158 017 (mobile phone). The former takes you on a tasting tour of Cadbury's, Myer, New Zealand Natural Ice Creamery, Chocolate Box, and Darrell Lea, and finishes off over chocolate cake at a cafe. This 2-hour tour leaves every Saturday at 12:30pm and costs A$22 (U.S.$15.40) (children under age 6 are free). The latter tour includes sampling plenty of ice cream and chocolate around town as you visit kitchens and talk to chefs; the tour finishes with afternoon tea at the Grand Hyatt. This tour leaves every Saturday at 2:30pm and also costs A$22 (U.S.$15.40). A new walk called the **Coffee and Café Walk** includes drinks and pastries, and revolves around Melbourne's groovy cafe society. It also costs A$22 (U.S.$15.40). Bookings are essential.

JEWELRY

Altman & Cherny. 120 Exhibition St., corner of Little Collins St., City ☎ **03/9650 9685.**

Even if you don't want to buy anything, it's worth coming here to see the Olympic Australia, the largest precious-gem opal in the world, which was found in Coober Pedy in South Australia in 1956 and is valued at U.S.$1.8 million. The store offers tax-free shopping for tourists armed with a passport and return airline ticket. Open Monday to Friday from 9am to 5:30pm and Saturday and Sunday from 9am to 4pm

✪ **Dinosaur Designs.** 562 Chapel St., South Yarra. ☎ **03/9827 2600.**

Taking the fashion world by storm, Dinosaur Designs makes a range of very artistic resin jewelry and modern homewares. Expect bold shapes and strong colors. None of it's cheap, but the odd item won't break the bank. Open Monday to Saturday from 10am to 6pm, and Sunday from noon to 5pm.

Portobello Lane of South Yarra. 405 Chapel St., South Yarra. ☎ **03/9827 5708.**

Robyn Meate, the proprietor here, specializes in locally produced and imported sterling silver jewelry with lots of beads and glass. Some of the designs are really interesting and intricate, and cost from A$40 to $200 (U.S.$28 to $140). Open Monday to Thursday from 10am to 6pm, Friday from 10am to 8pm, Saturday from 9:30am to 5pm, and Sunday from 1pm to 4pm.

8 Melbourne After Dark

Melbourne can be an exciting place after the sun has set. The pubs here are far better than the ones in Sydney, although they are definitely split between very trendy and very down to earth. Friday and Saturday nights will see most pubs packed to the rafters, and at lunchtime those that serve food are pretty popular, too. To find out what's hot and happening, check the entertainment guide included in *The Age* each Friday.

THE PERFORMING ARTS

Tickets and details on schedules for many shows are available by calling **Ticketek** at ☎ **1800/062 849** in Australia, or 61-3/9299 9079 (international number), or 13 28 849.

THE HEART OF MELBOURNE'S CULTURAL LIFE

Victorian Arts Center. 100 St. Kilda Rd. ☎ **03/9281 8000,** or 13 61 66 for ticket purchase; www.artscentre.net.au. Tickets for State Theatre A$40–$110 (U.S.$28–$77); Playhouse and Fairfax A$30–$45 (U.S.$21–$31.50); Concert Hall A$40–$80 (U.S.$28–$56).

The towering spire atop the Theatres Building of the Victorian Arts Center, on the banks of the Yarra River, crowns the city's leading performing arts complex. Beneath it, the State Theatre, the Playhouse, and the Fairfax present performances that represent the focal point of Melbourne's cultural life.

The **State Theatre,** seating 2,079 on three levels, can accommodate elaborate stagings of opera, ballet, musicals, and more. The **Playhouse** is a smaller venue that often hosts the Melbourne Theatre Company. The **Fairfax** is more intimate still, and is often used for experimental theater or cabaret.

Adjacent to the Theatres Building is the **Melbourne Concert Hall,** home of the Melbourne Symphony Orchestra and the State Orchestra of Victoria, and often host to visiting orchestras. Many international stars have graced this stage, which is known for its excellent acoustics.

Guided 1-hour **tours** of the Concert Hall and the theaters are offered Monday to Friday at noon and 2:30pm and Saturday at 10:30pm and noon. They cost A$9 (U.S.$6.30) for adults, A$6.50 (U.S.$4.55) for children, and A$20 (U.S.$14) for a family. Backstage tours on Sunday at 12:15pm cost A$12 (U.S.$8.40). Children under age 11 are not allowed. Call ☎ **03/9281 8152** between 9:30am and 5pm for information.

ADDITIONAL VENUES & THEATERS

Check *The Age* to see what productions are scheduled during your visit. Odds are that the leading shows will be produced in one of the following venues.

The **Athenaeum Theatre.** 188 Collins St., City (☎ **03/9650 3504,** or 03/9650 1500 for tickets), which dates from the 1880s, frequently hosts dramas and musicals The **Princess Theatre,** 63 Spring St., City (☎ **03/9299 9800**), is a huge facility that hosts major extravaganza productions. The theater was designed by colonial architect William Pitt and opened its doors in 1886; it still retains a dramatic marble staircase and ornate plaster ceilings. *Les Misérables* was showing at press time, to be followed by *Boy from Oz.*

Built in 1929, the **Regent Theatre,** 191 Collins St., City (☎ **03/9299 9800**), fell into disrepair, and its stage was dark for 25 years. Now, after a recent A$35 million (U.S.$24.5 million) renovation, it's been restored to its former glory. In 1999, an extravagant production of *Showboat* was staged, fresh from its sell-out season at the Star City in Sydney. Tickets are available in the United States through **ATS Tours** at ☎ **800/423-2880.** The theater offers a range of dining packages including a preshow meal in the Plaza Ballroom.

The **Forum Theatre,** 154 Flinders St., City (☎ **03/9399 9700**) hosts well-known bands and international comedians. Tables and chairs are set up in cabaret-style booths, from which you can order drinks and meals from the bar.

Part of the huge Crown complex, which includes the Crown Towers Hotel and Crown Casino, the **Crown Showroom,** 8 Whiteman St., Southbank (☎ **03/9292 8888**) has 900 seats and hosts a wide variety of performers and events.

The **Sydney Myer Music Bowl,** King's Domain, Alexandra Ave., City (☎ **03/9281 8360**), is an enormous outdoor entertainment center run under the auspices of the Victorian Arts Center Trust. It hosts opera, jazz, and ballet in the warmer months (and you can ice-skate here in the winter).

The ornate Spanish rococo-style design of the **Comedy Theatre,** 240 Exhibition St., City (☎ **03/9299 9800**), manages to create an intimate feeling, even though this venue seats more than 1,000 people. Plays and musicals usually fill the bill, but dance companies and comedians also appear, as do shows here as part of the Melbourne Festival and Melbourne Comedy Festival.

A fire destroyed the original **Her Majesty's Theatre,** 219 Exhibition St., City (☎ **03/9663 3211**), but the current structure still retains the original facade and the

Half-Price Tickets

Buy your tickets for entertainment events, including opera, dance, and drama, on the day of the performance from the **Half-Tix Kiosk** in Bourke Street Mall (☎ **03/9650 9420**). The booth is open Monday from 10am to 2pm, Tuesday to Thursday from 11am to 6pm, Friday from 11am to 6:30pm, and Saturday from 10am to 2pm. Tickets must be paid for in cash. The available shows are displayed each day on the booth door, and you can't get show information over the phone.

art deco interior added during a 1936 renovation. Musicals, such as the Australian premier of *Chicago,* frequent the boards.

The **Malthouse Theatre Company,** 113 Sturt St., South Melbourne (☎ 03/9685 5111), performs in two medium-sized theaters, the Merlyn and the Beckett, at this location. The Playbox Theatre Company of Monash University also calls this site home and runs productions of contemporary Australian theater.

THE CLUB & MUSIC SCENE

King Street is nightclub row in Melbourne. Nightclubs around here come and go.

✪ **Bobby McGee's Entertainment Lounge.** In the Rydges Melbourne Hotel, 186 Exhibition St. ☎ **03/9639 0630**. Cover A$5 (U.S.$3.50) Mon and Wed–Sat after 8pm; free for hotel guests.

If you want a fun night out, head for the restaurant section of Bobby McGee's, then hit the dance floor at the disco. The restaurant has good American-style food served by waiters in fancy dress, while the disco area is open from 5pm to the wee hours (the music, a mix of the popular dance hits of the moment, starts pounding at 9pm). The disco is popular with the 22-to-35 crowd after work, while the younger set flocks in after 10pm. Happy hours and drinks promotions vary according to the night. You'll see lots of business suits on Thursday and Friday nights, but dress is casual but smart on other nights.

✪ **The Comedy Club.** Level 1, 380 Lygon St., Carlton. ☎ **03/9348 1622.** Dinner and show Fri–Sat A$40–$45 (U.S.$28–$31.50) depending on performer; show only Thurs–Sat around A$20 (U.S.$14).

The Comedy Club is another Melbourne institution. Come here to see local and international comedy acts, musicals, and special shows. Check schedules before you go because they are seasonal and subject to change.

Heaven Nightclub. 195 King St. ☎ **03/9670 0980.** Cover A$10 (U.S.$7). Fri–Sat 9pm–7am.

This nightclub features some of Melbourne's top DJs spinning a mix of '70s, '80s, and '90s classics and dance hits. It attracts mostly folks in the 24-to-35 age bracket.

Monsoon's Nightclub. In the Grand Hyatt Melbourne, 123 Collins St. ☎ **03/9657 1234.** Cover A$15 (U.S.$10.50); free for house guests.

Dress up a bit if you want to blend in with the crowd at the upscale Monsoon's. Hotel guests and well-heeled locals dance to Top 40 tunes or check out visiting jazz or cabaret performers on Friday and Saturday nights (Thursday night is funk night). One Sunday and Wednesday every month the nightclub is also open for special theme nights.

WHERE TO SHARE A PINT

Bridie O' Reillys. 62 Little Collins St. (just off Exhibition St.). ☎ **03/9650 0840.**

One of Melbourne's best Irish bars, Bridie O' Reillys is a magnet for anyone who likes traditional dark wood decor and good beer. The pub is on two levels, and serves

---

Pub Crawls

Something fun to do if you want to have a few drinks and meet a few people is to join the young and relaxed guides from **City Pub Walks** (☎ **03/9384 0655,** or 0412/085 661 mobile phone). The 2½- to 3-hour walks stop off at a variety of interesting pubs and bars where you can sample the local brews (at your own expense). Tours leave from under the clocks at Flinders Railway Station at 6:30pm Tuesday and Thursday.

19 different beers on tap (7 of them Irish). There is live Irish music every night from around 9pm. The place gets quite crowded on weekends.

The Charles Dickens Tavern. 290 Collins St. (between Elizabeth and Swanston sts.). ☎ **03/9654 1821.**

Come here for a touch of Olde England in the heart of the city. The homey pub has two bars and a good pub-grub restaurant serving traditional roasts and pies and lighter meals of fish and pasta. The pub has a 24-hour license, but generally it's open daily from 10am to around 2am or 3am, depending on whether it has more than a handful of patrons.

Cricketers Bar. In the Windsor Hotel, 103 Spring St. ☎ **03/9653 0653.**

The locals come to this popular English-style pub in this five-star establishment hotel to lift a glass surrounded by the relics of Australia's summer passion. Glass cases are packed full of cricket bats, pads, and stumps, while the plush green carpets and solid mahogany woodwork give the place an air of tradition.

The Mitre Tavern. 5 Bank Place (between Queen and William sts. and Collins and Little Collins sts.). ☎ **03/9670 5644.**

If the owners put some carpets on the floor, this place could be almost as good as a traditional English pub. Still, it's an atmospheric, centrally located place, with an outdoor courtyard perfect for lunch on a sunny day. French fries, sushi, steak sandwiches, and nachos go for between A$5 and $8 (U.S.$3.50–$5.60).

The Prince St. Kilda. 29 Fitzroy St., St. Kilda. ☎ **03/9536 1111.**

This pub is a legend among the locals. Although it's recently been refurbished, it's kept its original rough-around-the-edges appearance. Bands play most nights, some of them big names. Pots of beer are just A$1 (U.S.70¢) Monday evenings from 8pm to 1am.

Young & Jacksons. At the corner of Flinders and Swanston sts. ☎ **03/9650 3884.**

You probably won't think that much of the rough and tumble downstairs area. You might want to check upstairs, though, for here resides the naked *Chloe;* a painting brought to Melbourne for the Great Exhibition in 1880. The pub, which was built in 1853 and started selling beer in 1861, has a few years on the *Chloe,* who was painted in Paris in 1875. She has a special place in the hearts of customers and has spawned hundreds of copies that have found their way to far-flung places worldwide.

A CASINO

Crown Casino. Clarendon St., Southbank. ☎ **13 21 38** in Australia, or 03/9292 6868.

Australia's largest casino is a plush affair open 24 hours. You'll find all the usual roulette and blackjack tables and so on, as well as an array of poker machines. There are some 25 restaurants and 40 bars on the premises.

9 Side Trips From Melbourne

DANDENONG RANGES

40km (24 miles) E of Melbourne

Melburnites traditionally do a "day in the Dandenongs" from time to time, topping off their getaway with a Devonshire tea of scones and jam in one of the many cafes on route. Up in the cool, high country you'll find native bush, famous gardens, the Dandenong Ranges National Park, historic attractions such as the Puffing Billy vintage steam train, and plenty of restaurants and cozy B&Bs. The **Dandenong Ranges National Park** is one of the state's oldest, having been put aside in 1882 to protect the region's mountain ash forests and lush tree-fern gullies.

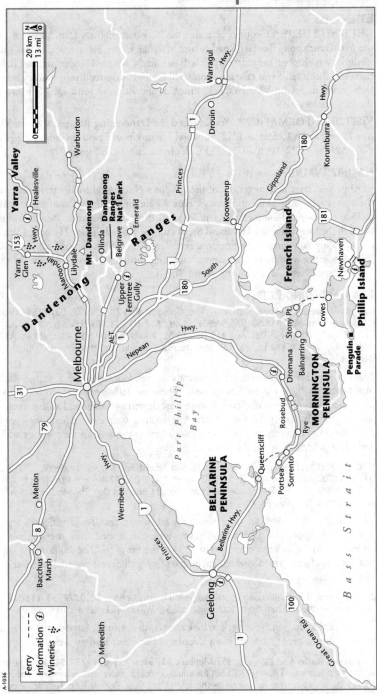

Side Trips from Melbourne

N

20 km
13 mi

Warragul
Hwy.

Drouin

Hwy.

Korumburra

180

Gippsland

Warburton

Yarra Valley

Healesville

Hwy.

153

Yarra Glen

Lilydale

Maroondah

Mt. Dandenong

Dandenong Ranges Nat'l Park

Olinda

Belgrave

Ranges

Emerald

181

Princes

Kooweerup

Dandenong

Upper Ferntree Gully

French Island

Newhaven

ALT 1

South

180

Stony Pt.

Cowes

Phillip Island

Melbourne

Hwy.

Nepean

Penguin Parade

Dromana

Balnarring

MORNINGTON PENINSULA

31

Port Phillip Bay

Rosebud

Rye

79

Bass Strait

Hwy.

Werribee

Queenscliff

BELLARINE PENINSULA

Portsea

Sorrento

Melton

8

Princes

Bellarine Hwy.

Bacchus Marsh

100

Meredith

Geelong

1

Great Ocean Rd.

Ferry − − − −   Information ⓘ   Wineries

A-1036

593

ESSENTIALS

GETTING THERE   Get there by taking the Burwood Highway from Melbourne to the **Mt. Dandenong Tourist Road,** which starts at Upper Ferntree Gully and then winds its way through the villages of Sassafras, Olinda, Mount Dandenong, and Kalorama to Montrose. If you take a turnoff to Sherbrook, or extend your journey into a loop taking in Seville, Woori Yallock, Emerald, and Belgrave you'll see a fair slice of the local scenery.

VISITOR INFORMATION   You can find the **Dandenong Ranges & Knox Visitor Information Center** at 1211 Burwood Hwy., Upper Ferntree Gully, VIC 3156 (☎ **03/9758 7522;** fax 03/9758 7533). It's open daily from 9am to 5pm.

NATURE WALKS

Most people come here to get out of the city for a pleasant bushwalk, so in that way the area is the equivalent of Sydney's Blue Mountains. Some of the better walks include the easy 2.5-kilometer (1½-mile) stroll from the Sherbrook Picnic Ground through the forest, and **the Thousand Steps and the Kokoda Track Memorial Walk,** a challenging rain-forest track from the Fern Tree Gully Picnic Ground up One Tree Hill. Along the way are plaques commemorating Australian troops who fought and died in Papua New Guinea during World War II.

FOR GARDENING BUFFS

National Rhododendron Gardens. The Georgian Rd., Olinda. ☎ **03/9751 1980.** Admission Sept–Nov A$6.50 (U.S.$4.55) adults, A$2 (U.S.$1.40) children 12–16, A$15 (U.S.$10.50) family of 5; Dec–Aug A$5 (U.S.$3.50) adults, A$2 (U.S.$1.40) children, A$12 (U.S.$8.40) family. Closed Christmas Day. Train to Croydon, and then bus no. 688 to the gardens.

From September to November, thousands of rhododendrons and azaleas burst into bloom in these magnificent gardens. There are 103 lovely acres in all, with a 3-kilometer (2-mile) walking path leading past flowering exotics and native trees, as well as great vistas over the Yarra Valley. A tearoom is open every day during spring, and on weekends at other times. Visitors flock here in summer for the glorious walks, and again in autumn when the leaves are turning.

William Ricketts Sanctuary. Mt. Dandenong Tourist Rd., Mount Dandenong. ☎ **03/9751 1300.** Admission A$5 (U.S.$3.50) adults, A$2 (U.S.$1.40) children 10–14, A$12 (U.S.$8.40) family of 4. Daily 10am–4:30pm. Closed Christmas Day. Train to Croydon, then bus no. 688 to the sanctuary.

This wonderful garden, set in a mountain ash forest, features clay figures representing the Aboriginal Dreamtime. They were all created over the lifetime of sculptor William Ricketts, who died in 1993 at the age of 94. The sculptures occupy just 2 acres of the gardens, which encompass fern gullies and waterfalls spread out over 33 acres.

Bonsai Farm. Mt. Dandenong Tourist Rd., Mount Dandenong. ☎ **03/9751 1150.** Free admission. Wed–Sun 11am–5pm. Transportation: See William Ricketts Sanctuary, above.

If you don't like to crane your neck to look at trees, then visit the large display of petite bonsais here. Some of them are many decades old and cost a pretty penny.

Tesselaar's Bulbs and Flowers. 357 Monbulk Rd., Silvan. ☎ **03/9737 9305.** Admission during tulip festival, A$9.50 (U.S.$6.60) for adults, children under age 16 free when accompanied by an adult; free for everyone the rest of the year. During Tulip Festival (approx. Sept 12 to Oct 11) daily 10am–5pm; rest of year Mon–Fri 8am–4:30pm, Sat–Sun 1–5pm. Take the train to Lilydale, then bus no. 679.

There are literally tens of thousands of flowers on display here, all putting on a flamboyantly colorful show in the spring, between September and October. Expect to see a dazzling variety of tulips, daffodils, rhododendrons, azaleas, fuschias, and ranunculi. Bulbs are on sale at discount prices at other times.

FOR TRAIN BUFFS

Puffing Billy Railway. Belgrave Station, Belgrave. ☎ **03/9754 6800** for 24-hour recorded information. Admission A$18 (U.S.$12.60) adults, A$10 (U.S.$7) children 4–16, A$51 (U.S.$35.70) family of 5. Operates daily except Christmas Day. Trains from Flinders Street Station in Melbourne carry passengers to Belgrave; then the Puffing Billy station is a short walk away.

For just about a century, the Puffing Billy steam railway has been chugging over a 13-kilometer (8-mile) track from Belgrave to Emerald Lake. Passengers take trips on open carriages and are treated to lovely views as the train passes through forests and fern gullies and over a National Trust–classified wooden trestle bridge. Trips take around an hour either way. Trains leave at 10:30am, 11:15am, noon, and at 2:30pm on weekdays; 10:30am, 11:45pm, 1:30pm, and 3:15pm on Saturday and Sunday. A further stretch of track to Gembrook was opened in 1998. Daily trips to Gembrook take an extra 45 minutes and cost A$25 (U.S.$15) for adults, A$14 (U.S.$9.80) for children, and A$72 (U.S.$50.40) for a family. Night trains also run on occasional Saturday nights.

WHERE TO DINE

Wild Oak Café. 232 Ridge Rd., Mount Dandenong. ☎ **03/9751 2033.** Main courses A$7.50–$10.80 (U.S.$2.45–$7.60). BC, DC, MC, V. Wed–Mon 10am–10pm. MODERN OZ.

For good home cooking at very reasonable prices, you can't beat this cozy cafe. The food is innovative and could include crumbed quail with oven-roasted eggplant, or parsnip tart. The restaurant has a roaring log fire in winter.

Churinga Café. 1381 Mt. Dandenong Tourist Rd., Mount Dandenong. ☎ **03/9751 1242.** Main courses A$12.95–$13.95 (U.S.$9.05–$9.75). AE, BC, DC, MC, V. Sat–Wed 10:30am–4:30pm. CAFE.

This is a nice place for a quick lunch or morning or afternoon tea. It's right opposite the William Ricketts Sanctuary and has nice gardens. You can get everything from curries and salads to traditional British fare. Devonshire tea costs A$6 (U.S.$4.20).

YARRA VALLEY

61km (36½ miles) E of Melbourne

The Yarra Valley is a well-known wine-growing region just east of Melbourne. It's dotted with villages, historic houses, gardens, craft shops, antiques centers, and restaurants, as well as dozens of wineries. There are some good bushwalks around here, and the Healesville Sanctuary is one of the best places in Australia to see native animals.

ESSENTIALS

GETTING THERE **McKenzie's Bus Lines** (☎ **03/9853 6264**) operates a bus service from Lilydale Railway Station to Healesville (catch a train from Melbourne's Spencer Street Station to Lilyvale; the trip takes about an hour). Buses connect with trains approximately 12 times a day; call for exact connection times.

If you're driving, pick up a detailed map of the area from the **Royal Automotive Club of Victoria** (☎ **03/9790 3333**) in Melbourne. Maps here are free if you're a member of an auto club in your home country, but remember to bring along your membership card. Alternatively, you can pick up a map at the tourist office. From

Melbourne, take the Maroondah Highway to Lilydale and on to Healesville. The trip takes around 1 hour and 15 minutes.

VISITOR INFORMATION   Pick up details on what to see and where to stay at the **Yarra Valley Visitor Information Center,** Old Court House, Harker Street, Healesville (☎ **03/5962 2600;** fax 03/5962 2040). It's open daily from 9am to 5pm.

EXPLORING THE VALLEY

There are three principal roads in the valley: the Melba Highway, Maroondah Highway, and Myers Creek Road, which together form a triangle. Within the triangle are three smaller roads, the Healesville Yarra Glen Road, Old Healesville Road, and Chum Creek Road, which all access wineries. Most people start their tour of the Yarra Valley from Lilydale and take in several ✪ **cellar-door tastings at vineyards along the route.**

Healesville Sanctuary. Badger Creek Rd., Healesville. ☎ **03/5957 2800.** Fax 03/ 5957 2870. www.zoo.org.au (same site as the Melbourne Zoo). Admission A$14 (U.S.$9.80) adults, A$7 (U.S.$4.90) children 4–15; Econo Ticket (2 adults and up to 4 children) A$38 (U.S.$26.60). Daily 9am–5pm (Jan 9am–6pm). Trains from Flinders Street Station to Lilydale, then bus no. 685 to the sanctuary.

Forget about seeing animals in cages—this preserve is a great place to spot native animals in almost natural surroundings. You can see wedge-tailed eagles flying free, dingoes going walkabout, and koalas, wombats, reptiles, and more, all while strolling through the peppermint-scented gum forest, which rings with the chiming of bell birds. The sanctuary was started in 1921 by Sir Colin McKenzie, who set it up as a center for preserving endangered species and to educate the public at the same time. There's a gift shop, a cafe serving light meals, and picnic grounds.

A NICE PLACE TO STAY & DINE

Sanctuary House Motel Healesville. Badger Creek Rd., (P.O. Box 162, Healesville, VIC 3777). ☎ **03/5962 5148.** Fax 03/5962 5392. 12 units. A/C TV. A$60–$75 (U.S.$42–$52.50) double. Additional person A$20 (U.S.$14) extra; children A$10 (U.S.$7) extra. AE, BC, DC, MC, V. Transportation: See the Healesville Sanctuary, above.

This place is very handy for visiting the sanctuary and even better if you want to relax and sample some good Yarra Valley wine. Just 400 meters (440 yd.) from the animals at the zoo, Sanctuary House is set in some 10 acres of beautiful bushland. The rooms are motel-style and come with all the essentials; there's also a pool, a Jacuzzi, a sauna, a half-court tennis court, a game room, and a phone booth. A casual restaurant on the premises serves three-course home-cooked meals for A$22 (U.S.$15.40) (reservations required by 4pm). Nonguests can dine here as well, but they also must reserve by 4pm. Meet your fellow guests in front of the log fire in the living area in cooler months. Two of the rooms are good for families.

PHILLIP ISLAND: PENGUINS ON PARADE

139km (83½ miles) S of Melbourne.

Philip Island's penguin parade, which you can see every evening at dusk, is one of Australia's most popular animal attractions. There are other less crowded places in Australia, places that also feel less staged, where you can watch home-coming penguins (Kangaroo Island in South Australia comes to mind), but at least the little guys and their nesting holes are protected from the throngs of curious tourists by guides and boardwalks. Phillip Island also offers nice beaches, good bushwalking, and a seagull rookery. If you have the time, you should spend at least 2 days here.

ESSENTIALS

GETTING THERE   Most visitors come to Phillip Island on a day trip from Melbourne and arrive in time for the Penguin Parade and dinner. Several tour companies run day trips to Phillip Island. Among them are **Gray Line** (☎ 03/9663 4455), which operates penguin trips daily, departing 1:30pm and returning at around 11:30pm. They cost A$79.50 (U.S.$55.65) for adults and A$39.75 (U.S.$27.85) for children. Gray line also offers full-day trips that include a visit to the Dandenong Ranges and a ride on the Puffing Billy Steam Train.

Another operator, **Down Under Day Tours** (☎ 03/9650 2600), offers a similar half-day tour for A$79.50 (U.S.$55.65) for adults and A$39.50 (U.S.$27.65) for children. The tour leaves at 1:30pm and returns at 11:30pm. This company also offers a day-long trip that combines a Melbourne sightseeing tour with the penguin tour for A$106 (U.S.$74.20) for adults, and A$53 (U.S.$36.50) for children, and a half-day combined Dandenong Ranges/Phillip Island tour costing A$96 (U.S.$67.20) for adults and A$48 (U.S.$33.60) for children.

An excellent budget option is a half-day trip with **Melbourne Sightseeing** (☎ 03/9663 3388). Tours depart Melbourne daily at 2pm and include visits to a cattle farm where you can hand-feed kangaroos, the Koala Conservation Centre, and a seal colony, as well as the Penguin Parade. The coach returns to Melbourne at 11pm. The trip costs A$49 (U.S.$55.30). For the same price, an express bus departs Melbourne at 5:30pm (returning at 11pm) and travels directly to the Penguin Parade.

If you're driving on your own, it's an easy trip (a bit over an hour) from Melbourne along the South Gippsland Highway and then the Bass Highway. A bridge connects the highway to the mainland.

V/Line trains run in summer from Flinders Street Station to Phillip Island via Dandenong. The trip takes just over 2 hours and costs A$13.40 (U.S.$9.40).

VISITOR INFORMATION   The **Phillip Island Information Center,** Phillip Island Tourist Road, Newhaven (☎ 1300/366 422 in Australia, or 03/5956 7447), is an attraction in itself, with interactive computer displays, relevant information, dioramas giving visitors a glimpse into the penguin's world, and a theaterette. It's open daily from 9am to 5pm (to 6pm in the summer).

EXPLORING THE AREA

Visitors approach the island from the east, pass through the town of Newhaven and then, just a little farther along, there's the Phillip Island Information Center.

The main town on the island, **Cowes** (pop. 2,400), is on the far north coast. It's worth taking a stroll along its Esplanade. The Penguin Parade is on the far southwest coast.

The tip of the west coast of the Summerland Peninsula ends in a particularly interesting rock formation called **The Nobbies.** This strange-looking outcropping can be reached at low tide by a basalt causeway. From here there are some spectacular views of the coastline and two offshore islands. On the farthest of these is a population of up to 12,000 Australian fur seals, the largest colony in Australia (bring your binoculars). This area is also home to thousands of nesting Silver Gulls.

On the north coast you might like to explore **Rhyll Inlet,** an intertidal mangrove wetland, where you can see wading birds such as spoonbills, oyster catchers, herons, egrets, cormorants, the rare bar-tailed Godwit, and the Whimbrel.

Bird-watchers will also love **Swan Lake,** another important breeding habitat for wetland birds.

Elsewhere, walking trails lead through heath and pink granite to **Cape Woolamai,** the island's highest point, where there are fabulous coastal views. From September to April, the cape is home to thousands of short-tailed shearwaters, or muttonbirds as they are sometimes called.

If you want to stay on a bit longer instead of just seeing the parade and dashing off (and I really advise it if you can spare the time), you could take one of the 15 different tours offered by Mike Cleeland and his **Island Nature Tours,** RMB 6080, Cowes, Phillip Island, VIC 3922 (☎ **03/5956 7883**).

Phillip Island Penguin Reserve. Summerland Beach, Phillip Island. ☎ **03/5956 8300.** Admission A\$9.50 (U.S.\$6.65) adults, A\$5 (U.S.\$3.50) children 4–13, A\$24.50 (U.S.\$17.15) family. Visitor center opens 10am; penguins arrive at sunset. Reservations for the Penguin Parade are essential in summer when tickets can be difficult to get, and on weekends and public holidays throughout the year.

The Penguin Parade takes place every night of the year at dusk, when hundreds of little penguins appear at the water's edge, gather together in the shallows, and waddle up the beach toward their burrows in the dunes. They're the smallest of the world's 17 species of penguins, standing just 33 centimeters (13 in.) high, and they're the only penguins that breed on the Australian mainland. Fences and viewing stands were erected in the 1960s to protect the nesting areas. Flash photography is banned because it scares the little guys. Wear a sweater or jacket, since it gets chilly after the sun's gone down. A kiosk selling food opens an hour before the penguins turn up.

If you didn't drive or come on a tour, the **Penguin Parade Bus** (☎ **03/5952 1042,** or 0417/360 370 mobile phone) will pick you up from your accommodation in time to see the action and bring you back again. It costs A\$18 (U.S.\$12.60) round-trip for adults and A\$11 (U.S.\$7.70) for children and includes a prebooked ticket for the Penguin Parade.

Koala Conservation Center. At Fiveways on Phillip Island Tourist Rd., Phillip Island. ☎ **03/ 5956 8300.** Admission A\$4 (U.S.\$2.80) adults, A\$1.50 (U.S.\$1.05) children, A\$10 (U.S.\$7) family. Daily 10am–5pm.

Koalas were introduced to Phillip Island in the 1880s, and at first they thrived in the predator-free environment. However, overpopulation, the introduction of foxes and dogs, and the clearing of the land for farmland, townships, and roads, have all taken their toll. Today you can still see a few koalas in the wild, and the best place to find them is at this sanctuary, which was set up for research and breeding purposes. Visitors can get quite close to them, especially on the elevated boardwalk, which lets you peek into their treetop home. For the best viewing, come around 4pm, when the ordinarily sleepy koalas are on the move.

WHERE TO STAY

Amaroo Park YHA Hostel. Corner of Church and Osborne sts., Cowes (97 Church St., Cowes, VIC 3922). ☎ **03/5952 2548.** Fax 03/5952 3620. E-mail: amaroo@nex.net.au. 100 beds. A\$34 to \$40 (U.S.\$23.80 to \$28) double. A\$17 (U.S.\$11.90) dorm bed (A\$14 /U.S.\$9.80 for YHA members). A\$7 to \$9 (U.S.\$4.90 to \$6.30) tent site. AE, BC, Dc, MC, V.

This clean and friendly youth hostel has the usual lounges, TV room, laundry, and barbecue area, and it serves up breakfast and cheap (A\$5/U.S.\$3.50) evening meals. It runs a free courtesy bus from Melbourne on Tuesday and Friday, leaving Queensbury Hill YHA, Howard Street, North Melbourne at 1pm. It also offers tours to the Penguin Parade for A\$17 (U.S.\$11.90), including the entry ticket.

Beach Park Tourist Caravan Park. 2 Mackenzie Rd., Cowes, Phillip Island, VIC 3922. ☎ **03/5952 2113.** Fax 03/5952 3107. 11 cabins, 50 powered campsites. A\$55 (U.S.\$38.50) cabin for two; A\$18 (U.S.\$12.60) campsite for two. Additional person A\$4 (U.S.\$2.80) extra at campsite; A\$5 (U.S.\$3.50) extra in cabin (except children under 3). BC, MC, V.

A 30-foot curtain of tea trees is all that separates this caravan park from the nearest beach. Cabins are quite large, with a balcony, a full kitchen with microwave, a bathroom with toilet and shower, and a TV. Each can sleep up to five people in a double bed and three bunks. Also on the site are communal bathrooms, a good heated outdoor pool, a children's playground, a coin-op laundry, barbecues, and a recreation room with Ping-Pong and billiards. Campsites have electrical power and sewer hookups.

Penguin Hill Country House B&B. At Backbeach and Ventnor rds. (RMB 1093, Cowes, Phillip Island, VIC 3922). ☎ and fax **03/5956 8777.** 3 units. A$120 (U.S.$84) double. Rates include cooked breakfast. BC, MC, V. Not suitable for children.

This private home with views over sheep paddocks to Bass Strait is within walking distance of the Penguin Parade. Each room has good views and is stocked with antiques (as is much of the house) and queen-size beds. Two have an attached bathroom with shower, and the third has a private bathroom across the hall. There's a TV and a phone in the cozy lounge. The hosts can pick you up from Cowes.

WHERE TO DINE

Isola di Capri, at the Esplanade and Thompson Avenue in Cowes (☎ **03/ 5952 2435**), offers good Italian food with main courses costing between A$8.50 and $17.50 (U.S.$5.95–$12.25). This is one of many restaurants and cafes in Cowes. You can also get good-value counter meals at the **Isle of White Hotel** (there's a buffet restaurant upstairs).

AROUND PORT PHILLIP BAY

West of Melbourne, the **Princes Freeway** (or M1) heads towards Geelong via a bypass at Werribee, while to the east, the **Nepean Highway** travels along the coast to the Mornington Peninsula as far as Portsea. If you have time to stay the night, you can combine the two options, heading first down to the Mornington Peninsula (see below) and then taking the car and passenger ferry from Sorrento to Queenscliff on the Bellarine Peninsula.

Theoretically, it's even possible to start off early from Melbourne, visit Geelong, tour the Great Ocean Road farther east (see chapter 14), stop off overnight, and then dash back to Melbourne, though I suggest that you slow down and enjoy yourself at a more leisurely pace.

WERRIBEE

This small country town is located 32 kilometers (19¼ miles) southwest of Melbourne, a 30-minute drive away. Trains run from Melbourne to Werribee station; a taxi from the station to the zoo will cost around A$5 (U.S.$3.50).

Victoria's Open Range Zoo at Werribee. K Rd., Werribee. ☎ **03/9731 9600.** Admission A$14 (U.S.$9.80) adults, A$7 (U.S.$4.90) children under 14, A$38 (U.S.$26.60) family. Daily 9am–5pm (entrance gate closes at 3:30pm). Safari tours hourly 10am–4pm.

From inside your zebra-striped safari bus you can nearly touch the mainly African animals that wander almost freely over the plains—no depressing cages here. This high-caliber open-air zoo is closely associated with the Melbourne Zoo. There is also a walk-through section featuring African cats, including cheetahs and monkeys.

Werribee Park Mansion. K Rd., Werribee. ☎ **03/9741 2444.** Park and picnic grounds free; admission to mansion A$10 (U.S.$7) adults, A$5 (U.S.$3.50) children 5–15, A$26 (U.S.$18.20) family. Nov–March daily 10am–5pm; Apr–Oct daily 10am–4pm. Closed Christmas Day.

Known as "the palace in the paddock," this 60-room Italianate mansion was built in 1877. It was quite the extravagant project in its day. In addition to touring the house, you may want to stroll around the grounds and have a picnic; the mansion is surrounded by 325 acres of bushland fronting onto the Werribee River. You can also prearrange to take one of the popular carriage rides that make their way through the property.

GEELONG

Victoria's second largest city, Geelong, lies 72 kilometers (43¼ miles) southwest of Melbourne. It's an industrial center, not really of note to visitors except as the home of the National Wool Museum. Geelong is a 45-minute drive from Melbourne. There's regular train service from Melbourne, and the museum is just a couple of blocks from the station.

You can pick up brochures and book accommodations through the **Geelong & Great Ocean Road Visitor Information Center,** Stead Park, Princes Highway, Geelong (☎ **1800/620 888** in Australia, or 03/5275 5797; www.greatoceanroad.org.au). The office is open daily from 9am to 5pm.

National Wool Museum. 26 Moorabool St., Geelong. ☎ **03/5227 0701.** Admission A$7 (U.S.$4.90) adults, A$3.50 (U.S.$2.45) children under 16 A$18 (U.S.$12.60) family. Daily 9:30am–5pm. Closed Christmas Day and Good Friday.

For Australians in colonial time, the sheep was the lifeblood of the nation, providing food and warm wool; profits to the landlords; and jobs to shearers, stockmen, and farmhands. This fascinating museum tells the story, from how sheepdogs work to how the sheep are sheared. You'll also see an interesting collection of gadgets used to create products from wool, such as a sock-knitting machine. There is also a reconstructed shearers' hut and a 1920s mill worker's cottage, as well as a specialty wool store, a gift shop, and a bistro.

THE MORNINGTON PENINSULA
80km (48 miles) south of Melbourne

The Mornington Peninsula, a scenic 40-kilometer (24-mile) stretch of windswept coastline and hinterland, is one of Melbourne's favorite day trips and weekend getaways. The coast is lined with good beaches and thick bush, consisting almost entirely of tea trees (early colonists used them as a tea substitute). The **Cape Schanck Coastal Park** stretches from Portsea to Cape Schanck. It's home to gray kangaroos, Southern Brown bandicoots, echidnas, native rats, mice, reptiles, bats, and many forest and ocean birds.

Along the route south you could stop off at the **Morning Peninsula Regional Gallery,** 4 Vancouver St., Mornington (☎ **03/5975 4395**), to check out the work of famous Australian artists, or visit **Arthurs Seat State Park** to take a short hike or ride a chairlift to a 305-meter (1,000-foot) summit offering glorious views over the surrounding bush. At Sorrento, take time out to spot pelicans on the jetty or visit the town's many galleries.

ESSENTIALS
GETTING THERE   From Melbourne, take the Mornington Peninsula Freeway to Rosebud, and then the Point Nepean Road. If you want to cross Port Phillip Bay from Sorrento to Queenscliff, take the **Queenscliff Sea Road Ferry** (☎ **03/5258 3255;** fax 03/5258 1877), which operates daily every 2 hours from 8am to 6pm. (There's an 8pm ferry on Fri and Sat from mid-Sept to mid-Dec, and daily from mid-Dec until Easter Thur.) Ferries from Queenscliff operate from 7am to 5pm (plus a 7pm ferry on days listed above). The fare is A$32 to $34 (U.S.$19.20 to $23.80) for cars, depending on season, plus A$3 (U.S.$2.19) for adults, A$2 (U.S.$1.40) for children ages 5 to 15,

and A$1 (U.S.70¢) for children age 4 and under. Passenger-only fares are A$7 (U.S.$4.90) for adults, A$5 (U.S.$3.50) for children ages 5 to 15, and A$1 (U.S.70¢) for children under age 4. The crossing takes 35 to 40 minutes.

VISITOR INFORMATION   The **Peninsula Visitor Information Center,** Point Nepean Road, Dromana (☎ **1800/804 009** in Australia, or 03/5987 3078), has plenty of maps and information on the area and can also help book accommodations. It's open daily from 9am to 5pm. You can get more information on this and all the other Victorian National Parks by calling ☎ 13 19 63, or via the Internet at www.parks.vic.gov.au.

FOR MAZE & GARDEN BUFFS

Ashcombe Maze & Water Gardens. Red Hill Rd., Shoreham, on the Mornington Peninsula. ☎ **03/5989 8387.** Admission A$7 (U.S.$4.90) adults, A$4 (U.S.$2.80) children. Daily 10am–5pm.

Here you'll find Australia's oldest and most famous maze, as well as extensive water and woodland gardens. There is even a rose maze, made of 1300 rose bushes, which is spectacular when in full bloom over the spring and summer months.

WHERE TO STAY

For super-cheap sleeps, head to the **Sorrento YHA Hostel,** 3 Miranda St., Sorrento, VIC 3943 (☎ and fax **03/5984 4323**). A dorm room here costs A$14 (U.S.$9.80) for YHA members and A$17 (U.S.$11.90) for nonmembers, and the two double rooms cost between A$40 and $60 (U.S.$28 to $42), depending on the season.

The Portsea Hotel. 3746 Point Nepean Rd., Portsea, VIC 3944. ☎ **03/5984 2213.** Fax 03/5984 4066. www.portseahotel.com.au. 34 units, 8 with bathroom (most with shower only). A$35 (U.S.$24.50) single without bathroom; A$60 (U.S.$42) double without bathroom; A$110 (U.S.$77) double with bathroom; A$140 (U.S.$98) bay view suite. AE, BC, DC, MC. V.

The rooms in this typical Australian motel right on the seafront are done up in country-style furnishings. The standard twin rooms are quite basic, and all share bathrooms. None have a TV, but all have tea- and coffee-making facilities. En suite doubles have a double bed and TV and an attached bathroom with shower. There's a reasonable bistro and three bars downstairs, as well as a terraced beer garden and another outdoor bar.

14

Victoria

by Marc Llewellyn

Australia's southernmost mainland state is astoundingly diverse. Within its boundaries are 35 national parks, encompassing every possible terrain, from rain forest and snow-capped mountain ranges to sun-baked Outback desert and a coast where waves crash dramatically onto rugged sandstone outcroppings.

Melbourne (see chapter 13) may be this rugged state's heart, but the mighty Murray River, which separates Victoria from New South Wales, is its lifeblood, providing irrigation for vast tracks of semidesert land.

Most visitors to Victoria start out exploring Melbourne's cosmopolitan streets and then visit a few local wineries before heading for the gold fields around the historic city of Ballarat. Lots of them only experience a fraction of Victoria as a blur whizzing by the window of their rental car, but this wonderful and not overly touristed region is worth spending some quality time on.

Visitors with more time might make their way inland to the mountains (perhaps for skiing or bushwalking at Mount Hotham or Falls Creek), or seek out the wilderness of the Snowy River National Park. Others head to the Outback, to the Grampians National Park, and onward to Mildura, through open deserts and past pink lakes and red sand dunes.

Lots of options await you, and because much of it is out in the country, you'll find prices for accommodations are very affordable, or you could rent a campervan and save even more on hotel bills. Whatever itinerary you choose, you're sure to find adventure and dramatic scenery.

EXPLORING THE STATE

VISITOR INFORMATION Pick up brochures and maps at the **Victorian Visitors Information Centre,** Melbourne Town Hall, Swanston Street, at the corner of Little Collins Street (☎ **1800/ 63 77 63** in Australia, or 03/9658 9955; fax 03/9650 1212), or call **the Victorian Tourism Information Service** (☎ **13 28 42**) from anywhere in Australia to talk to a consultant about your plans. The service, open daily from 8am to 6pm, will also send out brochures. If you need information along the way, look for blue road signs with a yellow information symbol.

GETTING AROUND If you fly into Melbourne and then want to drive around the rest of Victoria, the major car-rental companies are **Avis,** 400 Elizabeth St. (☎ 1800/225 533 in Australia, or 03/9663 6366); **Budget,** 11 Queens Rd. (☎ 13 27 27 in Australia; **Hertz,**

Victoria

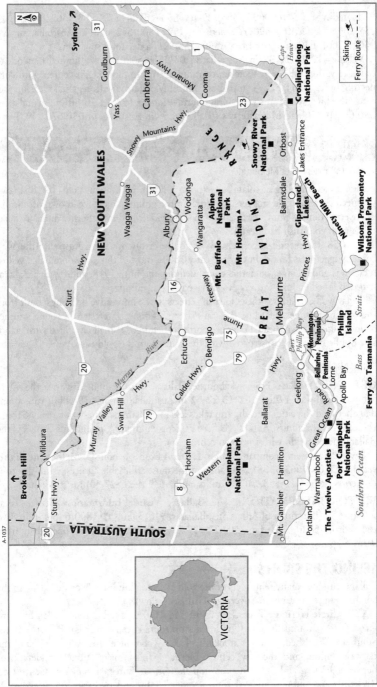

Skiing 🎿
Ferry Route - - - -

Sydney 🡵
[31]
Goulburn
Yass
Canberra
Cooma
Monaro Hwy.
[1]
Cape Howe
[23]
Croajingolong National Park

NEW SOUTH WALES
Snowy Mountains
Wagga Wagga
[31]
Snowy River National Park
Orbost
Lakes Entrance

Albury
Wodonga
Wangaratta
Mt. Buffalo ▲
Alpine National Park
Mt. Hotham ▲
Bairnsdale
Gippsland Lakes
Ninety Mile Beach

Sturt Hwy.
[16]
Freeway
Hume
GREAT DIVIDING RANGE
Princes Hwy.
Wilsons Promontory National Park

[20]
Murray River
Echuca
Bendigo
[75]
Hume
[79]
Melbourne
Bass Strait

Swan Hill
Murray Valley Hwy.
[79]
Calder Hwy.
Geelong
Bellarine Peninsula
Lorne
Apollo Bay
Mornington Peninsula
Port Phillip Bay
Phillip Island
Ferry to Tasmania

Mildura
Broken Hill 🡸
Sturt Hwy.
Horsham
Western Hwy.
[8]
Ballarat
Gramplans National Park
Great Ocean Road
Warrnambool
The Twelve Apostles
Port Campbell National Park
Southern Ocean

Mt. Gambier
Portland
Hamilton
[1]
[20]
SOUTH AUSTRALIA

A-1037

VICTORIA

603

97 Franklin St. (☎ 03/9698 2555); **Delta,** 85 Franklin St. (☎ 03/9662 2399, or 13 13 90); and **Thrifty,** 390 Elizabeth St. (☎ 1800/652 008 in Australia, or 03/ 9663 5200). Expect to pay from A$30 (U.S.$21) a day for a small car.

V/Line (☎ **13 22 32** in Australia, or 03/9619 5000) runs a limited network of trains to various places in Victoria, continuing trips to most major centers with connecting buses. Several bus companies connect Melbourne with regional areas of Victoria; the biggest operators are **Greyhound-Pioneer** (☎ 13 20 30 in Australia, or 03/9600 1687), and **McCafferty's** (☎ 13 14 99 in Australia, or 03/9670 2533).

1 Ballarat: Gold-Rush City

113km (68 miles) W of Melbourne

Ballarat, Victoria's largest inland city (pop. 90,000), is all about gold. In 1851, two prospectors found gold nuggets scattered on the ground at a place known, ironically, as Poverty Point. Within a year, 20,000 people had drifted into the area and Australia's El Dorado gold rush had begun.

In 1858, the second-largest chunk of gold ever discovered in Australia (the Welcome Nugget) was found, but by the early 1860s, most of the easily obtainable yellow metal was gone. Larger operators continued digging until 1918, and by then Ballarat had developed enough industry to survive without mining.

Today, you can still see the gold rush's effects in the impressive buildings, built from the miners' fortunes, that line Ballarat's streets. If you're interested in seeing another former mining town, head 1½ hours north to Bendigo, a small city filled with elaborate public buildings constructed with the gains from the gold rush.

ESSENTIALS

GETTING THERE   From Melbourne, Ballarat is a 1½-hour drive via the Great Western Highway. **V/Line** (☎ **13 22 32** in Australia, or 03/9619 5000) runs trains daily between the cities, and the trip takes less than 2 hours. One-way fare is A$13.40 (U.S.$9.40) for adults, A$6.70 (U.S.$4.70) for children. A public bus connects the Ballarat train station with the town center.

Several sightseeing companies offer day trips from Melbourne. **Melbourne Sightseeing** (☎ **03/9663 3388**), offers one of the most affordable choices, a full-day tour that costs A$77 (U.S.$53.90) for adults, and A$39 (U.S.$27.30) for children.

VISITOR INFORMATION   The **Ballarat Visitor Information Centre** is at 39 Sturt St. (the corner of Albert St.), Ballarat, VIC 3350 (☎ **1800/648 450** in Australia, or 03/5320 5741; fax 03/5332 7977; www.ballarat.com). It's open daily from 9am to 5pm.

SEEING THE SIGHTS

Ballarat contains many reminders of the gold-rush era, but it really comes to life in the colonial-era re-creation on **Sovereign Hill** (see below).

City Circle Heritage Tours (☎ **0500 544 169**) uses red double-decker buses to ferry visitors around the city. The seven-stop route covers Sovereign Hill, the Great Southern Woolshed, Eureka Stockade, Lake Wendouree, the Wildlife Park, the railway station, and the city center. Heritage Tours makes nine complete trips between 9:30am and 3:30pm (last stop 4:40pm at Eureka Interactive Centre) on weekends and public holidays from Sovereign Hill, and two trips on weekdays— one starting at 9:30am and another at 2pm from Sovereign Hill. Get off at one stop and catch another bus later. Tickets cost A$8 (U.S.$5.60) for adults, and A$4 (U.S.$2.80) for children.

✪ **Sovereign Hill Goldmining Township.** Bradshaw St. ☎ **03/5331 1944.** Admission (including mine tour and admission to Gold Museum) A$19.50 (U.S.$13.65) adults, A$9.50 (U.S.$6.65) children 5–15, A$52 (U.S.$36.40) families (2 adults and up to 4 children); free for children under 5. Daily 10am–5pm. Closed Christmas Day. Bus: From Ballarat catch the Buninyong bus.

Australia's best outdoor museum transports you back to the 1850s and the heady days of the gold rush. More than 40 stone and wood reproduction buildings, including shops and businesses on the re-created Main Street, sit on this 60-acre former gold-mining site. There are also tent camps around the diggings on the lowest part of the site, which would have been the outskirts of town. There's lots to see and do here, so expect to spend at least 4 hours.

The township bustles with actors in period costumes going about their daily business. In addition to seeing how miners and their families lived, visitors can pan for real gold, watch lessons in Victorian classrooms, ride in horse-drawn carriages, and watch potters, blacksmiths, and tanners make their wares.

On top of Sovereign Hill are the mine shafts. The fascinating tour of a typical underground gold mine takes around 45 minutes.

The **Voyage to Discovery** museum has various artifacts from the gold rush, dioramas of mining scenes, and interactive computer displays.

A restaurant and several cafes, coffee shops, and souvenir stores can be found around the site.

The Gold Museum. Bradshaw St. (opposite Sovereign Hill), Ballarat. ☎ **03/5337 1107.** Admission included with Sovereign Hill ticket; otherwise A$5.30 (U.S.$3.70) adults, A$2.60 (U.S.$1.75) children. Daily 9:30am–5:20pm.

This interesting museum houses a large collection of gold nuggets found at Ballarat, as well as alluvial deposits, gold ornaments, and coins. There are also gallery displays relating to the history of gold mining in the area.

Blood on the Southern Cross. At Sovereign Hill, Bradshaw St. ☎ **03/5333 5777.** Fax 03/5332 9740. Reservations required. Admission A$23.50 (U.S.$16.45) adults, A$12 (U.S.$8.40) children 5–15, A$65 (U.S.$45.50) families. Other packages include daytime entry to Sovereign Hill: A$40 (U.S.$28) adults, A$20.50 (U.S.$14.35) children, and A$111 (U.S.$77.70) families. Call ahead for information about other packages. 2 shows nightly Mon–Sat (times vary seasonally). Usually closed the first 2 weeks of August (but call first).

This 80-minute show re-creates the Eureka Uprising, one of the most important events in Australia's history, in a breathtaking sound-and-light show that covers Sovereign Hill's 25 hectares (62 acres). Bring something warm to wear, because it can get chilly.

After gold was discovered, the government devised a system of gold licenses, charging miners a monthly fee, even if they came up empty-handed. The miners had to buy a new license every month, and corrupt gold-field police (many of whom were former convicts) instituted a vicious campaign to extract the money.

When license checks intensified in 1854, even though most of the surface gold was gone, resentment flared; prospectors began demanding political reforms, such as the right to vote, parliamentary elections, and secret ballots.

The situation exploded when the owner of the Eureka Hotel murdered a miner and was let off scot free by the government. The hotel was burned down in revenge, and more than 20,000 prospectors joined together and burned their licenses in a huge bonfire, and built a stockade over which they raised a flag.

Troops arrived at the Eureka Stockade the following month, but by then only 150 miners remained behind its walls. The stockade was attacked at dawn, and in the 15-minute skirmish, 24 miners were killed and 30 wounded. The civil uprising forced the government to act. The licenses were replaced with miners rights and cheaper fees, and the vote was introduced to Victoria.

Eureka Stockade Centre. Eureka St. ☎ **03/5333 1854.** Admission A$8 (U.S.$5.60) adults, A$4 (U.S.$2.80) children, and A$22 (U.S.$15.40) families. Daily 9am–5pm. Closed Christmas.

You can't miss this building with its huge sail, signifying the flag of the southern cross, which was raised above the original miners' stockade. Relive the action of the battle through multimedia displays. The Contemplation Room, where you are asked to think about Australian history while listening to trickling water, is a bit too hokey for me.

Ballarat Fine Art Gallery. 40 Lydiard St. North, Ballarat. ☎ **03/5331 5622.** Admission A$4 (U.S.$2.80) adults, A$1(U.S.70¢) children 6–16. Daily 10:30am–5pm. Closed Good Friday and Christmas.

After you've learned the story of the Eureka uprising, you may find it moving to come here and see the original Eureka flag. This provincial gallery also houses a large collection of Australian art, including works by Sydney Nolan, Fred Williams, and Russell Drysdale. Look out for Tom Roberts' *Charcoal Burners* and Phillip Fox's *Love Story.*

WHERE TO STAY & DINE

The Ansonia. 32 Lydiard St. South, Ballarat 3350. ☎ **03/5332 4678.** Fax 03/5332 4698. 20 units. TV TEL. A$115 (U.S.$80.50) double; A$130 (U.S.$91) executive double; A$150 (U.S.$101.50) suite; A$180 (U.S.$126) family room; A$180 (U.S.$126) apt. AE, BC, DC, MC, V.

This boutique hotel in a restored Victorian building sports a glass atrium that runs the length of the property and is filled with plants and wicker chairs. Studio rooms are simply but comfortably furnished, and have nice polished floorboards. The executive doubles are larger and a little more plush. The two family rooms can sleep four people in two bedrooms. There is a comfortable library and sitting room, and plenty of flowers and art are scattered everywhere. Smoking is not allowed on the property.

The hotel restaurant acts as more of a cafe during the day and a Mediterranean-style restaurant at night. It serves up such fare as homemade pies, soups, curries, meat dishes, and a great gorgonzola soufflé on a bed of forest mushrooms.

The Sovereign Hill Lodge. Magpie St., Ballarat, VIC 3350. ☎ **03/5333 3409.** Fax 03/5333 5861. A/C TV TEL. A$98 (U.S.$68.60) double or family room; A$108–$125 (US$76–$87.50) heritage room. Additional person A$10 (U.S.$7) extra. A$18 (U.S.$12.60) dorm bed (A$16/U.S.$11.20 for YHA members). Ask about packages. AE, BC, DC, MC, V.

The colonial-style wooden buildings adjacent to the Sovereign Hill Goldmining Township were built to resemble an 1850s Government Camp. (Camps were used to control—and tax—the mine fields.) The Residence building has rooms with queen-size beds and a set of single bunks. The Offices building has heritage rooms with four-poster beds and plenty of pine furnishings, some with Jacuzzis. There are eight double rooms in the Superintendent's house, while the Barracks has dorm rooms that sleep up to eight people. There's a bar, 24-hour reception, and a game room on the grounds. Guests get a 10% discount off entry to Sovereign Hill.

WORTH A SPLURGE

Ballarat Heritage Homestay. 185 Victoria St., (P.O. Box 1360, Ballarat Mail Centre, VIC 3354). ☎ **1800/813 369** in Australia, or 03/5332 8296. Fax 03/5331 3358. www. ballarat.com./homestay.htm. 5 cottages, 1 B&B unit. TEL (available on request) TV. A$250–$320 (U.S.$175–$224) for 2 people for 2-night weekend stay; A$120–$150 (U.S.$175–$224) weekday night. Additional person A$25 (U.S.$17.50) extra, children under 18 A$15 (U.S.$10.50) extra. Rates include a cook-your-own breakfast. AE, BC, DC, MC, V.

If you'd enjoy staying in a historic cottage, you might want to try Ballarat Heritage Homestay. Some of these Victorian and Edwardian cottages date back to gold-rush days. All of them are very different. Three cottages have claw-foot bathtubs, and one has a Jacuzzi. Generally, each cottage has a queen, a double, and two single beds.

WHERE TO DINE

Lake Pavilion Restaurant Café. Wendouree Parade (across from the Botanical Gardens). ☎ **03/5334 1811.** Fax 03/5334 1665. Menu items A$7.50–$12.90 (U.S.$5.25–$9). AE, BC, MC, V. Daily 9am–6pm. Bus: 15 Mon–Sat. INTERNATIONAL.

I like this restaurant on the shores of Lake Wendouree and across from the Botanical Gardens. The Lake Pavilion was constructed in 1890 and still has that old-world atmosphere, with polished floorboards and high ceilings. Whether you eat indoors or outside, you have some good views across the gardens and the lake. The menu includes pizzas, focaccia sandwiches, various pasta dishes, salads, steaks, and seafood. It's licensed, but you can also bring your own wine (corkage fee A$5/U.S.$3.50 a bottle). A kiosk adjacent to the restaurant sells snacks.

Robin Hood Family Bistro. 33 Peel St. N. ☎ **03/5361 3433.** Fax 03/5331 7168. Reservations recommended Fri–Sat. Main courses A$8.95–$17.95 (U.S.$6.25–$12.55); salad bar A$5 (U.S.$3.50). AE, BC, DC, MC, V. Daily 11:30am–2pm and 5:30–8pm. AUSTRALIAN HOTEL BISTRO.

The Robin Hood is located in a big old pub—not exactly a place where you'd expect to find a bistro catering to healthy eating. But everything here is made with low-fat, low-cholesterol ingredients. On the menu you'll find steak-and-kidney pie, beef curry, and several types of steak. Not healthy so far, I hear you say, but there is an extensive salad bar and all main courses come with a healthy dollop of vegetables.

2 The Great Ocean Road: One of the World's Most Scenic Drives

Geelong: 75km (45 miles) SW of Melbourne; Torquay: 94km (56½ miles) SW of Melbourne; Port Campbell National Park: 285km (171 miles) SW of Melbourne; Peterborough 200km (120 miles) SW of Melbourne.

✪ **The Great Ocean Road**—which hugs the coast from Torquay, and onward through Anglesea, Lorne, Apollo Bay, and Port Campbell, until it ends at Peterborough—is one of Australia's most spectacular drives (many say it's the best). The scenery along the 106-kilometer (63½ -mile) route includes huge cliffs, ocean vistas, beaches, rain forests, and some incredible rock formations. The settlements along the highway are small, but they offer a number of choices of where to stay.

In the early years of the colony, some 163 ships sank along the coastline between Port Phillip Bay and Nelson while trying to navigate the Great Circle Route from England to Australia, earning the formidable coastline the title "The Shipwreck Coast."

The best way to travel along the Great Ocean Road is to drive yourself at a leisurely pace, stopping off wherever your fancy takes you. The main attractions are in the coastal **Port Campbell National Park,** so don't be surprised if you're not overly impressed until you get there. If you are traveling on to Adelaide, you could stop off for one night along the Great Ocean Road, and spend another night in the Coorong in South Australia.

ESSENTIALS

ORGANIZED TOURS   Melbourne Sightseeing (☎ 03/9663 3388) offers a bus trip featuring the highlights of the Great Ocean Road. The bus leaves Melbourne daily at 8:45am and returns at 9:15pm. It costs A$83 (U.S.$58.10) for adults (A$50/U.S.$35 if you have a YHA card), and A$42 (U.S.$29.40) for children

(A$38/U.S.$26.60 with a YHA card). The trip can be stretched out over 2 days, with overnight accommodations in the YHA in Lorne for A$129 (U.S.$90.30). **Grayline Sightseeing Tours** (☎ 02/9663 4455) also has daily trips.

Another option worth considering is a 2-day excursion with **Let's Go Bush Tours** (☎ 03/9662 3999), which departs Melbourne every Wednesday to Saturday. The trip is less rushed than others, and you get to stay in the company's own house, situated on the highest point of the Great Ocean Road. The trip costs A$89 (U.S.$62.30), including dinner, breakfast, and accommodations.

Wild-Life Tours (☎ 03/9747 1882) also offers a 2-day tour for A$69 (U.S.$48.30), a 3-day tour including the Grampians for A$120 (U.S.$84), and a one-way fare from Melbourne to Adelaide along the Great Ocean Road for A$119 (U.S.$83.30). Prices do not include accommodations or food.

V/Line (☎ 13 22 32 in Australia, or 03/9619 5000) runs a special combined train-coach Coast Link service as far as Warrnambool, via Geelong, Lorne, Apollo Bay, and Port Campbell. The train leaves Melbourne every Friday at 8:49am; you transfer to a bus at Geelong. The bus tours the Great Ocean Road, stopping off at various lookout points (and for lunch), and then carries on to Warrnambool. At 5:35pm, passengers catch the train back to Melbourne. There's an extra service every Monday in December and January. The trip costs A$66.40 (U.S.$46.50) for adults, and A$33.20 (U.S.$23.24) for children.

VISITOR INFORMATION   Most places along the route have their own information centers. If you're coming from Melbourne, stop at the **Geelong & Great Ocean Road Visitors Centre,** Stead Park, Princess Highway, Geelong, VIC 3220 (☎ 1800/620 888 in Australia, or 03/5275 5797; fax 03/5223 2969; www.greatoceanrd.org.au). You can book accommodations here. It's a good idea to book accommodations well in advance during summer. There's also a visitor center at the **National Wool Museum,** 26 Moorabool St., Geelong (☎ 03/5222 2900).

Along the route, the **Park Information Centre,** at Port Campbell National Park, Norris Street, Port Campbell (☎ 03/5598 6382), is another good place to pick up brochures. It also has some interesting displays and an audiovisual show of the area.

If you're approaching from the north, visit the **Camperdown Visitor Information Centre,** "Court House," Manifold Street, Princes Highway, Camperdown (☎ 03/5593 3390).

The information centers are open daily from 9am to 5pm (the one at the Wool Museum is closed Sundays).

EXPLORING THE COASTAL ROAD

Along the route you might want to stop off at **Torquay,** a township dedicated to surfing. The main surf beach here is much nicer than the one farther down the coast in Lorne. While here, you might want to stop off at **Surfworld,** Surfcoast Plaza Beach Road, West Torquay (☎ 03/5261 4606). It has interactive exhibits on surfboard design and surfing history, as well as the world's best surfers captured on video. Admission is A$5 (U.S.$3.50) for adults, A$3 (U.S.$2.10) for children, and A$13 (U.S.$9.10) for families. **Bells Beach,** just down the road, is world famous in surfing circles for its perfect waves.

Lorne has some nice boutiques and is a good place to stop for lunch or stay the night. Behind the town is a rain forest and a nice river estuary. The trip from Lorne to Apollo Bay is one of the most spectacular sections of the route, as the road narrows and twists and turns along a cliff edge with the ocean on the other side. **Apollo Bay** itself is a pleasant town that was once a whaling station. It has good sandy beaches and is much more low-key than Lorne.

Next, you come to the **Angahook-Lorne State Park,** which protects most of the coastal section of the Otway Ranges from Aireys Inlet, just south of Anglesea, to the Kennett River. It has plenty of well-marked rain-forest walks and picnic areas at Shelly Beach, Elliot River, and Blanket Bay. There's plenty of wildlife around here.

About 13 kilometers (8 miles) past Apollo Bay, just off the main road, you can take an elevated stroll through the rain forest on the **Maits Rest Rainforest Boardwalk.** A little farther along the main road, an unsealed (unpaved) road leads north past Hopetoun Falls and Beauchamp Falls to the settlement of **Beech Forest.** Seven kilometers (4¼ miles) farther along the main road, another unsealed road heads off south for 15 kilometers (9 miles) to the windswept headland and the **Cape Otway Lighthouse.** Built by convicts in 1848, the 100-meter- (328-ft.-) tall lighthouse is open to tourists daily. Entry costs A$5 (U.S.$3.50), but call Parks Victoria (☎ 03/5237 9240) beforehand because opening times vary.

Back on the main road, your route heads inland through an area known as **Horden Vale,** before running to the sea again at **Glenaire.** (There's good surfing and camping at Johanna, 6km/3½ miles north of here.) Then the Great Ocean Road heads north again to **Lavers Hill,** a former timber town. Five kilometers (3 miles) southwest of Lavers Hill is the small **Melba Gully State Park,** where you can spot glowworms at night and walk through a rain forest. Keep an eye out for one of the last **giant gum trees** that escaped the loggers—it's some 27 meters (88¾ ft.) in circumference and is estimated to be more than 300 years old.

The next place of note is **Moonlight Head,** which marks the start of the Shipwreck Coast, a 120-kilometer (72-mile) stretch of coastline running to Port Fairy, which claimed more than 80 ships in just 40 years at the end of the 19th century and the beginning of the 20th.

Just past Princetown starts the biggest attraction of the entire trip, the ✪ **Port Campbell National Park,** which with its sheer cliffs and coastal rock sculptures is one of the most immediately recognizable images of natural Australia. You can't miss the **Twelve Apostles,** a series of rock pillars that stand in the foam just offshore. Other attractions are the **Blowhole,** which throws up huge sprays of water; the **Grotto,** a baroque rock formation intricately carved by the waves; **London Bridge,** which looked quite like the real thing until the center crashed into the sea in 1990, leaving a bunch of tourists stranded on the wrong end; and the **Loch Ard Gorge.**

Port Fairy, a lovely fishing town once known as Belfast by Irish immigrants who settled here to escape the potato famine, is also on the Shipwreck Coast.

Not far past the town of Peterborough, the Great Ocean Road heads inland to Warrnambool and eventually joins the Princes Highway heading towards Adelaide.

WHERE TO STAY ALONG THE WAY

The **Great Ocean Road Accommodation Centre,** 136 Mountjoy Parade, Lorne, VIC 3232 (☎ **03/5289 1800**), rents out cottages and units along the route.

IN LORNE

Lorne is a good option for a night's rest. Although the beach and water are nothing special, there are plenty of restaurants.

✪ **Cumberland Lorne Conference & Leisure Resort.** 150–178 Mountjoy Parade, Lorne, VIC 3232. ☎ **1800/037 010** in Australia, or 03/5289 2400. Fax 03/5289 2256. 99 units. TV TEL. A$175–$240 (U.S.$122.50–$168) 1-bedroom apt., A$230–$250 (U.S.$161–$175) in summer; A$220–$240 (U.S.$154–$168) 2-bedroom apt., A$265–$285 (U.S.$186–$200) in summer; A$270–$290 (U.S.$189–$203) penthouse, A$315–$335 (U.S.$220.50–$235) in summer. Ask about packages. AE, BC, DC, MC, V.

This sporty resort, built in 1988 but already crumbling around the edges, stands out like a sore thumb from its location between the sea and the foothills of the Otway Ranges. Still, I highly recommend it, as it's a good value and quite luxurious. Every apartment has a queen-size bed and a fold-out sofa bed, a large kitchen, a laundry, a Jacuzzi, a balcony, and free in-house movies. All have large bathrooms with a shower-tub combination. More than half the rooms have panoramic ocean views, while the rest look out onto gardens. Two-bedroom apartments have two extra single beds, and split-level penthouses have two Jacuzzis and two balconies. There's an indoor heated pool, a spa, a sauna, a gym, barbecues, two squash courts, two tennis courts, and free use of bicycles, surfboards, and body boards. A kids' club makes life easier for Mom and Dad, and there's a good restaurant on the premises, too.

An off-season package—available any time except between December 24 and the end of January, and Easter—includes one night's accommodation and breakfast for two people for just A$158 (U.S.$110.60).

Great Ocean Road Cottages. 10 Erskine Ave. (P.O. Box 60), Lorne, VIC 3232. ☎ **03/5289 1070.** Fax 03/5289 2508. 10 cottages, 7 apts., dorms sleeping 33. A$95–$185 (U.S.$66.50–$129.50) cottages and A$100–$185 (US$70–$129.50) apts., depending on season. Dorm bed A$16 (U.S.$11.20) for YHA members and A$18 (U.S.$12.60) for nonmembers off-season, and A$16 (U.S.$11.20) for members and A$28 (U.S.$19.60) for nonmembers during peak periods (from Christmas to end of Jan, Easter, and public holidays). AE, BC, DC, MC, V.

This complex has it all, although with so many people around (and quite a few children), it can be a little noisy in summer. There's a set of self-contained cottages, set away from each other in a quiet patch of bushland, about a 5-minute walk from the town center. Each cottage is a two-story wooden hut with a double bed, two twin beds, and a pull-out mattress. Each cottage also has a bathroom and a full kitchen.

Also on the property is **Great Ocean Road Backpackers,** which offers dorm-style accommodations and a few family rooms. Just down the road is **Waverley House,** a historic mansion that has been divided into seven apartments. All of them are nice, but they vary enormously.

IN APOLLO BAY

Caravans costing from A$25 (U.S.$17.50) to A$40 (U.S.$28), and tent sites from A$12 (U.S.$8.40) to A$15 (U.S.$10.50) are available at the **Recreation Reserve** (☎ 03/5237 6577), located on the Great Ocean Road just 1 kilometer (half a mile) from the center of town. The **Surfside Backpackers YHA,** 7 Gambier St., Apollo Bay (☎ 03/5237 7263) is almost on the oceanfront and offers dorm beds for A$12 (U.S.$8.40) to A$15 (U.S.$10.50), and doubles from A$35 (U.S.$24.50).

Bayside Gardens. 219 Great Ocean Rd., Apollo Bay, VIC 3233. ☎ and fax **03/5237 6248.** 10 units. TV. A$55–$110 (U.S.$38.50–$77) 1-bedroom apts. Higher rates apply Christmas, January, Easter, and public holidays. 1-week minimum stay in Jan. BC, MC, V.

Right opposite the beach, with good ocean views from the front rooms, Bayside Gardens is a pleasant place to stay. The units all have a separate bedroom with a double bed, a lounge area, a full kitchen, and an attached bathroom with shower. Rooms at the front can be noisy if you're not used to living beside an ocean. Some units have fireplaces.

IN PORT CAMPBELL

The **Port Campbell Caravan Park,** Tregea St. (☎ 03/5598 6492; fax 03/55986 471) has campsites for A$10 (U.S.$7) to A$20 (U.S.$14) and 15 good cabins with their own bathroom and television from A$50 (U.S.$35) to A$80 (U.S.$56), depending on the season. The **Port Campbell Youth Hostel** (☎ and fax **03/5598 6305**) offers dorm beds for A$13 (U.S.$9.10) for YHA members and A$16 (U.S.$11.20) for nonmembers.

Macka's Farm. RSD 2305 Princetown Rd., Princetown, VIC 3269. ☎ **03/5598 8261.** Fax 03/5598 8201. Email: macka's@net.com.au. 3 units. A$85–$100 (U.S.$59.50–$70) double, depending on season. Additional person A$15 (U.S.$10.50) extra. AE, BC, DC, MC. V.

This working farm is located 4 kilometers (2½ miles) inland from the Twelve Apostles (continue on from the Twelve Apostles for 2 kilometers (1¼ miles) and turn off at the sign for Macka's Farm; it's another 4 kilometers (2½ miles) from there). Rooms sleep six to eight people in a mixture of singles and doubles. There's no TV, but who needs it when there are so many pigs, cows, ducks, and chickens running around. It's a great farm experience.

WHERE TO DINE IN LORNE

Arab Restaurant. Mountjoy Parade. ☎ **03/5289 1435.** Reservations recommended. Main courses A$10.50–$18.50 (U.S.$7.35–$12.95). AE, BC, MC, V. Christmas–Easter Mon–Fri 9am–9pm, Sat 8am–11pm, Sun 7:30am–10pm. Closed rest of year. INTERNATIONAL.

This popular bistro is not cheap, but the food is some of the best along this part of the coast. The house specialty is chicken Kiev, but you can also tuck into dishes such as chicken schnitzel and the fish of the day. The apple crumble is delicious.

Ozone Milk Bar. Mount Joy Parade. ☎ **03/5289 1780.** Main courses A$1.80–$4 (U.S.$1.25–$2.80). No credit cards. Daily 7am–6pm (to 11pm from Christmas–end of Jan). AUSTRALIAN MILK BAR.

An Ozzie icon, the milk bar is a kind of down-market cafe selling everything from milk shakes and pies to newspapers. This one sells good pies and quiche, a limp-looking and bland-tasting veggie burger I wouldn't recommend, chicken fillet burgers, cookies, ice cream, and small homemade cakes. The milk shakes are particularly good. You can sit inside or around three small tables outside. There's a Thai place next door, but it's very unwelcoming.

Marks. Mount Joy Parade. ☎ **03/5289 2787.** Main courses A$9–$17.50 (U.S.$6.50–$12.25). AE, BC, DC, MC, V. Daily noon–2:30pm (Sat–Sun only in winter) and 6–8:30pm. INTERNATIONAL.

Lorne's best restaurant is a classy joint with simple wooden chairs and tables in a cool, yellow-walled interior. Menu items include fried calamari salad, lamb's brains, spicy octopus, risotto, and the intriguing oven-baked, vine-wrapped goat cheese and macadamia nut parcel on eggplant pâté with red capsicum puree. The bar is open for coffee and alcoholic drinks all day.

3 The Murray River

Mildura: 544km (326¼ miles) NW of Melbourne; Albury-Wadonga: 305km (183 miles) N of Melbourne; Echuca: 210km (126 miles) N of Melbourne

The Murray is Australia's version of the Mississippi. Although it's a rushing torrent of white water at its source in the Snowy Mountains, by the time it becomes the meandering border between Victoria and New South Wales, it's slow-moving and a muddy brown.

The Murray was once used by Aborigines as a source for food and transportation, and later the water was plied by paddle steamers, laden with wool and crops from the land the Murray helped irrigate. In 1842, the Murray was discovered by explorers Hamilton Hume and William Howell on the first-ever overland trek from Sydney to Port Phillip, near Melbourne. On their trek, the explorers "suddenly arrived at the bank of a very fine river—at least 200 feet wide, apparently deep, the bank being 8 or 9 feet above the level, which is overflowed at the time of flood. . . . In the solid wood of a healthy tree I carved my name." You can still see the carved initials on a tree standing by the river bank in Albury, on the border between the two states.

Today, the Murray faces many problems: pollution, overuse, erosion of the river banks, and a great depopulation of the fish that once swam in its waters. These last two problems stem from the introduction of European carp into the Murray River. Since their release into the river system earlier this century, the carp have multiplied into countless millions, eating away at the river banks and turning the water a muddy brown, as well as seeing off most of the native aquatic inhabitants.

ESSENTIALS

GETTING THERE   Most visitors cross the river during an overland drive between cities. There are two routes to get to the Murray from Melbourne: Either take the Calder Highway to Mildura, a 6-hour drive, or take the 2½-hour route down the Midland Highway to Echuca. Traveling from Melbourne to Mildura is only practical if you're continuing on to Broken Hill, which is 297 kilometers (178 miles) north of Mildura. Those in a hurry to get to and from Sydney can travel via the Hume Highway to the river-straddling twin towns of Albury-Wadonga (it's about a 12-hour trip from Melbourne to Sydney on this route).

V/Line (☎ **13 22 32** in Australia, or 03/9619 5000) runs regular train services to Mildura, Echuca, and Albury-Wadonga.

VISITOR INFORMATION   The **Echuca and Moama and District Visitor Information Centre,** 2 Heygarth St., Echuca, VIC 3564 (☎ **1800/804 446** in Australia, or 03/5480 7555; fax 03/5482 6413) has plenty of maps and detailed information about local accommodations and Murray cruises. It's open from 9am to 5pm daily. The **Mildura Visitor Information & Booking Centre,** at 180–190 Deakin Ave., Mildura, VIC 3502 (☎ 1800/039 043 in Australia, or 03/5021 4424; fax 03/5021 1836; e-mail: tourism@mildura.vic.gov.au), offers similar services. It's open Monday to Friday from 9am to 5:30pm and weekends from 9am to 5pm. If you're passing through Albury, you might want to contact the **Gateway Visitors Information Centre,** Gateway Village, Lincoln Causeway, Wadonga, VIC 3690 (☎ **1800/800 743** in Australia, or 02/6041 3875; fax 02/6021 0322). It's open from 9am to 5pm daily.

RIVER CRUISES & OTHER FUN STUFF

IN MILDURA   Today Mildura is one of Australia's most important fruit-growing areas. There was a time, however, when this was just semiarid red-dust country. The area bloomed due to a little ingenuity and, of course, the Murray. The original irrigation system consisted of two imported English water pumps and the manual labor of hundreds of newly arrived immigrants, who were put to work clearing the scrub and digging channels through the new fields: Today, the hungry land soaks up the water.

Several paddle steamers leave from Mildura wharf. One of the nicest boats is the **PS Melbourne** (☎ **03/5023 2200;** fax 03/5021 3017), which was built in 1912 and is still powered by steam. It offers 2-hour trips leaving at 10:50am and 1:50pm. The trip costs A$17 (U.S.$11.90) for adults, and A$6 (U.S.$4.20) for children. Children under age 5 are free.

PS *Melbourne's* sister ship, the *Rothbury,* was built in 1881, but its steam-driven engine has been replaced by a conventional one. It churns out a day's winery cruise every Thursday from 10:30am to 3:30pm, stopping off at a winery for tastings and a barbecue lunch. The trip costs A$35 (U.S.$24.50) for adults and A$15 (U.S.$10.50) for children. The *Rothbury* has evening dinner cruises every Thursday from 7 to 10pm for the same price. You can also take the paddleboat to the zoo during school holiday periods (see below). It leaves Mildura Wharf at 9:50am Wednesday morning (returning at 3pm), and costs A$30 (U.S.$21) for adults and A$15 (U.S.$10.50) for children ages 5 to 14, including zoo admission.

If you have more time, I recommend an all-inclusive cruise on the *Murray Princess,* run by **Captain Cook Cruises** in Sydney (☎ 02/9206 1144; fax 02/9251 4725; www.captcookcrus.com.au). A 2-night weekend cruise costs from A$350 (U.S.$245) to A$490 (U.S.$343) per person, depending on the cabin. Longer cruises are also offered. Round-trip transfers from Adelaide cost A$50 (U.S.$35) to A$75 (U.S.$52.50).

On dry land, the **Golden River Zoo,** Flora Avenue, Mildura (☎ 03/5023 5540), is a pleasant place to see native animals. The zoo fronts onto the river 4 kilometers (2½ miles) from the city center down 11th Street. The animals here virtually follow you around (on the lookout for food) as you walk through their large enclosures. Admission is A$12 (U.S.$8.40) for adults, and A$6 (U.S.$4.20) for children, including a free barbecue lunch at noon and a free tractor train ride down to the river at 1:30pm. The zoo's open daily, except Christmas, from 9am to 5pm.

IN ECHUCA In Echuca, another paddle-steamer option is the *Emmylou* (☎ 03/5480 2237; fax 03/5480 2927), which offers various day trips that cost A$12 (U.S.$8.40) for adults for 1 hour, and A$15 (U.S.$10.50) for 1½ hours. Children pay half price. Overnight cruises are also available.

The **Port of Echuca** (☎ 03/5482 4248; fax 03/ 5482 6951) is definitely worth a look. The three-level red gum wharf was built in 1865 and is still used by paddle steamers. The Port owns the **PS** *Adelaide* (1866), the oldest operating wooden-hulled paddle steamer in the world, the **PS** *Pevensey* (1911), and the **PS** *Alexander Arbuthnot* (1923). One-hour cruises on the latter two are offered daily at 10:15am, 11:30am, 1pm, 2:15pm, and 3:30pm. They cost A$12 (U.S.$8.40) for adults, and A$5 (U.S.$3.50) for children. You can also take a look around the wharf on a guided tour, visiting a steam display showcasing various engines, the restoration sheds, a historic sawmill, a working blacksmith's shop, and a woodturner's workshop. Outside the port, in the **Echuca Port Precinct,** there are various things to do, including horse and carriage rides and old penny arcade machines in Sharpes Magic Movies, located in an old riverboat warehouse.

WHERE TO STAY
IN MILDURA

Mildura Grand Hotel Resort. Seventh St., Mildura, VIC 3500. ☎ **1800/034 228** in Australia, or 03/5023 0511. Fax 03/5022 1801. 112 units (20 with tubs, the rest with private showers). A/C MINIBAR TV TEL. A$81–$127 (U.S.$56.70–$88.90) double; A$127 (U.S.$88.90) "Grand Room" double; A$146–$420 (U.S.$102.20–$294) suite. Rates include breakfast. Ask about packages. AE, BC, DC, MC, V. Free parking.

This huge 19th-century hotel is right in the center of Mildura, overlooking the Murray. Standard double rooms are comfortable, and many have been recently refurbished. The 21 "Grand" rooms are a little bigger, and some have balconies and garden views. The State Suite (A$250/U.S.$175 per night) has also been refurbished, and matches anything you're likely to find in a five-star hotel.

Guests have use of laundry facilities, a pool, a sauna, a hot tub, a game room, a pool room, and five restaurants, including the excellent Stefano's, which serves Italian cuisine with zingy Asian accents.

Rosemont Guest House. 154 Madden Ave., Mildura, VIC 3500. ☎ **03/5023 1535.** Fax 03/5023 1535. 4 units. TV. A$45–$52 (U.S.$31.50–$36.40) double. Additional person A$10 (U.S.$7) extra. Rates include cooked breakfast. BC, MC, V.

This traditional B&B, a short walk from the river and the town center, offers very good value on modern rooms in a quiet central location. Double rooms are large enough for a family of three, with a queen-size bed and a spare single. The A$45 (U.S.$31.50) rooms are smaller and have two single beds. All rooms have their own showers. There is a communal lounge, dining room, guest kitchen, and laundry, as well as a pool and a barbecue in the garden.

IN ECHUCA

Echuca Gardens B&B and YHA. 103 Mitchell St., Echuca, VIC 3564. ☎ **03/5480 6522.** Fax 03/5482 6951. 3 units in B&B, 16 beds in hostel. B&B room A$100 (U.S.$70) weekdays, A$120 (U.S.$84) weekends. Rates include breakfast. Hostel $19 (U.S.$13.30) dorm bed (A$16/U.S.$11.20 for YHA members); A$32 (U.S.$22.40) twin or double. BC, MC, V.

In the evening guests gather around the piano at this popular two-story log cabin B&B. Or you may choose to relax in the hot tub in the front yard, surrounded by murals and landscaped water gardens. Rooms are decorated in native flower themes, and all have balconies. Two rooms have showers in the bathroom, and another has a shower on the second floor. It's a short stroll from the B&B to either the river or a state forest. The YHA here also has three basic dorm rooms. There's a basic twin room inside, and three tent-like cabins outside, one with a double bed, and the other with two singles.

IN ALBURY

Hume Country Golf Club Motor Inn. 736 Logan Rd., Albury, NSW 2640. ☎ **02/6025 8233.** Fax 02/6040 4999. 25 units. A/C TV TEL. A$75 (U.S.$52.50) double; A$85 (U.S.$59.50) family room; A$115 (U.S.$80.50) suite. Additional person A$10 (U.S.$7) extra. AE, BC, DC, MC, V.

This is a good place to stop if you're making the long trip north to Sydney. Just on the New South Wales side of the border, this motor inn has typical motel rooms with everything you'd expect, plus a toaster thrown in for good measure. There are also two very large family rooms, both of which sleep five; one has a separate bedroom. Suites are also large and come with a Jacuzzi tub. All rooms overlook the 27-hole golf course, where a round of golf costs A$15 (U.S.$10.50).

4 The Southeast Coast

The Princes Highway wanders down the coast from Sydney, just past Eden, then darts across into Victoria, passing through the logging town of Orbost, and then dipping down toward Lakes Entrance. The highway continues to the southwest, swooping in an arch to Melbourne.

This region's most interesting sights are **Wilsons Promontory National Park,** and—to a lesser extent—**Lakes Entrance.**

WILSONS PROMONTORY NATIONAL PARK
200km (120 miles) SE of Melbourne.

The Prom, as it's called, is Victoria's best-loved national park. Dipping down the Bass Strait, the park—which was named after a prominent London businessman— marks the southernmost point on Australia's mainland, and it's thought to have once been joined to Tasmania by a land bridge.

Visitors come here for the spectacular scenery: imposing granite mountains, thick forests, vast plains, and some of the country's best beaches. There are plenty of animals around, such as koalas, kangaroos, wallabies, possums, echidnas, wombats, and emus. You can hand-feed crimson rosellas at the capital of the Prom, **Tidal River,** but you'll

Hitting the Beach in Wilsons Promontory

There are 30 beaches in the park, some of which are easily accessible. **Norman's Beach** in Tidal River is the most popular, and it's the only one recommended for swimming. There's no snorkeling, and no lifeguards are on duty at these beaches, but they're gorgeous.

find little more here than the national park's **Tourist Information Center** (☎ 1800/350 552 in Australia, or 03/5680 9555) and its camping and caravan grounds.

There are plenty of trails leading away into the mountains. Following the longer trails can turn into a 2- or 3-day excursion, though shorter day hikes are possible. One of the best trails is the 1-hour **Mt Oberon walk,** which starts from the Mt. Oberon parking lot and offers superb views. Visitors also rave about the **Squeaky Beach Nature Walk,** a 1½-hour walk from Tidal River to the next bay and back. The best time to visit the park is from late September to early December, when all the bush flowers are in bloom.

Park entry costs A$8 (U.S.$5.60) for cars; you pay at the park entrance gate 30 kilometers (18 miles) north of Tidal River. The gate is open 24 hours, but if you arrive late and the collection station is closed, pay the following morning at Tidal River.

GETTING THERE   From Melbourne, take the South Gippsland Highway (B440), turning south at Meeniyan, and again at Fish Creek or Foster. The route is well sign-posted. Tidal River is 30 kilometers (18 miles) inside the park boundary. **Amaroo Park Backpackers** on Phillip Island (☎ 03/5952 2548) offers day trips to the park for A$30 (U.S.$21), and you can stay overnight at their cabin-tents at Tidal River. Public transportation directly to The Prom is nonexistent. One option is to take the **V/Line** (☎ 13 22 32 in Australia, or 03/9619 5000) bus from Melbourne to Foster (A$21.30/U.S.$14.90), 60 kilometers (36 miles) north of The Prom. In Foster, you could stay at the **Foster Backpackers Hostel,** 17 Pioneer St. Foster, VIC 3960 (☎ 03/5682 2614). It's a private home with a few spare rooms, where a dorm bed costs A$17 (U.S.$11.90) and two doubles cost A$40 (U.S.$28) each. The owner is also the "Prom Postie," who leaves each morning for Tidal River delivering the mail along the way, while tourists sit shotgun. The trip takes around 2 hours and costs A$10 (U.S.$7) each way.

WHERE TO STAY

The national park's **Tourist Information Center** operates 17 self-contained cabins that cost A$110 (U.S.$77) a night for two (they can accommodate up to six people; each additional person costs A$15/U.S.$10.50 extra), as well as 5 "Lorikeet" units that cost A$78 (U.S.$54.60) a night for two and A$112 (U.S.$78.40) for four. Very basic huts with no shower (you'll need to bring your own linen) cost A$42 (U.S.$29.40) for a 4-bed hut and A$63 (U.S.$44.10) for a 6-bed hut. For bookings call ☎ 03/5680 9500, or fax 03/568 09516.

Waratah Park Country House. Thomson Rd., Waratah Bay, VIC 3959. ☎ 03/5683 2575. Fax 03/5683 2275. 6 units. A/C TV TEL. A$75 (U.S.$52.50) including breakfast; A$106 (U.S.$74.20) Sun–Thurs (including 4-course dinner and breakfast); A$255 (U.S.$178.50) for weekend package, including 2 nights' lodging, 2 breakfasts, and 2 4-course dinners. All rates are per person. AE, BC, MC, V.

If you don't feel like roughing it, this is the only place in the park that will do. Rooms, with king-size beds and double spas, offer stunning views over Wilsons Promontory and a dozen or so islands. The hotel is next to the new Cape Liptrap Coastal Park, home to some 120 species of birds. It's a very friendly place, and the hosts will sit down with you and go through the things you want to do while you're in the area. The food here is excellent, too.

LAKES ENTRANCE
316km (189½ miles) E of Melbourne; 775km (491 miles) SW of Sydney

Lakes Entrance (pop. 4,200) is Victoria's fishing capital and a popular summer resort town. People come here for three things: the surrounding **national parks,** the vast **Gippsland Lakes** (Australia's largest enclosed waterway, separated from the coast by sand spits and dunes crossed by walkways), and the **beaches** (the most famous of which is Ninety Mile Beach).

The town is situated at the eastern end of the lake system and attracts lots of anglers, windsurfers, boaters, and water-skiers. If you're hurrying on down to Melbourne from Sydney, you might want to pull over here and admire the ocean views from **Jemmy Point,** 2 kilometers (1 mile) west of town on the Princes Highway.

GETTING THERE **V/Line** (☎ **13 22 32** in Australia, or 03/9619 5000) operates daily buses from Melbourne to Bairnsdale for around A$40 (U.S.$28), with a connection to Lakes Entrance for an another A$7.30 (U.S.$5.10).

VISITOR INFORMATION The **Lakes Entrance Visitor Information Centre** (☎ **03/5155 1966;** fax 03/5155 1324) is on the Princes Highway, just as you enter the town from the west.

WHERE TO STAY

Abel Tasman Motor Lodge. 643 Esplanade (Princes Hwy.), Lakes Entrance, VIC 3909. ☎ **03/5155 1655.** Fax 03/5155 1603. 17 units. A/C TV TEL. A$65–$95 (U.S.$45.50–$66.50) standard double; A$85–$110 (U.S.$59.50–$77) double with spa; A$95–$160 (U.S.$66.50–$112) family room; A$100–$200 (U.S.$70–$140) 2-bedroom apt.; A$150–$200 (U.S.$105–$140) penthouse (minimum 2-night stay required in penthouse). Rates are highest Christmas–end of Jan, and Easter week. AE, BC, DC, MC, V. Free parking.

The rooms at this modern motel, which was totally refurbished in 1998, are the best in Lakes Entrance. Standard rooms are furnished in typical motel style, and those on the top floor also have private balconies. All have views across the lake. The apartments were built in 1998 and are quite classy. The penthouse has a spa off one of three separate bedrooms. Guests have the use of a swimming pool, barbecues, and a coin-op laundry.

Deja Vu. Clara St. (P.O. Box 750), Lakes Entrance, VIC 3909. ☎ **03/5155 4330.** Fax 03/5155 3718. 6 units (4 with spa). TV. A$115 (U.S.$80.50) standard double; A$135–$175 (U.S.$94.50–$122.50) double with spa. Minimum 2-night stay required. Ask about midweek packages. Rates include cooked breakfast. AE, BC, DC, MC, V.

This waterfront retreat is set in six acres of rain forest and wetlands and offers panoramic ocean views. Rooms are large and comfortable; each has a sitting room and a balcony (from which you might spot pelicans, black swans, and other feathered friends). Four rooms have Jacuzzis. There is also a meditation room, and massages are available. Seafood platters are served on your balcony, or you can paddle a canoe to

---

Hitting the Beaches around Lakes Entrance

Most of **Ninety Mile Beach** is encompassed by the Gippsland Lakes Coastal Park—a bird-lovers paradise. Lake Entrance's beaches never get crowded, so grab a blanket and head for your own personal stretch of white sand. The swimming is fine here, but this is not the place for outstanding snorkeling.

the shops and restaurants in town. Tours of the area can be arranged. There's also a waterfront apartment with its own private beach; it costs A$240 (U.S.$168) for four people, or A$145 (U.S.$101.50) for two.

5 The High Country

Victoria's High Country is made up of the hills and mountains of the **Great Dividing Range,** which runs from Queensland, through New South Wales, and down to just before Ballarat, where the range drops away only to reappear in the dramatic mountains of the Grampians in western Victoria. The range separates inland Australia from the greener coastal belt. The highest mountain in the Victorian segment of the range is **Mt. Bogong,** which at just 1,988 meters (6,621 ft.) is minuscule by world mountain standards.

The main attractions of the High Country are its natural features, which include moorland and typical alpine scenery. It's also popular for its outdoor activities, including hiking, canoeing, white-water rafting, and rock climbing. The High Country is also the home of the **Victorian ski fields,** based around Falls Creek and Mt. Hotham.

SNOWY RIVER NATIONAL PARK

390km (234 miles) NE of Melbourne.

The Snowy River National Park, with its lovely river scenery and magnificent gorges, protects the largest of Victoria's forest wilderness areas. The Snowy River was once a torrent worthy of Banjo Patterson's famous poem, *The Man from Snowy River,* but since Snowy Mountain Hydro-Electric came along and erected a series of dams, it's become a mere trickle of its former self.

GETTING THERE & GETTING AROUND   There are two main access roads to the park, the **Gelantipy Road** from Buchan and the **Bonang Freeway** from the logging township of Orbost. **MacKillop's Road** (also known as Deddick River Road) runs across the park's northern border from Bonang to a little south of Wulgulmerang. Around MacKillop's Bridge, along MacKillop's Road, is some spectacular scenery and the best of the park's campgrounds, set beside some nice swimming holes and sandy river beaches. **Barry Way** leads through the main township of Buchan, where you'll find some of Australia's best caves.

VISITOR INFORMATION   The main place to get information on the Snowy River National Park and the Alpine National Park (see below) is the **Buchan Caves Information Centre,** in the Buchan Caves complex. It's open daily from 9am to 4:30pm. Closed Christmas.

EXPLORING THE BUCHAN CAVES

The ✪ **Buchan Caves** (☎ **03/5155 9264**) are set in a scenic valley that is particularly beautiful in autumn, when all the European trees are losing their leaves. Tourists can visit the Royal and Fairy caves (which are quite similar), with their fabulous stalactites and stalagmites. There are several tours daily: April to September at 11am, 1pm, and 3pm; October to March at 10am, 11:15am, 1pm, 2:15pm, and 3:30pm. Entry to one cave costs A$10 (U.S.$7) for adults, A$5 (U.S.$3.50) for children ages 5 to 16, and A$25 (U.S.$17.50) for a family of five.

To get there from the Princes Highway, turn off at Nowa Nowa (it's well signposted), or if you're coming south from Jindabyne (see chapter 6) follow the Barry Way, which runs alongside the Snowy River.

High Country Travel Tips

If you plan to go hiking in the High Country, make sure you have plenty of water and sunscreen, as well as a tent and a good-quality sleeping bag. As in any alpine region, temperatures can plummet dramatically. In summer, days can be very hot and nights very cold.

ALPINE NATIONAL PARK
333km (200 miles) NE of Melbourne; 670km (402 miles) SW of Sydney

Victoria's largest national park at 646,000 hectares, the Alpine National Park connects the High Country areas of Victoria and New South Wales. The park's scenery is spectacular, encompassing most of Victoria's highest mountains, wild rivers, impressive escarpments, forests, and high plains. The flora is diverse, ranging from eucalyptus and peppermint trees in the lowlands to blue gums, snow gums, and both mountain and alpine ash in the higher areas. In all, some 1,100 plant species have been recorded within the park's boundaries, including 12 not found anywhere else. Bushwalking here is particularly good in spring and summer, when the **Bogong High Plains** are covered in a carpet of wildflowers. Other impressive walking trails include a 5.7-kilometer (3½-mile) route past Bryce Gorge and The Bluff, a 200-meter- (356-ft.) high rocky escarpment with panoramic views from the top.

Most of Victoria's **ski areas** are in, or on the edge of, the Alpine National Park, and there are plenty of walking tracks—the best known of which is the **Alpine Walking track,** which bisects the park for 400 kilometers (240 miles) from Walhalla to the New South Wales border township of Tom Groggin.

Feel like the Man from Snowy River? **Snowy Mountain Rider Tours,** Karoonda Park, Gelantipy (☎ **03/5155 022;** fax 03/5155 0308), offers half-day rides in the Alpine National Park for A$50 (U.S.$3.50), and full-day tours for A$100 (U.S.$70), including lunch. Four- and five-day trips include tent accommodations and all meals, and cost A$420 (U.S.$294) and A$530 (U.S.$371), respectively.

GETTING THERE   The Alpine National Park can be accessed by several routes from Melbourne, including the Great Alpine Road (B500), the Kiewa Valley Highway (C531), and the Lincoln Road from Heyfield. Get to The Bluff from Mansfield along the Maroodah Highway.

There are plenty of access roads into the park, although some close in winter.

VISITOR INFORMATION   See "Visitor Information" under Snowy River National Park, above.

HITTING THE SLOPES: HIGH COUNTRY SKI RESORTS
The ski season here runs from the end of June to the end of September.

MT. HOTHAM
373km (224 miles) NE of Melbourne.

Mt. Hotham (1,750m/5,740 ft.) is an intimate ski resort significantly smaller than the one at Falls Creek (see below). Eight lifts offer runs for beginners to advanced skiers. The resort also offers some good off-piste (off-trail) cross-country skiing, including a route across the Bogong High Plains to Falls Creek. Some of the lifts are quite far apart, although there's a free zoo cart and bus transport system in winter along the main road. Resort entry costs A$11 (U.S.$7.70) per car per day, payable at the resort entry gates or at the Mount Hotham Resort Management office (see "Visitor Information," below). Ski tickets are available from **Mount Hotham Skiing Company** (☎ **03/5759 4444**). Full-day lift tickets cost A$42 (U.S.$29.40) for adults, and A$18 (U.S.$12.60) for children. Combined lift and ski-lesson tickets cost A$59 (U.S.$41.30) for adults, and A$31 (U.S.$21.70) for children.

GETTING THERE   From Melbourne, take the Hume Highway via Harrietville, or the Princes Highway via Omeo. The trip takes around 5½ hours (slightly quicker on the Hume Highway).

   Trekset Mount Hotham Snow Service (☎ **03/9370 9055**) runs buses from Melbourne to Mount Hotham daily during the ski season, leaving at 9am from Spencer Street Coach Terminal. The trip takes 6 hours and costs A$70 (U.S.$49) one-way or A$105 (U.S.$73.50) round-trip. You need to book in advance.

VISITOR INFORMATION   **Mount Hotham Resort Management,** Great Alpine Rd., Mt. Hotham (☎ **03/5759 3550**), is as close as you'll come to an information office. It has plenty of brochures. It's open daily from 8am to 5pm in the official ski season, and Monday to Friday from 9am to 5pm at other times.

WHERE TO STAY   The **Mt. Hotham Accommodation Service** (☎ **03/5759 3636;** e-mail: hotham@netc.net.com), can book rooms and advise you on special deals and what's available during both peak and off-peak periods. You'll find that in the snow season most places will want you to book for the whole week. Off-season prices are significantly lower. Most budget offerings are in so-called "Club Lodges," basically small backpacker abodes with shared rooms and facilities. These generally cost around A$40 (U.S.$28) per person weekdays and A$60 (U.S.$42) on weekends.

FALLS CREEK
375km (225 miles) NE of Melbourne.

One of Victoria's best ski resorts—and quite upscale—Falls Creek is situated on the edge of the Bogong High Plains overlooking the Kiewa Valley. It's the only alpine village in Australia where you can ski from your lodge to the lifts and back again from the ski slopes.

   The ski fields are split into two parts, the **Village Bowl** and **Sun Valley,** with 22 lifts in all, with a vertical drop of 267 meters (876 ft.). There are plenty of intermediate and advanced runs, as well as a sprinkling for beginners. You'll also find some of Australia's best cross-country skiing here. Australia's major cross-skiing event, the **Kangaroo Hoppet,** is held here on the last Saturday in August every year. Entry to the resort costs A$6 (U.S.$4.20). Full-day lift tickets cost A$64 (U.S.$44.80) for adults, and A$33 (U.S.$23.10) for children. Combined lift and ski-lesson tickets cost A$37 (U.S.$25.90) for adults, and A$29 (U.S.$20.30) for children. Call the **Falls Creek Ski Lifts** at ☎ **03/5758 3280;** fax 03/5758 3416) for details. The ski lifts can also organize accommodations.

GETTING THERE   **Pyles Coaches** (☎ **03/5754 4024**) runs buses to the ski resort from Melbourne every day during the ski season, departing Melbourne at 9am and Falls Creek at 5pm. The round-trip fare is A$100 (U.S.$70) for adults, and A$75 (U.S.$52.50) for children, and includes the resort entrance fee. The company also runs shuttle buses to and from Albury, just over the border in New South Wales.

VISITOR INFORMATION   The **Falls Creek Information Centre** is at 1 Bogong High Plains Rd., Falls Creek (☎ **03/5758 3490**). It's open daily from 8am to 5pm. Buy your lift tickets in the booth next door.

WHERE TO STAY   Falls Creek is a year-round resort, with a good range of accommodations available at all times, although it tends to fill up fast during the ski season.

There are few budget accommodations in Falls Creek, but room prices are significantly cheaper outside the ski season. The **Falls Creek Central Reservations booking office** (☎ **03/5757 2718**) can tell you what deals are on offer and can book accommodations for you. The best budget accommodation option is the **Frying Pan Inn** (☎ **03/5758 3390**), which is located right in the village next to the ski lifts. It offers bunks in four- or six-bed rooms; packages are available.

Mt. Buffalo National Park

350km (210 miles) NE of Melbourne.

Based around Mt. Buffalo, this is the oldest national park in the Victorian High Country, declared in 1898. The scenery around here is spectacular, with huge granite outcrops and plenty of waterfalls. As you ascend the mountain you pass through dramatic vegetation changes, from tall snow gum forests to subalpine grasslands. In summer, carpets of Silver Snow daisies, royal bluebells, and yellow Billy Button flowers bloom on the plateau. Animals and birds here include wallabies and wombats, gang-gang cockatoos, lyrebirds, and mobs of crimson rosellas, which congregate around the campsite at Lake Catani (popular for swimming and canoeing). Other popular sports in and around the park include advanced hang gliding and some very serious rock climbing. There are also more than 90 kilometers (54 miles) of walking tracks. Mt. Buffalo is also home to Victoria's smallest ski resort, with just five lifts and a vertical drop of 157 meters (515 ft.). There are also 11 kilometers (6½ miles) of marked cross-country ski trails. The entry to Mt Buffalo ski resort is A$9 (U.S.$6.30) per car. Full-day lift tickets cost around A$35 (U.S.$24.50) for adults, A$21 (U.S.$14.70) for children under age 15, and A$10 (U.S.$7) for children under age 8. Combined lift and ski-lesson packages cost A$35 (U.S.$24.50) for adults, and A$24 (U.S.$16.80) for children.

GETTING THERE   From Melbourne, take the Hume Freeway (M31) to Wangaratta, then follow the Great Alpine Road to Porepunkah. From there follow the Mount Buffalo Tourist Road.

VISITOR INFORMATION   The nearest visitor information center is in the town of Bright. Find the **Bright Visitor Information Centre** at 1A Delaney Ave., Bright (☎ **03/5755 2275**).

WHERE TO STAY   There are 55 campsites available around Lake Catani (☎ 03/5756 2328).

Mt. Buffalo Chalet. Mt. Buffalo National Park, VIC 3740. ☎ **03/5755 1500.** Fax 03/5755 1892. 97 units, 72 with bathroom (some with shower only). A$119 (U.S.$83.30) guest house room without bathroom; A$145 (U.S.$101.50) en suite room with bathroom; A$170 (U.S.$119) view room with bathroom; A$185 (U.S.$129.50) suite. All rates are per person, including guided walks, evening activities, park entry, and all meals. Higher rates Christmas to mid-Jan and Easter weekend. AE, BC, DC, MC, V.

This rambling mountain guest house was built in 1910 and retains a wonderful old-world feeling. Guest house bedrooms are simple and share bathrooms; they have tea and coffee but no TV. En suite rooms come with a shower, and some have tubs. View rooms have better furnishings and views across the valley. There's a large lounge room, and a game room, both with open fires. Meals are available for nonguests for A$35 (U.S.$24.50) for a three-course dinner. You'll also find a sauna, spa, tennis courts, a cafe, and a bar. During summer the chalet operates canoeing, mountain biking, and abseiling.

6 The Northwest: Grampians National Park

260km (161 miles) NE of Melbourne.

One of Victoria's most popular attractions, the rugged Grampians National Park rises some 1,000 meters (3,280 ft.) from the plains, appearing from the distance like some kind of monumental island. The park, which is an ecological meeting place of Victoria's western volcanic plains and the forested Great Dividing Range, contains one-third of all the wildflowers native to Victoria, and most of southeastern Australia's surviving Aboriginal rock art. Almost 200 species of birds, 35 different species of mammals, 28 species of reptiles, 11 species of amphibians, and 6 species of freshwater fish have been discovered here. Kangaroos, koalas, emus, gliders, and echidnas can be easily spotted.

There are some awesome sites in the Grampians, including **Reeds Lookout** and **The Balconies,** which are both accessible by road, and **Wonderland,** which offers walking tracks leading past striking rock formations and massive cliffs to waterfalls and more spectacular lookouts. The main town in the Grampians is **Halls Gap,** which is situated in a valley between the southern tip of the Mt. Difficult Range and the northern tip of the Mt. William Range. It's a good place to stock up on supplies. The Wonderland Range, with its stunning scenery, is close to Falls Gap. There are plenty of short strolls and longer bushwalks available.

You must visit the **Brambuk Aboriginal Living Cultural Centre** (☎ **03/ 5356 4452**), adjacent to the Park Visitor Centre (see below). It offers an excellent introduction to the area's Aboriginal history and to the accessible rock art sites. A 15-minute movie shown in the Dreamtime Theatre highlights the local Aboriginal history. Admission to the center is free; the movie costs A$4 (U.S.$2.80) for adults and A$2.50 (U.S.$1.75) for children. The center is open daily from 10am to 5pm.

ESSENTIALS

GETTING THERE   By car, the park is accessed from the Western Highway at Ararat, Stawell (pronounced "Storl"), or Horsham. Alternatively, you can access the southern entrance from the Glenelg Highway at Dunkeld. The western areas of the park are reached from the Henty Highway (A200).

V/Line (☎ **13 22 32** in Australia, or 03/9619 5000) has a daily train and bus service to Falls Gap from Melbourne (the train goes to Stawell, and a connecting bus takes you to your destination). The trip takes around 4 hours.

GETTING AROUND   Sealed (paved) roads include the **Grampians Tourist Road,** which cuts through the park from Dunkeld to Halls Gap; the **Mt. Victory Road** from Halls Gap to Wartook; and **the Roses Gap Road** from Wartook across to Dadswells Bridge on the Western Highway. Many other roads in the park are unsealed, but most are passable with a 2WD car.

Grampians National Park Tours (☎ **03/5356 6221**) offers all-day 4WD tours of the national park, stopping off at Aboriginal rock art sites, waterfalls, and lookouts. There's not much walking involved, but you certainly get the chance to spot native animals and ferret around among the native flora. The tour includes lunch and morning and afternoon tea, and costs A$75 (U.S.$52.50).

VISITOR INFORMATION   The **Grampians National Park Visitor Centre** (☎ **03/5356 4379**) is 2.5 kilometers (1½ miles) south of Halls Gap. It has plenty of maps and brochures, and the rangers here can advise you on walking trails and camping spots.

WHERE TO STAY

Camping is available at some 15 park campgrounds and is also permitted in more remote areas. Site permits cost A$6 (U.S.$4.20) per car and are available from the Visitor Centre.

You can hire a caravan or a cabin for the night at **Halls Gap Caravan Park** (☎ **03/5356 4251.** Caravans cost from A$34 to $41 (U.S.$23.80 to $28.70) and cabins from A$53 to $67 (U.S.$37.10 to $46.90), depending on the season. Another option is the **Halls Gap Lakeside Caravan Park** (☎ **03/5356 4281**), which is 5 kilometers (3 miles) from town on the shores of Lake Bellfield. Cabins cost from A$37 (U.S.$25.90) to A$63 (U.S.$44.10) (the more expensive units have air-conditioning and attached bathrooms), and holiday units (older-style permanent buildings with attached bathrooms and cooking facilities) cost from A$47 (U.S.$32.90) to A$60 (U.S.$42). The **Halls Gap YHA** (☎ **03/5356 6221;** fax 03/5356 6330) has 8-bed dorms, and one family room with a double bed and a set of bunks. Beds cost A$13 (U.S.$9.10) for YHA members and A$16 (U.S.$11.20) for nonmembers. A new hostel with 71 beds and several double and twin rooms is due to be completed on the same property toward the end of 1999.

The Mountain Grand Guesthouse and Business Retreat. Grampians Tourist Rd., Halls Gap, VIC 3381. ☎ **03/5356 4232.** Fax 03/5356 4254. E-mail: mtgrand@netconnect.co.au. 10 units. A/C. A$49 (U.S.$34.30) per person in twin share. Rates include breakfast. AE, BC, DC, MC, V.

A couple of years ago this old-fashioned guest house was pretty run-down, but a recent refurbishment by the new owners has brought it up to a comfortable 3½-star standard. These days it's selling itself as a business retreat, so the tourists who turn up get all those little corporate extras, such as exceptional service. The guest house specializes in a weekend-getaway package costing A$90 (U.S.$63) per person twin share, with a Devonshire tea, a three-course dinner, a buffet breakfast, a gourmet picnic lunch, and champagne and chocolates thrown in. The cheaper price of A$49 (U.S.$34.40) per person is generally available only on weekdays (though if you simply happen to be driving by on the weekend, it's worth checking whether there's a spare room for the cheaper price).

Recently renovated rooms are quite small, but furnished with nice country-style furniture and double beds. All have an attached bathroom. Larger family rooms, some of which will have a spa, are being renovated throughout 1999. There are several lounge rooms and conversation nooks, all with TVs; a guest laundry; a bar; a cafe; and a restaurant serving good home cooking at reasonable prices.

Canberra 15

by Marc Llewellyn

If you mention you're heading to Canberra, the capital of Australia, located in the Australian Capital Territory (ACT), most Australians will raise an eyebrow and say, "Why bother?" Even many Canberrans will admit that it's a great place to live, but they wouldn't want to visit.

So what is it about Canberra that draws so much lackluster comment? Simply put, Australians aren't used to having things so nice and ordered. In many ways, Canberra is like Washington, D.C., or any new town that was a planned community from the start: The roads are wide and in good order, the buildings are modern, and the suburbs are pleasant and leafy. Canberra is also the seat of government and the home of thousands of civil servants—enough to make almost any free-thinking Aussie with a hint of convict in him or her shudder.

But to me, Canberra's differences from other Australian cities are the very things that make it special. The streets aren't clogged with traffic, and there are plenty of opportunities for safe biking—try that in almost any other city center and you'll be dusting the sides of cars and pushed onto the sidewalks in no time. There are plenty of open spaces, parklands, and fascinating monuments, and there is an awful lot to see and do—from museum and gallery hopping to boating on Lake Burley Griffin. You can certainly pack a lot into a few days' visit.

Canberra was born after the Commonwealth of Australia was officially created in 1901. Melbourne and Sydney, even then jockeying for preeminence, each put in their bid to become the new Federal capital. In the end, Australian leaders decided to follow the example of their U.S. counterparts by creating a federal district; in 1908 they chose an undeveloped area between the two cities.

Designing the new capital fell to Chicago landscape architect Walter Burley Griffin, a contemporary of Frank Lloyd Wright. The city he mapped out was christened Canberra (a local Aboriginal word meaning "meeting place"), and by 1927, the first meeting of parliament took place. The business of government was underway.

1 Orientation

ARRIVING

BY PLANE   Ansett and Qantas both run frequent daily services to Canberra. The flight from Sydney is 40 minutes, and from Melbourne, 55 minutes.

The **Canberra Airport** is about 10 minutes from the city center. It has car-rental desks, a gift shop, a newsagent (newsstand), a currency exchange, a bar, and a bistro. The airport lacks lockers, showers, and a post office. **Canberra City Sites and Tours** (☎ 02/6294 3171, or 0412/625 552 mobile phone) meets most planes, but make sure you phone them before you arrive. They charge A$6 (U.S.$4.20) per person for a trip to city center hotels.

BY TRAIN   A nice way to see some of the countryside while you're in Australia is to take the train. **Countrylink** (☎ 13 22 32 in Australia) runs three *Canberra Xplorer* trains daily from Sydney to Canberra and return. The 4-hour trip costs A$58 (U.S.$40.60) in first class and A$43 (U.S.$30.10) in economy; children are charged half price, and a return trip costs double. Many people make use of Countrylink packages (call **Countrylink Holidays** at ☎ 13 28 29 in Australia), which can save you quite a bit of money. The Countrylink office in Sydney is at Wynyard CityRail Station.

From Melbourne, **V/Line's** (☎ 13 22 22 in Australia, or 03/9619 5000) **Canberra Link** involves a 5-hour bus trip and a 3½-hour train trip. One-way fares are A$47 (U.S.$32.90) for adults and A$23.50 (U.S.$16.45) for children.

Canberra's Railway Station is situated 3 kilometers (2 miles) southeast of Capital Hill.

BY BUS   **Greyhound Pioneer** (☎ 13 20 30 in Australia, or 07/3258 1600; fax 07/3258 1900; www.greyhound.com.au) runs eight services a day from Sydney to Canberra. Tickets cost A$33 (U.S.$23) for adults and A$19 (U.S.$13.30) for children; the trip takes 4 to 4½ hours. From Melbourne, tickets to Canberra cost A$54 (U.S.$38) for adults and A$44 (U.S.$31) for children, and the trip takes around 10 hours.

Murrays Australia (☎ 13 22 51 in Australia, or 02/9252 3590; fax 02/9252 3694) runs three services a day from Sydney to Canberra for A$28 (U.S.$20) for adults and A$15 (U.S.$11) for children. YHA members travel for A$19 (U.S.$13.30). Several sightseeing companies in Sydney, including **AAT King's, Murrays,** and **Australia Pacific Tours,** offer day trips to Canberra.

Intercity buses arrive at **Jolimont Tourist Centre,** at the corner of Northbourne Avenue and Alinga Street, in Canberra City.

BY CAR   The ACT is surrounded by the state of New South Wales. Sydney is 306 kilometers (183½ miles) northeast and Melbourne is 651 kilometers (390½ miles) southwest of Canberra. If you drive from Sydney via the Hume and Federal highways, the trip will take 3½ to 4 hours. From Melbourne, take the Hume Highway to Yass, then switch to the Barton Highway; the trip will take about 8 hours.

VISITOR INFORMATION

Canberra Visitors' Centre, 330 Northbourne Ave., Dickson (☎ **02/6205 0044;** fax 02/6205 0776; Web site: www.canberratourism.com.au; e-mail:canberravisitorscentre @msn.com.au), dispenses information and books accommodations. The office is open Monday to Friday from 9am to 5:30pm, and Saturday and Sunday from 9am to 4pm.

CITY LAYOUT

The first thing that strikes a visitor to Canberra is its parklike feel (amazing, since there was barely a tree on the original site). Half a dozen avenues radiate from **Capital Hill,** where the Parliament House stands. Each of these broad, tree-shaded streets leads to a traffic circle, from which yet more streets emanate. Around each hub, the streets form a pattern of concentric circles—not the easiest layout for visitors trying to find their way.

Canberra

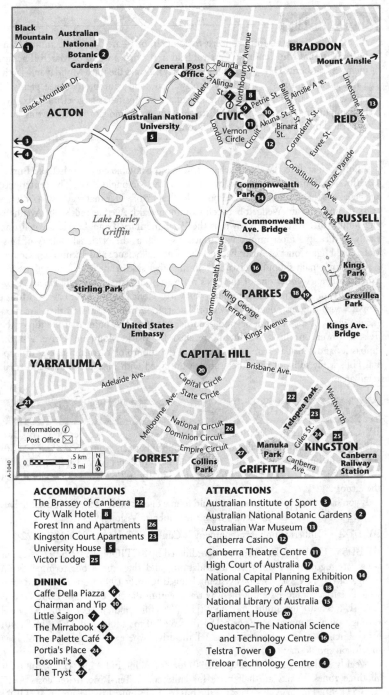

Black Mountain △ **1**
Australian National Botanic Gardens **2**
ACTON
Black Mountain Dr.
General Post Office ✉
Bunda St. **6**
Alinga St. **7**
Australian National University **5**
London
CIVIC
Vernon Circle
Circuit
Petrie St. **8** **9**
Akuna St. **10**
Binara St. **11**
BRADDON
Mount Ainslie →
Ballumbir St.
Ainslie Ave.
Northbourne Avenue
12
Coranderrk St.
REID
Euree St.
Limestone Ave.
13
Anzac Parade
Constitution Ave.
Lake Burley Griffin
Commonwealth Park **14**
Commonwealth Ave. Bridge
Commonwealth Avenue
RUSSELL
Parkes Way
15
16 **17**
PARKES
King George Terrace
Kings Ave.
Kings Park
18 **19**
Grevillea Park
Kings Ave. Bridge
Stirling Park
United States Embassy
YARRALUMLA
Adelaide Ave.
CAPITAL HILL
Brisbane Ave.
Capital Circle
State Circle
20
Melbourne Ave.
National Circuit
Dominion Circuit
Empire Circuit
26
27
Collins Park
FORREST
Manuka Park
GRIFFITH
Canberra Ave.
Telopea Park
Wentworth
22
23
Giles St.
24 **25**
KINGSTON
Canberra Railway Station

Information ⓘ
Post Office ✉
0 .5 km / .3 mi
N
A-1040

ACCOMMODATIONS
The Brassey of Canberra **22**
City Walk Hotel **8**
Forest Inn and Apartments **26**
Kingston Court Apartments **23**
University House **5**
Victor Lodge **25**

DINING
Caffe Della Piazza **6**
Chairman and Yip **10**
Little Saigon **7**
The Mirrabook **19**
The Palette Café **21**
Portia's Place **24**
Tosolini's **9**
The Tryst **27**

ATTRACTIONS
Australian Institute of Sport **3**
Australian National Botanic Gardens **2**
Australian War Museum **13**
Canberra Casino **12**
Canberra Theatre Centre **11**
High Court of Australia **17**
National Capital Planning Exhibition **14**
National Gallery of Australia **18**
National Library of Australia **15**
Parliament House **20**
Questacon–The National Science and Technology Centre **16**
Telstra Tower **1**
Treloar Technology Centre **4**

It's a Festival!

A host of free events—from concerts to competitions—are part of the annual **Canberra National Multicultural Festival** held in the first 3 weeks of March. The fun includes **Canberra Day** (a local public holiday), always the third Monday in March; a hot-air balloon fiesta; fireworks displays; food and wine promotions; plenty of music; and a large range of activities organized by Australia's large ethnic mix. Visitors might find it a little more difficult to book accommodations during this time, but you should always be able to find something.

Another of architect Walter Burley Griffin's most notable creations is **Lake Burley Griffin,** a man-made lake created by damming the Molonglo River. The centerpiece of the lake is the Captain Cook Memorial Jet, a spire of water that reaches 147 meters (482 ft.) into the air. Wedged between Commonwealth Avenue and Kings Avenue is the suburb of **Parkes,** also known as the **Parliamentary Triangle.** Here you'll find many of the city's most impressive attractions, such as the National Gallery of Australia, the High Court of Australia, and the National Science and Technology Center.

Canberra's main shopping district is on the other side of the lake, centered around **Northbourne Avenue,** one of the city's main thoroughfares. Officially labeled **Canberra City,** this area is more commonly known as **Civic.** Northeast of Civic is **Mount Ainslie,** with the Australian War Memorial at its foot; from its summit there are spectacular views of the city and beyond. Another good lookout point is at the top of the Telstra Tower on Black Mountain, reached by Black Mountain Drive. All the embassies and consulates are concentrated in the suburb of **Yarralumla,** east of Capital Hill, while most of the other suburbs are filled with pleasant homes and small retail areas.

2 Getting Around

BY CAR   **Advantage Car Rentals,** 74 Northbourne Ave. (corner of Barry Dr.), (☎ 1800/504 460 in Australia, or 02/6257 6888) has cars from A$35 (U.S.$24.50) per day, including 200 kilometers (120 miles) free per day. **Budget** (☎ 02/6257 1305), **Hertz** (☎ 02/6249 6211), and **Thrifty** (02/6247 7422) are located at the airport.

If you have your own wheels, you could follow one or more of the six **tourist drives** marked with signs; pick up details from the Canberra Visitors' Centre.

BY TAXI   Canberra's only taxi company is **Canberra Cabs** (☎ 02/6285 9222).

BY BUS   Canberra's bus system is coordinated by **ACTION** (☎ 02/6207 7611, or www.action.gov.au for timetable information), and the central bus terminal is on Alinga Street, in Civic. The bus system changed in early 1999 from a standard city-wide fare to a zoning system. One-way travel within the city center, or Zone One, is A$2 (U.S.$1.40) for adults and A$1 (U.S.70¢) for children ages 5 to 15. Travel through more than one zone costs A$4 (U.S.$2.80) for adults and A$2 (U.S.$1.40) for children. When you board the bus, tell the driver where you are going and ask how much you should pay.

Weekly Tickets cost A$17 (U.S.$11.90) for Zone One and A$34 (U.S.$23.80) for all three zones; tickets are half price for children. A **Ten-Ride ticket** costs A$17 (U.S.$11.90). Purchase all tickets on the bus, or from most newsagents or ACTION interchanges.

For timetable information, call ACTION Monday to Friday from 6:30am to 11:30pm, Saturday from 7:30am to 11pm, and Sunday from 8:30am to 6pm. Pick up bus route maps at bus interchanges, newsagents, and the Canberra Visitors' Center.

The **Canberra Explorer bus** (☎ **02/6295 3611**) makes 18 stops on a 2-hour circuit of the city, stopping off at the Australian War Memorial, Regatta Point, the National Gallery, the National Science and Technology Center, and Parliament Houses, the Botanical Gardens, Black Mountain Tower, and the National Aquarium, as well as many other places. Passengers can get off at any attraction along the route, and then board the next bus. Two-hour tickets cost A$9 (U.S.$4.90) for adults and A$6 (U.S.$3.50) for children. Four-hour, 6-hour, and full-day tickets are available, as well as a range of family passes and 2- and 3-day passes. Full-day tickets cost A$18 (U.S.$12.60) for adults and A$15 (U.S.$10.50) for children). There's full commentary on board. Buses leave daily from the Jolimont Tourist Centre, 65–67 Northbourne Avenue, and the Canberra Visitors' Centre every 2 hours from 8:40am (9am at the Jolimont Tourist Centre), to 5pm (4:40pm at the Visitors' Centre).

FAST FACTS: Canberra

American Express   The office at Centerpoint, Shop 1, 185 City Walk (at the corner of Petrie Plaza), Civic (☎ **02/6247 2333**), is open Monday to Friday from 8:30am to 5pm, and Saturday and Sunday from 9am to noon.

Business Hours   Banks are generally open Monday to Thursday from 9:30am to 4pm and Friday from 9:30am to 5pm. Stores and offices are open Monday to Friday from 9am to 5:30pm. Many shops stay open on weekends and until 9pm Friday.

Car Rentals   See "Getting Around," above.

Climate   The best time to visit Canberra is in spring (September to November) or autumn (March to May). Summers are hot and winters can get pretty cold.

Currency Exchange   Cash traveler's checks at banks, at American Express (above), or at Thomas Cook, at the Petrie Plaza entrance of the Canberra Centre (☎ 02/6257 2222), open Monday to Friday from 9am to 5pm and Saturday from 9:30am to 12:30pm.

Dentist   Canberra lacks a dental emergency referral service. A reputable dentist in the center of town is Lachland B. Lewis, Level 3, 40 Allara St., Civic (☎ 02/6257 2777 after hours, and 02/6295 2319 or 02/6295 9495 weekends).

Doctor   The Capital Medical Centre, 2 Mort St., Civic (☎ 02/6257 3766), is open Monday to Friday from 8:30am to 5pm. The Travellers' Medical & Vaccination Centre, Level 1, City Walk Arcade, 2 Mort St., (☎ 02/6257 7154) offers vaccinations and travel medicines.

Drugstores/Chemists   The Canberra Centre Pharmacy, Civic (☎ 02/6249 8074) is open general shopping hours.

E-mail   Cyberchino Café, 33 Kennedy St., Kingston (☎ 02/6295 7844), is open daily from 10am to midnight (Sat open from 8:30am). The National Library, Parkes Place, Parkes (☎ 02/6262 1111), has e-mail facilities available Monday to Thursday from 9am to 9pm, Friday and Saturday from 9am to 5pm, Sun from 1:30 to 5pm.

Embassies/Consulates   The **British High Commission** is located at Old Parliament House Annexe, Parkes (☎ 02/6270 6666). The **Canadian High**

Commission is at Commonwealth Ave., Yarralumla (☎ 02/6273 3844); the **U.S. Embassy** is found at Moonah Place, Yarralumla (☎ 02/6270 5000); and the **New Zealand High Commission** is at Commonwealth Ave., Yarralumla (☎ 02/6270 4211).

Emergencies Call **000** for an ambulance, the police, or the fire department.

Eyeglasses For repairs try OPSM Express, Shop 5, Lower Ground Floor, The Canberra Centre, Civic (☎ 02/6249 7344).

Hospitals For medical attention, go to the Canberra Hospital, Yamba Drive, Garran (☎ 02/6224 2222), or call the Accident & Emergency Department on 02/ 6244 2324 (24 hours).

Police See "Emergencies" above.

Post Office Find the Canberra GPO at 53–73 Alinga St., Civic (☎ 02/ 6209 1680). It's open Monday to Friday from 8:30am to 5:30pm. The Poste Restante address is ℅ Canberra GPO, ACT 2601.

Taxes There's no GST, no hotel tax, and no sales tax added to purchases in Canberra.

3 Accommodations You Can Afford

Canberra has a good scattering of moderately priced places. Many people travel to Canberra during the week, so many hotels offer cheaper weekend rates to put heads on beds. You should always ask about special deals. The rates given below are rack rates, or what the hotels hope to get on a good day—you can often get the room for less.

The Brassey of Canberra. Belmore Gardens, Barton, ACT 2600. ☎ **02/6273 3766.** Fax 02/6273 2791. E-mail: info@brassey.net.au. 95 units. MINIBAR TV TEL. A$135 (U.S.$94.50) double, or A$150 (U.S.$105) family room; A$160 (U.S.$112) heritage double, or A$210 (U.S.$147) family room; A$185 (U.S.$129.50) suite. Rates include full breakfast. AE, BC, DC, MC, V. Free parking. Bus: 310 or 311 (get off outside the National Press Club).

Rooms in this 1927 heritage-listed building, formally a boarding house for government officials visiting Canberra, are large, quiet, and somewhat plush. The garden bar and piano lounge are popular. Other good points include its proximity to Parliament House and other major attractions, and the hearty breakfasts served. My only complaints are that I found the staff to be a little inattentive, and the narrow corridors got crowded, especially during the breakfast and dinner rush. There's a A$12 (U.S.$8.40) lunch menu Monday to Friday from noon to 2pm.

City Walk Hotel. 2 Mort St., Civic, ACT 2601. ☎ **02/6257 0124.** Fax 02/6257 0116. E-mail: citywalk@ozemail.com.au. 55 units, 17 with bathroom. A$40–$55 (U.S.$28–$38.50) single; A$45 (U.S.$31.50) twin with shared bathroom; A$50 (U.S.$35) double with shared bathroom; A$60 (U.S.$42) double with bathroom. Additional person A$12 (U.S.$8.40) extra; children A$8 (U.S.$5.60) extra. A$18 (U.S.$13) dorm bed. BC, MC, V.

You can hardly get closer to the city center than this former YWCA-turned-budget-travel hotel. Being right near the Jolimont Tourist Centre bus interchange, it picks up a lot of business from backpackers and budget travelers arriving by bus from other parts of the country. The rooms are pretty basic, but clean. There are five double rooms with shared bathrooms, though three of these also have two extra single beds. Family rooms sleep up to seven people, all in one room (one has its own kitchen). There is also a guest lounge, laundry, a kitchen, an air-conditioned common room with TV and video, and tea and coffee facilities.

Forest Inn and Apartments. 30 National Circuit, Forrest, ACT 2603. ☎ **1800/676 372** in Australia, or 02/6295 3433. Fax 02/6295 2119. 102 units. A/C TV TEL. A$95 (U.S.$66.50) motel room; A$95 (U.S.$66.50) 1-bedroom apt.; A$130 (U.S.$91) 2-bedroom apt. AE, BC, DC, MC, V. Free parking. Bus: 310 or 311 (get off at the Rydges Hotel).

The Forest Inn is far from fancy, but it's close to the Manuka shops and restaurants and Parliament House. The outside of this 1960s property looks tacky, but the interior has been refurbished recently. The motel rooms are small and colorless, but clean; the apartments are nicer and have full-size kitchens, so for the same price I'd go for one of these. Two-bedroom apartments are perfect for families, and even the one-bedroom apartments have a single bed in the living room. The restaurant serves breakfast, but go to the Italian Club next door for good pasta.

Kingston Court Apartments. 4 Tench St., Kingston, ACT 2604. ☎ **02/6295 2244.** Fax 02/6295 5300. 36 units. A/C TV TEL. A$110 (U.S.$77) apt. for 2. Additional person A$15 (U.S.$10.50) extra; children A$5(U.S.$3.50) extra. AE, BC, DC, MC, V. Free parking. Bus: 237 or 238.

Kingston Court, situated about one kilometer (half a mile) from the Parliamentary Triangle and 6 kilometers (3½ miles) from Civic, is a good option if you're looking for the comforts of home. The apartments are modern and very spacious, and they come with a full kitchen, a washer and dryer, and a balcony. There is also a courtyard, a pool, a gas barbecue, and a half-court tennis court on the grounds.

University House. On the campus of the Australian National University, Balmain Crescent, Acton (G.P.O. Box 1535, Canberra, ACT 2601). ☎ **02/6249 5211.** Fax 02/6249 5252. 100 units. TV TEL. A$106 (U.S.$76) twin; A$111 (U.S.$78) suite; A$116 (U.S.$81) 1-bedroom apt.; A$161 (U.S.$113) 2-bedroom apt. Ask about package deals. AE, BC, DC, MC, V. Free secured parking. Bus: 434.

University House, situated less than 2 kilometers (1¼ miles) from the city center, offers a pleasant alternative to run-of-the-mill hotels in a similar price bracket. Twin rooms come with two single beds; suites have a sitting room and a queen-size bed; family rooms have either two sets of singles in two rooms, or one set and a queen. The one-bedroom apartments have a bedroom with a queen-size bed, a sitting room, and a kitchenette; and the two-bedroom apartments are huge, with two large bedrooms, a dining room, lounge room, and a full kitchen. All rooms have bathrooms with a shower and tub. Meals are served in Boffins Restaurant and the Cellar Bar. Breakfast, baby-sitting, and bicycles are available. University House also has tennis courts and easy access to walking and jogging tracks.

Victor Lodge. 29 Dawes St., Kingston, ACT 2604. ☎ **02/6295 7777.** Fax 02/6295 7777. 28 units, none with bathroom. A$39 (U.S.$27.50) single; A$49 (U.S.$34.30) double. A$19 (U.S.$13.30) dorm bed. Rates include continental breakfast. BC, MC, V. Free parking. Bus: 238, 265, 313.

Backpackers, parliamentary staff, and budget travelers frequent this friendly place, which is situated right next to Kingston shops and about a 15-minute drive from the city center. Rooms vary from dorms with three, four, or five beds, to modern, simple doubles. There are communal showers and toilets, a laundry, a guest refrigerator, a TV room, free tea and coffee, and a courtyard. The staff picks up guests from the train and bus stations daily and makes drop-offs into town every morning.

The owners also own the Best Western motel next door, which has stand-by rates of A$70 (U.S.$49) a double. Apparently, long-suffering parents often dump their teenage kids at the lodge and live it up at the motel. Bike hire is A$12 (U.S.$8.40) for a full day and A$8 (U.S.$5.60) for a half day after 2pm. It's a nice place overall, but you'll have to decide whether you want to put up with the short trek into the city.

4 Great Deals on Dining

Caffe Della Piazza. 19 Garema Place, Civic. **02/6248 9711.** Reservations recommended. Main courses A$11–$14 (U.S.$7.70–$9.80). AE, BC, DC, MC, V. Daily 10am–midnight. ITALIAN/CAFE.

Good eating isn't hard to find in Canberra, but this place is up there with the best. It's won several awards for its Italian-inspired cooking. The restaurant offers both indoor and outdoor dining in pleasant surrounds, and it's a good place to pop in for a light meal and a coffee, or something more substantial. Pastas cost around A$11 (U.S.$7.70), and the best-seller is the king prawn and chicken tenderloin salad. You need to book early on Friday or Saturday evenings.

Jehangir Indian Restaurant. 15 Swinger Hill Shops, Mawson. ☎ **02/6290 1159.** Main courses A$10–$12 (U.S.$7–$9). AE, BC, DC, MC, V. Tues–Fri noon–2:30pm; Mon–Sat 6–10:30pm. NORTH INDIAN.

Look no further for a good north Indian curry. The small dining room has no decor to speak of, but the curries are way above average and well worth making the trek to the suburbs if you have a car. The tandoori murg chicken is a favorite, as is the Fijian-style goat curry. The so-called Balti curries, usually served steaming and bubbling at your table, are not up to par. Vegetarian options are delicious. I like the Kofta—dumplings of potato, cottage cheese, raisins, and nuts in a thick saffron sauce. Mop up the meal with naan bread and basmati rice.

✪ **Little Saigon.** Alinga St. and Northbourne Ave., Civic. ☎ **02/6230 5003.** Main courses A$8–$12 (U.S.$5–$9). AE, BC, DC, MC, V. Daily 10am–3pm, and 5–10pm. VIETNAMESE.

A great budget option, this spacious restaurant has minimalist decor and floor-to-ceiling windows offering views of the busy city center as you eat. Tables are set up on either side of an indoor pond, and there's a bar in the back of the restaurant. The menu is vast, with lots of noodle dishes as well as spicy seafood, duck, chicken, pork, beef, and lamb selections. Soups, which go for just A$6.50 (U.S.$4.55), are the top attractions in this popular spot, which packs in locals and guests from nearby hotels alike.

The Palette Cafe. Beaver Gallery, 81 Denison St., Deakin. ☎ **02/6282 8416.** Main courses A$12–$16 (U.S.$8.40–$11.20). AE, BC, MC, V. Daily 10am–5pm. CAFE/MODERN AUSTRALIAN.

This is a great choice for lunch, especially since it's in the same building as Canberra's largest private art gallery. You can either eat inside, surrounded by artwork, or claim a table outside in the sunny courtyard. Standout dishes include grilled asparagus spears with Japanese scallops and almond hollandaise, and the chili-salted baby octopus. The Caesar salads are particularly good, as are the field mushrooms with a sauce of soy, Japanese rice wine, honey, and coriander.

Portia's Place. 11 Kennedy St., Kingston. ☎ **02/6239 7970.** Main courses A$9.80–$18.80 (U.S.$6.85–$13.15). AE, BC, DC, MC, V. Daily noon–2:30pm, Sun–Wed 5–10pm, Thurs–Sat 5–10:30pm. CANTONESE/MALAYSIAN/PEKING.

A small restaurant serving up excellent traditional cookery, Portia's Place does a roaring lunchtime trade. The best things on the menu are the lamb ribs with shang tung sauce, the King Island fillet steak in pepper sauce, the flaming pork (brought to your table wrapped in foil and bursting with flames), and the Queensland trout stir-fried with snow peas.

Tosolini's. Corner of London Circuit and East Row, Civic. ☎ **02/6247 4317.** Main courses A$12–$14 (U.S.$8–$14). AE, BC, MC, DC, V. Daily 7:30am–10:30pm. CAFE/MODERN AUSTRALIAN.

Since it's situated right next to the busy central bus terminal and close to the major shopping areas, Tosolini's really pulls in the passing crowd. You can sit out on the sidewalk terrace and watch the world go by. The eggs Benedict served here at breakfast could be the best A$7.50 (U.S.$5.25) you've ever spent. Lunchtime fare is almost as good. Both the battered flathead and the pan-fried broad bill (both local fish) are tasty, but Tosolini's really made its name with the pastas and focaccias. Dinner specials are a good value; for A$10 (U.S.$7), you get a pasta dish and a glass of wine. The popular A$12 (U.S.$8.40) theater special, served between 6pm and 7:30pm, includes a pizza or a large serving of risotto and a glass of wine.

✪ **The Tryst.** Bougainville St., Manuka. ☎ **02/6239 4422.** Reservations recommended. Main courses A$15–$18 (U.S.$11–$13). AE, BC, DC, MC, V. Daily noon–2:30, and 6–10:30pm. MODERN AUSTRALIAN.

The personal touches and the service really shine through at The Tryst, and the food is consistently delicious. The restaurant is tastefully decorated in an upscale cafe style, with the kitchen staff on show as they rustle up some of the capital's best tucker. It's also relaxed, feeling more communal than intimate on busy nights. My favorite dish is the Atlantic salmon served with beurre blanc sauce and potatoes, but the oven-roasted spatchcock (a small chicken) and traditional herb stuffing on stir-fried vegetables gets a big thumbs up, too. If you have room left for dessert, don't miss out on the sticky date pudding served with hot butterscotch sauce, pralines, and ice cream—it's as good as it sounds.

WORTH A SPLURGE

✪ **Chairman and Yip.** 108 Bunda St., Civic. ☎ **02/6248 7109.** Reservations required. Main courses A$16–$22 (U.S.$11.20–$15.40). AE, BC, DC, MC, V. Daily noon–3pm and 6–11pm. ASIAN AUSTRALIAN.

This is, without doubt, Canberra's best restaurant. Upbeat and popular with political bigwigs, it really is the place to see and be seen. The avant-garde Chairman Mao paintings adorning the wall are sought after but never sold, and the partly stripped walls reveal the previous layers of paint that once adorned Zorbas, the Greek restaurant that stood here for decades. The fish specials are good and spicy. I always go for the prawns with homemade chili jam, served on vermicelli noodles with mango salsa. Abalone and lobster also find their way onto the menu. The panna cotta is the signature dessert. The local newspaper, the *Canberra Times*, named it the best restaurant in Canberra.

✪ **The Mirrabook.** Sculpture Garden of the National Gallery of Australia, Parkes. ☎ **02/6273 2836.** Reservations recommended. Main courses A$17–$22 (U.S.$12–$16). AE, BC, DC, MC, V. Daily noon–2:30pm (but closing times vary depending on patronage). MODERN AUSTRALIAN.

If it's a nice day outside, plan your lunch around the Mirrabook. The restaurant sits on a lake edged with rushes and sculptures, and full of goldfish. Add smoke machines (they call it a fog sculpture) on the far bank to send mysterious white eddies across the lake's surface toward your lakeside table, and you have a charming fantasy world in which to dine. The menu changes regularly, but you might find a goat cheese tartlet or a warm lamb salad with grilled zucchini, eggplant, and capsicum. While the food is wonderful, the service on busy afternoons can be erratic.

5 Seeing the Sights

Australian Institute of Sport. Leverrier Crescent, Bruce. ☎ **02/6252 1111.** Tours A$8 (U.S.$6) adults, A$4 (U.S.$3) children, A$20 (U.S.$9.80) families; tours leave the AIS shop at 11:30am and 2:30pm daily. Bus: 432 from city center.

This institution provides first-class training and facilities for Australia's elite athletes. Tours, led by one of the institute's athletes, include visits to the gymnasium, basketball courts, and Olympic swimming pool to see training in progress. There is also a fascinating interactive sports display where visitors can test their sporting skills.

   Canberra fields rugby league, basketball, water polo, baseball, hockey, and soccer teams. Many of these matches are held at the **Institute at Bruce Stadium,** Battye Street (☎ **02/6253 2111** for more information).

✪ **Australian War Memorial.** At the head of Anzac Parade on Limestone Ave. ☎ **02/6243 4211.** Free admission. Daily 9am–5pm (when the Last Post is played), every day except Christmas Day. Guided tours at 10am, 10:30am, 11am, 1:30pm, and 2pm. Bus: 233, 302, 303, 362, 436, or 901.

This monument to Australian troops who gave their lives for their country is truly moving, and well worth a visit. Artifacts and displays tell the story of Australia's conflicts abroad. You won't soon forget the exhibition on Gallipoli, the bloody World War I battle in which so many ANZAC (Australian and New Zealand Army Corps) servicemen were slaughtered. The Hall of Memory is the focus of the memorial, where the body of the Unknown Soldier lies entombed after his remains were brought back from a World War I battlefield in 1993. There's a good art collection at the memorial, too. Throughout 1999 the War Memorial is being revamped.

✪ **Canberra Deep Space Communication Complex.** Tidbinbilla, 39km (23¼ miles) southwest of Civic. ☎ **02/6201 7838.** Free admission. Summer 9am–8pm; rest of year daily 9am–5pm. No public bus service, but several tour companies offer programs that include the complex.

This information center, which stands beside huge tracking dishes, is a must for anyone interested in space. There are plenty of models, audiovisual recordings, and displays, including a genuine space suit, space food, and archive film footage of the Apollo moon landings. The complex is still active and is tracking and recording results from the Mars Pathfinder; Voyager 1 and 2; and the Cassini, Soho, Galileo, and Ulysses space-exploration projects; as well as providing a vital link with NASA spacecraft. This is a great stop off on the way back from the Tidbinbilla Nature Reserve just up the road (see below).

High Court of Australia. Overlooking Lake Burley Griffin, Parkes Place. ☎ **02/6270 6811.** Free admission. Mon–Fri 9:45am–4:30pm. Closed holidays. Bus: 310, 313, 360, 361.

The High Court, an impressive concrete and glass building that overlooks Lake Burley Griffin and stands next to the National Gallery of Australia, was opened by Elizabeth II in 1980. It is home to the highest court in Australia's judicial system and contains three courtrooms, a video display, and a huge seven-story-high public hall. When the court is in session, visitors can observe the proceedings from the public gallery. Call for session details.

National Capital Planning Exhibition. On the lake shore at Regatta Point in Commonwealth Park. ☎ **02/6257 1068.** Free admission. Daily 9am–6pm (5pm in winter). Bus: 310, 313, 360, 361, 901.

If you want to find out more about Canberra's beginnings—and get a memorable view of Lake Burley Griffin, the Captain Cook Memorial Water Jet, and the Carillon in the bargain—then head here. The displays are well done, and a film provides an overview of the city's design.

National Gallery of Australia. Parkes Place. ☎ **02/6240 6502.** Free admission (except for major touring exhibitions). Daily 10am–5pm. Guided tours at 11am and 2pm daily, and every Sun at 11am there's a tour focusing on Aboriginal art. Bus: 310, 313, 360, 361, 901.

Linked to the High Court by a pedestrian bridge, the National Gallery showcases both Australian and international art. The permanent collection and traveling exhibitions are displayed in 11 separate galleries. You'll find paintings by big names such as Claude Monet and Jackson Pollock, and Australian painters Arthur Boyd, Sidney Nolan, Arthur Streeton, Charles Condor, Tom Roberts, and Albert Tucker. The exhibition of Tiwi Islander burial poles in the foyer is also interesting, and there's a large collection of Aboriginal bark paintings. A sculpture garden surrounds the gallery and is open to the public.

Parliament House. Capital Hill. ☎ **02/6277 3508.** Free admission. Daily 9am–5pm. Closed Christmas. Bus: 231, 234, 235, 901.

Conceived by American architect Walter Burley Griffin in 1912, Canberra's unmistakable centerpiece was designed to blend organically into its setting at the top of Capital Hill; only a national flag rises above the peak of the hill. In good weather, picnickers crowd the grass that covers the roof, where the view is spectacular. Free 50-minute guided tours are offered throughout the day. You must make reservations for gallery tickets if you want to see parliament in action. Call the sergeant-at-arms at ☎ **02/6277 4889.** (The public dining room is an inexpensive self-service option.)

Questacon—The National Science and Technology Centre. King Edward Terrace, Parkes. ☎ **02/6270 2800.** Admission A$8 (U.S.$6) adults, A$4 (U.S.$3) children, A$20 (U.S.$14) families. Daily 10am–5pm. Closed Christmas. Bus 310, 313, 360, or 361.

Questacon offers some 170 hands-on exhibits that can keep you and your inner child occupied for hours. Exhibits are clustered into six galleries, each representing a different aspect of science. The artificial earthquake is a big attraction. The center is great for kids, but give it a miss if you've already visited the Powerhouse Museum in Sydney.

Telstra Tower. Black Mountain Dr. ☎ **02/6248 1911.** Admission A$3 (U.S.$2) adults, A$1 (U.S.70¢) children. Daily 9am–10pm. Bus: 901 or 904.

The tower, which rises 195m (640 feet) above the summit of Black Mountain, incorporates open-air and enclosed viewing galleries that provide a magnificent 360° view over Canberra and the surrounding countryside. Those who dine in the pricey, revolving **Tower Restaurant** (☎ **02/6248 7096**) are thoughtfully entitled to a refund of their admission charge.

Tidbinbilla Nature Reserve. Tidbinbilla, 39km (23¼ miles) southwest of Civic. ☎ **02/6237 5120.** Admission A$8 (U.S.$6) per vehicle. Daily 9am–6pm (8pm in summer). Visitor center Mon–Fri 9am–4:30pm, Sat–Sun 9am–5:30pm. No public bus service, but several tour companies offer programs that include the reserve.

This is a great place to see native animals such as kangaroos, wallabies, koalas, platypus, and birds in their natural environment. Unlike other wildlife parks around

A Taste of the Grape

National Capital Wine Tours (☎ **02/6231 3330**) offers wine-tasting trips with gourmet lunches on Saturdays and Sundays for A$59 (U.S.$41.30), including hotel pick up. Tours leave at 10am, visit three local wineries, and return at 4pm.

the country, this one has plenty of space, so sometimes you'll have to look hard to spot the animals (I saw a few birds and not much else last time on a short visit, but on previous occasions I've almost been stomped on by kangaroos). A guide is available from the visitor's center. If you want to be sure of spotting animals, contact **Round About Tours** (☎ **02/6259 5999**), a company that runs day tours of the reserve for A$55 (U.S.$38.50), including a picnic lunch and afternoon tea. It also offers 2-hour kangaroo-spotting night tours for A$20 (U.S.$14).

Treloar Technology Centre. Corner of Vickers and Callan sts. ☎ **02/6241 8949.** Free admission. Floor tours A$15 (U.S.$10.50) adults, A$10 (U.S.$7) children (one week's advance notice needed). Sun and Wed 11am–4pm (other times by appointment). Bus: 500.

Aviation buffs will want to book a floor tour of this facility, which you have to do well in advance. Last time I was here the technicians in the workshop were stripping down a Spitfire, which was to be followed by a Lancaster bomber. Also on display are plenty of war relics: German V1 and V2 rockets (the V2 is 14m/46 ft. long and weighed 14 tons at launch), a Gallipoli landing craft, a Soviet T34 tank, Vietnam War helicopters, a Korean War Meteor, a Japanese Zero once flown by the 4th-ranked Japanese Ace (with 68 kills to his credit), miniature submarines, a Messerschmitt 163b Komet, and much more.

6 Outdoor Pursuits

BIKING   With 120 kilometers (72 miles) of bike paths, Canberra is made for exploring on two wheels. Rent a bike from **Mr. Spoke's Bike Hire** on Barrine Drive near the ferry terminal in Acton (☎ **02/6257 1188**). Bikes for adults cost A$8 (U.S.$6) for the first hour and A$7 (U.S.$5) for each subsequent hour; rates are A$7 (U.S.$5) for kids, going down to A$6 (U.S.$4) for each subsequent hour.

BOATING   **Burley Griffin Boat Hire,** on Barrine Drive near the ferry terminal in Acton (☎ **02/6249 6861**), rents paddleboats for A$9 (U.S.$6.50) per hour and canoes for A$15 (U.S.$11) per hour. **Row 'n' Ride,** near MacDermott Place Boat Ramp, Belconnen (☎ **02/6254 7838**), is open on weekends and school and public holidays and offers canoes from A$9 (U.S.$6.50) per hour, kayaks for A$10 (U.S.$7) per hour, and mountain bikes for A$9 (U.S.$6.50) per hour.

GLIDING   The **Canberra Gliding Club** (☎ **02/6257 1494** or 02/6452 3994) offers joy flights and trial instructional flights on weekends and public holidays from the Bunyan Airfield. Flights cost A$60 (U.S.$42).

GOLF   With 11 golf courses, Canberra offers varied opportunities for keen golfers. The nearest to the city center is the **Yowani Country Club** on the Federal Highway in the suburb of Lyneham (☎ **02/6241 3377**). Greens fees are A$35 (U.S.$25) for 18 holes and A$20 (U.S.$14) for 9 holes. Club rental is an additional A$13 to $20 (U.S.$9 to $14). Dress restrictions apply, and advance reservations are essential. The **Federal Golf Course,** Red Hills Lookout Road, Red Hill (☎ **02/6281 1888**), is regarded as the capital's most challenging course. Nonmembers are welcome on most weekdays. Greens fees are A$40 (U.S.$28) for 18 holes.

HORSEBACK RIDING   **National Equestrian Centre,** 919 Cotter Rd., Weston Creek, Canberra (☎ **02/6288 5555**), 15 minutes from Parliament House, offers trail rides through rolling rural countryside filled with kangaroos and cattle. Rides cost around A$21 (U.S.$14) for 1 hour, A$37 (U.S.$25) for 2 hours, A$51 (U.S.$35) for half a day (minimum 4 people), and A$95 (U.S.$67) for a full day (minimum 4 people).

SWIMMING   The indoor heated pool at the **Australian Institute of Sport,** Leverrier Crescent, in Bruce, a short drive northwest of Civic (☎ **02/6214 1281**), is open to the public at certain times during the day (call ahead to check schedules). Adults pay A$3.50 (U.S.$2.50), and children pay A$2 (U.S.$1.40). It's compulsory to wear swimming caps, which can be bought there for A$2.50 (U.S.$1.75). Use of the pool, spa, and sauna costs A$6 (U.S.$4).

TENNIS   The **National Tennis and Squash Centre,** Federal Highway, Lyneham (☎ **02/6247 0929**), has squash courts available for A$11.50 to $15.50 (U.S.$8–$11) per hour, depending on when you want to play. Tennis courts can be booked for A$9.50 to $14.50 (U.S.$7–$11). The **Australian Institute of Sport** (see "Swimming," above) also rents courts for A$8 (U.S.$6) per hour.

7 The Shopping Scene

The **Canberra Centre,** 4 square blocks between City Walk and Ballumbir Street between Petrie and Akuna streets in Civic, is the place to shop till you drop. You can spend hours browsing through the dozens of boutiques or the department stores in the three-story atrium. The **City Market** section, which includes a bakery, fruit and vegetable sellers, a deli, and more, is the place to take a break; it's open Monday to Thursday from 9am to 6pm, Friday from 9am to 9pm, and Saturday and Sunday from 9am to 5pm.

The centrally located **Gorman House Markets,** Ainslie Avenue (☎ **02/ 6249 7377**), are spread around the courtyard of a heritage building. You can pick up good arts and crafts here, as well as clothing, jewelry, essential oils, books, and secondhand clothes. There's often live music and puppet shows and great take-out foods. The markets are open Saturday from 10am to 4pm, and Sunday from noon to 4pm.

8 Canberra After Dark

The "Good Time" section in Thursday's *Canberra Times* has listings on what's on offer around town.

Of the pubs in town, the best in the city center are the British-style **Wig & Pen** on the corner of Limestone and Alinga Street (☎ **02/6248 0171**); the very popular **Moosehead's Pub** at 105 London Circuit in the south of the city (☎ **02/6257 6496**); and the **Phoenix,** at 21 East Row (☎ **02/6247 1606**), which has live music upstairs for a small cover charge.

The **Canberra Tradesmen's Union Club,** 2 Badham Street, Dickson (☎ **02/ 6248 0999**), sometimes has bands, too. It's located 4 kilometers (2½ miles) from Civic. Here you'll find rooms full of poker machines, several snooker tables, and bingo, which is played 20 times a week. Most people come here to drink at the bars, where beer is generally cheaper than in other places around the city. Here, too, is the Canberra Bicycle Museum, with about 60 unusual bicycles on display. You can also have dinner in one of the 10 restored trams.

✪ **Bobby McGee's, Rydge's Canberra Hotel, London Circuit** (☎ **02/ 6257 7999**), is a lively dance spot appealing to a variety of ages with a mixture of contemporary music and old favorites. Good American-style food is also served. Entry is free all nights except Monday and Friday, when it costs A$3 (U.S.$2.10).

If you're looking for a popular place with live entertainment, head for **Tilly's** (Divine Court Cafe), at Wattle and Brigalow streets, in Lyneham (☎ **02/6249 1543**). Jazz is the specialty, but phone to see what's on.

16

Tasmania: The Apple Isle

by Marc Llewellyn

The very name "Tasmania" has an exotic ring about it. It suggests an unspoiled place, considered for decades to be at the ends of the earth, with vast stretches of wilderness roamed by strange creatures like the Tasmanian Devil. Many mainland residents still half jokingly refer to their country cousins as rednecks. In truth, most Tasmanians are hospitable and friendly people, lacking the harsh edge that big cities can foster. Most also care passionately for the magnificent environment they've inherited, and lay scorn on the pockets of the population who still believe that anything that moves deserves a bullet and anything that stands still needs chopping down.

Visitors to Tasmania are surprised by its size, although compared to the rest of Australia the distances here are certainly more manageable. Dense rain forests, stony mountain peaks, alpine meadows, pine plantations, vast eucalyptus stands, and fertile stretches of farmland are all easily accessible, but you should still be prepared for several hours of concentrated driving to get you between the main attractions. Tasmania has two main drawing cards. First, there's the natural environment. More than 20% of the island has been declared a World Heritage Area, and nearly a third of the island is protected within its 14 national parks. Wherever you go, wilderness is always within reach, and although part of it can be viewed from the road, you really need to shake off your city clothes and step out into the bush to get the best out of it.

Tasmania's second drawing card is its history. Remains of the Aboriginal tribes that lived here for tens of thousands of years are evident in isolated rock paintings, engravings, stories, and a general feeling of spirituality that still holds tight in places that modern civilization has not yet reached.

Europeans discovered Tasmania (or Van Diemen's Land, as it was once known) in 1642, when the great seafarer Abel Tasman set anchor off its southwest coast; it wasn't identified as an island until 1798. Tasmania soon made its mark as a dumping ground for convicts, who were more often than not transported for petty crimes committed in their homeland. The brutal system of control, still evident in the ruins at Port Arthur and elsewhere, soon spilled over into persecution of the native population. Tragically, the last full-blooded Tasmanian Aborigine died in 1876, just 15 years after the last convict transportation. Most of the rest had already died of disease or had been hunted down and killed.

Tasmania

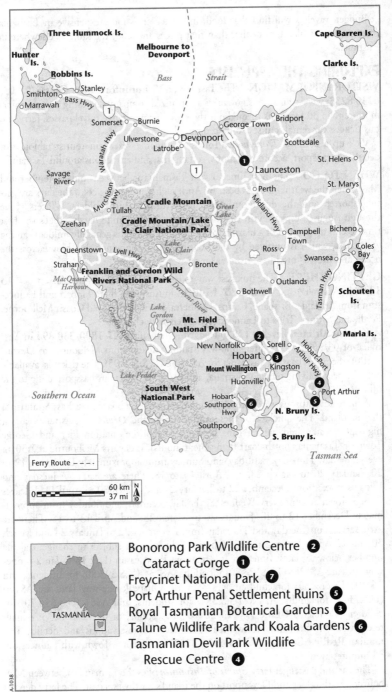

Three Hummock Is.

Cape Barren Is.

Hunter Is.

Melbourne to Devonport

Clarke Is.

Robbins Is.

Bass Strait

Stanley

Smithton

Bass Hwy

Marrawah

Somerset

Burnie

George Town

Bridport

Ulverstone

Devonport

Scottsdale

Latrobe

St. Helens

1 Launceston

Savage River

Perth

St. Marys

Waratah Hwy

Cradle Mountain

Great Lake

Midland Hwy

Tullah

Cradle Mountain/Lake St. Clair National Park

Campbell Town

Bicheno

Zeehan

Murchison Hwy

Lake St. Clair

Ross

Coles Bay

Queenstown

Lyell Hwy

Bronte

Swansea

7

Strahan

Franklin and Gordon Wild Rivers National Park

Outlands

Tasman Hwy

Schouten Is.

MacQuarie Harbour

Gordon River

Franklin R.

Derwent River

Bothwell

Lake Gordon

Mt. Field National Park

Maria Is.

New Norfolk

Sorell

2

Lake Pedder

Hobart

3

Hobart-Port Arthur Hwy

South West National Park

Mount Wellington

Kingston

4 Port Arthur

Southern Ocean

Huonville

5

Hobart-Southport Hwy

6

N. Bruny Is.

Southport

S. Bruny Is.

Tasman Sea

Ferry Route – – – –

0   60 km / 37 mi   N

TASMANIA

Bonorong Park Wildlife Centre **2**
Cataract Gorge **1**
Freycinet National Park **7**
Port Arthur Penal Settlement Ruins **5**
Royal Tasmanian Botanical Gardens **3**
Talune Wildlife Park and Koala Gardens **6**
Tasmanian Devil Park Wildlife Rescue Centre **4**

A-1038

Budget travelers will find that food, in particular, is more expensive in Tasmania than on the mainland, but other than that prices are about the same as elsewhere in Australia.

EXPLORING THE APPLE ISLE

VISITOR INFORMATION   The **Tasmanian Visitor Information Centre** (☎ **03/ 6230 8233;** www.tourism.tas.gov.au) is a privatized company operating visitor centers in more than 30 locations throughout the state. It can arrange travel passes, ferry and bus tickets, car rental, cruises, and accommodations.

Pick up a copy of *Travelways,* Tourism Tasmania's excellent tourist tabloid, for details on transport, accommodations, restaurants, and attractions around Tasmania.

WHEN TO GO   The best time to visit Tasmania is between mid-September and May, when the weather is at its best. By April nights are getting cold, the days are getting shorter, and the deciduous trees are starting to turn golden. Winters (June through August), especially in the high country, can be quite harsh—that's the best time to curl up in front of a blazing log fire. The east coast is generally milder than the west coast, which is buffered by the Roaring 40s —the winds that blow across the ocean and the 40° meridian, from as far away as Argentina.

GETTING THERE   The quickest way to get to Tasmania is by air. **Ansett** (☎ **13 13 00** in Australia) and **Qantas** (☎ **13 13 13** in Australia) fly to Hobart and Launceston from Adelaide, Brisbane, Cairns, Canberra, Darwin, the Gold Coast, Melbourne, Perth, and Sydney. Trips to Launceston are generally cheaper.

Kendell Airlines, Level 3, 118 Queens St., Melbourne (☎ **1800/338 894** in Australia, or 03/9670 2677) offers one-way standby tickets from Melbourne to Devonport on the north coast of Tasmania for A$98.50 (U.S.$68.95). The ticket is available only for people living outside Australia, and you must take your passport along to the office.

A more adventurous way to reach Tasmania is to take a boat across Bass Strait from the mainland. The quickest of these options is on the *DevilCat,* Australia's largest high-speed catamaran, which runs between Melbourne's Station Pier and George Town on Tasmania's north coast (trip time: 6 hours). It departs Melbourne at 7:30am every Tuesday, Thursday, Saturday, and Sunday from approximately December 12 to 20, January 26 to March 28, and April 13 to 18. There are extra Wednesday and Friday services from December 22 to January 24 and March 30 to April 11. It leaves George Town at 4pm every Wednesday, Friday, Saturday, and Sunday from approximately December 12 to 20, January 26 to March 28, and April 13 to 18. There are extra services on Tuesday and Thursday from December 22 to January 24 and March 30 and 11 April. The trip time is 6 hours. Schedules are subject to change; call the number below for latest timetable information. Peak season (Dec 13 to Jan 24) one-way fares are A$176 (U.S.$123.20) for adults, A$134 (U.S.$93.80) for students, and A$89 (U.S.$62.30) for children ages 3 to 16. Off-peak one-way fares are A$160 (U.S.$112) for adults, A$120 (U.S.$84) for students, and A$81 (U.S.$56.70) for children. Contact **TT-Line** (☎ **13 20 10** in Australia, or 03/9206 6233; e-mail: reservations@tt-line.com.au; www.tt-line.com.au) for reservations and details. **Tasmanian Redline Coaches** (☎ **03/6331 3233**) link George Town with Launceston, 35 minutes away.

The car and passenger ferry *Spirit of Tasmania* plies the Tasman Sea between Melbourne's Station Pier and Devonport on the island's northwest coast. The ferry departs Melbourne every Monday, Wednesday, and Friday at 6pm and arrives in Devonport the next day at 8:30am. Return trips leave Devonport every Saturday, Tuesday, and Thursday at 6pm. One-way adult fares range from A$103 to $380 (U.S.$72.10 to

$266) depending on the type of accommodation. To transport a car costs an extra A$40 (U.S.$28) or A$30 (U.S.$21) in winter. Prices are highest during the school-holiday periods of mid-December to January, and during the 2 weeks over Easter. Make reservations through **TT-Line** (see above). You can also book tickets by calling **Inta-Aussie** at ☎ **800/531-9222** in the United States or Canada. **Tasmanian Redline Coaches** (see below) connect with each ferry. Standard single fares are A$33.20 (U.S.$23.25) for adults and A$16.60 (U.S.$11.65) for children to Hobart, A$19.50 (U.S.$13.65) for adults and A$9.75 (U.S.$6.85) for children to Launceston.

   McCafferty's (☎ **13 14 99** in Australia) can organize coach travel from the eastern mainland states, with transfers to Tasmania by ferry.

GETTING AROUND   Regional airline **Tasair** (☎ **03/6248 5577;** fax 03/6248 5528) flies to most major settlements in Tasmania. **Par Avion** (☎ **03/6248 5390;** 03/6248 5117; www.tassie.net.au/~paravion) concentrates on the southwest World Heritage areas of the state and also operates tours.

   Bus service is provided by **Tasmanian Redline Coaches** (☎ 03/6231 3233), **Tasmanian Wilderness Travel** (☎ 03/6334 4442; fax 03/6334 2029; www.tassie.net.au/wildtour), **Tasmanian Tours & Travel Tigerland** (☎ 03/6231 3511; fax 03/6234 9241), and **Hobart Coaches** (☎ 1800/030 620 in Australia, or 03/6234 4077; fax 03/6234 8575).

   Driving a car from Devonport on the north coast to Hobart on the south coast takes less than 4 hours. From Hobart to Strahan on the west coast also takes around 4 hours, while the journey from Launceston to Hobart takes just under 3 hours. The **Royal Automobile Club of Tasmania (RACT),** at Murray and Patrick streets, Hobart TAS 7000 (☎ **13 27 22** in Australia), can supply you with touring maps.

   Several companies, including Hertz, rent campervans, but one of the cheapest is **Adventure Campervan Rentals** (☎ **03/6394 3563**), which rents two- or three-berth vans from A$35 (U.S.$24.50) a day.

   There are no passenger trains in Tasmania.

TOUR OPERATORS   Dozens of operators run organized hiking, horse trekking, sailing, caving, fishing, diving, cycling, rafting, climbing, kayaking, or canoeing trips in Tasmania. One of the best operators is **Peregrine Adventures** (☎ **03/6231 0977,** or 018/124 801; fax 03/6225 0946). They run rafting tours of the Picton and Huon rivers and 5- ,7- ,11- , and 13-day raft adventures on the Franklin River through World Heritage areas. Peregrine also has a 6-day East Coast Adventure involving walking, mountain biking, rafting, and snorkeling. Other good operators are **Rafting Tasmania** (☎ **03/6239 1080,** fax 03/6239 1090), and the **Roaring 40's Ocean**

Money-Saving Bus Passes

The cheapest way to get around by coach is to buy a **Tassie Wilderness Pass,** which can be used on a combined network of Tasmanian Redline Coaches and Tasmanian Wilderness Travel routes. Passes come in five categories: A 5-day pass costs A$99 (U.S.$69.30) and allows unlimited travel within 7 days of the first day of travel, a 7-day pass good for travel within 10 days is A$119.95 (U.S.$84), a 10-day pass good for travel within 14 days is A$149.95 (U.S.$105), a 14-day pass good for travel within 20 days is A$159.95 (U.S.$112), and a 30-day pass good for travel within 40 days is A$220 (U.S.$154). Passes are available through **Tasmanian Wilderness Travel,** 101 George St., Launceston (☎ **03/6334 4442**); **Tasmanian Redline Coaches** (see above); or by calling ☎ **1300/300 520** toll-free in Australia. Tasmanian Travel Centres and the Spirit of Tasmania also sell the passes.

National Park Passes

To visit a national park you will need a National Parks Pass. A 24-hour pass costs A$9 (U.S.$6.30) per car, or A$3 (U.S.$2.10) per person; a monthly pass is A$30 (U.S.$21) per vehicle. The best value pass is the Holiday Pass, which costs A$30 (U.S.$21) per car, or A$12 (U.S.$8.40) for backpackers, cyclists, bushwalkers, and motorcyclists. It provides entry into all Tasmania's national parks and is valid for 2 months from the date of issue. Buy passes at the entrance to most parks; at Tasmanian Travel and Information Centers; from many bus, ferry, and tour operators; and from the national parks head office at 134 Macquarie St., Hobart (☎ **03/ 6233 2621;** www.parks.tas.gov.au).

Kayaking Company (☎ **1800/653 712** in Australia). Both companies offer paddling expeditions that last from 1 to 11 days. **Tas-Trek,** based in Launceston (☎ **03/ 6398 2555,** or 018/132 649; fax 03/6398 1500) offers four-wheel drive excursions lasting from 1 to 10 days. (The company's 4-day Franklin River/World Heritage Tour is especially popular). **Tasmanian Expeditions,** also based in Launceston (☎ **1800/ 030 230** in Australia, or 03/6334 3477; fax 03/6334 3464) runs a whole range of cycling, trekking, and rafting trips around the country.

SUGGESTED ITINERARIES If I were planning my first trip to Tasmania, I'd pack my walking boots, raincoat, and shorts, and head off first to either Launceston or Hobart, the island's two main cities. I'd take in Freycinet National Park for its wonderful scenery and abundant wildlife, stop in at Port Arthur for its beautiful setting and disturbing convict past, and head to the central highlands for a tramp around Cradle Mountain. If I had more time, I'd drive to Strahan on the far west coast to discover the great southwest wilderness, take some time off to go trout fishing in the central lakes, and head off to the quaint coastal towns of the north.

1 Hobart

198km (119 miles) S of Launceston

Tasmania's capital (pop. 126,000) is an appealing place well worth visiting for a couple of days. Second in age only to Sydney, Hobart has a wonderful harbor and colonial cottages lining the narrow lanes of Battery Point. As with Sydney, Hobart's harbor is the city's focal point, attracting yachts from all over the world. Down by the waterfront, picturesque Salamanca Place bursts with galleries, pubs, cafes, and an excellent market on Saturdays. European settlement at Hobart took place in 1804, a year after Tasmania's first colony was set up at Risdon (10km/6 miles up the Derwent River).

Driving Safety

More car accidents involving tourists occur in Tasmania than virtually anywhere else in Australia. Many roads are narrow, and bends can be tight, especially in the mountainous inland regions. Marsupials are also very common around dusk, and many accidents occur when drivers hit the animals or swerve to avoid them. Be especially alert on dirt tracks, which can be very hazardous, especially when damp. You'll also notice plenty of signs warning about speed cameras, so keep an eye on the speedometer, or you're likely to be hit with a hefty fine.

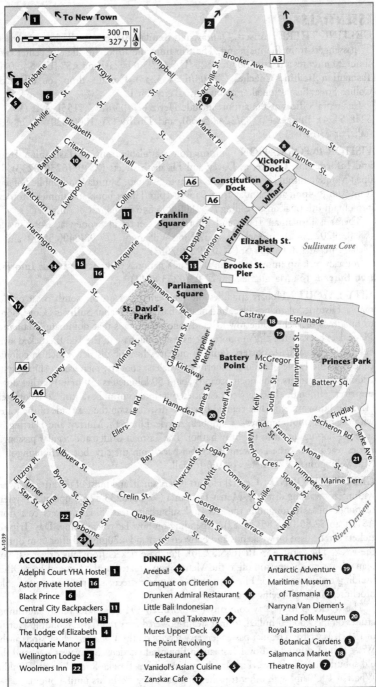

↑ **1**   ↖ **To New Town**

0 ————— 300 m / 327 y N

A-1039

↑ **2** ↗   ↑ **3**

Brooker Ave.   **A3**

Campbell   Sackville St.   Sun St.   Evans   St.

Brisbane St.   Argyle   **6**   St.   **7**   Market Pl.   Hunter   St.

4 Melville   Elizabeth   St.   **8**   **Victoria Dock**

5 Bathurst   Criterion St.   **10**   Mall   **A6**   **Constitution Dock**   **9**   **Wharf**

Murray   Liverpool   Collins   **A6**

Watchorn St.   St.   **11**   St.   **Franklin Square**   Despard St.   **Franklin**   **Elizabeth St. Pier**   *Sullivans Cove*

Harrington   Macquarie   **12**   Morrison St.   **Brooke St. Pier**

14   **15**   **16**   St.   Salamanca   **13**   **Parliament Square**

St. David's Park   Place   Castray   **18**   Esplanade

17 Barrack   **19**

Wilmot St.   Gladstone St.   Montpelier Retreat   **Battery Point**   McGregor St.   Runnymede St.   **Princes Park**

A6 Davey   Kirksway   Battery Sq.

A6 Molle   St.   -lie Rd.   Hampden   James St.   Stowell Ave.   Kelly   South   Rd.   Francis   St.   Secheron Rd.   Findlay St.   Clarke Ave.

Albuera St.   Rd.   Bay   **20**   Logan   Waterloo Cres.   Mona   St.   **21**

Fitzroy Pl.   Byron   St.   Newcastle St.   DeWitt   Cromwell St.   Colville   Sloane   Trumpeter   Marine Terr.

Turner   Erina   Sandy   Crelin St.   St. Georges   Napoleon

Star St.   **22**   Quayle   Bath St.   *River Derwent*

23   Osborne   Princes   St.   Terrace

ACCOMMODATIONS

Adelphi Court YHA Hostel **1**
Astor Private Hotel **16**
Black Prince **6**
Central City Backpackers **11**
Customs House Hotel **13**
The Lodge of Elizabeth **4**
Macquarie Manor **15**
Wellington Lodge **2**
Woolmers Inn **22**

DINING

Areeba! **12**
Cumquat on Criterion **10**
Drunken Admiral Restaurant **8**
Little Bali Indonesian
  Cafe and Takeaway **14**
Mures Upper Deck **9**
The Point Revolving
  Restaurant **23**
Vanidol's Asian Cuisine **5**
Zanskar Cafe **17**

ATTRACTIONS

Antarctic Adventure **19**
Maritime Museum
  of Tasmania **21**
Narryna Van Diemen's
  Land Folk Museum **20**
Royal Tasmanian
  Botanical Gardens **3**
Salamanca Market **18**
Theatre Royal **7**

ESSENTIALS

GETTING THERE **Ansett, Qantas,** and **Kendall Airlines** (book through Ansett) fly passengers from the mainland. The trip from the airport to the city center takes about 20 minutes and costs about A$25 (U.S.$17.50) by taxi and A$7 (U.S.$4.90) by **Tasmanian Redline Coaches** (☎ 03/6231 3233). Coaches drop you off at the Collins Street bus terminal or at any central city hotel.

Car-rental offices at the airport include **Hertz** (☎ 03/6237 1155), **Avis** (☎ 03/6248 5424), **Budget** (☎ 03/6248 5333), and **Thrifty** (☎ 1800/030 730 in Australia, or 03/6234 1341).

VISITOR INFORMATION Information is available from the **Tasmanian Travel and Information Centre,** at Davey and Elizabeth streets (☎ **03/6230 8233**). It's open Monday through Friday from 8:30am to 5:15pm, Saturday and public holidays from 9am to 4pm, and Sunday from 9am to 1pm (longer hours in summer). You can also obtain information by calling ☎ 1800/806 846 in the rest of Australia.

There's a Tasmanian Travel and Information Centre in Sydney, at 149 King St. (☎ 02/9202 2022); in Adelaide, at 32 King William St. (☎ 08/8400 5533); and in Melbourne, at 256 Collins St.(☎ 03/9206 7933).

You can pick up information on the state's national parks at the **Lands Information Bureau,** 134 Macquarie St., (☎ **03/6233 8011**).

CITY LAYOUT Hobart straddles the Derwent River on the south coast of Tasmania. Historic Salamanca Place and nearby Battery Point abut **Sullivans Cove,** home to hundreds of yachts. The row of sandstone warehouses that dominate **Salamanca Place** date back to the city's importance as a whaling base in the 1830s. Tucked away behind Princes Wharf, **Battery Point** is the city's historic district, which in colonial times was the home of sailors, fishermen, whalers, coopers, merchants, shipwrights, and master mariners. The open ocean is about 50 kilometers (30 miles) farther down the river, although the Derwent empties out into Storm Bay, just 20 kilometers (12 miles) downstream. The **central business district** is on the west side of the water, with the main thoroughfares—Campbell, Argyle, Elizabeth, Murray, and Harrington streets—sloping down to the busy harbor. The Tasman Bridge and regular passenger ferries reach across the Derwent River. Set back from the city, but overlooking it, is Mt. Wellington, 1,270-meters (4,166-ft.) tall.

GETTING AROUND Central Hobart is very small, and most of the attractions are within easy walking distance. **Metro Tasmania** (☎ 03/6233 4232) operates a system of public buses throughout the city and suburban areas. Single tickets cost from A$1.20 to $2.80 (U.S.85¢ to $2), depending on how far you're going. **Day-Tripper tickets** can be used on weekends and between 9am and 4:30pm and after 6pm during the week. They cost A$3.10 (U.S.$2.20). Purchase tickets from bus drivers. If you plan on busing about, stop off at the Metro Shop situated in the General Post Office building on the corner of Elizabeth and Macquarie streets and pick up a timetable, brochures, and sightseeing information.

The **Roche-O'May** ferry company (☎ 03/6223 1914) operates lunch and dinner cruises on the wooden-hulled, former steam-powered ferry the *Cartela* (built in Hobart in 1912), as well as a regular passenger ferry service on the *Wanderer,* which stops at the Wrest Point Casino, the Royal Tasmanian Botanical Gardens, Sullivans Cove, and the old suburb of Belle Reeve. The first ferry leaves from Brooke Street Pier on Franklin Wharf at 10:30am, with other trips heading out every 1½ hours until 4:30pm.

SPECIAL EVENTS The **Sydney-to-Hobart Yacht Race,** which starts in Sydney on December 26, fills the Constitution Dock Marina and general harbor area close to overflowing with spectators and party-goers when the ships eventually turn up in

Tasmania. The race takes anywhere from 2 to 4 days, and the sailors and fans stay on to celebrate New Year's Eve in Hobart. Food and wine lovers indulge themselves after the race during the month-long **Hobart Summer Festival,** which starts around December 28.

ENJOYING THE CITY & ENVIRONS

Simply strolling around the harbor and popping into the shops at **Salamanca Place** can keep you nicely occupied. Take a look around **Battery Point,** an area chock-full of colonial stone cottages just south of the harbor. The area gets its name from a battery of guns set up on the promontory in 1818 to defend the town against potential invaders (particularly the French). Today, there are plenty of tearooms, antiques shops, cozy restaurants, and atmospheric pubs interspersed between grand dwellings.

One of the houses worth looking into is **Narryna Van Diemen's Land Folk Museum,** 103 Hampden Rd. (☎ **03/6234 2791**). The museum depicts the life of upper-class pioneers and is open Monday through Friday from 10:30am to 5pm, Saturday and Sunday from 2 to 5pm (closed July). Admission is A$5 (U.S.$3.50) for adults and A$2 (U.S.$1.40) for children. The **Maritime Museum of Tasmania,** Secheron Rd. (☎ **03/ 6223 5082**), is one of the best museums of its type in Australia. It's open daily from 10am to 4:30pm, and admission is A$4 (U.S.$2.80); free for children under age 15.

The **National Trust** (☎ **03/6223 7570**) offers a 2-hour **Battery Point Heritage Walk** leaving at 9:30am every Saturday from the wishing well in Franklin Square. It costs A$10 (U.S.$7) for adults and A$2.50 (U.S.$1.75) for children ages 6 to 16 and includes morning tea.

For magnificent views over Hobart and across a fair-sized chunk of Tasmania, drive to **The Pinnacle** on top of Mt. Wellington, about 40 minutes from the city center. Take a warm coat, though; the wind in this alpine area can bite. An extensive network of walking trails offers good hiking around the mountain. Pick up a copy of *Mt. Wellington Day Walk Map and Notes* from the **Department of Environment Tasmap Centre,** on the ground floor of the Lands Building, 134 Macquarie St. (☎ **03/6233 3382**).

✪ **Antarctic Adventure.** 2 Salamanca Square. ☎ **03/6220 8220.** Admission A$16 (U.S.$11.20) adults, A$8 (U.S.$5.60) children 4–13, A$40 (U.S.$28) family of 4. Daily 10am–5pm. Closed Christmas.

Hobart is the last port of call for expeditions to Antarctica. You can experience the cold continent yourself at this highly recommended attraction. It doesn't look like much at first, but I promise you'll be sucked in. You can experience an Antarctic blizzard, climb all over heavy machinery, experience a downhill ski simulator (I'm not sure how that fits in), and get computer access to Antarctic weather conditions and communications. The photos and other displays are also interesting. The irresistible stuffed huskies in the souvenir shop will take a hefty bite out of your wallet.

Bonorong Park Wildlife Centre. Briggs Rd., Brighton. ☎ **03/6268 1184.** Admission A$8 (U.S.$5.60) adults, A$4 (U.S.$2.80) children under 15. Daily 9am–5pm. Closed Christmas. Bus: 125 or 126. Drive north on route 1 to Brighton; it's about 25 minutes north of Hobart and well signposted.

I don't think I've ever seen so many wallabies in one place as I saw here. There are lots of other native animals around, too, including snakes, koalas, Tasmanian Devils, and wombats. The Bush Tucker shed serves lunch, *billy tea* (basically, tea brewed up in a metal pot with a gum leaf thrown in), and *damper* (Australian-style campfire bread). Koala cuddling isn't allowed in Tasmania, but if you're around at feeding time, it's possible to stroke one—they're not as shy as you might think. Feeding times are 12:30pm and 3pm daily. The park is on the side of a steep hill, so travelers in wheelchairs or people who likes things flat are likely to fare badly.

Cadbury Chocolate Factory. Claremont, 12km (7 miles) north of Hobart. ☎ 1800/ 627 367 in Australia, or 03/6249 0333. Tours Mon–Fri 8am (summer only), 9am, 9:30am, 10:30am, and 1pm. A$10 (U.S.$7) adults, A$5 (U.S.$3.50) children, A$25 (U.S.$17.50) families.

Eat chocolates till they make you sick on this Willy Wonka–type trip. Book well ahead because chocolate tours are very popular. See "Organized Tours" below for information on how to get there by boat.

Cascade Brewery Tours. Cascade Rd. ☎ **03/6221 8300.** A$7.50 (U.S.$5.25) adults, A$1.50 (U.S.$1.05) children 5–16. Mon–Fri 9:30am and 1pm. Closed public holidays. Reservations essential. Bus: stop 18 on routes 44, 46, and 49.

Cascade Premium is one of the best beers in the country, in my opinion. To see how this heady amber nectar is produced, head to Australia's oldest brewery and tag along on a fascinating 2-hour tour, which includes a stroll through the grand old Woodstock Gardens behind the factory.

Fudge Factory and Historic Garden Tours. Island Produce Confectionery, 16 Degraves St., South Hobart. ☎ **03/6223 3233.** Tours A$6 (U.S.$4.20) adults, A$3 (U.S.$2.10) children, A$15 (U.S.$10.50) families (2 adults, 2 children). Mon–Fri 8am–4pm, Sat 10am–3pm. Tours begin at 10:30am (and 1:30pm during summer) Mon–Fri; reservations essential. (You can look around the gardens for free anytime if you make a purchase in the shop; there are always free samples of fudge.) Bus: 44, 46, or 49 to South Hobart and Cascade Rd.; get off at stop 16.

This is an interesting stopover if you're visiting either the Cascade Brewery or Mt. Wellington. Not only do you get a trip around a very successful fudge-making factory, but also a guided tour around the remains of the women's prison next door. The tales told around here will make the hairs on your neck stand on end—like the fact that 17 out of every 20 children born within the walls of the institution died soon after birth, and that women who died were simply tossed into an unmarked mass grave. All the proceeds of the tour literally go into a black hole: The factory's owner is excavating the convict-made drainage system for posterity.

Royal Tasmanian Botanical Gardens. On the Queens Domain, near Government House. ☎ **03/6234 6299.** Gardens, free; Conservatory A$2 (U.S.$1.40). Daily 8am–6:30pm (until 4:45pm in winter). Bus: 17.

Established in 1818, these gardens are known for the English-style plant and tree layouts, the Japanese garden dominated by a miniature Mt. Fuji, and the colorful seasonal blooming plants housed in the conservatory. A restaurant provides lunch and teas. A new visitor center opened in December 1998, along with a Sub-Antarctic plant house.

ORGANIZED TOURS & ACTIVE ENDEAVORS

A good introduction to the city is the daily **Hobart Historic Walk** (☎ **03/6225 4806;** fax 03/6225 4807). Guides lead visitors on a leisurely 2-hour stroll through historic Sullivan's Cove and Battery Point. Tours depart at 10am daily from September to May, and on request from June to August. They cost A$15 (U.S.$10.50) for adults, A$12 (U.S.$8.40) for students and seniors; children under age 12 are free.

Several companies run boat tours of the harbor. **Trans Derwent Ferry and Railway Harbour Cruises** (☎ **03/6223 5893**) offers a wide range of morning tea, lunch, afternoon, and dinner cruises. The company also runs Cadbury Factory Tours, which include coach transfers, a tour of the factory, a harbor cruise, and a 2-course lunch for A$30 (U.S.$21) for adults, and A$18 (U.S.$12.60) for children; these tours leave at 9:45am Monday through Thursday. Cruises depart from Franklin Wharf at the bottom of Elizabeth Street.

The **Cruise Company** (☎ **03/6234 9294**) operates river trips along the Derwent to the Cadbury Chocolate Factory at 10am daily, returning at 2:30pm. The trips (including entry and a guided tour of the factory) cost A$33 (U.S.$23.10) for adults, A$16 (U.S.$11.20) for children ages 5 to 15, and A$93 (U.S.$65.10) for a family of four. Children under age 5 are free. The boat also leaves from Brooke Street Pier. Also of interest is the company's 2-hour Ironpot Cruise (to the lighthouse of that name at the mouth of the Derwent). The scenic tour of the river leaves Brooke Street Pier at 2pm every Saturday, and costs A$20 (U.S.$14) for adults and A$10 (U.S.$7) for children.

THE SHOPPING SCENE

If you are in Hobart on a Saturday, don't miss the **Salamanca Market,** in Salamanca Place, which in my experience is the best in Australia. Some 200 stalls offer everything from fruit and vegetables to crafts. The markets are open from 8:30am to 3pm. Salamanca Place itself has plenty of craft and souvenir shops that are worth exploring, although you pay for the privilege of buying them in such a fashionable, high-rent area. The best bookshop in town, **Hobart Bookshop,** at 22 Salamanca Square (☎ **03/6223 1803**), is a beauty and sells a range of new and secondhand books, many relating to Tasmania. For great chocolate and the best licorice, head to **Darrell Lea,** shop 36 in the Cat & Fiddle Arcade between Collins and Liverpool streets. There are plenty of other interesting shops here, too. **Store hours** are Monday through Thursday from 9am to 6pm, Friday from 9am to 9pm, and Saturday from 9am to noon.

WHERE TO STAY

Hobart has some of the best hotels, guesthouses, and B&Bs in Australia. For something different, stay with a Tasmanian family either in town or at a farm in the country. Contact **Heritage Tasmania Pty Ltd.,** P.O. Box 780, Sandy Bay, TAS 7005. (☎ **03/6233 5511;** fax 03/6233 5510) for more information. The company can also arrange stays in boutique bed-and-breakfasts throughout Tasmania. Nightly bed-and-breakfast rates range from about A$60 (U.S.$42) to around A$160 (U.S.$112) for a double.

Astor Private Hotel. 157 Macquarie St., Hobart, TAS 7000. ☎ **03/6234 6611.** Fax 03/6234 6384. 21 units, none with bathroom. A$65–$80 (U.S.$45.50–$56) double, depending on season (lower rates in winter). Additional person A$25 (U.S.$17.50) extra. BC, MC, V.

Built in 1922 right in the heart of the city, this very homey three-story property fell from grace following a few years of neglectful management. That's all changed now, and minor renovations are gradually proceeding with the owner of the Central City Backpackers at the helm. It's a friendly place, with lots of natural wood. On the ground floor is the Astor Grill, an upscale fish and steak restaurant (main courses A$18 to $25/U.S.$12.60 to $17.50), and the Greek taverna, El Greco (main courses A$11.50 to $16/U.S.$8.05 to $11.20). There's a guest lounge with a TV and a laundry.

Black Prince. 145 Elizabeth St. Hobart, TAS 7000. ☎ **03/6234 3501.** Fax 03/6234 3502. TV. 10 units. A$50 (U.S.$35) double. AE, BC, DC, MC, V.

If you're looking for somewhere central, clean, tidy, and unfussy, then I recommend the Black Prince, an American-influenced pub with a 1950s bent. All rooms come with a shower and bathtub, and a TV. Room no. 8 is the landlord's favorite because "it's nearer to the stairs so you don't have to walk too far" (presumably beneficial when you've had a few too many beers). Downstairs, the American-style bar is popular, especially on weekends, while the American-influenced restaurant serves up budget-priced steaks and chicken dishes.

Customs House Hotel. 1 Murray St., Hobart, TAS 7000. ☎ **03/6234 6645.** Fax 03/6223 8750. 13 units, 2 with bathroom. A$65 (U.S.$45.50) double without bathroom; A$70 (U.S.$49) double with bathroom. Rates include continental breakfast. AE, BC, DC, MC, V.

You won't find a better value than the rooms above this historic sandstone pub overlooking the waterfront. Built in 1846, the property offers simple, colonial-style rooms. Four have water views overlooking the old sailing ship the *May Queen,* which used to carry wood up the Derwent River. Other rooms look across Parliament House. Guests make the best of a shared TV room. Downstairs, a friendly public bar overlooks the water, and at the back of the building is a popular seafood restaurant known for its scallops.

The Lodge on Elizabeth. 249 Elizabeth St., Hobart, TAS 7000. ☎ **03/6231 3830.** Fax 03/6234 2566. 13 units (some with shower only). A$85 (U.S.$58.50) standard double; A$115 (U.S.$80.50) deluxe double; A$125 (U.S.$87.50) spa room. AE, BC, DC, MC, V.

The Lodge on Elizabeth is located in the second-oldest building in Tasmania, with some parts of it dating back to 1810. Originally a gentleman's residence, it later became the first private boy's school in Tasmania. It's well situated, just a 12-minute walk from Salamanca Place, and is surrounded by restaurants. All rooms are decorated with antiques, and many are quite romantic, with four-poster beds. Standard rooms have just a shower, whereas the deluxe rooms come with more antiques and a large granite bathroom with tub. Complimentary drinks are served in the communal living room in the evenings, and a good continental breakfast buffet goes for A$9.50 (U.S.$6.65).

Wellington Lodge. 7 Scott St., Glebe, Hobart, TAS 7000. ☎ **03/6231 0614.** Fax 03/6234 1551. 5 units, 1 with bathroom (shower only). TV. A$85–$100 (U.S.$58.50–$70) double. Additional person A$30 (U.S.$21) extra. Rates include cooked breakfast. BC, MC, V. Free parking. The airport bus will drop you off here, as will any bus to the Aquatic Center. Children under age 11 not accepted.

This charming Victorian-style town house is just a 10-minute walk (through Hobart's Rose Garden) from the main shopping area and Salamanca Place. It was refurbished in 1997 and stocked with period antiques. One room has its own shower; the other four rooms share two baths. All rooms have wicker chairs and matching bedspreads and drapes. Complimentary port is served every evening in the guest lounge. Smoking is not permitted.

Woolmers Inn. 123–127 Sandy Bay Rd., Hobart, TAS 7000. ☎ **1800/030 780** in Australia, or 03/6223 7355. Fax 03/6223 1981. 31 apts. TV TEL. A$99 (U.S.$69.30) 1-bedroom apt; A$130 (U.S.$91) 2-bedroom apt. Additional person A$15 (U.S.$10.50) extra; children A$8 (U.S.$5.60) extra. Rates 10% higher Christmas–Jan. AE, BC, DC, MC, V. Free parking. Bus: Catch bus to Sandy Bay at the Elizabeth St. mall.

Situated 2 kilometers (1¼ mile) south of the city, Woolmers Inn offers quite cozy units with either one or two bedrooms with fully equipped kitchens. One unit is suitable for travelers with disabilities. Sandy Bay is Hobart's main suburb, featuring a "golden mile" of boutique shopping. It's halfway between the casino and the city, and within walking distance of Salamnca Place. You'll find a coin-op laundry and a travel center on the property. The inn will be upgraded throughout 1999.

SUPER-CHEAP SLEEPS

Jane Franklin Hall, a residential college of the University of Tasmania, 3 kilometers (2 miles) from the city center at 6 Elbowden St., South Hobart ☎ **03/6223 2000;** fax 03/6224 0598), offers 181 study-type bedrooms from December to February for A$35 (U.S.$24.50) for a single room, and A$45 (U.S.$31.50) for a double, including continental breakfast. The rooms are neat and tidy, with little else in them besides a bed and a desk. Bathrooms are shared, and there are free laundry facilities. A two- to three-course evening meal here costs just A$10 (U.S.$7). Credit cards: BC, MC, V.

Adelphi Court YHA Hostel. 17 Stoke St., New Town (postal address: YHA Tasmania, G.P.O. Box 174, Hobart, TAS 7001). ☎ **03/6228 4829.** Fax 03/6278 2047. 25 units, 2 with bathroom. A$19 (U.S.$13.30) per person twin/double without bathroom; A$48 (U.S.$33.60) double with bathroom. A$14 (U.S.$9.80) dorm bed. Non-YHA members pay A$3 (U.S.$2.10) per person extra. BC, MC, V. Free parking. Bus: 15 or 16 from Argyle St. to stop no. 8A, or any bus from Stop E at Elizabeth Street Mall to bus stop no 13.

The Adelphi, situated 3 kilometers (less than 2 miles) from the city center, is a typical clean and friendly Australian youth hostel. All dorm rooms sleep four people. It has a large game and TV room, a tour-booking desk, a kiosk, a communal kitchen, a dining room serving breakfasts from A$3 to $8 (U.S.$2.10–$5.60), a laundry, and a barbecue area. The hostel also rents bikes.

Central City Backpackers. 138 Collins St., Hobart, TAS 7000. ☎ **1800/811 507** in Australia, or 03/6224 2404. Fax 03/6224 2316. 60 units. A$19 (U.S.$13.30) twin per person; A$30 (U.S.$21) single; A$38 (U.S.$26.60) double. A$14 (U.S.$9.80) dorm bed. Cash only. 2-minute walk from central bus terminal.

This place is typical of backpacker-type accommodations—cheap and cheerful, a little frayed around the edges, but right in the heart of things. The central shopping district is right outside the door, and it's only a short walk to the harbor. There is a common room with e-mail and Internet access; and a pool table, a fully equipped kitchen, a dining room, and laundry facilities are on the premises.

WORTH A SPLURGE

✪ **Macquarie Manor.** 172 Macquarie St., TAS 7000. ☎ **1800/243 044** in Australia, or 03/6224 4999. Fax 03/6224 4333. 18 units (most with shower only). MINIBAR TV TEL. A$140 (U.S.$98) Heritage room; A$170 (U.S.$119) Heritage suite; A$185 (U.S.$129.50) Macquarie suite. Rates include cooked breakfast. AE, BC, DC, MC, V. Free parking. 2 blocks from central bus terminal.

As soon as you walk into this place, you'll know you want to stay. Macquarie Manor was built in 1875 as a doctor's surgery and residence. Extra rooms were added in 1950. Thick carpets and double-glazing keep the place very quiet, even though the Manor is on the main road. Rooms, which vary enormously, are comfortable and elegantly furnished. One room is suitable for people with disabilities. Most come with shower but no bathtub. The staff is very friendly and will be happy to escort you around the premises in search of your favorite room. Check out the delightful dining room, and the drawing room, complete with old couches and a grand piano. Smoking is not permitted.

WHERE TO DINE

Tasmania is known for its fresh seafood, including oysters, crab, crayfish, salmon, and trout. Once cheap, in recent years prices have crept up to match or even surpass those on the mainland. Generally, though, the food is good quality—as long as you avoid some of the cheaper fish-and-chips take-out joints on the waterfront (a budget favorite, **Flippers on Constitution Dock,** is an exception).

One of the best areas for cheap eats is **North Hobart,** especially along Elizabeth Street, near Burnett Street. Probably the best food court in town is **The Cat & Fiddle Food Court,** best accessed from Collins Street.

If you want to cook your own food or pack up a lunch for the day, then you'll need a supermarket. The most convenient is **Ralph's Super Seven,** 181 Campbell St. (☎ **03/6234 8077**)—about a 10-minute walk from the city center. It's open daily from 8am to 7pm.

⭐ **Areeba!** 7 Despard St., (behind the Customs House Hotel). ☎ **03/6224 4484.** Reservations recommended. Main courses A$15–$18.50 (U.S.$10.50–$12.95). AE, BC, DC, MC, V. Daily 5pm–late. MODERN MEXICAN.

The owner of this excellent Tex-Mex place learned his trade at a cooking school in Santa Fe and honed his skills in his own restaurant in Bali. Everything is fresh—even the corn chips are imported from the U.S. The decor is modern and colorful, and the bar is a great place for a predinner tequila. There's a good selection of fajitas, burritos, tacos, enchiladas, and salads on the menu. A favorite dish is the smoked chili prawns on buttermilk pancakes with salsa fresca.

Cumquat on Criterion. 10 Criterion St. ☎ **03/6234 5858.** Reservations recommended. Main courses A$9–$14 (U.S.$6.30–$9.80). No credit cards. Mon–Fri 8am–late. MIXED ASIAN/AUSTRALIAN.

This cafe is an excellent breakfast venue, offering everything from egg on toast to traditional porridge with brown sugar. On the menu for lunch and dinner you could find Thai beef curry, laksa, a daily risotto, and chermoula marinated fish. The sticky rice pudding is one of my favorite deserts. Vegetarians, vegans, and anyone on a gluten-free diet are well cared for, as is your average carnivore.

Drunken Admiral Restaurant. 17–19 Hunter St. ☎ **03/6234 1903.** Reservations required. Main courses A$15.90–$22.90 (U.S.$11.15–$13.95). AE, BC, DC, MC, V. Daily 6pm–late. SEAFOOD.

The Drunken Admiral, opposite the Hotel Grand Chancellor on the waterfront, is an extremely popular spot with tourists and can get quite raucous on very busy evenings. The main attraction is the famous seafood chowder, swimming with anything the fishmonger had to sell at the docks that morning. The large "Yachties" seafood grill is made up of plenty of squid, scallops, fish, mussels, and prawns; but there are plenty of simpler fish dishes on the menu, too. A rather uninspired all-you-can eat salad bar is spread out in a sailing dingy.

Little Bali Indonesian Café and Takeaway. 84A Harrington St. ☎ **03/6234 3426.** Reservations not accepted. Most main courses about A$7.50 (U.S.$5.25). No credit cards. Mon–Fri 11:30am–3pm and 5–9pm, Sat–Sun 5–9pm. INDONESIAN.

If you're looking for cheap and filling Indonesian-style beef, lamb, or vegetable curry, or some peanut-sauce satay, then you've come to the right place. Order your meal at the counter and either take it to go or grab a spot at one of the seven tables in this tiny place. All meals are served with rice and salad.

The Point Revolving Restaurant. In the Wrest Point Hotel Casino, 410 Sandy Bay Rd. ☎ **03/6225 0112.** Reservations recommended. Main courses from A$11.50 (U.S.$8.05) at lunch and from $21.50 (U.S.$15.05) at dinner. Set 3-course lunch menu A$25.50 (U.S.$17.85); set 3-course dinner menu A$48 (U.S.$33.60) or A$34 (U.S.$23.80) Sun–Thurs. AE, BC, DC, MC, V. Daily noon–2pm and 6:30–9:30pm. TASMANIAN/AUSTRALIAN.

This revolving restaurant on the 17th floor of the Wrest Point Hotel Casino is known for its spectacular harbor and mountain views. Criticism of its consistency has led to a complete review of its cuisine over the last couple of years, but fortunately its specialty prawns flambé in a curry sauce and the Caesar salad—both of which are prepared at your table—have remained through regular menu upgrades. The crêpes Suzette, a wonderful signature dessert, is also whipped up as you watch. The service is friendly and relaxed. This place is packed on weekends. The cheaper set dinner has fewer options.

Vanidol's Asian Cuisine. 353 Elizabeth St., North Hobart. ☎ **03/6234 9307.** Reservations recommended. Main courses A$11.90–$14.50 (U.S.$8.35–$10.15). Tues–Sun 6pm–late. BC, MC, V. ASIAN.

Another restaurant very popular with both locals and tourists, Vanidol's serves up a variety of Thai, Indonesian, and Indian dishes. The beef salad with basil, chili, and mint is very good as are the barbecue prawns served with a sweet tamarind sauce. The fish cooked in a light red curry sauce is another specialty. Smoking is not permitted between 6 and 9pm.

Zanskar Cafe. 39 Barrack St. ☎ **03/6231 3983.** Main courses A$6–$10 (U.S.$4.20–$7). No credit cards. Mon–Thurs 10am–9pm, Fri 10am–9:30pm, Sat and Sun 2–9pm. VEGETARIAN/VEGAN.

The decor here is as bright and colorful as the food. The owner formerly ran a wholefood cafeteria in California's Silicon Valley, so that explains the profusion of Mexican-style dishes on offer, especially on Saturday nights. Come here on Sunday for curry night. Meals are cheap and filling, with some great salads available from the salad bar.

WORTH A SPLURGE

✪ **Mures Upper Deck.** Between Victoria and Constitution Docks, Hobart. ☎ **03/6231 2121.** Reservations recommended. Main courses A$19.50–$25 (U.S.$13.65–$17.50). AE, BC, DC, JCB, MC, V. Daily noon–10pm. SEAFOOD.

This large and bustling waterfront restaurant offers great views of bobbing yachts as well as very fine seafood caught on the owner's own fishing boats. I recommend starting with a bowl of potato soup, or the signature Mures oysters topped with smoked salmon, sour cream, and salmon caviar. The most popular main courses are the blue-eye fillet Martinique—a Creole-inspired sweet fish curry with coconut cream and banana sauce—and the giant seafood platter for two. The best summer dessert on the menu is the restaurant's famous summer pudding, which almost bursts with berries. In winter, come here if only for the Granny Leatherwood Pudding—made of apples and Australian leatherwood honey beneath a bread-and-butter pudding top and served with cinnamon ice cream. The complex also includes Lower Deck, a very popular self-service family restaurant where you can dine very well for under A$15 (U.S.$10.50).

HOBART AFTER DARK

THE PERFORMING ARTS   Built in 1837, the 747-seat **Theatre** Royal, 29 Campbell St. (☎ **03/6233 2299**), is the oldest remaining live theater in the country. It's known for its excellent acoustics and its classical Victorian decor. Ticket prices vary depending on the performance, but A$25 (U.S.$17.50) is average.

PUBS & CLUBS   You may be interested in the **Hobart Historic Pub Tour** (☎ **03/ 6225 4806;** fax 03/6225 4807), which traces the city's early development through hotel drinking holes—an important part of life in Hobart early last century. The 2-hour tours take in four pubs and run Sunday to Thursday, starting at 5pm; they cost A$35 (U.S.$24.50), including a drink at each pub.

The popular **Irish Murphy's pub,** 21 Salamanca Place (☎ **03/6223 1119**) is my favorite drinking hole in Hobart. It's rustic and atmospheric, with stone walls and lots of dark wooden panels and beams. Local bands play Friday and Saturday evenings.

Knopwood's Retreat, 39 Salamanca Place (☎ **03/6223 5808**), opened in 1829 as a tavern and a brothel frequented by whalers. It's still a raucous place on Friday and Saturday evenings, when some 200 people cram inside its historic interior and up to 600 more spill out onto the streets. Light lunches are popular throughout the week, and occasionally you'll find jazz or blues on the menu.

A CASINO   **Wrest Point Casino,** in the Wrest Point Hotel, 410 Sandy Bay Rd. ☎ 03/6225 0112), was Australia's first legal gambling club. It offers blackjack, roulette, baccarat, keno, and so forth. The table games are open Sunday through

Thursday from 1pm to 2am, and Friday and Saturday from 1pm to 3am. Smart, casual attire is required (collared shirts for men).

2 Port Arthur: Discovering Tasmania's Convict Heritage

102km (61 miles) SE of Hobart.

Port Arthur, on the Tasman Peninsula, is one of Australia's prettiest harbors and houses the extensive remains of Tasmania's largest penal colony. It's the state's number-one tourist destination, and you really need to spend at least a whole day in this incredibly picturesque, yet haunting, place.

From 1830 to 1877 Port Arthur was one of the harshest institutions of its type anywhere in the world. It was built to house the settlement's most notorious prisoners, including those who had escaped from lesser institutions. Nearly 13,000 convicts found their way here, and nearly 2,000 died while incarcerated. Port Arthur was, and still is, connected to the rest of Tasmania by a narrow strip of land called **Eaglehawk Neck.** Guards and rows of dogs kept watch over this narrow path, while the authorities circulated rumors that the waters around the peninsula were shark infested. Only a few convicts ever managed to escape, and most of those either perished in the bush or were tracked down and hanged.

Look out for the blowhole and other coastal formations, including Tasman's Arch, Devil's Kitchen, and the Tessellated Pavement, as you pass through Eaglehawk Neck.

ESSENTIALS

GETTING THERE   Port Arthur is a 1½-hour drive from Hobart via the Lyell and Arthur highways. **Tasmanian Tours & Travel Tigerland** (☎ **03/6231 3511;** fax 03/6234 9241; www.tigerline.com.au; e-mail: info@tigerline.com.au) runs trips from Hobart to the former penal settlement every day except Monday; tours depart from 199 Collins St. at 9am and return around 5:30pm. Tours cost A$45 or $55 (U.S.$31.50 or $38.50) for adults and A$21 or $25 (U.S.$14.70 or $17.50) for children ages 4 to 16. Children under age 4 are free.

Experience Tasmania (☎ **03/6234 3336**) also runs coach trips from Hobart to Port Arthur every Monday, Wednesday, Friday, and Sunday, leaving the Cruise Company ferry offices on Franklin Wharf at 9:15am and returning around 5pm. Tours cost from A$40 to $55 (U.S.$28 to $38.50) for adults and from A$21 to $30 (U.S.$14.70 to $21) for children ages 5 to 16. Children under ages 5 are free. All three tours include a guided tour of the prison complex.

EXPLORING THE SITE

The **Port Arthur Historic Site** (☎ **03/6250 2363;** fax 03/6250 2494) is large and scattered with thirty 19th-century buildings. Most of the main structures were damaged during bushfires in 1877, shortly after the site ceased to be a penal institution. You can tour the remains of the church, guard tower, model prison, and several other buildings. It's best to tour the area with a guide, who can graphically describe what the buildings were originally used for. Don't miss the fascinating museum in the old lunatic asylum, which has a scale model of the prison complex, as well as leg irons and chains.

The historic site is open daily from 9am to 5pm; admission is A$16 (U.S.$11.20) for adults, A$8 (U.S.$4.55) for children ages 4 to 7. The admission price includes a walking tour and a boat cruise around the harbor, leaving eight times daily in summer. There is also a separate cruise twice a day to the Isle of the Dead off the coast of Port Arthur; some 1,769 convicts and 180 free settlers were buried here, mostly in mass graves with no headstones. The cruise costs an extra A$5 (U.S.$3.50) per person.

Something Spooky

Excellent **Ghost Tours** of Port Arthur by lantern light leave nightly at 9:30pm (8:30pm during winter). They cost A$12 (U.S.$8.40) for adults and A$6 (U.S.$4.20) for children. Reservations are essential; call ☎ **1800/659 101** in Australia.

A new **Visitor Centre** opened in January 1999. The main feature is the Interpretive Gallery, which takes visitors through the process by which convicts were sentenced in England and transported to Van Dieman's Land (Tasmania). The gallery contains a courtroom, a section of a transport ship's hull, a blacksmith's shop, a lunatic asylum, and much more. Allow around 5 to 6 hours to explore the site and the gallery.

EN ROUTE TO PORT ARTHUR

On the way to Port Arthur you might want to stop off at the historic village of Richmond and visit the Tasmanian Devil Park Wildlife Rescue Centre.

Richmond is just 26 kilometers (15½ miles) northeast of Hobart and is the site of the country's oldest bridge (1823), the best-preserved convict jail in Australia (1825), and several old churches, including St. John's Church (1836)—the oldest Catholic church in the country. Richmond also has lots of tearooms, craft shops, galleries, and antique stores.

The **Tasmanian Devil Park Wildlife Rescue Centre,** Port Arthur Highway, Taranna, 80 kilometers (48 miles) from Hobart (☎ **03/6250 3230**) houses plenty of orphaned or injured native animals. The park is open daily from 9am to 5pm. Admission is A$11 (U.S.$7.70) for adults and A$5.50 (U.S.$3.85) for children.

WHERE TO STAY & DINE

Port Arthur Caravan Park. C/o Port Arthur Post Office, Port Arthur, TAS 7182. ☎ **03/6250 2340.** Fax 03/6250 2509. 20 cabins, 8 dorm rooms, caravan sites. A$60 (U.S.$42) standard cabin; A$70 (U.S.$49) deluxe cabin. A$19 (U.S.$13.30) powered site with bathroom; A$14 (U.S.$9.80) powered site without bathroom; A$12 (U.S.$8.40) unpowered site. A$13 (U.S.$9.10) dorm bed for adults, A$8 (U.S.$5.60) dorm bed for children. Additional person A$13 (U.S.$9.10) extra (children A$9/U.S.$6.30 extra) in cabins; additional person A$6 (U.S.$4.20) extra (children A$3/U.S.$2.10 extra) in powered or unpowered sites. BC, MC, V.

This pleasant caravan and cabin park is at Garden Point, 1 kilometer (half a mile) before Port Arthur. It overlooks the ocean and is a 10-minute walk to the beach and a 40-minute walk to the historic site. The standard cabins sleep up to five people and come with a kitchenette. Deluxe cabins have a balcony, a full kitchen, and are closer to the ocean. Bunk rooms are very basic, and you need to provide your own linen.

Port Arthur Motor Inn. Port Arthur Historic Site, Arthur Hwy., Port Arthur, TAS 7182. ☎ **1800/030 747** in Australia, or 03/6250 2101. Fax 03/6250 2417. 35 units. MINIBAR TV TEL. A$110 (U.S.$77) double. Additional person A$15 (U.S.$10.50) extra. Children 11 and under stay free in parents' room. AE, BC, DC, MC, V. Free parking. Bus: Tigerline runs from Hobart (Mon–Fri only).

If you decide to stop over rather than drive all the way back to Hobart (remember: marsupials get killed all the time on the roads at night—and they can do a lot of damage to a rental car), then this is a good choice. The rooms are attractive and overlook the historic site. There is also a self-service laundry and a kids' playground. Port Arthur ghost-tour packages are available from here. The motel's restaurant is quite formal, but there's often something on the menu suitable for the budget conscious.

3 Freycinet National Park

206km (123½ miles) NE of Hobart, 214km (128½ miles) SW of Launceston.

If you only have time to visit one place in Tasmania, make sure it's Freycinet National Park. The Freycinet Peninsula hangs down off the eastern coast of Tasmania. It's a place of craggy pink granite peaks, spectacular white beaches, wetlands, heath lands, coastal dunes, and dry eucalyptus forests. This is the place to spot sea eagles, wallabies, seals, and pods of dolphins. From May to August, you can also see humpback and southern right whales during their migration to and from the warmer waters of northern New South Wales. The township of **Coles Bay** is the main staging post, and there are many bushwalks in the area. The walk to the spectacular **Wineglass Bay** will be one of the nicest you'll ever do.

ESSENTIALS

GETTING THERE   **Tasmanian Redline Coaches** (☎ 03/6231 3233) runs between Hobart and Bicheno, leaving Hobart Monday and Wednesday at 10am, Tuesday and Thursday at 12:30pm, Friday at 2pm, and Sunday at 10:30am. The trip takes about 4½ hours. From Launceston, buses leave Monday to Thursday at 2pm, Friday at 3:45pm, and Sunday at 11am, and take less than 3 hours. From Bicheno, catch a local bus run by **Bicheno Coach Services** (☎ 03/6257 0293, or 0419 570 293 mobile phone). Buses leave at 9am and 3pm Sunday to Friday, at 9am only on Saturday (there's no 3pm service). Buses also meet every coach from Hobart or Launceston, but you need to book in advance. Tickets cost A$5 (U.S.$3.50) one-way to Coles Bay, and A$6 (U.S.$4.20) to the start of the Wineglass Bay walking track. From Hobart it's about a 3-hour drive by car.

VISITOR INFORMATION   There is a **Visitor Information Centre** (☎ 03/6375 1333) on the Tasman Highway at Bicheno. Otherwise, the **Tasmanian Travel and Information Centre** in Hobart (☎ 03/6230 8383) can supply you with maps and details. Daily entry to the park costs A$2.50 (U.S.$1.75) per person, or A$8 (U.S.$5.60) per vehicle.

EXPLORING THE PARK

If you have time for only one walk, then head out from Freycinet Lodge on the 30-minute, uphill hike past spectacularly beautiful pink granite outcrops to **Wineglass Bay Lookout** for breathtaking views. You can then head down to Wineglass Bay itself and back up again. The walk takes around 2½ hours. A longer walk takes you along the length of **Hazards Beach,** where you'll find plenty of shell middens—sea shell refuse heaps—left behind by the Aborigines who once lived here. This walk takes 6 hours.

Not to be missed is a trip aboard **Freycinet Sea Charter's** vessel *Kahala* (☎ 03/6257 0355; fax 03/6375 1461), which offers whale watching between June and September, bay and game fishing, dolphin watching, diving, scenic and marine wildlife cruises, and sunset cruises. Half-day cruises cost A$60 (U.S.$42) per person with a minimum of four adults onboard. Full-day cruises cost A$100 (U.S.$70) per person.

WHERE TO STAY & DINE

Camping is available in the national park for A$10 (U.S.$7) per tent, but water is scarce. For inquiries, call the **Parks and Wildlife Service** (☎ 03/6257 0107). There are also two caravan parks: The **Bicheno Cabin and Tourist Park,** in Champ Street, Bicheno (☎ 03/6375 1117), offers on-site vans from A$30 (U.S.$21) a double, as well as backpacker rooms; and the **Bicheno Caravan Park,** on the corner of Burgess and Tribe streets, Bicheno (☎ **03/6375 1280**), has on-site vans for A$25 (U.S.$17.50).

Freycinet Backpackers. 2352 Main Rd., Coles Bay 7215. ☎ **03/6257 0100.** Fax 03/6257 0270. 24 twin-share rooms. A$14 (U.S.$9.80) per person first night, A$10 (U.S.$7) each subsequent night. MC, V. Reach hostel by public bus from Bicheno.

Set in the bush beside the ocean, this simple backpacker's establishment is 3 kilometers (2 miles) outside the national park and 7 kilometers (4¼ miles) from the main walking tracks. Rooms are basic, with little more than a set of bunk beds, a table and chair, a wardrobe, and a mirror. Guests make use of a self-catering kitchen, a coin-op laundry, and large dining and lounge areas. You can rent a bed quilt for A$4 (U.S.$2.80).

Silver Sands Resort. Peggy's Point, Bicheno 7215. ☎ **03/6375 1266**). Fax 03/6375 1168. 32 units. A$50 (U.S.$35) budget double; A$75 (U.S.$52.50) standard double with ocean view; A$79 (U.S.$55.30) standard double with pool view. AE, BC, DC, MC, V.

The budget rooms here are old and pretty scruffy; they come with either singles or a double bed, a TV ("if it works"), and a shower. Standard rooms are much nicer, with better furniture and a mixture of queen-size, double, and single beds. There's a pool, a guest laundry, a bar, and a seafood restaurant with reasonable meals averaging A$15 (U.S.$10.50).

WORTH A SPLURGE

✪ **Freycinet Lodge.** Freycinet National Park, Coles Bay 7215. ☎ **03/6257 0101.** Fax 03/6257 0278. E-mail: frey@trump.net.au. 60 units. A$160 (U.S.$112) standard cabin; A$185 (U.S.$129.50) spa cabin. AE, BC, DC, MC, V.

I can't praise this eco-friendly lodge enough. Comfortable one- and two-room cabins are spread unobtrusively through the bush and connected by raised walking tracks. Each has a balcony, and some have a huge spa. The main part of the lodge houses a lounge room and a truly excellent restaurant that sweeps out onto a verandah overlooking the limpid green waters of Great Oyster Bay. The menu here is excellent, and includes delicious Freycinet oysters. The lodge is right next to Hazards Beach, and it's an easy stroll to the start of the Wineglass Bay Walk.

4 Launceston

198km (119 miles) N of Hobart

Tasmania's second city is Australia's third oldest, after Sydney and Hobart. Situated at the head of the Tamar River, 50 kilometers (30 miles) inland from the state's north coast, and surrounded by delightful undulating farmland, Launceston (pop. 104,000) is a pleasant city crammed with elegant Victorian and Georgian architecture and plenty of remnants from convict days. Unfortunately, shortsighted local and state government officials are gradually chipping away at its great architectural heritage in favor of the usual parking garages and ugly concrete monoliths. The city is still one of Australia's most beautiful, however, with plenty of delightful parks and churches. It's also well placed as the gateway to the wineries of the Tamar Valley, the highlands and alpine lakes of the north, and the stunning beaches to the east.

ESSENTIALS

GETTING THERE   Both **Ansett** and **Qantas** fly to Launceston from Melbourne (trip time: 55 minutes) and Sydney (trip time: around 3 hours). Coaches meet flights throughout the day and do a run of the main city hotels for A$7 (U.S.$4.90).

Tasmanian Redline Coaches (☎ **03/6231 3233**) depart Hobart for Launceston several times daily. The trip takes around 2 hours and 40 minutes and costs A$19 (U.S.$13.30) one-way. Launceston is 1½ hours from Devonport. The trip from Devonport costs around A$13 (U.S.$9.10).

The driving time from Hobart to Launceston is just over 2 hours on Highway 1.

VISITOR INFORMATION The **Gateway Tasmania Travel Centre** is at the corner of St. John and Paterson streets (☎ **03/6336 3133;** fax 03/6336 3118; e-mail: gateway.tas@microtech.com.au). It's open Monday through Friday from 9am to 5pm, Saturday from 9am to 3pm, and Sunday and public holidays from 9am to noon.

EXPLORING THE CITY & ENVIRONS

Launceston is easily explored by foot. A must for any visitor is a stroll with ✪ **Launceston Historic Walks** (☎ **03/6331 3679**). Walks leave from the Gateway Tasmania Travel Centre Monday to Friday at 9:45am (weekend walks can also be arranged). The hour-long walk gives a fascinating insight into Launceston's history and costs A$10 (U.S.$7). **City Sights** (☎ **03/6336 3122**), on the corner of St. John and Paterson streets, runs daily city tours in replica trams. Tours cost A$23 (U.S.$16.10) for adults, and A$16 (U.S.$11.20) for children under age 16.

A must-see is ✪ **Cataract Gorge,** the result of violent earthquakes that rattled Tasmania some 40 million years ago. It's a wonderfully scenic area just 10 minutes from Launceston. The South Esk River flows through the gorge and collects in a small lake traversed by a striking yellow suspension bridge and the longest single-span chair lift in the world. The chair lift is open daily from 9am to 4:30pm August 13 to June 19; from June 20 to August 12 it operates on Saturdays and Sundays only. A ride costs A$5 (U.S.$3.50) for adults and A$3 (U.S.$2.10) for children under age 16. Outdoor concerts are sometimes held on the banks of the lake. The hike to Duck Reach Power Station takes about 45 minutes. Bring good footwear and a raincoat. Other walks in the area are shorter and easier. The Gorge Restaurant (see "Where to Dine," below) and the kiosk next door offer glorious views from the outdoor tables.

Tamar River Cruises (☎ **03/6334 9900**) offers lunch, afternoon, and evening buffet-dinner cruises up the Tamar River from Home Point Wharf in Launceston. The 4-hour lunch cruise costs A$48 (U.S.$33.60) for adults and A$24 (U.S.$16.80) for children and departs Monday through Saturday at 10am, and Sunday at 11am. A 2-hour afternoon cruise costs A$20 (U.S.$14) for adults and A$10 (U.S.$7) for children and departs Tuesday, Wednesday, and Thursday at 3pm. A 4-hour dinner cruise costs A$55 (U.S.$38.50) for adults and A$27.50 (U.S.$19.25) for children and departs Friday and Saturday at 7:15pm.

Mountain biking is popular in this area. Contact Tasmanian Expeditions (☎ **1800/030 230** in Australia, or 03/6334 3477; www.tassie.net.au/tas_ex/; e-mail: tazzie@tassie.net.au) for information on its 4- to 7-day trips along the east coast in summer.

You can rent bicycles from the youth hostel at 36 Thistle St. (☎ **03/6344 9779**) for A$11 (U.S.$7.70) per day for a touring bike or A$18 (U.S.$12.60) per day for a mountain bike.

The **Trevallyn State Recreation Area,** on the outskirts of Launceston off Reatta Road, is a man-made lake surrounded by a beautiful wildlife reserve with several walking tracks and boating down the South Esk River. There are also barbecue facilities, picnic areas, and even a beach. For something different, you could attempt a cable hang glide off a 18-meter (60-ft.) cliff while strapped into a harness and hooked onto a 198- meter (650-ft.) cable. Apparently it's so safe and easy that even the owner's dog has made the plunge. It's open for action daily from 10am to 5pm (winter until 4pm) and costs A$10 (U.S.$7).

OTHER ATTRACTIONS

Aquarius Roman Baths. 127 George St., ☎ **03/6331 2255.** Admission A$18 (U.S.$12.60) for 1, A$28 (U.S.$19.60) for 2 for baths and hot rooms. Treatments extra. Mon–Fri 8:30am–10pm, Sat–Sun 9am–6pm.

Adorned with works of art, gold, and Italian marble, this remarkable Romanesque structure is worth visiting just for the architectural experience. Indulge in warm, hot, and cold water baths; visit the steam room; or get a massage or a beauty makeover.

National Automobile Museum of Tasmania. 86 Cimitiere St. ☎ **03/6334 8888.** Admission A$7.50 (U.S.$5.25) adults, A$4 (U.S.$2.80) children under age 16, A$19 (U.S.$13.30) families. Daily 9am–5pm summer, 10am–4pm winter. Closed Christmas.

More than 80 classic automobiles and motorbikes are on display here, some unique to this exhibition. Children particularly enjoy the model car collection.

The Old Umbrella Shop. 60 George St. ☎ **03/6331 9248.** Free admission. Mon–Fri 9am–5pm, Sat 9am–noon.

Built in the 1860s, this unique shop is the last genuine period store in Tasmania and has been operated by the same family since the turn of the century. Umbrellas spanning the last 100 years are on display, while modern brollies and souvenirs are for sale.

Queen Victoria Museum & Art Gallery. Corner of Wellington and Paterson sts. ☎ **03/6331 6777.** Free admission. Mon–Sat 10am–5pm, Sun 2–5pm.

Opened in honor of Queen Victoria's Golden Jubilee in 1891, this museum houses a large collection of stuffed wildlife, including the extinct Tasmanian Tiger, or *Thylacine*. There are also temporary exhibits and historical items on display.

Waverley Woollen Mills. Waverley Rd. ☎ **03/6339 1106.** Tours A$4 (U.S.$2.80) adults, A$2 (U.S.$1.40) children, A$12 (U.S.$8.40) families. Tours daily 9am–4pm (there's usually a 20-minute wait).

Established in 1874 on a site 5 kilometers (3 miles) northeast of town, this business still uses a waterwheel to turn the looms that help make Woollen blankets and rugs. Tours show how the process works. Everything from woolen hats to ties is sold on the premises.

Penny Royal World & Gunpowder Mill. Off Bridge Rd. ☎ **03/6331 6699.** Admission A$19.50 (U.S.$13.65) adults, and A$9.50 (U.S.$6.65) children. Daily 9am–4:30pm. Closed Christmas.

This amusement park, with its sailboat, barges, and trams, and historic gunpowder mills, is large enough to occupy an entire day. Admission also includes a trip up Cataract Gorge and the Tamar River on a paddle steamer, the MV *Lady Stelfox*.

Shopping Tips

The **Design Centre of Tasmania,** on the corner of Tamar and Brisbane streets (☎ **03/6331 5506**) is a wonderful gallery on the edge of City Park where locally produced contemporary furniture and fine crafts are sold. It's open Monday through Friday from 10am to 6pm, Saturday from 10am to 1pm, and Sunday from 2 to 5pm.

If you're in Launceston on a Sunday, try to visit the **York Town Square Market,** at the rear of the Launceston International Hotel. There are plenty of craft items on sale. The market is open from 9am to 5pm.

WHERE TO STAY

Hillview House. 193 George St., Launceston, TAS 7250. ☎ **03/6331 7388.** Fax 03/6331 7388. 9 units. A$90 (U.S.$63) double; A$105 (U.S.$73.50) family room for 3. Rates include cooked breakfast. MC, V.

The rooms at this restored 1840–1860 farmhouse are nothing fancy but are quite comfortable. They come with a double bed, a TV, and a shower. Family rooms have an extra single bed. The hotel overlooks the city, and the large verandah and colonial dining room both have extensive views over the city and the Tamar River.

Innkeepers Colonial Motor Inn. 31 Elizabeth St., Launceston, TAS 7250. ☎ **03/6331 6588.** Fax 03/6334 2765. 64 units. A/C MINIBAR TV TEL. A$120 (U.S.$84) double; A$195 (U.S.$136.50) suite. Additional person A$15 (U.S.$10.50) extra. Lower weekend rates. Children under 3 free in parents' room. AE, BC, DC, MC, V. Free parking.

Those who desire tried-and-true motel lodging will feel right at home at the Colonial, a place that combines old-world ambiance with modern facilities. The rooms are quite large and have attractive furnishings. The motel attracts a large corporate clientele. The Old Grammar School that stands next door has been incorporated into the complex, with the **Quill and Cane Restaurant** operating in what once was a schoolroom, and **Three Steps On George,** Launceston's liveliest nightspot, making use of the former boys' gym.

Lloyd's Hotel. 23 George St., Launceston, TAS 7250. ☎ **03/6331 4966.** Fax 03/6331 5589. 18 units (some with shower only). A$54 (U.S.$37.80) double. Rates include cooked breakfast. Additional person A$20 (U.S.$14) extra. BC, MC, V. Free parking.

This older-style property offers comfortable lodging. It's very centrally located, and the owners are friendly and interesting. Each room comes with a refrigerator, and tea- and coffee-making facilities. Most rooms have a TV. All rooms come with a shower; some also have tubs.

Hotel Tasmania. 191 Charles St., Launceston, TAS 7250. ☎ **03/6331 7355** (one of those awful electronic switchboards). Fax 03/6331 5589. 18 units. A$58 (U.S.$40.60) double. Additional person A$17 (U.S.$11.90) extra. Rates include continental breakfast. BC, MC, V. Free on-street parking.

Situated right in the heart of town, this hotel offers simple rooms with modern furnishings, a TV, coffee- and tea-making facilities, and attached showers. All the rooms were renovated in 1998, which helped win the hotel the Australian Hoteliers Association for the best budget pub-style accommodation in Tasmania. Downstairs, there's a saloon-style bar with a cowboy theme. There's also a reasonable bistro and a family restaurant with the same menu. The Cactus Club nightclub has pool tables. Live bands play in the bar area Wednesday, Friday, and Saturday evenings, and daily Happy Hours run between 5:30pm and 7pm, and 9pm and 10pm.

WORTH A SPLURGE

✪ **Alice's Place & Ivy Cottage.** 129 Balfour St., Launceston, TAS 7250. ☎ **03/6334 2231.** Fax 03/6334 2696. 2 cottages (9 more also reviewed below). TV. Alice's Place A$170 (U.S.$119) cottage for 1 or 2, additional person A$50 (U.S.$35) extra; Ivy Cottage A$170 (U.S.$119) cottage for 1 or 2, additional person A$30–$50 (U.S.$21–$35) extra. Rates include breakfast ingredients. AE, DC, BC, MC, V. Free parking.

Also highly recommended, these two delightful cottages are next door to each other and belong to the same owner, the hard-working Helen Poynder. She made Alice's Place, which sleeps four, entirely from bits and pieces of razed historic buildings. Ivy Cottage, on the other hand, is a restored Georgian house (ca. 1831). Both places are furnished with antiques and fascinating period bric-a-brac. Kitchens are fully equipped, and both units have large spa baths. Both cottages share the same garden.

Also available for rent are five other spa cottages called Alice's Hideaways, which cost A$170 (U.S.$119) a night for one or two people, and four cottages collectively known as The Shambles, which cost A$140 (U.S.$98) for one or two.

✪ **York Mansions.** 9–11 York St., Launceston, TAS 7250. ☎ **03/6334 2933.** Fax 03/ 6334 2870. 5 units. TV TEL. A$162 (U.S.$113.40) 2-bedroom apt, additional person A$45 (U.S.$31.50) extra; A$178 (U.S.$124.60) 3-bedroom apt, additional person A$50 (U.S.$35) extra. Rates include breakfast provisions. AE, BC, DC, MC, V. Free parking.

I can't praise this place enough; it rivals the best accommodations found anywhere in the world. If you feel that where you stay is just as important to your visit as what you see, then you must stay here. Within the walls of the National Trust–classified York Mansions, built in 1840, are five very spacious apartments, each with a distinctly individual character. The Duke of York apartment resembles a gentleman's drawing room, complete with antiques, an extensive book collection, and a rich leather sofa. The light and airy Duchess of York unit has hand-painted silk panels. Each apartment is self-contained and has its own separate kitchen, dining room, living room, bedrooms, bathroom, and laundry. A CD player and large-screen TV are modern touches. The ingredients for a hearty breakfast can be found in the refrigerator. There's also a delightful cottage garden.

WHERE TO DINE

You'll find that most places to eat in Launceston don't have a fixed closing time. Rather, they shut up shop when the last customer has been served and has eaten.

✪ **Croplines Coffee Bar.** Brisbane Court, off Brisbane St. ☎ **03/6331 4023.** Coffees and teas A$1.60–$2.40 (U.S.$1.15–$1.70). Cakes under A$2 (U.S.$1.40). AE, BC, MC, V. Daily 8am–5:30pm.

If you crave good coffee, then bypass every other place in Launceston and head here. It's a little difficult to find, and you may have to ask directions, but basically it's behind the old Brisbane Arcade. The owners are dedicated to coffee, grinding their beans on the premises daily. If coffee's not your cup of tea, then try the hot chocolate—it's the best I've tasted anywhere.

Konditorei Cafe Manfred. 106 George St. ☎ **03/6334 2490.** Reservations not accepted. Light meals A$4–$5 (U.S.$2.80–$3.50); main meals A$9–$18 (U.S.$6.30–$12.60). AE, BC, DC, MC, V. Mon–Thurs 9am–5:30pm, Fri 9am–late Sat 10am–late. PATISSERIE.

This German patisserie has recently moved to larger premises to keep up with demand for its sensational cakes and breads. It's also added an à la carte restaurant serving up pastas and steaks. Light meals include croissants, salads, and cakes. You can eat inside or out.

O'Keefe's Hotel. 124 George St. ☎ **03/6331 4015.** Reservations recommended. Main courses A$10.50–$14.50 (U.S.$7.35–$10.15). AE, BC, MC, V. Daily 11:30am–2pm, 5:30pm–late. ASIAN/TASMANIAN.

This pub-based eatery earns high praise for its variety of well-prepared dishes. You can choose from such delicacies as Thai curry and laksa; seafood dishes such as scallops, prawns, and sushi; and plenty of pastas and grills. There's also a range of good salads. Small and large servings are available.

✪ **Shrimps.** 72 George St. (corner of Paterson St.) ☎ **03/6334 0584.** Reservations recommended. Main courses A$14–A$19 (U.S.$9.80–$13.30). AE, BC, DC, MC, V. Mon–Sat noon–2pm, 6:30pm–late. SEAFOOD.

Shrimps offers the best selection of seafood in Launceston. Built in 1824 by convict labor, its exterior is classic Georgian. Tables are small and well spaced, and the best meals are off the blackboard menu, which generally has at least eight fish dishes.

Usually available are wonderful Tasmanian mussels, whitebait, Thai-style fishcakes, and freshly split oysters. Everything is very fresh and seasonal.

Star Bar Cafe. 113 Charles St. ☎ **03/6331 9659.** Reservations recommended. Main courses A$10.50–$17.50 (U.S.$7.35–$12.25). AE, BC, MC, V. Mon–Wed 11am–11pm, Thurs–Sat 11am–midnight, Sunday noon–10pm. MEDITERRANEAN.

The Star Bar Cafe has often been commended as Tasmania's Best Bistro. It serves great-quality food, including such dishes as mee goreng, beetroot, and quail risotto; grilled octopus, steaks, and chicken livers; as well as the popular pizzas and breads cooked in the large wood-fired oven. Pizzas cost between A$12.50 and $16.50 (U.S.$11.55 to $8.75) and are big enough for two. In winter, guests congregate around a large open fire.

Worth a Splurge

Fee & Me Restaurant. Corner of Charles and Frederick sts. ☎ **03/6331 3195.** Reservations recommended. A$42 (U.S.$29.40) for 3 courses, A$48 (U.S.$33.60) for 4 courses, A$50 (U.S.$35) for 5 courses. AE, BC, DC, MC, V. Mon–Sat 7pm–late. MOD OZ.

What is perhaps Launceston's best restaurant is found in a grand old mansion. A five-course meal could go something like this: Tasmanian smoked salmon with salad, capers, and a soft poached egg; followed by chili oysters with a coconut sauce and vermicelli noodles; then ricotta and goat cheese gnocchi with creamed tomato and red capsicum; followed by Asian-style duck on bok choy with a citrus sauce; finally topped off with a coffee and chicory soufflé. This is just a guide, as the dishes change frequently. An extensive wine list has been designed to complement selections for each course.

5 Cradle Mountain & Lake St. Clair National Park

85km (51 miles) S of Devonport; 175km (105 miles) NW of Hobart.

The national park and World Heritage area that encompasses both Cradle Mountain and Lake St. Clair is one of the most spectacular regions in Australia and, after Hobart and Port Arthur, the most visited place in Tasmania. The 1,545-meter (5,067-ft.) mountain dominates the north part of the island, and the long, deep lake is to its south. Between them lie more steep slopes, button grass plains, majestic alpine forests, dozens of lakes filled with trout, and several rivers. **Mt. Ossa,** in the center of the park, is Tasmania's highest point at 1,617 meters (5,303 ft.). Australia's best-known walking trail, the **Overland Track** (see below), links Cradle Mountain with Lake St. Clair.

ESSENTIALS

GETTING THERE   Tasmanian Wilderness Transport (☎ **03/6334 4442;** fax 03/6334 2029) runs buses to Cradle Mountain from Hobart, Launceston, Devonport, and Strahan (see "Exploring the Apple Isle," earlier in this chapter for more details). One-way coach transfers from Launceston cost A$36.50 (U.S.$25.55) and leave at 7:30am (arriving at 11am) every Tuesday, Thursday, and Saturday. Coach transfers from Hobart leave at the same time (arriving at 3:30pm) on the same days and cost A$50 (U.S.$35). A special Overland Track service drops off passengers at the beginning of the walk and picks them up at the end; it costs A$69 (U.S.$48.30) round-trip from Hobart. All coaches have commentary on board.

    Maxwells Cradle Mountain–Lake St. Clair Charter Bus and Taxi Service (☎ and fax **03/6492 1431**) runs buses from Devonport and Launceston to Cradle Mountain from A$35 (U.S.$24.50) (depending on how many people are onboard) and travels to other areas within the park, such as the Walls of Jerusalem, as well as Lake St. Clair. Buses also run from Cradle Mountain campground to the start of the Overland Track; the fare is A$7 (U.S.$4.90) one-way.

VISITOR INFORMATION   The **Cradle Mountain Visitor Centre** (☎ **03/ 6492 1133;** fax 03/6492 1120; www.parks.tas.gov.au), is on the northern edge of the national park, just outside Cradle Mountain Lodge. It offers the best information on local walks and treks and is open from 8am to 5pm daily.

EXPLORING THE PARK

Cradle Mountain Lodge (see "Where to Stay," below) runs a daily program of guided walks, abseiling, rock-climbing, and trout-fishing excursions for lodge guests. The staff at the park headquarters (see "Visitor Information," above) can supply information on the numerous trails in the park. Be warned, though, that the weather changes quickly in the high country, so go prepared with wet-weather gear and always tell someone where you are heading. Of the shorter walks, the stroll to **Pencil Pines** and the 5-kilometer (3-mile) walk to **Dove Lake** are the most pleasant.

Between June and October, it's sometimes possible to cross-country ski in the park.

HIKING THE OVERLAND TRACK

The best- known hiking trail in Australia is the ✪ **Overland Track,** an 85-kilometer (45-mile) route between Cradle Mountain and Lake St. Clair. The trek takes from 5 to 10 days, passes through highland moors and dense rain forests, and traverses several mountains. Every summer up to 200 people a day start the trek. Lodging is in simple huts, spread along the route, that are available on a first-come, first-served basis. You can also camp if you take your own tent.

Tasmanian Expeditions (☎ **1800/030 230** in Australia, or 03/6334 3477; www.tassie.net.au/tas_ex/; e-mail: tazzie@tassie.net.au) offers 3-day walking tours around Cradle Mountain. The trips depart from Launceston and cost A$430 (U.S.$301), all-inclusive. The company also offers an 8-day full trek on the Overland Track for A$995 (U.S.$696.50) all-inclusive from Launceston.

Another alternative is to go on an organized trek with **Cradle Mountain Huts** (Box 1879, Launceston, TAS 7250. ☎ **03/6331 2006;** fax 03/6331 5525). The huts are heated and well equipped. A 6-day walk costs A$1,450 (U.S.$1,015) for adults and A$1,350 (U.S.$945) for children ages 12 to 16; rates are all-inclusive and include transfers to and from Launceston. Children under age 12 are not permitted.

WHERE TO STAY & DINE

✪ **Cradle Mountain Lodge.** P.O. Box 153, Sheffield, TAS 7306. ☎ **1800/132 469** in Australia, or 03/6492 1303. Fax 03/6492 1309. 2 lodge rooms (neither with bathroom), 96 self-contained cabins. Lodge rooms A$97 (U.S.$67.90) twin-share; Pencil Pine cabins A$174 (U.S.$121.80) per cabin; spa cabins A$225 (U.S.$157.50) per cabin. Additional person A$34 (U.S.$23.80) extra. Children under 3 free in parents' room. Ask about special winter packages. AE, BC, DC, MC, V. Free parking.

If you like luxury with your rain forests, then this award-winning lodge is the place for you. Cradle Mountain Lodge is simply marvelous. Just minutes from your bed are the giant buttresses of 1,500-year-old trees, moss forests, craggy mountain ridges, limpid pools and lakes, and hoards of scampering marsupials. The rooms are comfortable, the food excellent, and the staff friendly. The big open fireplaces are well worth cuddling up in front of for a couple of days at least. Each modern wood cabin has a potbellied stove as well as an electric heater for chilly evenings, a shower, and a small kitchen. There are no telephones or TVs—but who needs them! Spa cabins come with carpets, a spa tub, and a balcony with scenic views. Some have a separate bedroom. Two cabins have limited facilities for travelers with disabilities. Guests have the use of the casual and comfortable main lodge, where there is a large dining room, a guest lounge with TV and VCR, cozy bars, a tavern, and a cafe that serves lunch and snacks. Almost every room in the lodge has a blazing log fire.

In the evening, possums, Tasmanian devils, wombats, native cats, and wallabies wander the grounds; some critters even scamper onto the verandahs to claim food left out for them.

You can stop by for a meal, a drink, or Devonshire tea at the lodge even if you are not staying here.

Lemonthyme Lodge. Off Cradle Mountain Rd., Moina via Sheffield (Locked Bag 158, Devonport 7310). ☎ **03/6492 1112.** Fax 03/6492 1113. E-mail: lemonthyme@ southcom.co.au. 8 lodge rooms, none with bathroom, 5 self-contained 2-bedroom cabins, 14 luxury cabins, 7 with spa. A$85 (U.S.$59.50) double room; from A$170 (U.S.$119) cabin. Additional person A$25 (U.S.$17.50) extra in room and A$30 (U.S.$21) extra in cabin; children under 15 A$15 (U.S.$10.50) extra. 3-course dinner A$37.50 (U.S.$26.25) extra; breakfast from A$10–$14.50 (U.S.$7–$10.15); lunch from A$5.50 (U.S.$3.85). AE, DC, BC, MC, V. Free parking. Lodge is 70km (42 miles) sw of Devonport. Management can provide transfers, or you can take the Tasmanian Wilderness Transport coach, which drops you 8km (5 miles) from the lodge and management will pick you up. If you're driving, call for directions.

This remote lodge is the largest log cabin in the southern hemisphere and is perfect for anyone who wants to get away from it all. Lodge rooms are sparsely furnished and share bathrooms down the hall. The luxury cabins are much nicer and come with private balconies, nicely appointed bathrooms, minibars, and wood heaters. All meals are served in a rustic dining room, where there's a large open fire. Complimentary tea and coffee are available all day. There are plenty of walks from here, as well as fishing and four-wheel-drive trips.

Waldheim Cabins. Cradle Mountain Visitor Centre, P.O. Box 20, Sheffield, TAS 7306. ☎ **03/6492 1110.** Fax 03/6492 1120. 8 cabins, none with bathroom. A$55 (U.S.$38.50) 4-berth cabin for 2; A$65 (U.S.$45.50) 6-berth cabin for up to three; A$75 (U.S.$52.50) 8-berth cabin for up to 3. Additional person A$19 (U.S.$13.30) extra; children A$9 (U.S.$6.30) extra. BC, MC, V. Collect cabin keys from National Park Visitor Centre, just inside boundary of the park, 8am–5pm daily.

If you want a real wilderness experience, then head for these cabins run by the Parks and Wildlife Service and located just 5 kilometers (3 miles) from Cradle Mountain Lodge. Nestled between button grass plains and temperate rain forest, they are simple and affordable and offer good access to plenty of walking tracks. Each cabin is equipped with heating, single bunk beds, basic cooking utensils, crockery, cutlery, and a gas stove. They are serviced by two composting toilets and showers. Generated power is provided for lighting from 6 to 11pm only. Supplies and fuel can be bought at Cradle Mountain Lodge. Bring your own bed linen and toiletries.

6 The West Coast

Strahan: 296km (177½ miles) NW of Hobart, 245km (1472 miles) SW of Devonport.

Tasmania's west coast is wild and mountainous, with a scattering of mining and logging towns and plenty of wilderness. The pristine **Franklin and Gordon rivers** tumble through World Heritage Areas once bitterly fought over by loggers, politicians, and environmentalists, while the bare, poisoned hills that make up the eerily beautiful moonscape of **Queenstown** show what intensive mining and industrial activity can do. **Strahan,** the only town of any size in the area, is the starting point for cruises up the Gordon River and ventures into the rain forest.

ESSENTIALS

GETTING THERE **Tasmanian Wilderness Transport** (☎ 03/6334 4442) runs coaches to and from Strahan from Hobart, Launceston, Devonport, and Cradle Mountain every Tuesday, Thursday, and Saturday (and also Sunday to and from

Hobart). The cheapest way to travel between these places is with the Tassie Wilderness Pass (see "Exploring the Apple Isle," earlier in the chapter for details). The drive from Hobart to Strahan takes about 4 hours without stops. From Devonport, allow at least 3 hours. Although the roads are good, they twist and turn quite dramatically and are particularly hazardous at night when marsupials come out to feed.

VISITOR INFORMATION The **Strahan Visitors Centre,** on The Esplanade in Strahan (☎ **03/6471 7622**), is open daily from 10am to 6pm in winter and to 8pm in spring and summer. It has good information on local activities.

CRUISING THE RIVERS & OTHER ADVENTURES

Gordon River Cruises, P.O. Box 40, Strahan, TAS 7468 (☎ **03/6471 7187;** fax 03/6471 7317) offers a half-day trip daily at 9am year-round and also at 2pm in first three weeks of January.

Cruises take passengers across Macquarie Harbour and up the Gordon River past historic Sarah Island, where convicts—working in horrendous conditions—were once used to log valuable Huon pine, and through forests of tea tree, melaleuca, and sassafras. A stop is made at Heritage Landing, where you can get a taste of the rain forest on a half-hour walk. There is also a full-day cruise during the high season (October through March), which includes lunch and a guided tour through the convict ruins on Sarah Island. Half-day tours cost A$45 (U.S.$31.50) for adults, A$25 (U.S.$17.50) for children under age 14, and A$126 (U.S.$88.20) for families; and the full-day cruise costs A$61 (U.S.$42.70) for adults, A$31 (U.S.$21.70) for children, and A$166 (U.S.$116.20) for families. Cruises depart from the Main Wharf on The Esplanade, in Strahan.

World Heritage Cruises (☎ **03/6471 7174;** fax 03/6471 7431) offers daily trips from the beginning of September until the end of July, leaving Strahan Wharf at 9am and returning at 4:30pm. The company's MV *Wanderer II* stops at Sarah Island, Heritage Landing, and the salmon and trout farm at Liberty Point. Meals and drinks are available on board. Cruises cost A$44 (U.S.$30.80) for adults and A$20 (U.S.$14) for children under age 14.

West Coast Yacht Charters (☎ **03/6471 7422**) runs fishing trips from 9am to noon for A$40 (U.S.$28) (negotiable), with fishing gear, bait, and morning tea included; crayfish dinner cruises for A$50 (U.S.$35); and 2-day, 2-night sailing cruises for A$320 (U.S.$225) all-inclusive.

While cruises are the main attraction in the area, you can also enjoy jet-boat rides, "flightseeing" in a seaplane that lands on the Gordon River, helicopter flights, and four-wheel-drive tours.

The majestic **Montezuma Falls,** the highest (at 113 m/370½ ft.) in Tasmania, are located just 10 minutes outside Rosebery.

The **Queenstown Chairlift,** in Queenstown, is also interesting. It's open from 8am to 6pm daily and costs A$6 (U.S.$4.20) for adults, A$4 (U.S.$2.80) for children, and A$15 (U.S.$10.50) for families. The chairlift offers panoramic views across the surrounding starkness of the hillsides.

MINE TOURS & OTHER ATTRACTIONS

Zeehan's West Coast Pioneers Memorial Museum (☎ **03/6471 6225**), 42 kilometers (25 miles) north of Strahan, is worth a visit for its mining relics and fascinating local history. It's open daily, and admission is A$3 (U.S.$2.10) for adults, A$1 (U.S.70¢) children, and A$7 (U.S.$4.90) for a family.

Lyell Tours (☎ **03/6471 2388**) offers a unique underground mine tour through a working Queenstown mine. The tour takes around 3 hours and costs A$48 (U.S.$28).

Dune Buggy Rides

What's more fun than scooting across the sand in a dune buggy? **Four-Wheelers** (☎ **03/6471 7622,** or 0419/508 175 mobile phone; fax 03/6471 7020) offers exhilarating, 40-minute rides across the Henty Sand Dunes, about 10 minutes north of Strahan. Trips cost just A$30 (U.S.$21) for one adult and A$55 (U.S.$38.50) for two. Longer trips are also offered outside the hot summer months.

Children under age 12 are not permitted. Tours leave at 8:30am and 1pm daily and must be booked in advance because only six people go down at a time. The company also operates 1-hour Surface Tours of the mine for A$11 (U.S.$7.70) for adults and A$6.50 (U.S.$4.55) for children, and an all-day "four-wheel-drive tour with a difference" that leaves Queenstown and travels past lakes, forgotten towns, and industrial scenery, and ends up in the Bird River rain forest. This latter tour costs A$60 (U.S.$42) for adults and A$35 (U.S.$24.50) for children under age 16, including morning tea and lunch.

WHERE TO STAY

Gordon Gateway Chalets. Grining St., Strahan, TAS 7468. ☎ **03/6471 7165.** Fax 03/6471 7165. 12 units (most with shower only). TV. Jan–Apr A$110 (U.S.$77) double; May–Dec A$65 (U.S.$45.50). BC, MC,V.

These modern, self-contained units are on a hill with good views of the harbor and Strahan township. Each has cooking facilities, so you can save on meal costs. Two have a bathtub, and the rest have just a shower. Breakfast is provided on request for A$8.50 (U.S.$5.95) per person. Guests have the use of a self-service laundry, a barbecue area, and a children's playground. One unit has facilities for travelers with disabilities.

Strahan Cabin Park. Corner of Jones & Innes sts., Strahan, TAS 7468. ☎ **03/6471 7442.** Fax 03/6471 7278. 16 cabins. TV. Dec 24–Apr 30 A$73 (U.S.$51.10) per cabin, May 1–Aug 31 A$48 (U.S.$33.60), Sept 1–Dec 23 A$58 (U.S.$40.60). Children under 18 A$10 (U.S.$7) extra. AE, BC, DC, MC, V.

Of the two cabin parks in town—**Azza's Holiday Units** (☎ 03/6471 7253), next door, is the other—this is the better. Cabins are clean and simple and well spaced. Each comes with a small TV, heating, a sink, a refrigerator, a small oven, a shower, two bunk beds, and a double bed. For A$90 (U.S.$63) you could consider a family unit within the main house itself. The unit has two double bedrooms, four bunk beds, a spa, and a large lounge.

WORTH A SPLURGE

✪ **Ormiston House.** The Esplanade, Strahan, TAS 7468. ☎ **03/6471 7077.** Fax 03/6471 7007. 4 units. TV TEL. A$180–$210 (U.S.$126–$147) double. Additional person A$44 (U.S.$30.80) extra. Rates include breakfast. AE, BC, DC, MC, V.

Ormiston House is a five-star gem. Built in 1899 for the family that gave it its name, the present owners have made it into a sort of shrine to their predecessors. Each of the four rooms is styled to represent one of the original family members; there's even a history room up in the attic stocked with bits and pieces from the old days. Each room is intricately furnished and wallpapered in busy designs and comes with a good-sized private bathroom. There's a nice morning room and a restaurant serving good food, with main courses costing A$19 (U.S.$13.30) and a three-course meal going for A$41 (U.S.$28.70). The owners are very friendly and have plenty of time for their guests. Smoking is not permitted.

Index

Page numbers in italics refer to maps.

FROMMER'S® COMPLETE TRAVEL GUIDES

Alaska
Amsterdam
Arizona
Atlanta
Australia
Austria
Bahamas
Barcelona, Madrid & Seville
Belgium, Holland &
  Luxembourg
Bermuda
Boston
Budapest & the Best of
  Hungary
California
Canada
Cancún, Cozumel &
  the Yucatán
Cape Cod, Nantucket &
  Martha's Vineyard
Caribbean
Caribbean Cruises & Ports
  of Call
Caribbean Ports of Call
Carolinas & Georgia
Chicago
China
Colorado
Costa Rica
Denver, Boulder &
  Colorado Springs
England
Europe
Florida

France
Germany
Greece
Greek Islands
Hawaii
Hong Kong
Honolulu, Waikiki & Oahu
Ireland
Israel
Italy
Jamaica & Barbados
Japan
Las Vegas
London
Los Angeles
Maryland & Delaware
Maui
Mexico
Miami & the Keys
Montana & Wyoming
Montréal & Québec City
Munich & the Bavarian Alps
Nashville & Memphis
Nepal
New England
New Mexico
New Orleans
New York City
Nova Scotia, New Brunswick
  & Prince Edward Island
Oregon
Paris
Philadelphia & the
  Amish Country

Portugal
Prague & the Best of the
  Czech Republic
Provence & the Riviera
Puerto Rico
Rome
San Antonio & Austin
San Diego
San Francisco
Santa Fe, Taos &
  Albuquerque
Scandinavia
Scotland
Seattle & Portland
Singapore & Malaysia
South Pacific
Spain
Switzerland
Thailand
Tokyo
Toronto
Tuscany & Umbria
USA
Utah
Vancouver & Victoria
Vermont, New Hampshire
  & Maine
Vienna & the Danube Valley
Virgin Islands
Virginia
Walt Disney World &
  Orlando
Washington, D.C.
Washington State

FROMMER'S® DOLLAR-A-DAY GUIDES

Australia from $50 a Day
California from $60 a Day
Caribbean from $60 a Day
England from $60 a Day
Europe from $50 a Day
Florida from $60 a Day

Greece from $50 a Day
Hawaii from $60 a Day
Ireland from $50 a Day
Israel from $45 a Day
Italy from $50 a Day
London from $75 a Day

New York from $75 a Day
New Zealand from $50 a Day
Paris from $70 a Day
San Francisco from $60 a Day
Washington, D.C.,
  from $60 a Day

FROMMER'S® PORTABLE GUIDES

Acapulco, Ixtapa &
  Zihuatanejo
Alaska Cruises & Ports of Call
Bahamas
California Wine Country
Charleston & Savannah
Chicago

Dublin
Las Vegas
London
Maine Coast
New Orleans
New York City
Paris

Puerto Vallarta, Manzanillo
  & Guadalajara
San Francisco
Sydney
Tampa & St. Petersburg
Venice
Washington, D.C.

FROMMER'S® NATIONAL PARK GUIDES

Family Vacations in the
   National Parks
Grand Canyon

National Parks of the
   American West
Yellowstone & Grand Teton

Yosemite & Sequoia/
   Kings Canyon
Zion & Bryce Canyon

FROMMER'S® GREAT OUTDOOR GUIDES

New England
Northern California

Southern California & Baja
Pacific Northwest

FROMMER'S® MEMORABLE WALKS

Chicago
London

New York
Paris

San Francisco
Washington D.C.

FROMMER'S® IRREVERENT GUIDES

Amsterdam
Boston
Chicago

London
Manhattan

New Orleans
Paris

San Francisco
Walt Disney World
Washington, D.C.

FROMMER'S® DRIVING TOURS

America
Britain
California

Florida
France
Germany

Ireland
Italy
New England

Scotland
Spain
Western Europe

THE COMPLETE IDIOT'S TRAVEL GUIDES

Boston
Cruise Vacations
Planning Your Trip to Europe
Hawaii

Las Vegas
London
Mexico's Beach Resorts
New Orleans

New York City
San Francisco
Walt Disney World
Washington D.C.

THE UNOFFICIAL GUIDES®

Branson, Missouri
California with Kids
Chicago
Cruises
Disney Companion

Florida with Kids
The Great Smoky &
   Blue Ridge
   Mountains

Las Vegas
Miami & the Keys
Mini-Mickey
New Orleans

New York City
San Francisco
Skiing in the West
Walt Disney World
Washington, D.C.

SPECIAL-INTEREST TITLES

Born to Shop: Caribbean Ports of Call
Born to Shop: France
Born to Shop: Hong Kong
Born to Shop: Italy
Born to Shop: New York
Born to Shop: Paris
Frommer's Britain's Best Bike Rides
The Civil War Trust's Official Guide
   to the Civil War Discovery Trail
Frommer's Caribbean Hideaways
Frommer's Europe's Greatest Driving Tours
Frommer's Food Lover's Companion to France
Frommer's Food Lover's Companion to Italy
Frommer's Gay & Lesbian Europe

Israel Past & Present
Monks' Guide to California
Monks' Guide to New York City
New York City with Kids
New York Times Weekends
Outside Magazine's Guide
   to Family Vacations
Places Rated Almanac
Retirement Places Rated
Washington, D.C., with Kids
Wonderful Weekends from Boston
Wonderful Weekends from New York City
Wonderful Weekends from San Francisco
Wonderful Weekends from Los Angeles

WHEREVER YOU TRAVEL, *H*ELP IS NEVER FAR AWAY.

From planning your trip to

providing travel assistance along

the way, American Express®

Travel Service Offices

are always there to help

you do more.

American Express Travel Service
Offices are found in central locations
throughout Australia.